# BRITISH WATERCOL[illegible] AND DRAWINGS

## Lord Leverhulme's Collection in the Lady Lever Art Gallery

Jessica Feather

With contributions from
Heather Birchall
Caroline Georgiadis
Martin Hopkinson
Alex Kidson
Reyahn King
Christopher Newall
Sandra Penketh
Jane Sellars
Joseph Sharples
Tim Wilcox

Lady Lever ART GALLERY
National Museums Liverpool

LIVERPOOL UNIVERSITY PRESS

First published 2010 by
Liverpool University Press
4 Cambridge Street
Liverpool
L69 7ZU

and

National Museums Liverpool
127 Dale Street
Liverpool
L2 2JH



British Library Cataloguing-in-Publication data
A British Library CIP record is available

ISBN 978-1-84631-155-0

Unless otherwise stated, all photography is by Keith Sweeney and David Flower

Designed and typeset by
AW @www.axisgraphicdesign.co.uk
Printed and bound by DeckersSnoeck, Antwerp, Belgium

Cover:
**J. M. W. Turner,** ***Falmouth Harbour, Cornwall*** (detail)
LL 3771 (WHL 3507)

Watercolour with touches of gouache and scratching out on wove paper
15.6 x 23.2 cm
Date: c. 1812–14

# Contents

## Foreword

The Lady Lever Art Gallery was founded in 1922 by William Hesketh Lever, 1st Viscount Leverhulme, to house the best of his personal fine and decorative art collection. Formed over a period of forty years, the collection is now regarded as being of international significance. Part of Lever's gift included a group of around 400 British watercolours and drawings; following sales from the collection these now number approximately 300. In putting together his collection, Lever was determined to demonstrate the high quality of British art production of the eighteenth and nineteenth centuries; the British School of watercolour painting was an essential chapter in this story. Jessica Feather's introduction to this catalogue investigates Lever's approaches to collecting these watercolours and drawings, his taste and the relationships he developed with dealers to assist him in his acquisitions. The most significant of these dealers was James Orrock who had a particular influence on Lever's approach to collecting. This is considered along with Orrock's sometime predilection for forgery.

Some of the British drawings and watercolours were catalogued in 1928 by R. R. Tatlock, in a volume on the fine art collections commissioned by Lever before his death. Eighty years later, Jessica Feather's research adds considerably to our knowledge of the collection. The detailed entries consider the original context for the production, meaning and, where appropriate, the critical reception of each work. National Museums Liverpool are grateful to the author for first proposing this project and for her dedicated work, insight and enthusiasm in cataloguing the collection. We would also like to thank the guest researchers for their contributions. Indeed, many specialists have assisted with expert advice and we extend our thanks to all of them.

This publication would not have been possible without the generous support of many individuals and organisations. In particular we would like to thank: The Paul Mellon Centre for Studies in British Art, Lord Leverhulme's Charitable Trust, Marc Fitch Fund, The Alliance Family Foundation Ltd, The Martineau Family Trust, W/S Fine Art Ltd and Wirral Decorative and Fine Arts Society.

Sandra Penketh
Head of Lady Lever Art Gallery

Reyahn King
Director of Art Galleries

**Acknowledgements**

Many people have helped to bring this catalogue to fruition. I should particularly like to thank Charles Nugent and Andrew Wyld, who originally inspired me on the subject of watercolours, and have patiently answered my questions over a number of years. I am grateful to Amy Meyers and her colleagues at the Yale Center for British Art, New Haven, for providing me with a fellowship that allowed me time away from my desk in March 2006 to think about watercolours. Numerous people have helped with queries about specific artists. Most of these are credited in the footnotes but for generously giving up their time to lengthy discussions I am grateful to the following: John Christian, Lee Edwards, Donato Esposito, Annie Lyles, Richard Stephens, Ian Warrell and Stephen Wildman. I should also like to thank my fellow contributors for their interesting and insightful entries (signed with their initials). For their help in a variety of ways thanks must also go to Robin Emmerson, Conrad Feather, Alexandra Harris, Gavin Hunter, Rosie Jarvie, Moira Lindsay, Edward Morris, Jane Munro, Victoria Osborne, Pat and Robert Owen, Cecilia Powell, Kim Sloan, Greg Smith, Norma Watt, Henry Wemyss and Scott Wilcox.

I am grateful to a large number of staff within National Museums Liverpool for their help in realising this project. In my efforts to examine every work without its frame and mount I have been reliant on the patience and good spirits of colleagues in Handling and Transport, Keith Sweeney in Photography, Roy Irlam in Frames and Keith Oliver in Paper Conservation. I have received the support of former and current members of the Art Department at the Walker Art Gallery; I owe particular thanks to Ann Bukantas, Alex Kidson, Jon Murden and Karen Miller for their help in editing the text. I am also grateful to Johanna Booth for her assistance in obtaining comparative illustrations. Thanks must also go to James Hernandez and Alex Middleton in the Development Office for advice on sourcing funding for the publication. For allowing me to take up residence and for support in a number of ways, I am most grateful to Sandra Penketh, Sarah Lynch and all the staff of the Lady Lever Art Gallery. Several volunteers have also contributed towards this project at a number of stages: Frances MacMillan in the initial stages of documentation and Sam Schwab who assisted during a later period.

This project would not have been realised without the collaboration of Liverpool University Press. In particular I would like to thank Andrew Kirk and Helen Tookey for their help with the production process. Thanks must also go to the catalogue's designer Alan Ward, who has shown great patience in producing such an attractive volume.

Finally, special thanks must go to my mum and dad for all their support and words of wisdom.

Jessica Feather

## Notes to the reader

This catalogue excludes one work by Lawrence Alma-Tadema (1836–1912) and another by James Abbott McNeill Whistler (1834–1903) as these have been included in Edward Morris and Mark Evans, *Lady Lever Art Gallery: Port Sunlight: Catalogue of Foreign Paintings, Drawings, Miniatures, Tapestries, Post-Classical Sculpture and Prints* (Liverpool, 1983). The collection of around 70 architectural drawings for the design of the Lady Lever Art Gallery and Port Sunlight Village by the firm of William & Segar Owen have also been omitted due to their specialist nature.

The works in the catalogue are organised alphabetically according to artist.

Sections devoted to individual artists are categorised according to four groupings, in the following order:

1. Documented works, works where there is no reason to doubt the traditional attribution, as well as works which have been re-attributed. These works are described using the plain name of the artist and, as far as possible, are listed according to date and, where the date is approximately similar, according to inventory number.

2. Works where the attribution is less certain, although it is probably a work by the artist. These works are designated by the prefix 'attributed to'.

3. Versions of identified works by the artist, whether or not these are autograph, which are described with the prefix 'after'. These works are arranged by inventory number.

4. Works that are not accounted for by any of the above categories are described by the name of the artist in inverted commas. In the absence of evidence of authorship, these works are catalogued according to their attribution when they were purchased by Lever. The status of these items is examined in the individual entries, which are listed according to inventory number.

Each work possesses a Lady Lever (LL) inventory number which was assigned in the 1980s and 1990s. Before these LL numbers were allocated, each work was designated either with a WHL (William Hesketh Lever) number for pictorial art,[1] or an LP (Late Picture) number for those works acquired by the Trustees following Lever's death. The WHL Inventory was begun by Lever in 1913 and its numbering system was applied to all purchases made after this date as well as retrospectively to his existing art collections. These latter works had previously been assigned numbers that referred to the various homes and properties where Lever had displayed them. TM was used for Thornton Manor, H for the Hill, Hampstead and HH for Hulme Hall, Port Sunlight. The old inventory numbers for the works are given in parentheses beside each entry. These numbers can occasionally be found in older publications, including Tatlock's 1928 catalogue, which used the WHL sequence.

The entries attempt to collate the existing state of knowledge on each work, placing the watercolour or drawing within the context of the artist's career. In most cases, where these have proved to be available, biographical details about each artist are given within each entry. On occasions when there is more than one work by an artist, these details are given in the first entry. Where works are known to have been exhibited, information about their critical reception has generally been incorporated. The listing of exhibitions and literature is as comprehensive as possible. Where the original title of the work could be sourced, this has been retained. When this information has not been available, the title nearest to the period of the work's production has been kept, although this is generally the title of the work when it was purchased by Lever or latterly by the Trustees. On some occasions the title has been embellished or changed when its traditional form has been proven to be either unhelpful or incorrect; these instances are signposted within the footnotes. Many of the watercolours and drawings in this volume were previously undocumented and I am conscious that consequently some are catalogued here more extensively than others. However, it is hoped that the bare details given in some of these entries will at least provide a starting point for any future research.

I have examined and measured each work without its frame, and most items without their mount; on the occasions when it has not been possible to remove the mount, the work's sight size has been recorded. Dimensions are given in cm only, height before width. Inscriptions have been recorded as those made by the artist; all annotations are in unknown hands unless otherwise indicated. Minor inscriptions and labels on mounts and versos with no historical relevance have not been transcribed. Although condition notes have been recorded for some works, it has not been possible to provide this information for all items. I have attempted to

1 John Jackson's *Sketch of John Flaxman* (LL 2705, pp. 130–1) entered Lever's collection with the 'Flaxman Relics' as a Wedgwood item. It was therefore included in an inventory (of non-pictorial art) that was created after May 1914. Works in this inventory were designated by the prefix 'X'.

provide information on watermarks as well as the type of paper used for some works; however, I am conscious that no thorough scientific examination of the papers or other supports used has been undertaken. I have made only a few remarks about frames, although those that are contemporary are generally emphasised.

All auctions listed took place in London unless otherwise stated.

Prices are given in guineas or pounds, shillings and pence, as recorded in contemporary documents, and no attempt has been made to make them consistent.

Lever is referred to throughout using this name, although he was styled Baron Leverhulme of Bolton-le-Moors from 1917, and Viscount Leverhulme of the Western Isles from 1922.

The two watercolour societies (the SPWC and NSPWC as detailed below) altered their names at various points; references have been made to the name of the society at the particular date as cited.

The following abbreviations have been used:

1904 Inventory: MS *Inventory of Pictures, Watercolour Drawings, Furniture and China purchased by Mr. W. H. Lever from Mr. J. Orrock, November 1904, and, it is mutually agreed these remain at 48 Bedford Square at Mr. Orrock's risk, 'til April or May 1905*

1910 Inventory: typed *Inventory & Valuation for Fire Insurance of Pictures, Watercolour Drawings & Decorative Furniture Purchased from James Orrock, Esq., 48 Bedford Square* [by Tom Cox, dated 5 September 1910]

1912 Inventory: typed *Inventory and Valuation of Pictures, Furniture, China, Silver and Glass removed from 48 Bedford Square July 1912*

1897–1902 TM Inventory: MS *Inventory of Furniture, China &c. at Thornton Manor, Thornton Hough, Cheshire for W. H. Lever Esq^re^* [dated from between Lever's purchase of Hoppner's painting *The Duchess of Rutland*, 20 March 1897, and the creation of the music room in 1902]

1905 TM Inventory: typed *Inventory & Valuation of Pictures, Engravings, Coloured Prints, Watercolours, Sketches & Drawings at Thornton Manor, Thornton Hough, Cheshire* [dated May 1905]

1906 TM Inventory: typed *Inventory and Valuation of Pictures, Engravings, Coloured Prints, Watercolours, Sketches & Drawings at Thornton Manor, Thornton Hough, Cheshire* [dated November 1906]

1907 TM Inventory: typed *Inventory and Valuation of Pictures, Engravings, Watercolours, Coloured Prints, Sketches & Drawings at Thornton Manor, Thornton Hough, Cheshire* [dated January 1907]

1907 Hill Inventory: typed *Inventory and Valuation of Pictures, Watercolours, Engravings, Coloured Prints, Sketches & Drawings known to be at The Hill, London* [dated January 1907]

1911 Hill Inventory: typed *Particulars of Pictures, Watercolours, Engravings &c. The Property of Sir William H. Lever Bart. at The Hill Hampstead, London* [dated 31 December 1911]

1912 Hill Inventory: typed *Inventory and Valuation – The Hill Pictures* [dated 31 December 1912]

1915 Hill Inventory: typed *Sir W. H. Lever, Bart., The Hill, Hampstead Heath, N.W., Valuation for Fire Insurance. Pictures, Drawings & Engravings* [by Tom Cox, dated 3 August 1915]

WHL Inventory: typed *General Inventory of Pictures, 1925* [1913–25]

ARA: Associate of the Royal Academy

LLAG files: files situated within the Lady Lever Art Gallery archive; unless otherwise indicated all inventories and other documentation cited in this catalogue are located in this archive

Milner: Frank Milner, *Turner: Paintings in Merseyside Collections* (Liverpool, 1990)

NSPWC: New Society of Painters in Water-Colours (1832–63), thereafter known as the Institute of Painters in Water-Colours and, from 1883, as the Royal Institute of Painters in Water-Colours

*ODNB*: *Oxford Dictionary of National Biography*, ed. H. G. C. Matthew and Brian Harrison (Oxford, 60 vols, 2004)

PRB: Pre-Raphaelite Brotherhood

RA: Royal Academy (1768–) or Royal Academician

RCA: Royal College of Art

SPWC: Society of Painters in Water-Colours (founded 1804), known as the Society of Painters in Oils and Water-Colours, 1812–21, and as the Royal Society of Painters in Water-Colours from 1881. From 1832 the institution was also known as the Old Water-Colour Society.

Tatlock: R. R. Tatlock, *English Painting of the XVIIIth to XXth Centuries with some examples of the Spanish, French and Dutch Schools, together with a collection of Historic and Modern Sculpture* (London, 1928)

Wilton: Andrew Wilton, *J.M.W. Turner: His Art and Life* (New Jersey, 1979)

## Glossary

**Cartoon**: A full-scale drawing of the principal forms of a composition, for a painting, fresco, stained-glass window or tapestry. The more modern use of the term describes a humorous or sarcastic representation of a current topic, often political.

**Chalk**: 1. Natural chalks in various colours are derived from earths. Natural black chalk is a mineral, a species of carbonaceous shale whose main ingredients are carbon and clay. Natural white chalk is of two varieties: carbonate of calcium or soapstone (steatite). Natural red chalk is made from the red ochre variety of haematite. Although chalk can be shaved to a point, it soon wears down, and therefore produces a softer line than the one made by *pencil*. 2. Fabricated chalks or *pastels* are made from powdered pigments combined with non-greasy binders. They are used in the form of finger-length sticks. The marks made by pastels are opaque and they tend to be used on specially prepared papers.

**Charcoal**: This is produced by reducing wood to carbon in heated chambers from which oxygen is excluded in order to prevent combustion occurring. Charcoal was cut into pieces and used in holders. Charcoal drawings are often sprayed with fixative to prevent them from smudging.

**Crayon**: In the seventeenth and eighteenth centuries the term was used to describe both *chalk* and *pastel* drawings and seems generally to have denoted the use of colour. By the late eighteenth and early nineteenth centuries, modern wood-encased crayons began to be developed. Modern crayons are made from colours combined with oily, waxy or greasy binding media, or with combinations of water-soluble and fatty binders.

**Drypoint**: A member of the class of prints known as intaglio (whereby the paper receives the ink from the incised lines and not from the surface of the plate). In drypoint, the line is scratched directly into the plate with a metal point, which is pulled across the surface and not pushed as in an *engraving*. The metal residue displaced from the scratched line and thrown up on either side is called the 'burr'. The line has a rich, velvety texture when inked but the burr is fragile and wears away with each impression. Drypoint is often used in combination with other techniques, especially *etching*.

**Engraving**: A term sometimes used of all intaglio prints (see *drypoint*) but more appropriately used to define those made with a tool called a 'graver' or 'burin', a small metal rod with a sharpened point. It is pushed across the plate, rather than pulled as in *drypoint*. An engraving can generally be distinguished from an *etching* by the ends of the lines: these taper into a point in engravings but are blunt and rounded in an etching.

**Etching**: A type of intaglio print (see *drypoint*) in which the lines are bitten by acid into a metal plate. The plate is first covered with a thin layer of ground, composed of waxes, gums and resins. The plate is then drawn on using a metal point, which exposes the metal. It is then immersed in a bath of acid, which bites into the plate through the exposed lines. The depth of the line, and therefore its darkness when printed, is determined by the length of time the plate is immersed. An etched line, being drawn and bitten unevenly by acid, is slightly irregular, in contrast to an engraved line, which being cut is sharp and clean.

**Gouache**: Lead white mixed with *watercolour* pigment to make it opaque. Lead white has a propensity to discolour (it blackens on exposure to hydrogen sulphide), and was gradually replaced by the more stable zinc white or 'Chinese White' manufactured by Windsor and Newton in 1834. A watercolour can be painted entirely in gouache, or the use of gouache can be restricted to highlights, especially in white. The term 'bodycolour', instead of gouache, can also be used.

**Gum arabic**: A vegetable gum derived from the acacia tree and used in the manufacture of watercolours. Its chief value is in assisting the paint in adhering to the paper. In the Victorian period, extra gum arabic was applied on top of areas of *watercolour*. When dry, the gum became a transparent film, causing a darker tone and richer effect.

**Heightening**: A term describing the addition of highlights by adding white *gouache* or white *chalk*.

**Lithograph**: A type of print based on the principle that grease and water repel one another. A suitable surface (usually stone or zinc) is drawn on in a greasy medium. It is then dampened with water which only settles on the unmarked areas. The surface is then rolled over with greasy printing ink, which only adheres to the drawn marks, the water repelling it from the rest of the surface.

**Mezzotint**: A form of tonal *engraving*, in which unlike line engraving the artist works from dark to light. The plate is ground all over using a toothed, chisel-like tool known as a 'rocker', which creates a dense mesh of small burred dots. If inked at this stage the plate would print a deep velvety black. The artist scrapes away at the burred dots in proportion to the lightness of tone required.

**Paper**: All paper is made from cellulose fibre, which is derived from plants. Until the nineteenth century the only source of fibre for paper was cotton and linen rags. Hand-made paper is made in a mould with a fine wire grid as its base. The mould is dipped into liquid pulp, and then removed for drying. Until c. 1750 all paper produced in Europe was laid paper, which shows the chain pattern impressed by the mould's wire grid. By the end of the eighteenth century, watercolourists preferred the smooth surface of wove paper, produced by using a wire mesh woven like a piece of fabric. Handmade wove papers included those made by the manufacturers Whatman and Creswick.

**Pastel**: See *chalk*

**Pencil**: Made of graphite, a crystalline form of carbon. A graphite pencil leaves a shiny deposit on the *paper*, while the appearance of black *chalk* is duller in tone.

**Pen and ink**: Ink could be diluted and used as a wash. It could be used on its own, or as reinforcement to a finished *watercolour*. It could be applied with a brush, a reed or quill pen. A reed pen was made from fine canes or bamboo-like grasses. The quill pen was usually cut from goose or swan feathers which were hardened by being placed in hot sand before being cut as quills. Carbon ink was generally made from soot dissolved in water, often with a binder such as *gum arabic*. Indian ink was a waterproof form of carbon ink in which a type of resin had been dissolved. Bistre was a brown ink made by extracting soluble tars from wood soot. Sepia was made from an extraction of the cuttle-fish, although the term is also used to refer to dark brown ink in general.

**Pentimenti**: From the Italian meaning alteration. This term is used to describe visible corrections made by the artist in the course of their work

**Photogravure**: A photomechanical process of reproducing an image; it combines photography and *etching*. The gelatine in the photographic negative of the image functions as the acid resist when the image is etched. There are two types of photogravure. Hand photogravure, popular in the late nineteenth century, entails the photographic transfer of the image to a copper plate, prepared with aquatint to provide tone, into which the design is etched. Machine photogravure is a commercial process which uses a cylinder rather than the plate; a cross-line screen is used instead of aquatint to provide tone.

**Remarque proof**: Sketch made by the artist on the margin of an etched plate, often unrelated to the main composition. In the seventeenth century, the practice was begun as a way of testing the strength of etching acid on a plate; in the nineteenth century 'remarque proofs', in which the remarque served no purpose at all, were specially created as collectible rarities.

**Scratching out**: A method of creating a highlight by removing an area of *watercolour* with a knife, the end of a brush or even a fingernail, to expose the paper beneath.

**Sfumato**: The use of general gradations of tone to create form. The term is used in relation to oil paintings and drawings. The word comes from the Italian *fumo* meaning smoke; sfumato describes the blending of tones as if seen through smoke.

**Silverpoint**: This technique was commonly used in Italy in the fifteenth and early sixteenth centuries, but briefly revived in the late nineteenth century. An instrument with a point of silver (or another metal such as gold) was used for drawing on a prepared paper. The silver point reacted chemically with the ground on the paper, producing a line.

**Stipple**: The production of tiny spots of *watercolour* using the point of a fine brush.

**Stopping out**: A means of preserving a highlight by masking a selected area of *watercolour* pigment with an agent such as *gum arabic*, in order to stop that area being hidden by subsequent layers of *wash*.

**Vignette**: A small, decorative engraving or design, mainly used in book illustration. Its chief feature is that it has no defined border and thus appears to emerge from the page.

**Wash**: An application of colour (*watercolour* or ink) over a larger field than can be easily covered by the brush with one stroke. A wash must be continued while the colour is still wet and show no joins. Washes can also be run into one another when still wet, often described as 'wet-on-wet' working.

**Watercolour**: A finely ground pigment combined with a water-soluble binding agent, usually *gum arabic*. Water is used to spread and dilute the colour, and it subsequently evaporates. The gum arabic binds the pigment to the surface of the support, which is most commonly *paper*. The brilliancy of pure watercolour derives from the white of the paper showing through the transparent pigment. As the watercolour painting has its technical origins in the 'tinted' or 'stained' drawing, it is sometimes called a water drawing, and therefore the terms 'watercolour' and 'drawing' are sometimes used interchangeably.

**Watermark**: Devices used by paper manufacturers, the earliest being found in Italian paper of the late thirteenth century. The device is made of wire and sewn onto the mould; it leaves an impression on the paper by making it thinner and thus more translucent. Watermarks can be seen most easily when the sheet is viewed with light behind it.

## Introduction: Lever as a collector of British watercolours and drawings

The majority of the 334 British watercolours and drawings included in this catalogue were collected by the wealthy industrialist, philanthropist and social reformer William Hesketh Lever (1851–1925), later 1st Viscount Leverhulme, between 1896 and his death.[1] Lever, the son of a Bolton wholesale grocer, was a partner in the family business Lever & Co. by the age of 21. By 1888 his own firm, Lever Brothers, under his stewardship, was producing soap on a large scale from its factory in Port Sunlight, Merseyside.[2] At this point the company had expanded rapidly and Lever was an extremely successful businessman who was on his way to becoming the leading soap manufacturer in Britain. At the time of his death, despite some fluctuations in its financial position, Lever Brothers was one of the largest international companies in the world and Lever, as its only ordinary shareholder, was an enormously rich man.

Lever first started buying contemporary British oil paintings in the second half of the 1880s for Lever Brothers to use as soap advertisements, but it was not until the 1890s that he began to assemble a significant art collection for his home, Thornton Manor on Wirral, into which he had moved in 1888. He ultimately amassed an art collection that included outstanding groups of English furniture, Chinese porcelain, Wedgwood pottery, classical and contemporary sculpture as well as eighteenth- and nineteenth-century British painting and nineteenth-century watercolours and drawings. Lever gave the best pieces from this collection to the Lady Lever Art Gallery in the model village of Port Sunlight, a custom-designed building whose commission reflected Lever's strongly held beliefs in the moral and educational value of art and which opened to the public in 1922.[3]

The British watercolours and drawings in the Lady Lever Art Gallery are a chronologically and qualitatively diverse group, spanning the late eighteenth to the early twentieth centuries, although the most numerous and best examples are concentrated in the nineteenth century. They have until now received little attention as a distinct group, with their history absorbed within more general discussions of the development of Lever's Victorian and eighteenth-century painting collections.[4] To a large degree, the picture of Lever as a collector that emerges from examining his acquisitions of watercolours and drawings follows that which can be seen from a study of his collections as a whole. It is an image of a Northern industrialist collector, generally old-fashioned in his tastes, whose essentially business-like but amateurish and decorative-led approach to collecting led to an eclectic mix of works in both type and quality.[5] Additionally, the amount of money that he was prepared to spend follows a broadly upward trajectory, in line with the progress of his business career and his increasing wealth. In terms of its content, the watercolours and drawings collection also follows the more general development of Lever's taste, first in the late 1890s in contemporary, if well-established, Victorian painting and then later, largely as a result of the influence of the amateur collector, dealer and watercolourist James Orrock (1829–1913), in earlier British art.

1 For information on Lever, see 2nd Viscount Leverhulme, *Viscount Leverhulme: By His Son* (London, 1927). For details of his collecting and building ventures, see Edward Morris (ed.), *Lord Leverhulme: Founder of the Lady Lever Art Gallery and Port Sunlight on Merseyside: A Great Edwardian Collector and Builder* (exh. cat., London, Royal Academy, 1980) and Edward Morris, 'Art and Business in Edwardian England: The Making of the Lady Lever Art Gallery', *Journal of the History of Collections*, vol. 4, no. 2 (1992).

2 For Lever and Lever Brothers, see Charles Wilson, *The History of Unilever* (Cambridge, 3 vols, 1954–68), especially vol. I.

3 For details of Port Sunlight village and the building of the Lady Lever Art Gallery, see Edward Hubbard and Michael Shippobottom, 'Architecture', in Morris (ed.), *Lord Leverhulme*, particularly pp. 150–75. See also Shippobottom, 'The Building of the Lady Lever Art Gallery', *Journal of the History of Collections*, vol. 4, no. 2 (1992), pp. 175–93. For Lever's views on art, see his speech at the opening of the Lady Lever Art Gallery, quoted in Leverhulme, *Viscount Leverhulme*, p. 288.

4 See especially Edward Morris, 'Paintings and Sculpture', in Morris (ed.), *Lord Leverhulme*, pp. 13–37. On Lever's Victorian paintings, see Edward Morris, *Victorian and Edwardian Paintings in the Lady Lever Art Gallery* (London, 1994), pp. xiii–xx. On Lever's collection of eighteenth-century painting, see Alex Kidson, 'Lever and the Collecting of Eighteenth-century British Paintings', *Journal of the History of Collections*, vol. 4, no. 2 (1992), pp. 201–09 and Kidson, *Earlier British Paintings in the Lady Lever Art Gallery* (Liverpool, 1999), pp. 11–14.

5 For the characteristics of Lever as a collector, see Edward Morris's introduction in the *Journal of the History of Collections*, vol. 4, no. 2 (1992), pp. 169–73.

Although the majority of works included in the current catalogue were among those that Lever transferred to the Gallery in 1922, they do not represent the sum of his collecting in this area. While the finest examples may have been given to the Gallery,[6] Lever collected at least several thousand watercolours and drawings that were hung in his private homes and businesses;[7] around 600 works not placed in the Gallery were sold by the executors of his estate in sales during 1925–26, immediately after his death (see Appendices 2–3). Others, the exact number of which is unknown, remained in the possession of his son, the 2nd Viscount Leverhulme (1888–1949), and his descendants (see Appendix 9). A further sizeable group of just over 100 works belonging to the Gallery were sold by the Trustees between 1958 and 1961 with the intention of raising further funds for the Lady Lever Art Gallery (see Appendices 4–8).[8] In order to gain an understanding of the nuances of Lever's taste, it is important to consider the contents of these sales alongside the present Gallery collection. These sales do in broad terms reflect the emphasis of the current collection on watercolourists favoured by Orrock as well as High and later Victorian drawings and watercolours; only a tiny proportion of material is by artists following an eighteenth-century tradition.[9] However, the sales are significantly more revealing than the present collection when it comes to exploring Lever's earliest forays into collecting watercolours and drawings.

Lever's earliest interest in watercolours and drawings as decorative furnishings emerges most dramatically, not from the present group, but by looking at the works sold off from Lever's homes between 1925 and 1926. Some of Lever's earliest purchases, before around 1893 when he started to assemble a significant private collection of paintings, were cheap, illustrative drawings and watercolours, often of a literary and comic nature.[10] The 1925–26 sales included four works by Hablot Knight Browne (1815–82), two of which were illustrations to Dickens, one of Lever's favourite authors; five drawings by Harry Furniss (1854–1925), three of which were sketches of Lever's political hero, William Ewart Gladstone (these were among 16 drawings of Gladstone by a variety of artists hung in the Picture Gallery at Thornton Manor); 39 works by George Cruikshank (1792–1872), including at least eight illustrations to Shakespeare, Lever's other favourite author;[11] 18 items in total by the cartoonists John Leech (1817–64), Phil May (1864–1903) and Linley Sambourne (1844–1910) as well as 26 works by the cartoonist and journalist Francis Carruthers Gould (1844–1925). These sales also contained 14 watercolours by the caricaturist Thomas Rowlandson (1756–1827), with such titles as *The Village Alehouse* and *Flirtation* suggesting their humorous tone. Many of these works were hung at Thornton Manor between 1897 and 1902 alongside prints

6 This is the opinion of Lever's son; see Leverhulme, *Viscount Leverhulme*, p. 285.

7 The exact number is difficult to determine as the WHL Inventory does not list the media for all works; this estimate is based on those works listed as a watercolour or drawing in this inventory, which includes 1,000 watercolours by Orrock alone. Lever owned a total of twelve houses between his marriage in 1874 and his death in 1925 but his art collection was housed principally at Thornton Manor, Wirral, and The Hill, London.

8 W. G. Constable is reported to have advised the Trustees on these 1958–61 sales, which were seen as a means of getting rid of 'forgeries, imitations or works by minor artists' (Morris, 'Paintings and Sculpture', p. 24). Other factors were also considered; for example, a substantial number of drawings and watercolours by Burne-Jones were sold, no doubt because that artist was deemed to be sufficiently represented in that medium by the works that would remain.

9 I have used the phrase 'eighteenth-century tradition' to include a few works that date from after 1800 but that can be described as eighteenth-century in style and intention. Only around 5 per cent of the present collection conforms to this description. These include works collected by Lever by or attributed to the following artists: Richard Cosway, John Robert Cozens, Thomas Girtin, William Hamilton, Ozias Humphry, Julius Caesar Ibbetson, John Jackson, Joshua Reynolds, George Romney, Thomas Rowlandson, Paul Sandby, Samuel Shelley, J. M. W. Turner and Francis Wheatley. A further five watercolours were added by the Trustees, one each by John White Abbott, Francis Towne and Paul Sandby, and two by John 'Warwick' Smith. The 1925–26 sales do contain a number of works by a wider variety of eighteenth-century artists. These include a drawing by Alexander Cozens, seven drawings and watercolours by John Downman, four drawings by Thomas Gainsborough, a gouache by Daniel Gardner, two drawings by George Morland and one drawing by Richard Wilson. This eighteenth-century material represents a similar proportion to that which remains in the existing collection.

10 In 1893 Lever bought Frederic Leighton's oil painting *Psamathe* (LL 3630), which seems to have been his first major purchase (see Morris, *Victorian and Edwardian Paintings*, pp. xv and 68). The earliest surviving TM Inventory 1897–1902 does not give values for these items. However, in the TM Inventory for 1907, the majority are valued at £5 or £10, and rarely exceed this latter figure.

11 Lever's son described his father's love of Shakespeare and Dickens 'above all other authors' (Leverhulme, *Viscount Leverhulme*, p. 273).

and watercolours, the latter mostly by minor late Victorian artists.[12] All these items may have been bought as early as the 1880s.[13] This type of work was mostly considered unsuitable for the Lady Lever Art Gallery, and in the existing collection only a handful of purchases made at a later date of some of the same artists, such as Gould's *Sir Isumbras at the Ford* (LL 3856) and Rowlandson's *The Social Day* (LL 3989), hint at Lever's early interests. It was not until the second half of the 1890s that Lever began to develop a taste for more significant watercolour and drawing purchases. Up until that point the low cost of these items was the overwhelming factor in determining Lever's acquisitions to decorate his home, although his personal interest in the literature of Dickens and the politics of Gladstone, for example, explains some of the choices made within a certain price bracket.

Lever's earliest recorded important acquisitions of British drawings and watercolours were in 1896.[14] Lever had started to collect major paintings by contemporary, if well-established, Victorian artists such as Frederic Leighton, John Everett Millais and Edward Burne-Jones around 1893; his watercolour and drawing acquisitions a few years later reflect this burgeoning interest. In 1896 his purchases included a magnificent chalk head study by Burne-Jones, entitled *Study for West Wind* (LL 3788) costing £36 15s and a beautifully crafted, highly finished watercolour by Helen Allingham, *Old Cottage, Pinner* (LL 3654) bought for £53 11s.[15] These two examples demonstrate, in line with his purchases of Victorian paintings, Lever's cautious conservatism in what he bought: Burne-Jones was considered quite old-fashioned by the mid-1890s, and Allingham, although at the peak of her career, was firmly entrenched in the artistic establishment having been made the first full woman member of the Society of Painters in Water-Colours in 1890. Although the 1896 purchases reflect Lever's growing acquisition of Victorian oils, it was precisely these paintings, along with an increasing interest in earlier British painting, which took precedence among Lever's purchases at this stage. By contrast, Lever's collecting of watercolours and drawings was underdeveloped at this period.

If they are unusual in some respects, these two purchases from 1896 do demonstrate more general trends in Lever's collecting practice. Both works were bought through London dealers; the Burne-Jones directly from the Fine Art Society, and the Allingham by commissioning F. W. Fox at Agnew's to bid on his behalf at auction. Both these methods of acquisition were favoured by Lever throughout his life, although from 1904 onwards he tended to buy mostly at auction. He rarely seems to have bought an item without seeing it, or at least its photograph, beforehand and he would often visit the sale room prior to the auction making notes against the lots in the catalogue.[16] He seldom purchased works direct from artists themselves unless they were his friends, citing the fact that they would inflate their prices once they recognised his name[17] but it may also have been out of a curious shyness.[18] The 1896 campaign also demonstrated Lever's increasing tendency, particularly after the purchase of his first London home in 1893,[19] to buy in London rather than from the provincial dealers from whom he had bought in earlier years.

12 TM Inventory 1897–1902, LLAG files.

13 Lever did not move into Thornton Manor until 1888 but his son described him buying etchings and a few modern watercolours during the 1880s. Thornton Manor provided Lever with the 'wall space for larger pictures' (Leverhulme, *Viscount Leverhulme*, pp. 277–78).

14 The earliest invoices have been found from this date (LLAG files). Although not all invoices survived, looking at the earliest inventory of works at Thornton Manor, 1897–1902, suggests that no other significant purchases were likely to have been made before this date.

15 This information derives from invoices in the LLAG files.

16 Leverhulme, *Viscount Leverhulme*, p. 279.

17 See Morris, 'Paintings and Sculpture', p. 34.

18 This is the opinion of Morris, 'Paintings and Sculpture', p. 34.

19 Lever's first London address was 10 Norfolk Street.

Lever began to acquire important earlier British watercolours and drawings on a larger scale during the period 1904–13. The most significant influence on the character of Lever's collection during this period was his friendship with James Orrock, whom Lever had met by the mid-1890s.[20] Orrock was born in Edinburgh, where he studied dentistry, practising in Nottingham before moving permanently to London in 1866 to pursue his artistic interests.[21] Once established in London, Orrock began collecting on a considerable scale, concentrating on the so-called classic age of British painting and watercolours, a tradition beginning in the early 1750s with Richard Wilson and Joshua Reynolds and ending in 1851 with the death of J. M. W. Turner. Within this school of British art, Orrock especially favoured landscapes and watercolours, viewing both as particularly indigenous to the United Kingdom. As a watercolourist himself and a member of the Institute of Painters in Water-Colours from 1875, Orrock campaigned tirelessly to protect and encourage the art of watercolour, a practice particularly close to his heart.[22] Orrock's intention to establish the primacy of the British school and his championing of the campaign, between 1870 and 1890, to create a gallery of British art were to have an important influence on Lever in his creation of the Lady Lever Art Gallery, where one of his prime objectives was to show that 'English Art throughout the centuries had not been second to the art of any nation in the world'.[23]

Lever's purchases from Orrock dominated the period 1904–13. It was during these years that Lever Brothers suffered from financial difficulties and Lever spent relatively little on works of art;[24] but he bought Orrock's entire house collection (including pictures, furniture and porcelain) on three occasions for what seemed to him to be 'bargain' prices. The first time was in 1904 for £45,000, which coincided with Lever's purchase of a new London home, The Hill, Hampstead, earlier the same year; the fact that Lever had been offered the collection at several earlier points for £100,000 strongly suggests that the timing of the purchase was linked to Lever's intention to find pictures for his new home as well as pointing to Lever's commercial acumen in holding out for a lower price.[25] Two subsequent purchases *en bloc* were made in 1910 for £43,000, which coincided with Lever's plans to open Hulme Hall in Port Sunlight as an art gallery and museum, and in 1912 for £15,000, perhaps as Lever's plans for a larger art gallery had started to form. Lever's purchasing from Orrock during this period was significant, leading to the exclusion, in the case of watercolours and drawings, of purchases from any other dealer. It was not until late in 1913, after Orrock's death in May, that Lever purchased a handful of minor works from two other London dealers, B. T. Batsford and Nicholl's.[26]

In total Lever purchased 1,240 watercolours from Orrock, of which 1,000 were watercolours and drawings by the dealer himself. Only 87 of these Orrock purchases survive

---

20 Lever's first recorded purchases from Orrock were in 1896 when he bought some satinwood furniture as well as several paintings by William Etty and Thomas Lawrence. Alex Kidson has suggested that the tone of the correspondence at this time suggests that the men were already 'more than polite acquaintances' (see Kidson, *Earlier British Paintings*, pp. 11–12). A letter from 25 June 1896 between Orrock and Lever is quoted in Lucy Wood, *The Lady Lever Art Gallery Catalogue of Commodes* (London, 1994), p. 36, n. 188.

21 See Christopher Beetles, 'Orrock, James (1829–1913)', *ODNB*, vol. 41, pp. 968–99. See also Byron Webber, *James Orrock, R.I.: Painter, Connoisseur, Collector* (London, 2 vols, 1903). This is a hagiographical account which Edward Morris has suggested may have been paid for by Orrock himself (Morris, verbally June 2008). For the most recent writing on Orrock and all his activities, see Edward Morris, 'James Orrock, dentist, artist, patron, collector, dealer, curator, connoisseur, forger, propagandist', *Visual Culture in Britain*, vol. 6, no. 2 (2005), pp. 85–98.

22 Orrock played an important part in the great debate of 1886–87 on the durability of watercolours. See Morris, 'James Orrock', p. 91 for details.

23 Leverhulme, *Viscount Leverhulme*, p. 288. Lucy Wood has pointed out that Orrock 'generally spoke specifically of the importance of English art (despite his own Scottish origins) ... although when proposing the creation of a gallery of native art talked in terms of British art as a whole' (*Catalogue of Commodes*, p. 33, n. 172).

24 See Wilson, *History of Unilever*, vol. I, pp. 115–210.

25 Lever relates this offer in a letter to the dealer F. W. Fox, 8 June 1904, LLAG files.

26 Lever purchased architectural illustrations by John Gendall (LL 3885) and Charles James Richardson (LL 3879–3880) and two views of Chester by George Shepherd (LL 3889 and LL 3993) from B. T. Batsford. He also bought a political cartoon based on Millais's painting of *Sir Isumbras at the Ford* by Gould (LL 3856) from Nicholl's. Lever's relationship with Batsford was the more developed. He later bought the majority of his collection of Old Master drawings from Batsford. These came either through the Earl of Pembroke's collection (sold at Sotheby's, July 1917) or through the artist Edward John Poynter (his sale, Sotheby's, April 1918). See Edward Morris and Mark Evans, *Lady Lever Art Gallery: Port Sunlight: Catalogue of Foreign Paintings, Drawings, Miniatures, Tapestries, Post-Classical Sculpture and Prints* (Liverpool, 1983), pp. 27–56.

in the Lady Lever Art Gallery, including five of Orrock's own watercolours: most of the remainder were sold by Lever's executors soon after his death and others in the 1958–61 sales. However, the watercolours that do survive give a general flavour of the characteristics of Orrock's collection. He was not particularly interested in eighteenth-century watercolourists, and his collection showed a preference for the nineteenth-century watercolour school. In particular, the present collection reveals Orrock's championing of what he called 'the four pillars of the English Watercolour Art':[27] J. M. W. Turner (seven works), David Cox (17 works), Peter DeWint (15 works) and George Barret Junior (five works).[28] There are also nine watercolours originally attributed to William Henry Hunt who was described by Orrock as a 'prentice pillar'.[29] Orrock also collected a large number of works by Thomas Collier, one of a later generation of watercolourists whose style was influenced by Cox; five works by this artist from Orrock's collection survive in the Lady Lever Art Gallery. The works by Orrock's favourite watercolour specialists correspond to over a fifth of the present collection, an indication of the great extent (despite considerable losses) to which the dealer's influence and concern to promote particular artists still permeates the Lady Lever Art Gallery's collection.

Lever made some important and valuable watercolour purchases from Orrock, especially in the 1904 sale, including DeWint's *View in Epping Forest* (LL 3800) as well as several significant Henry Hunt watercolours, *Young Salts* (LL 3972), *Thrush's nest and a basket of primroses* (LL 3859) and *Jim Crow* (LL 3974). He also purchased a group of Turner watercolours from this sale: *Minehead* (LL 3782), *Portsmouth* (LL 3783), *Lancaster from the Aqueduct* (LL 3774) and *Bolton Abbey* (LL 3777), which had formerly belonged to John Ruskin (1819–1900).[30] Despite these significant acquisitions, Orrock's collections included a substantial number of works, both paintings and watercolours, which were of poor quality and dubious authenticity, a fact noted by contemporaries. Charles Holmes, writing at the time of the 1904 sale, described the pictures as offering 'in a good many cases only a very general indication of authorship'.[31] Although many of these works were disposed of in both the 1925–26 and 1958–61 sales, a great number still remain in the collection. The following 13 watercolours in the collection bought in the 1910 sale (out of a total of 58 works) are now considered to be forgeries, imitations or copies: Cox (10 works, over half of the holdings by this artist), DeWint (one work), Anthony Vandyke Copley Fielding (one work), and Myles Birket Foster (one work). Therefore over a fifth of the acquisitions from the 1910 sale are not genuine; before works were sold by the Trustees the proportion was higher still. None of the admittedly smaller representation of watercolours from the 1912 sale (13 in total) has been proved to be anything other than genuine, which is in contrast to the number of non-autograph works deriving from this sale in the oils collection. Given the preponderance of watercolour fakes and copies in the 1910 sale, it seems unlikely that there were none in the 1912 sale, but this can only be speculative given that the works obtained in the latter sale and now sold off remain largely unidentified and unlocated.

The sizeable number of watercolours previously attributed to Cox in the 1910 sale provides an interesting example of Orrock's business dealings with Lever. The Lady Lever Art Gallery holds ten watercolours purchased from Orrock in 1910 as by Cox (see pp. 66–69) but that now appear to be forgeries, that is, works that attempt deliberately to deceive rather than just imitate. Although in several different hands, they all bear what purports to be

27 This phrase is quoted from Orrock's essays in *The Art Journal* in Webber, *James Orrock*, for example vol. I p. 106.
28 These numbers of works have been calculated according to the work's original attribution when it was purchased by Lever from Orrock.
29 Quoted from Orrock's fifth essay in *The Art Journal* in Webber, *James Orrock*, vol. I p. 147.
30 Like many of the works in the 1904 Orrock sale, most of these watercolours were bought in by two Norwich dealers, A. Smith and Boswell, on behalf of Orrock and then sold to Lever at a later date. See the individual entries on these works for details.
31 C. J. Holmes, 'Notes on Mr. Orrock's English Pictures', *The Burlington Magazine*, vol. 5 (July 1904), p. 414.

Cox's signature and are inscribed and dated in the 1840s. In common with numerous oil paintings of equally doubtful authenticity purchased by Lever in the 1910 sale, the source of these watercolours is obscure. Orrock may have produced some of these paintings himself or employed others to do so and accusations linking the dealer with forgery were made at the time.[32] Charles Nugent has recently argued that although the 'Cox' watercolours are not in Orrock's own style, the circumstantial evidence strongly suggests that the dealer had access to 'some sort of factory of anonymous artists' that was producing Cox fakes.[33] However he acquired these 'fakes', Orrock's *modus operandi* does appear to have been duplicitious, tending to disguise a rather large number of dubious works under cover of a couple of star items.[34] In this case the ten 'Cox' forgeries were acquired alongside a number of genuine Coxes and after Orrock had whetted Lever's appetite with Cox's late masterpiece, *Peace and War* (LL 3948), acquired in 1904.[35] For Lever's part, he seems to have been willing to be duped; even as late as 1916, after Orrock's death, he wrote echoing the dealer's philosophy that repetitions and plagiarisms could be an advantage if the copy was of a good original.[36] Perhaps Lever's continued dealings with Orrock reflected the genuine affection and trust he seems to have felt for the latter, whom he never treated in the same way as he did other dealers;[37] but that is to underestimate Lever as a shrewd businessman and it was more likely to have been a reflection of a strategy that he could understand, that of operating on a large scale and keeping the prices low, even if it was at the expense of some quality.

Orrock did not just impact upon the contents of Lever's collection. He was also an important factor in the way that Lever displayed his art works. Orrock arranged his late eighteenth-century home at 48 Bedford Square, London, in the way that he hoped the new 'National Gallery of British Art' would be organised, by mixing British pictures and furniture. In particular, as photographs of his home showing double or even triple hung works demonstrate (fig. i), Orrock appears to have displayed (rather than stored) many of his watercolours in frames without roller blinds and therefore at least partially exposed to light.[38] He had previously entered into the great debate on the permanence of watercolours in 1886–87 and believed that watercolours should generally be placed out of direct sunlight but were quite safe hanging on domestic walls, or in exhibitions. In contrast, many curators and scientists thought they should be kept in portfolios and cabinets.[39] Although we do not know if Lever was aware of Orrock's views on the durability of watercolours, he would presumably have witnessed his methods of display at first-hand through visiting his widely renowned Bedford Square house.[40] It is not surprising then that Lever, who shared Orrock's taste and commitment to raising the profile of British art, should have carried over the latter's approaches towards the display of watercolours in his own homes and subsequently in the Lady Lever Art Gallery. For example, a photograph of the Adam drawing-room at

fig. i. The front drawing room at James Orrock's home, 48 Bedford Square. The photograph shows Peter DeWint's *View in Epping Forest, near High Beech, Essex* (LL 3800) directly above the commode. Above the DeWint is George Cattermole's *Divine Service in the Baron's Chapel* which was sold from the Lady Lever Art Gallery in 1958. Photograph from Byron Webber, *James Orrock, R.I.: Painter, Connoisseur, Collector* (London, 2 vols, 1903), vol. I, facing p. 140.

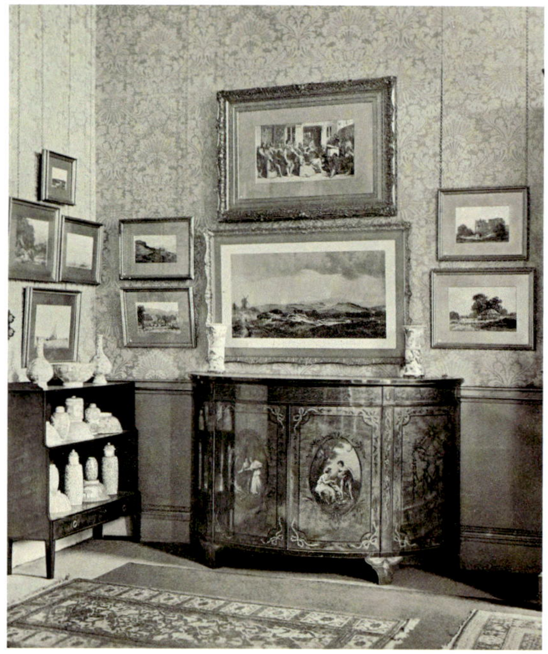

32 W. G. Rawlinson, the expert on Turner prints, allegedly found Orrock forging a Turner; quoted by C. J. Holmes, *Self and Partners* (London, 1936), pp. 207–08. See also the discussion in Morris, 'James Orrock', pp. 92–95. For the suggestion that Orrock had access to a 'studio' which produced at least Constable forgeries, see Charles Rhyne, 'Constable Drawings and Water-colours in the Collections of Mr. and Mrs. Paul Mellon and the Yale Center for British Art', *Master Drawings* (winter 1987), pp. 406–07.

33 This suggestion is made by Charles Nugent, 'David Cox Jr. and the Problem of Cox Forgeries', in Scott Wilcox (ed.), *Sun, Wind, and Rain: The Art of David Cox* (exh. cat., New Haven, Yale Center for British Art, and Birmingham, Birmingham Museums and Art Gallery, 2008–09), pp. 138–39.

34 Morris has described Orrock as imitating 'the rather unscrupulous greengrocer in hiding a considerable amount of bruised apples behind a few of impeccable quality' (Morris, 'Paintings and Sculpture', p. 25).

35 There is no surviving invoice for this work but its first listing in Lever's collection was in the 1904 Inventory.

36 Letter to F. W. Fox, 20 July 1916, about some pictures at Christie's, quoted in Morris, 'Paintings and Sculpture', p. 25.

37 See Morris, 'Paintings and Sculpture', p. 24.

38 This is also suggested by those surviving original frames on Orrock purchases in the Lady Lever Art Gallery, none of which is furnished with a roller-blind mechanism.

39 Morris, 'James Orrock', p. 91.

40 Orrock's collection at 48 Bedford Square was also widely illustrated in publications such as Walter Shaw Sparrow's 1904 *The British Home of Today*, Byron Webber's 1903 biography of Orrock as well as in long articles on the collection in *The Art Journal* of 1892 and *The Magazine of Art* of 1904.

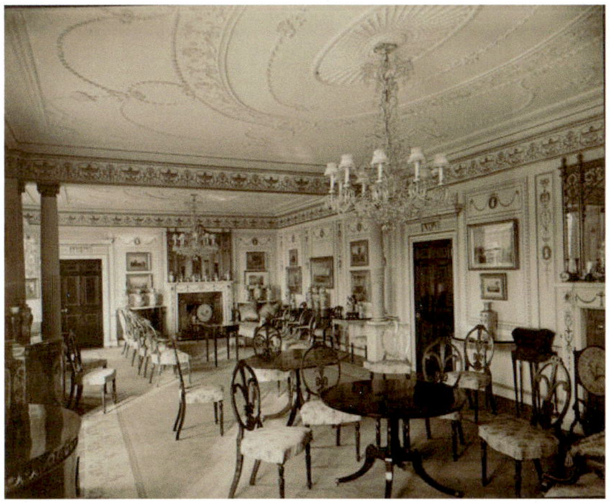

fig. ii. The Adam drawing room at The Hill, 1915. Photograph courtesy of Leverhulme Family Archive.

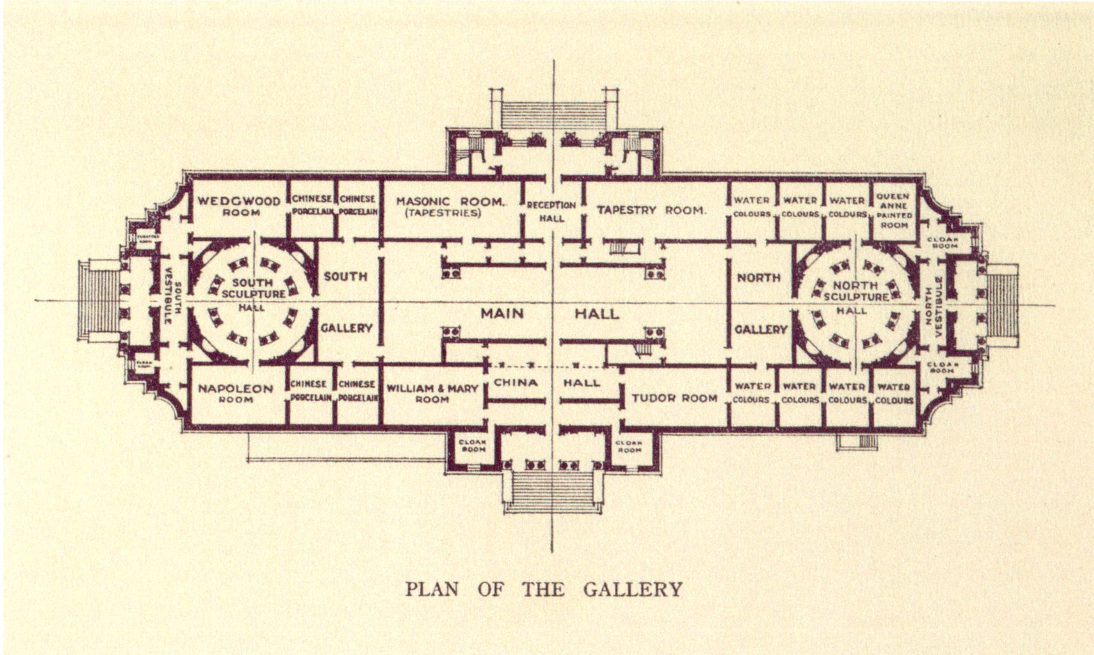


fig. iii. Plan of the Lady Lever Art Gallery from the brochure produced for the opening of the Gallery by HRH Princess Beatrice, 16 December 1922.

The Hill from 1915 showed Lever combining large numbers of framed watercolours with late eighteenth-century English furniture and inset medallions of Wedgwood jasperware (fig. ii). Although no photographs have been located which would illustrate the way in which Lever displayed watercolours in the Lady Lever Art Gallery, a number of facts are suggestive.[41] The allocation of seven 'watercolour' rooms as illustrated in the first guide to the Lady Lever published in 1922 (fig. iii), as well as the listing of particular works in this and later versions, reveals that large numbers were semi-permanently displayed. A guide to the collection dating from between 1929 and 1930 lists over 70 watercolours displayed in six rooms, with concentrations of works by Turner, DeWint, Cox and Hunt as well as works by Pre-Raphaelite artists and those closely linked to them.[42] The west gallery over the main hall contained *Lady Hamilton* by 'Romney' and drawings by Burne-Jones, as well as works by Cosway, Constable, Mulready and Landseer.[43] These works were probably displayed in frames for long periods of time, as attested by the fading of some of these watercolours. The same guide also describes the furniture and decorative art in each room and it seems likely that the same mixture of pictures and objects was in place when the gallery first opened in 1922.

Following Orrock's death in 1913, Lever never found an adviser whom he trusted in the same way. From 1915 until his own death in 1925, Lever's purchases were generally made on his behalf at auction by F. W. Fox, who had left Agnew's in 1903 to set up in partnership with Stephen Thomas Gooden. Lever relied increasingly on Fox's judgements, which were generally sound in that he knew whether an attribution was correct or not.[44] However, Fox lacked the ability as an adviser and perhaps the expertise that might have encouraged Lever

---

41 Lever was heavily involved in the details of the display of works of art within the Lady Lever Art Gallery and was known to have visited the building at least 23 times between February 1920 and its opening in December 1922. This figure is quoted in Shippobottom, 'Building of the Lady Lever Art Gallery', p. 184.

42 C. Reginald Grundy and Sydney L. Davison, *Illustrated Guide to the Lady Lever Collection*, published by the Trustees, undated (copy in LLAG files). The dating of this publication is based on its inclusion of the recently purchased painting *David Garrick in the Green Room*, then thought to be by William Hogarth but now attributed to Pietro Longhi, which was purchased in 1929. The absence of Johann Zoffany's painting *Robert Baddeley as Moses in 'The School for Scandal'*, purchased in December 1930, strongly suggests that the catalogue was produced before this latter date.

43 Grundy and Davison, *Illustrated Guide*, p. 35.

44 This is also true with regard to Lever's paintings collection (see Kidson, 'Lever and the Collecting of Eighteenth-Century British Paintings', pp. 203–04).

to move away from his established taste for mid- and later Victorian material and the canon of artists promoted by Orrock, the two lines of interest that he continued to pursue in these later years.[45]

Between 1915 and 1924 Lever continued to buy the work of mid- to later, well-established Victorian artists and, in a move that was reminiscent of his large bulk purchases from Orrock, he purchased over a hundred drawings by Burne-Jones in the artist's studio sale of 1919 (although many of these were sold in the 1925–26 sales). By this stage the building of the Lady Lever Art Gallery was well under way and it is clear that Lever was buying finished works of art of 'gallery quality' as well as broadening the range of his collection.[46] He made purchases that added to the late Victorian material, and included artists such as Simeon Solomon not already represented in the collection (he purchased Solomon's *Girl at a Fountain* [LL 3881] in 1917), as well as significant pictures by others who were, buying Dante Gabriel Rossetti's *Pandora* (LL 3647) in 1919 and Hubert Herkomer's *Alfred Tennyson* (LL 3793) in 1922. Lever also collected works by artists who had been favoured by Orrock, purchasing a handful of watercolours and drawings by Constable, and more works by Cox, DeWint and Turner. He also bought some late eighteenth-century material, in the form of Francis Wheatley and Rowlandson watercolours and a handful of Richard Cosway drawings, to redress Orrock's preference for nineteenth-century watercolours.

Despite these attempts to broaden both the existing representation of artists and the spread of their oeuvre, Lever's choices were not especially novel and were made within the existing parameters of his interests. His purchase of *The Death of Procris* (LL 3661) by George Owen Wynne Apperley in 1916 signals a rare moment of more progressive taste. Although the artist was well-established by this date, the symbolist qualities of the work were a new departure both for Apperley and for Lever; for the latter this purchase was akin to his patronage of the New Sculpture.[47] Despite this occasional glimpse of a more adventurous collector, Lever was essentially conservative in his choices, choosing to purchase artists who had a well-established reputation, both at exhibition and in the sale rooms, and whose work often had an excellent provenance. This also affected the type of work he chose by such artists. He can be contrasted in this respect to the collector Sir Hickman Beckett Bacon (1855–1945), who was acquiring British watercolours around the period 1895–1914.[48] Both Lever and Bacon bought watercolours by Turner. Lever was prepared to pay relatively high prices to acquire two watercolours by the artist with an exceptional provenance (they were from Ruskin's collection), paying £2,367 for *Dudley* (LL 3923) in 1919 and £2,583 for *Lucerne* (LL 3772) in 1924. However, Bacon was unusual for his time in buying late ethereal Turners, which only became fashionable (and their prices raised accordingly) with the advent of abstract painting in the 1940s and 1950s.[49]

From 1915 until his death Lever bought watercolours and drawings almost every year (he made no purchases in 1921 due to financial problems) but these were on a much smaller scale than the purchases *en bloc* made from Orrock during the period 1904–13. However, in

45 Fox was a Master of the Fine Art Trade Guild and a President of the Fine Art Provident Institution. Fox's partner, Gooden, died in 1909 and Morris has expressed the opinion that it may well have been Gooden who possessed the knowledge of late eighteenth- and early nineteenth-century British pictures (see Morris, 'Paintings and Sculpture', p. 34).

46 Lever asked the architects William & Segar Owen of Warrington to prepare plans for a new art gallery at Port Sunlight in June 1913. For more details of the commission see Shippobottom, 'Building of the Lady Lever Art Gallery', pp. 175–93.

47 For details of Lever's patronage of the New Sculpture, see Andrew Clay, Edward Morris, Sandra Penketh and Timothy Stevens, *British Sculpture in the Lady Lever Art Gallery* (Liverpool, 1999), pp. x–xxvi.

48 For an introduction and visual overview of Bacon's collection of watercolours, see Eric Shanes, *The Golden Age of Watercolours* (London, 2001), especially pp. 11–16.

49 Although it is almost impossible to tell what Bacon paid for particular items because the descriptions are so vague, in most cases it was less than £100 and in some cases £20. I am grateful to Tim Wilcox for kindly supplying me with this information and to Sir Nicholas Bacon for allowing me to publish it.

contrast to the 'bargain' bulk purchases made from Orrock, which sometimes resulted in the acquisition of dubious works, Lever spent significant sums to secure certain highly prized watercolours. In 1918, for example, he purchased Frederick Walker's *The Fishmonger's Shop* (LL 3444) from Christie's, a highly praised work from his rival Joseph Beecham's collection, for £1,076.[50] This was the largest amount he had yet spent on a watercolour, where the numbers of pounds were usually only in double figures, and rivalled the amount he spent on the much larger oil by the same artist, *The Bathers*, which Lever purchased in the same year for £2,265. Nevertheless, Lever, who always had an eye for a bargain, never gave Fox *carte-blanche* to bid above the odds for a picture and this watercolour was purchased well within the limit of £1,500 set by Lever.[51] In the same sale, Fox lost his bid for Walker's watercolour *Marlow Ferry*, where the limit was also set at £1,500 but the work sold for 1,600 guineas.[52] In the early 1920s, towards the end of his life, Lever was forced to hand over the day-to-day management of Lever Brothers as a result of some disastrous business ventures.[53] This gave him more time to focus on his art collecting and it was in these final years that he sourced some of his most significant and costly watercolour acquisitions, including Ford Madox Brown's *Cordelia's Portion* (LL 3640) (£609) and Turner's *Lucerne* (£2,583) both in 1924.

Lever's own assessment of the watercolours and drawings in his collection is difficult to fathom because he rarely made any personal comments on his art works in correspondence, or discussed what prompted him to opt for one object over another. An evaluation of the significance of this part of the collection for Lever in contrast to other aspects, such as earlier British painting, is only possible through examining his relative expenditure, as well as other indirect sources of evidence. He does not appear to have become interested in significant watercolour and drawing purchases until 1896, at least a couple of years later than Victorian and eighteenth-century British paintings, and even then the relative amounts of money he was prepared to spend were modest in comparison with his expenditure on oils. However, between 1904 and 1913, the relative spending on watercolours was akin to that spent on earlier British painting; in both cases, Lever's acquisitions in these areas were dominated by 'bargain' bulk buys from Orrock. Similarly, following Orrock's death, from 1915 onwards, these two aspects of the collection tell a similar story, with Lever prepared to spend significant sums of money, although always within limits, to secure works of exceptional pedigree. Other sources also reveal the extent to which Lever viewed the British drawings, and particularly watercolours, as an integral part of his collection and, later, his Gallery displays. Lever's son described the 'Old English watercolour school' as 'perhaps his [father's] favourite school of painting'.[54] Certainly Lever's allocation of seven rooms to watercolours in the Lady Lever Art Gallery, including a large representation of Orrock's favourite artists, suggests the degree to which he viewed this aspect of the collection as playing a crucial role in disseminating his and Orrock's vision of the superior position of British art within the European canon.

Following Lever's death in 1925 his son, the 2nd Viscount Leverhulme, and the Gallery's first curator Sydney Davison continued to make purchases on behalf of the Trustees.[55]

---

50 Bought at Christie's, 29 November 1918 (lot 89). For contemporary comments on this watercolour, see the entry in this catalogue.

51 Letter from F. W. Fox to Lever, 29 November 1918, LLAG files.

52 Ibid. Lever did give Fox the flexibility to give 10 per cent above the amount set in his limit. This is cited, for example, in a letter from Lever to Fox, 18 November 1918, LLAG files.

53 Wilson, *History of Unilever*, vol. I, pp. 253–66.

54 Leverhulme, *Viscount Leverhulme*, p. 279.

55 Sydney Davison was the Lady Lever Art Gallery's first curator; he was in post between 1922 and his retirement in 1957 (see *Museums Journal*, vol. 58, p. 265, quoted in a letter from Susan Nicholson, honorary archivist of the Bromborough Society, to Sarah Lynch, 21 July 2008, with Davison correspondence, LLAG files). Andrew Carlyle Tait was the first assistant curator. He worked for Lever at Hulme Hall Museum and Art Gallery from 1914 (an extract from his diary on 26 May 1939 refers to 'My twenty fifth anniversary of work at Port Sunlight', MS Diary, 1939, LLAG files). It is not known precisely at what date he transferred officially to the Lady Lever Art Gallery. He retired from the position of assistant curator in October 1946 (see *Museums Journal*, vol. 46, p. 175, quoted in letter from Susan Nicholson).

These items were bought sporadically between 1928, when the Trustees acquired 26 small pencil studies (LL 10301–10326) for Edward John Gregory's oil painting of *Boulter's Lock, Sunday Afternoon* (LL 3149), already in the collection, and the late 1940s by which time a further ten watercolours had been added.[56] In acquiring watercolours for the Lady Lever Art Gallery, the Trustees intended not only to broaden the existing collection but also to uphold Lever's aims, as moulded by Orrock, to represent the best of British art and craftsmanship.[57] To that end, they bought watercolours by artists who were not already represented. The tone of the correspondence between Leverhulme and Davison during this period reveals that the acquisition process was one of negotiation between the two men, with dealers making suggestions based on their clients' known preferences.[58] No significant art historical advice was sought by either and this surely explains the conservative although sound purchases made during these years. These included watercolours by the contemporary artists William Russell Flint (LL 3792) and Philip Wilson Steer (LL 3882) from the dealer Lockett Thomson, as well as historic watercolours by John White Abbott from Agnew's (LL 3926) and by Paul Sandby (LL 3992) and Francis Towne (LL 3769) from the Fine Art Society. These last three purchases made in the late 1940s were a valiant but limited attempt to fill the gaps left by Orrock's favouring of a particular canon of nineteenth-century artists.

Since at least 1978, when Merseyside County Council took over its running,[59] the Lady Lever Art Gallery has operated as a 'closed collection', making no new acquisitions to a group of works that largely represent the taste of one man. There are two exceptions to this rule. On occasion it has acquired works, either by gift or purchase, that were not included in the original gift to the Gallery and were retained by the Leverhulme family. In 1989, for example, the 3rd Viscount Leverhulme presented the Gallery with eight drawings (LL 3406–3407, LL 3431–3436) by the architectural draughtsman Thomas Raffles Davison that had not been considered appropriate for the original 1922 gift. Similarly, in 2001, following the death of the 3rd Viscount Leverhulme, the Gallery purchased Raffles Davison's portrait of the painter *Sir David Murray* (LL 10335) as well as George John Pinwell's *Study for 'A Seat in St James's Park'* (LL 10334). On rare occasions, the Lady Lever Art Gallery has acquired works that had previously been sold. The only instance of this in the watercolour collection is Apperley's *The Death of Procris*, which was sold in 1958 and purchased again in 1989 because it so clearly illuminates, in a way that the then current watercolour collection could not, a more progressive aspect to Lever's otherwise traditional taste. Notwithstanding these conservative tendencies, it was Lever's commitment to pursuing acquisitions of British watercolours and drawings that has left its mark on the existing rich and varied collection published here, in full, for the first time.[60]

56 The painting *Boulter's Lock, Sunday Afternoon* is illustrated in this catalogue, see p. 109.

57 See, for example, Sydney Davison, letter to the 2nd Viscount Leverhulme, 23 May 1939, where these intentions are formally stated (Purchases and Acquisitions, 1923–45, LLAG files).

58 See the correspondence between the 2nd Viscount Leverhulme and Sydney Davison (Purchases and Acquisitions, 1923–45, LLAG files).

59 In 1986 the Gallery was given 'national' status and became part of a group of eight museums collectively managed as National Museums and Galleries on Merseyside; from 2003 this has been known as National Museums Liverpool.

60 R. R. Tatlock's *English Painting of the XVIIIth to XXth Centuries with some examples of the Spanish, French and Dutch Schools, together with a collection of Historic and Modern Sculpture* (London, 1928) includes sections on the British watercolours and drawings but is limited in its scope. The catalogue does not contain works acquired after 1928, the entries are limited to a title, and sometimes a description of the work, and not all items are illustrated.

## JOHN WHITE ABBOTT

1764 Exeter–1851 Exeter

### Peamore

LL 3926 (LP 66)

Watercolour with pen and dark grey ink on five sheets of wove paper
38.8 x 53.6 cm (sight); two larger sheets joined horizontally 23.2 cm from lower edge, respectively 23.2 x 37.3 cm (bottom) and 15.4 x 37.3 cm (top), joined vertically to three smaller sheets right of centre, respectively 23.2 x 16.1 cm (bottom), 10.5 x 16.1 cm (middle), 5 x 16.1 cm (top)
Date: 1802

Inscr: JWA [monogram] 1802 (watercolour, bottom right); Sept 4 1802 (pencil, bottom left)

Prov: Fine Art Society, 1946; bt. by Agnew's 10 September 1946 (£52); bt. from Agnew's by the Trustees, 14 February 1947 (£56)

Exh: London, Agnew's, *74th Annual Exhibition of Water-colour Drawings*, 1947 (cat. 84)

John White Abbott was brought up in Exeter as part of the city's ruling class. His father died while he was still a child and his uncle James White (1744–1825), a lawyer interested in the arts, brought him up as his son and heir. Abbott practised as a surgeon and an apothecary but was also an accomplished amateur artist and one of the best pupils of Francis Towne (see pp. 181–82). He may have met Towne through his uncle, who was one of the artist's close friends. The exact period of Abbott's tuition from Towne is not certain, although teacher and pupil must have maintained close contact in the late 1780s as the watercolours from Towne's 1786 Lake District tour appear to have influenced Abbott's early drawing style.[1] Abbott painted consistently from before the 1790s until at least the 1840s, and when in 1825 he inherited his uncle's property of Fordland, near Exeter, he was able to dedicate himself exclusively to painting. Although he made tours in various parts of the country, including Scotland, the Lake District, Lancashire, Derbyshire and Warwickshire, the majority of his work was produced near his home town of Exeter. Abbott exhibited landscape oils at the Royal Academy on several occasions but he never sold a picture.

Although Abbott's formal training under Towne came to an end in the 1790s, the two artists remained friends and collaborated together well into the younger artist's adulthood.[2] Throughout their careers both Abbott and Towne went on sketching trips to Peamore, a small estate about three miles south of Exeter and within an hour's walking distance of the city. The estate was famous locally for the beauty of its hilly grounds which gave views of Exeter but both Abbott and Towne preferred the lower ground, with its dense woodlands near the lake and quarry. In 1792 the Revd John Swete described the estate: 'the chief Beauty of Peamore lies in the undulating form of its grounds, rising and falling in the regular alternation of hills and dales - in its woods, groves and trees - and in a Quarry, which surrounded by a thicket of high towering, Oaks, beech &c is one of the grandest and most romantic objects in the Country'.[3]

LL 3926 is one of a group of large and very intricate studies of woodlands made by Abbott between c. 1799 and 1810 on estates around Exeter, in particular at Peamore but also at Ugbrooke Park and Canonteign. There are other drawings by Abbott of Peamore in the Courtauld Institute of Art Gallery, London, the Fitzwilliam Museum, Cambridge (dated 1799) and the Royal Albert Memorial Museum, Exeter (dated 1803). Richard Stephens has pointed out that by contrast to the generalised depictions of his older mentor Towne, Abbott's early nineteenth-century woodland studies tended to be more focused on the structures of individual trees.[4] Towne's *Trees in Peamore Park* (dated 1804) in the Whitworth Art Gallery, Manchester, for example, is highly coloured and atmospheric, in contrast to the more linear approach of LL 3926.

Many of Abbott's drawings were made using multiple pieces of paper: for LL 3926 he used five sheets.[5] It is likely that the two largest sheets (the central portion of the drawing) were sketched on the spot, whereas the right third of the drawing, consisting of three small sheets of paper, was added later. Abbott would have used pencil for his sketches on the spot, adding the ink and wash later; in this case, the pen and ink lines do not all flow across the vertical join. The central portion of the work on its own acted as a nature study of three trees; by adding the right-hand sheets, with their detailed foreground and more generalised background, Abbott created a more conventional pictorial framework for the original study.[6]

1 1786 is the date of Abbott's earliest known drawing (auctioned in the 1970s). I am grateful to Richard Stephens for this information.

2 Abbott's 1791 sketching tour to Cumbria and Scotland has been identified by Richard Stephens as the period when he came of age artistically; email correspondence, August 2007.

3 M. Rowe and T. Gray (eds), *Travels in Georgian Devon: The Illustrated Journals of the Reverend John Swete (1789–1800)* (Exeter, 4 vols, 1997–2000), vol. I, p. 56.

4 Richard Stephens, email correspondence, September 2007.

5 Abbott was not the only artist to have used multiple pieces of paper for his works and while it may seem unusual now, it was not viewed as remarkable by contemporaries in an age where paper production was still in its infancy in Britain. Paul Oppé pointed to the fact that smaller sheets were easier to manipulate outdoors, and this practical reason may indeed be part of the explanation. A. P. Oppé, 'John White Abbott of Exeter (1763–1851)', *Walpole Society*, vol. 13 (1924–25), p. 77.

6 Richard Stephens, email correspondence, September 2007.

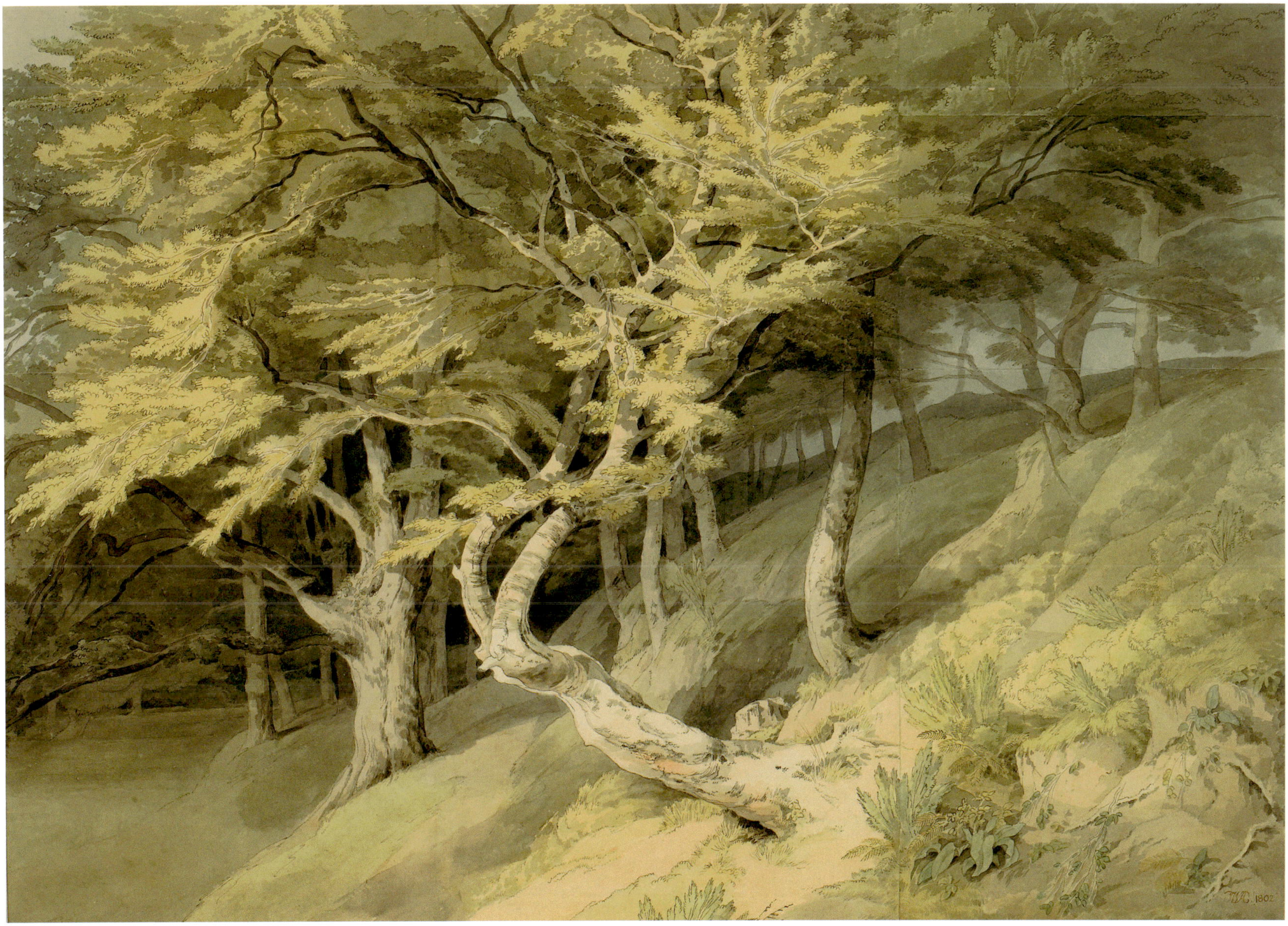

LL 3926

## HELEN ALLINGHAM

1848 Burton on Trent–1926 Haslemere, Surrey

### In Witley Village

LL 3655 (WHL 3159)

Watercolour, touched with gum arabic with scratching out and cutting out on wove paper
26.3 x 37.7 cm (sight)
Date: either 1884 or by spring 1885

Inscr: H Allingham (watercolour, bottom left)

Prov: Charles Churchill, Weybridge, 1903;[7] his sale, Christie's, 16 February 1917 (lot 3); bt. by Gooden and Fox for Lever (£32 15s)

Exh: London, Fine Art Society, *Surrey Cottages*, 1886 (cat. 22); Brisbane, Queensland Art Gallery and tour of Australia and New Zealand, organised by the Empire Art Loan Exhibitions Society, *Exhibition of British Watercolours 1850–1914*, 1952–53 (cat. 1)

Lit: H. Allingham and M. B. Huish, *Happy England* (London, 1903), pp. 77–78

Helen Allingham (née Paterson) studied at the Birmingham School of Design and from 1867 at the Royal Academy Schools. She began working as a commercial artist, producing illustrations for *The Graphic* and *Cornhill* magazines. In 1874, following her marriage to the Irish poet William Allingham, she abandoned black-and-white illustration (possibly as a result of her new-found financial security) and chose to concentrate on watercolours of the English countryside. In 1875 she was elected an associate of the SPWC, becoming their first full woman member in 1890 once the prohibition on women joining was withdrawn; she was a regular exhibitor there and at the Fine Art Society following her first one-woman show there in 1886.

In 1881 the Allingham family moved to the village of Witley, Surrey. It was here that the artist developed her trademark cottage scenes. The Allinghams and their Surrey social circle, which included the poet Alfred Tennyson and the garden designer and writer Gertrude Jekyll, shared an interest in preserving the countryside, in particular its vernacular architecture. In the last quarter of the nineteenth century, following the effects of agricultural depression and a consequent rural exodus, these cottages (and the unspoilt, idyllic version of rural life they represented) were seen to be increasingly under threat from demolition and abandonment. A back-to-the-land movement grew up among middle- and upper-class urban dwellers, some of whom, like the Allinghams, moved into these cottages; others bought the artist's watercolours (as the dramatically successful sales of her subjects at exhibition testify). Helen Allingham is known to have worked outdoors, sketching the cottages, including those that had been condemned to demolition.

The Lady Lever work was one of the watercolours of particular cottages that Allingham exhibited in her solo show, appropriately named *Surrey Cottages*, at the Fine Art Society in 1886. The catalogue suggested a date for the watercolour of 1884, and certainly the work would have been completed before the spring of 1885 when the cottage was demolished by its owner and replaced by a more modern dwelling.[8] The watercolour is typical of Allingham's subject-matter at this period in depicting a cottage and its male dweller returning home carrying a load of ripe bracken; a small girl holds open the gate of the property, and a female figure, possibly her mother, waits in a doorway behind. Although it is an accurate depiction of the cottage, it is also an idealised image of rural plenitude and blissful family life in the tradition of Allingham's mentor and friend Myles Birket Foster (see pp. 98–99). Allingham's vision was shored up by the marketing approach taken by her dealers, the Fine Art Society, whose managing director, Marcus Huish, published a book on the artist in 1903 entitled *Happy England*. Her wistful vision of an endangered rural life, combined with a largely Pre-Raphaelite attention to detail, was echoed in his comments on LL 3665. He wrote that it showed: 'a loving fidelity to nature, as if the artist … was looking upon the likeness of an old friend for the last time, and wished to perpetuate every lineament and feature'.[9]

7 LL 3655 was recorded in Churchill's collection in H. Allingham and M. B. Huish, *Happy England* (London, 1903), p. 77.

8 Ibid., pp. 77–78.

9 Ibid., p. 78.

### Old Cottage, Pinner

LL 3654 (WHL 1497, TM 78)

Watercolour, touched with gum arabic with scratching out and cutting out on wove paper
28.6 x 38.5 cm (sight)
Date: early 1890s

Inscr: H Allingham (watercolour, bottom right)

Prov: William Barlow, 1894; Christie's, 27 March 1896 (lot 76); bt. by Agnew's for Lever (£53 11s) as *3 Old Cottages Pinner*[10]

In 1888, due to the declining health of her husband William, Helen Allingham and her family returned from Surrey to London where they set up home in Hampstead. William Allingham died in 1889, leaving his wife with little money and three children to support. She continued to produce large numbers of watercolours; in 1889 she exhibited 79 paintings in a solo show at the Fine Art Society entitled *On the Surrey Border* and her output remained high in the following years. Having a young family to look after, Allingham made painting excursions close to home, taking trips to Pinner and Amersham (places within a short railway journey from London) in the early 1890s with her friend the artist Kate Greenaway (see pp. 104–107).

LL 3654 is one of many watercolours which Allingham painted of Pinner cottages, and dates from the early 1890s. It is also one of a number of images (the others now in private collections) that she painted of this particular cottage, which has since been demolished.[11] A number of works with similar titles, one of which may be this watercolour, were exhibited at the Fine Art Society and the Royal Society of Painters in Water-Colours between 1891 and 1894. By the 1890s Allingham was no longer using recognisable models such as her own children, and the young girl in the picture cannot be identified.[12] LL 3654 is typical of the many watercolours the artist made representing women and children standing in doorways and (sometimes open) gateways of cottages; this was such a common trope in her work that it has prompted art-historical discussion about the way in which Allingham's paintings functioned within middle-class notions of women's role and the domestic sphere.[13]

10 Label on the back of the frame. LL 3654 may be the *Old Cottage* listed as being in the housekeeper's room in the 1897–1902 TM Inventory. It is listed in the 1905 TM Inventory as being in the refreshment room, valued at £53 11s.

11 Annabel Watts, email correspondence, March 2007.

12 LLAG files: Annabel Watts, letter, 10 August 2006.

13 See, for example, Anne Helmreich, 'The marketing of Helen Allingham: the English cottage and national identity', in Steven Adams and Anna Gruetzner Robins (eds), *Gendering Landscape Art* (Manchester, 2000), pp. 45–60.

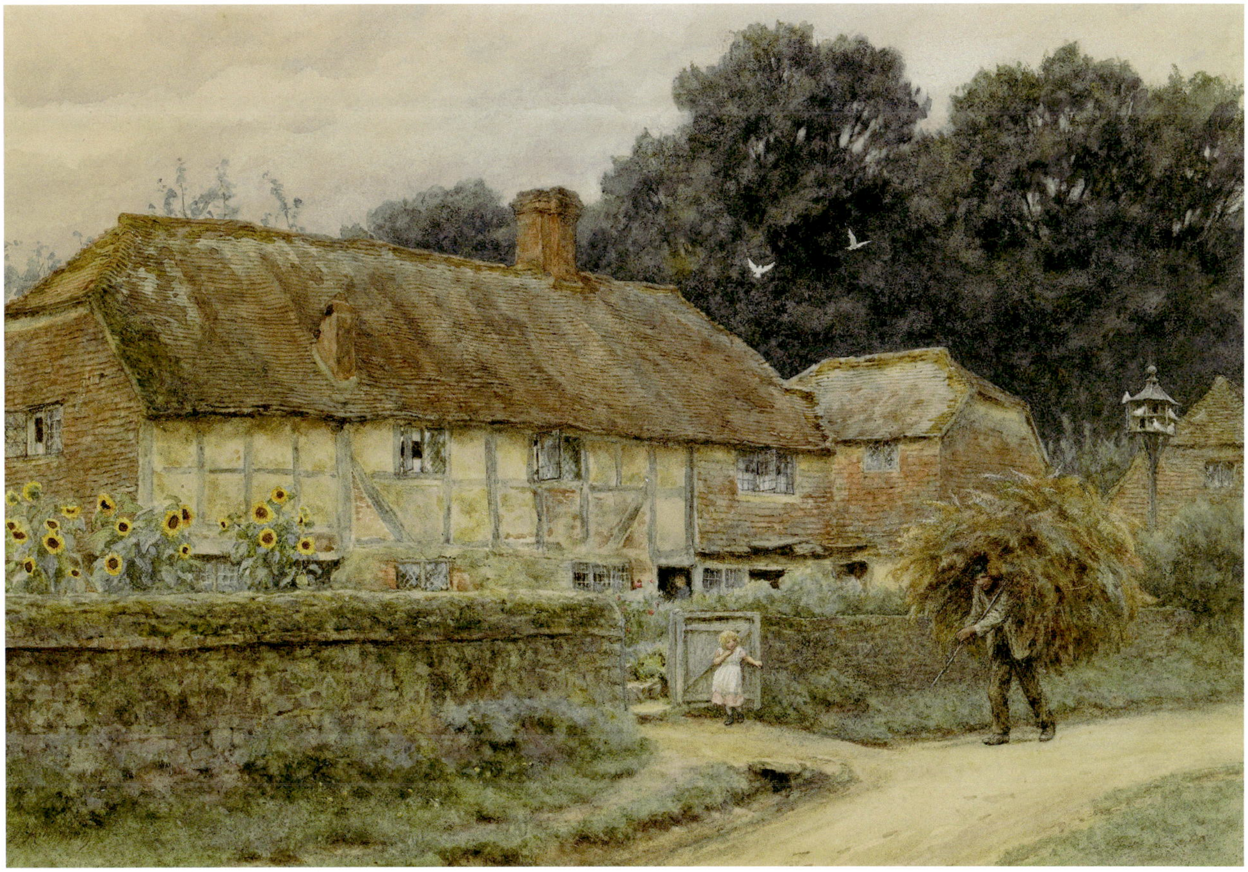

LL 3655

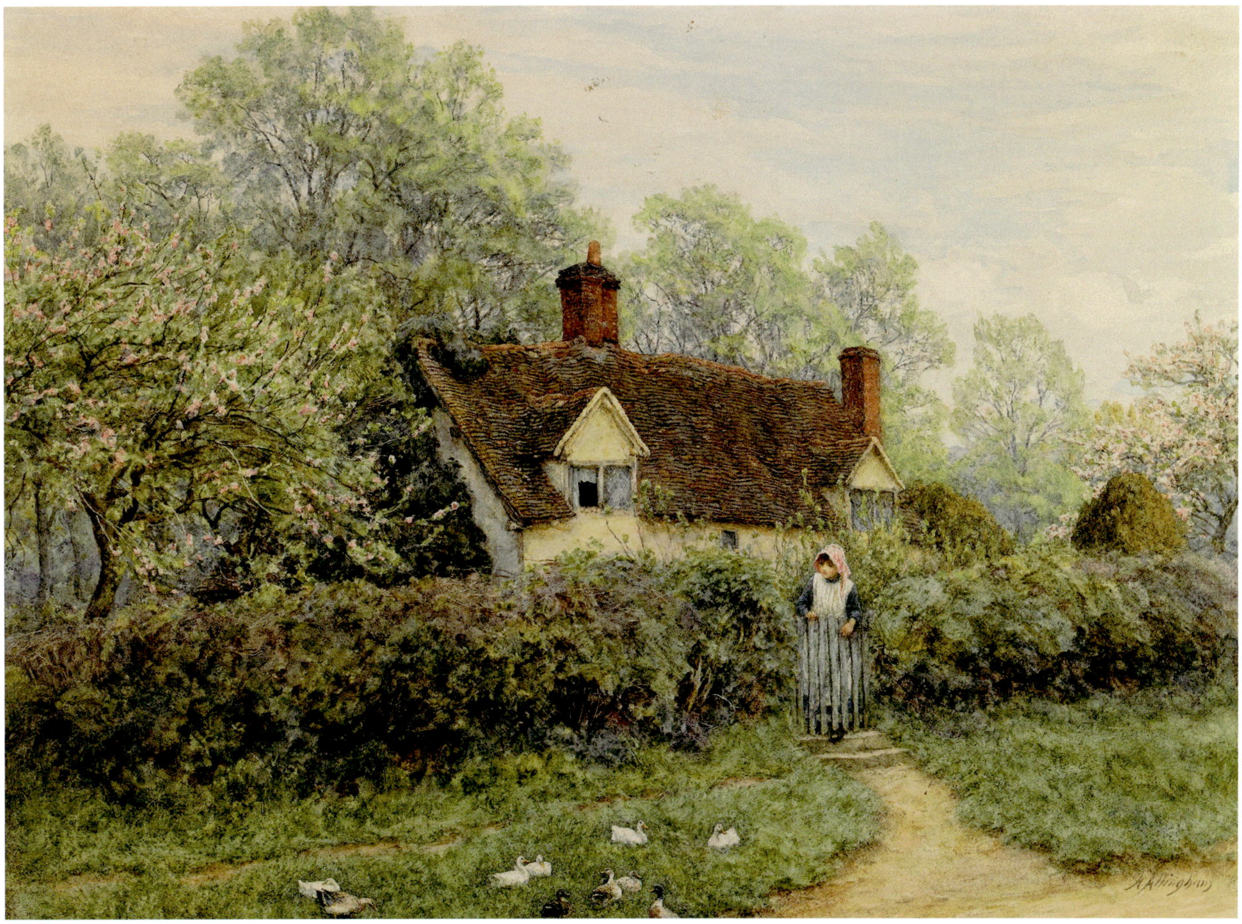

LL 3654

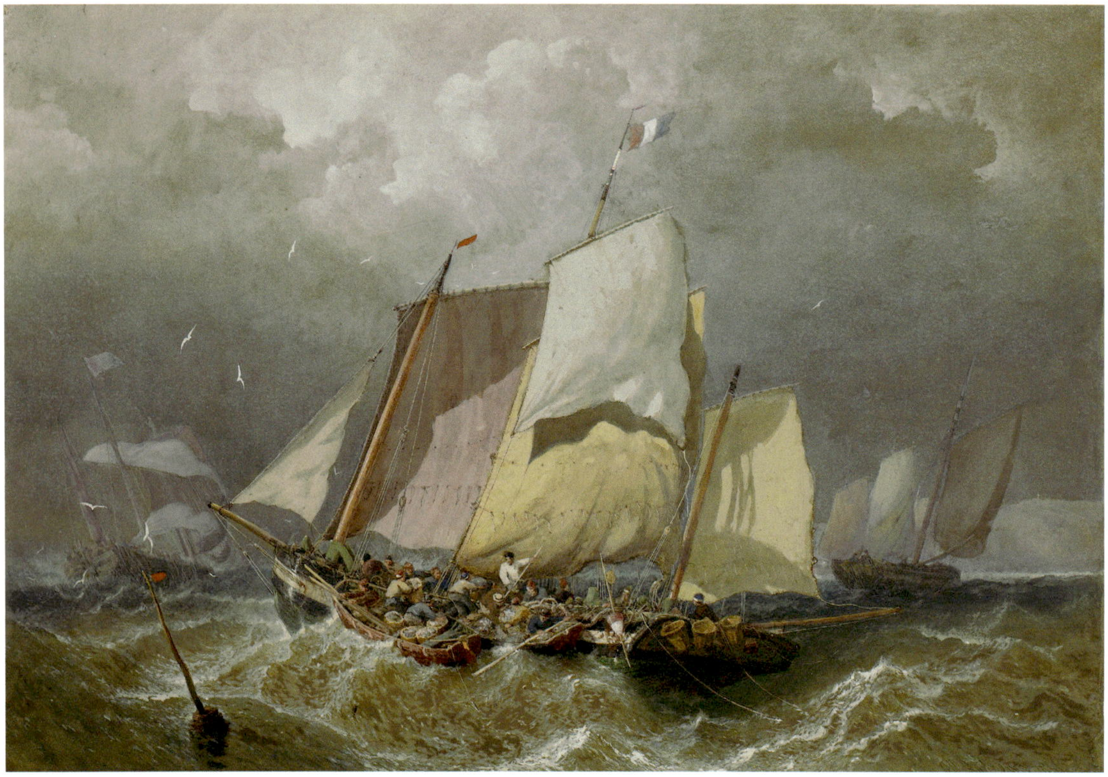

LL 3809

## GEORGE HENRY ANDREWS
1816 Lambeth, London–1898 London

### A French Lugger
LL 3809 (LP 53)

Gouache with extra gum arabic and white heightening on blue paper
52.7 x 74.3 cm (torn irreg.)
Date: 1866

Inscr: G H Andrews 1866 (watercolour, bottom right)

Prov: bt. from Grindley & Palmer, 14 North John Street, Liverpool by the Trustees, August 1939 (£35)

Andrews was an agricultural engineer and marine artist who contributed to the *Illustrated London News* and *The Graphic.* He exhibited from 1840 until his death, and was elected an associate of the SPWC in 1856 and a member in 1878. He accompanied the Prince of Wales to North America in 1860 as Special Artist, and also recorded the Franco-Prussian War (1870–71).

In subject-matter and technique LL 3809 is typical of Andrews's highly finished, exhibition-size watercolours of this period (see, for example, his *Storm in the North Sea*, also dated 1866, in the Victoria & Albert Museum).[14] The scene shows fishermen engaged in the difficult operation of transferring their catch from a lugger, a small sailing vessel, into two smaller boats in hazardous weather conditions. The image of the three-masted lugger is an accurate one, to be expected of an artist engaged primarily in marine subject-matter as well as in pictorial war reportage; but despite this technical accuracy, the work's focus (and the appeal of this type of watercolour at exhibition) was the human drama on display. The tricolour flag at the head of the main mast would appear to be French, although it is unclear why it has been reversed. It has been suggested that this could have been to alert the men on land to the fact that the lugger was ready to offload its fish.[15] The known popularity of this type of boat in France during this period has prompted the suggestion that the view could represent the cliff-lined French channel coast.[16]

14 A watercolour by Andrews was exhibited at the SPWC in 1866 (no. 22) as *Wreck of an East Indiaman Eighty Years Ago* but this title does not match LL 3809.

15 Sam Davidson, verbally, 12 February 2007.
16 Ibid.

## GEORGE OWEN WYNNE APPERLEY
1884 Ventnor, Isle of Wight–1960 Tangier, Morocco

### The Death of Procris
LL 3661 (WHL 2820)

Watercolour and gouache with some stopping out over pencil, on wove paper laid down on card
78.9 x 134 cm (trimmed irreg.)
Date: 1915

Inscr: Wynne Apperley. / FECIT. 1915 (watercolour, bottom right on cartouche)

Prov: bt. from the Royal Institute of Painters in Water-Colours exhibition by Lever, 1916 (£125); sold by the Trustees at Christie's, 6 June 1958 (lot 1); bt. by Goldschmidt and Vellekoup (3 gns); bt. from Goldschmidt and Vellekoup by Charles Cholmondeley August 1986; his sale, Christie's, 23 June 1989 (lot 147); bt. back by the Lady Lever Art Gallery (£63,064)

Exh: London, Royal Institute of Painters in Water-Colours, 1916 (cat. 430); London, Barbican Art Gallery, *The Last Romantics: The Romantic Tradition in British Art, Burne-Jones to Stanley Spencer*, 1989 (cat. 179)

Lit: 'Current Art Notes, The Royal Institute of Painters in Water-colour', *The Connoisseur*, vol. 45 (May 1916), pp. 56–58, illus. p. 56

Apperley, who came from a sporting and military family, was largely self-taught, although he studied briefly at Herkomer's school, Bushey from 1903 to 1904. Subsequently he left to tour Italy, the first of many such travels in search of subjects for watercolour landscapes which were the focus of his early career. In 1905 he exhibited his first work at the Royal Academy, and subsequently showed widely, including a successful one-man show at the Leicester Galleries in 1908. In 1914, by now married with children, he visited Spain for the first time; two years later he left his family and moved to Granada, later marrying the daughter of a Spanish stonemason.[17] Although he painted some landscapes and subject pictures, portraits of Spanish women and gypsies occupied Apperley for the remainder of his career. He gained a reputation in Spain and was elected a Distinguished Member of the Royal Academy of Fine Arts in Malaga in 1951.

The principal source for the Lady Lever work is the story of Cephalus and Procris from Ovid's *Metamorphoses* (VII, 752–65), a couple whose marriage ends in tragedy as a result of their mutual mistrust and jealousy. Procris follows her husband when he goes hunting, suspecting he has a lover; Cephalus, hearing a noise in the bushes, throws his spear and mistakenly kills his wife. Apperley's watercolour shows the dead Procris, with Cephalus kneeling covering his face in his hands with grief. LL 3661 remains largely true to the Greek myth; Cephalus's hunting dog, a gift from Procris is depicted in the right foreground, although the spear mentioned in the original narrative has been exchanged for

17 The circumstances surrounding Apperley's move to Spain are obscure. In 1916 he was declared medically unfit for military service and moved to Spain apparently for his health. It remains unclear why his wife refused to join him.

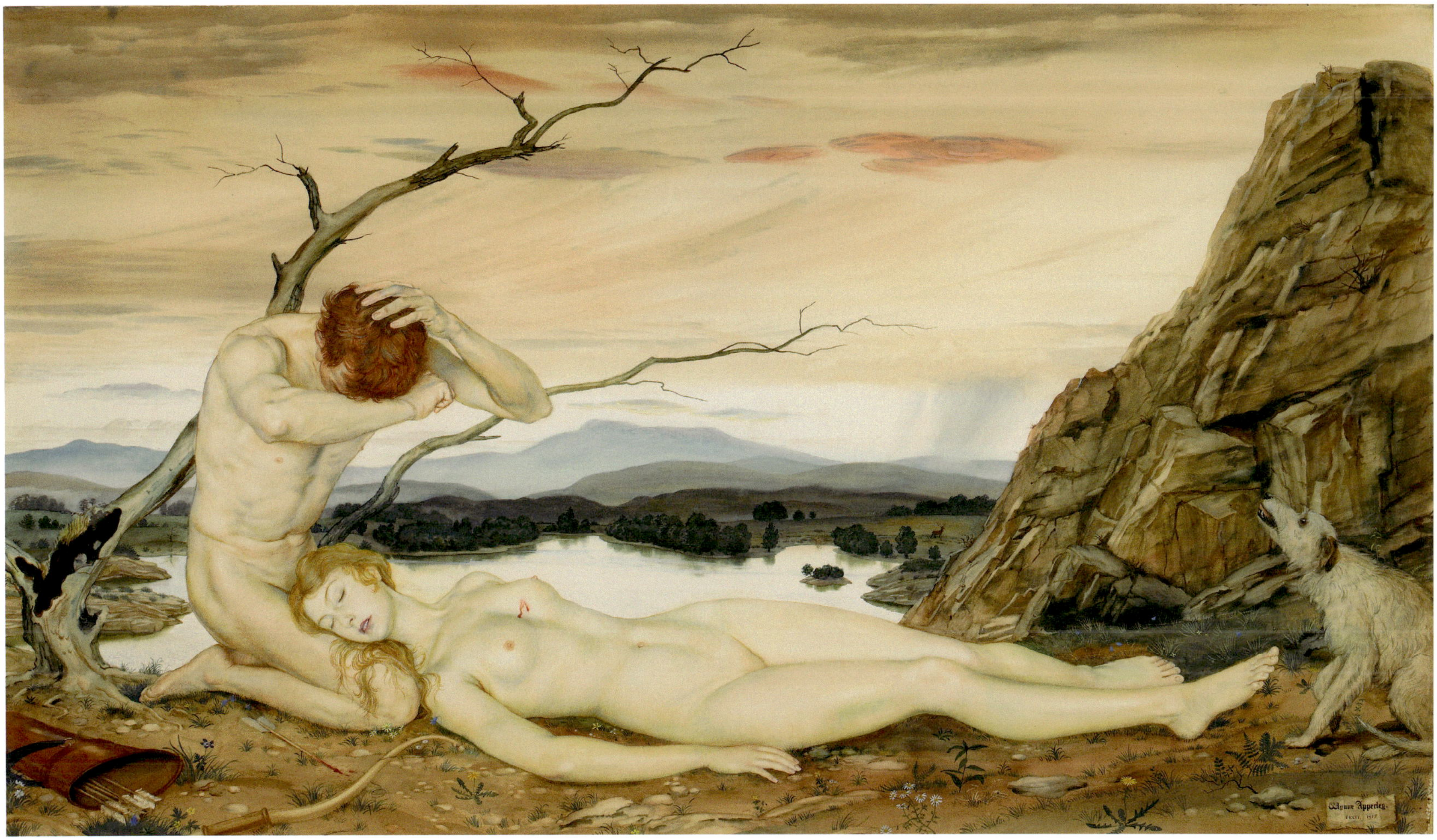

LL 3661

a bow and arrow. Of the numerous depictions of this subject, the artist may have seen Piero di Cosimo's painting *A Satyr mourning over a Nymph* (National Gallery, London) which has a strikingly similar composition to LL 3661 (fig. 1).[18]

*The Death of Procris* is one of a number of imaginative figure subjects that Apperley painted c. 1914–16, where he eschewed his previously bold watercolour technique in favour of a tighter manner influenced by Renaissance painting. The watercolour is reminiscent in technique of his painting of three water nymphs, *Summer Night* (Sotheby's, 2 December 2002, lot 102) which has a similar recumbent female as its focus. The landscape in LL 3661 is imagined but may be partially based on Apperley's trip to Spain in 1914. As with the main female figure in *Summer Night*, the features of Procris are based on those of Apperley's first wife Hilda whom he painted on numerous occasions following their marriage in 1907 (see, for example, Sotheby's, 14 October 1987, lot 79).

When exhibited at the Royal Institute of Painters in Water-Colours in 1916, LL 3661 was described in *The Connoisseur* as a success in an otherwise disappointing exhibition. Its reviewer admired the simplicity of the watercolour's setting '[al]though the background is painted with the minuteness of a Pre-Raphaelite landscape'.[19] He described 'The feeling of death [which] is subtly and beautifully suggested, not only by the rigidity of the figure, but in the austere and cold brilliance of the work'.[20]

A watercolour sketch for the picture that possesses all the main features of the final work aside from Cephalus's dog is in a private collection.[21]

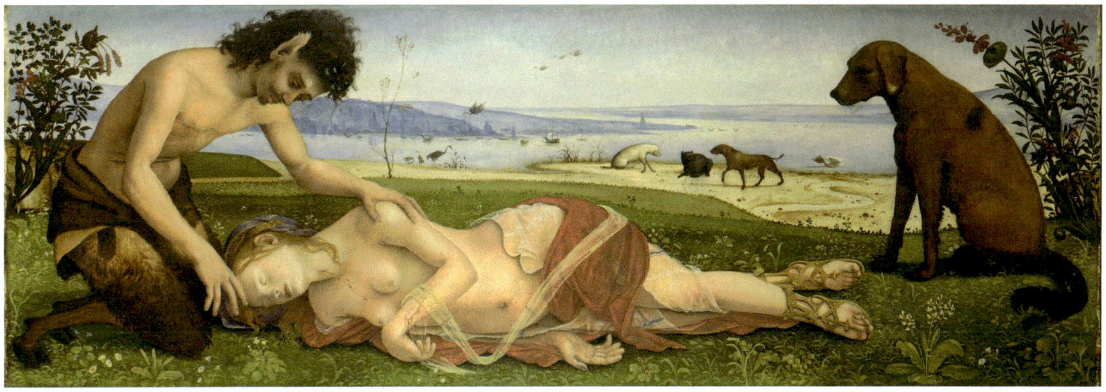

fig. 1. Piero di Cosimo, *A Satyr mourning over a Nymph*, c. 1495, oil on poplar, 65.4 x 184.2 cm, © The National Gallery, London

18 C. Baker and T. Henry, *The National Gallery Complete Illustrated Catalogue* (London, 1995), p. 529.

19 *The Connoisseur*, vol. 45 (May 1916), pp. 56–58.

20 Ibid.

21 John Christian (ed.), *The Last Romantics: The Romantic Tradition in British Art, Burne-Jones to Stanley Spencer* (exh. cat., London, Barbican Art Gallery, 1989), p. 139, incorrectly states that this sketch is in the Lady Lever collection. It was sold by Charles Cholmondeley to a private collector in 1998.

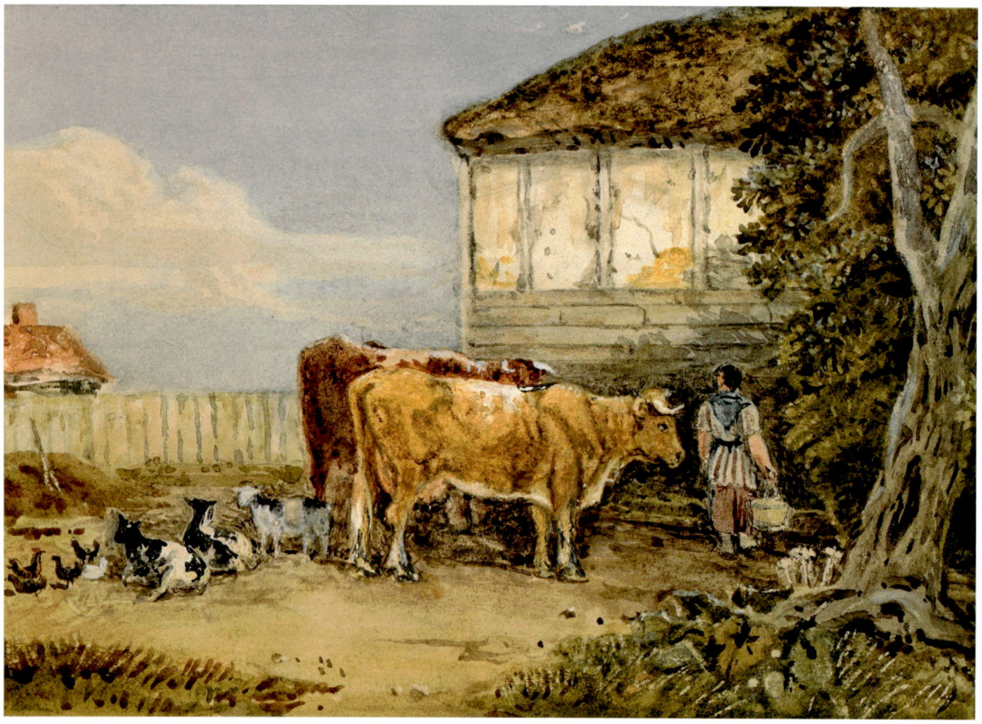

LL 3928

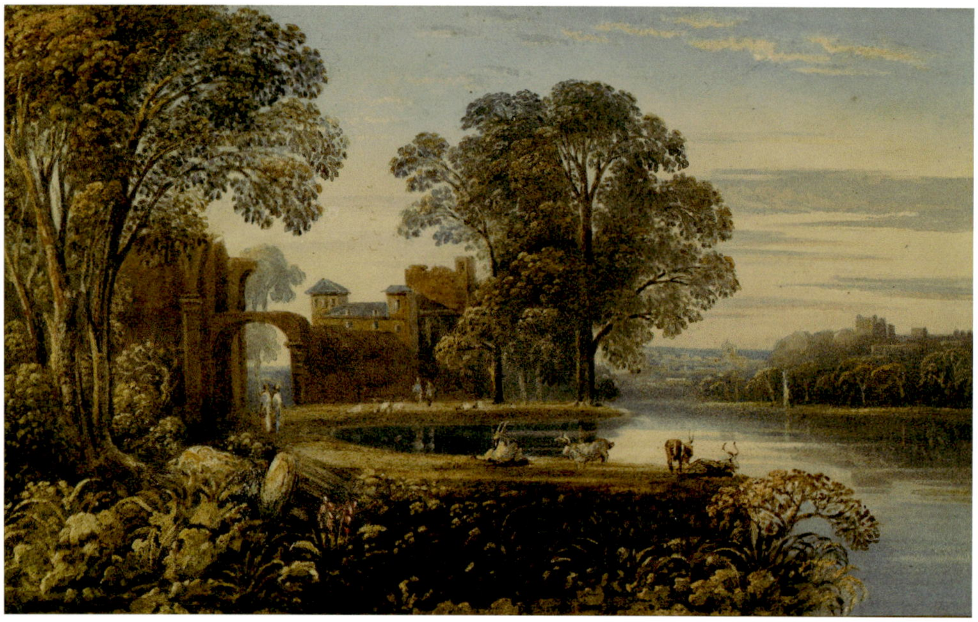

LL 3931

**GEORGE BARRET JUNIOR**
1767 London–1842 London

**Cows in a Farmyard**
LL 3928 (WHL 725, HH 397)

Watercolour, gouache and scratching out on wove paper
18.3 x 25.5 cm
Date: probably before 1825

Prov: bt. from James Orrock by Lever, 1910

The son of the Irish-born painter George Barret ([?]1732–1784), the younger George was almost certainly taught by his father. Barret Junior exhibited at the Royal Academy from 1800, showing occasional oil paintings but concentrating on watercolours after 1803. One of the 16 founder members of the SPWC, he exhibited nearly 600 watercolours at their exhibitions. Mallalieu described his career as 'remarkably uneventful';[22] the artist certainly travelled little, and his early subjects were mostly topographical landscapes found in the Thames valley, the Home Counties, and an occasional view in Wales. From around 1825 he began to concentrate on idealised, Claudean landscapes, frequently set in moonlight, sunset or sunrise, and these became the staples of his exhibited work for the rest of his career. In 1840 he published a small treatise entitled *The Theory and Practice of Water-Colour Painting*. Although held in high regard by his colleagues, he did not make (or at least retain) much money in his lifetime, and died leaving his family destitute. All five of his watercolours in the Lady Lever collection belonged to the artist, collector and art dealer James Orrock (see pp. xiv–xvii; 146–49) who had a high regard for Barret and owned numerous other works by him. He described Barret in *The Art Journal* as the 'last of the Four Pillars of the Great English School of Watercolour Painters ... [who] like Claude, Poussin, Turner, and Wilson, [was] imbued with an irresistible feeling for classical landscape...'[23]

*Cows in a Farmyard* is characteristic of Barret's early watercolours produced in the Home Counties and around London. It probably pre-dates 1825.

**A Classical River Scene**
LL 3931 (WHL 762, HH 389)

Watercolour, gum arabic with scratching out and stopping out on wove paper
14.5 x 23.2 cm (sight)
Date: probably mid- to late 1820s

Prov: bt. from James Orrock by Lever, 1910

From the mid-1820s Barret began to exhibit watercolours of idealised landscapes at the SPWC, taking the seventeenth-century painters Claude Lorrain, Nicolas Poussin and Gaspar Dughet as his inspiration. LL 3931 combines elements of this classical form of painting (the repoussoir trees, the 'stump' of a classical column, the staffage and goats), although the buildings appear to be a combination of ancient and modern. The care with which the foreground foliage is depicted, using the techniques of stopping and scratching out, demonstrates Barret's interest, apparent from an early stage of his work, in painting flowers and plants. As in *Cows Watering at a Pool: Sunset* (p. 9), Barret has applied gum arabic liberally over the watercolour washes, a technique typical of his work from the mid-1820s, used to create the richly textured effect, in keeping with the Arcadian world he was trying to recreate. This highly finished work

22 Huon Mallalieu, 'Barret, George (1767–1842)', *ODNB*, vol. 4, pp. 38–39.

23 Quoted in Byron Webber, *James Orrock, R.I.: Painter, Connoisseur, Collector* (London, 2 vols, 1903), vol. I, p. 137.

may have been exhibited and its assigned title is similar to several listed as appearing in the SPWC's exhibitions between the mid- and late 1820s.

**A Lake Scene**
LL 3929 (WHL 761, HH 372)

Watercolour over pencil, with touches of gouache and scratching out on wove paper
13.8 x 25 cm (sight)
Date: after 1825

Prov: bt. from James Orrock by Lever, 1910

This work is an invented scene, influenced by Claude Lorrain and other idealising landscape painters and is typical of Barret Junior's work after 1825.

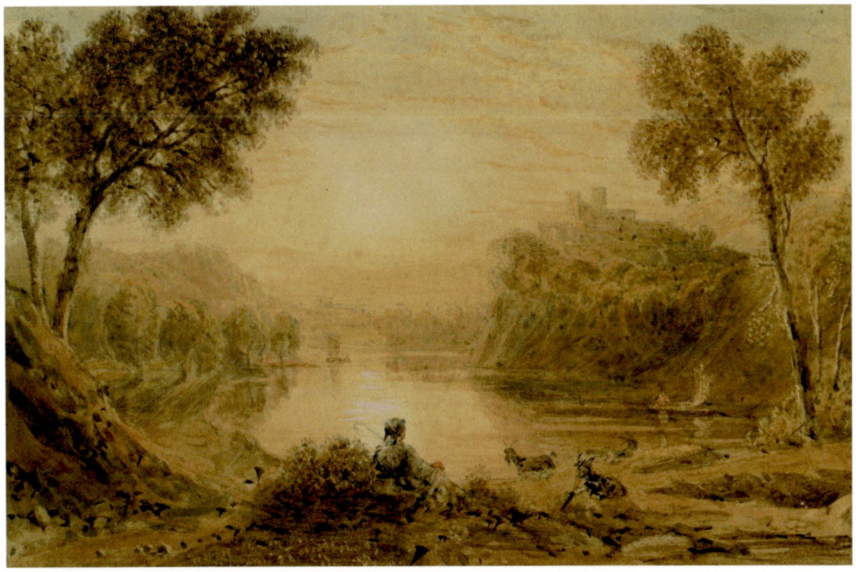
LL 3929

**A landscape with lake, with two figures, one on horseback**
LL 3930 (WHL 870, HH 379)

Watercolour over pencil, gum arabic with touches of gouache on wove paper
13.5 x 19.6 cm (sight)
Date: probably after 1825

Prov: bt. from James Orrock by Lever, 1910

This watercolour, like *A Lake Scene* (above), is an idealised, Italianate landscape scene which probably dates from after 1825.

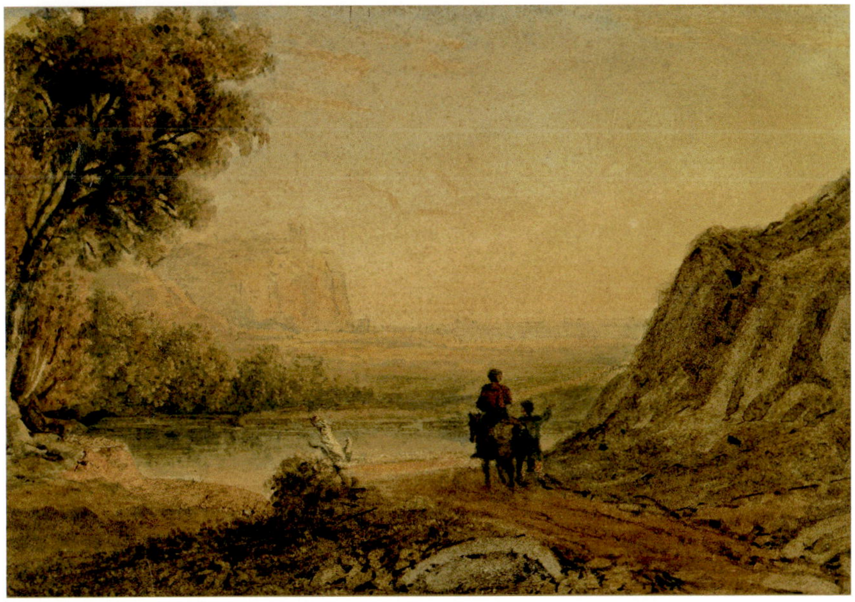
LL 3930

**Cows Watering at a Pool: Sunset**
LL 3927 (WHL 865, HH 390)

Watercolour, gouache and gum arabic on wove paper
18.6 x 26.2 cm
Date: probably mid-1830s to early 1840s

Prov: bt. from James Orrock by Lever, 1910

This work is a typical treatment of one of the artist's favourite subjects from the early 1820s onwards, cows watering at sunset. As he wrote in *The Theory and Practice of Water-colour Painting*: 'The setting sun is acknowledged by the generality of the admirers of nature to be one of the most fascinating of her appearances'.[24] LL 3927 probably dates from between the mid-1830s and the early 1840s and may have been exhibited, possibly with one of the appended poetic quotations that Barret increasingly used in the SPWC catalogues.

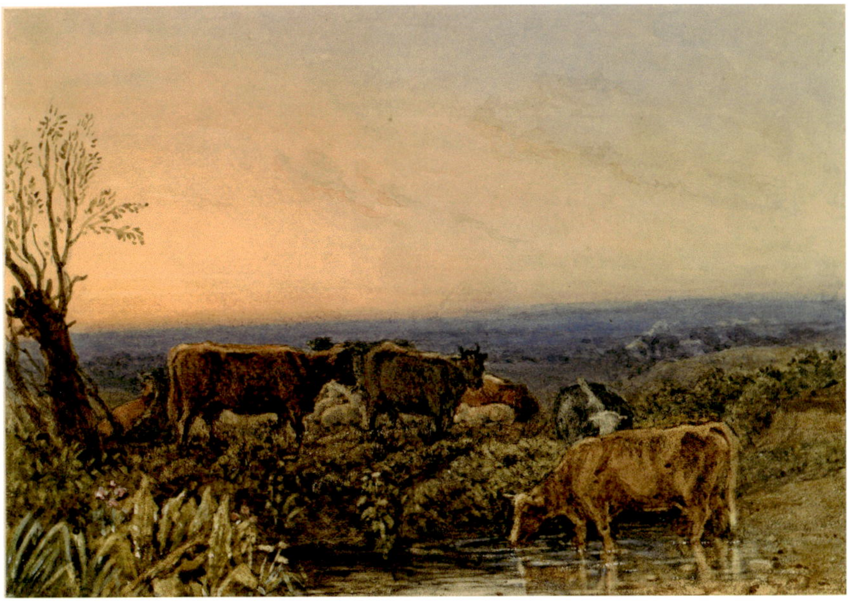
LL 3927

24 George Barret, *The Theory and Practice of Water-colour Painting* (London, 1840), p. 104.

## WILLIAM BENNETT

1811 place of birth unknown–1871 Clapham Park, London

**Stream and Rocky Landscape**[25]
LL 3808 (WHL 369, H 423)

Watercolour with extra gum arabic on wove paper
38.2 x 50.2 cm (sight)
Date: probably late 1840s or 1850s

Prov: in Lever's collection by 1912[26]

William Bennett may have been a pupil of David Cox (see pp. 59–65)[27] and he certainly sketched with the older artist in North Wales in the later 1840s. He exhibited at the New Society of Painters in Water-Colours from 1848, in which year he was elected an associate, becoming a full member in 1849. Bennett assumed a prominent position at the Society's exhibitions throughout the 1850s and was described by contemporaries as the chief exponent of Cox's boldness of handling.[28]

This watercolour probably dates from the late 1840s or 1850s, given the similarity in subject-matter and technique to other watercolours inscribed by the artist with a date from this period (see, for example, *A Rocky Stream*, Christie's, 9 May 1984 [lot 4], signed and dated 1855). A handwritten note on an earlier mount suggested that LL 3808 depicted Glen Nevis, near Fort William, on the west coast of Scotland.[29] Bennett was probably in Scotland in the early 1850s (his *The Pass of Glencoe* was exhibited at the New Society of Painters in Water-Colours in 1852)[30] but he also spent time in North Wales in the late 1840s and again in the 1850s, and this non-specific view, with its brooding mountains in the background, might also be located there. LL 3808 exhibits the vigour of handling apparent in Cox's watercolours of Welsh subjects from the 1840s.

25 1912 Hill Inventory, valued at £6.
26 Ibid. It is not listed in the 1906 TM Inventory so must have been acquired after this date.
27 F. Gordon Roe, *David Cox* (London, 1924), p. 48.
28 He was called 'the New Society's David Cox' in *The Art Journal* (1871), p. 155.

29 LLAG files: note on accession card.
30 *The Pass of Glencoe*, 1852, watercolour over pencil, 55.2 x 76.9 cm, Victoria & Albert Museum.

LL 3808

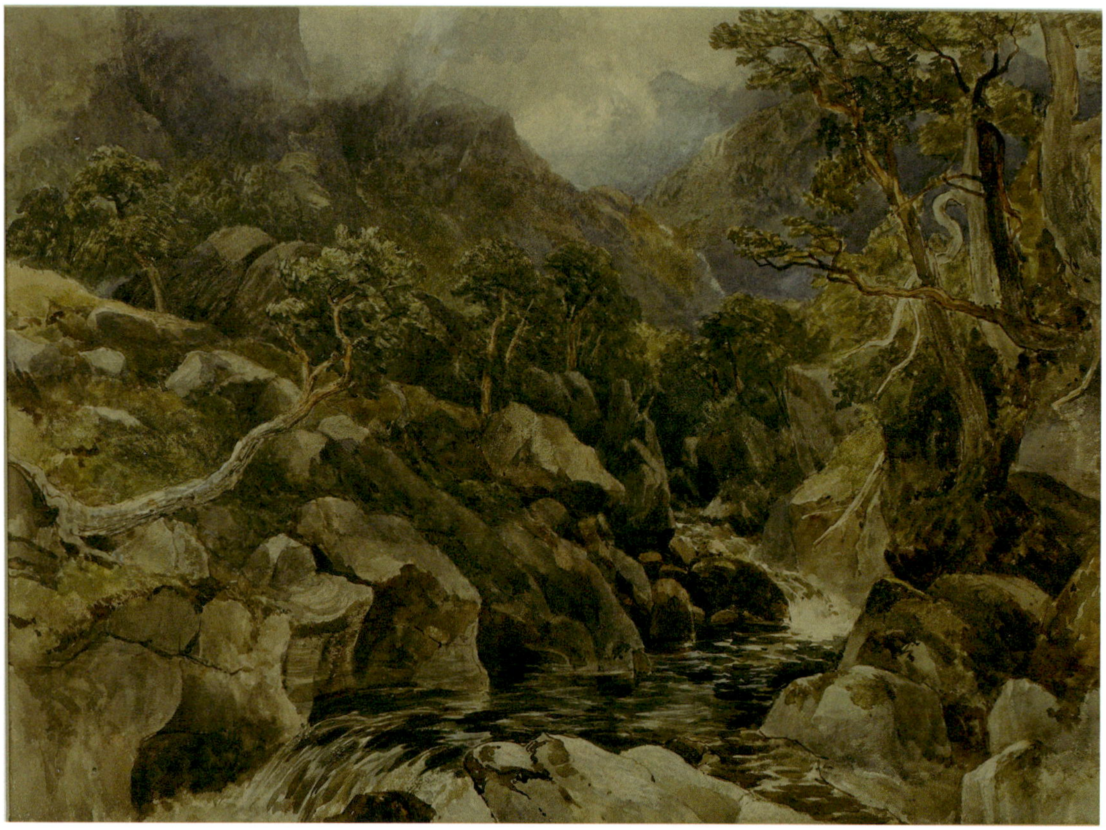

## AFTER RICHARD PARKES BONINGTON

1802 Arnold, near Nottingham–1828 London

**The Belfry, Bergues**
LL 3876 (WHL 3528)

Watercolour over pencil on wove paper
7.1 x 5 cm (sight)
Date: after 1824 and possibly after 1831

Prov: A. Sargent; Christie's, 16 May 1918 (lot 23); bt. by Gooden and Fox (34 gns with LL 3872–75, and 3877) for Lever (£37 9s 8d)

Bonington's father moved his family to Calais in 1817, where the young artist was taught to paint in watercolour by the Anglo-French artist Louis Francia. Between 1820 and 1822 Bonington attended classes at the Ecole des Beaux-Arts in Paris and embarked on a series of tours of Normandy. In 1825 he visited London where he worked with Eugène Delacroix (1798–1863) at Westminster Hall, later sharing a studio with him in Paris. The following year, Bonington commenced a tour of northern Italy and Switzerland. In the final two years of his life his primary subject-matter for both oils and watercolours was views of Venice and illustrations to medieval and Renaissance history and the literary works of Scott and Goethe. His works were shown at the British Institution from 1826 to 1829 and at both the Salon and the Royal Academy in 1827 and 1828. Despite his premature death from tuberculosis, Bonington was instrumental in encouraging the practice of watercolour painting among French artists.

Bonington's view of the famous sixteenth-century belfry of Bergues, south of Dunkirk, was originally published in his collection of lithographs, *Restes et fragmens [sic] d'architecture du moyen age*, which appeared in 1824.[31] Given that others of the group of small watercolours with which LL 3876 is framed (see also below under Prout, pp. 156–57, and Stanfield, p. 177) were culled from contemporary landscape annuals, the source of this copy is perhaps more likely to have been the reduced engraving made by W. J. Cooke published in *The Gem* for 1831, *La tour du marché at Bergues near Dunkirk on the River Colne*. LL 3876 is a somewhat slapdash copy, compressing the height of the portion of the belfry that is visible and distorting the strong verticals of the corner turrets. The gap between the houses is enlarged and figures in the left foreground omitted.

The belfry, considered the finest in France, was destroyed by dynamite on 16 September 1944. A simplified replica was completed in 1961.

31 A. Curtis, *Catalogue de l'oeuvre lithographié et gravé de R.P. Bonington* (Paris, 1939), unpag. (cat. 6).

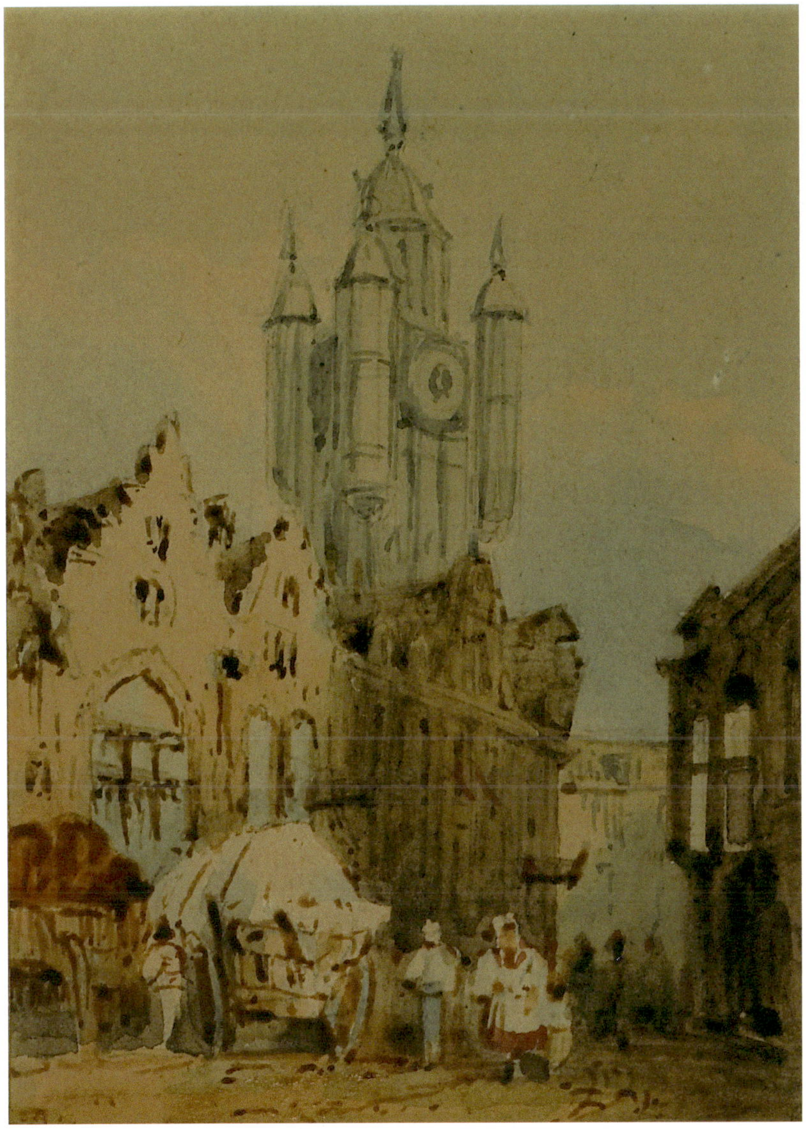

LL 3876

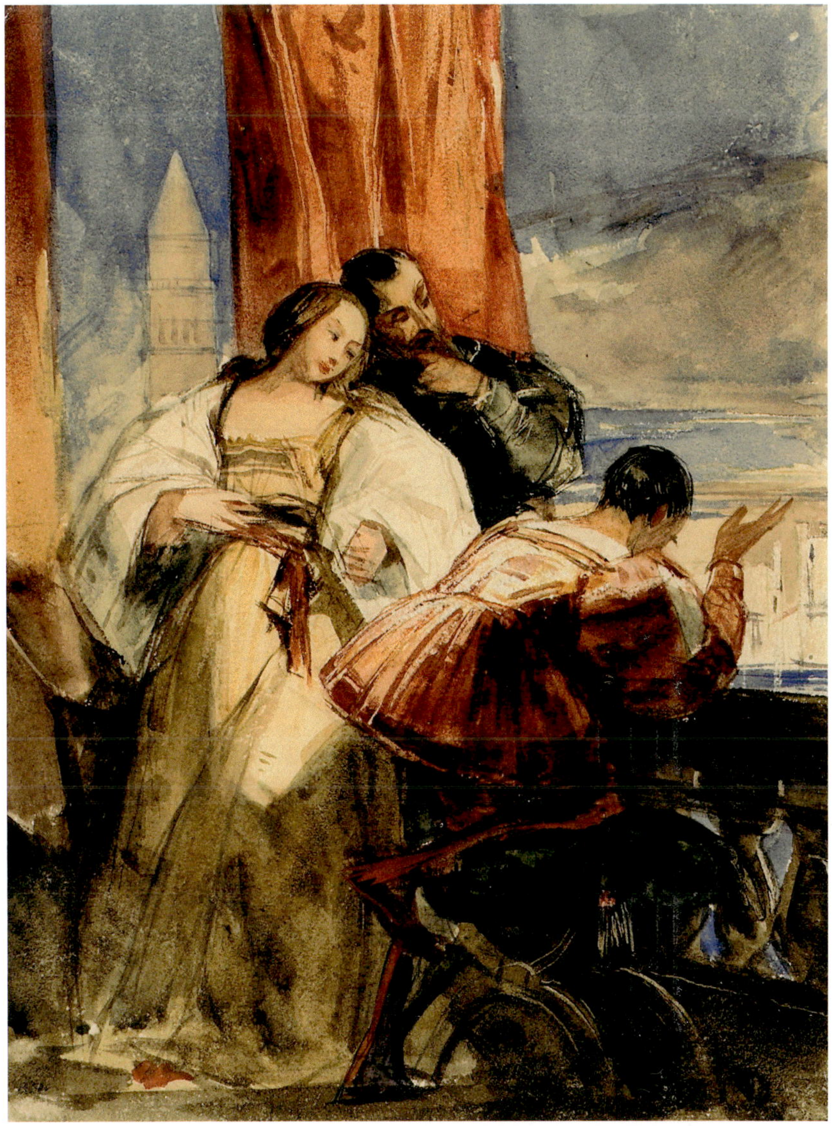

LL 3932

fig. 2

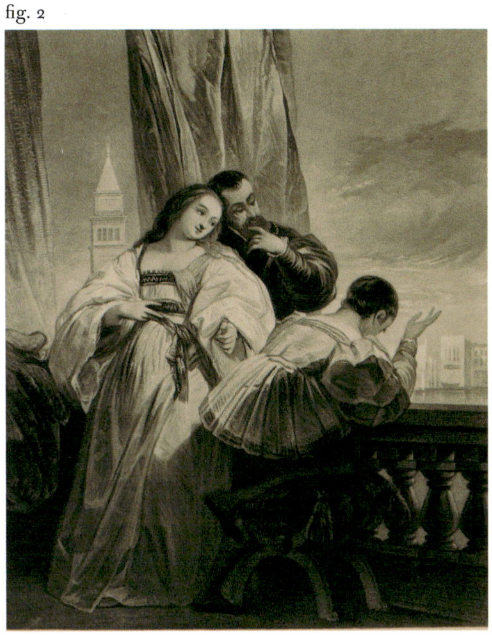

fig. 3

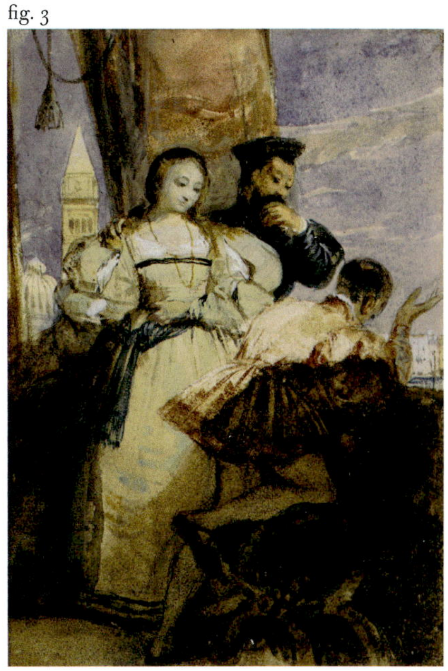

fig. 2. H. Quilley, After Richard Parkes Bonington, *Scene in Venice*, nineteenth century, mezzotint on paper, 25.8 x 20.9 cm (plate), © The Trustees of the British Museum

fig. 3. Richard Parkes Bonington, *On a Venetian Balcony*, c. 1826–27, watercolour and gouache on wove paper, 16.2 x 11.2 cm, Culture & Sport Glasgow (Museums)

Other copies of Bonington's print by various unidentified artists exist. An oil, by an artist who may have been an associate of Bonington, is in the Wallace Collection.[32] A small watercolour of the same view was sold at the American Art Association, New York on 2 February 1927 (as *Street in Amsterdam*) with the (false?) signature 'C. Stanfield'.

TW

### On the Balcony, Venice
LL 3932 (WHL 4155, HH 389)

Watercolour with gouache and scratching out on wove paper
18.8 x 13.7 cm
Date: nineteenth century, possibly c. 1826–36

Prov: J. P. Heseltine, 1920; his sale, Sotheby's, 25 March 1920 (lot 96); bt. by Gooden and Fox (£58) for Lever, March 1920 (£59 9s)

Exh: London, Burlington Fine Arts Club, *Catalogue of an Exhibition of Pictures and Drawings by Richard Parkes Bonington and his Circle*, 1937 (cat. 85); Hamburg, Kunsthalle and tour of Scandinavia, organized by the British Council, *British Painting from Hogarth to Turner*, 1949–50 (cat. 11); Geneva, Musée Rath and Zurich, Cabinet des Estampes de l'Ecole Polytechnique Fédérale, organized by the British Council, *L'Aquarelle Anglaise 1750–1850*, 1956 (cat. 12)

Lit: 'Current Art Notes, Our Plates', *The Connoisseur*, vol. 88 (August 1931), p. 125, illus. p. 101; Andrew Shirley, *Bonington* (London, 1940), p. 117

*On the Balcony, Venice* was purchased by Lever as an autograph work by Bonington and was subsequently catalogued by Shirley with the same attribution.[33] Patrick Noon has suggested that the Lady Lever work is a copy of an untraced oil painting which was in the artist's 1829 studio sale.[34] This oil was reproduced in mezzotint by H. Quilley (fl. 1834–35) (fig. 2) and it was also depicted as an ornament in John Frederick Lewis's watercolour *An Interior* (Tate). There is another watercolour version of the composition by Bonington in Glasgow Museum and Art Gallery which differs slightly from the oil in minor details of costume and pose (fig. 3).[35] LL 3932 is less close to this than to the oil, as reproduced in Quilley's engraving. There is a copy of the Glasgow watercolour in the Fogg Art Museum, Harvard University.[36] Another oil sketch that relates closely to the Lady Lever composition was with the Redfern Gallery in 1962; this is also thought by Noon to be a copy.[37]

In the Glasgow watercolour the figures are wearing sixteenth-century costumes; in LL 3932 the fashion is not as specific, although the page's short pleated gown with slashed sleeves was of a type popular in the 1530s and 1540s.[38] Noon has dated the Glasgow work to c. 1826–27.[39] Bonington had spent much of 1826 in Venice, and in subsequent months produced many genre pictures of Venetian subjects. In both the Glasgow work and LL 3932 the campanile of St Mark's is depicted in the background, but in the Glasgow work the basilica itself is seen as well. During his time in Venice, Bonington came into contact with Venetian Renaissance painting, whose colouring and expressive techniques can be seen in each of the versions of this balcony piece (for example in the deep red of the drapery). Nevertheless, the composition is too informal to relate to any specific sixteenth-century painting, and no specific source can be identified.

Noon has suggested the Lady Lever and Fogg copies may have been painted by Lewis Brown, a Bordeaux wine merchant of British descent who was both an expert copyist and an ardent collector of Bonington's watercolours from at least 1826 until his own death a decade later.[40] After Brown's death, his watercolours were auctioned at sales in Paris in 1837, 1839 and 1843.[41] The mezzotint by Quilley and three reproductive prints after the Glasgow version indicate the popularity of the image throughout the nineteenth century.[42]

## BRITISH SCHOOL
Late nineteenth century

### Three profiles after antique sculpture
LL 2912

Pencil and black chalk with white heightening on green paper
36.8 x 53.2 cm
Date: probably 1860s–1890s

Prov: found in the Gallery at an unknown date

LL 2912–LL 2942 and LL 2969–LL 2970 were found, wrapped together, in the Lady Lever Art Gallery. They were inventoried in 1996 but are likely to have been in the gallery from a much earlier date. A number of them are annotated with the names of two of Lever's elder sisters, Emily and Jane Lever. It is not clear, however, whether the annotation is a contemporary signature or a suggested attribution. Nevertheless it is likely that all these works have the same provenance and they may be by various members of Lever's immediate family.[43] On this view, the works are likely to date from the 1860s to the end of the nineteenth century.

The sources for the subject-matter of many of these works are unknown, but they cover a wide range of themes that would have appealed to amateur artists, from classical to literary subjects. Some of them are copies after prints (themselves after known paintings) and it is possible that they derive from late nineteenth-century drawing manuals. Lever's own collection of classical sculptures may also have provided inspiration.[44]

### Head after sculpture of Homer
LL 2913

Pencil and black chalk on green paper
47.6 x 35.4 cm.
Date: probably 1860s–1890s

Prov: found in the Gallery at an unknown date

32 S. Duffy, *Richard Parkes Bonington* (London, 2003), pp. 88–89 (cat. 36).
33 WHL Inventory; Andrew Shirley, *Bonington* (London, 1940), p. 117.
34 Patrick Noon, email correspondence, July 2006. The oil painting was lot 108 in Bonington's posthumous sale, Sotheby's, 29–30 June 1829, and subsequently belonged to Lord Charles Townshend, figuring as lot 50 in his sale, Christie's, 6 May 1836.
35 Shirley, *Bonington*, p. 117; Marion Spencer, *RP Bonington* (exh. cat., Nottingham, Castle Museum, 1965), pp. 32–33 (cat. 243) describes LL 3932 as a version of the Glasgow work. See also Patrick Noon, *Richard Parkes Bonington 'On the Pleasure of Painting'* (exh. cat., New Haven, Yale Center for British Art and Paris, Petit Palais, 1991–92), p. 249 (cat. 124).
36 Patrick Noon, email correspondence, July 2006.
37 LLAG files: photograph of oil sketch; Patrick Noon, email correspondence, August 2007.
38 Pauline Rushton, email correspondence, November 2007.
39 Shirley dated LL 3932 to 1828.
40 Noon, *Richard Parkes Bonington*, p. 249.
41 Shirley, *Bonington*, pp. 134–36, and 141–42 lists three sales for Brown: 109 watercolours were in his sale in Paris, Place de la Bourse, 17–18 April 1837; the second sale was at Pierret, 12–13 March 1839 and included at least 33 watercolour lots; a final sale in 1843 included 24 lots (media unidentified).
42 The mezzotint is signed on the plate 'Quilly' without any initial and is not dated. The British Museum attributes the print to H. Quilley on the basis of stylistic similarity to a mezzotint of a scene from *As You Like It* published in 1835 and lettered H. Quilley; Noon, *Richard Parkes Bonington*, p. 249.
43 Lever had eight sisters: Elizabeth, Eliza Emma, Mary, Jane, Emily, Alice, Hariette and Lucy Ann; information from Gavin Hunter, Leverhulme Family Archive.
44 For this, see Geoffrey B. Waywell, *The Lever and Hope Sculptures, Ancient Sculptures in the Lady Lever Art Gallery, Port Sunlight and A Catalogue of the Ancient Sculptures formerly in the Hope Collection, London and Deepdene* (Berlin, 1986); it should be noted, however, that none of Lever's purchases of classical sculpture pre-dated 1900.

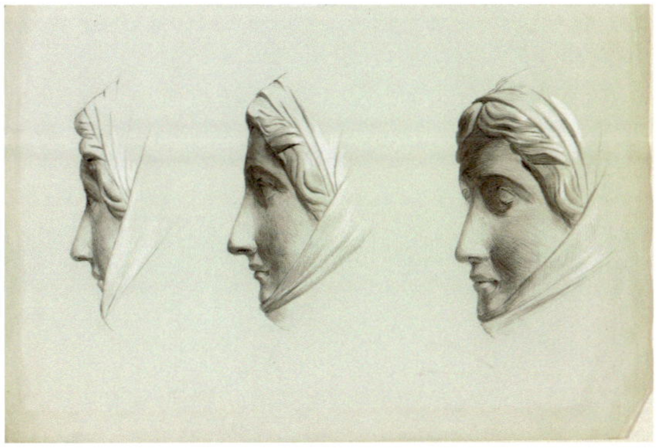

LL 2912

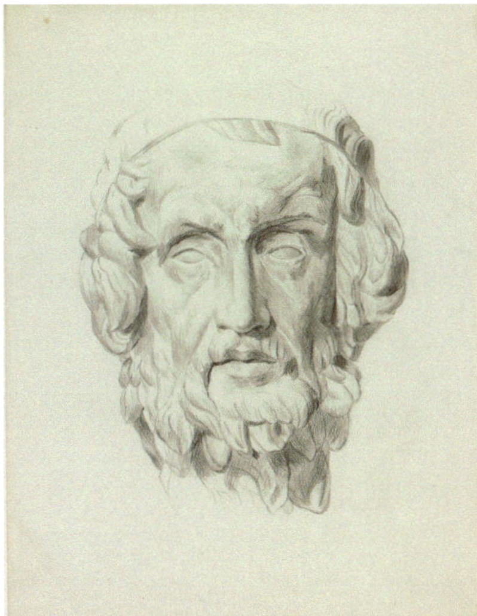

LL 2913

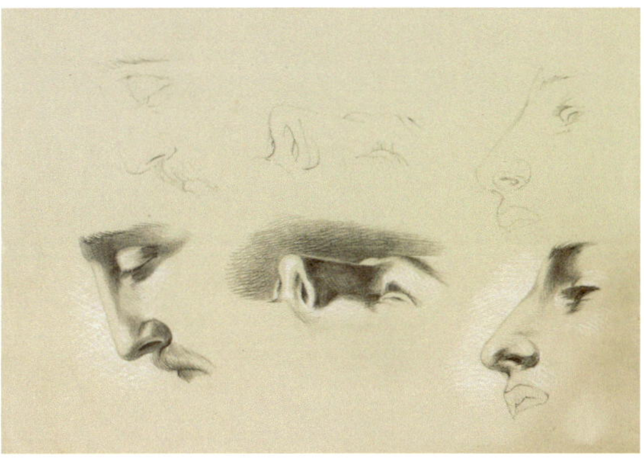

LL 2914

**Six profile studies of a [?] male head**
LL 2914

Pencil with white heightening on paper
26.8 x 38 cm
Date: probably 1860s–1890s

Annot: Emily Lever[45] (pencil, verso, top right)
Prov: found in the Gallery at an unknown date

It is not clear whether the annotation is a contemporary signature or a suggested attribution.

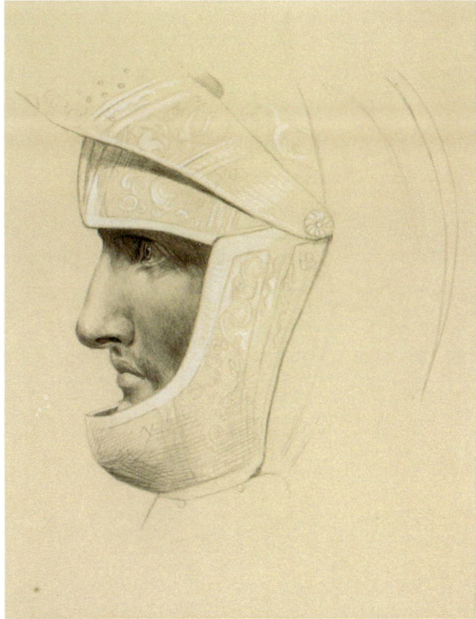

LL 2915

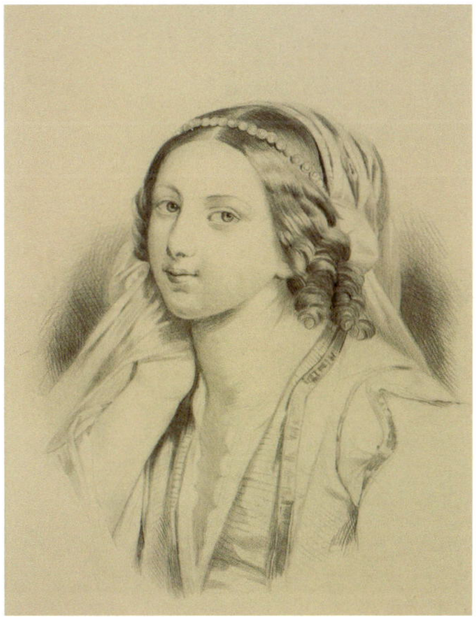

LL 2916

**Head of a knight in profile**
LL 2915

Pencil and black chalk with white heightening on paper laid down on card
37.2 x 27.7 cm
Date: probably 1860s–1890s

Prov: found in the Gallery at an unknown date

**Head of a woman in [?] oriental dress**
LL 2916

Pencil on paper laid down on card
43.5 x 31 cm
Date: probably 1860s–1890s

Prov: found in the Gallery at an unknown date

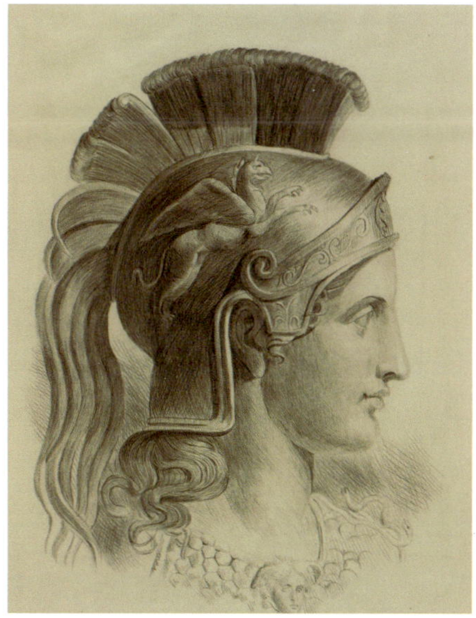

LL 2917

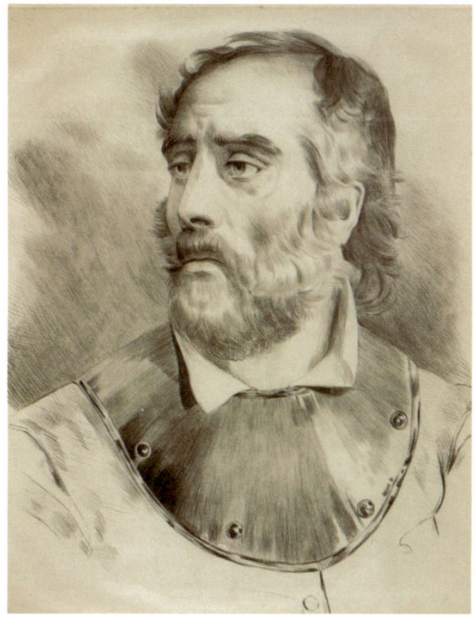

LL 2918

**Head of a soldier after an antique sculpture**
LL 2917

Pencil and black chalk with gum arabic on buff paper laid down on card
47.7 x 34.6 cm
Date: probably 1860s–1890s

Prov: found in the Gallery at an unknown date

**Head and shoulders of a man in armour**
LL 2918

Pencil and black chalk with gum arabic on paper laid down on card
54.1 x 41.8 cm
Date: probably 1860s–1890s

Prov: found in the Gallery at an unknown date

45 Emily Lever was born in 1847 and died in 1939; information provided by Gavin Hunter, Leverhulme Family Archive.

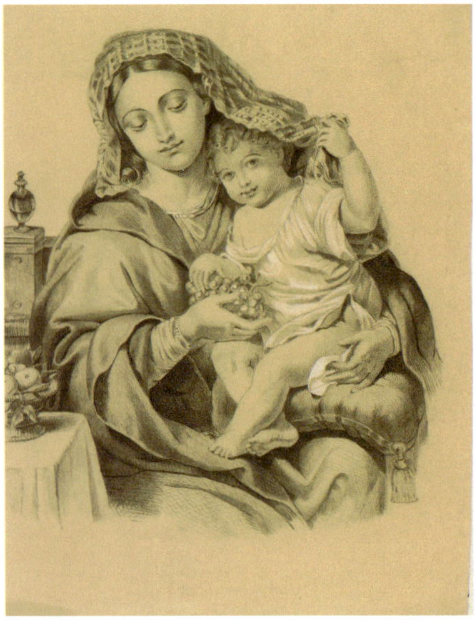

LL 2919

## Mother and child
LL 2919

Pencil and black chalk, with touches of [?] black watercolour and white heightening on buff paper
48.8 x 34.3 cm
Date: probably 1860s–1890s

Prov: found in the Gallery at an unknown date

This work may be after a seventeenth-century painting but no source has been located.

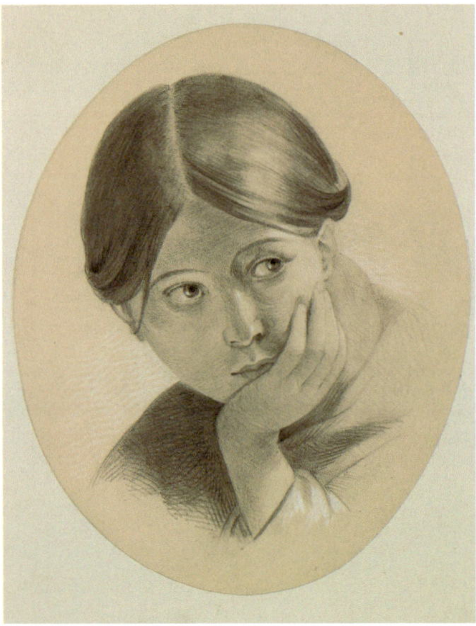

LL 2920

## Portrait of a girl
LL 2920

Pencil with white heightening on paper cut in oval and laid down on card
29.9 x 23.9 cm (cut in oval)
Date: probably 1860s–1890s

Annot: <u>Miss</u> [?] <u>Lever</u> (pencil, on card lower right)
Prov: found in the Gallery at an unknown date

It is not clear whether the annotation is a contemporary signature or a suggested attribution.

LL 2921

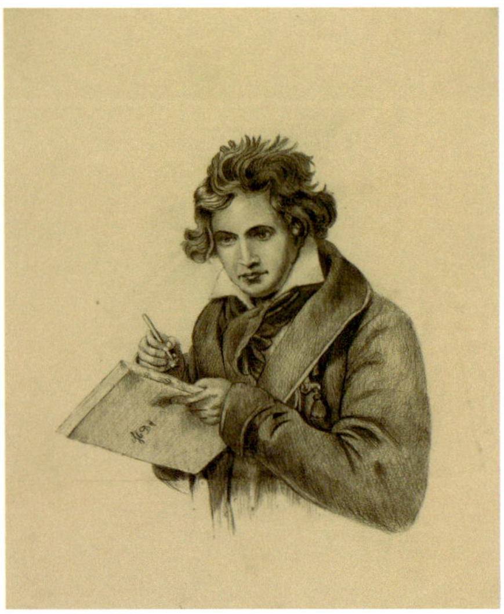

## Portrait of Ludwig Van Beethoven
LL 2921

Pencil and black chalk on paper
32.4 x 27.3 cm
Date: probably 1860s–1890s

Prov: found in the Gallery at an unknown date

This work is based on Joseph Carl Stieler's famous portrait of the composer which was painted c. 1819–20 (in the Beethoven-Haus, Bonn). Silke Bettermann has suggested that LL 2921 may be derived from the lithograph after the painting by Friedrich Dürck (1809–84), published in 1826 in Vienna and quite widely distributed around Europe in the nineteenth century.[46]

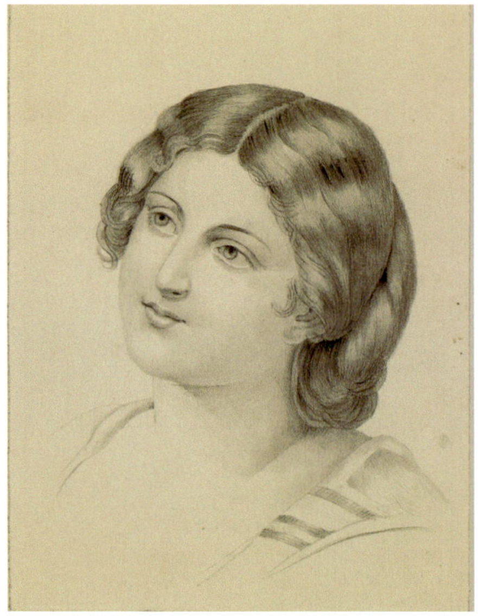

LL 2922

## Head of a woman in classical style
LL 2922

Pencil with touches of black chalk, black watercolour and gouache on paper
21.5 x 15.5 cm
Date: probably 1860s–1890s

Prov: found in the Gallery at an unknown date

This work is similar in technique and subject-matter to LL 2929 (p. 16), which is annotated 'Jane Lever'. It may be by the same hand.

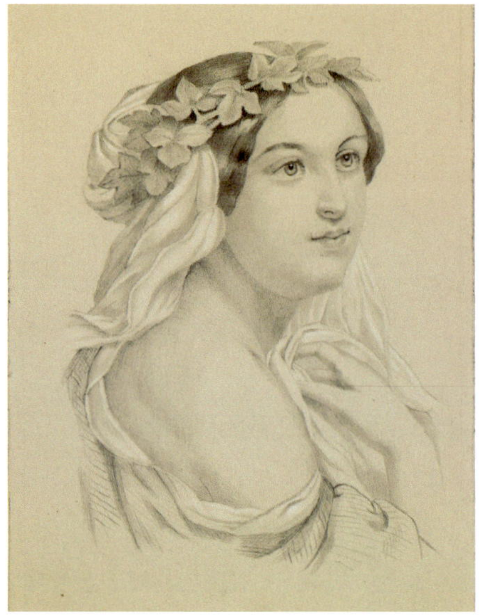

LL 2923

LL 2924

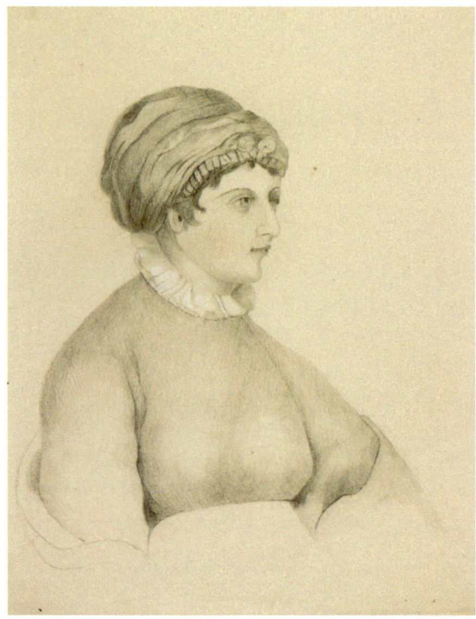

46 Correspondence with Silke Bettermann, Beethoven-Haus, Bonn, July 2007.

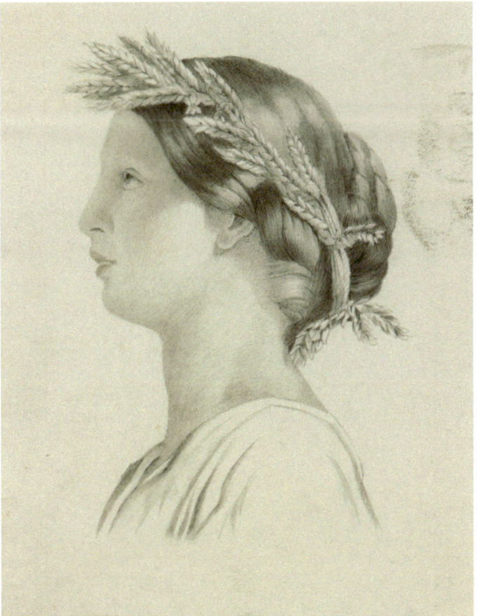

LL 2925

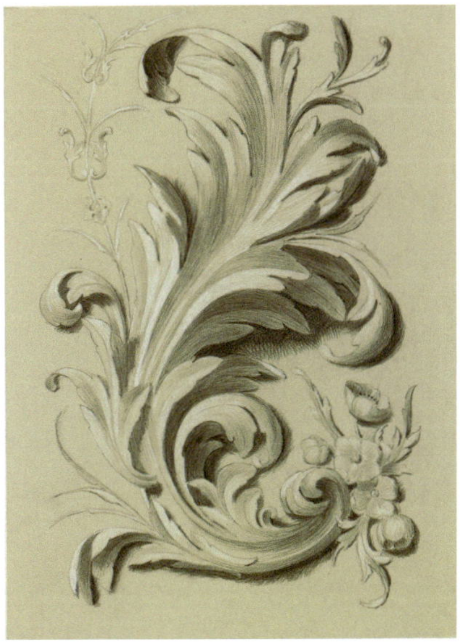

LL 2926A
LL 2926B

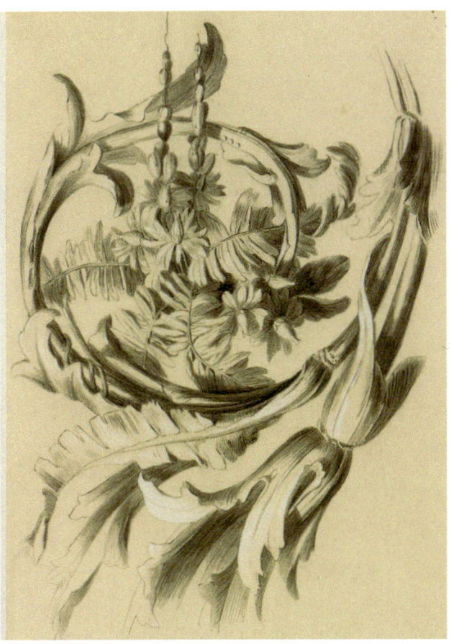

**Head of a woman wearing wreath and drapery**
LL 2923

Pencil with black watercolour and white heightening on paper
22 x 15.3 cm
Date: probably 1860s–1890s

Prov: found in the Gallery at an unknown date

This work is similar in technique and subject-matter to LL 2929 (p. 16), which is annotated 'Jane Lever'. In common with LL 2922 (p. 14), it may be by the same hand.

**Portrait of a woman wearing headdress**
LL 2924

Pencil, black and coloured chalks with white heightening on paper
35.5 x 29.7 cm
Date: probably 1860s–1890s

Prov: found in the Gallery at an unknown date

**Head of a woman in profile, wearing wreath**
LL 2925

Pencil, with coloured chalks, black watercolour and touches of gouache on paper
23.8 x 17.9 cm
Date: probably 1860s–1890s

Prov: found in the Gallery at an unknown date

The work has been marked by a footprint (unknown) at the top right edge.

**Floral design**
LL 2926A

Pencil with black chalk and white heightening on paper laid down on card
40.4 x 27.4 cm
Date: probably 1860s–1890s

Prov: found in the Gallery at an unknown date

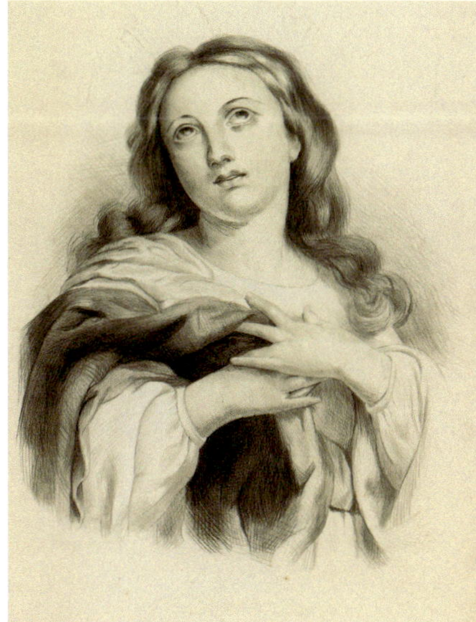

LL 2927

**Floral design**
LL 2926B

Watercolour over pencil with touches of black chalk
27.8 x 22.3 cm
Date: probably 1860s–1890s

Annot: E. Lever (pencil, verso)

Prov: found in the Gallery at an unknown date

It is not clear whether the annotation is a contemporary signature or a suggested attribution, nor to which of Lever's sisters this refers.

**Head and shoulders of the Virgin**
LL 2927

Pencil and black chalk with gum arabic on paper
48.8 x 32.6 cm

Date: probably 1860s–1890s

Prov: found in the Gallery at an unknown date

This work is based on the figure of the Virgin from Bartolomé Esteban Murillo's *Immaculate Conception of Los Venerables* (c. 1678, Museo del Prado, Madrid). Murillo's painting was in the Soult sale of 1852 which attracted considerable notice[47] and a reproduction or illustration made at that time may have been the source on which the present drawing was based.

47 See, for example, 'Sale of the Soult Pictures', *Athenaeum* (29 May 1852), pp. 609–10.

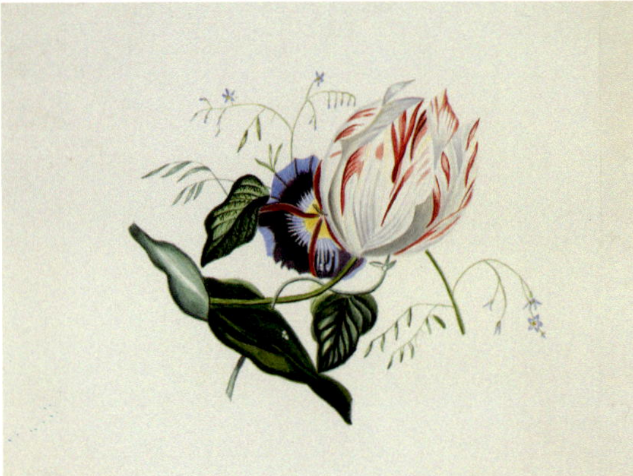

LL 2928

**Flowers**
LL 2928

Watercolour on paper
26.1 x 36.1 cm
Date: probably 1860s–1890s

Prov: found in the Gallery at an unknown date

**Head and shoulders of a woman wearing wreath, face turned to viewer**
LL 2929

Pencil, black chalk and black watercolour with white heightening on paper
22 x 15 cm
Date: probably 1860s–1890s

Annot: Jane Lever[48] (pencil, bottom right)
Prov: found in the Gallery at an unknown date

**Unfinished sketch after Ary Scheffer's *Dante and Beatrice***
LL 2930

Pencil on paper
50.3 x 36.2 cm
Date: probably 1860s–1890s

Prov: found in the Gallery at an unknown date

This is a very faint unfinished sketch after Ary Scheffer's painting of 1851, *Dante and Beatrice* (Museum of Fine Arts, Boston). It is based on a later engraving by Butterworth and Heath published in *Leisure Hour*. An impression of the print (unaccessioned) was found with the drawing (fig. 4).

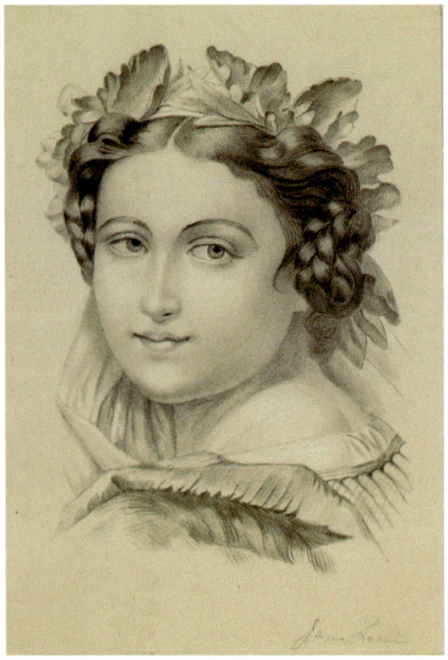

LL 2929

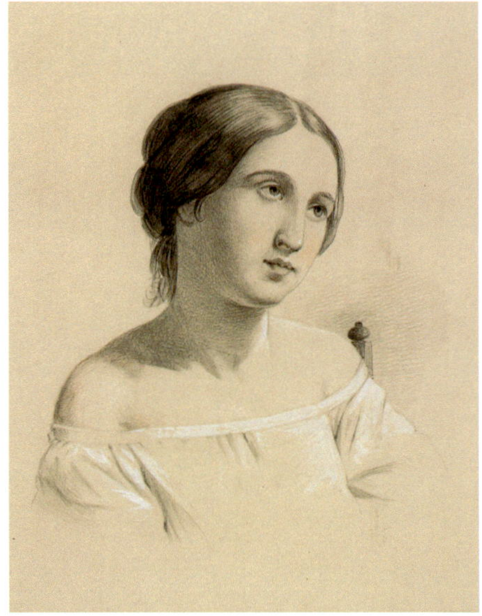

LL 2931

LL 2930

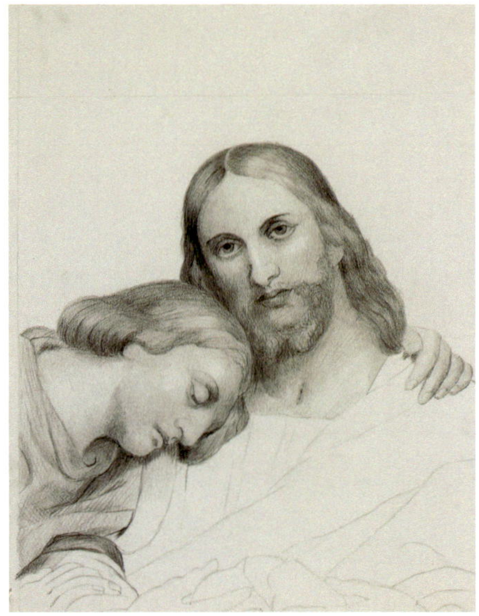

LL 2932

LL 2933

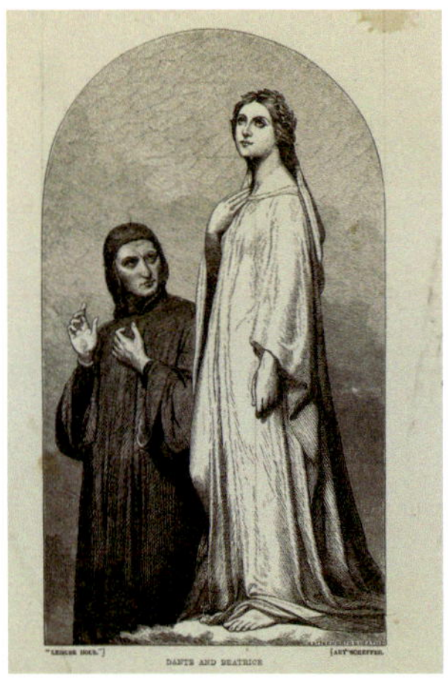

fig. 4. Butterworth and Heath, After Ary Scheffer, *Dante and Beatrice*, nineteenth century, engraving on paper, 27.5 x 18.8 cm, reproduced in *Leisure Hour*, National Museums Liverpool, Lady Lever Art Gallery

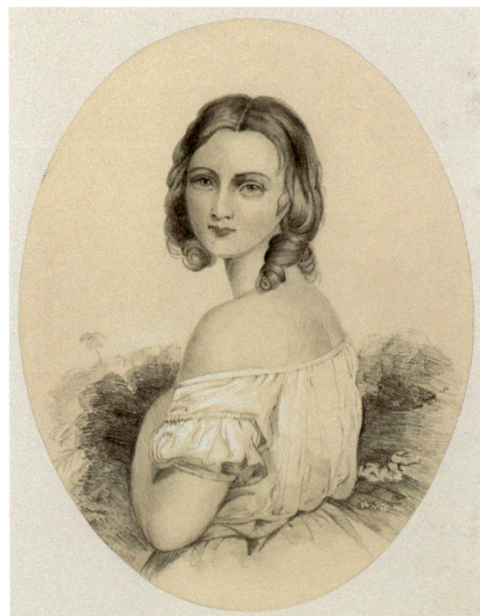

48 Jane Lever was born in 1845 and died in 1871; information provided by Gavin Hunter, Leverhulme Family Archive.

**Portrait of a girl, head and shoulders, wearing dress off the shoulders**
LL 2931

Pencil, black and coloured chalks with white heightening on paper laid down on card
33 x 25.4 cm
Date: probably 1860s–1890s

Prov: found in the Gallery at an unknown date

**Figure of Christ with a man**
LL 2932

Pencil on card
23.9 x 17.4 cm
Date: probably 1860s–1890s

Annot: From an [?] engraving of a painting by Ary Scheffer (pencil, verso)

Prov: found in the Gallery at an unknown date

The annotation on the reverse of LL 2932 is probably in the artist's hand. Neither the print nor the painting after which it was made has been identified.

**Portrait of a young girl with ringlets, wearing dress off the shoulders, head turned to face viewer**
LL 2933

Pencil with coloured chalks and white heightening on paper laid down on card
36 x 27.4 cm (cut in oval)
Date: probably 1860s–1890s

Prov: found in the Gallery at an unknown date

**Women and three children in Italianate landscape**
LL 2934

Pencil with white heightening on paper laid down on card
27.6 x 37.1 cm
Date: probably 1860s–1890s

Prov: found in the Gallery at an unknown date

The composition suggests that this drawing may be based on a print after a painting, although the latter has not been identified.

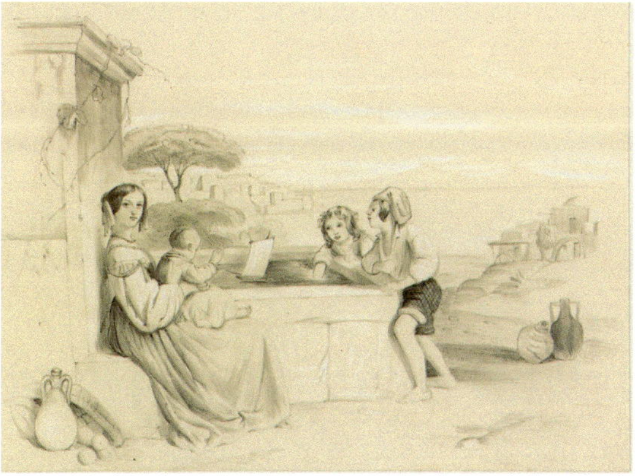

LL 2934

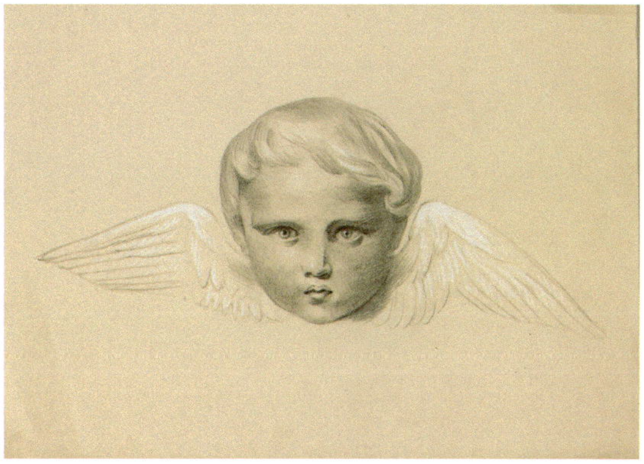

LL 2935

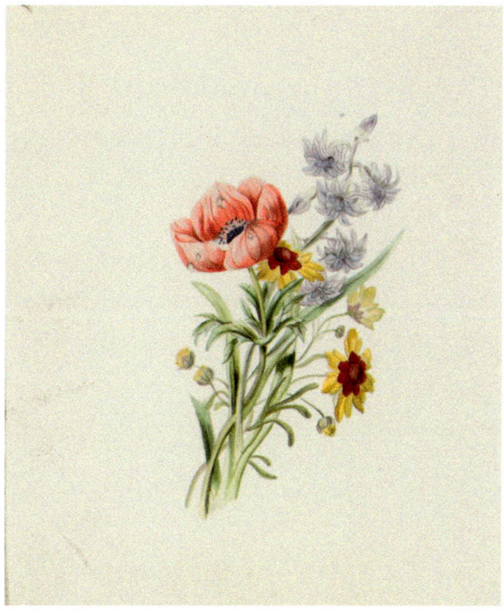

LL 2936

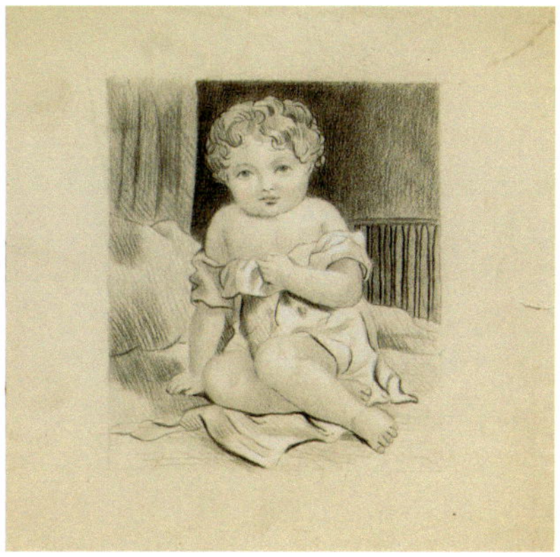

LL 2937

**Winged head of a boy**
LL 2935

Pencil with white heightening on paper
26.9 x 37.3 cm
Date: probably 1860s–1890s

Annot: Emily Lever (pencil, verso, top left)

Prov: found in the Gallery at an unknown date

It is not clear whether the annotation is a contemporary signature or a suggested attribution.

**Study of wild flowers**
LL 2936

Watercolour over pencil on paper
27.7 x 22.3 cm
Date: probably 1860s–1890s

Prov: found in the Gallery at an unknown date

**Young child on a bed**
LL 2937

Pencil, black and coloured chalks with white heightening on paper
17.6 x 15.3 cm (image); 25.4 x 25.3 cm (sheet)
Date: probably 1860s–1890s

Prov: found in the Gallery at an unknown date

**Portrait of a man, head and shoulders, wearing bow tie**
LL 2938

Pencil with black watercolour on paper
26.5 x 21.9 cm
Date: probably 1860s–1890s

Prov: found in the Gallery at an unknown date

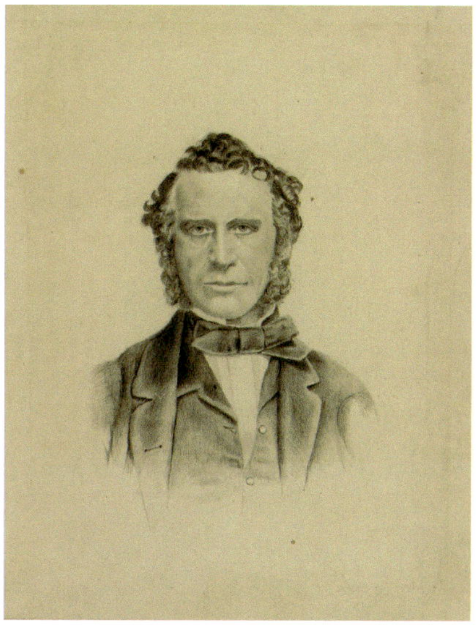

LL 2938

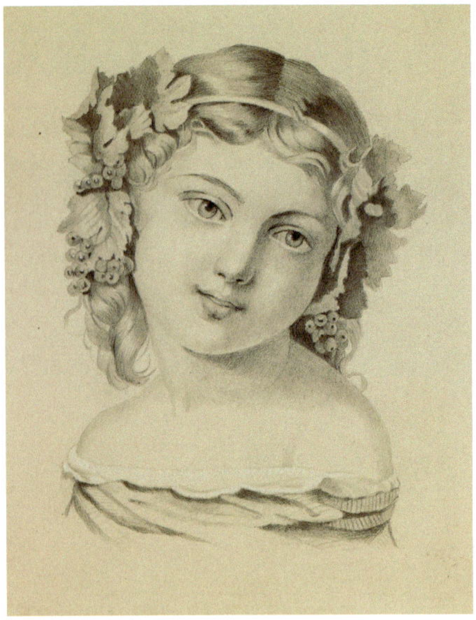

LL 2939

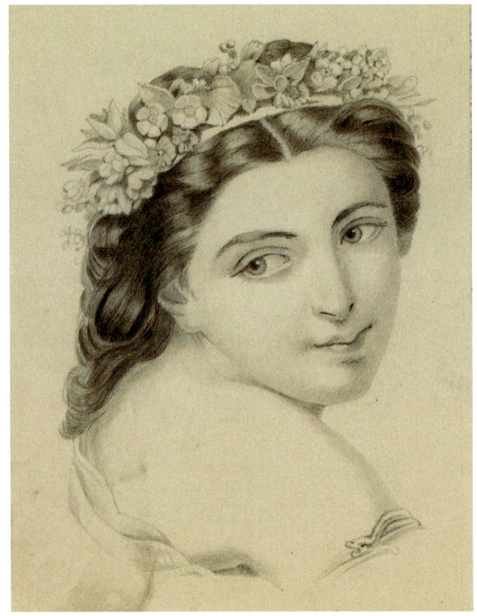

LL 2942

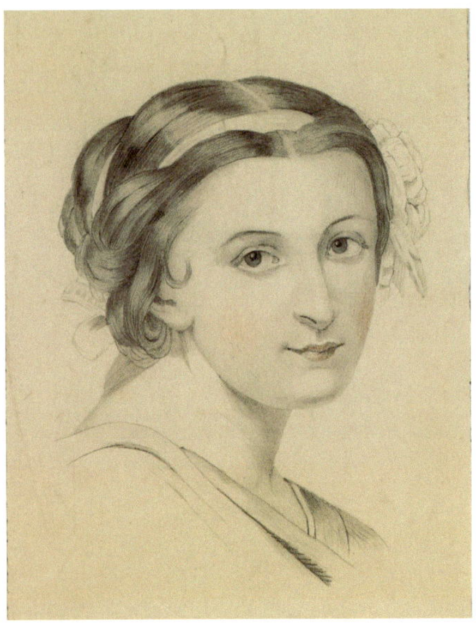

LL 2940

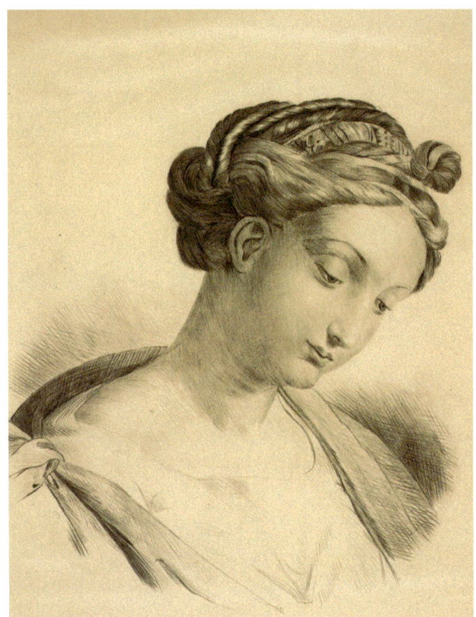

LL 2969

LL 2941

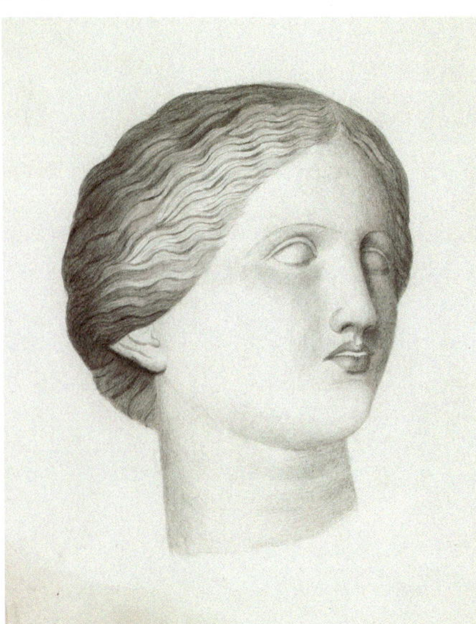

LL 2970

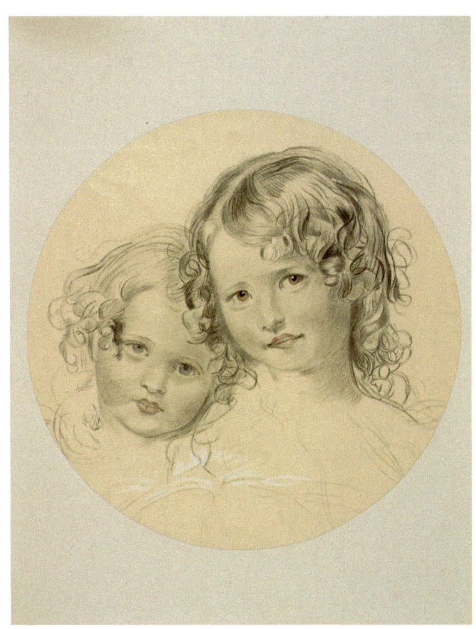

**Head of a Bacchante**
LL 2939

Pencil and black chalk with white heightening on paper
22.1 x 16.1 cm
Date: probably 1860s–1890s

Prov: found in the Gallery at an unknown date

**Portrait of a young woman, head and shoulders, wearing floral hair piece**
LL 2940

Pencil with coloured chalks and touches of gouache on paper
22.8 x 15.3 cm
Date: probably 1860s–1890s

Prov: found in the Gallery at an unknown date

**Head of a woman after an antique sculpture**
LL 2941

Pencil and black chalk on paper
39 x 27.8 cm
Date: probably 1860s–1890s

Annot: Emily Lever (pencil, verso)

Prov: found in the Gallery at an unknown date

It is not clear whether the annotation is a contemporary signature or a suggested attribution.

**Portrait of a girl as a Bacchante**
LL 2942

Pencil with black watercolour and chalk, with touches of gouache on paper
22.4 x 15.1 cm
Date: probably 1860s–1890s

Prov: found in the Gallery at an unknown date

The work is marked by a footprint (unknown) at lower left.

**Portrait of a woman, with plaited hair, head and shoulders, face looking downwards**
LL 2969

Pencil with black chalk and gum arabic on buff paper laid down on card
43 x 34.3 cm
Date: probably 1860s–1890s

Prov: found in the Gallery at an unknown date

**Portrait of two girls**
LL 2970

Pencil and black chalk with touches of watercolour and gouache on cream paper cut in oval and laid down on card
40.4 x 40.2 cm (cut in oval)
Date: probably 1860s–1890s

Prov: found in the Gallery at an unknown date

The head of the girl on the left is based on the portrait of Laura Anne in Thomas Lawrence's *The Calmady Children* (1823, Metropolitan Museum of Art, New York), but the head on the right appears freely invented (unless a print after an unidentified variant of Lawrence's work was the source for LL 2970).[49]

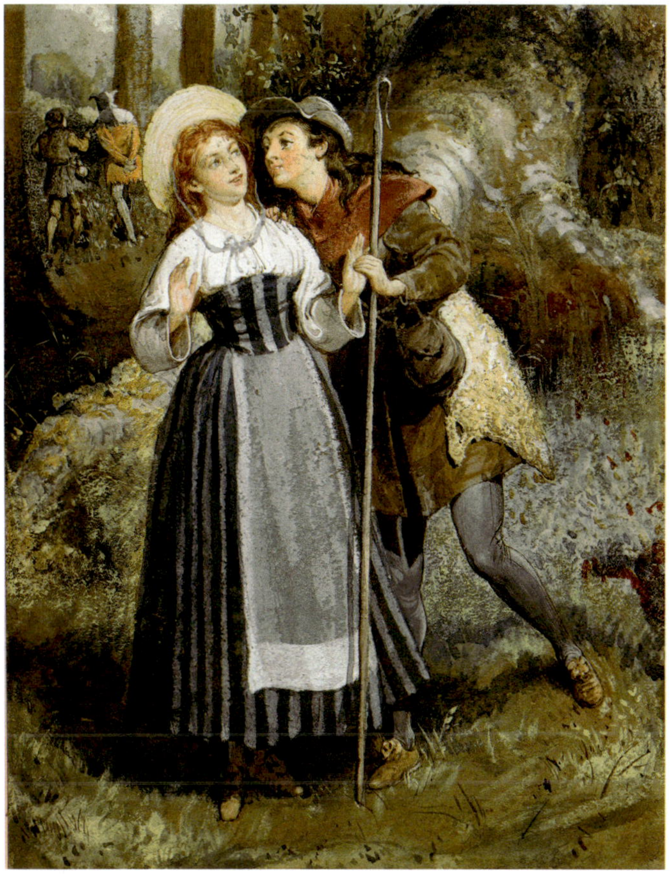

LL 3933

## VALENTINE WALTER LEWIS BROMLEY

1848 London–1877 Fallowes Green, Harpenden

**Rosalind and Celia**
LL 3933 (WHL 4702)

Gouache with watercolour on oatmeal paper
21.6 x 16.6 cm
Date: probably 1860s or 1870s

Annot: V. W. Bromley (pencil, on mount, bottom left)[50]

Prov: Sir Cuthbert Quilter; his sale, Christie's, 22 June 1923 (lot 126); bt. by Gooden and Fox (15 gns with WHL 4701) for Lever (£16 2s 10d)[51]

Bromley was taught by his father, an engraver, and in 1867 was elected an associate of the Institute of Painters in Water-Colours. He was also a member of the Society of British Artists and acted as an art correspondent for the *Illustrated London News*. He worked regularly as an illustrator and produced an important series of illustrations of Shakespeare (for the publishers Cassell, Petter and Galpin) and the Bible (for the *Illustrated London News*).

LL 3933 depicts the characters of Celia and Rosalind from Shakespeare's play *As You Like It*. The two women are cousins who have fled from the court of Duke Frederick, Celia's father and Rosalind's uncle. To ensure their anonymity, Rosalind has dressed as a man, Ganymede (the figure on the right) while Celia has assumed the guise of a shepherdess called Aliena (on the left). In the background the right-hand figure is Touchstone, the court jester who has fled with the girls. It is not clear whether Bromley's picture is intended to represent a particular scene from the play.

Works based on literary themes, especially from Shakespeare, were popular with middle-class art audiences and buyers during the Victorian period; the image may have been intended for engraving, but it has not been possible to link it to a particular publication. On stylistic grounds the work is consistent with other Bromley watercolours dating from the 1860s and 1870s (see, for example, *A Lady with a Falcon*, Sotheby's, 1 March 1984, lot 477).[52]

49 For versions of the painting, see Kenneth Garlick, 'A catalogue of the paintings, drawings and pastels of Sir Thomas Lawrence', *Walpole Society*, vol. 39 (1962–64), p. 47. It is unclear, however, whether any of these is a variant, as distinct from a study or a copy.

50 Comparison with Bromley's signature on other finished watercolours and engravings suggests that this inscription is not by him.

51 WHL 4701, E. Bale, *Maréchal Niel Roses in a Glass*, a watercolour dated 1873, was sold at the Anderson Galleries, New York, 2–4 March 1926 (see appendix 2).

52 *A Lady with a Falcon*, watercolour, signed and dated 1866, 31.5 x 20.5 cm.

## FORD MADOX BROWN
1821 Calais-1893 London

### The Nosegay
LL 3639 (WHL 3405)

Watercolour, gum arabic, white highlights and black chalk on paper
23.3 x 15.9 cm (sight)
Date: 1865-67

Inscr: FMB [monogram] 67 (watercolour, bottom left)

Prov: sold by the artist to T. H. McConnel of Manchester (£31 10s); his sale, Capes and Dunn, 30 July 1872 (lot 244); J. Kendrick Pyne, 1897; George Moore, 1910; bt. from the Leicester Galleries by Lever, 1918 (£75)[53]

Exh: London, Grafton Galleries, *Exhibition of the Works of Ford Madox Brown*, 1897 (cat. 181) as 'pastel study'; London, New Gallery, *3rd Exhibition of Fair Women*, 1910 (cat. 180); Port Sunlight, Lady Lever Art Gallery, *The Pre-Raphaelites - Their Friends and Followers*, 1948 (cat. 17); Brisbane, Queensland Art Gallery and tour of Australia and New Zealand, organised by the Empire Art Loan Exhibitions Society, *Exhibition of British Watercolours 1850-1914*, 1952-53 (cat. 11); Port Sunlight, Lady Lever Art Gallery and tour, *Pre-Raphaelite Drawings*, 2006-2008 (no cat. no.)

Lit: Ford Madox Hueffer, *Ford Madox Brown: A Record of his Life and Work* (London, 1896), p. 440; Virginia Surtees (ed.), *The Diary of Ford Madox Brown* (New Haven and London, 1981), p. 207; Mary Bennett, *Artists of the Pre-Raphaelite Circle: The First Generation* (London, 1988), pp. 36-37, illus. p. 36; Frank Milner, *The Pre-Raphaelites: Pre-Raphaelite Paintings and Drawings in Merseyside Collections* (Liverpool, 1995), p. 103; Dianne Sachko Macleod, *Art and the Victorian Middle Class: Money and the Making of Cultural Identity* (Cambridge, 1996), p. 447[54]

Although Brown was never a member of the Pre-Raphaelite Brotherhood, he was sympathetic towards their ambitions to reform English painting. He studied in Bruges and Ghent, and between 1837 and 1839 attended the Antwerp Academy, studying under the historical painter, Gustave, Baron Wappers. In 1844 Brown settled in London, following his marriage to his cousin, Elizabeth Bromley. In the same year he competed unsuccessfully for the Westminster Hall Decorations. Traveling to Basle and Rome in 1845-46, Brown came into contact with the German Nazarene painters led by Peter Cornelius and Johann Friedrich Overbeck. The meticulous detail and fresco-like colouring of Brown's early paintings, for example, *The Seeds and Fruits of English Poetry* (1845-51, 1853) reflect the influence of these artists. Brown taught Dante Gabriel Rossetti for a few weeks in 1848 and thereafter became a mentor to the PRB. The Pre-Raphaelite taste for everyday subjects with moral implications are reflected in two of his most famous paintings, *Work* (1852, 1856-65) and *The Last of England* (1852-55). Struggling to sell his own paintings, Brown identified with the desperation of the couple in the latter painting who are forced to emigrate to survive. Through his friendship with Rossetti, he became a founder member of the decorating firm Morris, Marshall, Faulkner and Co. in 1861, for which he designed furniture and stained glass.

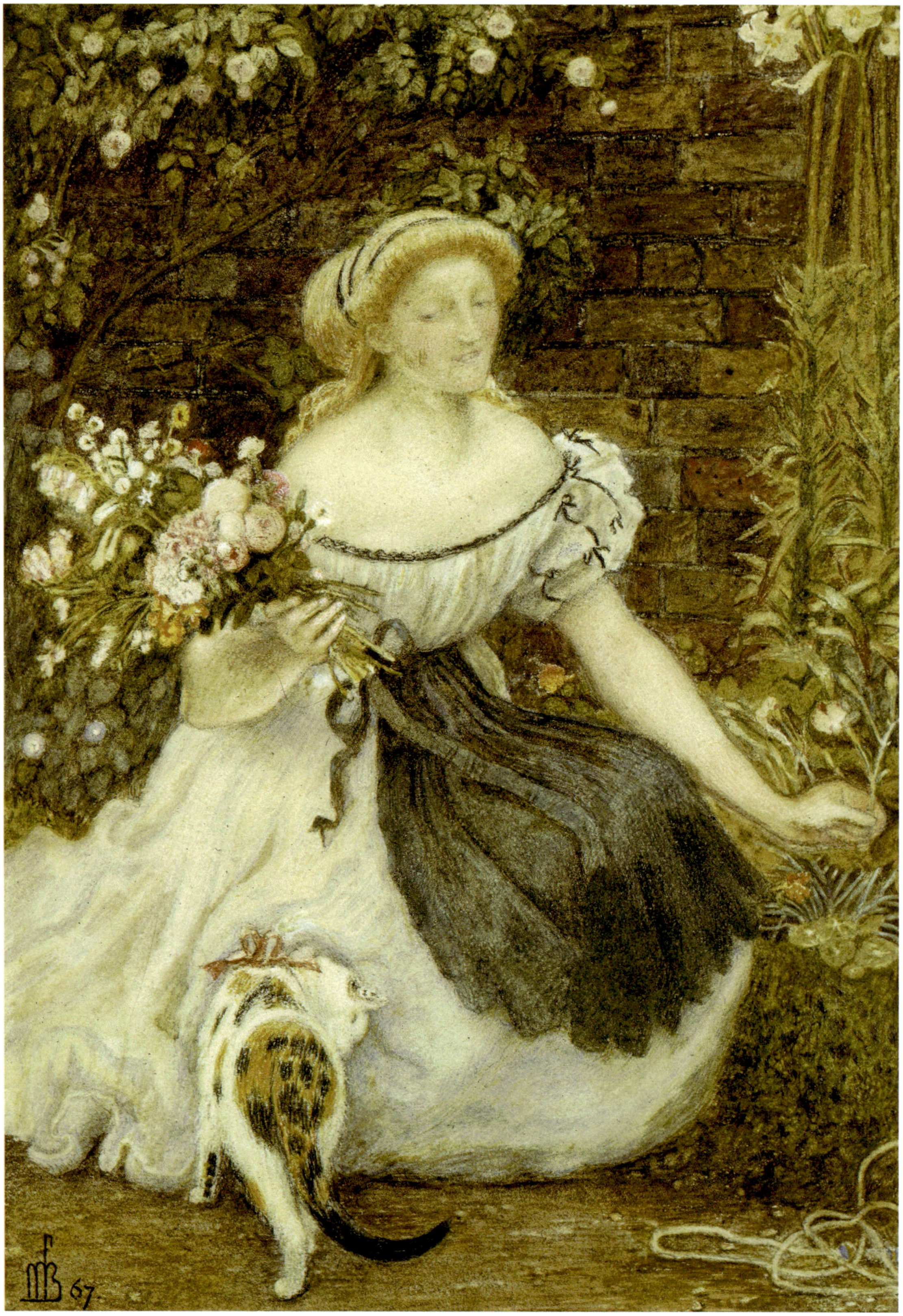

LL 3639

53 LLAG files: invoice, 7 January 1918.
54 I am grateful to Mary Bennett for her help in compiling the literature sections for all the Ford Madox Brown entries in this catalogue.

Brown's last major commission, received in 1878, was a series of murals for Manchester Town Hall depicting the history of the city.

This watercolour shows a young girl gathering flowers into a posy in a garden, her tortoiseshell cat attempting to distract her attention from the array of flowers and scents that surround her. The model was the artist's daughter, Catherine, who had appeared as a babe in arms in Brown's painting *Pretty Baa Lambs* (1851–59, Birmingham Museums and Art Gallery), but is here 17 years old.[55] Brown used LL 3639 as the basis for a finished watercolour, now in the Ashmolean Museum, Oxford, which was commissioned by the Manchester calico printer, Frederick Craven (1818–94) (fig. 5). The face of the girl in the latter is much idealised compared to the Lady Lever sketch, and the apron is pulled further across her skirt. Brown's diary records the number of hours he spent working on the girl's head and shoulders, her muslin dress and apron, and also the cat. The latter caused some frustration, and he recorded on 28 September 1865 'Tried to work at the Cat. Spoilt it'.[56] At the same time as painting *The Nosegay* Brown was progressing on a much larger oil painting, *The Coat of Many Colours* (1866, Lady Lever Art Gallery, LL 1633), which had been commissioned by George Rae in 1863.

Frederick Craven particularly admired the early watercolour school, and owned works by David Cox, George Cattermole, Samuel Prout and J.M.W. Turner.[57] However he also had a taste for contemporary watercolour artists and bought two watercolours by Rossetti, *Washing Hands* (1865, location unknown) and *Hesterna Rosa* (1865, Delaware Art Museum, Wilmington). Craven probably first came to Brown's attention in a letter he received from Rossetti on 21 March 1865 in which Rossetti announced that his patron 'wants water-colours' and remarked that Craven hoped to make Brown's acquaintance on his next visit to London.[58] Although Brown did not meet Craven when he was next in the city, just over two months later he received a commission from him to produce a companion piece for a watercolour of a boy praying by William Henry Hunt, Hunt's death the year before having prevented him from completing the commission.[59] Rossetti, who had already produced a number of works for Craven, probably recommended Brown for the task, and he advised his friend in a letter of 26 June 1865 that Craven wished the work to feature 'a golden haired female party',[60] but gave him no further instruction as to the subject. Rossetti gave Brown the dimensions of Hunt's watercolour (18½ by 12½ in.), so that he could match it, and said that Craven would willingly send him an outline sketch so as to 'give an idea of the size of head etc.'.[61]

The young female in Brown's watercolour who gathers flowers in a fashionably low-cut dress was an unusual companion to Hunt's devout young boy, his confinement and pious expression contrasting with the pleasure the girl gains from her fertile surroundings. Brown paid particular attention to the flowers in *The Nosegay,* and wrote to George Rae that he was progressing slowly on *The Coat of Many Colours* owing to the 'necessity of painting some flowers from nature in a drawing which otherwise could not be done till they blossom again next year'.[62] Although there is no evidence that Brown saw Hunt's watercolour, it is tempting to see the discarded rope in the bottom left of *The Nosegay* as a deliberate echo of the rosary at the feet of the boy in Hunt's work. *The Nosegay* has some allusions to an earlier painting by Brown, *Stages of Cruelty* (1856–57, Manchester Art Gallery), in which a young woman is seated on a garden wall teasingly avoiding the attentions of her suitor who looks at her adoringly, despite his uncomfortable position on the other side of the wall. Craven was clearly satisfied with the watercolour and went on to commission further works from Brown, including *Elijah and the Widow's Son* (1868, Victoria & Albert Museum) and two versions of *The Finding of Don Juan by Haidee* (a watercolour dating from 1868–70 is now in the National Gallery of Victoria, Melbourne; an oil version of 1878 is in the Musée d'Orsay, Paris).

This study for the finished watercolour was sold to T. H. McConnel who, having seen the watercolour he had made for Craven, asked Brown to work up the drawing. On receipt of the work he described it as a 'brilliant cheerful drawing and will be satisfactory until I can get some more important drawings from you'.[63]
HB

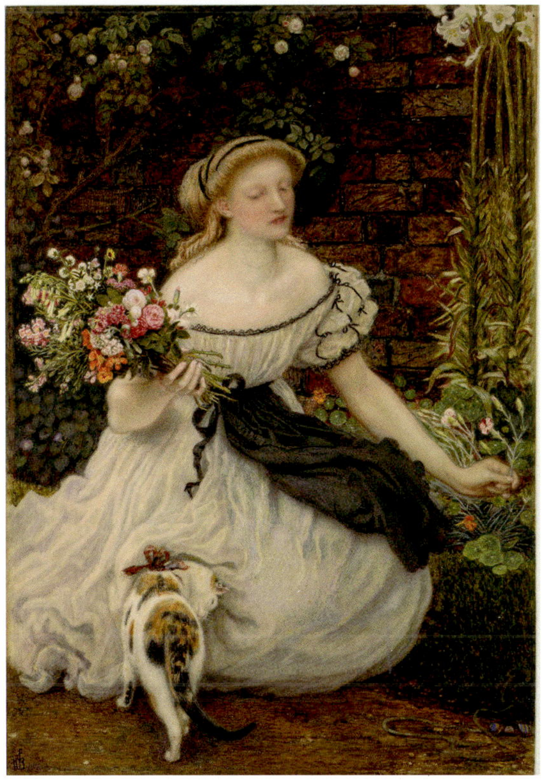

fig. 5. Ford Madox Brown, *The Nosegay*, 1865, watercolour and oil on paper, 47.5 x 31.9 cm, Ashmolean Museum, University of Oxford

55 Catherine Madox Brown (1850–1927) attended Queen's College, a girl's school in Harley Street, London, and was trained as an artist by her father. She also worked as his model and studio assistant. Her first exhibition was in 1869 and thereafter she chiefly painted in watercolours. See Jan Marsh and Pamela Gerrish Nunn, *Pre-Raphaelite Women Artists* (London, 1998), pp. 129–31.

56 Virginia Surtees (ed.), *The Diary of Ford Madox Brown* (New Haven and London, 1981), p. 204.

57 Rossetti described Craven to Brown as 'a very good paymaster and not a haggler at all – a grave, and (let us say in a whisper) rather stupid, enthusiast, of all the inarticulate business-type, with a mystic reverence for the English Water-colour school, D. Cox, Hunt, etc. Besides this, I think a thoroughly good fellow. Not a *very* rich man, I should fancy'; Oswald Doughty and John Robert Wahl (eds), *Letters of Dante Gabriel Rossetti* (Oxford, 4 vols, 1965), vol. II, p. 560. For more information about Frederick Craven, see Dianne Sachko Macleod, *Art and the Victorian Middle Class: Money and the Making of Cultural Identity* (Cambridge, 1996), p. 407.

58 Doughty and Wahl (eds), *Letters of Dante Gabriel Rossetti*, vol. II, p. 548.

59 The pendant picture is thought to be *Devotion*, now in the collection of Manchester Art Gallery, although this work is dated much earlier at 1836–42. Hunt's watercolour shows a young boy kneeling in an enclosed space, a rosary at his feet, and his hands positioned in prayer.

60 Doughty and Wahl (eds), *Letters of Dante Gabriel Rossetti*, vol. II, pp. 558–59.

61 Ibid., p. 559.

62 Brown to Rae, letter, 25 July 1865, quoted by Mary Bennett, *Artists of the Pre-Raphaelite Circle: The First Generation* (London, 1988), p. 37.

63 J. A. McConnel to Brown, letters, 8 March, 11 April 1867 (artist's family papers) quoted by Bennett, *Artists of the Pre-Raphaelite Circle*, p. 37.

## Cordelia's Portion
LL 3640 (WHL 4746, LP 9)

Watercolour, gouache and pastel on paper
70.5 x 107.3 cm
Date: 1866 (retouched in 1867, 1872 and 1883)

Inscr: FMB [monogram] 66 72 (watercolour, bottom left)

Prov: commissioned by Frederick Craven of Manchester, November 1865;[64] his sale, Christie's, 18 May 1895 (lot 45); bt. by Rowley (£210); Edgar Wood of Manchester, 1909; by descent to W. H. Wood; his sale, Christie's 2 May 1924 (lot 76); bt. by Gooden and Fox (580 gns) for Lever

Exh: London, 37 Fitzroy Square [artist's studio], 19–21 November 1866; London, Dudley Gallery, *3rd Watercolour Exhibition*, 1867 (cat. 249); Leeds, Royal Infirmary, *National Fine Arts Exhibition, Gallery of British Living Painters in Oil*, 1868 (cat. 234); Manchester, Manchester Academy, *Jubilee Exhibition*, 1909 (cat. 77); Manchester, Manchester City Art Gallery, *Ford Madox Brown and the Pre-Raphaelites*, 1911 (cat. 89); London, Tate Gallery, *Loan Exhibition of Works by Pre-Raphaelite Painters from Collections in Lancashire*, 1913 (cat. 10); Bath, Victoria Art Gallery, *Autumn Loan Exhibition of Works by Pre-Raphaelite Painters from Collections in Lancashire*, 1913 (cat. 26); Birkenhead, Williamson Art Gallery, *Loan Collection of Oil Paintings &c., on the occasion of the opening of the building*, 1928 (cat. 7); Port Sunlight, Lady Lever Art Gallery, *The Pre-Raphaelites - Their Friends and Followers*, 1948 (cat. 18); Belfast, Ulster Museum, *Shakespeare in Pictures*, 1964 (cat. 5); London, Tate Gallery, *The Pre-Raphaelites*, 1984 (cat. 239)

Lit: 'Mr Madox Brown's "Cordelia"', *The Reader*, vol. 7, no. 205 (1 December 1866), p. 977; 'The Dudley Gallery', *Nature in Art*, vol. 2 (1 March 1867), pp. 83–84; 'The General Exhibition of Watercolour Drawings (second notice)', *The London Review* (2 March 1867), p. 260; Ford Madox Hueffer, *Ford Madox Brown: A Record of his Life and Work* (London, 1896), pp. 197, 207, 214, 221–25, 232, 235–36, 441; Hippolyte Taine, *Notes sur l'Angleterre* (Paris, 3rd edn, 1871), pp. 352–53, trans. Edward Hymans, *Taine's Notes on England, 1860–1870* (London, 1957), pp. 262–63; Ernest Chesneau, *La Peinture anglaise* (Paris, 1882), p. 103; Sadakichi Hartmann, *Shakespeare in Art* (Boston, 1900), pp. 223–34; William Michael Rossetti, *Rossetti Papers, 1862–1870* (London, 1903), pp. 197, 224; W. Graham Robertson, *Time Was* (London, 1931), p. 168; John Sweeney (ed.), *The Painter's Eye: Notes and Essays on the Pictorial Arts by Henry James* (London, 1956), p. 250; Oswald Doughty and John Robert Wahl (eds), *Letters of Dante Gabriel Rossetti* (Oxford, 4 vols, 1965), vol. II, pp. 580–81, no. 652 DGR to FMB 19 November 1865; Deborah Cherry, 'An Annotated Edition of the Diary and Selected Letters of Ford Madox Brown, 1850–1870', unpublished PhD thesis (University of London, 1977), pp. 121–22, 130–31, 135–36; Helen O. Borowitz, '"King Lear" in the Art of Ford Madox Brown', *Victorian Studies*, vol. 21, no. 3 (spring 1978), p. 330 and *passim*; Christine Poulson, 'A Checklist of Pre-Raphaelite Illustrations of Shakespeare's Plays', *The Burlington Magazine*, vol. 122, no. 925 (April 1980), pp. 244–250; Virginia Surtees (ed.), *The Diary of Ford Madox Brown* (New Haven and London, 1981), pp. 207, 209–18; Dan H. Laurence (ed.), *Shaw's Music* (London, 3 vols, 1981), vol. II, pp. 525–26, 776; Martin Meisel, *Realizations: Narrative, Pictorial and Theatrical Arts in Nineteenth-Century England* (Princeton, 1983), pp. 404, 417, illus. fig. 195; Mary Bennett, *Artists of the Pre-Raphaelite Circle: The First Generation* (London, 1988), pp. 42–45, illus. p. 42, illus. col. pl. 12; Teresa Newman and Raymond Watkinson, *Ford Madox Brown and the Pre-Raphaelite Circle* (London, 1991), pp. 150, 193, illus. fig. 122; Frank Milner, *The Pre-Raphaelites: Pre-Raphaelite Paintings and Drawings in Merseyside Collections* (Liverpool, 1995), p. 107, illus. p. 106; Diane Sachko Macleod, *Art and the Victorian Middle Class: Money and the Making of Cultural Identity* (Cambridge, 1996), p. 407; Kenneth Bendiner, *The Art of Ford Madox Brown* (University Park, PA, 1998), pp. 27, 37, 40, 43, 71, 95, 113, 119, illus. fig. 52

The tragic story of King Lear preoccupied Brown throughout his career, and he was keen to illustrate all the episodes from Shakespeare's play in which the king's virtuous and moral daughter, Cordelia, played a role. In 1865, one year before beginning *Cordelia's Portion*, Brown exhibited at his solo exhibition 16 pen-and-ink studies depicting scenes from the play, which he had produced in 1844 while living in Paris.[65] LL 3640 was the result of Brown's intention, acknowledged in the accompanying catalogue to the 1865 exhibition, to use these outline drawings as the foundation for more finished designs.[66] LL 3640 in particular resembles *France Claims the Dispossessed Cordelia* (1844, Whitworth Art Gallery, Manchester), although the sensuous colouring and fluid gestures in the later watercolour contrast to the austere nature of the early composition.

Frederick Craven, who had a particular enthusiasm for English watercolours, commissioned *Cordelia's Portion* as a pendant to *The Return of Tibullus to Delia* which he had commissioned from Rossetti for £235.[67] Although Craven had requested an upright two-figure subject, Brown was unenthusiastic and suggested instead the 'declaration scene in the first act with a dozen figures'.[68] Craven eventually gave in to Brown's proposal and they agreed a price of £525. The completed work was delivered to Craven on 23 November 1866, eleven months after Brown had begun the composition. Although he continued to make alterations for Craven until the early 1870s, his patron was clearly impressed: 'the subject is finely conceived - broad in treatment and beautiful in colour - I thank you for making it for me with so much earnestness of purpose and for doing me so much justice'.[69]

The Lady Lever watercolour illustrates Act I, scene I of the play in which the King of France takes the disinherited Cordelia for his wife. Holding her arm to his heart, France declares his purpose: 'Fairest Cordelia, that art most rich, being poor / Most choice, forsaken, and most loved, despised, / These and thy virtues here I seize upon.' King Lear, slumped in his throne, dominates the composition, his state of mind reflected in both his contorted posture and crazed expression. A large map of the kingdom lies beneath his feet, different sections marked with the names of each of his daughters, though it is torn across the part marked 'Cordelia'. On the left-hand side of the throne, Cordelia's sisters, Goneril and Regan, accompanied by their husbands, the Dukes of Albany and Cornwall, exchange sour looks, their fingers interlaced in the interstices of the crown. Standing beside the throne the Duke of Burgundy bites his fingers in an agitated manner, his thoughts preoccupied with his decision to withdraw his suit towards Cordelia following her disinheritance. Cordelia looks away from her more impassioned suitor, the King of France (her expression contrasts with that in the Whitworth drawing in which she appears downcast). Meanwhile, in the background, Kent lingers in the doorway and subsidiary figures look over the back of the king's high throne in an attempt to witness the unfolding events.

Characteristically, Brown compresses an abundance of action into a confined space. The costumes and artefacts are painted with a Pre-Raphaelite diligence and attention to historical detail, from the imperial griffins carved into the throne and Roman table to the costumes worn by each of the figures. His family and friends were his principal models, Brown's daughter, Catherine, playing Cordelia and his wife, Emma, her evil sister, Goneril. Brown captures the raw emotions of each of the players in the unfolding drama. There were 21 productions of *King Lear* staged in London during the nineteenth century, and Borowitz conjectures that the theatricality of Brown's watercolour may demonstrate his awareness, in particular, of the production by William Charles Macready (who regularly moved his audiences to tears), which had first been performed in London in 1838.[70] Like Macready, Brown recreates the past in his watercolour (previous productions of the play had paid scant attention to Shakespeare's original text), dressing his characters as early Britons and exaggerating their expressions and gestures. The obvious theatricality of Brown's composition captivated Sir Henry Irving, who had an engraved copy of this watercolour in his dressing room, and, in 1892, commissioned Brown to design the sets and costumes for his production of *King Lear* at the Lyceum, London.

Brown was an extremely competent watercolourist and the critic F. G. Stephens recalled that his work in this medium 'secured

64 Brown was paid £130 on account on 22 November 1865; £130 on 25 April 1866, and again on 22 July 1866; final payment about September 1866 unrecorded; the work was finished in November 1866, and retouched in 1867, 1872 and 1883.

65 The exhibition was held at 191 Piccadilly and it included 100 of his works, including *Last of England* and *Work*. Brown completed 18 studies in total; 16 are now in the collection of the Whitworth Art Gallery, and two are owned by Birmingham Museums and Art Gallery. The catalogue accompanying the Piccadilly Exhibition is reproduced in Kenneth Bendiner, *The Art of Ford Madox Brown* (University Park, PA, 1998), pp. 131–56. Brown's interest in Shakespeare and the influence of the German illustrator Moritz Retzsch (1779–1857) on his sketches of Lear is detailed in Helen O. Borowitz, '"King Lear" in the Art of Ford Madox Brown', *Victorian Studies*, vol. 21, no. 3 (spring 1978), pp. 309–34.

66 These designs also formed the basis for *Lear and Cordelia* (1848–54, Tate), *The Parting of Cordelia and her Sisters* (1854, private collection) and an etching Brown made for *The Germ* in March 1850, vol. 3.

67 Rossetti's watercolour is dated 1867. See Virginia Surtees, *Dante Gabriel Rossetti 1828–1882: The Paintings and Drawings: A Catalogue Raisonné* (London, 2 vols, 1971), vol. I, p. 25. Rossetti wrote to Brown on 19 November 1865 to inform him that Craven hoped their watercolours would be a similar size (although Brown's watercolour ended up being much bigger). Rossetti was not able to begin his watercolour as quickly as he was still preoccupied with other commissions; Doughty and Wahl (eds), *Letters of Dante Gabriel Rossetti*, vol. II, p. 580.

68 Quoted in Bennett, *Artists of the Pre-Raphaelite Circle*, p. 43.

69 Ibid.

70 Borowitz, 'King Lear', p. 319.

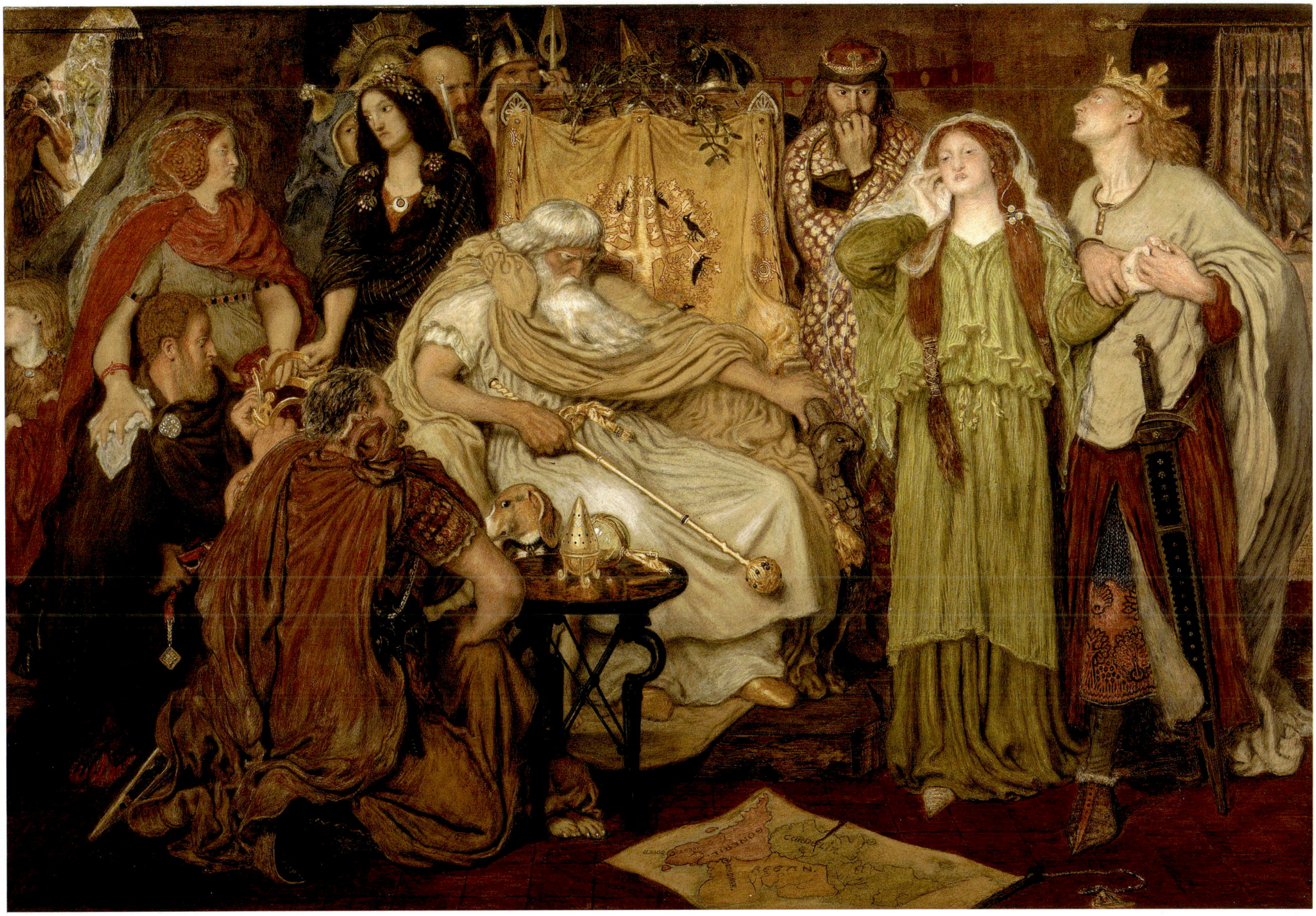

LL 3640

him a world of admirers'.[71] However, in 1867, when LL 3640 was exhibited at the Dudley Gallery, the superabundance of detail perplexed the critic of the *Saturday Review* who complained:

> That Mr. Madox Brown is an artist of real genius every good judge must be ready to admit, but his energy is not accompanied by moderation and good taste ... There is an overcrowding and obtrusiveness of minor detail which, though common in the [Pre-Raphaelite] school to which Mr. Madox Brown belongs, is a fault and hindrance. What is the use of the dog's paws under the table? The picture would have been better without them, and the dog's head does not easily explain itself; many spectators fail to see what it is.[72]

(Craven also questioned whether the dog was crucial to the composition.) The awkward composition, in part, reflects the influence of the German Nazarene painters, Peter Cornelius and Fredrich Overbeck, whose primitive style Brown was familiar with from his early art training on the Continent. However, there were few precedents to the jewel-like colouring in Brown's watercolour. Craven, in particular, found some of the colouring garish and insisted that Brown tone down Albany's cheek, and complained that there was 'too much red in the hair and face of Goneril'.[73] The dazzling colours may reflect Brown's contemporary preoccupation with producing stained glass for Morris and Co.

Three other versions of this scene exist. They include an oil sketch (1867–75, Fitzwilliam Museum, Cambridge),[74] a version in chalk and wash dated 1869 (Manchester Art Gallery),[75] and a finished oil dated 1875–80 (Southampton Art Gallery).[76]

HB

71 *Portfolio*, vol. 24 (1893), p. 70.

72 *Saturday Review* (2 March 1867), quoted by Bendiner, *Art of Ford Madox Brown*, p. 43.

73 Quoted by Bennett, *Artists of the Pre-Raphaelite Circle*, p. 44.

74 55 x 77 cm.

75 74.5 x 107 cm.

76 79.5 x 111.8 cm.

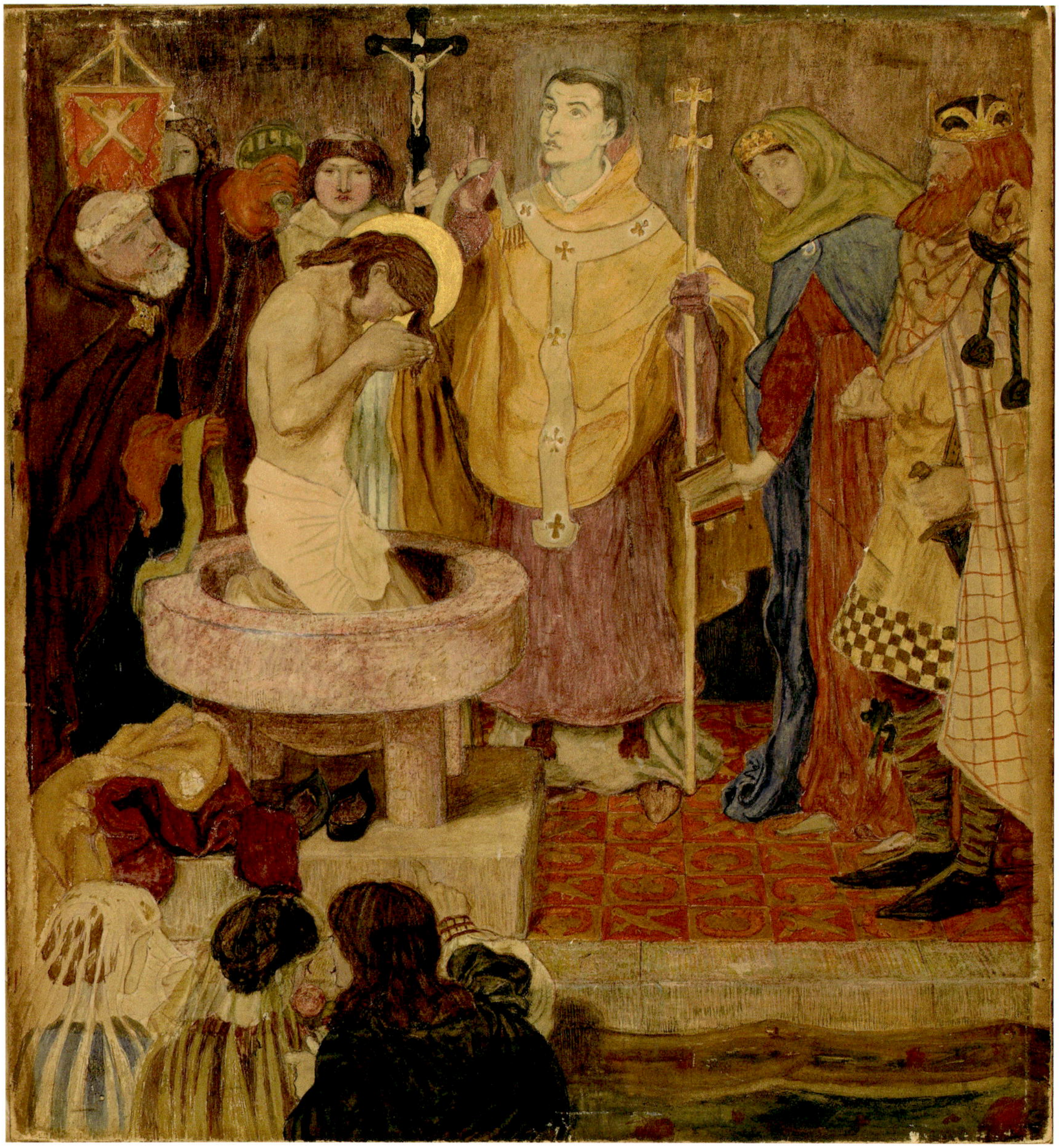

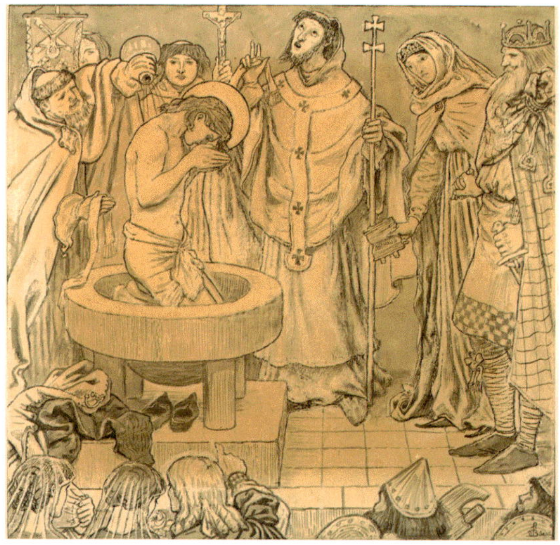

fig. 6. Ford Madox Brown, *The Baptism of St Oswald* (cartoon for stained glass), 1864, chalk and wash on paper, 47.2 x 48 cm, V&A Images/Victoria and Albert Museum

LL 3645

## AFTER FORD MADOX BROWN

### The Baptism of St Oswald
LL 3645 (WHL 2766)

Watercolour with gilt [on nimbus] on paper
56 x 51 cm
Date: after 1864, before 1877

Prov: possibly artist's executors' sale, T. G. Wharton, London, 29–31 May 1894 (lot 281 or 282);[77] bt. by Rathbone (£3) and (£6); Harold Rathbone, who sold it from the exhibition at the Bluecoat School, Liverpool, to Lever in May 1916 (£30)

Exh: Liverpool, Bluecoat School, exhibition title unknown, 1916 (cat. no. unknown);[78] Port Sunlight, Lady Lever Art Gallery, *The Pre-Raphaelites – Their Friends and Followers*, 1948 (cat. 12); China and East Berlin, British-China Friendship Association, *British Watercolour Painting during Three Centuries*, 1963 (cat. 104)

Lit: Mary Bennett, *Artists of the Pre-Raphaelite Circle: The First Generation* (London, 1988), pp. 53–54, illus. p. 53; Frank Milner, *The Pre-Raphaelites: Pre-Raphaelite Paintings and Drawings in Merseyside Collections* (Liverpool, 1995), p. 98, illus. p. 98

This watercolour was made after a cartoon (fig. 6), now in the Victoria & Albert Museum, for a stained-glass window depicting the life of St Oswald for St Oswald's Church in Durham, where the saint was buried.[79] St Oswald (c. 605–642), who is primarily known for introducing Christian missionaries to Northumbria, helped by St Aidan (Oswald would succeed St Aidan as King of Northumbria) is depicted here kneeling in a large stone font, the clothing he has removed surrounding its base. The priest, who pours holy water over him from a bottle, and a monk partake in the ceremony, while the King of Northumbria holds the Queen's left hand (in her right hand she possibly carries a copy of the Bible) and their attendants observe. One spectator, accompanied by two veiled women, gestures from his position below the platform towards the holy ritual.

77 Lots 281 and 282 were printed as 'Moses' and 'Zachariah', but in an annotated copy of the sale catalogue (now owned by the artist's descendants) this has been crossed out and replaced with 'unfinished painting the Baptism' and 'do do' (Bennett, *Artists of the Pre-Raphaelite Circle*, p. 52). This is supported by the fact that '281' is also chalked on the reverse of LL 3645 but, as Bennett points out, Rathbone also purchased a cartoon of Zachariah (now in Birmingham Museums and Art Gallery) at the sale (ibid., p. 53).

78 This exhibition is cited in Bennett, *Artists of the Pre-Raphaelite Circle*, p. 52.

79 All six cartoons were exhibited in the artist's 1865 exhibition. They became part of a three-light window set at the west end of the church. The panels were positioned within decorative work by Webb, and roundels of angels by Morris.

The Lady Lever work and the cartoon differ primarily in the appearance of the priest in the act of baptising St Oswald: his expression is rapturous in the latter, whereas in LL 3645 it conforms to the formality of the blessing. In addition the two soldiers in the bottom right are omitted in LL 3645, and the floor has plain rather than patterned tiles. Harold Rathbone, who sold the watercolour to Lever in 1916, suggested that the Browns' daughter, Catherine, created this replica. Although Catherine, like her sister, Lucy, was to become a competent watercolourist, the awkwardness of the figures and loosely painted background in this design may indicate her hand rather than that of her father. In addition the colouring is muted, and the figures extremely pale, which contrasts to the sensuous colouring that often characterises Brown's watercolours, for example, *Cordelia's Portion* (pp. 22–23).

The manufacture of stained glass had been within the remit of Morris, Marshall, Faulkner and Co. from its inception in 1861, and the majority of the partners produced designs, including Burne-Jones and Philip Webb. The firm aimed for simplicity in their designs, and avoided the harsh colours used by early stained-glass manufacturers. Brown produced nearly 130 subjects and single-figure designs for the firm up until 1874, many portraying early English saints. In 1864, the year he made the cartoon of St Oswald, Brown worked on windows for Bradford Cathedral and churches in Guernsey, Glasgow, Northamptonshire and the Isle of Wight.[80] He generally retained the copyright for his inventions, considering his work in the medium to contain 'invention, expression, and good dramatic action'[81] which could be translated into his historical pictures. Indeed, Brown referred back to his early cartoon, and LL 3645, while he was working on the murals for Manchester's new Gothic town hall which he began in 1877. In these, St Edwin, who was supposedly baptised in Manchester,[82] replaces St Oswald kneeling in the font. The priest has a strong resemblance to the equivalent figure in LL 3645, and his expression and gestures were clearly intended to resemble those in the earlier work.

HB

80 For a complete list of Brown's stained-glass designs, see A. C. Sewter, *The Stained Glass of William Morris and his Circle* (New Haven and London, 2 vols, 1974–75).

81 Quoted in Linda Parry (ed.), *William Morris* (London, 1997), p. 130.

82 The subject was justified for inclusion in the mural scheme on the grounds that Manchester formed part of Edwin's kingdom of Northumbria and Deira; see Julian Treuherz, 'Ford Madox Brown and the problem of the Manchester Murals', in J. H. G. Archer (ed.), *Art and Architecture in Victorian Manchester* (Manchester, 1985), p. 187.

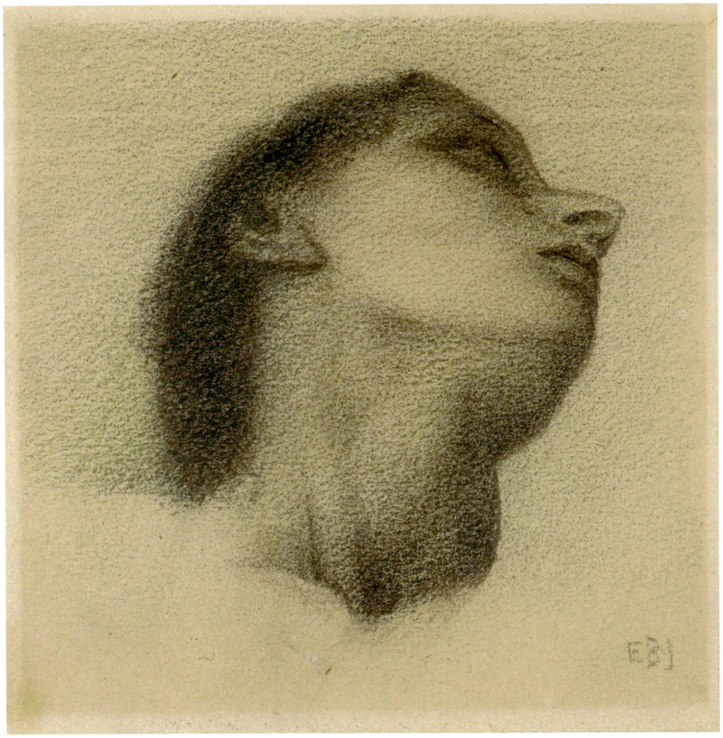

LL 3787

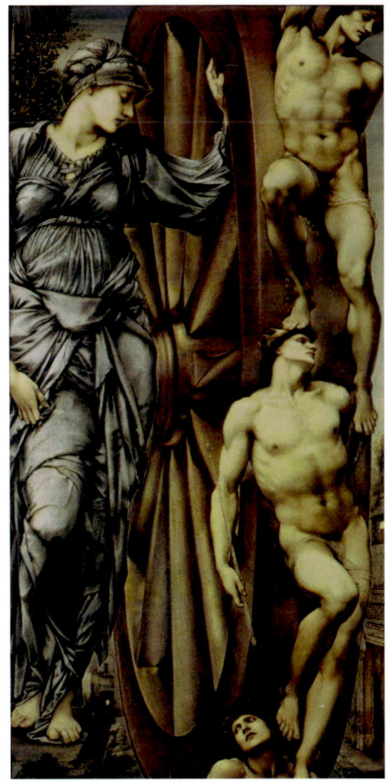

fig. 7. Edward Burne-Jones, *The Wheel of Fortune*, 1875–83, oil on canvas, 199 x 100 cm, Musée d'Orsay, Paris/Bridgeman

## EDWARD BURNE-JONES

1833 Birmingham–1898 Fulham, London

**Study for the head of the king in *The Wheel of Fortune***

LL 3787 (WHL 3931)

Green pastel and pencil on wove paper
14.8 x 14.7 cm (image); 15.7 x 15.5 cm (sheet)
Date: c. 1870–71

Inscr: EBJ (pastel, bottom right)

Prov: by descent to Philip Burne-Jones; his sale, Christie's, 5 June 1919 (lot 90); bt. by Gooden and Fox (10 gns) for Lever

Exh: Port Sunlight, Lady Lever Art Gallery, *The Pre-Raphaelites – Their Friends and Followers*, 1948 (cat. 83)

As a boy, Burne-Jones showed the scholarly qualities that would later influence his art, whose subject matter mainly took its inspiration from medieval legend and classical myth. In 1853 he went up to Exeter College, Oxford, intending to enter the church. At Oxford he met his lifelong friend and collaborator William Morris and the two bonded over their mutual passion for the Middle Ages. Inspired by seeing Pre-Raphaelite pictures and reading Ruskin they resolved to devote themselves to art. Burne-Jones was virtually self-taught as an artist, although he did receive a few lessons from Dante Gabriel Rossetti (see pp. 164–66) whom he met in 1856; his early watercolours and small pen drawings show the older artist's influence.

In 1861, together with Rossetti and Ford Madox Brown (see pp. 20–23), Burne-Jones helped Morris found the decorating firm of Morris, Marshall, Faulkner and Co.; from then on he supplied Morris with an endless stream of designs which included stained glass and tapestries. In the 1860s he evolved his own characteristic style, with his work influenced by the simplicity of form and richness of colour of the Venetian painting he had seen on a trip to Italy with Ruskin in 1862. In 1864 he was elected an associate of the SPWC and, despite some hostility towards his figurative subject-matter, began to gain patrons. In 1867, now married to Georgiana and with two children, he settled at The Grange in Fulham. In 1870, when criticisms were made of the nudity of one of his figures, he resigned from the SPWC.

The next seven years were spent in relative isolation, although he made two final visits to Italy in 1871 and 1873 where he studied the work of Michelangelo, Mantegna, Leonardo da Vinci and Botticelli, artists who were to influence his mature style. In 1877 Burne-Jones showed

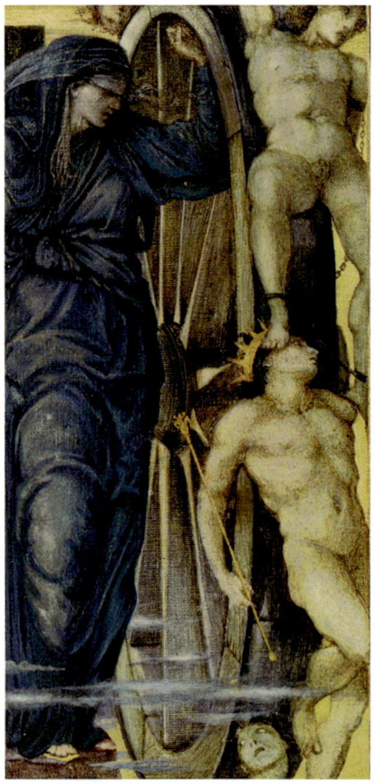

fig. 8. Edward Burne-Jones, *Fortuna: The Triumph of Love, or Amor Vincit Omnia*, 1871, watercolour and gouache heightened with gold on canvas, laid on paper, 33 x 19.7 cm, © Christie's Images Ltd, 2008

eight paintings at the opening exhibition of the Grosvenor Gallery, where he was acclaimed as the leader of a rising national school of art, and he continued to exhibit there until 1887 when he transferred to the New Gallery. In later years he produced many illustrations for books published by Morris at the Kelmscott Press, notably *Chaucer* (1896). By the time he had accepted a baronetcy in 1894, Burne-Jones had also gained a considerable reputation in France. In the last decade of his life, with paintings such as *The Sleep of Arthur in Avalon* (1881–98), Burne-Jones was to return to his earlier preoccupations with Arthurian legend and with the Gothic style.

LL 3787 is a study for the head of the figure of the king in Burne-Jones's monumental painting *The Wheel of Fortune* (1875–83, Musée d'Orsay, Paris, fig. 7).[83] Burne-Jones's composition depicted the huge and statuesque Fortune with her wheel alongside the helpless mortal figures representing a slave, a king and a poet. The final painting was begun in 1875 but developed from an idea generated in the summer of 1870 from the unfinished oil, the so-called Troy triptych (where the figure of Fortune is depicted on one of the intermediate panels of the predella).[84]

83 Stephen Wildman and John Christian, *Edward Burne-Jones: Victorian Artist-Dreamer* (exh. cat., New York, Metropolitan Museum of Art, Birmingham, Birmingham Museums and Art Gallery, and Paris, Musée d'Orsay, 1998–99), pp. 153–55 (cat. 52), illus. col. See also Leslie Parris (ed.), *The Pre-Raphaelites* (exh. cat., London, Tate Gallery, 1984), pp. 236–37 (cat. 155), illus. b&w.

84 This work is arguably more correctly referred to as a polyptych. For the Troy triptych, see Wildman and Christian, *Edward Burne-Jones*, pp. 152–53 (cat. 50).

There are at least five other versions of *The Wheel of Fortune* in various media and John Christian has suggested that the Lady Lever work is probably a study for the early 1871 watercolour version, exhibited at the Dudley Gallery in 1872 (until recently in the Watts Gallery, Compton, Surrey, fig. 8).[85] It is in this version that the angle of the king's head is most similar to the Lady Lever drawing. Although the Lady Lever work must date from c.1870–71, Burne-Jones's use of chalk on a relatively heavy paper, giving a grainy texture to the shadows and background, is typical of the artist's finished 'presentation' drawings produced in the mid-1860s (see, for example, his *Head of a Man in a Renaissance Cap*, Birmingham Museums and Art Gallery).[86] The fact that the artist initialled the Lady Lever drawing suggests that he conceived of it as a finished drawing. Numerous studies exist for the figures and drapery in the painting, including one for the torso of the king (British Museum)[87] but LL 3787 is the only known study for this figure's head.

### Female head study for *The Wheel of Fortune*
LL 3816 (WHL 3904)

Pencil on wove paper
22 x 12.4 cm
Date: early 1870s

Inscr: EBJ / 1873 (pencil, lower right)

Prov: by descent to Philip Burne-Jones; his sale, Christie's, 5 June 1919 (lot 69); bt. by Gooden and Fox (11 gns with LL 3817, WHL 3903, WHL 3905) for Lever (£11 16s 9d)

Exh: London, Burlington Fine Arts Club, *Exhibition of Drawings and Studies by Sir Edward Burne-Jones, Bart.*, 1899 (cat. 43); Port Sunlight, Lady Lever Art Gallery, *The Pre-Raphaelites - Their Friends and Followers*, 1948 (cat. 85); Sheffield, Mappin Art Gallery, *Burne-Jones*, 1971 (cat. 108); Port Sunlight, Lady Lever Art Gallery and tour, *Pre-Raphaelite Drawings*, 2006–2008 (no cat. no.)

This drawing is one of a number of studies that Burne-Jones made in the first half of the 1870s for the head of the figure of Fortune in *The Wheel of Fortune*. Burne-Jones first started thinking about this composition in 1870 with his so-called Troy triptych and in his main oil of the subject begun in 1875 (Musée D'Orsay, Paris, fig. 7) (see the previous entry for a discussion of these and other versions). In the final painting, Fortune is depicted wearing a classical-style head-dress. In the early 1870s (the inscribed dates on Burne-Jones's drawings should always be treated with a certain degree of caution) the artist produced a number of drawings of a female model with a bowed head, sometimes swathed, sometimes with elaborate plaits and other times combining the two.[88] By the time of the 1875 composition Burne-Jones had decided on a classical type of head-dress that owes an obvious debt to Michelangelo's Libyan and Erythraean Sibyls on the Sistine Chapel ceiling, which he had spent time sketching on his visit to Rome in 1871.
LL 3816 is a working study, demonstrating Burne-Jones's attempts to perfect every element of the design of his final paintings. The elaborate head-dress depicted here is not replicated in the final painting, where Fortune's head-covering has been simplified and may be the 'quaint little bonnet' designed by Mrs Comyns Carr, wife of one of the directors of the Grosvenor Gallery.[89]
The identity of the model in LL 3816 is not known, but appears to be the same as in another head study dated 1872 (Musée du Louvre, Paris).[90]

85 John Christian, verbally, January 2008. The versions include a gouache in blue grisaille of c. 1870 in Tullie House Museum and Art Gallery, Carlisle, for which see John Christian, 'La Roue de Fortune de Burne-Jones', *Revue du Louvre et des musées de France* (March 1984), pp. 204–11, illus. fig. 3; also Martin Harrison and Bill Waters, *Burne-Jones* (London, 1973), p. 105 (fig. 147); a gouache of c. 1871–85 belonging to the London Borough of Hammersmith and Fulham public libraries, currently on loan to Leighton House, John Christian, *Burne-Jones* (exh. cat., London, Hayward Gallery and tour organised by the Arts Council, 1975–76), p. 49 (cat. 124); and a gouache of c. 1882 in the National Museum of Wales, Cardiff, Harrison and Waters, *Burne-Jones*, p. 133 (cat. 190). There is a smaller oil of 1885 in the National Gallery of Victoria, Melbourne. The ex Watts Gallery version is watercolour on canvas, 33 x 19.7 cm (Christian, 'La Roue de Fortune', illus. fig. 4). It was sold at Christie's, 5 June 2008 (lot 39).

86 Stephen Wildman, *Visions of Love and Life: Pre-Raphaelite Art From The Birmingham Collection, England* (exh. cat., Birmingham, Birmingham Museums and Art Gallery and US tour organised by Art Services International, 1995–96), p. 244 (fig. 73), illus. b&w.

87 Christian, *Burne-Jones*, p. 50 (cat. 126). Although its inscribed date of 1879 may be incorrect, this study, with its use of hard pencil in Burne-Jones's Florentine manner, is of a different style to LL 3787 and is typical of his drawings from the 1870s.

### Two female head studies (framed together)
LL 3822A–B (WHL 3883)

### Female head turned half left
LL 3822A

Pencil on wove paper
24.8 x 17.1 cm (sight)
Date: probably c.1873

Inscr: EBJ 18/70 (pencil, bottom right)

### Female head turned half right
LL 3822(B)

Pencil on wove paper
21.7 x 15.3 cm (sight)
Date: 1872

Inscr: EB-J / 1872 / a portrait (pencil, bottom right)

88 See, for example, Hilary Morgan, *Burne-Jones, The Pre-Raphaelites and Their Century* (exh. cat., London, Peter Nahum Gallery, 2 vols, 1989), vol. I, pp. 71–72 (cats. 52–53), illus. vol. II, pls. 36–37.

89 Eve Adam (ed.), *Mrs J. Comyns Carr's Reminiscences* (London, 1926), p. 62.

90 Illustrated in Wildman and Christian, *Edward Burne-Jones*, p. 155 (cat. 53). There are two further studies for the head of Fortune in monochrome oil of a later date, taken from a different model (see Christian, 'La Roue de Fortune', figs. 10 and 11).

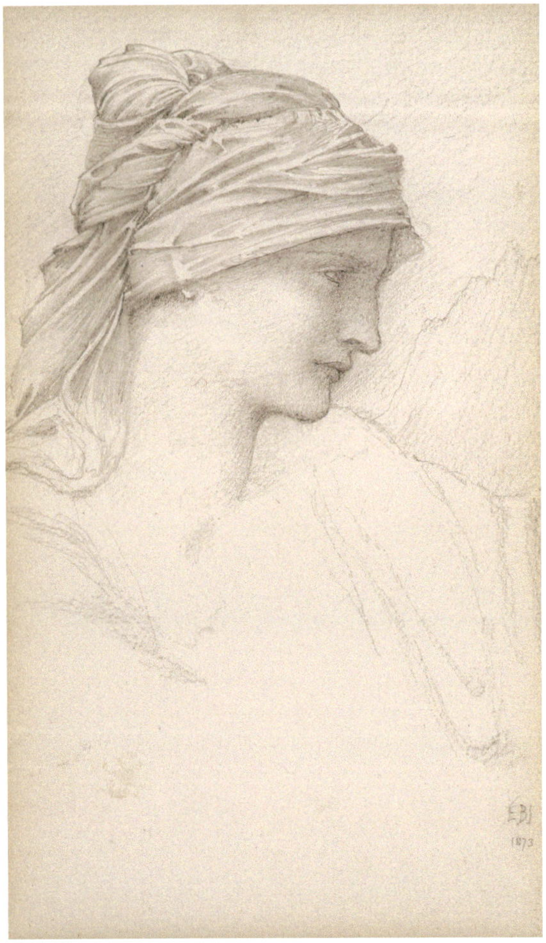

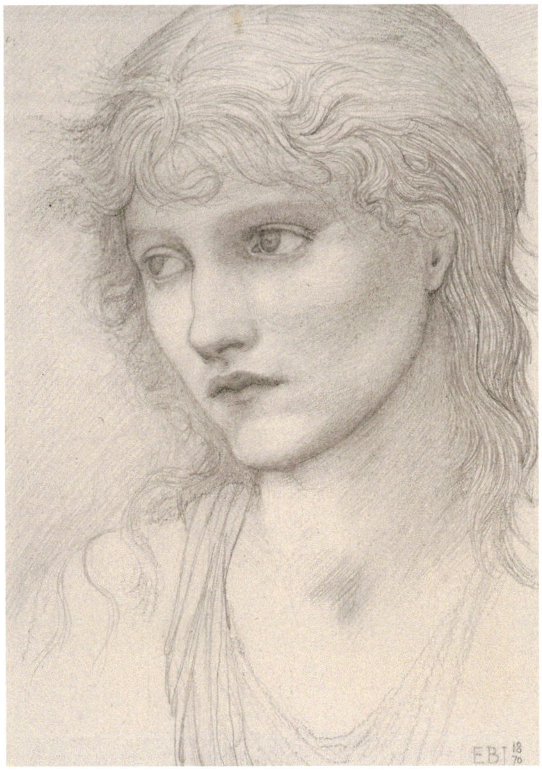

LL 3822A

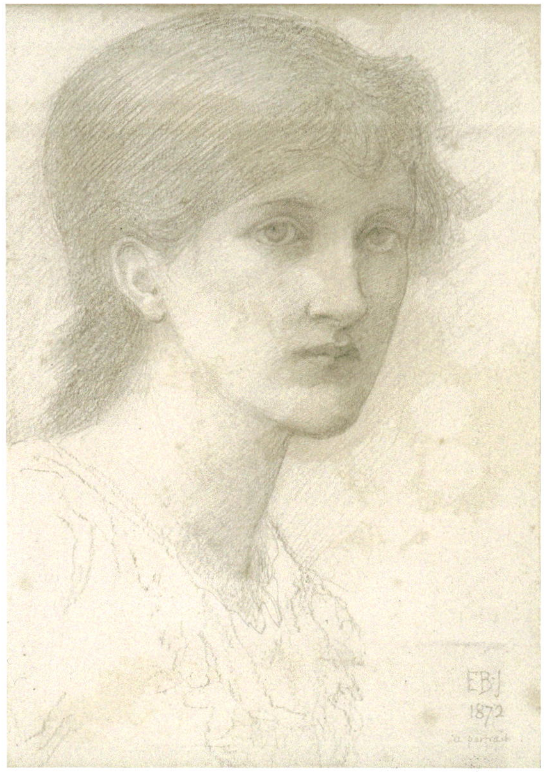

LL 3822B

LL 3816

Prov: by descent to Philip Burne-Jones; his sale, Christie's, 5 June 1919 (lot 50); bt. by Gooden and Fox (£29 8s with WHL 3884-85) for Lever (£30 2s 9d)

Exh: Port Sunlight, Lady Lever Art Gallery, *The Pre-Raphaelites - Their Friends and Followers*, 1948 (cats. 71i and 71ii); Sheffield, Mappin Art Gallery, *Burne-Jones*, 1971 (cat. 58)

Unlike LL 3813A and B (p. 33), which are also framed together, these two drawings are not from the same model. LL 3822A, although inscribed 1870, is stylistically consistent with a slightly later date of c. 1873 and may be another example of the artist retrospectively inscribing a work and misremembering the date (see LL 3816, p. 26, and LL 3815, pp. 34-35). The work is in the artist's Florentine mode; here, the sinuous lines of hair captured in hard pencil show the influence of Botticelli. The drawing does not appear to be related to a painting and may be one of many examples by the artist which he drew for its own sake where he revelled in the act of drawing, of capturing a particular pose or the expression of a model.

LL 3822B, like LL 3822A, does not appear to relate to a painting. Inscribed 'a portrait' and with the artist's initials, it may have been intended as a gift to the (unidentified) model (the inscription could represent some sort of private joke), although why the work then remained in Burne-Jones's possession is a puzzle.

## St John the Evangelist
LL 10327 (WHL 3898)

Pencil on wove paper
25.2 x 17.8 cm
Date: 1873

Annot: Evangelist.1873 (pencil, verso, lower left)

Prov: by descent to Philip Burne-Jones; his sale, Christie's, 5 June 1919 (lot 53); bt. by Gooden and Fox for Lever (4 gns with WHL 3899-3901)

Exh: Port Sunlight, Lady Lever Art Gallery, *The Pre-Raphaelites - Their Friends and Followers*, 1948 (cat. 84)

Lit: A. Charles Sewter, *The Stained Glass of William Morris and his Circle - A Catalogue* (New Haven and London, 2 vols, 1974-75), illus. vol. I, pl. 437 (window); vol. II, pp. 43-44

This work is a preliminary drawing for the central light for the St John window on the south transept west wall of Jesus College chapel, Cambridge. The drawing depicts St John the Evangelist holding a pen and book, although in the window he is represented with his distinguishing attribute of an eagle. The window was part of a decorative scheme for the chapel, with Burne-Jones designing 11 windows for its nave and transepts between 1872 and 1876. In the St John window, which was completed by 1875, the Evangelist stands in the central light with a sibyl on either side (this format was repeated in three other windows). All the windows in the scheme use single figures in individual lights,

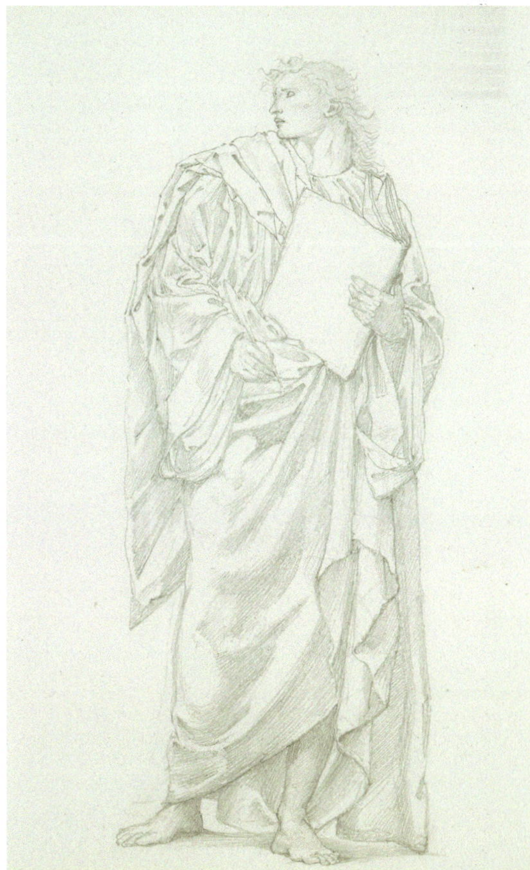

LL 10327

a form typical of Burne-Jones's stained-glass designs in the 1870s and influenced by his study of the Italian Renaissance masters. The cartoon for the figure of St John (untraced) was made in late 1873 and the Lady Lever drawing is likely to date from earlier the same year.[91] With its use of a fine hard pencil line the drawing is typical of the sketches the artist made during the 1870s, and given its dimensions, appears to have been made on the page of a sketchbook. The monumental size and sculptural qualities of the draped figure in LL 10327 show the influence of Michelangelo whose Sistine Chapel ceiling the artist had studied on his 1871 trip to Italy.

**Nude female figure: study for Venus from the Pygmalion series**
LL 3817 (WHL 3902)

Pencil on wove paper
26.7 x 17.2 cm (sight)
Date: probably mid-1870s

Inscr: 79 (pencil, top right)

Prov: by descent to Philip Burne-Jones; his sale, Christie's, 5 June 1919 (lot 69); bt. by Gooden and Fox (11 gns with WHL 3903, LL 3816 and WHL 3905) for Lever (£11 16s 9d)

Exh: Port Sunlight, Lady Lever Art Gallery, *The Pre-Raphaelites – Their Friends and Followers*, 1948 (cat. 86); Sheffield, Mappin Art Gallery, *Burne-Jones*, 1971 (cat. 104); Port Sunlight, Lady Lever Art Gallery and tour, *Pre-Raphaelite Drawings*, 2006–2008 (no cat. no.)

Burne-Jones first set about depicting subjects from the Pygmalion myth in the late 1860s for a proposed illustrated edition of William Morris's cycle of narrative poems, *The Earthly Paradise*.[92] When this failed to materialise, he embarked on a series of four small oil paintings of *Pygmalion and the Image*, which were commissioned in 1868 and completed in 1870 (Lloyd Webber collection).[93] These distil the story told in Morris's poem (originally derived from Ovid's *Metamorphoses*) of the sculptor Pygmalion, who fell in love with the image of perfection he had made in marble; on his praying to Venus, she brought the sculpture to life as Galatea, whom Pygmalion later married. Burne-Jones began a second, larger set of the oils in 1875 which were finished in time for exhibition at the Grosvenor Gallery in 1878 (Birmingham Museums and Art Gallery).[94]

The Lady Lever drawing is a sketchbook study for the figure of Venus in the third picture of the Pygmalion series, *The Godhead Fires*. This picture (in both earlier and later oils) shows the figure of Venus bringing the sculpture to life as Galatea. It seems most likely that the Lady Lever drawing relates to the 1875 version (see fig. 9): in the earlier oil the figure of Venus is shown heavily draped, whereas later she is depicted covered only in diaphanous material, presumably to give her a more unearthly appearance. There are other dated female nude drawings from the mid-1870s that show that the artist returned to the live model for his figures in the 1875 version (see, for example, a female nude study for Galatea in the second picture from the cycle, *The Hand Refrains*, Christie's, 5 March 1993, lot 43) and it is probable that LL 3817 is another example of him doing this. Stylistically also, this work is more likely to relate to the second cycle: its use of soft pencil, and the model's graphically modelled torso showing the influence of Michelangelo, are typical of Burne-Jones's drawings from the mid-1870s. It is worth noting, however, that the position of the model's left arm as well as the angle of her head relate more closely to the position of Venus in the earlier version; it may be that LL 3817 was a nude study produced in the mid-1870s but before the artist changed his mind about the positioning of the figure.

**Head of a woman with furrowed brow, probably a study for Medusa**
**Verso: study of male nude**
LL 3811 (WHL 3910)

Pencil on wove paper
Recto 25.4 x 16.6 cm (sight); verso 23.1 x 10.7 cm (sight)
Date: probably 1875 or 1877

Prov: by descent to Philip Burne-Jones; his sale, Christie's, 5 June 1919 (lot 73); bt. by Gooden and Fox (8 gns with LL 3934A–B) for Lever (£8 12s 3d)

Exh: Port Sunlight, Lady Lever Art Gallery, *The Pre-Raphaelites – Their Friends and Followers*, 1948 (cat. 88)

Lit: Kurt Löcher, *Der Perseus-Zyklus von Edward Burne-Jones* (Stuttgart, 1973), nos. 4k–l; pls. 60–61

This drawing was acquired by Lever with the title *Perseus series. Head for Medusa – a study from Mrs Drummond*.[95] The attitude of the model's face (her furrowed brow) and flailing hair suggests that this is probably a study for the head of the gorgon Medusa for the artist's Perseus series.[96] Based on the Greek legend, this was a commission from the young politician Arthur Balfour in 1875 to decorate his London drawing room, although Burne-Jones was left to come up with the subject matter. He quickly designed a scheme of ten subjects, with decorative borders of William Morris wallpaper. Full-scale cartoons were begun in 1877 and completed in 1885 but only four of the cartoons were ever painted in oils.[97] The Lady Lever drawing can be loosely compared to the cartoon for the fourth episode of the story, *The Finding of Medusa*, a scene showing Perseus approaching Medusa with the help of his magic mirror. The figure of the gorgon is depicted full face, Burne-Jones emphasising her legendary terrible stare, while her sisters crouch behind her hiding underneath their wings. The oil painting for this scene was never made but the full-scale cartoon of c. 1882 is in Southampton Art Gallery (fig. 10) and there is a later version of 1890 now in the Staatsgalerie Stuttgart.[98] At a later stage in the cycle, Burne-Jones would add the snakes, which according to the myth were entangled in Medusa's hair. Many of the sketches for this series date from 1875 and 1877 (one sketchbook in Birmingham inscribed July 1875 contains 18 studies for the series)[99] and the Lady Lever drawing probably dates from around this period.

The original identification of the model as Mrs Margaret Drummond, who was the younger sister of the architect and metal-worker W. A. S. Benson, may be correct. Burne-Jones met the Benson family around 1877 at a Wagner rehearsal at the Albert Hall, where he is said to have described Margaret as a 'young girl whose head was of a type that he knew would be helpful to him in his Perseus pictures'.[100] A comparison of LL 3811 with another *Female Head Study* (Tate) said to be Mrs Drummond, although from a different angle, suggests that the models with their strong features and prominent noses are one and the same.

The sketch of the male nude on the verso of LL 3811 is one of the many hundreds of drawings the artist produced from the live model. Nevertheless, its conjunction with the study on the recto suggests that it too may bear some relationship to the Perseus series, for which many male nude studies were made in two sketchbooks now in Birmingham (the one mentioned above, and another that contains at least 16 studies for the series).[101] Unfortunately, it has not been possible to lift the modern mount on LL 3811, so any sketchbook page numbers have been obscured, nor has it been possible to obtain exact measurements for the works; nevertheless, the approximate dimensions suggest that this could be a sheet from either of these two sketchbooks.

91 See Sewter, *Stained Glass of William Morris*, vol. II, p. 44 for the entry in Burne-Jones's account book.

92 For details of the preparatory pencil drawings produced at this time, see Wildman, *Visions of Love and Life*, p. 301 (cat. 105).

93 The poem was published as text alone in 1868–70. See Harrison and Waters, *Burne-Jones*, pp. 98–99, illus. pls. 20–23; also Nicholas Tromans, Peter Cormack et al., *Pre-Raphaelite and Other Masters: The Andrew Lloyd Webber Collection* (exh. cat., London, Royal Academy, 2003), pp. 84–85 (cats. 49a–d). See also Wildman, *Visions of Love and Life*, pp. 301, 304, 306 and 308 (fig. 93, 96, 97, and 99), illus. b&w.

94 Wildman, *Visions of Love and Life*, pp. 301–09 (cats. 105, 106, 107, 108), illus. col.; also Wildman and Christian, *Edward Burne-Jones*, pp. 216–21 (cats. 87a, 87b, 87c, 87d), illus. col.

95 WHL Inventory, p. 566.

96 See Wildman and Christian, *Edward Burne-Jones*, pp. 221–34 (cats. 89–98).

97 The incomplete oil set is now in the Staatsgalerie, Stuttgart.

98 See Wildman and Christian, *Edward Burne-Jones*, p. 226 (cat. 91), illus. col. See also Anne Anderson et al., *The Perseus Series: Sir Edward Coley Burne-Jones* (Southampton, 1998), pp. 26–27, illus. col.

99 The 1875 sketchbook (1952.P.5), now reduced to 21 pages, also contains male nude studies for *The Romaunt of the Rose*. Most pages measure 25.5 x 18.3 cm.

100 G[eorgiana] B[urne]-J[ones], *Memorials of Edward Burne-Jones* (London, 2 vols, 1904), vol. II, p. 80.

101 This sketchbook (1952.P.4) is reduced to 21 pages; most of these measure 26.3 x 17.7 cm. Its drawings can be dated to between 1875 to 1879.

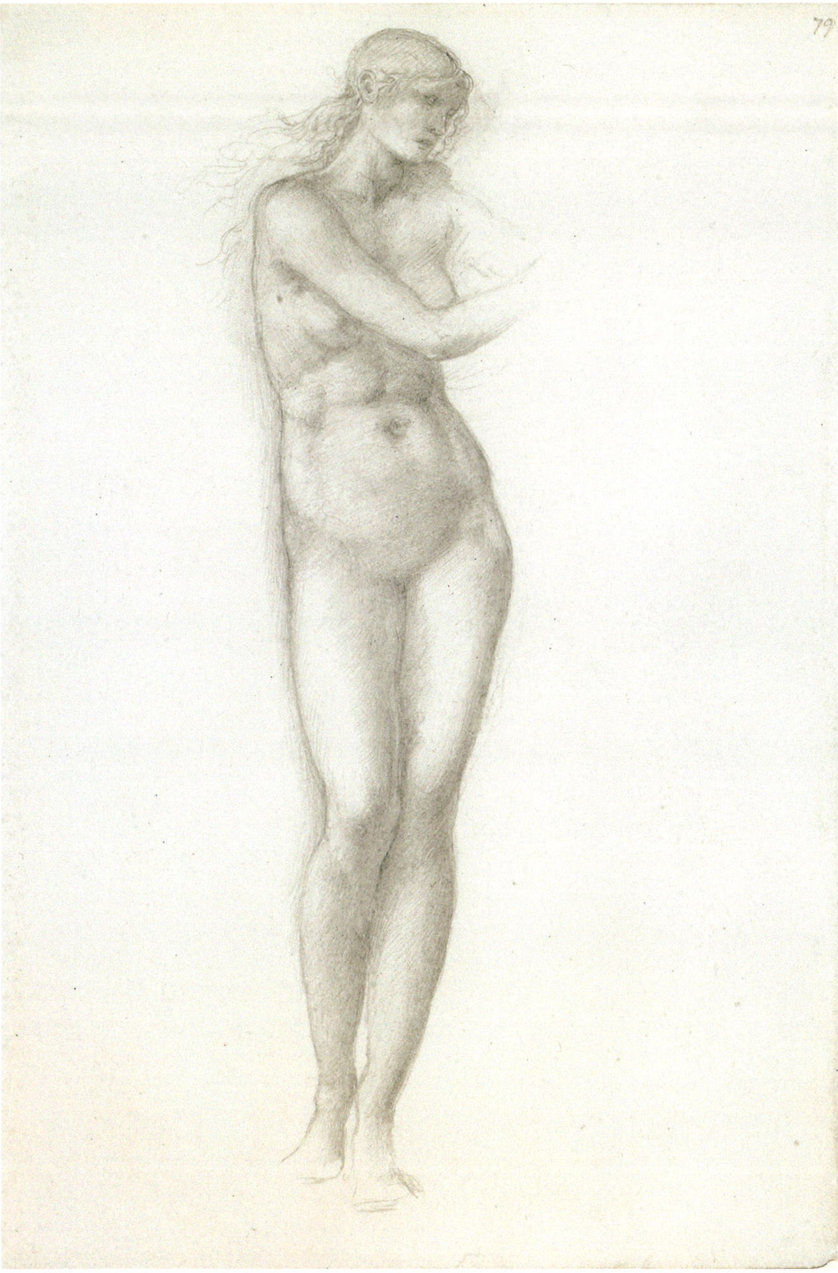

LL 3817

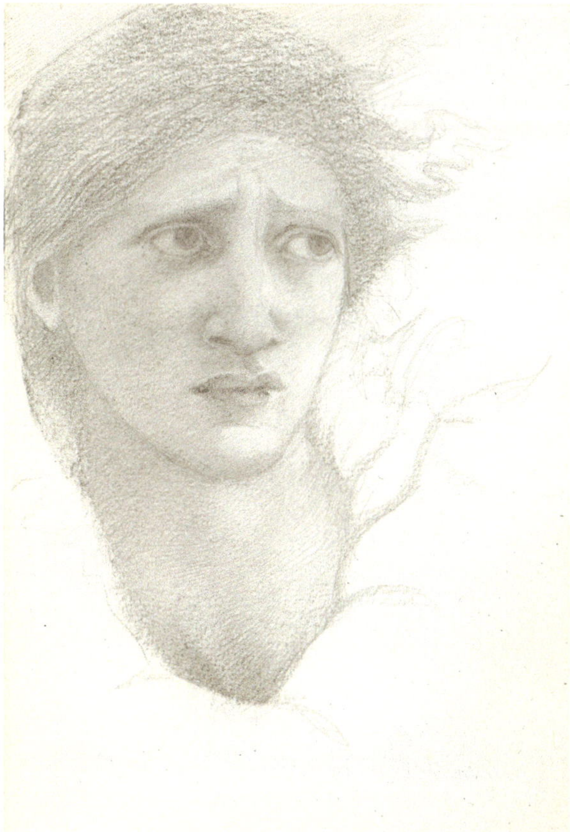

LL 3811

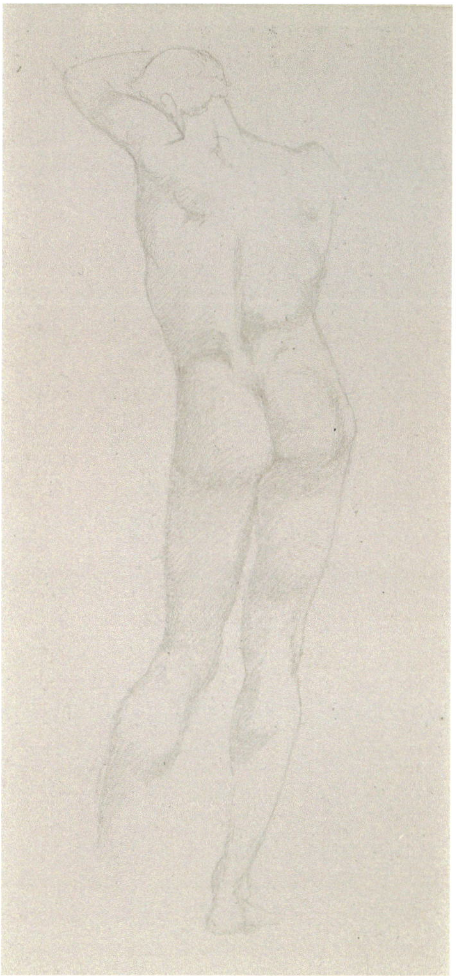

LL 3811 (verso)

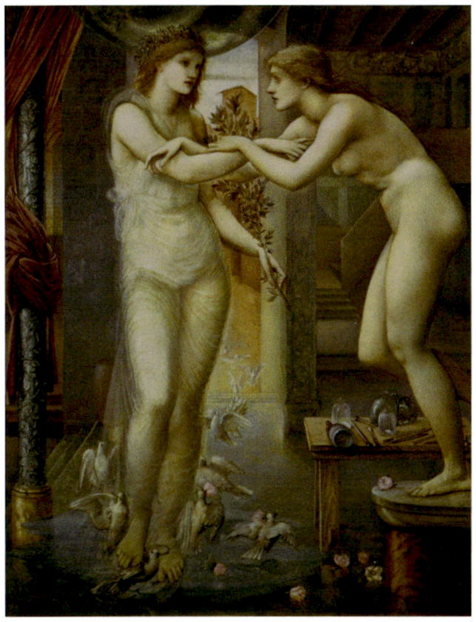

fig. 9. Edward Burne-Jones, *Pygmalion and the Image: The Godhead Fires*, 1875–78, oil on canvas, 99 x 76.3 cm, Birmingham Museums and Art Gallery

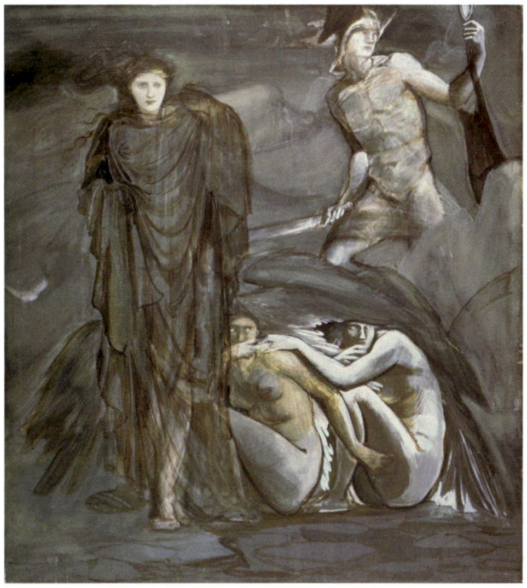

fig. 10. Edward Burne-Jones, *The Perseus Series: The Finding of Medusa*, c. 1882, gouache on paper, 152.5 x 137.7 cm, Southampton City Art Gallery/Bridgeman

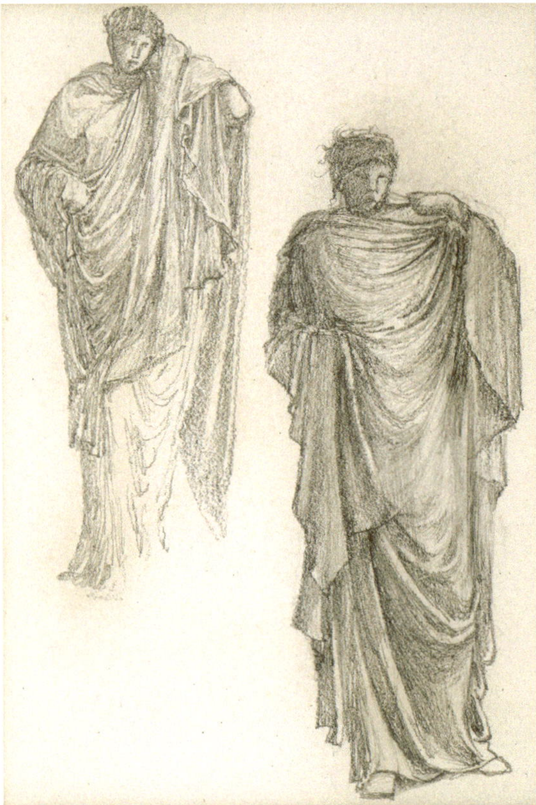

LL 3934A

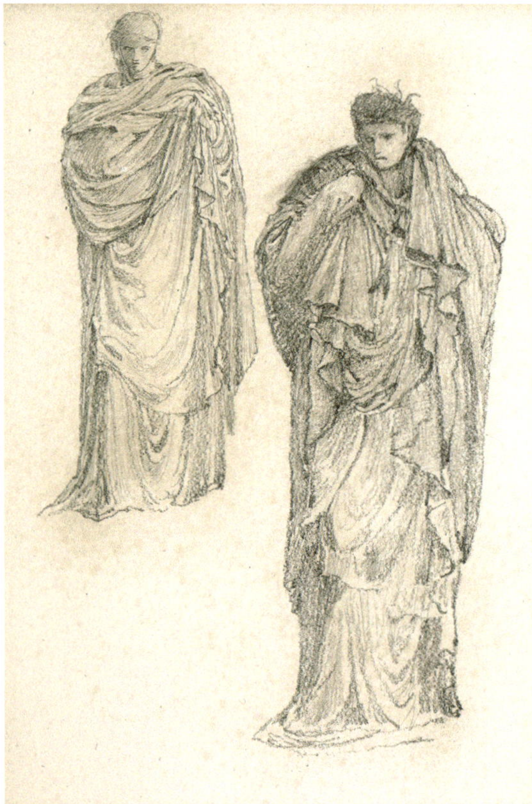

LL 3934B

**Two studies of a draped Medusa for *The Finding of Medusa* (framed together)**
LL 3934A–B (WHL 3909)

**Study of a draped Medusa**
LL 3934A

Pencil on wove paper
25.3 x 16.8 cm (sight)

**Study of a draped Medusa**
LL 3934B

Pencil on wove paper
25.3 x 16.7 cm (sight)
Date: probably c. 1875–79

Prov: by descent to Philip Burne-Jones; his sale, Christie's, 5 June 1919 (lot 73); bt. by Gooden and Fox (8 gns with LL 3811) for Lever (£8 12s 3d)

Exh: Port Sunlight, Lady Lever Art Gallery, *The Pre-Raphaelites – Their Friends and Followers*, 1948 (cat. 87); London, Hayward Gallery and tour organised by the Arts Council of Great Britain, *Burne-Jones: The Paintings, Graphic and Decorative Work of Sir Edward Burne-Jones, 1833–98*, 1975–76 (cat. 166)

Lit: Kurt Löcher, *Der Perseus-Zyklus von Edward Burne-Jones* (Stuttgart, 1973), nos. 4k–l; pls. 60–61

Both sheets are studies for the draped figure of Medusa in the fourth episode of Burne-Jones's Perseus cycle, *The Finding of Medusa* (fig. 10) (see also pp. 28–29). The scene in the cartoon shows Perseus, sword in hand, approaching Medusa with the help of a magic mirror; Medusa raises a hand to her head as it is about to be cut off by the invisible Perseus. Both sets of Lady Lever studies show Burne-Jones, with characteristic attention to detail, working out the placement of Medusa's hands and the folds of her gown. The artist's painstaking insistence on getting such details correct is emphasised by the existence of similar drawings in the Beaverbrook Art Gallery, Fredericton, and in a sketchbook in Birmingham Museums and Art Gallery.[102] Both the Lady Lever and Beaverbrook studies are approximately the same dimensions and are likely to be sketchbook pages, possibly from the same Birmingham sketchbook. LL 3934A and B are for the earlier version of the cartoon (now in Southampton); as that was completed c. 1882, these probably date from c. 1875–79, around the same time as many other drawings for the series. They are examples of a recurrent theme in the artist's work, his delight in the decorative effect of folds of drapery, although it is worth noting that later draped figures such as LL 3818 (p. 39) are Gothic in influence, contrasting with the Italianate qualities of these drawings from the 1870s.

102 One of the drawings now in the Beaverbrook Art Gallery belonged to Lever. It measures 26.4 x 17.5 cm. It was purchased by Lever at the artist's sale, Christie's, 5 June 1919 (part of lot 53); sold at Christie's, 6 June 1958 (part of lot 25); bought Brown for Lord Beaverbrook. See Katharine A. Lochnan, Douglas E. Schoenherr and Carole Silver (eds), *The Earthly Paradise: Arts and Crafts by William Morris and His Circle from Canadian Collections* (exh. cat., Toronto, Art Gallery of Ontario and tour 1993–94), pp. 67–68 (cat. A:20 a), illus. p. 67. The Birmingham sketchbook (1952.P.4) contains 21 drawings mostly for the Perseus Series and contains sheets measuring approximately 26.3 x 17.7 cm.

**Dies Domini**
LL 3784 (WHL 3920)

Pencil, with silver and gold enamel paint, touches of pastel and scratching out on wove paper laid down on canvas
112.5 x 112.5 cm (circular); three sheets; top inner sheet 52.5 x 102 cm (semicircular); bottom inner sheet 49.5 x 102 cm (semicircular); outer ring diameter 4.75–5.75 cm (variable)
Date: c. 1874–75 (probably retouched 1880)

Prov: by descent to Philip Burne-Jones; his sale, Christie's, 5 June 1919 (lot 81); bt. by Gooden and Fox for Lever (£75 6s 9d plus an additional £24 for the frame)

Exh: London, Whitechapel Art Gallery, *Spring Exhibition*, 1901 (cat. 234); Port Sunlight, Lady Lever Art Gallery, *The Pre-Raphaelites – Their Friends and Followers*, 1948 (cat. 43); Sheffield, Mappin Art Gallery, *Burne-Jones*, 1971 (cat. 23)

Lit: Philip Burne-Jones, 'Notes on some unfinished works of Sir Edward Burne-Jones', *The Magazine of Art* (1900), pp. 159–67; A. Charles Sewter, *The Stained Glass of William Morris and his Circle – A Catalogue* (New Haven and London, 2 vols, 1974–75), illus. vol. I, pl. 510 (window), vol. II, pp. 66–67

This work is the cartoon for the upper part of the east window of the church of St Michael and St Mary Magdalene at Easthampstead, Berkshire.[103] The window, commissioned in 1874 and completed in 1876, takes the Last Judgement as its subject. The composition is spread out over three vertical lights below (for which the cartoons are in Birmingham Museums and Art Gallery) and a rose window surrounded by six foils each containing an angel.[104] The Lady Lever work, depicting Christ sitting in judgement (Dies Domini) is the cartoon for this rose window. The window itself dates from the middle period of his stained-glass designs and represents a transitional stage, the beginning of his practice of treating a large window as a continuous picture that unites all the separate parts which found full expression in his windows of the 1880s and 1890s, such as his only other design using the same subject, the west window of St Philip's, Birmingham.[105]

Burne-Jones had returned from a trip to Italy in 1871, and the statuesque figure and sculptural design of LL 3784 reflect the influence of Michaelangelo, whose Sistine Chapel ceiling he had studied on that visit. A preliminary pen-and-ink design for the whole composition (Royal Academy of Arts, London) is dated 18 June 1874, although the cartoons are referred to in Burne-Jones's account book in 1875.[106] In 1880 Burne-Jones added colour to the cartoons of the lights (exhibiting them at the Grosvenor Gallery in 1881) as well as to some of the cartoons for

103 See Wildman and Christian, *Edward Burne-Jones*, p. 14 for a colour illustration of the window.
104 For the cartoons of the three lights, see Wildman and Christian, *Edward Burne-Jones*, pp. 178–79 (cat. 71), illus. col.
105 See Harrison and Waters, *Burne-Jones*, p.117.
106 Wildman and Christian, *Edward Burne-Jones*, pp. 178–79 (cat. 71).

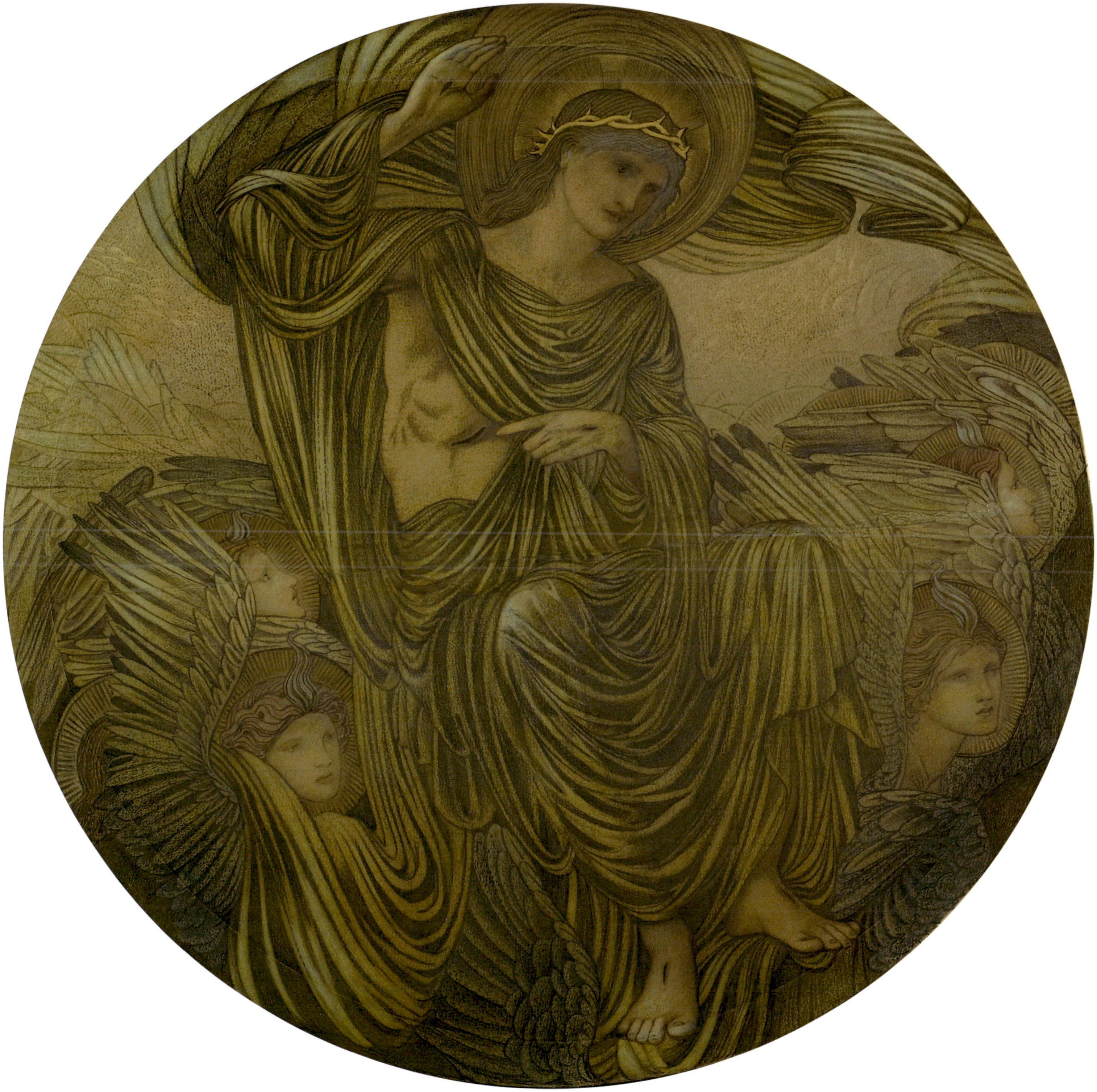

LL 3784

windows at Brampton, Cumberland, and it is probable that he re-touched LL 3784 at the same time.[107] In the same year Burne-Jones made a copy of *Dies Domini* for George Howard, later the 9th Earl of Carlisle and a patron of the artist, who may have seen the cartoon in the artist's studio.[108]

107 Autograph work record, Fitzwilliam Museum, Cambridge.
108 Ibid. Sewter, *Stained Glass of William Morris*, vol. II, p. 67 incorrectly identifies the Earl of Carlisle's watercolour as the original cartoon and LL 3784 as another version in pastel.

In this watercolour (now untraced), Christ's features and those of the surrounding angels have become more humanised.[109] Fortunée de Lisle in 1904 described the colour scheme of this watercolour as 'very simple, a harmony of blue and of ivory flesh tones'.[110] Lever owned an impression of the photogravure based on this watercolour.[111]

109 The work is illustrated in black and white in Malcolm Bell, *Sir Edward Burne-Jones: A Record and Review* (London, 1899), pp. 60–61 and is recorded in Tatlock, p. 122 as being 44 inches in diameter (the same size as LL 3784). It was exhibited at the Grosvenor Gallery in 1881 and the New Gallery in 1892–93 and 1899. It was sold from the Earl of Carlisle's collection at Sotheby's, 10 May 1922 (lot 96).

110 Fortunée de Lisle, *Burne-Jones* (London, 1904), pp. 122–23.
111 LLAG files: LL 2978 (WHL 953), published by the Berlin Photographic Company in 1900.

**Two studies for Fortitude**
LL 3821a and b (WHL 3913)

**Nude full-length study for Fortitude, holding long shield and sword**
LL 3821a

Pencil on wove paper
25.3 x 17.1 cm
Date: probably 1870s

Inscr: EBJ 1889 (pencil, bottom left); FORTITUDO (pencil, vertically along left-hand side of figure)

**Head study for Fortitude, wearing helmet**
LL 3821b

Pencil on wove paper
20.4 x 15.3 cm (sight)
Date: probably 1870s

Inscr: EB-J 1880 / Fortitude (pencil, with decorative flourish, lower right)

Prov: by descent to Philip Burne-Jones; his sale, Christie's, 5 June 1919 (lot 74); bt. by Gooden and Fox (8 gns with WHL 3911 and 3912) for Lever

Exh: Port Sunlight, Lady Lever Art Gallery, *The Pre-Raphaelites – Their Friends and Followers*, 1948 (cat. 91)

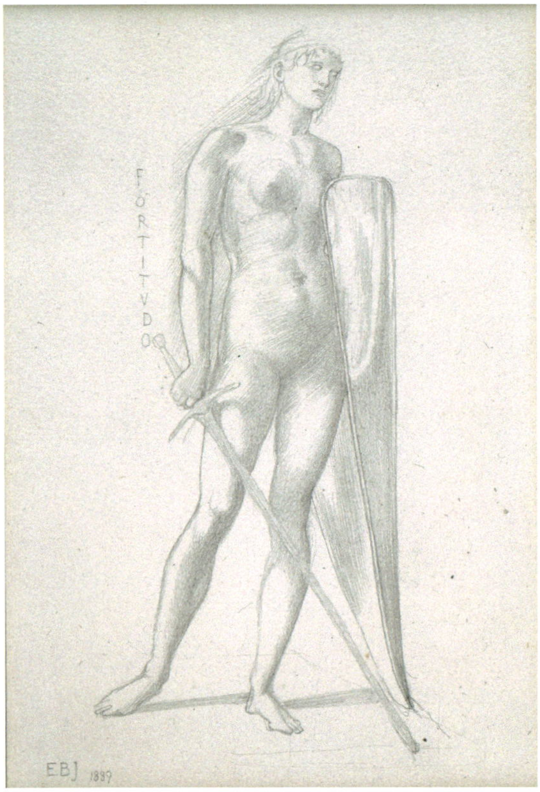


LL 3821a

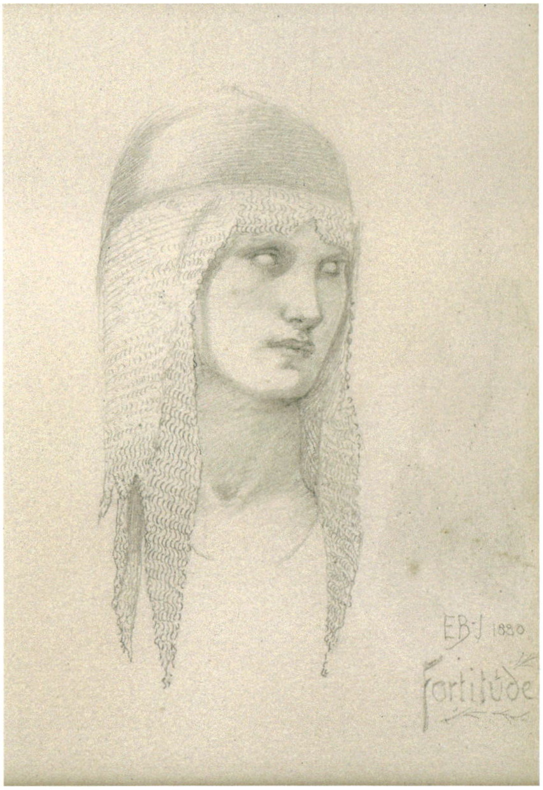


LL 3821b

Both works are preliminary drawings made from a professional model for the figure and head of Fortitude. Burne-Jones made several known stained-glass window designs which included a figure of Fortitude but the Lady Lever drawings do not directly relate to them.[112] However, they are similar to a Frederick Hollyer photograph of an independent watercolour composition (c.1875) depicting a clothed female full-length figure of Fortitude holding a shield and sword.[113] It is possible that both drawings are studies for this composition: the stance of the model in LL 3821a is repeated, and LL 3821b is very similar both in the position of the head and the type of helmet. The Lady Lever drawings, despite their inscribed dates, are in the fine, hard pencil style associated with Burne-Jones's drawings in the 1870s and it is likely that, as with many other works, the artist dated them retrospectively, misremembering the date.[114]

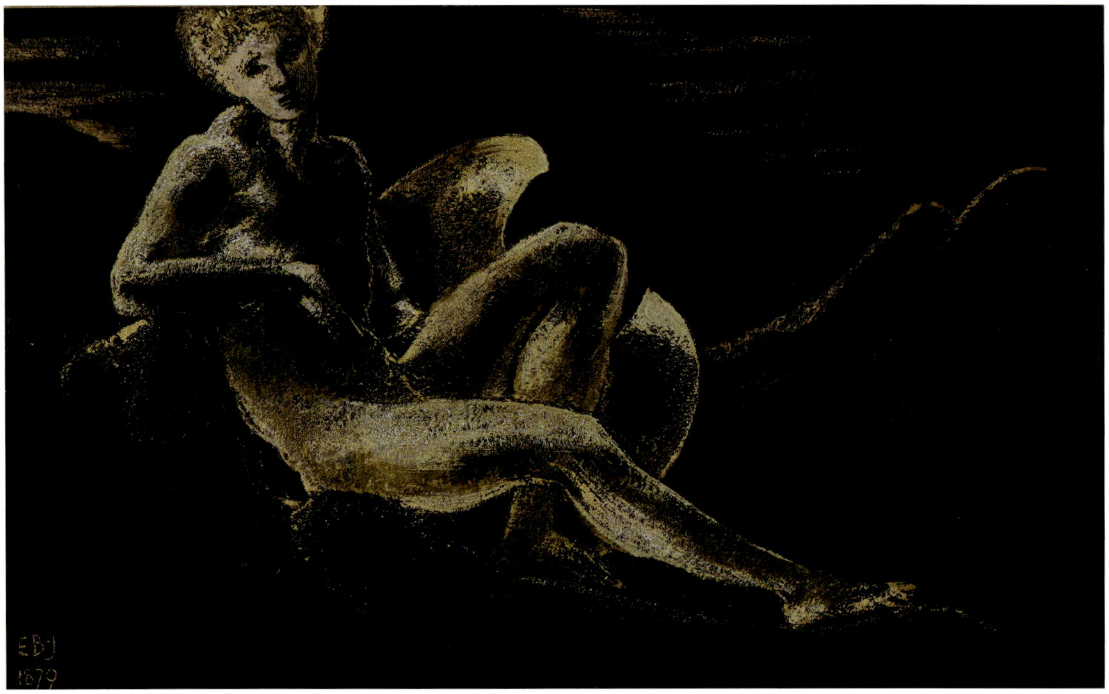


LL 3919

**Nude reclining seated male figure with shield**
LL 3819 (WHL 3979)

Bronze metallic paint on wove paper painted with black gouache
15.9 x 25 cm (sight)
Date: 1879

Inscr: EB-J / 1879 (bronze metallic paint, bottom left)

Prov: by descent to Philip Burne-Jones; his sale, Christie's, 5 June 1919 (lot 141); bt. by Gooden and Fox (14 gns with WHL 3978) for Lever (£15 1s 6d)

Exh: London, Burlington Fine Arts Club, *Exhibition of Drawings and Studies by Sir Edward Burne-Jones, Bart.*, 1899 (cat. 112); Port Sunlight, Lady Lever Art Gallery, *The Pre-Raphaelites – Their Friends and Followers*, 1948 (cat. 76)

112 These are listed in Sewter, *Stained Glass of William Morris*, vol. II, p. 294. They include a window in Jesus College Chapel, Cambridge, although this figure is more male in appearance and holds a differently shaped shield and a 'pole' instead of a sword. This figure is very similar to a depiction identified as a scale drawing for a window in St Patrick's Church, Dublin (Birmingham Museums and Art Gallery), illus. in Harrison and Waters, *Burne-Jones*, p. 122. They also include a window formerly in St Cuthbert's, Newcastle upon Tyne (now in the Laing Art Gallery, Newcastle) which does depict a female figure of Fortitude, but the cartoon for this window (now in a private collection) reveals that there is no direct relationship to the Lady Lever drawings.

113 This photograph is in John Christian's collection.

114 John Christian, verbally, January 2008.

In technique LL 3819, with its use of bronze metallic paint on coloured paper, seems characteristic of Burne-Jones's drawings of the 1890s (see LL 3818 and LL 3820, pp. 39), so its inscribed date of 1879 is a puzzle. Nevertheless, the artist did use gold paint for his figures around 1880; his panel painting, *Cupid's Hunting Ground*, commissioned by Sir Hugh Grosvenor (c. 1882, Delaware Art Museum, Wilmington) is a notable example. Furthermore, a comparison with the Lady Lever's two later works reveals just how different the artist's style has become by the 1890s, where the paint is applied delicately, with a lightness of touch befitting the ethereal nature of the subjects; in LL 3819, his handling of the medium is clumsy. On balance then, it appears as if the inscribed date is correct and that LL 3819 is an early and anomalous example of a technique that became characteristic of Burne-Jones's very late work. Although the subject-matter appears as if it could be related to the artist's Perseus Series – a number of male nudes with shields occur in the Birmingham sketchbooks,[115] which would be in keeping with the date of 1879 – the figure does not relate to any known drawings and appears to be an independent composition.

**Two female head studies (framed together)**
LL 3813A AND B (WHL 3907)

**Girl's head, profile to right**
LL 3813A

Pencil on wove paper
20.7 x 16.7 cm (sight)
Date: late 1870s or early 1880s

**Girl's head, half turned to right**
LL 3813B

Pencil on wove paper
20.9 x 16.8 cm (sight)
Date: late 1870s or early 1880s

Prov: by descent to Philip Burne-Jones; his sale, Christie's, 5 June 1919 (lot 71); bt. by Gooden and Fox for Lever (15 gns with WHL 3906 and WHL 3908)[116]

Exh: Port Sunlight, Lady Lever Art Gallery, *The Pre-Raphaelites – Their Friends and Followers*, 1948 (cat. 94)

Both drawings appear to be taken from the same model, who appears again in two pencil studies now in the Lloyd Webber collection.[117] None of these can be related to a particular painting

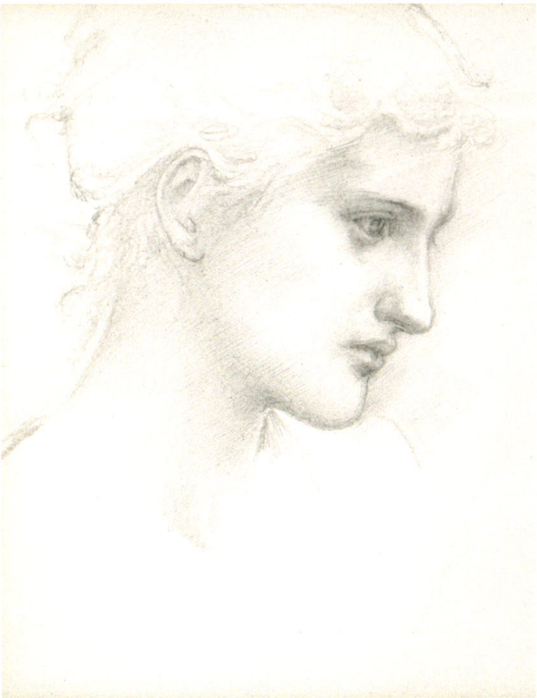

LL 3813A

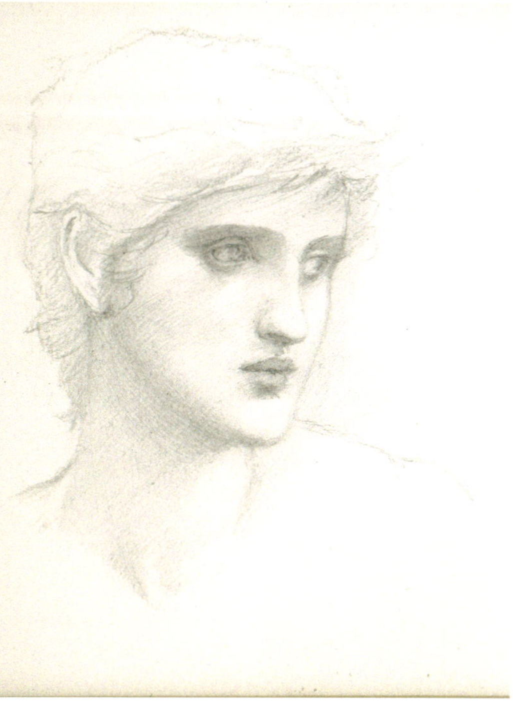

LL 3813B

and seem to be independent drawings of an unidentified model whose face intrigued the artist. The drawings are typical of Burne-Jones's use of a fine but soft pencil employed in the late 1870s and early 1880s.

**Head study for mermaid in *The Depths of the Sea***
LL 3935 (WHL 3917)

Pencil on wove paper
31.7 x 22.1 cm
Date: 1886

Inscr: E-B-J (with flourish through J) 18/86 (pencil, bottom right)

Prov: by descent to Philip Burne-Jones; his sale, Christie's, 5 June 1919 (lot 78); bt. by Gooden and Fox for Lever (£94 10s with WHL 3918 and WHL 3919)

Exh: London, Burlington Fine Arts Club, *Exhibition of Drawings and Studies by Sir Edward Burne-Jones, Bart.*, 1899 (cat. 62); Port Sunlight, Lady Lever Art Gallery, *The Pre-Raphaelites – Their Friends and Followers*, 1948 (cat. 89); Port Sunlight, Lady Lever Art Gallery and tour, *Pre-Raphaelite Drawings*, 2006–2008 (no cat. no.)

This drawing is a study for the head of the mermaid in Burne-Jones's painting *The Depths of the Sea* (private collection, fig. 11), exhibited at the Royal Academy in 1886, the artist's first and only exhibit at Burlington House.[118] The picture depicted a mermaid who, having captured the body of a drowning sailor, drags him down to the depths of the sea, her smile showing that she was unaware that he was already dead.

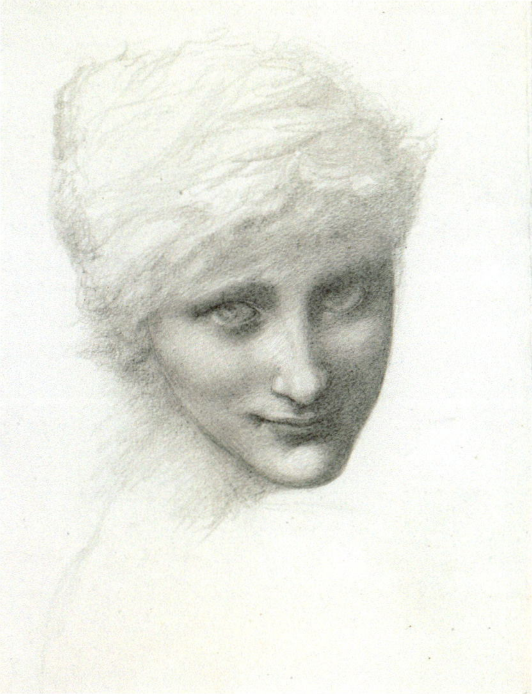

LL 3935

Burne-Jones's interest in the subject of the sea may have been prompted by his purchase of a house at Rottingdean, a village on the Sussex coast in 1880, where he was to spend most of his holidays from then on. The proximity of the sea inspired a number of paintings including mermaids, although it was typical, as in this case, for the artist to give the subject a literary twist. The painting was executed early in 1886, with Burne-Jones striving to make the picture

115 See, for example, the study for a male nude at the Court of Phineus, p. 19 in the 1875 Birmingham sketchbook (1952.P.5) illustrated in Wildman and Christian, *Edward Burne-Jones*, p. 233 (cat. 98).

116 LLAG files: WHL 3906 was given to the Misses Lever, Hesketh Grange, Thornton Hough, Cheshire, 28 August 1922; WHL 3908 was sold in the USA in 1926 (see appendix 2).

117 Tromans, Cormack et al., *Pre-Raphaelite and Other Masters*, illus. p. 80 (cats. 45 a, b).

118 Wildman and Christian, *Edward Burne-Jones*, pp. 264–66 (cat. 119), illus. col. There is a watercolour version dated 1887 in the Fogg Art Museum, Cambridge, Massachusetts and a preliminary compositional sketch in watercolour in the Ashmolean Museum, Oxford (illus. Harrison and Waters, *Burne-Jones*, p. 142, figs. 206 and 207).

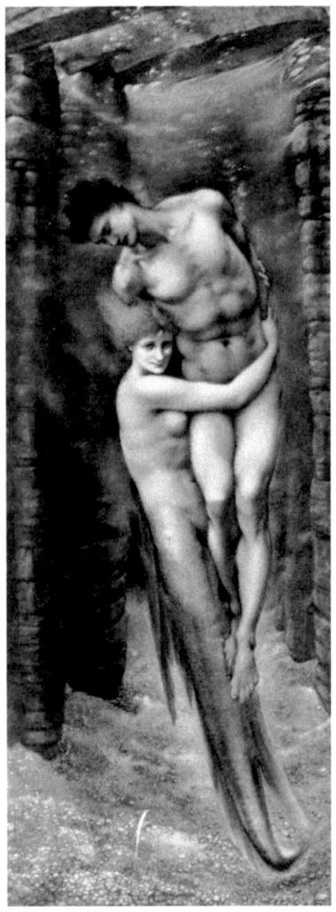

fig. 11. Edward Burne-Jones, *The Depths of the Sea*, 1886, oil on canvas, 197 x 75 cm

look naturalistic, to this end borrowing a studio property containing a large tank.[119]

Although Burne-Jones's drawings were sometimes dated retrospectively, this study inscribed 1886 was probably executed early that year, in preparation for the picture. The study relates closely to the painting, with the model's head posed at the same angle; in the final work, the artist has altered her hair, adding mermaid's tresses which float upwards in the sea water. The use of cross-hatching in the drawing to create a softer, *sfumato* effect shows a move away from the artist's linear drawing style of the 1870s, although the work does not reveal the same expressive qualities seen in his very late drawings such as those for *Sponsa de Libano* (LL 2908 and LL 3788, pp. 36–37).

The identity of the model has provoked some speculation, one of the suggestions being that she was Laura Lyttelton, the daughter of Sir Charles Tennant, who had become a visitor to the Burne-Jones household and such a source of fascination that the family called her the 'Siren'.[120] Georgiana, Burne-Jones's wife, encouraged this by writing: 'We always associated "The Depths of the Sea" with our dear "Siren", for the face of the mermaid had some likeness to her strange charm of expression'.[121] Another suggestion by Lady Lewis, a friend of the artist, was that the model was based on a young girl whom she and Burne-Jones saw in 1886 while on a walk together through the woods. Lady Lewis wrote: 'He was as under a spell, and when we came home at once made a drawing of her from memory ... he never altered it, but used it for the head of the mermaid'.[122] Despite these speculations, LL 3935 has all the marks of a study done from a professional model.[123]

The ambiguous expression of the model was replicated in the painting, drawing praise from critics who drew a parallel with Leonardo da Vinci's enigmatic heads. A critic from *The Times* wrote that her 'look of triumph that is neither human nor diabolic ... [is] almost worthy of Leonardo da Vinci'.[124]

119 Wildman and Christian, *Edward Burne-Jones*, pp. 264–66.
120 Burne-Jones, *Memorials of Edward Burne-Jones*, vol. II, pp. 148–49.
121 Ibid., p. 166.
122 Ibid., p. 307.

### Study of female head to right
LL 3812 (WHL 3916)

Charcoal on Japanese paper
35.2 x 22.4 cm
Date: 1889

Inscr: EBJ / 1889 (pencil, bottom right)

Prov: by descent to Philip Burne-Jones; his sale, Christie's, 5 June 1919 (lot 76); bt. by Gooden and Fox for Lever (11 gns with WHL 3914 and WHL 3915)

Exh: London, Burlington Fine Arts Club, *Exhibition of Drawings and Studies by Sir Edward Burne-Jones, Bart*, 1899 (cat. 4); Port Sunlight, Lady Lever Art Gallery, *The Pre-Raphaelites – Their Friends and Followers*, 1948 (cat. 90); Sheffield, Mappin Art Gallery, *Burne-Jones*, 1971 (cat. 79)

In subject-matter LL 3812, with its depiction of a female head wearing a head-dress, can be compared to LL 3816 (pp. 26–27), identified as a study for the figure of Fortune in *The Wheel of Fortune*.[125] Nevertheless, some crucial differences suggest that LL 3812 is not a study for this composition. Here the model is in complete profile, looking fully to the side and not down in the manner of the figure of Fortune. Of equal importance, while LL 3816 employs Burne-Jones's fine pencil technique of the 1870s, LL 3812, dated 1889 in the artist's hand, is in charcoal, giving the work a softer, more *sfumato* effect, typical of his drawings in the late 1880s. Given this date it is far too late to be a study for any *Wheel of Fortune* composition (the last version, in the Hammersmith and Fulham Library's collection, was finished in 1885). The work is therefore likely to be an independent presentation-style drawing, but one which was inspired by the artist's earlier studies of swathed heads and elaborate hairstyles in relation to the figure of Fortune. It is notable that the drawing combines a head-dress with elaborate plaits, elements that appear separately and together in other drawings in the early 1870s and that we know Burne-Jones was considering for the figure of Fortune (see the entry on LL 3816). The elaborate coiffure of LL 3812 shows the influence of Michelangelo's so-called Ideal or Divine Heads drawings (*teste divine*) of the 1520s, which Burne-Jones may have seen in photographs.[126]

123 Wildman and Christian, *Edward Burne-Jones*, p. 265.
124 *The Times*, 8 May 1886, p. 8; quoted in Wildman and Christian, *Edward Burne-Jones*, p. 265.
125 See LL 3787 (pp. 25–26) for a discussion of Burne-Jones's painting *The Wheel of Fortune*, and other versions of the same composition.
126 It is known that Burne-Jones began to accumulate photographs of Renaissance paintings and drawings in the early 1870s. Some of his albums are in the collection of University College London.

### Head study for *The Summons* (from the Holy Grail tapestries)
LL 3815 (WHL 3869)

Charcoal with black chalk on Japanese paper
31.1 x 21.1 cm (sight)
Date: probably c. 1890–91

Inscr: EB-J / 1893 / study for LAMORAK / [? one] subject of the / ROUND TABLE / for the Tapestries of the / MORTE D'ARTHUR (pencil, lower right)

Prov: by descent to Philip Burne-Jones; his sale, Christie's, 5 June 1919 (lot 17); bt. by Gooden and Fox for Lever (£26 5s with LL 2908, LL 3814 and WHL 3868)

Exh: London, Fine Art Society, *Edward Burne-Jones: Studies and Drawings*, 1896 (cat. 114); Port Sunlight, Lady Lever Art Gallery, *The Pre-Raphaelites – Their Friends and Followers*, 1948 (cat. 51); Sheffield, Mappin Art Gallery, *Burne-Jones*, 1971 (cat. 15)

Between 1890 and 1895 the firm of Morris & Company worked on a commission to decorate the dining room of Stanmore Hall, Middlesex, home of the Australian mining engineer William Knox D'Arcy.[127] William Morris and Burne-Jones, in one of their final and most successful collaborations, devised a scheme which was to be a series of six narrative tapestries with verdure panels underneath. The subject was the Arthurian legend of the search and discovery of the Holy Grail based loosely on the fifteenth-century text, Malory's *Morte d'Arthur*. The story had inspired the two friends ever since their collaboration on murals for the Oxford Union in 1857, which had drawn on various episodes from the text.

Burne-Jones had begun designs for the tapestries by the end of 1890, and after the basic composition of each subject had been established, began work on many studies for individual figures.[128] LL 3815 is a portrait study that relates closely to the first tapestry of the series, *The Knights of the Round Table Summoned to the Quest by a Strange Damsel (The Summons)*.[129] This scene, which conflated various episodes from Malory's text, depicts King Arthur sitting at the round table with his knights on the morning of Pentecost, when a damsel appears calling upon them to take up the quest for the Holy Grail, the vessel believed to have been used by Christ at the Last Supper. The tapestry shows writing on the empty chair, in Burne-Jones's own words, 'where no man can sit but the one who can achieve the adventure. Lancelot is opposite the chair, and points to

127 The firm of Morris, Marshall, Faulkner & Co. was reorganised and renamed in 1874.
128 Wildman and Christian, *Edward Burne-Jones*, p. 298.
129 Weaving of the original commission took until 1895, but various repetitions of the tapestries were made after this date. See Wildman and Christian, *Edward Burne-Jones*, pp. 298–305 (cats. 145–51); also Oliver Fairclough and Emmeline Leary, *Textiles by William Morris and Morris & Co. 1861–1940* (London, 1981), pp. 107–08. A repetition of the first scene, *The Summons*, was made in 1898–99 (now Birmingham Museums and Art Gallery, fig. 12).

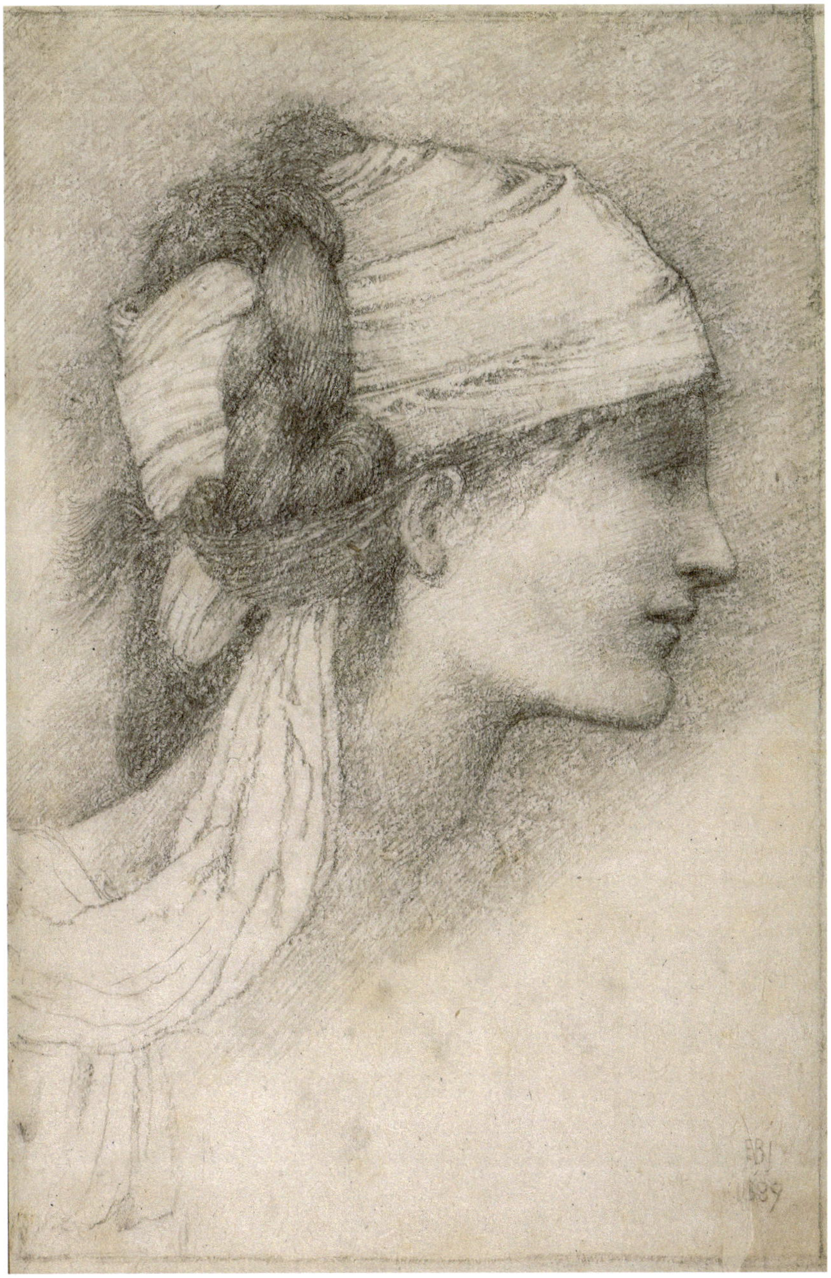

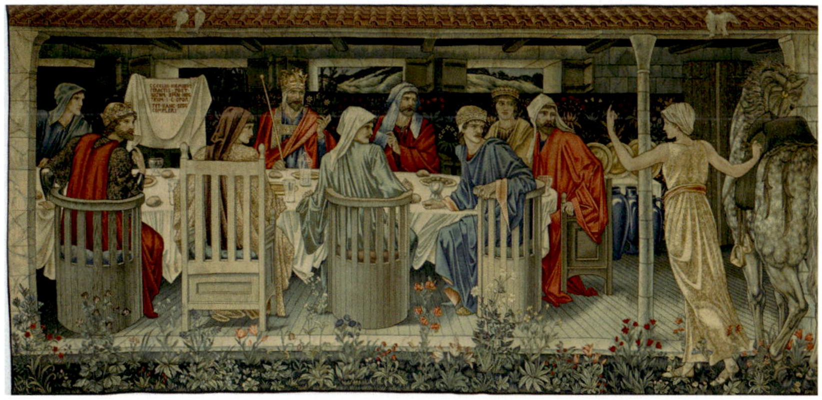

fig. 12. Edward Burne-Jones, *The Knights of the Round Table Summoned to the Quest by a Strange Damsel (The Summons)*, woven 1898–99, wool and silk tapestry on cotton warp, 245 x 535 cm, Birmingham Museums and Art Gallery

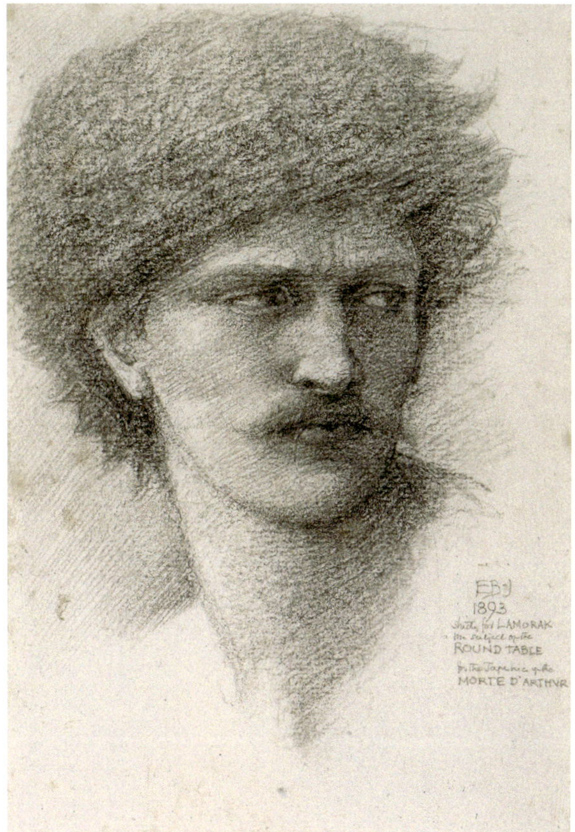


LL 3812 LL 3815

himself as if asking if he is to sit there. Gawain and Lamorak and Percival and Bors are all there.'[130]

The Lady Lever study relates closely to a similar drawing (itself formerly in the Lady Lever Art Gallery) in the Metropolitan Museum, New York, which is inscribed Gawain.[131] In the tapestry, it is not clear which of the two figures in the centre foreground, one dressed in blue and the other in green, is intended to be Gawain and which Lamorak, although it is evident that Burne-Jones used the same model for both. A possible explanation for this confusion may be that the present sheet, during the selection process for the Fine Art Society exhibition of 1896, was annotated incorrectly by Burne-Jones who reviewed hundreds of his works, adding dates and titles in preparation for the exhibition. There are other examples of the artist making mistakes on this occasion, and it is possible that the work is in fact a preliminary study for Gawain, although at an even earlier stage than the New York work where, as in the tapestry, he wears a head-dress.[132] On the occasion of the Fine Art Society exhibition, Burne-Jones inscribed the date 1893 on a large group of drawings associated with the *Holy Grail* tapestries, although as weaving of the tapestries was begun in 1891, it is likely that this study dates to c. 1890–91. In its use of black chalk and cross-hatching to create soft shadowing, LL 3815 is characteristic of the materials and techniques used by Burne-Jones in his very late drawings (see also LL 3814, pp. 38–39).

130 Burne-Jones, *Memorials of Edward Burne-Jones*, vol. II, p. 208.
131 Wildman and Christian, *Edward Burne-Jones*, pp. 299-300 (cat. 146); *Study for the head of Gawaine* WHL 3868, sold from the Lady Lever Art Gallery, Christie's, 6 June 1958 (lot 22). See Appendix 2.
132 A study for the second scene, *The Arming and Departure of the Knights* (Edmonton Art Gallery, Alberta), has been misdated to 1863. See Lochnan, Schoenherr and Silver (eds), *The Earthly Paradise*, pp. 72–73 (cat. A:24).

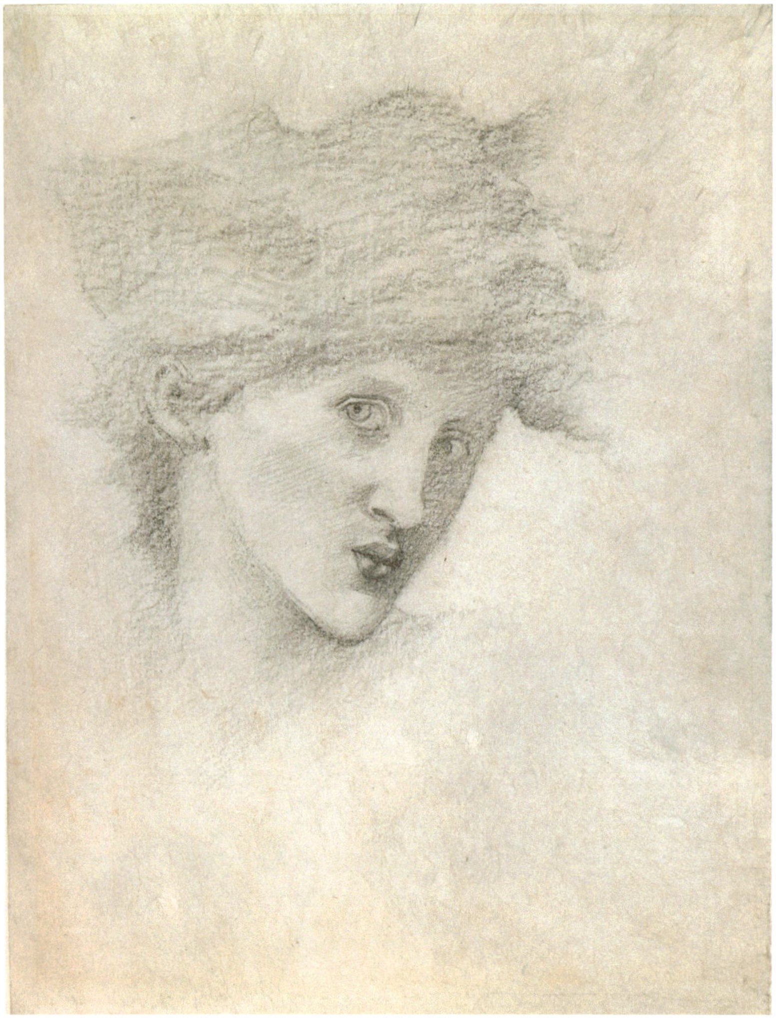

LL 2908

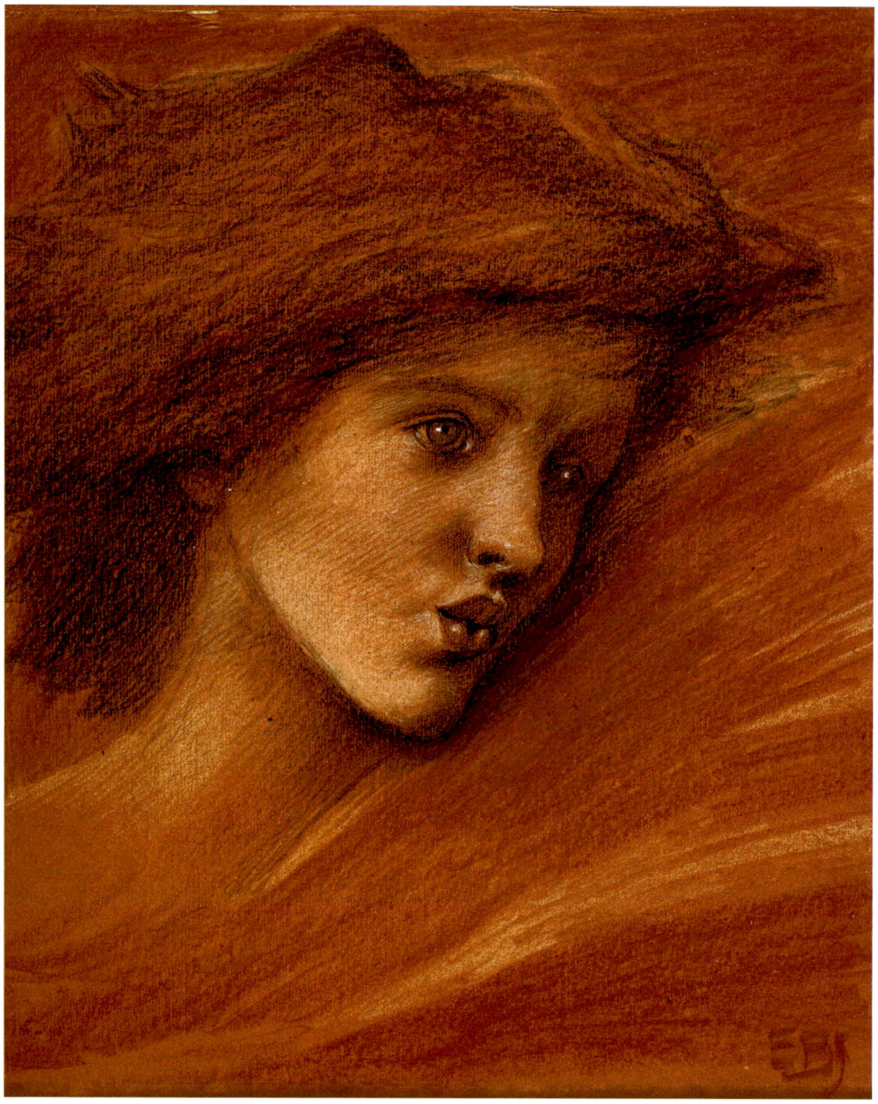


LL 3788

**Study of a female head for *Sponsa de Libano***
LL 2908 (WHL 3870)

Black chalk on Japanese paper
30.9 x 23.5 cm
Date: c. 1891

Prov: by descent to Philip Burne-Jones; his sale, Christie's, 5 June 1919 (lot 17); bt. by Gooden and Fox for Lever (£26 5s with LL 3814, LL 3815 and WHL 3868)

Exh: Port Sunlight, Lady Lever Art Gallery, *The Pre-Raphaelites – Their Friends and Followers*, 1948 (cat. 82); Sheffield, Mappin Art Gallery, *Burne-Jones*, 1971 (cat. 204)

**Study of a female head for *Sponsa de Libano***
LL 3788 (WHL 737, H 331)

Coloured chalks and watercolour on salmon-pink wove paper
34.7 x 29 cm
Date: c. 1891

Inscr: EBJ (red chalk, bottom right)

Prov: bt. from the Fine Art Society by Lever, 30 June 1896 (£36 15s)

Exh: Port Sunlight, Lady Lever Art Gallery, *The Pre-Raphaelites – Their Friends and Followers*, 1948 (cat. 81); Sheffield, Mappin Art Gallery, *Burne-Jones*, 1971 (cat. 203); Port Sunlight, Lady Lever Art Gallery and tour, *Pre-Raphaelite Drawings*, 2006–2008 (no cat. no.)

Around 1876 Burne-Jones produced a sequence of five large pencil drawings, which were recorded in his work record as 'designs from the Song of Solomon – for painting on panel some day'.[133] The first four subjects from the series focus on Solomon's love for his Bride of Lebanon, whom he ultimately reveals to the world. The third sheet (Birmingham Museums and Art Gallery) illustrates the following verse from the Song of Solomon: 'Awake O North Wind, and come thou South, blow upon my garden that the spices thereof may flow out'.[134] The design depicts these two winds above, surrounded by swirling draperies, and below there is the figure of Solomon's beloved. Towards the end of his career, Burne-Jones returned to the same subject and composition in a large, highly mannered watercolour, signed and dated 1891 and exhibited at the New Gallery in that year with the title *Sponsa de Libano* (The Bride of Lebanon) (Walker Art Gallery, Liverpool; fig. 13).[135]

Both LL 2908 and LL 3788 relate to the face of the wind on the far left of this watercolour (they are also similar to the design of c. 1876 but the attitude and position of the face is much more closely related to the later watercolour). Burne-Jones probably began and finished *Sponsa de Libano* in the same year, 1891, and it is likely that these two drawings, in the artist's expressive late drawing style, must have been executed quite rapidly around the same time.[136] With their sensuous modelling, both drawings seem to

133 Quoted in Wildman and Christian, *Edward Burne-Jones*, pp. 188–90 (cats. 82 and 83). These have usually been associated with designs for needlework, although only one embroidery is known (see ibid.)

134 Song of Solomon, 4:16; Wildman and Christian, *Edward Burne-Jones*, p. 118 (cat. 82), illus. b&w.

135 New Gallery, 1891 (cat. 34). The work was purchased by the Walker Art Gallery from the Liverpool Autumn Exhibition, 1896 (cat. 924). The spelling of the title *Sponsa de Libano* is recorded as written in a letter from Burne-Jones to the curator of the Walker Art Gallery, 28 August 1896, held in Walker object files.

136 Burne-Jones, *Memorials of Edward Burne-Jones*, vol. II, p. 215.

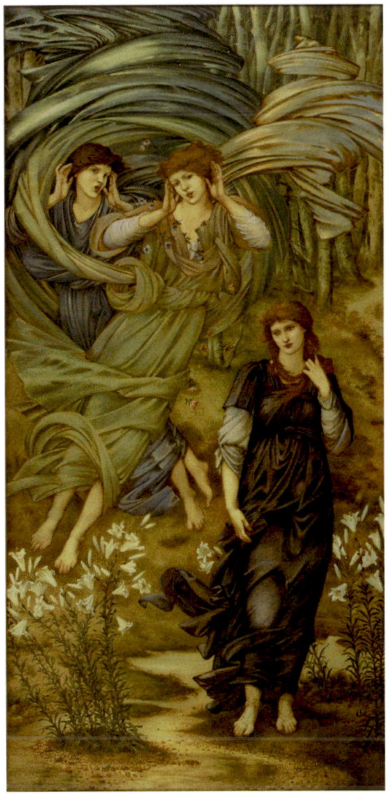

fig. 13. Edward Burne-Jones, *Sponsa de Libano*, 1891, watercolour and gouache on paper, 325.7 x 158 cm, National Museums Liverpool, Walker Art Gallery

have been done from life and the artist later described the model as 'a little Houndsditch Jewess, self-possessed, mature and wordly, and only about twelve years old'.[137] LL 2908 is the weaker drawing with the model's right cheekbone appearing flattened. In contrast, LL 3788 is a bravura expression of Burne-Jones's abilities in the medium of chalk (which he increasingly used during the 1880s and 1890s) to produce a highly finished, presentation-style drawing, indicated by the presence of his signature. Both drawings have been incorrectly recorded in the WHL Inventory as studies for 'The West Wind'; although it is not clear whether the left-hand figure is the 'South' or 'North' Wind mentioned in the biblical passage, the idea of a 'West Wind' seems to be a mistake in this context.[138]

## St Gabriel
LL 3785 (WHL 3922)

Watercolour, gouache and pastel over pencil on brown paper in four pieces laid down on canvas
278.2 x 53.1 cm (image); 289 x 60.7 cm (sheet)
Date: probably c. 1892–93

Inscr: ROTTINGDEAN / St. Margarets Ch. (gouache over pencil, top left); EGO.SUM.GABRIEL.ARCHANGELUS / NUNTIUS. MAGNAE. LAETITIAE. [I am the Archangel Gabriel / the messenger of great joy] (black pastel, under main subject); PRO UNICA FILIA MARGARITA IN HAC [AE deleted] S. MARGARITAE AEDE [for his only daughter Margaret in this, St Margaret's Church] (white pastel, under predella)

137 Ibid.
138 WHL Inventory, p. 556.

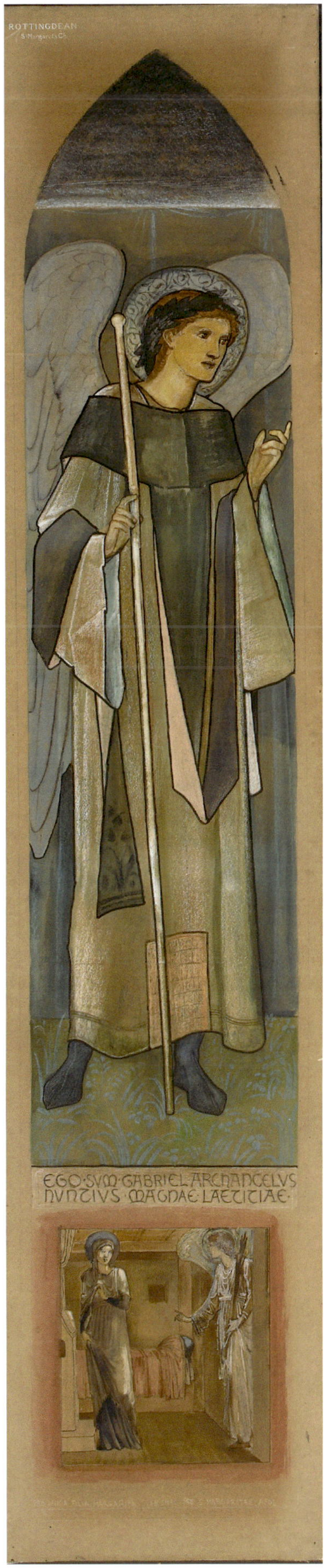


LL 3785

Prov: by descent to Philip Burne-Jones; his sale, Christie's, 5 June 1919 (lot 82); bt. by Gooden and Fox for Lever (£79 10s with LL 3786 and WHL 3921)[139]

Exh: Port Sunlight, Lady Lever Art Gallery, *The Pre-Raphaelites – Their Friends and Followers*, 1948 (cat. 44)

Lit: A. Charles Sewter, *The Stained Glass of William Morris and His Circle – A Catalogue* (New Haven and London, 2 vols, 1974–75), illus. vol. I, pl. 617, vol. II, pp. 163–64

## St Raphael
LL 3786 (WHL 3923)

Watercolour, gouache and pastel over pencil on brown paper in four pieces laid down on canvas
279 x 53.3 cm (image); 289 x 61 cm (sheet)
Date: probably c. 1892–93

Inscr: ROTTINGDEAN / St Margaret's Ch (gouache over pencil, top left); EGO. SUM. RAPHAEL. ARCHANGELUS / CUSTOS. INFANTIUM. DOMINI [I am the Archangel Raphael / the custodian of the children of the Lord] (black pastel, under main subject); 4 PARVULORUM instead of / infantium (white pastel, right, adjacent to predella)

Prov: by descent to Philip Burne-Jones; his sale, Christie's, 5 June 1919 (lot 82); bt. by Gooden and Fox for Lever (£79 10s with LL 3785 and WHL 3921)

Exh: Port Sunlight, Lady Lever Art Gallery, *The Pre-Raphaelites – Their Friends and Followers*, 1948 (cat. 46)

Lit: A. Charles Sewter, *The Stained Glass of William Morris and His Circle – A Catalogue* (New Haven and London, 2 vols, 1974–75), illus. vol. I, pl. 618, vol. II, pp. 163–64

LL 3785 and LL 3786 are cartoons for, respectively, the left and right lancets of the east window in St Margaret's Church, Rottingdean, East Sussex.[140] From 1880 Burne-Jones owned a house in the village of Rottingdean that he used as a retreat by the sea to escape from the pressures of life in London; the church was across the green from the house. The window depicts the three archangels: St Gabriel with the Annunication beneath (LL 3785), St Raphael with the Guardian angel leading the young boy Tobias beneath (LL 3786), with the central lancet depicting St Michael, and underneath his slaying of the dragon. In the window the inscription, which is begun under the predella of the cartoon for St Gabriel, continues under the three panels so that in full it reads: 'pro unica filia Margarita in hac S. Margaritae aede feliciter nupta Edwardus Burne Jones pictor dedicavit' (the painter Edward Burne Jones dedicated [this] to his only daughter Margaret happily married in this St Margaret's Church). In September 1888 the artist's daughter Margaret, with whom he had an extraordinarily close relationship, married the classical scholar J. W. Mackail in a small ceremony at the church. The windows were instated in the autumn of 1893. Burne-Jones's

139 WHL 3921, the central panel depicting St Michael, was sold at Christie's, 6 June 1958 (lot 9), bt. by Agnew's (£29 8s) and is now with Sir Brandon Rhys Williams (see Sewter, *Stained Glass of William Morris*, vol. II, p. 164).
140 Sewter, *Stained Glass of William Morris*, vol. I, illus. pl. 618. The church contains no fewer than seven windows designed by Burne-Jones; this is the earliest of them (see Sewter, vol. II, pp. 163–64).

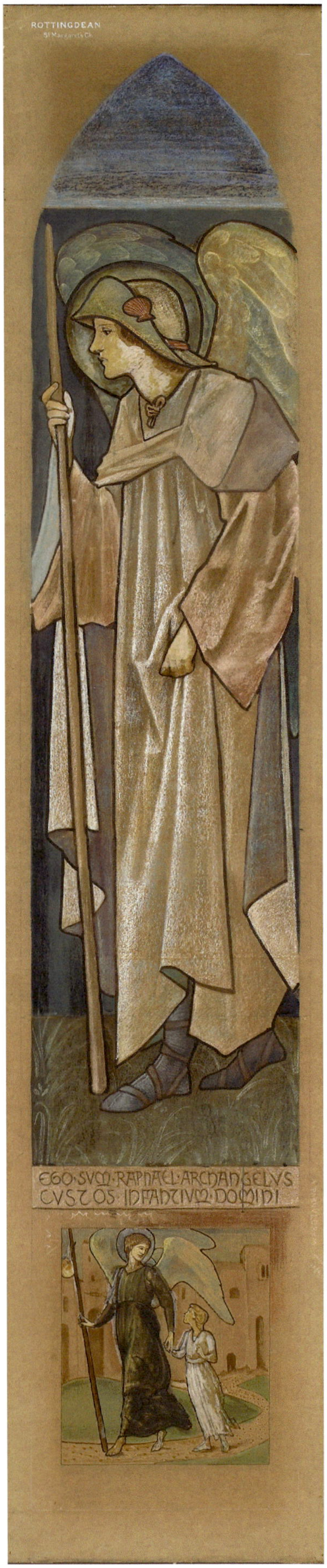

LL 3786

wife, Georgiana, recalled: 'one day we went over to the little church and watched the workmen putting in the last light of the window that he had given as a record of our daughter's marriage there'.[141] As the windows were given by Burne-Jones, there is no record of the cartoons in the account books, making them impossible to date precisely, but it is likely that they date from c. 1892–93.[142] Both designs, with their strong linear compositions and colouring of blues and greens, are typical of Burne-Jones's late stained-glass cartoons. It is worth noting that on the final version of the window, the inscription under the figure of Raphael has been changed to include the word 'parvulorum' instead of 'infantium'. As the words have approximately the same meaning (child and infant respectively), it seems that the change was made for visual reasons: parvulorum being the lengthier word, it fitted better with the layout of the inscription.

**Study of a woman's head, profile to left**
LL 3810 (WHL 3877)

Pencil on wove paper
43.1 x 34.4 cm
Date: 1890s

Prov: by descent to Philip Burne-Jones; his sale, Christie's, 5 June 1919 (lot 33); bt. by Gooden and Fox for Lever (£16 3s)

Exh: Port Sunlight, Lady Lever Art Gallery, *The Pre-Raphaelites – Their Friends and Followers*, 1948 (cat. 95); Port Sunlight, Lady Lever Art Gallery and tour, *Pre-Raphaelite Drawings*, 2006–2008 (no cat. no.)

In technique, LL 3810 can be compared to the many pencil studies that Burne-Jones made for his large canvas of *The Car of Love* dating from the 1890s (for example, *Study for The Car of Love*, 1895, in the Cecil Higgins Art Gallery, Bedford).[143] Like many of the studies from this period, however, it does not seem to be related to a particular painting and is probably an independent drawing. It has been suggested that the model may have been Venetia Benson[144] and there is certainly a likeness to identified drawings of her from this period in which she wears her hair piled up in the same distinctive style (see, for example, Christie's, 9 June 2004 [lot 19, figs. 4 and 5]). Venetia was the second daughter of the painter Alfred William Hunt who had married the architect and metal-worker W. A. S. Benson in 1886 (see entry for LL 3811, p. 28).

141 Ibid., p. 239.
142 Sewter, *Stained Glass of William Morris*, vol. II, p. 12.

**Study of a female head, smiling**
LL 3814 (WHL 3871)

Black chalk, with black pastel on Japanese paper
36 x 32.4 cm (sight)
Date: 1890s

Prov: by descent to Philip Burne-Jones; his sale, Christie's, 5 June 1919 (lot 17); bt. by Gooden and Fox for Lever (£26 5s with LL 2908, LL 3815 and WHL 3868)

Exh: Port Sunlight, Lady Lever Art Gallery, *The Pre-Raphaelites – Their Friends and Followers*, 1948 (cat. 79); Sheffield, Mappin Art Gallery, *Burne-Jones*, 1971 (cat. 59)

143 Evelyn Joll, *Cecil Higgins Art Gallery Watercolours and Drawings* (Bedford, 2002), p. 49.
144 LLAG files: this suggestion was made in a note from Martin Levey, 1986.

LL 3810

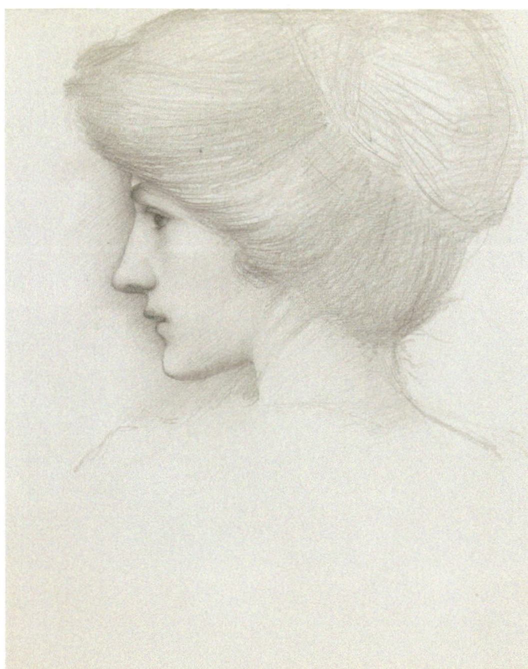

LL 3814

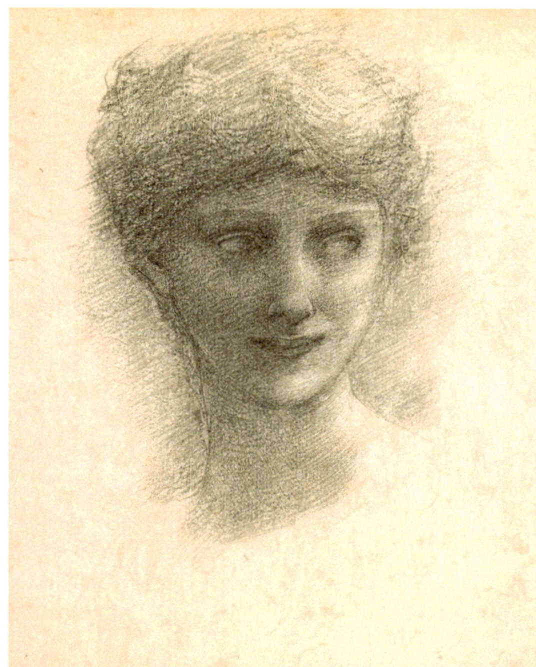

In its use of black chalk, pastel and cross-hatching to create soft shadowing and modelling, LL 3814 is typical of drawings produced by Burne-Jones in the 1890s (the same materials and techniques are used in LL 3815, pp. 34–35, for example).[145] In this respect, it contrasts with the crisp outlines of drawings from the 1870s (see, for example, LL 3822A, pp. 26–27). In the mid-1890s Burne-Jones produced numerous individual female head studies for his huge oil painting of *The Sirens* (c. 1891–98, Ringling Museum of Arts, Sarasota, Florida) and although LL 3814 does not directly relate to any one figure in the painting, it is possible that this is a drawing produced around this time with a view to being used in the final painting.[146]

## Draped Female Figure
LL 3818 (WHL 3975)

Gold paint on wove paper painted with black gouache
24.7 x 16.6 cm (sight)
Date: 1896

Inscr: EB-J 1896 (gold paint, bottom right)

Prov: by descent to Philip Burne-Jones; his sale, Christie's, 5 June 1919 (lot 139); bt. by Gooden and Fox for Lever (18 gns)

Exh: London, Burlington Fine Arts Club, *Exhibition of Drawings and Studies by Sir Edward Burne-Jones, Bart.*, 1899 (cat. 123); [?] London, White City, *Japan-British Exhibition*, 1910 (cat. 89 or 97);[147] [?] London, Bermondsey Settlement, *Bermondsey Settlement Picture Exhibition* (date and cat. no. unknown)[148]

## Girls Dancing
LL 3820 (WHL 3977)

Gold and bronze paints on wove paper painted with black gouache
25.1 x 17.2 cm
Date: 1896

Inscr: EB-J / 1896 (gold paint, bottom right)

Prov: by descent to Philip Burne-Jones; his sale, Christie's, 5 June 1919 (part of lot 140 with WHL 3976); bt. Gooden and Fox (£35 14s for the pair) for Lever (£35 15s 6d)

Exh: London, Burlington Fine Arts Club, *Exhibition of Drawings and Studies by Sir Edward Burne-Jones, Bart*, 1899 (cat. 21); Port Sunlight, Lady Lever Art Gallery, *The Pre-Raphaelites – Their Friends and Followers*, 1948 (cat. 63); Brisbane, Queensland Art Gallery and tour of Australia and New Zealand, *Exhibition of British Watercolours 1850–1914*, organised by the Empire Art Loan Exhibitions Society, 1952–53 (cat. 13); New York, Metropolitan Museum of Art, *Edward Burne-Jones: Victorian Artist-Dreamer*, 1998 (cat. 168)

By the 1890s the elderly and ailing Burne-Jones had become acutely aware that his work was waning in popularity.[149] The artist's highly personal literary vision was perceived as unfashionable by the late Victorian art world, which had seen the rise of realism with the founding in 1886 of the New English Art Club. His last large-scale finished painting, *Love Leading the Pilgrim* (1877, 1896–97, Tate), returned unsold after it was exhibited at the New Gallery in 1897, something that would have been unheard of in earlier years.[150] It was in this context that the artist, who otherwise made little concession to changes in taste, began from 1890 to produce on a regular basis small drawings in gouache and gold paint on coloured paper for which he found there was a market. In appearance these resemble fifteenth-century Italian silverpoint drawings, reminding us that Burne-Jones had a thorough knowledge of Old Master techniques, aided by several trips to Italy as well as his extensive library of books and photographs. LL 3818 and LL 3820 are examples of a particular type of this late drawing where he used gold paint on a prepared black ground.

Neither Lady Lever work is a study for a related painting; like many of his drawings using these techniques, they were intended as independent pieces, although they do rely on motifs used in the artist's earlier work. They are both good examples of Burne-Jones's long-standing fascination with drapery. LL 3820 showcases the artist's delight in the effect of clinging drapery on the female form. This image draws on the artist's fascination for early Renaissance art. In 1871, for example, he is said to have admired Ghirlandaio's 'sweet girls running, and their dresses blown about' and on his 1873 trip to Italy he made careful studies of such figures from the fifteenth-century floor of Siena Cathedral.[151] The figures in LL 3820 are based directly on the two left-hand figures in a pencil illustration for the poem *The Parlement of Foules* (c. 1892–95), one of the few designs for the Kelmscott Chaucer (1896) which was not engraved.[152] The pair to LL 3820, formerly in the Lady Lever Art Gallery, was used as a design for a repoussé silver plaque by Robert Catterson Smith, who had translated Burne-Jones's drawings into outlines for the Kelmscott Chaucer.[153]

LL 3818 is similarly an independent work of art, although Burne-Jones's treatment of the subject relates closely to the Gothic folds and heavy drapery of the female figures in late paintings such as *The Wedding of Psyche* (1895, Musées Royaux des Beaux-Arts, Brussels) and

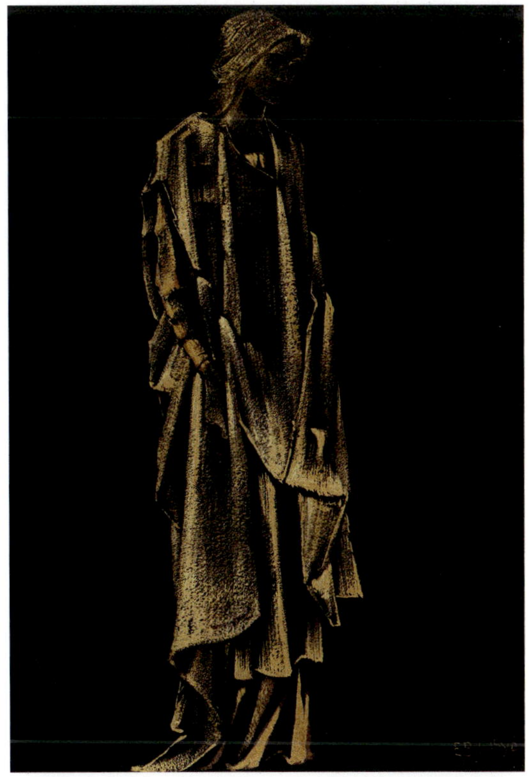

LL 3818

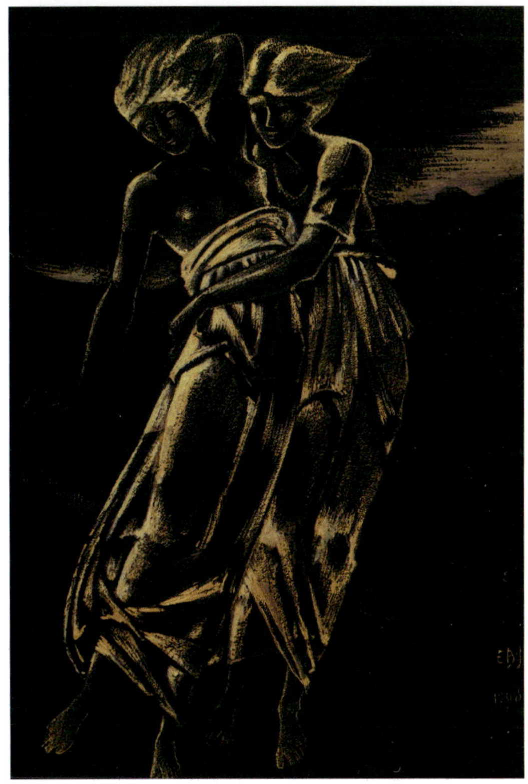

LL 3820

*The Sleep of Arthur in Avalon* (1881–98, Museo de Arte de Ponce, Puerto Rico), pieces that demonstrated Burne-Jones's revived interest in medievalism towards the end of his life.[154]

145 John Christian and Stephen Wildman, verbally, February 2008.
146 Wildman and Christian, *Edward Burne-Jones*, pp. 321–22 (cats. 157–58).
147 This reference is cited in the LLAG files: it has not been possible to confirm it.
148 This reference is cited in the LLAG files. The work is not listed in the 1912 exhibition of this name.
149 See Wildman and Christian, *Edward Burne-Jones*, pp. 317–18.
150 Ibid., p. 318, illus. p. 182 (cat. 74).
151 Burne-Jones, *Memorials of Edward Burne-Jones*, vol. II, p. 21; Duncan Robinson, 'Burne-Jones, Fairfax Murray, and Siena', *Apollo*, vol. 102 (November 1975), p. 348, figs. 2 and 4.
152 Wildman and Christian, *Edward Burne-Jones*, pp. 311–12 (cat. 155), illus. p. 311.
153 This was one of two plaques exhibited at the Arts and Crafts Exhibition Society, London, 1896 (cats. 109 and 110), illus. *The Studio*, vol. 9 (1896), p. 119.
154 See Wildman and Christian, *Edward Burne-Jones*, pp. 126–28, (cat. 41) and p. 316, fig. 107.

## WILLIAM CALLOW

1812 Greenwich–1908 Great Missenden, Buckinghamshire

### The Market Square, Frankfurt

LL 3789 (WHL 734, HH 352)

Watercolour over pencil, with extra gum arabic, and stopping out on wove paper
17.7 x 25.6 cm
Date: probably 1852, 1860 or 1863

Inscr: Frankfort / August 17 (pencil, bottom left)

Annot: 16475 / Frankfort / J. Holland (label on verso of frame)

Prov: bt. from James Orrock by Lever, 1910

Lit: J. Reynolds, *William Callow R.W.S.* (London, 1980), p. 191

Callow was trained as an engraver by a brother of Copley Fielding (see pp. 92–96), before moving to Paris in 1827 where he shared a studio with Thomas Shotter Boys. It was with Boys that Callow roamed the streets of Paris, sketching the picturesque old houses and churches that formed his standard subjects throughout his career. Through Boys Callow absorbed the technique used by Bonington (see pp. 10–12) of using paint on an extremely fine brush, giving his watercolours a distinctive calligraphic quality. Until 1841, when Callow left Paris to live in London, he divided his time between England and the Continent, having been appointed in 1834 as drawing master to the family of King Louis-Philippe. Throughout his career he made numerous sketching tours in Central Europe. He retired to Great Missenden in 1854, although he continued to teach. He was elected associate of the SPWC in 1838 and a member in 1848.

The inscription on LL 3789 suggests that it may have been drawn on the spot, at least in pencil outline, with watercolour added later. The date of the watercolour is uncertain. It is stated to have been inscribed under an old mount: 'Frankfort, Aug. 27, 1835'.[155] However, there is no mention in Callow's autobiography of having visited Frankfurt in 1835.[156] He first records visiting Frankfurt in the autumn of 1838, although he seems to have only passed through briefly.[157] He may have spent more time in the city during his honeymoon tour in 1846, although on 17 August of that year, the date inscribed on the Lady Lever sketch, he and his wife were in Venice.[158] LL 3789 is most likely to date from trips made in 1852, 1860 or 1863. In August 1852 Callow and his wife spent the month in Germany, travelling home via Kassel and Frankfurt.[159] They returned to Germany in the autumn of 1860, when they made a journey from Coblenz up the Moselle; and were there again in August 1863, when Callow visited Queen Victoria at Rosenau, near Coburg: various works titled *Market Place, Frankfurt* were exhibited at the summer exhibitions of the SPWC in 1863 and 1864, suggesting that Callow had renewed his acquaintance with the city during the early 1860s. Callow returned often to the same composition at a later date and it is possible that later, more highly finished versions of this work may exist, although none are known.

The Lady Lever watercolour depicts one of Frankfurt's market squares adjacent to the Cathedral, or the parish church of St Bartholomew as it was known since the eighteenth century. The south transept of the largely Gothic cathedral can be seen to the right of the picture; in the foreground is the bread market, and to the far left, the city weighing machine, used by merchants to weigh their goods publicly before standard measurements were introduced.[160]

LL 3789 was listed in James Orrock's collection as by James Holland, and was re-attributed to Callow only after it had been acquired by Lever.[161]

### The Market Place, Malines

LL 3790 (LP 60)

Watercolour, with extra gum arabic over pencil, with touches of gouache and cutting out on wove paper
50.9 x 74.6 cm (sight)
Date: 1883–84

Inscr: William / Callow 1884 (watercolour, bottom right); W Callow / 188[3?] (watercolour, bottom right); [?] Van der (watercolour, on placard of building, far left)

Prov: Thomas Barlow, 1908; bt. from the Fine Art Society by the Trustees, 27 July 1943 (£70 17s 6d)

Exh: London, Leicester Galleries, *Exhibition of Watercolours by William Callow*, 1907 (cat. 60); London, Fine Art Society, *Exhibition of Early English Watercolours and Drawings*, 1943 (cat. 13)

Lit: H. M. Cundall (ed.), *William Callow R.W.S., F.R.G.S: An autobiography* (London, 1908), illus. p. 70; J. Reynolds, *William Callow R.W.S.* (London, 1980), pp. 149, 191, illus. pl. 97

Callow may have first visited the city of Malines, half-way between Brussels and Antwerp, in 1841, and he described sketching in the city in 1844, producing further material in 1850 and again in 1854. It was during the autumn 1844 trip that he made a watercolour sketch, now in the Victoria & Albert Museum (fig. 14), which was used as a basis for the Lady Lever work,[162] a large studio piece painted some forty years later when Callow was resident in Great Missenden. A comparison with the sketch shows that Callow added much of the foreground detail in the final watercolour: only the two nuns appear in the earlier work, although in the later one they face outwards. The final watercolour is signed and dated 1884 and possibly 1883 (the last digit in the latter date is difficult to decipher); the work may well have been begun in 1883 and retouched the following year. Such a large, highly finished piece was presumably intended for exhibition and may have been shown at the Royal Society of Painters in Water-Colours in 1884 or 1885.[163]

The Lady Lever work depicts the main civic buildings in the market square, Malines. The Clothmakers' Hall, with the red roof in the far left foreground, was built in the late Middle Ages, when Malines gained wealth and power as a result of its lucrative cloth trade.[164] Alongside it is the Palace of the Great Council, which was designed in Neo-Gothic style. Malines was briefly the capital of the Low Countries in the early sixteenth century: when political power moved to Brussels, it became important as a religious centre and in 1559 it was proclaimed an archdiocese of Belgium. LL 3790 is typical of Callow's technique, which changed little over the course of his career, in using paint on a fine brush which gives a linear quality to the work. The watercolour shows his interest, in common with his contemporary Thomas Shotter Boys and the older artist Samuel Prout (see p. 155), in depicting the decorative effects of masonry and other architectural details.

155 LLAG files.
156 H. M. Cundall (ed.), *William Callow, R.W.S., F.R.G.S.: An autobiography* (London, 1908), pp. 28–29.
157 Ibid., p. 70.
158 J. Reynolds, *William Callow R.W.S.* (London, 1980), pp. 84–85.
159 Cundall, *William Callow*, p. 107.

160 I am grateful for the help of Xanthe Brooke and Wolfgang Cillessen for help in identifying the precise location.
161 It had been re-attributed by 1928; Tatlock, p. 125.

162 Reynolds, *William Callow*, p. 149 refers to a photograph of a drawing in the Witt library inscribed Malines. Maison de Conseil and dated Sept 17.41. The Victoria & Albert Museum sketch is also inscribed Sep 17 but with the year 1844 and it seems possible that the date has been recorded incorrectly from the photograph. Callow recorded in his autobiography, published immediately after his death, that he visited Malines in the autumn of 1844 en route to revisiting the Rhine and the Moselle (Cundall, *William Callow*, p. 91). A sketch of the *Palais de Justice, Malines*, dated 27 September 1850, is in the Tate; Bristol Museum and Art Gallery has a drawing of Malines signed and dated 1854. Neither of these works relates to LL 3790.
163 Two works with the title *On the Market Place at Malines* were exhibited at the RSPWC in the summer of 1884 and the winter of 1885. The SPWC renamed itself after receiving its royal charter in 1881.
164 The Clothmakers' Hall was altered in neo-Gothic style between 1900 and 1911. It subsequently became the Town Hall.

fig. 14. William Callow, *Malines: Maison de Conseil*, 1844, pencil and watercolour on paper, 26.6 x 36.6 cm, V&A Images/ Victoria and Albert Museum

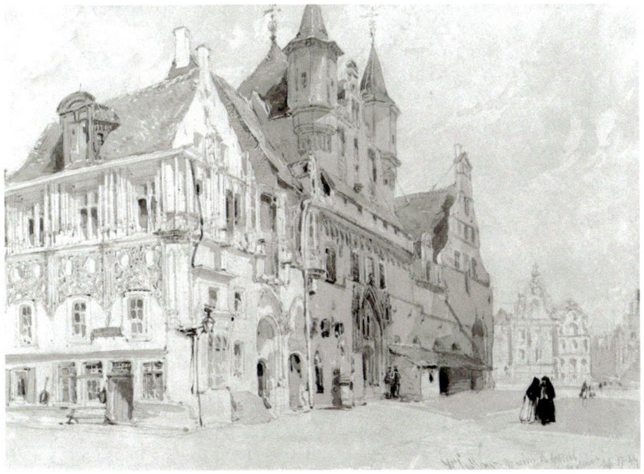

LL 3790

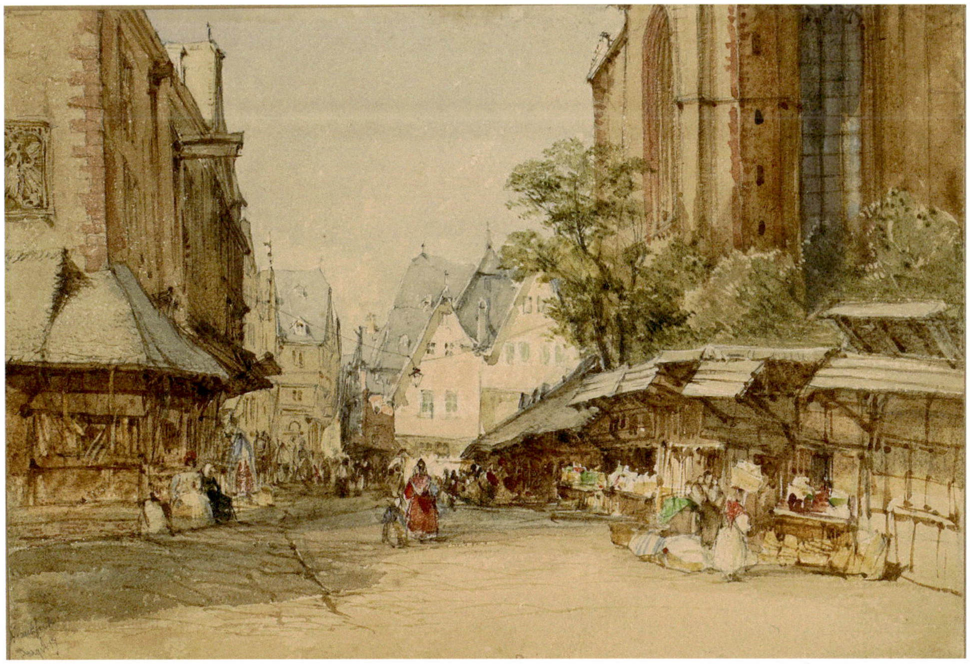

LL 3789

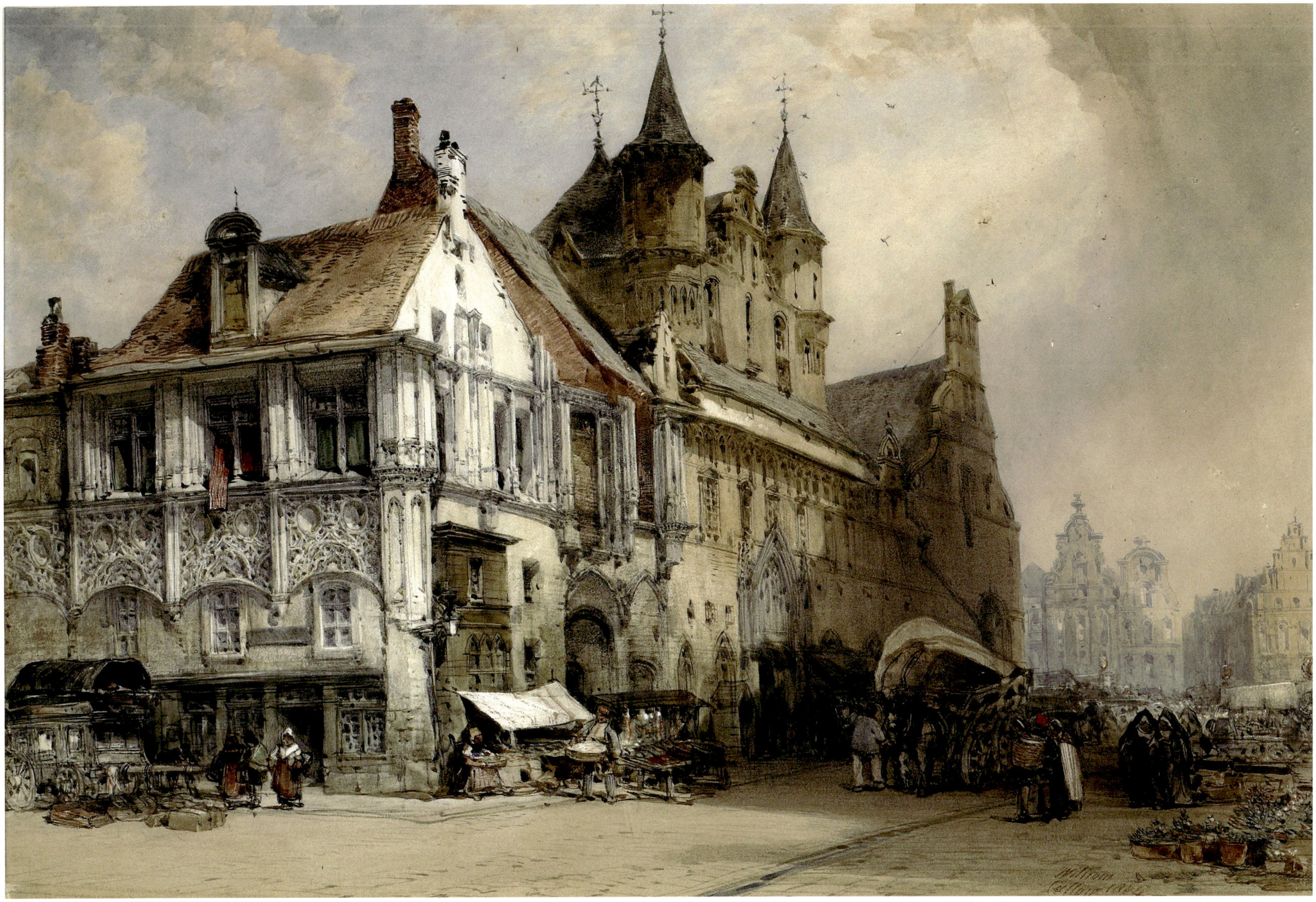

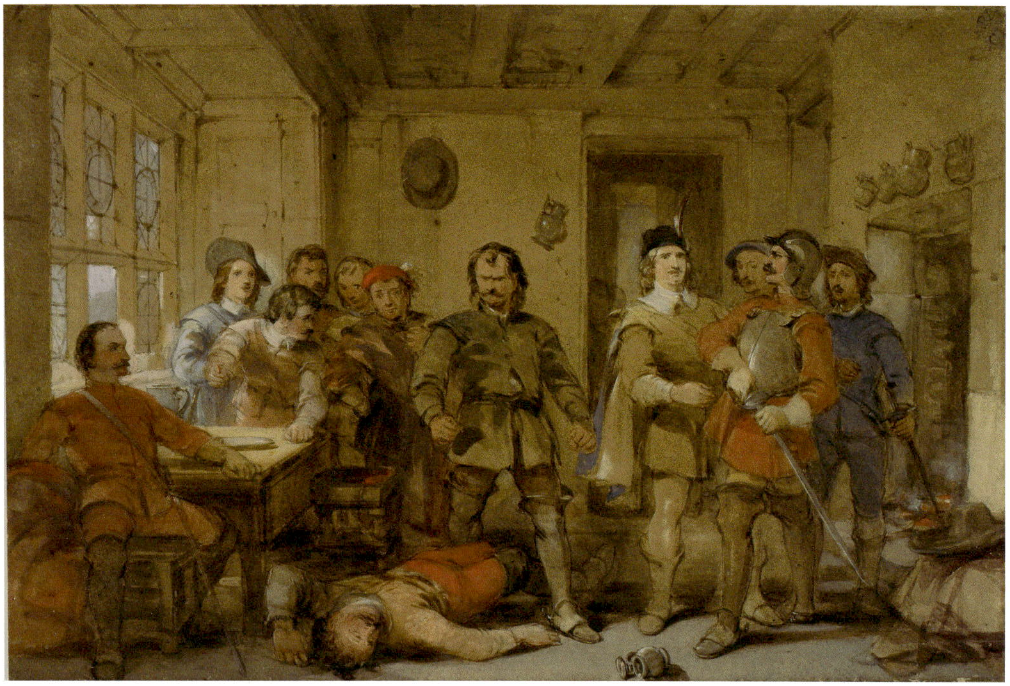

LL 3823

## GEORGE CATTERMOLE

1800 Dickleburgh, near Diss, Norfolk–1868 London

**A Quarrel in the Guardroom**
LL 3823 (WHL 759, HH 342)

Watercolour with touches of gouache, chalk and white heightening on wove paper
39.7 x 58.5 cm
Date: 1830s, possibly 1831

Annot: PA / CH (ink stamp, top right corner)
Prov: bt. from James Orrock by Lever, 1910[165]
Exh: [?] London, SPWC, 1831 (cat. 415)

Cattermole had moved permanently to London from Norfolk by at least 1819. Soon afterwards he began work as an architectural draughtsman for the antiquary John Britton, contributing illustrations to his numerous publications. He also illustrated volumes I (1841) and II (1844) of his brother Richard's *The Great Civil War of Charles I and the Parliament.* Cattermole exhibited at the Royal Academy between 1819 and 1827 and at the British Institution in 1827, but the majority of his exhibited works were shown at the SPWC between 1822 and 1850. He was elected an associate of the Society in 1822 and became a full member in 1833. In 1852, he briefly and unsuccessfully experimented with oil painting. He exhibited 11 works at the *Exposition Universelle* in Paris in 1855 which were received with great acclaim, and he was awarded a medal of honour.

Cattermole specialised in watercolours depicting subjects of historical genre, often based on authors such as Walter Scott and Shakespeare, whom he read from an early age, but also purely imaginary pieces. In LL 3823 the figures are wearing the standard military dress of the 1640s, 'buff coats' made from thick oxhide for protection from weapons; the figure on the right wears military armour over his. The scene depicts the aftermath of a fight, with a male figure lying recumbent on the floor. Cattermole included an overturned vessel in the foreground to suggest the drama of the recent incident, a device he used in other works (see, for example, *When Did You Last See Your Master?*, Sotheby's, London, 16 July, 1992 [part of lot 31]). Although LL 3823 is clearly set in the Civil War period of the 1640s, it cannot be linked to Richard Cattermole's publication on the Civil War nor to any work of fiction. LL 3823 may be the work exhibited at the SPWC in 1831 as *The Guard Room* and its style is certainly consistent with other finished watercolours from this period (see, for example, *Salvator Rosa among the Banditti*, exh. SPWC, 1838).[166] The frieze-like composition of the figures was one Cattermole used throughout his career (see, for example, *Scene of Ancient Monastic Life*, 1850, Victoria & Albert Museum).[167]

165 1910 Inventory, p. 44, valued at £40.

166 *Salvator Rosa sketching amongst the Banditti of the Abruzzi*, watercolour and gouache, 54.8 x 76.2 cm, exh. SPWC 1838 (cat. 165), signed with monogram, Whitworth Art Gallery, Manchester.

167 *A Scene of Monastic Life*, watercolour, signed with monogram and dated 1850, 31.7 x 45.4 cm, Victoria & Albert Museum.

## ATTRIBUTED TO THOMAS CHEESMAN

1760–1834/5, places of birth and death unknown

**Emma, Lady Hamilton**
LL 3938 (WHL 2613)

Black and coloured chalks on paper
45 x 35.5 cm (sight)
Date: probably before 1797

Prov: Jeffery Whitehead; his sale, Christie's, 6 August 1915 (lot 51); bt. by Frank Partridge (15 gns) for Lever (£17 6s 6d)

Lever acquired LL 3938 as a portrait by Richard Cosway (see pp. 53–54) of his wife Maria. The sitter bears no resemblance to Maria Cosway as she appears in other portraits and the drawing style is completely uncharacteristic of Richard Cosway.[168]

The re-identification of the sitter as Lady Hamilton (1765–1815) and the attribution itself both derive from a stipple engraving, currently known only in a modern reproduction, which is stated to be by Cheesman, after his own drawing, published on 10 February 1797.[169] The engraving is closely comparable to LL 3938 even though it is in reverse and exhibits some significant differences. These differences, which include the treatment of the hair and the angle of the sitter's gaze, seem explicable in terms of a printmaker improving upon his own original drawing as he went along. No original impression of Cheesman's print, however, has been traced[170] and the attribution must be regarded as tentative; nevertheless, the likeness to Lady Hamilton as she appears in other portraits appears to confirm the subject of the drawing.

Cheesman, who worked in London, trained under the engraver Francesco Bartolozzi and is known for his sentimental, literary and religious subjects. His work exhibits a wide range of moods and styles. One of his best-known prints, published on 1 August 1789, was after Romney's painting of *Emma Hart, Lady Hamilton, as the Spinstress*. If Cheesman drew Emma from the life, it must have been some years before 1797: she had lived in Naples since 1786 and had visited London only once in the meantime, in the summer of 1791, to celebrate her marriage to Sir William Hamilton.
AK

168 Stephen Lloyd kindly confirmed this, verbally, 31 January 2008.

169 Information from the caption to Plate V in G. P. B. Naish (ed.), *Nelson's Letters to his Wife* (London and Colchester, 1958), illustrating the engraving; the caption titles the work *Lady Hamilton*.

170 It is not listed in Freeman O'Donoghue, *Catalogue of Engraved British Portraits Preserved in the Department of Prints and Drawings in the British Museum* (London, 5 vols, 1908–25), nor referred to in John Ingamells, *National Portrait Gallery Mid-Georgian Portraits 1760–1790* (London, 2004).

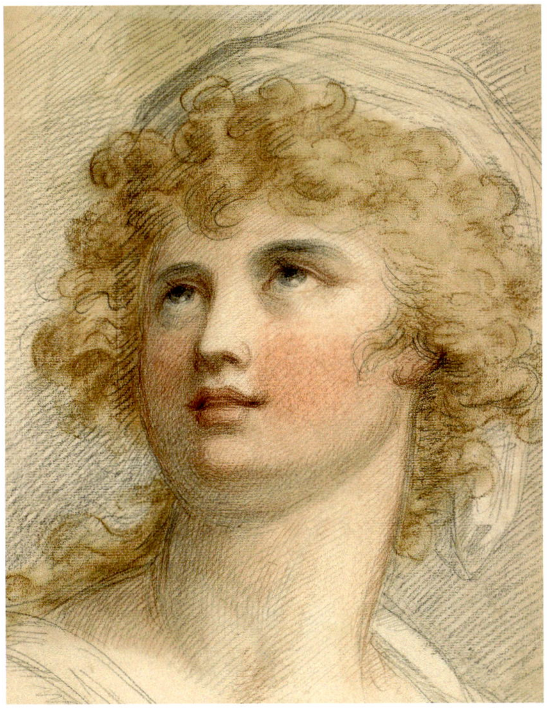

LL 3938

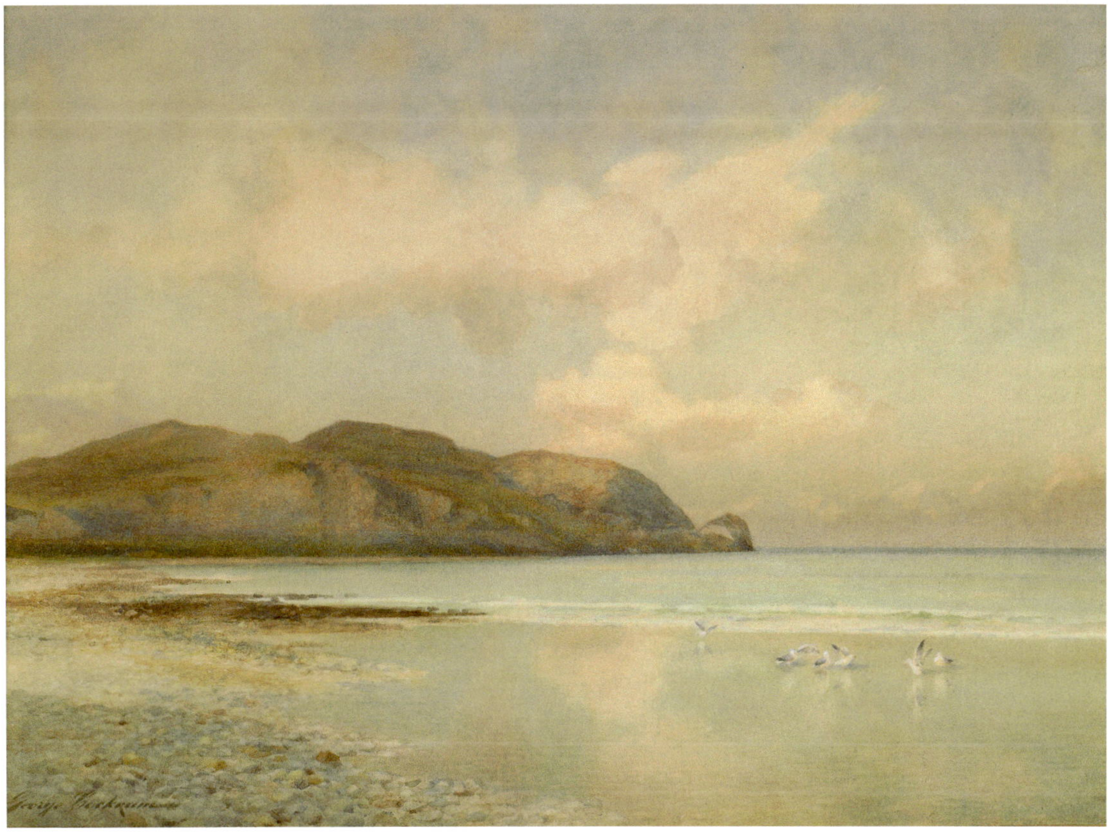

LL 3825

## GEORGE COCKRAM

1861 Birkenhead–1950 Rhosneigr, Anglesey

**The Little Orme from Penrhyn Bay**
LL 3825 (LP 50)

Watercolour with touches of gouache on wove paper
45.6 x 60.3 cm (sight)
Date: 1890s onwards

Inscr: George Cockram (watercolour stamp, bottom left)

Prov: given by Sir William Hulme Lever, 2nd Viscount Leverhulme, 10 October 1938

Cockram studied at the Liverpool School of Art under John Finnie (1829–1907) between 1876 and 1884. He first exhibited at the Royal Academy in 1883 and subsequently at numerous other societies, including the Liverpool Autumn Exhibitions at the Walker Art Gallery, the Royal Cambrian Academy and the Royal Institute of Painters in Water-Colours. Between 1881 and 1887, Cockram lived in Liverpool but in the early 1890s he moved to Anglesey where he lived for the remainder of his life. In the following decades Cockram produced large numbers of watercolours of seashore and mountain subjects, often based on North Welsh landscapes. Cockram died after being burnt by a paraffin heater in his studio at Rhosneigr, Anglesey.[171]

LL 3825 depicts the limestone headland, the Little Orme, situated at the end of Llandudno Bay, Conway, on the North Welsh coast, viewed from Penrhyn Bay. The watercolour's high finish and smooth surface is characteristic of Cockram's work from the 1890s onwards. No record can be found of LL 3825 being exhibited at the Liverpool Autumn Exhibitions or the Royal Cambrian Academy.[172]

171 *The Times*, 29 September 1950; *Manchester Guardian*, 28 September 1950; *Liverpool Post*, 28 September 1950.

172 LLAG files: a note describes LL 3825 as having been purchased by [the 2nd] Lord Leverhulme from an unknown exhibition.

## THOMAS COLLIER

1840 Glossop, Derbyshire–1891 Hampstead, London

### A Welsh Mountain Side

LL 3829 (WHL 221, H 485)

Watercolour over pencil, with extra gum arabic on paper
26.9 x 51.2 cm
Date: mid- to late 1860s

Inscr: T. Collier (watercolour, bottom right)

Prov: artist's sale, Christie's, 24–25 March 1892 (lot 33, as *Study in Wales*); bt. by James Orrock (11 gns); bt. from Orrock by Lever, 1912[173]

Exh: Brisbane, Queensland Art Gallery and tour of Australia and New Zealand, *Exhibition of British Watercolours 1850–1914*, organised by the Empire Art Loan Exhibitions Society, 1952–53 (cat. 23)

Lit: Adrian Bury, *The Life and Art of Thomas Collier, R. I.* (Leigh-on-Sea, 1944), p. 71, illus. pl. 11

After studying at the Manchester School of Art, Collier followed in the footsteps of David Cox (see pp. 59–65), spending the years 1864–69 at Betws-y-Coed in North Wales. Following brief periods in Birmingham and Manchester, Collier moved to London in the early 1870s, where in 1879 he built a home and studio in Hampstead, living there until his death. After being rejected twice as a member of the SPWC, he was elected an associate of the Institute of Painters in Water-Colours in 1870 and a full member in 1872. Collier did not exhibit a large number of works, but at the 1878 Paris *Exposition Universelle* he was awarded the French Legion of Honour for his watercolour of *Arundel Castle from the Park*.[174]

With its mountainous subject-matter and relatively detailed technique (in contrast to later works such as LL 3828, p. 46), LL 3829 is characteristic of the watercolours Collier was making in the mid- to late 1860s. During this period, Collier was based at Betws-y-Coed, and the watercolour shows the inspiration of the late Welsh landscapes of this area's most famous artistic resident, David Cox. Collier relished painting outdoors and the Lady Lever watercolour was probably painted while the artist was on one of his sketching excursions in the vicinity. It contrasts, for example, with a more highly worked watercolour from this period, *Welsh Mountain Landscape* (1869, Birmingham Museums and Art Gallery).[175] The slightly sloping handwritten signature is also characteristic of Collier's earlier work (the artist predominantly used a stamp in later years).

*A Welsh Mountain Side* belonged to James Orrock (see pp. xiv–xvii, 146–49) who collected Thomas Collier's work, having discovered it at an exhibition of the Birmingham Society of Artists in the late 1860s.[176]

### Study of Waterdocks

LL 3824 (WHL 337, H 164)

Watercolour over pencil on wove paper
24.5 x 36 cm
Date: 1870s, or 1880s

Inscr: Thos Collier (stamp, bottom left)

Prov: James Orrock, 1907; bt. by Gooden and Fox for Lever, 1907 (£25)[177]

Lit: Adrian Bury, *The Life and Art of Thomas Collier, R. I.* (Leigh-on-Sea, 1944), p. 71, illus. pl. 83

This work is typical of Collier's watercolour sketches made outdoors late on in his career. These watercolours were characterised by a loose, fluid technique akin to the work of the early nineteenth-century watercolourists David Cox and Peter DeWint (pp. 76–89), rather than the more precise techniques of contemporaries such as William Henry Hunt (see pp. 120–27). LL 3824 undoubtedly dates from Collier's London period (after 1870), but there is little to differentiate the watercolours he produced in the 1870s from those of the 1880s and the work may date from either decade.

LL 3824 depicts a canal in the middle ground, with several figures around a higher and lower lock, but there is not enough detail to suggest a location.

### Waterfall - A Scotch River in Spate - a sketch[178]

LL 3826 (WHL 367, H 188)

Watercolour over pencil on wove paper
25.5 x 35.7 cm
Date: mid- to late 1870s

Inscr: Thos Collier (stamp, bottom right)

Prov: artist's sale, Christie's, 24–25 March 1892 (lot 182); bt. by James Orrock (£11 0s 6d); bt. from Orrock by Lever at an unknown date

Lit: Byron Webber, *James Orrock, R.I.: Painter, Connoisseur, Collector* (London, 2 vols, 1903), vol. II, p. 4; Adrian Bury, *The Life and Art of Thomas Collier, R. I.* (Leigh-on-Sea, 1944), p. 71, illus. pl. 41

On his sketching trips outdoors, Collier was drawn repeatedly to depicting the harsher aspects of nature and this watercolour is one of a number where he painted the subject of a rushing, swollen river (see also, for example, *A River in Spate*, Sheffield Museums and Art Gallery).[179] The title of the work is probably the original and may indicate that it was made on a trip to Scotland, although there is no record of such a visit. The vigorous handling and use of fluid washes suggest a date of the mid- to late 1870s.

### Study of Trees in Parham Park

LL 3827 (WHL 335, H 193)

Watercolour over pencil, with scratching out on wove paper
24.1 x 34.7 cm
Date: mid- to late 1870s

Inscr: Aug (pencil, bottom left); Thos Collier (ink, bottom left)

Prov: [?] artist's sale, Christie's, 24–25 March 1892 (lot 25, as *Parham Park*); bt. by McLean (5 gns); [?] James Orrock, 1907; [?] bt. by Gooden and Fox for Lever, 1907 ([?] £25)[180]

Exh: Perth, Art Gallery of Western Australia and Australian tour, *Exhibition of Early British Water-colours*, organised by the Empire Art Loans Exhibition Society, 1948–49 (cat. 156)

Lit: Adrian Bury, *The Life and Art of Thomas Collier, R. I.* (Leigh-on-Sea, 1944), p. 71, illus. pl. 44

Although LL 3827 was identified in the WHL Inventory as a view of Barham Park, this must be an error for the work represents Parham Park, the ancient deer park surrounding the Elizabethan house in West Sussex.[181] Collier visited the Sussex Downs during the middle and late 1870s, when he made sketches for various versions of *Arundel Castle from the Park*, and LL 3827 is likely to date from this period.[182] The watercolour shows Collier's concern to capture the essence of the landscape, with broad, fluid washes; both technique and subject-matter were heavily influenced by David Cox and Peter DeWint.

173 1912 Inventory, valued at £50.
174 Present location unknown; illus. Adrian Bury, *The Life and Art of Thomas Collier, R. I.* (Leigh-on-Sea, 1944), pl. 8.
175 Scott Wilcox and Christopher Newall, *Victorian Landscape Watercolors* (exh. cat., New Haven, Yale Center for British Art, Cleveland, Cleveland Museum of Art and Birmingham, Birmingham Museums and Art Gallery, 1992–93), p. 139 (cat. 75).
176 Bury, *Life and Art of Thomas Collier*, pp. 24–25.
177 LLAG files: note on accession card. No documentation has been found to confirm this provenance.
178 This title derives from the WHL Inventory. See also Bury, *Life and Art of Thomas Collier*, p. 71, where the title of the work is referred to as *A Scottish River in Spate*.
179 Illus. Bury, *Life and Art of Thomas Collier*, pl. 29.
180 LLAG files: note on accession card. No documentation has been found to confirm this provenance.
181 The WHL Inventory titles the work *Study of Trees in Barham Park, with sheep and Water in foreground*. Bury, *Life and Art of Thomas Collier*, p. 71, recorded the work as *Study of Trees, Parham Park*.
182 For the various dated versions of *Arundel Castle from the Park*, including one in the collection of Frederick Nettlefold, dated 1874, and one dated 1878 in the Victoria & Albert Museum, see the entry on the version in the Fitzwilliam Museum, Cambridge in Wilcox and Newall, *Victorian Landscape Watercolors*, p. 147 (cat. 83).

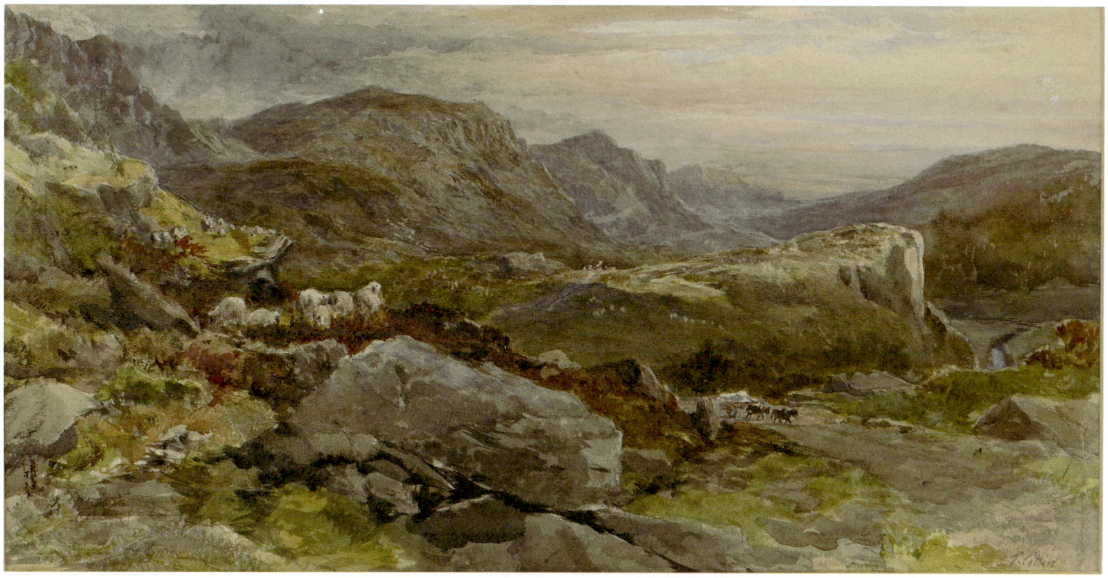

LL 3829

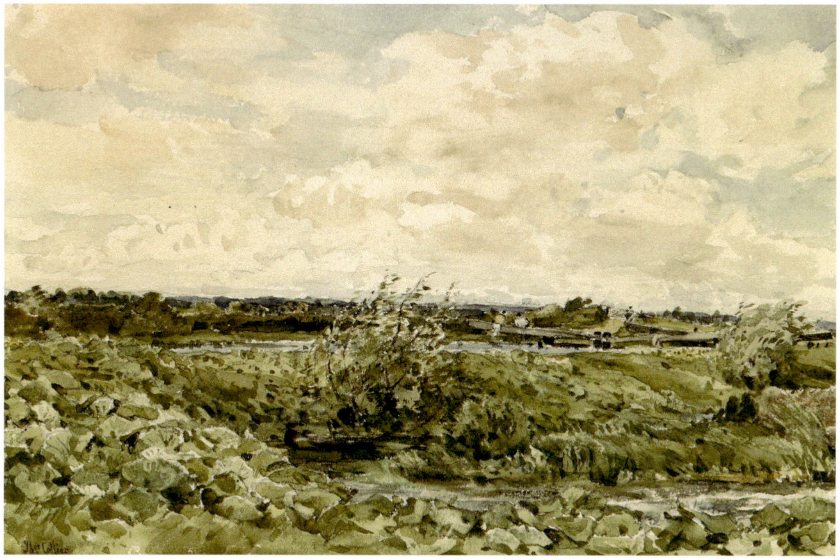

LL 3824

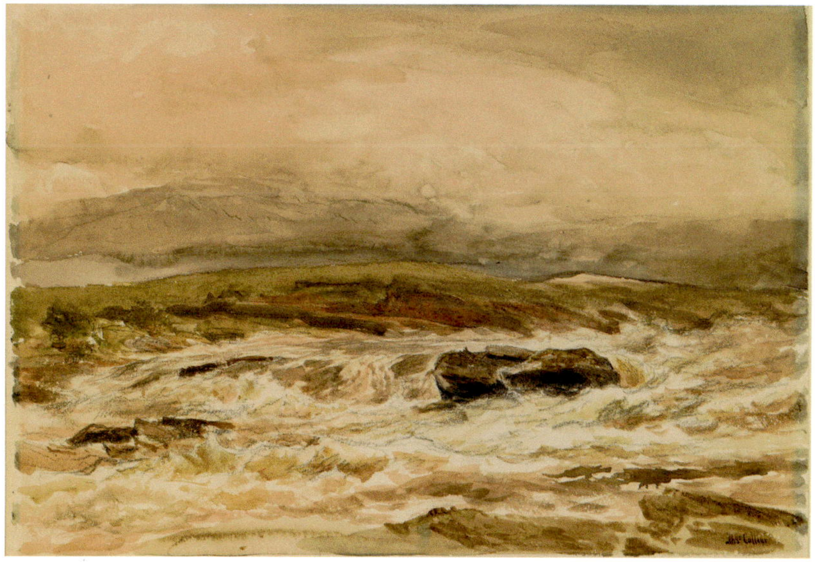

LL 3826

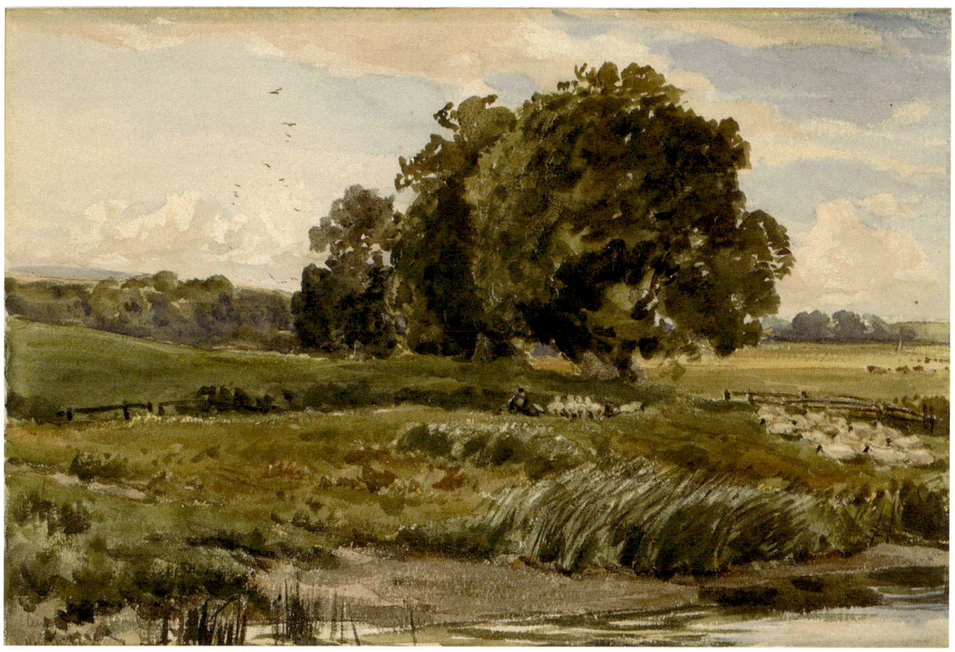

LL 3827

**Three Small Moorland Scenes**[183]
LL 3828 (WHL 220, H 475)

**Moorland Scene**
LL 3828A

Watercolour over pencil, with extra gum arabic on wove paper
9.7 x 15.8 cm (sight)
Date: 1880s

**Moorland Scene**
LL 3828B

Watercolour over pencil on wove paper
9.7 x 13.3 cm (sight)
Date: 1880s

**Moorland Scene**
LL 3828C

Watercolour over pencil, with extra gum arabic on wove paper
9.7 x 15.8 cm (sight)
Date: 1880s

Prov: [?] James Orrock, 1907; [?] bt. by Gooden and Fox for Lever 1907 ([?] £25)[184]

Lit: Adrian Bury, *The Life and Art of Thomas Collier, R.I.* (Leigh-on-Sea, 1944), p. 71

These three watercolours (which came into Lever's possession as a group) are typical of Collier's favourite subject-matter: moorland scenes under wide open skies. They are characteristic of the very sketchy technique used by the artist late on in his career in the 1880s.[185] In 1883 Collier described his working method and this might aptly be applied to these works: 'I always paint a subject as simply and as direct from nature as possible, using the fewest numbers of colours I can'.[186] The watercolours are characteristic of the artist's work in capturing the effects of stormy weather in the sky. This particular skill was celebrated by the artist's friend and collector of his work, James Orrock, who described Collier as: 'the finest of sky painters, especially of rain and cumulus clouds, while possessing more mastery of direct modelling and pearl-grey shadows in his skies and landscapes than any member of our brotherhood ... In moorland, with brilliant skies full of "accident", he has never had a rival.'[187] Collier travelled widely and it has not been possible to identify the locations depicted in these works.

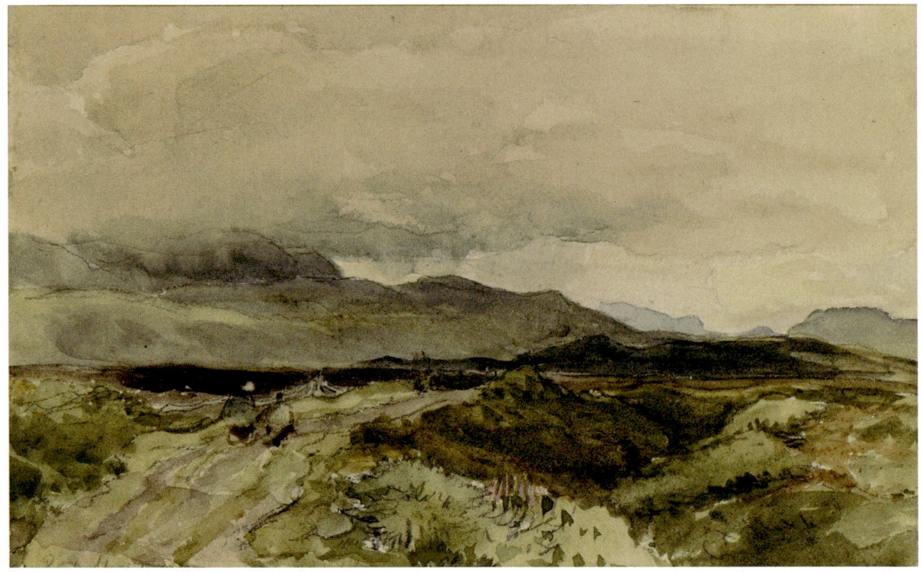

LL 3828A

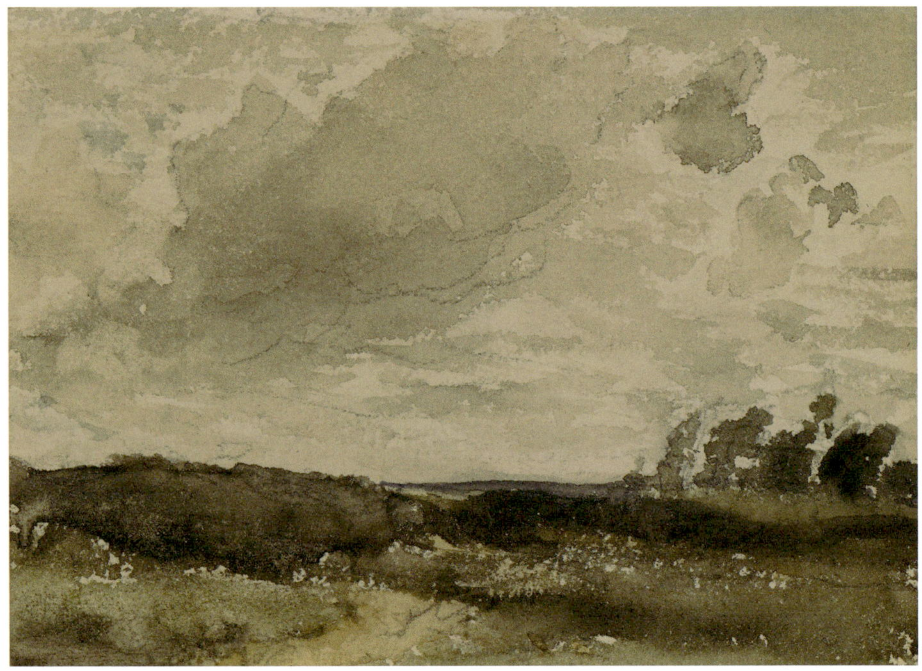

LL 3828B

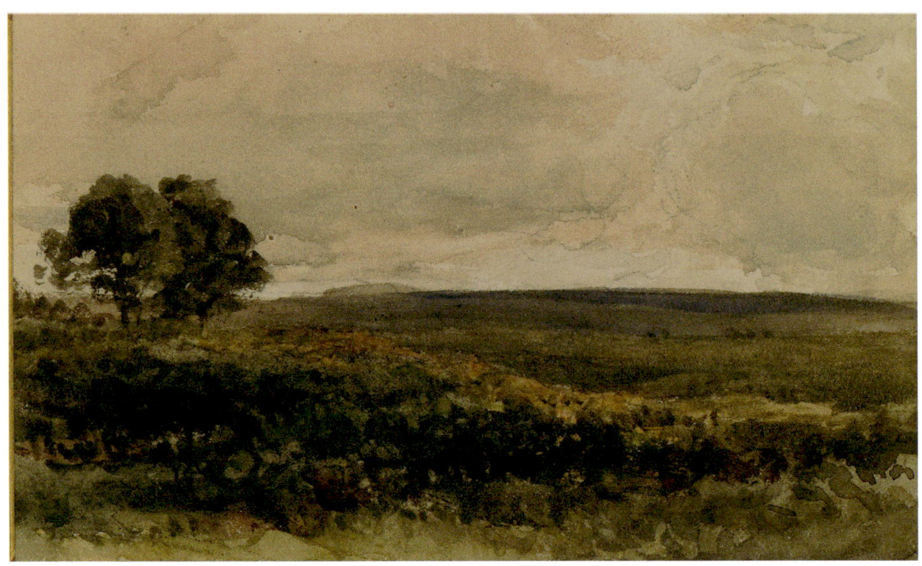

LL 3828C

183 Listed in WHL Inventory as *Three Landscapes (in one frame)*.
184 LLAG files: note on accession card. No documentation has been found to confirm this provenance.
185 See, for example, a very sketchy watercolour by Collier in the British Museum: *A river bank* (1904, 0530.6), dated 'July 1885', 25.7 x 35.7cm.
186 Quoted by Scott Wilcox, 'Collier, Thomas', *Macmillan Dictionary of Art* (London, 34 vols, 1996), vol. VII, p. 569.
187 Quoted by Bury, *Life and Art of Thomas Collier*, p. 25.

## JOHN CONSTABLE

1776 East Bergholt, Suffolk–1837 Hampstead, London

### East Bergholt Church: South-East View[188]

LL 3936 (WHL 324, H 151)

Watercolour over pencil, with touches of gum arabic and gouache, with scratching out on paper
39.7 x 60 cm
Date: 1811

Inscr: John Constable / feby.1811. (ink, bottom left)

Annot: A / South East View of / East Bergholt Church / in the County of Suffolk. / a Drawing by J. Constable Esqr. / and presented in testimony of Respect / to the Revd. Durand Rhudde. D.D. / the Rector. Febry. 25 / 1811 (ink, on backboard verso, a decorative label, lettered by John Dunthorne) (fig. 15)[189]

Prov: given by Ann Constable, the artist's mother, to Revd Durand Rhudde, 1811; James Orrock; his sale, Christie's, 4 June 1904 (lot 17); bt. by Lever (£35 14s)[190]

Exh: London, Royal Academy, *Winter Exhibition*, 1906 (cat. 167); London, Tate Gallery, *Constable: Paintings, Watercolours and Drawings*, 1976 (cat. 101)

Lit: 'Current Art Notes, Our Plates', *The Connoisseur*, vol. 90 (1932), p. 125, illus. p.105; R. B. Beckett (ed.), *John Constable's Correspondence* (Ipswich, 6 vols, 1962–68), vol. I, pp. 56–59; Reg Gadney, *Constable and his World* (London, 1976), p. 28; Leslie Parris, Ian Fleming-Williams and Conal Shields, *Constable: Paintings, Watercolours and Drawings* (exh. cat., London, Tate Gallery, 1976), p. 36, illus. pl. 10; Malcolm Cormack, *Constable* (London, 1986), p. 72, illus. pl. 65; Graham Reynolds, *The Early Paintings and Drawings of John Constable* (New Haven and London, 2 vols, 1996), vol. I, pp. 156–57, illus. vol. II, pl. 893

Constable, the son of a wealthy miller, devoted his career to the study of landscape, producing hundreds of pencil and watercolour sketches and many finished oil paintings. Although he moved to London in 1799 to study at the Royal Academy Schools, he was to return to his place of birth, the village of East Bergholt, frequently until 1816, and the Stour valley was to have a strong presence in his art throughout his life. In 1809 Constable embarked upon a seven-year courtship of Maria Bicknell, the granddaughter of the Revd Rhudde, rector of East Bergholt; despite opposition from Maria's family, the couple finally married in 1816. In the early 1820s he was to extend his repertoire of places, making a visit to Salisbury in the summer of 1820. He also found new inspiration in Hampstead Heath during the 1820s, producing hundreds of sky studies. Constable became an associate of the Royal Academy in 1819, gaining full membership only in 1829. In the 1830s, plagued by grief at the death of Maria in 1828 and persistent ill health, Constable's outdoor sketching was limited, but he did draw at Worcester, Petworth and Arundel.

LL 3936 is a copy of an original watercolour (not located) that Constable had given to his mother at an unknown date.[191] The work is intriguing on one level for the light it sheds on Ann Constable's involvement in her son's difficult courtship of Maria Bicknell, a relationship that was opposed by Maria's family, with the most ardent resistance coming from her grandfather, the Revd Rhudde. Around 1810 Constable's mother could see that her son's attachment to Maria was entering a critical stage and decided that he should make another version of the watercolour to give to the rector, in an attempt to gain his favour. Constable received the original in London around 18 January 1811 and as the inscription on the back reveals (fig. 15), the copy was sent to the Revd Rhudde on 25 February.[192] The rector, after initially thinking the watercolour was a gift from Mrs Constable, wrote to thank her son on 16 March, enclosing a bank note for him to buy 'some little article by which you may be reminded of me, when I am no more'.[193] Nevertheless, despite these efforts, the following year the rector began his serious opposition to the marriage; it was not until 1816, when the artist had become more financially secure, that he felt able to ignore this antagonism and the couple were wed.

The church of St Mary's was only a short distance away from East Bergholt House, the Constable family home – they had a pew in the church, and its congregants and services featured strongly in the life of the young artist. He made over 40 drawings and paintings of the church in his early years, including two exhibited works, more than any other specific subject. The architecture of St Mary's was described as late Perpendicular by Pevsner and was built on a wide, open plan typical of the period.[194] The Lady Lever drawing showing the building from the south-east reveals two unusual features of its exterior: a sundial over the south porch (on the left of the watercolour) with the inscription (not visible) 'Ut umbra sic vita' ('Even as a shadow is our Life'); and a little eighteenth-century cupola at the west end (at the far end of the drawing). Constable's inclusion of a sunset and the figure of a lone woman in the graveyard lends a romantic touch to the watercolour, making it more than an architectural study.

With its broad, even washes LL 3936 is closely related to two other watercolour views of the church, one in the National Gallery of Canada, Ottawa, and another, almost a replica, in the Victoria & Albert Museum, which show the building from the east.[195] The former drawing is inscribed by the artist with a date of 1805, a fact that led Beckett to suggest that the original on which LL 3936 is based could be dated to that year.[196] However, as Reynolds has convincingly argued, the manner of these watercolours was preserved by Constable for a number of years (with the Lady Lever work showing that he was still using this style in 1811) making the precise dating of uninscribed examples impracticable.[197]

LL 3936 is a rare example of an early, exhibition-style watercolour by Constable. Watercolour was not the artist's preferred medium and he showed very few at the Royal Academy (a handful in 1805–06 and then again in 1832–36). Although neither LL 3936 nor the original watercolour was exhibited, the high finish and size suggests that the Lady Lever work was of this type. In this early period Constable's few exhibited watercolours, such as *The 'Victory' in the Battle of Trafalgar* (Victoria & Albert Museum) exhibited at the Royal Academy in 1806 reveal the influence of Girtin's colour schemes and broad washes;[198] Constable had studied his fellow artist's drawings at the home of Sir George Beaumont, to whom he was introduced in 1795. The style of LL 3936 can be contrasted with the artist's later use of watercolour in exhibited works, adopted from the late 1820s, where he employed separate, broken touches, showing something of the influence of David Cox (pp. 59–65) (see, for example, *Old Sarum* exhibited at the Royal Academy in 1834).[199] The Lady Lever work is also remarkable for its good condition; the pigment in the sky, for example, is notably well-preserved.

LL 3936 was bought by Lever from James Orrock (see pp. xiv–xvii, 146–49). Orrock had formed one of the most inauthentic collections of Constable's work; it is one of the few examples of a genuine Constable that Lever acquired from him.[200]

188 This is the title given in the WHL Inventory, p. 58.
189 This hand has been identified as John Dunthorne in Graham Reynolds, *The Early Paintings and Drawings of John Constable* (New Haven and London, 2 vols, 1996), vol. I, p. 157. Dunthorne lived in East Bergholt and acted as the village constable, plumber and glazier. He was also a keen amateur artist who became Constable's first mentor and painting companion.
190 WHL Inventory.
191 Reynolds records the original as being in the possession of Constable's sister Ann in 1843. See Reynolds, *Early Paintings*, vol. I, p. 157. The original is based on a black-and-white chalk drawing in the collection of C. F. Merriam. See Reynolds, *Early Paintings*, vol. I, p. 67 (cat. 05.59); illus. vol. II, pl. 303.
192 R. B. Beckett (ed.), *John Constable's Correspondence* (Ipswich, 6 vols, 1962–68), vol. I, pp. 56–57.
193 Ibid., vol. II, p. 48.
194 Leslie Parris and Ian Fleming-Williams, *Constable* (exh. cat., London, Tate Gallery, 1991), p. 86.
195 Reynolds, *Early Paintings*, vol. I, p. 62 (cats. 05.13 and 05.14), vol. II, pls. 253 and 255.
196 Leslie Parris, Ian Fleming-Williams and Conal Shields, *Constable Paintings, Watercolours and Drawings* (exh. cat., London, Tate Gallery, 1976), p. 77 (cat. 101).
197 Graham Reynolds, *Catalogue of the Constable Collection at the Victoria and Albert Museum* (London, 1960), p. 56.
198 Reynolds, *Early Paintings*, vol. I, p. 71 (cat. 06.1), vol. II, pl. 307.
199 Graham Reynolds, *The Later Paintings and Drawings of John Constable* (New Haven and London, 2 vols, 1984), vol. I, p. 257 (cat. 34.1), vol. II, pl. 913. This is now in the Victoria & Albert Museum.
200 The oil *Cottage at East Bergholt* (LL 3120) is a spectacular example of a genuine Constable owned by Orrock and purchased by Lever but there were many others that were inauthentic and were sold off in sales by the Trustees after Lever's death.

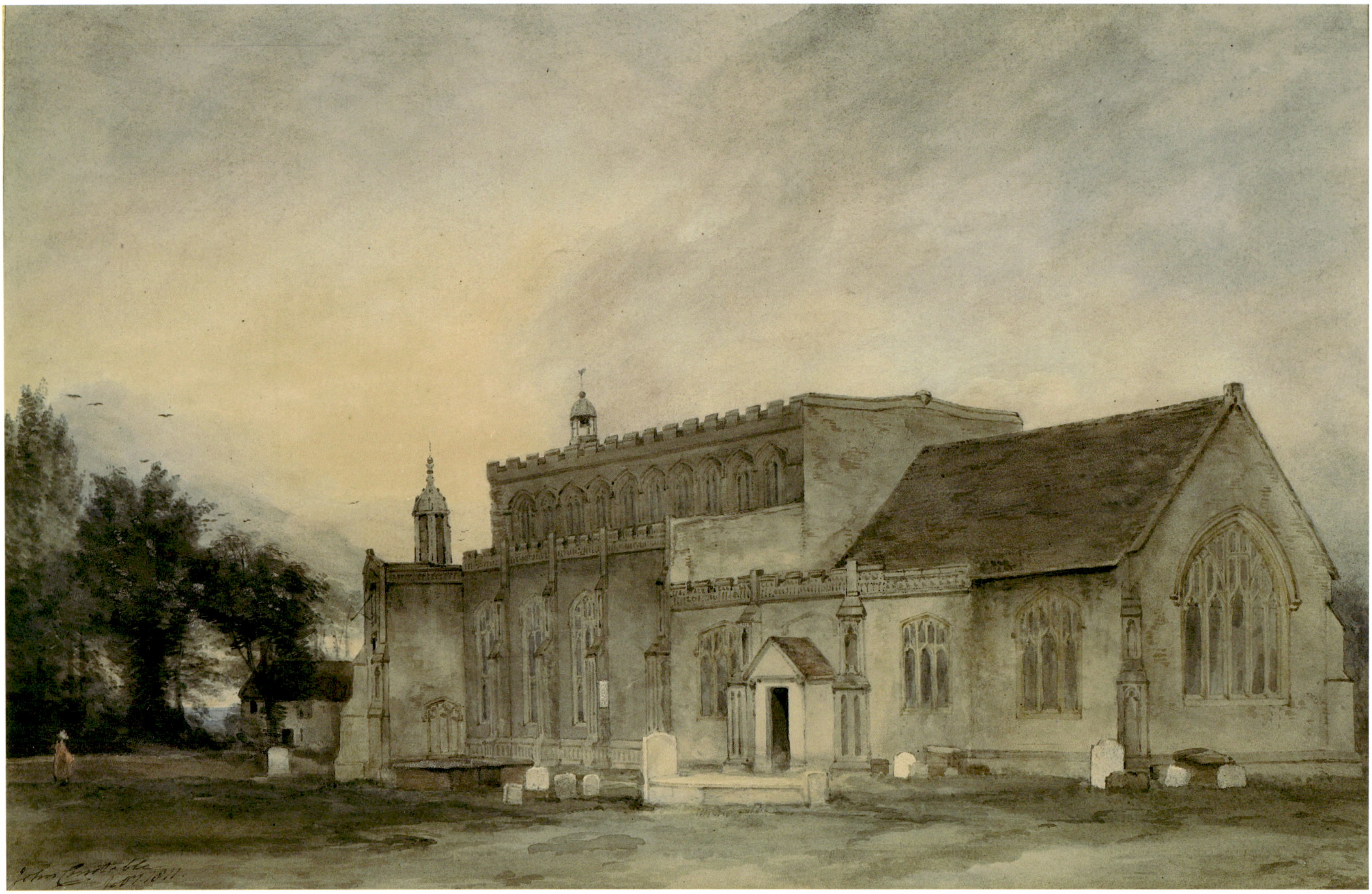

LL 3936

fig. 15. Label on backboard of *East Bergholt Church: South-East View* (LL 3936)

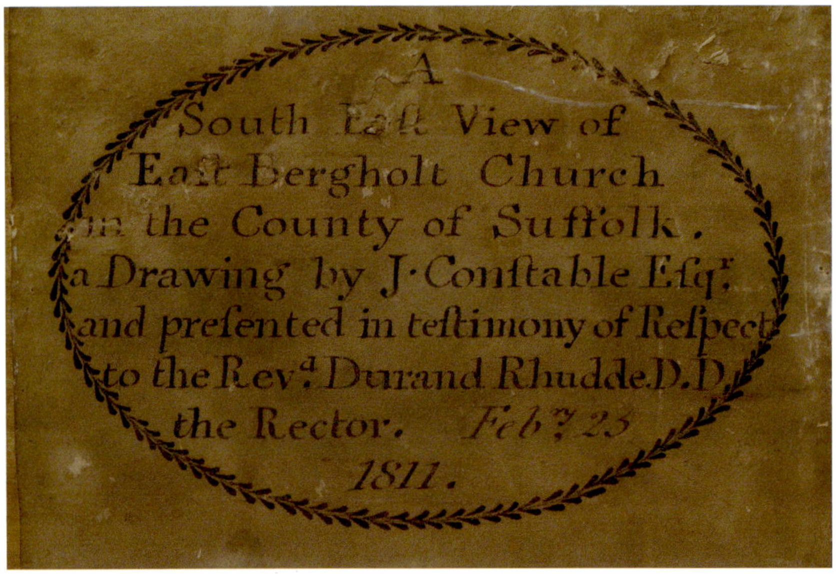

## Salisbury Cathedral from Long Bridge[201]
LL 10337 (WHL 3384)

Pencil on wove paper
23.2 x 33.4 cm
Date: 1829

Inscr: [...] 11.1829 (pencil, bottom left corner)

Prov: by descent to Isabel Constable; her sale, Christie's, 17 June 1892 (probably lot 151); bt. by Murray;[202] Charles Fairfax Murray; his sale, Christie's, 14 December 1917 (lot 7); bt. by Gooden and Fox (9 gns with WHL 3383) for Lever (£9 14s)[203]

Exh: London, Tate, Washington, National Gallery of Art and San Marino, Huntington Art Collections, *Constable: The Great Landscapes*, 2006–2007 (cat. 58)

Lit: Selby Whittingham, *Constable & Turner at Salisbury* (London, 1976), p. 52, illus. fig. 35; Leslie Parris, *The Tate Gallery Constable Collection* (London, 1981), pp. 140, 142, 144; Ian Fleming-Williams and Leslie Parris, *The Discovery of Constable* (London, 1984), pp. 36–37; Graham Reynolds, *The Later Paintings and Drawings of John Constable* (New Haven and London, 2 vols, 1984), vol. I, p. 203 (cat. 29.13), illus. vol. II, pl. 714

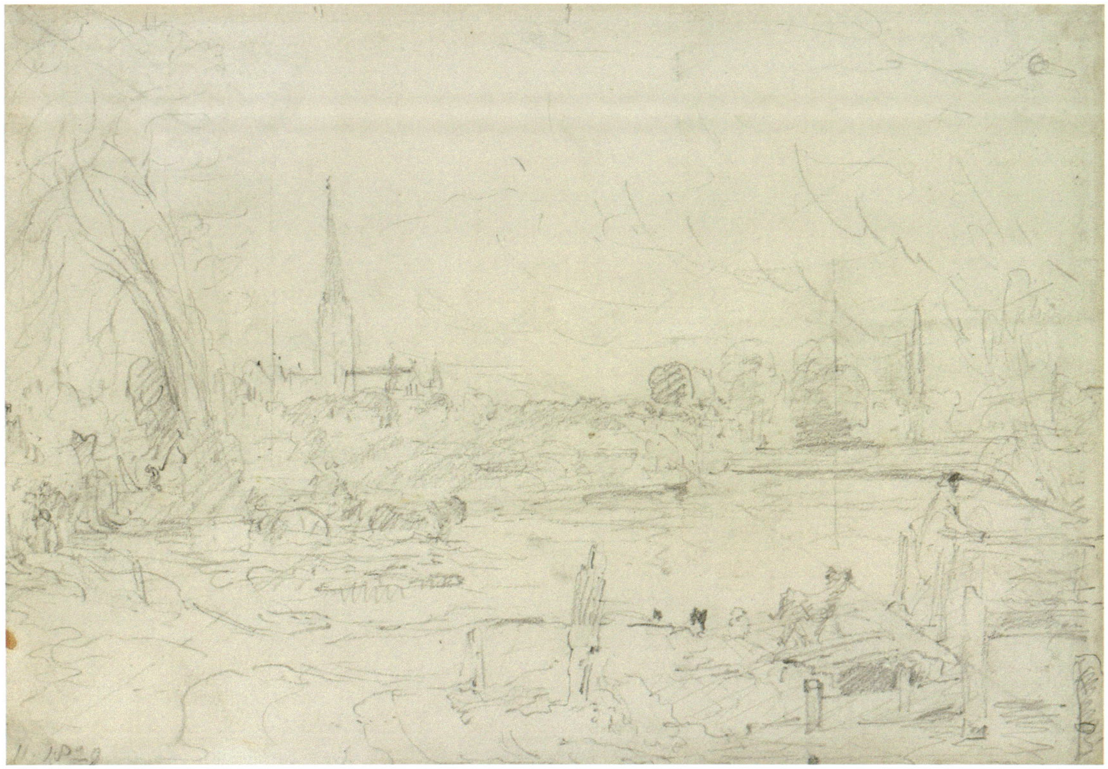

LL 10337

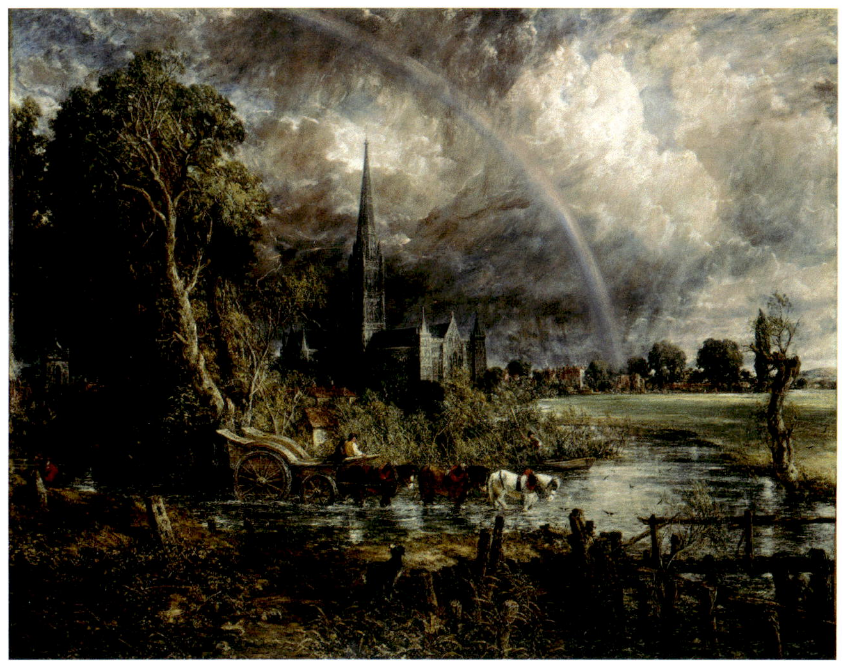

fig. 16. John Constable, *Salisbury Cathedral from the Meadows*, 1831, oil on canvas, 151.8 x 189.9 cm, © The National Gallery, London. On loan from a private collection since 1983

Constable made his first visit to Salisbury in 1811 to visit Dr John Fisher, the bishop, whom he had first met at Dedham. While there, he renewed his friendship with the bishop's nephew, also named John, and it was this relationship that drew the artist back to Salisbury a number of times in the 1820s, when he stayed with John Fisher at his home. While at Salisbury the view of the cathedral became an important subject for Constable and he drew it numerous times. LL 10337 was completed on one of the artist's last visits to the town in 1829 and is on a page from the larger sketchbook of 1822 Whatman paper used mainly at Salisbury in that year.[204] Squared up for transfer using horizontal, vertical and diagonal lines, it is one of three compositional drawings (and three small oil sketches derived from them) for his greatest painting of the scene, *Salisbury Cathedral from the Meadows*, exhibited at the Royal Academy in 1831 (private collection, fig. 16).[205]

Constable seems to have discussed with Fisher the possibility of making a large painting of the cathedral from across the River Avon, looking across the meadows, on his visit to Salisbury in July 1829.[206] During that visit he made a number of studies of the cathedral from this viewpoint; two drawings in particular were later worked up as small oil sketches, presumably trial compositions for the final painting. The first is a view from Long Bridge on the northern branch of the River Nadder (Fitzwilliam Museum, Cambridge) and the second was taken from a spot further up river (formerly Paul Mellon Collection, Upperville, Virginia).[207]

LL 10337 is inscribed with a truncated date, '11 1829' and this could mean that it was done on either 11 July or in November. Despite the ambiguity, it has recently been convincingly suggested that the former date seems unlikely.[208] Constable only arrived in Salisbury on 7 July and this would have meant that the two pencil drawings and their related oil sketches would have had to have been completed within three days.[209] In addition, the oil sketch relating to the Lady Lever work (Tate) is larger and quite different in style to the other pair of oil sketches, suggesting a period of time between the

201 LL 10337 is recorded in the WHL Inventory as *A View of Salisbury Cathedral from the River (sketch for the large picture).*
202 Lot 149 was *4 Sketches for the Large Salisbury* bt. by Murray (£1 5s) and lot 151 was *2 Sketches for the Large Salisbury* bt. by Murray (5s). The fact that Lever acquired the work with one other from Murray's sale suggests lot 151 is the more likely.
203 WHL 3383 is recorded in the WHL Inventory as John Constable, *Salisbury Cathedral, a watercolour sketch for the large picture*. It was sold in New York, 2 March 1926 (lot 77) ($150).
204 Reynolds, *Later Paintings*, vol. I, p. 213.
205 Reynolds, *Later Paintings*, vol. I, p. 225 (cat. 31.1); illus. vol. II, pl. 792. For a detailed interpretation of the painting, its reception and preparatory material, see Parris and Fleming-Williams, *Constable*, pp. 360–67 and Anne Lyles (ed.), *Constable: The Great Landscapes* (exh. cat., London, Tate, Washington, National Gallery of Art and San Marino, Huntington Art Collections, 2006–2007), pp. 178–83.
206 Beckett, *Constable's Correspondence*, vol. VI, pp. 250–51.
207 Reynolds, *Later Paintings*, vol. I, p. 209 (cats. 29.43 and 29.42) and vol. II, pls. 741 and 740.
208 Parris and Fleming-Williams, *Constable*, p. 363.
209 Ibid.

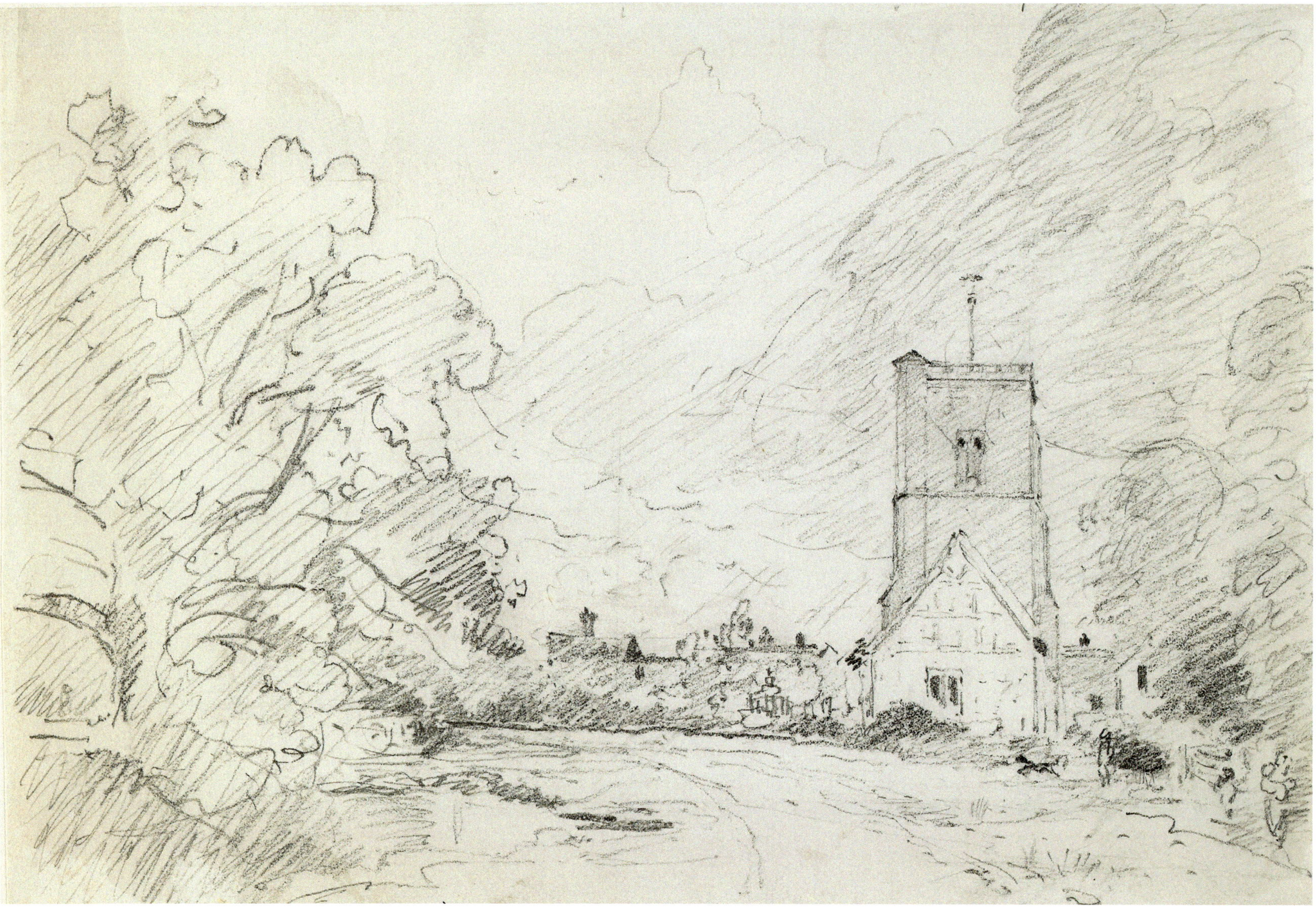

LL 10341

LL 3925

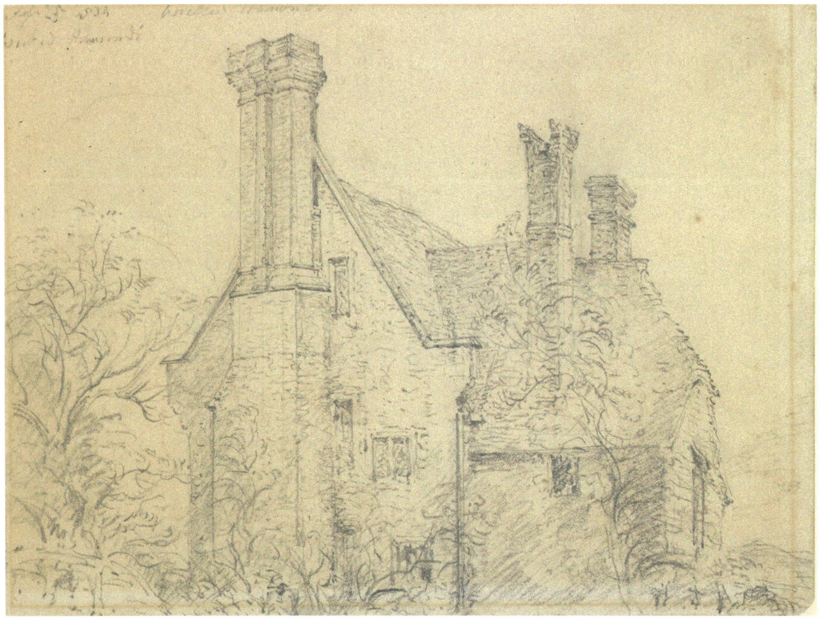

LL 3925 (verso)

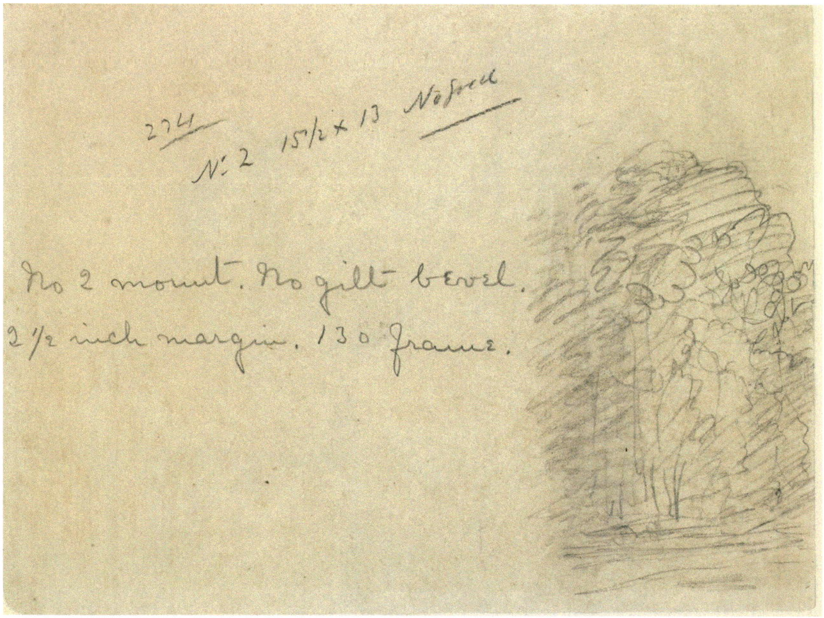

completion of this one and the others.[210] LL 10337 is the nearest of the three sketches to the final composition. It is, like the Fitzwilliam sketch, a view of the cathedral from Long Bridge but the scene has been extended to the right to reveal a man (possibly Fisher) and dog crossing the bridge.[211] In contrast to both earlier sketches, the motif of the wagon fording the river is in place. Both a further full-size oil sketch (Guildhall Art Gallery, London) and the final painting show that Constable was playing around with aspects of the composition at these stages, in particular the figure of the man and dog, but the main elements are in place by the time of the Lady Lever sketch.[212]

This drawing, along with LL 10341, LL 3925 and LL 3937 (see the following entries), were all in the collection of the artist and collector Charles Fairfax Murray who bought extensively at the sale of Constable's works at Christie's in 1892.[213]

### A Church and Cottage
LL 10341 (WHL 3385)

Pencil on wove paper
23 x 33.3 cm
Date: probably 1829

Annot: 20 (pencil, top right, verso)

Prov: Mrs MacKinnon, Calcutta;[214] her sale, Christie's, 17 June 1892 (probably lot 168, as *Stratford &c (four in one frame)*); bt. by Murray (14s); Charles Fairfax Murray; his sale, Christie's, 14 December 1917 (lot 10); bt. by Gooden and Fox (5 gns with LL 3925 and LL 3937) for Lever (£5 7s 6d)

Lit: Graham Reynolds, *The Later Paintings and Drawings of John Constable* (New Haven and London, 2 vols, 1984), vol. I, p. 210 (cat. 29.48), vol. II, pl. 748

LL 10341 was purchased by Lever with the title *Stratford Church*, and described in the WHL Inventory as the church of Stratford St Mary.[215] However, Reynolds has stated that this identification is incorrect: 'that building has aisles on either side of the nave'.[216] The drawing is on a page of the larger sketchbook of 1822 Whatman paper used mainly during Constable's stays with his friend John Fisher at Salisbury in 1829 (see LL 10337, p. 49).[217] On this basis, Reynolds has suggested that the church may be located in that area.[218]

*A Church and Cottage* is one of the many pencil sketches which the artist produced throughout his career, preferring the medium to chalk, pen or brush. This work is a good example of the range of mark-making, both tonal and more linear, that the artist could accomplish with pencil. While the hurried nature of the marks suggests that the sketch was drawn on the spot (and we know that Constable favoured this method of working), the subject is carefully composed, suggesting that this was a work that Constable might have intended to be seen by others. The drawing's inclusion in the 1829 sketchbook used mainly at Salisbury suggests that Constable might have shown it to Fisher and his family. It contrasts, for example, with LL 3925 (see the next entry) which is not a fully articulated composition and is far less self-conscious in design.

### Wicked Hammond's House
### Verso: A slight sketch of trees
LL 3925 (WHL 3388)

Pencil on wove paper
20.8 x 27.3 cm
Date: 1834

Inscr: Sep. 25 1834 Wicked Hamonds / Wicked Hammond's (pencil, top left)

Annot: 274 / No. 2 15 ½ x 13 No [illeg. word] (pencil, upper centre, verso); no 2 mount. no gilt bevel / 2 ½ inch margin. 130 frame. (pencil, left centre, verso)

Prov: Mrs MacKinnon, Calcutta;[219] her sale, Christie's, 17 June 1892 (probably lot 179); bt. by Murray (4s); Charles Fairfax Murray; his sale, Christie's, 14 December 1917 (lot 10); bt. by Gooden and Fox (5 gns with LL 10341 and LL 3937) for Lever (£5 7s 6d)

Lit: R. B. Beckett (ed.), *John Constable's Correspondence* (Ipswich, 6 vols, 1962–68), vol. III, p. 120, illus. pl. 4; Harold Day, *John Constable Drawings* (Eastbourne, 1975), p. 129, pl. 132; Graham Reynolds, *The Later Paintings and Drawings of John Constable* (New Haven and London, 2 vols, 1984), vol. I, pp. 264–65 (cats. 34.48, 34.49), vol. II, pls. 958 and 959

In July 1834 Constable visited West Sussex for the first time, staying at Arundel with the wealthy brewer George Constable (no relation), with whom he had struck up a friendship. On that occasion he was introduced to the third Earl of Egremont who invited him to stay at Petworth, an invitation that the artist took up in September, joining C. R. Leslie (Constable's friend and biographer) and a houseful of other guests. Constable returned to Sussex again to stay with George Constable at Arundel in July 1835.

LL 3925 was drawn towards the end of Constable's stay at Petworth in September 1834 and is on a page from the larger sketchbook of 1828 Whatman paper used in that year.[220] Leslie wrote that the Earl of Egremont 'ordered one of his carriages to be ready every day, to enable Constable to see as much of the neighbourhood as possible'.[221] He went on to describe their visit to this particular house:

> I recollect spending a morning with him, he drawing the outside, while I was sketching the interior, of a lonely farm-house, which was the more picturesque from its being in a neglected state, and which a woman we found in it told us was called 'wicked Hammond's house'; a man of that name, strongly suspected of great crimes, having formerly been its occupant. She told us that in an old well in the garden some bones had not long ago been found, which the doctor said were 'the arm bones of a Christian'.[222]

Constable, by contrast to his friend, was attracted to the ramshackle exterior and LL 3925 is similar in subject matter and composition to a number of sketches produced on his trips to Sussex, where picturesque barns and old farmhouses dominate the page – see, for example, *A Sussex barn* from September 1834 (Huntington Art Collections, San Marino) and *The ruins of the Maison Dieu, Arundel* from 1835 (Victoria & Albert Museum).[223]

Constable's trips to the Sussex countryside provided fresh inspiration for the increasingly frail artist. So enthusiastic was he at seeing the different landscape for the first time that he felt momentarily disloyal to his more usual subjects, writing to George Constable that 'I have never seen such scenery as your county affords; I prefer it to any other for my pictures'.[224] This enthusiasm is indicated by the large number of works he produced during the 1834–35 trips, almost filling four sketchbooks as well as a further 50 drawings and watercolours. In style LL 3925 is typical of the fluent and inventive manner in which Constable employed pencil in these mature outdoor sketches. While others such as *The ruins of the Maison Dieu, Arundel* (referred to above) showed greater tonal contrast, the Lady Lever work is more linear but exhibits the vigour of execution and bravura mark-making that characterise many

210 Ibid.
211 Both Fleming-Williams and Parris have made the connection between the man and dog in LL 10337 and the Tate sketch, with another drawing of 1829 showing Archdeacon Fisher and his dogs about to cross a footbridge (Reynolds, *Later Paintings*, vol. I, p. 204 [cat. 29.19] and vol. II, pl. 723). See Leslie Parris, *The Tate Gallery Constable Collection* (London, 1981), p. 142 and Leslie Parris, Ian Fleming-Williams and Conal Shields, *Constable: Paintings, Watercolours and Drawings* (exh. cat., London, Tate Gallery, 1976), p. 98.
212 See Reynolds, *Later Paintings*, vol. I, p. 227 (cat. 31.2) and vol. II, pl. 793 for the full-size sketch. There has been some debate over the authenticity of this work largely due to some awkward passages but it is now accepted as genuine (see Parris and Fleming-Williams, *Constable*, p. 364). A notable inclusion in the final painting, but not in the full-size sketch, is the rainbow. For an interpretation of this see Parris and Fleming-Williams, *Constable*, p. 367.
213 Christie's, 17 June 1892. Many of the works Fairfax Murray acquired from this sale were given to the Fitzwilliam Museum, Cambridge.
214 In the auctioneer's copy of the sale catalogue, Christie's archives, she is recorded as the vendor although most of the contents of the sale were consigned by Isabel Constable.
215 WHL Inventory, p. 435.
216 Reynolds, *Later Paintings*, vol. I, p. 210. The church of St Mary in the village of Stratford, which was westwards along the river Stour from East Bergholt, featured regularly in Constable's paintings of the valley, although it was usually shown in the middle distance. An early tinted drawing of the church confirms the different architecture. See Reynolds, *Early Paintings*, vol. I, p. 18 (cat. 98.5), vol. II, pl. 58.
217 Reynolds, *Later Paintings*, vol. I, p. 210.
218 Ibid.
219 In the auctioneer's copy of the sale catalogue, Christie's archives, she is recorded as the vendor although most of the contents of the sale were consigned by Isabel Constable.
220 Reynolds, *Later Paintings*, vol. I, p. 265.
221 C. R. Leslie, *Memoirs of the Life of John Constable* (London, 1845), p. 258.
222 Ibid.
223 Reynolds, *Later Paintings*, vol. I, pp. 264 (cat. 34.44) and 276 (cat. 35.10); vol. II, pls. 955 and 996.
224 Quoted in Reynolds, *Catalogue of the Constable Collection*, p. 19.

of his outdoor sketches of this period (see, for example, *Arundel Mill and Castle* [1835, Victoria & Albert Museum]).[225] This frenetic pencil work may to some extent suggest the haste with which Constable completed these sketches, but it also surely indicates his excitement at the experience of new scenery.[226] In contrast to LL 10341 (pp. 50-51) this sketch is very much of a private nature, intended as an observational exercise and not as a finished composition.

Annie Lyles has suggested that the sketch of trees on the verso of LL 3925 might be an extension of a drawing on a right-hand sketchbook page.[227] It does not, however, relate to any of the pages identified as being part of the larger 1834 sketchbook.[228]

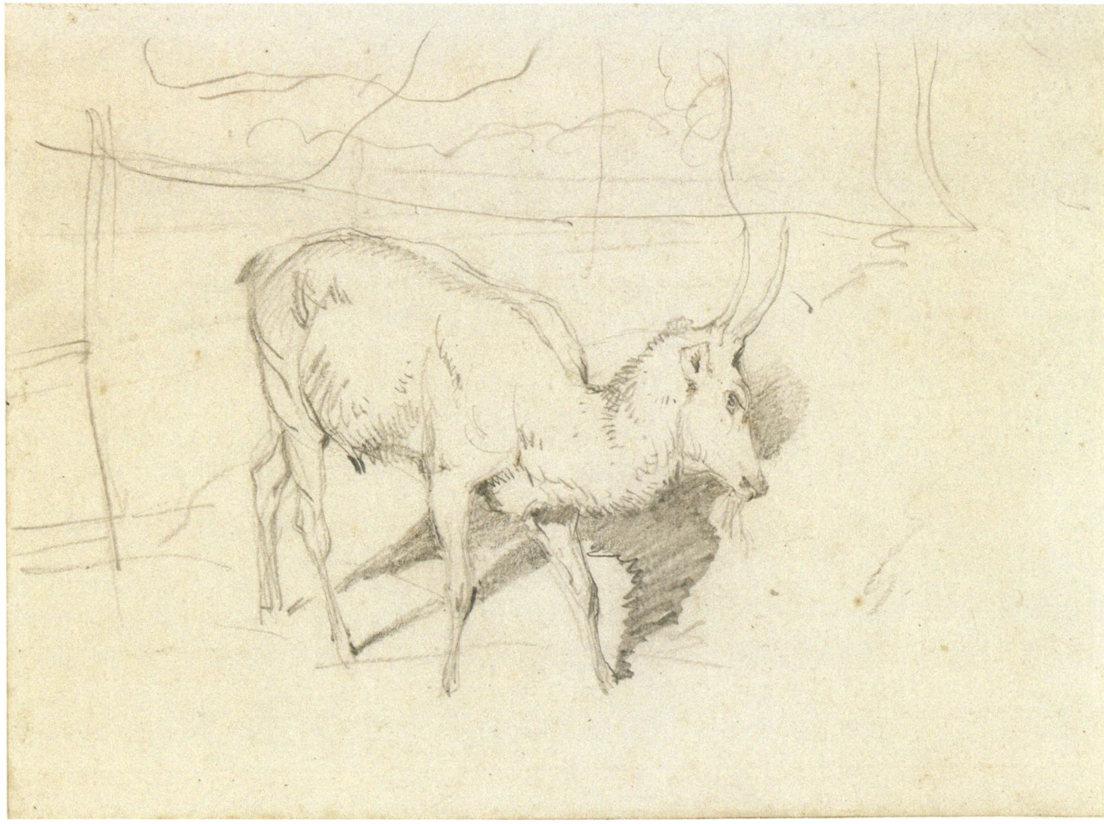

LL 3937

## 'JOHN CONSTABLE'

**Drawing of a deer (recto); Drawing of a chained dog (verso), on a page from a sketchbook**
LL 3937 (WHL 3386 and 3387)

Pencil on wove paper
22.5 x 17 cm
Date: nineteenth century

Prov: Charles Fairfax Murray; his sale, Christie's, 14 December 1917 (lot 10); bt. by Gooden and Fox (5 gns with LL 10341 and LL 3925) for Lever (£5 7s 6d)

LL 3937 was purchased by Lever as Constable although Reynolds later described the drawing of the chained dog as 'hardly acceptable as a work' by the artist.[229] This assessment has been confirmed by Annie Lyles and has been extended to the drawing of the deer.[230]

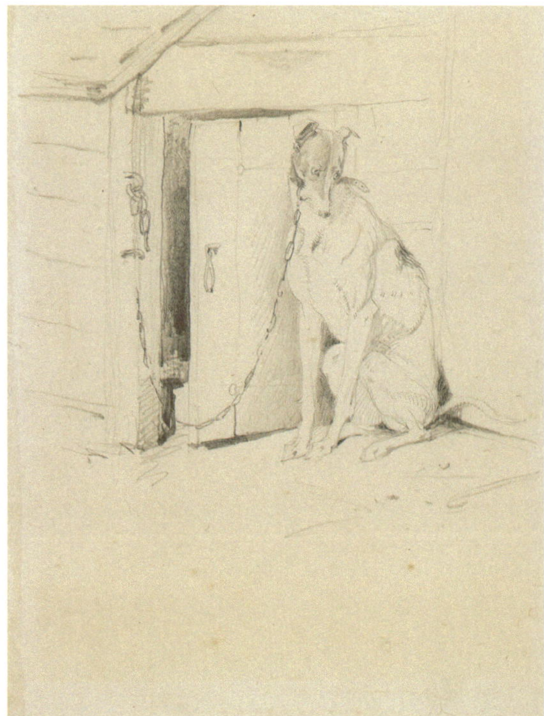

LL 3937 (verso)

225 Reynolds, *Later Paintings*, vol. I, p. 276 (cat. 35.11); vol. II, pl. 997.
226 Reynolds, *Catalogue of the Constable Collection*, p. 20.
227 Annie Lyles, verbally, January 2008.
228 These sketchbook pages are listed in Reynolds, *Later Paintings*, vol. I, p. 301.

229 WHL Inventory, p. 435, where WHL 3386 is described as a goat and WHL 3387 as a deer-hound; Reynolds, *Later Paintings*, vol. I, p. 12 (cat. 17.34).
230 Annie Lyles, email correspondence, January 2008, suggesting John Frederick Lewis as a possible attribution.

## THOMAS SIDNEY COOPER
1803 Canterbury–1902 Vernon Holme, near Canterbury

**A Cow and Five Sheep**
LL 3830 (WHL 1501, TM 82)

Watercolour on wove paper
25.1 x 32.3 cm
Date: 1887

Inscr: T Sidney. Cooper R.A / 1887 (watercolour, bottom right)

Prov: unknown, but bt. by Lever before 1902[231]

Exh: Port Sunlight, Hulme Hall, *Coronation Art Exhibition*, 1902 (cat. no. unknown)[232]

Lit: Stephen Sartin, *Thomas Sidney Cooper, 1803–1902* (Leigh-on-Sea, 1976), p. 76 (cat. 466)

Cooper trained at the Royal Academy Schools from 1823 and subsequently moved to Brussels, where he met Eugène Verboeckhoven (1798–1881), who introduced him to the work of seventeenth-century Dutch animal painters such as Aelbert Cuyp and Paulus Potter. Following this meeting Cooper began to specialise in paintings of cattle and sheep. He returned to London in 1831, exhibiting at the Royal Society of British Artists and at the British Institution, although primarily at the Royal Academy (from 1833 to 1902 he exhibited 266 works there without a break). He was elected an associate of the Royal Academy in 1845 and a full member in 1867. In the 1860s Cooper moved back to Canterbury, where he opened an art school and gallery at the end of the decade.

Throughout the 1870s and 1880s, Cooper painted large numbers of oil paintings of placid pastoral scenes, as well as snow subjects. LL 3830 is one of only a few known watercolours produced in 1887, although it is typical of Cooper's later smaller work in this medium in featuring a single cow, either standing or lying down, beside a group of sheep in a typically flat Kentish landscape, which provided the backdrop for much of Cooper's work. It does not appear to relate to any known oil painting. It is likely that LL 3830, as with other of Cooper's small late watercolours, was produced to meet the demand of late Victorian collectors on limited budgets.[233]

231 LL 3830 did not feature in the studio sale of Cooper's work, held at Christie's, 12–15 April 1902, and must have been purchased by Lever before this.

232 The reference to this exhibition is recorded on the accession card, LLAG files. The exhibition, held in honour of the king's coronation, is described in *Progress*, vol. 3 (July 1902), pp. 230–37. No catalogue of this exhibition has been located either in the Lady Lever archives, the Port Sunlight Museum archives or the Unilever archives.

233 Kenneth Westwood, email correspondence, February 2007.

LL 3830

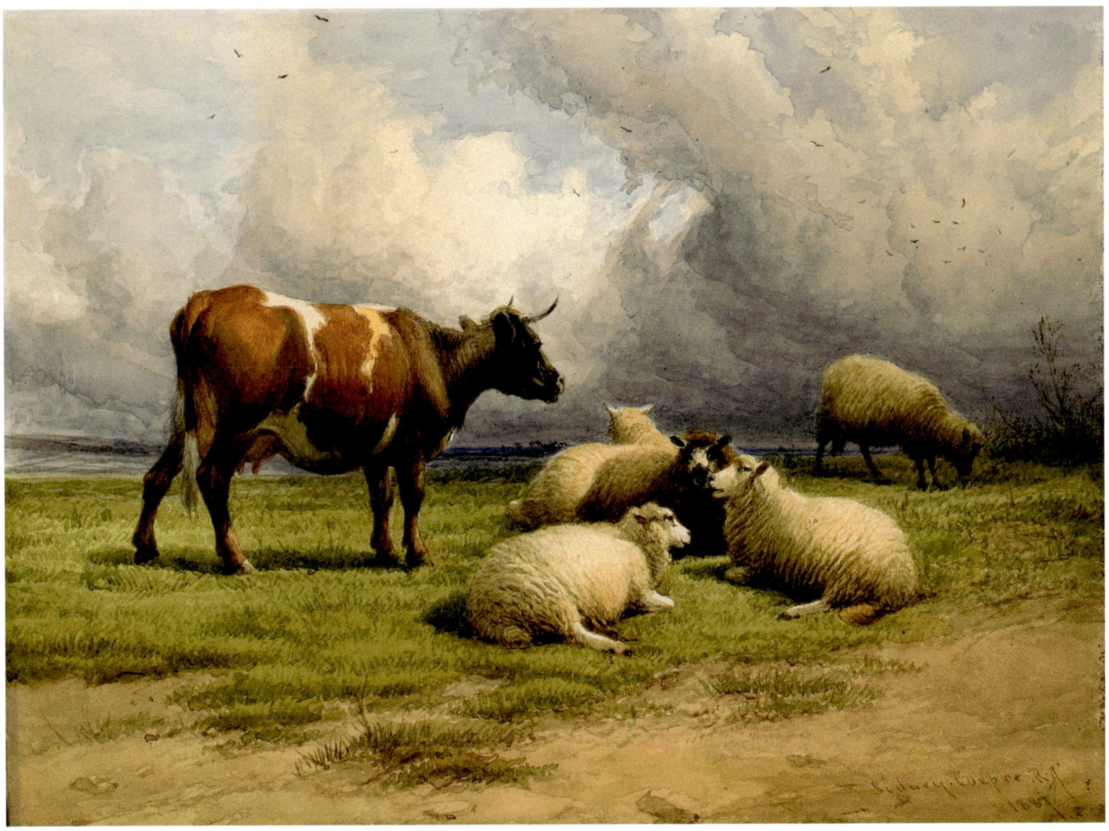

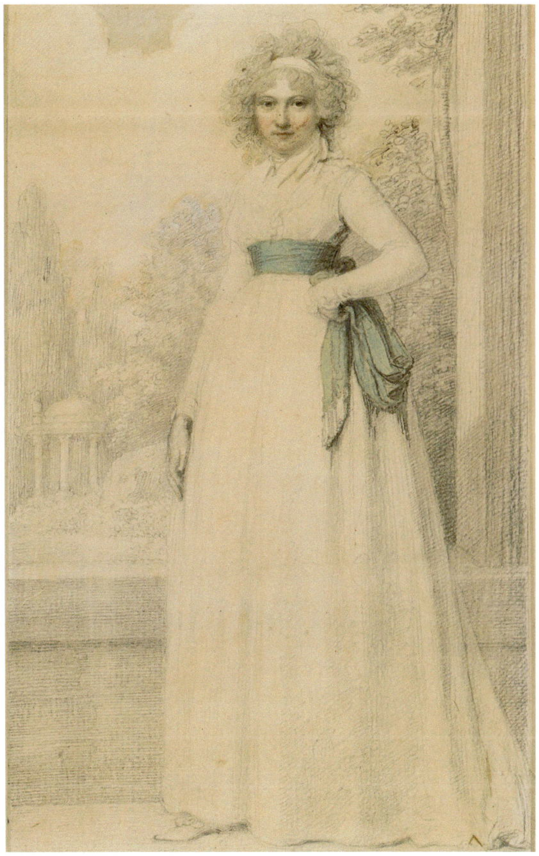

LL 3945

## RICHARD COSWAY
1742 Okeford, Devon–1821 London

**Miss Hayes**
LL 3945 (WHL 3219)

Pencil and watercolour on paper laid down on original wash-line mount
23.3 x 14.1 cm (image), 31.5 x 22.1 cm (mount)
Date: 1794

Inscr: Richd Cosway R.A. Primarius Pictor serenissimi Wallie Principis Fecit. London 1794 (pencil, at bottom, in mount border)

Prov: E. H. Hodgkin, 1911;[234] his sale, Christie's, 29 June 1917 (lot 11); bt. by Gooden and Fox (40 gns) for Lever (£44 2s)

Cosway, like Sir Joshua Reynolds, was the son of a Devon schoolmaster. Showing precocious promise as a draughtsman, he was sent at the age of 12 to London, where he studied at the drawing school of William Shipley and won prizes for drawing offered by Shipley's Society for the Encouragement of the Arts. He set up on his own in 1760, and became the leading miniaturist and portrait draughtsman of his age, as well as a painter in oils and a noted collector. Celebrated for his wit and as a man of fashion (as well as for his smallness in stature), Cosway became even more famous after his marriage in 1781 to the

234 A photograph of the work is no. 47 in a photographic album of Hodgkin's stock dating from 1911 and the work is no. 350 on a list of Hodgkin's stock preserved with the album (private collection).

captivating, artistically talented and cosmopolitan Maria Hadfield. The two moved in high society and were cultivated by the Prince of Wales, who made Cosway his Principal Painter in 1785, an appointment referred to in the artist's inscription on LL 3945. Cosway continued to draw and paint throughout his life but his activities as a collector and man of taste dominated his later years.[235]

LL 3945 is a characteristic portrait drawing by Cosway of the 1790s, with its restricted use of colour, manneristic treatment of the figure and addition of a wash-line border. Drawings of this type represent Cosway's conscious adaptation to a smaller format of the full-length society portraits of his contemporaries - perhaps especially Gainsborough here in the handling of the parkscape in the background.[236] The drawing is in indifferent condition with extensive patches of discolouration. Nothing has been established about the sitter.[237]
AK

235 Stephen Lloyd, *Richard & Maria Cosway, Regency Artists of Taste and Fashion* (exh. cat., Edinburgh, Scottish National Portrait Gallery, 1995).
236 Stephen Lloyd, verbally, 31 January 2008.
237 LL 3945 was not one of Cosway's engraved works and is not mentioned in the inventory of 1820 which lists debts outstanding on many of his portraits. See Stephen Lloyd, 'The Cosway Inventory of 1820: Listing Unpaid commissions and the Contents of 20 Stratford Place, Oxford Street, London', *Walpole Society*, vol. 66 (2004), pp. 163–217. No sitter of the name Miss Hayes is recorded in the archive of the National Portrait Gallery, and she is not recorded as having sat to such contemporaries as Romney, Lawrence or Hoppner.

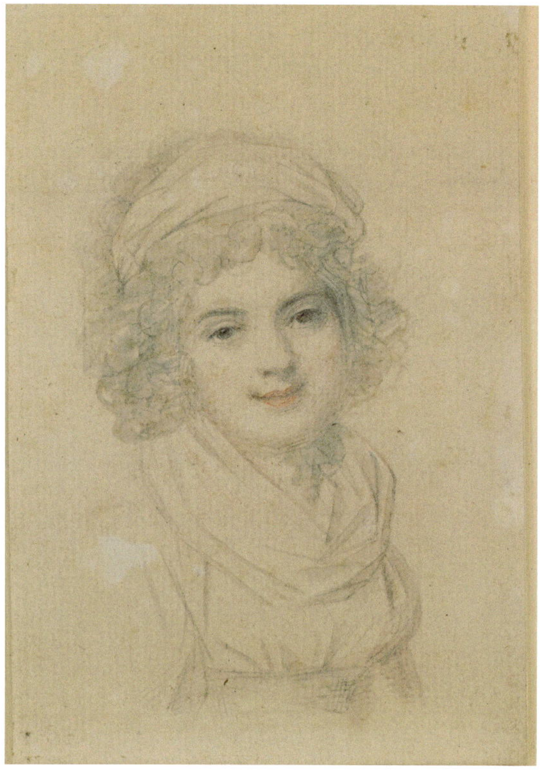
LL 3940A

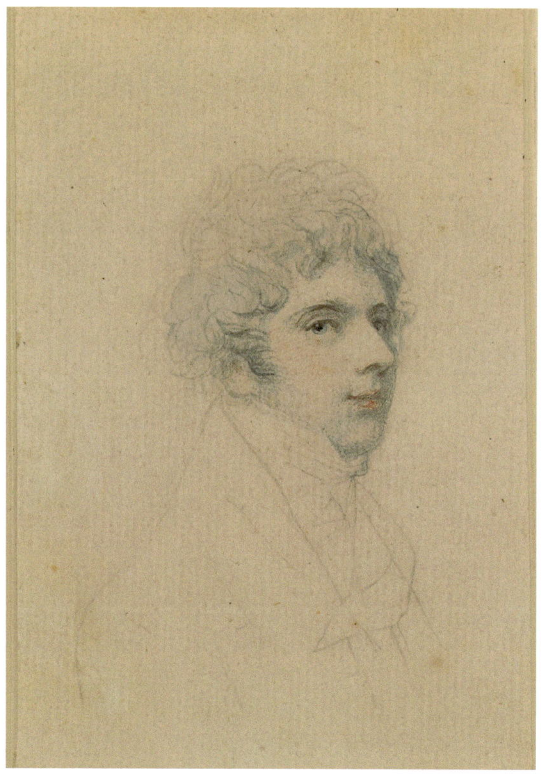
LL 3940B

## ATTRIBUTED TO RICHARD COSWAY

**A Pair of Portraits of a Lady and a Gentleman**
LL 3940 (WHL 2612–2612A)

**Portrait of a Lady**
LL 3940A

Pencil and watercolour on laid paper
11.4 x 7.7 cm (sight)
Date: c. 1790–95

**Portrait of a Gentleman**
LL 3940B

Pencil and watercolour on laid paper
11.4 x 7.7 cm (sight)
Date: late 1790s or early 1800s

Prov: Jeffery Whitehead; his sale, Christie's, 6 August 1915 (part of lot 19); bt. by Frank Partridge (9 gns) for Lever

Lot 19 of the Whitehead sale, which Partridge bought for Lever, was described in the sale catalogue as 'R. [*sic*] Shelley: A study of three children, A Lady in a black dress and Heads of a Lady and a Gentleman, two on one mount'. LL 3940 is the third component of this item (for the first two see LL 3943 and LL 3944, pp. 170–71, under Samuel Shelley; all four of the above works appear to have been re-mounted and framed, either by Partridge or immediately after their acquisition by Lever, with two further works, for which see LL 394, p. 55).[238]

Although they were subsequently attributed within Lever's collection to Samuel Shelley,[239] LL 3940A–B have recently been recognised as authentic works by Cosway. Small, sketch-like portrait drawings of this type are not common in his work but other instances are known.[240] However, it is unclear that the two drawings were made as a pair. The costume of the woman indicates a date of about 1790–95; that of the man seems later, perhaps by as much as a decade. The handling of the eyes also differs slightly, those of the man being emphasised while those of the woman are undifferentiated within the face as a whole. Neither sitter can be identified.
AK

238 On the reverse of the frame is a diagram drawn in pencil indicating the intended positioning within the mount of the six works.
239 LLAG files: the attribution was made by Lever's first assistant curator, A. C. Tait.
240 Stephen Lloyd, verbally, 31 January 2008; a group of similar drawings is in the Huntington Art Collections, San Marino, California.

# AFTER RICHARD COSWAY

## Mrs Robinson

LL 3941[241]

Pencil on paper
10.1 x 7.5 cm
Date: by 1915

Inscr: R. Cosway (pencil, lower left); H. Meyer (pencil, lower right)
Prov: acquired by Lever, August 1915[242]

The actress Mrs Robinson (1758–1800) was born Mary Darby in Bristol, the daughter of an American seaman. She married at the age of 15, and with the encouragement of David Garrick and Richard Brinsley Sheridan went on the stage in 1776, making her debut at Sheridan's Drury Lane Theatre as Juliet in Shakespeare's *Romeo and Juliet*. Her career blossomed and her performances as Perdita in *The Winter's Tale* in the 1779–80 season brought her to the attention of the Prince of Wales, with whom she had a liaison in 1780, and who made her give up her career as an actress. After her affair with the Prince was over, she was taken up by Col. Banastre Tarleton, the celebrated cavalry commander in the American War of Independence, but her health was undermined following the miscarriage of their baby; she spent the years 1784–88 convalescing in France and after her return to London she lived a less public life, making a literary career. A volume of her collected *Poems* was published in 1791 and she also wrote several novels and a play. At the height of her fame many portraits were made of her, including celebrated works by Sir Joshua Reynolds, Thomas Gainsborough and George Romney.[243]

The source for LL 3941, Cosway's miniature portrait on ivory of Mrs Robinson (private collection), appears to show her in her early twenties,[244] but it may have been revisited in connection with the publication of the *Poems*; the artist was one of the many leading cultural figures who subscribed to the volume[245] and it included a stipple engraving by Van Assen after a different portrait of her by Cosway, which depicted her in the character of Laura Maria[246] (a fictive name Mrs Robinson had given to herself in poems published in *The World* shortly before). It is tempting to wonder whether Van Assen's engraving was deemed inadequate, either by Mrs Robinson or by Cosway, and whether the engraving by J. Condé which was made from the earlier miniature and published in the *European Magazine* in November 1792 was undertaken as a kind of damage-limitation exercise. Condé's print was subsequently re-used for portraits of Mrs Robinson by two early nineteenth-century engravers, Edwin Roffe (who titled his version of the image *Melania*, presumably in order to distinguish it from *Laura Maria*)[247] and Henry Meyer, whose engraving was titled *Perdita*, a name by which the sitter had become more generally known following her success in Shakespeare's role.

LL 3941 is closely related to Meyer's engraving, an impression of which was with the present work when Lever acquired it (fig. 17).[248] It is unclear whether LL 3941 could be Meyer's original drawing on which he based his engraving (which is the same size), but the treatment of the inscriptions militates against this and it seems more likely to be a drawn copy of the engraving made with intention to deceive.[249]
AK

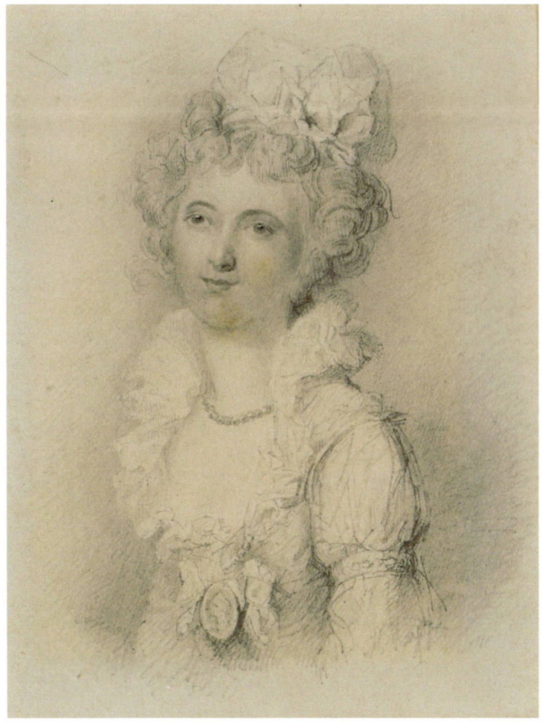

LL 3941

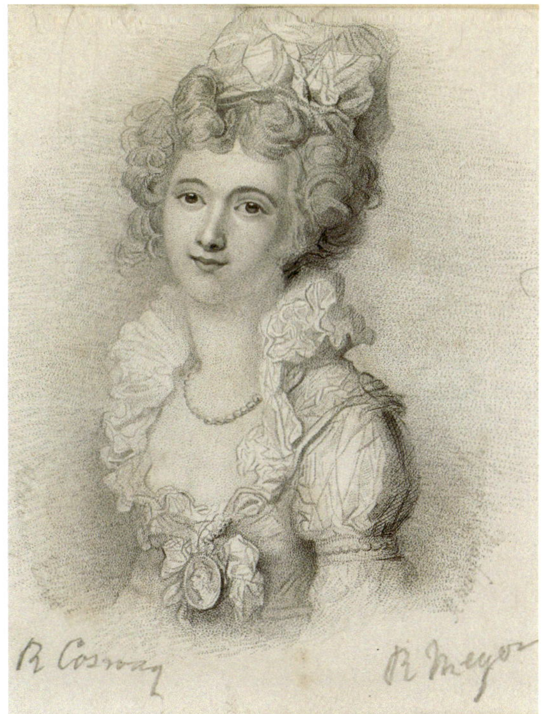

fig. 17. Henry Meyer, After Richard Cosway, *Mrs Robinson (Perdita)*, c.1815, engraving on paper, 10 x 7.5 cm (sight), National Museums Liverpool, Lady Lever Art Gallery

241 The WHL number of LL 3941 is impossible to determine.
242 The provenance of LL 3941 before its appearance in Lever's collection is unknown. Either just before, or just after it came to him, it was framed up, together with an impression of Meyer's print of *Mrs Robinson* (LL 3942), in one frame with four other small drawings that Frank Partridge had purchased for Lever from the Jeffery Whitehead sale at Christie's, 4–10 August 1915 (see LL 3940A–B and LL 3943–44); however, LL 3941–42 do not appear on Partridge's account for these purchases. It seems possible that he 'slipped them in' as a douceur (for which see also the discussion of LL 3986A–F, pp. 159–60).
243 John Ingamells, *Mrs Robinson and her Portraits* (London, 1978).
244 A photograph is in the Witt Library, Courtauld Institute of Art; on the mount it is dated 'c. 1780'.
245 Ingamells, *Mrs Robinson*, p. 22.
246 F. Daniell, *The Engraved Works of Richard Cosway, R.A. with a Memoir of Cosway by Sir Philip Currie* (London, 1890), p. 31.
247 Daniell, *Engraved Works of Richard Cosway*, p. 31, gives the title *Melania* to Condé's engraving but as published in the *European Magazine* the latter is titled simply *Mrs Robinson*.
248 LL 3942 in the collection.
249 In LL 3941 the inscriptions are added very faintly within the shaded area each side of the figure, not as they appear, outside the image, in impressions of the print; in the version of the print acquired with LL 3941 by Lever, the inscriptions are overwritten in pencil as if to suggest that it too is a drawing; and both works have hitherto been accessioned as drawings (of a sitter named Miss Meyer) in LLAG files. Stephen Lloyd kindly discussed LL 3941 and 3942, verbally, 31 January 2008.

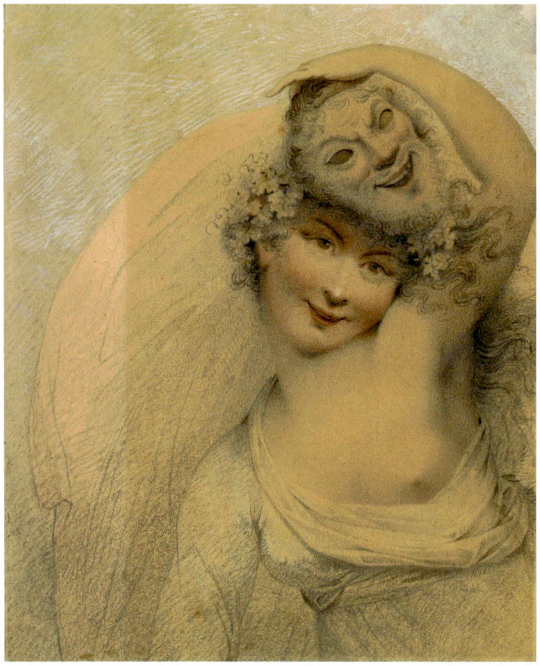

LL 3939

## 'RICHARD COSWAY'

**Comedy**
LL 3939 (WHL 3220)

Pencil and watercolour touched with white gouache on paper
22.8 x 14 cm
Date: by 1911

Prov: F. H. Hodgkin, 1911;[250] Christie's, 29 June 1917 (lot 12); bt. by Gooden and Fox (28 gns) for Lever (£30 17s 6d)

Lever acquired LL 3939 as by Cosway but doubts have been expressed that it is an autograph work by him.[251] Despite the delicacy of some of the draughtsmanship, the head, neck, shoulder and armpit of the figure are anatomically weak and the relationship between them unconvincing, as is that between the figure and the background drapery, and this drapery and the rest of the work. The whole has the air of being a pastiche, with the actress's face perhaps carrying a remote suggestion of Reynolds's portraits of Mrs Abington.[252] A photograph taken of the work about 1911 indicates that the white hatching in the upper portion of the work was added after that date.
AK

250 A photograph of the work is no. 30 in a photographic album of Hodgkin's stock dating from 1911 and the work is no. 278 on a list of Hodgkin's stock preserved with the album (private collection).
251 LLAG files: Stephen Lloyd, letter, October 1992 and again Lloyd, verbally, 31 January 2008.
252 As suggested by Stephen Lloyd.

## FREDERICK GEORGE COTMAN
1850 Ipswich–1920 Felixstowe

**An extensive landscape with rocks, a castle, possibly Bamburgh, beyond**
LL 3831 (WHL 881, HH 439)

Watercolour on wove paper
22 x 34.5 cm (sight)
Date: 1892

Inscr: F.G.Cotman 1892 (watercolour, lower left)
Prov: F. Anstead Browne, Abbey Green, Chester;[253] James Orrock; bt. from Orrock by Lever, 1910[254]

Cotman was born in St Clements, Ipswich, the youngest child of Henry Edmund Cotman and Maria Taylor, and nephew of the distinguished watercolour artist John Sell Cotman (see pp. 57–58). During his lifetime comparisons were often drawn between the works of Cotman and his uncle and he was a highly successful and popular artist.[255]

At the age of 15 Cotman became pupil and assistant to W. Thompson Griffiths, headmaster of Ipswich School of Art. However, the apprenticeship was short-lived; Cotman was dismissive of Griffiths's artistic and teaching abilities and in 1868 he began his studies at the Royal Academy where he remained until about 1875. A talented pupil, Cotman was awarded four silver medals and one gold, the latter in 1873 for *The Death of Eucles* (exh. RA 1874; Ipswich Town Hall). From 1871 Cotman was a regular exhibitor at the Academy, painting portraits, landscape, genre and historical subjects both in oils and watercolours. His early works were admired and purchased by prominent artistic figures of the day including Frederic, Lord Leighton (1830–96), Henry Tanworth Wells (1828–1903) and George Frederick Watts (1817–1904). While still studying at the Academy, Cotman was engaged by Leighton to help paint *The Daphnephoria* (1874–76, Lady Lever Art Gallery, LL 3632) and by Wells to assist with a portrait of *Lord Hatherley, Lord High Chancellor* (1869).

Cotman began his professional career and established his reputation by painting fashionable portraits, and he soon attracted important patrons, for example, the Duke of Westminster, for whom Cotman painted a number of pictures, including the large portrait group of *The Marchioness of Westminster, Lady Theodora Guest and Mr Guest playing dummy whist* (exh. RA 1882; private collection). Cotman showed great proficiency in painting children and often incorporated them in his genre scenes. The first major acquisition of one of his works by a public institution was of one such domestic genre scene, *One of the Family* (1880, Walker Art Gallery, Liverpool), today probably the artist's best-known work.

By 1882 Cotman was predominantly painting

253 Label on the back of the frame; noted in LLAG files.
254 1910 Inventory, p. 66, valued at £3.
255 'The man who can emerge from the shadow of a great predecessor [J. S. Cotman], and who … can establish himself as a popular favourite, has certainly more than ordinary strength of personality and unusual steadfastness of purpose'; quoted by N. Watt, 'F. G. Cotman', *Norfolk Fair* (May 1984), p. 56.

LL 3831

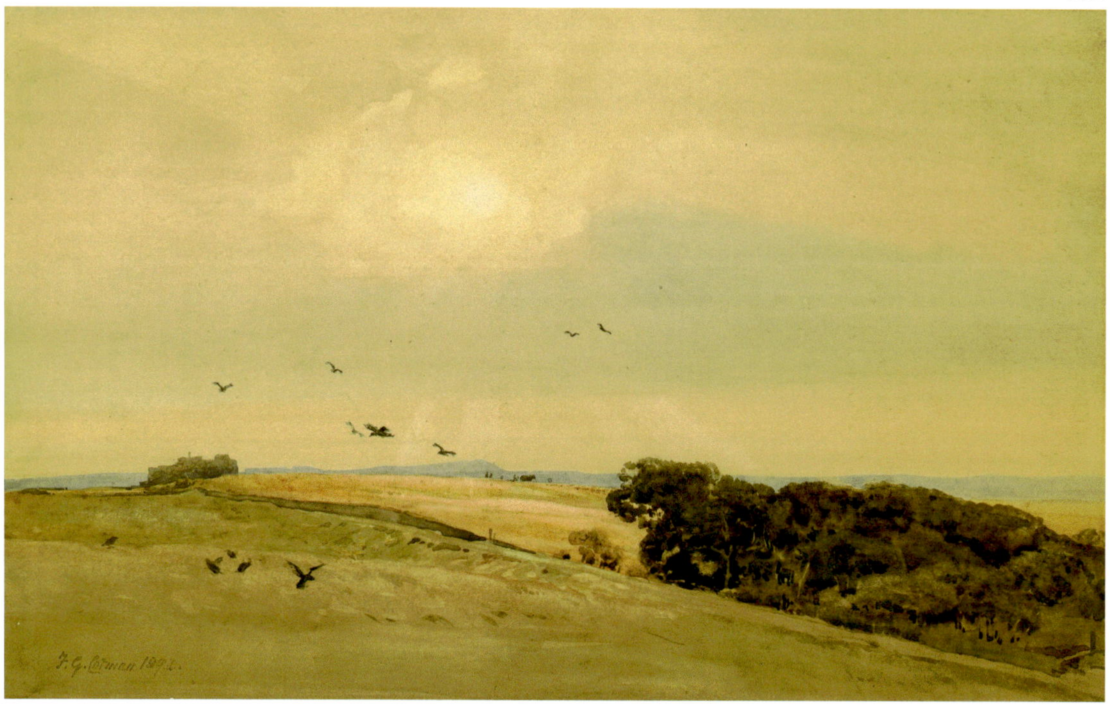

landscapes. That year he was elected member of the Institute of Painters in Water-Colours and in 1883 he became a member of the Institute of Painters in Oil-Colours. Undoubtedly influenced by Turner's atmospheric studies, Cotman's landscapes of the 1880s and 1890s reflect a similar preoccupation. He 'revelled in capturing atmospheric effects of nature – the hazy sun-drenched countryside, evening river mists and rainbows'.[256] LL 3831, with shafts of sunlight breaking through a hazy sky and a landscape delineated by strong swathes of colour, is a fine example of his work of this period. While the view remains unidentified, the outline of the castle recalls that of the Norman fortress of Bamburgh Castle on the Northumbrian coast; the deep blue on the skyline may show the North Sea and the undulations in this otherwise flat passage may represent the Farne islands. Cotman's account book shows that he sent 'Bamburgh Castle Morning £18' to Northampton in 1892,[257] a price that would suggest a watercolour. Cotman was highly proficient in both watercolour and oil and would often paint subjects in both media. He painted an oil of *Bamburgh Castle, Evening*, exhibited both in 1891 and 1892.[258]

Cotman stopped exhibiting in 1916, hampered by ill health and his fading eyesight, although he continued to paint occasionally, embracing a freer, impressionist style.

CG

256 Watt, 'F. G. Cotman', p. 59.

257 Norma Watt, letter to the compiler, 28 January 2008; a copy of Cotman's account book is held at the Castle Museum, Norwich.

258 Ibid.

LL 3946

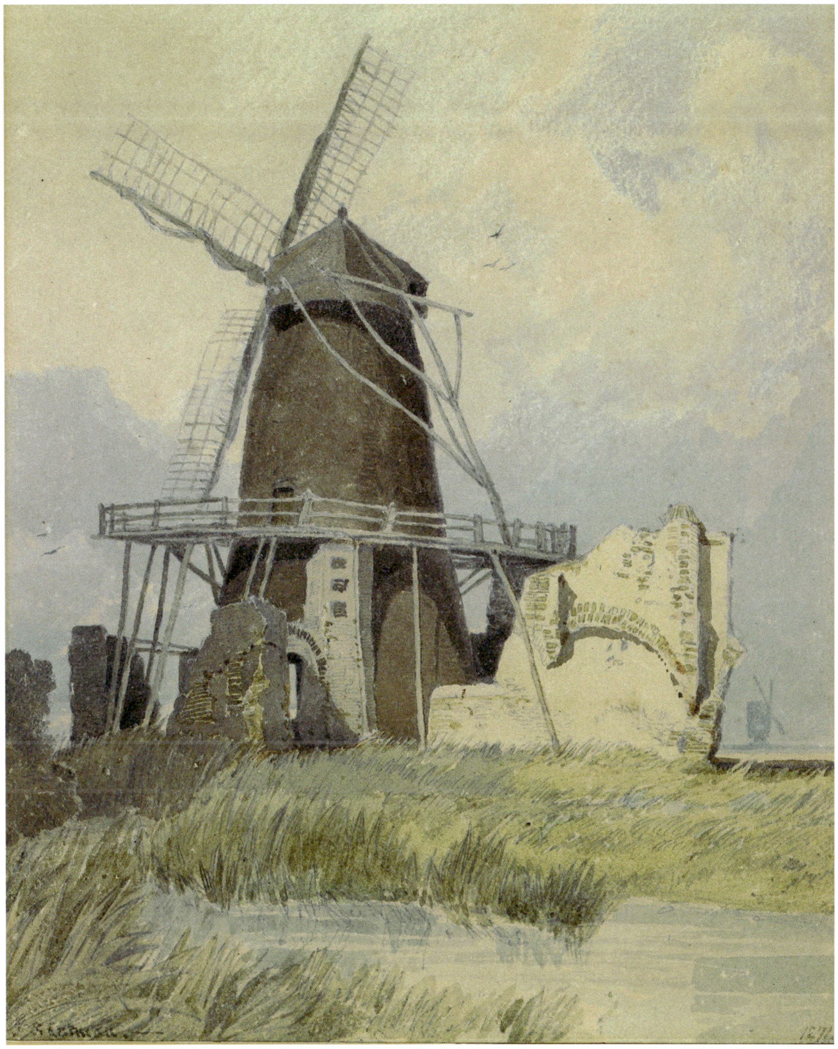

## JOHN SELL COTMAN

1782 Norwich–1842 London

**The Mill, St Benet's Abbey**

LL 3946 (LP 67)

Watercolour with scratching out over pencil on wove paper
28.2 x 22.4 cm (sight)
Date: early 1820s

Inscr: J.S.Cotman (watercolour, bottom left); 1876 (watercolour, bottom right)

Prov: bt. from the Fine Art Society by the Trustees, 11 March 1947 (£189)

Lit: Andrew W. Moore, *John Sell Cotman, 1782–1842* (Norwich, 1982), p. 104, n. 3

Cotman was born in Norwich and attended the city's grammar school. When he left to pursue an artistic career in London in 1798 he had received no formal instruction in drawing, but was soon noticed by Dr Thomas Monro, who gave him encouragement and introduced him to his circle of watercolour specialists, including Thomas Girtin (p. 102) and John Varley (pp. 206–207). Cotman exhibited at the Royal Academy in 1800, before leaving for a tour of Wales. A second tour, made in company with Paul Sandby Munn, followed in 1802. The early watercolours have the brooding intensity of Girtin, coupled with a sense of drama and corresponding variety of touch derived from Turner (pp. 182–203). During three periods of residence with the Cholmeley family in Yorkshire between 1803 and 1805 Cotman developed the linear clarity and subtle handling of overlapping colour washes which became his lasting contribution to English watercolour painting. Sidelined by the newly founded SPWC, Cotman returned to Norwich in 1806, where he played a leading role in the Norwich Society of Artists and took numerous pupils. Married in 1809 and soon with a young child, Cotman published etchings to gain an income. From 1812 he taught the six daughters of Yarmouth banker Dawson Turner and concentrated on drawings for publication, culminating in 1822 with the two folio volumes of *The architectural antiquities of Normandy*. Cotman eventually joined the SPWC in 1825, contributing British and continental scenes often criticised for their garish colour. When appointed Drawing Master of King's College School, London in 1834 he at last attained a secure and respectable position, but he had little time to enjoy his status; he died in London in 1842.

Cotman published an etching of St Benet's Abbey, seen from the east, in 1813, later collected in his 1818 volume, *A series of etchings illustrative of the architectural antiquitites of Norfolk*.[259] He was later to paint a richly coloured watercolour of the site, dated 1831.[260] LL 3946 can be dated midway between these two points, somewhere in the early 1820s. The inscription '1876' in the lower right corner is the number in the sequence of drawings and watercolours Cotman lent to pupils to copy. Begun in 1806, when he first advertised his services as a teacher in Norwich, the series continued to be added to, not only by Cotman himself, but also by his children, right up until his death, with numbers extending well beyond 2,000. The dating is further confirmed by the technique; the extensive use of scratching in the sky was employed by Cotman most conspicuously in a number of the landscape watercolours he made of subjects from his tours of Normandy, of which the last took place in 1820.[261] These marked a return to painting after a gap of several years when he had produced very little in the medium, having concentrated instead on architectural drawing and printmaking.

The remains of St Benet's Abbey stand close to the north bank of the river Bure, south of Horning in Norfolk. In LL 3946 Cotman's view is from the south, diminishing the bulk of the gatehouse, which is virtually all that survived in his time. From the middle of the eighteenth century it sheltered a large tower mill; the combination of modern technology and ancient architecture was recognised as one of the most outstanding expressions of the picturesque in Norfolk, and painted by all the Norwich School artists.[262]

TW

259 Andrew W. Moore, *John Sell Cotman, 1782–1842* (Norwich, 1982), p. 152.

260 Norwich Castle Museum, 211.217.947; Moore, *John Sell Cotman*, p. 104. Moore also records drawings of the abbey and windmill in the British Museum and Leeds City Art Gallery, but none directly related to LL 3946.

261 See, for instance, *Domfront* in the Spooner Collection, Courtauld Institute of Art Gallery, dated 1823. M. Broughton, *The Spooner Collection of British watercolours* (exh. cat., London, Courtauld Institute of Art, San Marino, Huntington Art Collections and Grasmere, the Wordsworth Trust, 2005–2006), pp. 200–01 (cat. 64).

262 See M. Allthorpe-Guyton, *John Thirtle 1777–1839. Drawings in Norwich Castle Museum* (Norwich, 1977), p. 42 (cat. 23).

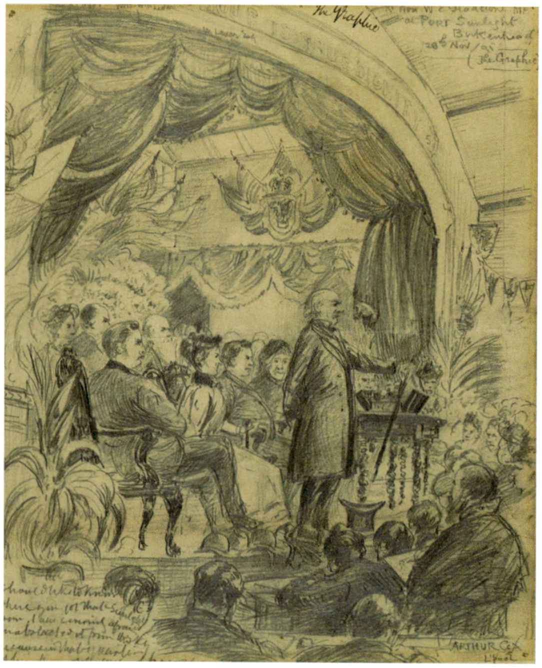

LL 3832A

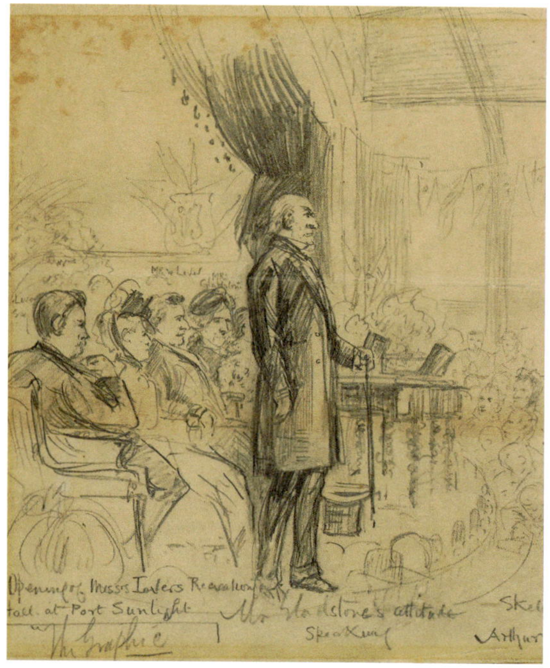

LL 3832B

## CHARLES ARTHUR COX

Dates and places of birth and death unknown

**Rt. Hon W. E. Gladstone at Port Sunlight**
LL 3832A (WHL 1702, TM 345, LP 3)

Pencil on paper
28.3 x 22.1 cm
Date: 1891

Inscr: ARTHUR COX / L'pool (pencil, bottom right); J. D. Lever! (pencil, top, far left); Mrs W. H. Lever! (pencil, top left); W. Lever Esq (pencil, top centre); The Graphic (ink, top centre); Rt. Hon W. E. Gladstone M.P. / at Port Sunlight / Birkenhead / 28th Nov / 91 - / (The Graphic) (pencil, top right); I should like to know / where you got that Sunlight / from. I am seriously afraid / you abstracted it from [illeg.] / because in that quarter it / has been of late very scarce (pencil, bottom left); [?LAB]OUR IS TRUE DIGNITY (pencil, on arch over stage, partially hidden by mount)

Prov: acquired by Lever before 1906;[263] deposited at the Lady Lever Art Gallery in 1925, presumably by Sir William Hulme Lever, 2nd Viscount Leverhulme

Cox's sketch depicts Gladstone making his speech at the opening ceremony of Gladstone Hall on 28 November 1891. The hall was the first community building to be opened in Port Sunlight, the model village built by Lever for his workers. Designed by William Owen (1846–1910) as a workers' canteen and recreational hall, it was completed in 1891.[264]

Lever invited his great political hero William Ewart Gladstone to formally open the building. The presence of the Liverpool-born former Prime Minister at this event was a great coup for Lever; it gave his soap-making business and new model village the official stamp of approval.[265]

Lever, like Gladstone, was a Liberal. He became involved in politics shortly after moving to Wirral in 1888 and stood as the Liberal candidate for local seats in 1892, 1894, 1895 and 1900. He was finally successful in 1906 when he stood for the Wirral constituency. Lever's outstanding achievement as an MP was to campaign for an old-age pension.

In LL 3832A we see Gladstone centre stage leaning on his cane as he makes his address. Behind him sit the VIP guests including, on the front row from the left, James Darcy Lever (Lever's brother), Mrs W. H. Lever, Lever and Mrs W. E. Gladstone. Reporters and illustrators sit near the stage recording the event. Lever's own speech on the day praised Gladstone's policies of reducing duty on goods to encourage business enterprise, specifically the removal of duty on soap and paper in 1853 and 1861 respectively. As Lever summarised, 'no trade in the country owes so much to yourself as the industry we are engaged in'.[266] Lever's approach to the care of his employees and business policies epitomised for Gladstone a new spirit of industry. He noted that the day was one 'to inspire great thankfulness

263 LL 3832A is listed in the 1906 TM Inventory, p. 17, valued at £2. It hung in the ballroom lobby along with LL 3832B and LL 3855. At least 12 images of Gladstone were displayed in this space, a reflection of Lever's great enthusiasm for the Liberal leader.

264 E. Hubbard and M. Shippobottom, *A Guide to Port Sunlight Village* (Liverpool, 1988), pp. 33–35.

265 Gladstone went on to secure a fourth term as Prime Minister, 1892–94.

266 2nd Viscount Leverhulme, *Viscount Leverhulme by His Son* (London, 1927), p. 55.

for the past, more hopefulness for the future'.[267] Lever found the whole event deeply moving. Years later he told his son, 'I could not sleep much that night; I had to walk up and down the park thinking of him. He made an extraordinary impression.'[268]

The sketch was reproduced in *Black and White*, 5 December 1891.

SP

**Mr Gladstone's Attitude Speaking**
LL 3832B (WHL 1703, TM 346, LP 4)

Pencil on paper
24.7 x 22.1 cm
Date: 1891

Inscr: Arthur Cox (pencil, bottom right); Mr. Gladstone's attitude / speaking (pencil, bottom centre); Opening of Messrs Levers Recreation / Hall at Port Sunlight (pencil, bottom left); The Graphic (pencil, bottom left); Sketch 2 (pencil, bottom right); W H Lever / Esq / (pencil, centre left); MR W Lever / MRS / Gladstone (pencil, centre); [illeg.] (pencil, top right)

Prov: acquired by Lever before 1906;[269] deposited at the Lady Lever Art Gallery in 1925, presumably by Sir William Hulme Lever, 2nd Viscount Leverhulme

This sketch is a companion to LL 3832A. It concentrates on the central group of figures observed from a closer viewpoint. The artist has made an error in noting the guests sitting behind Gladstone. James Darcy Lever is at the extreme left, not William Hesketh Lever as the inscription implies.

SP

267 Ibid., p. 56.
268 Ibid.
269 LL 3832B is listed in the 1906 TM Inventory, p. 17, valued at £2. It hung in the ballroom lobby along with LL 3832A and LL 3855.

LL 3957

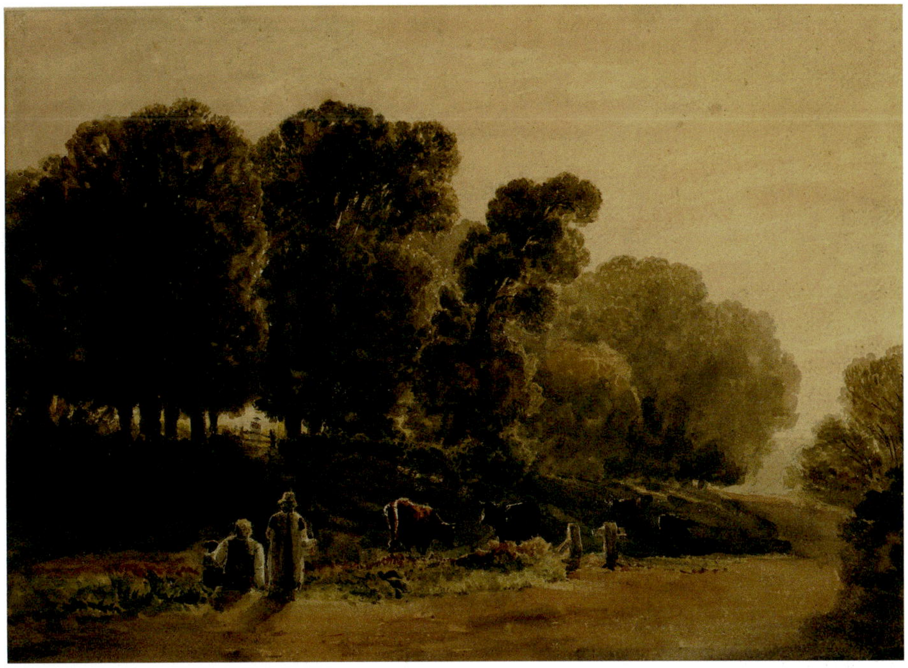

**DAVID COX**
1783 Birmingham–1859 Harborne, Birmingham

**Road Through a Park**[270]
LL 3957 (WHL 804, HH 366)

Watercolour with gum arabic over pencil on wove paper
41.1 x 55.8 cm
Date: c. 1810

Prov: bt. from James Orrock by Lever, 1910[271]

Exh: Perth, Art Gallery of Western Australia and Australian tour, *Exhibition of Early British Water-colours*, organised by the Empire Art Loans Exhibition Society, 1948–49 (cat. 100, as by DeWint); China and East Berlin, British-China Friendship Association, *British Watercolour Painting during Three Centuries*, 1963 (cat. 76)

Lit: 'Current Art Notes, Our Plates', *The Connoisseur*, vol. 88 (1931), p. 345, illus. p. 309

The son of a metal-worker, Cox took drawing lessons from Joseph Barber in Birmingham, after which he was briefly apprenticed to a miniature painter named Albert Fieldler. Around 1800 he spent a lengthier period employed in painting scenery for the New Theatre, Birmingham. Cox travelled to London in 1804 at the promise of similar employment but when this came to nothing, encouraged by John Varley (see pp. 206–207) he decided to make a living as a professional watercolourist and drawing master. He published the first of a series of drawing manuals in 1811. Around 1814 Cox moved with his family to Hereford to accept a teaching position at Miss Croucher's School for Young Ladies. He lived at Hereford until 1827, when he and his family moved back to London. In 1841 he retired from his teaching practice to live at Harborne, near Birmingham, chiefly to concentrate on his oil painting. In June 1853 Cox suffered a stroke that affected his vision and coordination and seriously limited the amount of new work he could undertake. Cox first exhibited at the Royal Academy in 1805, and from 1809 until its collapse in 1812 with the Associated Artists in Water-Colours, becoming its president in 1812. In 1813 he was elected a member of the SPWC, where he exhibited almost every year until his death.

LL 3957 was purchased by Lever as by Peter DeWint[272] and was illustrated in *The Connoisseur* in 1931 with that attribution. With its broad blocks of tonal wash and the treatment of the trees (influenced by Varley and Girtin), the work does resemble certain early works of DeWint (see, for example, LL 3799, pp. 76–77). However, it is now thought to be an early work by Cox, dating from his London period before he moved to Hereford in 1814.[273] Scott Wilcox has suggested a date of c. 1810; it would be impossible to be more precise as there are so few dated drawings from that period.[274]

270 The full title in the 1910 Inventory is *Road through a park, with row of tall trees on a bank, cattle and figures in foreground – a sketch*.
271 1910 Inventory, valued at £80.

272 WHL Inventory, p. 125.
273 Re-attribution proposed by Andrew Wyld and Charles Nugent, verbally, 2005 and Scott Wilcox, verbally, 2007. Charles Nugent has pointed to the treatment of the figures as being particularly characteristic of Cox.
274 Scott Wilcox, email correspondence, May 2007.

## Kenilworth Castle
LL 3950 (WHL 342, H 412)

Watercolour with extra gum arabic and scratching out over pencil on wove paper
41.2 x 54.7 cm
Date: 1820s

Inscr: D. Cox / 1830 (watercolour, bottom left)

Prov: in Lever's collection by 1912[275]

Exh: [?] London, SPWC, 1821 (cat. 113, as *Caesar's Tower and part of Leicester Buildings*); [?] London, Earl's Court, *Victorian Era Exhibition*, 1897 (cat. 174, as *Kenilworth*); Perth, Art Gallery of Western Australia and Australian tour, *Exhibition of Early British Water-colours*, organised by the Empire Art Loans Exhibition Society, 1948–49 (cat. 90)

Lit: Trenchard Cox, *David Cox* (London, 1947), pp. 26–27, illus. p. 28

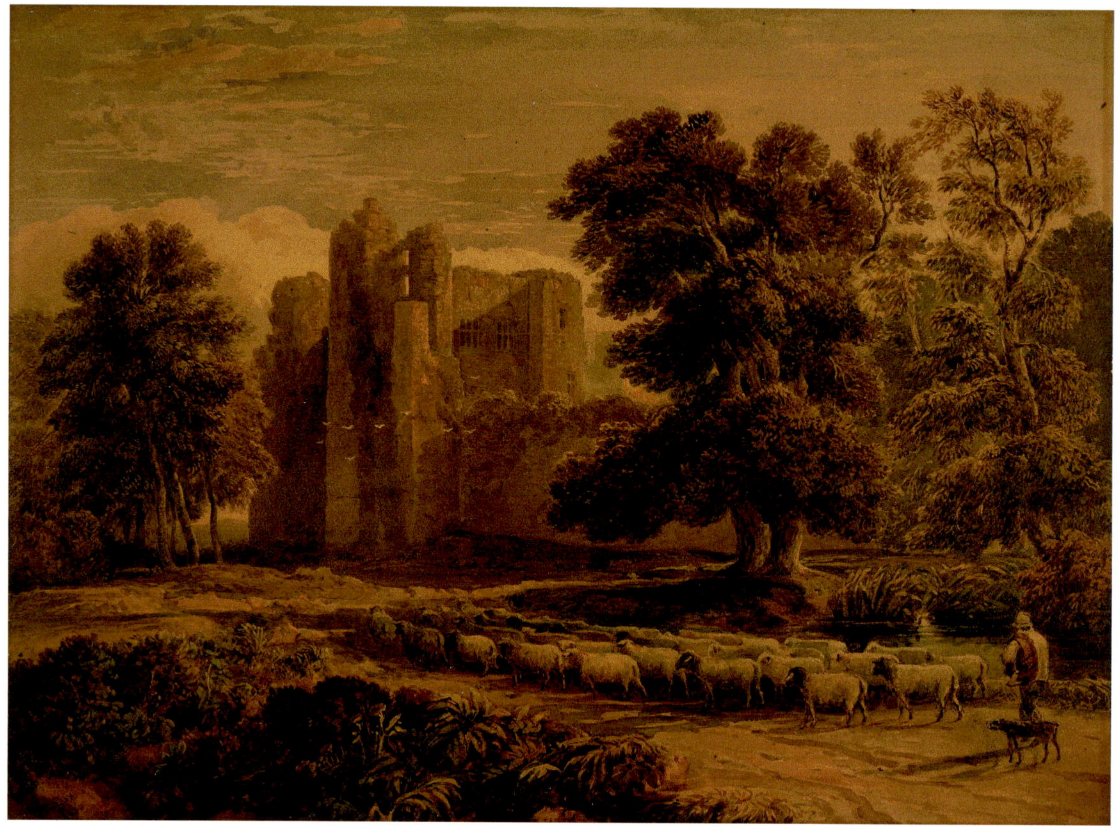

LL 3950

Cox made a number of drawings and watercolours of the ruins of Kenilworth Castle in Warwickshire. By the 1830s the medieval and Elizabethan castle had firmly entered the popular imagination thanks to the publication of Sir Walter Scott's best-selling historical novel *Kenilworth* in 1821, and it provided inspiration for writers and artists alike. In fact Cox's earliest recorded watercolour of the subject dates from 1806–07 (Birmingham Museums and Art Gallery, fig. 18).[276] Another version of the same composition dated 1807 depicts Windsor Castle in the background (Victoria & Albert Museum, fig. 19). One of Cox's biographers, N. Neal Solly, described how in 1806 or 1807, after Cox completed 'his copy of the Gaspar Poussin in Simpson's shop, he made a large drawing, about 16 x 20, in rivalry of that work, the subject being a composition, with a flock of sheep and a man and dog, also some trees and Kenilworth Castle'.[277] It has been suggested that the Birmingham *Kenilworth* (which is the right size) is that drawing.[278] It is possible that the 'Gaspar Poussin' concerned is *Landscape with a Shepherd and his Flock* (c. 1670, National Gallery, London) whose composition bears a close similarity to the Birmingham work.[279] The painting was in the collection of William Young Ottley in 1801 and could have been on show in Simpson's shop in 1806–07.[280]

fig. 18. David Cox, *Kenilworth Castle*, c. 1807, watercolour over pencil on wove paper, 35.9 x 50.3 cm, Birmingham Museums and Art Gallery

fig. 19. David Cox, *In Windsor Park*, 1807, watercolour over pencil on wove paper, 35.5 x 50.5 cm, V&A Images/Victoria and Albert Museum/Bridgeman

fig. 20. David Cox, *Kenilworth Castle*, c. 1857–59, watercolour on 'Scotch' paper, 51 x 72.7 cm, Worcester City Museums Collection

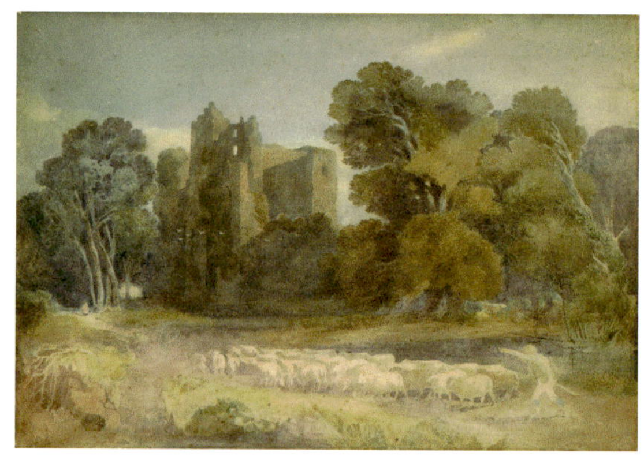

fig. 18

fig. 19

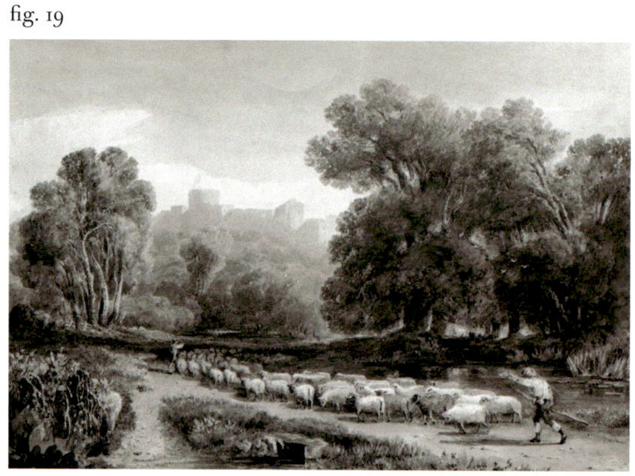

fig. 20

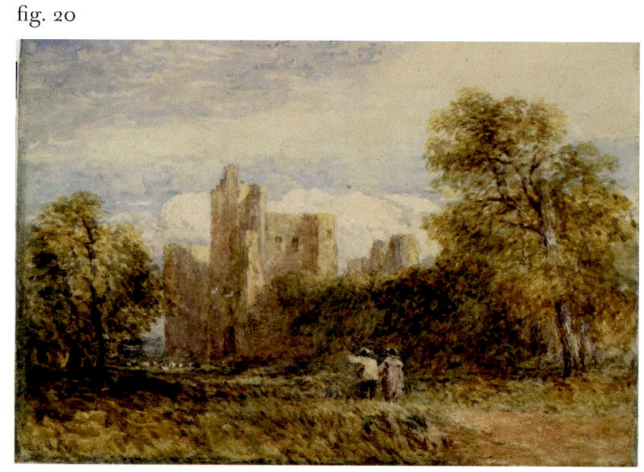

275 1912 Hill Inventory.

276 Stephen Wildman (ed.), *David Cox 1783–1859* (exh. cat., Birmingham, Birmingham Museums and Art Gallery and London, Victoria & Albert Museum, 1983–84), p. 48 (cat. 3).

277 N. Neal Solly, *Memoir of the Life of David Cox* (London, 1873), p. 16. See also William Hall, *A Biography of David Cox: With Remarks on His Worlds and Genius* (London, 1883), p. 15.

278 Wildman (ed.), *David Cox 1783–1859*, p. 48. Solly's description of this drawing as 'no later than 1806 or 1807' (Solly, *Life of David Cox*, p. 16) could refer to the Birmingham *Kenilworth* or another as yet unknown work, but the photographic illustration (pl. 5) shows the Lady Lever work. It seems odd that Solly would have misdated the Lady Lever picture when it was clearly inscribed 1830, and it may be the case that the wrong work was illustrated.

279 NG 68: catalogued and illus. in Humphrey Wine, *National Gallery Catalogues: The Seventeenth Century French Paintings* (London, 2001), pp. 152–53.

280 The painting was offered by Ottley at Christie's, 16 May 1801 (lot 21) but failed to meet the reserve price set; it was sold at Christie's, 25 April 1818 (lot 126) to Holwell Carr. See Wine, *National Gallery Catalogues*, pp. 152–53.

LL 3950 is a later reworking of the Birmingham picture. In the Lady Lever watercolour, the Arcadian elements have been toned down, the drover no longer has his arm outstretched, and he has gained a dog by his side. Although the signature seems genuine, it was probably added later as the work dates stylistically from the 1820s.[281] The watercolour depicts the keep, also known as Caesar's Tower, in the background; the other portions of the castle represented may be part of the Leicester Buildings, although they are not depicted accurately. LL 3950 may be the *Caesar's Tower and part of Leicester Buildings* shown at the SPWC in 1821. Cox returned to the same subject and composition in a version from c. 1857–59 now in Worcester City Museum and Art Gallery (fig. 20). In this version the drover and sheep have been replaced by two figures, and the tighter handling exhibited in the Lady Lever work has given way to Cox's characteristically late, loose brushstrokes.

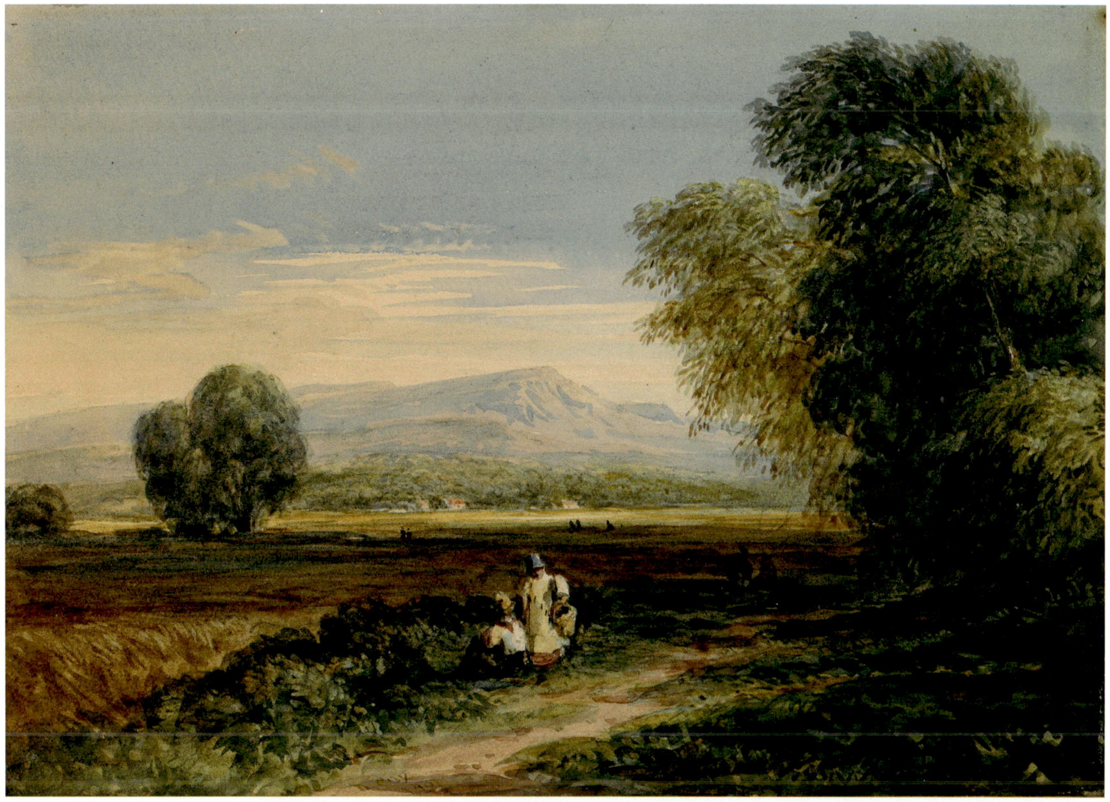

LL 3835

### Landscape with Hills in Distance
LL 3835 (WHL 340, H 413)

Watercolour with extra gum arabic, with stopping out on wove paper
18.8 x 26.3 cm
Date: 1831

Inscr: D. Cox / 1831 (watercolour, bottom edge, centre)

Prov: Ralph Bernal, 1853;[282] Edwin Henry Lawrence, London;[283] in Lever's collection by 1915[284]

Exh: Swansea, Glynn Vivian Art Gallery, *David Cox (1783–1859)*, 1953 (cat. 28)

An old label on the back of the frame gives the title of LL 3835 as *A View in Wales with children in foreground*.[285] Cox exhibited other views of Wales at the SPWC in 1831 suggesting that he was in Wales just before or during this year and, although the location has not been identified, it is quite possible that the mountainous scenery is Welsh. The work is dated in the Hill Inventory to 1858; this is clearly a mistake as LL 3835 is in Cox's crisp, neat style from a much earlier period.

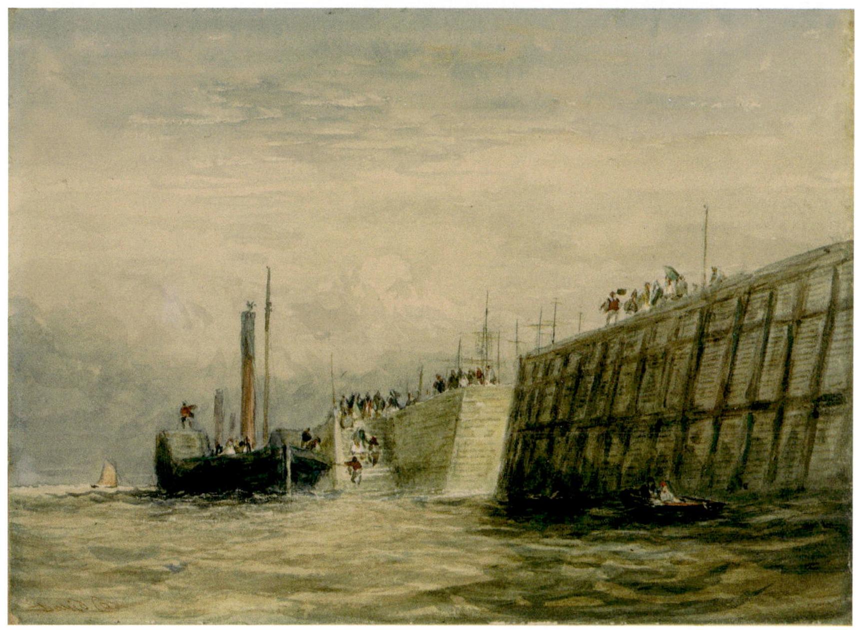

LL 3840

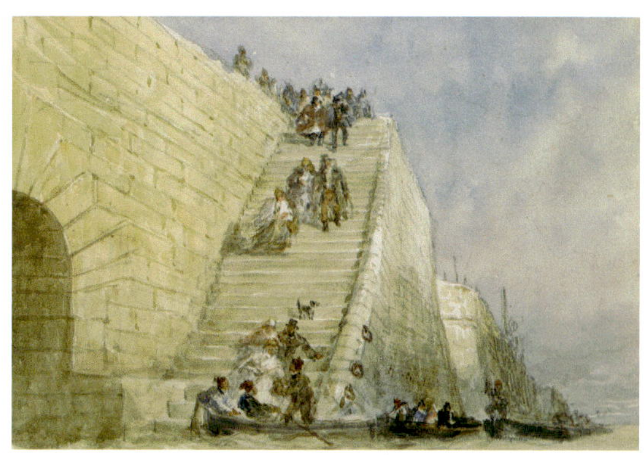

fig. 21. David Cox, *The Old Pierhead, Liverpool*, c. 1839–41, watercolour over pencil on wove paper, 18.5 x 25.7 cm, Whitworth Art Gallery, Manchester

281 Scott Wilcox, verbally, March 2006.
282 LLAG files: label on back of frame.
283 LLAG files: label on back of frame.
284 LL 3835 is listed in the 1915 Hill Inventory as *Landscape with hills in the distance* in the corridor to music room, valued at £20. This work does not appear to have been purchased in any of the large Orrock sales; no invoice for the work has been found.
285 LLAG files.

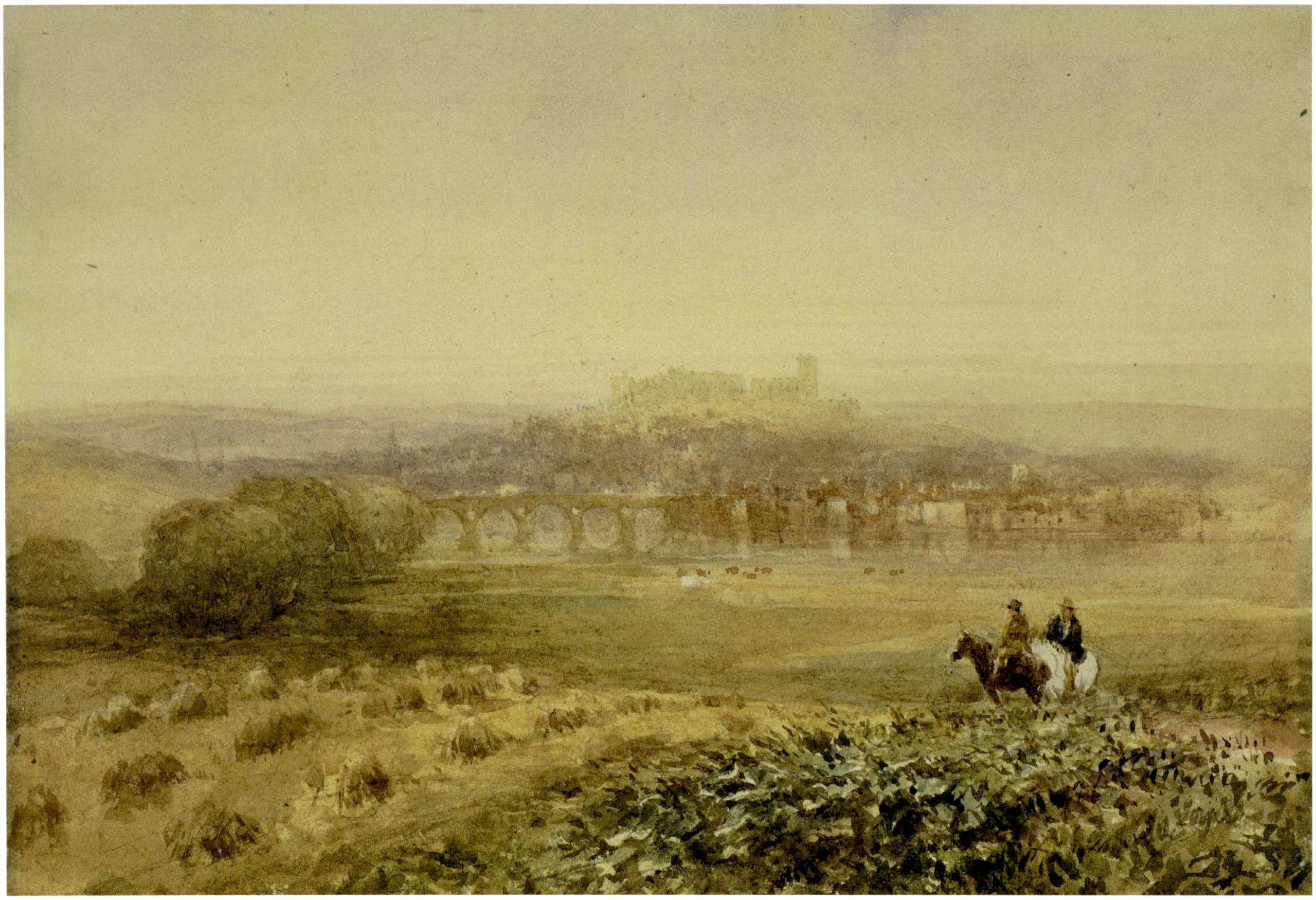

LL 3845

### George's Dock, Liverpool
LL 3840 (WHL 3302)

Watercolour with touches of gouache over black chalk on wove paper
20.3 x 28.1 cm
Date: early to mid-1830s

Inscr: David Cox (watercolour, bottom left)

Prov: James Gresham, Ashton-on-Mersey; his sale, Christie's, 12–16 July 1917 (lot 12, as *The Old Landing Stage Liverpool*); bt. by Gooden and Fox (£65 2s) for Lever (£66 14s 6d)

LL 3840 was formerly titled *The Old Landing Stage, Liverpool*;[286] in fact there was no landing stage until 1847 and the work depicts the landing steps at George's Dock at low water with passengers waiting to embark on the moored Woodside ferry steamer, which went across the river to Woodside, near Birkenhead.[287] The entrance shown is that of George's Dock Slip, a mooring point for smaller boats; in the far distance, but not visible in this view, would have been George's Basin.

LL 3840 can be dated on stylistic grounds to the early to mid-1830s. Cox probably visited Liverpool on a number of occasions during this period. His sister Mary Ann was married to a music teacher living in Manchester, and his friend Charles Barber (1784–1854), son of his teacher Joseph Barber, lived in Liverpool and was successively treasurer, secretary and twice president of the Liverpool Academy. Solly described a trip Cox made to Liverpool in July 1835, when he stayed at the house of Samuel Eglington, secretary of the Liverpool Academy, 'with whom he was on very friendly terms'.[288] It is possible that the Lady Lever watercolour was made on this occasion. Another watercolour by Cox (Whitworth Art Gallery, Manchester, fig. 21) depicts the landing steps at Seacombe Slip, with a view looking towards George's Dock.[289]

### Lancaster
LL 3845 (WHL 358, H 430)

Watercolour with touches of gouache and gum arabic over pencil on wove paper
19.1 x 27.4 cm
Date: mid-1830s

Prov: in Lever's collection by 1915[290]

Cox's trips to the town of Lancaster began in 1834 when he became attracted by the subject of travellers crossing the sands (see LL 3841 below). LL 3845 presents a tourist's view of Skerton Bridge with the town and castle beyond. Its translucent washes and delicate handling are typical of Cox's style in the mid-1830s. Another watercolour by Cox in the British Museum is taken from the same viewpoint, and belongs to the same period, although this time there are cows in the foreground.[291]

286 This title is given in the WHL Inventory, also by Tatlock, p. 71.

287 Sam Davidson, verbally, March 2007. Steam ferries were well established by the early 1830s. The different coloured funnels indicated the different steamers; red indicated the Birkenhead ferries, including Woodside, and those further south. Seacombe, Egremont and New Brighton ferries, to the north, adopted white funnels.

288 Solly, *Life of David Cox*, p. 78.

289 The Whitworth work, *The Old Pierhead, Liverpool*, watercolour over pencil, 18.5 x 25.7 cm, although similar in style to LL 3840 has been dated by Charles Nugent to 1839–41. This is based on the exhibition of a work titled *A Pier at Liverpool* at the SPWC in 1840 (cat. 244). The SPWC exhibit is probably too late to be the Lady Lever work.

290 1915 Hill Inventory, corridor to music room, valued at £60. The work is here titled *Lancaster – a sketch – harvest time*.

291 *Lancaster*, watercolour, 18.4 x 28.5 cm, British Museum (1878, 1228.75).

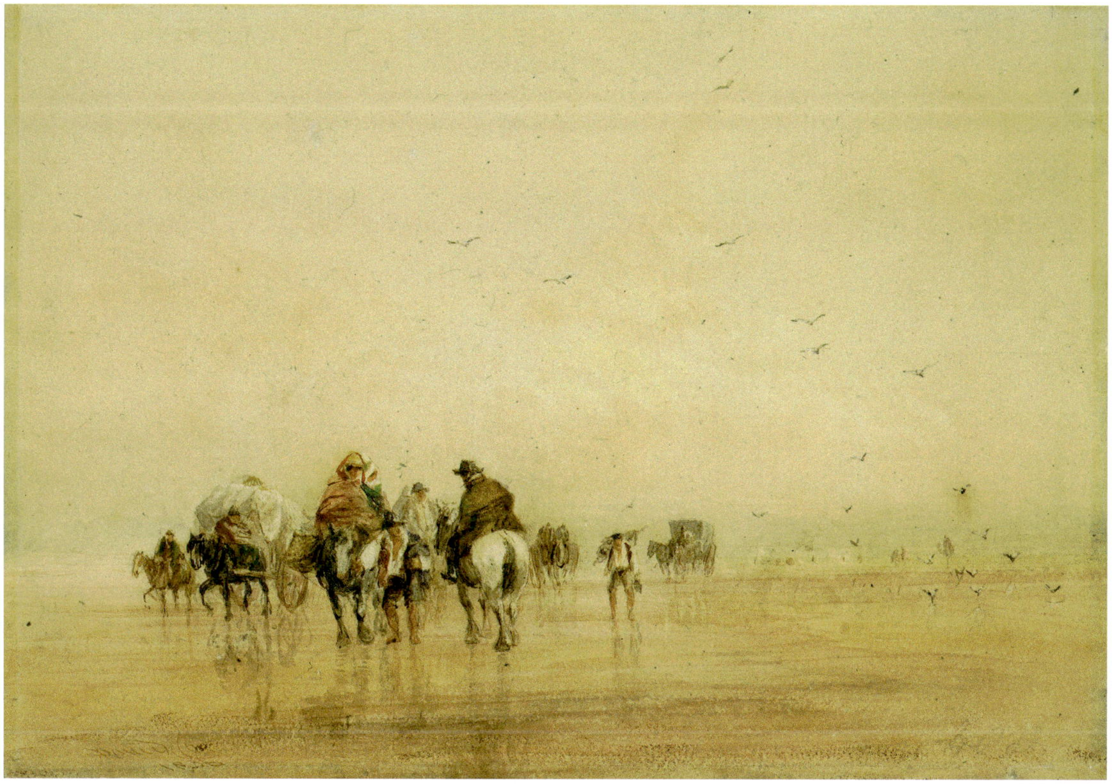

LL 3841

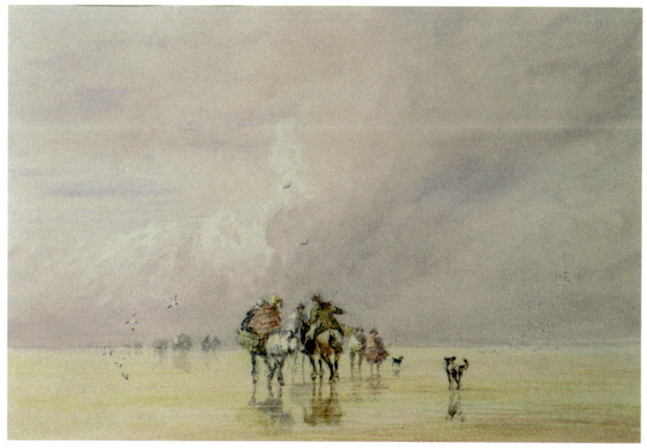

fig. 22. David Cox, *Crossing Lancaster Sands*, c. 1835–40, watercolour on wove paper, 26 x 36.8 cm, Towneley Hall Art Gallery and Museum, Burnley, Lancashire/Bridgeman

## Crossing Lancaster Sands
LL 3841 (WHL 200, H 472)

Watercolour with touches of gouache over pencil on wove paper
18.8 x 26.4 cm
Date: 1836

Inscr: David Cox / 1836 (watercolour, bottom left)

Prov: bt. from James Orrock by Lever, 1912[292]

Exh: Birmingham, Birmingham Museum and Art Gallery, *Special collection of works by David Cox*, 1890 (cat. 324); Lancaster, Storey Institute Art Gallery, *Summer Exhibition of Oils and Watercolours*, 1929 (cat. 12); Lancaster, Storey Institute Art Gallery, *Festival of Britain*, 1951 (cat. 12)

Cox first visited Lancaster and Ulverston Sands in 1834, returning in 1835 and again in 1840. Between 1835 and 1847 he produced more than 20 drawings (and a smaller number of oil paintings) of people going to market, crossing, or preparing to cross the treacherous sands that stretch across the head of Morecambe Bay at low tide. The present work could be the *Lancaster Sands – Market People returning from Ulverstone* exhibited at the SPWC in 1836 (cat. 119).[293] LL 3841 is most similar in composition and style to *Lancaster Sands* in Towneley Hall Art Gallery and Museum, Burnley (c. 1835–40, fig. 22). In the Lady Lever work, the pigment in the sky has faded greatly with the watercolour losing much of its atmospheric effect.

292 1912 Inventory.
293 Sold for 35 guineas. LL 3841 could also be any one of three 'Lancaster Sands' subjects exhibited at the Liverpool Academy in 1836 (cats. 500, 518 and 532).

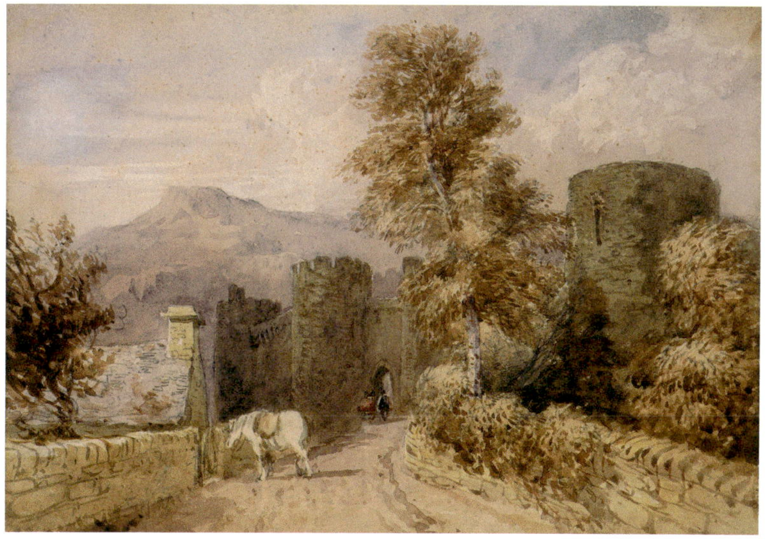

LL 3836

## The White Pony[294]
LL 3836 (WHL 816, HH 357)

Watercolour with touches of gouache over pencil on wove paper
21.3 x 29.4 cm
Date: probably mid- to late 1830s

Prov: bt. from James Orrock by Lever, 1910[295]

Exh: Swansea, Glynn Vivian Art Gallery, *David Cox 1783–1859*, 1953 (cat. 37)

Although the handling of the horse is poor, the work appears to be autograph, and probably dates from the mid- to late 1830s.[296] Charles Nugent has identified the scene as Mill Gate in Conwy town walls.[297]

294 In the WHL Inventory, LL 3836 is titled *The white pony: A Welsh road with round towers of a castle, figures and cottage.*
295 1910 Inventory, in drawing room, valued at £10.

296 Date suggested by Andrew Wyld, verbally, May 2005.
297 Charles Nugent, verbally, May 2007.

## A Road in North Wales with Figures[298]

LL 3833 (WHL 825, HH 340)

Watercolour with extra gum arabic, with touches of gouache over black chalk on wove paper
18.7 x 27.1 cm
Date: mid- to late 1840s

Prov: bt. from James Orrock by Lever, 1910[299]

Exh: Brisbane, Queensland Art Gallery and tour of Australia and New Zealand, *Exhibition of British Watercolours 1850–1914*, organised by the Empire Art Loan Exhibitions Society, 1952–53 (cat. 33, as *Entrance to Bettws-y-Coed Churchyard*); Birmingham, Birmingham Museum and Art Gallery, *Centenary Exhibition of the Works of David Cox 1783–1859*, 1959 (cat. 90); Swansea, Glynn Vivian Art Gallery, *Art in Wales – a survey of four thousand years to AD 1850*, 1964 (cat. 211)

While living at Harborne, Cox spent every summer between 1844 and 1856 at Betws-y-Coed and its surroundings. The small Caernarvonshire village contained numerous attractive subjects, including its old church, which provided the inspiration for one of his major oil paintings, *The Welsh Funeral* (1848, Birmingham Museums and Art Gallery).[300] LL 3833 has been mistakenly described as a study for *The Welsh Funeral*.[301] It is easy to see how this confusion arises as the central recess in both images give the works a similar composition, although in LL 3833 there is no church. While not directly related to *The Welsh Funeral*, the watercolour, in Cox's characteristically sketchy style of this period, is likely to have been done during one of the artist's summer visits to Betws-y-Coed and its vicinity. It may even depict the village churchyard although it has not been possible to confirm this. LL 3833 was previously documented as inscribed with Cox's initials and dated '46'[302] and while this is no longer visible, the loose, broad washes of colour and use of black chalk are consistent with Cox's style of the mid- to late 1840s.

298 The title in the 1910 Inventory is *A road in North Wales, with figures, stone walls and dark trees – in the manner of De Wint*.
299 1910 Inventory, in Mr Orrock's drawing room, valued at £15.
300 Wildman, *David Cox 1783–1859*, p. 17 (cat. 115), illus. b&w.
301 John Rowlands, *Centenary Exhibition of the Works of David Cox 1783–1859* (exh. cat., Birmingham, Birmingham Museum and Art Gallery, 1959), p. 24 (cat. 90).
302 Ibid. and also in LLAG files.

## Peace and War

LL 3948 (WHL 318, H 206)[303]

Watercolour with extra gum arabic and touches of gouache on oatmeal paper
60.6 x 86.6 cm
Date: 1848

Inscr: David Cox / 1848 (watercolour, bottom left)

Annot: Peace and War / 4 David Cox (ink, label on backboard, verso)[304]

Prov: Mr Bickerstaff, Preston;[305] William Quilter, 1873; his sale, Christie's, 8 April 1875 (lot 114); [?] bt. in;[306] Quilter's sale, Christie's, 18 May 1889 (lot 121); bt. Agnew's (700 gns); bt. from James Orrock by Lever, 1904[307]

Exh: London, SPWC, 1848 (cat. 154); [?] Ventnor, venue and exhibition title unknown, 1871 (cat. no. unknown);[308] Liverpool, Liverpool Art Club, *David Cox exhibition*, 1875 (cat. 58); London, Royal Academy, *Exhibition of works of the Old Masters and Deceased Masters of the British School, including a collection of watercolours*, 1908 (cat. 225)

Lit: N. Neal Solly, *Memoir of the Life of David Cox* (London, 1873), pp. 85–86, 152, 259, 325; F. Gordon Roe, 'David Cox's Peace and War', *The Connoisseur*, vol. 90 (July 1932), pp. 20–24, illus. p. 21; F. Gordon Roe, *Cox The Master* (Leigh-on-Sea, 1946), pp. 76–80; Trenchard Cox, *David Cox* (London, 1947), pp. 85–86

One of Cox's most enigmatic subjects, *Peace and War* demonstrates the artist's fascination with portraying the contrasting relationship between the peaceful aspects of the countryside and the sombre spectre of war. LL 3948 depicts a line of soldiers on the right, representing war; they are watched by a group of country folk, symbolising peace. In the background is Lympne Castle and church, Kent; the castle had been a fortified residence of the medieval Archdeacons of Canterbury, and so hints at ancient wars. In the background are just visible a few of the Martello towers on the Kent and Sussex coast, built between 1804 and 1812 as defensive forts to guard against possible invasion from Napoleonic France.

In 1848, on the occasion of the work's exhibition at the SPWC, Cox was reported to have considered changing its title to 'Dungeness Bay', which described the view more accurately, but decided to retain 'Peace and War', suggesting that he was keen to enhance its potentially symbolic resonances.[309] Nevertheless, despite its enigmatic qualities, Cox does not appear to have intended any firm historical associations to have been made and his inspiration for the work seems to have been a trip in early 1838 when he accompanied his sickly wife to Seabrook, near Hythe, Kent. While his wife benefited from the sea air, the artist was able to make sketches around the Kentish coast, including the barracks at Hythe. At the beginning of May he described a visit made to Lympne Castle: 'It is very small, but stands on a bold situation overlooking Romsey [*sic*] Marshes. The atmosphere has been very clear for more than a week, and we can see the French coast quite distinct. Today it was more clear than I have ever before seen it, and the sea of a most beautiful colour.'[310]

The Lady Lever *Peace and War* is one of a number of versions of the subject. In the early 1840s Cox painted a watercolour in which he transferred the scene from Lympne to the grander setting of Lancaster Castle and its surroundings (Art Institute of Chicago, fig. 23). He also painted a version in oils in 1846, with troops marching towards the town of Lancaster, which was owned by Lever.[311] In LL 3948 Cox returned to the setting of Lympne Castle; there is also a smaller, seemingly unfinished watercolour of the composition which may date from a number of years before the Lady Lever work (Birmingham Museums and Art Gallery, fig. 24).[312]

Solly, one of Cox's biographers, reported that the subject of the Lady Lever drawing was inspired by the sight of William James Müller's painting of *The Baggage Wagon or Passage of Troops over a Common* (1845) which Cox may have seen in preparation when he took lessons in oil painting from Müller in 1839.[313] However, aside from the subject-matter of troops crossing the countryside, there is no compositional relationship between Müller's painting and any of Cox's versions of *Peace and War*. Furthermore, as Roe pointed out, Cox was 'attracted by themes with a military motif long before Müller painted his *Baggage Wagon*'.[314] In 1838, for example, Cox exhibited works with the following titles at the SPWC: *Rocky Scene – Infantry on the March* (cat. 125) and *Stirling Castle – Cavalry on the March* (cat. 395). Roe's comment that Müller's *Baggage Wagon* may have 'stimulated rather than originated Cox's interest in subjects of this nature' seems fair.[315]

LL 3498 is a highly finished work, to be expected of an exhibition piece. Its technique is characteristic of Cox's broader watercolour style of the mid- to late 1840s.

303 1907 Hill Inventory as 'Orrock collection per Gooden and Fox, valued at £1200'.
304 LLAG files: A. C. Tait's notes suggest that this is probably the handwriting of the artist and that 'the use of the numeral 4 suggests this is the fourth version'.
305 George Redford, *Art Sales* (London, 2 vols, 1888), vol. I, p. 204.
306 Christie's auctioneer's copy of the sale catalogue is annotated with the purchaser's name Eley and the price 950 gns, both crossed through. The work was most probably bought in.
307 1904 Inventory, as *Peace and War*, 23 x 33$^3/_8$ in.
308 F. Gordon Roe, *Cox The Master* (Leigh-on-Sea, 1946), p. 79. It has not been possible to verify the details of this exhibition.
309 Solly, *Life of David Cox*, p. 152.
310 Quoted in Solly, *Life of David Cox*, p. 86.
311 WHL 9 (H 437). It was sold for $2,500 at the Anderson Galleries, New York, 17 February 1926 (lot 52) and again Sotheby's, 11 March 1987 (lot 109); its present whereabouts are unknown.
312 Wildman, *David Cox 1783–1859*, p. 90 (cat. 77).
313 Solly, *Life of David Cox*, p. 259.
314 F. Gordon Roe, 'David Cox's Peace and War', *The Connoisseur*, vol. 90 (July 1932), p. 23.
315 Ibid.

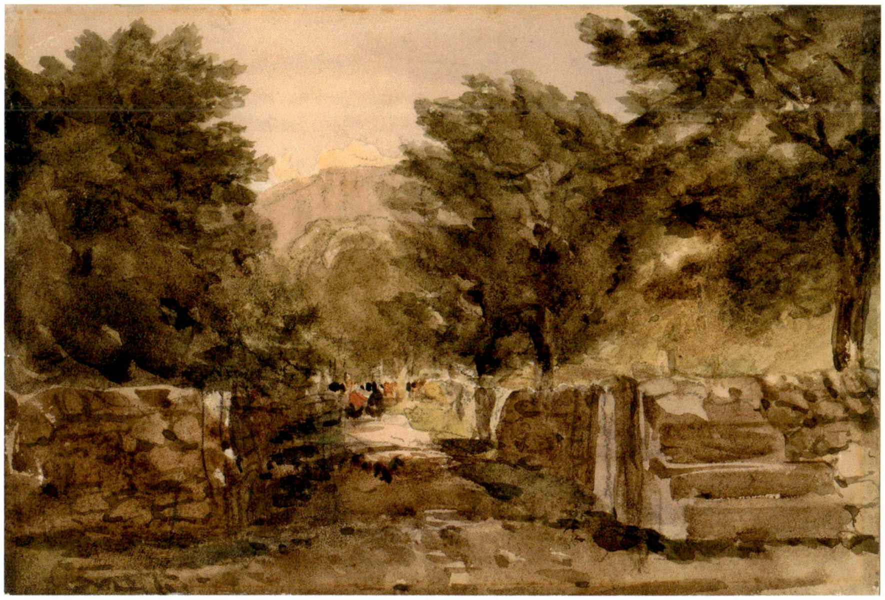

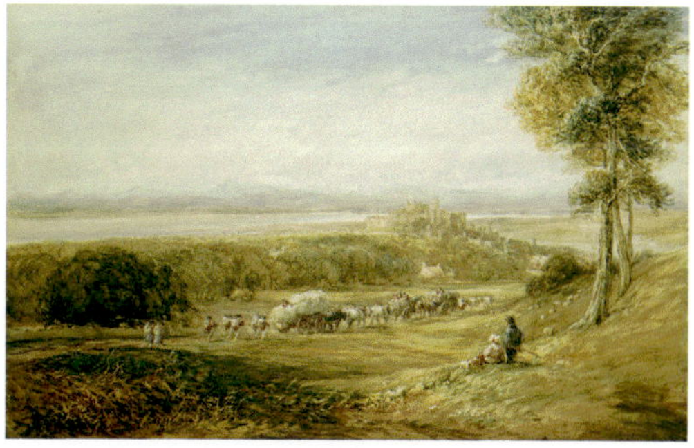

fig. 23. David Cox, *Lancaster: Peace and War*, 1842, watercolour and gum arabic, with gouache over pencil on wove paper, 49.7 x 76 cm, Art Institute of Chicago

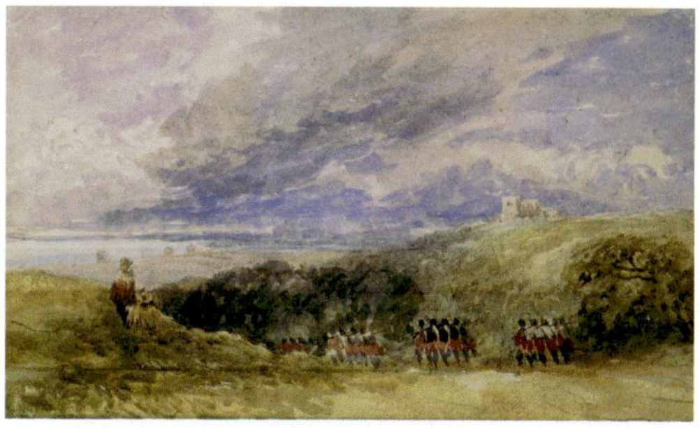

fig. 24. David Cox, *Peace and War: Lympne Church and Castle*, c. 1838, watercolour over black chalk on 'Scotch' paper, 28 x 46.2 cm, Birmingham Museums and Art Gallery

LL 3833

LL 3948

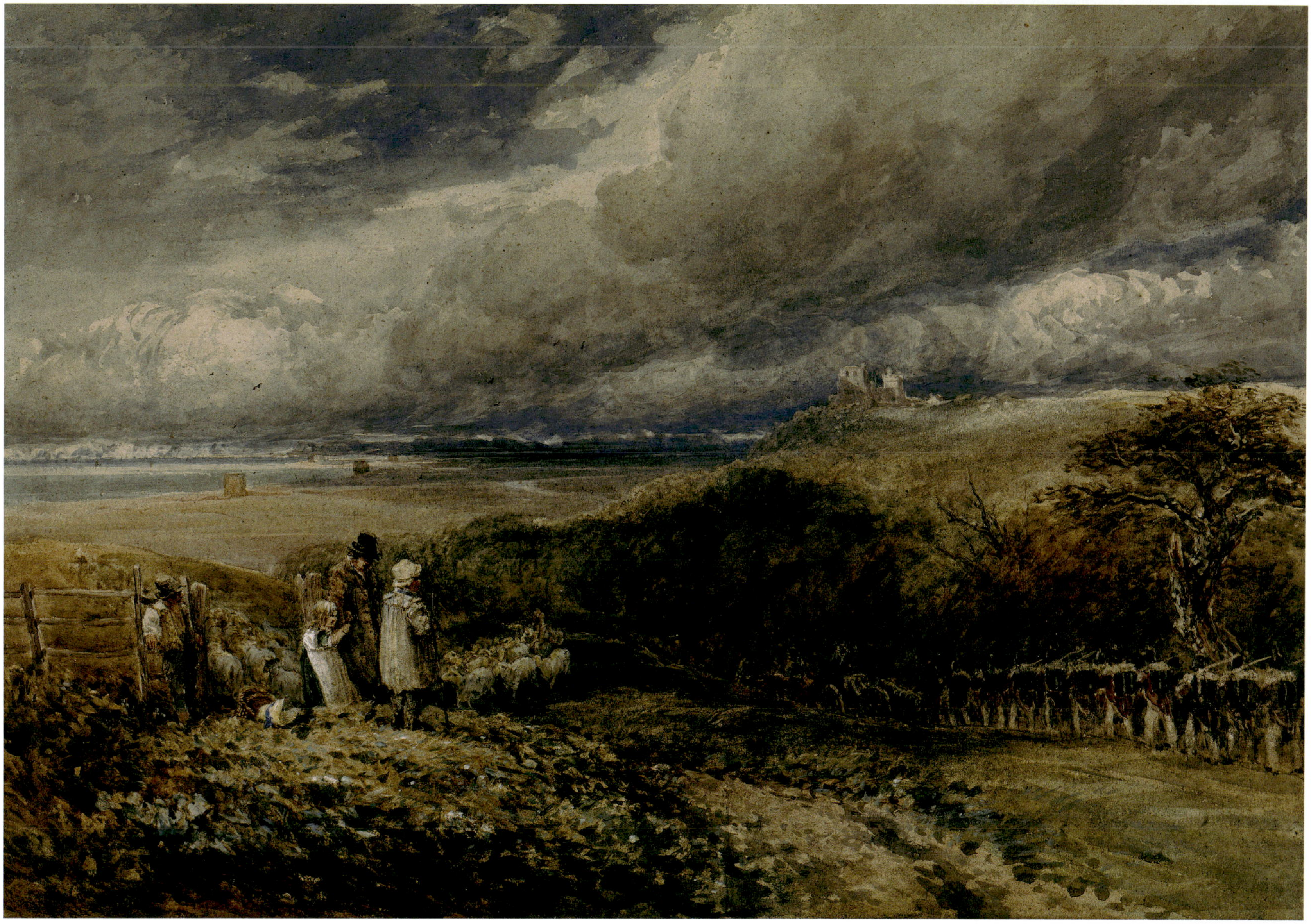

## AFTER DAVID COX

### Barden Tower, Yorkshire[316]

LL 3838 (WHL 826, HH 338)

Watercolour with gum arabic, with touches of gouache and black chalk over pencil on wove paper
24.6 x 33.5 cm (sight)
Date: probably c. 1903–10

Inscr: David Cox. 1846. (watercolour, bottom left)

Annot: Barden Tower on the Wharfe / Property of J. Orrock R.I (pencil, verso, upper centre [by James Orrock]); 39131 (pen and ink, verso, lower left)

Prov: bt. from James Orrock by Lever, 1910

This and the nine following watercolours are forgeries of the hand of David Cox (1783–1859), that is, works that attempt deliberately to deceive rather than just imitate.[317] There were a large number of forgeries of Cox Senior's work being produced by the end of the nineteenth century and several different hands have been identified. Many of the Lady Lever examples are by one hand in particular, the so-called 'pink Cox faker' (the watercolours have sometimes faded to a pinkish tone) or the 'soft hand' (the outlines in the watercolours have been intentionally softened in imitation of Cox's later style). They all bear what purports to be the signature of David Cox and are inscribed and dated in the 1840s. In common with other forgeries by the 'soft hand' they have many of the features of Cox's later style, including the imitation of a signature from his later period, where the final 'd' arches back over the Christian name; although in the case of the Lady Lever works these signatures are often excessively laboured.[318]

In the case of the first five works, the Cox prototypes on which the copyist based their work have been discovered. In several cases (such as the present work and LL 3952 below) the copyist probably used a published or engraved image to work from, and there are other instances (for example LL 3844 below) where the work may have been copied from an original watercolour.

All the Lady Lever Cox forgeries were acquired by Lever in 1910 from the artist, collector and dealer James Orrock (see pp. xiv–xvii, 146–49), together with three genuine Coxes (LL 3833, LL 3836 and LL 3957), and following Lever's purchase from him in 1904 of Cox's fine late watercolour, *Peace and War* (LL 3948).[319] In common with many other of the dubious paintings that Lever acquired from Orrock, the provenance of these 'Cox' works remains obscure. Alex Kidson has suggested with regard to some of these paintings that Orrock had painted them himself 'or employed associates to paint [them] for him or had obtained [them] earlier from known forgers'.[320] Suggestions linking Orrock's name with forgery are not new and have been described elsewhere.[321] Most recently, Charles Nugent has argued that the circumstantial evidence strongly points to Orrock having had access to 'some sort of factory of anonymous artists' which was producing Cox fakes.[322]

LL 3838 is a copy after an original composition by Cox, *Barden Tower*, signed and dated 1836 (British Museum, fig. 25). The work was illustrated in *The Studio*'s Special Summer Number of 1903, and it is most likely that the copyist used this source.[323] The copyist's weak draughtsmanship is revealed in comparing his painting of the dogs, figures and horses with that of the original and he has not even attempted to depict Cox's sky. Interestingly, the forger has chosen to inscribe and date the work 1846 in keeping with the dates of the rest of the Lady Lever copies.

Cox produced many drawings of the famous beauty spot Barden Tower when he visited Yorkshire on numerous occasions from the 1830s until c. 1847. On his 1846 trip to Yorkshire, the signed date of this work, Solly reports that Cox went to Barden three times.[324]

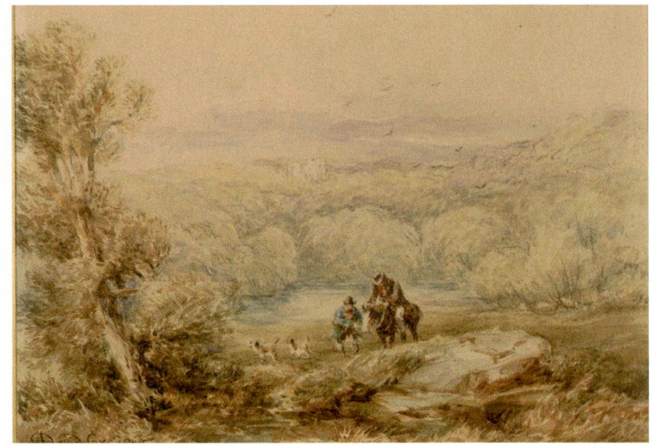

LL 3838

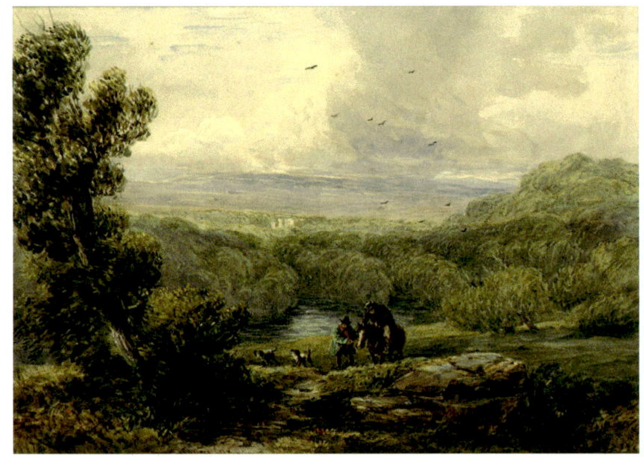

fig. 25. David Cox, *Barden Tower*, 1836, watercolour on paper, 19.9 x 27 cm, © The Trustees of the British Museum

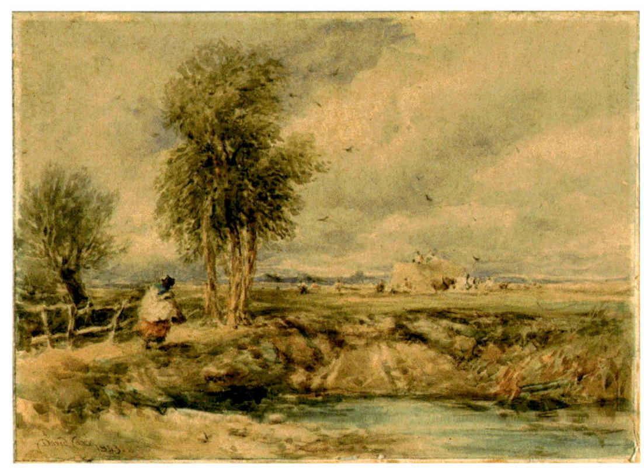

LL 3839

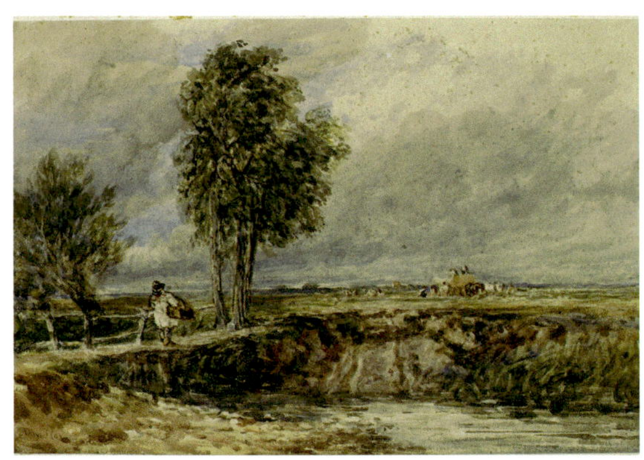

fig. 26. David Cox, *Crossing the Bridge: A Windy Day*, 1842, watercolour on 'Scotch' paper, 37 x 54.5 cm, Birmingham Museums and Art Gallery

316 The full title given in the WHL Inventory is *Barden Tower, Yorkshire, and a farmer on horseback, and figure with two dogs in foreground*.

317 I am grateful for the help of Andrew Wyld, Charles Nugent, Scott Wilcox and Stephen Wildman with the attribution of these works.

318 This discussion is informed by Charles Nugent, 'David Cox Jr and the Problem of Cox Forgeries', in Scott Wilcox (ed.), *Sun, Wind, and Rain: The Art of David Cox* (exh. cat., New Haven, Yale Center for British Art and Birmingham, Birmingham Museums and Art Gallery, 2008–09), especially pp. 138–39.

319 Charles Nugent has pointed out that Orrock's tactic was to tempt the buyer with genuine works, and include forgeries alongside them as part of the purchase; ibid.

320 Alex Kidson, *Earlier British Paintings in the Lady Lever Art Gallery* (Liverpool, 1999), p. 13.

321 The assertion that Orrock forged at least one Turner was made by W. G. Rawlinson and quoted by C. J. Holmes, *Self and Partners* (London, 1936), pp. 207–08. For the suggestion that Orrock had a 'studio' that produced Constable forgeries, see C. Rhyne, 'Constable Drawings and Watercolours in the Collections of Mr and Mrs Paul Mellon and the Yale Center for British Art', *Master Drawings* (winter 1987), pp. 406–07.

322 Nugent, 'David Cox Jr'; he is not suggesting that Orrock himself produced these forgeries, as his own watercolour style is known from signed works.

323 Charles Holme (ed.), 'Masters of English Landscape Painting', *The Studio*, Special Number (summer 1903), pl. 31.

324 Solly, *Life of David Cox*, p. 143.

## The Hayfield[325]
LL 3839 (WHL 817, HH 345)

Watercolour with touches of gouache and black chalk on oatmeal paper
23.7 x 33.2 cm (trimmed irreg.)
Date: probably c. 1897–1910

Inscr: David Cox / 1843. (watercolour, bottom left)

Prov: [?] James Orrock, 1897; bt. from Orrock by Lever, 1910

Exh: [?] London, Earl's Court, *Victorian Era Exhibition*, 1897 (cat. 178 or 179, as *The Hayfield*)[326]

LL 3839 is a copy after an original watercolour by Cox (Birmingham Museums and Art Gallery, fig. 26). The original was owned by J. Arthur Kenrick in 1925;[327] it is not known where it was before that date and it is tempting to think that before 1910 it could have belonged to James Orrock and that he could have provided it for the forger (see also LL 3844) who used it to make a copy for the 1897 *Victorian Era Exhibition*. Nevertheless, the original was also illustrated in *The Studio*'s Special Summer Number of 1903, and it is also conceivable that the copyist used this source.[328] Like many of the Lady Lever 'Cox' forgeries, the work has a heavily laboured signature.

## On the Beach[329]
LL 3842 (WHL 828, HH 334)

Watercolour with touches of gouache over pencil on wove paper
15.1 x 19.3 cm (sight)
Date: mid-nineteenth to early twentieth century

Inscr: David Cox (watercolour, bottom right)

Prov: bt. from James Orrock by Lever, 1910

LL 3842 has been recorded as inscribed with a date of 1847, in addition to the signature, although it is not possible to see this with the current mount in place.[330] The work is a direct copy of an original drawing by David Cox, now only known in its engraved form by Robert Brandard as *Sea Coast*, which was produced in 1834.[331]

## Valle Crucis Abbey[332]
LL 3844 (WHL 819, HH 348)

Watercolour with touches of gouache over pencil on [?] oatmeal paper
22 x 30.2 cm
Date: possibly early twentieth century

Inscr: David Cox. / 1847. (watercolour, bottom right)

Prov: bt. from James Orrock by Lever, 1910

LL 3844 is a direct copy after a sepia wash drawing now in Birmingham Museums and Art Gallery (fig. 27)[333] (a variant of the subject was used as an illustration for Plate XI of Thomas Roscoe's *Wanderings and Excursions in North Wales* of 1836).[334] The work was bequeathed to Birmingham in 1927 by the collector James Richardson Holliday. Charles Nugent has observed that 'It is not known where the Birmingham drawing was in 1910, but it is tempting to believe that Orrock owned it at that date and provided it for the forger, and later sold it to Holliday'.[335]

Valle Crucis Abbey, or the 'Valley of the Cross', is named after Eliseg's Pillar, a ninth-century memorial cross that stands close to the Abbey near Llangollen in north-east Wales. The Abbey was founded in 1201 by the Cistercian order but fell into decline after the dissolution of the monasteries in 1538. The ruins of Valle Crucis became a subject for many nineteenth-century watercolourists including David Cox, who depicted the Abbey on a number of occasions throughout his career and exhibited watercolours of the subject at the SPWC in 1826, 1837 and 1841.

## Changing Pastures[336]
LL 3952 (WHL 797, HH 339)

Watercolour with touches of gouache over pencil on wove paper
16.9 x 26.4 cm
Date: probably c. 1903–10

Inscr: David Cox. / 1847. (watercolour, bottom left)

Prov: bt. from James Orrock by Lever, 1910

LL 3952 is a direct copy of the oil painting *Changing Pasture*, signed and dated 1850 (location unknown).[337] The work was illustrated in *The Studio*'s Special Summer Number of 1903 and it is likely that the copyist used this as a source.[338]

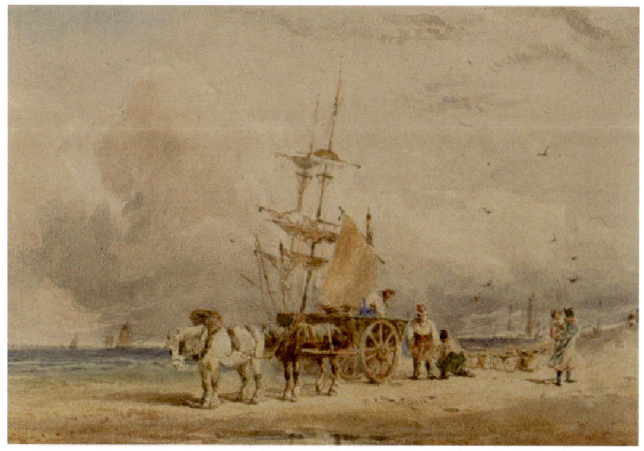

LL 3842

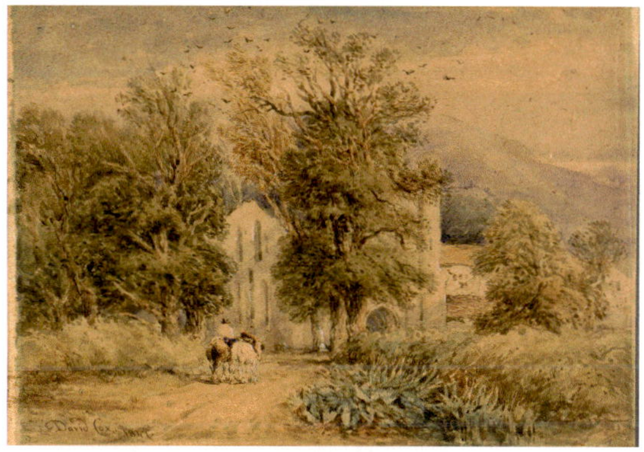

LL 3844

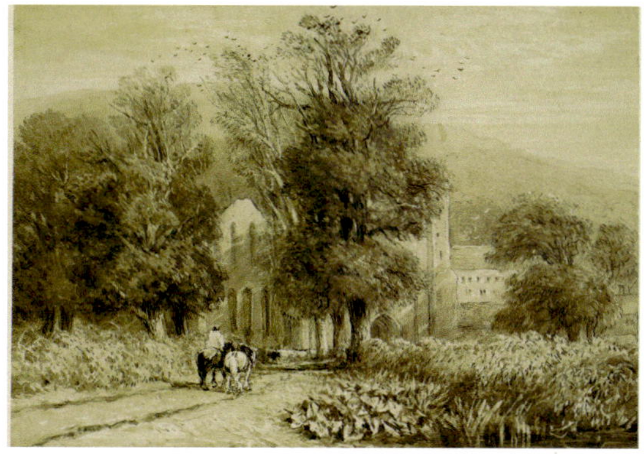

fig. 27. David Cox, *Valle Crucis Abbey*, late 1830s, sepia wash on wove paper, 25.7 x 34.8 cm, Birmingham Museums and Art Gallery

LL 3952

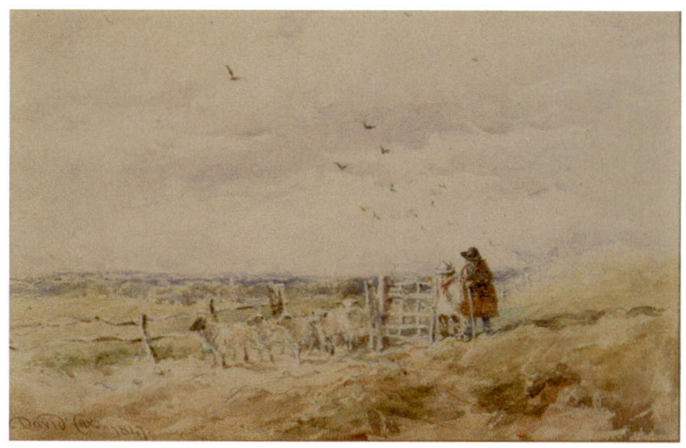

325 The title given in the WHL Inventory is *A rustic bridge in Wales, with woman crossing to a hayfield – windy day*. See also LLAG files: an unidentified note in the object file points out, 'but there is no indication that it depicts a Welsh scene. It is one of Cox's ordinary hayfield subjects, and the "bridge" is merely a rustic fence beside a pond and can scarcely represent a bridge, even indirectly. James Orrock has written in ink on the backboard of the picture "The Hayfield" [no longer visible] and this might be used as a title.' The title *The Hayfield* was used in *The Studio*'s illustration of the original watercolour.

326 Two watercolours were exhibited with the title *The Hayfield* as cats. 178 and 179 in the *Victorian Era Exhibition* of 1897. As Orrock was identified as the owner of these loans, it seems likely that these were LL 3839 and LL 3951.

327 It was presented to Birmingham Museums and Art Gallery in 1925.

328 Holme (ed.), 'Masters of English Landscape Painting', pl. 54. In 1903 the work was with Agnew's.

329 The WHL Inventory gives the title as *On the Beach, with figures loading a cart drawn by two horses, a sailing vessel beyond*. The work has more recently been known as *On the Beach, Hastings*, but this appears to be based on an assertion in the object file. See LLAG files, note by A. C. Tait based on Solly, *Life of David Cox*, p. 78.

330 LLAG files: recorded by A. C. Tait in object file.

331 The engraving is entitled *Sea Coast: From an Original Drawing by D. Cox*. There is an impression of the print in the British Museum.

332 LL 3844 was entitled in the WHL Inventory, *A road with a ruin and trees and a man with two horses*.

333 See Wildman, *David Cox 1783–1859*, illus. p. 66 (cat. 39).

334 Cox supplied half of the illustrations for this volume, which were engraved alongside works by Cattermole and Copley Fielding. This and a later companion volume on South Wales were often used by Cox forgers as a source of material; see Nugent, 'David Cox Jr'.

335 Ibid., p. 138.

336 The WHL Inventory gives the full title as *Changing pastures, two figures with sheep passing a gateway*.

337 There is another version of this subject, dated 1847, in Birmingham Museums and Art Gallery.

338 Holme (ed.), 'Masters of English Landscape Painting', pl. 8.

## 'DAVID COX'

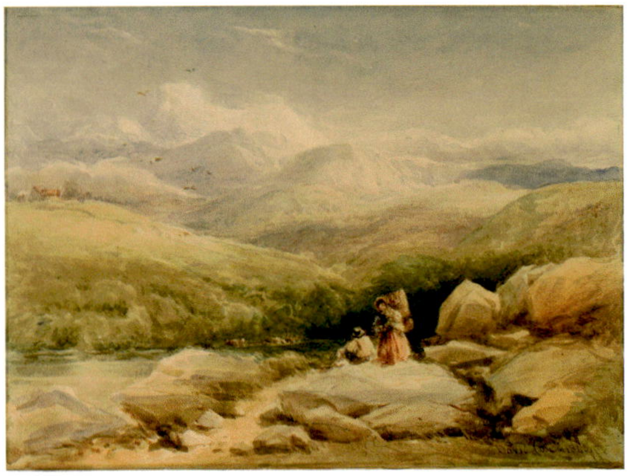

LL 3834

### In the Welsh Hills[339]
LL 3834 (WHL 789, HH 361)

Watercolour with extra gum arabic with touches of gouache over pencil on wove paper
26.7 x 35.8 cm (trimmed irreg.)
Date: mid-nineteenth to early twentieth century

Inscr: David Cox. 1845. (watercolour, bottom right)
Prov: bt. from James Orrock by Lever, 1910
Exh: Swansea, Glynn Vivian Art Gallery, *David Cox (1783–1859)*, 1953 (cat. 50)

Unlike the five preceding works, there does not appear to be an exact prototype for this one. LL 3834 is a mixture of various Cox compositions.[340]

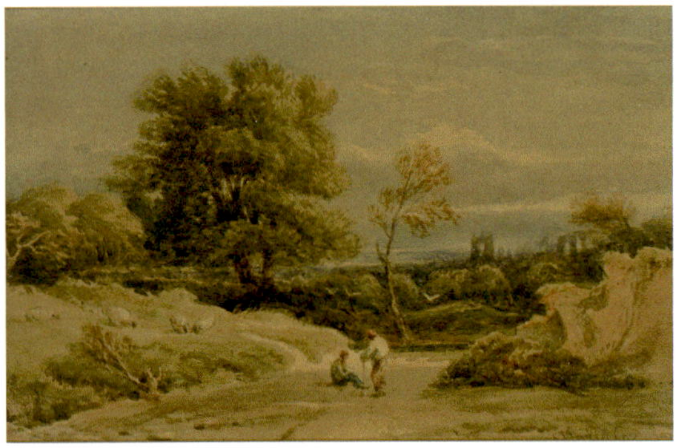

LL 3837

### Landscape with ruins in the distance[341]
LL 3837 (WHL 790, HH 401)

Watercolour with extra gum arabic over pencil on wove paper
14.8 x 23.7 cm (sight)
Date: mid-nineteenth to early twentieth century

Inscr: David Cox. 1846 (watercolour, bottom right)
Prov: bt. from James Orrock by Lever, 1910

Cox did produce watercolours of classical style landscapes but not as late as the 1840s, when this work is dated. The copyist has here tried to imitate Cox's early style.

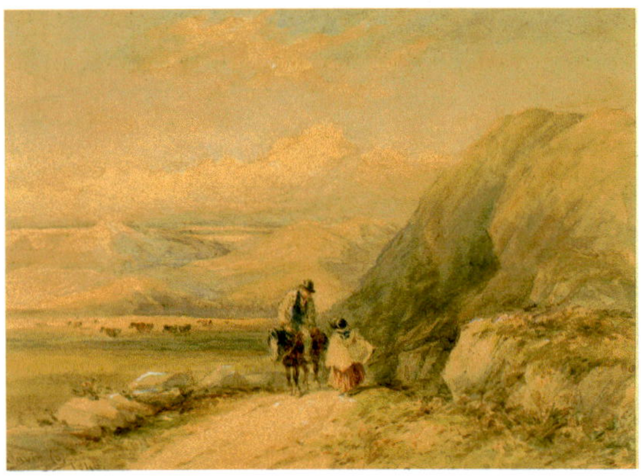

LL 3843

### Friendship in the Welsh Hills[342]
LL 3843 (WHL 822, HH 346)

Watercolour with extra gum arabic and touches of gouache over pencil on [?] oatmeal paper
22.6 x 30.6 cm (sight)
Date: mid-nineteenth to early twentieth century

Inscr: David Cox. / 1848. (watercolour, bottom left)
Prov: bt. from James Orrock by Lever, 1910

The motif of a female wayfarer asking the way from a man on a horse was one used by Cox in a number of pictures.[343] In this case, no work with exactly the same composition has been located.

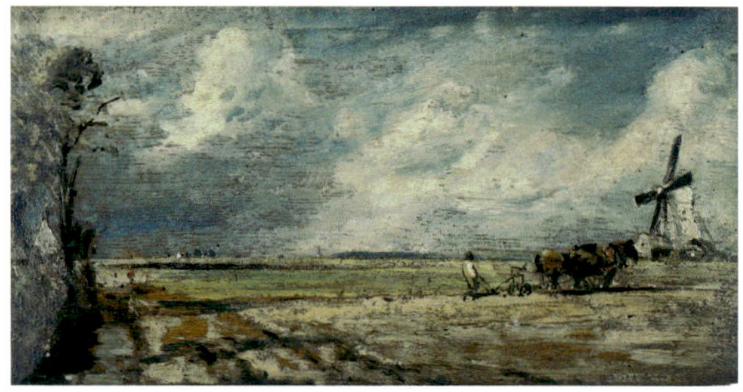

fig. 28. John Constable, *Spring. East Bergholt Common*, c. 1809–16, oil on panel, 19 x 36.2 cm, V&A Images/Victoria and Albert Museum

LL 3947

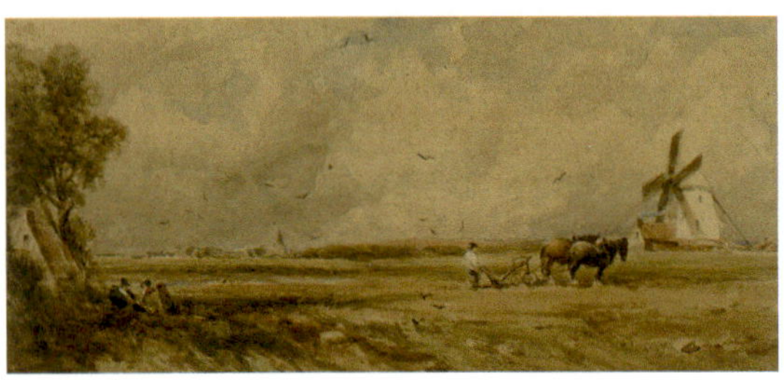

### Landscape with windmill and man ploughing
LL 3947 (WHL 821, HH 363)

Watercolour with extra gum arabic and touches of gouache, with scratching out over pencil and black chalk on oatmeal paper
21.8 x 51.9 cm (sight)
Date: mid-nineteenth to early twentieth century; probably by 1897

Inscr: David Cox. 1847. (watercolour, bottom right)
Prov: [?] James Orrock, 1897; bt. from Orrock by Lever, 1910
Exh: [?] London, Earl's Court, *Victorian Era Exhibition*, 1897 (cat. 193, as *Ploughing*);[344] [?] Windsor, Eton College, exhibition title unknown, 1933 (cat. 9);[345] Birmingham, Birmingham Museum and Art Gallery, *Centenary Exhibition of the Works of David Cox 1783–1859*, 1959 (cat. 92)
Lit: F. Gordon Roe, *Cox The Master* (Leigh-on-Sea, 1946), p. 155; Trenchard Cox, *David Cox* (London, 1947), p. 102, illus. p. 111

LL 3947 is a direct copy of a print after a Constable oil sketch, *Spring. East Bergholt Common* (Victoria & Albert Museum, fig. 28).[346] The sketch was engraved by David Lucas for *English Landscape Scenery*: LL 3947 includes the rooks that were added by Constable at the final proof stage of the mezzotint.[347] *English Landscape Scenery* was first published in June 1830, with another edition in 1832, but the mezzotint continued to be reproduced in publications well into the early twentieth century and beyond. If, as seems likely, LL 3947 was the *Ploughing* exhibited at the *Victorian Era Exhibition* in 1897 then the work would have been completed by this date. LL 3947 is by a different hand from the majority of the other Cox copies in the Lady Lever collection.

339 The title given in the WHL Inventory is *In the Welsh Hills, with two figures and cows in a stream.*
340 Scott Wilcox, verbally, March 2006.
341 The WHL Inventory gives the full title as *Pastoral Landscape, with figures on a sand road – summer.* As this description is rather vague, and it does not really look as if the scene is summer, it has been renamed for this catalogue for the purposes of clarity.
342 The WHL Inventory gives the full title as *Friendship in the Welsh Hills, a farmer on horseback chatting to a woman walking beside him.*
343 See, for example, *Asking the Way – "Take the left Road"* (private collection), and *Keep the Left Road* (Birmingham Museums and Art Gallery), both illus. in Gérald Bauer, *David Cox 1783–1859* (Arcueil, 2000), pp. 60 and 121.
344 *Ploughing* (cat. 193) was exhibited in 1897 as belonging to James Orrock; LL 3947 is likely to be this work.
345 This exhibition is cited in the LLAG files, but there is no record of it in Eton College's archives. The exhibition may have been held in the Drawing Schools (the school's art department) but it is not recorded in the *Eton Chronicle* (the school's magazine) for 1933 . I am grateful to Penny Hatfield, Eton College's archivist, for providing this information.
346 Reynolds, *Catalogue of the Constable Collection*, p. 91 (cat. 122), illus. pl. 94.
347 Both oil sketch and the first published state of the print were illustrated in Andrew Shirley, *The Published Mezzotints of David Lucas after John Constable R.A.* (Oxford, 1930), illus. pl. VII, facing p. 164.

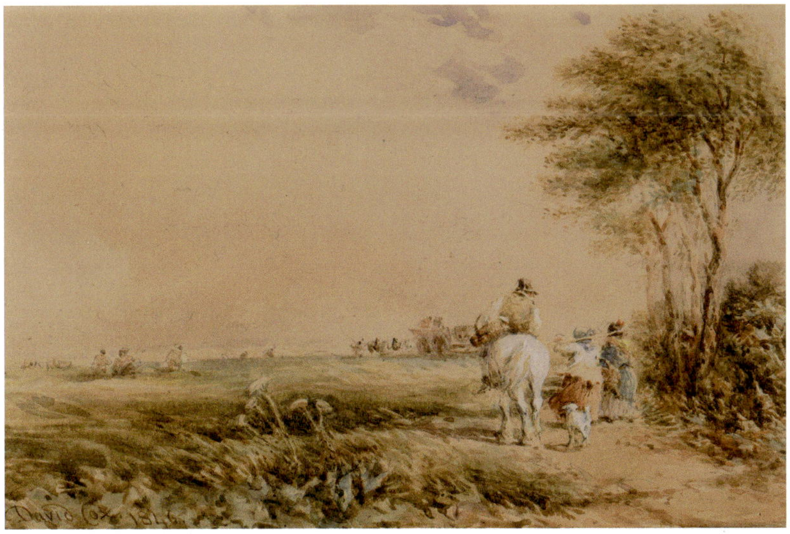

LL 3951

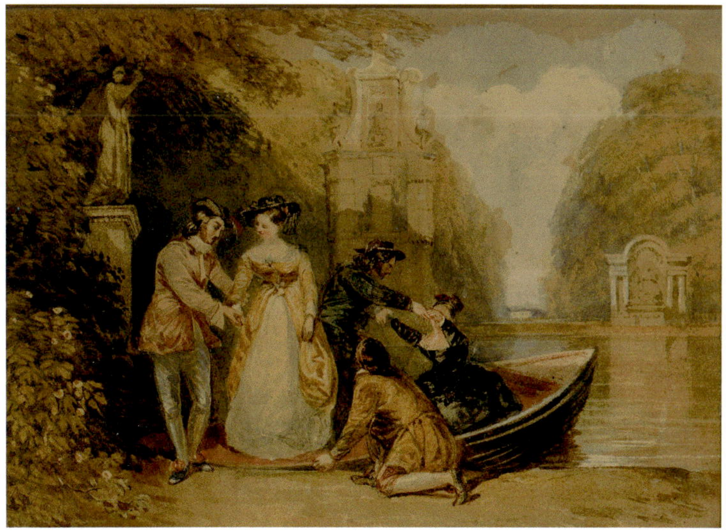

LL 3949

## ATTRIBUTED TO DAVID COX JUNIOR

1809 Dulwich, London–1885 London

### Going to the Hayfield[348]

LL 3951 (WHL 815, HH 347)

Watercolour with extra gum arabic, with touches of gouache over pencil on wove paper
18 x 27.5 cm (sight)
Date: late nineteenth to early twentieth century; probably by 1897

Inscr: David Cox. / 1846. (watercolour, bottom left)

Prov: [?] James Orrock, 1897; bt. from Orrock by Lever, 1910

Exh: [?] London, Earl's Court, *Victorian Era exhibition*, 1897 (cat. 178 or 179, as *The Hayfield*)[349]

Cox titled many of his works *Going to the Hayfield*, first exhibiting the subject at the SPWC in 1839; he used a similar composition repeatedly, returning to the motif of a man on a horse accompanied by two figures. It is therefore unsurprising that the same subject and motifs were chosen by Cox copyists. LL 3951 relates most closely to an oil painting of the subject dating from 1849, illustrated in Solly's *Memoir of the Life of David Cox* (published in 1873). It is possible that the copyist based his work on this published illustration.[350] If, as seems likely, LL 3951 was exhibited at the *Victorian Era Exhibition* in 1897 then the work would have been completed by this date.

### A Watteau scene, with figures landing from a boat[351]

LL 3949 (WHL 794, HH 395)

Watercolour with touches of gouache and extra gum arabic over pencil on wove paper
19.7 x 26.7 cm (sight)
Date: 1830s

Annot: David Cox / 18[?3]9 (watercolour, bottom left)

Prov: bt. from James Orrock by Lever, 1910

Exh: Birmingham, Birmingham Museum and Art Gallery, *Centenary Exhibition of the Works of David Cox 1783–1859*, 1959 (cat. 64)

David Cox Junior was the only son of David Cox (1783–1859). The family moved to Hereford in 1814 where young David was taught to paint and draw by his father, accompanying him on sketching trips to France and Belgium in 1826 and 1829. The younger Cox exhibited four watercolours at the Royal Academy, the first in 1827. In 1841 he took over the family teaching practice and in the same year was elected an associate of the New Society of Painters in Water-Colours, only changing his allegiance to the SPWC (the Old Water-Colour Society) in 1848. Cox Junior's reputation was inevitably overshadowed by that of his father, and his work has often been unfairly dismissed as little more than 'banal prettiness'.[352]

The younger Cox generally signed his work 'Junior' but there were occasions when he did not, and these cases, where they do not bear the stamp commissioned by the artist's heirs, can create problems of attribution.[353] LL 3949, which is signed 'David Cox', is a case in point. It was purchased by Lever as David Cox Senior, but more recently it has been attributed to his son and the suggestion made that the signature (which is in an unknown hand) has been added.[354] Historical costume pieces such as LL 3949 were a feature of both Cox Senior and Junior's work: the elder Cox, for example, produced a number of watercolours in the 1830s of romantic re-creations of life at Haddon Hall, Derbyshire. A combination of subject-matter and style suggest that LL 3949 may be by Cox Junior. In the central middle ground of LL 3949 is the Diana Fountain at Hampton Court, designed originally by Inigo Jones in the mid-1630s.[355] It can hardly be coincidental that Cox Junior published a book of lithographs in 1840, *Six Views of Hampton Court*, which contained similar costume pieces set within the grounds of the palace. In addition, although LL 3949 resembles the work of the elder Cox, the handling of the figures does not have the sureness of touch of Cox Senior's work. The work can be dated to the 1830s, before the emergence of the more detailed touch and richness of palette that characterised Cox Junior's watercolours from the 1840s, such as *Powis Castle* (Birmingham Museums and Art Gallery).

348 The WHL Inventory gives the title as *A Harvest scene with a man on a white horse, two women and a dog*.

349 Two watercolours were exhibited with the same title in this exhibition. As Orrock was identified as the owner of these loans, it seems likely that these were LL 3951 and LL 3839.

350 Solly, *Life of David Cox*, p. 197 and illus. facing p. 189, pl. xviii. It is described as dated 1849, measuring 28 x 34 in., and in the collection of Mr Mayou, Edgbaston, Birmingham.

351 1910 Inventory.

352 Trenchard Cox, *David Cox* (London, 1947), p. 118. For a discussion of Cox Junior's contemporary and subsequent reputation and a bibliographical summary, see Nugent, 'David Cox Jr', pp. 129–39.

353 In 1886, on the occasion of Cox Junior's studio sale held at Christie's, 14 and 15 April, the artist's widow and children commissioned the dealers John and William Vokins to make a stamp identifying his work. See Nugent, 'David Cox Jr', p. 133.

354 LL 3949 was catalogued by Tatlock, p. 129, as by David Cox Senior. It was also attributed to David Cox Senior in Birmingham's Cox exhibition of 1959. The attribution to David Cox Junior was proposed by Charles Nugent and Andrew Wyld, verbally, May 2005.

355 The high rusticated base seen on the fountain in Cox's work was added in 1712. For the history of the fountain, see John Harris, 'The Diana Fountain at Hampton Court', *The Burlington Magazine*, vol. 3 (July 1969), pp. 444–47.

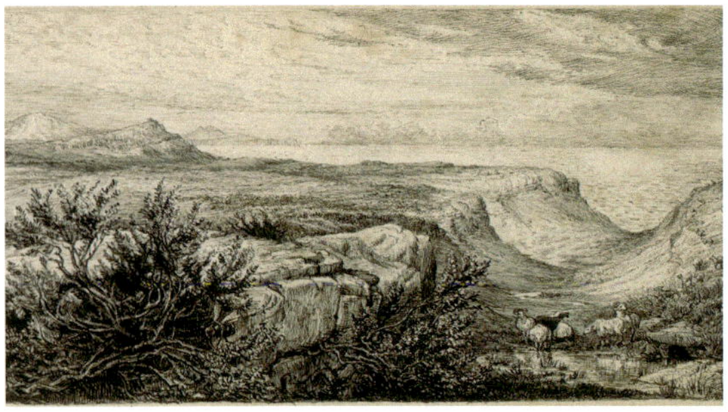

LL 2958

## EDWARD W. COX

1826 place of birth unknown–1899 Birkenhead, Wirral, Merseyside[356]

### On Jura's Heath

LL 2958

Pen and ink, watercolour with gum arabic on wove paper
15.7 x 30.8 cm (trimmed irreg.)
Date: mid- to late nineteenth century

Annot: On Jura's Heath / pen drawing by E.W Cox, F.S.A / The Bebington Antiquary (ink, label on back of frame)

Prov: unknown[357]

Cox was a local historian and antiquarian, and a regular contributor to the *Transactions of the Historic Society of Lancashire and Cheshire.* He was also an amateur artist and some of his works were engraved for these volumes in the 1880s.

It seems unlikely that Cox based the work on a visit to the island of Jura, in the Hebrides. The title may be a quotation from the poem *The Mermaid* by John Leyden (1775–1811) which includes the lines: 'On Jura's heath how sweetly swell / The murmurs of the mountain bee'.

356 Obituary in *The Liverpool Mercury*, 3 February 1899, p. 9.

357 LLAG files: LL 2958 is described as 'found in the gallery'. The work was not included in Tatlock's 1928 catalogue, and therefore may have been transferred to the gallery's collection from one of Lever's homes after this date. The work was not accessioned until after the Lady Lever Art Gallery was transferred to the care of Merseyside County Council in 1978.

## JOHN ROBERT COZENS

1752 London–1797 London[358]

### The Gulf of Salerno: Raito from Vietri[359]

LL 3953 (WHL 770, HH 410)

Watercolour over pencil on wove paper laid down on original wash-line mount
37 x 52.9 cm (image), 40 x 56.1 cm (original mount)
Date: 1790

Inscr: Jn.o Cozens.1790 (ink, bottom left on mount)

Annot: Mr Hawkins / 16032 (ink over pencil, verso)

Prov: bt. from James Orrock by Lever, 1910

Exh: London, Special Art Palace, *Franco-British Exhibition*, 1908 (cat. 492, as *Coast Scene*)

Lit: C. F. Bell and T. Girtin, 'The Drawings and Sketches of John Robert Cozens: A Catalogue with an Historical Introduction', *Walpole Society*, vol. 23 (1935), pp. 59–60

John Robert Cozens was given lessons in drawing by his father, the artist, theorist and drawing master Alexander Cozens (1717–86). The younger Cozens exhibited landscape drawings at the Society of Artists annually between 1767 and 1771. A recently discovered album from this early period reveals that he made landscape studies from sites around London, as well as a brief trip to Derbyshire in 1772. In 1776 Cozens visited Switzerland and Italy with the classical scholar and antiquarian Richard Payne Knight (1751–1824), and many of his finest watercolour views from that trip convey the grandeur and the sublimity of the mountainous scenery. In 1782 he embarked on his second trip to Italy, this time as one of the entourage of the writer and wealthy patron of the arts William Beckford (1760–1844). Little is known of Cozens's career over the decade following his return to London in 1783, although he produced a number of versions of earlier Swiss and Italian compositions as well as rarer views of English subjects. By 1794 Cozens was suffering from an incurable mental illness and spent the rest of his life under the care of Dr Thomas Monro.

Cozens filled at least seven sketchbooks while travelling in Italy as draughtsman to William Beckford between 4 June 1782 and 27 October 1783.[360] Although many were later worked up for other patrons, these pencil sketches with grey and blue ink washes were produced with the primary intention of providing nearly a hundred finished watercolours for Beckford.[361] LL 3953 is based on a sketch the artist made on 23 September 1782 inscribed 'From Vietri', which was squared up for transfer (fig. 29).[362] The view is of the buildings of the Marina di Vietri in the foreground; in the middle distance to the right is the village of Raito, halfway up the slope of Monte Pertuso.[363] Cozens and Beckford had parted company earlier in September in Naples, but the artist continued to travel the countryside recording sites his patron had requested, which included the dramatic coastline between Vietri and Salerno. The same sketchbook contains a number of other views of the coastline from subsequent days.

The Lady Lever work is one of four known finished watercolour versions based on the same sketch: the others are in the Tate (fig. 30), the Laing Art Gallery, Newcastle upon Tyne, and the Hickman Bacon collection.[364] They are of a comparable size to the Lady Lever work and are broadly similar in composition, although there are slight variations, for example, among the trees in the right foreground (in both the Hickman Bacon and Lady Lever works these are extended up to the picture plane). The works are broadly similar in colour, all employing Cozens's characteristically restricted palette of soft blues, greens and greys, with touches of ochre on the roofs of buildings, but it is difficult to make an instructive comparison as LL 3953 has substantially faded.

As with other popular compositions based on his Italian and Swiss trip, only one of these watercolours belonged to Beckford; the rest were presumably worked up for other patrons. It is unlikely, given the late date inscribed on the work, that LL 3953 was the one done for

358 No record has been found of Cozens's place of birth. However, it was likely to have been in London as his father was employed as drawing master to Christ's Hospital between 1750 and 1754 and therefore must have been resident in London in 1752. See Kim Sloan, 'Cozens, John Robert (1752–1797)', *ODNB*, vol. 13, pp. 886–89.

359 The full title given to LL 3953 in Bell and Girtin is: *Part of Vietri and Raito (which is on the brow of the hill on the right with Monte Pertuso above it, castle and House-tops at Marina di Vietri in the foreground)*: C. F. Bell and T. Girtin, 'The Drawings and Sketches of John Robert Cozens: A Catalogue with an Historical Introduction', *Walpole Society*, vol. 23 (1935), p. 59. The work was titled by Tatlock, p. 71, as *A Swiss Lake-Veitri* [*sic*]; this derived from James Orrock whose 1910 Inventory listed it as *A Swiss Lake*.

360 Bell and Girtin, 'Drawings and Sketches of John Robert Cozens', p. 4. The sketchbooks are now in the Whitworth Art Gallery, Manchester.

361 Beckford eventually tired of these watercolours, selling them at auction at Christie's, 10 April 1805.

362 The verso of the sketch has a detailed topographical description in Cozens's handwriting.

363 LLAG files: letter from Bell, 7 September 1933.

364 The Tate version is the only one apart from LL 3953 that is signed. The Laing Art Gallery version is illustrated in *The Old Water-Colour Society's Club: Twentieth Annual Volume* (1942), pl. 8. The Hickman Bacon version is reproduced in colour in Eric Shanes, *British Watercolours from the Hickman Bacon Collection* (exh. cat., Tokyo, Odakyu Grand Gallery, and Osaka, Navio Museum of Art, 1990–91), p. 33 (cat. 14).

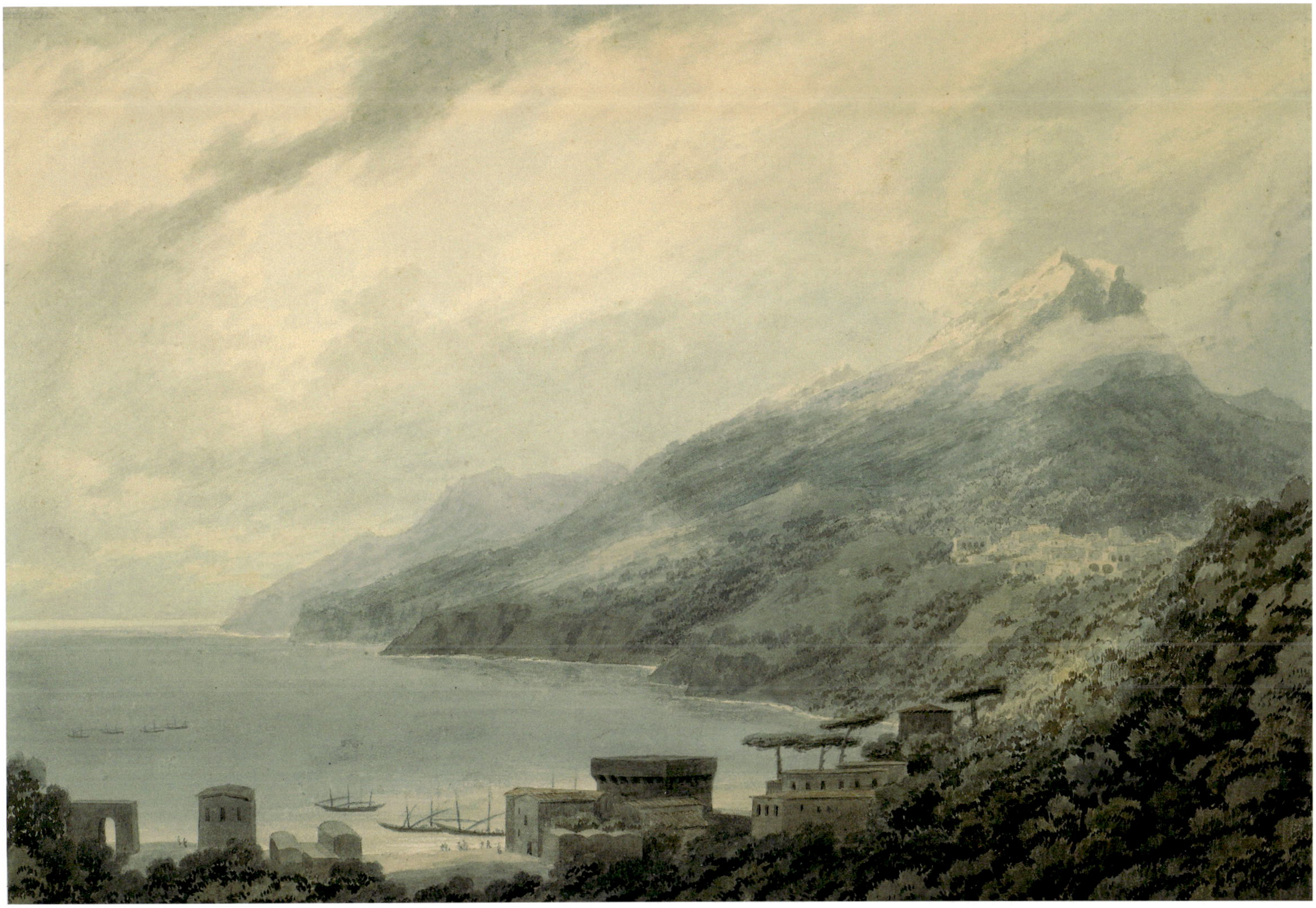

LL 3953

Beckford but it is not known who may have commissioned it.[365]

LL 3953 is characteristic of Cozens's use of a softer, tonal system drawing on a palette of greys and grey-greens which became standard for the artist in the years around 1790 and contrasts with more richly coloured Beckford compositions such as his view of *Lake Albano and Castel Gandolfo* (Leeds City Art Gallery). It was this subtle tonal contrast that enabled the artist to evoke space and atmosphere and represented one of his substantial contributions to the development of watercolour painting. A comparison with other versions of the watercolour, for example, the Tate's version, suggests that the sky in LL 3953, now considerably faded, was once an important feature of the composition, and far more evocative of atmospheric effects.

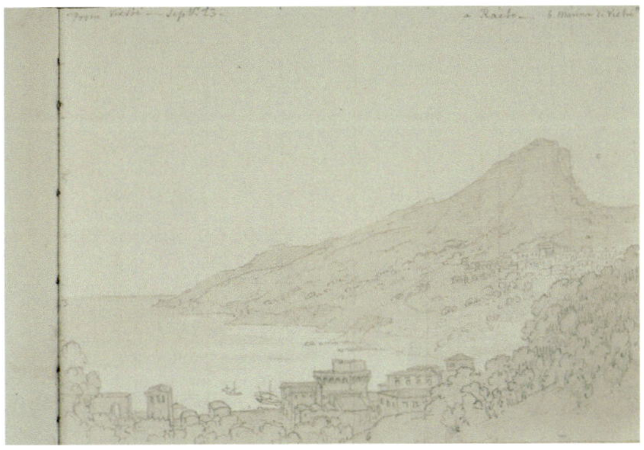

fig. 29

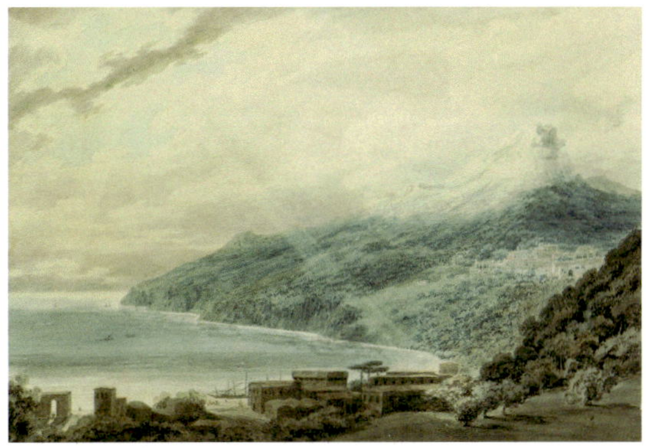

fig. 30

There is a copy of the composition in the Victoria & Albert Museum that has been attributed to Girtin.[366]

fig. 29. John Robert Cozens, *The Gulf of Salerno: Raito from Vietri*, 1782, pencil and grey watercolour on paper, 17.8 x 24.1 cm, Whitworth Art Gallery, Manchester

fig. 30. John Robert Cozens, *The Gulf of Salerno: Raito from Vietri*, c. 1790, watercolour over pencil on paper, 37.1 x 53.7 cm, © Tate, London, 2009

365 It is unclear which version might have been owned by Beckford. Bell stated that the Hickman Bacon work was Beckford's but does not give any evidence for this; LLAG files: letter from Bell, 7 September 1933.

366 This work was described in Bell and Girtin, 'Drawings and Sketches of John Robert Cozens', p. 60 (cat. 270) as a copy by an unknown artist bought at the C. R. Leslie sale, Christie's, 27 April 1860 (lot 398) when it was catalogued as a view in Sicily by Cozens. The suggested attribution to Girtin, of which there is a note in an unidentified hand in LLAG files, is also recorded on a label on the modern mount, recto, lower left, V&A No. (FA 498).

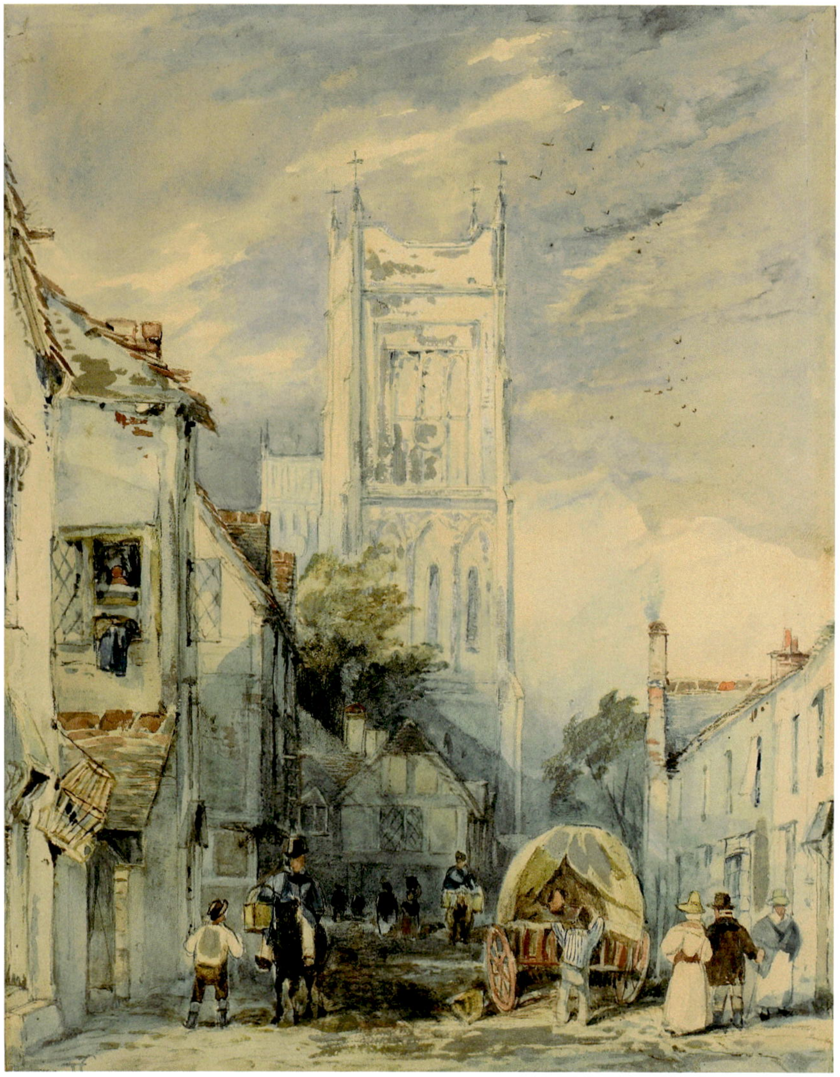

LL 3846

## THOMAS CRESWICK
1811 Sheffield–1869 London

**Street Scene with Church Tower**
LL 3846 (WHL 275, H 389)

Watercolour with touches of gouache on wove paper
23.3 x 17.8 cm
Date: possibly 1830s

Inscr: TC [monogram] (watercolour, bottom left)

Prov: in Lever's collection by 1912[367]

Creswick painted landscapes in both oil and watercolour, studying under Joseph Vincent Barber in Birmingham, where his contributions to the exhibitions of the Birmingham Society of Arts in the mid-1820s attracted considerable attention. He moved to London in 1828, where he showed two paintings at the Royal Academy that year. He exhibited at the Academy until his death, being elected an associate in 1842 and a full member in 1851. Creswick was also known as a book illustrator and from c. 1838 was one of the first members of the Etching Club.

LL 3846 may be compared stylistically with Creswick's oil, *Ballymahon, County Longford*, dated 1836 (in the artist's hand) (Sotheby's, 10 July, 1973, lot 119), which is a similarly composed street scene, using the same narrow, portrait format, and which displays the same stocky figure-types. LL 3846 may be *A Street Scene* of 1831 exhibited at the *London International Exhibition* of 1873.[368] It has not been possible to identify the location, although it may be East Anglia.[369]

367 1912 Hill Inventory, valued at £15.

368 Thomas Oldham Barlow, *A Catalogue of the Works of Thomas Creswick, R.A., exhibited at the London International Exhibition, 1873* (London, 1873), p. 2 (cat. 3).

369 This suggestion has been made by Professor Christopher Wilson of University College London, email correspondence, June 2006.

## THOMAS RAFFLES DAVISON
1853 Stockton-on-Tees, Durham–1937 London

**Royal Marines Memorial, the Mall**
LL 3406 (WHL 2157)

Ink on paper laid down on board
40.8 x 28.1 cm (image), 45.6 x 33.2 cm (sheet)
Date: c. 1910

Inscr: T Raffles Davison delt (ink, bottom left, on image); ROYAL MARINES MEMORIAL IN THE MALL (ink, bottom left, beneath image); ADRIAN JONES SCULPTOR (ink, bottom right, beneath image)

Prov: bt. from the artist by Lever, 16 March 1915;[370] by descent to 3rd Viscount Leverhulme; presented by 3rd Viscount Leverhulme, 1986[371]

Raffles Davison was trained as an architect, but his skill as a draughtsman led him to spend most of his career travelling the country making his so-called 'rambling sketches'. He made some 15,000 of these, largely of architectural subjects.[372] Many of these pen-and-ink drawings ended up as illustrations in the weekly magazine *The British Architect*, of which he was editor for nearly forty years. He also made perspective drawings of projected buildings for other architects. In 1914 he took a leading part in the founding of the London Society, whose chief aim was to raise awareness among the general public about the future development of London as a city.

LL 3406–3407 and LL 3431–3436 are a selection of pen-and-ink drawings that Raffles Davison made of existing London monuments and public spaces. Although the WHL Inventory identifies them all as illustrations for 'Beautiful London', the article which Raffles Davison wrote in 1914 to launch the London Society, only one drawing (LL 3407) can be firmly linked to this. Like many of his drawings, they may have been used as illustrations in the weekly magazine *The British Architect*.

The drawings were purchased from Raffles Davison in 1915 and were the first of some hundred drawings that Lever purchased from the artist up until 1918. Fairly soon after this first purchase, Lever commissioned Raffles Davison to make illustrations of Port Sunlight, its buildings and village, which were published in 1916.[373] Raffles Davison also made drawings of the proposed Lady Lever Art Gallery, one of which was exhibited at the Royal Academy in

370 WHL Inventory. There is no invoice recording Lever's purchase of LL 3406-07 and LL 3431-36.

371 LLAG files. No correspondence appears to survive relating to the 3rd Viscount's gift of LL 3406-07 and LL 3431-36.

372 For Raffles Davison, see A. Stuart Gray, *Edwardian Architecture: A Biographical Dictionary* (London, 1985), p. 160; D. Barclay Niven and W. T. Plume, 'The Late T. Raffles Davison: Two Appreciations', *The Builder*, vol. 152 (14 May 1937), p. 1024; see also Gavin Stamp, *The Great Perspectivists* (London, 1982).

373 The WHL Inventory states that these were purchased by Lever from Raffles Davison, 9 January 1917. See T. Raffles Davison, *Port Sunlight* (London, 1916).

1917.[374] In 1918 Raffles Davison made drawings, subsequently purchased by Lever, of Lews Castle and the Island of Lewis.[375] On this occasion he probably stayed with Lever and was recorded as being one of the guests at a party at Lews Castle.[376]

Raffles Davison's known interest in depicting London during the period leading up to and following the launch of the London Society in 1914 suggests that the present group dates from c. 1910–14. The costume on the figures in LL 3432 certainly suggests a date of c. 1910. However, it cannot be assumed that all the works date from the same year; in particular LL 3406 may well date from several years earlier. The drawing depicts the Royal Marines Memorial in the Mall, London, unveiled in 1903 to commemorate the officers and men of the Royal Marines who were killed in action during the wars in South Africa and China in 1899–1900. Raffles Davison depicts the back of the sculpture showing a wounded marine with his comrade standing over him defending him with his rifle and bayonet; on the pedestal are carved dolphins on each corner symbolising naval service. The sculpture was made by Adrian Jones (1845–1938), who executed a number of statues and memorials including his most famous work, *Quadriga Peace*, on top of the Wellington Arch at Hyde Park corner.

### St Margaret's Church, Westminster
LL 3432 (WHL 2160)

Brown ink over pencil on paper laid down on board
45.4 x 32.2 cm (image); 53.3 x 38.1 cm (sheet)
Date: c. 1910

Inscr: T Raffles Davison (ink, bottom left); S. Margaret's Church Westminster (ink, bottom right)

Prov: bt. from the artist by Lever, 16 March 1915; by descent to 3rd Viscount Leverhulme; presented by 3rd Viscount Leverhulme, 1986

This drawing shows the west front of St Margaret's, the parish church of the Houses of Parliament. Founded in the twelfth century, the church is situated in the grounds of Westminster Abbey. The costumes of the figures suggest a date of c. 1910.

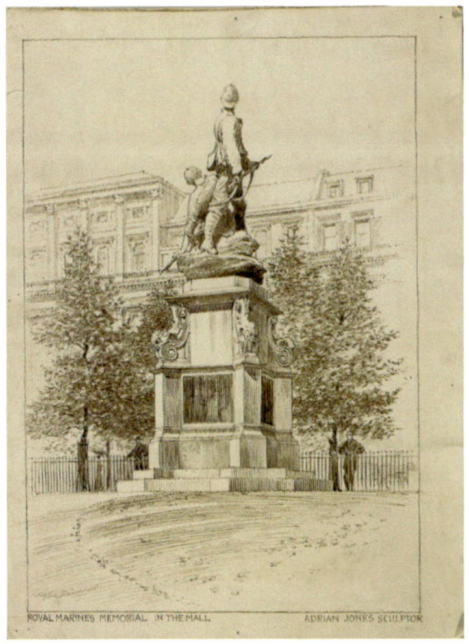


LL 3406

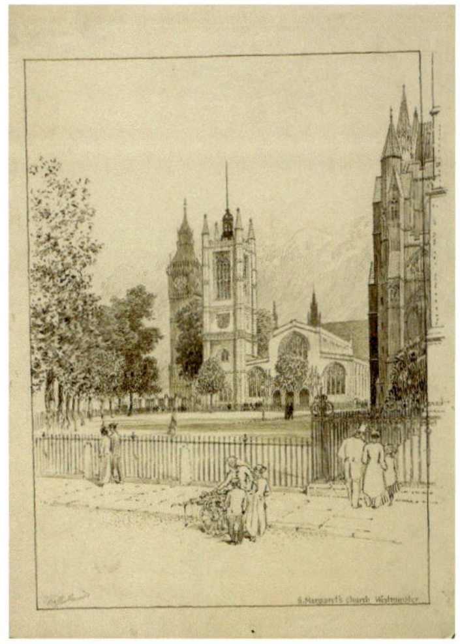

LL 3432

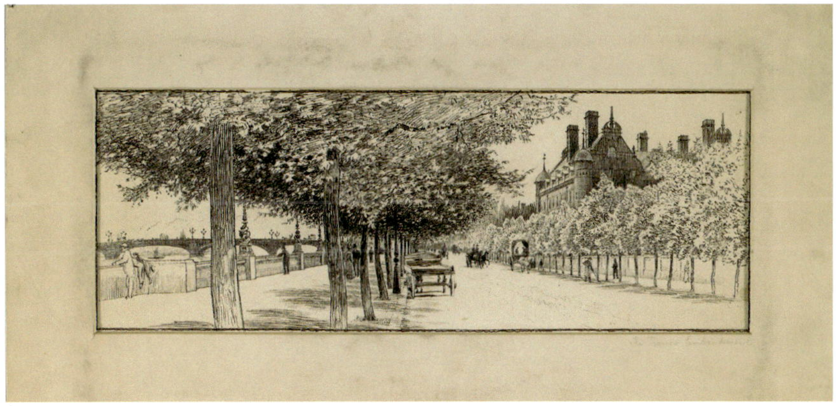

LL 3407

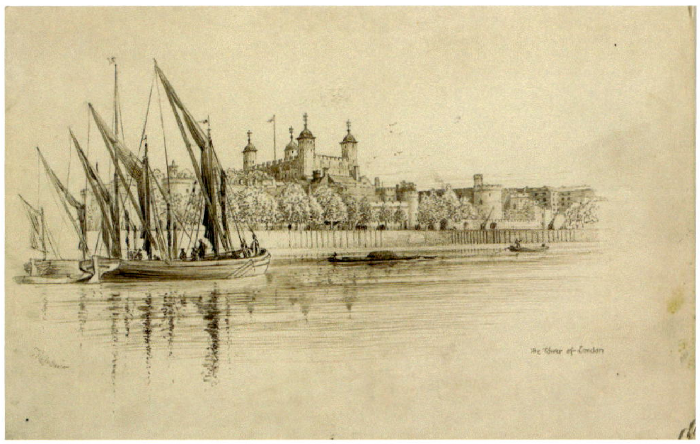

LL 3433 LL 3431

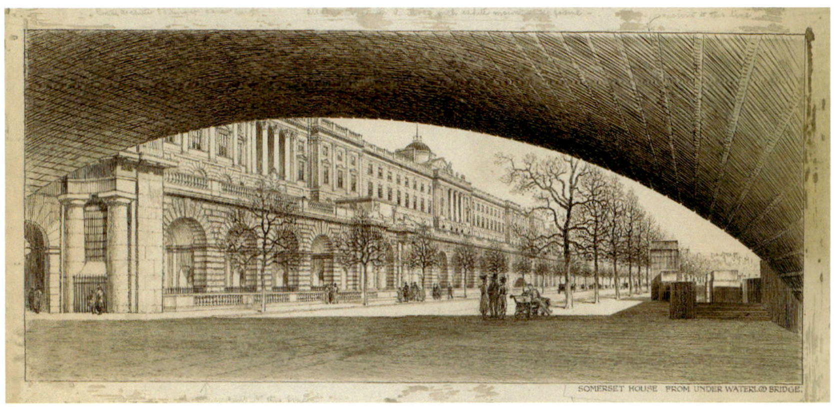


374 This was a drawing of one of the sculpture halls. *Building News*, vol. 112 (1917), p. 395.

375 WHL Inventory. The island of Lewis was purchased by Lever in the autumn of 1917. For Lever's involvement in the Hebrides see Leverhulme, *Viscount Leverhulme*, pp. 208–21.

376 See W. Hulme Lever (2nd Viscount Leverhulme), *Loose Leaves from the Lews* (privately published, 1918), unpag. There is a copy of this in the archives of the Port Sunlight Museum.

**The Thames Embankment**
LL 3407 (WHL 2152)

Ink over pencil on paper laid down on board
16.7 x 45.3 cm (sight)
Date: c. 1910–14

Annot: The Thames Embankment (pencil, on mount, bottom right)

Prov: bt. from the artist by Lever, 16 March 1915; by descent to 3rd Viscount Leverhulme; presented by 3rd Viscount Leverhulme, 1986

Lit: Thomas Raffles Davison, 'Beautiful London', *Journal of the Royal Institute of British Architects* (1914), illus. p. 452

This drawing is described in the WHL Inventory as 'the Thames Embankment Gardens, looking toward Waterloo Bridge'. It illustrated Raffles Davison's article 'Beautiful London' in 1914.[377] This publication set out the aims of the London Society, which intended to 'stimulate the desires and ambitions of the whole body of London citizens for the most perfect development of the city'.[378] Although this drawing was not mentioned specifically in the text, an image of the tree-lined gardens was a suitable illustration for a manifesto that talked about ideal public space.[379]

**The Tower of London**[380]
LL 3431 (WHL 2161)

Brown ink over pencil on paper laid down on board
36.8 x 53.8 cm (sheet)
Date: c. 1910–14

Inscr: T Raffles Davison (ink, lower left); The Tower of London (ink, lower right)

Prov: bt. from the artist by Lever, 16 March 1915; by descent to 3rd Viscount Leverhulme; presented by 3rd Viscount Leverhulme, 1986

This work is a view of the Tower taken from the south-west.[381] Raffles Davison probably made this sketch either from a boat on the river or from the south bank of the Thames using a telescope.[382]

**Somerset House from under Waterloo Bridge**
LL 3433 (WHL 2154)

Ink over pencil on paper laid down on board
34.1 x 76.4 cm (image), 40.2 x 82.3 cm (sheet)
Date: c. 1910–14

Inscr: T Raffles Davison (ink, bottom left, on image); SOMERSET HOUSE FROM UNDER WATERLOO BRIDGE (ink, bottom right, below image); British Architect 33 King st Covent Garden (pencil, top left, above image)[383]

Prov: bt. from the artist by Lever, 16 March 1915; by descent to 3rd Viscount Leverhulme; presented by 3rd Viscount Leverhulme, 1986

This drawing especially shows Raffles Davison's skills as a perspectivist; here he has drawn Somerset House from an unusually low and difficult angle from under Waterloo Bridge. The inscription above the image in the artist's hand suggests that the work may have been intended as an illustration for the weekly magazine *The British Architect*, of which Raffles Davison was editor.

**Westminster Hall**
LL 3434 (WHL 2155)

Ink over pencil, with a touch of watercolour on paper laid down on board
50.7 x 58.5 cm (image), 55.4 x 62 cm (sheet)
Date: c. 1910–14

Inscr: T Raffles Davison / delt. (ink, bottom left, on image); Westminster Hall (ink, bottom right, below image)

Prov: bt. from the artist by Lever, 16 March 1915; by descent to 3rd Viscount Leverhulme; presented by 3rd Viscount Leverhulme, 1986

This drawing is described in the WHL Inventory as 'the interior of Westminster Hall looking east'. Westminster Hall was the oldest part of the Palace of Westminster, dating from the eleventh century. The artist has taken a low viewpoint so that the piece is dominated by the Hall's vaulted hammer-beam roof. LL 3434 has heavy adhesive staining on the edges of the paper from an earlier mount.

**The Victoria Memorial**
LL 3435 (WHL 2153)

Ink over pencil on paper laid down on board
53.8 x 97.3 cm (image), 59.2 x 103.9 cm (irreg.) (sheet)
Date: c. 1911–14

Inscr: T Raffles Davison / delt. (ink, bottom left, on image); THE VICTORIA MEMORIAL AS COMPLETED SIR THOMAS BROCK R.A SCULPTOR SIR ASTON WEBB R.A ARCHITECT (ink, below image)

Prov: bt. from the artist by Lever, 16 March 1915; by descent to 3rd Viscount Leverhulme; presented by 3rd Viscount Leverhulme, 1986

This drawing shows the Victoria Memorial at the centre of Queen's Gardens in front of Buckingham Palace, London. Just visible is the statue of Queen Victoria facing towards the Mall; on the pinnacle is the figure of Victory. The sculpture is the most celebrated work of Sir Thomas Brock (1847–1922); the surround was designed by the architect Sir Aston Webb (1849–1930). The Memorial was unveiled in 1911 and Raffles Davison's drawing must therefore date from after this. LL 3435 is in poor condition. The support has snapped 27 cm from the left edge, 77 cm from the right edge. The paper has broken away from the board upper left, approximately 7 cm from the top edge, 45.5 cm from the bottom edge.

**The Victoria Embankment**
LL 3436 (WHL 2156)

Ink over pencil on paper laid down on board
33.9 x 59.6 cm (image), 46 x 73.9 cm (sheet)
Date: c. 1910–14

Inscr: T. Raffles Davison delt (ink, bottom left, on image); The Victoria Embankment (ink, bottom right, on image)

Prov: bt. from the artist by Lever, 16 March 1915; by descent to 3rd Viscount Leverhulme; presented by 3rd Viscount Leverhulme, 1986

This work is described in the WHL Inventory as 'the Victoria Embankment, looking east'. The view is taken from the old pedestrian footpath across Hungerford Bridge. The present-day Embankment underground station is in the foreground to the left, with beyond it the Hotel Cecil, the Savoy Hotel; on the right in the distance is Waterloo Bridge. Cleopatra's Needle is shown in the middle distance. LL 3436 has heavy adhesive staining on the edges of the paper from an earlier mount.

**Portrait Study of Sir David Murray**
LL 10335 (WHL 3667)

Pencil, black and brown crayon on paper
36 x 26.1 cm
Date: probably 1918 or 1919

Inscr: Sir David Murray / R A (pencil, bottom right)

Prov: bt. from Gooden and Fox by Lever, March 1920;[384] by descent to 3rd Viscount Leverhulme; Leverhulme Collection sale, Thornton Manor, Sotheby's, 26–28 June 2001 (lot 449); bt. by the Lady Lever Art Gallery (£800)

The subject is the Scottish painter David Murray (1849–1934). In his youth he had studied at the Glasgow School of Art and became well known as a painter of Scottish highland scenes. He moved to London in 1882 and made a sketching trip to Picardy in northern France in 1886, after which his subject-matter in oils and watercolour consisted of southern English landscapes and Continental scenes. His work from the 1890s onwards shows the influence of Corot and the French Barbizon school. Murray was elected an associate of the Royal Academy in 1891 and a full member in 1905.

Murray was a personal friend of Lever's, spending two summers with him at Lews Castle on the island of Lewis in the Outer Hebrides. This was probably in 1918 or 1919, as Murray sent paintings of Hebridean subjects to the Royal Academy exhibitions in 1919, 1920 and 1921.[385] Lever purchased at least two paintings by Murray: one of these was *Scenting the Summer Air: Golden Gorse*, bought in 1917 (LL 3129) and

377 Thomas Raffles Davison, 'Beautiful London', *Journal of the Royal Institute of British Architects* (1914), pp. 452–71, illus. p. 452.
378 Ibid., p. 454.
379 Ibid.
380 The WHL Inventory gives the title *The Tower of London, from the river: group of barges to left*.
381 This has been identified by Jane Spooner, Curator (Historic Buildings) Historic Royal Palaces, email correspondence, August 2008.
382 Spooner, email correspondence, August 2008.
383 There are various framing notes in pencil, top centre and right edge, above image and bottom centre edge, below image.

384 WHL Inventory.
385 Edward Morris (ed.), *Lord Leverhulme: Founder of the Lady Lever Art Gallery and Port Sunlight on Merseyside: A Great Edwardian Collector and Builder* (exh. cat., London, Royal Academy, 1980), p. 66.

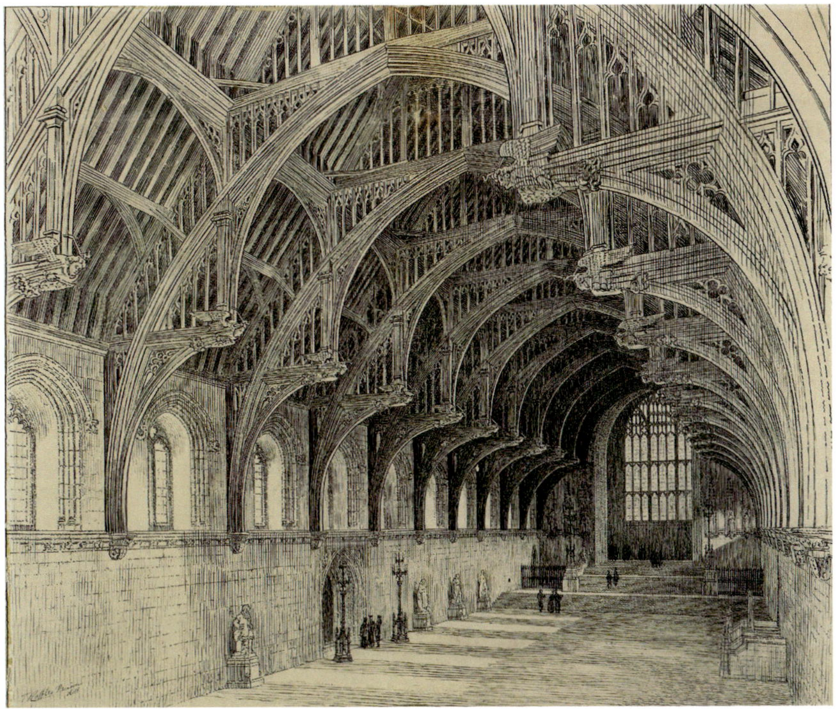

LL 3434

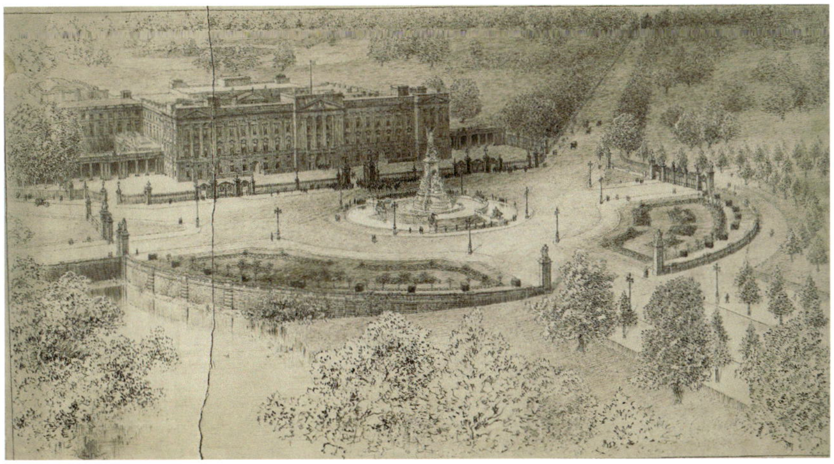

LL 3435

LL 3436

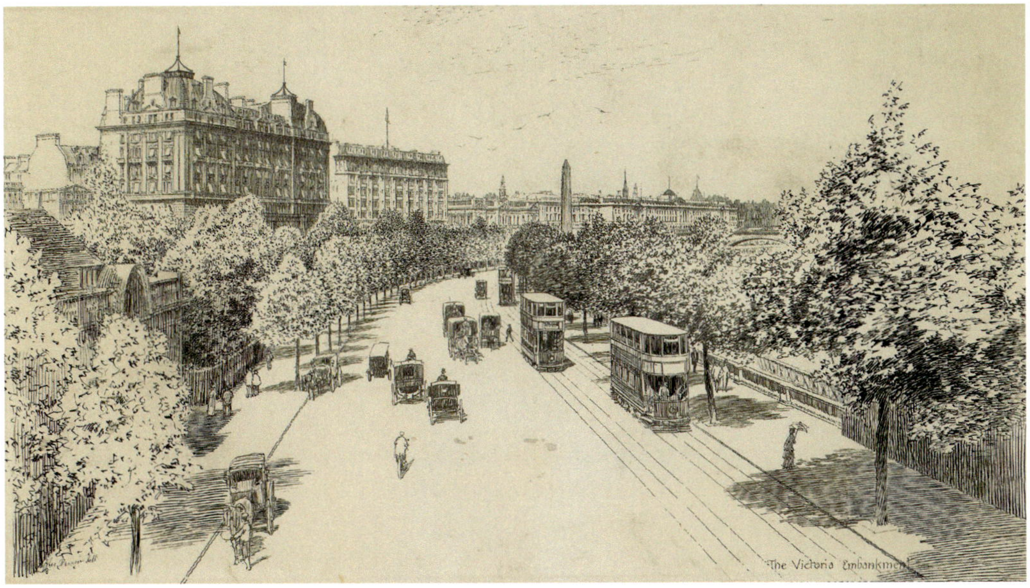


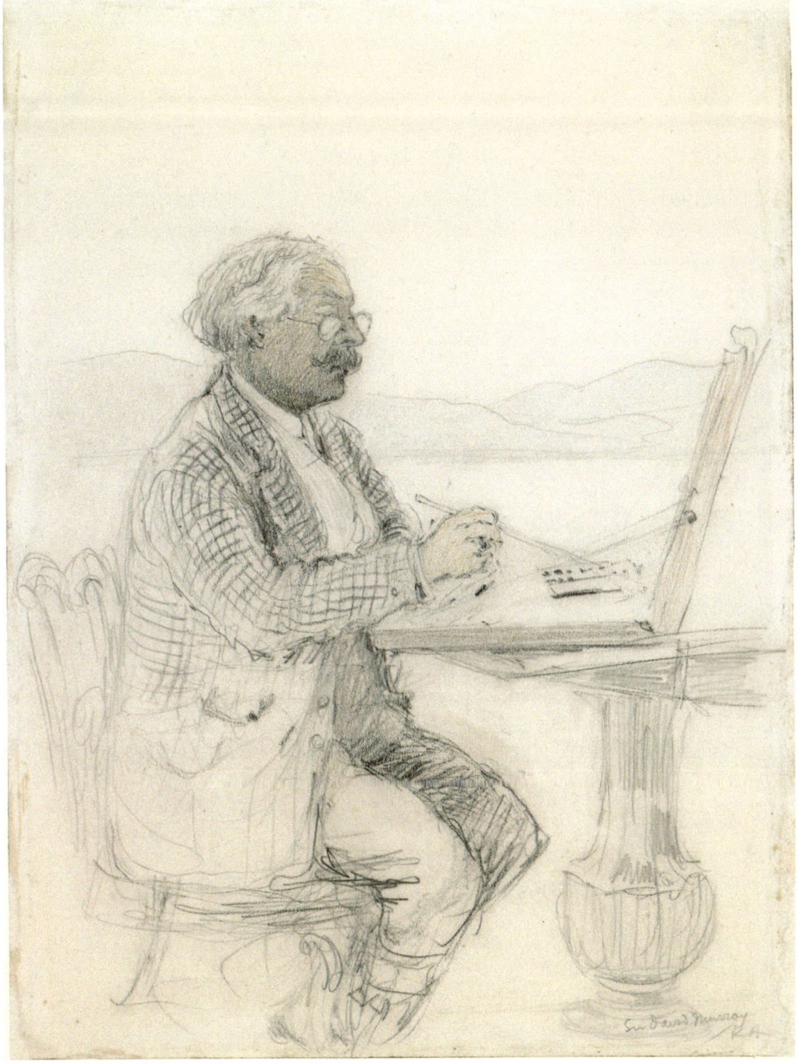

LL 10335

the other was a Hebridean subject, sold from the collection in 1926.[386]

LL 10335 depicts the artist working outdoors using a portable easel; there are the suggestions of mountains in the background. Raffles Davison is known to have made drawings of Lews Castle and the island of Lewis in 1918 and it is possible that this sketch was made that summer when Murray was also staying with Lever.[387] Murray was only knighted in 1918 and so the inscription on the drawing in Raffles Davison's hand, which reads Sir David Murray / RA, would suggest that the work was made in the summers of 1918 or 1919 as the work was purchased by Lever in early 1920.

The vigorous quality of the pencil marks and the unfinished nature of certain areas of the composition suggest this was a sketch done from life.

386 LL 3129 (WHL 3143), oil on canvas, signed and dated 1916; see Edward Morris, *Victorian and Edwardian Paintings in the Lady Lever Art Gallery* (London, 1994), pp. 92–93; also Morris (ed.), *Lord Leverhulme*, pp. 65–66 (cat. 27). The Hebridean subject sold from the collection was titled *In the Bay of Stornoway* (WHL 4429), 114.3 x 130.8 cm.

387 See LL 3406, pp. 72–73.

## PETER DEWINT[388]

1784 Hanley, Stoke-on-Trent, Staffordshire–1849 London

### Landscape with Cottage and Figure[389]

LL 3900 (WHL 296, H 386)

Watercolour over pencil on wove paper
23 x 34.4 cm
Date: c. 1810

Prov: bt. from James Orrock by Lever, 1912

DeWint was the son of a doctor from New York who had settled in Stoke-on-Trent, although the family were of Dutch extraction. He moved to London in 1802 to begin an apprenticeship with the engraver John Raphael Smith, purchasing his freedom with 18 oil paintings in 1806. He took lessons from John Varley (see pp. 206–207) and also attended Dr Monro's Academy, where he encountered Girtin's work (see p. 102). He entered the Royal Academy schools in 1809. Around this time he was working in oils as much as watercolours but his work in the former medium was less successful, and for the rest of his career he concentrated on watercolours. He was made an associate member of the SPWC in 1810 and a full member the following year, exhibiting over 400 drawings there until his death. DeWint established himself as a drawing master, spending his summers travelling around England and Wales teaching wealthy provincial families. His tours included repeated trips to the Lake District, Wales and Shropshire as well as Lincoln and the surrounding countryside. He made only one tour abroad, to Normandy in 1828. DeWint famously rarely signed or dated his works, contributing to difficulties in attribution and dating.[390]

From its style, LL 3900 dates from early in DeWint's career. The broad blocks of wash show that he had assimilated Girtin's technique and his treatment of the trees reveals the influence of his teacher John Varley. Andrew Wyld has suggested a date for the work of c. 1810.[391]

The subject-matter, depicting a run-down cottage, is conventionally picturesque. The location is uncertain, but given the mountains in the background, it may be the Lake District or North Wales.[392]

### Kneeton-on-the-Hill[393]

LL 3799 (WHL 317, H 162)

Watercolour, extra gum arabic, with scratching out on wove paper
54.5 x 80.3 cm
Date: c. 1815–16

Prov: James Orrock; his sale, Christie's, 4 June 1904 (lot 50); bt. by Gooden and Fox for Lever, 1907[394]

Exh: [?] Windsor, Eton College, exhibition title unknown, 1933 (cat. 10);[395] Lincoln, Usher Gallery, *Exhibition of the works of Peter DeWint*, 1937 (cat. 54)

Lit: Charles Holme (ed.), 'Masters of English Landscape Painting', *The Studio*, Special Number (summer 1903), pl. 29 (titled *Sunlight and Shade*); *The Connoisseur*, vol. 90 (July 1932), illus. p. 53

LL 3799 is a view of Kneeton village, near Newark, Nottinghamshire, from the surrounding countryside.[396] The fourteenth-century tower of Kneeton Church is visible in the centre background. Harriet DeWint wrote in her *Memoir* that her husband 'was partial to river scenery and studied much on the borders of the Trent about Newark and Nottingham'.[397] Although there is no precise chronology of DeWint's visits to the area, he exhibited paintings of Nottinghamshire subjects between 1807 and 1815. The relatively muted colour tones and broad blocks of wash suggest a date of c. 1815–16.

This large-scale, finished watercolour is a conventional depiction of a rustic and picturesque subject. It is a tranquil image of the countryside in the early evening showing a farmer leading his cart and horse home from the fields, the time of day suggested by the shadows of the cows created by the low sun. In the background to the right are hayricks in a field, a hint of the agricultural activity in the area and the time of year. The foliage in the right foreground is typical of that found in many of DeWint's agricultural scenes and would have been worked up from on-the-spot studies.

A preliminary watercolour study taken from a sketchbook contains all the main elements of the final work (fig. 31). Nevertheless, in LL 3799 DeWint has changed the proportions of the work to make it longer and narrower, adding a thin strip on the right-hand side containing two cows and the haystacks in the background.

fig. 31. Peter DeWint, *Kneeton-on-the-Hill*, c. 1815–16, watercolour over pencil on paper, 40.6 x 61.3 cm, V&A Images/Victoria and Albert Museum

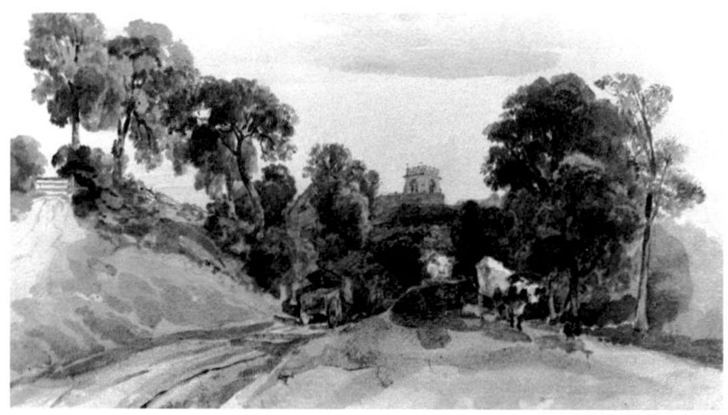

388 DeWint's name is spelt in this catalogue as one word, following the example of Hammond Smith in his monograph, *Peter DeWint 1784–1849* (London, 1982). Smith based his decision to do this on the evidence of DeWint's signature on a number of documents. The same spelling has been adopted in the most recent publication on DeWint: John Lord (ed.), *Peter DeWint 1784–1849: 'For the common observer of life and nature'* (exh. cat., Lincoln, The Collection, 2007).

389 1912 Inventory (no. 39) listed as *Landscape, cottage & figures*, valued at £50.

390 The difficulties over the attribution of DeWint's work are complicated by the fact that he had a large number of pupils, some of whom were good, and their work is often confused with genuine DeWints. There are dated drawings by DeWint which, based on style, enable the tentative dating of others. Equally there are those which have a *terminus ante quem* because it is known when they were exhibited, engraved or sold. Nevertheless, his style does not fit into strict chronologies, leading to difficulties in dating some of his works.

391 Andrew Wyld, verbally, July 2006.

392 LLAG files: a note on the accession card in an unidentified hand suggests that this may be a 'Welsh scene'.

393 Later inventories of Lever's collection list the title as *Kneeton-on-the-Hill near Hoveringham on Trent*.

394 1907 Hill Inventory, listed as *Kneeton-on-the-Hill*, valued at £500, Orrock Collection as per Gooden and Fox.

395 This exhibition is cited in the LLAG files, but there is no record of it in Eton College's archives. The exhibition may have been held in the Drawing Schools (the school's art department) but it is not recorded in the *Eton Chronicle* (the school's magazine) for 1933. I am grateful to Penny Hatfield, Eton College's archivist, for providing this information.

396 LLAG files: letter from George L. Neale, 3 January 1957, confirming this identification.

397 Harriet DeWint, *A Short Memoir of the Life of Peter DeWint and William Hilton RA*, reprinted in Lord (ed.), *Peter DeWint*, p. 85.

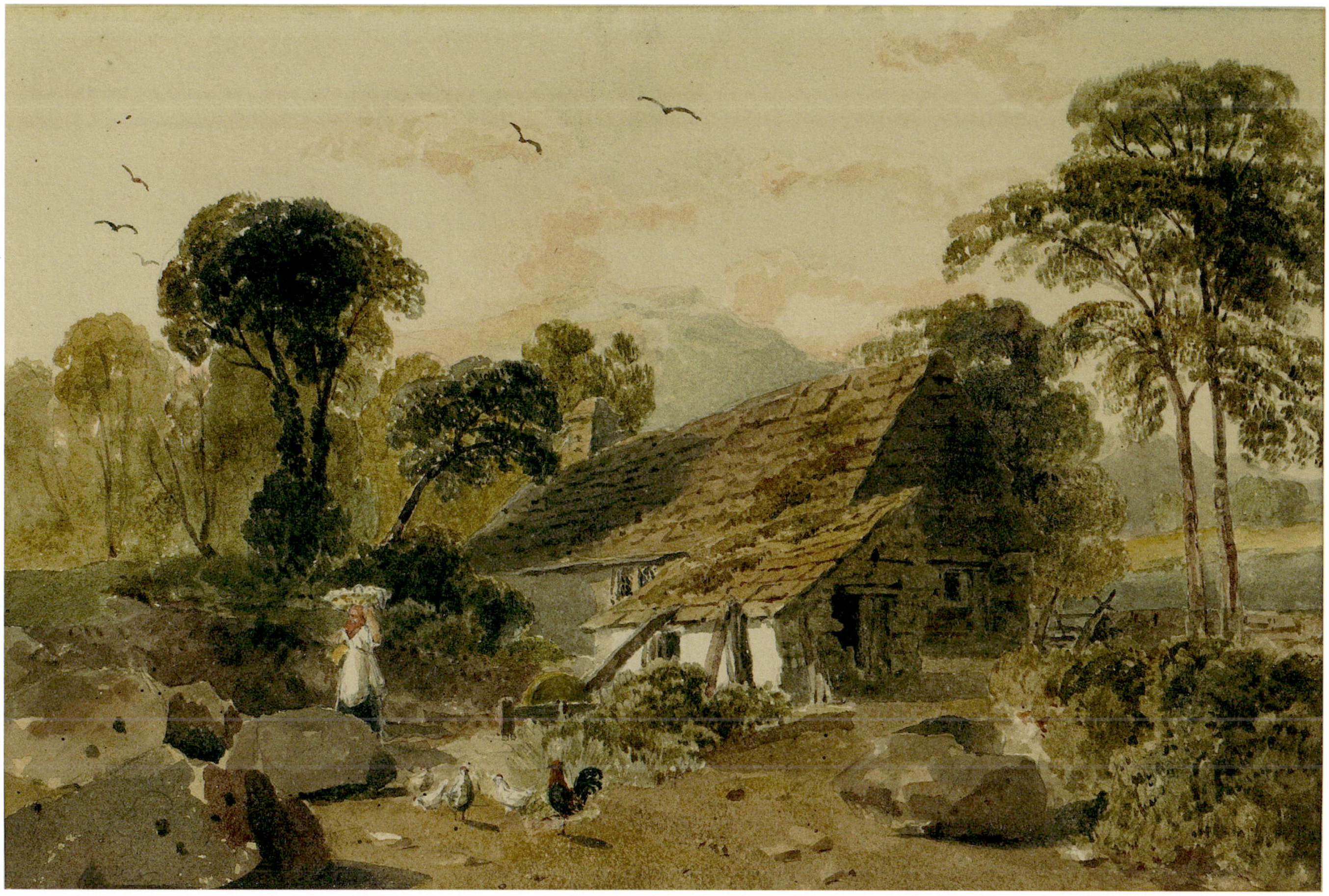

LL 3900

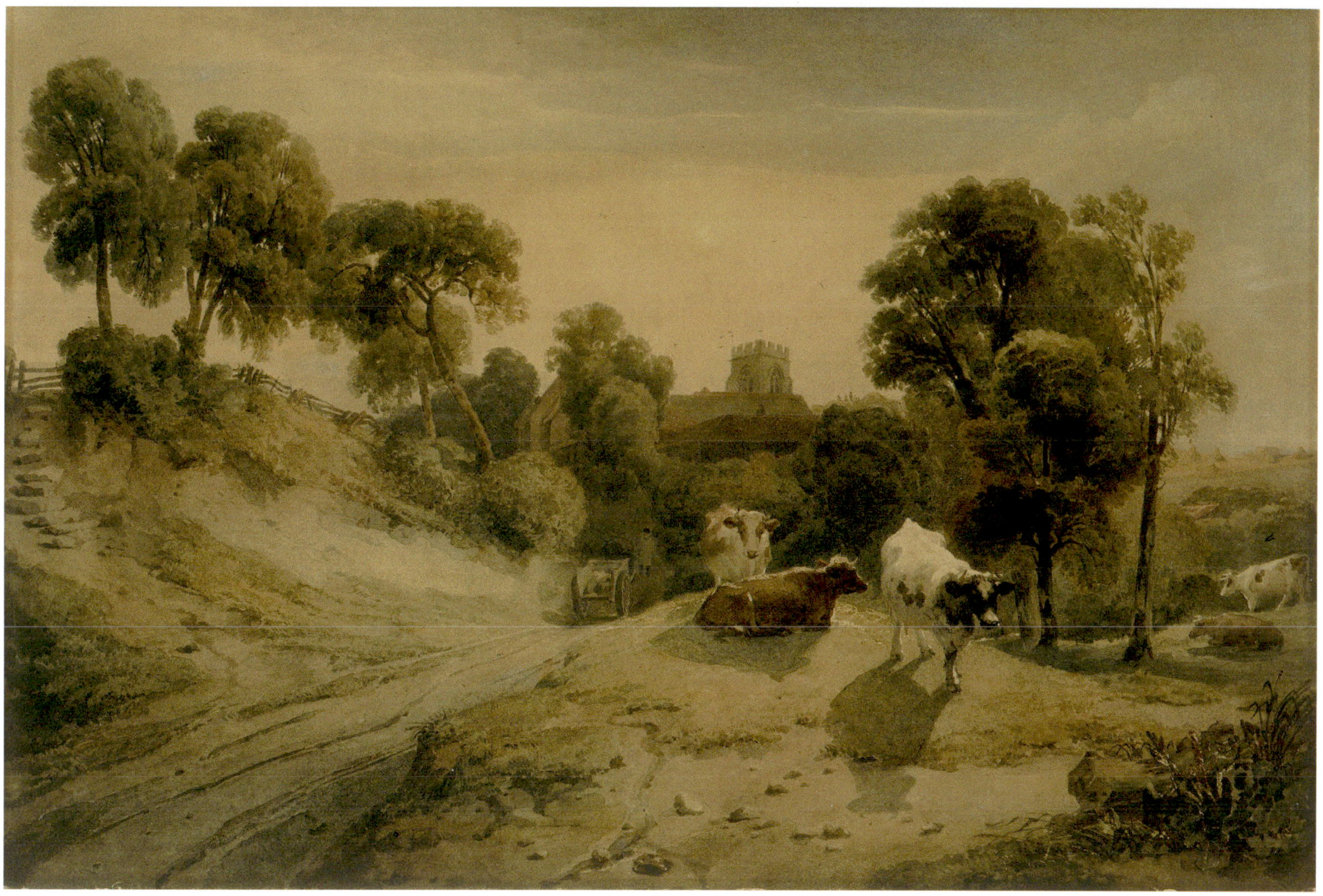

LL 3799

### The Hayfield
LL 3894 (WHL 329, H 415)

Watercolour over pencil, touches of gouache and gum arabic with cutting out on wove paper
24.7 x 68.4 cm
Date: c. 1815–20

Prov: bt. from James Orrock by Lever, 1912[398]

Exh: Lincoln, Usher Gallery, *Exhibition of the works of Peter DeWint*, 1937 (cat. 42)

LL 3894 is one of numerous harvesting and haymaking scenes that DeWint made throughout his career, many of which were painted in Lincolnshire. The watercolour conforms to the flat, open landscapes of Lincolnshire, and yet the lack of distinctive topographical detail means that it is hard to confirm its precise location. The work is typical of DeWint's use of a long, narrow panoramic format. Along with the composition, where two thirds of the space is dominated by the sky, this serves to emphasise the vast, open nature of the landscape. In the left foreground DeWint has included a still-life group with a large stoneware jar and tools, which adds incidental detail to the scene. On stylistic grounds Tim Wilcox has suggested a date for LL 3894 of c. 1815–20.[399]

In LL 3894 much of the colour has faded and the original tones have been distorted or lost.

### A Distant View of Ullswater
LL 3801 (WHL 3790)

Watercolour with extra gum arabic over pencil, with scratching out on wove paper
59.1 x 98.3 cm
Date: probably 1820s

Prov: C. D. Rudd, Ardnamurchan, Argyll, 1919;[400] his sale, Christie's, 2 May 1919 (lot 46, as *Derwentwater, a woody foreground, with cattle on a road; the lake in the distance*); bt. by Gooden and Fox for Lever (£753)

Exh: [?] London, SPWC, 1825 as *Distant View of Ulles [sic] Water, Cumberland* (cat. 14); Lincoln, Usher Gallery, *Exhibition of the works of Peter DeWint*, 1937 (cat. 118, as *Derwentwater*); Grasmere, Dove Cottage, *The Lake District Discovered 1810–1850; The Artists, The Tourists, and Wordsworth*, 1983 (cat. 18, as *Derwentwater*)

Although bought by Lever with the title *Derwentwater* and known since then under this title, LL 3801 appears to be the final composition based on a preliminary pen-and-ink compositional sketch, inscribed in the artist's hand a Distant view of Ullswater (The Collection, Lincoln, fig. 32).[401] In the final watercolour, the following topography has been identified which points to the view being Ullswater: in the far background the highest hills depicted are part of the Helvellyn ridge and, to the left, the hill with the long ridge that drops down to the little peak is Place Fell, while the rounder hill below is Hallin Fell.[402] DeWint spent many summers in the Lake District, a location recommended by writers such as the Revd William Gilpin as having all the elements of the picturesque and the sublime, and approximately a quarter of DeWint's exhibited views are of Lake District subjects. He may have painted the view while staying with his patron William, 1st Earl of Lonsdale, at Lowther Castle, not far from Ullswater, near Penrith.

The work's earthy colour palette suggests that it probably dates from the 1820s.[403] With its large size and highly finished technique, LL 3801 was probably exhibited at the SPWC, and it might be the *Distant View of Ulles [sic] Water, Cumberland* exhibited at the SPWC in 1825.[404] The detailed foreground foliage features in many of DeWint's watercolours from throughout his career.[405]

### Felling trees in a park - a sketch
LL 3803 (WHL 811, HH 382)

Watercolour over pencil on wove paper
24.5 x 35 cm
Date: probably 1820s

Prov: bt. from James Orrock by Lever, 1910[406]

With its loose pencil marks and fluid watercolour washes, LL 3803 is an example of DeWint's early sketching style. The large amount of pencil under-drawing may indicate that this was completed outside, with the watercolour added later in the studio. Tim Wilcox has suggested that the work can be dated to the 1820s.[407] The subject-matter, woodcutters felling trees and a wagon towing the timber away, may show the influence of DeWint's contemporary John Linnell (1792–1882) who painted the theme of woodcutters on a number of occasions.

The work has faded generally overall; in particular the original green pigment of the trees is shown in a strip at the top right edge which was obscured by an earlier mount.

### Timber Sawing
LL 3905 (WHL 355, H 431)

Watercolour on paper
16.7 x 25.6 cm
Date: probably 1820s

Prov: bt. from James Orrock by Lever, 1912[408]

In common with LL 3803 (above), this work takes as its subject-matter woodcutters sawing timber. A female figure wearing a bonnet sits on a log on the left of the painting, a stoneware jar suggesting that she has brought refreshment for the workers. As with the other Lady Lever woodcutting subject, DeWint may have been influenced by the work of his contemporary, John Linnell. The earthy colour palette and relatively broad treatment of the trees suggests a date of the 1820s.[409]

### Near Lowther Castle[410]
LL 3892 (WHL 301, H 404)

Watercolour, with gouache, extra gum arabic and scratching out on wove paper
71.3 x 105.6 cm
Date: probably mid- to late 1820s

Prov: Arthur Sanderson;[411] James Orrock, 1903;[412] bt. from Orrock by Lever, 1912[413]

Exh: Lincoln, Usher Gallery, *Exhibition of the works of Peter DeWint*, 1937 (cat. 67)

Lit: Byron Webber, *James Orrock, R.I.: Painter, Connoisseur, Collector* (London, 2 vols, 1903), vol. I, illus. facing p. 128; Charles Holme (ed.), 'Masters of English Landscape Painting', *The Studio*, special number (Summer 1903), illus. facing p. xii.

LL 3892 is a distant view of Lowther Castle, near Penrith in the Lake District, home of one of DeWint's major patrons William, 1st Earl of Lonsdale. Here the castle is only just visible in the far background, on a hillside; the view is taken from the north near Clifton.

The work is similar in style to the Lady Lever's *A Distant View of Ullswater* (LL 3801 above), notably employing the same earthy colour palette and tightly controlled technique. With this comparison in mind, LL 3892 probably dates

398 1912 Inventory, p. 4 (no. 47), valued at £150.
399 Tim Wilcox, verbally, May 2005. A note in LLAG files by A. C. Tait states that the work 'has a pencil date on the back, 1839, but this appears to have been added in recent years'. This inscription is no longer visible.
400 WHL Inventory. At least five lots in DeWint's studio sale, Christie's, 22–27 May 1850, are possible candidates for the work (lots 52, 97, 209, 373 and 405).
401 David Scrase, *Drawings & Watercolours by Peter DeWint* (exh. cat., Cambridge, Fitzwilliam Museum, 1979), p. 16 (cat. 38), pl. 22.
402 Email correspondence with Alex Black of the Wordsworth Trust, Dove Cottage, Grasmere, June 2007.
403 Tim Wilcox, email correspondence, April 2008.
404 *Distant View of Ulles [sic] Water, Cumberland* (cat. 14); sold to the Marquis of Ailesbury [*sic*] for 60 gns.
405 See, for example, *Bray on Thames from the Towing Path* (c. 1849, Tate), illus. in Lord (ed.), *Peter DeWint*, p. 71 (cat. 74).
406 1910 Inventory, valued at £15.
407 Tim Wilcox, verbally, May 2005.
408 1912 Inventory (no. 36), listed as *Landscape - Timber sawing*, 6¼ x 10 in., valued at £8.
409 Tim Wilcox, email correspondence, April 2008.
410 At least eight lots in DeWint's studio sale, Christie's, 22–27 May 1850, are possible candidates for the work (lots 217, 259, 269, 278, 297, 341, 344 and 348).
411 LLAG files: recorded on accession card. This information appears to have been known at least by the time of Sydney L. Davison (curator of the Lady Lever Art Gallery 1922–57) according to correspondence dating from 1946 in the Guildhall Art Gallery files; Jeremy Johnson, Curator, Guildhall Art Gallery, email correspondence, April 2008.
412 Illustrated in Webber, *James Orrock*, vol. I, facing p. 128.
413 1912 Inventory, valued at £1,200, as *Nr. Lowther Castle.*

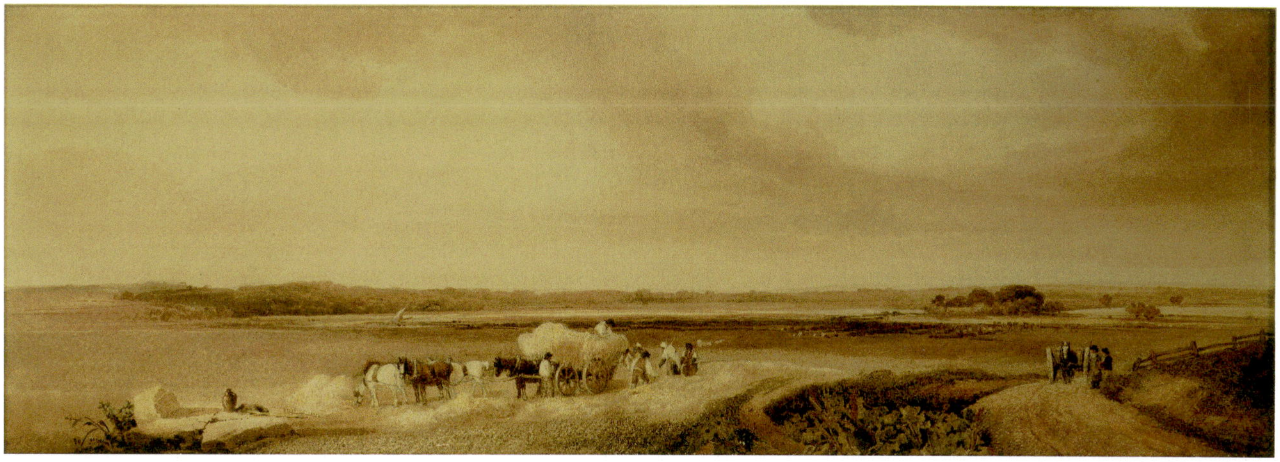

LL 3894

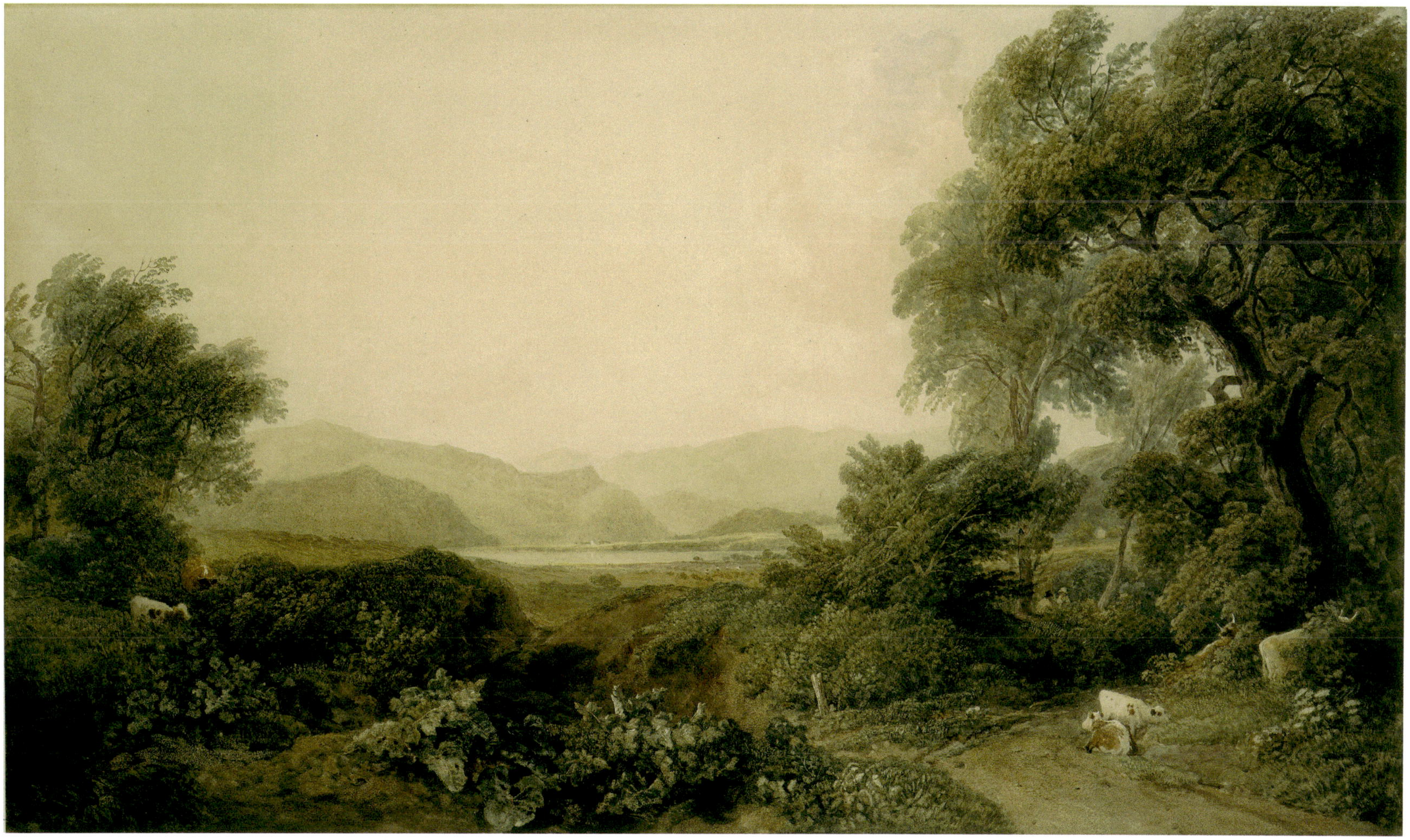

LL 3801

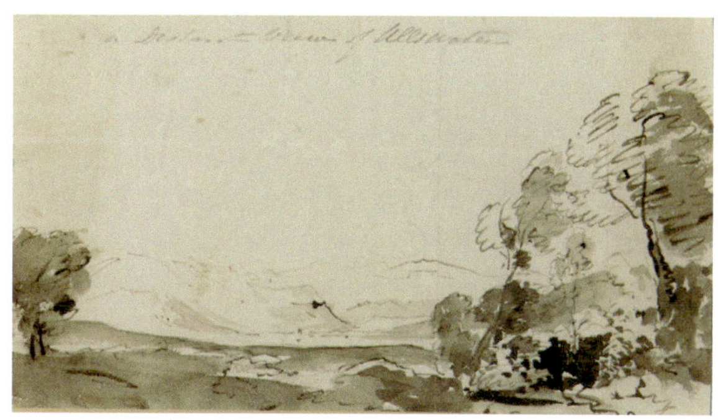

fig. 32. Peter DeWint, *A Distant View of Ullswater*, date unknown, possibly 1820s, pen and brown ink with grey wash on paper, 10.6 x 18 cm; 11.5 x 19 cm (two sheets), The Collection: Art and Archaeology in Lincolnshire (Usher Gallery, Lincoln)

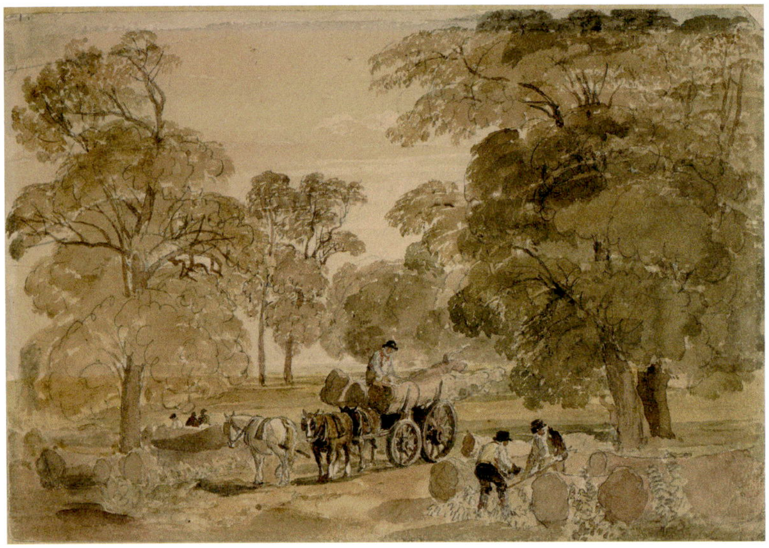

LL 3803

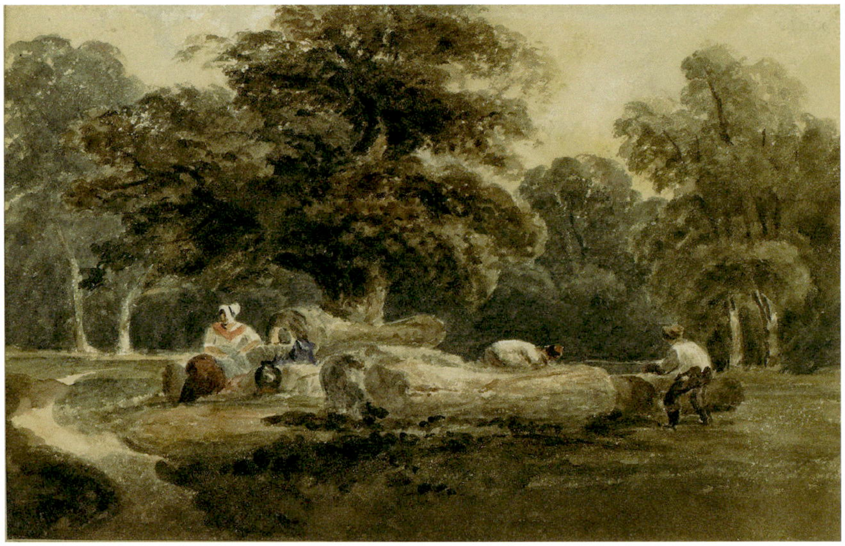

LL 3905

LL 3892

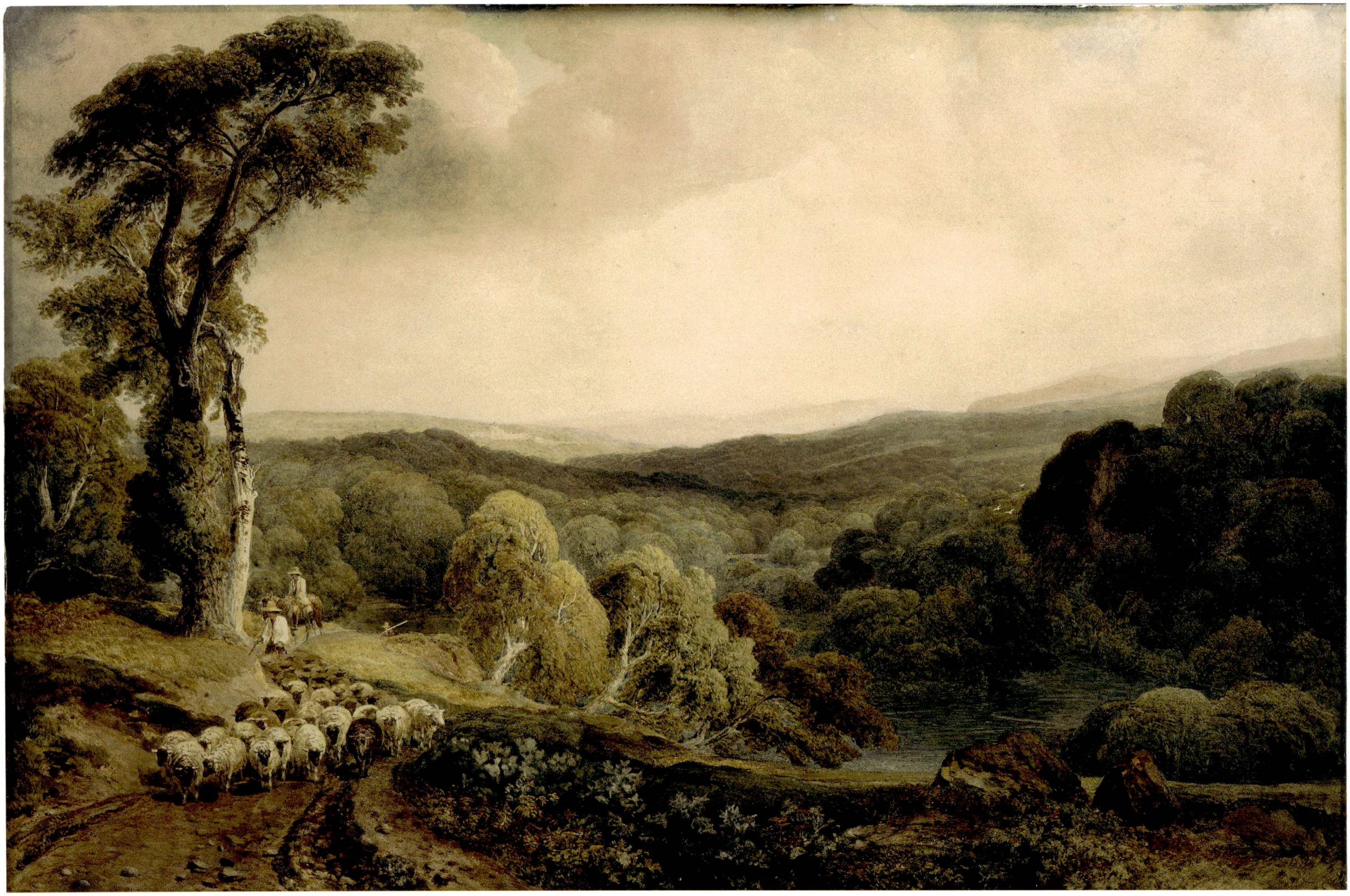

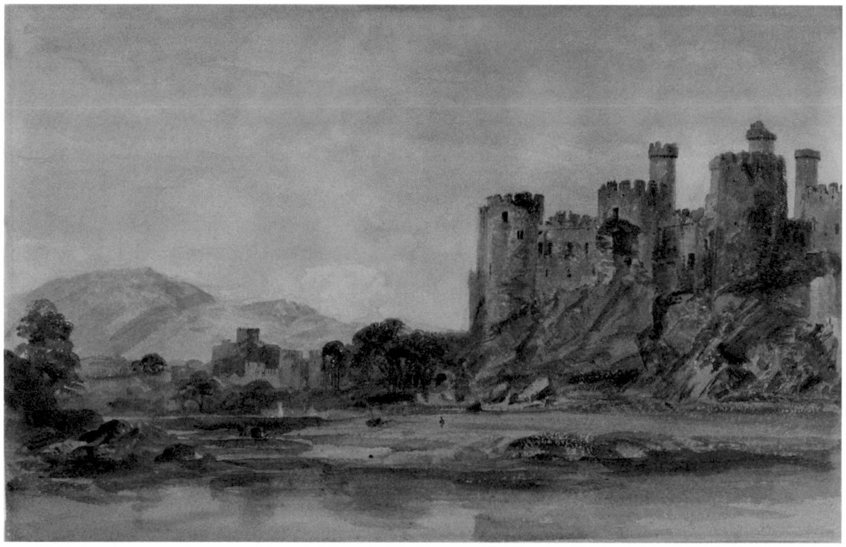

LL 3896

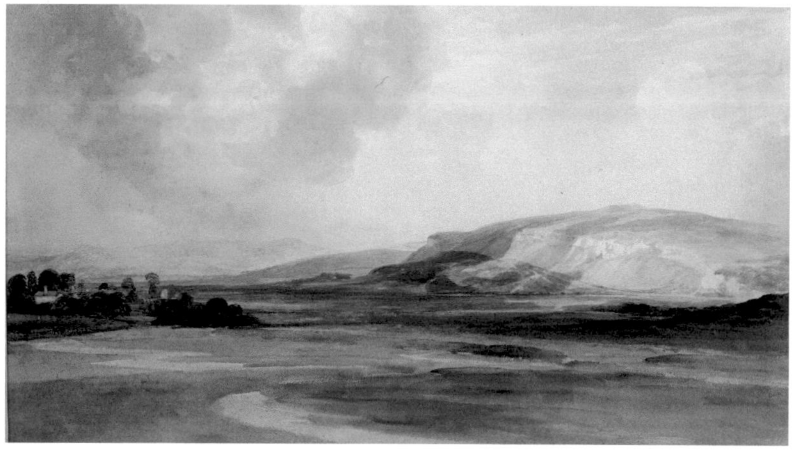

LL 3895

LL 3898

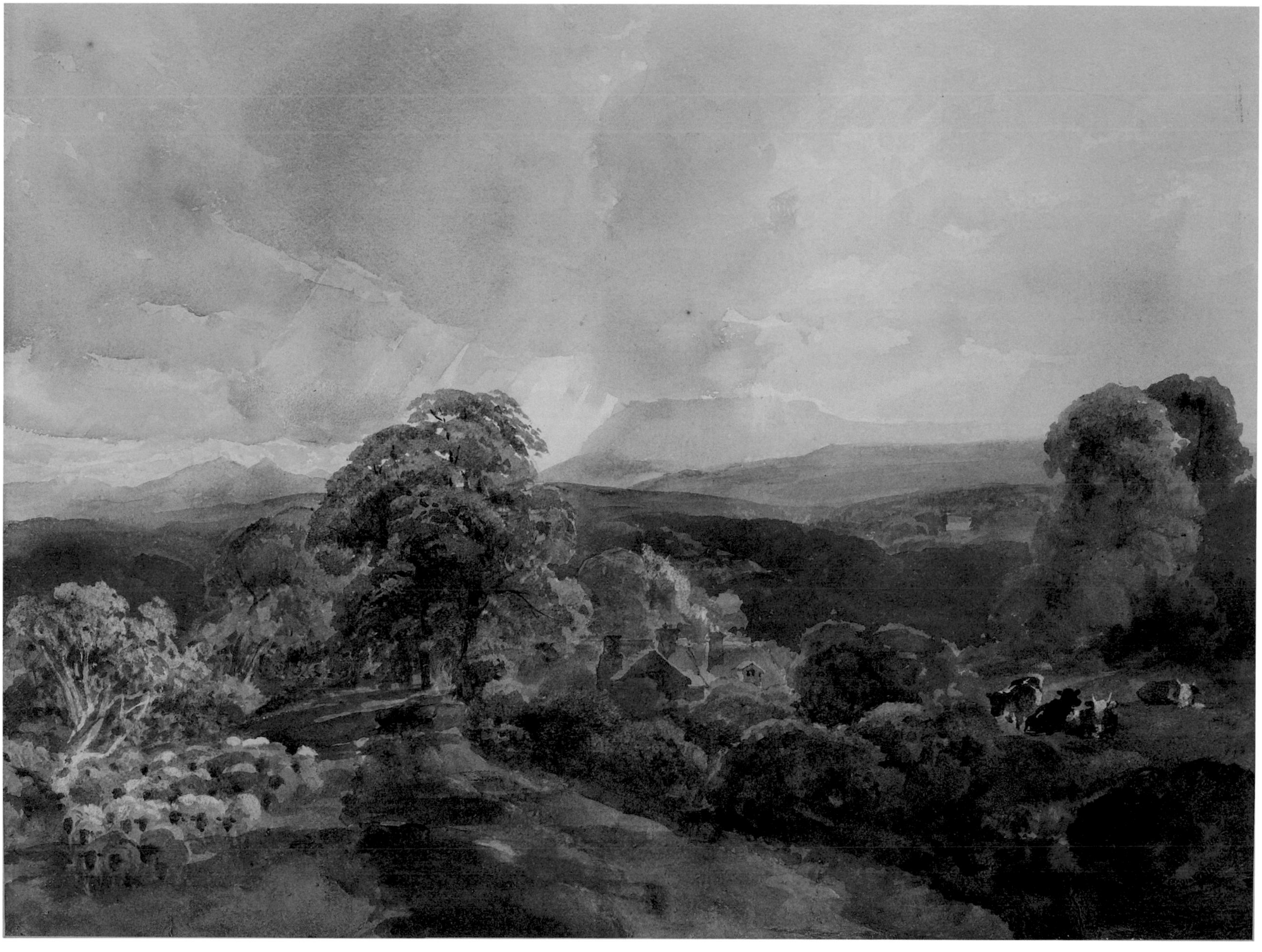

from the mid- to late 1820s.[414] DeWint was exhibiting views of the castle and its park at the SPWC by the mid-1830s and it is certainly possible that he was visiting the area before this, although it is not known exactly when. The work has the appearance of a finished exhibition watercolour, although no titles at the SPWC from this period match this description.

There is a replica of the subject of roughly the same size in the Guildhall Art Gallery, London.[415]

### Conway Castle[416]
LL 3896 (WHL 3506)

Watercolour over pencil, with gouache on wove paper
30.1 x 46.2 cm
Date: c. 1830

Prov: John Henderson, 1873;[417] his sale, Christie's, 16 February 1882 (lot 95); bt. by W. Permain (£31 10s); A. R. Johnston; his sale, Christie's, 3 May 1918 (lot 40); bt. by Gooden and Fox (£54 12s) for Lever (£57 6s 6d)

Exh: London, Burlington Fine Arts Club, *Drawings and Sketches by the late David Cox and the late Peter DeWint*, 1873 (cat. 64)

LL 3896 is a view of Conwy Castle, North Wales, from the south-east side looking north-west. In the far distance on the high ground is 'tower 13', the highest point of the town walls, and in the middle, to the left of the trees, is the Mill Gate that stands between towers 18 and 19.[418]

This is one of a number of finished watercolour studies that DeWint made of castles including Caernarfon and Conwy on his trips to North Wales during the 1830s.[419] On stylistic grounds Tim Wilcox has suggested that the work can be compared to the Usher Gallery's *Dieppe Castle from the Beach* (c. 1828–30), although the latter is a more highly finished exhibition watercolour.[420] On this basis LL 3896 can be dated to c. 1830.[421] A *Conway* was exhibited at the SPWC in 1831, and though that would have been a more finished work it is possible that LL 3896 could have been a sketch for it. According to Harriet DeWint's *Memoir*, 'His last visit into the ... districts of Carnarvon [*sic*] and Merioneth was in the autumn of 1835'.[422] DeWint continued to exhibit North Wales subjects throughout the late 1830s and 1840s.

### A stormy day near the coast – a sketch
LL 3895 (WHL 806, HH 362)

Watercolour over pencil, with scratching out on wove paper
42 x 72.5 cm (sight)
Date: mid- to late 1830s

Prov: bt. from James Orrock by Lever, 1910[423]

Exh: Lincoln, Usher Gallery, *Exhibition of the works of Peter DeWint*, 1937 (cat. 120)

With its long washes of watercolour, this work is typical of DeWint's sketching manner from the mid- to late 1830s.[424] The combination of mountains and the coast suggest that this may be a North Wales subject, although the precise location has not been identified. The work could have been made on DeWint's trip to North Wales in the autumn of 1835.[425] Given the degree of pencil under-drawing and DeWint's known preference for working from nature, it is possible that this watercolour was completed outdoors. The drawing is badly faded overall.

### Sockbridge Hall
LL 3898 (WHL 371)

Watercolour with scratching out on Creswick paper laid down on another sheet of paper
36.2 x 46.7 cm
Date: mid-1830s or later

Annot: Sackbridge Hall, near Lowther / Saddleback in the distance / P. DeWint 1833 (ink, on backing paper, verso, centre); IMPROVED / DRAW^G. PAPER / ROUGH / THOMAS CRESWICK (blind-embossed manufacturer's stamp, lower right corner)

Prov: James Orrock; bt. from Orrock by Gooden and Fox for Lever, 1907[426]

LL 3898 has been titled *Sackbridge Hall* at least since Lever's acquisition of the work in 1907, but no record can be found of a house with this name. Given the identification of the mountain of Saddleback, or Blen Cathra, in the background to the left, the work almost certainly depicts a view of Sockbridge Hall in the village of Tirril, near Penrith in the Lake District. It would have been easy enough for the title to have been recorded incorrectly either at the point of its record in the 1907 Hill Inventory or at some stage before. Here the Hall is just visible among the trees in the foreground.

The watercolour is an example of DeWint's use of liquid washes of pigment on a slightly dampened paper, which adds a limpid quality to the piece. The work is on a buff-coloured Creswick paper, a type preferred by DeWint and used for many of his non-exhibition watercolours as its rough textured surface was well suited to the broad, fluid washes of colour employed in many of these sketches.[427] In LL 3898 he has chosen a dark green pigment to cover up the lower right corner of the drawing that contains Creswick's blind-embossed stamp. DeWint has used a sharp knife to scratch away areas of the pigment, adding highlights to areas such as the sheep and trees in the left foreground.

Tim Wilcox has dated the work to the mid-1830s or later, and as with many of DeWint's watercolours that do not seem to have been exhibited, it is difficult to be more precise.[428] The work would almost certainly have been made during one of DeWint's regular stays with his patron William, 1st Earl of Lonsdale, at Lowther Castle, which was not far from Sockbridge Hall.

### Landscape, cattle in stream, with sluice gate[429]
LL 3893 (WHL 217, H 484)

Watercolour with scratching out on [?] Creswick paper
33.2 x 50.8 cm
Date: probably 1830s or early 1840s

Prov: possibly James Orrock, 1904;[430] bt. from Orrock by Gooden and Fox for Lever, 1907[431]

The attribution of this work has been confirmed by Andrew Wyld and Henry Wemyss.[432] In subject-matter, LL 3893 (along with LL 3897) displays DeWint's keen interest in river scenery, a passion described by Harriet DeWint in her *Memoir* of her husband. John Ellis has suggested that LL 3893 depicts the countryside around Grantham in south Lincolnshire and shows one

414 LLAG files: a note on the accession card suggests that LL 3892 may be the *Distant View of Lowther Castle* exhibited at the SPWC in 1836 (cat. 103). However, its style is too consistent with LL 3801 to be dated much later than the late 1820s. Furthermore, this work was sold for 15 gns to a Miss Thompson, too small a sum to make LL 3892 a likely candidate for it.
415 *Near Lowther Castle*, watercolour, 28¼ x 42¾ in., sold by Richard Johnson, Christie's, 30 May 1895 (lot 144); presented to Guildhall Art Gallery by Miss T. A. C. Durning-Lawrence, 1946.
416 The spelling of Conway is contemporary, as listed in Lever's invoice; today it is generally spelt Conwy.
417 A *Conway Castle, North Wales* belonging to John Henderson was lent to the Burlington Fine Arts Club's exhibition in 1873 (cat. 64). At 11 ⅞ x 18 ¼ in., its dimensions agree with those of LL 3896.
418 Email correspondence with John Kenyon, April 2008.
419 No other watercolours or pencil studies relating to the subject of Conwy have been found, although based on several known studies relating to Caernarfon it is likely that there was more than one.
420 Illus. Lord (ed.), *Peter DeWint*, pp. 106–07 (cat. 18).
421 Tim Wilcox, verbally, May 2005.
422 Harriet DeWint, *A Short Memoir of the Life of Peter DeWint*, reprinted in Lord (ed.), *Peter DeWint*, p. 85.
423 1910 Inventory, valued at £50.
424 This date has been suggested by Andrew Wyld and Charles Nugent, verbally, July 2003.
425 Harriet DeWint, *A Short Memoir of the Life of Peter DeWint*, reprinted in Lord (ed.), *Peter DeWint*, p. 85, described her husband's 'last visit into the mountainous districts of Carnarvon [*sic*] and Merioneth ... in the autumn of 1835'. This does not seem to have been his last visit to North Wales, as DeWint was exhibiting North Wales subjects at the SPWC well into the 1840s.
426 1907 Hill Inventory, as *Sackbridge Hall*, Orrock collection per Gooden and Fox, valued at £170.
427 DeWint tended to use a smoother Whatman paper for his larger exhibition watercolours. For DeWint's use of paper, see Peter Bower, 'Peter DeWint and Thomas Creswick's Paper: "Signed all over"', in Lord (ed.), *Peter DeWint*, pp. 71–77.
428 Tim Wilcox, verbally, May 2005.
429 This title has been given to the work in 2008 to distinguish LL 3893 from the other scenes of cattle in a stream.
430 This is based on LL 3893 being the work referred to in the 1904 Inventory (no. 100) as *Cattle in a Stream*, 12½ x 19 in. (and see n. 435) but this could also refer to LL 3897.
431 This is based on LL 3893 being the work referred to in the 1907 Hill Inventory, p. 1, as *Cattle in a Stream*, valued at £300, Orrock collection as per Gooden and Fox (and see n. 435) but this could also refer to LL 3897.
432 Andrew Wyld, verbally, September 2003; Henry Wemyss, verbally, September 2006.

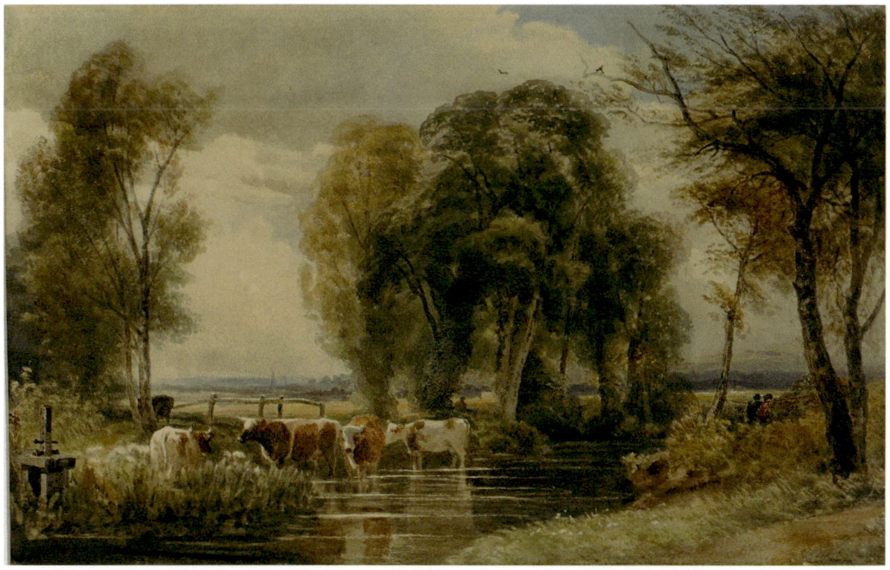

LL 3893

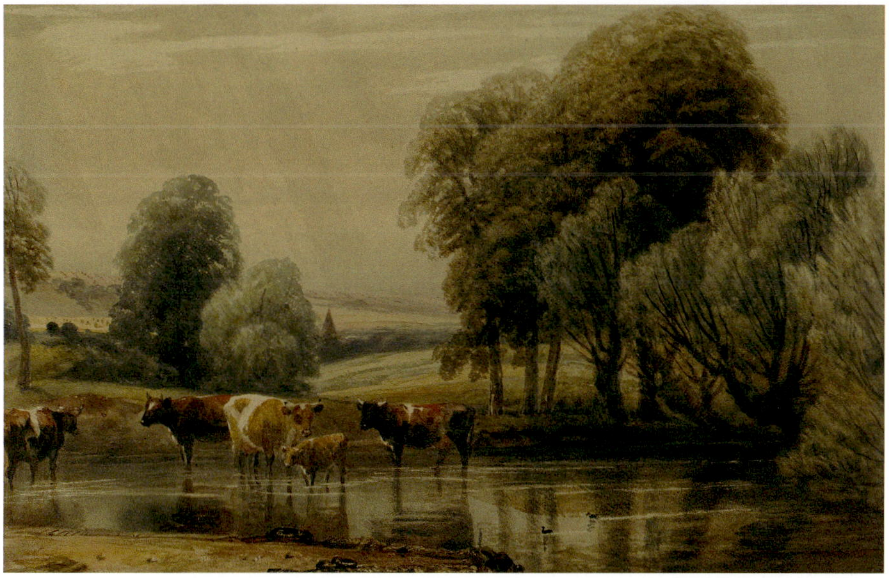

LL 3897

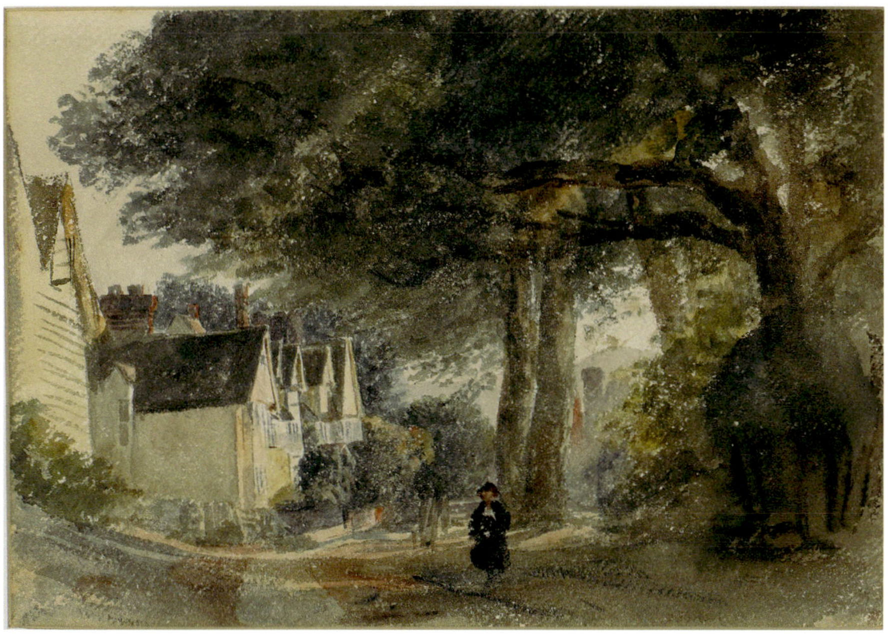

LL 3899

of the small watercourses that fed the Grantham Canal, constructed by an Act of Parliament of 1793 to link Grantham to the River Trent at Nottingham.[433] In the far left foreground is a sluice gate by means of which water might be fed into the canal as required. If this location is correct, the spire in the background is probably the church of St Wulfran, Grantham. On the same basis, the higher ground in the far right background may be Harlaxton.

LL 3893 probably dates from the 1830s or early 1840s. It shows the beginnings of a slightly spiky treatment of the trees, which became more apparent in DeWint's works of the 1840s. Equally, the watercolour demonstrates a more contrasting colour palette, in comparison to the more earthy colouring of works of the 1820s (see, for example, LL 3905, pp. 78, 80).

**Landscape with willows, cows and calf in a stream**
LL 3897 (WHL 206, H 218)

Watercolour over pencil, with scratching out on wove paper
33·3 x 49·5 cm
Date: probably 1830s or early 1840s

Prov: James Orrock, 1903;[434] probably bt. from Orrock by Lever, 1904;[435] in Lever's collection by 1912

Lit: Byron Webber, *James Orrock, R.I.: Painter, Connoisseur, Collector* (London, 2 vols, 1903), vol. I, illus. facing p. 122.

John Ellis has suggested that LL 3897 represents the upper reaches of the River Brant, a tributary of the River Witham in Lincolnshire.[436] If this is the case, in the middle distance is the bowed and crocketed spire of the church of St Vincent, Caythorpe.[437] In the far distance on the hills there are groups of sheaves of corn, indicating that this is autumn.

LL 3897 has stitching marks across the top of the paper, which indicates that it was once part of a sketchbook, and it is possible that this piece with its pencil under-drawing was begun outside and completed later in the studio. Much of the original pigment in the sky has been lost; it is only just possible to decipher where the artist imagined rays of sunshine streaming through the clouds onto the fields below.

In style and subject-matter the work is very similar to LL 3893 and probably dates from the

433 John Ellis, verbally, May 2007.
434 Webber, *James Orrock*, vol. I, facing p. 122.
435 The 1904 Inventory lists a work under no. 100 titled *Cattle in a Stream*, 12½ x 19 in. This work could be LL 3897. By the time of the 1912 Hill Inventory, p. 25 (no. 218), a more specific title lists *A landscape, with willows and four cows and calf in a stream*. The latter definitely refers to LL 3897. However, the 1904 reference could equally refer to LL 3893, which is the same size as LL 3897 and also shows cattle in a stream. There is only one reference in the 1904 Inventory to a *Cattle in a Stream* subject.
436 John Ellis, verbally, June 2007.
437 Ibid.

1830s or early 1840s (see entry on LL 3893 for a discussion of style). The work is approximately the same size as LL 3893 and the two watercolours may derive from the same sketchbook.[438]

### A lane scene with houses and a figure
LL 3899 (WHL 175, H 183)

Watercolour on [?] Creswick paper
24.5 x 34.6 cm (sight)
Date: probably c. 1838 or 1840s

Prov: probably James Orrock, 1904;[439] in Lever's collection by 1911
Exh: London, Earl's Court, *Victorian Era Exhibition*, 1897 (cat. 3)

A suggestion that LL 3899 is a view in Tunbridge Wells in Kent derives from an inscription in an unknown hand on the back of the mount.[440] If this is Tunbridge Wells it may depict one of the nearby villages rather than the town itself.[441] On stylistic grounds Tim Wilcox has suggested that LL 3899 dates from the 1840s.[442] However, a *Lane Scene* was exhibited at the SPWC in 1838 (cat. 303), and given that LL 3899 was referred to under this title when first inventoried by Lever the possibility exists that it is that work.

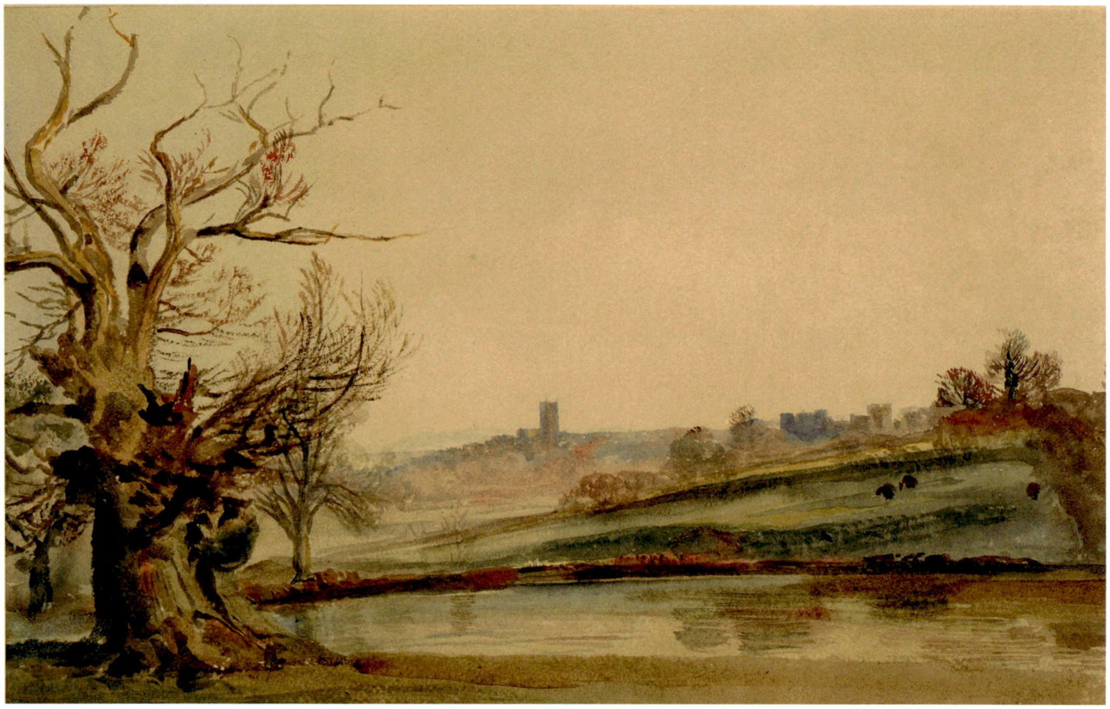

LL 3901

### Ludlow from the Teme
LL 3901 (WHL 808, HH 375)

Watercolour over pencil on [?] Creswick paper laid down on card
29.4 x 46 cm
Date: c. 1838 onwards

Annot: 15442 Distant View of Ludlow. / P. DeWint 27. Dec. 1838 (ink, on backing card, verso, upper left)
Prov: bt. from James Orrock by Lever, 1910[443]

The annotation on the backing card of LL 3901 is correct in stating that the view is of Ludlow. The work depicts the Shropshire town as seen from the river Teme, near to Oakley Park: in the background to the left is the prominent tower of St Laurence's Church and to the right is Ludlow Castle.[444] The magnificent blasted or 'stricken' oak in the foreground may in fact have been drawn by DeWint in Oakley Park, near to Oakley Hall, and then placed in this riverside view.[445]

DeWint visited the neighbourhood of Ludlow on many occasions from at least c. 1829–30.[446] He had been introduced to the area by Lord Robert Henry and Lady Harriet Clive of Oakley Park who had become friends and patrons. Harriet DeWint in her *Memoir* wrote that among the other pleasures of the neighbourhood of Ludlow, 'Oakley Park and its venerable oaks were a constant source of admiration' and DeWint made several studies of trees in Oakley Park, including one exhibited at the SPWC in 1841.[447]

The annotation on the backing card seems to be based on another on the back of the drawing, now obscured by the card, but the latter is also recorded as 27 December 1838 in the object file.[448] Although it is rare to find DeWint's watercolour sketches dated at all, the precision of the date in this case suggests that this was the artist's original inscription (or at least based on it). The dates of DeWint's visits to Ludlow are not fully known; he seems to have been there in 1829 or 1830 but may have been visiting before this date. Equally he only started exhibiting works of Ludlow subjects from 1841 but may have been there and making sketches during the 1830s. The use of sharper, more contrasting colours is characteristic of DeWint's later work from the late 1830s and 1840s. On the basis that we cannot dismiss the record of the date unless further evidence comes to light, LL 3901 can be dated to c. 1838 onwards.

The economy of the washes used in LL 3901 is typical of many of DeWint's watercolour sketches throughout his career. It is worth noting that the pigments in the sky do not appear to have faded (a common accusation against DeWint's work) and the work is probably close to the artist's intention. Here an expansive sky, painted in a warmish hue created by the mixing of an off-white pigment with buff paper underneath, serves to emphasise the brighter colours in the rest of the composition.

438 No stitching marks have been found on LL 3893 but it is possible that the work has been trimmed.
439 1904 Inventory (no. 118), as *Cottage Scene*, 9¾ x 13¾ in. *Cottage Scene* has the same dimensions as a work listed in the 1911 Hill Inventory, p. 21 (no. 183), as *A lane scene, with old houses, trees and a woman on the road*, a title that appears to describe LL 3899. The 1904 Inventory also lists (no. 92) *A road scene – with cottage*, but the dimensions of this work, 9½ x 13¼ in., are slightly smaller than LL 3899.
440 LLAG files: this inscription is recorded as *A Lane Scene – Tunbridge Wells* in the object file.
441 Ian Beavis, Tunbridge Wells Museum and Art Gallery, email correspondence, March 2008.
442 Email correspondence, April 2008.
443 1910 Inventory, listed as *The Stricken Oak – a sketch*, 11¼ x 17 in., valued at £35. Works in DeWint's studio sale, Christie's, 22–27 May 1850, that are possible candidates for LL 3901 include lots 368 and 402.
444 LLAG files: identification confirmed by Professor Stuart Wright in a letter to Henry Wemyss, August 2006.
445 This has been suggested by Wright, correspondence, August 2006.
446 Harriet DeWint, *A Short Memoir of the Life of Peter DeWint*, reprinted in Lord (ed.), *Peter DeWint*, pp. 85–86. Harriet DeWint states that it was from Shropshire that DeWint first went to Wales.
447 Ibid., p. 86. Several studies of trees in Oakley Park were exhibited at the Centenary Exhibition of DeWint's work, 1884 (cats. 124–27); see Smith, *Peter DeWint*, p. 162. The location of the work exhibited at the SPWC, 1841, *Study of an Oak Tree at Oakley Park – The Seat of the Hon. Robert Henry Clive, M.P.* (cat. 165; sold, 30 gns) is now unknown.
448 LLAG files.

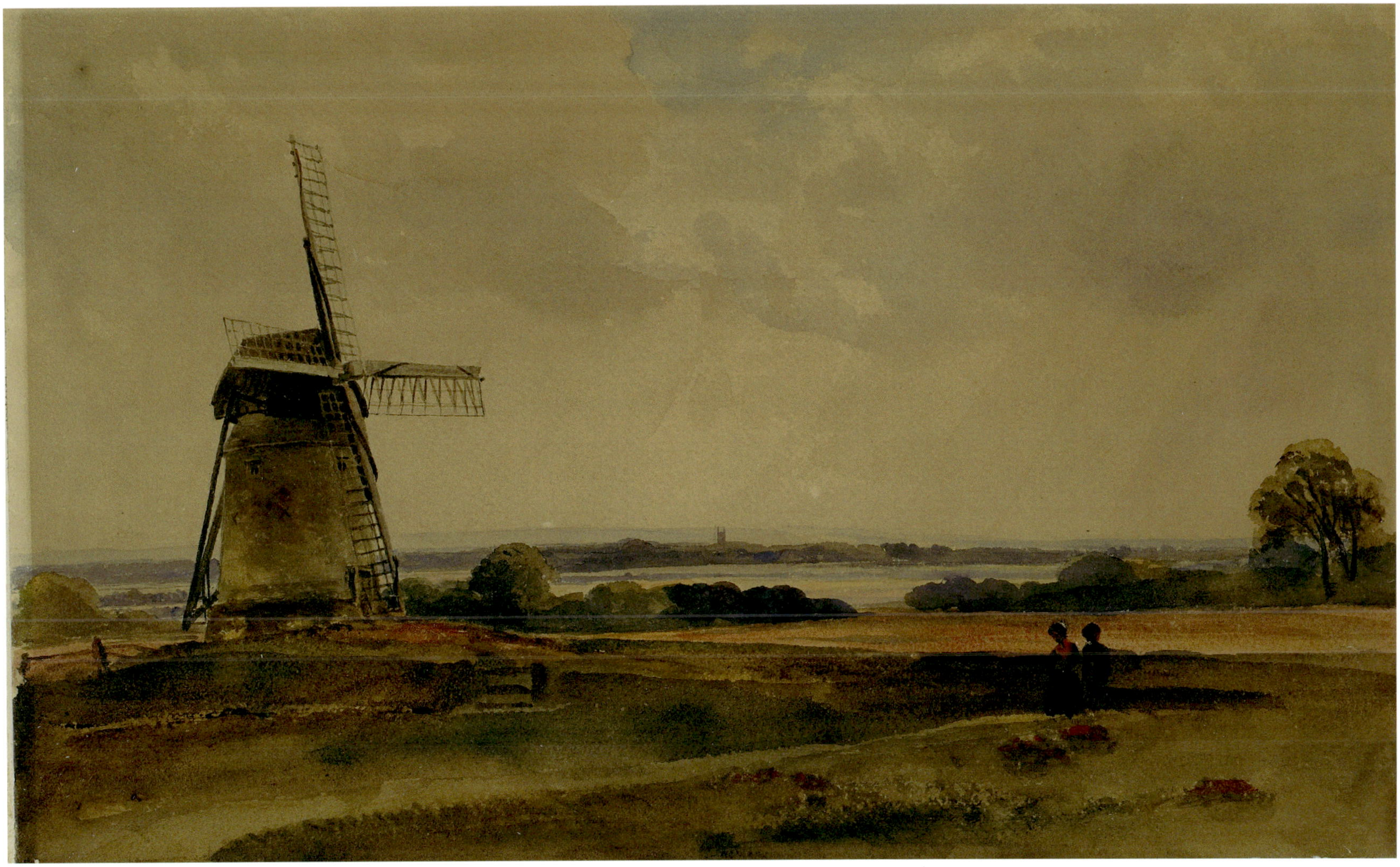

LL 3956

**The Windmill**
LL 3956 (WHL 809, HH 367)

Watercolour with touches of gouache on wove paper
29.3 x 46.4 cm
Date: c. 1840

Prov: James Orrock, 1878;[449] bt. from Orrock by Lever, 1910[450]

Exh: Nottingham, Midland Counties Art Museum, *Opening Exhibition*, 1878 (cat. 124)

LL 3956 is a finished watercolour in DeWint's fluid wet-on-wet technique. The choice of brighter, contrasting colours is characteristic of the artist's mature style and Tim Wilcox has suggested a date for the work of c. 1840.[451] Another version of this work of almost exactly the same size has been known as *Yaxley, near Peterborough*, and is said to have been inscribed with the name Mr Heathcote.[452] Although DeWint visited his patron and one of his most competent amateur pupils, John Moyer Heathcote (1806–90), at Conington Castle, Huntingdonshire in the late 1830s and early 1840s, it has not been possible to confirm that the view in the watercolours is related to this location.[453] In particular, the small tower visible in the distance does not appear to relate to any known building in Peterborough. Nevertheless, DeWint exhibited a number of East Anglian subjects at the SPWC in the late 1830s and early 1840s and both versions may depict a view in the area. It is possible that LL 3956 may be *A Windmill in the Fens* exhibited at the SPWC in 1842 (cat. 109).

Although the other version of LL 3956 has been attributed to DeWint, its weaker handling overall raises the possibility that it may be a copy by a contemporary, possibly a pupil of the artist.[454]

449 This work is listed in the exhibition catalogue for the *Opening Exhibition* at Midland Counties Art Museum, Nottingham, in 1878 as contributed by James Orrock. Information supplied by Nicholas Alfrey, Nottingham University, email correspondence, March 2009.

450 1910 Inventory, listed as *The Windmill – a sketch*, 11¼ x 17 in., valued at £35.

451 Email correspondence, April 2008.

452 LLAG files: this version belonged to Mr John Simpson in 1985. In correspondence between June and September 1985, Mr Simpson stated that its dimensions were 10¾ x 17¾ in., and that he had purchased it at auction from Sotheby's. He described two annotations, one, 'Yaxley', on the gold mount, and a second, 'back of the old mount pencil name of Mr. Heathcote'. It is this reference probably to the Heathcote family of Conington Castle that caused Mr Simpson to think that the Yaxley in question was Yaxley, near Peterborough (there is also a Yaxley in Suffolk). Without seeing this annotation, it is not possible to say whether this is a signature or a much later suggestion of ownership and attribution. The work was subsequently for sale at Sotheby's, London, 15 November 1990 (lot 119) as *Yaxley, near Peterborough*, 27 x 45 cm. Its current location is unknown.

453 No windmill can be traced on a site at Yaxley near Peterborough. John Ellis has identified the type of mill represented as a post-mill.

454 LLAG files: photograph supplied by Mr Simpson. The recorded annotation may have intended to suggest that the work was by John Moyer Heathcote (see n. 452). Heathcote's style is known and there are several examples of his work in the British Museum, but without seeing the original this could not be confirmed.

### Landscape, cattle in stream with bridge[455]
LL 3802 (WHL 349, H 409)

Watercolour, with gouache and scratching out on [?] Creswick paper
30.5 x 45 cm
Date: early 1840s

Prov: bt. from James Orrock by Lever, 1912

Exh: Lincoln, Usher Gallery, *Exhibition of the works of Peter DeWint*, 1937 (cat. 97, as *Landscape Near Ludlow*)

This watercolour's attribution had been questioned by Jane Farrington,[456] but more recently DeWint's authorship has been accepted by Charles Nugent.[457] Despite the title used in the Usher Gallery's 1937 exhibition, the work does not appear to show Ludlow in Shropshire. Nugent has suggested that the view may be of Brougham Castle, Penrith;[458] however, this does not appear to be likely as there is no church with a tower near Brougham, and the castle sits in a valley, not on a hill, as in LL 3802.[459] The combination of the spiky treatment of the trees with touches of bright colour within a generally more muted scheme suggests that the watercolour dates from the early 1840s. John Ellis has suggested that the object held by the man in the foreground may be a net for catching eels.[460] There is another version of the composition in a private collection, although this appears from a photograph as if it may be a later copy.[461]

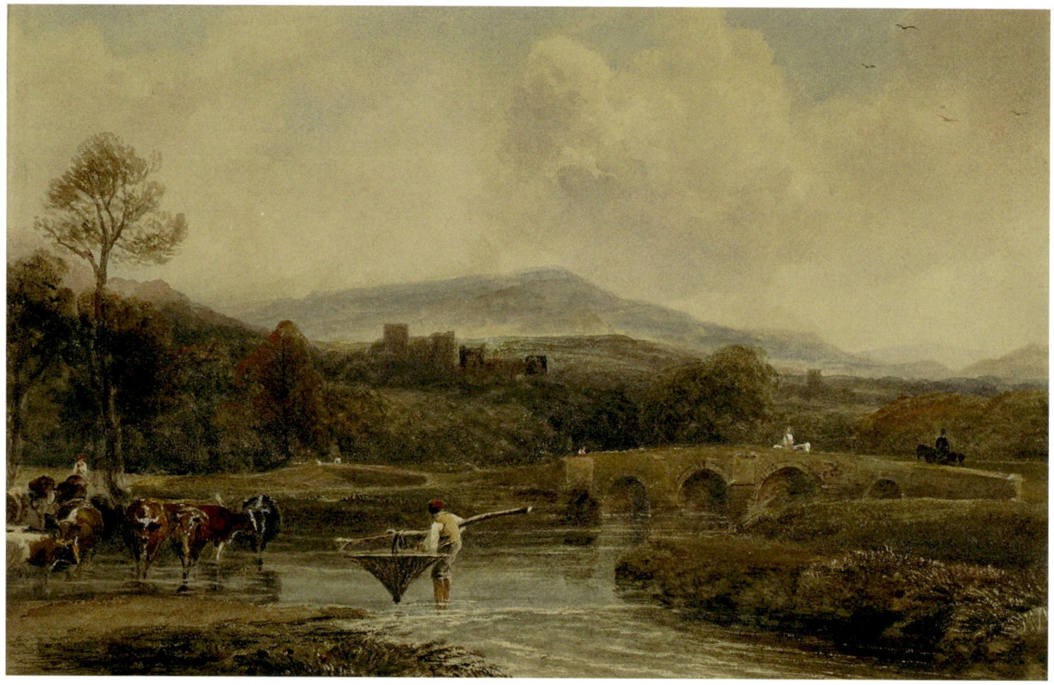

LL 3802

### Atcham Church, near Shrewsbury
LL 3902 (WHL 801, HH 364)

Watercolour over pencil, with scratching out and stopping out on wove paper
21 x 36.7 cm
Date: probably 1841-44

Prov: DeWint's studio sale, Christie's, 22-27 May 1850 (part of lot 193); bt. by Smith (£1 7s the pair);[462] bt. from James Orrock by Lever, 1910[463]

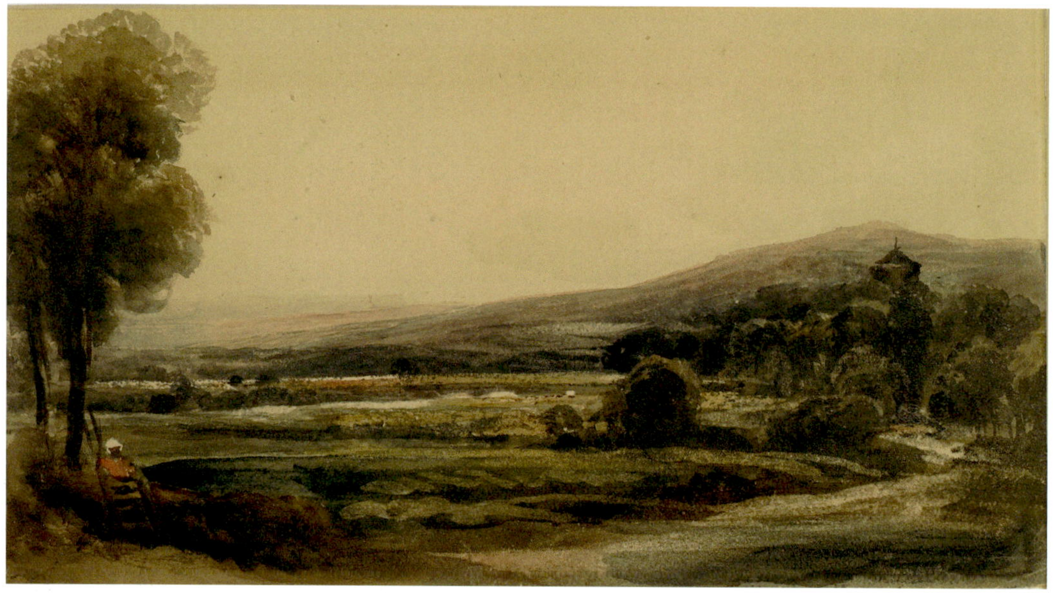

LL 3902

LL 3902 is a view of Atcham Village on the river Severn, south of Shrewsbury, Shropshire.[464] The distinctive building on the right is Atcham church, while behind it is the hill known as the Wrekin. DeWint appears to have been visiting Shropshire on a regular basis between 1841 and

LL 3903

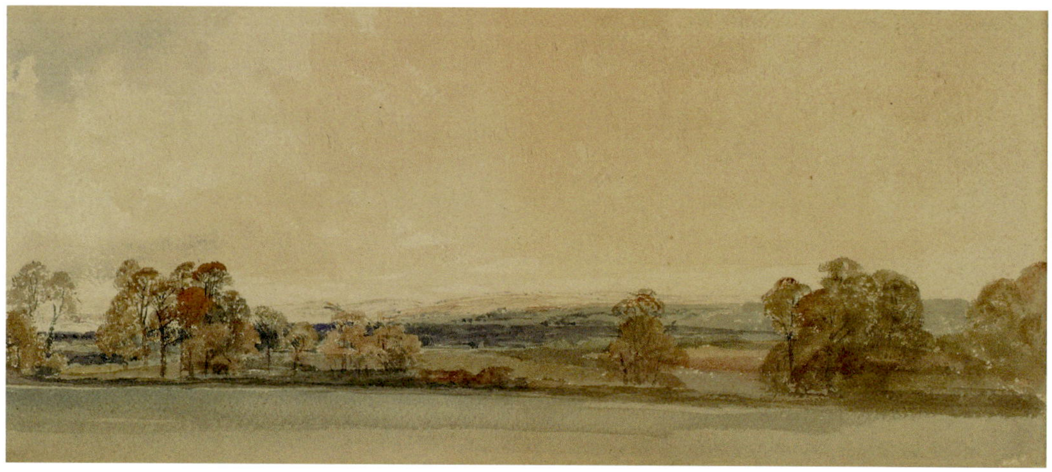

455 1912 Inventory (no. 29) listed as *Landscape, stream, cattle, bridge*, 11¾ x 17¼ in., valued at £150.
456 LLAG files: Jane Farrington, letter to Edward Morris 1981, describing LL 3802 as 'suspect'.
457 Charles Nugent, verbally, August, 2007.
458 Ibid.
459 John Goodall, English Heritage, verbally, May 2007.
460 John Ellis, verbally, June 2007.
461 This version is in a private collection in the UK. LLAG files: photograph donated by owner on a visit to the Lady Lever Art Gallery, c. 1987.
462 Lot 193 is listed as *Atcham Church, near Shrewsbury*; and *Wreck of the Pomone off the Needles* in Smith, *Peter DeWint*, p. 144.
463 1910 Inventory, listed as *A hilly landscape with a winding river and two trees on left*, 8 x 14¼ in., valued at £25.
464 The location was identified by Tim Wilcox, email correspondence, April 2008.

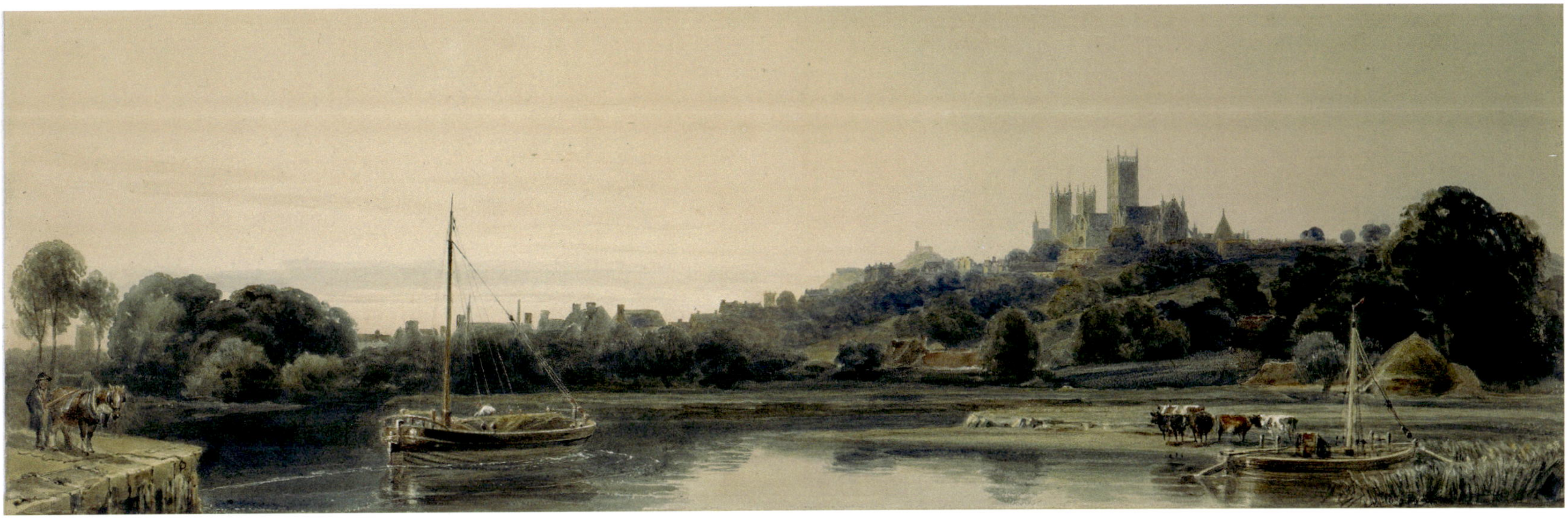

LL 3955

1844, exhibiting views of Shropshire subjects at the SPWC each year in this period. This work probably dates from within that timespan.[465] It was probably made while he was staying with one of his Shropshire patrons, R. H. Cheney of Badger, near Atcham.

This watercolour is distinctive for its lively use of stopping and scratching out techniques.

**Autumnal Landscape**
LL 3903 (WHL 805, HH 368)

Watercolour on [?] Creswick paper
21.3 x 46.4 cm
Date: probably 1840s

Prov: bt. from James Orrock by Lever, 1910[466]

LL 3903 depicts a flat stretch of country, with low-lying hills in the background. This was the sort of landscape DeWint depicted in many of his Lincolnshire subjects, although in this case the location is unknown. Here the panoramic view is emphasised both by the artist's application of paint in long, sweeping washes as well as the narrow format. The work's complete lack of narrative incident turns it into an exercise in colour and form. On stylistic grounds Tim Wilcox has suggested that LL 3903 dates from the 1840s: this opinion is based on the sharp colour palette and the spiky forms of the trees.[467]

465 A *View on the Severn, Shropshire* was exhibited at the SPWC in 1843 (cat. 86) and was sold for 30 gns to George Constable. LL 3902 is a possible candidate for this exhibited work but could not then be the work sold in DeWint's sale in 1850. On the balance of the recorded titles, LL 3902 appears more likely to be the latter.

466 1910 Inventory, listed as *A landscape, with stretch of low-lying country, fringed with a line of autumnal trees – sketch*, 8¼ x 18 in., valued at £10.

467 Tim Wilcox, email correspondence, April 2008.

**Lincoln: a view of the town and cathedral from the river**[468]
LL 3955 (WHL 807, HH 373)

Watercolour, with touches of gouache over pencil, with scratching out on wove paper
30 x 91 cm
Date: 1840s

Prov: William Dell, 1899;[469] R. E. Tatham, 1908;[470] his sale, York Street, Portman Sq., 1909 (lot no. unknown) sold for 1,050 gns;[471] bt. from James Orrock by Lever, 1910[472]

Exh: London, Agnew's, *Thirty-Fourth Annual Exhibition of Selected High-Class Water-Colour Drawings*, 1900 (cat. 112); London, Special Art Palace, *Franco-British Exhibition*, 1908 (cat. 495); Lincoln, Usher Gallery, *Exhibition of the works of Peter DeWint*, 1937 (cat. 103)

Lit: *The Art Journal* (1900), illus. p. 125

DeWint first visited Lincoln in the summer of 1806 with his fellow apprentice, William Hilton, whose family lived in the city. It was on this occasion that he met William's sister Harriet, whom he was to marry in 1810. With his marriage, DeWint was to create the foundations for a relationship with the city and the surrounding countryside that was to last for most of his career. In 1814 he bought Hilton House on the top of Motherby Hill, near the junction of Drury Lane and Union Road.[473] This was where the couple passed most of their summers until the death of Harriet's mother in 1835, when the house was let to tenants; in 1846 DeWint sold the property. Harriet describes in her *Memoir* how her husband found delight in both Lincoln and its neighbourhood: 'the long extensive distances with their ever varying effects, the flats bordering the river covered with cattle, the groups of cattle in the Brayford, the cornfields and the hayfields, and above all the magnificent cathedral seen from so many points, afforded him unceasing delight'.[474]

LL 3955 depicts one of the artist's favourite views of the city, from the southern, Washingborough bank of the River Witham. The watercolour shows Lincoln Cathedral, whose building had begun in 1092, and Lincoln Castle, built by William the Conqueror from 1068, immediately to its left. In the very far left corner is the Saxon tower of the Church of St Mary-le-Wigford.[475] The sailing barges in the foreground would have carried cargoes of corn and wool downstream to Boston for export, returning with seaborne cargoes from that port.

The watercolour's use of gouache to highlight areas such as the cows is typical of DeWint's work in the 1840s.[476] The style is similar, for example, to his *Nottingham*, exhibited at the SPWC in 1848.[477] With its highly finished appearance, LL 3955 is likely to have been exhibited and there are several candidates for it among the works DeWint showed at the SPWC in the late 1840s.[478]

DeWint depicted this same view at many stages in his career including an early

468 The title given in the 1910 Inventory is *Lincoln: A view of the town and Cathedral from the river, with boats and cattle*, 11½ x 35½ in., valued at £1,000. LL 3955 may be *Lincoln*, lot 460 in DeWint's studio sale, Christie's, 22–27 May 1850.

469 1910 Inventory, p. 48.

470 Ibid.

471 LLAG files. There is no lot no. recorded for the 1909 sale.

472 Tatlock, p. 141 records that LL 3955 was 'from the collection of J. Rushton in 1913 (?)' but this is a mistake. See also LLAG files: a note records the *Lincoln* in the Rushton collection as measuring 21 x 34½ in.

473 Smith, *Peter DeWint*, pp. 21–22. Smith quotes documents in Lincoln Castle for this piece of information.

474 Harriet DeWint, *A Short Memoir of the Life of Peter DeWint*, reprinted in Lord (ed.), *Peter DeWint*, pp. 84–85.

475 This has been identified by John Ellis, verbally, June 2007.

476 This has been suggested by Tim Wilcox, email correspondence, April 2008.

477 Illus. in Lord (ed.), *Peter DeWint*, p. 172 (cat. 75).

478 LL 3955 may have been one of the following works exhibited at the SPWC: 1847 (cat. 125): *View on the Witham, near Lincoln*, sold to Lewis Pocock, 30 gns; 1848 (cat. 147): *Lincoln*, sold; 1849 (cat. 139): *View of Lincoln, from below the Lock 'Now fades the glimmering landscape on the sight, / And all the air a solemn stillness holds.'*

watercolour now in a private collection as well as one from c. 1825 in the Usher Gallery, Lincoln.[479] Of the numerous works taken from this viewpoint, LL 3955 is among the most successful in using a particularly long, narrow format that accentuates the sense of space and light in this elegant river scene. It is a device that may have been strategic as it would have made DeWint's works stick out from the squatter watercolours on the walls of the SPWC.[480] The Usher's 1937 exhibition included a sepia sketch for this work from Geoffrey Harmsworth's collection, now untraced.[481]

479 *Lincoln Cathedral from the River*, illus. Scrase, *Drawings & Watercolours by Peter DeWint*, p. 7 (cat. 15); *Lincoln Cathedral from the River* (c. 1825, Usher Gallery, Lincoln), illus. in A. Wilton and A. Lyles, *The Great Age of British Watercolours, 1750–1880* (exh. cat., London, Royal Academy of Arts, 1993), pl. 284 (cat. 115).
480 Tim Wilcox, *The Triumph of Watercolour: The early years of the Royal Watercolour Society 1805–55* (exh. cat., London, Dulwich Picture Gallery and Manchester, Whitworth Art Gallery, 2005), p. 57.
481 G. Harmsworth, *Exhibition of the Works of Peter DeWint* (exh. cat., Lincoln, Usher Gallery, 1937), p. 25 (cat. 156).

## View in Epping Forest, near High Beech, Essex[482]

LL 3800 (WHL 316, H 157)

Watercolour, with extra gum arabic and touches of gouache on wove paper
45.7 x 83.2 cm
Date: possibly late 1840s

Annot: View in Epping Forest, near High Beech, Esse[...] / P. DeWint 18[...] (ink, on a label on the frame, verso; part of the label torn away)

Prov: James Orrock; his sale, Christie's, 4 June 1904 (lot 49); bt. in (1,020 gns);[483] bt. from Gooden and Fox by Lever, 1907[484]

Exh: [?] London, SPWC, 1847 (cat. 41)

Lit: Charles Holme (ed.), 'Masters of English Landscape Painting', *The Studio*, Special Number (summer 1903), pl. 28 (titled *Near Epping Forest*)

Although LL 3800 is not obviously recognisable as Epping Forest, DeWint seems to have visited Essex, not far from his base in London, in the late 1840s, as he exhibited a handful of works with titles referring to the area at the SPWC from 1846 to 1848.[485] DeWint's son-in-law, Paul Tatlock, who was married to his daughter Helen, came from High Beech, Essex, and it is possible that the artist visited the couple there.[486]

LL 3800 has the attention to detail and 'tight' formal qualities present in many of DeWint's panoramic landscapes from the late 1830s onwards. With its large dimensions, it may be the *View in Epping Forest, near High Beech, Essex* exhibited at the SPWC in 1847.[487] This work was described favourably by a reviewer in the *Athenaeum* as showing 'the effect of the passing storm and the bursting forth of the light [which] are given with great truth. It shows how much may be done in the application of such effects to forms of very unpromising character'.[488] LL 3800, which now has severe losses of pigment in the sky, may once have exhibited the brooding atmospheric qualities of some of DeWint's best work.

482 WHL Inventory lists LL 3800 as *A view in Epping Forest with Cornfield and sandhills, windmill and figures on a road near High Beech*.
483 1904 Inventory (no. 101), listed as *View in Epping Forest*, 18 x 32½ in.
484 1907 Hill Inventory, listed as *View in Epping Forest*, Orrock collection per Gooden and Fox.
485 A handwritten note in the WHL Inventory (made by A. C. Tait?) states 'This does not represent any scene in Epping Forest, but has been known for a long time under this title'.
486 Paul Tatlock's origins are mentioned in Harriet Helen Tatlock's addendum to her grandmother's *Memoir*. See Harriet DeWint, *A Short Memoir of the Life of Peter DeWint*, reprinted in Lord (ed.), *Peter DeWint*, p. 89. There is no conclusive evidence that Helen and Paul remained in Essex, but there is nothing to suggest otherwise.
487 This work was sold for 40 gns to George Constable Senior of Arundel, Sussex. It has not been possible to trace the early provenance of LL 3800.
488 *Athenaeum* (1 May 1847), p. 471.

LL 3800

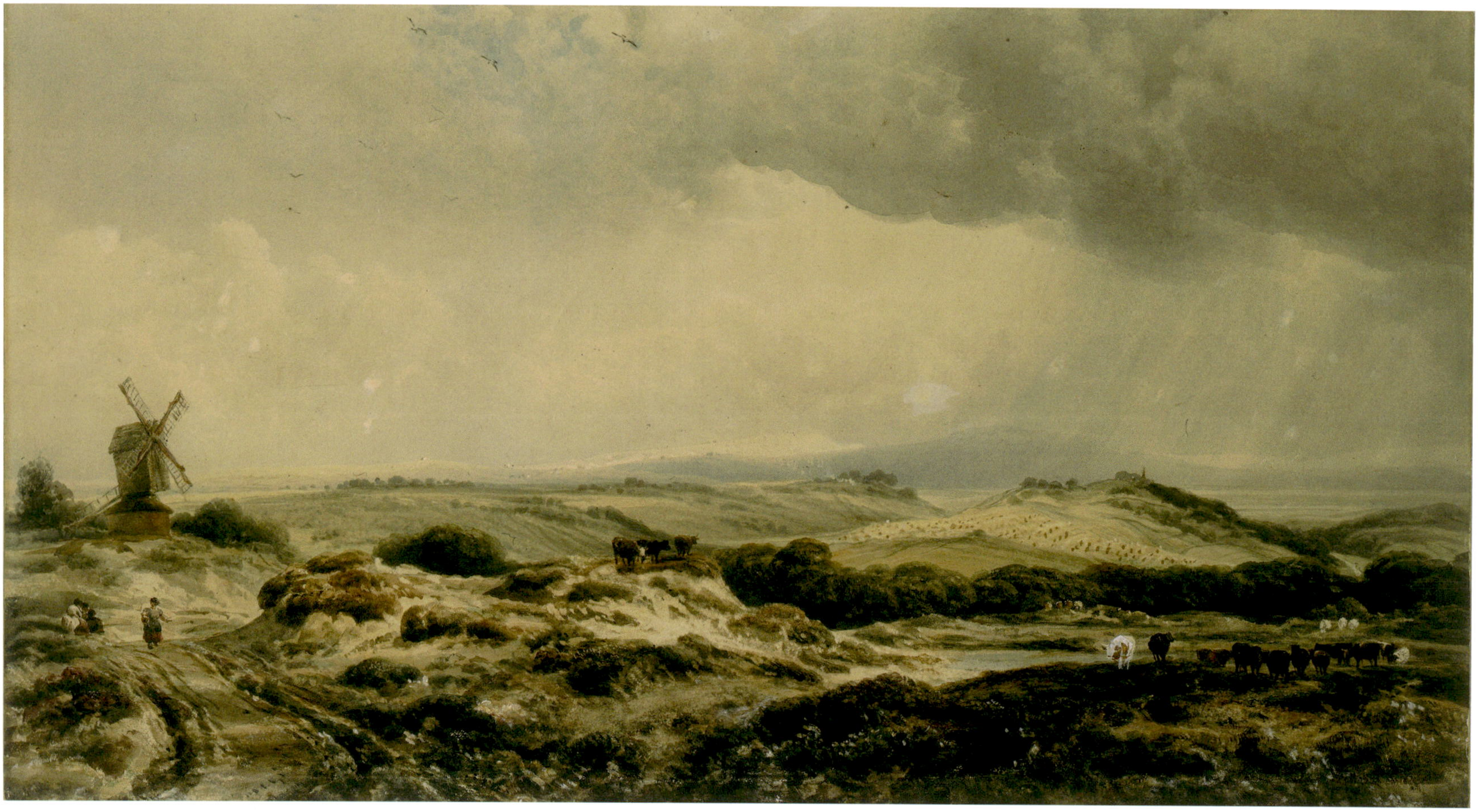

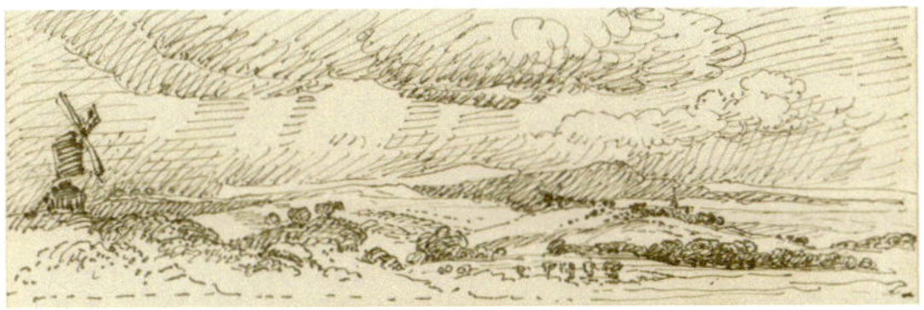

fig. 33. Peter DeWint, *Near Epping*, date unknown, possibly late 1840s, pen and brown ink on paper, 7.1 x 20.9 cm, Fitzwilliam Museum, Cambridge

A preliminary ink sketch in the same narrow format (Fitzwilliam Museum, Cambridge, fig. 33) has all the main features of the watercolour, although DeWint moved the church spire (on the right) further back in the finished composition.

### Still Life on a Table

LL 3904 (WHL 768, HH 438)

Watercolour with extra gum arabic over traces of pencil on wove paper
24 x 32.4 cm
Date: c. 1810–49

Inscr: <u>6</u> or 3 or <u>8</u> [?] (black chalk, bottom right)

Prov: bt. from James Orrock by Lever, 1910[489]

Exh: Lincoln, Usher Gallery, *Exhibition of the works of Peter DeWint*, 1937 (cat. 139)

Although landscape was DeWint's preferred genre, his output also included a small number of still-lifes. These were not exhibited but they seem to have been produced throughout his career, both to 'keep his hand in' but also as examples for his many pupils to follow.[490] LL 3904 is typical of these still-lifes in that DeWint's chosen range of domestic objects, including an earthenware bowl, a piece of cloth and a turnip, provide a variety of shapes, colours and textures that would test the abilities of his pupils.

Andrew Wyld has suggested that LL 3904 is by DeWint himself;[491] similar works are clearly by his pupils. In this case, the slightly weak handling of the black urn may suggest the work of a pupil, and it is quite possible that a student worked on the same sheet as DeWint. Unless these still-lifes are inscribed with a date, it is generally difficult to date them and this is the case with LL 3904.

489 1910 Inventory, 9½ x 13 in., valued at £5.

490 Walter Armstrong, *Memoir of Peter DeWint* (London, 1888), p. 41.
491 Andrew Wyld, verbally, July 2003.

LL 3904

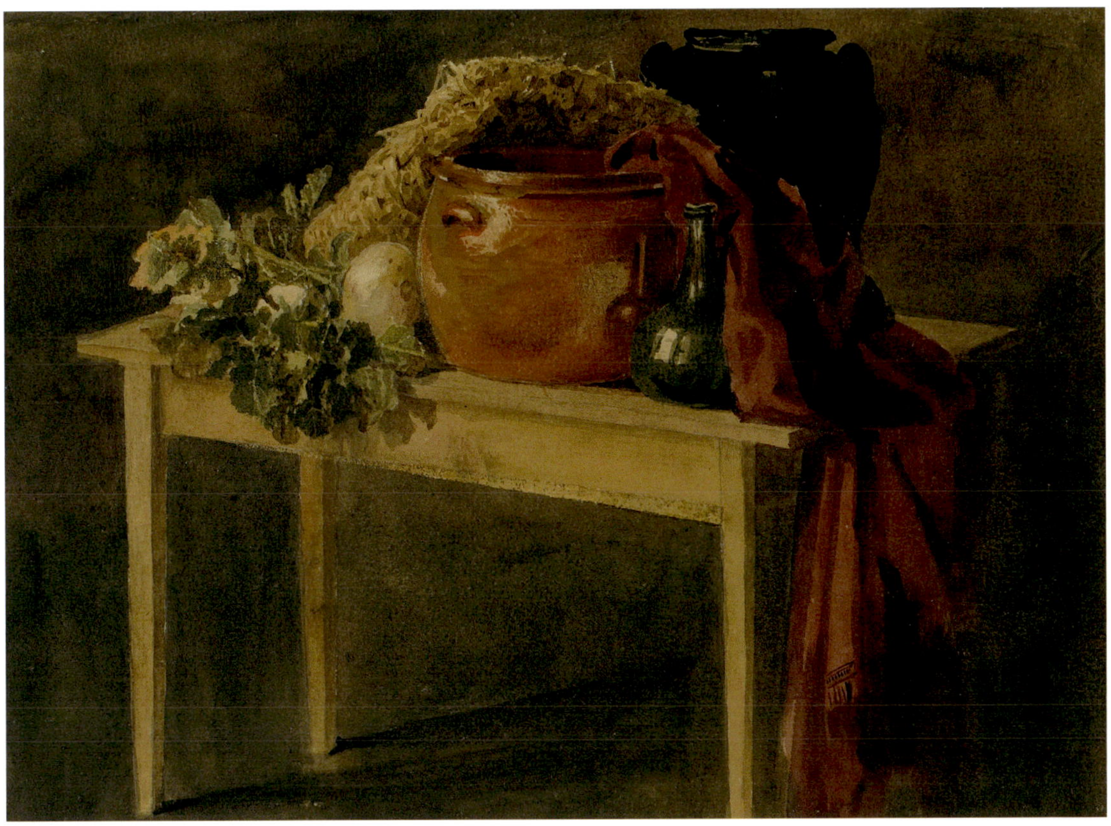

## AFTER PETER DEWINT

### Entrance to Haddon Hall

LL 3954 (WHL 802, HH 369)

Watercolour with extra gum arabic, over pencil on wove paper
16.8 x 24.7 cm (sight)
Date: nineteenth century

Prov: [?] Miss H.H. Tatlock;[492] James Orrock; bt. from Orrock by Lever, 1910

Lever acquired LL 3954 as by Peter DeWint from James Orrock in 1910, along with numerous other watercolours by the artist. However, it has recently been identified as a version of a larger and more finished watercolour by the artist (fig. 34).[493] The weak handling of the tower and the figures has led Harriet Drummond and Noel Annesley to suggest that the Lady Lever work is not autograph.[494] Nevertheless, it does display many elements of DeWint's style and is likely to be by a contemporary, possibly one of his many pupils.

492 1910 Inventory lists LL 3954 as *Entrance to Haddon Hall*, 6¾ x 9¾ in., valued at £40, and describes it as 'from collection of Miss H. H. Tatlock'. Miss Harriet Helen Tatlock was the artist's grand-daughter and inherited a sizeable number of his works by descent. However, it is known that she owned the original after which this is a copy, and it may be that James Orrock either deliberately or mistakenly conflated the provenance of the original, which was published in Holme (ed.), 'Masters of English Landscape Painting', with the Lady Lever work. It remains possible, however, that she did also own LL 3954, in which case it would seem likely that LL 3954 was copied for her from the original when it was in her possession.
493 Up until recently this was in the Loyd Collection, Lockinge, Berkshire; see Leslie Parris, *The Loyd Collection of Paintings and Drawings at Betterton House, Lockinge near Wantage, Berkshire* (London, 1967), p. 56 (cat. 87). It was for sale at Christie's, 5 June 2007 (lot 7), bt. in. Parris stated that 'a photograph of a less finished version (whereabouts unknown) of this drawing is in the Witt library'. I could find no photograph of any version apart from the Lady Lever work in the Witt library, and while the 'other version' may have been mislaid, it seems more likely that Parris was referring to the Lady Lever version.
494 Verbally, May 2007. This is also the opinion of Andrew Wyld, verbally, July 2003.

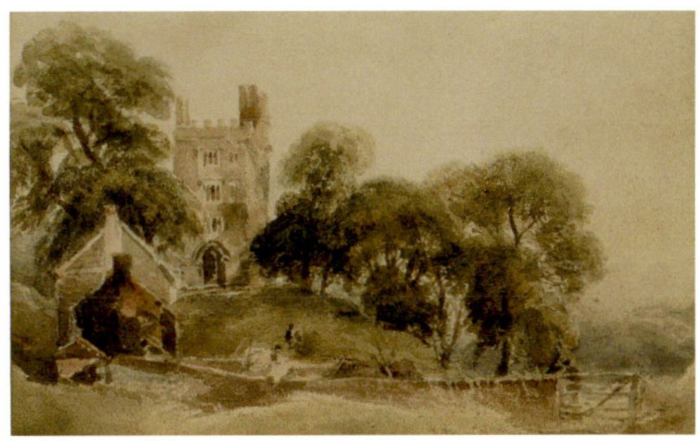

LL 3954

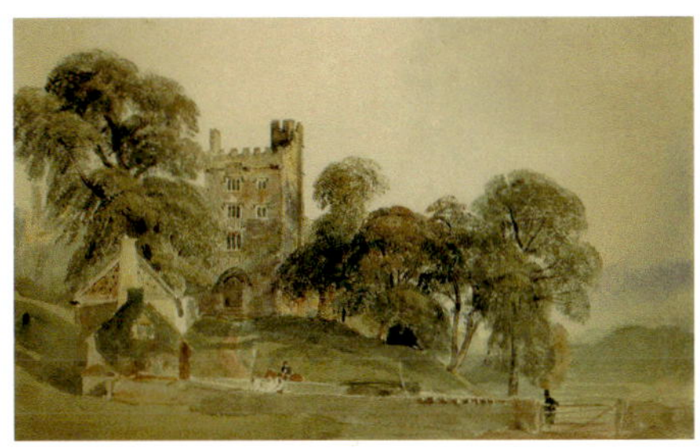

fig. 34. Peter DeWint, *Haddon Hall*, Derbyshire, ?1840s, watercolour, 29 x 46.3 cm, © Christie's Images Ltd 2007

## 'PETER DEWINT'

### View in Staffordshire, near Stone
LL 3577 (WHL 3804)

Watercolour with extra gum arabic and scratching out on wove paper laid over a stretcher
21.4 x 32.6 cm
Date: nineteenth century

Annot: Peter DeWint an eminent watercolour painter, / was born at Stone in Staffordshire, in 1784. He / Studied under John Raphael Smith, the engraver. / In 1807 he entered the schools of the Royal / Academy. He joined the Water-Colour Society / as an Associate in 1810, becoming a full member / in 1812. Peter DeWint also painted in oils / occasionally. He died in London in 1849. (ink, on a label pasted on to the stretcher, verso)

Prov: S. Stern; his sale, Christie's, 9 May 1919 (lot 144); bt. by Gooden and Fox (£39 18s) for Lever (£40 18s)

LL 3577 bears some of the hallmarks of DeWint's style, notably his earthy colour palette punctuated by small touches of flaming red, here on the figure. However, the poor handling overall suggests that the work is not by the artist.[495] The work may be by a contemporary imitator, possibly one of DeWint's many pupils.

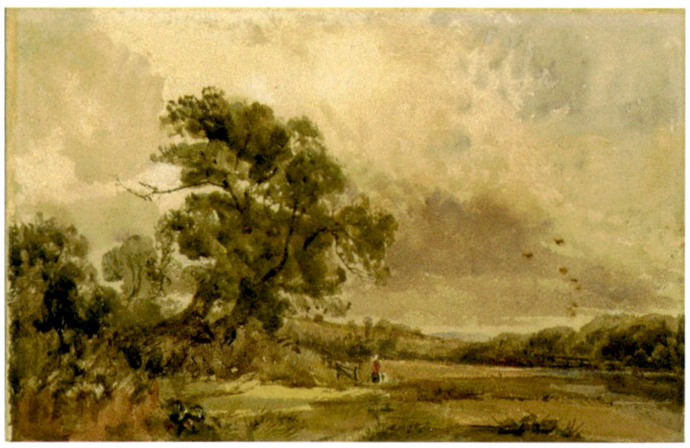

LL 3577

495 Andrew Wyld and Charles Nugent, verbally, July 2003.

## GEORGE HAYDOCK DODGSON
1811 Liverpool–1880 London

### Fête champêtre
LL 3958 (WHL 315, H 391)

Gouache and watercolour with extra gum arabic over pencil on wove paper
50.3 (arched top) x 89.6 cm
Date: 1849

Inscr: GH Dodgson / 1849 (watercolour, bottom left)

Prov: Edward Duncan; his sale, Christie's, 9–12 March 1883 (lot 143); bt. by J. & W. Vokins (145 gns); James Orrock, his sale, Christie's, 4 June 1904 (lot 194), unsold; bt. from Orrock by Lever, 1912[496]

Exh: London, SPWC, 1849 (cat. 131, as *A Sunshine Holiday*); London, SPWC, *Winter Exhibition*, 1880 (cat. 431, as *A Sunshine Holiday*); Manchester, Manchester Art Gallery, *Jubilee Exhibition*, 1887 (cat. 1656, as *A Sunshine Holiday*)

Lit: J. L. Roget, *A History of the 'Old Water-Colour' Society* (London, 2 vols, 1891), vol. II, p. 308; Byron Webber, *James Orrock, R.I.: Painter, Connoisseur, Collector* (London, 2 vols, 1903), vol. II, p. 254, illus. p. 98

Dodgson took some of his first lessons in watercolour in Liverpool from Andrew Hunt, father of the watercolourist Alfred William Hunt. In 1827 Dodgson was apprenticed to railway engineer George Stephenson, but on completing his articles in 1835 he turned to art. He exhibited oils and watercolours in London before being elected to the New Society of Painters in Water-Colours in 1842. In 1848 he became an associate of the SPWC, and a full member in 1852. For the first decade of his membership he exhibited primarily generalised 'poetic' landscapes, evocative of moods either of gaiety or melancholy. After 1860 his work was in the main topographical, favouring the Thames valley, Whitby and, towards the very end of his life, the Gower peninsula.

Dodgson's particular strength was the combining of figures with landscape, or rather the artificial landscape of the English park, in which architectural elements such as steps, balustrades and terraces give shape and structure to the space. LL 3958 is perhaps the outstanding example of this strand in his work; Roget certainly implies this, citing the high price fetched when the work was sold from the collection of fellow SPWC member Edward Duncan in 1883. The two artists had reason for fellow-feeling, since both had previously been members of the New Society of Painters in Water-Colours and were elected to the senior body on the same day in 1848.

The title by which the work became known, *A Fête champêtre*, makes an explicit reference to Watteau, the supposed inventor of the genre, though Dodgson's figures are dressed in the costume of cavaliers, a garb that had been revived as a sign of Tory privilege since the middle of the eighteenth century. Its original title, *A Sunshine Holiday*, is certainly somewhat stilted, but skilfully makes reference both to the light Dodgson preferred to paint and the festive atmosphere. 'Of summer days, that here enjoy an undisputed reign, the artist seems to have made a special study' commented Roget.[497]

Another watercolour also titled *A Fête champêtre* was sold in the artist's studio sale at Christie's on 25 March 1881 (lot 13).
TW

496 1912 Inventory, valued at £50.

497 J. L. Roget, *A History of the 'Old Water-Colour' Society* (London, 2 vols, 1891), vol. II, p. 306.

LL 3958

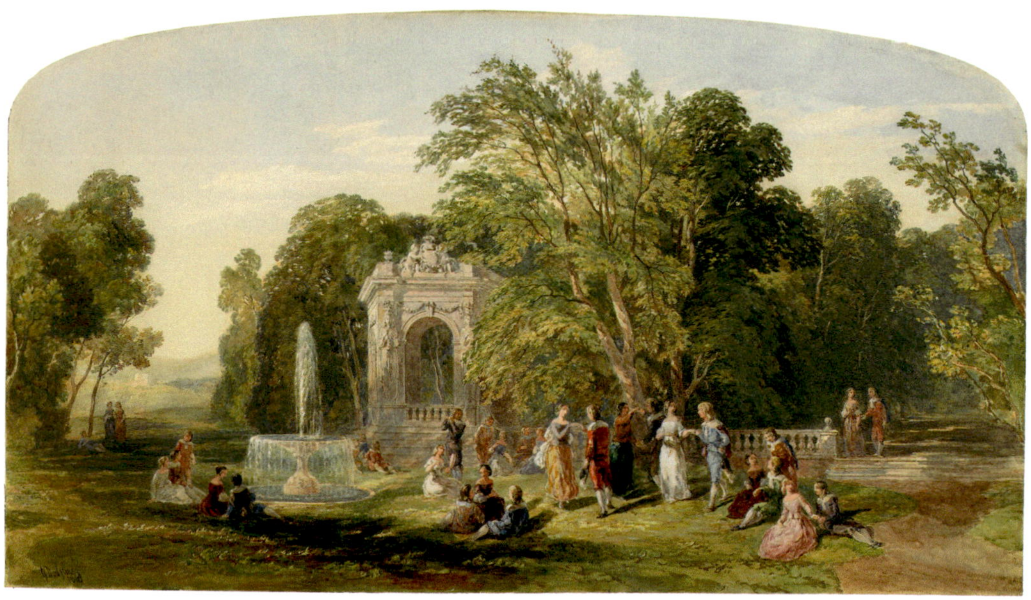

## Crossing the Stream

LL 3847 (WHL 274, H 384)

Watercolour and gouache over pencil on [laid?] paper
15.2 x 23 cm (trimmed irreg.)
Date: c. 1840–80

Inscr: GHD [monogram] (watercolour, bottom left)
Prov: acquired by Lever in 1912[498]

The subject is typical of the English pastoral that was an abiding theme in Dodgson's exhibits at the SPWC. In 1848, his first year as an associate, he showed *Crossing the Brook*, followed the next year by *The Ford*. The idiosyncratic handling, with little dabs of paint, was apparently due to a nervous condition attributed to overwork during Dodgson's early years as an engineer. The mannerism became more pronounced in later life, but was already present in his earliest productions, as *The Times*'s reviewer noted in 1846: 'The "dotty" touch of this artist causes his works to be recognised at a glance, and his little avenues and flights of steps, so well conceived and so well executed, invariably produce a sensation of tranquil pleasure in the observer'.[499] The dating of LL 3847 cannot, therefore, be established with certainty.
TW

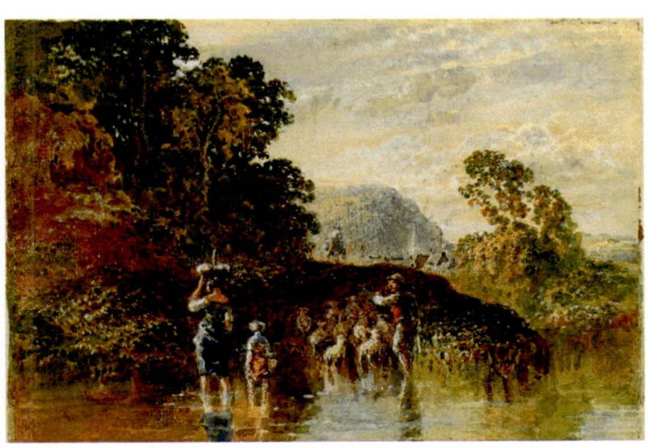

LL 3847

498 Listed in the 1912 Hill Inventory but not in the 1911 Hill Inventory. A label of the framemakers Dolman on the reverse of LL 3847 refers to 'Miss T. R.'; presumably a previous owner.
499 *The Times*, 27 April 1846, p. 5.

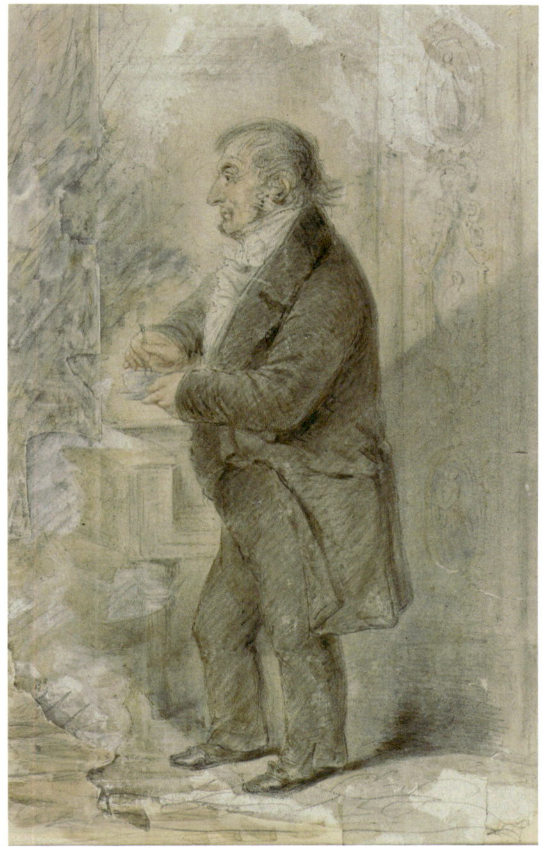

LL 3971

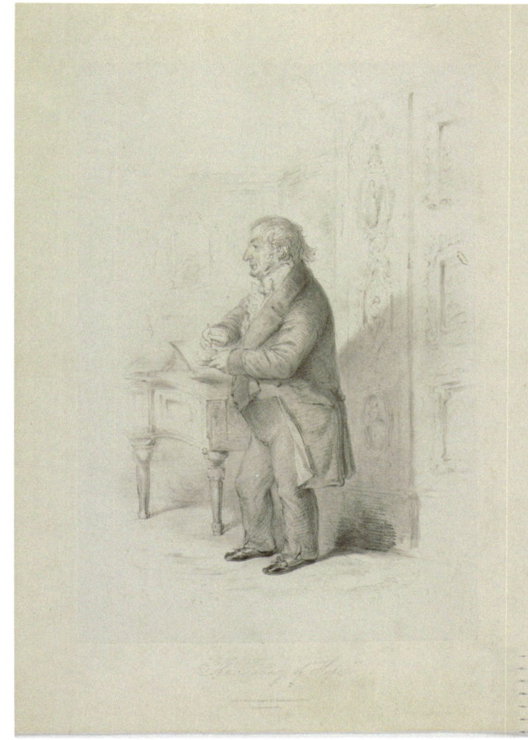

fig. 35. J. Hogarth, after Count Alfred D'Orsay, *The Fallacy of Hope*, 1851, lithograph on paper, 40.5 x 30 cm, National Museums Liverpool, Lady Lever Art Gallery

## AFTER COUNT ALFRED D'ORSAY

1801 Paris–1852 Paris

### J. M. W. Turner

LL 3971 (WHL 739, HH 696)

Pencil and watercolour on paper
25.9 x 16.4 cm (sight)
Date: possibly after 1851

Prov: bt. from James Orrock by Lever, 1904
Lit: R. J. B. Walker, 'The Portraits of JMW Turner: A Check-List', *Turner Studies*, vol. 3, no. 1 (summer 1983), p. 29

Lever purchased LL 3971 as a portrait of J. M. W. Turner by William Henry Hunt (see pp. 120–127) and it was subsequently catalogued by Tatlock with the same attribution.[500] However, the drawing has since been re-attributed as a copy after a drawing by Count D'Orsay (untraced).[501] It may be from a lithograph published 1 January 1851 by J. Hogarth based on the original (fig. 35).[502]

Alfred Guillaume Gabriel D'Orsay was the second son of a general in Napoleon's army, and in 1821 the young Count joined the army of the restored Bourbon monarchy. In 1822, after meeting the married Countess of Blessington (with whom he embarked on an affair), D'Orsay resigned his commission, and he spent the years up until 1829 travelling on the continent with her family. By this time the party included his own wife, Lady Harriet Gardiner, a marriage which was purely a financial arrangement. By 1829 Lord Blessington had died, D'Orsay was estranged from his wife, and he had returned to London with Lady Blessington. In London D'Orsay, or the 'prince of dandies' as he was known, presided over Lady Blessington's fashionable salon at Gore House, where they entertained many of the political and literary celebrities of the time, including by 1840 Disraeli, Dickens and Thackeray. D'Orsay's wide circle of friends provided him with ready material for his artistic work as a sculptor and a painter, and he specialised in portraiture. D'Orsay made 297 known portrait drawings, many of which were lithographed by Richard Lane.[503]

500 Tatlock, p. 132 and illus. pl. 89.
501 D'Orsay's drawing was owned by Elhanan Bicknell and in his sale, Christie's, 29 April–1 May 1863 (lot 74); bt. by Holmes (£52 10s).
502 R. J. B. Walker, 'The Portraits of JMW Turner: A Check-List', *Turner Studies*, vol. 3, no. 1 (summer 1983), p. 29, suggests that LL 3971 may be the original, although it is unclear whether he saw the drawing. Frank Milner, *Turner: Paintings in Merseyside Collections* (Liverpool, 1990) mistakenly refers to LL 3971 as a lithograph but he does attribute it as 'after D'Orsay' (caption to frontispiece).

503 Willard Connely, *Count D'Orsay: The Dandy of Dandies* (London, 1952), p. 563.

By 1849 D'Orsay had fled to France to escape his creditors, closely followed by Lady Blessington who died shortly after her arrival, with D'Orsay following not long afterwards.

D'Orsay's drawing was one of the relatively few images of Turner (see pp. 182–203), who was not depicted by illustrious artist contemporaries such as Lawrence and Beechey.[504] In LL 3971, as with other Turner portraits, the image has been captured surreptitiously and does not represent a formal sitting; the artist is depicted wearing his usual wool coat and linen cravat in a moment of repose, stirring his tea, located in a grand drawing room, adjacent to a piano. Walker has suggested that this may be Lady Blessington's or Elhanan Bicknell's house.[505] The drawing shows Turner in profile, emphasising his prominent nose; Turner was self-conscious about his appearance from an early age, and avoided depicting himself in profile in an early self portrait (Tate) of c. 1799. The original drawing has been dated to c. 1845–49, when Turner was in his seventies, and captures his short, stout stature as well as the unkempt appearance often described by contemporaries.[506] The drawing gained fame through its publication as a print, and was described by a writer in the *Athenaeum* in 1858 as: 'The best sketch of him we know is Count D'Orsay's clever drawing of him at some soirée, with a tea-cup in his hand'.[507]

LL 3971 has been framed with an impression of the lithograph by Hogarth, titled *The Fallacy of Hope*. The title is a reference to a poem, *The Fallacies of Hope*, which, although possibly imaginary, was referred to by Turner first in 1812 and then on numerous occasions as the source of the poetry appended to many of his paintings.[508] The phrase was famously associated with Turner into the 1840s and 50s, and may have been used in the case of this print to suggest Turner's mortality.

504 Walker lists 51 portraits of Turner. He makes this point in the introduction to his article, p. 21.

505 Walker, 'Portraits of JMW Turner', p. 29. Elhanan Bicknell was a wealthy whaling entrepreneur and patron of Turner in the 1830s and 1840s. He had a large house in Herne Hill, south-east London, where Turner was a regular guest.

506 Walker, 'Portraits of JMW Turner', p. 29; these contemporary descriptions are mentioned on p. 21.

507 *Athenaeum* (13 March 1858), p. 344.

508 For this argument and a discussion of possible sources for the phrase, see Jerrold Ziff, 'John Langhorne and Turner's "Fallacies of Hope"', *Journal of the Warburg and Courtauld Institutes*, vol. 27 (1964), pp. 340–42.

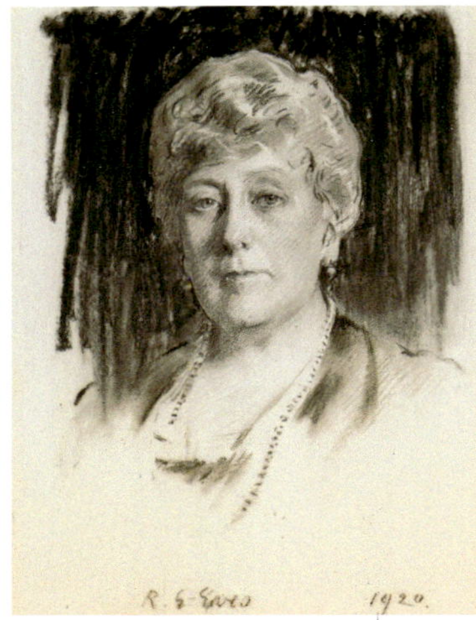


LL 3848

## REGINALD GRENVILLE EVES

1876 London–1941 Middleton-in-Teesdale, Durham

### H.R.H. The Princess Beatrice

LL 3848 (LP 59)

Charcoal and pencil on paper
58.2 x 45.5 cm
Date: 1920

Inscr: R. G. Eves 1920 (charcoal, bottom)

Prov: bt. from the artist's widow by the Trustees, 1941 (£26 5s)

Exh: location unknown, The Pastel Society, exhibition title and date unknown (cat. 2);[509] Manchester, Manchester Art Gallery, *Royal Society of Portrait Painters exhibition*, 1925 (cat. 10)

A successful portrait artist, Eves studied at the Slade School. He exhibited widely and became an associate of the Royal Academy in 1934 and a full member in 1939. He was employed as an official war artist by the War Artists Advisory Committee in 1940.

Eves made several portraits of members of the Royal Family. In the same year as making this drawing of Princess Beatrice he made studies of the Duke of Windsor (King Edward VIII).[510] Princess Beatrice, fifth daughter and youngest child of Queen Victoria, was born in 1857. When her father, Prince Albert, died in 1861, Beatrice became a constant companion to her mother, eventually acting as the Queen's unofficial secretary, dealing with both general and political correspondence. She married Prince Henry of Battenberg in 1885. After her mother's death in 1901 Beatrice continued to carry out public duties,[511] one of which was the official opening of the Lady Lever Art Gallery on 16 December 1922.[512] This drawing was presumably purchased because of this historical connection.
SP

509 This is cited in the LLAG files. It has not been possible to trace this exhibition.

510 There are chalk and oil studies in the National Portrait Gallery, NPG 4138 and NPG 4169.

511 See Matthew Dennison, *The Last Princess: The Devoted Life of Queen Victoria's Youngest Daughter* (London, 2007).

512 National Museums Liverpool, *Lady Lever Art Gallery Guide* (Liverpool, 2007), p. 12; 2nd Viscount Leverhulme, *Viscount Leverhulme*, p. 284.

## ANTHONY VANDYKE COPLEY FIELDING

1787 Sowerby Bridge, Yorkshire–1855 Worthing, Sussex

### Ben Vorlich and Loch Lomond

LL 3959 (WHL 270, H 388)

Watercolour over pencil with white heightening and gum arabic, with stopping out and scratching out on wove paper
18.9 x 26.5 cm
Date: 1836

Inscr: CF/1836 (pencil, bottom right); Ben Vorlich (pencil, top left)

Prov: bt. from James Orrock by Lever, 1912[513]

Exh: Perth, Art Gallery of Western Australia and Australian tour, *Exhibition of Early British Water-colours*, organised by the Empire Art Loans Exhibition Society 1948–49 (cat. 105); Hove, Hove Museum of Art, *Festival exhibition of work by Sussex artists, past and present*, 1951 (cat. 36)

Fielding, one of five brothers, all of whom became artists, was taught by his father, the portrait and landscape painter Nathan Fielding. The family lived in various locations in the north of England: in 1804 in Ambleside in the Lake District, then a spell in Manchester. In 1807 Copley and his father came to live in Liverpool. From there Copley made a tour of North Wales, then settled in London. He was given free lessons by John Varley (see pp. 206–207), and in 1810 was elected associate of the SPWC. In 1813 Fielding married the sister of Varley's wife; due to her delicate health, and that of their eldest daughter, they moved to the south coast and lived in Kent and then in Brighton, Hove and Worthing. Fielding never travelled abroad; as a result perhaps of his brothers' presence as painters and printmakers in Paris, watercolours by Copley were shown at the Paris Salon in 1824 and made a great impression, alongside the works of Constable (pp. 47–52) and Bonington (pp. 10–12).

When the SPWC relaunched itself in 1821 Fielding was first secretary, then deputy president and finally, from 1831, president. Each year he contributed 40 or more paintings, concentrating on the English coast and the mountain scenery of Wales, the Lake District and Scotland. Ruskin, who was an admirer and went to Fielding for lessons, was perhaps right in his comment in the first volume of *Modern Painters*, that 'had he painted five rather than five hundred such … he might … have been one of our greatest artists'.[514]

Fielding made his first trip to Scotland in 1823. There are several inscribed drawings from that year in the British Museum, including one of *Loch Lomond from Luss*, dated Aug 25–23.[515] The view in LL 3959 appears to be the narrow, northern end of the loch, looking north-west

513 1912 Inventory, p. 1, as *Loch Katrine*, valued at £80.

514 E. T. Cook and A. Wedderburn (eds), *The Works of John Ruskin* (London and New York, 39 vols, 1903–12), vol. III, p. 532.

515 1904-3-7-14.

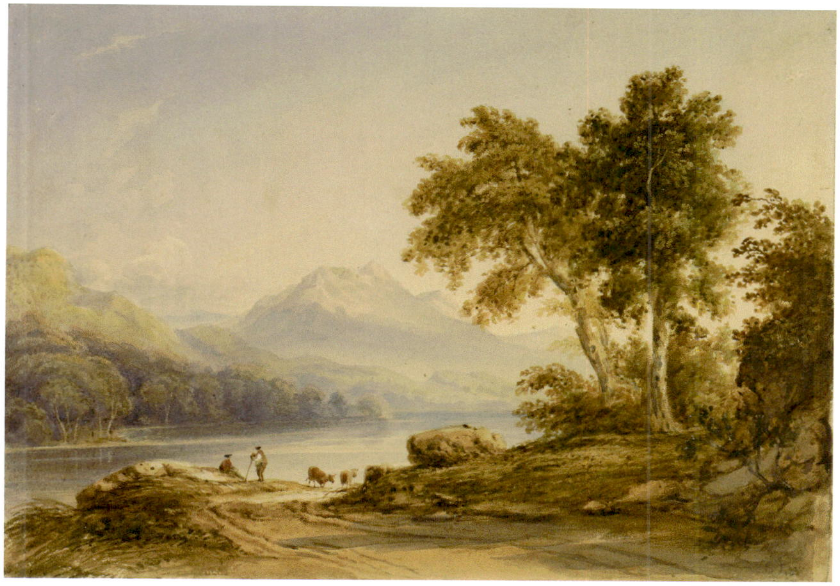

LL 3959

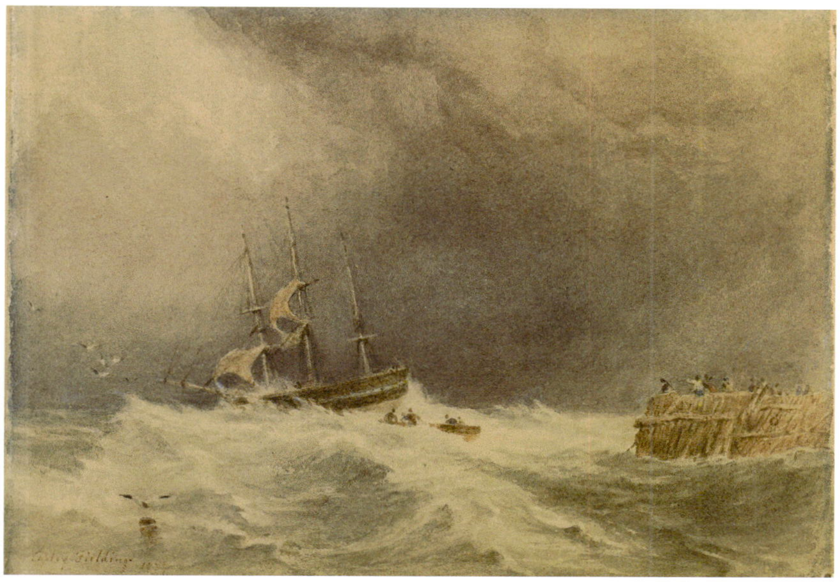

LL 3850

towards Ben Vorlich. It was a view Fielding was to paint many times. In the SPWC exhibition of 1824, the first to include Scottish subjects by him, he showed *View of Ben Vorlich and mountains, at the head of Loch Lomond, from near the Point of Farkin – an effect after rain* (cat. 21), as well as another watercolour simply entitled *Loch Lomond* (cat. 57) among 17 works derived from the recent tour.[516] The same features were named in the titles of a further eight watercolours exhibited between 1826 and 1854.

A watercolour of *Ben Vorlich with Loch Lomond*, dated 1840, is in the collection of Harrow School.[517] A watercolour titled *View of Ben Vorlich, looking up Loch Lomond* was exhibited at the SPWC in 1850 (cat. 219). An oil on canvas of this subject was with Patterson Gallery in 1968,[518] while a small oil on panel was sold at Sotheby's, London in 1985.[519]

Lever acquired LL 3959 as a view of Loch Katrine, but it was subsequently confused in the gallery with LL 3791, being identified on the frame under the title *A Mountain Lake*.[520] It was under this title that it was lent to the Festival of Britain exhibition at Hove Museum in 1951 and it was presumably also this work that was lent to the Empire Art Society *Exhibition of early English watercolours* that toured Australia in 1948–49.
TW

516 A British Museum sketch, 1904-3-7-18, inscribed Ben Lomond & Point of Farkin Aug 25 was evidently made nearby on the same day. It depicts a less obstructed view towards the head of the loch.

517 C. Leder, *In search of the picturesque; watercolourists in Wales and Scotland* (exh. cat., Harrow, Harrow School, Old Speech Room Gallery, 1996) unpag., (cat. 19).

518 Photograph: Witt Library, Courtauld Institute of Art.

519 Sotheby's, 17 July 1985 (lot 596).

520 Tatlock, p. 129, correctly catalogued LL 3959 under its original title of *Loch Katrine*, so the confusion appears to postdate this.

## A Shipwreck near a Jetty
LL 3850 (WHL 717, HH 371)

Watercolour over pencil on wove paper
13.4 x 18.6 cm
Date: 1837

Inscr: Copley Fielding 1837 ([?] ink, bottom left)
Prov: bt. from James Orrock by Lever, 1910[521]

Although this work has always been known in the Lady Lever collection as *A Shipwreck*, the description is premature. In over 1,700 works exhibited at the SPWC, Fielding only showed one vessel defeated by the waves. That was in 1835, and the work in question, *Shipwreck under Beachy Head*, could well have been a beach scene with the remains of a wreck, since the commemoration of destruction – and the loss of life almost inevitably entailed – was not to Fielding's taste.

In 1837, the date inscribed on LL 3850, Fielding introduced a new vein of material into his annual submissions to the SPWC, namely, the coast of Yorkshire. Given the reputation of Scarborough and Bridlington, or Burlington as it was then called, as spa towns, alongside his professional commitments, he may well have taken his delicate wife and daughter for a change of air. The 1837 exhibition included *The old pier at Burlington, Yorkshire, during a gale* (cat. 96) and *Burlington Quay* (cat. 113). LL 3850 could possibly be one of the 1838 exhibits: *Vessel off Burlington Pier, Yorkshire* (cat. 72). However, the *Bridlington Harbour* in the Wallace Collection, dated 1839, though broadly similar in composition, shows a wooden jetty of different construction.[522]

Similar subjects continued for the next decade. In the first volume of *Modern Painters*, published in 1843, Ruskin praised Fielding as the greatest living sea painter after Turner, but deprecated the monochrome tonality in which he painted stormy weather, unrelieved by any point of colour, even the red of a sailor's cap.[523] He could well have had such a work as LL 3850 in mind when he wrote those lines. An undated watercolour in the Whitworth Art Gallery, Manchester, titled *Boats in a storm, Bridlington harbour*, shows a wooden pier with a hut at its seaward end, which may be the other arm of the harbour wall to that depicted in LL 3850.
TW

521 1910 Inventory, valued at £35.

522 J. Ingamells, *The Wallace Collection. Catalogue of pictures, I: British, German, Italian, Spanish* (London, 1985), p. 89 (cat. 691).

523 A. Sumner, *Ruskin and the English watercolour from Turner to the Pre-Raphaelites* (exh. cat., Manchester, Whitworth Art Gallery, 1989), p. 30 (cat. 42).

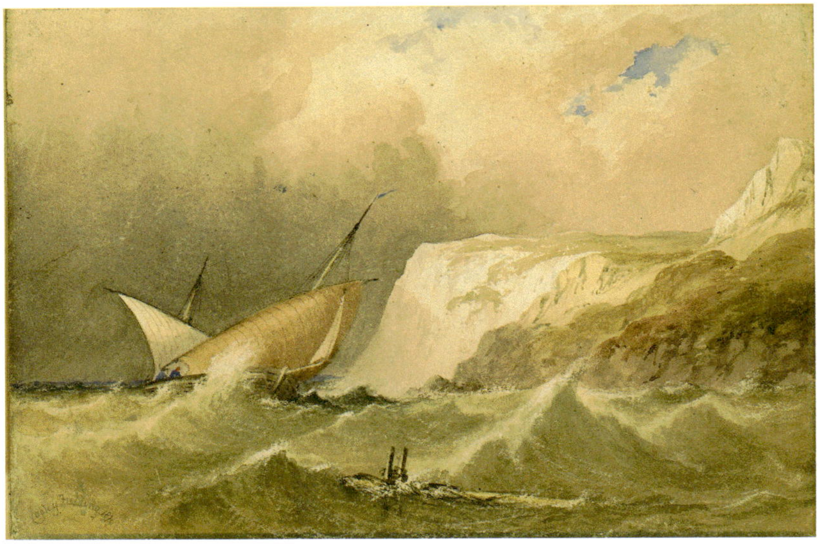

LL 3961

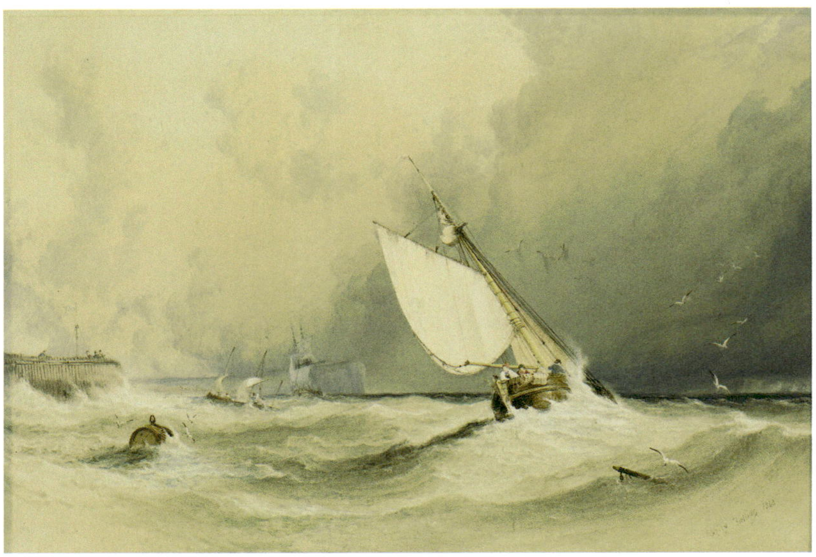

LL 3851

LL 3960

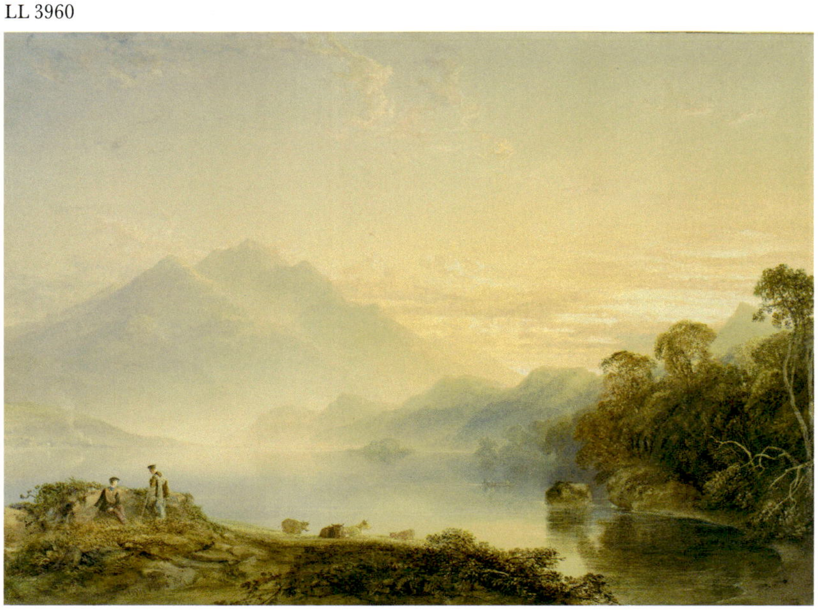

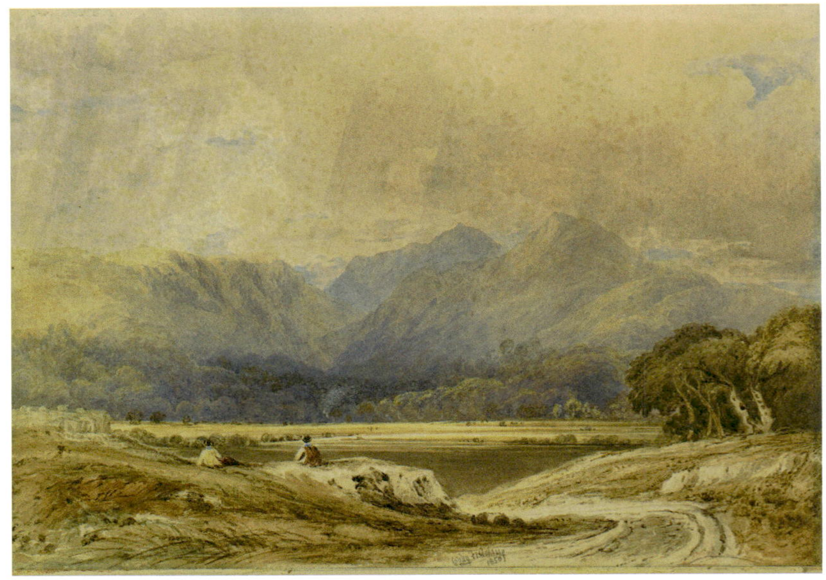

LL 3791

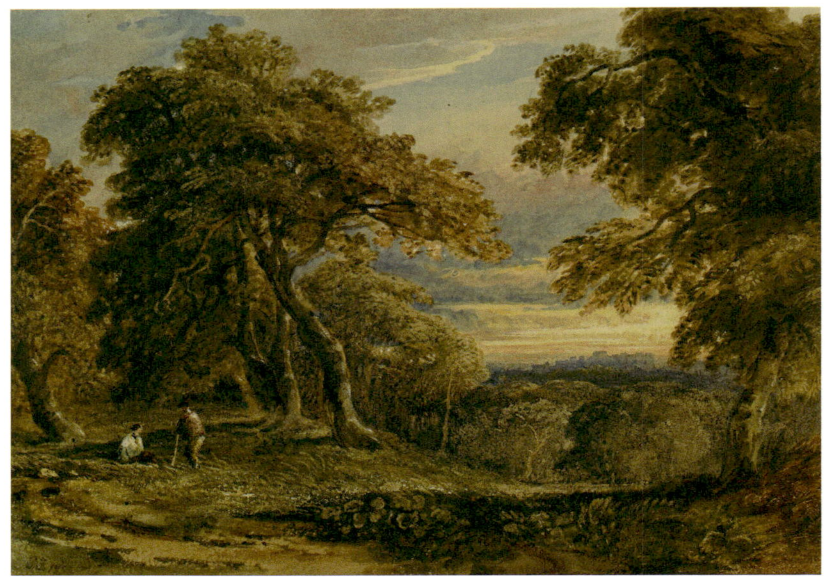

LL 3852

LL 3849

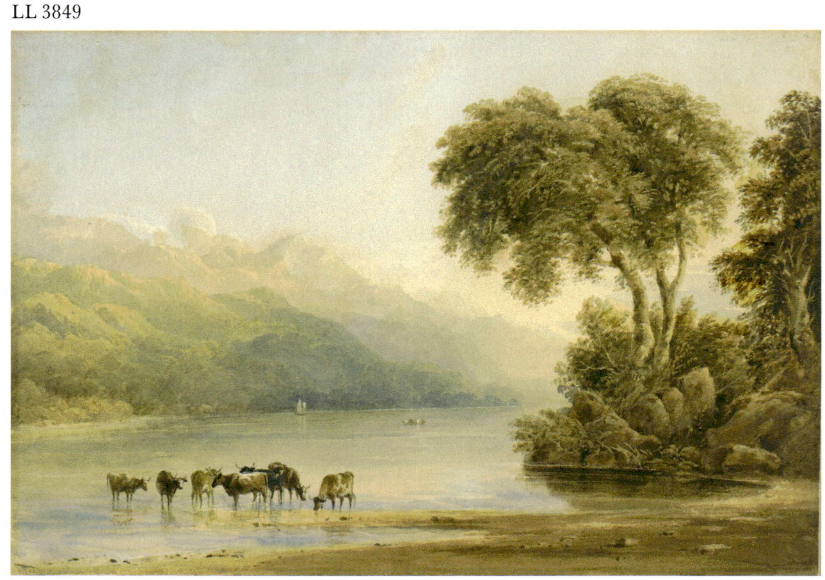

### Coast Scene, Luccombe, Isle of Wight
LL 3961 (WHL 751, HH 414)

Watercolour with touches of gouache and scratching out on wove paper
17.9 x 27.3 cm
Date: 1839

Inscr: Copley Fielding 1839 (pencil, bottom left, over a faint bowed line)

Annot: Coast at Luccomb [*sic*] / Isle of Wight (pencil, verso)

Prov: bt. from James Orrock by Lever, 1910[524]

Luccombe, a hamlet on the south-east coast of the Isle of Wight, is noted for its cliffs and secluded beach, to which the only access is down a narrow gully or 'chine'. Fielding exhibited coastal scenes around the eastern shores of the Isle of Wight first in 1823, and then intermittently until the end of his life. They were almost all small works, priced at 10 guineas or less. LL 3961 is consistent with such productions; it may not be of the highest quality, but the doubt recently cast on its authenticity[525] is probably unwarranted. LL 3961 does not appear to have been exhibited. The titles of watercolours that mention Luccombe, shown at the SPWC in 1832, 1833 and 1844, were all beach scenes, not the vessels battling a stiff breeze that are depicted here.
TW

### Ships at sea off Folkestone harbour, storm approaching
LL 3851 (WHL 727, HH 349)

Watercolour, gouache and gum arabic with scratching and stopping out on wove paper
41.5 x 61.4 cm
Date: 1843

Inscr: Copley Fielding 1843 (watercolour, bottom right)

Prov: bt. from James Orrock by Lever, 1910[526]

Fielding moved to the Kent coast in 1818. From 1819 he exhibited watercolours of Folkestone and Sandgate and the series continued unabated until the end of his life. If shipping off British coasts became one of his most recognisable offerings year after year in the SPWC, more must have been set off Folkestone than at any other location. One of the earliest, dated 1820 and shown in 1821 as *Vessels at the entrance of Folkestone harbour in a stormy day*, sold to the bishop of Ferns.[527] In 1843, the year LL 3851 was painted, Fielding's largest submission, priced at 60 guineas, was *The Folkestone cliffs, looking towards Dover – sun-rise*. LL 3851, until now known only as *Fishing smack in a squall*,[528] shows the coast from slightly further to the west, with the distinctive rising silhouette of Shakespeare Cliff in the distance. It could possibly have been another of Fielding's 42 exhibits that year, *Folkestone, Kent* (cat. 350), priced at 22 guineas. This sold to the eminent collector Richard Ellison, but was not among the portion of his collection bequeathed to the Victoria & Albert Museum.
TW

524 1910 Inventory, valued at £35.
525 Charles Nugent, verbally, 2006; note in LLAG files.
526 1910 Inventory, valued at £250.
527 Christie's, 9 July 1985 (lot 141).
528 Tatlock, p. 129.

### Ben Venue and the Trossachs seen from Loch Achray[529]
LL 3960 (WHL 813, HH 350)

Watercolour with gum arabic and scratching out on wove paper laid down on card
43.8 x 62.9 cm
Date: 1845

Inscr: Copley Fielding 1845 (watercolour, bottom left)

Annot: Ben Venue & the Trossachs / seen from Loch Achray (pencil, verso, by a later hand)

Prov: bt. from James Orrock by Lever, 1910[530]

To judge by the large number of repetitions, this view of Ben Venue seen towering above the tranquil waters of Loch Achray, a small expanse of water barely a mile long, was a favourite both of Fielding and of his clientele. John Ruskin copied a Fielding watercolour of this loch after one of his lessons with the artist in 1834–35.[531]

Fielding first exhibited a watercolour of the scene in 1828. No drawing directly related to LL 3960 survives, but his presence in the area is documented in a drawing inscribed Glenfinlas from near Loch Achray, and dated Aug 18–23.[532] In both 1836 and 1837 Fielding exhibited two variations of the view of Ben Venue and Loch Achray in the same year, both of relatively modest proportions. A larger version, with the lake and mountain depicted in early morning light, was bought by the Art Union in 1840 for 15 guineas (originally priced at 20 guineas) and may be the watercolour of that date formerly in the Nettlefold collection.[533] LL 3960, larger still, is dated 1845 but does not appear to have been exhibited. The streaks of white at the extreme right and the misty distance may also be intended to evoke the morning, though the direction is more north than east. Its composition is essentially a reprise of a watercolour dated 1842, previously with Agnew's, although there the two figures are seated. The man in profile leaning on his staff, a motif found repeatedly in the watercolours of Copley Fielding, derives from prints after Gaspar Dughet and subtly underscores the Arcadian atmosphere of the whole scene.[534]
TW

529 Titled *Scotch Lake Scene* by Tatlock, p. 129.
530 1910 Inventory, valued at £350.
531 R. Hewison, *Ruskin, Turner and the Pre-Raphaelites* (exh. cat., London, Tate Gallery, 2000), p. 47 (cat. 22).
532 British Museum: 1904-3-7-16.
533 C. Grundy, *Catalogue of the Nettlefold collection of pictures* (London, 2 vols, 1935), vol. II, illus. facing p. 62.

### A Mountain Lake
LL 3791 (WHL 746, HH 409)

Watercolour over pencil with touches of gouache and gum arabic, with scratching out on paper
18.5 x 27 cm
Date: 1850

Inscr: Copley Fielding / 1850 (pencil, bottom centre)

Prov: bt. from James Orrock by Lever, 1910[535]

Two mountain peaks rise in the distance beyond an expanse of water approached by a single track. The prominence of the date and signature suggest that this was one of Fielding's exhibits at the SPWC in 1850 or 1851. The majority of his submissions in these years were titled with the names of Scottish lochs and mountains in combination. It is likely that LL 3791 will in time be recognised as one of these.[536]
TW

### Landscape with Windsor Castle in the distance
LL 3852 (WHL 729, HH 365)

Watercolour with gum arabic, stopping out and scratching out on paper
17.5 x 25.2 cm (sight)
Date: 1854

Inscr: C.F. 1854 (watercolour, bottom left)

Annot: Windsor Forest, sunset / C. Fielding (pencil, verso, [? by a later hand])

Prov: bt. from James Orrock by Lever, 1910[537]

Exh: [?] Windsor, Eton College, exhibition title unknown, 1933 (cat. 7)[538]

534 See, for instance, *A forest with a waterfall*, engraved by W. Woollett and J. Browne after Dughet; Anne French, *Gaspar Dughet called Gaspar Poussin 1615–75* (exh. cat., London, Iveagh Bequest, Kenwood, 1980), p. 55 (cat. 55).
535 1910 Inventory, p. 51, as *A Mountain Lake: sunshine breaking through storm clouds*, valued at £20. A Dolman frame-makers' label on the reverse of LL 3791 is inscribed Miss L.S.R., 15/16 Batter [...] (possibly Battersea) which may refer to an earlier owner.
536 Sometime after Tatlock, p. 129, correctly catalogued LL 3791 under the title *A Mountain Lake*, the work became confused in the gallery with LL 3959, being framed and re-inventoried under the title *Loch Katrine*.
537 1910 Inventory, p. 47, valued at £15.
538 This exhibition is cited in the LLAG files, but there is no record of it in Eton College's archives. The exhibition may have been held in the Drawing Schools (the school's art department) but it is not recorded in the *Eton Chronicle* (the school's magazine) for 1933. I am grateful to Penny Hatfield, Eton College's archivist, for providing this information.

The silhouette of Windsor Castle is seen on the skyline, framed by trees. The view is from the south, in the woodland of Windsor Great Park. The subject, tackled by watercolour painters from Sandby (p. 169) and Turner (pp. 182–203) down to David Cox (pp. 59–65) and Turner of Oxford (p. 205), was first treated by Fielding in a small exhibit of 1830, *Distant view of Windsor Castle from the park*. He continued to produce variations on the theme until the end of his life, as the late date of 1854 on LL 3852 testifies. An example exhibited in 1847 and bought by Richard Ellison is now in the Victoria & Albert Museum.[539] The last exhibited watercolour of this subject appeared in 1852, but another watercolour of Windsor has the inscription last drawing.[540] The castle inspired one of Fielding's grandest productions, a view of *Windsor Castle from the park* over one metre in width.[541]
TW

**A Scottish loch, with cattle**
LL 3849 (WHL 350, H 408)

Watercolour over pencil, with gum arabic and stopping out and scratching out on wove paper
24.5 x 36.4 cm
Date: c. 1823–55

Prov: bt. from James Orrock by Lever, 1912[542]

Reference to the collection of drawings in the British Museum from Fielding's 1823 Scottish tour suggests that this watercolour may represent a part of Loch Lomond. A drawing inscribed Ben Lomond from the upper part of Loch Lomond has the same characteristics, looking across a narrow part of the loch with lower hills beside the water and higher peaks rising behind.[543] Such features could be recognised in many other Scottish views, and the identification can only remain tentative. The unruffled lake surface with drinking cattle and the pale morning light (assuming the view is towards the north-east) convey an atmosphere of tranquillity with which Loch Lomond was often associated.

Fielding exhibited a large number of views of Loch Lomond, in different aspects. One example, dated 1833, was sold at Sotheby's, 13 March 1990 (lot 92).
TW

539 1024-1873.
540 Sotheby's, 17 November 1988 (lot 128).
541 Sotheby's, 10 July 1997 (lot 124), 64.8 x 100.8 cm.
542 1912 Inventory, as *Scotch loch with cattle in foreground*, valued at £75.
543 British Museum: 1904-3-7-11.

## 'ANTHONY VANDYKE COPLEY FIELDING'

**Landscape with a ruined castle and figures**
LL 3853 (WHL 757, HH 404)

Watercolour with traces of gouache and scratching out on wove paper
13.8 x 21.1 cm (sight)
Date: mid-nineteenth century

Inscr: A.V.C.F (watercolour, bottom left)
Prov: bt. from James Orrock by Lever, 1910[544]

The principal subject can perhaps be better described as a fortified manor house than a castle. Such ruins never formed part of Fielding's repertoire of landscape subjects, and it may be that, despite the initials (not a typical form of signature for Fielding), this is the work of a lesser-known contemporary, perhaps Henry Gastineau (1791–1876), who was an indefatigable recorder of just such scenes.
TW

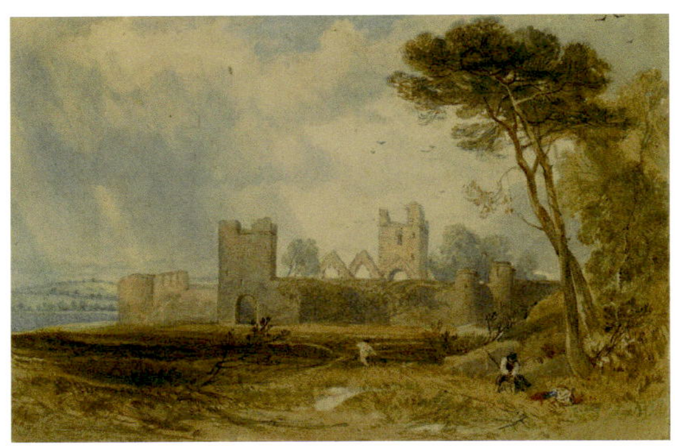

LL 3853

544 1910 Inventory, valued at £10.

## J. FISHER
Dates and places of birth and death unknown

**A Rustic Beauty**
LL 3962 (WHL 305, H 181)

Watercolour and gouache over pencil, heightened with gum arabic and scratching out, on wove paper
44.6 x 37.4 cm (oval)
Date: 1848

Inscr: J. FISHER / 1848 (watercolour, right centre)
Annot: Clare Leeds / 1890 (pencil, verso)
Prov: E. Bacchus; his sale, Christie's, 20 March 1897 (lot 140, as *A child gathering flowers*); bt. Agnew's (18 gns); acquired by Lever by 1912[545]

The artist of LL 3962, whose first name is unknown, would appear to be the same J. Fisher who painted a portrait miniature of a young girl with mid-brown hair, holding a spaniel (Christie's, 5 June 2007, lot 170), in which similar broad strokes of watercolour are heightened with drier strokes and scratching out. His miniatures have been described as 'most attractive ... the colouring is fresh and the draughtsmanship good, the work slightly reminiscent of Sir W. C. Ross';[546] this is certainly an apposite characterisation of this larger-scale work depicting a young girl carrying flowers in her poke bonnet.

The inscription on the reverse could well refer to the otherwise unidentified owner of the work in 1890;[547] it is not out of the question that she is identical with the sitter forty-two years earlier.
CG

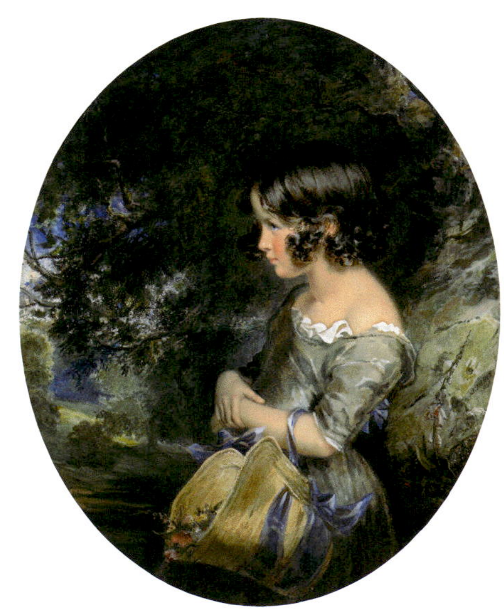

LL 3962

545 1912 Hill Inventory, titled *A Rustic Beauty: a girl carrying flowers in her poke-bonnet, with blue ribbons in a landscape, oval.*
546 Daphne Foskett, *A Dictionary of British Miniature Painters* (London, 1987), p. 540.
547 She cannot be the Duchess of Leeds of the day, whose name was Frances.

## WILLIAM RUSSELL FLINT

1880 Edinburgh–1969 London

### The Three Green Domes, San Simeone Piccolo

LL 3792 (LP 27)

Watercolour on wove paper
50.4 x 67.7 cm
Date: 1929

Inscr: W. RUSSELL FLINT (watercolour, bottom left); Three Green Domes, Venice / (San Simione [*sic*] Piccolo) / W. Russell Flint / 1929 (Loading Milk in Foreground) (pencil, verso)

Prov: sold by Russell Flint with 11 other watercolours to D. Croal Thomson, Barbizon House, December 1929 (£1,050);[548] bt. from Lockett Thomson, Barbizon House by the Trustees, 30 January 1930 (£150)[549]

Exh: London, Barbizon House, *Recent Venetian Water-Colours by W. Russell Flint A.R.A., R.W.S.*, 1932 (cat. 1); [?] Rochdale, Rochdale Art Gallery, exhibition title unknown, 1938 (cat. 9)[550]

Lit: Ralph Lewis and Keith S. Gardner, *Sir William Russell Flint R.A., P.P.R.W.S. 1880–1969* (Newton Abbot, Bristol and Guildford, 1988), p. 102

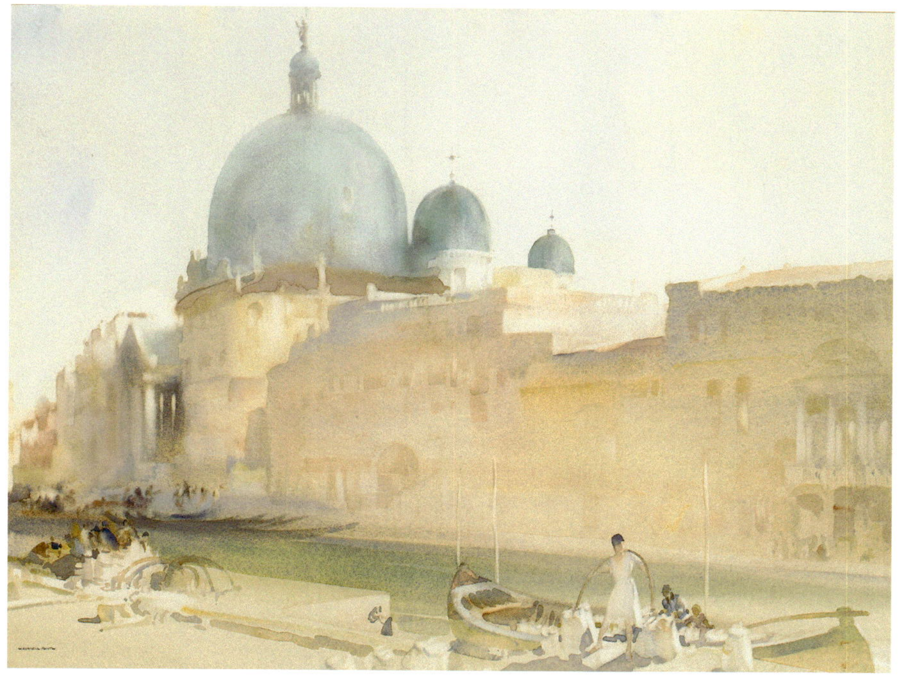

LL 3792

The son of Francis Wighton Flint, a graphic designer and watercolourist, William Russell Flint received his initial artistic training as a lithographer and designer with Banks & Co. in Edinburgh for six years from 1894. He settled in London in 1900, where he initially worked as a medical illustrator, while studying part-time at Heatherley's Art School. Flint worked as an illustrator for the *Illustrated London News* between 1903 and 1907, and it was in this field that he first established a reputation with his illustrations for Henry Rider Haggard's *King's Solomon's Mines*, published by Cassell & Co. in 1907.

After he married the artist Sibylle Sueter, Flint made the first of many visits to Italy, where he settled in Rome in 1912, taking a studio in the Villa Strohl-Fern, the centre of much lively artistic life. The cityscapes and architecture of Italy provided him with regular subject-matter for his watercolours for the rest of his career. Flint's immense artistic facility was recognised by election as an associate of the Royal Society of Painters in Water-Colours in 1914, and as a full member in 1919. He was president of the Society from 1936 to 1956. Flint was also elected a member of the Royal Academy in 1933, and was awarded the very rare distinction of a lifetime retrospective in 1962. Flint's accomplishments as an etcher, in a style deriving from Whistler, led to his election as a member of the Royal Society of Painter-Etchers and Engravers in 1933, and he was awarded a silver medal at the 1913 Paris Salon for his illustrations to Mallory's *Morte d'Arthur*, published in four volumes in 1910–11 by P. L. Warner. His work was extremely popular and was finally recognised by the grant of a knighthood in 1947.

Flint's watercolours of partially dressed or nude, lissom and curvaceous girls were widely collected and much reproduced in contemporary journals, and sold in large editions in high-quality photographically reproduced prints. Today he is better known for this part of his oeuvre, for which the models were frequently Spanish or gypsy girls, than for his oils and topographical watercolours. Flint was noted for his use of antique paper, which enhanced the qualities of his subtle but very free washes. His watercolours are generally notable for the vibrancy of their light.

This watercolour was one of a group of Venetian views that the artist exhibited at his one-man show at Barbizon House in 1930, the results of his trip to Italy the previous two winters. Flint had first visited Venice on the return leg of his honeymoon in the winter of 1905. Other known visits were in 1963, 1964 and 1965. The small baroque church of San Simeone Piccolo, correctly San Simeone e Giuda Apostoli, with its prominent copper dome, lies on the north-west side of the Grand Canal, almost opposite Venice's railway station. It was designed by Giovanni Scalfarotto (1690–1764) in a style indebted to Longhena, the architect of Santa Maria della Salute at the other end of the canal, and was built between 1718 and 1738.[551] The church was in part modelled on the Pantheon in Rome. Although the church was painted by both Canaletto (c. 1738, National Gallery, London [NG 163] – also a drawing in the Royal Collection)[552] and Guardi (c.1780, Museo Thyssen-Bornemisza, Madrid, and other pictures),[553] it was not particularly favoured as a subject by later artists. It is very unlikely that Flint ever saw Turner's 1840 watercolour of the church looking down the canal towards its northern end made in his 'Grand Canal and Giudecca' sketchbook.[554]

Flint adopted an oblique view, an approach often used by John Singer Sargent in his Venetian watercolours. His style is closer to that of Turner than of Sargent, but far more independent of the work of the early nineteenth-century painter than the watercolours of Hercules Brabazon Brabazon (1821–1906), the most productive English painter of views of Venice contemporary with Flint. In the foreground Flint introduced a milkwoman loading or unloading milk in an improbably spotless graceful white dress. She is similar in type to many he painted in his watercolours of Spanish and Provençal interiors. On at least one of his trips to Venice, Flint took photographs,[555] but there is no evidence from the surviving prints that he made use of photography in preparation for this watercolour. However, it is possible that he made pencil sketches, as the view of the church that he painted suggests that he may have conceived the subject while on a boat on the Grand Canal.
MH

548 Victoria & Albert Museum: William Russell Flint Archive AAD9/43. Russell Flint's notebook, 'Pictures Oct 1927 – Sept 1933', where it was priced at £105; Barbizon House paid for the 12 watercolours in two instalments, £550 on 15 February 1930 and £500 on 15 March 1930.

549 LLAG files: invoice.

550 This is cited in the LLAG files. Rochdale Art Gallery has no archival record of this exhibition. Yvonne Hardman, email correspondence, March 2009.

551 A concise description of the church is given in Umberto Franzoi and Dina De Stefano, *Le Chiese di Venezia* (Venice, 1976), pp. 76–78.

552 J. G. Links, *Canaletto* (Oxford, 1999), pp. 105, 112, pl. 92; W. G. Constable, revised by J. G. Links, *Canaletto. Giovanni Antonio Canal 1697–1768* (Oxford, 2 vols, 1976), vol. I, pp. 348 (cat. 320), 522 (cat. 468); vol II, pls. 114, 203.

553 Luigiana Rossi Bortolatto, *L'opera completa di Francesco Guardi* (Milan, 1974), p. 121 (cats. 534–38) and pp. 134–35 (cat. 766); also Antonio Morassi, *Guardi* (Venice, 2 vols, 1976), vol. I, pp. 418–20 (cats. 578–83, 590) for various paintings of the church by Guardi.

554 Ian Warrell, *Turner and Venice* (exh. cat., London, Tate, 2004), p. 150 (cat. 94), illus. pl. 152.

555 Some of his photographs are in the William Russell Flint Archive in the Victoria & Albert Museum, AAD9.

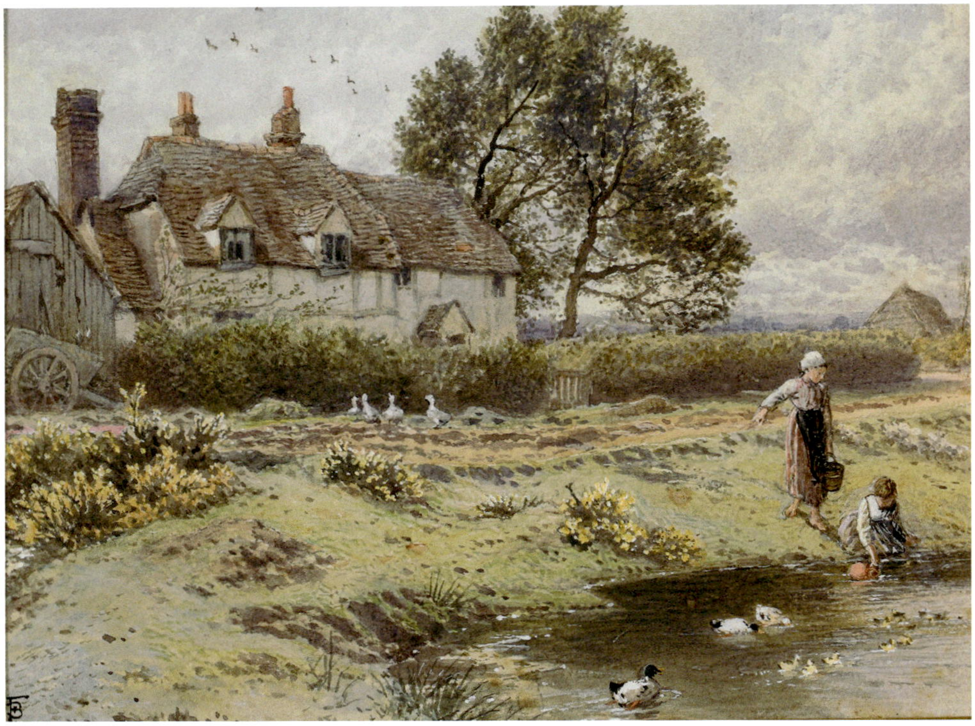

LL 3963

## MYLES BIRKET FOSTER

1825 North Shields–1899 Weybridge, Surrey

**On the Common, Hambledon, Surrey**
LL 3963 (WHL 3550)

Watercolour over pencil, heightened with touches of gouache on wove paper
15.5 x 20.6 cm (sight)
Date: probably mid-1860s

Inscr: MBF [monogram] (watercolour, bottom left)

Prov: James Barrow, Waterloo, Liverpool, 1895; his wife, Sarah A. Barrow, 1902; her sale, Samuel Lever's Rooms, Liverpool, 17 May 1918 (lot 178); bt. by Phillips and MacConnal for Lever (£138 12s)[556]

Myles Birket Foster was the fifth son of Myles Birket Foster and his wife, Ann, both from wealthy Quaker families. His early childhood was spent in London and he was educated first at a Quaker boarding school in Tottenham, Middlesex, and c. 1835–40 at Isaac Brown's Academy, Hitchin, Hertfordshire, where his natural talent as a landscape painter was encouraged. At the age of 16 he was apprenticed to the leading wood-engraver, Ebenezer Landells, with whom he remained until 1846. His drawings, published in the *Illustrated London News*, *Punch* and other magazines, brought him to the notice of the influential publisher and engraver, Henry Vizetelly, who commissioned of him a series of vignettes for *The Boys' Country Year Book* (1847) and employed him to illustrate H. W. Longfellow's *Evangeline*. Birket Foster's illustrations for *Evangeline* were much admired for their grace and elegance and he became the most sought-after poetry illustrator of his day. Relatively late in his career, about 1859, he began to paint watercolours, meeting with immediate success. He was elected an associate of the SPWC that same year, and was made a full member in 1862.

In 1862 Birket Foster published the phenomenally successful *Pictures of English Landscapes*, a series of scenes of idyllic Surrey villages and children in flowery country lanes that were perfectly attuned to the Victorian taste for sentiment and prettiness. He had a genuine attachment to Surrey, where he lived in Hambledon for a few years up until 1865. He exhibited numerous views of Hambledon Common and its sandpits between 1863 and 1896. In 1865 he moved to Witley, and in 1893 to Weybridge, also in the county.

The subject of this work has been identified by Anthony Oxley as Oakhurst Cottage, Hambledon, near Godalming.[557] A more distant view, titled *Landscape with Cattle*, is in the Victoria & Albert Museum. On stylistic grounds, the work can probably be dated to the mid-1860s.[558] LL 3963 lacks the blue sheen that is evident in earlier pictures such as *Downhill* (exhibited at the SPWC in 1861, now in the Victoria & Albert Museum).

LL 3963 was formerly in the collection of James Barrow (1831–1902), a prominent and wealthy sugar merchant who lived in the prosperous Waterloo area of Liverpool. Barrow, who inherited his father's business, also owned John Brett's *The Stonebreaker* (1857–58, Walker Art Gallery, Liverpool), and in 1889 gave the Walker two paintings by the popular local painter Thomas Huson. Barrow and his wife were much involved in the local community and believed in distributing their wealth to benefit local causes, Barrow as one of the three donors endowing the Gladstone Chair of Classic and Ancient History at Liverpool University and his widow establishing the Chair of French there in his memory in 1905.[559]
CG

556 LLAG files: invoice dated 24 May 1918.

557 Anthony Oxley, email correspondence, April 2009.

558 Ibid.

**Holy Trinity Church on the banks of the River Avon, Stratford-upon-Avon**
LL 3965 (WHL 736, HH 403)

Watercolour heightened with touches of gouache on wove paper
7 x 10.2 cm (trimmed irreg.)
Date: probably late 1860s or early 1870s

Inscr: MBF [monogram] (watercolour, bottom left)

Prov: bt. from James Orrock by Lever, 1910[560]

Birket Foster may have visited Stratford-upon-Avon on two occasions in the late 1860s and early 1870s; he exhibited two watercolours of the subject at the SPWC in 1868 and 1871. He also visited Stratford in 1875, while on a sketching tour of Oxfordshire. Although the scale and detail of this charming view recalls Birket Foster's pictures that were reproduced as vignettes to illustrate volumes of poetry and novels in the mid-1870s, this work's rectangular shape as well as the sharp brush-strokes in the foreground suggest that it may date from the artist's earlier trips to Stratford.[561]

The church depicted in LL 3965 is unidentified in Orrock's 1910 Inventory,[562] but the work has more recently been catalogued as *The Church, Stratford-upon-Avon*.[563] Both architecturally and topographically there is a clear resemblance to Holy Trinity Church in Stratford-upon-Avon, which dates from 1210 and was built on the site of a Saxon monastery, but more significantly is known as 'Shakespeare's church' as it is the place of William Shakespeare's baptism and burial. Birket Foster had an interest in theatre, putting on plays in his large studio; Holy Trinity Church would have been a natural subject for the artist.[564]
CG

559 I am grateful to Professor Tim Unwin for providing biographical details of Mr and Mrs James Barrow.

560 1910 Inventory, valued at £25.

561 Anthony Oxley, email correspondence, April 2009.

562 The title in the 1910 Inventory is given as *A riverside church, with figures, sheep, sunset*. Tatlock, p. 129 gives the title as *Riverside Church, with Figures and Sheep*.

563 LLAG files: note in accession files in an unknown hand.

564 Anthony Oxley, email correspondence, April 2009.

## Seaweed Gatherers
LL 3964 (WHL 1528, TM 112)

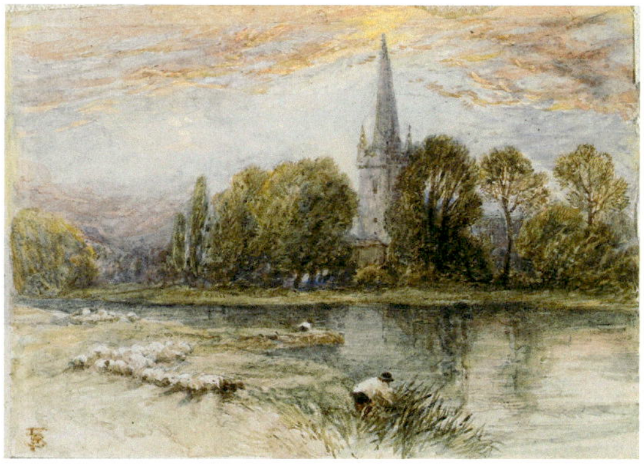

LL 3965

Watercolour heightened with touches of gouache and scratching out on wove paper
15 x 22.3 cm (sight)
Date: probably early 1870s

Inscr: MBF [monogram] (watercolour, bottom left)

Prov: Sir John Fowler; his sale, Christie's 6 May 1899 (lot 12); bt. by Agnew's (£63) for Lever (£73 10s)[565]

Exh: Perth, Art Gallery of Western Australia and Australian tour, *Exhibition of Early British Water-colours*, organised by the Empire Art Loans Exhibition Society, 1948–49 (cat. 153)

Lit: J. Reynolds, *Birket Foster* (London, 1984), p. 211

While the principal subject of LL 3964 is the figures collecting seaweed and a single horse pulling their wagon across the seashore, the scene is dominated by an endless sunlit sky. Birket Foster did not often paint seascapes, but when he did, as in LL 3964, they often depict a dramatic, almost impressionistic sky, as in *Return of the Lifeboat, with St Michael's Mount in the distance* (Cecil Higgins Art Gallery, Bedford) and *The Ferry, Walberswick* (c. 1894, private collection).[566]

Birket Foster made a series of pictures with the theme of 'The Gatherers' in the mid-1860s.[567] These were mostly larger in format than the Lady Lever work, one example being *Lilac Gatherers* (Godalming Museum). LL 3964 probably dates from the early 1870s, when his figure groups tended to be reduced in size. Anthony Oxley has suggested that the work may have been inspired by a visit to Morecambe Bay.[568] A picture by the artist titled *Morecambe* was exhibited at the SPWC in 1871.

Birket Foster's early years were spent as a wood-engraver and he was therefore used to drawing with pen, pencil or even a slight wash upon a box-wood block that had been coated with white. It is probable that he would have prepared his paper with a covering of Chinese white. His use of Chinese white is particularly significant in reference to his technique in painting skies, the white mixture making the blue colours sufficiently tacky to hold the imprint of the hair-strokes of his brush, creating the texture and movement of clouds scudding across the skies.[569]
CG

565 LLAG files: invoice.
566 J. Reynolds, *Birket Foster* (London, 1984), p. 180, illus. pl. 106.
567 Anthony Oxley, email correspondence, April 2009.
568 Ibid.
569 For further discussion of Birket Foster's technique see M. Hardie, *Watercolour Painting in Britain* (London, 3 vols, 1979), vol. III, p. 112.

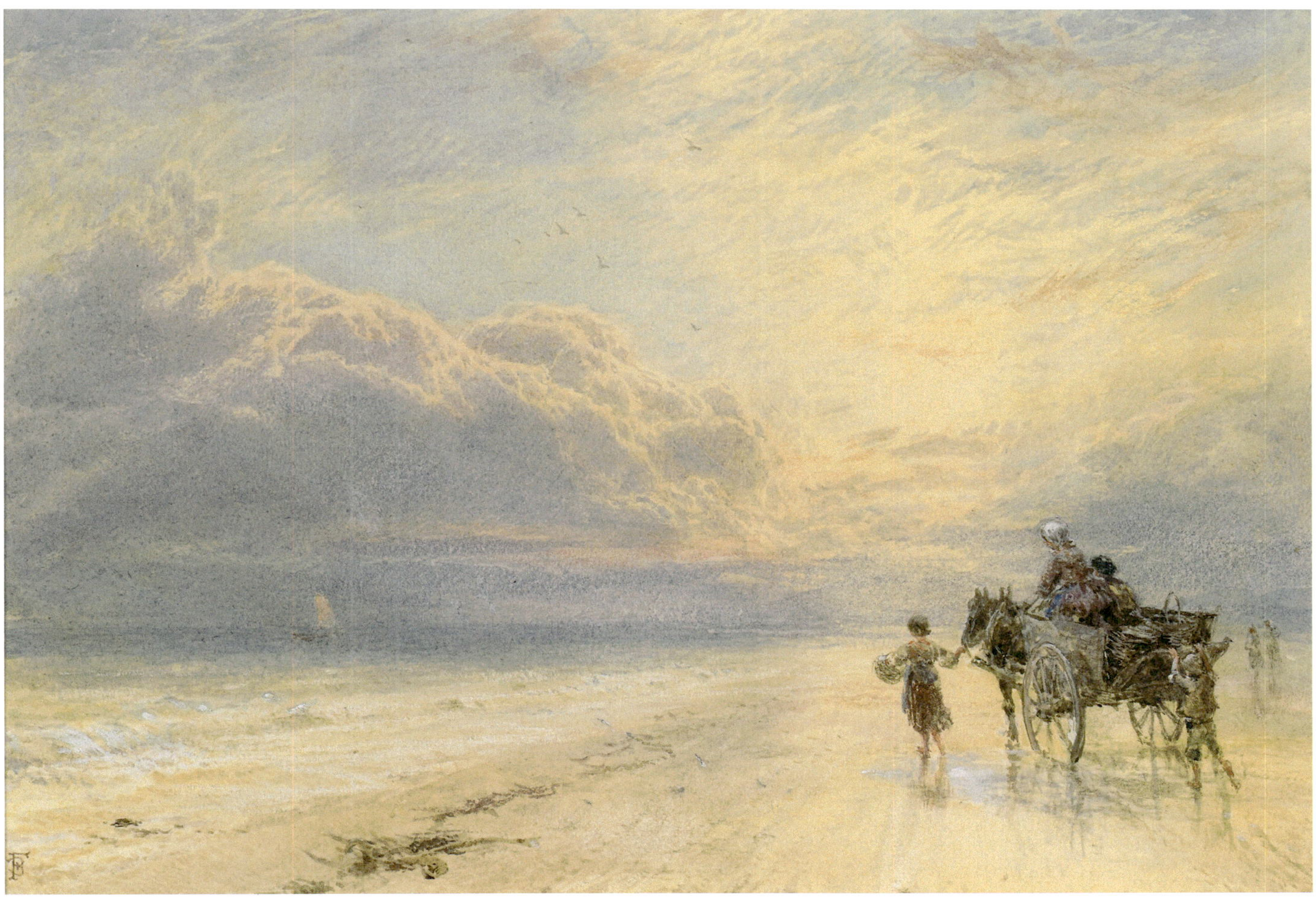

LL 3964

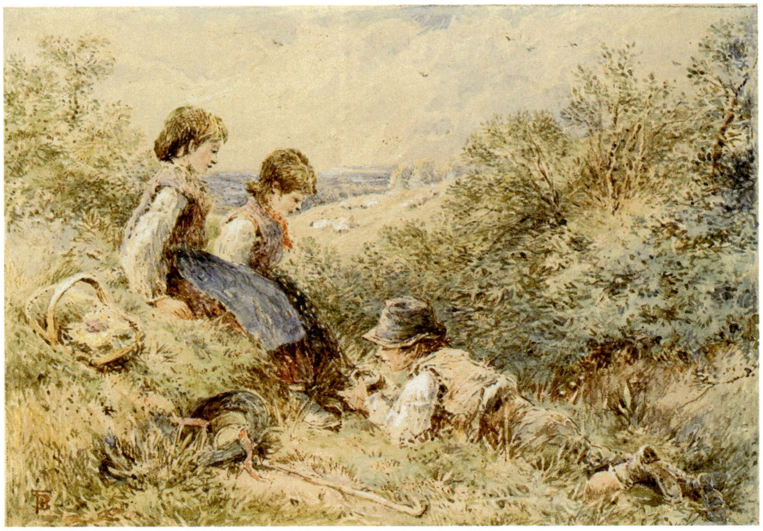

LL 3854

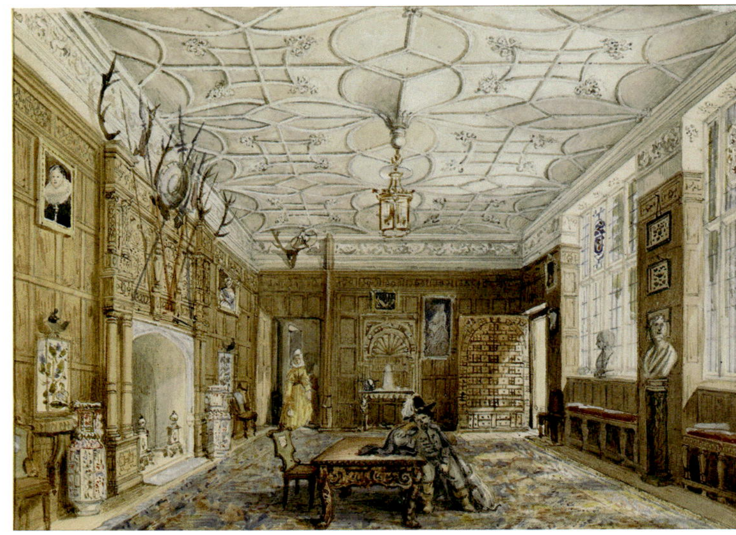

LL 3885

**AFTER MYLES BIRKET FOSTER**

**The Bird's Nest**
LL 3854 (WHL 740, HH 370)

Watercolour heightened with gouache over pencil on wove paper
10.5 x 15.1 cm (sight)
Date: nineteenth century

Inscr: MBF [monogram] (watercolour, bottom left)
Prov: bt. from James Orrock by Lever, 1910[570]
Lit: *Country Life* (23 August 1956), illus. p. 388

Birket Foster made a number of sketches of children studying a bird's nest, a subject that well suited the contemporary taste for sentimental rustic scenes. In this picture the three children have thrown aside their basket, bonnet, cap and crook to examine a nest, while beyond the figure group, white sheep are clustered on a hill, and the distance glows with the blues and greens of a valley.

The immense popularity of Birket Foster's subject-matter and sheer demand for his work led to it being extensively copied. Birket Foster's work was widely faked even during his lifetime. Indeed the artist was often asked to advise on the authenticity of a watercolour that he was purported to have painted and the fakes were so numerous that he was forced to charge a small fee for giving his opinion. His style lent itself to reproduction in the form of chromolithographs and most copies were made after subjects that had been printed, as he commented in a letter to his brother-in-law, Robert Spence, advising on the authenticity of a questionable watercolour: 'I cannot of course say without seeing it whether the drawing is mine or not. There is a subject which might bear that title that was Chromolithographed years ago. The forgeries are generally selected from the published prints.'[571]

LL 3854 is probably after a lithograph (identical, although the colours are a little darker) produced by George Rowney & Co.[572] The harsh, unblended tones and clumsy sheep mark LL 3854 as a copy. A further copy is in the Russell-Cotes Art Gallery and Museum, Bournemouth.
CG

570 1910 Inventory, valued at £50.
571 Newcastle upon Tyne Libraries: Robert Spence family letters.

572 A. B. Daryll, *Rustic England* (London, 1906), illus. pl. 19 (titled *Birds' Nesting on the Common*).

**JOHN GENDALL**
1789 Exeter–1865 Exeter

**The Hall, Forde House, Devon**
LL 3885 (WHL 230)

Watercolour and gouache over pencil on wove paper
21.6 x 30.1 cm
Date: 1847 or earlier

Prov: bt. from B. T. Batsford by Lever, 1913 (5 gns)

The young John Gendall was employed as a domestic servant in Exeter, where his drawings were seen by a salesman from the London publisher and printseller Rudolph Ackermann. Gendall moved to London and worked for Ackermann from 1811 to 1824, travelling and making topographical watercolours for publication as prints. In 1824 he returned to Exeter, where he spent the rest of his life in business as a picture dealer, framer and art teacher, while continuing to work as an artist. He first exhibited at the Royal Academy in 1818, and showed views of the Devon countryside there between 1846 and 1863.

Tatlock catalogued LL 3885 as a work by Charles James Richardson (1806–71).[573] However, a lithograph of the watercolour dated 1 September 1847 in S. C. Hall's *The Baronial Halls and Picturesque Edifices of England* (London, 1848) is identified on the plate as being after Gendall.

Forde House, just outside Newton Abbot, was built in the early seventeenth century by the lawyer Sir Richard Reynell.[574] The figures in LL 3885 wear costume consistent with the period of the architecture, but the bust between the windows and the cases of stuffed birds flanking the fireplace strike an early Victorian note.
JoS

573 Tatlock, pp. 135–36.
574 *Country Life* (14 March 1908), pp. 378–83; B. Cherry and N. Pevsner, *Devon* (Harmondsworth, 1989), pp. 589–90.

## JOHN GILBERT

1817 Blackheath, Kent–1897 Blackheath, Kent

**The Return of the Victors**
LL 3966 (WHL 3161)

Watercolour and gouache, heightened with gum arabic, over traces of pencil on wove paper
37.1 x 64.8 cm
Date: 1872

Inscr: John Gilbert, A.R.A. 1872 (watercolour, bottom left)

Prov: John Henderson; his sale, Christie's, 16 February 1882 (lot 116); bt. by W. Permain (£115 10s); Charles Churchill, Weybridge; his sale, Christie's, 16 February 1917 (lot 27); bt. by Gooden and Fox (£78 15s) for Lever (£81 18s)

Exh: London, SPWC, *Winter Exhibition*, 1872 (cat. 177)

Lit: John Oldcastle, 'Our Living Artists. Sir John Gilbert RA', *The Magazine of Art* (1878), pp. 131–34; 'Sir John Gilbert, RA, PRWS: A Memorial Sketch', *The Magazine of Art* (1898), pp. 53–64; Randall Davies, 'Sir John Gilbert, RA', *The Old Water-Colour Society's Club: Tenth Annual Volume* (1933), pp. 20–43

John Gilbert's career as an artist began in the late 1830s, when he worked principally as an illustrator. In this capacity he was immensely prolific, producing designs for woodblock engravings for many contemporary novels and also contributing many thousands of illustrations for the *Illustrated London News* from the time of its founding in 1842. As an illustrator to literary texts, Gilbert is principally remembered for his designs for Longfellow's *Poetical Works* (1854, 1855) and for an illustrated complete works of Shakespeare (1856–58). In due course he took to watercolour, sending works to the London exhibitions. His *Don Quixote giving advice to Sancho Panza*, shown at the British Institution in 1841, is an early instance of his particular fondness for literary subjects, and from this time on the works of Cervantes served as a great inspiration. Gilbert was a natural and instinctive draughtsman – he supposedly escaped a career in a commercial office because he habitually drew when he was supposed to be doing business. Because he failed to gain admission to the Royal Academy Schools and therefore had no formal training beyond a few lessons from the painter of still-life subjects George Lance, he was free to develop his own individual and distinctive technique. This was essentially linear, even when colour was applied, and was a method that lent itself to rapid production, even when superficially the work appears ornately detailed.

In addition to the historical and literary subjects that were his stock in trade, he also treated themes of his own invention, often showing figures in an indeterminate antiquated setting and engaged in some unspecific or imaginary event. *The Return of the Victors* is a subject of this kind. A cavalcade of troops, mounted and wearing full battle armour, and carrying spears decorated with pennants and regimental colours, is seen returning in victory from a battle or campaign. They pass in frieze-like arrangement and the mass of figures and horses fills the entire picture space. The soldiers are accompanied by a group of three maidens, two dressed in flowing white robes and one in black. One holds the bridle of a grey horse upon which is mounted a soldier who bends forward to glimpse the girl's face. With the maidens is a child who brings garlands of laurel with which the soldiers will be crowned as victors. The troops are led by a band of frolicking children who dance in celebration, and a group of musicians who trumpet the victory.

John Gilbert's career as a watercolourist is closely associated with the SPWC, of which association he was a stalwart. He was elected an associate in 1852 and a member in 1854. In 1871 he was elected president of the Society, in 1881 obtaining permission for it to be styled the Royal Society of Painters in Water-Colours. He was represented in its summer exhibitions every year from 1852 until his death, and also most years at the winter exhibitions intended for sketches and more informal works, which were instituted in 1862. *The Return of the Victors* was included in the Society's winter exhibition in 1872–73. Exhibited works aside, a large part of his production went directly to dealers, his drawings being always in demand and found to be readily saleable.

On occasions he made oil and watercolour versions of the same subject. The oil version of *The Return of the Victors* was made six years after the drawing, in 1878, and was exhibited at the Royal Academy in 1879. It entered the collection of George McCulloch, and is now in Birmingham Museums and Art Gallery.
CN

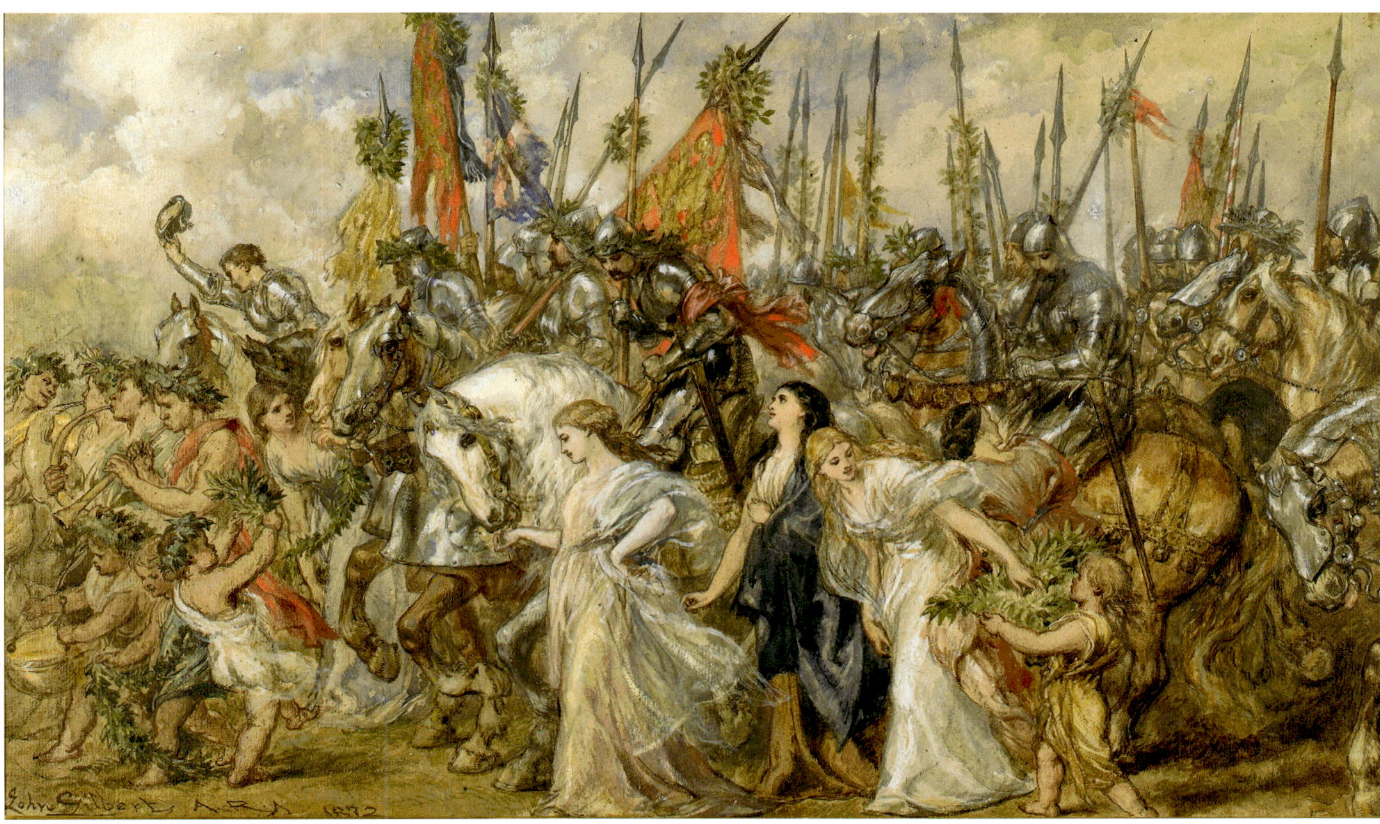

LL 3966

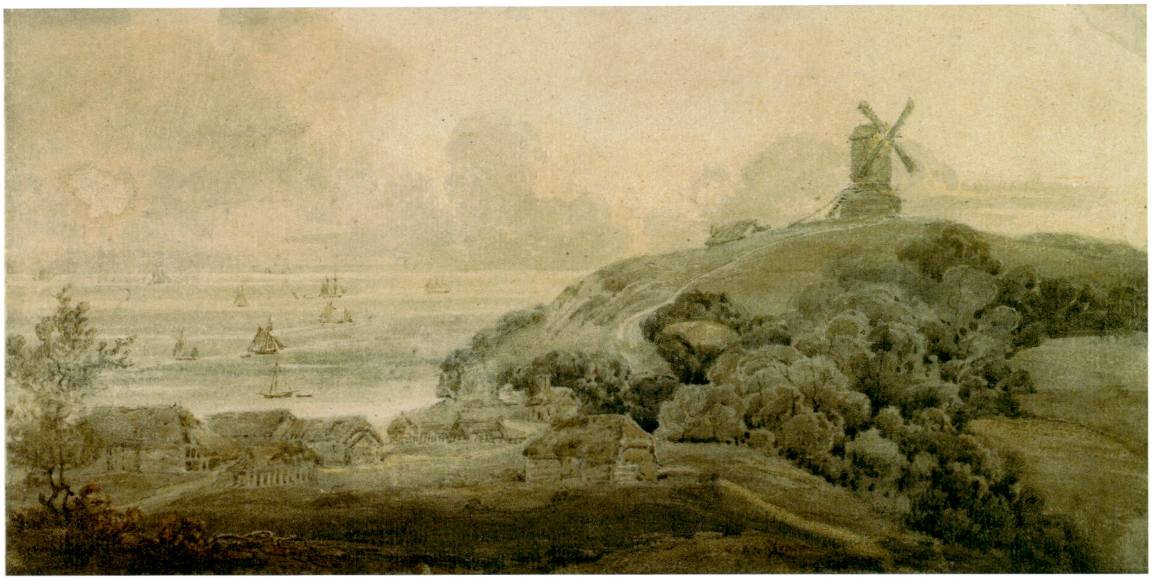

LL 2944

## THOMAS GIRTIN

1775 Southwark, London–1802 London

**Landscape with windmill on hilly ground by the sea**[575]
LL 2944 (WHL 767, HH 408)

Watercolour with gum arabic over pencil on laid paper
16.3 x 32.6 cm
Date: probably c. 1797–98

Prov: bt. from James Orrock by Lever, 1910[576]

Exh: Hove, Hove Museum and Art Gallery, *The Romantic Windmill*, 1993 (cat. 18)

Girtin, the son of a brush-maker, was apprenticed to the topographical watercolourist Edward Dayes from 1789 and seems to have served the full seven years required. In 1794 he toured the Midlands with the antiquarian James Moore; in the same year he exhibited for the first time at the Royal Academy, and was to exhibit there throughout his career. Between mid-1794 and 1797 Girtin worked alongside J. M. W. Turner (see pp. 182–203) copying drawings by J. R. Cozens (see pp. 70–71) and others which were in the possession of Dr Thomas Monro. In 1796 he made tours to the North of England, visiting the West Country the following year. In 1798 and 1800 he made trips to North Wales. Between 1799 and 1801 Girtin attended meetings of 'The Brothers', a sketching society, which included such artists as Robert Ker Porter and Louis Francia. Between 1801 and 1802 he visited Paris to explore the possibility of exhibiting his London panorama, the *Eidometropolis*, there; this proved unrealistic and the work was exhibited in London in the summer of 1802. Nevertheless, while in Paris Girtin did produce panoramic sketches for *Twenty Views in Paris and its Environs*, which were published in 1803 following the artist's death. Along with his friend and rival Turner, Girtin is credited with having led the revolution in watercolour painting of the 1790s.

LL 2944 was re-titled in Tim Wilcox's 1993 catalogue as *A windmill by the coast at Harwich*.[577] It is unlikely that Girtin ever visited Harwich and Wilcox has suggested that the watercolour may have been based on earlier eighteenth-century engravings of the port, citing the example of a view from 1730 when a post-mill stood up above the town on Beacon Hill.[578] Although this print does have general similarities with LL 2944, it is hard to imagine the context in which Girtin would have been copying early eighteenth-century engravings of Harwich. More convincing is Greg Smith's recent suggestion that the Lady Lever work may be a copy after an old master print.[579] He has compared LL 2944 to Girtin's *View of a Town on an Estuary* (Rhode Island School of Design, Providence), which is of a similar size to the Lady Lever work and has been identified as being a copy of a print by Chatelain after a picture then attributed to Rembrandt.[580] It is known that Girtin was in the habit of copying old master prints while at Dr Monro's and LL 2944 certainly seems to show the general influence of Dutch seventeenth-century landscapists such as Salomon van Ruysdael, who often employed the panoramic mode for their coastal scenes. It is possible that an as yet unidentified old master print is also the source here.

Following Girtin's tour to the West Country in 1797 and the challenge of depicting the coastal scenery this provided, his work shows a preference for a wide-angled, panoramic view (see, for example, his *Lyme Regis, Dorset* of c. 1797 in the Yale Center for British Art, New Haven).[581] The proportions of LL 2944 are as much as two to one, greatly enhancing the panoramic effect of the composition, and on this basis the work seems likely to date from c. 1797–98 rather than the earlier date of 1795–97 suggested by Wilcox.[582] It is this interest in the panoramic mode that encouraged the broader treatment with the brush and suppression of detail, apparent in Girtin's work from the late 1790s and visible in the Lady Lever watercolour.

LL 2944 has faded substantially overall, and in particular blue, probably indigo, pigments have disappeared from the sky, indicated by evidence of the original colours along the top left edge.[583] Although some of this fading must be due to general exposure to light (the remaining pigment may have been covered by an old mount) it is also probably due to the particularly fugitive pigments that Girtin adopted.[584]

575 WHL Inventory gives the title as *A Windmill by the sea coast, the after glow of sunset*.

576 1910 Inventory, p. 51, as *A windmill by the sea coast*, valued at £20.

577 Tim Wilcox (ed.), *The Romantic Windmill: The Windmill in British Art from Gainsborough to David Cox, 1750–1850* (exh. cat., Hove, Hove Museum and Art Gallery, 1993), p. 58 (cat. 18).

578 Ibid. This engraving is illustrated in Kenneth G. Farries, *Essex Windmills, Millers and Millwrights* (Edinburgh, 3 vols, 1984), vol. III, p. 113.

579 Greg Smith, email correspondence, January 2008.

580 Malcolm Cormack et al., *Selection II: British Watercolors and Drawings from the Museum's Collection* (exh. cat., Providence, Museum of Art, Rhode Island School of Design, 1972), unpag. (cat. 43).

581 On Girtin's use of the panoramic mode, see Greg Smith (ed.), *Thomas Girtin: The Art of Watercolour* (exh. cat., London, Tate, 2002), pp. 143–45.

582 Greg Smith, email correspondence, January 2008.

583 LLAG files: conservation treatment report by Catherine Rickman, 22 February 1993.

584 For Girtin's use of fugitive pigments, see Smith (ed.), *Thomas Girtin*, pp. 95–96.

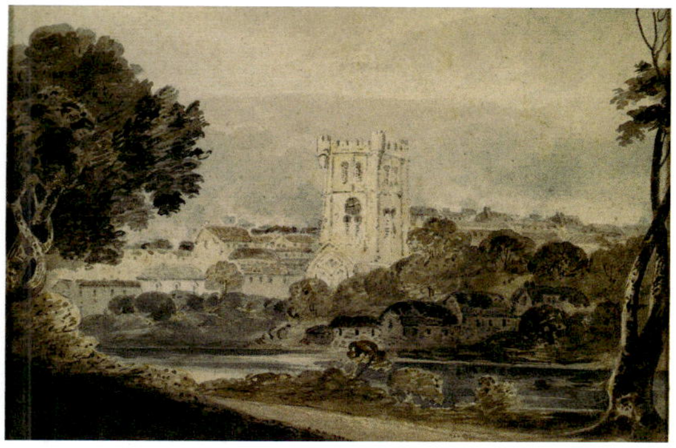

LL 3447

## 'THOMAS GIRTIN'

### View of a Town
LL 3447

Watercolour over pencil on laid paper
18.1 x 27.3 cm (sight)
Date: late eighteenth or early nineteenth century

Prov: unknown[585]

This watercolour has a number of stylistic links to Girtin, but is much too crudely painted to be his work. It shows Girtin's influence in combining broad, horizontal washes with a linear, dot-and-dash technique, created by using the point of a brush. This broken line, which was used so effectively by Girtin, is employed in LL 3447 to give graphic form to the church and surrounding houses. Although the work has faded, particularly in the sky, it shows the influence of the limited, more naturalistic palette of browns, dark greens, greys, ochres and blues that the artist adopted from the late 1790s.

LL 3447 is not thought to be copied from any known Girtin composition, nor does the church bear any similarity to one on a site known to have been visited by the artist. Greg Smith has suggested that the work may be by a pupil, although it is not by any identifiable hand such as Amelia Long or Lady Sutherland.[586] Whether by a pupil or not, the work is certainly by a contemporary imitator rather than a later artist.[587] It is possible that LL 3447 may be by William Pearson (1772–1849), who was Girtin's closest follower, but not enough is known about Pearson's style to make this suggestion any more than tentative.[588]

585 LLAG files: LL 3447 is described as being 'found in the gallery'.
586 Greg Smith, email correspondence, January 2008.
587 Ibid.
588 LL 3447 is very close in style to a photograph of a watercolour in the Witt Library, Courtauld Institute of Art, of a *Landscape near Lakenham*, previously attributed to John Crome but with a handwritten note by Timothy Clifford attributing it to Pearson. Another possibility is that LL 3447 could be by Franz Joseph Manskirsch (1770–1827). Both artists are mentioned in Iolo A. Williams, *Early English Watercolours and some Cognate Drawings by Artists born not later than 1785* (London, 1952), pp. 107–08, as imitators of Girtin's style but little is known about their careers, and the stylistic links between their work and Girtin's have not been fully explored. For more discussion of Girtin's followers, see Thomas Girtin and David Loshak, *The Art of Thomas Girtin* (London, 1954), pp. 121–23.

## WARWICK GOBLE
1862 place of birth unknown–1943 place of death unknown

### Mr and Mrs Gladstone
LL 3855 (WHL 1706, TM 349, LP 5)

Watercolour, gouache and black chalk over pencil on buff-coloured paper
30.7 x 23.6 cm (sight)
Date: 1891

Inscr: WARWICK GOBLE (watercolour, bottom right)

Prov: acquired by Lever before 1906;[589] deposited at the Lady Lever Art Gallery in 1925, presumably by Sir William Hulme Lever, 2nd Viscount Leverhulme

Like LL 3832A and LL 3832B by Charles Cox (see pp. 58–59) this work depicts the opening of Gladstone Hall in Port Sunlight Village on 28 November 1891 when William Ewart Gladstone was guest of honour. Goble's work was perhaps intended to be reproduced as a half-tone illustration but there is no record of it ever being produced in this way. The content differs slightly from the depictions of the event by Cox. Here Gladstone stands without cane and only the key guests are depicted behind him. From left to right they are James Darcy Lever, Mrs W. H. Lever, Mrs J. D. Lever (?), Lever and Mrs W. E. Gladstone.
SP

LL 3855

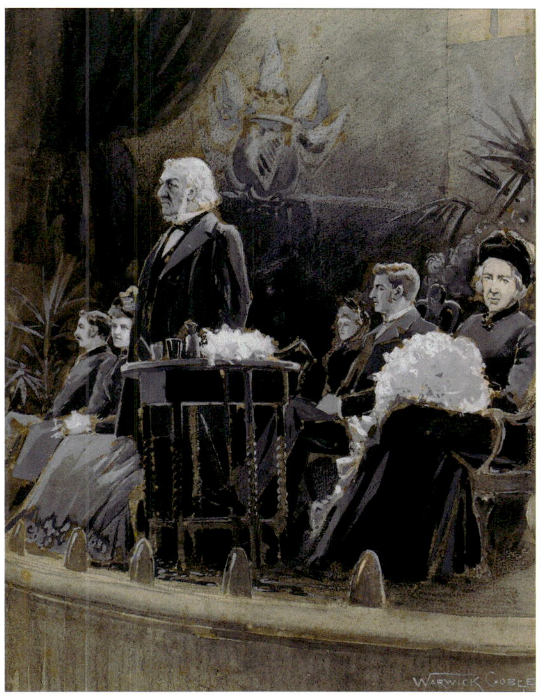


589 1906 TM Inventory, valued at £2, ballroom lobby along with LL 3832A and LL 3832B.

## FRANCIS CARRUTHERS GOULD
1844 Barnstaple, Devon–1925 Porlock, Somerset

### Sir Isumbras at the Ford
LL 3856 (WHL 1169)

Pen and ink over pencil on paper
19.2 x 25.4 cm (sight)
Date: 1912

Inscr: F.C.G (ink, bottom right); HOME RULE / WELSH / DISESTABLISHMENT / FRANCHISE (ink, on figures); AUTUMN / SESSION (ink, lower left); Westminster Gazette / Oct 8. 1912 (ink, bottom left, on mount); Sir Isumbras at the Ford / (after Sir John Millais's picture) (ink, bottom centre, on mount)

Prov: bt. from Nicholl's, London by Lever, 26 June 1913 (£8 8s)[590]

Exh: [?] London, Brook Street Gallery, exhibition title unknown, 1913 (cat. no. unknown)[591]

Gould established the political cartoon in Britain's daily press. Following a short spell as a stockbroker, during which time he began to acquire a reputation among his friends and colleagues for his caricatures, he started working for the *Pall Mall Gazette*, to which he regularly contributed cartoons and sketches. In 1893 Gould joined the staff of the newly founded Liberal newspaper, the *Westminster Gazette*. His daily cartoon appeared on the front page, a position never previously occupied by a satirical strip. Among Gould's unique strengths were his ability to 'accentuate the salient features of the political situation of the moment',[592] his frequent targets including Sir William Harcourt, the Duke of Devonshire and Lord Rosebery; the latter described Gould as 'one of the most remarkable assets of the Liberal Party'.[593] In 1901 *The Studio* ran a feature on Gould in their section 'Studio-Talk', the reviewer acknowledging that the subject of his feature had the 'most notable style at present in English caricature'.[594]

The publication of this cartoon in the *Westminster Gazette* on 8 October 1912 was timely, coinciding with the failure of three bills in Parliament, a disaster that secured the fall from power of Lord Asquith four years later. George V's speech nine months before Gould's cartoon was published had included three measures, all business that had festered since Gladstone's term in office: a Government of Ireland Bill, Welsh disestablishment Bill and a fourth Reform Bill. The first, in particular, was the subject of fierce opposition in Ulster, and civil war over the issue in Ireland was a real possibility until the outbreak of the First World War in August 1914, when affairs at home became far less urgent and the Bill was shelved.

590 WHL Inventory, p. 179. There is no invoice for this work.
591 This reference is cited in the LLAG files. It has not been possible to confirm that it is correct.
592 H. C. G. Matthew, 'Gould, Sir Francis Carruthers (1844–1925)', *ODNB*, vol. 23, pp. 68–69.
593 Mark Bryant and Simon Heneage, *Dictionary of British Cartoonists and Caricaturists 1730–1980* (Aldershot, 1994), p. 94.
594 'Studio-talk', *The Studio*, vol. 23 (1901), pp. 196–220.

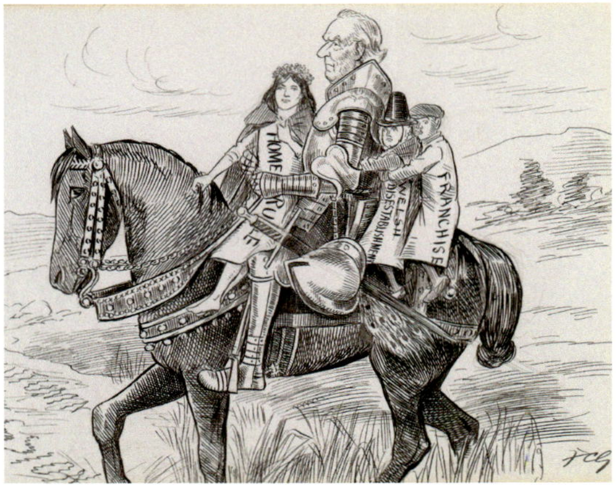


LL 3856

Gould was a staunch Liberal and his sympathy with their cause is reflected in the presentation of Asquith in this cartoon as a chivalrous knight protecting the Irish colleen bearing the words Home Rule on her white robe. He is also shown heroically rescuing on his charger a girl in a traditional black-crowned Welsh hat labelled Welsh / Disestablishment, and a young boy in a cloth cap with Franchise written across him. In the bottom left the words Autumn Session are written into the stream. (In A. W. Lloyd's cartoon *Women and Children First*, published in *News of the World* on 12 February 1928, Lloyd refers both to Millais's painting and Gould's cartoon, and 1928 Session forms part of the water the horse navigates through.) Although clearly referring to Millais's painting, Gould takes some liberties with his composition. The horse is placed in a roughly outlined landscape setting, rather than crossing a ford, and he adds an extra figure clutching on to the knight. Although the features of the knight do not obviously resemble those of Asquith, the intense expression on his unusually large head demonstrates the prime minister's firm resolve regarding the three issues about to be put before Parliament.

Millais's large painting *Sir Isumbras at the Ford* (Lady Lever Art Gallery, LL 3625, fig. 45, p. 139) was a popular choice for political cartoonists, the painting being familiar to their middle-class audience owing to the scandal surrounding its exhibition at the Royal Academy in 1857. As with *Bubbles*, which Millais painted in 1886, the portrayal of an armoured knight rescuing two children appealed to popular tastes but, with the exception of a satire made by Sir John Illingworth for *Punch* in 1948 (see LL 2955, pp. 129–30), few artists treated the subject with the seriousness Millais had intended. In his biography of Millais, John Guille Millais, the artist's son, quoted from Frederick Stephens's *Notes on the Grosvenor Gallery*, 1885:

> The appearance of *Sir Isumbras*, produced a tremendous sensation. Satires, skits, jokes, deliberate analyses and criticisms – most of them applied to purposes and technical aims not within the artist's intention when the picture was in hand – crowded the columns of the comic as of the more serious journals. Utter ruin and destruction were prophesied of the artist who, somewhat rashly, had followed a technical purpose, but whose success in that respect cannot now be questioned.[595]

Frederick Sandys was the first artist to produce a satirical print of the subject. Appearing in the *Cornhill Magazine* in May 1857, it was aptly titled *A Nightmare*. Sandys portrayed Ruskin as the ass, branded J. R. Oxon, carrying Millais as an armoured knight, with William Holman Hunt clinging to him and Dante Gabriel Rossetti in the place of the young girl. The artists caricatured in Sandys's print possibly welcomed the free publicity. In 1865 Rossetti wrote to Ford Madox Brown, certainly alluding to Sandys's interpretation of *Sir Isumbras*, that to advertise his forthcoming exhibition he should be presented as 'Brown Mad Ox crossing a Ford marked British Art with you holding on to his horns with a palette and brushes, and *R.A.* and *Public Press* waving red flats to frighten him on either bank ...'[596]

The appeal of Millais's painting to political cartoonists did not deter Lever, who purchased it from the McCulloch sale in 1913, the year after the publication of Gould's cartoon. Lever's acquisition was given extensive coverage in *The Times*, the reviewer describing in detail the history of the painting and, in particular, Millais's struggle to paint the horse accurately.[597]
HB

595 John Guille Millais, *The Life and Letters of Sir John Everett Millais* (London, 2 vols, 1899), vol. I, pp. 312–13.

596 Doughty and Wahl (eds), *Letters of Dante Gabriel Rossetti*, vol. II, p. 542.

597 *The Times*, 26 June 1913, p. 5.

## KATE GREENAWAY
1846 London–1901 London

**Boy with basket of vegetables, little girl and kitten**
LL 3656 (WHL 1748, TM 392)

Watercolour with brush and ink on paper
30.6 x 22.6 cm (sheet), 24.5 x 18.2 cm (image)
Date: c. 1880

Inscr: K.G (watercolour, lower left); '8' (pencil, bottom edge, centre)

Prov: Frederic, Lord Leighton; his sale, Christie's, 14 July 1896 (lot 257); bt. by Agnew's (17 gns with LL 3657); in Lever's collection by 1905[598]

Exh: Birkenhead, Birkenhead Art Gallery, *Opening Loan Exhibition*, 1912 (cat. no. unknown)[599]

Kate Greenaway was one of the most celebrated children's book illustrators of her age, whose work, with its lightness, simplicity and mild sentiment, dramatically changed the art of the picture book. In a career that lasted over thirty years she made illustrations for more than 150 books and 90 periodicals, as well as 49 exhibited paintings. For many modern critics her work represents the essence of a Victorian childhood, and her influence on book illustration continues to this day.

Greenaway was born in Hoxton, London, the daughter of a draughtsman and wood-engraver, John Greenaway, and Elizabeth, a seamstress and milliner. Other members of her family also worked in the book trade as engravers and binders. By the age of 11, as befitted a girl growing up in an artistic family surrounded by illustrated books and engravings, Greenaway had learnt to draw. In 1858 she attended Finsbury School of Art, moving on to the Central School of Art in South Kensington in 1864 and the Slade in 1871, with classes at Heatherley's School of Art in the evenings. She was a diligent student who concentrated on the refinement of her use of line, and on life drawing, at a time when women artists were only just beginning to gain access to drawing from the nude.

From 1868 she worked freelance, taking commissions from, for example, *The People's Magazine*, *Little Folks*, *Illustrated London News* and *Cassell's Magazine*, for illustrations to other writers' work, and for Christmas and Valentine cards for Marcus Ward & Co. But Greenaway nurtured an

598 Both LL 3656 and LL 3657 were listed in the 1905 TM Inventory, p. 18, both valued at £10, alongside numerous other works by Kate Greenaway. There is no invoice for these works.

599 The exhibition contained a number of works of art on loan from Lever, Dr Nazeby Harrington, the vice-chair of the Libraries and Museums Committee, having been given carte blanche to choose what he wanted from Lever's collection. There does not appear to have been a published catalogue of the exhibition, and this work is not listed in press notices about the display. It is recorded as having been lent to Birkenhead in the LLAG files: accession card. From information supplied by Colin Simpson, Curator, the Williamson Art Gallery, Birkenhead. The Williamson Art Gallery and Museum opened to the public in 1928 and replaced the Birkenhead Art Gallery which had occupied a converted library space in Hamilton Street.

ambition to write and illustrate her own books for children, inspired by memories of her own happy childhood. Her desire to do this coincided with a market for children's books that was booming under the influence of Forster's Education Act of 1870. In 1877–78 she was making fanciful drawings of children to illustrate her own verses, which her father showed to the colour printer Edmund Evans, who worked with Walter Crane and Randolph Caldecott. This introduction resulted in her first book, *Under the Window, Pictures and Rhymes for Children*,[600] which was an immediate success and sold more than 100,000 copies. The technical novelty of her designs was made possible by Evans's new colour printing techniques, which allowed her to use delicate pale tones and much white. However, the book's universal appeal lay with Greenaway's depiction of a visionary dream world of childhood, above all in the stylised manners, attitudes and activities of the children in their quaint old-fashioned clothes. This first success led to many more children's classics, including *Kate Greenaway's Birthday Book for Children* (1880), *Mother Goose or the Old Nursery Rhymes* (1881), *Language of Flowers* (1884), *Marigold Garden* (1885) and a series of *Kate Greenaway's Almanacks*, published each year (except 1896) from 1883 to 1897.

In 1890, influenced by John Ruskin, her friend and mentor, Greenaway stopped illustrating books and pursued a gallery career. In her later years she was beset by financial difficulties, in part caused by the incessant plagiarism of her illustrations. Her later painting style never achieved the same level of popularity as the drawings she made for her children's books.

LL 3656 is recorded in the WHL and TM inventories as *Girl with basket of vegetables, child and kitten*, although it is more likely, given the rural costume of smock and hat, that the figure carrying the basket of beets and turnips is intended to be a boy. The figures represent a romanticised view of rural life in an industrial age, which was a significant part of the appeal of Greenaway's art. The drawing is not identified as a particular book illustration. It was one of 150 works that she showed at her first exhibition at the Fine Art Society in 1891, for which she cleared a substantial number of old drawings, illustrations and paintings from her studio cupboards.[601] Lord Leighton, from whose collection LL 3656 derived, is known to have bought two drawings from the 1891 exhibition;[602] it is therefore possible that LL 3656 and LL 3657 (p. 106), acquired as a pair, were these two.[603]

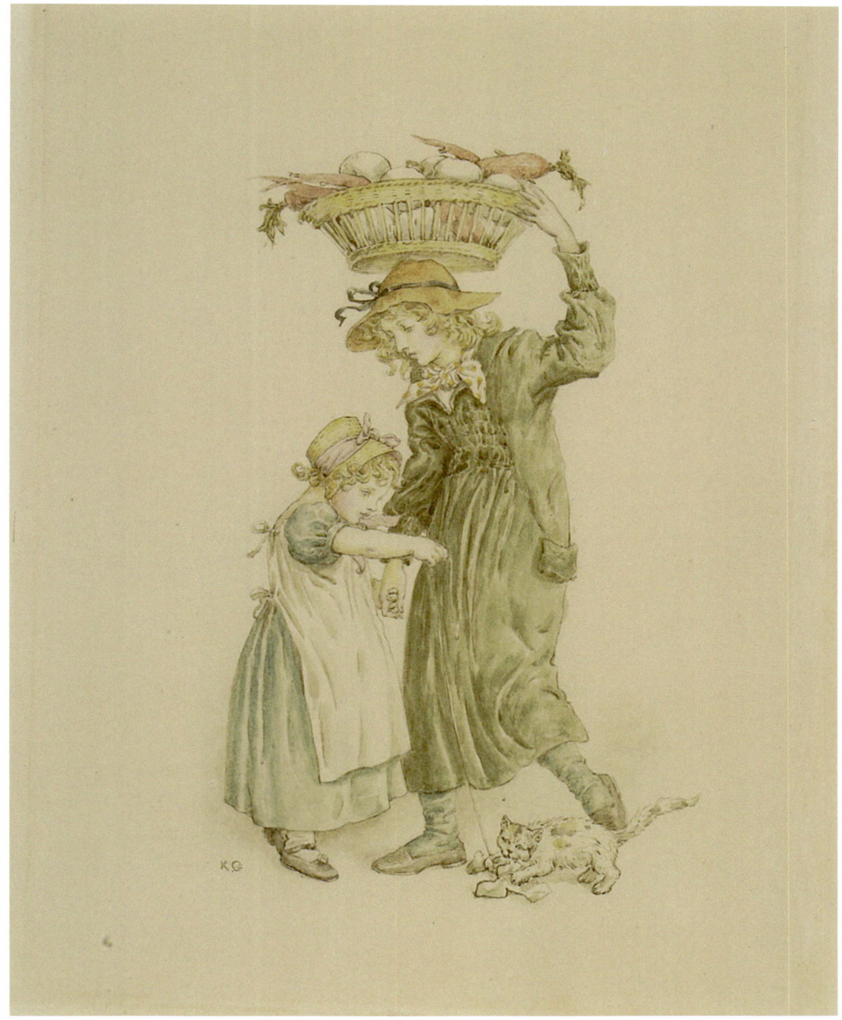

LL 3656

The subject of LL 3656 derives from Greenaway's recollections of childhood times spent with her mother's family in the countryside at Rolleston near Newark, Nottinghamshire. Many of her illustrations stemmed from her detailed memories of this place, as described in autobiographical notes that she made a few years before she died.[604] It has also been claimed by Greenaway's biographers that she possessed a photographic memory.

Greenaway's style in LL 3656, with its delicate lines, minimal shading, sparse layout and pastel colours, has a captivating freshness that sat well alongside the new Aesthetic Movement. The archaic costumes, with their loose, fluid lines, reflect elements of the so-called Aesthetic dress of the period. The boy does not wear working boots, as he would have done in reality; instead his feet are shod in the loose, fanciful slippers that Greenaway favoured for most of her figures. The work can be dated to around 1880.

Greenaway's art had certain technical weaknesses that were frequently criticised. Despite her rigorous study, she never quite mastered the accurate depiction of the human form, as exemplified here in the awkward rendition of the boy's limbs. Critics also noted that despite the carefree and joyful world of childhood that Greenaway depicted, her children usually wore sad expressions, as seen here on the boy's face. This treatment of the children in her drawings was at odds with her much-quoted assertion that her own childhood had been one of unadulterated happiness: 'I had such a happy time when I was a child, and curiously, was so very much happier than my brothers and sisters, with exactly the same surroundings.'[605]
JaS

600 Engraved and printed by Edmund Evans, George Routledge and Sons (London and New York, 1878).
601 Rodney Engen, *Kate Greenaway, A Biography* (London and Sydney, 1981), pp. 170–71.
602 M. H. Spielmann and G. S. Layard, *Kate Greenaway* (London, 1905), p. 180.
603 Records of sales from the 1891 exhibition do not survive in the Fine Art Society archives to identify Leighton's purchases.
604 Spielmann and Layard, *Kate Greenaway*, pp. 8–20 and *passim*.
605 Ibid., p. 17, quoting from a letter to Miss Violet Dickinson.

## The Promenade
LL 3657 (WHL 1750, TM 394)

Watercolour with pen and ink on paper
20 x 19.6 cm (sheet), 13.3 x 13.3 cm (image)
Date: c. 1885

Inscr: K.G. (ink, lower left); 'When we went out with Grandmama / Mama said – For a treat / Oh dear – how stiff we had to walk / As we went down the street' (pencil, lower centre)

Prov: Frederic, Lord Leighton; his sale, Christie's, 14 July 1896 (lot 257); bt. by Agnew's (17 gns with LL 3656); in Lever's collection by 1905[606]

Exh: Bolton, Bolton Art Gallery, *Kate Greenaway 1846–1901*, 1975–76 (cat. 16)

This is a preliminary drawing for the coloured engraved illustration *When We Went Out With Grandmama*, on page 15 of *Marigold Garden* (1885). *Marigold Garden* was the last major book of Greenaway's own verses and pictures, produced when she was beginning to tire of making drawings that were being plagiarised by others, and suffering from a lack of confidence in her abilities that was largely induced by Ruskin's criticism of her work. On 26 May 1885 he wrote to her, 'I've been thinking rather sorrowfully over the *Marigold Garden*, which is no garden, but a mystification ... I mourn over you not showing me things till it's too late to do anything less, or more.'[607] Publication was greeted by some complimentary reviews, but sales in England only reached 6,500.

*Marigold Garden* contained a number of inconsistent styles and page designs; some figures were set in fully drawn gardens, while others, as in LL 3657, were left adrift in space. The drawing does, however, display the diluted influence of both the Aesthetic movement and Japanese prints, filtered to Greenaway through other artists such as Walter Crane. The Japanese influence is seen in the use of outline, the flatness of the space and the blocks of strong colour and stylised pattern seen in the grandmother's costume.

Greenaway placed great emphasis on the details of her figures' costumes throughout her work. Her mother had taught her dressmaking skills, and it was her practice to make the clothes for her models herself. It is also likely that she looked at fashion plates for inspiration. In general, she dressed her figures in the Regency fashion (1811 to 1820) with features from Aesthetic dress, fashionable dress of the 1880s and rural dress; an amalgam of styles that defined the picturesque nature of her imaginary world. For example, at first glance the costumes in LL 3657 appear to date from the early 1820s, but Grandmama's gown mixes the loose 'Greek' lines of late eighteenth-century dress with the higher waistline of later fashions. Her bonnet is the wrong shape for the 1820s, although it has the ostrich feather trim favoured at the time, and the muff she carries is too small. Similarly, the little boy wears a 'skeleton suit', close-fitting and tightly buttoned with a high waist, with completely the wrong style of hat for the period.[608]
JaS

606 Both LL 3656 and LL 3657 were listed in the 1905 TM Inventory, p. 18, both valued at £10, alongside numerous other works by Kate Greenaway. There is no invoice for these works.

607 Spielmann and Layard, *Kate Greenaway*, p. 151.

## Out for a Walk
LL 3658 (WHL 1518, TM 102)

Watercolour, with extra gum arabic and touches of gouache on Bristol board
18.3 x 14.3 cm (sheet), 17.5 x 13.5 cm (image)
Date: no earlier than 1890 and possibly early 1890s

Inscr: K Greenaway (ink, bottom left)

Prov: acquired by Lever between 1902 and 1905[609]

Exh: Bolton, Bolton Art Gallery, *Kate Greenaway 1846–1901*, 1975–76 (cat. 29)

LL 3658 is one of the later, more highly finished watercolours that Greenaway made for exhibition and sale from about 1890, when she gave up book illustration in favour of gallery work.

Greenaway exhibited her work from the age of 22, showing first at the Dudley Gallery, Piccadilly, in 1868, a watercolour and six little drawings on wood.[610] She exhibited in group shows at the Royal Society of British Artists, 1870, 1872–75; at the Royal Academy, 1877–80, 1890, 1895; at the Royal Institute of Painters in Water-Colours, 1893, 1895–97; and at the *World's Columbian Exposition*, Chicago, 1893. It was at the Fine Art Society in London that she had a series of one-woman shows in 1891, 1894 and 1898, with a posthumous retrospective in 1902. Greenaway found these exhibitions stressful, and not as financially rewarding as her book illustration work had been. For example, for her third Fine Art Society exhibition in 1898, she produced 127 pictures, 66 of which sold for a total of £1,024 16s, from which she made a profit of £645.[611] The 1898 exhibition included a number of paintings of the same type as LL 3658, each of them selling for 35 guineas.

A new influence on Greenaway in the period when LL 3658 was produced was fellow painter and illustrator, Helen Allingham (see pp. 4–5), whose nostalgic watercolour visions of rural England brought her great success. The two artists met initially at the Slade, then in 1889 (the year Greenaway became a member of the Royal Institute of Painters in Water-Colours) they rekindled their friendship and for a couple of years went on painting expeditions together in the Surrey countryside.[612] Allingham's one-woman show at the Fine Art Society in 1886 probably supplied the initial inspiration for Greenaway's own solo show in 1891; certainly, Allingham's denser, richer use of watercolour had an effect on Greenaway's working methods, as exemplified in LL 3658.

The contemporary appeal of the Lady Lever work came from the image of a pretty little child as a miniature adult, aping her mother with her elegant fur-lined coat and flower-trimmed hat, taking her toy horse 'out for a walk'. The rustic setting, with the red brickwork, green painted door and shutters and the crumbling stone steps, is one that Greenaway depicted on a number of occasions, with a nod towards William Morris's style of architecture. Another instance of this was in her watercolour *The Fable of the Girl and her Milk Pail*, a pronouncedly Pre-Raphaelite work exhibited at the Fine Art Society in 1893.[613]
JaS

608 From information supplied by Beatrice Behlen, Senior Curator of Costume, Museum of London.

609 1905 TM Inventory, 'Mrs Lever's bathroom'; it is not listed in the 1897–1902 TM Inventory; no invoice has survived.

610 Spielmann and Layard, *Kate Greenaway*, p. 44 (list of Greenaway's work exhibited at the Dudley Gallery, 1868–79).

611 Ibid., p. 224.

## Ready for the Party
LL 3659 (WHL 3547)

Watercolour, with extra gum arabic and touches of gouache on paper laid down on card
32.6 x 26.8 cm (sheet), 23 x 17 cm (image)
Date: late 1890s

Inscr: K.G. (watercolour, bottom left)

Prov: Alice H. Cooke, North Bank, Muswell Hill; her sale, Christie's, 24 May 1918 (lot 19); bt. by Gooden and Fox (£28 7s) for Lever (£29 1s 3d)

Exh: Bolton, Bolton Art Gallery, *Kate Greenaway 1846–1901*, 1975–76 (cat. 30)

LL 3659 probably dates from the late 1890s, when Greenaway was producing her more densely coloured and detailed paintings for exhibition. The stiffly posed image of the little girl, dressed up like a doll in her best party clothes, bears a strong resemblance to others produced at this time. It is particularly close in the choice of pose and the details of costume to portraits commissioned by Stuart Montague Samuel of his daughters; Samuel was a wealthy banker and MP who became a friend and patron of the artist. In 1896, for example, Greenaway painted a portrait of Vera Evelyn Samuel[614] dressed in a frilled, summer version of the party outfit in LL 3659. Samuel owned another version of LL 3659 entitled *Baby in White*, which was even closer in

612 Ibid., pp. 172–73.

613 Bryan Holme, *The Kate Greenaway Book* (London, 1976), illus. p. 133.

614 Engen, *Kate Greenaway*, illus. p. 196.

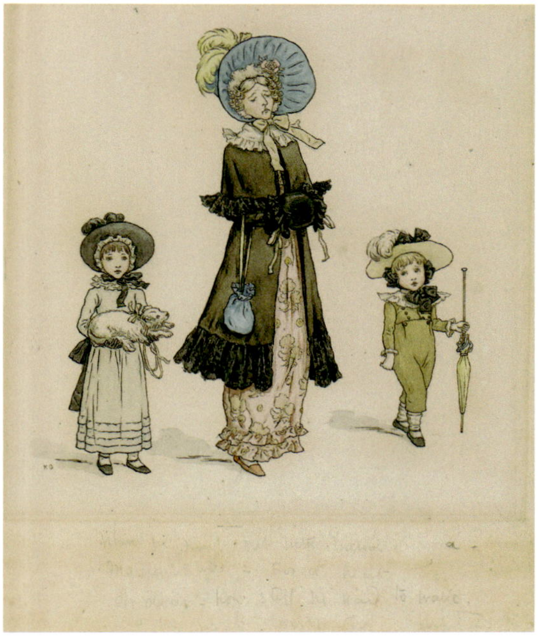

LL 3657

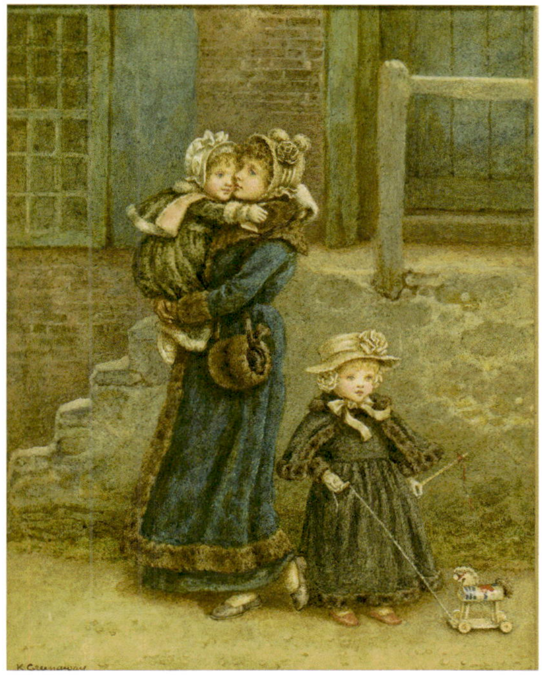

LL 3658

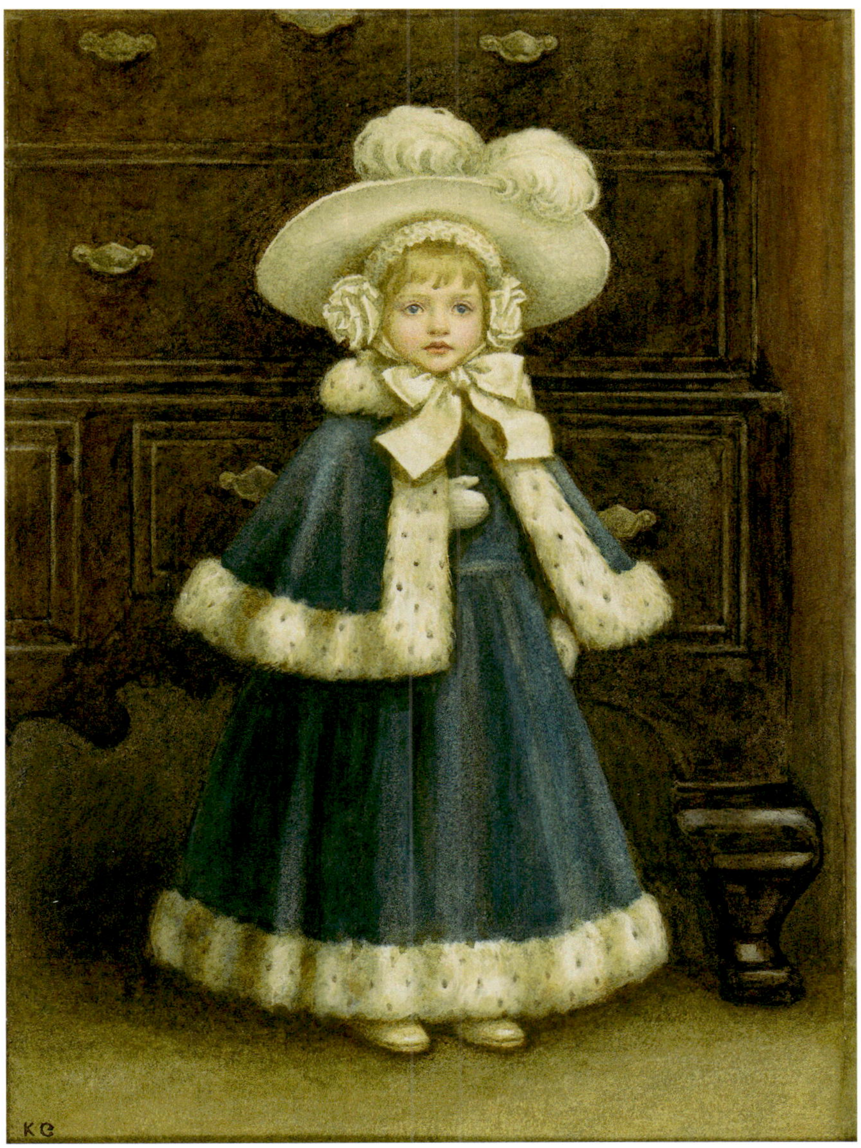

LL 3659

composition and showed a little girl against a background of spring flowers.[615]

The costume portrayed in LL 3659 is, like that in LL 3657, anachronistic. The dress, and particularly the hat, is very similar to that worn by the four-year-old Princess Victoria in a watercolour of 1823 in the collection at Dulwich Picture Gallery. The deep blue colour, however, is more in keeping with the Aesthetic taste in the late nineteenth century for rich colours in dress.

Several photographs survive of Greenaway in her studio at her Norman Shaw designed house at 39 Frognal, Hampstead. In one she sits beside an easel on which is displayed a painting of a child wearing the same costume as in LL 3659.[616] In another view of the studio, the large chest of drawers that appears in the background of LL 3659 can be seen.[617]

During her third Fine Art Society exhibition in 1898, Greenaway wrote to her friend Violet Dickinson: 'The large pencil and chalk drawings I fear do not take at all. The little ones sell, and the dressed up babies.'[618] The need to make money and satisfy her purchasers' preferences led Greenaway to produce a large number of pictures of 'dressed up babies' in her last decade. She also experimented with painting in oils but struggled with the medium. An avid exhibition-goer herself, with an undying admiration for the Pre-Raphaelites, she expressed her views on the 'New Art' in her letters to Ruskin, bemoaning the fickleness of the picture-buying public: 'I fear the exhibition [1898] won't be in the least successful; there seems to me [to be] very few pictures [that] sell now - or a person is popular for just a little time'.[619]

Greenway's last years were marred by ill health and professional uncertainty. She died aged 55 of breast cancer on 6 November 1901. In fact, Greenaway enjoyed long popularity in her own lifetime and her far-reaching influence on children's book illustration has been commemorated annually since 1955 by the Kate Greenaway Medal, founded by the Library Association and awarded for distinguished illustration in books for children.
JaS

615 Spielmann and Layard, *Kate Greenaway*, illus. facing p. 222.
616 Ibid., illus. facing p. 17.
617 Ibid., illus. facing p. 146.
618 Ibid., p. 226.
619 Ibid., p. 228, quoting a letter to John Ruskin dated 12 January 1898.

## EDWARD JOHN GREGORY
1850 Southampton-1909 Great Marlow, Buckinghamshire

### Study for *Boulter's Lock, Sunday Afternoon*
LL 3906[620]

Watercolour, gum arabic, with gouache and scratching out on paper, squared up in pencil for transfer
73.5 x 48.6 cm
Date: probably 1880s or early 1890s

Prov: artist's studio sale, Christie's, 31 January 1910 (lot 44); bt. by Cox (£8 8s 6d) for Lever

Gregory showed a natural aptitude for art at a young age, and attended life classes in Southampton, where he met Hubert Herkomer (pp. 115–16), who became a lifelong friend. He subsequently attended the South Kensington Art School and the Royal Academy Schools. Between 1871 and 1875 Gregory worked as an illustrator for *The Graphic* alongside Herkomer. Gregory was elected to the Institute of Painters in Water-Colours in 1871 and remained an active member throughout his life, serving as president from 1898 until his death. He first exhibited at the Royal Academy in 1875 and was elected an associate in 1879. Gregory did not produce large numbers of works, only exhibiting 55 times at the Institute of Painters in Water-Colours and showing 34 pictures at the Royal Academy throughout his career. His most celebrated painting, *Boulter's Lock, Sunday Afternoon* (Lady Lever Art Gallery, fig. 36), exhibited at the Royal Academy in 1897, probably secured his election as an Academician in 1898.[621]

Boulter's Lock, near Maidenhead on the upper Thames, was a popular site during the Thames boating craze in the 1890s. The lock had extremely heavy river traffic; for example, in 1894 a record number of 129 launches and almost 1000 smaller boats passed through in one day and the *Lock to Lock Times*, admittedly with a vested interest in representing the large numbers of spectators, reported that there was a crowd of two to three thousand alongside the bank and Mill Bridge.[622] Gregory's painting, then, seems to be a relatively faithful depiction of the chaotic frenzy of boats pouring out from the lock, watched by numerous spectators on the bridge. As Edward Morris has noted, the lock and its surroundings as well as the representative sample of boats are generally painted with great accuracy.[623] When it was first exhibited in 1897 contemporary reviewers of the picture were mainly enthusiastic, although some could be more equivocal, *The Art Journal* for example, wrote: 'The bewilderment which a first glance at the work produces, is due to the variegated hues demanded by the subject, and, more still, to a certain want of atmosphere, of light, and of shadow. But there is no denying the actuality and vividness of the crowding forms so well grouped and presented'.[624]

Gregory's painting, as contemporary reviewers emphasised, was the result of many years of deliberation, and was probably begun some time in the early 1880s.[625] It was commissioned by Gregory's long-time patron and collector of his work, the Manchester industrialist Charles Galloway, who in 1892 listed it as one of the pictures 'not at present hanging at Thorneyholme', his house in Cheshire, and we can assume it was nearing completion by this date.[626] The painting was acquired by Lever on Galloway's death, at the Christie's sale of his collection in 1905.[627] Gregory produced at least five known oil studies (of which the Lady Lever Art Gallery now owns three) and at least two watercolour sketches for the composition; LL 3906 is one of these watercolour compositional sketches.[628] The other was a finished watercolour with a quite different composition that was shown at the 1883 Royal Institute of Painters in Water-Colours exhibition, suggesting that the Lady Lever work dates from after this, although it would be difficult to be more precise about its date.[629] LL 3906 includes many elements that were retained in the final composition, including the triple-oared rowing boat, the punt, canoe and two launches (one steam and one electric), although the placement of some of these in the final painting was altered (in the case of the canoe and the steam boat for example).

620 LL 3906 was accidentally omitted from the WHL inventory.
621 For details of the painting see Morris, *Victorian and Edwardian Paintings*, pp. 41–45. For a discussion of the painting in its social and art-historical context, see Lisa Tickner, 'Messing About in Boats: E.J. Gregory's Boulter's Lock: Sunday Afternoon (R.A. 1897)', *Oxford Art Journal*, vol. 25, no. 2 (2002), pp. 1–28.
622 *Lock to Lock Times*, 30 June 1894, p. 5; quoted by Tickner, 'Messing About in Boats', p. 12.
623 Morris, *Victorian and Edwardian Paintings*, p. 42.
624 'The Royal Academy', *The Art Journal* (1897), pp. 179–80, quoted in Tickner, 'Messing About in Boats', p. 3. For further discussion of the painting's critical reception, see Morris, *Victorian and Edwardian Paintings*, p. 43. For details of the painting's exhibition abroad see Tickner, 'Messing About in Boats', p. 15.
625 *The Times*, 1 May 1897. Morris, *Victorian and Edwardian Paintings*, p. 43 suggests a tentative date of 1882.
626 Galloway's commissioning of the painting was originally reported in Gregory's 'Obituary', *The Art Journal* (1909), p. 255. See Tickner, 'Messing About in Boats', p. 8.
627 For further details see Morris, *Victorian and Edwardian Paintings*, p. 44.
628 Lever owned five oil studies for the composition. Three of these are in the Lady Lever collection, two were sold at Knight, Frank and Rutley, London, 15–18 June 1926 (lots 76 and 77). See Morris, *Victorian and Edwardian Paintings*, pp. 42–44, and p. 45, n. 1.
629 This is illustrated in Charles J. Galloway, *Catalogue of Paintings and Drawings at Thorneyholme, Cheshire* (Knutsford, 1892), facing p. 74 (no. 267).

### Twenty-six studies for *Boulter's Lock, Sunday Afternoon*
LL 10301–LL 10326 (WHL 1502, TM 83, LP 21A–Y)
Date: probably 1880s or early 1890s

Prov: artist's studio sale, Christie's, 31 January 1910 (lot 5); bt. by Cox (£1 5s) for Lever; by descent to 2nd Viscount Leverhulme; from whom aquired by the Trustees, 1928

### Seated man
### Verso: Landscape study with figures
LL 10301 (LP 21A)

Pencil on paper
32.4 x 22.5 cm

LL 10301–10326 are 26 of the many pencil sketches that Gregory made for individual figures in his painting *Boulter's Lock, Sunday Afternoon* (see LL 3906 above), revealing the artist's painstaking working processes and attention to detail. A further 26 studies were acquired for the Walker Art Gallery in 1989 (WAG 10779, 10787–10812).[630] Some of these studies appear to have been drawn using models in the studio; these may on occasion have been Gregory's relatives.[631]

The male figure in LL 10301 does not appear to be directly related to any of the figures in the painting. The landscape on the verso is unrelated to the painting.

### Female figure leaning on hand rail of bridge
LL 10302 (LP 21B)

Pencil on paper
32.3 x 22.6 cm

LL 10302 is a study for the female figure in the far right-hand corner on Mill Bridge.

### Female figure, holding paddle
LL 10303 (LP 21C)

Pencil on paper, with touch of purple crayon
26 x 17.9 cm (torn irreg.)

LL 10303 is an individual figure study of the female canoeist included in one of the oil sketches now in the Lady Lever Art Gallery (LL 3578, fig. 37). It may relate to the figure of the female canoeist to the left of the punt in the final painting, although in this the position of the woman's body has been altered, so that her left side faces the viewer.

630 These were exhibited at *Themes and Variations: Boulter's Lock*, London, Maas Gallery (1970), along with 20 other studies.
631 LLAG files: correspondence, 19 January 1984. H. R. Evans, Gregory's great-nephew, claimed that his mother and grandmother had modelled for *Boulter's Lock, Sunday Afternoon*. See also Tickner, 'Messing About in Boats', p. 23. Tickner has observed that the 'Ada' referred to on WAG 10788 was Boulter's sister-in-law, Ada Joyner.

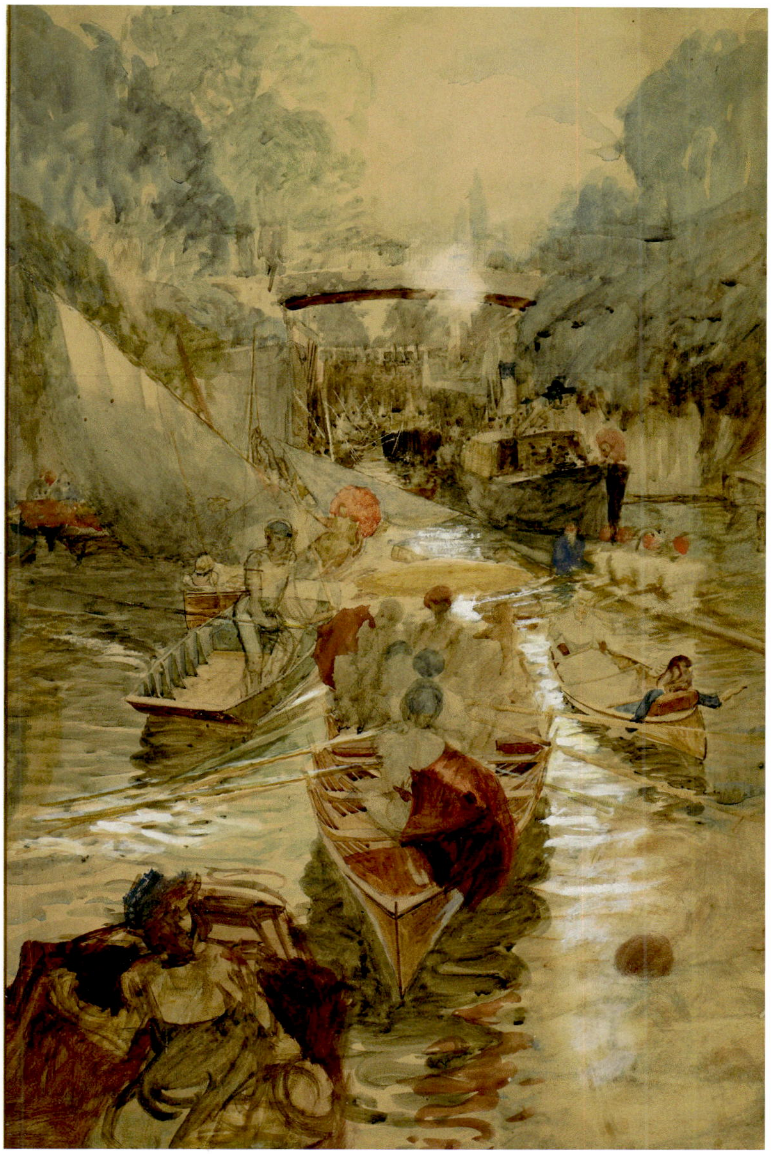

LL 3906

fig. 36. Edward John Gregory, *Boulter's Lock, Sunday Afternoon*, c. 1882–97, oil on canvas, 215 x 142 cm, National Museums Liverpool, Lady Lever Art Gallery

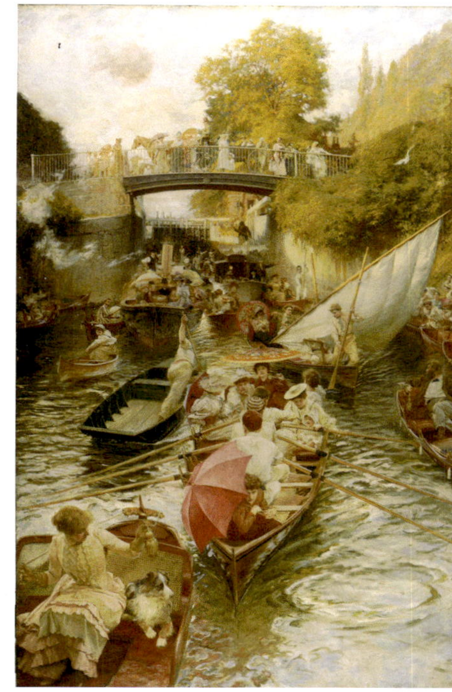

fig. 37. Edward John Gregory, *Study for Boulter's Lock, Sunday Afternoon*, c. 1882–97, oil on canvas laid on board, 40.5 x 66 cm, National Museums Liverpool, Lady Lever Art Gallery

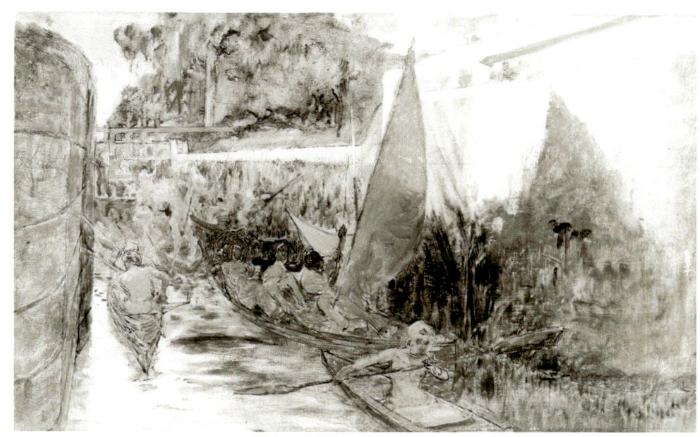

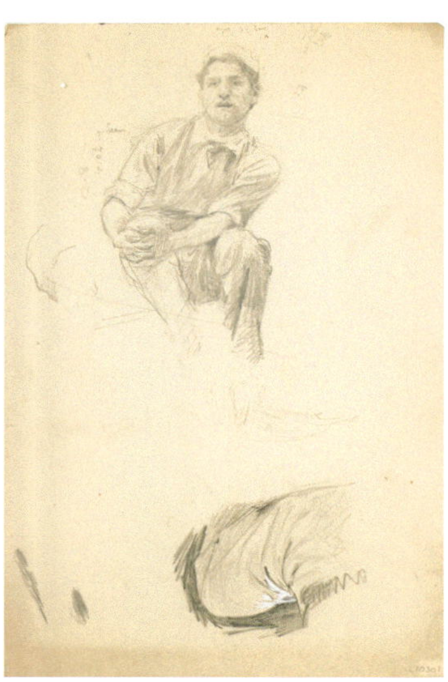

LL 10301

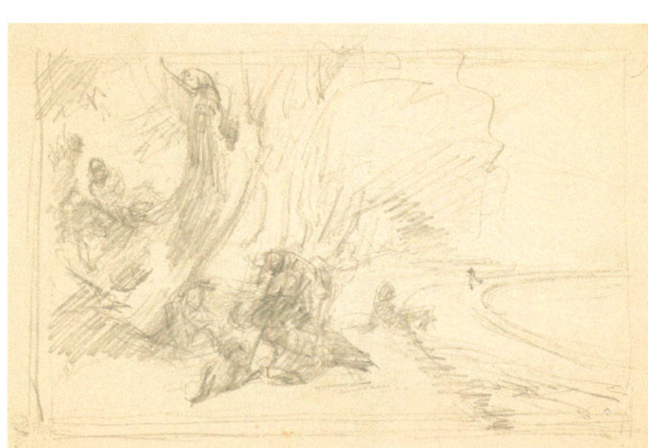

LL 10301 (verso)

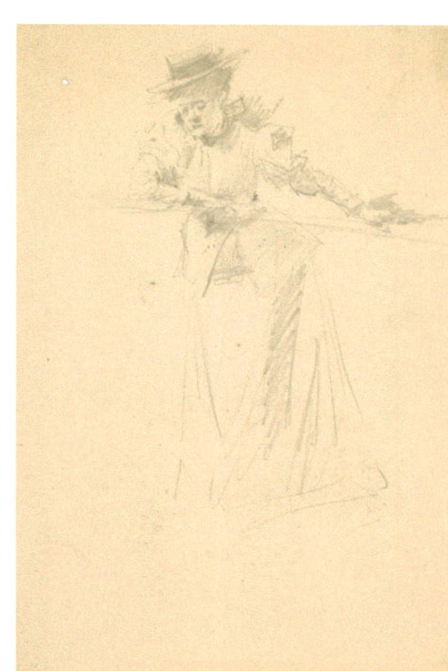

LL 10302

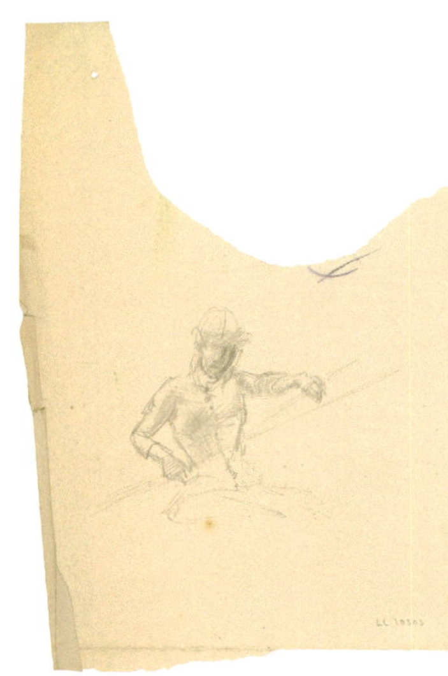

LL 10303

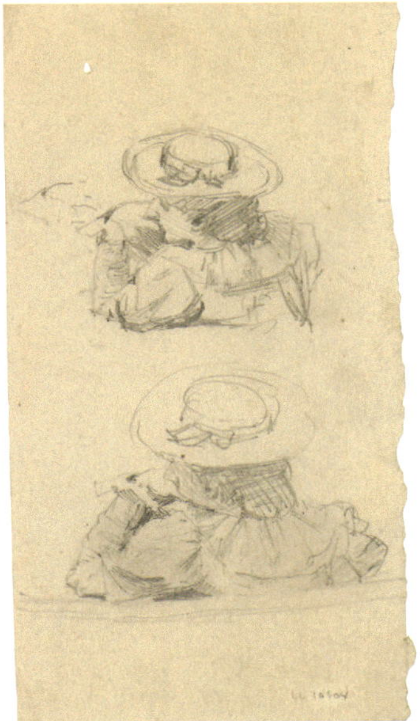

LL 10304

LL 10304 (verso)

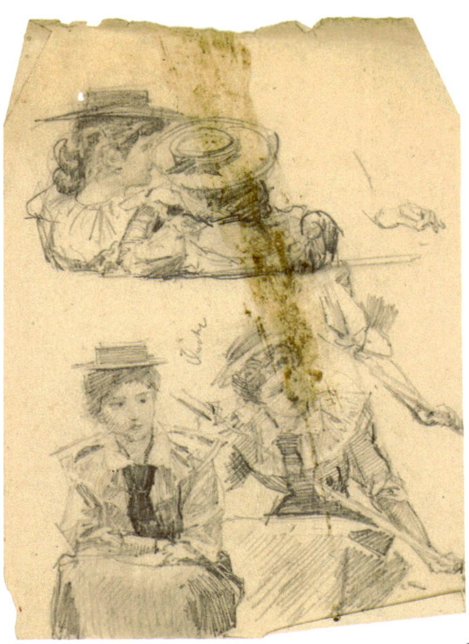

LL 10305

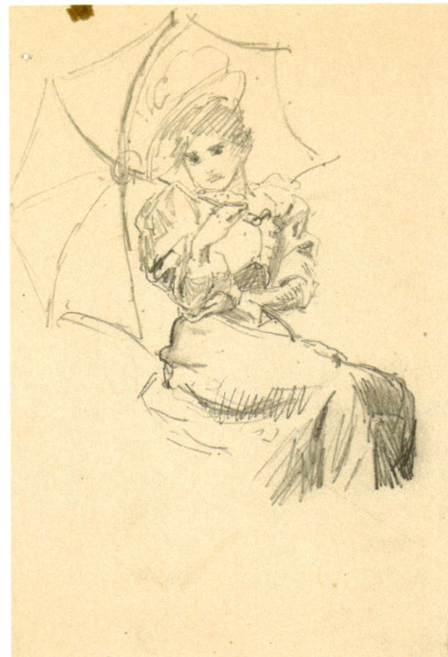

LL 10306

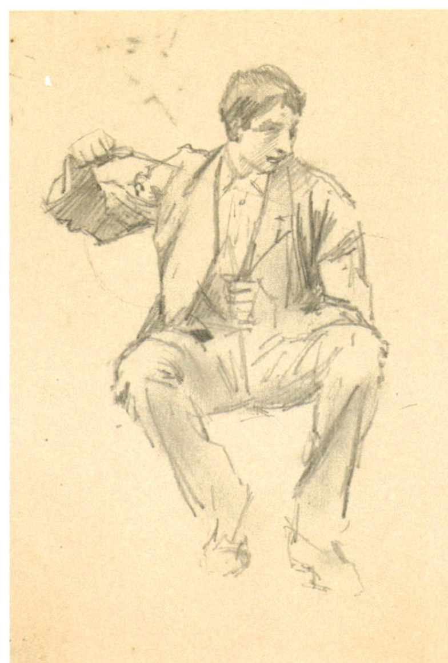

LL 10307

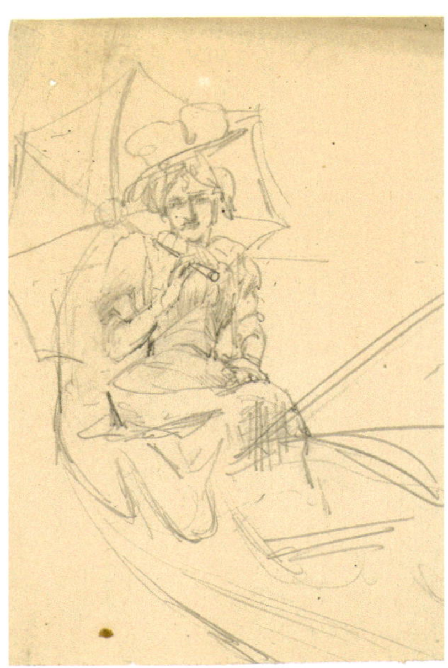

LL 10308

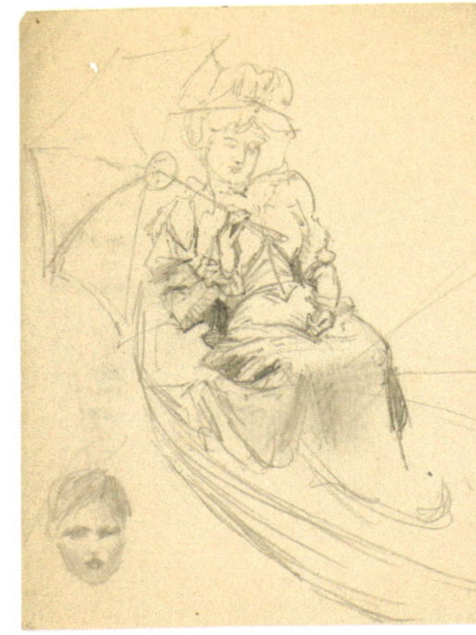

LL 10309

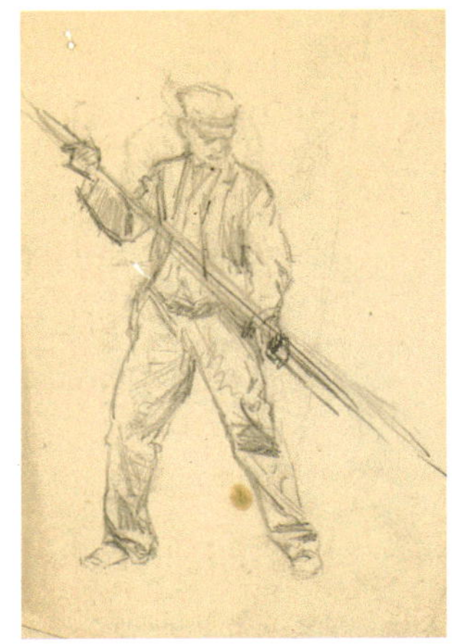

LL 10310

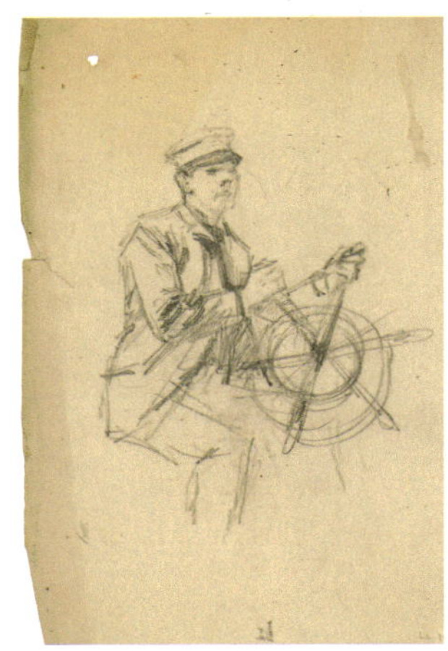

LL 10311

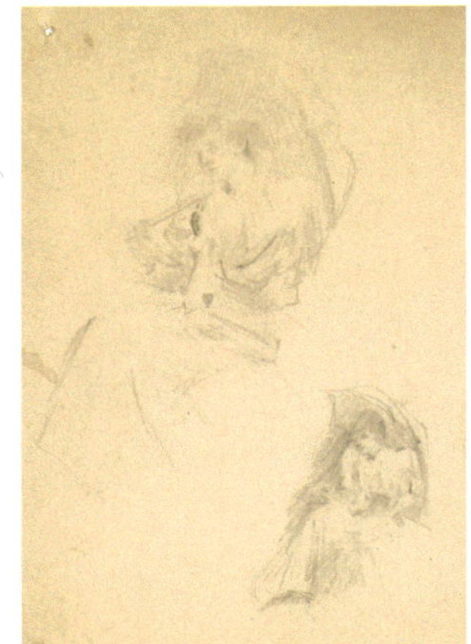

LL 10312

**Two studies of head and shoulders of female figure, wearing hat**
**Verso: graph and mathematical calculations**
LL 10304 (LP 21D)

Pencil on paper
25.4 x 13.5 cm (torn irreg. down right edge)

LL 10304 does not appear to relate to any figure in the final composition. The verso shows a graph and calculations, though it is not clear that these relate to the painting.

**Studies of female figures and an arm holding a paddle**
LL 10305 (LP 21E)

Pencil on paper
25.4 x 19 cm (torn and folded irreg.)

The model for the figure in the upper half of the drawing on the right is the same as that for the figure in LL 10304. The two drawings in the lower half may relate to the figure of the canoeist in the final painting. The study has an unidentified stain running across the recto.

**Seated female figure holding parasol, with arm supporting her elbow**
LL 10306 (LP 21F)

Pencil on paper, with slight adhesive stains on the recto, top left edge and bottom right edge
25.5 x 19.4 cm (torn irreg.)

This is a study for the female figure at the stern of the sailing boat holding a parasol.

**Seated male figure pulling line**
LL 10307 (LP 21G)

Pencil on paper
25.6 x 21.4 cm (torn irreg.)

This is a study for the male figure pulling a line at the stern of the sailing boat, although in the final painting he is wearing a hat.

**Seated female figure holding parasol, with hand on her lap**
LL 10308 (LP 21H)

Pencil on paper, with a slight adhesive stain, bottom left edge
25.5 x 19.3 cm (torn and folded irreg.)

This study is very similar to LL 10306, although the model's hand is now placed on her lap instead of under the elbow of her other arm. The sketch may be for the female figure at the stern of the sailing boat.

**Seated female figure holding parasol, with hand on lap; sketch of head in bottom left corner**
LL 10309 (LP 21I)

Pencil on paper
25.3 x 25.4 cm (torn and folded irreg.)

This study is very similar to LL 10306 and 10308 and may relate to the female figure at the stern of the sailing boat.

**Standing male figure holding pole**
LL 10310 (LP 21J)

Pencil on paper, with a slight adhesive stain lower centre
28.1 x 18.8 cm (torn and folded irreg., with some additional tears centre and top left)

This study relates to the male figure standing astride the roof of the Immisch, or electric launch, in the background just under Mill Bridge.[632] It has been suggested that this figure is either a second attendant or the lock-keeper, helping boats out of the lock.[633]

**Seated male figure holding steering wheel**
LL 10311 (LP 21K)

Pencil on paper
30.8 x 20.9 cm (torn and folded irreg., with an additional tear top left, possibly where work has been pinned)

Inscr: [various mathematical calculations] (pencil, bottom edge); [illeg. word] / steerer (pencil, lower centre); apx scale of launch boat (pencil, right edge); above boater (pencil, left edge)

This study probably relates to the male figure sitting down and steering the Immisch launch. The male figure steering the steam launch is standing up.

**Seated female figure holding parasol; with a smaller sketch of the same figure**
LL 10312 (LP 21L)

Pencil on paper
29.6 x 21cm (torn irreg., with an additional tear top left, possibly where work has been pinned)

This study is probably for the female figure holding a parasol in the stern of the sailing boat, as depicted in LL 10306, and LL 10308–09. Here, Gregory has depicted her from a different angle.

632 Tickner, 'Messing About in Boats', p. 9.
633 Tickner, 'Messing About in Boats', p. 10. There is another study for this figure in the Herbert Art Gallery, Coventry.

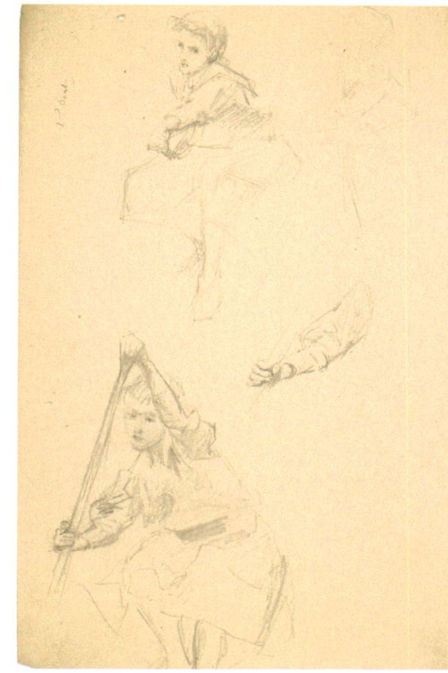

LL 10313

**Two studies of young girl rowing; study of arm holding paddle**
LL 10313 (LP 21M)

Pencil on paper
32.4 x 22.6 cm (torn irreg., with an additional tear top left, possibly where work has been pinned)

Inscr: 2nd seat (pencil, upper left)

The top study relates closely to the figure of the female canoeist in the final painting.

LL 10314

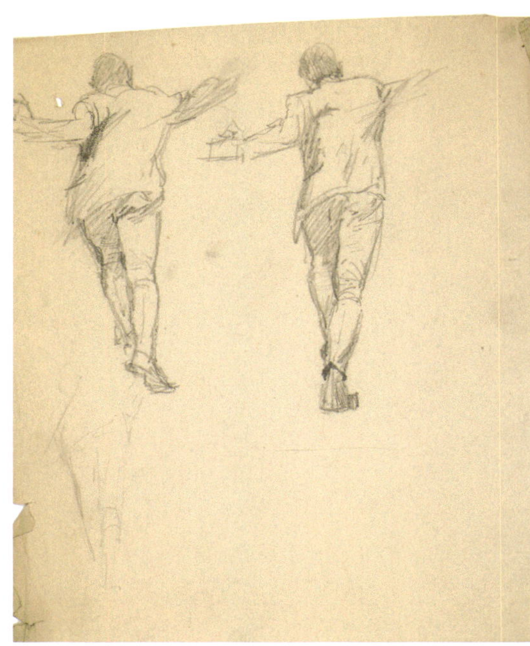

**Two studies for figure of male punter**
LL 10314 (LP 21N)

Pencil on paper
28.9 x 26 cm (torn and folded irreg., with an additional tear top left, possibly where work has been pinned)

Both sketches are studies for the figure of the male punter in the finished painting, who leans forward with his back to the viewer, left leg forward, right leg backwards.

**Three studies of boys rowing, one wearing a cap; study of legs**
LL 10315 (LP 21O)

Pencil on paper
32.3 x 22.6 cm (torn irreg.)

The study of the figure wearing a cap relates to the figure of the boy in a boat at the far right of the painting. The other studies may relate to other figures in this section of the painting.

**Four studies of a boy rowing**
LL 10316 (LP 21P)

Pencil on paper
32.4 x 22. 7 cm (torn irreg.)

These studies are from the same model wearing the cap who features in LL 10315.

**Six sketches of a boy**
**Verso: female figure rowing**
LL 10317 (LP 21Q)

Pencil on paper, with some oil paint
32.5 x 22.6 cm

Inscr: In all of these / except last head reach / is greater than / that / of shoulder (pencil, lower left edge); [illeg. word] of head / abou 3" in front of seat (pencil, upper right edge)

The studies on the recto are all for the same figure. They probably relate to the boy wearing a cap also seen in LL 10315 and LL 10316. The model on the verso has a similar pose to that of the female canoeist in the final painting.

**Sketches of male figure astride rail**
LL 10318 (LP 21R)

Pencil on paper
37.9 x 28.1 cm (torn and folded irreg., with an additional tear top left, possibly where work has been pinned)

Inscr: if move over / this is wider (pencil, lower right); line too / high (pencil, far right edge); would be more hollow (pencil, right edge, above head); white line (pencil, upper right, at waist of figure)

This figure, apparently a young boy, does not seem to relate to any in the final painting. The rail may be that of Mill Bridge. Gregory may have originally thought about placing a figure of a young boy balancing on the rail of the bridge.

**Study of seated man with moustache**
LL 10319 (LP 21S)

Pencil on paper
35.6 x 25.5 cm

Inscr: 27 (blue crayon, verso, top right)

The distinctive features of this model, here seated, do not seem to relate to any figure in the painting.

**Four studies of a seated man wearing a boater, looking behind**
LL 10320 (LP 21T)

Pencil on paper
38.4 x 27.9 cm (torn and folded irreg. with an additional tear top left, possibly where work has been pinned)

This study does not appear to relate to any figure in the painting.

**Sketches of two female figures rowing, one wearing a hat**
LL 10321 (LP 21U)

Pencil on paper
26 x 19.1 cm (torn and folded irreg. with an additional tear top left, possibly where work has been pinned)

These two figures do not appear to relate to any figures in the painting.

**Three studies of female figures, two holding paddle**
LL 10322 (LP 21V)

Pencil on paper
27.8 x 20.5 cm (torn irreg. with an additional tear top left, possibly where work has been pinned)

The two female figures centre and bottom are similar in pose to the female figure in LL 10303. They relate to the figure of the female canoeist in the oil study, LL 3578 (see fig. 37, p. 109).

**Studies of men's legs**
LL 10323 (LP 21W)

Pencil on paper, with some adhesive stains that have leaked through from the verso
29.3 x 18.4 cm (torn and folded irreg. with additional tears left edge, centre and top left, possibly where work has been pinned)

Inscr: too long (pencil, centre)

These studies of men's legs from behind may relate to the figure of the male punter in the finished painting, although their configuration is not quite the same as it is in that work.

**Study for figure of a male punter**
LL 10324 (LP 21X)

Pencil on paper
28.9 x 21.1 cm (torn and folded irreg. with an additional tear top left, possibly where work has been pinned)

This study for the figure of the male punter in the final painting relates closely to the sketches for the same figure in LL 10314 and LL 10325–26.

**Three studies for figure of male punter; additional head sketch**
LL 10325 (LP 21Y)

Pencil on paper
36.5 x 26.3 cm (torn and folded irreg. with an additional tear top left, possibly where work has been pinned)

These studies are similar to LL 10314, LL 10324 and LL 10326.

**Three studies for figure of male punter; additional leg sketch**
LL 10326

Pencil on paper
25.9 x 20.9 cm (torn irreg. with an additional tear top left, possibly where work has been pinned)

Inscr: Gaiters (pencil, verso, top centre)

These studies are similar to LL 10314 and LL 10324–25. LL 10326 does not poccess an LP number because the Gregory sketches were miscounted when these numbers were allocated.

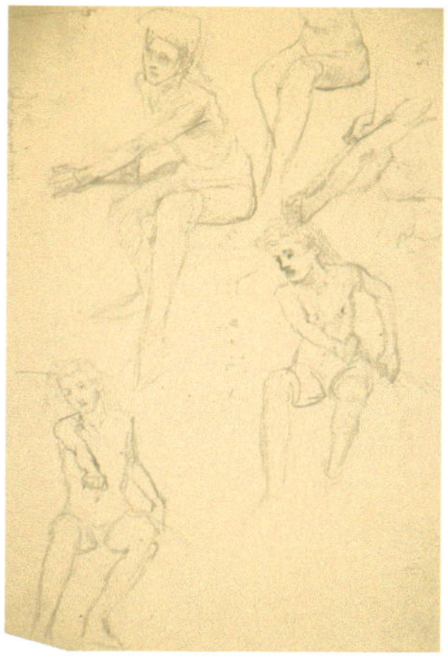

LL 10315

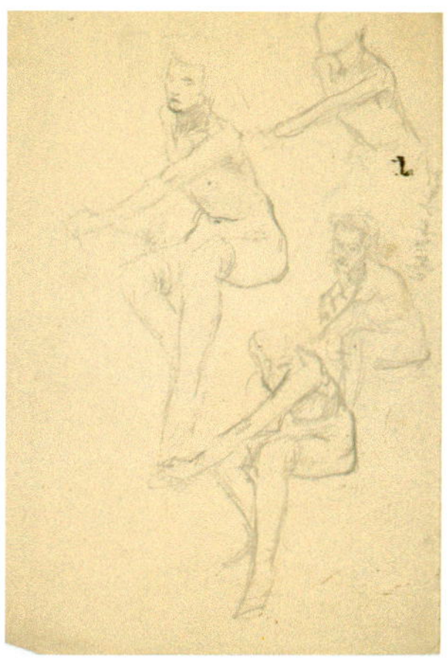

LL 10316

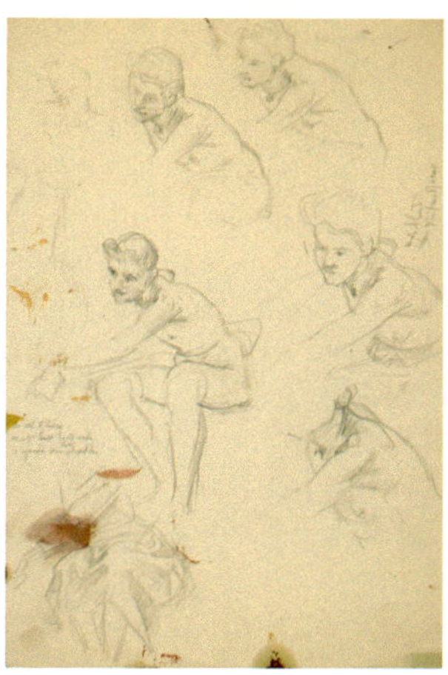

LL 10317

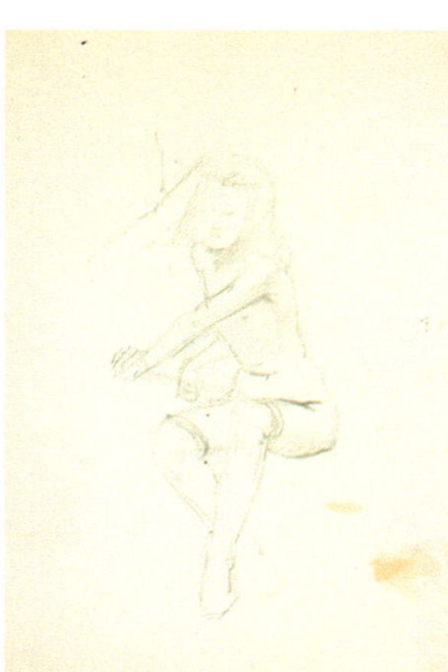

LL 10317 (verso)

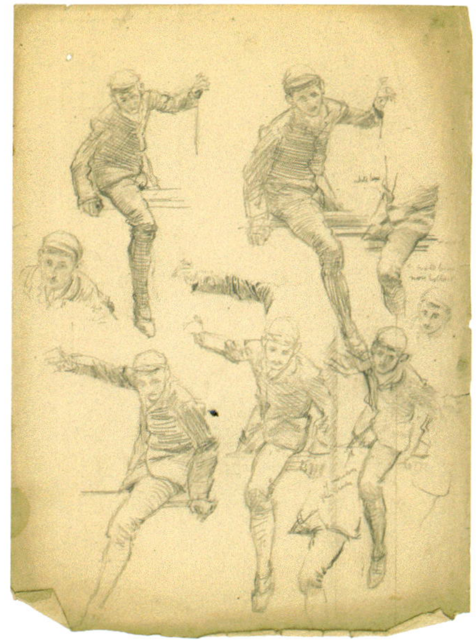

LL 10318

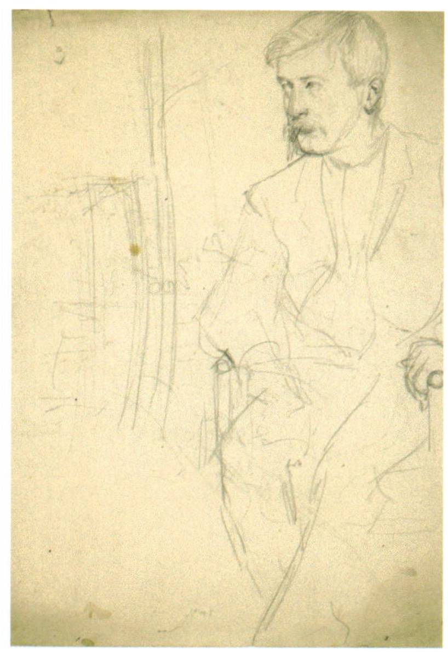

LL 10319

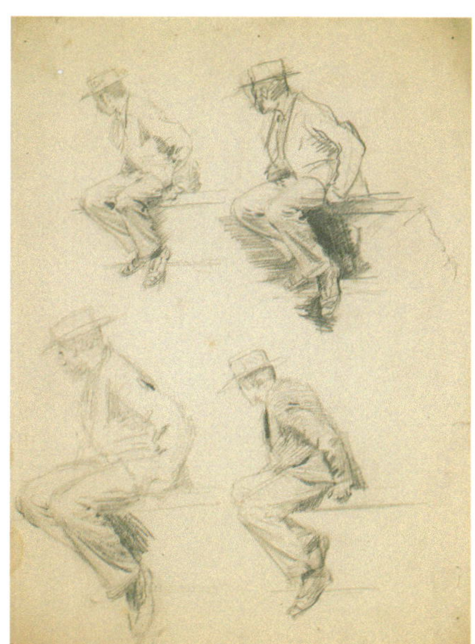

LL 10320

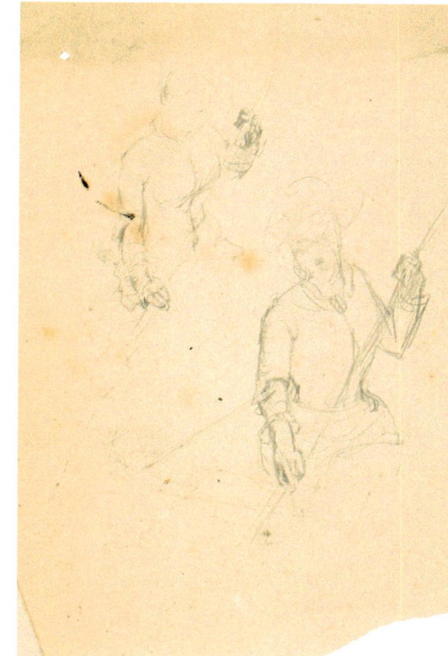

LL 10321

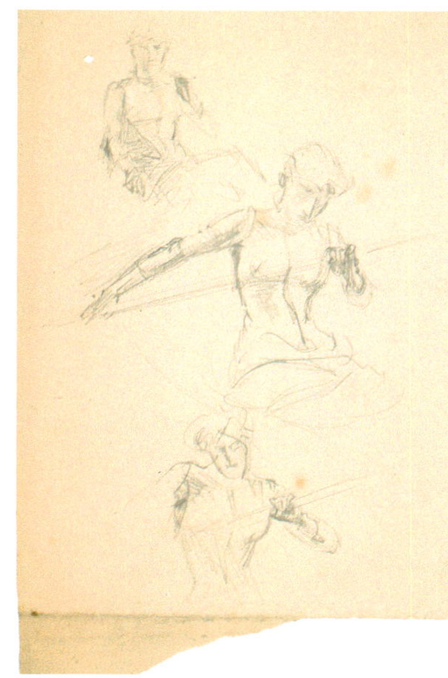

LL 10322

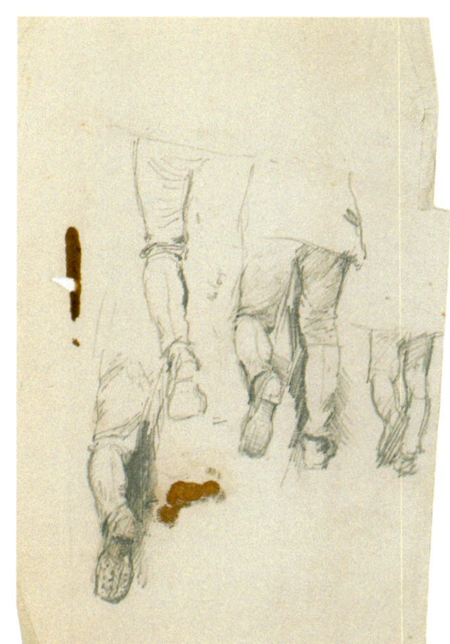

LL 10323

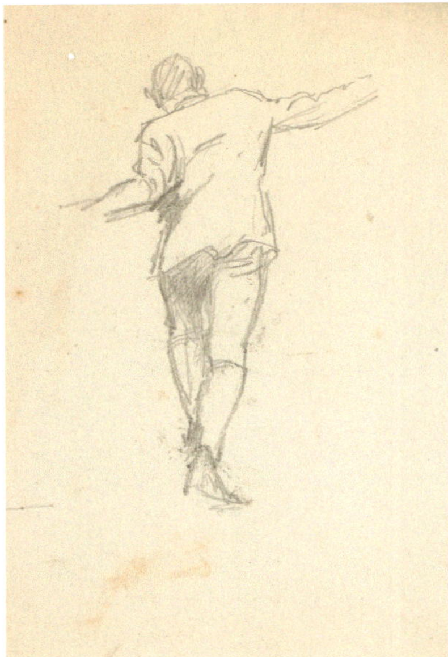

LL 10324

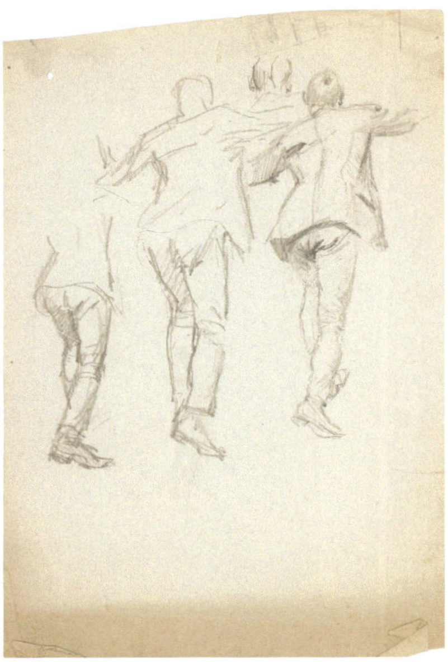

LL 10325

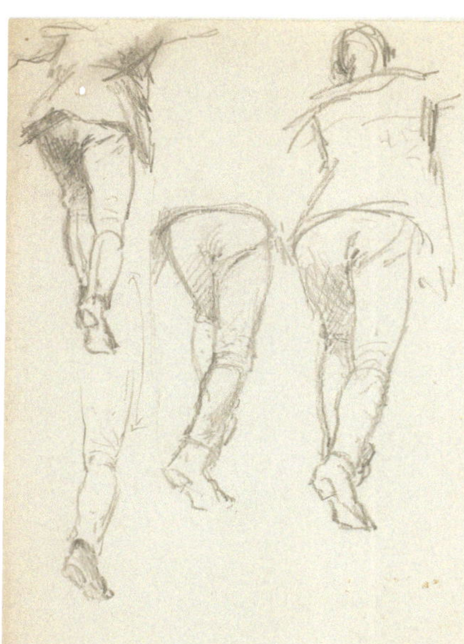

LL 10326

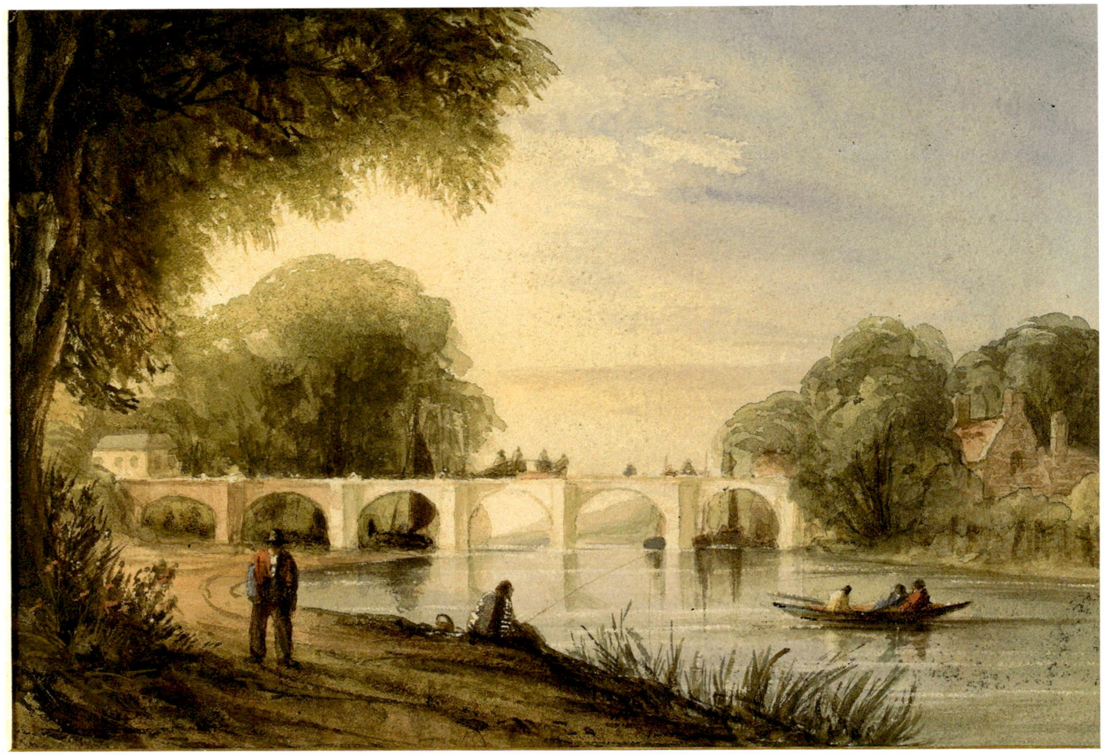

LL 3967

## ROBERT HINDMARSH GRUNDY

1816 Bolton–1865 Liverpool

**River scene with bridge of six arches**
LL 3967 (LP 42)

Watercolour, gum arabic, touches of gouache, with pencil and scratching out on paper
16.5 x 24.5 cm (sight)
Date: probably late 1820s or early 1830s

Prov: Cecil Reginald Grundy, 1924; given by him to the Trustees, 31 January 1935

Lit: *The Connoisseur*, vol. 69 (July 1924), illus. p. 126

Robert Hindmarsh Grundy was the son of John Grundy (1780–1843) of Bolton, Lancashire, a cotton mill owner who was a talented amateur miniature painter.[634] As a boy he won prizes for his drawings but did not become a professional artist, instead joining his eldest brother, John Clowes Grundy, in Manchester in the picture-dealing and print-publishing business. It was in this capacity that he met the artists Samuel Prout (p. 155) and David Cox (pp. 59–65). Cox became a life-long friend, and Grundy accompanied him on several sketching trips.[635] In the late 1830s Grundy moved to Liverpool, setting up his own art dealership at the corner of Church Street and Post Office Place. In 1847, along with his brother, he was one of the founder members of the Printsellers Association, established to guarantee the quality and authenticity of prints in the market place. He continued to paint in an amateur capacity.

LL 3967 probably dates from the late 1820s or early 1830s, when Grundy was based in Manchester. The figures in particular show the influence of David Cox, with whom Grundy was making sketching trips during this period. Although it has not been possible to identify the precise location, the watercolour may depict countryside outside Manchester. This work belonged to Cecil Reginald Grundy, editor of *The Connoisseur*, who was born in Liverpool.[636]

634 There is limited biographical material on Grundy. The main source for this entry is a typed sheet initialled *C. R. G.* (presumably the donor) in the LLAG files. He is also mentioned in Roe, *David Cox*, p. 49, where the correspondence between Grundy and Cox is also recorded, pp. 49–64.

635 A letter to Grundy from David Cox, dated 17 August 1835, gives a series of detailed instructions as to how to travel from Manchester to join the artist at Flookborough or Cartmel, where Cox was painting his earliest drawings of Ulverston sands; Roe, *David Cox*, p. 51–54.

636 It is not thought that Cecil Reginald Grundy was any relation to the artist.

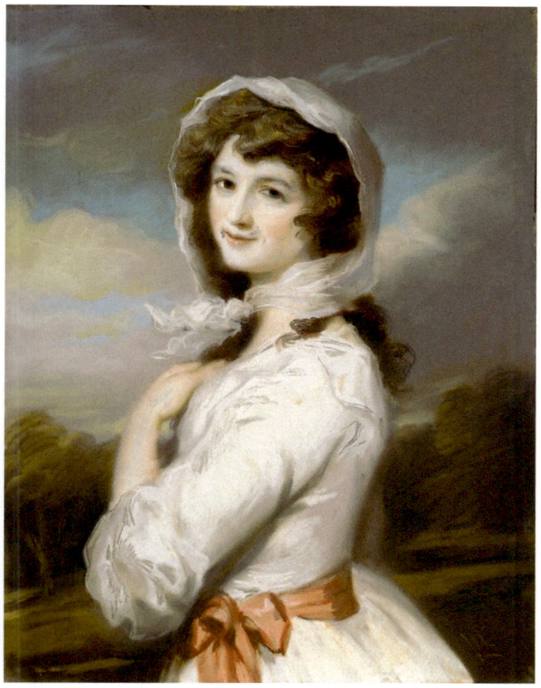

LL 3804

## 'WILLIAM HAMILTON'

1750/1 Chelsea, London–1801 London

**Miss Adelaide Paine**
LL 3804 (WHL 4695)

Pastel on paper, laid down on a wooden stretcher
80 x 64 cm
Date: probably early twentieth century

Prov: Robert Dell [?or Bell], Paris, 1911;[637] Messrs. Colnaghi; their sale, Christie's, 15 June 1923 (lot 96); bt. by Gooden and Fox (£262 10s) for Lever (£269 1s 3d)

Exh: Paris, Galeries Brunner, *Exposition des Pastellistes Anglais du XVIIIe siècle*, 1911 (cat. 63)

Lit: R. R. M. Sée, *English Pastels 1750–1830* (Paris, 1911), illus. facing p. 134

The attribution and identification of the sitter are given as at the time of the work's exhibition in 1911 and subsequent acquisition by Lever, but neither is plausible. William Hamilton is hardly known as a pastellist and in any case no work by him is known in a style remotely resembling this one, while it has not been possible to trace anyone in the period by the name of Adelaide Paine.[638] LL 3804 is loosely based on Romney's half-length portrait of the actress Mrs Jordan as Peggy in Garrick's *The Country Girl* dating from 1786–87 (sold at Sotheby's, 16 November 1988 [lot 68]) and it has every appearance of being a bold forgery dating from the early twentieth century when works by Romney and his imitators were in heavy demand with collectors. The operation to market it evidently involved its appearance in Sée's book as well as the commissioning of a mezzotint by H. Scott Bridgewater – an impression of which Lever also acquired[639] – while besides the manipulation of the source, the very names of the chosen artist and sitter give the impression of having been concocted to evoke association with people in Romney's circle. 'William Hamilton', although a real artist, also evokes the name of the celebrated connoisseur and ambassador to Naples who married Romney's adored model Emma Hart in 1791;[640] 'Adelaide' – a common name in the nineteenth century but very rare in the eighteenth century – was the name of the consort of King William IV, who previously had had a long association with Mrs Jordan; 'Paine' may have been a recollection of the eighteenth-century architects of that name with whom Romney had been associated in the 1770s.[641]

The two visible damages around the mouth of the sitter have been caused by lead-white oxidisation.[642]
AK

637 An exhibition label on the reverse gives the spelling of the owner's name as Bell and his address as 9 rue Pasquier Paris 9, but Dell is given on a label on the frame and in later documentation in LLAG files.

638 No sitter of this name is recorded in the archives of the National Portrait Gallery and no one of this name appears in, for example, P. H. Highfill, K. A. Burnim and E. A. Langhans, *A Biographical Dictionary of Actors, Actresses, Musicians, Dancers, Managers and Other Stage Personnel in London, 1660–1800* (Carbondale, IL, 16 vols, 1973–93).

639 WHL 4719, acquired by Lever from Gooden and Fox in 1923.

640 A work in oils identified as a portrait of Lady Hamilton, closely related both to LL 3804 and Romney's *Mrs Jordan*, is in a private collection in the UK (communicated by David Moore-Gwyn, Sotheby's, February 2005, LLAG files).

641 Romney's portrait *James Paine Junior with a Pomeranian dog* of 1777 was one of the most impressive of his works to emerge at the sale of Miss Romney, the artist's grand-daughter, at Christie's, 24–25 May 1894, where it was acquired by Agnew's; it was subsequently exhibited at the Grafton Gallery's exhibition of Romney's works in the autumn of 1900; see T. H. Ward and W. Roberts, *Romney* (London and New York, 2 vols, 1904), vol. II, p. 115.

642 LLAG files: conservation note by Keith Oliver, National Conservation Centre.

## HUBERT VON HERKOMER

1849 Waal, Bavaria, Germany–1914 Budleigh Salterton, Devon

**Alfred Tennyson, Poet Laureate**[643]
LL 3793 (WHL 4384)

Watercolour, gum arabic with scratching out on wove paper laid down on a stretcher (paper has a 2.5 cm strip added at bottom edge)
90.8 x 70.5 cm (including extra strip of paper)
Date: 1879

Inscr: HH 79 (watercolour [?stopped out], lower right edge)

Prov: by descent to Lady Herkomer; her sale, Christie's, 21 July 1922 (lot 68); bt. by Gooden and Fox (150 gns) for Lever (£165 7s 6d)

Exh: London, Grosvenor Gallery, *Summer Exhibition*, 1879 (cat. 49); London, Whitechapel Art Gallery, *Spring Exhibition*, 1901 (cat. 49); London, Royal Academy, *Winter Exhibition*, 1922 (cat. 195)[644]

Lit: J. Saxon Mills, *Life and Letters of Sir Hubert Herkomer, C.V.O, R.A.: A Study in Struggle and Success* (London, 1923), pp. 101–03, illus. between pp. 102 and 103; *NY Art News*, 13 June 1931, p. 17; Lee MacCormick Edwards, *Herkomer: A Victorian Artist* (Aldershot, 1999), p. 88.

Herkomer was the only child of a builder and woodcarver and his wife, a gifted pianist and music teacher. Following a brief spell in America between 1851 and 1857, the family emigrated to England, settling in Southampton. In 1863 Herkomer spent two years at the Southampton School of Art, where he met the artist Edward John Gregory (see pp. 108–14), who became a life-long friend; this was followed by a period of several months training at the Munich Academy and, in 1866 and 1867, summer terms at the National Art Training School in South Kensington, London (later the Royal College of Art). In the summer of 1869 Herkomer exhibited for the first time at the Royal Academy (a watercolour), where he was to show work almost every year until his death; in the same year he also exhibited at the Dudley Gallery. In 1870 his celebrated black-and-white work, which often depicted the urban poor, began to appear in *The Graphic*. In 1873 Herkomer moved to Bushey, Hertfordshire, a haven for artists not far from London, but also in close proximity to Watford, the home town of his first important patron Clarence Fry. Although he continued to exhibit his celebrated genre scenes depicting the poor and disadvantaged throughout his career (for example, *Eventide: A scene in the Westminster Union* [exh. RA 1878; Walker Art Gallery, Liverpool]), he focused primarily on portraiture from the 1880s. Herkomer was elected an associate of the Royal Academy in 1879 and a full member in

643 This is the title as listed in the Grosvenor Gallery exhibition catalogue for 1879.

644 Tatlock, p. 131 refers to LL 3793 having been exhibited at Southampton Art Gallery. Since the present Southampton Art Gallery only opened in 1939, this may mean Southampton School of Art, where Herkomer had been a pupil and where he continued to send works to be shown. Alternatively, it could have been at the Tudor House Museum, which opened in 1912 and held exhibitions of pictures (no records for this exist).

1890. He established an art school at Bushey, which flourished from 1883 to 1904. He was a multi-faceted individual who was often in the public eye because of his lecturing and writing; he also experimented in other art forms, writing plays and designing stage sets, and latterly making films. He was awarded a knighthood in 1907.

LL 3793 belongs to a group of portraits of important cultural figures that Herkomer painted from 1877 onwards, including Richard Wagner (now destroyed) and John Ruskin (National Portrait Gallery).[645] These were portraits that were not commissioned; Herkomer intended them to hang in his own home as a gallery of great men.[646] All three works were painted in watercolour, the medium with which Herkomer felt most comfortable at this point, and which he returned to throughout his career.[647]

Herkomer stayed with the Tennyson family at their home, Farringford, on the Isle of Wight in December 1878, having obtained an introduction through Tennyson's son Hallam.[648] By this date Tennyson (1809–92) had reached the pinnacle of his career: he had been appointed Poet Laureate in 1850 and Queen Victoria had come to admire his work. Herkomer was enchanted by Tennyson, taking 'long walks over the moors, in all weathers, with this great student of nature', and he referred to him as 'Alfred the Great'.[649] The artist was convalescing from a serious illness at the time, and he always remembered the kindness he received from Tennyson's wife, Emily, 'that angelic lady'.[650] Nevertheless Tennyson was 'an unwilling sitter' and the final portrait was worked up from a chalk drawing (fig. 38).[651]

LL 3793 was described as a 'striking portrait' when it was exhibited at the Grosvenor Gallery in 1879, although the *Athenaeum* described it as 'a bold and powerfully painted bust with an extremely unfortunate resemblance to a well-known picture by Mr Watts. The flesh will not bear that searching examination which this composition necessitates.'[652] Herkomer, who was unusual among his contemporaries for being active as a printmaker as well as a painter, made an etching from this portrait in 1879, which was illustrated in *The Magazine of Art* in 1893.[653] There is an impression of this print in the British Museum (fig. 39).[654]

In 1879, the same year as this watercolour, Herkomer received his earliest commission for a portrait, that of the British diplomat, Lord Stratford de Redcliffe; from the early 1880s Herkomer decided to focus on portrait painting, and his reputation for a bold portrait style continued to soar well into the late 1890s.[655] LL 3793 is characteristic of his early style, which favoured sombre, plain backgrounds and harmony of tone, which gave way in later years to looser brushstrokes and brighter colours.[656]

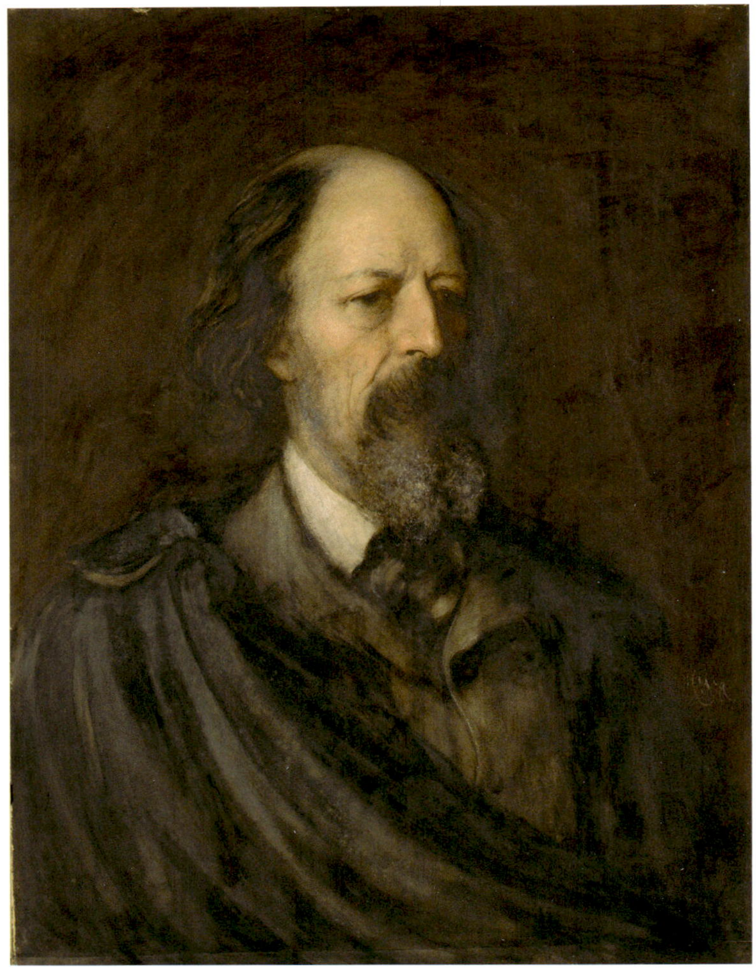

LL 3793

fig. 38. Hubert Herkomer, *Lord Alfred Tennyson*, 1878–79, charcoal on paper, 84 x 49 cm, Tennyson Research Centre, Lincoln

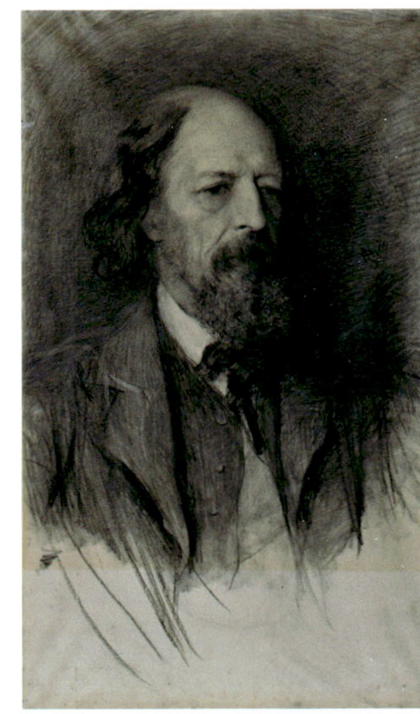

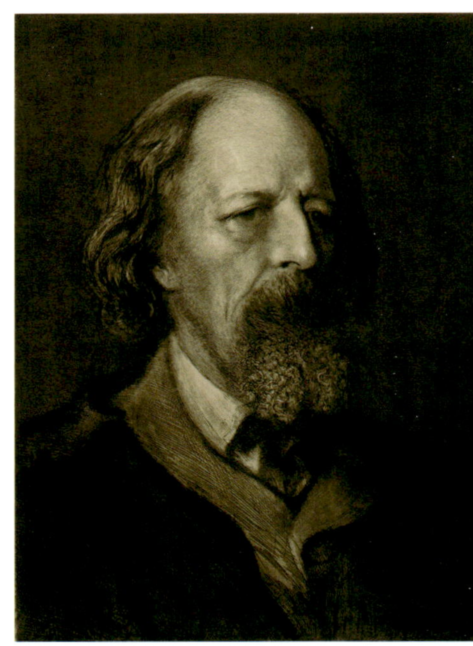

fig. 39. Hubert Herkomer, *Lord Alfred Tennyson*, 1879, etching and aquatint on paper, 59 x 43.9 cm (plate), © The Trustees of the British Museum

645 The 1877 portrait of Wagner is illustrated in Lee MacCormick Edwards, *Herkomer: A Victorian Artist* (Aldershot, 1999), p. 88.
646 Edwards, *Herkomer*, p. 87.
647 Ibid.
648 J. Saxon Mills, *Life and Letters of Sir Hubert Herkomer, C.V.O, R.A.: A Study in Struggle and Success* (London, 1923), p. 101.
649 Quoted by Mills, *Herkomer*, p. 101; Llanelli, Mansel Lewis Collection: Herkomer to Mansel Lewis, letter, 25 December 1878, quoted in Edwards, *Herkomer*, p. 88.
650 Mills, *Herkomer*, p. 101.
651 Edwards, *Herkomer*, p. 88. This chalk drawing is mentioned in Herkomer to Mansel Lewis, letter, 25 December 1878 (Llanelli, Mansel Lewis Collection). I am grateful to Lee Edwards for providing me with access to this documentation. This seems to have been the 'copy' given to the Tennyson family in 1880 and referred to in Mills, *Herkomer*, p. 101, as the 'portrait of the poet in black and white'. This drawing is now in the Tennyson Research Centre, Lincoln, and is inscribed on the back of the frame in Hallam Tennyson's handwriting: 'This is the original black and white sketch made at Farringford 1879 and presented by H Herkomer to Emily Tennyson and Hallam Tennyson'. A further smaller 'head and shoulders' study in ink and gouache over pencil (40 x 51 cm), signed HH (bottom left) is in a private collection.
652 *The Academy: A Weekly Review of Literature, Science and Art*, vol. 15 (February 1879), p. 311; *Athenaeum* (3 May 1879), p. 576.
653 'Our Illustrated Note-Book', *The Magazine of Art* (1893), p. 178.
654 The impression in the British Museum is a remarque, published proof.
655 Edwards, *Herkomer*, p. 91.
656 Edwards, *Herkomer*, p. 90.

## JAMES HOLLAND

1799 Burslem, Staffordshire–1870 London

### St Sévérin, Paris

LL 3858 (WHL 750, HH 421)

Watercolour over pencil with white heightening and scratching out on wove paper
26 x 16.7 cm
Date: 1831

Inscr: J Holland / Paris 1831 (watercolour, bottom right)

Annot: RUE ST SÉVÉRIN, PARIS / BY / B. 1800 JAMES HOLLAND D. 1870 / From the collection of James Orrock, Esq., R.I. / BRITISH SCHOOL, 1831 W.H.L.750 (ink, on mount)

Prov: bt. from James Orrock by Lever, 1910[657]

Exh: Nottingham, Nottingham University Art Gallery, and London, Agnew's, *Thomas Shotter Boys Centenary Exhibition*, 1974 (cat. 146)

Lit: 'Current Art Notes, Our Plates', *The Connoisseur*, vol. 86 (November 1930), p. 332, illus. col. p. 295

James Holland, son of Martha Holland, was born in Burslem in the potteries of Stoke-on-Trent. Aged 12 he was apprenticed as a painter to the Longport Hall pottery. In 1819, having completed his apprenticeship, he left Stoke for London. By 1824 he had given up pottery painting and had a flower painting accepted at the Royal Academy. He went on to exhibit regularly at the Royal Academy, the Society of British Artists, the British Institution and the SPWC. From 1832 he became recognized predominantly for his architectural and continental views in both oil and watercolour, especially those of Venice.[658] Holland was involved in 1862 in the introduction of new Winter Exhibitions at the SPWC to exhibit sketches rather than finished drawings. He died on 13 February 1870 and the contents of his studio were sold at auction on 26 May that year.[659]

This watercolour of 1831 marks the beginning of Holland's career as a painter of continental views. In this year Holland and fellow artist John Scarlett Davis travelled together to Paris where they drew similar views of streets and buildings, and thereafter Holland travelled to the continent regularly.

The work has been titled *A Normandy Street Scene*.[660] However, comparison with other images, such as Thomas Shotter Boys's view of 1839, reveal that it depicts the rue St Sévérin in Paris with the church of St Sévérin – the oldest church on Paris's Left Bank – on the right-hand side. A similar view was taken as late as 1923 by photographer Eugène Atget with the high wall on the right-hand side, minus the ruined arch in the foreground. The distinctive architecture of

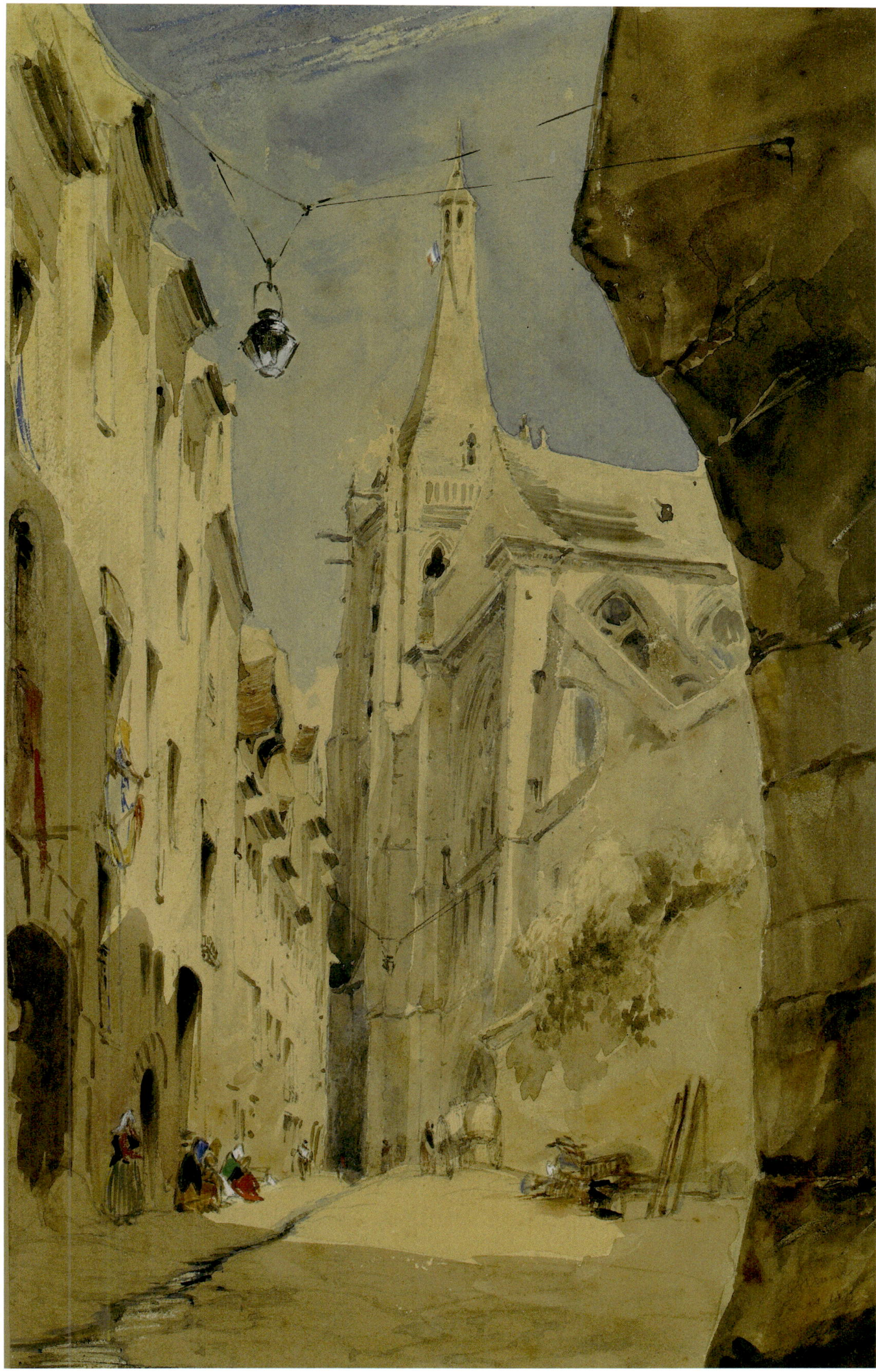

LL 3858

the church and spire remains today although the large wall abutting it has been replaced by a fenced garden that allows a clearer view of the church. In Holland's version a diminutive French flag flies from the spire.
RK

657 1910 Inventory, p. 52, as by Prout, titled *A Normandy Street Scene with figures*, valued at £40.
658 The Lady Lever Art Gallery has four Venetian scenes by Holland in oil: LL 3735–37 and LL 3744.
659 Steve Bond, *James Holland: the Forgotten Artist* (Leek, 1999).
660 LLAG files. See also Tatlock, p. 131.

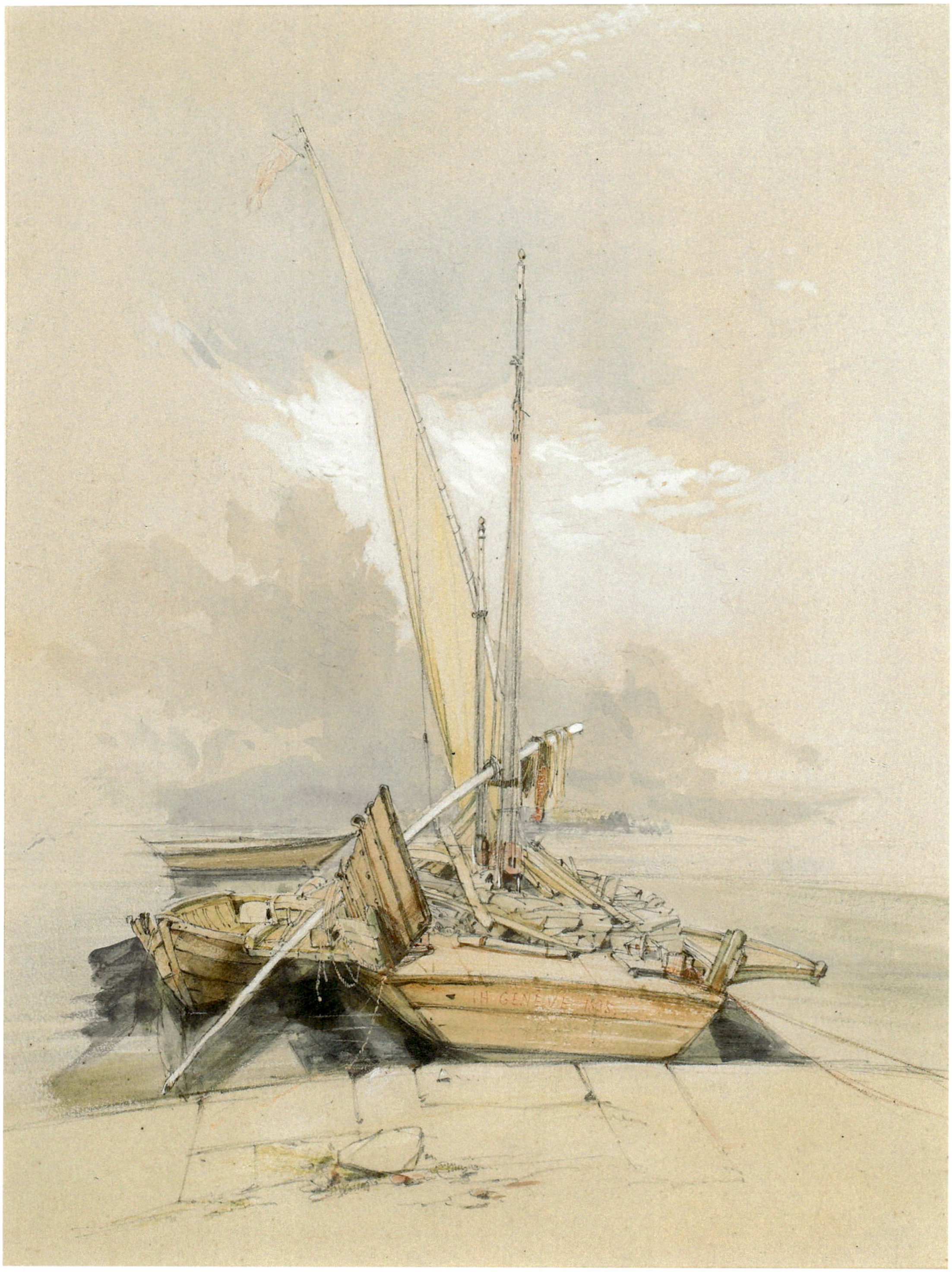

LL 3968

**Boats at a Quayside, Lake Geneva**
LL 3968 (WHL 721, HH 418)

Watercolour and pencil with gouache on buff wove paper
30.1 x 22.5 cm
Date: 1835

Inscr: I H GENÊVE 1835 (watercolour, on boat)

Prov: bt. from James Orrock by Lever, 1910[661]

Holland made a number of drawings of boats at various European ports from 1835 to 1866. Titled by Tatlock *Boats on the Quayside, Rotterdam*,[662] LL 3968 is in fact a study of boats on Lake Geneva. The boats are of a specific type used on this lake and the artist has inscribed the location on the boat nearest the viewer.

Holland made his first trip to Venice in 1835 via France and Switzerland. He stayed at the Hôtel d'Europe in Geneva from 26 October, presumably awaiting the passports issued on 29 October that enabled him to continue his journey into Italy.[663] This drawing surely dates from these waiting days or from his return stay in Geneva in mid-November.

LL 3968 is related to the central section of the oil painting *Head of Lake Geneva* (Graves Art Gallery, Sheffield), possibly exhibited at the Society of British Artists in 1843 as *Lake of Geneva*. Although the oil is later than the drawing we know that Holland liked to keep studies or sketches from his remark that 'parting with a sketch was like parting with a tooth: once sold, it could not be replaced'.[664] Holland retained six drawings of Geneva till his death, at least two of which were of boats on the lake.[665]

Holland became known for the use of opaque colour in his watercolour technique. This preference is shown in this early study in his use of opaque white against buff paper in the sky.
RK

661 1910 Inventory, p. 52, as *Boats at a Quayside – a Sketch*, valued at £5.

662 Tatlock's entry relates to a large picture exhibited at the Royal Academy in 1849 that is not in the Lady Lever Art Gallery's collection. Lever attempted to buy it in 1917.

663 Bond, *James Holland*, p. 28.

664 Cited by Roget, *History of the 'Old Water-Colour' Society*, vol. I, p. 251, n. 3.

665 *Catalogue of the whole of the Remaining Works of the late James Holland*, Christie's, 26 May 1870, lots 78, 278, 327, 353, 394 and 419; of these the first and last, respectively *Boats on the Lake of Geneva*, bt. by J. & W. Vokins (£3 5s) and *Study of Boats, Geneva*, bt. by Hall (£1 13s) seem to be the best candidates for LL 3968.

## OZIAS HUMPHRY

1742 Honiton, Devon-1810 London

### John Flaxman

LL 3924 (WHL 3414A)

Pastel on paper, laid down on canvas
60.7 x 50.6 cm
Date: after 1794 and probably before 1797

Prov: H. C. Seppings Wright; his sale, Christie's, 25 January 1918 (lot 53); bt. by Gooden and Fox (8 gns with WHL 3415)[666] for Lever (£6 18s 9d)

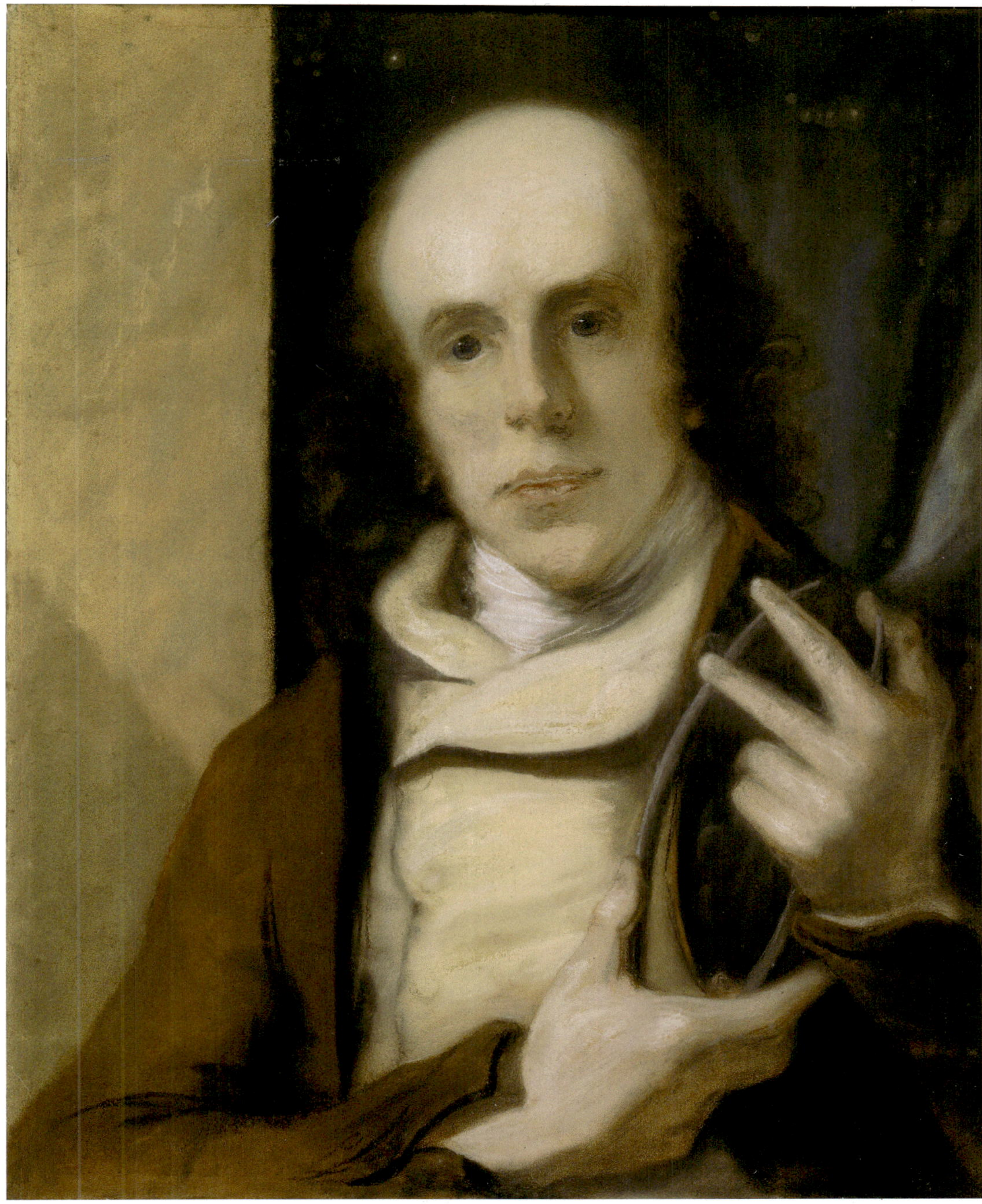

LL 3924

Humphry studied drawing at William Shipley's Academy and was then apprenticed to the miniaturist Samuel Collins in Bath. In 1764 he moved to London where he set up a successful practice specialising in miniatures. He travelled to Italy between 1773 and 1777. Humphry's subsequent career was more chequered; his attempts to paint in oils proved disappointing, although he was elected an associate of the Royal Academy in 1779. The deterioration of his eyesight in 1791 compelled him to change direction and he began to concentrate on drawing in crayon (he was appointed portrait painter in crayons to the king in 1792). By 1797 he had almost completely lost his sight and the remainder of his life was spent trying to garner financial support for his old age.

The subject of the Lady Lever portrait is the sculptor, illustrator and decorative designer John Flaxman (1755–1826). Humphry made a number of portraits of Flaxman including a miniature painting dating to c. 1770[667] and a chalk drawing that is signed and dated 1778 (Yale Center for British Art, New Haven).[668] On the basis of the sitter's age, LL 3924 dates from the 1790s: it shows a distinct likeness to Romney's portrait *John Flaxman Modelling the Bust of William Hayley*, which was begun in 1795.[669] Since Flaxman was in Rome between 1787 and 1794 and Humphry did not return to Rome after 1777, the Lady Lever portrait must have been made after 1794 and probably before 1797 when Humphry's vision began seriously to deteriorate.[670]

LL 3924 is one of a number of pastel portraits that Humphry made of artists during the 1790s when he specialised in this medium. These included a portrait of George Stubbs, probably exhibited at the Royal Academy in 1794 (Walker Art Gallery, Liverpool).[671] In both portraits the sitters are presented as fashionably dressed gentlemen,[672] although Flaxman is also depicted holding callipers, the tools of his trade, an indication of the esteem in which he was held as a sculptor by the mid-1790s.[673]

666 WHL 3415 was another Humphry pastel, *Portrait of the Rev Penneck in dark dress*. This was sold at the Anderson Galleries, New York, 3 March 1926 (lot 194).

667 Illus. G.C. Williamson, *Life and Works of Ozias Humphry, R.A.* (London, 1918), facing p. 84.

668 Patrick Noon, *English Portrait Drawings and Miniatures* (exh. cat., New Haven, Yale Center for British Art, 1979–80), p. 58 (cat. 64), illus.

669 Alex Kidson, *George Romney 1734–1802* (exh. cat., Liverpool, Walker Art Gallery, London, National Portrait Gallery, and San Marino, Huntington Art Collections, 2002), p. 229 (cat. 145).

670 There is no mention of Flaxman sitting for Humphry in Humphry's letters and papers, Royal Academy Library, nor in Humphry's accounts and notebook in the British Library, Add. MSS 22947-22952.

671 Edward Morris and Timothy Stevens, *Early English Drawings and Watercolours in the Walker Art Gallery* (Liverpool, 1968), pp. 26–27 (cat. 52), pl. 1.

672 Both sitters wear coats with high collars and high-necked stocks typical of the fashion for men during the 1790s.

673 For biographical details of Flaxman's career, see David Bindman (ed.), *John Flaxman* (exh. cat., London, Royal Academy, 1979); also Sarah Symmons, 'Flaxman, John (1775–1826)', *ODNB*, vol. 20, pp. 4–10.

## WILLIAM HENRY HUNT

1790 London–1864 London

### Portrait of an Old Man

LL 3969 (WHL 741, HH 1460)

Watercolour over pencil, with reed pen and brown ink, gum arabic and scratching out on oatmeal paper
32.9 x 24.6 cm (sight)
Date: mid-1820s

Prov: Charles Frederick Huth, 1895; his sale, Christie's, 6 July 1895 (lot 41, as *Portrait of the Artist*); bt. by J. & W. Vokins (£31 10s); T. Agnew, 1911; Christie's, 9 June 1911 (lot 72, as *The Artist*); bt. by Gooden and Fox (24 gns) for Lever (£26 9s 3d)

Exh: Wolverhampton, Wolverhampton Art Gallery, *William Henry Hunt: 1790–1864*, 1981 (cat. 123)

Lit: 'Current Art Notes, Our Plates', *The Connoisseur*, vol. 88 (August 1931), p. 125, illus. p. 81; J. Witt, *William Henry Hunt (1790–1864): Life and Work, with a Catalogue* (London, 1982), p. 186 (cat. 473), illus. pl. 37

Hunt, the son of a London manufacturer, was a sickly child. He was born with a physical disability and was deemed too weak to follow his father's profession as a skilled craftsman. He was apprenticed to John Varley (see pp. 206–207) between 1804 and 1811, spending some of this period at the Royal Academy Schools and Dr Thomas Monro's 'Academy'. Although at first Hunt painted in oils as well as watercolours, following his election to full membership of the SPWC in 1826 he focused almost exclusively on painting in that medium, exhibiting there every year until his death. His early works included watercolour portraits in miniature and landscapes, including a number of Bushey, Hertfordshire, where he spent time at the country home of his patron, Dr Monro. During the 1830s and 1840s Hunt became well-known for his highly detailed still-lifes in watercolour and gouache of fruit, flowers, nests and eggs (he was nicknamed 'Bird's Nest Hunt'). It was also during this period that he began to specialise in genre scenes, particularly figures in domestic settings. Hunt's meticulous and pioneering watercolour techniques of the 1830s and 1840s appealed to John Ruskin and he took lessons from the artist in 1854 and 1861.

LL 3969 was acquired by Lever as a self-portrait by Hunt. [674] There is a passing resemblance to the artist, but it has recently been suggested convincingly that stylistic considerations rule this identification out.[675] The pen work, watercolour washes and the coarse paper are all characteristic of Hunt's work in the mid-1820s, but by the time the artist was the age of the sitter, that is around 50, his technique and materials had altered substantially.[676] The use of the reed pen in particular derives from Hunt's training at the Monro 'Academy', where he learned to copy the pen-and-ink drawings of Canaletto. In his monograph on the artist Witt suggested a date for the work based on style of c. 1825.[677]

The sitter in another pen-and-ink drawing from the same period (Birmingham Museums and Art Gallery, fig. 40) has similar facial features and hair to the figure in the Lady Lever drawing and may be the same model.[678] In both drawings he wears a coat, breeches and gaiters of a type often worn by the middling sort in the country.[679] It has been suggested that the sitter may be Hunt's future father-in-law, Mr Holloway, a miller and farmer, which would be in keeping with the costume worn.[680] The Holloways lived near Bramley, Basingstoke, in Hampshire, and Hunt often rented a cottage near them as they were relatives on his mother's side. Hunt did not marry the miller's daughter Sarah until 1830 but if the theory about the sitter is correct, it remains possible that LL 3969 was painted in the mid-1820s during one of Hunt's extended visits to the area.[681]

This work belonged to Charles Frederick Huth (1806–95), a merchant and banker who owned a large collection of watercolours described by *The Art Journal* in 1857 as a 'curious, interesting, and valuable collection'.[682]

674 The WHL Inventory described the work as *Portrait of the Artist by himself.* The resemblance to Hunt can be seen by comparing the work to a photograph of the artist in his sixties or seventies (National Portrait Gallery); illus. J. Witt, *William Henry Hunt (1790–1864): Life and Work, with a Catalogue* (London, 1982), pl. 1.

675 See T. Jones, *William Henry Hunt 1790–1864* (exh. cat., Wolverhampton, Wolverhampton Art Gallery, 1981), p. 60. Witt, *William Henry Hunt*, p. 187, described the work as 'most unlikely to be a self portrait'.

676 Jones, *William Henry Hunt*, p. 60.

677 Witt, *William Henry Hunt*, p. 187.

678 This has been suggested by Jones, *William Henry Hunt*, p. 60. The Birmingham work was exhibited at the SPWC, 1824 (cat. 286) as *A Miller in his Mill*; see Witt, *William Henry Hunt*, p. 168 and pl. 36.

679 Pauline Rushton, email correspondence, September, 2007.

680 Witt, *William Henry Hunt*, p. 168 (cat. 272).

681 The precise chronology of Hunt's visits to Bramley is not known but he was likely to have been visiting his future relations here by the mid- to late 1820s.

682 *The Art Journal* (1857), p. 91; quoted by Macleod, *Art and the Victorian Middle Class*, pp. 432–33.

### Girl Seated by a Fireside

LL 10338 (WHL 262, H 383)

Watercolour and gouache, with scratching out over pencil on paper
27.2 x 19.2 cm (sight)
Date: c. 1830

Inscr: W HUNT (watercolour, bottom right)

Prov: bt. from James Orrock by Lever, 1912[683]

Lit: J. Witt, *William Henry Hunt (1790–1864): Life and Work, with a Catalogue* (London, 1982), p. 187 (cat. 474)

Stylistically, this drawing marks the beginning of a middle phase in Hunt's career, in which he moved away from the translucent watercolour washes of his earlier period towards a greater use of gouache, creating a more fragmented, stippled effect. Witt dated this phase of Hunt's style to 1830–45, although he also acknowledged how difficult it was to apply such demarcations to the dating of Hunt's drawings.[684] Witt himself dated this drawing to c. 1825–30 but it shows a heavier use of gouache and techniques such as scratching out than, for example, the well-known watercolour portrait of the painter James Holland, dated 1828, a work which does embody Hunt's early phase.[685] LL 10338 has more in common with Hunt's works of the 1830s, such as LL 3972 and 3973 below (p. 122). The style of the girl's hair, shape of her sleeves, pantaloons and shoes point to a date for the work of c. 1830.[686]

The subject of this drawing is a young girl, her face lit by the glow of a fire. Hunt returned to this theme throughout his career, as well as painting figures with their faces illuminated either by candle or lamplight. The model in LL 10338 cannot be identified.

683 1912 Inventory, listed in back room, valued at £15. See also LLAG files: a note records the former existence of a Dolman framemaker's label on the back of the frame inscribed Miss G. S. R. 8 [torn]; presumably an earlier owner.

684 Witt, *William Henry Hunt*, p. 43.

685 This work is now in the Victoria & Albert Museum; see Witt, *William Henry Hunt*, p. 192 (cat. 526), col. pl. 9.

686 Pauline Rushton, email correspondence, February 2010.

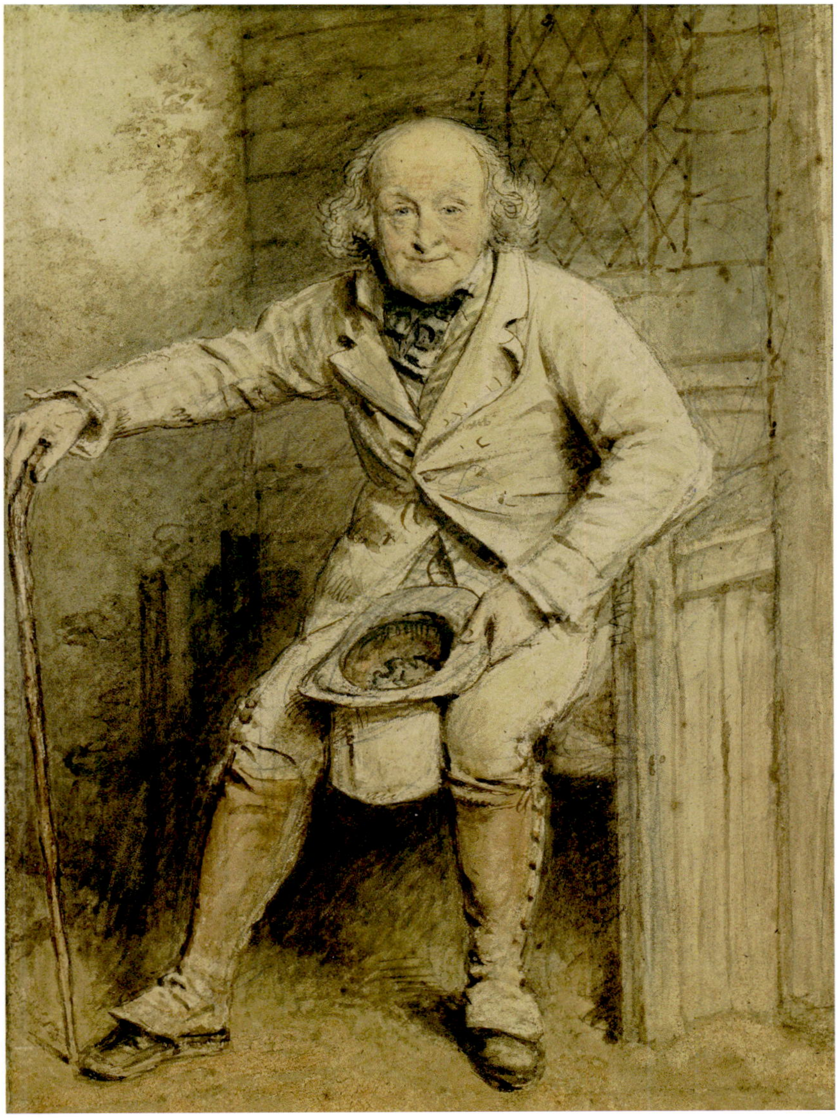

LL 3969

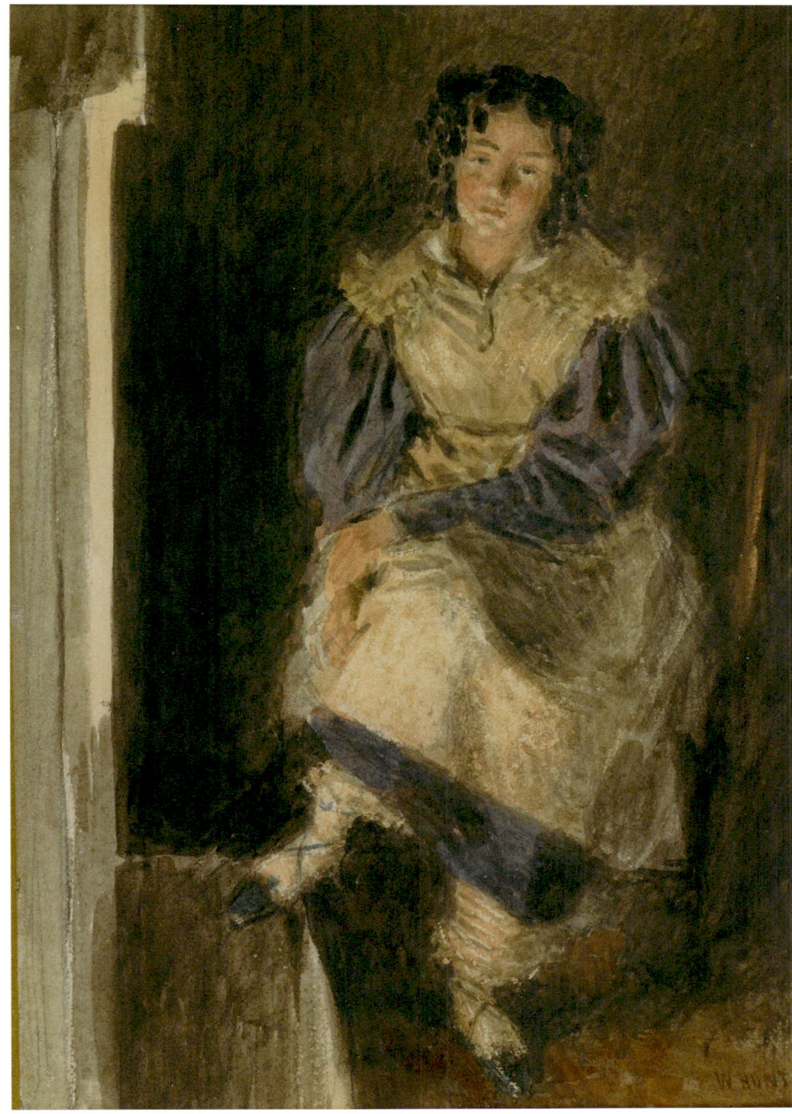

LL 10338

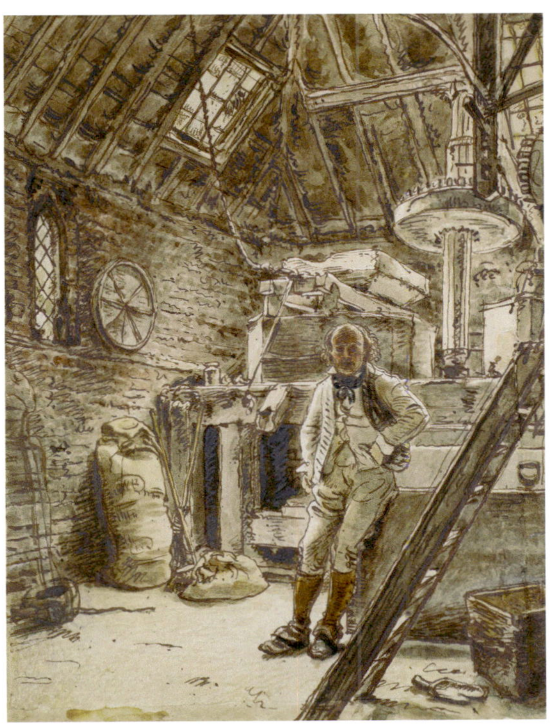

fig. 40. William Henry Hunt, *A Miller in his Mill*, exh. 1824, reed pen, ink and watercolour on paper, 38.7 x 30.3 cm, Birmingham Museums and Art Gallery

## Young Salts
LL 3972 (WHL 266, H 225)

Watercolour with gum arabic and scratching out on wove paper
27.3 x 18.9 cm (probably cut down)
Date: 1830–35

Prov: Ralph Bernal; his sale, Christie's, 21–23 April 1853 (lot 151, as *Sailor Boys*); bt. by Lawrence (£35 14s); Edwin Henry Lawrence, London; his sale, Christie's, 4–6 May 1892 (lot 304, as *Pick-a-Back, On the Seashore*); bt. by Gooden and Fox (£141 15s); James Orrock; his sale, Christie's, 4 June 1904 (lot 27); bt. in (£204 15s); bt. from Orrock by Lever, November 1904[687]

Exh: London, Agnew's, *27th Annual Exhibition of High-Class Water-colour Drawings*, 1893 (cat. 12, as *Young Salts*); London, Earl's Court, *Victorian Era Exhibition*, 1897 (cat. 202)

Lit: James Orrock, 'William Henry Hunt', *The Art Journal* (1895), pp. 12–16; J. Witt, *William Henry Hunt (1790–1864): Life and Work, with a Catalogue* (London, 1982), p. 187 (cat. 475)

This drawing shows the development in technique that occurred in Hunt's watercolours in his so-called middle phase (see LL 10338, p. 120). *Young Salts* is more stylistically advanced than LL 10338; the watercolour is built up more thickly and covered with layers of gum arabic. Even more extensively than in that slightly earlier watercolour, Hunt has employed a knife to scratch out highlights as well as using a fine brush to create a stippling effect on such areas as the boys' faces.

*Young Salts* is one of many watercolours by Hunt from the 1830s that use children as models. The younger boy is almost certainly John Swain and the older one his brother William.[688] Hunt met the Swain brothers around 1830 on one of his winter visits to Hastings, and subsequently employed them both as models in his studio in London until the mid-1840s.[689] 'Hunt's boys', as they became known, posed for many of the artist's most successful comic and sentimental drawings of children. Hunt dressed the boys in a variety of costumes; in LL 3972 they wear fishermen's smocks. There is a larger variant of this watercolour in the Duke of Norfolk's collection at Arundel Castle,[690] in which the same two models are depicted, here with the older boy looking inwards towards an additional third boy. Witt dated the Lady Lever work to between 1830 and 1835; more recently, on the basis of the Arundel work being signed and dated 1830, Craig Englund has suggested that LL 3972 could be from as early as 1830.[691]

LL 3972 is one of at least 18 Hunt watercolours purchased by Lever from James Orrock between 1904 and 1912 (five examples that Lever acquired from Orrock in 1904 alone are now no longer in the Lady Lever collection).[692] Orrock (see pp. xiv–xvii, 146–49) was a major collector and champion of the artist's work both during Hunt's lifetime and after his death. His article on Hunt in *The Art Journal* of 1895 extolled the virtues of an artist who 'From the capabilities of watercolours ... extracted a greater number of nature's truths than any other painter, Cox not excepted'.[693]

The pigments in LL 3972 have faded overall. This is particularly visible in the sky where, as the result of the removal of an earlier mount, the original pigments are exposed at the edges.

687 1904 Inventory, p. 5 (no. 105), listed in the drawing room.

688 This identification has been suggested by Craig Englund, email correspondence, September 2007. John Swain, the younger brother, was used more often as a model by Hunt. Among the watercolours he appears in is *A Shrimper* (Whitworth Art Gallery, Manchester). The identification of the older brother is more problematic, as he was depicted less frequently, but it is based on his similarity to the figure of a boy in *The Eavesdropper* (private collection); Englund, email correspondence.

689 William Collingwood in his 'Reminiscences of William Hunt', *The Magazine of Art* (1898), p. 503, stated that there were three Swain brothers. However, Craig Englund has recently shown this to be incorrect: according to baptismal records in Hastings, there were four brothers. He has suggested that only two of them, William and John, can have been Hunt's models (Hunt bequeathed £10 each to them in his will). See Craig W. Englund, 'Constructed Naturalism in the Watercolors of William Henry Hunt', *Huntington Quarterly* (winter, 1990), pp. 82–83, n. 24.

690 This watercolour measures 24½ x 20½ in. Craig Englund, email correspondence, September 2007.

691 Witt, *William Henry Hunt*, p. 187. LLAG files record that the drawing has been trimmed so that the date is no longer legible; they also record the former presence of a signature (W. HUNT); this was not visible at the time of Witt's catalogue, published in 1982.

692 1904 Inventory, p. 5; 1910 Inventory, pp. 46, 52; 1912 Inventory, pp. 3, 4, 7, 9, 10.

693 James Orrock, 'William Henry Hunt', *The Art Journal* (1895), p. 12.

## A Hastings Fisherman[694]
LL 3973 (WHL 3063)

Watercolour over pencil, with gum arabic, gouache and scratching out on wove paper
38.9 x 26.2 cm (sight)
Date: probably early 1830s

Inscr: W. HUNT (watercolour, bottom right)

Prov: W. Y. Baker, Aspen House, Brixton Hill, London; his sale, Christie's, 9 November 1916 (lot 194); bt. by Gooden and Fox for Lever (£39 5s 6d)

Exh: Wolverhampton, Wolverhampton Art Gallery, *William Henry Hunt: 1790–1864*, 1981 (cat. 71)

Lit: J. Witt, *William Henry Hunt (1790–1864): Life and Work, with a Catalogue* (London, 1982), p. 187 (cat. 476)

This is one of a number of drawings of single figures of fishermen and smugglers that Hunt made in the late 1820s and early 1830s.[695] In the main these were based on the artist's trips to Hastings, where he had begun to visit by 1814 and to which he returned frequently after this date.[696] Although there is nothing in the appearance of the work to confirm that this is a fisherman from Hastings, given the regularity of Hunt's visits to the town it is likely that this is the case.

In LL 3973 the subject is a fisherman in characteristic clothing. Hunt generally worked in the studio at home, and the sketchy nature of the background (even for Hunt, where the detail tended to be concentrated on his figures) suggests that the model was probably posed against an artificial backdrop.[697]

The work is similar in technique to *Young Salts*, using extensive scratching out and stippling of paint, particularly on the subject's face. Although Witt dated the work to c. 1835, Craig Englund has recently suggested that it was more likely to have been completed c. 1831–32, when Hunt painted most of his fishermen subjects.[698]

694 This title is given in the WHL Inventory, p. 387.

695 A number of works with these titles were exhibited at the SPWC between 1829 and 1833.

696 It is not known when exactly Hunt first visited Hastings, but he first exhibited views of Hastings at the SPWC in 1814 (cats. 210 and 229).

697 For Hunt's working methods, see Jones, *William Henry Hunt*, p. 28. Jones has argued that Hunt had no choice but to work from home because of the deformity of his legs (p. 34).

698 Witt, *William Henry Hunt*, p. 187; Craig Englund, email correspondence, September 2007. *A Fisherman* was exhibited at the SPWC in 1831 (cat. 260), and another work with the same title was exhibited in 1832 (cat. 165) along with *An Old Fisherman* (cat. 167).

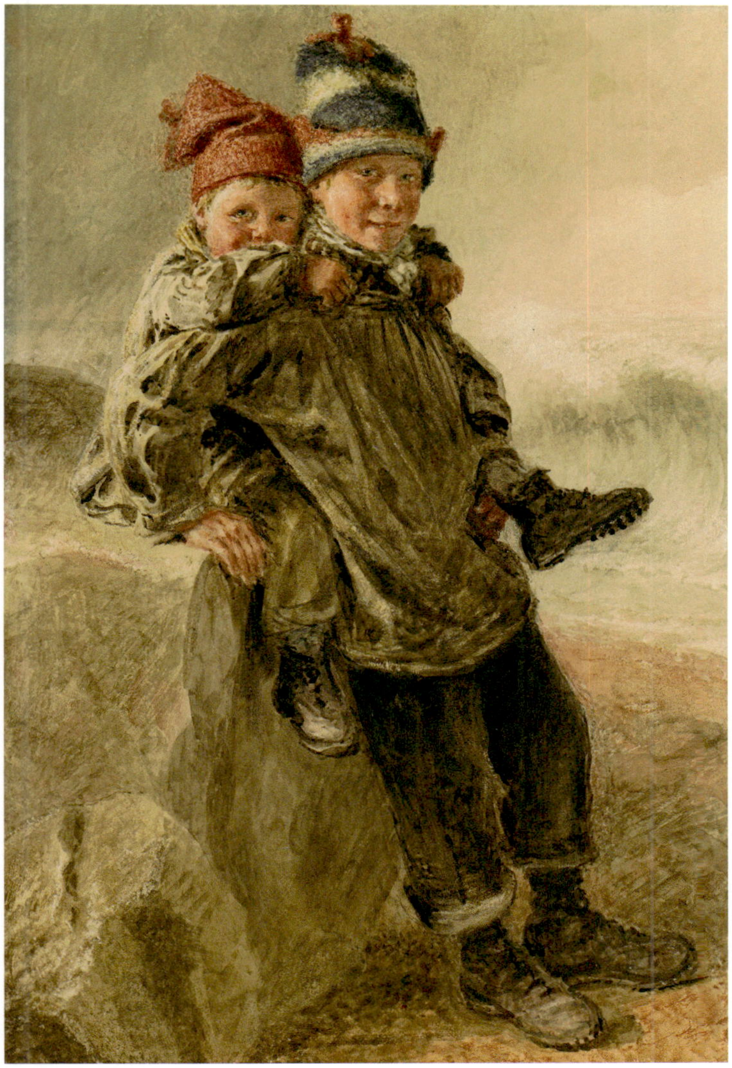

LL 3972

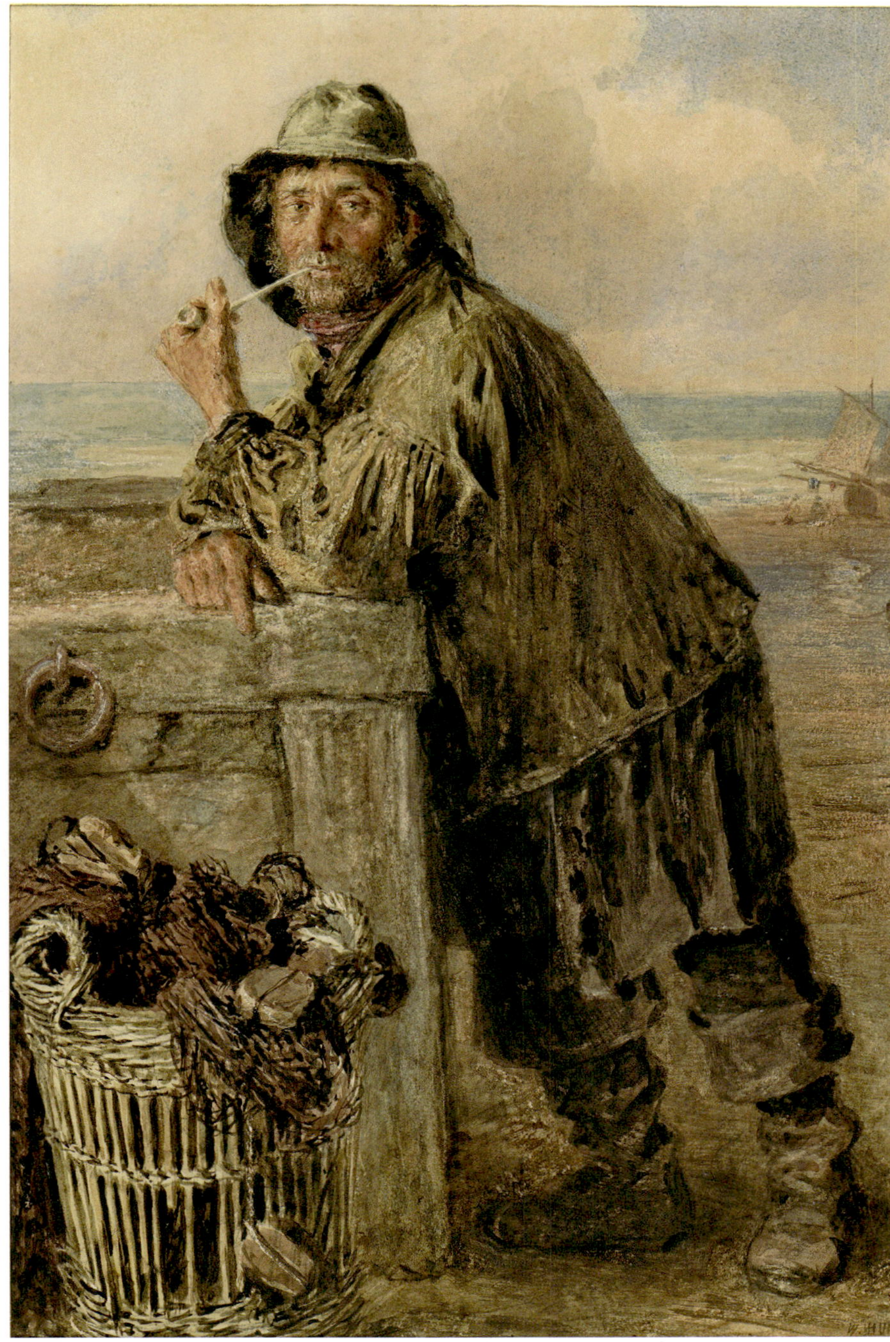

LL 3973

LL 10339

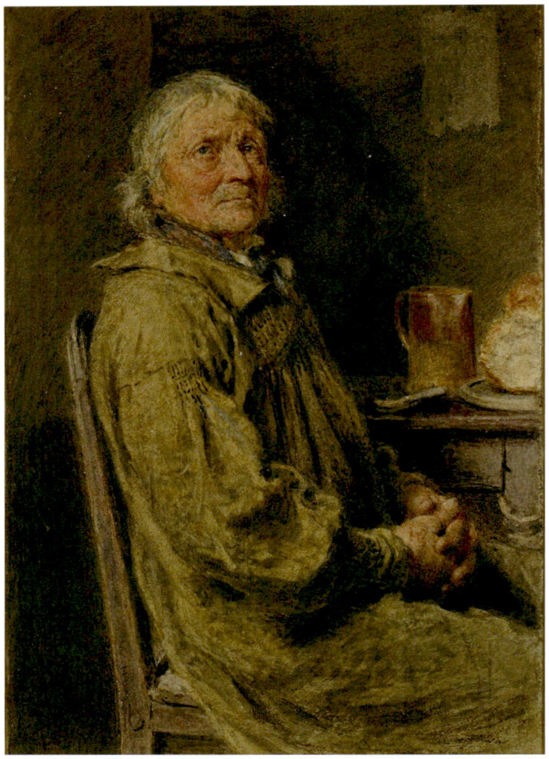

LL 10340

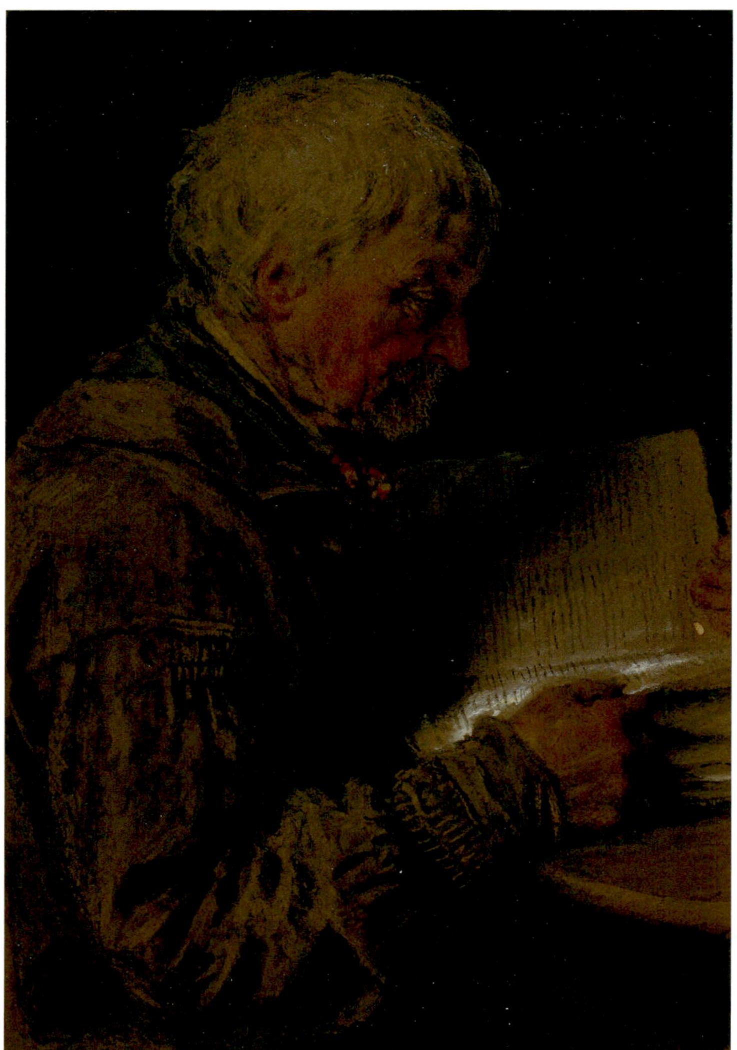

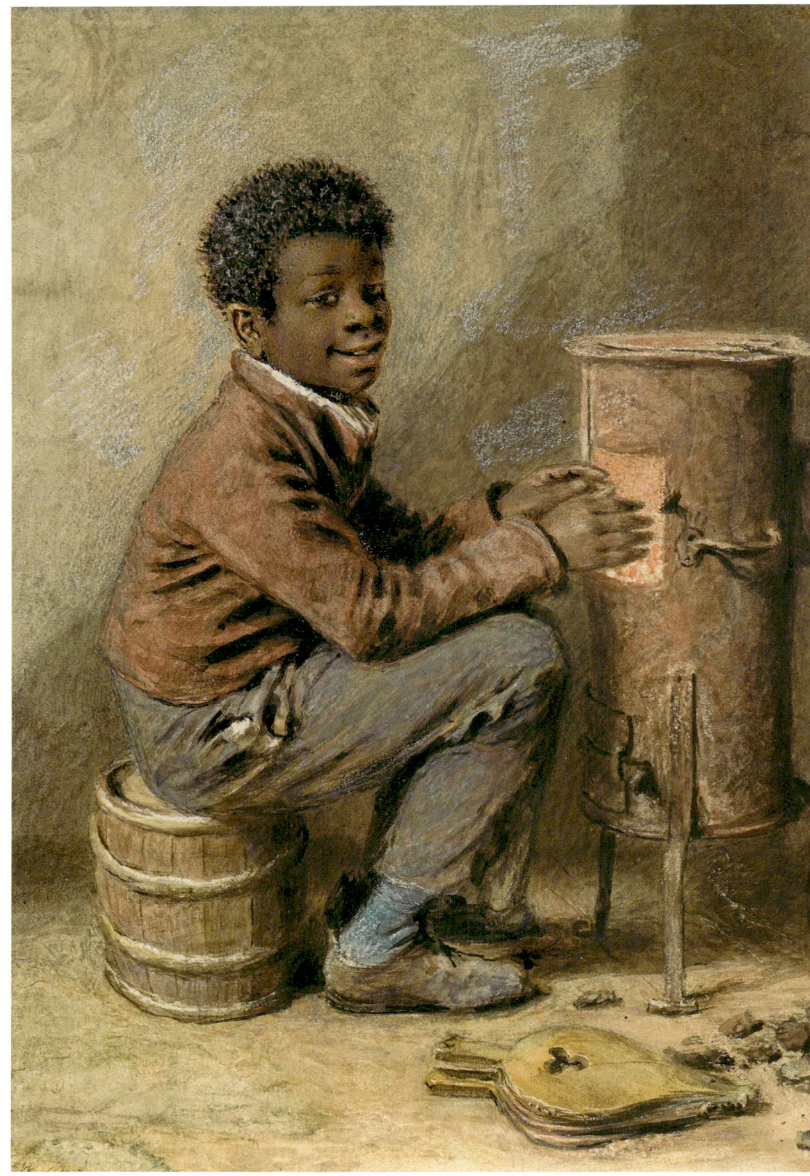

LL 3974

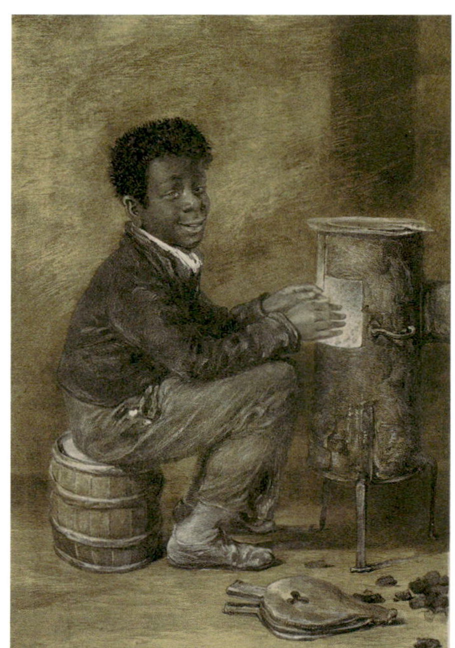

fig. 41. Thomas Fairland, After William Henry Hunt, *Master James Crow – Out of his Element* (plate eight from *Hunt's Comic Sketches*), lithograph printed in black with sepia tint-stone, 47.5 x 30.4 cm (sheet), © The Trustees of the British Museum

## The Blessing
LL 10339 (WHL 265, H 222)

Watercolour, heightened with white, gum arabic and scratching out on paper
27.5 x 19.2 cm
Date: 1836 or c. 1840

Inscr: W HUNT (watercolour, lower left, on chair); W HUNT 18 [3?] 6 (scratched out, bottom left corner)

Prov: James Orrock, 1878;[699] his sale, Christie's, 4 June 1904 (lot 200); bt from Orrock by Lever, November 1904[700]

Exh:[701] Nottingham, Midland Counties Art Museum, *Opening Exhibition*, 1878 (cat. 140, as *Asking a Blessing*); London, Fine Art Society, *Exhibition of Prout and Hunt*, 1879–80 (cat. 171); Manchester, *Royal Jubilee Exhibition*, 1887 (cat. 1730); London, Burlington House, *Exhibition of Works by the Old Masters, and by Deceased Masters of the British School; including a Collection of Watercolour Drawings illustrating the Progress of the Art of Watercolour in England*, 1891 (cat. 113); London, Earl's Court, *Victorian Era Exhibition*, 1897 (cat. 195)

Lit: James Orrock, 'William Henry Hunt', *The Art Journal* (1895), pp. 12–16, illus. p. 12; J. Witt, *William Henry Hunt (1790–1864): Life and Work, with a Catalogue* (London, 1982), p. 187 (cat. 478)

This watercolour shows an elderly man wearing a country labourer's smock, his hands clasped together in a gesture of thanks for the meal he is about to eat. It is one of several similar works depicting single figures in simple acts of faith (see also LL 10340 below; Hunt may have used the same model for the two works).[702] Works like these satisfied a growing demand for sentimentalised images of rustic life. Hunt himself was seemingly more comfortable with such subject-matter. In correspondence with a friend, he lamented not being able to make a drawing as requested of a particular genteel lady, saying 'I think I could have made a nice drawing of her if she had been one of my tramp girls'.[703]

The work was described in 1895 by James Orrock, at that time its owner, as a 'splendid drawing ... probably Hunt's masterpiece'.[704] John Ruskin also singled out *The Blessing* for praise. He described the work, along with two others, as 'things that the old painter was himself unspeakably blessed in having power to do. The strength of all lovely human life is in them.'[705]

Witt dated LL 10339 to c. 1840, although given the consistency of Hunt's technique over the period from 1830 to the mid-1840s the work could easily date from 1836, as indicated by the partially decipherable inscription.[706]

699 Lent by Orrock to the Midland Counties Art Museum, *Opening Exhibition* in 1878. Information supplied by Nicholas Alfrey, Nottingham University, email correspondence, March 2009.
700 1904 Inventory (no. 104), listed in drawing room.
701 The WHL Inventory records that LL 10339 was exhibited in 1877, 1887 and 1897.
702 Another drawing on a similar theme is *The Old Salt*, illus. *The Art Journal* (1895), p. 15; the model in this work appears to be the same as that in LL 10339.
703 Quoted by Roget, *History of the 'Old Water-Colour' Society*, vol. II, p. 190.
704 Orrock, 'William Henry Hunt', p. 14.
705 John Ruskin, *Notes on Prout and Hunt*, in Cook and Wedderburn (eds), *Works of John Ruskin*, vol. XIV, pp. 373–84 and 440–54, quoted in Witt, *William Henry Hunt*, p. 254.
706 It is not clear if Witt saw LL 10339, or whether he relied on information supplied from LLAG files and was not made aware of this inscription.

## An old man reading the Bible
LL 10340 (WHL 724, HH 360)

Watercolour, heightened with white, gum arabic and scratching out on paper
28.5 x 19.5 cm
Date: c. 1835–45

Prov: bt. from James Orrock by Lever, 1910[707]

Lit: J. Witt, *William Henry Hunt (1790–1864): Life and Work, with a Catalogue* (London, 1982), p. 187 (cat. 481)

In common with *The Blessing* (LL 10339 above) this work depicts an elderly man engaged in a devotional act. The model may be the same. Witt dated this work to c. 1845. However, Hunt's technique here is very similar to that in *The Blessing*, and such a late dating for LL 10340 should therefore be questioned. It is more appropriate to suggest a date c. 1835–45.

## Jim Crow
LL 3974 (WHL 320, H 148)

Watercolour, heightened with white, gum arabic, chalk and scratching out over pencil on wove paper
34.3 x 24 cm
Date: c. 1837

Inscr. W. HUNT (watercolour, bottom left; the date has been obscured as the work has been trimmed)

Prov: bt. from the SPWC exhibition by Lady Rolle, 18 Upper Street (20 gns); B. Johnson;[708] James Orrock; Christie's, 4 June 1904 (lot 24); bt. from Orrock by Lever, November 1904[709]

Exh: London, SPWC, *Summer Exhibition*, 1837 (cat. 62); Manchester, *Royal Jubilee Exhibition*, 1887 (cat. 1724); Wolverhampton Art Gallery, *William Henry Hunt: 1790–1864*, 1981 (cat. 117); Manchester, Manchester Art Gallery, and Birmingham, Birmingham Museums and Art Gallery, *Black Victorians: Black People in British Art 1800–1900*, 2005–06 (cat. 60)

Lit: J. Witt, *William Henry Hunt (1790–1864): Life and Work, with a Catalogue* (London, 1982), p. 187 (cat. 477)

In the 1830s Hunt exhibited numerous watercolours of children, mainly single figures, in humorous or sentimental scenes. Many of these were images of white children imitating adult behaviour (including punning titles such as *A Young Shaver – Giving Himself (H)Airs*).[710] At least two were of black children, namely LL 3974, which was exhibited at the SPWC in 1837 under the title *Jim Crow*, and a companion piece, *Miss Jem-ima Crow*, exhibited at the SPWC in 1839 (location unknown).

Although the subject appears to be a genre piece, the title of LL 3974 is a reference to a popular music hall act called 'Jump Jim Crow' performed by the actor Mr Rice in London from 1836.[711] The act involved the blacked-up singer performing a dance, accompanied by a simple song sung in 'negro' dialect. Hunt, who was fascinated by the theatre as a spectacle, would have been aware of this performance: and his choice of title, as with all his titles, is carefully considered.[712] However, the actual subject-matter and pose bear no relation to the theatrical act. Hunt, as with all his drawings, would have painted the image from a living model, here surrounded by studio props. Hunt probably took his sitter from the large numbers of black boys employed as domestic servants in early nineteenth-century London.

This drawing, along with around 20 other watercolours of children, was later lithographed by Thomas Fairland and published in the volume *Hunt's Comic Sketches* in 1843 (fig. 41).[713] When published, *Jim Crow* was re-titled *Master James Crow – Out of his Element*, a reference to the climate of the boy's supposed homeland.[714]

LL 3974 is similar in technique to other Hunt drawings produced in the 1830s, although Tom Jones has suggested that the addition of white chalk is unique and probably not in Hunt's hand.[715]

707 1910 Inventory, listed in the drawing room, valued at £30.
708 Jones, *William Henry Hunt*, p. 56 (cat. 117).
709 1904 Inventory (no. 108), listed in the drawing room.
710 Exhibited at the SPWC, London, 1841 as *Giving himself (H)Airs* (cat. 105), now in the Williamson Art Gallery, Birkenhead; see Jones, *William Henry Hunt*, pp. 62–63 (cat. 128); Witt, *William Henry Hunt*, p. 168 (cat. 270)
711 Roget, *History of the 'Old Water-Colour' Society*, vol. II, p. 193.
712 See Jones, *William Henry Hunt*, pp. 50–51, for a discussion of Hunt and the theatre. Jones (pp. 62–63) relates that Hunt wrote to J. J. Jenkins, the secretary of the SPWC, that he was particular about titles.
713 Thomas Fairland, *Hunt's Comic Sketches* (London, 1843), pl. 8.
714 Given Hunt's reported particularity with regard to titles (see n. 712 above) it is likely that Hunt suggested the title of the print.
715 Jones, *William Henry Hunt*, p. 57.

## The Ballad Seller
LL 3970 (WHL 313, H 154)

Watercolour, heightened with white, with gouache and gum arabic, over pencil on wove paper
42.5 x 28.4 cm (sight)
Date: c. 1840

Inscr: W. HUNT (watercolour, bottom right)

Annot: The Ballad-Seller / W Hunt / LM 1195 Hunt (pencil, on mount, verso) (L. B Mozeley's hand?)

Prov: Elhanan Bicknell; his sale, Christie's, 29 April–1 May 1863 (unknown lot);[716] 'Maj. R.', 14 London Rd, Reading; his sale, Christie's, 27 May 1865 (lot 126, as *The Ballad Singer*);[717] bt. by Agnew's (188 gns); Sir John Fowler; his sale, Christie's, 6 May 1899 (lot 17); bt. by Agnew's (£105); in Lever's collection by May 1905[718]

Exh: [?] Windsor, Eton College, exhibition title unknown, 1933 (cat. 4);[719] Wolverhampton, Wolverhampton Art Gallery, *William Henry Hunt: 1790–1864*, 1981 (cat. 133)

Lit: J. Witt, *William Henry Hunt (1790–1864): Life and Work, with a Catalogue* (London, 1982), p. 187 (cat. 479)

LL 3970 is another of Hunt's figure studies using children as models (see LL 3974, p. 125). In this case the young girl poses as a ballad seller, with her song sheets in the basket by her side. It has been suggested that the artist's model may have been his daughter, Emma, although this is more likely to be the case for LL 3794 below (where the sitter has different features).[720] Witt dated the work to c. 1840.

716 Christie's copy of the 27 May 1865 catalogue states that this work was in Bicknell's sale; it has not been possible to identify this work in his sale catalogue and it may be that it was listed under another title. One possible candidate is lot 250, *Two Girls with Basket* bt. by Agnew's (£192 3s); LL 3970 may have been cut down.

717 LLAG files: a note deriving from the Christie's 1899 catalogue states that L. B. Mozeley was the vendor of LL 3970 in 1865 but his name does not appear in Christie's auctioneer's copy of the 27 May 1865 sale catalogue. It is possible that Mozeley was responsible for the annotation quoted above. It is unclear who 'Maj. R.' was but his name is given in Christie's records.

718 1905 TM Inventory, as *The Ballard Seller* [*sic*] by W. Hunt, valued at £100, listed on the landing to Mr Lever's dressing room.

719 This exhibition is cited in the LLAG files, but there is no record of it in Eton College's archives. The exhibition may have been held in the Drawing Schools (the school's art department) but it is not recorded in the *Eton Chronicle* (the school's magazine) for 1933 . I am grateful to Penny Hatfield, Eton College's archivist, for providing this information.

720 Jones, *William Henry Hunt*, p. 66 (cat. 133).

## Cottage girl seated with a pitcher
LL 3794 (WHL 728, HH 415)

Watercolour with gum arabic on wove paper
27.7 x 19.1 cm
Date: c. 1844

Inscr: W HUNT (watercolour, bottom right)

Prov: [?] William Waring, 1902;[721] bt. from James Orrock by Lever, 1910[722]

Exh: Manchester, Manchester Art Gallery, *Royal Jubilee Exhibition*, 1887 (cat. 1695)

Lit: J. Witt, *William Henry Hunt (1790–1864): Life and Work, with a Catalogue* (London, 1982), p. 187 (cat. 480)

LL 3794 is another of Hunt's many watercolours depicting single figures of children. Here the young girl poses with a large pitcher. Witt has suggested that the model was Hunt's daughter, Emma, aged about 13. The sitter certainly bears a strong resemblance to a number of works where the artist specified that the model was his daughter, such as *The Artist's Daughter Holding a Jug* (private collection, London).[723] Witt has suggested a date for the work of c. 1844.

721 Tatlock, p. 132

722 1910 Inventory, as *A Cottage Girl with a Pitcher*, listed in the back drawing room, valued at £40.

723 Illus. Witt, *William Henry Hunt*, pl. 95 (cat. 518).

## Thrush's nest with eggs and a basket of primroses[724]
LL 3859 (WHL 212, H 179)

Gouache and watercolour, with gum arabic on paper laid down on board
32.3 x 42.5 cm
Date: c. 1850–60

Inscr: W HUNT (watercolour, lower right)

Prov: James Orrock; his sale, Christie's, 4 June 1904 (lot 23); bt. by Smith (190 gns) (bt. in);[725] bt. from Orrock by Lever, November 1904[726]

Lit: J. Witt, *William Henry Hunt (1790–1864): Life and Work, with a Catalogue* (London, 1982), p. 208 (cat. 690)

LL 3859 is one of the numerous still-life subjects that began to dominate Hunt's output from the mid-1840s. Although these included fruit and flower subjects, it was his depictions of bird's nests such as LL 3859 that earned him the nickname 'Bird's Nest Hunt'.

This drawing shows Hunt's extensive use of gouache, a medium that he began to rely on increasingly as his career progressed. Hunt's innovation, which he developed in conjunction with this new subject-matter, was to apply highlights in Chinese white mixed with gum arabic over which he would paint watercolour washes: it is this technique that gives areas like the flowers and the eggs their brilliant luminosity. This method of using a hard priming of Chinese white was adopted by Hunt's successors, such as John Frederick Lewis and Myles Birket Foster (see pp. 98–99) as well as by the Pre-Raphaelite Brotherhood.

Hunt's still-lives were carefully composed studio products, although as with all his subject-matter the artist placed great emphasis on painting them directly from nature. A later description reported Hunt selecting pieces of turf, having them dug up to be re-arranged in the studio; they were then decked with moss, nests and flowers, and were kept intact until the painting was finished.[727] Few preliminary drawings exist for any of Hunt's still-lives, suggesting that he generally worked on the finished watercolour without this kind of preparation.

Witt dated LL 3859 to c. 1850. This dating may have been based on the exhibition of *Primroses and Bird's Nest* at the SPWC in 1851 (cat. 398). However, Hunt exhibited a further two works with very similar titles at the SPWC in 1859 and 1863.[728] Given the consistency of Hunt's technique over the period c. 1850–60, it is possible that this work is considerably later than 1850.

724 The WHL Inventory titled the work *Thrush's Nest with eggs and a basket of primroses against a mossy bank*. Tony Parker, World Museum Liverpool, has confirmed that the nest and eggs are most likely to be those of a blackbird, which is a type of thrush.

725 LLAG files.

726 LL 3859 seems likely to be *Thrush's nest*, 12 x 16¼ in., in the 1904 Inventory, listed in the drawing room.

727 Collingwood, 'Reminiscences of William Henry Hunt', quoted in Jones, *William Henry Hunt*, p. 31.

728 *Bird's Nest and Primroses*, exh. 1859 (cat. 203); *Primroses and Bird's Nest*, exh. 1863 (cat. 266).

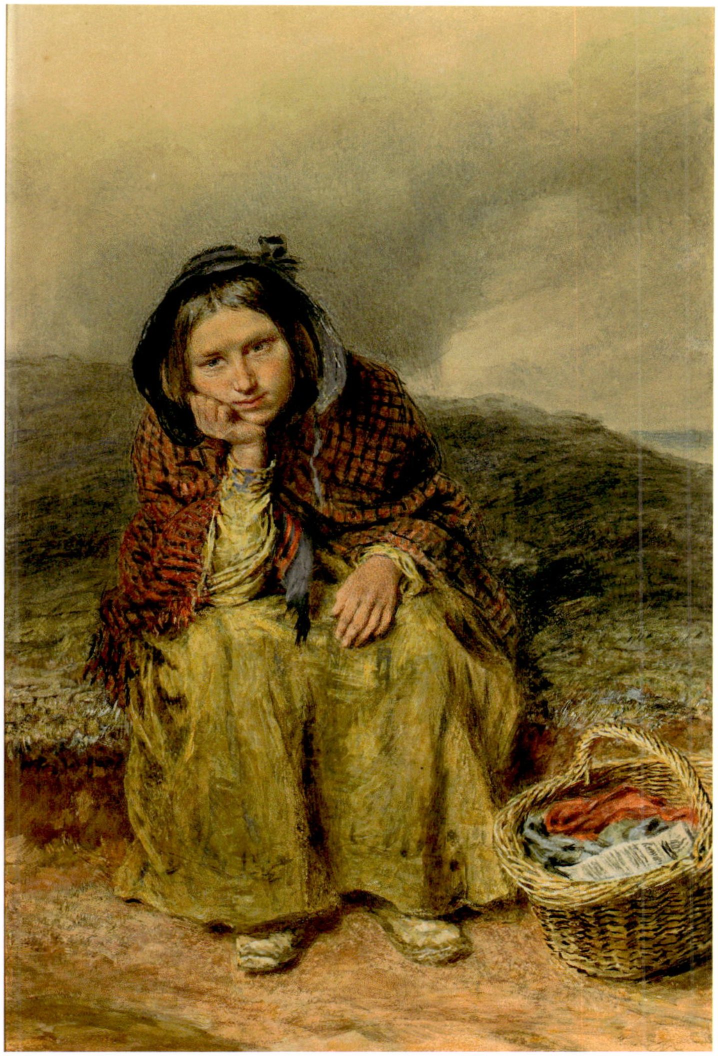

LL 3970

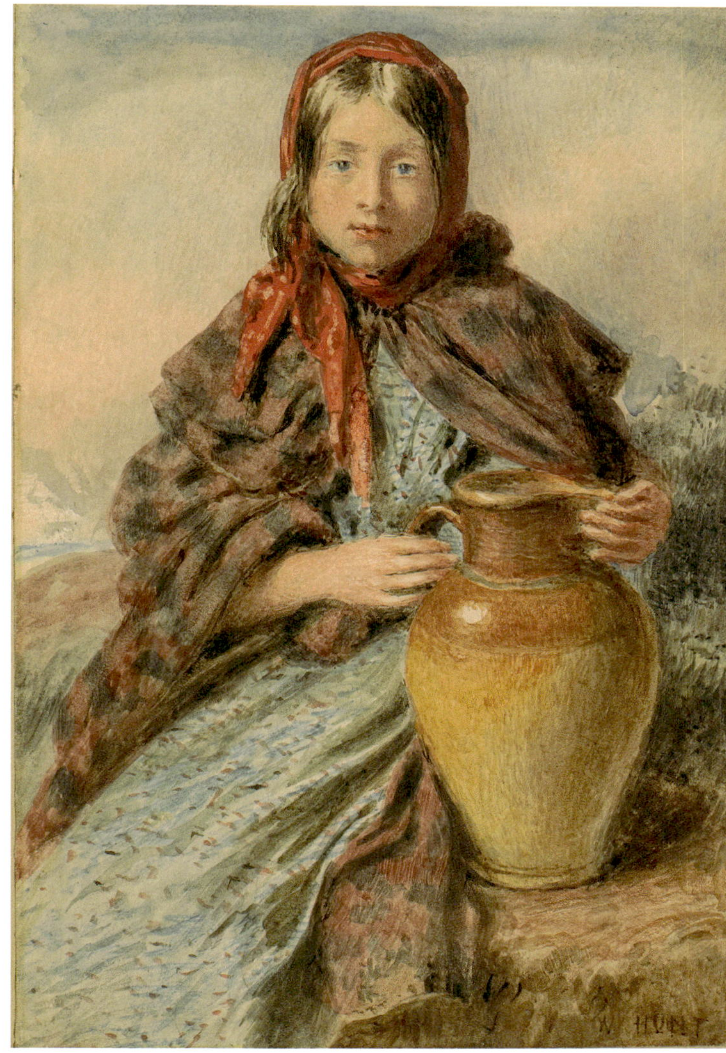

LL 3794

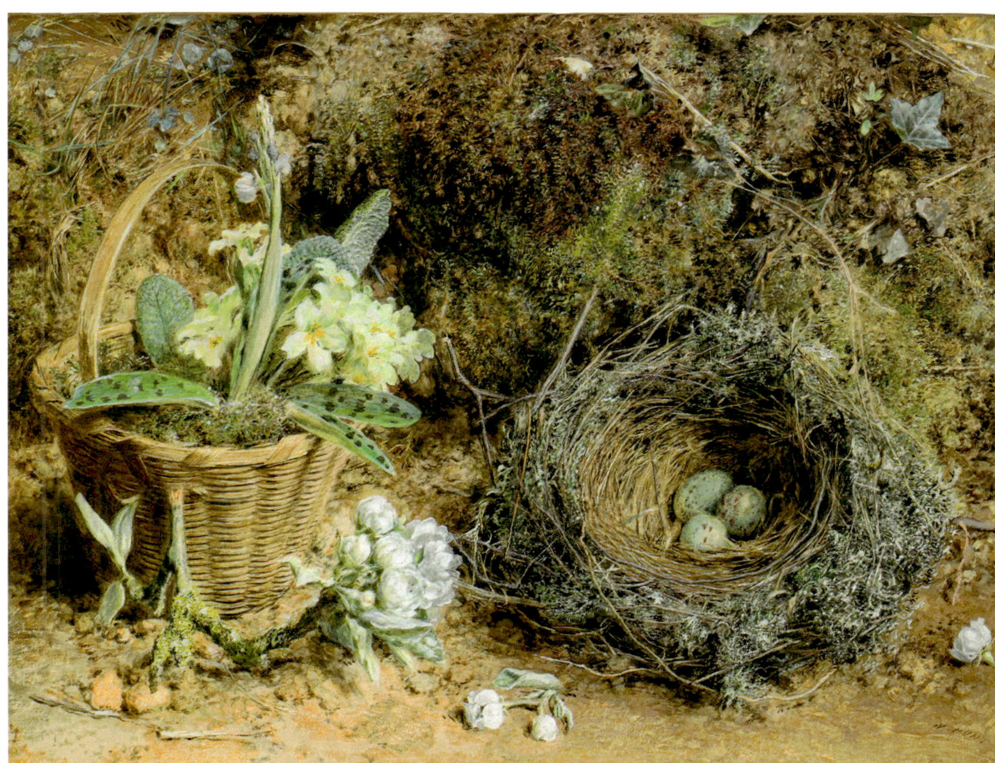

LL 3859

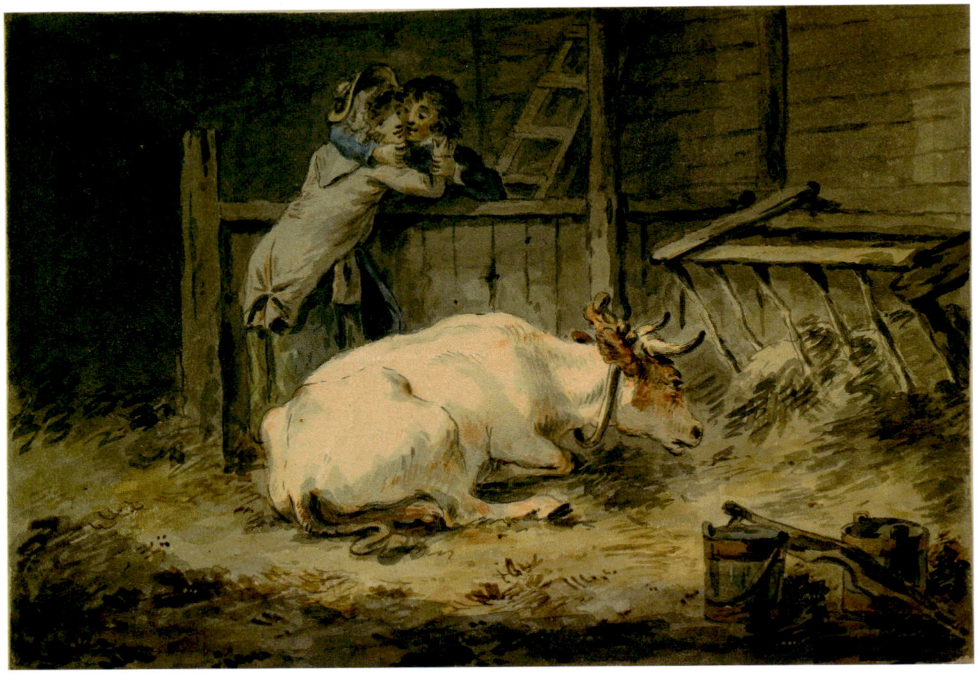

LL 3976

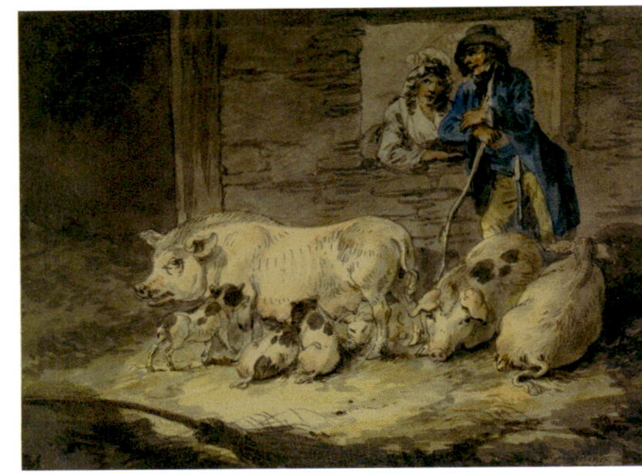

fig. 42. Julius Caesar Ibbetson, *Pigs: Sow with her litter*, c. 1788–93, watercolour with black crayon on paper, 13.2 x 18.4 cm, Birmingham Museums and Art Gallery

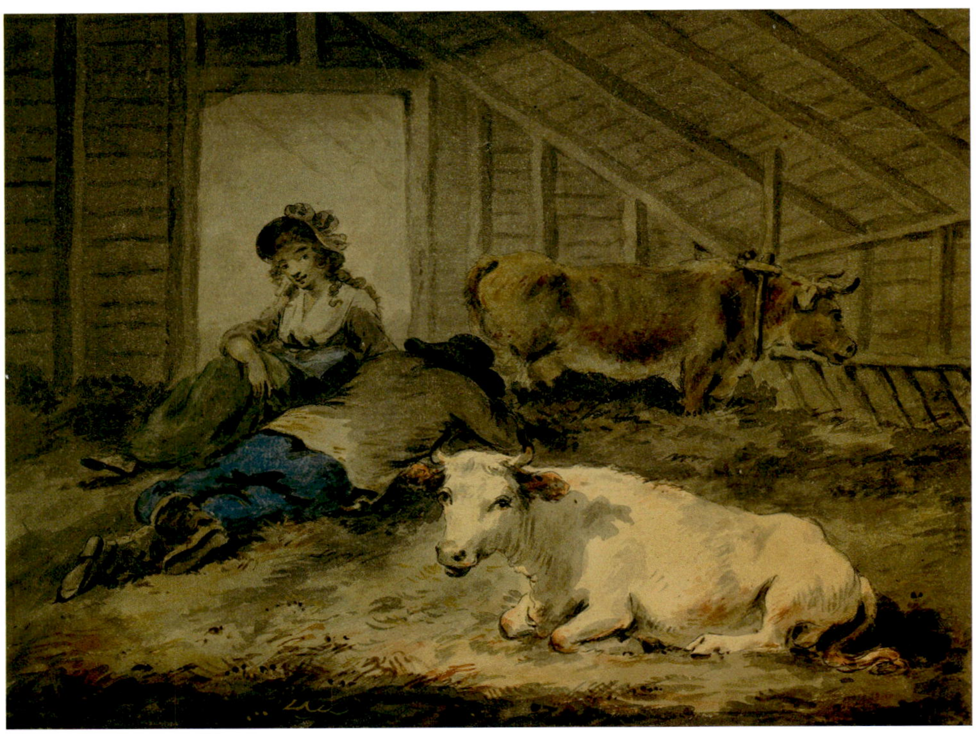

LL 3975

## JULIUS CAESAR IBBETSON

1759 Leeds–1817 Masham, North Yorkshire

**Courtship in a Cowshed**
LL 3975 (WHL 1530, TM 114)

Watercolour and gouache on laid paper, laid down on original wash-line mount
13.9 x 18.8 cm (image); 16.7 x 21.6 cm (mount, trimmed irreg.)

**Courtship in a Cowshed**
LL 3976 (WHL 1531, TM 115)

Watercolour and gouache on laid paper, laid down on original wash-line mount
13.5 x 19.6 cm (image), 16.2 x 22.5 cm (mount)
Date: probably late 1780s or early 1790s

Prov: in Lever's collection by 1906[729]

Exh: Perth, Art Gallery of Western Australia and Australian tour, *Exhibition of Early British Water-colours*, organised by the Empire Art Loans Exhibition Society, 1948–49 (cat. 42)[730]

Lit: LL 3975: 'Current Art Notes, Our Plates', *The Connoisseur*, vol. 90 (December 1932), p. 410, illus. p. 385; LL 3976: 'Current Art Notes, Our Plates', *The Connoisseur*, vol. 91 (February 1933), p. 120, illus. p. 111

Ibbetson was apprenticed to a ship painter in Hull, although in 1777 he prematurely ended his contract, moving to London where he worked as a picture restorer for an art dealer. This gave him an unusual opportunity, as an entirely self-taught artist, to study the seventeenth-century Dutch masters, who were to have an important influence on both his oils and watercolours. He exhibited landscape and genre scenes at the Royal Academy consistently from 1785 but failed to be elected as a member. He made tours to Wales and the Isle of Wight in the late 1780s and early 1790s, but despite commissions from some patrons was nearly destitute by the middle of the decade. In 1798 he moved to Liverpool and then later to the Lake District, settling in Yorkshire around 1805.

The artist's watercolours engage with a wide range of sometimes unusual subject-matter, including smuggling and ice-skating scenes, showing his debt to Dutch genre painters, and depictions of industrial scenes inspired by his trip to Wales with Colonel Greville and John 'Warwick' Smith (see pp. 173–74) in 1792. He also produced more conventional scenes, in common with his contemporaries Francis Wheatley (see p. 216) and George Morland, of rustic workers engaged in cottage industries, in line with the contemporary taste for the picturesque. LL 3975 and LL 3976 belong to an equally conventional but slightly different strand of this rustic idyll,

729 The works are listed in the 1906 TM Inventory as '*Shippons* by Ibbetson *(a pair)*', hanging in the ballroom, valued at £10 for the pair. They appear again in the 1907 TM Inventory as *Courtship in a Cowshed (Shippons)*, hanging in the entrance lobby to the ballroom, valued at £20 for the pair. They do not appear in the 1905 TM Inventory, suggesting that they were purchased after this date but before the 1906 TM Inventory.

730 Only LL 3976 was lent to this exhibition.

in which farmhands and their sweethearts are depicted engaged in amorous encounters.

The works are part of a tradition of 'before' and 'after' imagery of amorous couples made familiar in British art by Hogarth, which are gently humorous in intent. They are among several delicately handled watercolours by the artist of roughly the same size depicting similar subjects. A sketch depicting a couple with pigs is in Birmingham Museums and Art Gallery (fig. 42) and a further watercolour of a dairymaid and her companion is recorded as being in H. Towlson's collection.[731] Another watercolour, similar in style and size, is in the Fitzwilliam Museum, Cambridge, although this work depicts a lone farm girl alongside three pigs.[732] Considering their size and the known popularity of this type of subject-matter within a growing market for prints, it is likely that all these works were conceived as designs for colour engravings, although no impressions are known.[733] The Fitzwilliam watercolour is signed and dated 1793 and the Lady Lever works probably date from the late 1780s or early 1790s.[734] With their muted colour palette consisting of browns and greys, with splashes of brighter colour, applied in thin washes, the technique of these watercolours is consistent with that advocated by Ibbetson in his treatise, *A Process of Tinted Drawing*, published in 1795.

731 Rotha Mary Clay, *Julius Caesar Ibbetson 1759–1817* (London, 1948), p. 118, described as measuring 9 x 8 in. It has not been possible to trace the H. Towlson collection.
732 *Pigs* (no. 1381), 13.2 x 18.5 cm.
733 Clay, *Julius Caesar Ibbetson*, p. 118.
734 Correspondence with James Mitchell, September 2006.

## LESLIE GILBERT ILLINGWORTH
1902 Barry, Glamorgan–1979 Hastings

**Crossing the Ford: 'The Children's Bill'**
LL 2955

Pen and ink over pencil on paper
35.3 x 28.3 cm (sight)
Date: 1948

Inscr: ILLINGWORTH (pen and ink, bottom right); The / Children / Bill (pen and ink, on book)

Prov: unknown[735]

Illingworth demonstrated a precocious talent for drawing, and in 1920 won a scholarship to study under Sir William Rothenstein at the Royal College of Art. The following year his first political cartoon appeared in the *Western Mail* and in 1921, having given up his studies at the RCA, he began working full-time for the Welsh newspaper. By the age of 22 Illingworth was contributing cartoons to a range of magazines, including *London Life* and *Strand,* while also studying under Henry Tonks at the Slade (for a brief spell he also studied in Paris at the Académie Julien). On 27 May 1931 his work first appeared in *Punch* and six years later his cartoons began appearing as whole pages (as the cartoon after this drawing appeared in *Punch*). Illingworth began working formally for the magazine in 1945 when he was appointed second cartoonist under E. H. Shepard. In 1949, one year after the cartoon after LL 2955 was published, he became *Punch*'s principal cartoonist. During the 1960s Illingworth mainly worked for the *Daily Mail,* at the same time contributing to the *Sun* and *News of the World*. Illingworth did not retire from newspaper cartooning until 1976, three years before his death.

The enduring popularity of Millais's painting *Sir Isumbras at the Ford* (Lady Lever Art Gallery, LL 3625, fig. 45, p. 139) is evident from

735 LL 2955 was inventoried in 1996, having previously been kept in LLAG files as a piece of documentation. It was certainly in the collection before 1986 and may have been donated or bequeathed by the artist.

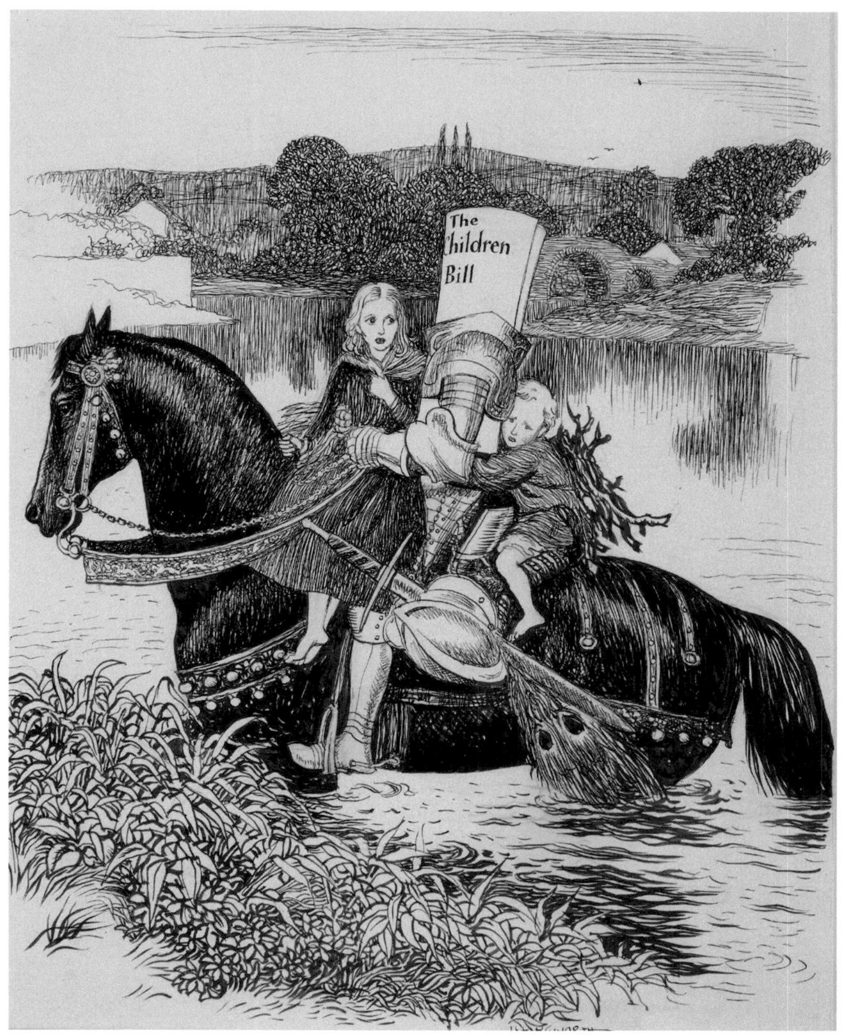


LL 2955

this pen-and-ink drawing for the cartoon that appeared between 'H. J's Belles Lettres' and a poem about poachers in *Punch*, 18 February 1948. Since the publication of Gould's cartoon in the *Westminster Gazette* in 1912 (see LL 3856, pp. 103–104), a number of caricaturists had derived their work from Millais's painting. The edition of *News of the World* published on 12 February 1928 contained A. W. Lloyd's cartoon titled *Women and Children First*, a comment on the Franchise Bill and Agricultural Credits which Stanley Baldwin attempted to push through Parliament in 1928. Six years later *Sir Isumbras* was chosen as the subject of an amusing take-off for an article in the *Daily Express* of 13 January 1934; Millais's chivalrous knight was humorously renamed Sir Isumbrook.

Illingworth's cartoon appeared under the heading 'The Children Bill' (which also replaces the head of the knight), and explanatory note: 'Crossing the Ford, the second Reading of the Bill to provide better care for neglected children was moved in the House of Lords last week'.[736] Illingworth adapted Millais's painting of a chivalrous knight rescuing two children to comment on the Bill passed in 1948 by the Labour leader, Clement Attlee, which aimed to provide better care for neglected children and, significantly, establish a children's committee and children's officer in each local authority. He may have been familiar with Millais's painting from engravings made after the subject, or from visits to the Lady Lever Art Gallery where it had been on display since 1922.[737] Readers of *Punch* may have recalled A. W. Lloyd's cartoon, inspired again by Millais's painting, published in *Punch* in 1934. Titled *The Minister of Transport Carries the Bairns Across*, Lloyd was commenting on the Road Traffic Bill which introduced driving tests and made other improvements to road safety. In 1948, the year Illingworth's cartoon was published, the public was reminded of Millais's painting as it appeared in an exhibition celebrating the centenary of the Pre-Raphaelite movement held at the Lady Lever Art Gallery.

William Hewison, *Punch*'s art editor from 1960 to 1984, described Illingworth's 'faultless pen-and-ink technique, a technique which is essentially naturalistic yet masterly in its variety of textures, arrangement of tones, and subtle atmospheric perspective'.[738] Illingworth's illustration is exceptional for the attention it pays to Millais's original painting, including the wild staring eyes of the girl and anxious look of the young boy. In addition he portrays the background with an almost Pre-Raphaelite obsession with detail, the bridge to the left of the knight and arrangement of foliage echoing that in the final painting. Millais's painting had caused mockery from the outset owing to his well-publicised struggle to accurately portray the horse, but here Illingworth observes the seriousness of Millais's subject. The Christian chivalric values represented by Millais's *Sir Isumbras at the Ford* are reflected in Illingworth's sensitivity to the Liberal cause and their achievement in passing the Children Bill successfully through Parliament.
HB

736 The description accompanying this cartoon was quite exceptional and, as a result, the meanings behind many of Illingworth's satires appear fairly opaque to modern readers.

737 The painting had also been included in a number of exhibitions since its acquisition by the LLAG, including at the Walker Art Gallery in 1922, and Royal Academy in 1934.

738 W. Hewison, *The Cartoon Connection* (London, 1977), pp. 68–69.

## JOHN JACKSON
1778 Lastingham, Yorkshire–1831 London

### Sketch of John Flaxman
LL 2705 (X 1961)

Pencil and brown wash on off-white laid paper
19 x 14 cm
Date: probably c. 1810

Inscr: J Jackson (pen and brown ink, centre, verso)

Prov: Probably Mrs Flaxman; Frederick Rathbone, 1912; bt. from Rathbone by Lever, 3 July 1914 with a letter from Josiah Wedgwood to Mrs Flaxman (£12 for both)[739]

Lit: Mrs Stewart Erskine, 'Some Flaxman Relics', *The Art Journal* (1912), pp. 81–83; W. G. Constable, *John Flaxman 1755–1826* (London, 1927), pp. 9 and 117

LL 2705 was acquired by Lever as by John Jackson and his authorship is confirmed by a comparison between the signature verso (fig. 43) and other samples by the artist.[740] John Jackson initially worked as a painter of miniatures on ivory, based at York and Whitby. The miniatures were poorly executed but he showed promise as a portrait painter, and by 1800 had won the patronage of the 1st Earl of Mulgrave, who introduced him to the 5th Earl of Carlisle and Sir George Beaumont. By 1804 Jackson had settled in London and was admitted to the Royal Academy Schools the following year. He found success not just as a portrait painter but also as a copyist. He was elected an associate of the Royal Academy in 1815 and a full member in 1818.

The subject of the Lady Lever sketch is the sculptor, decorative designer and illustrator John Flaxman (1755–1826). He was depicted on a number of occasions by Jackson, including a celebrated portrait painted for Lord Dover that was described at the Royal Academy dinner in 1827 by Thomas Lawrence as 'a great achievement of the English School'.[741] However, LL 2705 does not relate directly to any known painting of the artist. It is not known precisely when this sketch was drawn but as Jackson only moved permanently to London in 1804 it must

739 LLAG files: this letter (LL 2698) has been authenticated as having been written by Josiah Wedgwood I (1730–95) by Robin Emmerson, verbally, April 2008. It is undated and reads: 'Mr Wedgwood presents his compliments to Mrs Flaxman / and has the honor [*sic*] to present her with the portrait of / the first artist of the age which from her knowledge / of his many other good qualities he flatters himself / will be favourably received / Greek St., Sunday morning.' The portrait of Flaxman referred to in the letter seems to have been erroneously assumed to be LL 2705, though the date of Wedgwood's death rules this out. This confusion may have taken place in Mrs Flaxman's time; the fact that the letter was addressed to Mrs Flaxman, and that both the letter and the sketch came into Lever's collection together, strongly suggests that she owned the sketch. The conflation of the sketch with the portrait referred to in the letter had certainly been made by 1912 when the two (sketch and letter) were illustrated together in *The Art Journal* (1912), pp. 81–83.

740 See, for example, John Jackson's signature on his pencil copy of Thomas Gainsborough's self portrait, Victoria Art Gallery, Bath.

741 Richard and Samuel Redgrave, *A Century of British Painters*, ed. R. Todd, 3rd edn (London, 1947 [1866]), p. 245; the location of this portrait is unknown.

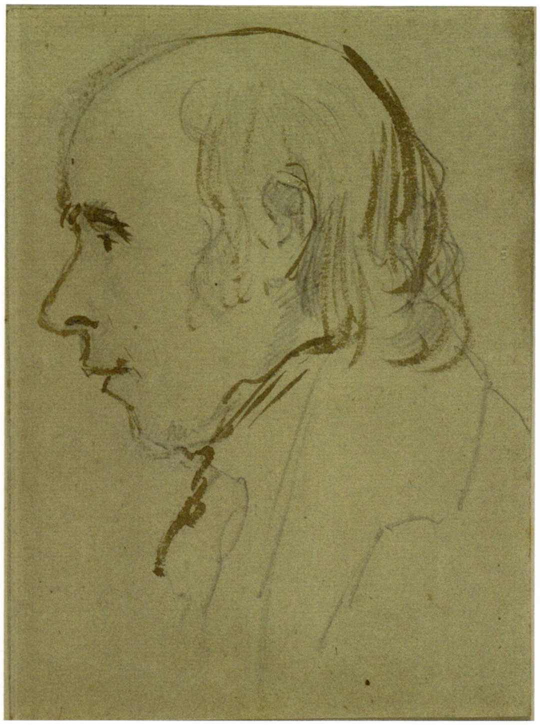

LL 2705

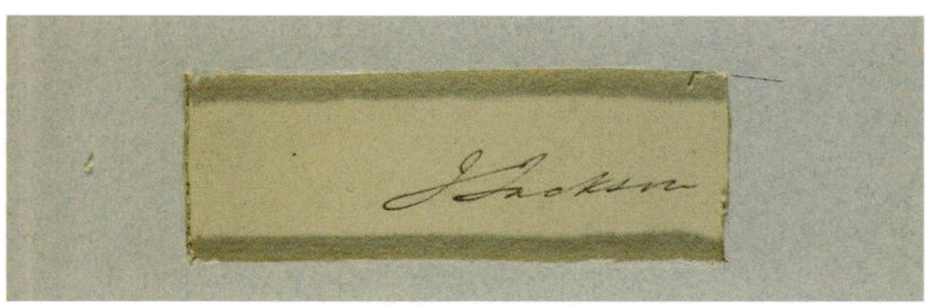


fig. 43. John Jackson's signature on verso of his *Sketch of John Flaxman* (LL 2705)

have been made after this date. Jackson probably met Flaxman through the Royal Academy; Jackson had entered its schools in 1805. LL 2705 probably dates from c. 1810, around the time when Flaxman was appointed Professor of Sculpture at the Royal Academy.[742] This dating is also suggested by the appearance of the sitter who seems to be substantially older than in Romney's portrait *John Flaxman Modelling the Bust of William Hayley* (Yale Center for British Art, New Haven), which was begun in 1795 when Flaxman was 40.[743]

LL 2705 is a lively sketch that has the characteristics of having been drawn from life; pentimenti on the sitter's forehead and chin show Jackson to have changed his mind about their shape.

742 Alex Kidson kindly discussed LL 2705, verbally, August 2007. This dating has also been suggested by Sarah Symmons, email correspondence, 14 February 2008.

743 Kidson, *George Romney*, p. 229 (cat. 145).

## EDWIN HENRY LANDSEER
1802 London–1873 London

### A Dead Stag
LL 3860 (WHL 3544)

Pen and brown ink with watercolour over pencil on wove paper
22.5 x 31.4 cm (sight)
Date: c. 1825–30

Prov: the artist's sale, Christie's, 8–15 May 1874 (lot unknown);[744] James Orrock; his sale, Christie's, 25 April 1895 ([?] lot 162);[745] [?] bt. by Pryce (6 gns); G. R. Macdougall, Bournemouth; his sale, Christie's, 24 May 1918 (lot 2, with LL 3861); bt. by Gooden and Fox for Lever (£4 4s the pair)

### Two Dead Stags
LL 3861 (WHL 3545)

Pen and brown ink over pencil on wove paper
25.2 x 35.8 cm (sight)
Date: c. 1825–30

Prov: the artist's sale, Christie's, 8–15 May 1874 (lot unknown);[746] James Orrock; his sale, Christie's, 25 April 1895 ([?] lot 159);[747] [?] bt. by Pryce (6 gns); G. R. Macdougall, Bournemouth; his sale, Christie's, 24 May 1918 (lot 2, with LL 3860); bt. by Gooden and Fox for Lever (£4 4s the pair)

Exh: London, Royal Academy, *Paintings and Drawings by Sir Edwin Landseer 1802–1873*, 1961 (cat. 155, as *Morning*)

Landseer, the son of an engraver, was educated at home by his father and as a young child was producing drawings and etchings of animals. In 1815 he exhibited his first painting at the Royal Academy, and the same year became a pupil of Benjamin Robert Haydon. In 1816 he entered the Royal Academy Schools, where he was nicknamed 'little dog boy' by Henry Fuseli, the keeper of the schools, suggesting that by this point Landseer's reputation as an animal painter was beginning to take shape. In 1824 he made his first trip to the Highlands of Scotland: the country was to have a huge impact on his life and art and he returned year after year. These expeditions inspired some of his most famous paintings of deer-hunting and highland life. By 1831, when Landseer was elected a full Royal Academician, he had established a reputation as the foremost animal painter of his day. The year

744 Candidates are lots 381, 387 and 392, bt. by Agnew's; and 386 and 393 bt. by 'Lord F.'.

745 There are 4 candidates for LL 3860-61 in Orrock's sale: lots 159, 160, 162 and 163; the present tentative identifications follow those in LLAG files. Lot 159 was titled *a Study for 'Morning'* and was bt. by Pryce (6 gns); lot 160 was *A Dead Stag*, bt. in (4½ gns); lot 162 was *A Study for 'Life in the Old Dog'*, bt. by Pryce (6 gns); and lot 163 was *Two Dead Stags*, bt. by Wiseman (6 gns).

746 Candidates are lots 389 and 390, bt. by Agnew's; and 398, bt. by Guinness.

747 See n. 745 above.

LL 3860

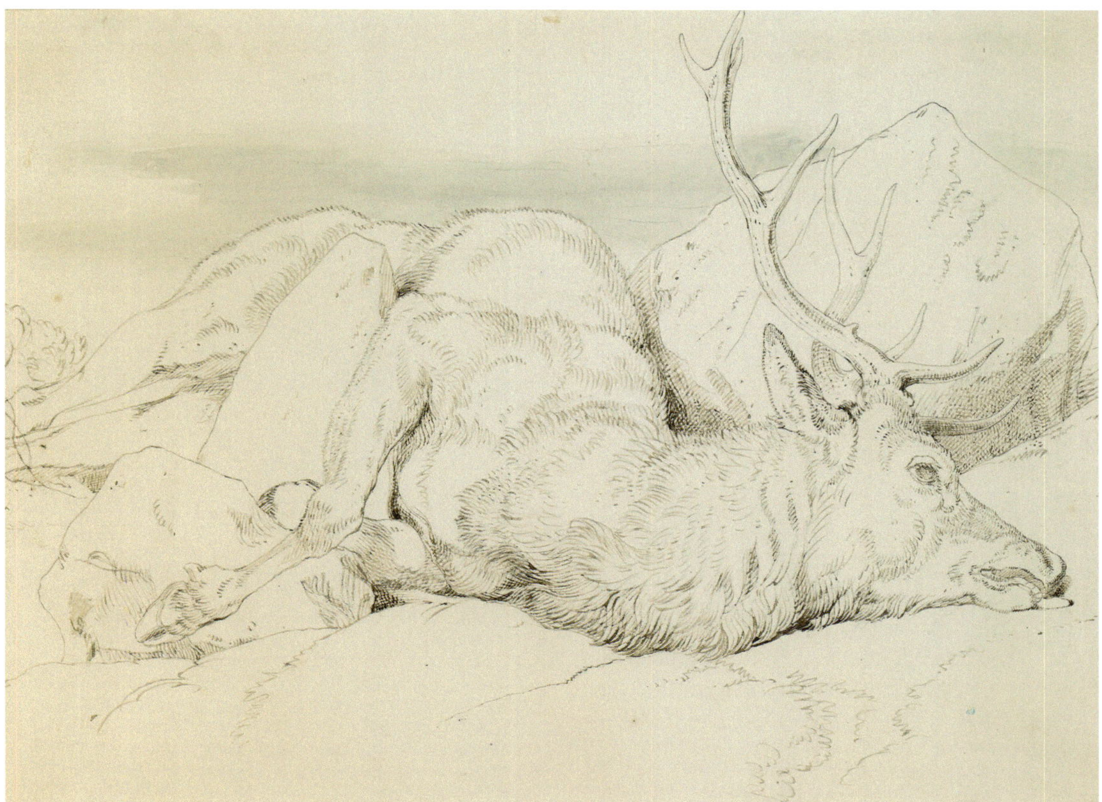

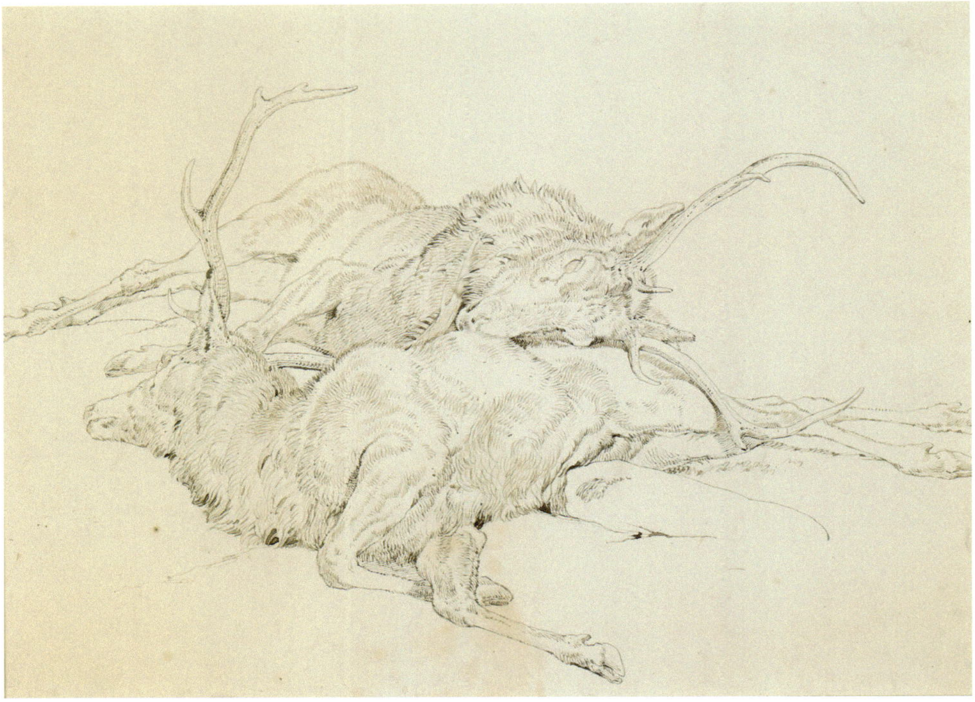

LL 3861

1840 heralded a new direction in Landseer's art, with the tight detail of his earlier style giving way to a broader method of painting, and his works becoming more weighty in tone. It was from the 1840s and 1850s that some of his most enduring images, such as the iconic painting *The Monarch of the Glen* (exh. RA, 1851; private collection) derive. Landseer continued painting until his death, producing some of his most complex compositions in later years, despite the onset of dementia.

Both drawings date from the period c. 1825-30 when Landseer spent the summer and autumn staying with aristocratic hosts in the Highlands of Scotland.[748] This period inspired a number of sporting pictures such as *The Death of the Stag in Glen Tilt* (1824-30, Blair Castle) that contained groups of figures, in this case the Duke of Atholl, his grandson and keepers, alongside the body of a dead stag. Landseer's paintings of deer did not always include the figures of his aristocratic patrons and friends: in the late 1820s and early 1830s he exhibited a range of oil paintings of the contorted bodies of dead deer, without the presence of humans.

Paintings such as *Dead Deer and Deerhound*, exhibited at the Royal Academy in 1827 (private collection) and said to be based on a real incident, show hunting as a way of life, and death as natural, but equally reveal Landseer's compassion for the tragic consequences. His engagement with his subject-matter is revealed in a description by the 6th Earl of Tankerville (1810-90), later a friend of the artist, but who on first sighting mistook him for a poacher: 'He was busily engaged in grallocking his deer. This he did with great quickness and dexterity ... He next let the head hang over, so as to display the horns, and then, squatting down on a stone opposite, took out of his pocket what I thought would be his pipe or whisky flask; but it was a sketch-book!'[749] LL 3860 and LL 3861 have been mistakenly associated with, respectively, the paintings *The Life's in the Old Dog Yet* (c. 1838, private collection) and *Morning* (exh. RA 1853, Philadelphia Museum of Art). In fact, although similar to the contorted stags represented in many of Landseer's oil paintings, the Lady Lever drawings are not believed to be studies for particular paintings but independent finished works, among numerous others similar in technique where the artist repeatedly explored dead stags in contorted positions.[750] Both drawings demonstrate Landseer's understanding of anatomy, an interest signalled by his early écorché (flayed) studies of animals, and encouraged by his teacher Benjamin Robert Haydon.

748 Richard Ormond, email correspondence, July 2007.

749 The Earl of Tankerville, *The Chillingham Wild Cattle. Reminiscence of Life in the Highlands*, privately printed (1891), p. 24; quoted by Richard Ormond, *The Monarch of the Glen: Landseer in the Highlands* (exh. cat., Edinburgh, National Galleries of Scotland, 2005), p. 84.

750 LLAG files list LL 3860 as *A Study for 'Life in the Old Dog'*. LL 3861 was catalogued in Derek Hill and John Woodward, *Paintings and Drawings by Sir Edwin Landseer 1802-1873* (exh. cat., London, Royal Academy of Arts, 1961), p. 30 (cat. 155) as a study for the painting *Morning* (exh. RA, 1853, cat. 69). However, Richard Ormond has pointed out (email correspondence, June 2007) that the Lady Lever drawings have been identified with these paintings in error. See his *Monarch of the Glen*, p. 53 for an illustration of *The Life's in the Old Dog Yet*; see his *Edwin Landseer* (exh. cat., Philadelphia, Philadelphia Museum of Art and London, Tate Gallery, 1981-82), p. 179 for prints after *Morning* and its companion piece *Night*. The pose in LL 3861 is particularly close to that in another Landseer drawing, in the British Museum, inscribed Glenfeshie / 1827. EL.

## EDWARD LEAR

Holloway, London 1812-San Remo, Italy 1888

### Finale

LL 3977 (LP 64)

Pen and sepia ink with watercolour and gouache over pencil on wove paper
36.5 x 54 cm
Date: 1864, possibly added to at a later date

Inscr: Fin[ale] (obscured by ink blot) / 4.30 P.M.& 11 AM / 16. + 17. December / 1864 (pen and ink over pencil, bottom left corner); Immense "Splash" of / sea foam (pen and ink over pencil, bottom left edge); sea (pen and ink over pencil, bottom left edge, towards centre); (53) (pen and ink over pencil, bottom right corner); 52 (pencil, bottom right); [illeg. word] (pen and ink, bottom right); white (pen and ink over pencil, centre); black / gray / black / sharp black (pen and ink, centre, on grey rock); a green / okr earth / stone (pen and ink over pencil, lower left); Rusty (pen and ink over pencil, lower left); w. foam (pen and ink over pencil, lower left); oker / oker / gray / oker / brown (pen and ink over pencil, centre left); green / gray / pale / oker / far (pen and ink over pencil, upper left); wall / perpendikular (pen and ink over pencil, left edge)

Prov: bt. from the Fine Art Society by the Trustees, March 1946 (£70 18s 6d with LL 3769)

Exh: London, Fine Art Society, *Winter Exhibition of Early English Watercolours and Drawings*, 1945-46 (cat. 11); Port Sunlight, Lady Lever Art Gallery, *The Pre-Raphaelites - Their Friends and Followers*, 1948 (cat. 122)

As an artist Lear was almost wholly self-taught; his first employment was as an ornithological draughtsman. Between 1831 and 1837 he worked for Lord Stanley, later 13th Earl of Derby, making drawings of the animals and birds in his menagerie at Knowsley Hall, near Liverpool. By the time he was 25 Lear had abandoned his ornithological career to become a landscape painter and he took up his patron's offer to send him to Rome, where he spent the next ten years. Aside from brief intervals in England, including a year in 1850 spent as a student at the Royal Academy Schools, Lear was to spend the rest of his life abroad; after Rome he lived in Corfu and finally San Remo. He travelled widely in Italy, Greece, southern France and also further afield, including Egypt, Palestine and Lebanon, India and Ceylon. Lear attempted to establish himself as a serious landscape painter in oils and exhibited at the Royal Academy and the British Institution during the 1850s, but his two most ambitious canvases were a commercial failure. During the last decade of his life he was occupied with a scheme to illustrate the poems of Tennyson. Lear's failures as an artist were somewhat offset by his success as a comic writer and illustrator; he published songs, limericks, stories and alphabets which were accompanied by his idiosyncratic, humorous illustrations.

LL 3977 was produced during the winter of 1864, which Lear spent in Nice. Shortly after his arrival in December, he embarked on a walking trip along the coast into Italy. On 16 and 17 December he was in the town of Finale Ligure where, excited by the landscape, he wrote in his

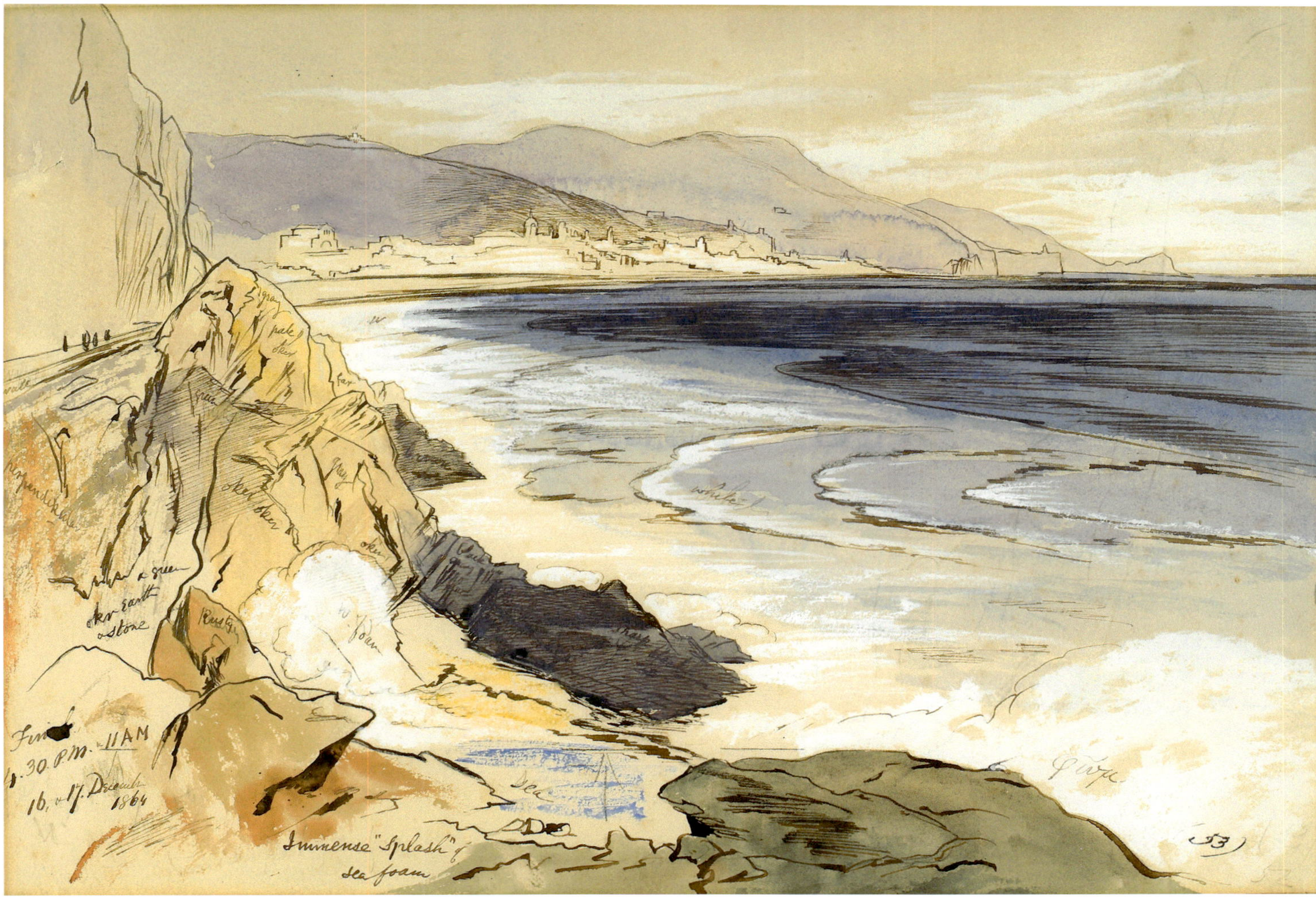

LL 3977

diary: 'The rolling sea was magnificent'.[751] He had returned to Nice by New Year's Eve 1864 with a folio of 144 drawings. The Lady Lever watercolour, which represents the rocky Ligurian coastline with the town of Finale in the distance, is typical of the many thousands of vigorous, freely handled landscape sketches produced while Lear was on his travels from the late 1840s onwards. On each of his trips he made hundreds of pencil sketches of the landscape, recording the precise location, date and often the time of day of the drawing, with extensive colour notations, often spelt in his idiosyncratic, phonetic manner. Sometimes months or years later he 'penned-out' the drawing in ink, a version of the eighteenth-century technique of the 'tinted' drawing, and added colour washes to the sketch based on the notes he had made. He also numbered the works in a sequence, which would begin again when he moved onto another country. LL 3977 was not intended for sale but functioned as a study that the artist may have shown to potential patrons and from which he may have intended to work up finished watercolours as well as oil paintings.

Another drawing, numbered 52 (Houghton Library, Harvard University, fig. 44) and inscribed 4.15 pm was sketched just slightly earlier on the same afternoon, from a viewpoint further away from the town. Lear may have believed the earlier sketch, with its rugged outcrop of rocks creating a strong vertical contrast to the horizontal hills in the background, to be the more powerful composition. This is suggested by the fact that Lear copied this drawing in pen with slight variations about 1874 and then again, as a grey and black wash drawing, as an illustration for Tennyson's *Poems* in 1885.[752]

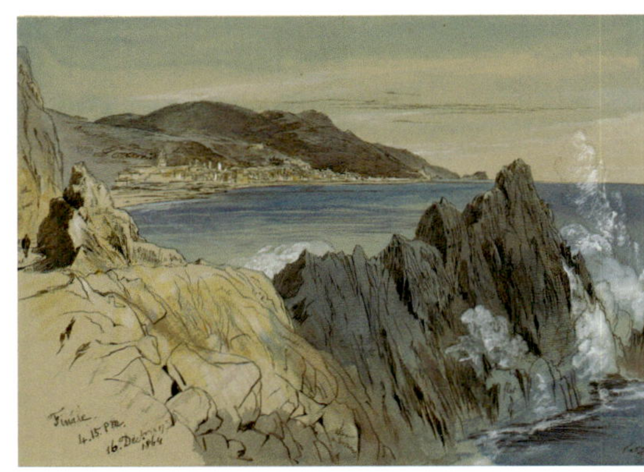

fig. 44. Edward Lear, *Finale*, 1864, watercolour, sepia ink and Chinese white over pencil on tan paper, 37 x 54 cm, Houghton Library, Harvard University, Cambridge, Massachusetts, MS Typ 55.26 (939)

751 Diary, 16 December 1864 (MS), Houghton Library, Harvard University, quoted by Vivien Noakes, *Edward Lear 1812–1888* (exh. cat., London, Royal Academy, 1985), p. 117.

752 Philip Hofer, *Edward Lear as a Landscape Draughtsman* (London, 1967), p. 33. The pen-and-ink copy is illustrated in Hofer, pl. 65, although it is mistakenly captioned as the illustration for Tennyson. The 1885 drawing was conceived as an illustration to Tennyson's poem *The Daisy* but was not published until after Lear's death in *Poems by Alfred, Lord Tennyson* (London and New York, 1889), illus. between pp. 41 and 43. For an explanation of the Tennyson project, see R. Pitman, *Edward Lear's Tennyson* (Manchester and New York, 1988), pp. 27–31 and Noakes, *Edward Lear*, pp. 129–36. Both Lear's later copies of *Finale* are thought to be in the Houghton Library, Harvard University, although recent efforts to locate them have proved unsuccessful.

## WILLIAM LEIGHTON LEITCH
Glasgow 1804-London 1883

**Town and Castle of Paramythia, Albania**[753]
LL 3863 (WHL 763, HH 388)

Watercolour with white heightening over pencil on wove paper
19.4 x 29.1 cm (sight)
Date: c. 1838

Inscr: W.L Leitch. 1855 (watercolour, bottom left)
Prov: bt. from James Orrock by Lever, 1910

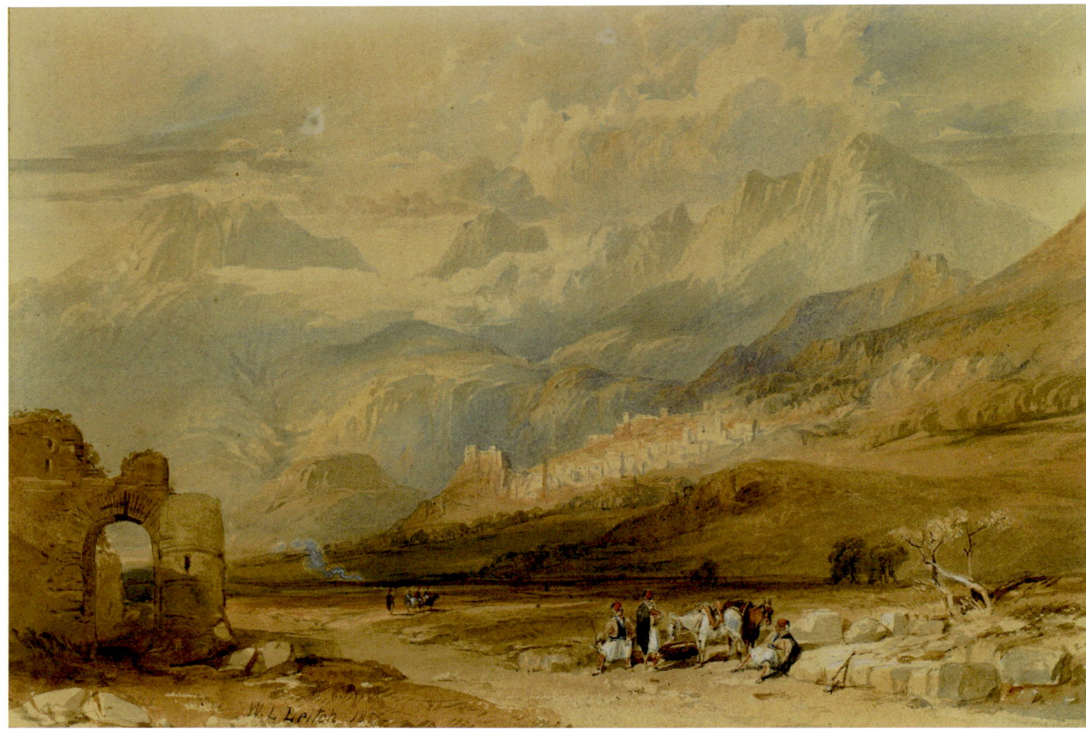

LL 3863

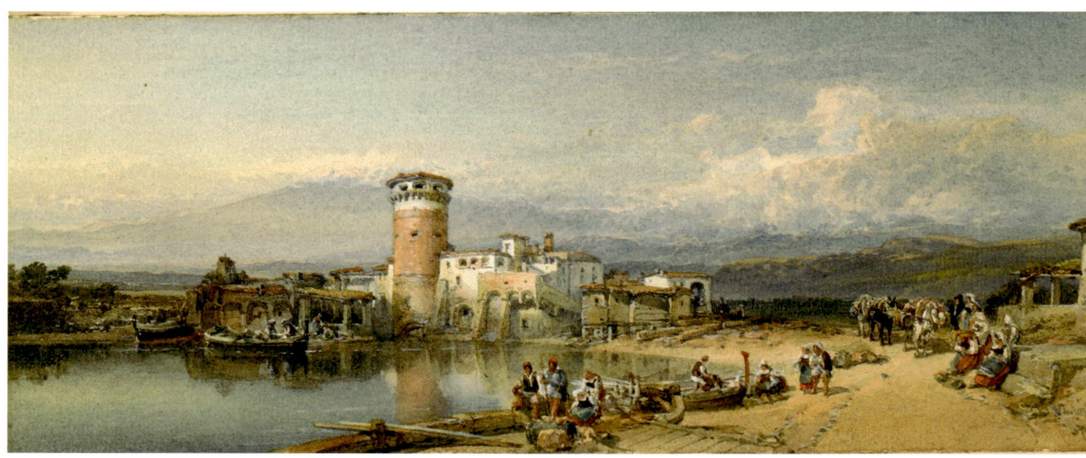

LL 3862

Leitch came from humble beginnings, working as a sign painter in Glasgow before a stint in the 1820s designing scenery at the Glasgow Theatre Royal. Here he learnt his art from stage scenery designed by Alexander Nasmyth and David Roberts, who had been employed before him. In the 1830s Leitch moved to London, initially working as a scene painter although he gradually turned his attention towards producing oil paintings and watercolours. Leitch's work was seen by a stockbroker who subsequently paid for him to make a four-year trip to Italy between 1833 and 1837, looking after the artist's family in his absence. Leitch returned to London with numerous sketches from nature and finished watercolours, a wealth of teaching experience and introductions to aristocratic families. These connections quickly led to his acquiring a circle of aristocratic pupils, and in 1846 he became drawing master to Queen Victoria, continuing lessons with her until 1865. From the 1860s Leitch painted only in watercolours, exhibiting works at the British Institution, the Society of British Artists and the New Society of Painters in Water-Colours (later known as the Institute of Painters in Water-Colours), where from 1873 until his death he served as vice-president.

Towards the end of 1837 or early in 1838 Leitch was employed by the publishers Fisher & Son to make drawings of scenes in Albania from sketches they supplied.[754] LL 3863 was one of a handful of Leitch's drawings engraved by W. Floyd for the publication *Constantinople and the scenery of the seven churches of Asia Minor* (1838).[755] The two volumes, which contained descriptions of each site with illustrations mainly by Thomas Allom, belonged to a growing amount of illustrated travel literature on the Near East in the second quarter of the nineteenth century. Leitch's image was accompanied by a lengthy text, which described the fortress of Paramythia, 'towering above the town ... reposing on a vast rock in some places one thousand feet above the plain, and having the town spread over an inclined plain on the side of the mountain just under it'.[756] Given the fact that Leitch based his watercolour on a sketch supplied by the publishers, it is unsurprising that the work relies on conventional forms of depicting sublime landscape, and exhibits only cursory interest in the present inhabitants of the town shown in traditional dress in the foreground. This was in stark contrast to the detailed figure drawings of Near Eastern subjects produced by John Frederick Lewis who lived in Constantinople and Cairo in the 1840s. The inscribed date of '1855' on LL 3863 is a puzzle, given that the drawing must have been made c. 1838 around the time of the original commission; it seems likely that the artist annotated the drawing latterly.

Both LL 3863 and LL 3862 (p. 135) belonged to James Orrock (see pp. xiv-xvii, 146-49) who was a pupil of Leitch over a period of four years.[757]

753 WHL Inventory titled *Mountain Landscape with ruins and figures.*
754 A. MacGeorge, *Wm. Leighton Leitch, Landscape Painter: A Memoir* (London, 1884), p. 94.
755 *Constantinople and the scenery of the seven churches of Asia Minor* (London and Paris, 1838). LL 3863 is engraved in vol. II, facing p. 82.
756 Ibid., p. 82.
757 MacGeorge, *Wm. Leighton Leitch*, pp. 67-68.

**A Sicilian Village**[758]
LL 3862 (WHL 777, HH 396)

Watercolour and gouache with white heightening over pencil on wove paper
13.4 x 33.6 cm
Date: 1879

Inscr: WL. Leitch / 1879 (watercolour, lower right corner)

Annot: No. 3 [illeg.] Near Giardini. Sicily / W.L. Leitch. 124 Alexandra Road / St Johns Wood. N. W. (ink, on mount verso)

Prov: bt. from James Orrock by Lever, 1910

As part of his extended trip to Italy Leitch visited Sicily between October and December 1835.[759] He produced many sketches from this visit, using them to work up finished watercolours many years later, and he was still exhibiting views of Italy at the exhibitions of the Institute of Painters in Water-Colours during the 1870s and 1880s. LL 3862 is one such example and, despite the slightly different title recorded on the verso, may be the *Tower at Giardini, Sicily* exhibited at their 1879 exhibition.[760] *A Sicilian Village* exhibits Leitch's standard watercolour technique of laying on flat washes of colour and using gouache very sparingly, methods that found their root in the eighteenth-century 'tinted' drawing. Leitch found his inspiration in the Old Masters and in Turner's early watercolours, and saw the latter's later works and those of the Pre-Raphaelites as misguided. When exhibited, Leitch's watercolours such as LL 3862 would have been admired but viewed as thoroughly conservative by the last quarter of the nineteenth century.[761]

758 The full title given in the WHL Inventory is *A Sicilian Village, near Lake, with figures*.
759 MacGeorge, *Wm. Leighton Leitch*, pp. 54-55.
760 MacGeorge, *Wm. Leighton Leitch*, p. 118. A work of this title was exhibited as no. 344. It is possible that '44' is the illegible part of the inscription on the verso of the mount.
761 For the context in which Leitch was operating as a watercolourist, see Wilcox and Newall, *Victorian Landscape Watercolors*, p. 25.

## WILLIAM HESKETH LEVER

Bolton 1851-London 1925

**Nauders, Tyrol**[762]
LL 3864 (WHL 1675, TM 279, LP 23)

Pencil with touches of gouache on wove paper, laid down on board
24.9 x 37.8 cm (sight)
Date: c. 1867

Annot: Oct Nov 1867 (pencil, on backboard)

Prov: by descent to Sir William Hulme Lever, 2nd Viscount Leverhulme; given by him to the Trustees, 1929[763]

Exh: London, Royal Academy, *Lord Leverhulme*, 1980 (cat. 396)

LL 3864 is a faithful copy of a James Duffield Harding lithograph *Nauders, Tyrol* (a village in Austria) published in *Harding's Sketches at Home and Abroad* (1836).[764] Harding (1798-1863) was well known as a watercolourist and teacher and his volumes of lithographs were widely disseminated and copied. The attribution to William Hesketh Lever stems from a letter from the 2nd Viscount Leverhulme dated 19 July 1929, where he wrote: 'The drawing by my father was probably done when he was not less than twelve and not more than fourteen years of age'.[765] However, the annotation in an unknown hand on the backboard suggests that the work was made when Lever would have been 16. Another similar if more cumbersome pencil drawing, *Neath*, signed by Lever and likely to have been copied from a lithograph, is in the Leverhulme family archive.[766] LL 3864, along with two other drawings produced by Lever when a boy, were shown at the Museums Conference held in the Lady Lever Art Gallery on 29 October 1928.[767] Lever's son described his father's childhood interest in drawing at school, when it was 'the fashion to teach pupils to copy pictures rather than to practise freehand'. He described the 'natural talent' that his father's drawings showed 'for using a pencil. These copies indicate an obvious enthusiasm for drawing, and a painstaking sincerity coupled with a considerable degree of skill.'[768]

762 WHL Inventory titled *Alpine Village Scene*.
763 LL 3864 was offered to the gallery on 28 March 1929. The fact that Lever inventoried it as part of his own collection at Thornton Manor (at least by 1910-11) suggests that he regarded it without the modesty due to it.
764 J. D. Harding, *Harding's Sketches at Home and Abroad* (London, 1836), p. 35.
765 LLAG files.
766 I am grateful to Gavin Hunter, Honorary Archivist to the Leverhulme family, for allowing me access to the Leverhulme Archive.
767 LLAG files. These two drawings are listed in the WHL Inventory as *Shore scene with shipping* (WHL 1674) and *Lynton* (WHL 1676).
768 Quoted in Morris (ed.), *Lord Leverhulme*, p. 181 (cat. 396).

LL 3864

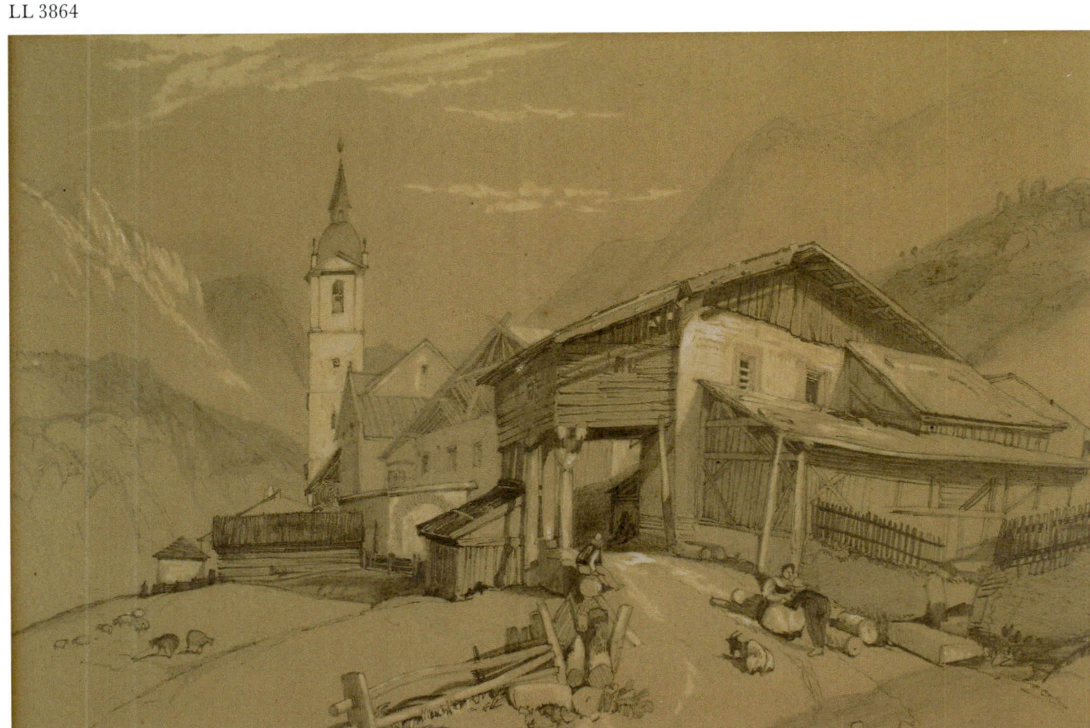

## JAMES DROMGOLE LINTON
1840 London–1916 London

**David Rizzio**
LL 3865 (WHL 864, HH 428)

Watercolour with gum arabic, heightened with white over pencil on wove paper
48.2 x 34.8 cm
Date: 1888

Inscr: JDLinton 1888 (watercolour, bottom right)

Prov: bt. from James Orrock by Lever, 1910[769]

Lit: Walter Wood, *Mary Queen of Scots, illustrated by Sir James Dromgole Linton and James Orrock* (London, 1906), illus. pl. 9, facing p. 44

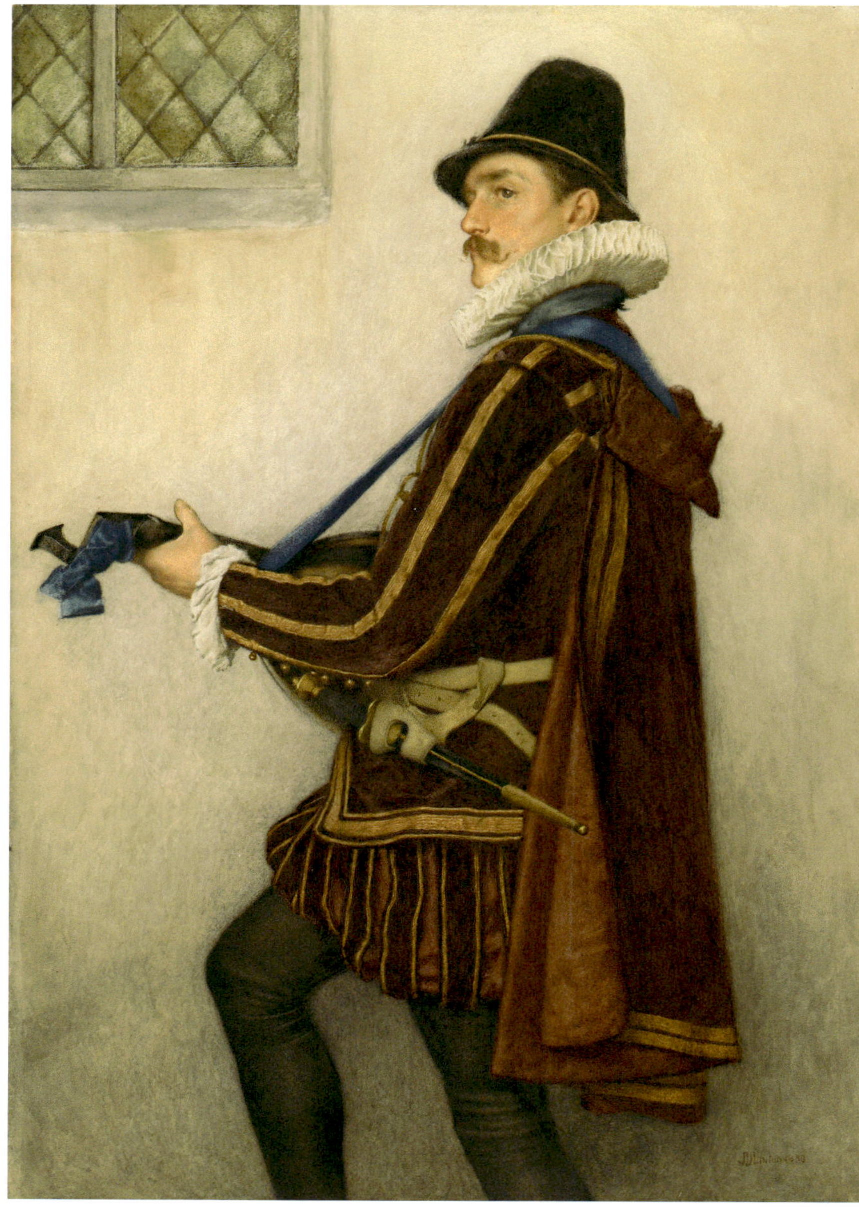

LL 3865

The WHL Inventory identifies LL 3865 as one of five pictures of associates of Mary, Queen of Scots purchased by Lever in 1910 from James Orrock. The others depicted *Janet Forster (Mary Seton)*, *Earl Murray*, *Lord Darnley* and *Lord Lindsay* and were sold at Christie's, 6 June 1958 (in pairs, as lots 67 and 69). Together with Linton's *Mary, Queen of Scots* (LL 3866 below, which Lever already owned) these five watercolours had been reproduced as part of a collaboration between Sir James Dromgole Linton and James Orrock to illustrate the life of Mary, Queen of Scots, accompanied by a history written by Walter Wood. While Orrock provided the landscape pictures, Linton's contribution, the six portraits apart, included a series of dramatic set pieces, among them a picture of Mary's execution reminiscent of Paul Delaroche's *Execution of Lady Jane Grey* (1833, National Gallery, London). Wood's text is notable for its rather melodramatic treatment of Mary's life.

Following the death of her father, James V, Mary was less than one year old when she was crowned Queen of Scotland in 1543. By the early 1560s Mary faced the problem of a country torn by Catholic and Protestant factions. A devout Catholic, she was regarded with suspicion by many of her subjects as well as by Elizabeth, the Protestant Queen of England, who feared her as she was the great-granddaughter of Henry VII and, to many English Catholics, the rightful heir to the English throne. Mary was conciliatory; she tolerated the Protestant lords and retained James Stewart, the Earl of Moray and leader of the Scottish Protestants, as her chief advisor, but she further alienated Elizabeth in 1565 by marrying Henry Stuart, Lord Darnley, who was a Catholic and also an English subject and another claimant to the English throne. Darnley proved an unsatisfactory husband and Mary refused to crown him consort. Frustrated by his lack of power and increasingly jealous of Mary's friendship with her private secretary, David Rizzio, Darnley entered into agreement with the key members of the Protestant nobility to murder Rizzio.[770] At the time of the murder, Mary was heavily pregnant and gave birth to James, future king of Scotland, on 19 June 1566. James's birth was met with great general rejoicing and temporarily helped to repair Mary's reputation, but this was again damaged the following year when she was implicated in the murder of Darnley. One of Mary's lords, James Hepburn, 4th Earl of Bothwell, who was widely held responsible for the assassination, abducted Mary as she returned to Edinburgh after visiting her son. She was taken to Dunbar castle where Bothwell allegedly imprisoned and raped her.

They then married according to the Protestant rites on 15 May 1567. Mary was widely perceived as having married her husband's murderer and public revulsion followed which culminated in uprising. Mary was imprisoned at Lochleven Castle where she was forced to abdicate in favour of her one-year-old son, James, with Moray as regent. On 2 May 1568 Mary escaped Lochleven, but her army was defeated at the Battle of Langside on 13 May and against all advice she fled to England to seek assistance from Queen Elizabeth. Elizabeth held her captive for the next nineteen years. As both Catholic and heir to the English throne, Mary, whether with or without her knowledge and consent, became the focus of numerous plots to assassinate Elizabeth and was eventually implicated in one such attempt

769 1910 Inventory, one of *Five studies of figures in costume for Mary Queen of Scots*, valued at £15 each.

770 Walter Wood, *Mary Queen of Scots, illustrated by Sir James Dromgole Linton and James Orrock* (London, 1906), pp. 8–9, reflects that the fate of Rizzio must have been a cause of the corruption of the English monarchy: 'Who, for instance, can read of the murder of Rizzio, without thinking both of its effect on the Queen during her pregnancy, and of its influence on her child and his descendants? Cowardice and deceit came into the family with James … It may be that the historian should detect the shade of Rizzio behind Charles the First on the Scaffold at Whitehall.'

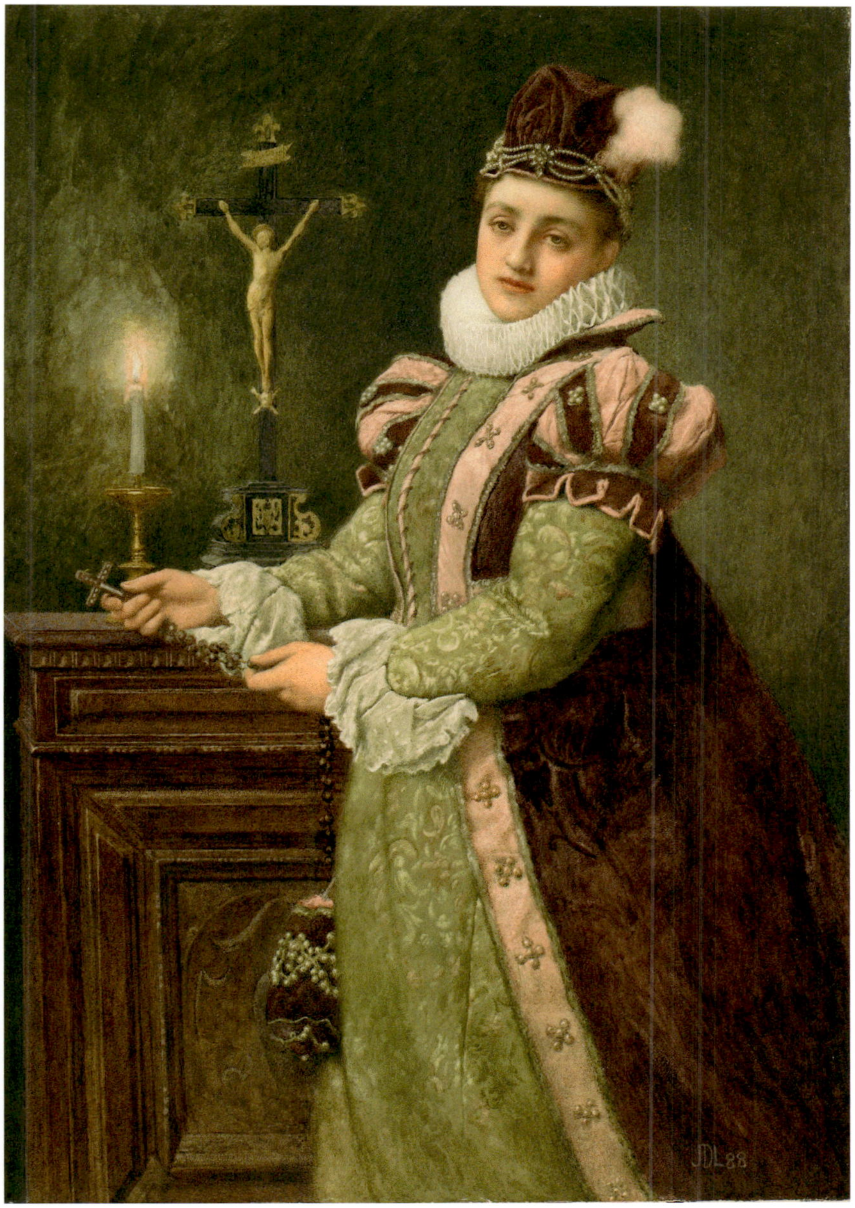

LL 3866

known as the 'Babington Plot'. She was tried for treason and beheaded on 8 February 1587.

After studying at J. M. Leigh's School in Newman Street, Linton began his artistic career as a black-and-white illustrator for *The Graphic*. He started exhibiting in 1863, first at the Dudley Gallery and later at the Royal Academy (1865) and other London exhibitions. He soon established himself as a popular and successful artist and his achievements were recognised by the Institute of Painters in Water-Colours where he was made an associate in 1867, a member in 1870, and was elected president twice (1884–98 and 1909–16). He was knighted in 1885. His work, primarily watercolours and oils of historical scenes and figure subjects, was greatly influenced by the medieval and Stuart subject-matter of George Cattermole (see p. 42) and of his brother Charles and shows a delight in colourful costume and rich draperies.

In LL 3865 Rizzio is depicted as an elegant and poised courtier and the lute that he holds may be a direct reference to his position as one of Mary's musicians. The conception of Rizzio, and expecially of his costume, owes more to Wood's Victorian reinterpretation of his role in Mary's story than a commitment to historical accuracy. Nevertheless, his face would appear to have been based upon the most recognisable image of Rizzio, a slight portrait probably intended as a miniature by an unknown contemporary artist that was widely known through engravings (for example, that of Charles Wilkin, published in 1814). In fact, this contemporary image is generally held to be inaccurate, since contemporary accounts of Rizzio disparaged his appearance.
CG

### Mary, Queen of Scots
LL 3866 (WHL 306, H 178)

Watercolour heightened with white over pencil on wove paper
48 x 34.4 cm
Date: 1888

Inscr: JDL '88 (watercolour, bottom right); JO [monogram] (stamp, verso, on paper glued to backboard)

Prov: Jordan Art Gallery, 1897;[771] bt. from James Orrock by Lever, 1907[772]

Lit: Walter Wood, *Mary Queen of Scots, illustrated by Sir James Dromgole Linton and James Orrock* (London, 1906), illus. as frontispiece

This picture of Mary, Queen of Scots, while influenced by Francis Clouet's soft-featured portraits of the young Mary in France, is essentially a late Victorian re-interpretation of the subject. Her rich dress is an inaccurate rendering of Elizabethan costume and the pose and expression a highly sentimentalised portrayal of Mary's tragic and difficult life. The picture was used as the frontispiece to Wood's history of the life of Mary, Queen of Scots and the accompanying text reflects a similarly emotive and empathetic approach to the subject: '[Mary's] story has made a world-wide appeal to the imagination of men, affecting Schiller and Alfieri no less than the historians; but the mystery of her life remains unsolved. None can estimate correctly her real nature, nor give true measure of her character.'[773] Linton has attempted to bring a greater degree of characterisation to his picture of Mary than is apparent in the other portraits of the series. While Mary's expression is thoughtful and introspective, her costume and bearing present the trappings of a dignified queen; meanwhile, the crucifix on the altar and rosary in her hands recall her Catholic beliefs, which provoked the mistrust that led ultimately to her downfall.

It has been suggested that the likeness for this portrait was taken from Ada Caroline Price (born 1868), wife to Edmund Meredith Crosse. Linton would appear to have been a family friend and it is also possible that Crosse (of Crosse and Blackwell) would have known Lever.[774] There is evidence that Lever owned LL 3866 before passing it to Orrock,[775] and purchased it back before going on to acquire from him the remaining portraits in the series (see LL 3865 above).
CG

771 Label on verso.
772 1907 Hill Inventory.
773 Wood, *Mary Queen of Scots*, foreword, facing frontispiece.
774 LLAG files: H. T. Fowle, grandson of Ada Crosse, letter to Lucy Wood, 9 September 1991.
775 Wood, *Mary Queen of Scots*, foreword, states that the portrait of Mary Queen of Scots was then (1906) in Lever's possession.

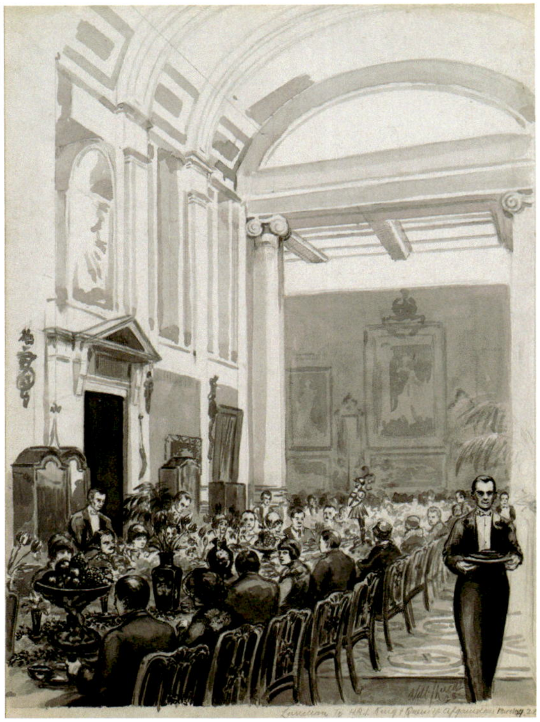

LL 3978

## WILLIAM JAMES LUCAS
dates and places of birth and death unknown

**The King and Queen of Afghanistan at the Lady Lever Art Gallery**
LL 3978

Watercolour over pencil with touches of gouache on wove paper
51.5 x 38.3 cm
Date: 1928

Inscr: Will | Lucas / 28. (pencil, bottom right); Luncheon To H.R.I. King + Queen of afganistan March 29.28 (pencil, bottom right)

Prov: presumably acquired or commissioned by the Trustees in 1928

Lucas was a local painter and etcher who exhibited regularly at the Liverpool Autumn Exhibitions between 1924 and 1930. He lived in Port Sunlight village.

King Amanullah (1892–1960) and Queen Surayya (1899–1968) of Afghanistan visited Port Sunlight on 29 March 1928 as part of a general tour of Europe and the United Kingdom. They were greeted at the west entrance of the Lady Lever Art Gallery by Lord and Lady Leverhulme and a Guard of Honour before making the short journey to the Lever Brothers factory at the opposite end of the village. After a tour of the site they returned to the Lady Lever Art Gallery where a lunch was held in the Main Hall. The event was described in great detail in the *Port Sunlight News*:

The tables were very beautifully decorated with pink carnations and roses and between the King and Queen, who faced each other across the central table, was a lovely bed of lilies of the valley, from which arose Onslow Ford's silver *chef d'oeuvre* of *St George and the Dragon*.[776] Rare specimens, from the Lady Lever collection, of Oriental pottery of the famous periods were among other decorations of the long length of tables which accommodated some hundred and fifty guests.[777]

This view looks to the south end of the Main Hall where Sir David Wilkie's portrait of Queen Victoria (LL 3598) was originally hung. The portrait to its left is Franz Xavier Winterhalter's portrait of Prince Albert (LL 3525).

Amanullah was king of Afghanistan from 1919 to 1929. His reign was marked by independence from the United Kingdom and rapid modernisation. Queen Surayya campaigned for women's rights and in particular the right of all Afghan women to have an education. The rapid pace of change inevitably produced strong reactions. Shortly after their return from Europe, King Amanullah was forced to abdicate. He and his wife lived the rest of their lives in exile in Europe.
SP

776 *St George and the Dragon* by Edward Onslow Ford (LL 3145) was purchased by William Hesketh Lever in 1911. Ford was one of Lever's favourite artists and the two became good friends.

777 The royal visit is described in full in *Port Sunlight News*, 11 April 1928, pp. 114–20.

## JOHN EVERETT MILLAIS
1829 Southampton–1896 London

***Sir Isumbras at the Ford*: sketch for the composition**
LL 3604 (WHL 2740)

Pencil on paper
12.2 x 17.1 cm
Date: c. 1856

Inscr: slate colour (pencil, right edge)

Prov: [?] Fine Art Society, 1901; Mrs G. E. Turner, 90 Clifton Hill, St John's Wood; her sale, Christie's, 31 January 1913 (lot 76): bt. in (8 gns); bt. from Geraldine Turner by Lever, 1916 (15 gns)[778]

Exh: [?] London, Fine Art Society, *Millais*, 1901 (cat. 31, as *Original Sketch for Sir Isumbras*); Birmingham, Birmingham Museum and Art Gallery, *The Pre-Raphaelite Brotherhood*, 1947 (cat. 187); Port Sunlight, Lady Lever Art Gallery, *The Pre-Raphaelites - Their Friends and Followers*, 1948 (cat. 138); Liverpool, Walker Art Gallery and London, Royal Academy, *Millais*, 1967 (cat. 361); Bolton Museum and Art Gallery and tour, organised by the Arts Council, *The Drawings of John Everett Millais*, 1979 (cat. 58); Port Sunlight, Lady Lever Art Gallery and tour, *Pre-Raphaelite Drawings*, 2006–2008 (no cat. no)

Lit: John Guille Millais, *The Life and Letters of Sir John Everett Millais, P.R.A.* (London, 2 vols, 1899), vol. I, illus. p. 312; Mary Bennett, *Artists of the Pre-Raphaelite Circle: The First Generation* (London, 1988), pp. 132, 136, illus. p. 136

Millais came to London from Jersey with his parents in 1838, and entered Sass's drawing school in the same year. A child prodigy, he enrolled at the Royal Academy Schools in 1840, their youngest-ever pupil. He exhibited his first work, *Pizarro Seizing the Inca of Peru*, in 1846 at the age of 16. He met William Holman Hunt at the Royal Academy Schools and, together with Dante Gabriel Rossetti, they formed the Pre-Raphaelite Brotherhood. Following the attack on his painting *Christ in the House of his Parents*, exhibited at the Royal Academy in 1850, Ruskin wrote to *The Times* defending the young artist. In 1853 Ruskin invited Millais to accompany him and his wife Effie to Glenfinlas in Scotland. Millais and Effie fell in love and, following the annulment of her marriage to Ruskin, were married in 1855. From this period Millais abandoned painting with microscopic attention to nature, and began to produce more saleable works in a looser style. By the 1870s he was earning £30,000 a year, and had established a reputation as the country's leading society portraitist. Disraeli, Gladstone and Carlyle were among his numerous sitters at his studio in Palace Gate, Kensington. At the same time Millais produced illustrations for many popular magazines and books, including the *Cornhill Magazine*. In 1885 Millais became the first English artist to be made a Baronet. He died in 1896, a few months after being elected president of the Royal Academy.

Although Millais's painting *Sir Isumbras at the Ford* (Lady Lever Art Gallery, LL 3625, fig. 45,

778 There is a letter in the LLAG files from Geraldine E. Turner to Lever acknowledging his cheque for £15 15s. Her address is recorded as 90 Clifton Hill, St John's Wood.

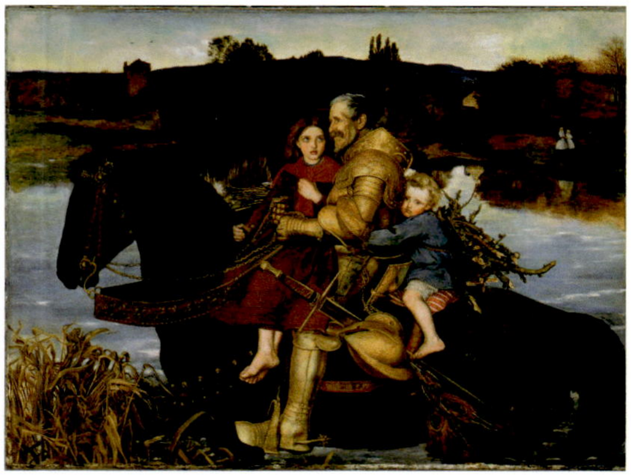

fig. 45. John Everett Millais, *Sir Isumbras at the Ford*, 1857, oil on canvas, 125.5 x 171.5 cm, National Museums Liverpool, Lady Lever Art Gallery

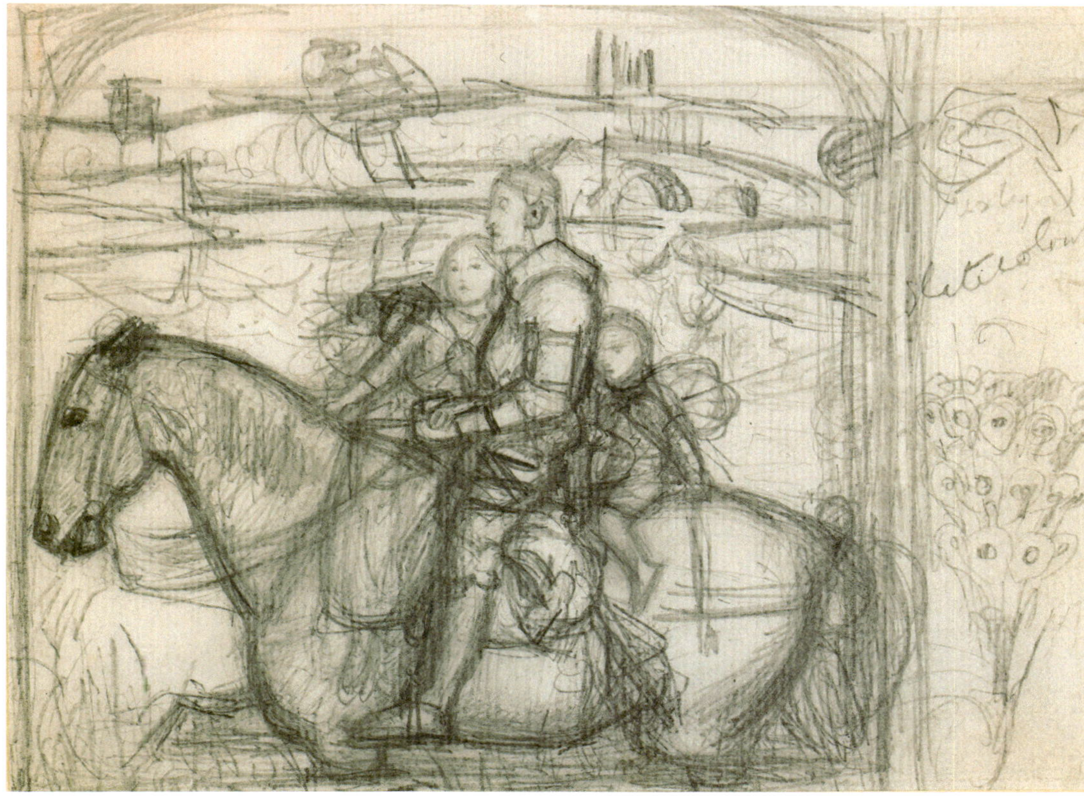

LL 3604

LL 3603

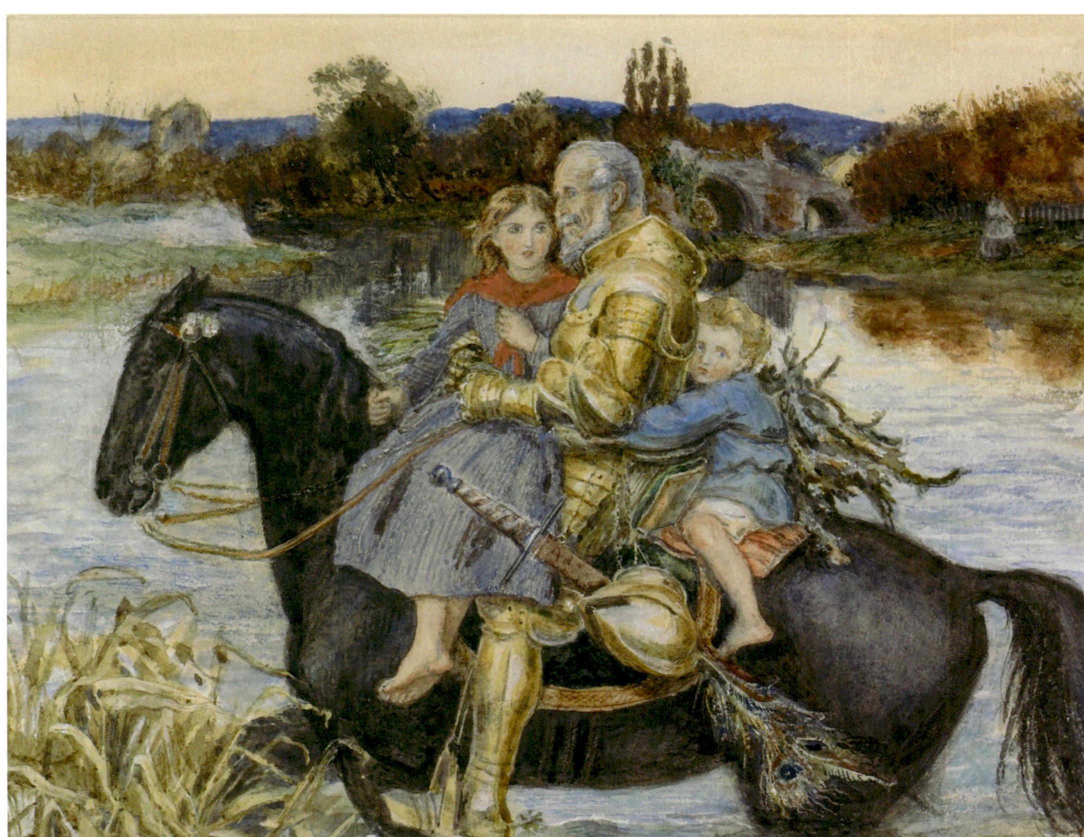

p. 139) had been exhibited at the Royal Academy in 1857, over thirty years later the artist was still making alterations to the composition. The original studies for the painting, of which LL 3604 is one of a number held in public collections, are often the most reliable sources for establishing the appearance of the original composition. In contrast to the finished work, in this early conception of the subject the horse ridden by Sir Isumbras fills the entire length of the canvas. Millais repainted the horse at least four times in an attempt to create a faithful likeness. The pencil lines along the right-hand edge of this drawing demonstrate Millais's attempts to work out how far the creature's tail should extend. It also appears from this pencil sketch that Millais may have considered a square rather than a rectangular format, with an arched top. The final painting, which has vertical folds, one at the left and two down the right-hand side, demonstrate that Millais continued to struggle with the shape of the composition.

Sir Isumbras was the hero of a medieval romance and, in conformity with the numerous paintings of chivalrous knights exhibited at the Royal Academy in the mid-nineteenth century, he was expected to be both chivalrous and dashing.[779] From this sketch it is evident that Millais intended Sir Isumbras to appear younger and more debonair than he does in the finished painting. In the poem upon which Millais loosely based his subject, Isumbras is described as being in his youth when he ferries the woodcutters' children across the river. Julie Codell has suggested that Millais later chose to give the knight an aged appearance as a result of a 'desire to move away from idealizing the knight' and make him appear more realistic.[780] Further

779 Christine Poulson illustrates a number of these paintings by the Pre-Raphaelites and their contemporaries in *The Quest for the Grail: Arthurian Legend in British Art, 1840–1920* (Manchester and New York, 1999).

780 Julie F. Codell, 'Sir Isumbras, M. P: Millais's Paintings and Political Cartoons', *The Journal of Popular Culture*, vol. 22, no. 3 (winter 1988), pp. 29–47.

studies of the head of the knight are in the collections of the Ashmolean Museum, Oxford, and the Whitworth Art Gallery, Manchester, the sketch in the latter collection again portraying a younger looking hero. The model for the knight in LL 3604 and the Whitworth study has not been identified, but Colonel Campbell, an officer quartered in Perth, is recorded as being the sitter in the finished painting. J. G. Millais, who recounts in detail the history of *Sir Isumbras* in his biography of his father, recalls that Nellie Salmon modelled for the young girl (M. H. Spielmann believed it was Millais's daughter, Alice Gray, although this is hardly likely given that Millais only married Effie in 1855).[781] J. G. Millais also recalled that the artist's son Everett modelled for the boy, though this again is hardly possible since Everett Millais was born only one year before the painting was exhibited.

The Lady Lever drawing reveals that Millais thought carefully about the relationship between the woodcutters' children and the knight. In the drawing the girl holds on to the knight's hand, whereas in the painting she holds together the two ends of her shawl. (Her gaze is also altered in the final work.) In addition, the young boy has his arm on the back of the horse in the drawing but, in the painting, they appear to be tightly wrapped around the knight. The words 'slate colour', written in the margin, are directed at the load on his back which appear as a bundle of faggots in the painting, alluding to the occupation of his father.

Millais painted *Sir Isumbras* in Perthshire and, according to his wife Effie, went on daily excursions for around a fortnight from the end of October to the beginning of November to the Bridge of Earn, to paint the old medieval bridge and the Ochill hills from under the bridge. The medieval stone bridge is sketched in lightly in the top right of the composition, as well as the medieval tower of Elcho Castle located on the south bank of the River Tay.[782] The main features of the background are sketchily drawn, but in their final form, which suggests that this study was made after Millais had begun painting the landscape.[783]

HB

781 Marion H. Spielmann, *Millais and His Works: With Special Reference to the Exhibition at the Royal Academy* (London, 1898), p. 96

782 Millais, *Life and Letters*, vol I, p. 306.

783 Bennett, *Artists of the Pre-Raphaelite Circle*, p. 132.

## Study for *Sir Isumbras at the Ford*
## LL 3603 (WHL 20)

Gouache with gum arabic and white heightening on paper
14 x 17.7 cm
Date: probably 1863

Inscr: JEM [monogram] (gouache, bottom right)

Prov: sold by the artist, 7 December 1863, to Agnew's; sold by Agnew's to Samuel Mendel, 30 December 1863; bt. back from Mendel by Agnew's, 12 February 1872; sold by Agnew's to John Heugh, 11 March 1872; his sale, Christie's, 24 April 1874 (lot 32); bt. by Agnew's (with *Vale of Rest*, £220 10s 1d); sold to John Knowles, 1 May 1874; his sale, Christie's, 19 May 1877 (lot 52); bt. by J. & W. Vokins (95 gns); J. Grant Morris; his sale, Christie's, 23 April 1898 (lot 47); bt. by Laurie (£294); Arthur Sanderson, 1904; his sale, Christie's, 3 July 1908 (lot 16); bt. by Agnew's (125 gns); sold by Agnew's to Mrs George McCulloch, 14 July 1908; George McCulloch; his sale, Christie's, 30 May 1913 (lot 213); bt. by Gooden and Fox (£357) for Lever (£365 18s 6d)

Exh: Bradford, *Exhibition of Fine Arts: Works of Art in the Cartwright Memorial Hall*, 1904 (cat. 463); London, Royal Academy, *Collection of George McCulloch*, 1908 (cat. 310); Birmingham, Birmingham Museum and Art Gallery, *The Pre-Raphaelite Brotherhood*, 1947 (cat. 94); Port Sunlight, Lady Lever Art Gallery, *The Pre-Raphaelites – Their Friends and Followers*, 1948 (cat. 139); Brisbane, Queensland Art Gallery and tour of Australia and New Zealand, *Exhibition of British Watercolours 1850–1914*, organised by the Empire Art Loan Exhibitions Society, 1952–53 (cat. 72); Liverpool, Walker Art Gallery and London, Royal Academy, *Millais*, 1967 (cat. 364); Bolton Museum and Art Gallery and tour, organised by the Arts Council, *The Drawings of John Everett Millais*, 1979 (cat. 61)

Lit: A. C. R. Carter, 'The Chief Picture Sales of 1898', *The Art Journal* (1898), p. 308; Mary Bennett, *Artists of the Pre-Raphaelite Circle: The First Generation* (London, 1988), pp. 136–37, illus. p. 136

In 1859 Millais wrote that '[Gambart] overwhelms me with small commissions, ... which all pay mightily well'.[784] To support his growing family Millais produced numerous watercolour studies of his illustrations and paintings, the former fetching between £15 and £25 and the latter anything up to £100.[785] In order to maintain their rarity, the copies were rarely dated and, in addition, were never identical to the original paintings. It is thought that this watercolour postdates the exhibition of Millais's painting *Sir Isumbras at the Ford*. D. T. White certainly commissioned a small version of *Sir Isumbras*, as a letter dated 20 July 1859 from Millais to his wife, Effie, indicates: 'The Knight leaves by carrier today and I go up to town with a little sketch of it for White ...'[786] LL 3603 is probably the watercolour version that Effie records in her account book under 1863 which was sold in that year to another dealer, Agnew's.[787]

784 Quoted in Malcolm Warner, 'The Professional Career of John Everett Millais to 1863' (unpublished PhD thesis, Courtauld Institute of Art, London, 1985), p. 123. Rossetti also wrote about the advantage of producing watercolour copies. In a letter to James Smetham on 13 November 1864 he wrote: 'The great thing with dealers now is to get men of name to make moderate sized watercolours for mounting. Of these they make portfolios ... and sell the collection together to cotton spinners and the like. It is far more profitable to them, & to the artists too, than anything else can be'; William E. Fredeman (ed.), *The Correspondence of Dante Gabriel Rossetti* (Cambridge, 7 vols, 2002–06), vol III, p. 212.

785 Malcolm Warner, *The Drawings of John Everett Millais* (exh. cat., Bolton Museum and Art Gallery and tour, organised by the Arts Council, 1979), p. 15.

786 Millais, *Life and Letters*, vol. I, p. 348.

787 Bennett, *Artists of the Pre-Raphaelite Circle*, p. 136.

Millais's painting appeared in the catalogue accompanying the Royal Academy exhibition of 1857 as *A Dream of the Past: Sir Isumbras at the Ford*.[788] It is likely that Millais devised the theme of the painting with *Punch*'s art critic, Tom Taylor, whose poem on the medieval romance was published in the accompanying catalogue to the exhibition.[789] From the outset the depiction of the horse tormented Millais. He worked outdoors in the stable yard at Annat Lodge, his wife's Perthshire home, against the biting Scottish weather in order to accurately paint the creature, only relieved by wine and soups brought to him by Effie.[790] The publisher, Gambart, who saw the painting before the Royal Academy exhibition, offered Millais £800 for it but complained that the horse was too small.[791] Millais's reworking was disastrous, and Taylor identified the horse in the poem with the name 'Grande Destrere', foreseeing the bewilderment of the critics. His efforts at mollification were short-lived, however, and the reviewers for the *Athenaeum* and *The Times* gleefully described the horse as 'monstrous' and 'impossible', respectively.[792] The horse was subsequently repainted after the 1857 exhibition, and again at the time it was exhibited at the Grosvenor Gallery in 1886, but never wholly successfully. In a letter to Effie, Millais despaired that 'I find all men dislike the great size of the Knight picture – Farrer, Gambart, White, all. They say it is too large for a room, and almost all the purchasers are without galleries.'[793]

The proportions of the horse are more realistic in this watercolour than in the painting as it appears today after numerous reworkings. LL 3603 also reveals Millais's original intention for the horse to have plain leather trappings (the trappings were made more ornamental on the recommendation of R. H. Benson, who bought the painting in 1887).[794] Millais was highly competent with the watercolour medium, and LL 3603 shows his ability to produce minute touches with the pigment. His works in this medium were always a modest size, and he never attempted to produce watercolours on the scale of his contemporaries, William Holman Hunt and Ford Madox Brown.

HB

788 Millais's paintings *News from Home* (private collection) and *Escape of a Heretic* (Museo de Arte de Ponce, Ponce, Puerto Rico) were included in the same exhibition.

789 Both artist and poet may have been inspired by *Sir Isumbras* from the *Thornton Romances* which had been published by the Camden Society in 1844.

790 Millais, *Life and Letters*, vol. I, p. 309.

791 The painting was sold eventually to the novelist, Charles Reade, in 1858 for £400 on condition that Millais made further alterations.

792 Quoted in Bennett, *Artists of the Pre-Raphaelite Circle*, pp. 132–33.

793 Letter from Millais to Effie, May 1857, quoted by Warner, *Drawings of John Everett Millais*, p.109.

794 At this time Millais also retouched the horse, and strengthened the neck and girth.

## Study for the figures in *The Black Brunswickers*

**Verso: a slight pencil outline of the same figures, on the same scale in reverse**
LL 3644 (LP 12)

Pencil on wove paper
19.7 x 12 cm
Date: c. 1860

Prov: F. M. Barwell, 1898; S. W. Barwell;[795] his sale, Christie's, 22 November 1926 (lot 54); bt. by Bird (£10 10s); bt. by Gooden and Fox for the Trustees (£11 1s 6d)

Exh: London, Royal Academy, *Millais*, 1898 (cat. 225); Port Sunlight, Lady Lever Art Gallery, *The Pre-Raphaelites – Their Friends and Followers*, 1948 (cat. 144); Port Sunlight, Lady Lever Art Gallery and tour, *Pre-Raphaelite Drawings*, 2006–2008 (no cat. no.)

Lit: Mary Bennett, *Artists of the Pre-Raphaelite Circle: The First Generation* (London, 1988), p. 149, illus. p. 149

This sheet, which has studies on both sides of the paper, is one of a number Millais made of the entangled lovers in his painting of 1860, *The Black Brunswickers* (Lady Lever Art Gallery, LL 3643, fig. 46). The study on the verso is only lightly drawn, whereas on the recto Millais has added firmer outlines and shading. The painting was intended as a companion to *A Huguenot* (Makins Collection) which Millais had exhibited eight years earlier. Both imagine scenes of love in adversity at different moments within history, the first set in sixteenth-century Paris and the latter in 1815, shortly before the Battle of Waterloo. The critics and public alike favoured the pathos of such subject-matter, and Millais hoped that a buyer would be forthcoming after the cool reception of his 'mood pictures', *The Vale of Rest* (Tate) and *Spring (Apple Blossoms)* (Lady Lever Art Gallery, LL 3624), which had been exhibited at the Royal Academy in 1859.

The recto of this drawing shows Millais's original conception for *The Black Brunswickers* with the soldier positioned to the right of his lover (a deliberate echo of *A Huguenot*).[796] Although Millais eventually reversed the positions of the lovers, a sketch for the painting in the Ashmolean Museum, Oxford, similarly situates the soldier on the right side of the woman; this study is adjacent to a sketch of the lovers in *A Huguenot*. In both LL 3644 and the finished painting the woman, anxious for the life of her lover, pushes the door closed in an attempt to prolong his stay, while her left arm is placed firmly across his chest. The placement of the soldier's right hand around the door knob in this study contrasts with further studies at Tate and in the Ashmolean, and also with the final painting, in which the soldier has his left arm raised and in the act of opening the door.

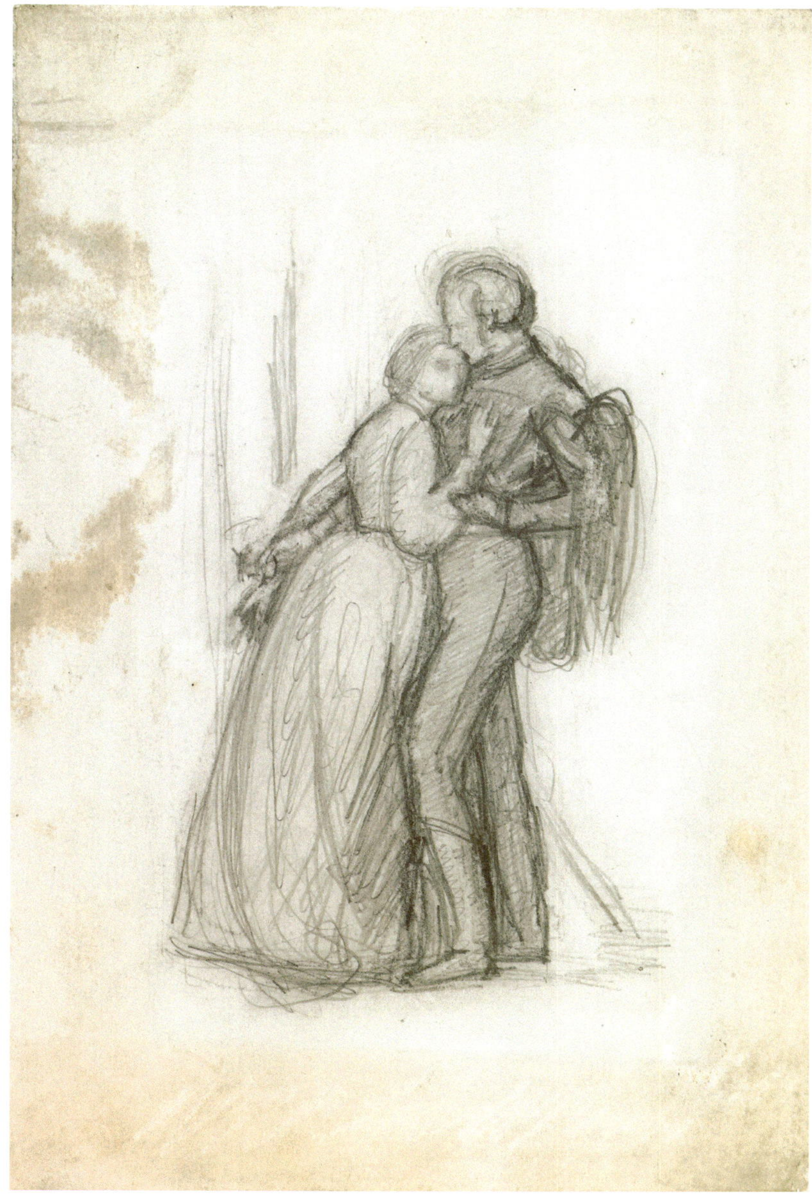

LL 3644

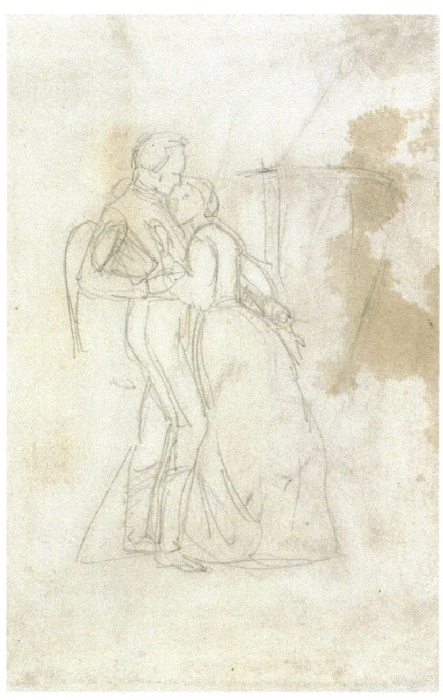

LL 3644 (verso)

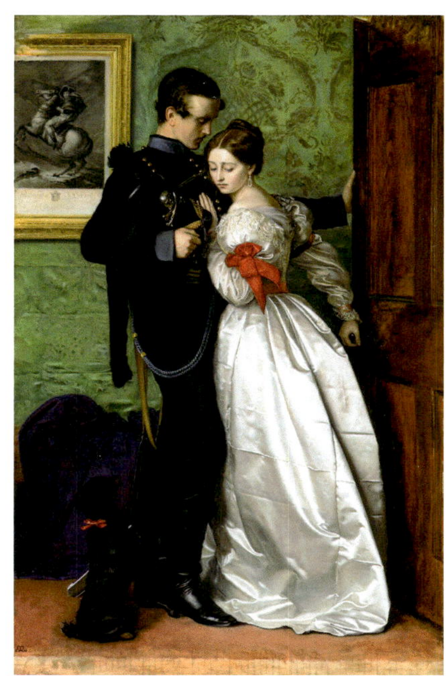

fig. 46. John Everett Millais, *The Black Brunswickers*, 1860, oil on canvas, 104 x 68.5 cm, National Museums Liverpool, Lady Lever Art Gallery

795 Bennett, *Artists of the Pre-Raphaelite Circle*, p. 149, gives Mrs A. L. Bickmore, Tonbridge, as a possible owner after F. M. Barwell.

796 Millais also originally intended to portray the woman in the action of sewing a crape on to the soldier's arm as a token of mourning, again in order for viewers to make the comparison with *A Huguenot*, in which a Catholic woman binds a white cloth around the arm of her Huguenot lover in order to hide his true identity.

The Brunswickers had been formed with the purpose of defeating the Napoleonic forces following their occupation of Germany, Napoleon being represented by an engraving after Jacques-Louis David's painting *Napoleon Crossing the Alps* that hangs on the wall in the finished painting. Their heroic deaths caught the imagination of the Victorians, and their dangerous exploits were grimly detailed in the British press.[797] Millais chose a private soldier who he spotted on parade at Albany Street Barracks to model for the Brunswicker; his physique described by the artist as 'a splendid type of masculine beauty'.[798] This sketch reveals that Millais may have already begun to research his distinctive attire, which consisted of a black broadcloth uniform with a silvered death's head badge worn in the hat. The model for the woman was Kate Dickens, the younger daughter of Charles Dickens (Millais formed a lasting friendship with Kate Dickens, and he painted a striking portrait of her in 1880.)[799] She began modelling from January 1860 when she was 21, her visits to his studio always chaperoned, and her path never crossing that of the model for the Prussian soldier who held on to a lay figure, while Kate Dickens leaned against a wooden stake. Millais intended the work to record an episode during the Duchess of Richmond's ball which was held in Brussels on 15 June 1815, the night before the Battle of Quatre Bras (during which the Brunswickers suffered severe casualties). This explains the ball gown she wears in the painting, although Millais may not have conceived this idea while he was working on the sketch as she appears in a plain crinoline.

Further studies for *The Black Brunswickers* are held in the collections of Tate, Birmingham Museums and Art Gallery and the Ashmolean. In addition two watercolour versions exist, one in the British Museum and a half-length in the Whitworth Art Gallery, Manchester.

HB

797 Their heroic charges could also be witnessed on stage in J. H. Amherst's highly successful play *The Battle of Waterloo*, which was performed at Astley's in 1824, and throughout the following decades.

798 Unfortunately the soldier died of consumption the following year; Millais, *Life and Letters*, vol. I, p. 353.

799 See Lucinda Hawksley, *Katey: The Life and Loves of Dickens's Artist Daughter* (London, 2007), p. 197.

## WILLIAM JAMES MÜLLER

Bristol 1812–Bristol 1845

### Near Wallenstadt[800]

LL 3867 (WHL 798, HH 358)

Watercolour with gum arabic, touches of gouache and scratching out, over pencil on paper
15.5 x 25 cm
Date: probably late 1830s

Prov: bt. from James Orrock by Lever, 1910[801]

Exh: Bristol, City Art Gallery, *William James Müller*, 1962 (cat. 44)

Lit: Cyril G. E. Bunt, *The Life and Work of William James Müller of Bristol* (Leigh-on-Sea, 1948), p. 13, illus. pl. 2, p. 65

Müller grew up in Bristol, participating in the artistic life of the city and was apprenticed to the landscape artist James Baker Pyne (see pp. 158–59). He first exhibited at the Royal Academy in 1833, and in the same year made two trips to Wales. Müller travelled widely: in 1834 he left for a seven-month sketching tour on the Continent before returning to Bristol in early 1835. In 1838 and 1839 he embarked on an extended trip to Greece and Egypt, and on his return to England in 1839 settled in London where he joined a society of artists known as the Clipstone Street Academy. In 1843 he embarked on his final trip, an eight-month tour to Lycia, Turkey. Müller exhibited paintings at the British Institution and the Royal Academy in 1845, but was rejected as an associate at the latter institution. Müller had already been ill the previous year and now exhausted from over-exertion and profoundly dejected, his health suffered. In May 1845 he returned to Bristol where he died at the age of 33.

LL 3867 does not bear any specific resemblance to the scenery of Lake Wallenstadt, where Müller spent a week or so during his visit to Switzerland in 1834.[802] In fact, Müller did not produce finished watercolours of this sort during these tours, instead concentrating on pencil drawings and watercolour sketches done on the spot (there are examples in the Tate, Birmingham Museums and Art Gallery and the Huntington Art Collections, San Marino, California).[803] The work probably dates from the late 1830s, when Müller worked up these subjects to meet the demands of patrons.[804] In 1834 Müller had spent several days sketching chalets at the village of Splügen[805] and it is possible that LL 3867 relates to a (now unknown) sketch of this area.

800 LL 3867 is titled *Near Walbonstadt [sic], Switzerland* by Tatlock, p. 134.

801 There are three possible candidates for LL 3867 in Müller's studio sale, Christie's, 1 July 1850, lots 93, 277, and 296; a less likely possibility is lot 44 in the Müller sale at Christie's, 1 April 1859, *Swiss Cottage Near Wallenstadt*.

802 Müller's visit to the area near Lake Wallenstadt is described in N. Neal Solly, *Memoir of the Life of William James Müller* (London, 1875), p. 37.

803 See Francis Greenacre and Sheena Stoddard, *W. J. Müller, 1812–1845* (exh. cat., Bristol, Museum and Art Gallery, 1991), pp. 92–93.

804 Sheena Stoddard, email correspondence, August 2007.

805 Solly, *William James Müller*, p. 38.

### The White House

LL 3868 (WHL 776, HH 411)

Watercolour on wove paper
35.6 x 53.5 cm (shaped as an arch, later altered to make rectangle)
Date: 1840s

Prov: bt. from James Orrock by Lever, 1910

Although the location is uncertain, LL 3868 dates from the 1840s when Müller was sketching outdoors, both in oil and watercolour. The generalised treatment of the trees and the unfinished sky suggest that this was a watercolour done on the spot. The work may derive from an excursion made when he was living in London in the early 1840s, or even from his visit to Lynmouth, Devon from July to September 1844. Despite the watercolour's rectangular appearance, the two top corners have been added to an original arch shape. This curved format is probably Müller's original; he used oval canvases for oils towards the end of his life, and there are some examples among his watercolours too.[806] Both LL 3868 and LL 3979 below are characterised by Müller's mature watercolour technique, which with its use of a large brush to add broad washes of colour is in contrast to some of his more tightly handled watercolour studies of the early and mid-1830s such as *The Lagoon, Venice* (1834, Tate).[807]

806 See, for example, *Interior of my room at Makri* (1844) in Greenacre and Stoddard, *W. J. Müller*, p. 159 (cat. 166), illus. col. pl. 42; also *Eel baskets on the Thames* (c. 1843), in Greenacre and Stoddard, *W. J. Müller*, p. 131 (cat. 121), illus. b&w.

807 N02340; watercolour and pencil, 11.6 x 41.4 cm; Greenacre and Stoddard, *W. J. Müller*, p. 93 (cat. 61), illus. b&w.

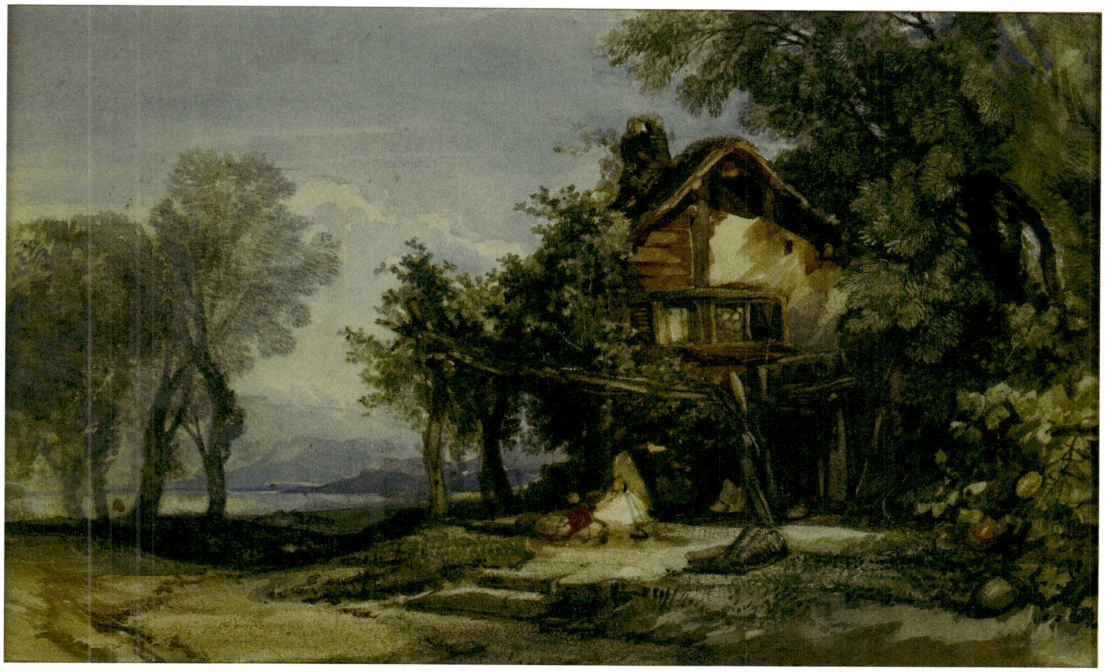

LL 3867

LL 3868

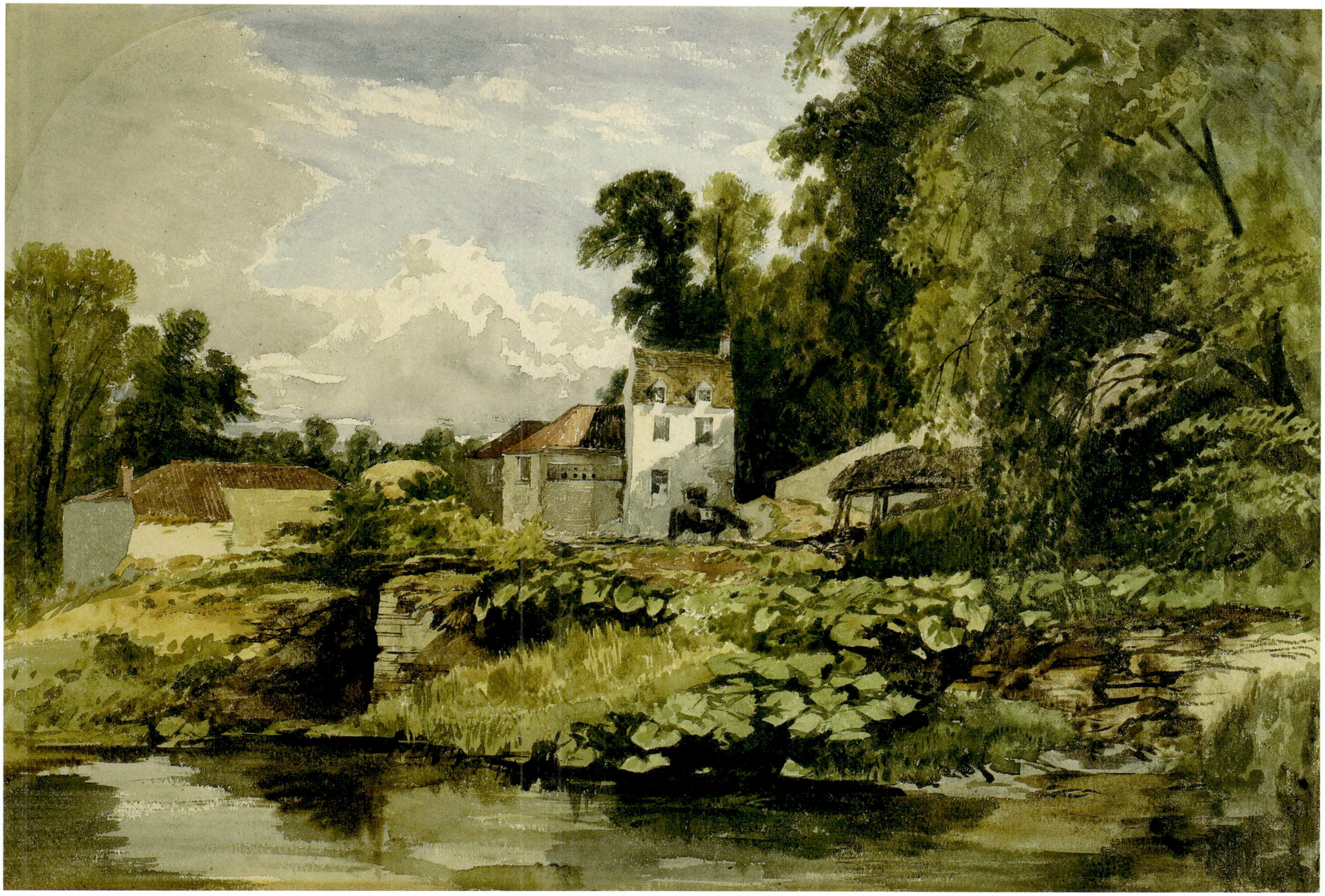

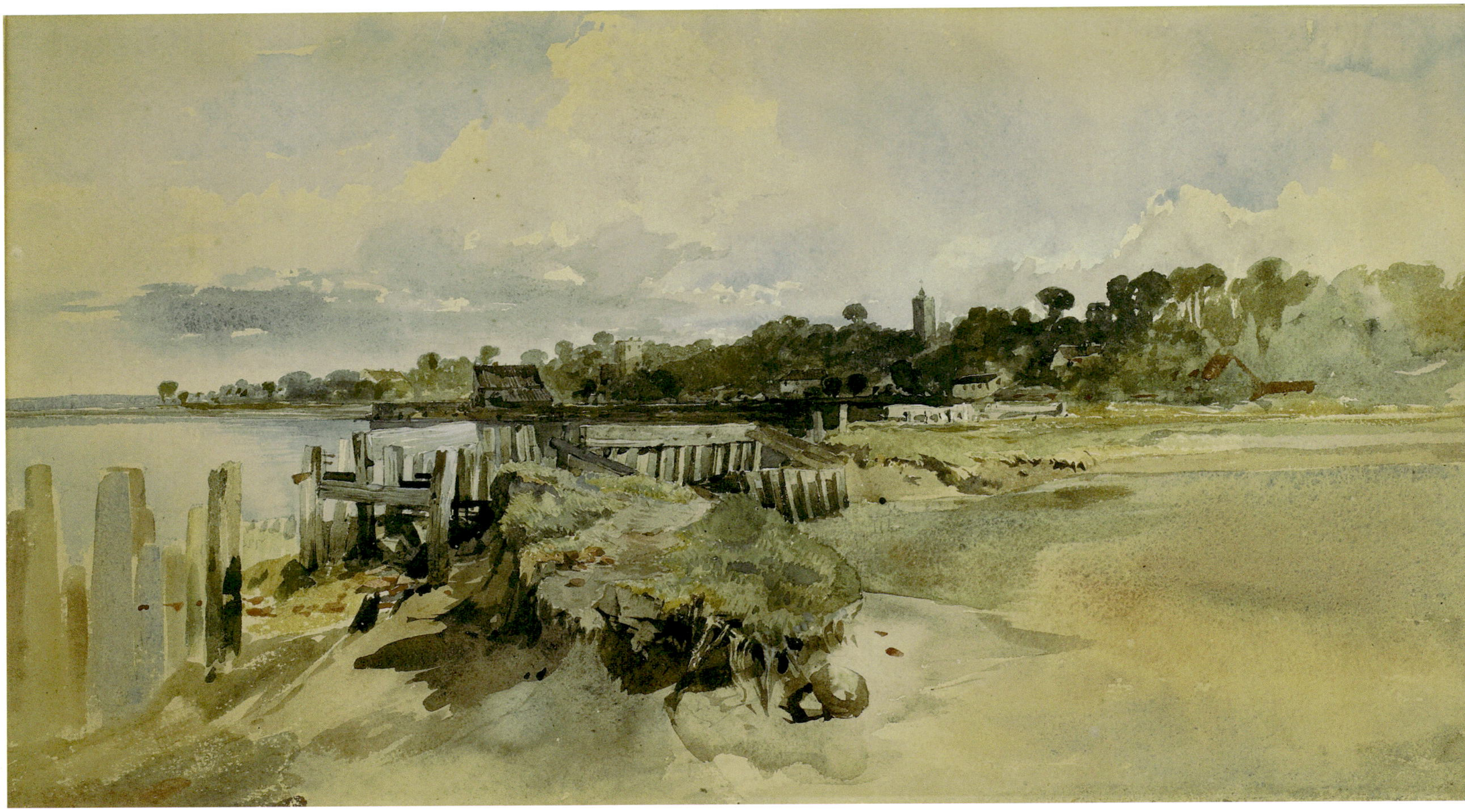

LL 3979

**Gillingham, Kent from the Medway**[808]
LL 3979 (WHL 753, HH 355)

Watercolour over pencil on wove paper
27 x 50.5 cm (sight)
Date: early 1840s

Prov: bt. from James Orrock by Lever, 1910[809]

Exh: Perth, Art Gallery of Western Australia and Australian tour, *Exhibition of Early British Water-colours*, organised by the Empire Art Loans Exhibition Society, 1948–49 (cat. 138)

LL 3979 is a view of the town of Gillingham, Kent, seen from the edge of the River Medway at low tide.[810] The tower of Gillingham church is visible among the trees in the background. LL 3979 dates from the early 1840s, when Müller was based in London and often took boating excursions down the Thames to the Medway with James Chisholm Gooden, a fellow watercolourist, and other friends. They would embark at Blackwall in a hired boat and sail to the mouth of the Thames and then up the Medway to Gillingham. The party would sketch by day before landing at riverside inns for the night. Müller made at least two sketches a day and Gillingham in particular was the subject of numerous oil paintings (for example, *Young Anglers*, 1843, Walker Art Gallery, Liverpool).[811]

Several features of LL 3979 indicate that this was a watercolour sketch made outdoors and would have been completed in a few hours: the limited colour palette, the use of blotting in the middle distance on the beach and among the trees in the background, as well as the generalised treatment of the forms. All these elements show the artist concerned to capture the essence of the scene. Müller often wrote about the pleasure he got from sketching and although he aspired to recognition as an oil painter, it was as a rapid and fluent sketcher (both in oils and watercolours) that he made his contemporary reputation. In 1875 his biographer Nathaniel Neal Solly wrote that the artist's standing rested on his sketches rather than his finished works.[812]

808 In the WHL Inventory, the work is titled *A river side-study from nature*.
809 There are four possible candidates for the work in the Müller sale at Christie's, 1 April 1859, lots 29, 43, 90 and 108.
810 This has been identified by Beverley Williams of the Royal Engineers Museum, Gillingham, Kent, email correspondence, June 2007.
811 The Walker work is also known as *Gillingham, Kent*. For other examples, see Greenacre and Stoddard, *W. J. Müller*, p. 126.
812 Solly, *William James Müller*, p. 233.

## AFTER WILLIAM MULREADY
1786 Ennis, co. Clare, Ireland–1863 London

**Study of a female nude**
LL 3795 (WHL 3390)

Black and red chalks on paper
46.3 x 33.6 cm
Date: possibly after 1857

Annot: ESK (in an oval, embossed blind-stamp, recto, lower left)

Prov: Charles Fairfax-Murray; his sale, Christie's, 14 December 1917 (lot 23); bt. by Gooden and Fox (7 gns) for Lever (£7 10s 9d)

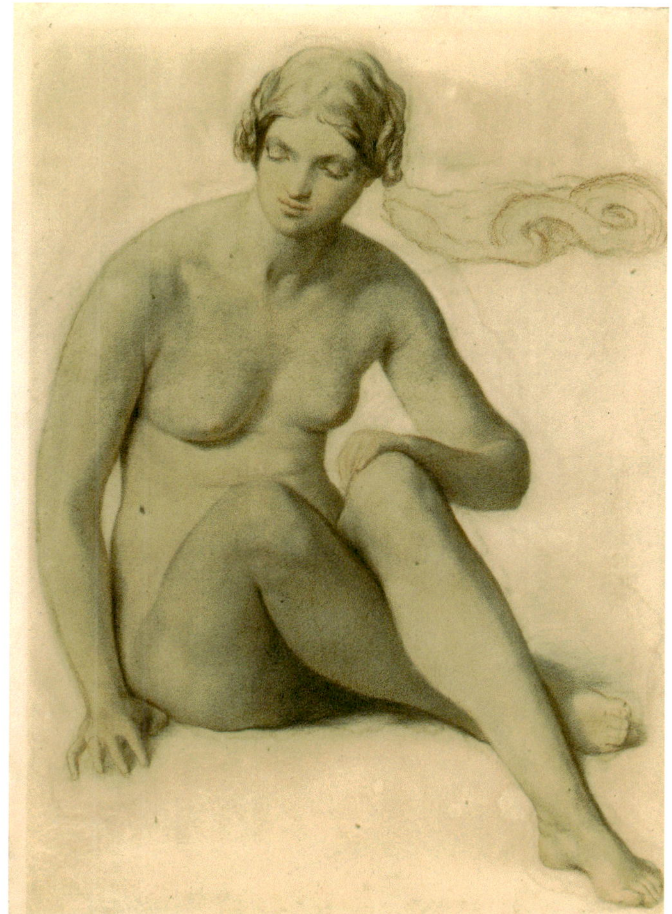

LL 3795

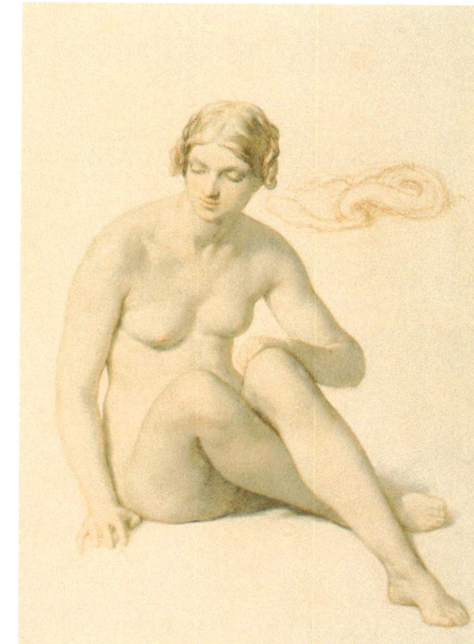

fig. 47. William Mulready, *Study of Female Nude*, 1840s or 1850s, black and red chalks on paper, 48.4 x 35.9 cm, V&A Images/Victoria and Albert Museum

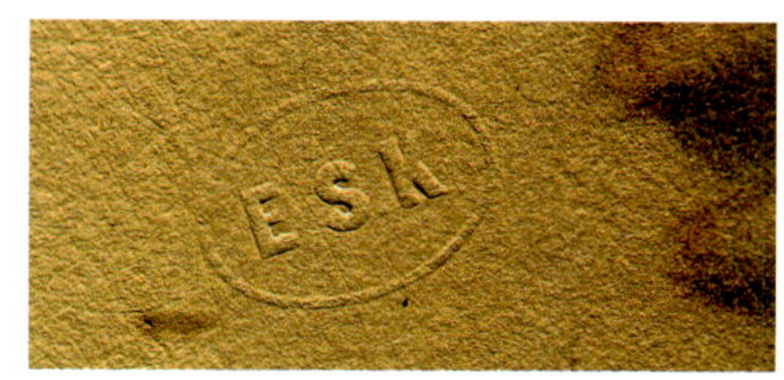


fig. 48. 'ESK': embossed blind-stamp, on recto lower left of *Study of a female nude* (LL 3795)

Lever purchased this drawing as by Mulready and it was subsequently catalogued by Tatlock with the same attribution.[813] A strikingly similar drawing with the same serpent motif and of comparable size is in the Victoria & Albert Museum (fig. 47) as part of the Sheepshanks gift and was probably purchased by John Sheepshanks (1787–1863) directly from the artist.[814] It arrived in the Victoria & Albert Museum in 1857, and one suggestion may be that LL 3795, which although a good copy lacks the delicacy of the Sheepshanks drawing, was copied after that date by a student at the South Kensington Art Schools (from 1863 the National Art Training School). LL 3795 was certainly made after 1829, the date of the watermark of the original. The Lady Lever drawing has the embossed stamp 'ESK' on the paper (fig. 48): one possibility, which supports the former suggestion, is that this mark stood for '[Board of] Education South Kensington' (or 'Examined South Kensington') and was applied to drawings by students who had sat the South Kensington School's examinations.[815]

Around 1791 Mulready moved with his family to London. He was admitted to the Royal Academy Schools in 1800 following tuition by the neo-classical sculptor Thomas Banks. His subject-matter during the first decade of his career was diverse and included landscapes, interiors in the Dutch style, literary scenes, history paintings and portraits. By 1816, the year when he was elected to membership of the Royal Academy, he was painting elaborately composed domestic genre scenes. His exquisite painting technique, with thin washes and stippling of brilliant pigments, inspired the Pre-Raphaelites, who nominated him to the Hogarth Club. Mulready's reputation was high in his own lifetime and he received a number of honours and awards, including chevalier in the Légion d'Honneur following his contribution of nine paintings to the 1855 *Exposition Universelle* in Paris.

Mulready attached particular importance to drawing, producing academic life-studies of both male and female nudes throughout his career. The artist soon gained fame as a draughtsman; in 1806 he received the Royal Academy's silver medal for draughtsmanship. Despite its watermark of 1829, the Victoria & Albert Museum's drawing dates from the 1840s or 1850s when Mulready started to use red and black chalks, producing studies of nudes in a variety of poses and lights, working not only at the Royal Academy's Life School but also at the Kensington Life Academy. The original drawing demonstrates the artist's exquisite skill in using subtle tones of light and dark to create the flesh tones and soft, rounded forms of the female body.

LL 3795 belonged to Charles Fairfax-Murray (1849–1919), who had been a studio assistant to Rossetti, Burne-Jones and William Morris during the 1860s and 1870s. Murray turned increasingly to art-dealing in the late 1870s, buying Italian Old Masters as well as Victorian paintings and drawings.

813 WHL Inventory, p. 436. See also Tatlock, p. 134, where the work is titled *Eve*.

814 The Sheepshanks gift of over 500 oils, drawings and sketches by Mulready was given to the Victoria & Albert Museum in 1857. The Victoria & Albert Museum drawing (F.A.74) measures 48.4 x 35.9 cm; the paper is dated with a watermark of 1829.

815 As yet, there is no generally accepted explanation of this 'ESK' stamp. Stephen Calloway has suggested that 'ESK' stood for '[Board] of Education, South Kensington' (email correspondence, February 2008) although he has agreed that 'Examined South Kensington' seems equally plausible. In both cases, it is odd that there is no record of this acronym in the Royal College of Art archives (Neil Parkinson, email correspondence, October 2007). It is not that of any known paper manufacturer and was not listed by Fritz Lugt (Rhea Blok, Fondation Custodia/Collection Fritz Lugt, Paris, email correspondence, October 2008). Lugt did record that the artist and collector Edward Sherard Kennedy (fl. 1863–90) used 'ESK', although this was a perforated mark; it is possible, however, that he used more than one. There is no record of LL 3795 in Kennedy's sales (Christie's, 3 February 1894 and 13 February 1894).

## HENRY NINHAM

1793 Norwich–1874 Norwich

**The Staircase, Strangers' Hall, Norwich**
LL 3980 (WHL 2197)

Watercolour over pencil, with touches of gouache on wove paper
32.6 x 23.1 cm (sight)
Date: nineteenth century

Prov: bt. from B. T. Batsford by Lever, 8 June 1915 (£3 3s)

Henry Ninham was trained by his father, a heraldic painter and copperplate engraver whose business he continued. He drew old Norwich buildings and exhibited architectural and street views at the Norwich Society of Artists between 1816 and 1831. He also produced prints and published collections of Norwich and Norfolk views.

Ninham made a number of views of Strangers' Hall: in 1846 it was reported that he had engraved parts of it and would 'shortly publish an etching of the interior'[816] and there are over 20 representations of the building by him in the Castle Museum, Norwich. These include an oil and a related pencil study that show the staircase from much the same viewpoint as LL 3980.[817]

Strangers' Hall – a former house, now a museum – was built at various dates from the early fourteenth century onwards. The staircase and the bay window containing it were added in 1627 for the mayor, Francis Cock.[818]
JoS

816 *Archaeological Journal* (1846), p. 197.
817 Castle Museum, Norwich, 1946.141:F and 1929.89.4:F. I am grateful to Norma Watt for her help with this entry.
818 N. Pevsner and B. Wilson, *Norfolk 1: Norwich and the North-East* (London, 1997), pp. 272–74.

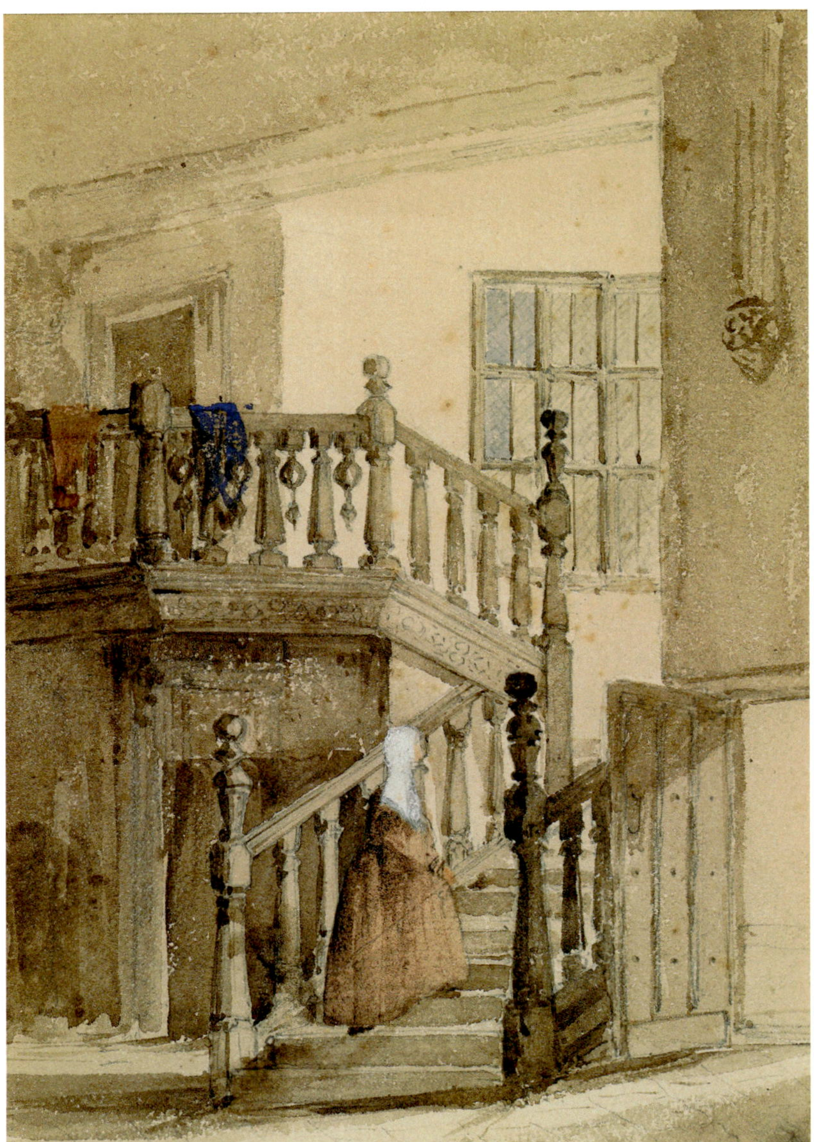

LL 3980

## JAMES ORROCK

1829 Edinburgh–1913 Shepperton-on-Thames, Middlesex

**Landscape with sheep and ruins**
LL 2989

Watercolour, gum arabic, touches of gouache with black chalk and pencil on wove paper
12.5 x 17.3 cm (sight)
Date: 1851

Inscr: Sep. 1851. J.O. (pencil, bottom left)

Annot: Study Old / Ruins (pencil, on mount, verso) 1169 (blue crayon, on mount, verso)/ No. 5 (red crayon, on mount, verso)

Prov: probably bt. from James Orrock by Lever, 1910[819]

The artist, collector and part-time art dealer James Orrock initially trained in dentistry and medicine, studying in Edinburgh and Leicester.[820] In 1853 his marriage prompted a move to Nottingham where he established a dental practice. During this period Orrock studied drawing and painting at the Nottingham School of Design and began collecting watercolourists from an older generation, including Anthony Vandyke Copley Fielding, Peter DeWint and David Cox.[821] In 1866–67 he abandoned his practice to move to London with the intention of focusing on his art. He took lessons from William Leighton Leitch (see pp. 134–35) and joined the Institute of Painters in Water-Colours as associate in 1871 and as a member in 1875. In London Orrock began to collect on a large scale, concentrating on British paintings and favouring works by artists such as Reynolds, Gainsborough and Constable. In the 1880s and 1890s he wrote and lectured extensively, championing the British landscape tradition and the medium of watercolour. He produced a large number of works, mainly watercolours which are close stylistically to the work of Cox and DeWint, whose work he favoured and collected. His watercolours were exhibited at Dowdeswell's in New Bond Street in 1886 and 1887 and again at Agnew's in 1889.[822] Orrock's practice as a dealer has been clouded by assertions made by contemporaries that he was forging works himself, or more recently that he

819 LL 2989 was probably one of the large number of watercolours acquired by Lever from Orrock in 1910, listed (but not identified by title) in the 1910 Inventory, pp. 69–71. LLAG files: a note on the accession card also indicates that LL 2989 and LL 3981–83 were originally held by Lever Brothers (i.e. presumably at the soap factory in Port Sunlight) and were transferred to the gallery at a later, unknown date.
820 For biographical detail on Orrock and also lengthy quotations from his writings on art, see Webber, *James Orrock*. For an interpretation of Orrock's collecting activities, see Edward Morris, 'James Orrock, dentist, artist, patron, collector, dealer, curator, connoisseur, forger, propagandist', *Visual Culture in Britain*, vol. 6, no. 2 (2005), pp. 85–98.
821 Webber, *James Orrock*, vol. I, p. 16.
822 Morris (ed.), *Lord Leverhulme*, p. 22.

had links to a forgery factory.[823] Lever bought the entire contents of Orrock's art collection on three separate occasions, in 1904, 1910 and 1912, and received a substantial number of fakes as a result (see for example, 'After David Cox' and 'David Cox', pp. 66–69).[824]

LL 2989-90 and LL 3981-83 are among about 1,000 drawings and watercolours and about 60 paintings by Orrock himself which were acquired by Lever in 1910 and 1912.[825] Most of these were sold or given away after Lever's death in 1925.[826]

LL 2989 is inscribed on the mount Study Old Ruins; the structure on the far right may in fact be one of the round corner towers of the fourteenth-century moated Scotney Castle, Kent. In 1851, the study's inscribed date, Orrock may have been resident in Leicester studying dentistry as a pupil assistant to Mr Williamson;[827] at the same time he took watercolour lessons from John Burgess of Leamington. During this period Orrock travelled about the countryside filling sketchbooks, often with John Burgess, and the two may have visited Scotney Castle. With its loose, free drawing style and liberal use of black chalk and pencil under-drawing, this watercolour sketch bears a strong resemblance to some of David Cox's watercolours of Wales from the 1840s, which combine lively marks in pencil or black chalk with wash (see, for example, *Watermill at Trefriw, near Llanrwst* in Birmingham Museums and Art Gallery).[828] Orrock's watercolours throughout the 1860s and 1870s continued to show his affinity with Cox's work but this is a particularly early example.

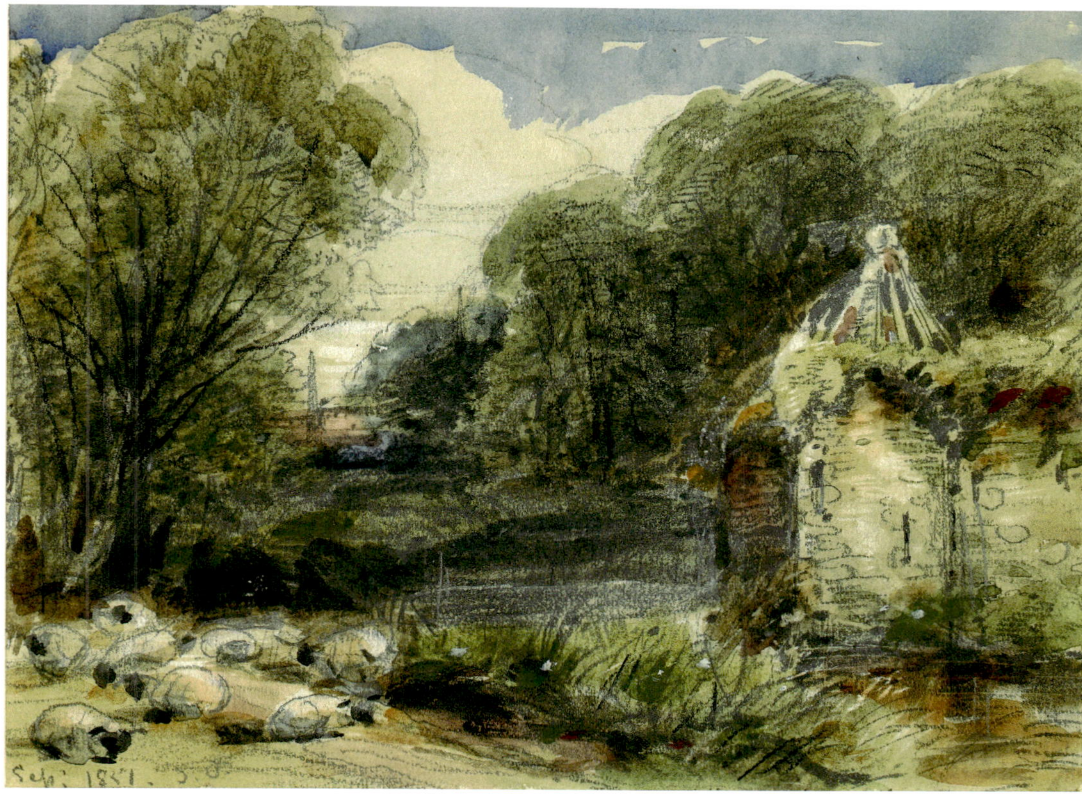

LL 2989

LL 3983

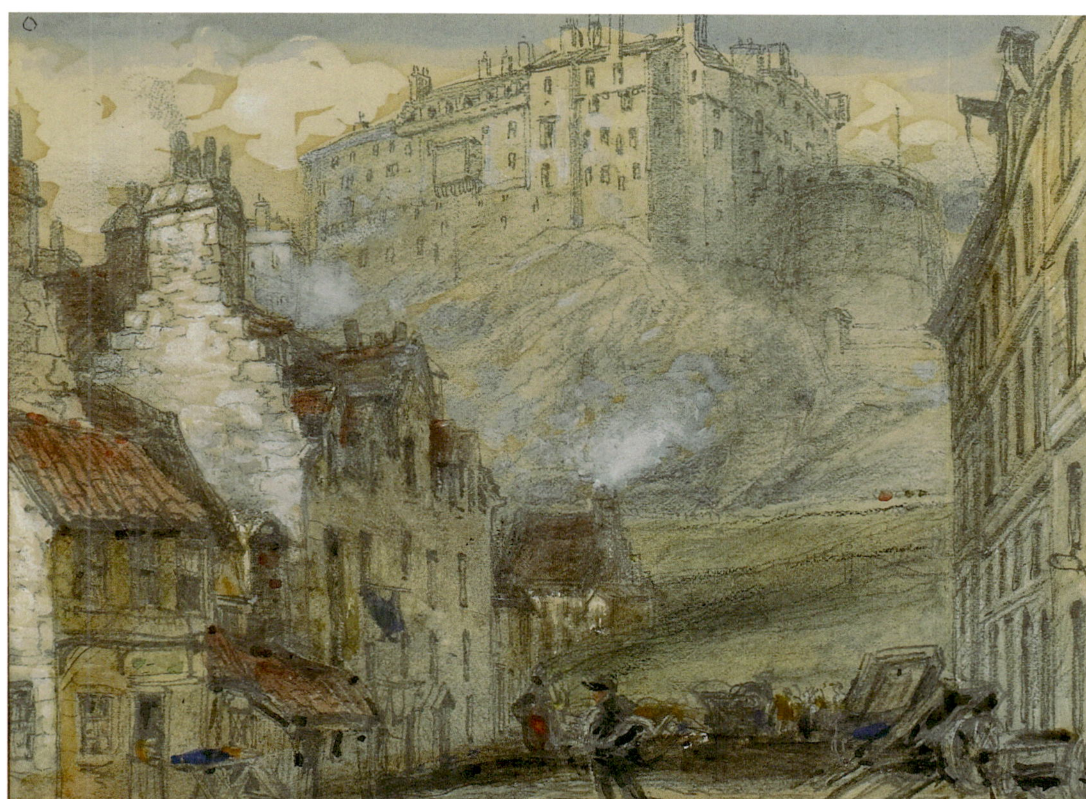

823 The assertion that Orrock forged at least one Turner was made by W. G. Rawlinson and quoted in C. J. Holmes, *Self and Partners* (London, 1936), pp. 207–08. For the suggestion that Orrock had a 'studio' that produced Constable forgeries, see Rhyne, 'Constable Drawings'; Nugent, 'David Cox Jr'.

824 This was particularly the case with Lever's third bulk purchase from Orrock in 1912. About 30 imitations of the work of Constable, Cox, Crome and other artists of that period formerly owned by Orrock remain in the Lady Lever Art Gallery; see the individual entries in Kidson, *Earlier British Paintings*.

825 1910 Inventory; 1912 Inventory.

826 One painting by Orrock, *Sandpits, Milford, Surrey* (LL 3134), still remains in the Lady Lever Art Gallery. See Morris, *Victorian and Edwardian Paintings*, pp. 100–01.

827 Orrock's precise chronological movements are not certain; it is known, however, that he was in Leicester c. 1850 before his marriage in 1853 and subsequent move to Nottingham.

828 Wildman, *David Cox*, p. 120 (cat. 122), illus. b&w.

## Edinburgh Castle from the Vennel
LL 3983 (HH 1412)

Pencil, watercolour with touches of gouache and traces of black chalk on wove paper
12.9 x 17.7 cm (sight)
Date: probably 1851

Inscr: 1851 (pencil, bottom left corner, partially obscured by mount); Edinb (pencil, bottom right)

Prov: probably bt. from James Orrock by Lever, 1910[829]

Lit: Byron Webber, *James Orrock, R.I.: Painter, Connoisseur, Collector* (London, 2 vols, 1903), vol. I, illus. pp. 4–5

LL 3983 is illustrated in Byron Webber's 1903 biography of James Orrock, where it is titled *Edinburgh Castle, From the Grassmarket*.[830] In fact, it represents a view of the castle from the Vennel, an area of Edinburgh city centre nearer to the castle than the Grassmarket. If the inscribed date of 1851 is correct, Orrock could have made this sketch in Edinburgh: following time studying at the Leicester Dispensary for the Study of Surgical Operations, Orrock returned to Edinburgh briefly to finish his medical studies before moving to Nottingham around 1853.[831] Webber described Orrock as filling his sketchbook with numerous drawings of Edinburgh, although he does not give a date for this.[832] In 1903, when this work appeared in Webber's monograph, it was described as a pencil sketch and was illustrated lacking the gouache now present; presumably Orrock added this prior to selling it probably around 1910.

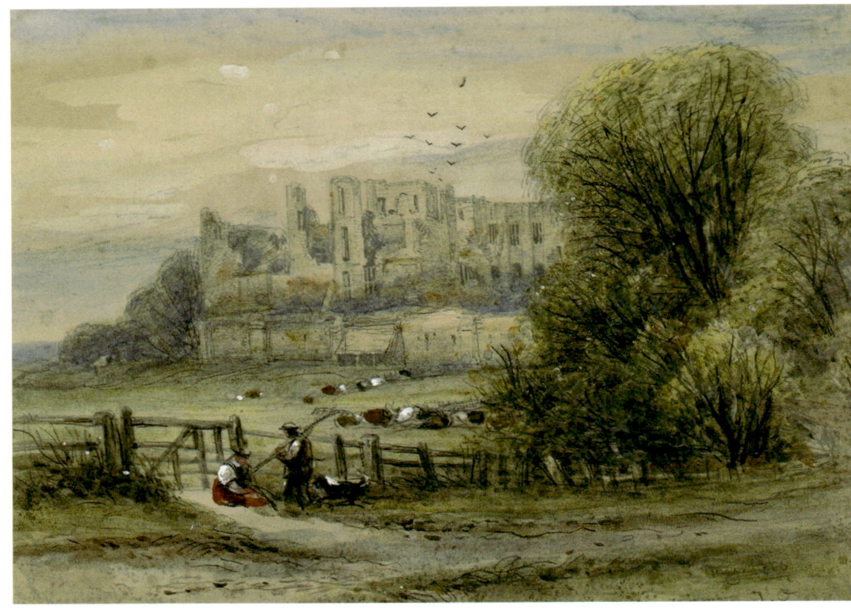

LL 3981

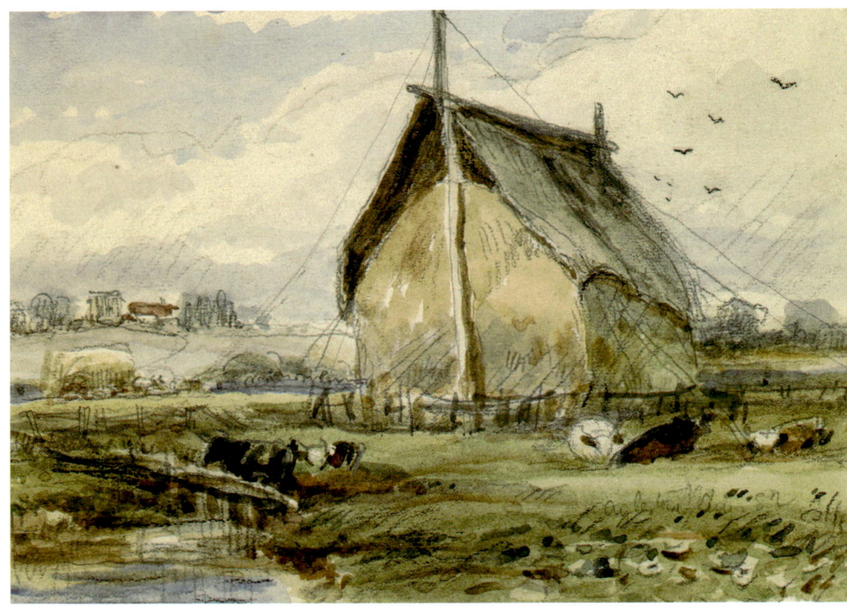

LL 2990

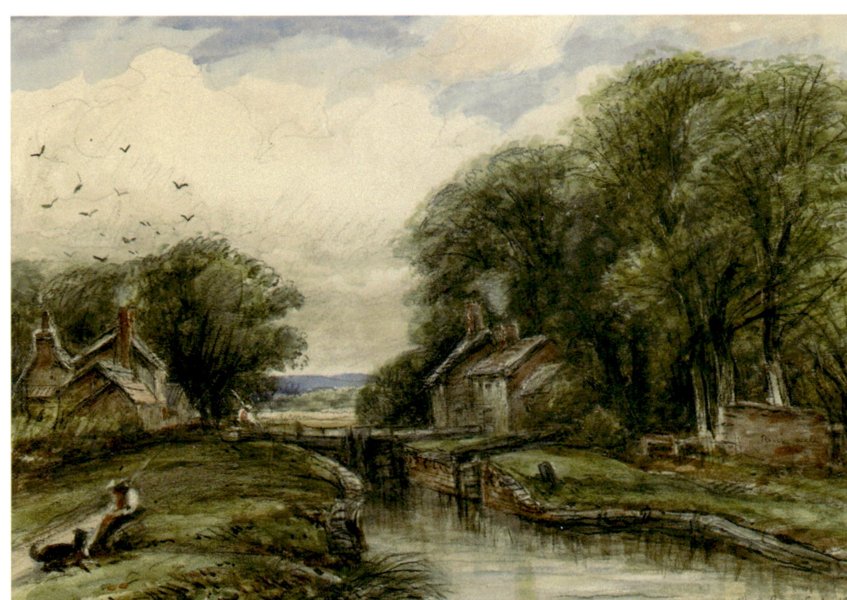

LL 3982

829 LL 3983 was probably one of the large number of watercolours acquired by Lever from Orrock in 1910, listed (but not identified by title) in the 1910 Inventory. LLAG files: a note on the accession card also indicates that LL 3983, LL 2989 and LL 3981-82 were originally held by Lever Brothers (i.e. presumably at the soap factory in Port Sunlight) and were transferred to the gallery at a later, unknown date.

830 Webber, *James Orrock*, vol. I, facing p. 4.

831 Orrock's precise chronological movements are not certain but it is known that he returned to Edinburgh briefly after a period of study in Leicester. The date of c. 1853 is based on his marriage to Susan Gould in this year, after which he is known to have moved to Nottingham.

832 Webber, *James Orrock*, vol. I, p. 12.

**Kenilworth**
LL 3981 (HH 851)

Pencil with black and coloured chalks, watercolour, gum arabic and touches of gouache on wove paper
25 x 35.8 cm (sight)
Date: 1880

Inscr: Kenilworth JO (pencil, bottom left); May 1880 / J.Orrock R I (pencil and black crayon, bottom right)

Prov: probably bt. from James Orrock by Lever, 1910[833]

LL 3981 depicts the ruined castle of Kenilworth, Warwickshire, made famous by the publication of Walter Scott's novel of 1821. Here, Orrock was following in the footsteps of his favourite artists, J. M. W. Turner, Peter DeWint and David Cox, all of whom painted the castle (for Cox's *Kenilworth*, see p. 60). Orrock shows the castle from the south, with the keep to the right, the so-called Leicester's Building at centre, and the Great Hall range to the left. The drawing is inscribed May 1880 and may have been based on a sketch made on an excursion by Orrock who had moved to London permanently by 1866. As with LL 3983, the pencil sketch may have been made on the spot, with watercolour and black chalk added later in the studio. The drawing style, with its loose line and liberal use of black chalk, resembles that of David Cox in the 1840s.

**Aylestone**
LL 2990[834]

Watercolour, touches of gum arabic, with black chalk and pencil on wove paper
12.3 x 17 cm (sight)
Date: 1882

Inscr: aylestone aug. 82 / Jas. Orrock (pencil, bottom right)

Annot: 535 (blue crayon, on mount, verso); Nº.4 (red crayon, on mount, verso)

Prov: probably bt. from James Orrock by Lever, 1910[835]

Aylestone (inscribed on the sketch) is a village south-west of Leicester. Orrock lived in the Midlands during the early part of his career, studying and working in Leicester and Nottingham, when he would have had opportunities to visit and sketch around Aylestone. LL 2990 is inscribed aug. 82, long after Orrock had moved to London, but it is possible that he may have returned to sketch familiar haunts during the 1880s. The watercolour depicts a haystack, covered with canvas to keep off the elements, supported at both ends. This was quite common practice in the 1880s and 1890s, although it was subsequently overtaken by the use of a permanent open-sided structure known as a dutch barn.

**Shardlow Lock, with the Lock-keeper's Cottage**
LL 3982 (HH 984)[836]

Watercolour, gum arabic, with white and black chalks, pencil and scratching out on wove paper
24.6 x 34.4 cm (sight)
Date: 1883

Inscr: J. Orrock R I (pencil, bottom left corner); Brick wall (pencil, lower right, on wall); Shardlow. Sep.1883 / Notts. (pencil, bottom right corner)

Prov: probably bt. from James Orrock by Lever, 1910[837]

Shardlow, a small village on the Nottinghamshire-Derbyshire border, is where the Trent and Mersey Canal meets the River Trent, and in the late nineteenth century was a thriving canal port, used to transport raw materials and goods such as pottery from Stoke-on-Trent. In common with LL 2990 and LL 3981 (above), LL 3982 is inscribed and dated in the 1880s, by which time Orrock had moved to London. The Trent was a frequent subject for Orrock throughout his career and it seems likely that he returned to familiar haunts to make a pencil sketch, probably adding watercolour later in the studio. It contrasts with much larger and more highly finished watercolour drawings made by Orrock that must have been intended for sale and exhibition from the point of execution (see, for example, *Old Mill Near Danbury, Essex*, Leverhulme Collection sale, Thornton Manor, Sotheby's, 26–28 June 2001 [lot 419]).

## JOHN BERNARD PARTRIDGE
1861 London–1948 London

**Study for the principal figure in an illustration to Robert Browning's *Rabbi Ben Ezra***
LL 2971 (LP 74)

Black, white and coloured chalks over pencil on blue paper
36.8 x 25.5 cm (sight)
Date: c. 1912–15

Prov: given to the Trustees by Lady Partridge through the National Art Collections Fund, 22 November 1949[838]

This drawing is a study for the watercolour illustrated on the cover and opposite page 26 in the edition of Robert Browning's *Rabbi Ben Ezra and other poems from Dramatis Personae*, published by Hodder & Stoughton in 1915. The poem was first published in *Dramatis Personae* (London, Chapman & Hall, 1864). The subsidiary studies are ideas for the figure's hands and drapery. The figure of a man looking upwards in accordance with Browning's text, and lifting a very large bowl of red wine with his arms outstretched above his head, illustrated the following lines from stanzas XXIX and XXX:

What through the earlier grooves
Which ran the laughing loves
Around thy base, no longer pause and press?
What though, about thy rim,
Scull-things in order grim
Grow out, in graver mood obey the sterner stress?

Look not thou down but up!
To uses of a cup
The festal board, lamp's flash and trumpet's peal,
The new wine's foaming flow,
The Master's lips a-glow!
Thou, heaven's consummate cup, what need'st thou with earth's wheel.

The twelfth-century Spanish biblical scholar, Abraham ibn Ezra, was ostensibly the subject of this long poem. However, Browning simply used him to express his very positive Epicurean, yet Deist views on aging.

The son of Michael Partridge (1805–73), Professor of Anatomy at the Royal Academy and later president of the Royal College of

833 LL 3981 was probably one of the large number of watercolours acquired by Lever from Orrock in 1910, listed (but not identified by title) in the 1910 Inventory. A note on the accession card also indicates that LL 3981, LL 2989 and LL 3982-83 were originally held by Lever Brothers (i.e. presumably at the soap factory in Port Sunlight) and were transferred to the gallery at a later, unknown date.

834 It has not been possible to determine the HH number for LL 2990.

835 LL 2990 was probably one of the large number of watercolours acquired by Lever from Orrock in 1910, listed (but not identified by title) in the 1910 Inventory. A note on the accession card describes LL 2990 as being found in the gallery.

836 LLAG files: Charles S. Rhyne questioned the attribution of LL 3982 to Orrock in a letter to Edward Morris, 10 October 1983. However, this was on the basis of a photograph, on which he does not appear to have seen the signature, bottom left.

837 LL 3982 was probably one of the large number of watercolours acquired by Lever from Orrock in 1910, listed (but not identified by title) in the 1910 Inventory. A note on the accession card also indicates that LL 3982, LL 2989, LL 3981 and LL 3983 were originally held by Lever Brothers (i.e. presumably at the soap factory in Port Sunlight) and were transferred to the gallery at a later, unknown date.

838 *National Art-Collections Fund Forty-sixth Annual Report, 1949* (1950), p. 25, no. 1543. A list of all 175 drawings presented by the National Art Collections Fund to 62 museums and galleries throughout Britain can be found at http://www.artfund.org/tag/Sir+Bernard+Partridge, consulted 12 January 2008. Other galleries in the North West given drawings by Partridge include the Haworth Art Gallery, Accrington; the Williamson Art Gallery, Birkenhead; Blackburn Museum and Art Gallery; the Grundy Art Gallery, Blackpool; Tullie House Museum and Art Gallery, Carlisle; Manchester City Art Gallery; the Whitworth Art Gallery, Manchester; Gallery Oldham; Salford Museum and Art Gallery; the Atkinson Art Gallery, Southport; the Astley Cheetham Art Gallery, Stalybridge; and Warrington Museum and Art Gallery.

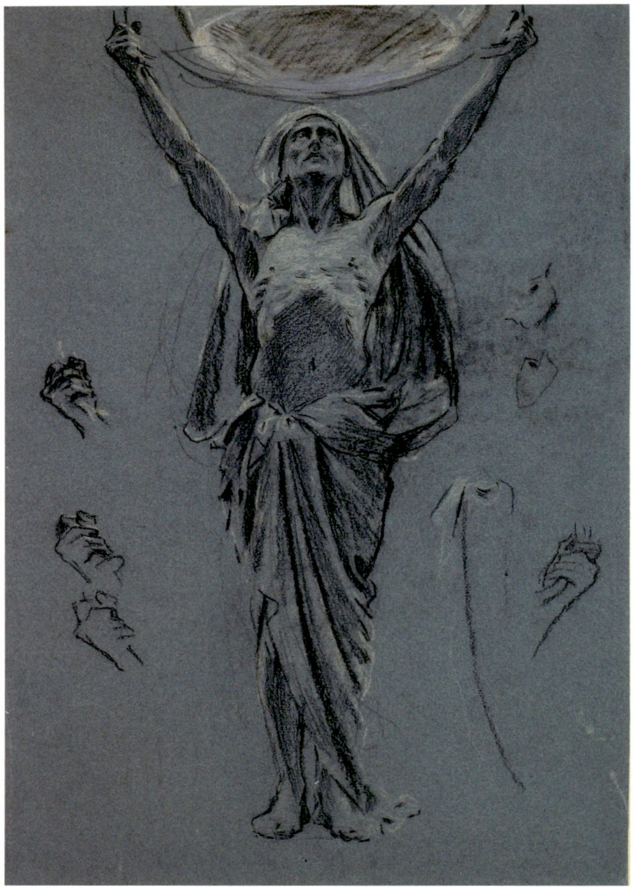

LL 2971

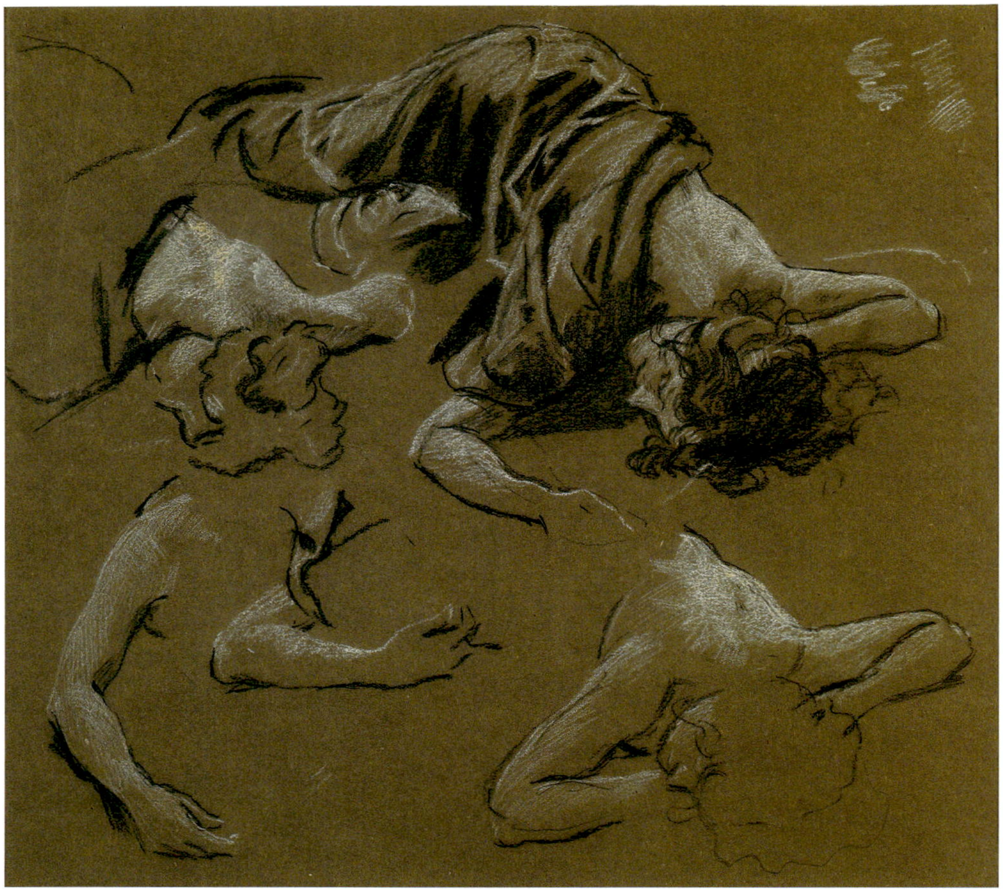

LL 3869

LL 3870

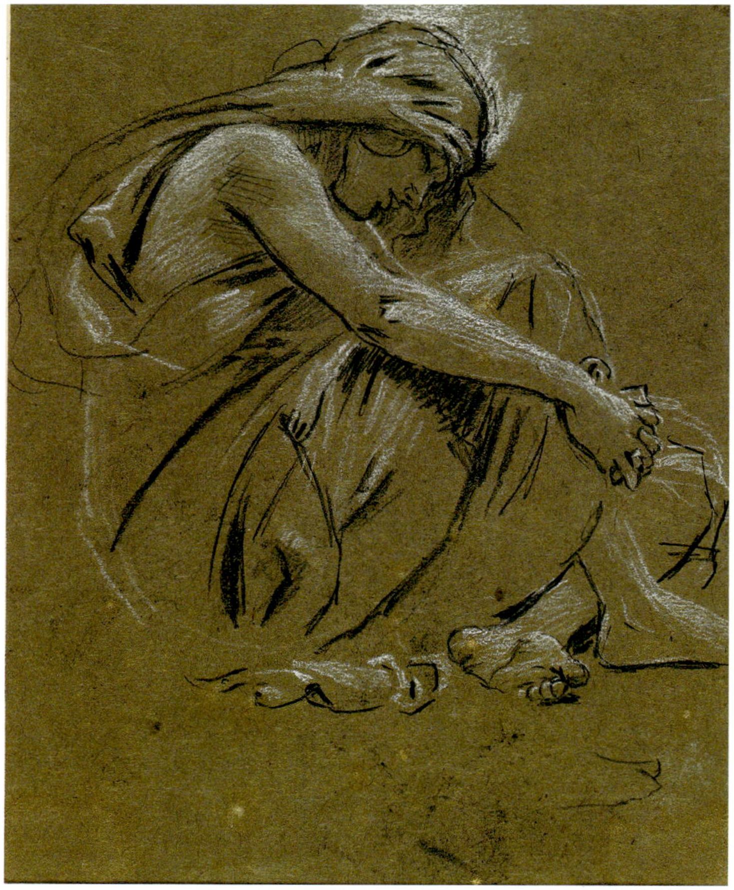

LL 2972

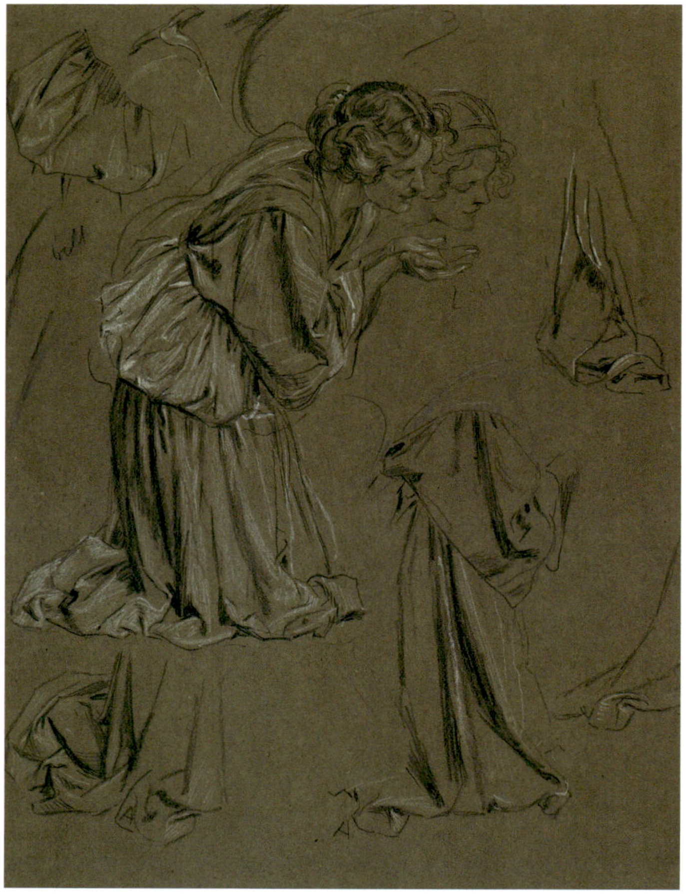

Surgeons, John Bernard Partridge was also a nephew of John Partridge (1789–1872), Portrait-Painter Extraordinary to Queen Victoria. He attended West London School of Art, where he said that he learnt nothing.[839] Partridge initially worked for two years as a stained-glass designer and church decorator for Lavers, Barraud and Westlake. He was an assistant to Philip Westlake, brother of one of the partners, 'who taught me pretty well all I ever learned'.[840] Partridge also acted professionally under the name of Bernard Gould with Henry Irving and Johnstone Forbes-Robertson. He was a member of F. R. Benson's company, a repertory company formed in 1883, which initially toured the provinces. Irving used Partridge's skills as a painter to publicise several of his productions at the Lyceum Theatre through studies in gouache in a series of *Souvenirs*. Partridge also painted several portraits of Irving in some of his most famous roles.

On the recommendation of Gerald Du Maurier and Frederick Anstey, Partridge was taken onto the staff of *Punch* in 1891, where he served under Edward Linley Sambourne. He succeeded Sambourne as second cartoonist in 1901, and nine years later became the magazine's principal cartoonist. From providing jokes he moved on first to theatrical cartoons and finally to political cartoons in 1899. Partridge was renowned for the excellence of his likenesses. He also worked for *Moonshine*, *Society*, *Judy* and, in particular, *Ladies' Pictorial*, as well as for several other magazines. Partridge was also very active as a book illustrator. His poster designs included work for the 1908 Olympic Games.

Although today Partridge is largely remembered only for his caricatures, he pursued a parallel career as a painter, watercolourist, pastellist and draughtsman, exhibiting at the Royal Academy and the New English Art Club, of which he was elected a member in 1893. His talent was recognised by his election in 1896 as a member of the Royal Institute of Painters in Water-Colours. Partridge also exhibited 12 works in the Liverpool Autumn Exhibitions. He was given a one-man show by the Fine Art Society in December 1902, which included most aspects of his work.[841] He was knighted in 1925.

Partridge was one of four artists whose drawings were used to advertise Sunlight Soap c. 1924–25 for Lever Brothers in a series of historical subjects evidently inspired by Ford Madox Brown's murals in Manchester Town Hall. Partridge's drawing was of *An Old English Market Place*, in which the figures were dressed in eighteenth-century costume. Spencer Pryse contributed *Phoenicians trading with the Ancient Britons*, Harold Nelson *Quality Tests in the Middle Ages* and Maurice Greiffenhagen *The Beginning of Imperial Trade*.[842] Partridge also provided advertising designs for Selfridge & Co.[843]

On LL 2971 there are three pin marks where the drawing has at one time been pinned on a board or to the wall.
MH

839 Percy V. Bradshaw, *The Art of the Illustrator: Bernard Partridge and his Works* (Forest Hill, 1917), p. 4.
840 Ibid.
841 *Catalogue of an exhibition of paintings & drawings by Bernard Partridge R.I.* (exh. cat., London, Fine Art Society, 1902).
842 Sydney R. Jones, *Art and Publicity: Fine Printing and Design* (London, 1925), p. 40.
843 Percy V. Bradshaw, *Art in Advertising* (Forest Hill, 1925), p. 411.
844 PR.1978.16.e.
845 FAO/346.

### Study for a sleeping female figure
LL 3869 (LP 75)

Black and white chalk on brown paper
25.5 x 28.8 cm (sight)
Date: c. 1912–15

Prov: given to the Trustees by Lady Partridge through the National Art Collections Fund, 22 November 1949

This drawing is a study for the woman dressed in a mauve robe at the bottom right corner of Partridge's illustration to Browning's *Rabbi Ben Ezra* (for further details see LL 2971 above). This figure is immediately below the sleeping female figure in an orange robe, for which the Lady Lever Art Gallery also owns a drawing (below). The other studies on this sheet are alternative sketches for the woman in a mauve robe.
MH

### Study for a sleeping female figure clasping her knees
LL 3870 (LP 76)

Black and white chalk on brown paper
21.5 x 17.7 cm (sight)
Date: c. 1912–15

Prov: given to the Trustees by Lady Partridge through the National Art Collections Fund, 22 November 1949

This drawing is a study for the woman dressed in an orange robe in the lower right of Partridge's watercolour illustrating Browning's *Rabbi Ben Ezra*. In the finished watercolour Partridge added a garland of flowers.

Another drawing for this watercolour, for the figure in the centre left foreground, is in the collection of Glasgow Museum and Art Gallery,[844] which also owns two other drawings for different watercolours reproduced in the book. Worcester City Museum and Art Gallery also owns a drawing[845] for one of the watercolours in the book.
MH

### Study of a kneeling woman for an illustration to Robert Browning's *Apparent Failure*
LL 2972 (LP 73)

Black and white chalk over pencil on brown paper
38 x 29 cm (sight)
Date: 1912–13

Inscr: belt (black chalk over pencil, upper left); A (black chalk, lower left, on edge of robe); A (black chalk, lower centre, at corner of robe)

Prov: given to the Trustees by Lady Partridge through the National Art Collections Fund, 22 November 1949

This drawing, dateable to 1912–13, is for the figure of the angel in the watercolour, signed and dated 1913, with which Partridge illustrated Browning's poem *Apparent Failure* reproduced opposite page 78 in Robert Browning, *Rabbi Ezra and other poems from Dramatis Personae* (Hodder & Stoughton, 1915). The subsidiary drawings on this sheet are alternative studies for the angel's drapery. The drawing illustrates the following lines:

It's wiser being good than bad,
It's safer being meek than fierce,
It's fitter being sane than mad.
My own hope is, a sun will pierce
The thickest cloud earth ever stretched,
That, after Last, returns the First.
Though a wide compass round be fetched,
That what began best, can't end worst,
Nor what God blessed once, prove accurst.

Browning's poem argues for hope and against the pessimism often found in the mid-Victorian period. Partridge's watercolours are suitably symbolist in style, in keeping with the mystical character of Browning's verse.

LL 2972, with its three companions (above) reveals Partridge as a highly accomplished draughtsman working in an academic style derived from such artists as Edward Poynter and Herbert Draper.
MH

## GEORGE JOHN PINWELL

1842 London–1875 London

### Study for *A Seat in St James's Park*

LL 10334 (WHL 4381)

Watercolour with gouache, over pencil on paper
23.4 x 31.9 cm (trimmed irreg.)
Date: 1869

Prov: [?] Edward Dalziel, 1876;[846] [?] J. Dalziel, 1895;[847] Harold T. Hartley, 1897–1900;[848] William Newall; his sale, Christie's, 30 June 1922 (lot 59); bt. by Gooden and Fox for Lever (£20); by descent to 3rd Viscount Leverhulme; Leverhulme Collection sale, Thornton Manor, Sotheby's, 26–28 June 2001 (lot 414); bt. by the Lady Lever Art Gallery (£7,000)

Exh: [?] London, SPWC, *Winter Exhibition*, 1875 (cat. 401); London, Deschamps Gallery, *Exhibition of Works by the late G.J. Pinwell*, 1876 (cat. 205); [?] Birmingham, Royal Society of Artists, *Thirtieth Spring Exhibition*, 1895 (cat. 346); [?] London, Earls Court, *Victorian Era Exhibition*, 1897 (cat. 4); London, New Gallery, *Exhibition of pictures, ancient and modern, by artists of the British and Continental schools*, 1897–98 (cat. 222A)

Lit: G. C. Williamson, *George J. Pinwell and His Works* (London, 1900), p. 19, illus. p. 31

In 1861 Pinwell left home to study art, at first attending evening classes at St Martin's School of Art and subsequently at Heatherley's Academy. From 1863 until his untimely death at the age of 33, Pinwell worked for the leading engraving firms of the period. These included J. W. Whymper, Joseph Swain and the Dalziel brothers, and he produced more than 500 illustrations for books and periodicals. From 1865 onwards, when he first exhibited at the Dudley Gallery, Pinwell increasingly worked in watercolours and oils, hoping to establish himself as a painter of merit. His work received consistently favourable notices and he was chosen as an associate of the SPWC in April 1869, being elected to full membership in 1870. In common with his contemporaries, Frederick Walker (see pp. 211–15) and John William North, Pinwell's work dealt with figurative subjects in domestic and landscape settings, which were presented in a poetic manner.

LL 10334 is a study for the highly finished watercolour *A Seat in St James's Park*, exhibited at the SPWC in 1869 (fig. 49).[849] In common with many of Pinwell's watercolours, the subject was based on an earlier periodical illustration, in this case for *Once a Week* (26 June 1869), and LL 10334 must date from shortly after this appeared.[850] The subject depicted is a group of individuals from disparate classes and occupations (as suggested by their different clothes) seated on a bench in St James's Park, London.[851] Contemporary life subjects such as this were unusual in Pinwell's oeuvre, as he more generally tended towards literary and historical subjects such as *Gilbert à Becket's Troth* (see below). LL 10334 bears a close resemblance to the final picture in compositional terms, although in the finished painting Pinwell used watercolour applied over opaque white to give a highly finished effect of the frostiness of a wintry day, something that is not as emphasised with the warmer tones of the Lady Lever work. The successful reception of the final watercolour is suggested by the fact that just after its exhibition at the SPWC, Pinwell was elected to full membership of the Society.

A less-finished study for *A Seat in St James's Park* (Cecil Higgins Art Gallery, Bedford, fig. 50) shows that, at an earlier stage, Pinwell was experimenting with variants of the composition and the figures.[852] The final composition was engraved in 1870.

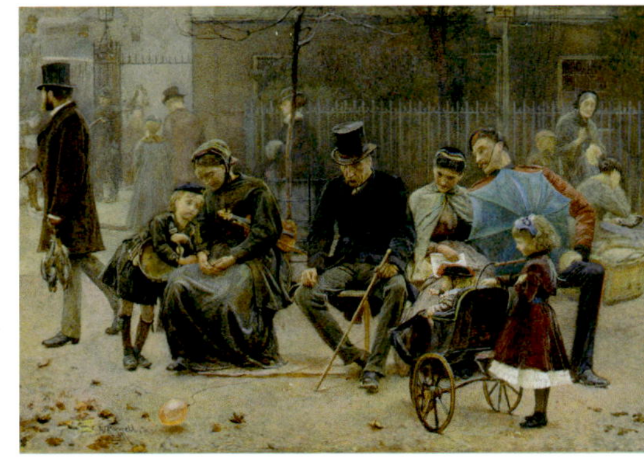

fig. 49. George John Pinwell, *A Seat in St James's Park, London*, 1869, watercolour and gouache over pencil on paper, 40.6 x 59 cm (sight), Art Gallery of New South Wales, Sydney

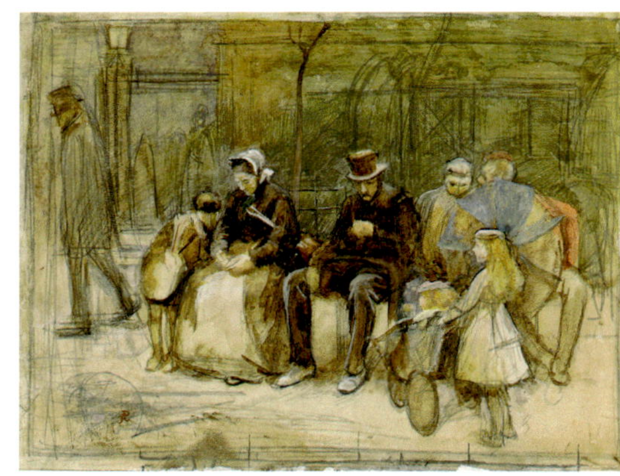

fig. 50. George John Pinwell, *Study for 'A Seat in St James's Park', London*, 1869, watercolour and gouache over pencil on paper, 19.3 x 23 cm, Trustees of the Cecil Higgins Art Gallery, Bedford

846 Lent by Dalziel to the 1876 exhibition as *The Park Seat* (cat. 205), 8 x 12 in.; see G. C. Williamson, *George J. Pinwell and His Works* (London, 1900), pp. 73–93.

847 *Seat in St James's Park. sketch* (cat. 346) was lent by Miss J. Dalziel to the Birmingham Royal Society of Artists exhibition in 1895.

848 Williamson, *George J. Pinwell*, p. 90.

849 *A Seat in St James's Park*, signed lower left G.J. Pinwell / 69, watercolour and gouache over pencil, 40.6 x 59 cm (sight). Prov: Edward Dalziel 1876–86; Christie's, 19 June 1886 (lot 58); bt. through J. & W. Vokins for the Art Gallery of New South Wales, Sydney.

850 There is an impression of this engraving in the Victoria & Albert Museum.

851 For an interpretation of the finished watercolour, see P. W. Trimpe, *George John Pinwell: A Victorian Artist and Illustrator* (New York, 2001), pp. 34–39. Trimpe argues that the painting is a commentary, although a far from radical one, on the economic and physical difficulties faced by people living in an industrialised society, in contrast to the elegance of the St James's district. She argues that the figures on the park bench share a sense of fatigue and dejection and that the whole overall emotion expressed in the composition is one of discontent. This is a fact emphasised by the sparseness of the trees and the huddling of the group, suggesting the rawness of a cold winter day.

852 *Study for 'A Seat in St James's Park'*, watercolour, pencil and gouache on paper, 19.3 x 23 cm. Prov: H. S. Reitlinger; Leicester Galleries; bt. by Cecil Higgins Art Gallery, November 1957. See Evelyn Joll, *Cecil Higgins Art Gallery Watercolours and Drawings* (Bedford, 2002), p. 200.

LL 10334

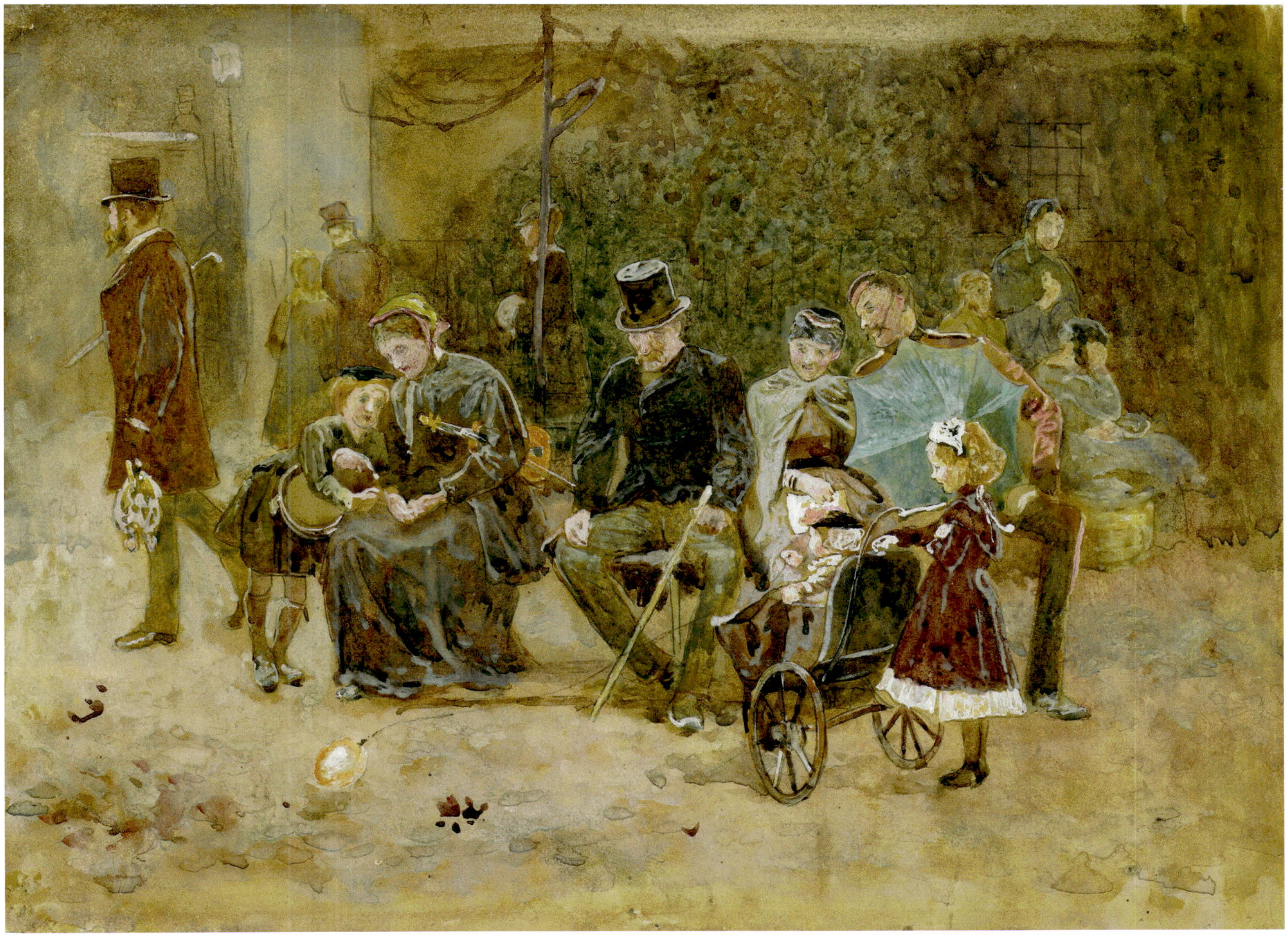

LL 3984

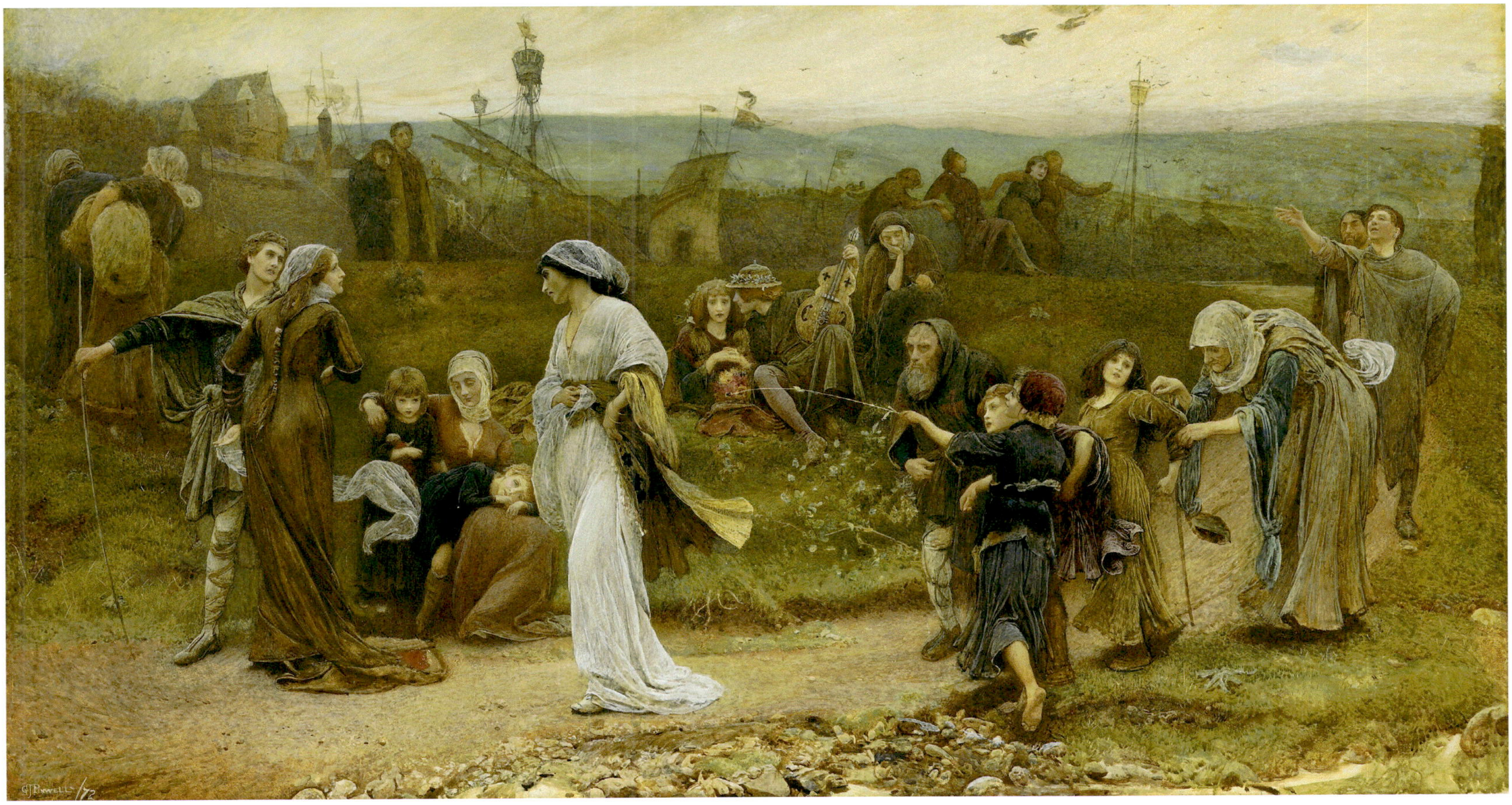

**Gilbert à Becket's Troth - the Saracen Maiden entering London at Sundown**[853]
LL 3984 (WHL 4380)

Gouache with gum arabic and scratching out, over pencil on paper stretched over canvas
57.5 x 109.3 cm
Date: 1872

Inscr: GJPINWELL / 72 (gouache, bottom left)

Prov: bt. by George Boulton from the 1872 SPWC exhibition (£420);[854] John Jaffray, 1895-1900;[855] William Newall, 1906;[856] his sale, Christie's, 30 June 1922 (lot 57); bt. by Gooden and Fox for Lever with WHL 4381 (£992 18s for the pair)

Exh: London, SPWC, *Summer Exhibition*, 1872 (cat. 127); London, Deschamps Gallery, *Exhibition of Works by the late G. J. Pinwell*, 1876 (cat. 80); Manchester, Manchester Art Gallery, *Royal Jubilee Exhibition*, 1887 (cat. 1504); Birmingham, Royal Society of Artists, *Thirtieth Spring Exhibition*, 1895 (cat. 446); London, Burlington House, *Exhibition of Works by the Old Masters and Deceased Masters of the British School*, 1906 (cat. 197); Munich, *Victorianische Malerei Von Turner bis Whistler*, 1993 (cat. 74)

Lit: G. C. Williamson, *George J. Pinwell and His Works* (London, 1900), p. 21, illus. frontispiece; C. Newall, *Victorian Watercolours* (London, 1987), p. 88, illus. p. 90; P. W. Trimpe, *George John Pinwell: A Victorian Artist and Illustrator* (New York, 2001), pp. 33-34

Pinwell was admired, alongside his technical proficiency as a watercolourist, for his poetic images of historical and literary subjects. In 1895 the art critic and collector Harry Quilter wrote:

> If ever there was a dreamer of dreams 'born out of his due time', it was George Pinwell, and his art is one of the most peculiar which has marked modern days. This is indeed a very strange, half-real, half-poetical world with which he is concerned, and many of his compositions are analogous ... to one of those old North-country ballads which commencing quietly with a maiden seated at her spinning wheel, or a page riding across the heather, end in shame and death.[857]

The Lady Lever watercolour is one of these works, based on a poem by Robert Buchanan (1841-1901) which relates the twelfth-century romance of the Saracen maiden who fell in love with the crusader Gilbert à Becket.[858] Having helped him to escape captivity in the Holy Land, she followed him to England. Although she only knew that his name was Gilbert and that he lived in London, she persevered in searching and eventually found him.

In LL 3984 Pinwell depicts the point in the narrative where the maiden, having arrived in London, is surrounded by hostile and indifferent townsfolk. This crowded scene draws attention to the different reactions of the various groups of people, but their gestures draw the viewer's attention to the isolated and poignant figure of the maiden. Her heroic qualities are emphasised by her white, classical-style robes and statuesque beauty which mark her out from the townsfolk, who are dressed in medieval costume and painted in the darker browns and blues that dominate the rest of the picture. The face of the Saracen maiden was reported to have been based on the features of Pinwell's favourite model, his sister, Mrs Walker.[859]

The work was shown at the SPWC in 1872, Pinwell's first exhibited work as a full member. By this time Pinwell was well established as a painter in watercolours and *Gilbert à Becket's Troth* was seen by contemporaries and by his biographers as one of his most successful works. *The Art Journal* in 1872 praised it as 'a work of great self-possession to entertain such a subject, but it is a triumph to carry such a theme to an issue so felicitous'.[860] The technical demands of such a large-scale, multi-figured work were admired by the artist's biographer in 1900 who wrote, 'as a composition he never surpassed it'.[861] In common with LL 10334 (pp. 152-53), it was based on an earlier illustration, published in *Once a Week* (14 May 1864).[862]

LL 3984 reveals the particularly linear qualities that made Pinwell so successful in his earlier years as an illustrator. In technique, it is typical of his highly wrought exhibition watercolours from the late 1860s and 1870s where watercolour is applied in a stippling fashion over opaque white.

Four works related to the final watercolour were exhibited at the Deschamps Gallery exhibition in 1876; one of these was an almost life-size compositional study in watercolour and gouache (now private collection, Brighton).[863]

853 The current title is the exhibited title from the SPWC exhibition of 1872, quoted in *The Art Journal* (1875), p. 92.
854 Williamson, *George J. Pinwell*, p. 21.
855 Lent by Jaffray to the Birmingham exhibition in 1895; still owned by him in 1900; Williamson, *George J. Pinwell*, p. 21.
856 LLAG files: lent by W. Newall to the Burlington House exhibition in 1906.
857 Harry Quilter, *A Catalogue of Pictures and Sketches by George Mason and George Pinwell* (Birmingham, 1895), pp. 10-11.
858 R.W. Buchanan, *The North Coast and Other Poems* (London, 1867).

859 Williamson, *George J. Pinwell*, p. 40.
860 Quoted by C. Newall, *Victorian Watercolours* (London, 1987), p. 88.
861 Williamson, *George J. Pinwell*, p. 21.
862 Trimpe, *George John Pinwell*, p. 33.
863 The compositional sketch, *Study for Gilbert à Becket's Troth*, was cat. 36 in the 1876 exhibition; prov: Christie's, 16 March 1876 (lot 111); bt. by P. Waller (11 gns); bt. by P. Rose and A. Gallichan, 1975. It measures 53.3 x 96.5 cm and is signed G. J. Pinwell. LLAG files: information given in correspondence in 1988 between A. Gallichan and Lucy Wood. There is also a black-and-white photograph of the work. The other three works in the 1876 exhibition were *Study for Gilbert à Becket's Troth, in Mrs Pinwell's collection* (cat. 116); *Study for Gilbert à Becket's Troth, in Mrs Pinwell's collection* (cat. 135) and *Sketch - Gilbert à Becket's Troth* (cat. 170).

## SAMUEL PROUT
1783 Plymouth-1852 London

**Street Scene, Bayeux, Normandy**
LL 3871 (WHL 756, HH 423)

Watercolour with white gouache on buff-coloured wove paper
27.2 x 20.7 cm
Date: 1820-52

Prov: bt. from James Orrock by Lever, 1910[864]

Lit: *The Connoisseur*, vol. 74 (June 1932), p. 401

Prout was the son of a ship's outfitter in Plymouth naval dockyard. He received his first drawing lessons from the headmaster at the grammar school. The antiquarian publisher John Britton met Prout in Plymouth in 1801 and employed him to make sketches on a tour of Cornwall; Prout learned quickly, and soon became one of Britton's principal draughtsmen, travelling the country and working up drawings by other members of his extensive team. He first exhibited watercolours in London in 1803, but his income was earned chiefly by supplying drawings and watercolours to the amateur market and through prints for copying. Prout was elected to the SPWC in 1819 and made his first continental tour the same year. His exhibits of French street scenes, then of the Rhine and, from 1825, of Venice were highly sought after. Prout was named Painter in Water-colours in Ordinary to George IV in 1829, the year steel engravings of his views in Italy and Switzerland illustrated the first issue of a new cultural phenomenon, the *Landscape Annual*. He was praised by Ruskin in the third edition of *Modern Painters I* (1846) for his rendition of Gothic stonework: 'there is nothing but the work of Prout which is true, living, or right, in its general impression, and nothing, therefore, so inexhaustibly agreeable'.[865] Through his many volumes of lithographs Prout remained a standard for students and copyists for the better part of the nineteenth century.

LL 3871 has previously been known as *Street in Normandy*.[866] The location is identifiable as Bayeux, from the twin turreted towers of the eleventh-century cathedral with their slender spires. Prout frequently exhibited views of Normandy at the SPWC from 1820 on, but only once was Bayeux represented, in 1828. A watercolour of the town, in which the north turret is viewed along the length of the rue des Cuisiniers, was sold at Sotheby's, 10 July 1980, lot 183 (as *The Cathedral at Rouen from the rue St Malo*). The quality of LL 3871 is not high, but as there is no lithograph or engraving of this subject, it is here accepted as a work by Prout.
TW

864 1910 Inventory, valued at £40.
865 Cook and Wedderburn (eds), *Works of John Ruskin*, vol. III, p. 217.
866 Tatlock, p. 135.

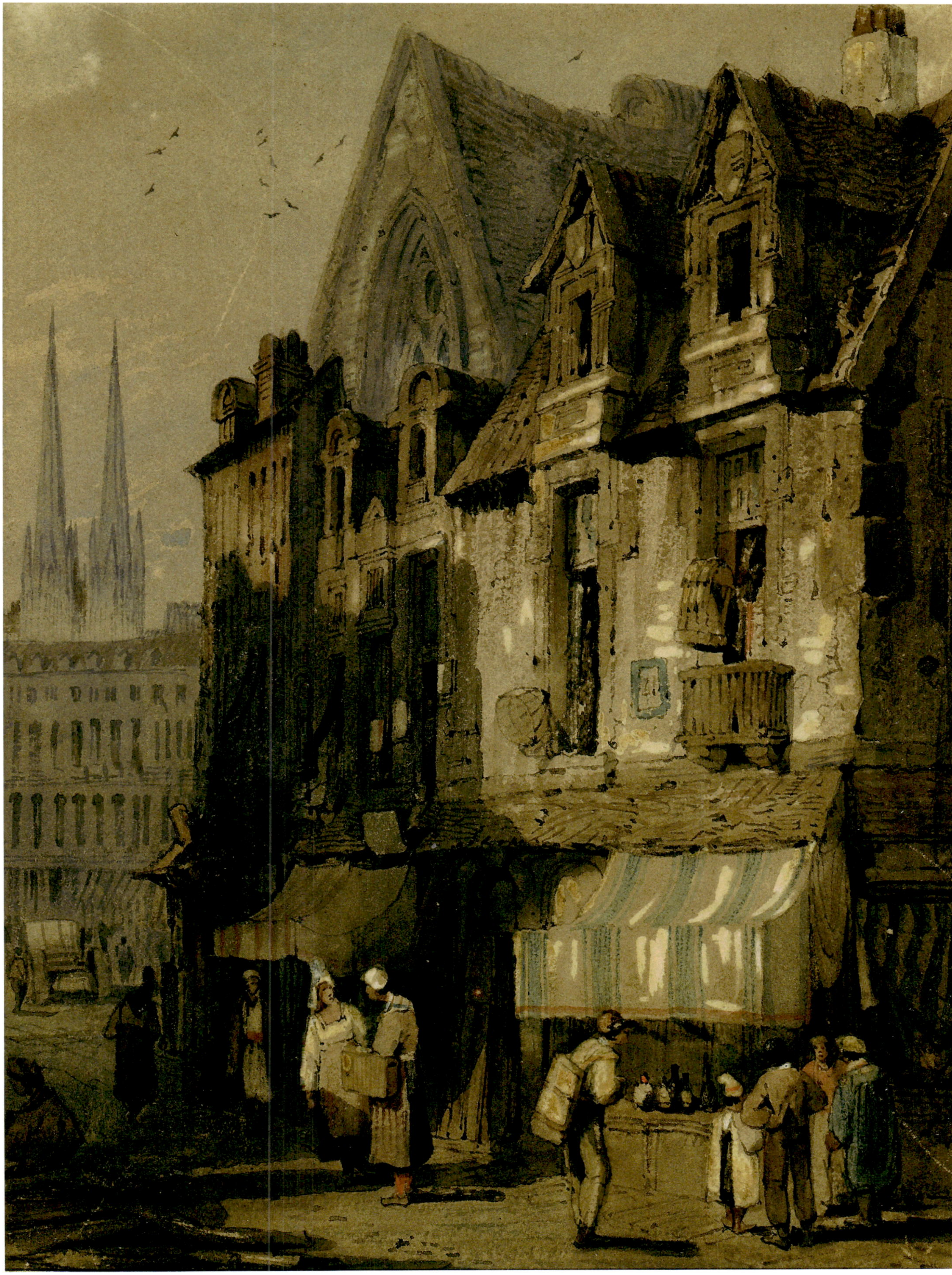

LL 3871

## AFTER SAMUEL PROUT

### Four Continental Scenes
LL 3872, 3873, 3875, 3877
Date: c. 1830–70

Prov: A. Sargent; Christie's, 16 May 1918 (lot 23, as *A View on the Grand Canal Venice; and six other small views, in one frame*); bt. by Gooden and Fox (34 gns with LL 3874, 3876 and 3878) for Lever (£37 9s 8d)

### Canal Scene, Venice
LL 3872 (WHL 3524)

Watercolour, gouache and pen and ink on wove paper
7.1 x 5.1 cm (sight)

This and the three following works are part of a group of seven topographical watercolours of continental views framed together. They were catalogued by Tatlock as the work of John Skinner Prout (1806–76),[867] rather than his uncle Samuel Prout, to whom all had previously been attributed. Now that sources of most have been identified, it appears that they are all anonymous copies of engravings from the popular *Landscape Annuals* of the 1830s. For the other three works in the set, see Bonington (pp. 10–12) and Stanfield (p. 177).

This canalside scene, with baroque palace in the foreground and a Gothic church and campanile in the distance, is likely to be based on an engraving of Venice after Prout, but the source has not been identified. His watercolours were reproduced in numerous publications apart from the *Landscape Annuals*, and the image may have been taken from a collection using the work of several artists.
TW

867 Tatlock, p. 135.

### The Temple of Peace, Rome
LL 3873 (WHL 3525)

Watercolour, pencil and white gouache on paper
7 x 5.1 cm (sight)

This watercolour is a copy of the engraving by James B. Allen after Samuel Prout for Robert Jennings's 1831 *Landscape Annual*, *The Tourist in Italy*, with a text by Thomas Roscoe (pl. 15). Most of the elements of the print are faithfully, if summarily, rendered in the copy, apart from two small figures in the middle ground, which have been omitted.

The foreground building, standing in the Forum, is now better known as the Basilica of Constantine. The distant belfry is that of the church of S. Francesco Romana. Prout's original drawing of this subject is in the British Museum.[868]
TW

868 1889-5-26-19.

### Palaces on the Grand Canal
LL 3875 (WHL 3527)

Watercolour and pen and ink on paper
9.4 x 13.9 cm (sight)

LL 3875 is a copy of the steel engraving in the second of Robert Jennings's *Landscape Annuals*, published late in 1830 for the year 1831.[869] The engraving, by William Smith, is entitled *Barbarigo and Pisani Palaces, Venice* on the plate; in the list of plates it appears as no. 3: *Titian's House, The Pisani and Barbarigo Palaces*. The central building is the late fifteenth-century Palazzo Pisani-Moretta. To its left is the Palazzo Barbarigo della Terrazza. This once contained 17 paintings by Titian, now in the Hermitage, St Petersburg, but the reference to 'Titian's house' presumably denotes the building further to the left.

The print measures 9.6 x 14.5 cm, virtually the same dimensions as this watercolour copy, which follows it closely in most respects, although some of the foreground activity and figures are omitted. A watercolour version of the subject by Prout, similar except for a covered gondola drawn up in front of the palace to the left, was sold at Christie's, 14 July 1987 (lot 212).
TW

869 R. Lockett, *Samuel Prout, 1783–1852* (London, 1985), p. 78, illus. fig. 28.

LL 3872

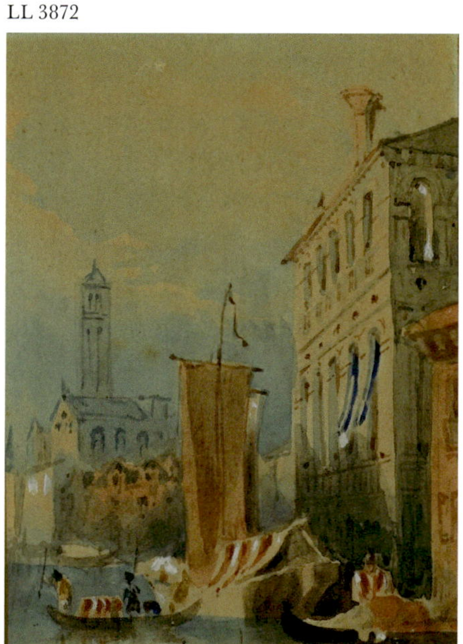

LL 3873

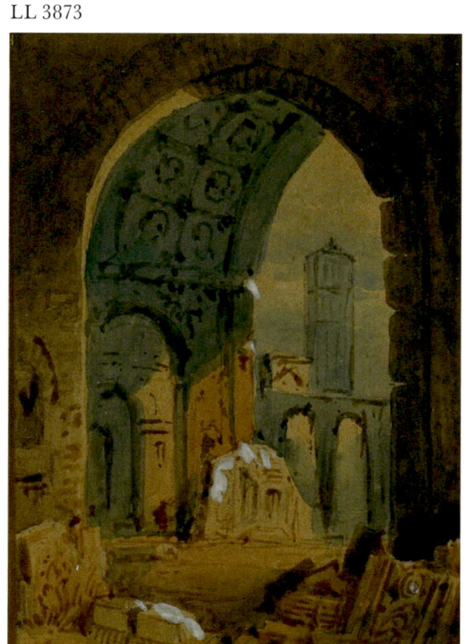

LL 3875

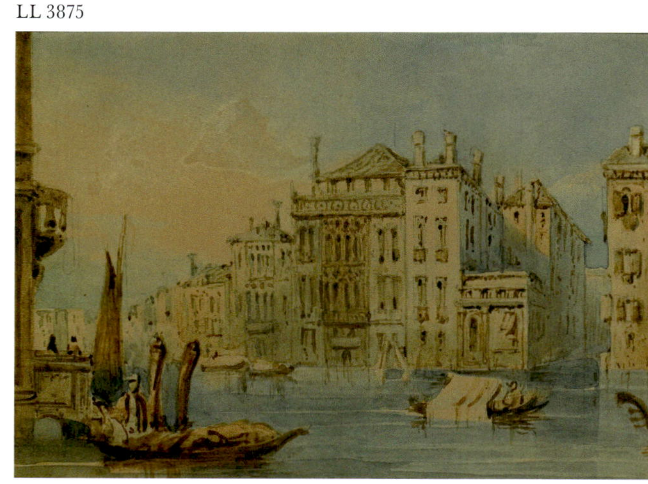

**The Fish Market, Rome**
LL 3877 (WHL 3529)

Watercolour, pencil and gouache with pen and ink on wove paper
8 x 5.3 cm (sight)

This watercolour is a copy of the engraving by W. R. Smith after Samuel Prout for Robert Jennings's 1830 *Landscape Annual.* The engraving appears as the last plate in the volume, dated Oct 28 1829. The basket in the print has fish displayed in it, and stands beside some clay or metal vessels; more fish are laid out on the wall to the right of the figures.

The columns were previously part of the Porticus of Octavia, built by Emperor Augustus in honour of his sister; they were later thought to have formed part of a Temple of Minerva, and this name is given to some of the watercolour versions. The fish market was established under the columns of the porch in the twelfth century and continued in this location until Prout's lifetime.[870] Several variants of the composition in watercolour are known; those in the Shipley Art Gallery, Gateshead, and in the Harris Museum and Art Gallery, Preston, have different foregrounds with new groups of figures. There is a further version previously with Agnew's. A watercolour in Leeds City Art Gallery, closely related to the print, is more likely to be a copy of the engraving.
TW

870 A. Macadam, *Rome and its environs* (London, 1985), p. 225.

LL 3877

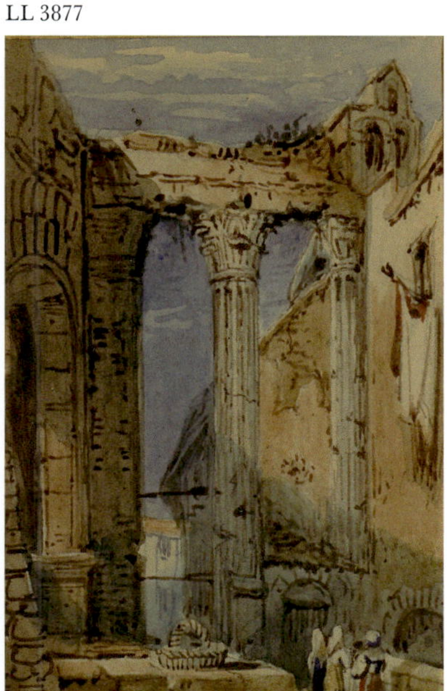

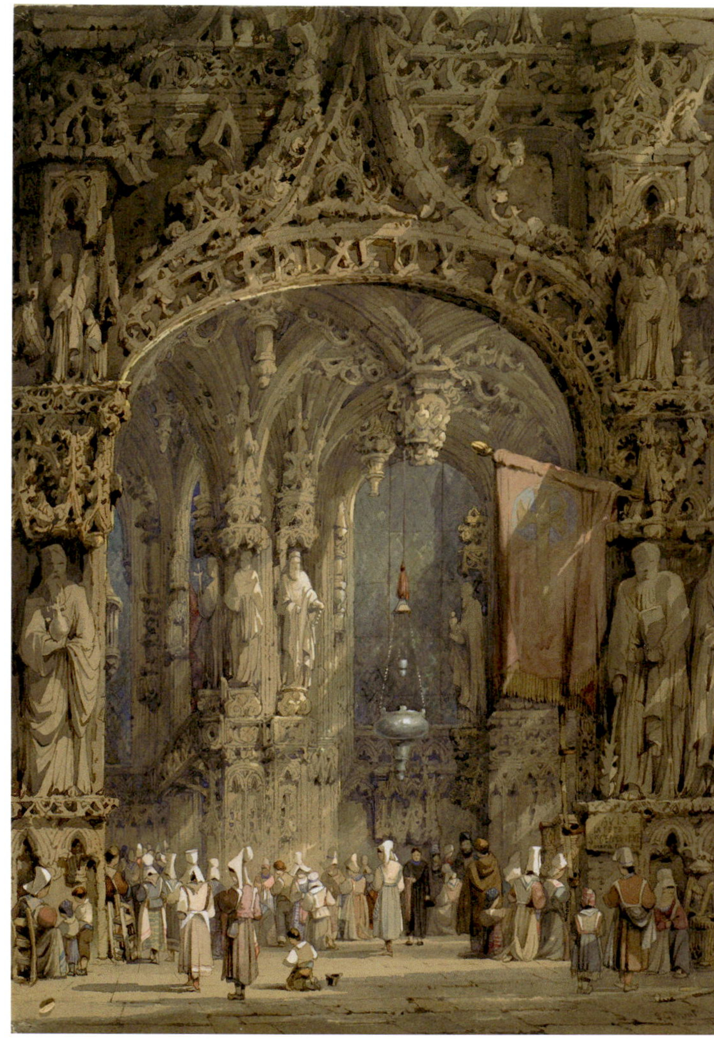

LL 3796

**SAMUEL GILLESPIE PROUT**
1822 London–1911 place of death unknown

**Cathedral Interior, Fête of St Geneviève**
LL 3796 (WHL 307, H 387)

Watercolour, gouache and pen and ink on wove paper
47.6 x 33.3 cm
Date: probably 1846

Inscr: S. G. PROUT (watercolour, bottom right); AVIS / LA FETE DE / STE GENEVIEVE / aura lieu [illeg.] (watercolour, on panel against right hand column)

Prov: bt. from James Orrock by Lever, 1912[871]

The youngest of Samuel Prout's four children, Samuel Gillespie was given his mother's maiden name to precede his father's. He seems to have intended to follow his father in the profession of artist, and made a tour of France in 1846.[872] His style relied heavily on his father's, although without fully gaining parental approval.[873] He made some largely unsuccessful attempts to earn a living as a teacher of drawing, but his later life was occupied chiefly in charitable work. In 1871 he was one of the first to bring relief to starving Parisians after the siege of Paris.

The location of this highly elaborate late Gothic chapel awaits identification. Sainte Geneviève is the patron saint of Paris, but this chapel does not exist in any church in the capital. The medieval abbey dedicated to her was deconsecrated during the Revolution and demolished in 1808. The feast day of the saint is celebrated on 3 January; the notice of the event would have been of significance not only in Paris itself. The subject was presumably sketched during Prout's French tour of 1846; his watercolours of this scale and level of ambition date mainly from the beginning of his career as an artist, during the later 1840s.
TW

871 1912 Inventory, valued at £35.
872 Hardie, *Watercolour Painting in Britain*, vol. III, p. 12, referring to F. Gordon Roe, 'Some letters of Samuel Prout', *The Old Water-Colour Society's Club: Twenty-fourth Annual Volume* (1946), p. 46.

873 Lockett, *Samuel Prout*, p. 94, n. 3.

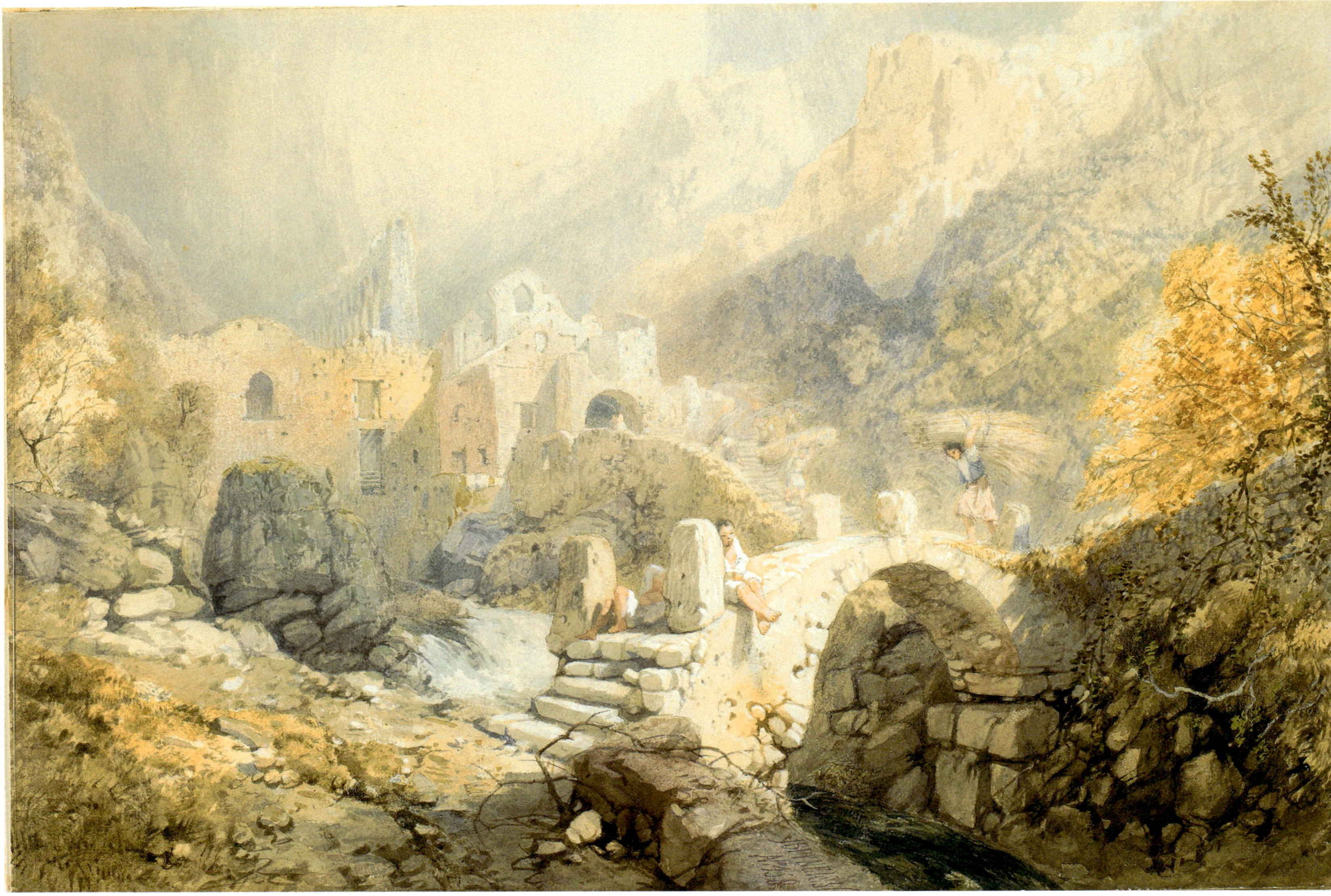

LL 3797

## JAMES BAKER PYNE
1800 Bristol–1870 London

### Val di Ferriera, near Amalfi
LL 3797 (LP 49)

Watercolour and gouache on wove paper
33.9 x 50.8 cm
Date: 1856

Inscr: JBPYNE1856 / No. 458 (watercolour, bottom centre, on rock)

Prov: bt. from Grindley & Palmer, 14 North John Street, Liverpool by the Trustees, 23 July 1938 (12 gns)

Pyne was born in Bristol. He worked for a lawyer while teaching himself to paint and exhibited his first picture in 1824. He was already well enough established in 1827 to take William James Müller (see pp. 142–44) as an apprentice. Around 1835 Pyne moved to London; he exhibited at the Royal Academy, but after 1840 was committed to the Society of British Artists, where he showed oils and watercolours and served as vice-president. Pyne made a first Continental tour in 1846. Paintings of the Lake District commissioned by William Agnew in 1849 led to two volumes of lithographs, published in 1853 and 1859. Pyne spent most of the years 1851–53 in Italy, travelling with William Evans of Bristol. The large group of works he completed for Agnew on his return further consolidated his reputation and provided material that he continued to draw on for the rest of his career.

Thanks to Pyne's own meticulous record-keeping, the subject of this previously unidentified watercolour can be established as the Val di Ferriera, in the rocky mountainous territory behind the coastal town of Amalfi in southern Italy. Pyne's entry for this work in his *Picture memoranda* reads, 'Val di Ferriera, or Valley of the Forge nr Amalfi. A painting in water colours (elaborate) commenced on the spot and finished in London Oct 1856. One of the above series.'[874] In August 1856 Pyne contracted with the London and Manchester picture dealer William Agnew to paint 35 watercolour landscapes of continental scenes at a price of £70 each, or £2,400 for the entire series. This agreement followed hard on the heels of an earlier one, made in June the same year, for a number of oil paintings. Two other watercolours from the series, numbered 451 and 455, depicting further scenes in the vicinity of Naples, are in the Whitworth Art Gallery, Manchester.[875]

The watercolour series included subjects mainly in Germany, the Italian Lakes and around Rome and Naples, the very places most popular with Victorian travellers, and of which the

874 National Art Library, Victoria & Albert Museum: *Picture memoranda*; MS L/1947/1562, vol. 1.

875 C. Nugent, *British watercolours in The Whitworth Art Gallery, The University of Manchester. A summary catalogue of drawings and watercolours by artists born before 1880* (Manchester, 2002), p. 222.

watercolourist William Callow (see pp. 40–41) also made something of a speciality.[876] While catering to a well-established market, Pyne, as this view near Amalfi demonstrates, was also interested in exploring scenery away from the well-trodden tourist tracks. The village appears to be in ruins. The two foreground figures are very poorly dressed and sitting idly on the ancient bridge; their inactivity only emphasises the contrast with the approaching figure, heavily laden with a burden of what is probably scrub, gathered for firewood. For Pyne, the challenge of the image was perhaps as much technical as moral; the sheer intensity of the Italian light bleaches surfaces and makes even the towering cliffs look insubstantial. In his *Picture memoranda* Pyne notes in relation to several of the Italian watercolours the use of an opaque white, used either neat, or mixed with Chinese (lead) white. While the SPWC had long frowned on the use of this opaque pigment, Pyne would have been aware that such censure was being severely challenged by the praise heaped on the contemporary work of John Frederick Lewis, in which gouache is freely used. One of Lewis's colleagues, Alfred Downing Fripp, had also used solid white in his depictions of Italian architecture, to create an effect even more dazzling than Pyne's own.[877]
TW

876 See the list of Callow's exhibited works in Reynolds, *William Callow*, pp. 209–36.
877 For example, in *The monastery of San Rocco, Olevano*, in the Victoria & Albert Museum; Hardie, *Watercolour Painting in Britain*, vol. II, pl. 223.

## 'SIR JOSHUA REYNOLDS'

1723 Plympton, Devon–1792 London

**Six Fancy Heads of Women**
LL 3986A–F (WHL 2624)
Date: possibly early twentieth century

Prov: bt. from Frank Partridge by Lever, 11 August 1915 (£16 10s)[878]

**A woman in a white hat with blue hatband**
LL 3986A

Pencil, pen and watercolour on wove paper, torn at the edges
9.6 x 6.9 cm

Inscr: J. Reynolds (brown ink, bottom centre)

**A woman in a straw hat with a red hatband**
LL 3986B

Pencil, pen and watercolour on wove paper with curved corners
12.8 x 8.9 cm

Inscr: Mrs Ingestre / J. Reynolds / 1789 (brown ink, lower centre)

**A woman in profile to the left in a white bonnet with red ribbon**
LL 3986C

Pencil, pen and watercolour on wove paper, torn at the corners
8.1 x 6.1 cm

Inscr: J. Reynolds (brown ink, lower centre)

**A woman to the right in a blue dress**
LL 3986D

Pencil, pen and watercolour on laid paper, torn at the corners
10.8 x 7.3 cm

**A woman to the left**
LL 3986E

Pencil, pen and watercolour on laid paper, torn at the corners
6.8 x 4.5 cm

**A young woman in a white bonnet with pink hatband**
LL 3986F

Pencil, pen and watercolour on wove paper, torn at the edges
11.5 x 8.2 cm

Inscr: for portrait / J Reynolds / 1789 (brown ink, lower centre)

878 LLAG files: copy of invoice.

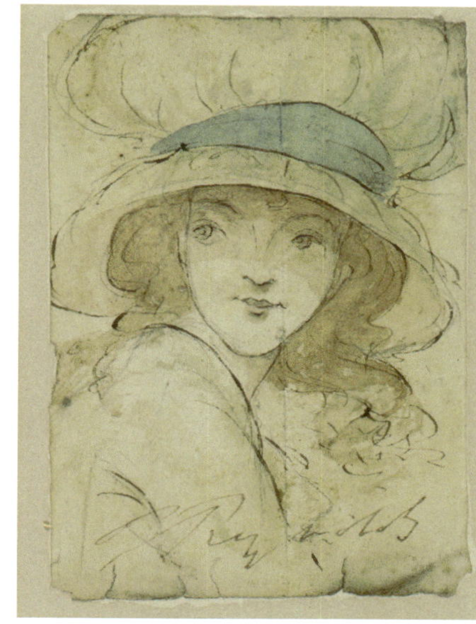

LL 3986A

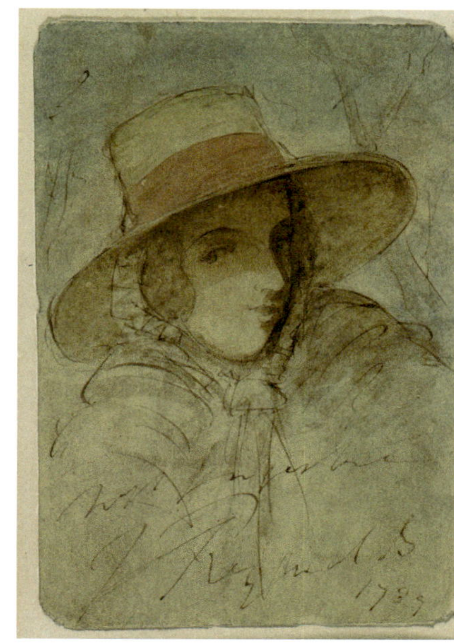

LL 3986B

LL 3986C

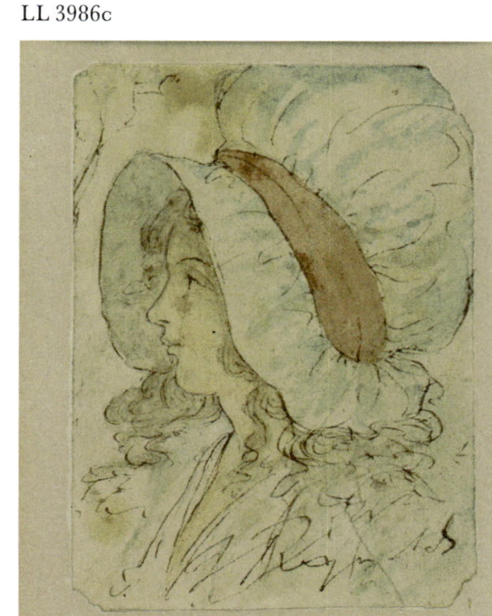

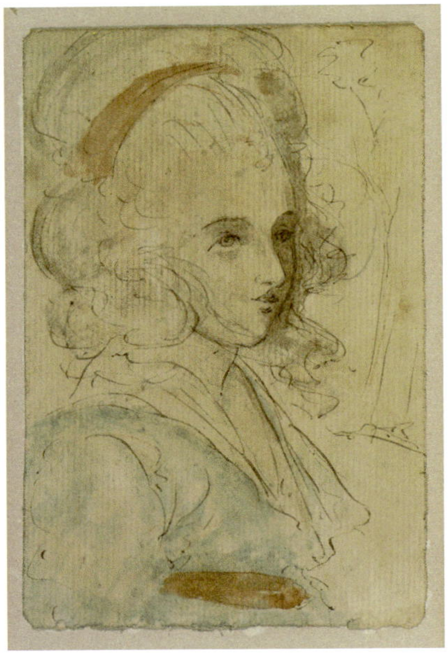

LL 3986D

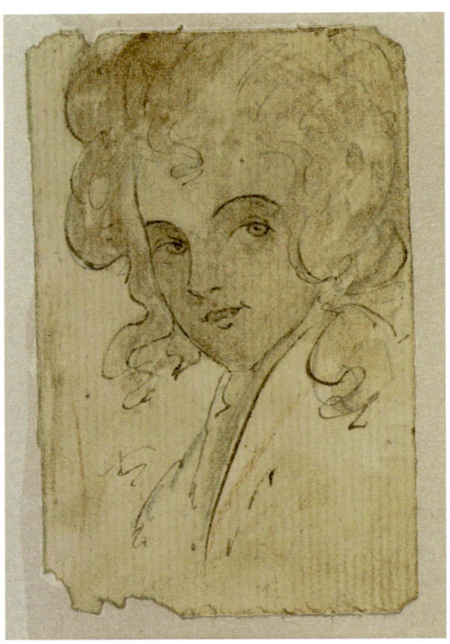

LL 3986E

LL 3986F

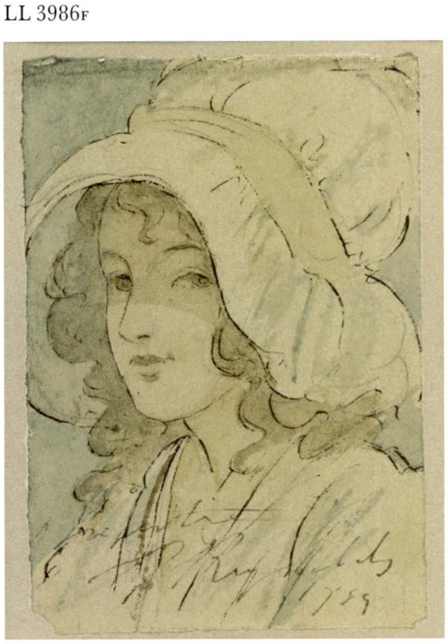

These six drawings are not only uncharacteristic of Reynolds's draughtsmanship at any stage of his life (let alone in 1789, when his painting technique was becoming ever broader and richer and his eyesight was failing); they are also foreign to his practice of portraiture. Having studied with Thomas Hudson in the early 1740s, Reynolds developed a profound understanding of Italian art and the Grand Manner during a visit to Italy between 1749 and 1752, and during the 1750s emerged as the leading portraitist in London. He was elected first president of the Royal Academy in 1768, a position he resigned briefly in 1790 but then resumed until his death. Even in his lifetime he was viewed as the intellectual figurehead of the British school and an artist of European stature. His drawing style is much more 'Baroque' in character than these works and in any case he rarely made preparatory sketches for portraits – as these are clearly intended to be understood – preferring to work directly on the canvas. The six drawings are clearly meant to represent six different female sitters and there is an artful element of differentiation in their basic mode of production, but although there is a faint recollection of a work such as *Penelope Boothby* (a much younger sitter) the character of the heads in general is much closer to the more rustic types of artists such as Wheatley or J. R. Smith. No-one named Mrs Ingestre is recorded as sitting to him;[879] while simple comparison of the handwriting on these drawings with Reynolds's autograph leaves no doubt that these are inauthentic works; they hardly even merit the description of forgeries. However, several other drawings in a similar style are recorded and LL 3986A–F may well be part of an early twentieth-century scam to create a new market for Reynolds drawings.[880]

Lever acquired LL 3986A–F from the dealer Frank Partridge at the same time as he took receipt of many other drawings, miniatures and enamels that Partridge had bought for him from the sale of Jeffery Whitehead's collection at Christie's, 4–10 August 1915. Although it was assumed from the moment they were first accessioned within Lever's collection that these six drawings had been owned by Whitehead, there is no trace of them in the sale catalogues, and it seems possible that Partridge could have slipped them in among Lever's consignment as a douceur.[881]

AK

879 See A. Graves and W. V. Cronin, *A History of the Works of Sir Joshua Reynolds P.R.A.* (London, 3 vols, 1899–1901); E. Waterhouse, *Reynolds* (London, 1941); David Mannings and Martin Postle, *Sir Joshua Reynolds: A Complete Catalogue of his Paintings* (New Haven and London, 2 vols, 2000).

880 Sketches by the same hand in the British Museum were shown in an exhibition of forgeries held in the Department of Prints and Drawings in 1960, a photograph of a similar drawing in a private collection in 1971 is in the Witt Library, and a further work titled *Mrs Meyrick* was auctioned at Lempertz, Cologne, 20 May 2006 (lot 1291).

881 Unless they are part of lot 689, 'nine portraits of ladies', not otherwise identified, which were purchased at the sale by Partridge.

## JOHN INIGO RICHARDS

1731 London–1810 London

### Orpington Church, Kent

LL 3805 (LP 41)

Watercolour, with pen and ink, with an ink border around the image, on laid paper, laid down on a further sheet of paper of the same size
21.5 x 28.8 cm (trimmed irreg.)
Date: 1768, with an added signature of 1775

Inscr: J. Richards. / 1775 (brown ink, bottom left corner); ORPINGTON. 1768. (black ink, centre, under image)[882]

Prov: Cecil Reginald Grundy, 1924; given by him to the Trustees, January 1935[883]

Lit: *The Connoisseur*, vol. 77 (March 1927), illus. p. 169, p. 185; *The Connoisseur*, vol. 78 (August 1927), p. 250

From 1759 Richards was a successful stage designer at Covent Garden, London, and between 1777 and 1803 he was the theatre's principal painter. From 1762 he exhibited landscapes and ruin subjects at the Society of Artists of Great Britain. From 1769 to 1783 he exhibited at the Free Society of Artists, and was also a founding member of the Royal Academy, where between 1769 and 1809 he exhibited capriccios and landscapes. In 1786 Richards was elected secretary of the Royal Academy, where he frequently clashed with Joseph Farington. He continued to design for the theatre until his death in 1810.

LL 3805 is one of a set of four watercolours by Richards depicting churches in north-west Kent.[884] It shows the parish church of All Saints, Orpington (an early Gothic structure, endowed by the Archbishop of Canterbury in 1173) with a funeral being conducted in the foreground. The present existence and location of the other three watercolours is unknown but they are illustrated in various volumes of *The Connoisseur*: *Downe Church, Kent* included figures attending a christening party in the foreground and dates from 1775;[885] *Hayes Church, Kent* is from the same year and includes a wedding procession;[886] *St Mary Cray, Kent* is the fourth work and dates from 1778 and includes a small figure, wearing black, possibly the vicar.[887]

All four works were engraved in 1786 and published by Pollard and Jukes.[888] Intriguingly, the Orpington engraving that relates closely to the Lady Lever watercolour has had its

882 There is a watermark on the backing paper but it has not been possible to identify this. There is a photograph of this in the LLAG files.

883 LLAG files: recorded on accession card.

884 *The Connoisseur*, vol. 77 (March 1927), p. 185.

885 Ibid., p. 169.

886 *The Connoisseur*, vol. 78 (August 1927), p. 213.

887 *The Connoisseur*, vol. 69 (May 1924), p. 41.

888 In 1927 Dr F. William Cock reported having a series of engravings of the watercolours. See *The Connoisseur*, vol. 78 (August 1927), p. 250. The engravings of *Hayes*, *St Mary Cray* and *Orpington* are included in the British Library's Kings Topographical Collection XVIII 1–62, Kent, Part 4.

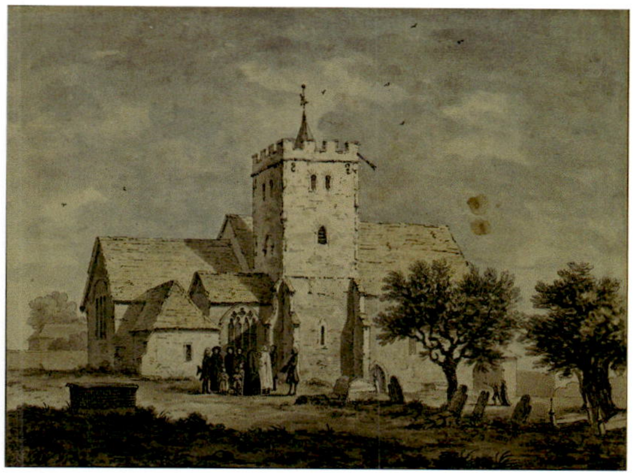

LL 3805

foreground figures altered. In the print, the grave remains open and a coffin is being carried towards it by female pall bearers. *The Connoisseur* described it as a funeral of a single woman, 'the pall being white, and its black strings held by girls as pall bearers'.[889] *Orpington* is the only watercolour to have been signed and dated twice; the most likely explanation being that Richards produced it in 1768 as a one-off, and then in 1775 when he began to conceive of it as a series to be engraved, added the later signature and date. This explanation is supported by the observation in *The Connoisseur*, in a piece probably written by its editor and owner of the four watercolours, Cecil Grundy, that in each work except *Orpington* the figures have been added later, suggesting that Richards may have added them in order to make the other three works similar to *Orpington*, and therefore part of a set.[890]

With its restricted colour palette, LL 3805 is typical of late eighteenth-century topographical watercolours by artists such as Michael Angelo Rooker (1746–1801) and Thomas Hearne (1744–1817).

889 *The Connoisseur*, vol. 78 (August 1927), p. 250.
890 *The Connoisseur*, vol. 77 (March 1927), p. 185.

## CHARLES JAMES RICHARDSON
1806 London–1871 London

### The Garden Porch, Coombe Abbey
LL 3879 (WHL 232)

Watercolour over pencil on wove paper, laid down on card
26.7 x 17.1 cm (sight)
Date: 1840 or earlier

Prov: bt. from B. T. Batsford by Lever, 2 September 1913 (£4 4s)

Charles James Richardson was an architect, architectural draughtsman and collector of architectural drawings. He was Sir John Soane's pupil from 1824 to 1830, then his assistant until Soane died in 1837. He designed housing for the 5th Earl of Harrington's South Kensington estate and for other London landowners, but his major achievement was as a pioneering student of Elizabethan and Jacobean architecture, on which he published important illustrated books. His interest in the architecture of the sixteenth and seventeenth centuries informed his own designs, published as *Picturesque Designs for Mansions, Villas, Lodges, etc.* (London, 1870).

LL 3879 and LL 3880 (see below) were lithographed and reproduced side by side as plate 14 in Richardson's *Architectural Remains of the Reigns of Elizabeth and James the First* (London, 1840).[891] They were presumably made for this purpose.[892] An engraving based on LL 3879 illustrates an article about Coombe Abbey by Richardson in *The Builder*.[893]

Coombe (or Combe) Abbey, a medieval building with seventeenth-century and later additions, is near Coventry in Warwickshire. The picturesque garden porch was attached to the east wing, which was demolished and rebuilt by William Eden Nesfield in the 1860s. Nesfield incorporated the re-erected porch into his design,[894] but his new wing was itself demolished in the 1920s.
JoS

891 In the published version of LL 3879 there is a female figure emerging from the door.
892 Victoria & Albert Museum: comparable architectural watercolours by Richardson for publication are contained in four albums: 3301, 1–26; 3302, 1–27; 3303, 1–31 and 3304, 1–32.
893 *The Builder*, vol. 4 (3 January 1846), pp. 5–7.
894 Victoria & Albert Museum: D1386-1907.

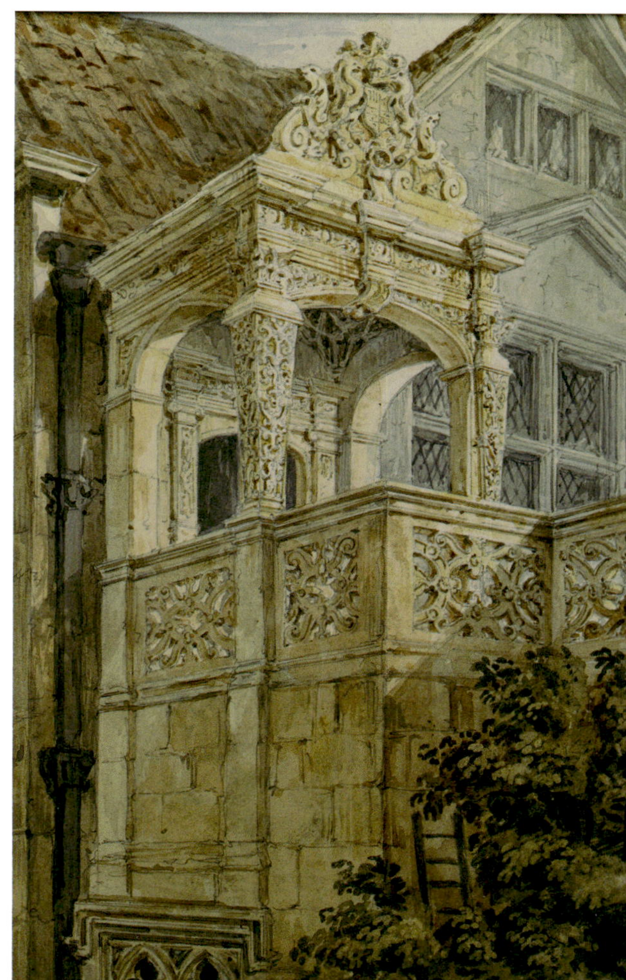

LL 3879

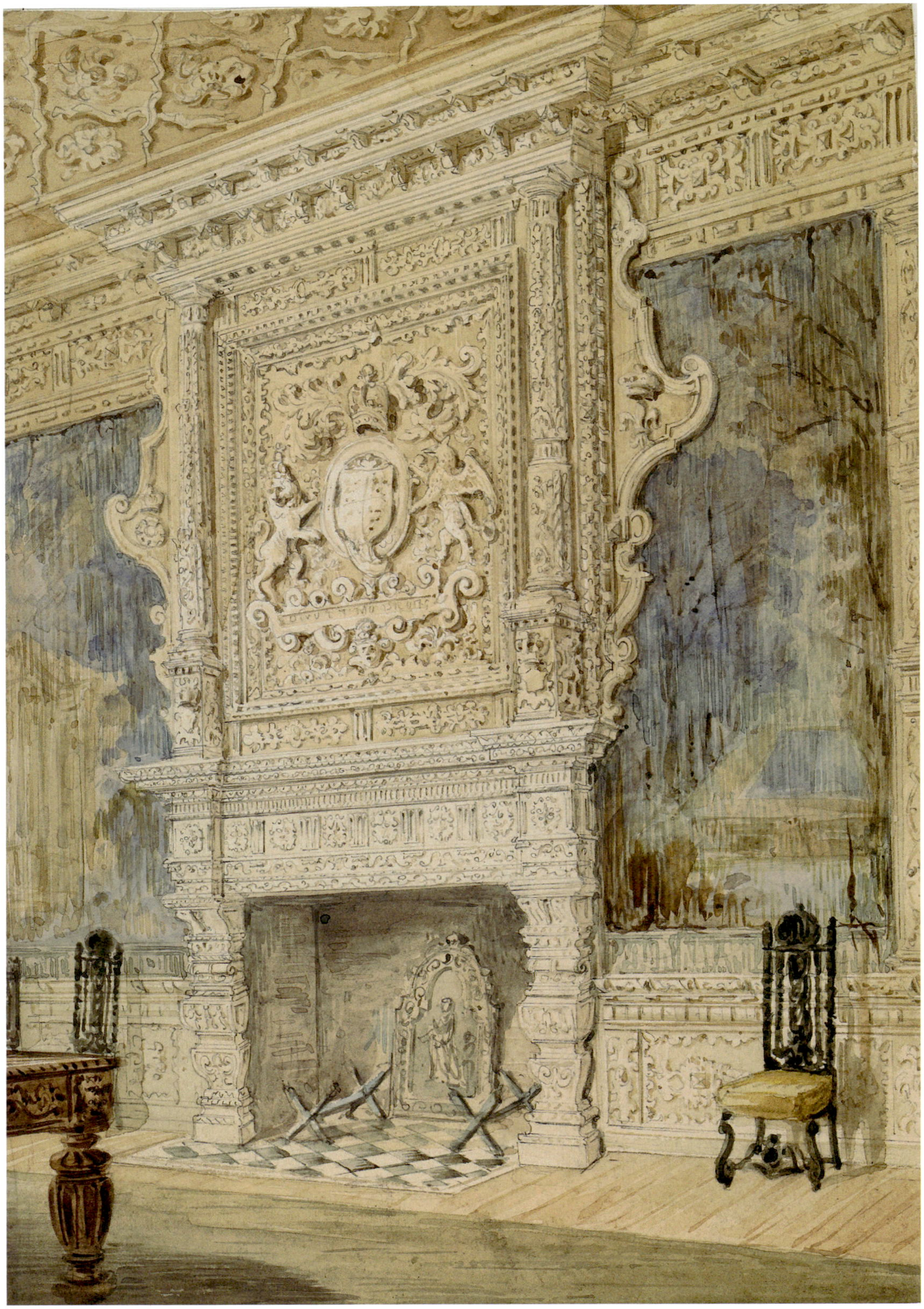

LL 3880

**Fireplace, Coombe Abbey**
LL 3880 (WHL 233)

Watercolour over pencil on wove paper
27.5 x 20.2 cm (sight)
Date: 1840 or earlier

Prov: bt. from B. T. Batsford by Lever, 2 September 1913 (£5 5s)

Like LL 3879 (see above), LL 3880 was reproduced in Richardson's *Architectural Remains of the Reigns of Elizabeth and James the First* (London, 1840). A lithograph showing the same fireplace in its wider setting is in S. C. Hall's *The Baronial Halls and Picturesque Edifices of England* (London, 1848), where the decoration of the room is said to have been carried out for a visit by Queen Elizabeth I (Richardson believed it was associated with Princess Elizabeth, daughter of James I, who lived at Coombe as a child). The room was in the north-east corner of the north wing, on the upper floor.

Large parts of Coombe Abbey were demolished after the house was sold in 1923, and original decorative features were removed.[895] Panelling from this room was with the dealers White Allom in April 1924, and a chimneypiece from Coombe, very similar to the one shown in LL 3880 but with a different overmantel, was with the same dealers in 1928.[896]
JoS

895 See J. Harris, *Moving Rooms: the trade in architectural salvage* (New Haven and London, 2007) and R. Moore, *A History of Coombe Abbey* (Coventry, 1983).
896 LLAG files: correspondence. See also the advertisement in *The Connoisseur*, vol. 82 (December 1928), p. 24.

## THOMAS MILES RICHARDSON

1784 Newcastle upon Tyne–1848 Newcastle upon Tyne

### Newcastle upon Tyne and Gateshead from the Ropery Banks

LL 3988 (WHL 4426)

Watercolour, gum arabic and chalk over pencil on wove paper
32.3 x 50.2 cm
Date: c. 1816–33

Annot: Newcastle-Upon-Tyne and Gateshead from Ropery Banks (pencil, upper left, verso)

Prov: S. H. Fraser; his sale, Christie's, 20 December 1922 (lot 7); bt. by Gooden and Fox (90 gns) for Lever (£99 4s 6d)

Exh: Newcastle upon Tyne, Newcastle Institute, *Second Annual Exhibition of Pictures of the Newcastle Institute for the Promotion of the Fine Arts* 1833 (cat. no. unknown)

Richardson was the central figure in the establishment of an independent community of artists in early nineteenth-century Newcastle. When his father, a schoolmaster, died in 1806, Richardson took over his job. In 1813 he decided to pursue the career of an artist, teaching and producing drawings and engravings of local antiquities. Richardson exhibited oils and watercolours in London, and was then instrumental in founding the Newcastle Institute in 1822. The more ambitious Northern Academy began its brief life in 1828, drawing exhibitors from across the country, but was wound up in 1831. Richardson's subject-matter was found mainly in the north of England and the Scottish borders. He was extremely active as a teacher in and around Newcastle and fathered six artist sons in two marriages; the best-known, Thomas Miles Junior, painted large panoramic landscapes that have often been confused with his father's.

Richardson had one of his earliest successes with a huge oil depicting a distant view of *Newcastle from Gateshead Fell*, purchased by the town council in 1816.[897] LL 3988 is in some senses a sequel to that work, though more an urban than a rural view. It shows the Tyne, looking westwards, with Newcastle to the right and Gateshead to the left, and although first exhibited in 1833 it may have been painted some years earlier. The Ropery Banks had long been a vantage point from which to view the growing city. Spoil from the local collieries was first deposited there in the middle of the sixteenth century. In the 1820s, however, this open ground outside the city's walls saw new roads and new housing built around it.[898] Richardson was surely aware that such open spaces, with their historic connections to the development of the city, would continue to be encroached with the advance of industrialisation. Around the time of the work's exhibition in 1833, a similar view but made from the bottom of the bank near the river was engraved in aquatint by W. H. Timms after Henry Perlee Parker, Richardson's associate in the promotion of the arts in the city.[899]
TW

897 P. Usherwood, *Art for Newcastle. Thomas Miles Richardson and the Newcastle Exhibition 1822–1843* (exh. cat., Newcastle upon Tyne, Laing Art Gallery, 1984), p. 54 (cat. 41).

898 Eneas Mackenzie, *Historical Account of Newcastle upon Tyne: Including the Borough of Gateshead* (Newcastle upon Tyne, 1827), pp. 182–86.

899 See *A view of Newcastle & Gateshead from the Ropery Bank on the Road going to Shields* in Usherwood, *Art for Newcastle*, pp. 47–53.

## WILLIAM RICHARDSON

date and place of birth unknown–1877 London

### Helmsley Castle, Yorkshire

LL 3987 (WHL 2196)

Watercolour over pencil on wove paper
17.1 x 27 cm
Date: 1844

Inscr: W. RICHARDSON / 1844 (watercolour, bottom centre)

Prov: bt. from B. T. Batsford by Lever, 8 June 1915 (3 gns)

William Richardson the painter may have been the same William Richardson who in 1836 applied to become an associate of the Institute of British Architects, describing himself as 'architect of York'; he was duly elected, but defaulted in 1848.[900] The painter William Richardson produced watercolours of architectural subjects, including those lithographed as illustrations to Edward Churton's *The Monastic Ruins of Yorkshire* (York, 1843, 1856). He exhibited landscapes and views of buildings in Yorkshire and elsewhere, from various London addresses, at the Royal Academy 1842–69, at the Society of British Artists 1844–77 and at the British Institution 1845–52.

LL 3987 was reproduced in S. C. Hall's *The Baronial Halls and Picturesque Edifices of England* (London, 1848), having presumably been painted for this purpose. The published plate is dated 1 March 1846. In the watercolour, the treatment of the architectural setting is highly finished while the figures and furniture are only roughly sketched in. The figures in the published version are different. The subject is a room in the mansion built by Edward Manners in the second half of the sixteenth century, within the medieval walls of Helmsley Castle.[901]
JoS

900 Victoria & Albert Museum: RIBA nomination papers, Av1, p. 44.

901 J. Clark, *Helmsley Castle* (London, 2004).

LL 3988

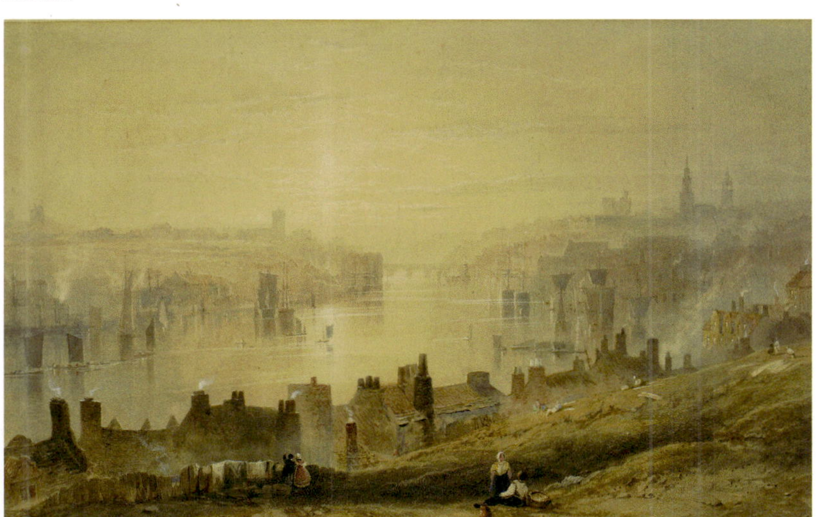

LL 3987

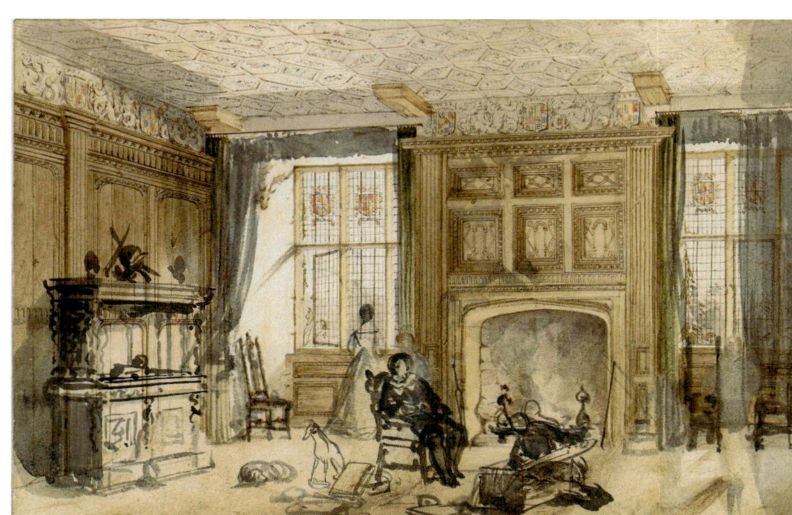

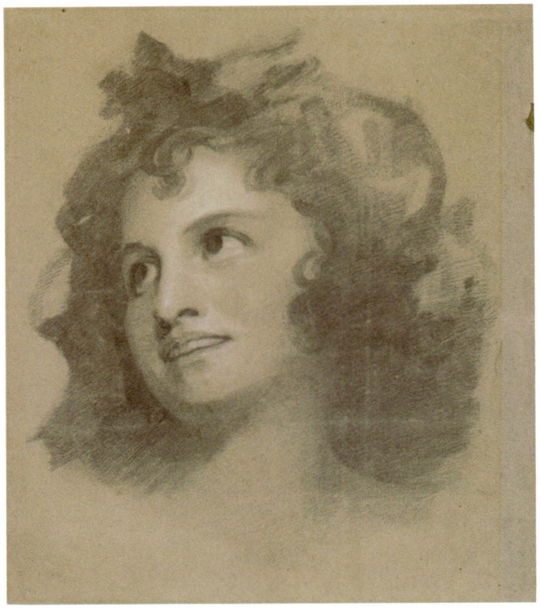

LL 3806

## AFTER GEORGE ROMNEY

1734 Beckside, Lancashire–1802 Kendal, Westmorland

**Emma Hart, Lady Hamilton, as Euphrosyne**
LL 3806 (WHL 4428)

Pencil and black and white chalk on grey paper
44.5 x 39.8 cm
Date: possibly late nineteenth century

Prov: Dr Thomas Munro;[902] Mrs Athelstan Coode; Christie's, 20 December 1922 (lot 28); bt. by Gooden and Fox (£84) for Lever (£88 4s)

This drawing is closely related to an oval oil sketch by (or at least traditionally attributed to) Romney, measuring 55 x 41 cm, currently untraced but in Lever's day successively in the well-known collections of Jeffery Whitehead and G. Harland Peck. Many copies of it in oil are known. Despite its celebrity in the Victorian and Edwardian period, when it was widely exhibited and frequently reproduced,[903] the oil sketch is not documented in Romney's own lifetime, although it may be the *Portrait of a lady as Euphrosyne, head only* which was lot 67 in the artist's posthumous studio sale (Christie's, 27 April 1807) and fetched 5 guineas. Its familiarity dated from its exhibition at the Royal Academy's *Old Masters* exhibition in 1879, and was at least in part generated by the identification of the model as Lady Hamilton, for the Victorian public the most prized of all Romney's sitters. This identification was later contested.[904]

George Romney was one of the leading portraitists in England between 1762, when he came to London from Lancashire, and 1798, when he retired. Despite or perhaps because of the fact that he was never a member of the Royal Academy nor exhibited there, he was the principal rival to Sir Joshua Reynolds from around 1775 onwards. He met the future Lady Hamilton in 1782 when she was Emma Hart, the mistress of his friend and patron Charles Greville, and over the next nine years she modelled for dozens of his fancy heads and female portraits in literary and mythological guises. Romney was never happier than when painting her, and in the late nineteenth century it was generally assumed that they had been lovers, giving the artist an honoured, if tangential place in the Lady Hamilton legend that grew up in that period.

Lever acquired LL 3806 as an autograph work by Romney, but it is not at all characteristic of his draughtsmanship, and he virtually never made pencil studies for his portraits, least of all his vibrant fancy heads. It exhibits slight variations in detail from the oil: the face is more broadly shaped, the gaze of the eyes is less upward, and a couple of extra curls are provided which smooth out the outline of the head. The provenance given in the 1922 sale catalogue (the surname was perhaps deliberately misspelt) raises the intriguing possibility that the drawing is a product of the circle of students around Dr Thomas Monro, the patron in the 1790s of J. R. Cozens, Girtin and Turner. However, this seems extremely unlikely, and the style of the drawing is much more consonant with a late Victorian origin. LL 3806 may have been made in connection with, or from, one of the engravings that appeared between 1898 and 1900.
AK

902 The drawing was described in the 1922 sale catalogue as 'from the collection of Dr. Thomas Munro' and the previous lot consigned by the same vendor was a landscape by Dr Thomas Munro.

903 For exhibitions down to 1900, and the four reproductions that appeared in the period 1898–1900, see T. H. Ward and William Roberts, *Romney* (London, 2 vols, 1904), vol. II, p. 183. The painting was subsequently shown in Paris in 1909 and in Rome in 1911.

904 Ward and Roberts, *Romney*, vol. II, p. 183, wrote that it 'certainly does not represent Lady Hamilton; it is much more likely to be a study of the head of Mrs Crouch the actress'; however, this judgement itself seems questionable.

## DANTE GABRIEL ROSSETTI

1828 London–1882 Birchington-on-Sea, Kent

**Pandora**
LL 3647 (WHL 4029)[905]

Pastel on paper
100.8 x 66.7 cm, on two joined sheets; 46.9 x 66.7 cm (top); 53.9 x 66.7 cm (bottom)
Date: 1878

Inscr: DGR [monogram] / 1878 (pastel, bottom left corner); ULTIMA / MANET / SPES (pastel, on casket)

Frame: gilt and oak with ribbed sides with engraved circles and squares on the sides; the flat has a border of circles and lozenges[906]

Prov: artist's executors' sale, Christie's, 12 May 1883 (lot 52); bt. by Smith (£120 15s); L. R. Valpy;[907] his sale, Christie's, 26 May 1888 (lot 102); bt. by Scott (£157 10s); Sir George A. Drummond, Montreal, Canada; his sale, Christie's, 26 June 1919 (lot 128); bt. from Gooden and Fox by Lever, June 1919 (£204 9s 9d)

Exh: Port Sunlight, Lady Lever Art Gallery, *The Pre-Raphaelites – Their Friends and Followers*, 1948 (cat. 176); London, Tate Gallery, *The Pre-Raphaelites*, 1984 (cat. 250); Liverpool, Walker Art Gallery and Amsterdam, Van Gogh Museum, *Dante Gabriel Rossetti*, 2003–04 (cat. 146); Port Sunlight, Lady Lever Art Gallery and tour, *Pre-Raphaelite Drawings*, 2006–2008 (no cat. no.)

Lit: Virginia Surtees, *Dante Gabriel Rossetti 1828–1882: The Paintings and Drawings: A Catalogue Raisonné* (London, 2 vols, 1971), vol. I, p. 126 (cat. 224 R I A); Mary Bennett, *Artists of the Pre-Raphaelite Circle: The First Generation* (London, 1988), pp. 180–82, illus. p. 181

Rossetti, the son of an Italian political refugee and Dante scholar, was famous as an artist and poet. As a young man he read widely and studied at Sass's drawing academy from 1841. He entered the Royal Academy Schools in 1845, although he did not finish his course. In 1848, with William Holman Hunt and John Everett Millais (see pp. 138–42), he helped found the Pre-Raphaelite Brotherhood. His work as part of this circle addressed the medieval and romantic ideals of Pre-Raphaelitism rather than the 'Truth to nature' precept followed by his fellow painters. During the 1850s his work centred on themes of doomed romantic love from Dante and the Arthurian romances. He also produced a series of intense drawings of Elizabeth Siddal, his pupil, model and later wife (they married in 1860). In 1857 he collaborated with William Morris and Edward Burne-Jones (see pp. 25–39) on the Arthurian mural decorations of the Oxford Union Society; later, he worked with them again in Morris, Marshall, Faulkner & Co., designing stained glass. The 1860s saw a change of subject-matter and style, with Rossetti producing depictions of beautiful women in languorous poses, in a style heralding Aestheticism and the beginnings of Art Nouveau and Symbolism.

905 Tatlock, p. 111, confuses some of the details (inscriptions, date and provenance) with those of the earlier oil painting of the same title.

906 Bennett, *Artists of the Pre-Raphaelite Circle*, p. 180. For details on Rossetti's frames, see Alistair Grieve, 'The Applied Art of D.G. Rossetti – I. His Picture-Frames', *The Burlington Magazine*, vol. 115 (January 1973), pp. 16–24.

907 Leonard Valpy was a solicitor based in London who began to patronise Rossetti in 1867. For details of Valpy's biography and collecting habits, see Macleod, *Art and the Victorian Middle Class*, p. 483.

Between 1868 and his death, despite declining health and an increasingly reclusive life, Rossetti produced some of his most powerful paintings including *Dante's Dream* (1871, Walker Art Gallery, Liverpool).

The Lady Lever pastel represents Pandora, one of various mythological figures envisaged as the first woman on earth. She is given a casket by Jupiter which she is told not to open. In some versions of the Greek myth her husband Prometheus opens the box; in others (as with Rossetti's depiction) it is Pandora herself who opens the casket. In both versions, all the evils and disasters are let loose to rush into the world, leaving only hope safe in the box.

LL 3647 is a later version of the Pandora subject, which Rossetti first conceived in 1869. He produced two pastel three-quarter length studies and two further head studies which resulted in an oil painting of a three-quarter length figure in 1871 (private collection).[908] In 1874 he was still hoping to paint a full-length figure, although this does not seem to have materialised.[909]

In 1869, the date when he first designed the composition for the oil version, Rossetti wrote an accompanying sonnet, later published in his *Poems* of 1870:[910]

What of the end, Pandora? Was it thine,
The deed that set these fiery pinions free?
Ah! Wherefore did the Olympian consistory
In its own likeness make thee half divine?
Was it that Juno's brow might stand a sign
For ever? And the mien of Pallas be
A deadly thing? And that all men might see
In Venus' eyes the gaze of Proserpine?

What of the end? These beat their wings at will,
The ill-born things, the good things turned to ill,-
Powers of the impassioned hours prohibited.
Aye, clench the casket now! Whither they go
Thou mayst not dare to think: nor canst thou know
If Hope still pent there be alive or dead.

The oil version of Pandora was one of a number of subject pictures from 1868 onwards for which Jane Morris was the model, and her same distinctive features appear in LL 3647. Rossetti retained studies of her in his studio, presumably using them for his later version.[911] Jane, the wife

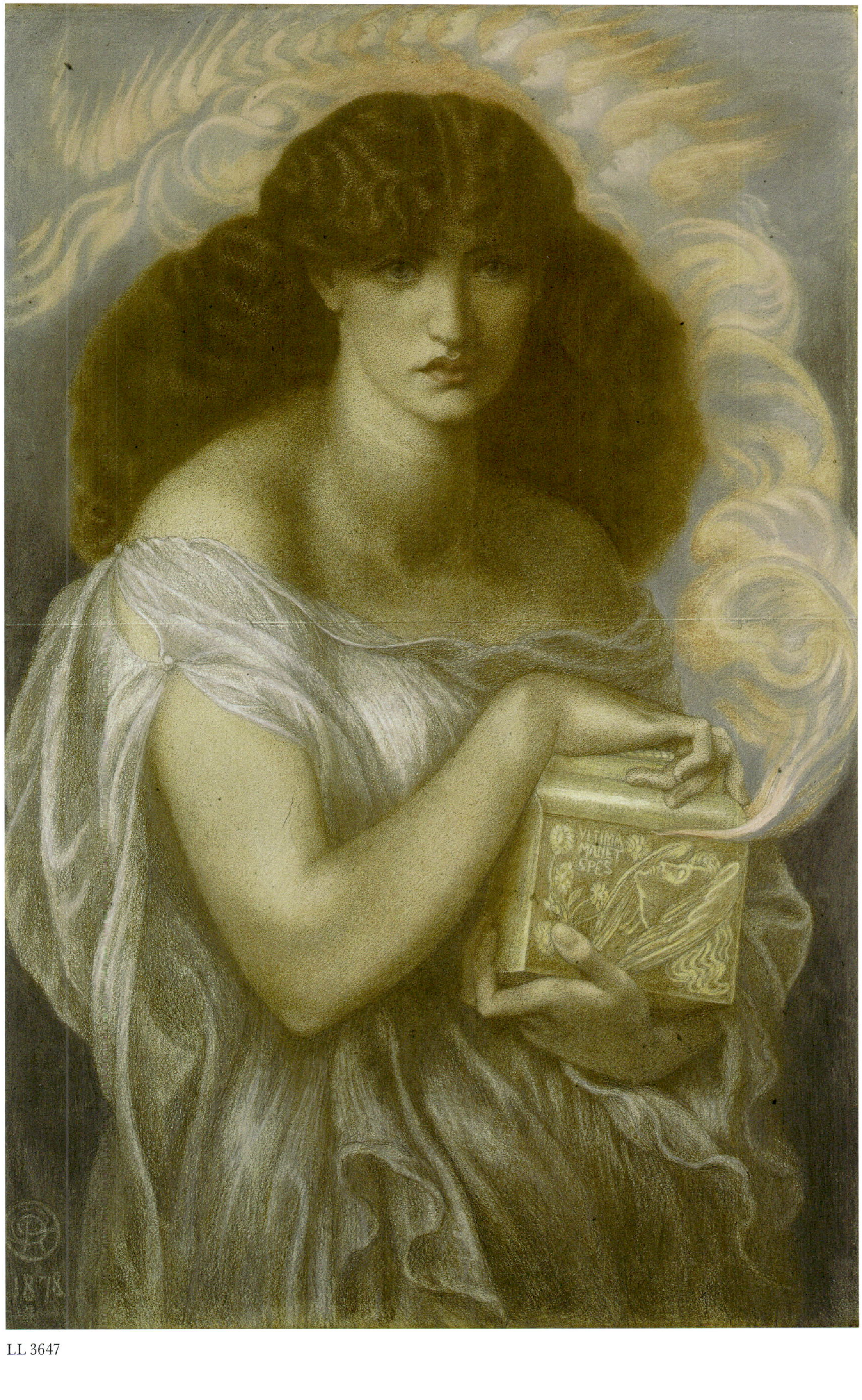

LL 3647

908 Surtees, *Dante Gabriel Rossetti*, vol. I, pp. 125–26, lists these studies as 224A-D; the oil painting is 224.
909 Bennett, *Artists of the Pre-Raphaelite Circle*, p. 180.
910 William Michael Rossetti, *The Collected Works of Dante Gabriel Rossetti* (London, 2 vols, 1897), vol. I, p. 360.
911 William Michael Rossetti, *Dante Gabriel Rossetti as Designer and Writer* (London, 1889), p. 80, quoted by Bennett, *Artists of the Pre-Raphaelite Circle*, p. 182.

of William Morris, developed an increasingly intimate personal and artistic relationship with Rossetti following the death of Elizabeth Siddal in 1862 and the Morrises' move back to central London after 1865. In March 1878 Rossetti wrote to Jane: 'I have taken up the Pandora drawing again with a fresh system of bogies round the head, and have now made it very complete indeed'.[912] Some writers have suggested an autobiographical interpretation of this piece, consistent with its inscription Ultima Manet Spes ('Hope remains last'), that Jane Morris represented a final hope to Rossetti.[913]

In February 1879 Rossetti wrote that he had produced the subject of Pandora (along with Proserpine) in replica, 'for the market as I wouldn't part with the originals, but haven't spotted a buyer yet'.[914] Another version of LL 3647, dated 1879 (Fogg Art Museum, Harvard University), was made for Theodore Watts-Dunton, who had helped Rossetti in providing legal advice.[915] The Lady Lever version has broader features in the face. In contrast to the oil, the features of Jane Morris in both later versions have become exaggerated; her bare arm and uncovered, oversized shoulders find their source in Michelangelo, while her hands have 'become almost talons', giving her a grotesque aspect.[916] Mary Bennett has suggested that 'Both versions ... replace the doom-laden introspection of the earlier idea with a writhing menace, which reflects the troubled thoughts of the artist's last years'.[917]

912 John Bryson and Janet Troxell (eds), *Dante Gabriel Rossetti and Jane Morris: Their Correspondence* (Oxford, 1976), no. 28 (8 March 1878), quoted by Bennett, *Artists of the Pre-Raphaelite Circle*, p. 182, n. 9.

913 This argument is expressed in Julian Treuherz, Elizabeth Prettejohn and Edwin Becker, *Dante Gabriel Rossetti* (exh. cat., Liverpool, Walker Art Gallery and Amsterdam, Van Gogh Museum, 2003–04), p. 209 (cat. 146).

914 Bryson and Troxell (eds), *Dante Gabriel Rossetti*, no. 52 (15 February 1879).

915 Surtees, *Dante Gabriel Rossetti*, vol. I, p. 126 (cats. 224 R I and 224 R IA), lists LL 3647 as a 'study', but it is in fact an earlier version of the Fogg Art Museum *Pandora*.

916 L. Parris (ed.), *The Pre-Raphaelites* (exh. cat., London, Tate Gallery, 1984) (cat. 250); Bennett, *Artists of the Pre-Raphaelite Circle*, pp. 180–82.

917 Bennett, *Artists of the Pre-Raphaelite Circle*, p. 182.

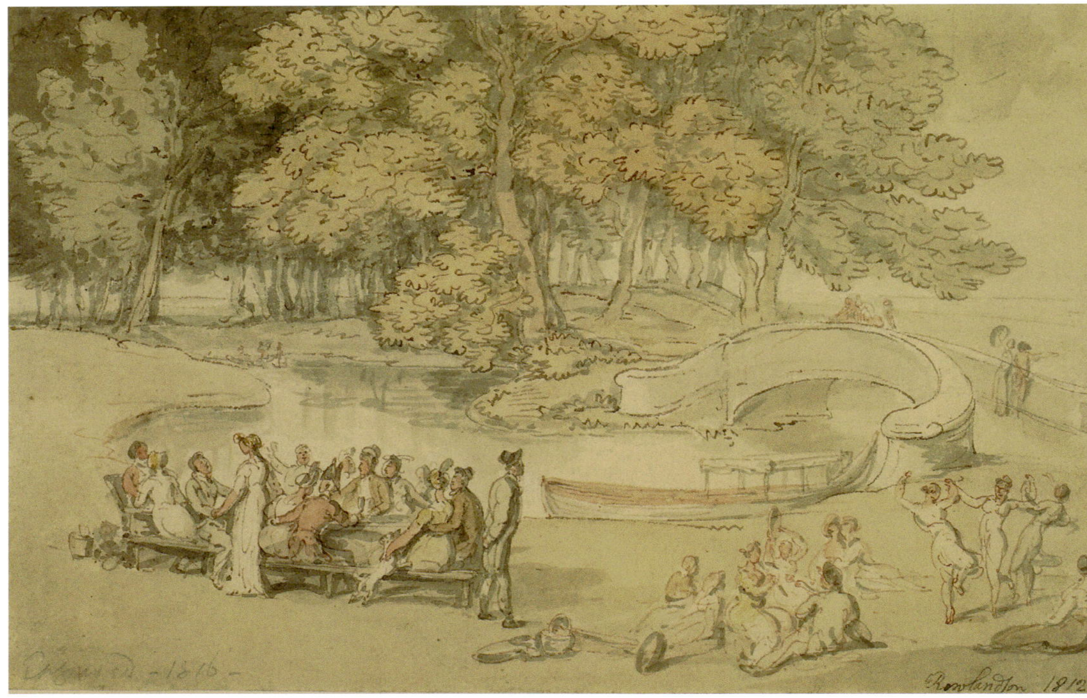


LL 3989

**THOMAS ROWLANDSON**
1756 London–1827 London

**The Social Day**
LL 3989 (WHL 4176)

Watercolour over pencil, with pen and brown and red inks laid down on original wash-line mount, with a further wash-line mount added later
14.5 x 23.5 cm (image); 15.9 x 24.9 cm (original wash-line mount); 19.2 x 28.2 cm (later wash-line mount)
Date: 1812

Inscr: Rowlandson 1812 (watercolour, bottom right)

Annot: Engraved-1816- (pencil, bottom left); "The social Day"/ (Engraved-1816-) (pencil [same hand], lower centre, on later wash-line mount);[918] T. Rowlandson / 12 x18 / keep [illeg.] (pencil, partially rubbed out, bottom right corner, on later wash-line mount); j; p; H ([? stamp], lower centre, on later wash-line mount)

Prov: J. P. Heseltine; his sale, Sotheby's, 25 March 1920 (lot 168); bt. by Gooden and Fox for Lever (£31 19s 6d)

Lit: F. Gordon Roe, *Rowlandson, The Life and Art of a British Genius* (Leigh-on-Sea, 1947), pl. 32

Rowlandson was the only son of a wool and silk merchant who went bankrupt when Thomas was still a child. He was brought up by his wealthy aunt and uncle in Soho, London. He entered the Royal Academy as a student in 1772 and first exhibited there in 1775. In 1778 he left the Academy, setting up on his own in Wardour Street. Rowlandson produced an enormous number of watercolours, using his characteristic technique of pen and ink outlines and flat washes of colour, in the tradition of such contemporaries as Francis Towne (pp. 181–82). His work included humorous subjects that owed much to the influence of John Hamilton Mortimer (1740–79), and caricatures.

LL 3989 is an example of one of Rowlandson's landscapes which, with their elegant composition and rococo treatment, owe much to his visit to Paris while still a student in 1774 as well as to the influence of Gainsborough. LL 3989 combines a landscape setting with the depiction of a number of figures, drawn with Rowlandson's usual deftness of touch, some enjoying a picnic, others playing music, and three figures dancing on the far right (perhaps a reference to the 'Three Graces'). While the work retains the mannered rococo treatment characteristic of Rowlandson's landscapes throughout his career, the drawing displays the elongated neo-classical figures that can be seen in his work after 1800.

A version of this drawing, titled *The Social Day*, was etched and published in *Rowlandson's World in Miniature*, published by R. Ackerman in 1816.[919] The plates were published in eight monthly numbers; *The Social Day* was published on 1 August 1816. The composition of the etching

918 The hand could be that of J. P. Heseltine but a comparison with examples known to be his handwriting has not been conclusive. It does not appear to be Lever's.

919 Joseph Grego, *Rowlandson: The Caricaturist* (London, 2 vols, 1880), vol. II, pp. 316–17, illus. p. 316.

remains largely the same as the Lady Lever drawing, although variations give the print more of a sense of caricature, emphasising the drinking and frivolity taking place in the scene. In the etching the centrally placed male figure, walking in the direction of the music makers, holds a tureen, which may contain wine; also a small table has been placed adjacent to the diners, which is overspilling with bottles and other containers; subtle changes, but implying greater frivolous excess than in the drawing.

Both the etching and the Lady Lever drawing may be connected to a poem by Peter Coxe (?1753–1844) titled *The Social Day*, first published in 1823, but announced in the press in 1813. The poem described the various 'polite' pleasures to be derived from a social party at Highgrove, Gloucestershire; the setting of the drawing certainly could be the grounds of a country house, and it may be intended to be Highgrove. It is possible that Rowlandson knew Coxe, and that they had discussed the poem, which pokes fun at these 'polite' pleasures, at least by the time of the etching in 1816.[920] Lever may have been aware of the connection as a first edition copy of the poem was in his private library.[921]

920 Rowlandson and Coxe may have socialised in similar artistic and literary circles. Kim Sloan has pointed out that John Jackson (see pp. 130–31) painted both figures (email correspondence, February 2007). The portrait of Coxe is in Birmingham Museums and Art Gallery and that of Rowlandson is in the National Portrait Gallery, London.

921 Sold Anderson Galleries, New York, 22 February 1926, *The Art Collections of the Late Viscount Leverhulme, Part Four, The Art Library* (lot 94).

## CHARLES PROSPER SAINTON

1861 London–1914 New York

### Three silverpoint drawings

LL 3886–3888

Date: 1897

Prov: in Lever's collection by 1906[922]

### An Idyll

LL 3886 (WHL 1652, TM 245)

Silverpoint and pencil on commercially prepared board

24.7 x 38 cm

Inscr: C Sainton 97 (silverpoint, bottom left)

Exh: London, Fine Art Society, *"Fancies". A series of silver-point drawings by Charles Prosper Sainton*, 1897 (cat. 6)

### A Nymph

LL 3887 (WHL 1653, TM 246)

Silverpoint and pencil on commercially prepared board

33.4 x 15.3 cm

Inscr: C Sainton 97 (pencil, bottom left); C Sainton (silverpoint, bottom right)

Exh: London, Fine Art Society, *"Fancies". A series of silver-point drawings by Charles Prosper Sainton*, 1897 (cat. 5)

922 LL 3886–3888 are listed in the 1906 TM Inventory, but do not appear in the 1905 TM Inventory.

LL 3886

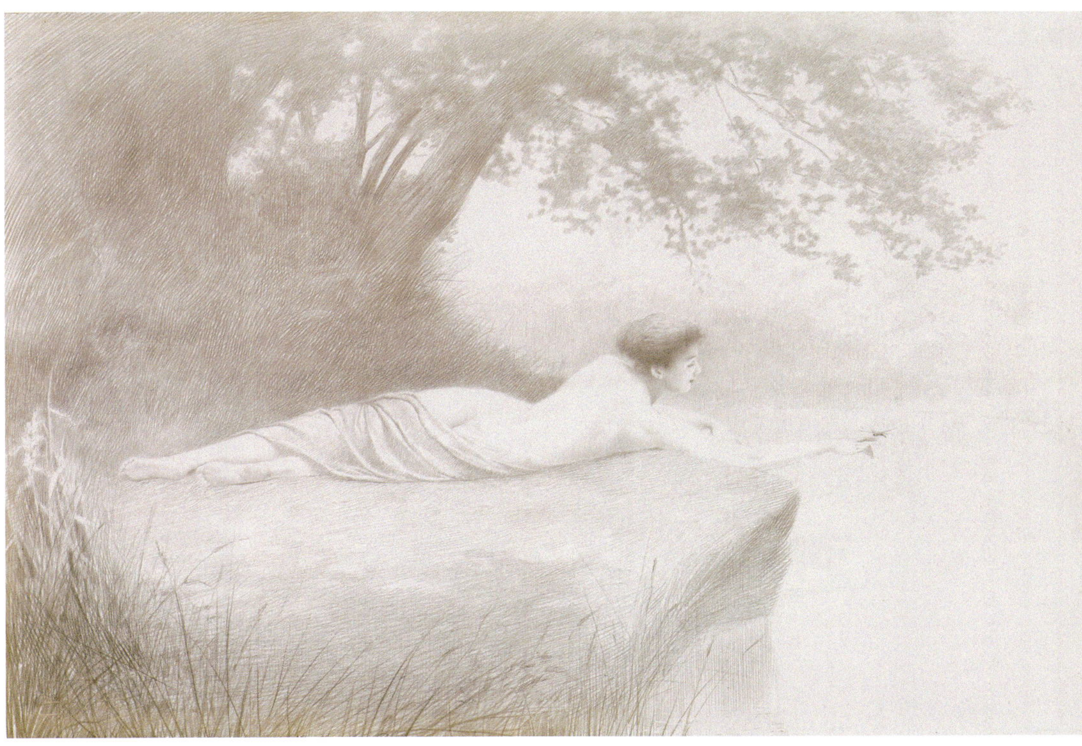

### La Belle du Village

LL 3888 (WHL 1654, TM 247)

Silverpoint and pencil on commercially prepared board

48 x 32.8 cm

Inscr: CSainton 97 (silverpoint, lower right, adjacent to image)

Exh: London, Fine Art Society, *"Fancies". A series of silver-point drawings by Charles Prosper Sainton*, 1897 (cat. 4)

Charles Prosper Sainton was the son of the well-known Toulouse-born violinist and composer, Prosper Philip Sainton, Professor at the Royal Academy of Music, who settled in London in 1845. His mother was the leading singer Helen Dolby, to whom Mendelssohn dedicated his *Six Songs, Op. 57* and who was the composer's choice as contralto for his oratorio *Elijah*.[923] Charles Prosper Sainton was educated at Harrow, where he was captain of the cricket team. He attended the Slade School of Art with Alphonse Legros for five years, before going on to study under the watercolourist, Michele Gordigiani (1830–1909) in Florence and Paris. Sainton practised as a medallist and miniaturist as well as painting a small number of oils, and making at least one drypoint which was based on one of his watercolours. Encouraged by the dealers Dowdeswell & Dowdeswell, he travelled

923 Barbara Clark, 'Philip Prosper Sainton Hon. A.R.C.M 1891–1967', http://www.musicweb-international.com/sainton, consulted 11 January 2008.

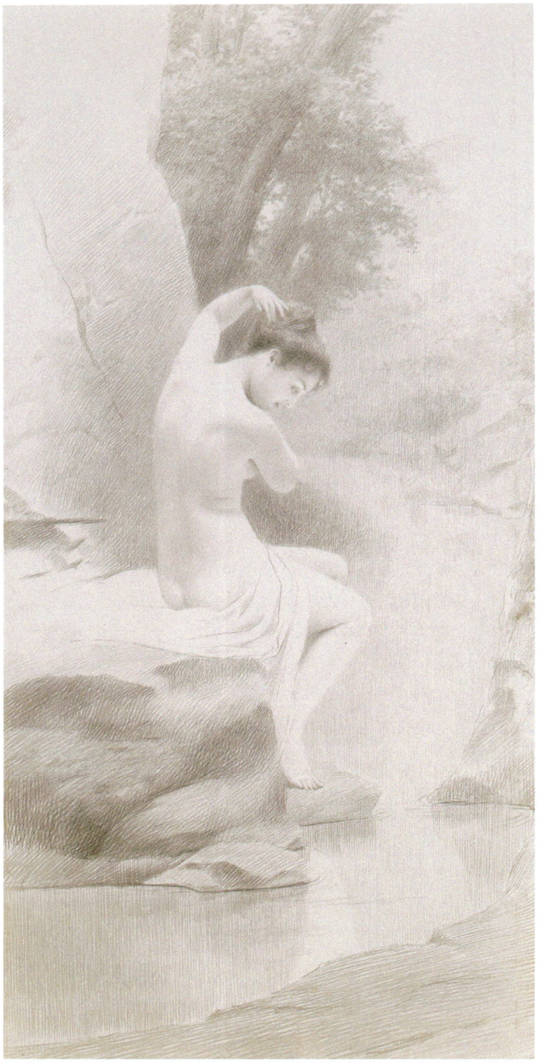

LL 3887

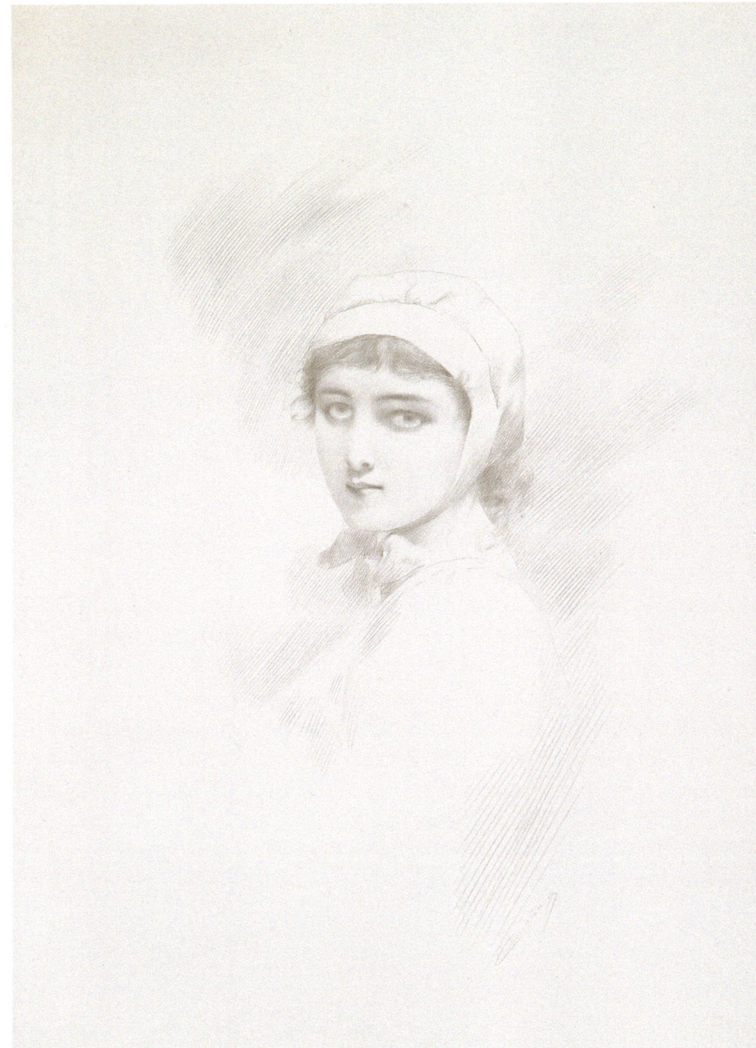

LL 3888

to France for three months in 1890, where he painted and drew French country folk. Sainton exhibited widely in London. He began exhibiting at the Royal Academy in 1887 and at the Paris Salon in 1888. Catalogues of no less than ten one-man exhibitions between 1891 and 1913 survive.[924] Sainton was elected a member of the Royal Institute of Painters in Water-Colours in 1897 and a member of the Royal Miniature Society in 1904. However, he was best known for his watercolours and drawings, particularly in silverpoint,[925] which he first exhibited in 1888, and goldpoint, which attracted the patronage of Edward VII, when Prince of Wales, and of Queen Alexandra, to whom he taught silverpoint. The earliest record of their purchases of Sainton's work is 28 October 1893.[926] The Royal family's interest in him continued into the next reign: shortly after his coronation King George V purchased one of his works at the Royal Institute of Painters in Water-Colours.[927] Several works of his are still in the Royal Collection.[928] He died in the Presbyterian Hospital, New York. A memorial exhibition was held in the Brook Street Gallery in 1925.[929]

A study for *An Idyll* was reproduced in *The Artist* (September 1897), p. 410. The dealer Nathan published reproductions of Sainton's works from 1892. Very deceptive facsimiles were issued of ten of the silverpoints, which were exhibited at the Fine Art Society in July 1897, including all the present works. The facsimiles were sold individually by the Fine Art Society in a portfolio for 8 guineas and at 1 guinea each individually.

Sainton explained his technique in the catalogue to his November 1892 exhibition at the Burlington Gallery.[930] 'Silver Point is simply a drawing, made upon paper, prepared with a wash of opaque-white, with a pencil or stylus of pure silver, fixed in a wooden holder. These drawings are permanent.'[931] This technique was practised in Italy in the fifteenth and early sixteenth century, but then fell into disuse until the second half of the nineteenth century. Alphonse Legros was the primary figure in its revival. In *The Artist*, George C. Williamson praised 'the ethereal lightness of Sainton's silverpoints ... In actual technique the charm largely consists in the fact that the shadows only are represented, the cold gleam of the paper giving all the lights of the figure.'[932]
MH

924 Some of these are recorded by Patricia de Montfort, *Exhibition Culture in London 1878–1908*, http://www.exhibitionculture.arts.gla.ac.uk/person_exhlist.php?pid=970 consulted 11 January 2008. Sainton showed first with Dowdeswell & Dowdeswell from 1889, before moving to the Fine Art Society from 1892 to 1897, and the Continental Gallery from 1898 to 1901. Sainton was also given exhibitions by the Burlington Gallery in 1892, the Quest Gallery in 1903, and the Brook Street Gallery in 1908 and 1913.

925 Sainton was taught silverpoint by Legros. George C. Williamson, 'Charles P. Sainton', *The Artist* (September 1897), pp. 410–19.

926 The Queen lent two miniatures and the Prince of Wales (later George V) one miniature to *Picture miniatures (Paintings in ivory): and Water Colours: and Studies in Oil; and in Pencil by Charles Sainton R.I.* (exh. cat., London, 1903), cats. 2, 3 and 4, unpag.

927 Obituary in *New York Times*, 5 December 1914.

928 Delia Millar, *The Victorian Watercolours and Drawings in the Collection of Her Majesty The Queen* (London, 2 vols, 1995), vol. I, pp. 777–78. Another example is in the collection of the Hunterian Art Gallery, Glasgow.

929 See 'Sainton Memorial Exhibition', *The Connoisseur*, vol. 73 (September 1925), p. 56. A catalogue of this exhibition has not been found.

930 See also 'Dowdeswell's Gallery', *The Artist* (1 January 1890), p. 11, which noted that most of Sainton's drawings in his 1889 Dowdeswell & Dowdeswell exhibition were purchased.

931 *Charles P. Sainton* (exh. cat., London, Burlington Gallery, 1892), unpag.

932 Williamson, 'Charles P. Sainton', p. 414.

## PAUL SANDBY
1731 Nottingham–1809 London

**Landscape with Overthrown Cart**[933]
LL 3992 (LP 61)

Watercolour over pencil with touches of gouache on wove paper
19.5 x 29.4 cm (sight)
Date: 1770s

Prov: bt. from the Fine Art Society by the Trustees, 27 July 1943 (£37 16s)

Exh: London, Fine Art Society, *Exhibition of Early English Watercolours and Drawings*, 1943 (cat. 146)

The son of a textile artisan and the younger brother of Thomas Sandby (1721–98), Paul Sandby was appointed draughtsman to the military survey in Scotland in 1747. During a five-year period at the survey, along with the maps for which he was employed, he produced many pen-and-wash landscape drawings and figure studies. Around 1752 Sandby was in London and had embarked on giving lessons to amateurs, a practice he was to continue for the rest of his career. During the 1760s he produced many watercolour and gouache views of Windsor Castle and its surroundings, where his brother was employed as draughtsman to the Ranger of the Great Park. He was a founding-member of the Royal Academy in 1768, exhibiting there annually until his death. The same year he was appointed to the position of drawing-master to the Royal Military Academy at Woolwich. Credited by one of his obituarists with being the 'father of modern landscape painting in water-colours',[934] he also helped to popularise aquatint, his *Twelve Views in South Wales* (1775) being among the first works in this medium made in Britain. Towards the end of his life Sandby worked more frequently in gouache, yet by the 1790s, when set against the work of artists like John Robert Cozens (see LL 3953, pp. 70–71) and John 'Warwick' Smith (see LL 3995, p. 173), his style seemed old-fashioned.

The great rock depicted in the background of LL 3992 does not appear to be a precise spot. It does bear some resemblance to Dumbarton Rock, situated on the Clyde estuary in the west of Scotland, which Sandby first visited in 1747, and which he depicted in a gouache of about 1779–80 (National Gallery of Canada, Ottawa).[935] However, in Ottawa's view of Dumbarton the rock is depicted as two conjoined hills, not the great mound as seen in LL 3992, suggesting that this is not Dumbarton. The Lady Lever work dates from the 1770s, a period when Sandby began to combine the topography that had dominated his work in the 1750s and 1760s with picturesque elements.[936] In LL 3992 the rock, town and estuary suggest topographical detail, with the incident of the farmer and his broken cart lending a picturesque aspect. The watercolour is a good example of the looser use of line in Sandby's landscapes from the 1770s and 1780s contrasting with the much tighter technique of many of his Windsor architectural subjects from the previous decade. The motif of several horses nuzzling one another was used by Sandby in a number of works throughout his career (see, for example, his *Northeast view of Wakefield Lodge in Whittlebury Forest, Northamptonshire* of 1767; Yale Center for British Art, New Haven).[937]

933 LL 3992 was titled *Landscape and River Scene* on the invoice from the Fine Art Society, 27 July 1943.

934 Quoted by Jane Roberts, *Views of Windsor: Watercolours by Thomas and Paul Sandby from the Collection of Her Majesty Queen Elizabeth II* (exh. cat., Amsterdam, Rijksmuseum and tour, 1995–97), p. 7.

935 I am grateful to Andrew Wyld and Susan Sloman for this suggestion, email correspondence, July 2006. For the Ottawa work, see Douglas E. Schoenherr, *British Drawings from the National Gallery of Canada* (exh. cat., Ottawa, National Gallery of Canada and Canadian tour, 2005–2008), pp. 42–43 (cat. 9). This drawing is based on a much earlier official military drawing now in the National Library of Scotland, Edinburgh.

936 Date suggested by Luke Herrmann, email correspondence, January 2008.

937 John Baskett, *Paul Mellon's Legacy: A Passion for British Art* (exh. cat., New Haven, Yale Center for British Art and London, Royal Academy, 2007), p. 256 (cat. 33), illus. col.

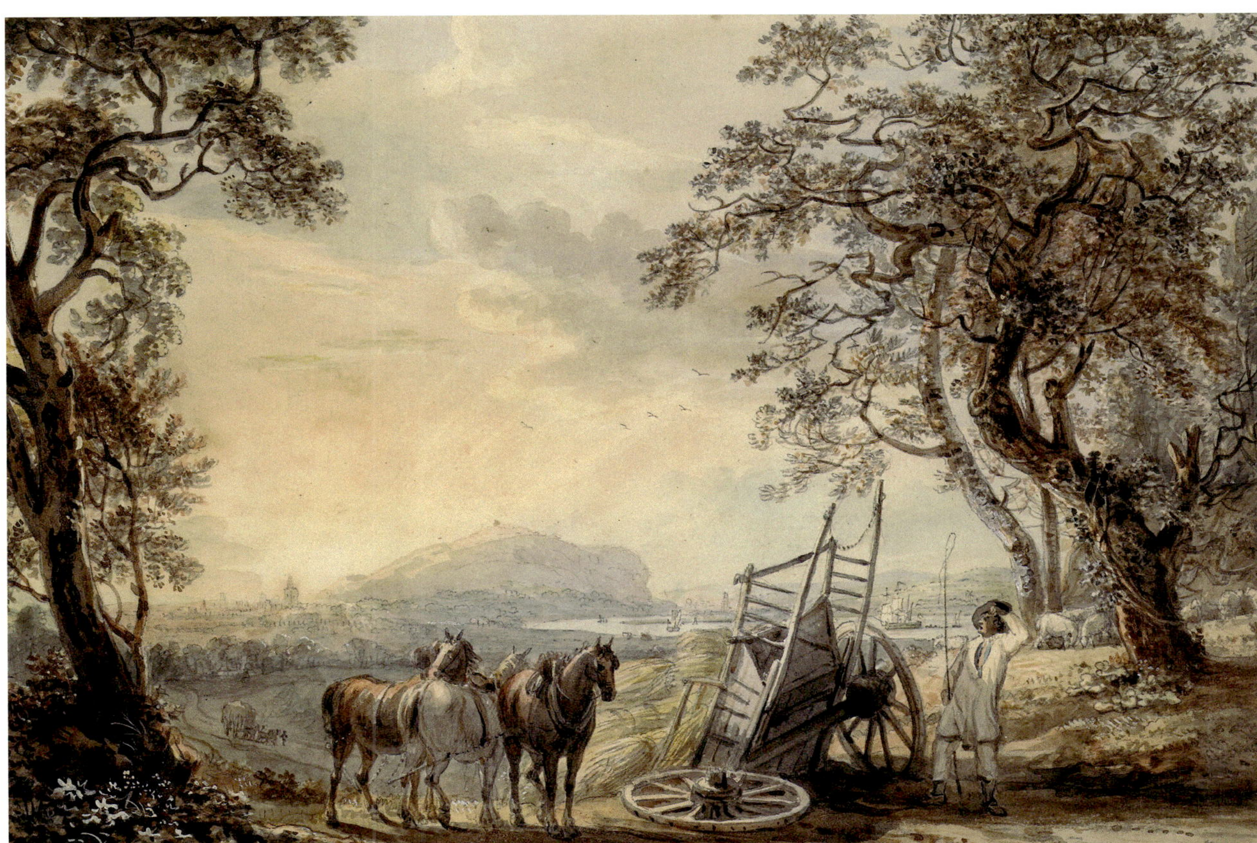

LL 3992

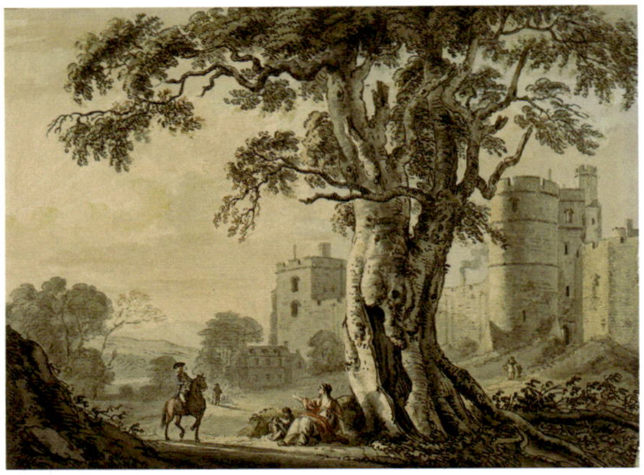

LL 3991

## AFTER PAUL SANDBY

**An Old Castle, with Horseman**[938]
LL 3991 (WHL 291, H 152)

Watercolour, pen and brown ink on laid paper
20.8 x 28. 5 cm
Date: 1798–c. 1809

Inscr: PS / 1781 (brown ink, on tree)
Prov: bt. from James Orrock by Lever, 1904

LL 3991 was purchased by Lever as a work by Paul Sandby purporting to date from 1781 but it is a direct copy of a watercolour by the artist (Sotheby's, London, 16 July 1987 [lot 99]) which is signed and dated PS / 1798 at bottom left. The composition is a capriccio view, typical, as Luke Herrmann has pointed out, of Sandby's work from the 1790s onwards; the contorted beech tree is a motif used often by the artist during this period (see, for example, *An Ancient Beech Tree* in the Victoria & Albert Museum which is signed and dated 1794).[939] The subject is not an exact topographical representation but contains various elements relating to views of Windsor Castle and its forest. The buildings recall Sandby's view of *Castle Hill with the Henry III Tower and the Mary Tudor Tower seen from the south* of c. 1765 (Royal Collection) whereas the foreground with its combination of tree and man on horseback is reminiscent of *Roadway through Windsor Forest* (Victoria & Albert Museum); in reality the combination of these two views would have been impossible.[940] Sandby had many pupils and followers and it is not possible to be conclusive but in its use of pen and ink and loose style, the work closely resembles that of his student Charles Waller of Woolwich.[941]

938 WHL Inventory, titled *An Old Castle, with horseman & woman seated beneath a beech tree in foreground.*
939 V&A No. (FA 383); Luke Herrmann, email correspondence, January 2008.
940 See Roberts, *Views of Windsor*, pp. 88–89 (cat. 26), illus. col. (RL 14541). *Roadway through Windsor Forest* (Dyce 748) is illustrated in Luke Herrmann, *Paul and Thomas Sandby* (London, 1986), p. 118 (cat. 31).
941 There is little literature on Sandby's pupils and followers. A reference to Waller appears in Bruce Robertson, *The Art of Paul Sandby* (exh. cat., New Haven, Yale Center for British Art, 1985), p. 103. There are examples of Waller's work in the Laing Art Gallery, Newcastle-upon-Tyne (TWCMS: C13207) and the Yale Center for British Art (Robertson, *Art of Paul Sandby*, p. 87, cat. 136).

## 'SAMUEL SHELLEY'

1750 Whitechapel, London–1808 London

**Portrait of a Lady in a Black Dress and Hat**
LL 3944 (WHL 2611)

Pencil and watercolour on laid paper, torn at the corners and edges
13 x 9 cm
Date: possibly c. 1788–90

Inscr: 53 (pencil, top right).
Prov: Jeffery Whitehead; his sale, Christie's, 6 August 1915 (part of lot 19); bt. by Frank Partridge (9 gns) for Lever

Lot 19 of the Whitehead sale, which Partridge bought for Lever, was described in the sale catalogue as 'R. [*sic*] Shelley: *A study of three children*, *A Lady in a black dress* and *Heads of a Lady and a Gentleman, two on one mount*'. LL 3944 is the second component of this item (for the first see LL 3943 below; for the last two, see LL 3940, p. 54: all four of the above works appear to have been re-mounted and framed, either by Partridge or immediately after their acquisition by Lever, with two further works, for which see LL 3941, p. 55).[942]

No artist by the name of R. Shelley is recorded and LL 3944 was re-attributed soon after its acquisition to Samuel Shelley,[943] whose well-known miniatures, however, bear little stylistic resemblance to the draughtsmanship of this work. Shelley did also occasionally make portrait drawings but of those that are known, none provides positive corroboration for the attribution of LL 3944.[944] The work is in a very damaged condition, having been backed onto a second sheet whose edges and corners themselves are torn; the scribbled foliage running down the left-hand side and much of the hatching represents an attempt to disguise this. The right-hand edge of the original work too appears to have been extended by approximately 1 cm and the extent of the repair and retouching is so considerable that it is difficult to determine the extent and nature of the original's handling.

The identity of the sitter is unknown, but the black jacket and hat, which suggest that she is in mourning, are from about 1788–90.
AK

942 On the reverse of the frame is a diagram drawn in pencil indicating the intended positioning within the mount of the six works: LL 3944 at upper centre is designated by the figure 53, which is also inscribed on the drawing at top right and appears to be an unidentified stock or collection number.
943 LLAG files: the attribution was made by Lever's first assistant curator, A. C. Tait.
944 Other artists proposed for authorship of LL 3944 include Cosway (e.g. by Jacob Simon, verbally, 15 February 2008; Stephen Lloyd, verbally, 31 January 2008, although expressing reservations, had also declined to rule out this possibility) and J. R. Smith (e.g. by Hugh Belsey, verbally, February 2008; although the medium is somewhat uncharacteristic for him, Smith certainly did have a line in pretty women in large black hats, as in the oils *A Visit to Grandfather* (R.A. 1787; sold Sotheby's, 19 November 1986, lot 73) and *Family Group* (sold Sotheby's, 24 November 1999, lot 730) and the pastel *A Lady* (sold Christie's, 17 November 2005, lot 9)).

**Study of three children**
LL 3943 (WHL 2610)

Watercolour and pencil on laid paper
10.2 x 8.1 cm
Date: possibly c. 1800

Prov: Jeffery Whitehead; his sale, Christie's, 6 August 1915 (part of lot 19); bt. by Frank Partridge (9 gns) for Lever

Lot 19 of the Whitehead sale, which Partridge bought for Lever, was described in the sale catalogue as 'R. [*sic*] Shelley: *A study of three children*, *A Lady in a black dress* and *Heads of a Lady and a Gentleman, two on one mount*'. LL 3943 is the first of these items (for the second, and further discussion, see LL 3944 above).[945]

As with LL 3944, the drawing was re-attributed in Lever's collection to the miniaturist Samuel Shelley. The two works, however, are not by the same hand and would appear, from the costumes worn by the sitters, to date from some years apart, LL 3943 being perhaps dateable to around 1800. Of the two it has arguably the better claim to be by him but even so the attribution remains fanciful. The drawing has the character of a study for a larger portrait (rather than a miniature, which was Shelley's customary product). The sitters are unidentified.

The eyes of the right-hand child appear to have been slightly strengthened and enlarged for effect by a later hand.
AK

945 With LL 3944 and four other works acquired at the same time, LL 3943 was immediately remounted and reframed as part of an ensemble of six. LL 3943 was placed at the bottom centre, under LL 3944. On the reverse of the frame, where an MS diagram was drawn in pencil for the framer to work to, LL 3943 was designated as 'No Name'. The re-attribution from 'R. Shelley' to Samuel Shelley was made by A. C. Tait, Lever's first assistant curator.

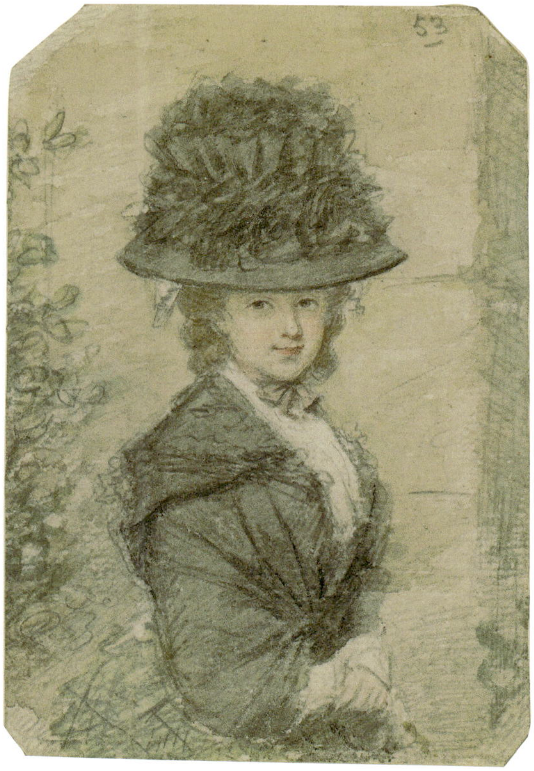

LL 3944

## 'GEORGE SHEPHERD'

1784 London–1862 London

**The Falcon Inn, Lower Bridge Street, Chester**[946]

LL 3993 (WHL 1213)

Watercolour over pencil with touches of gouache and gum arabic on wove paper

38.8 x 50.3 cm

Date: 1825

Inscr: Chester. Bridge Street 1825 (pencil, bottom right); GS [monogram, on its side] delt. (watercolour, bottom right); J JONAS FALCON INN HOME BREWED ALE (watercolour, on inn façade); WINE/ SPIRITS (watercolour, on inn façade)

Annot: Bridge Street [Corner of Cuppin Street] (crossed out) Chester / by G. Shepheard / 1825 (pencil, verso, on backboard; by A. C. Tait)

Exh: Perth, Art Gallery of Western Australia and Australian tour, *Exhibition of Early British Water-colours*, organised by the Empire Art Loans Exhibition Society, 1948–49 (cat. 61)

946 WHL Inventory, titled *Bridge Street, Chester.*

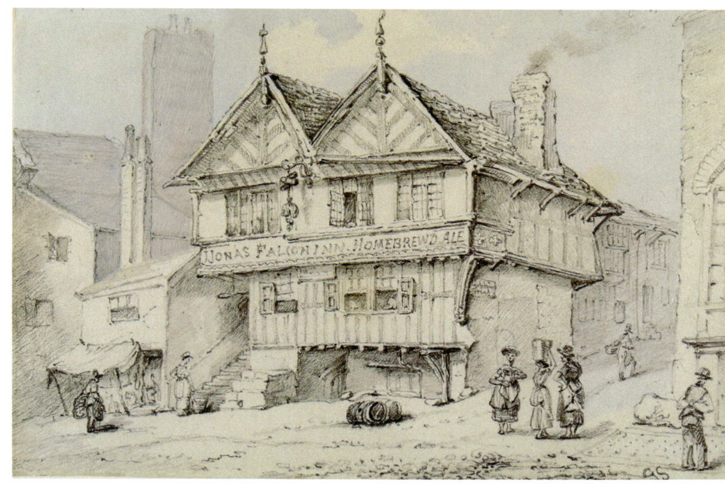

fig. 51. Attributed to George Shepheard, *Study for The Falcon Inn, Lower Bridge Street, Chester*, 1825, blue wash over pencil on paper, 17.4 x 25.7 cm, Grosvenor Museum, Chester

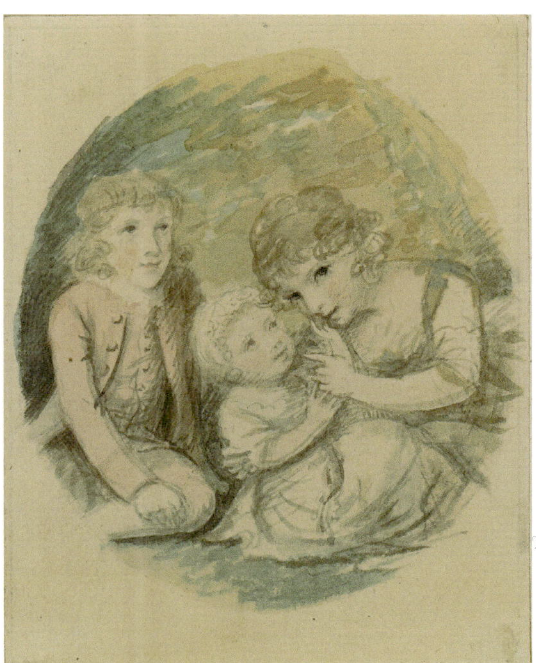

LL 3943

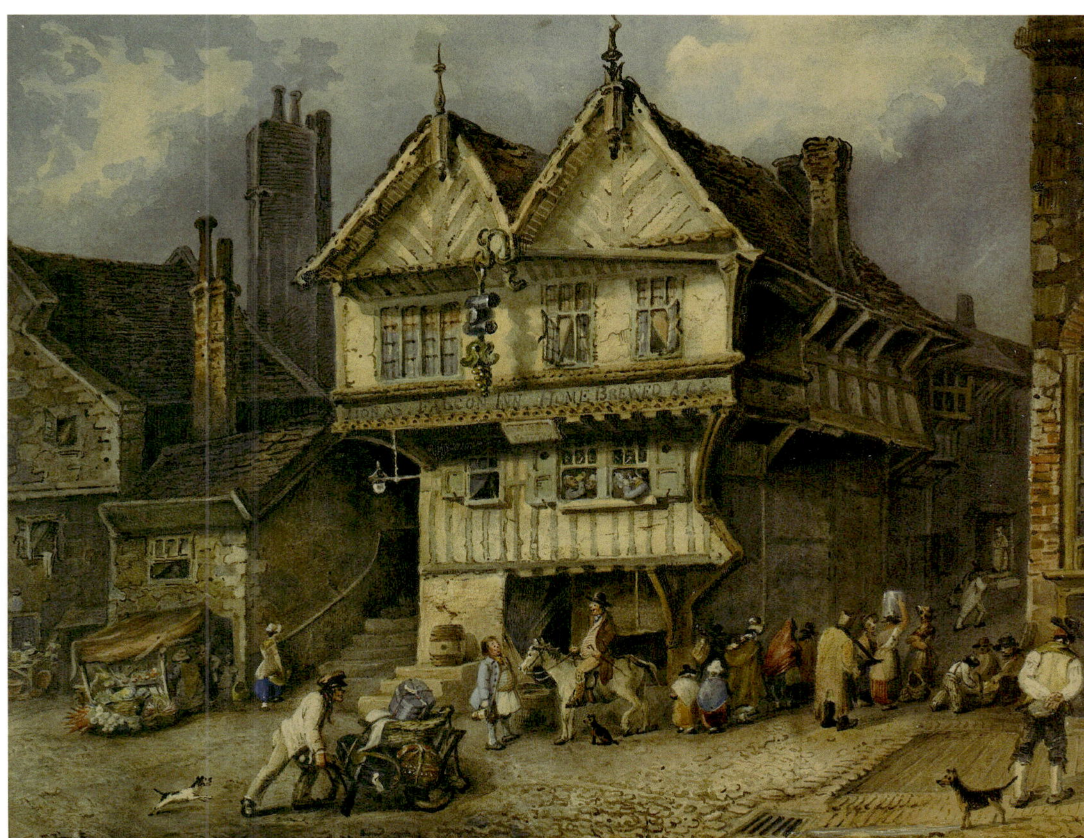

LL 3993

### Old Houses and St Olave's Church, Lower Bridge Street, Chester[947]
LL 3889 (WHL 1214)

Watercolour over pencil with touches of gouache, gum arabic and scratching out on wove paper
36.5 x 52.7 cm
Date: 1829

Inscr: D Williams (watercolour, on shop front)

Annot: In Lower Bridge Strt Chester / Drawn by G. Shepheard 1829 (pencil, verso, on backboard; by A. C. Tait)

Prov: bt. from B. T. Batsford by Lever, 2 September 1913 (£7 7s for pair)[948]

Both LL 3993 and LL 3889 were acquired by Lever as by George Shepherd, who is now thought to be the same artist as George 'Sidney' Shepherd (previously thought to be the latter's father).[949] Nevertheless, A. C. Tait, assistant curator at the Lady Lever Art Gallery between 1922 and 1946, attributed the watercolours to George Shepheard (1770 Guildford, Surrey–1842 London) who is known to have visited Wales in the 1820s, which could have coincided with trips to Chester.[950] Three pencil studies in the Grosvenor Museum, Chester, are by the same hand as the Lady Lever works; one in pencil and watercolour is a study for *The Falcon Inn* and is inscribed Chester July 8. 1825 (fig. 51). These too have previously been attributed to George Shepheard.[951] However, the works of these artists remain too little known for it to be possible to arrive at any conclusive attribution.

Many early nineteenth-century artists, including Thomas Shotter Boys and William Callow (see pp. 40–41), were attracted by the sixteenth- and seventeenth-century half-timbered houses of Chester. In the Lady Lever watercolours, the artist combines accurate architectural detail (which can be verified by comparing the works with etchings made in 1814–17 by George Batenham [active 1794, d. 1833])[952] with evocative depictions of the town's inhabitants. Although the figures in both works are slightly caricatured, details such as the shop sign boards are carefully recorded, creating a strong sense of place.[953]

947 WHL Inventory, titled *Lower Bridge Street, Chester*.
948 LLAG files: LL 3993 and LL 3889 are described as 'Two drawings of Chester, one being of the Falcon Inn which has been very much restored'.
949 Lucy Peltz, 'Shepherd, George Sidney (1784–1862)', *ODNB*, vol. 50, pp. 244–45.
950 LLAG files: A. C. Tait's notes are recorded on the accession card.
951 In an unknown hand on the mounts, verso.
952 See Thomas Hughes, *Ancient Chester: A Series of Illustrations of the Streets of this Ancient City, taken sixty years since* (London and Manchester, 1880), pls. 11 and 16, where the Batenham etchings are reproduced. I am grateful to Peter Boughton for this reference.
953 The Falcon Inn was listed as belonging to Jeremiah Jonas in *Pigot and Co.'s Commercial Directory, Cheshire* (Chester, 1822–23), p. 5.

LL 3889

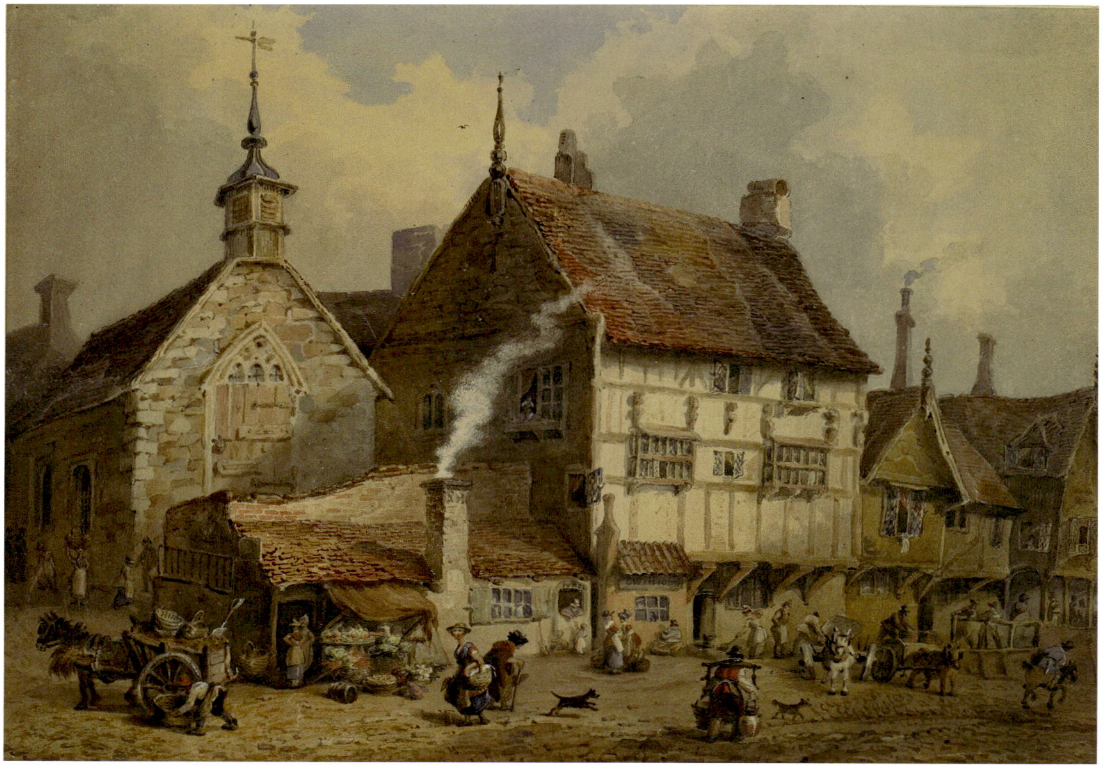

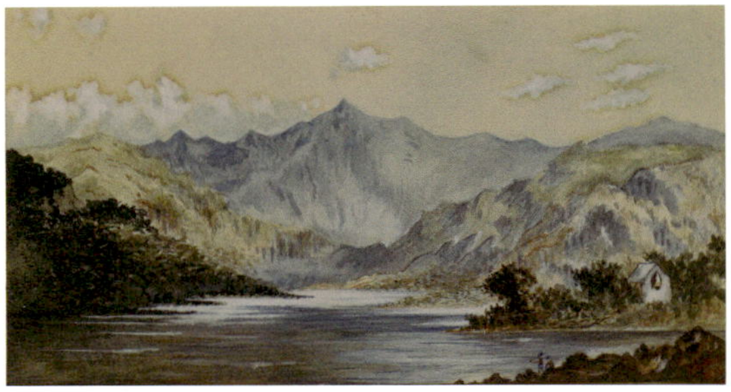

LL 3994

## JONATHAN SIMPSON
1850 Bolton–1937 Bolton

### Haweswater, Cumberland
LL 3994 (WHL 1525, TM 109)

Watercolour and gouache on wove paper
10.9 x 20.9 cm (sight)
Date: 1871

Inscr: J. SIMPSON. / 1871 (gouache, bottom right)

Prov: in Lever's collection by 1902[954]

Jonathan Simpson was a close personal friend of Lever, having met him at the school run by the Misses Aspinwall in Wood Street, Bolton, when the two were young boys.[955] Simpson was articled to a local surveyor, James Lomax, and he had his own architectural practice in Bolton.[956] He designed a number of houses for Lever, one in Bolton at the end of 1879 as well as three cottage blocks at Port Sunlight, and would have been an important influence on Lever's taste.[957] Simpson is described in the 2nd Lord Leverhulme's biography of his father as

> the closest personal friendship of my father's life ... Many interests and traits in common bound the two men together – art in general and architecture in particular, the collecting of old furniture and pictures, the associations and recollections of boyhood and youth, and last, but not least, a keen sense of humour which, in each case, was of very much the same type.[958]

Simpson joined Lever on many trips, including a trip to the Inner and Outer Hebrides in 1884,[959] and a round-the-world trip between 1923 and 1924.[960]

The title *Haweswater, Cumberland* was used to describe the work in the WHL Inventory, compiled in Lever's lifetime. The work was subsequently re-titled *Glenquare*, which appears to be a fictional place, and it is not known why the title was changed.[961]

954 1897–1902 TM Inventory, listed under art works in back corridor as *Haweswater Cumberland*. The watercolour may have been a gift from Simpson. It is not included in Tatlock, perhaps because it was a work by a friend and not by a professional artist.
955 2nd Viscount Leverhulme, *Viscount Leverhulme*, p. 15.
956 Hubbard and Shippobottom, *Guide to Port Sunlight Village*, p. 101.
957 Ibid., pp. 35 and 88.
958 2nd Viscount Leverhulme, *Viscount Leverhulme*, p. 306.
959 Ibid., p. 37.
960 Ibid., p. 306.
961 Glenquare is inscribed on the mount; in the absence of information as to why the title was changed, the decision has been made to revert to the original title.

## JOHN 'WARWICK' SMITH
1749 Irthington, Cumbria–1831 London

**Llanberis Copper Mines**
LL 3995 (LP 30)

Watercolour over traces of pencil on wove paper
14.3 x 22.5 cm (sight)
Date: probably 1792

Prov: [?] George Greville, 2nd Earl of Warwick; [?] by descent to the Hon. Robert Fulke Greville; [?] by descent to Lady Louisa Finch-Hatton;[962] bt. from Leon Kashnor, The Museum Book Store, 45 Museum Street, London, by the Trustees, 17 June 1930 (£6 with LL 3996)[963]

Exh: London, Royal Society of Painters in Water-Colours, *John 'Warwick' Smith: A Retrospective Exhibition of Views in Wales 1786–1806*, 1928 (cat. 164); Perth, Art Gallery of Western Australia and Australian tour, *Exhibition of Early British Water-colours*, organised by the Empire Art Loans Exhibition Society, 1948–49 (cat. 29)

Lit: *The Connoisseur*, vol. 91 (March 1933), illus. p. 191

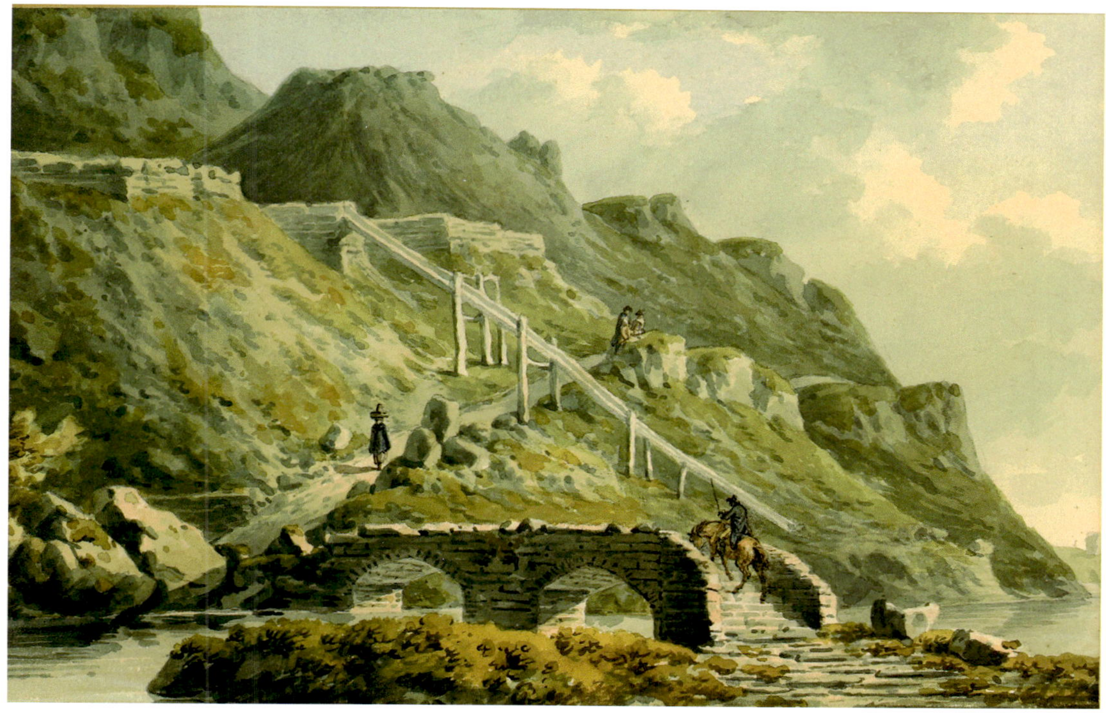

LL 3995

John Smith's father was gardener to the sister of Captain John Bernard Gilpin, an amateur artist. Gilpin and his artist sons William and Sawrey gave Smith lessons in drawing, and he was one of a number of artists who accompanied William Gilpin on his sketching tours over the period 1770 to 1776. While in Derbyshire around 1775, Smith met George Greville, 2nd Earl of Warwick, who was to become his patron, sending him to Italy in 1776, where he met the artists William Pars, John Robert Cozens (see pp. 70–71), Thomas Jones and Francis Towne (see pp. 181–82). Smith's Italian watercolours, which he continued to produce following his return to England in 1781, are often viewed as some of his finest works, combining dramatic perspective with a tour-de-force of handling. Once back in England Smith lived in Warwick: his sobriquet either derived from the place name, or from his patron. Subsequently, Smith travelled widely, making trips to Perthshire, the Isle of Man, the Lake District and Wales.

On the basis of dated drawings often inscribed 'taken on the spot', Smith seems to have visited Wales almost annually between 1784 and the late 1790s, with a final trip in 1806. During these tours, he produced Welsh views for Lord Warwick's family, all of a similar small size, which number well into the hundreds. LL 3995 is reported to have been inscribed and dated on the original mount July 14, 1792 and Llanberis Copper Mines, close to the Upper Lake, Caernarvonshire[964] and this was corroborated by Basil S. Long who recorded (based on dated drawings) that Smith was at the pass of Aberglaslyn and Llanberis on 14 July 1792.[965] It is likely then that LL 3995 dates from 1792 when Smith made an extended tour to Wales accompanied by the 2nd Earl of Warwick and Julius Caesar Ibbetson (see pp. 128–29). Fifteen of Smith's drawings from this year were subsequently published in *A Tour to Hafod in Cardiganshire* in 1810.[966]

LL 3995 depicts Llanberis copper mine; including the chute from the dressing floor used to load the ore on to boats on the lake. The ore was taken to the foot of Llyn Padarn, from where it was taken by road to Caernarfon. Llanberis was one of a number of copper mines in Snowdonia, although its output was small compared to Parys in Anglesey. Mines like Parys and Llanberis became part of the picturesque tour for artists and travellers alike in the late eighteenth century, and 'Warwick' Smith depicted the mines at Parys on a number of occasions from the mid-1780s and 1790s.[967] Smith is said to have produced further views at or near Llanberis in 1797 and 1806 although these drawings have not been located.[968]

Smith first exhibited with the SPWC in 1806, and by the time of his last exhibit in 1823, his style was viewed as old-fashioned. Nevertheless, earlier in his career he was viewed by contemporaries as at the forefront of changing methods of watercolour painting. George Barret wrote that Smith 'greatly improved upon this meagre style of colouring', by which he meant the prevailing style of pen-and-ink line with wash,

> by first forwarding his subjects with a grey tint composed with blue, red and yellow, so far as to produce the general effect, having previously subdued the white paper, from the horizon downwards, with a slight wash of the same tint. His drawings thus prepared, he proceeded to colour them with a degree of force that had never been attempted before, in a chaste style, as he possessed an excellent eye, and a strong feeling for the true and sober hues of Nature.[969]

Smith's Welsh views are characterised by their grey and blue colour scheme touched with ochre, and flashes of stronger blues and reds on his figures.

962 This provenance is as given in *A Retrospective Exhibition of Views in Wales 1786–1806* (exh. cat., London, Royal Society of Painters in Water-Colours, 1928), pp. 3–4.

963 LLAG files: a copy of the sale invoice is in the 'Purchases by Trustees 1925–1945' file.

964 LLAG files: these inscriptions on the mount are recorded on the accession card. The accession card also records A. C. Tait's note that the mount was 'marked with numbers in pencil – 36 upper left and 87 lower left corner. Date repeated on back, smaller.' It has not been possible to lift the modern mount to confirm this. Tait was Lever's first assistant curator.

965 Basil S. Long, 'John Warwick Smith (1749–1831)', *Walker's Quarterly*, no. 24 (1927), p. 10.

966 For details of the itinerary of this tour to Wales, see Long, 'John Warwick Smith', p. 10.

967 There are two views by 'Warwick' Smith of Parys Mines in the National Museums and Galleries of Wales, Cardiff, dated 1785 and 1790.

968 Long, 'John Warwick Smith', p. 12 records drawings at or near Llanberis dated '3 August 1797' and '8 June 1806'.

969 George Barret, *Theory and Practice of Water-Colour Painting* (London, 1840), pp. 30–31.

**Ellesmere - on the Verge of Ellesmere Lake**
LL 3996 (LP 29)

Watercolour over traces of pencil on wove paper
13.7 x 20.4 cm (sight)
Date: probably late 1790s

Prov: [?] George Greville, 2nd Earl of Warwick; [?] by descent to the Hon. Robert Fulke Greville; [?] by descent to Lady Louisa Finch-Hatton;[970] bt. from Leon Kashnor, The Museum Book Store, 45 Museum Street, London, by the Trustees, 17 June 1930 (£6 with LL 3995)[971]

LL 3996 is said to have been inscribed: Ellesmere - on the Verge of/ Ellesmere Lake. Adjoining are the Earth Mounds of its former Castle - the only traces of its site - Shropshire.[972] The small town of Ellesmere in northern Shropshire on the Welsh border would have provided 'Warwick' Smith and others with picturesque views and points of topographical interest en route to North Wales. The paper has a watermark of 1794 and it is likely that Smith visited on one of his Welsh tours of the late 1790s.[973] The work depicts the thirteenth-century church of St Mary's, overlooking the Mere. The mound from the former motte and bailey castle can be seen to the left.

970 This provenance is suggested on the basis of that given for LL 3995.
971 LLAG files: a copy of the sale invoice is in the 'Purchases by Trustees 1925–1945' file.
972 LLAG files: recorded on accession card as inscribed on the mount. A. C. Tait recorded that 'on the lower left-hand corner of mount is the pencil number 441 and on the lower left corner 35, also in pencil: on upper left corner the number 369 is printed with a hand stamp', but he made no mention of another inscription. It has not been possible to lift the modern mount in order to check this.
973 LLAG files: the date of the watermark was recorded on the accession card, probably by A. C. Tait. It has not been possible to check this against the work.

LL 3996

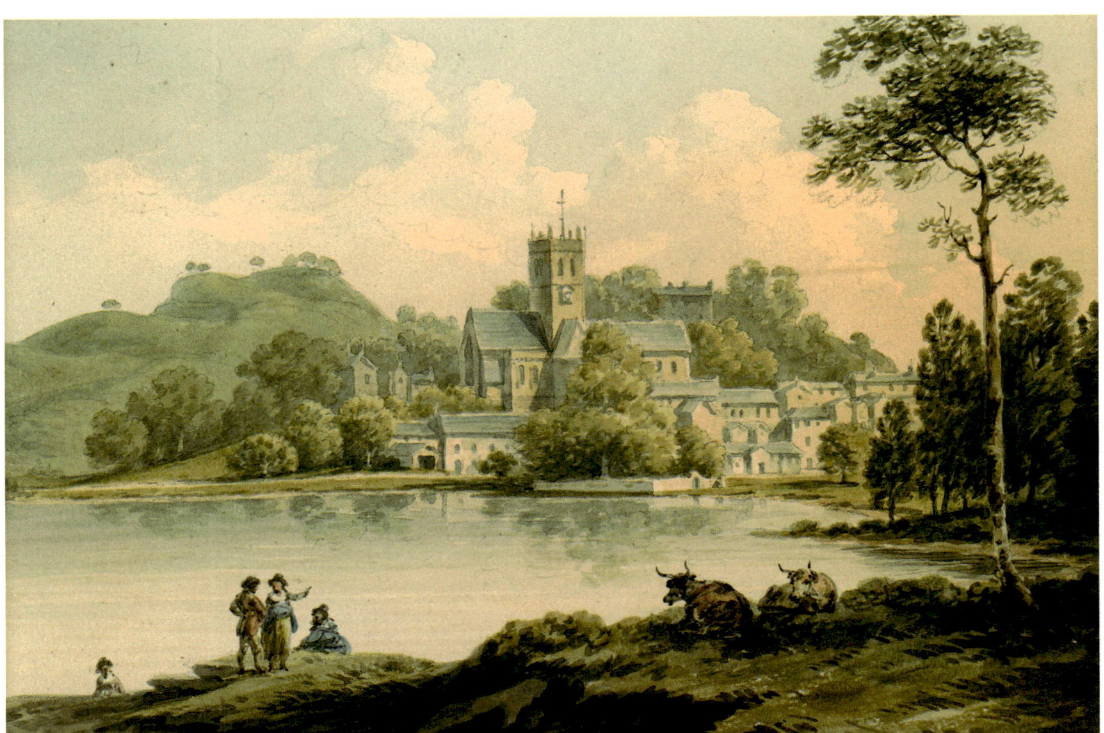

**SIMEON SOLOMON**
1840 London–1905 London

**Girl at a Fountain**
LL 3881 (WHL 3352)

Watercolour, extra gum arabic and white heightening on paper laid down on board
33 x 25.5 cm
Date: 1865

Inscr: SS [monogram] / 65 (watercolour, lower left)

Prov: William Coltart, Birkenhead, 1885; Mrs Eleanor Tong Coltart; her sale, Brown & Brown, Liverpool, 30 October 1917 (lot 71); bt. by Lever, 1917 (£48 10s 5d)

Exh: London, Royal Academy, *Winter Exhibition*, 1906 (cat. 183); Birmingham, Birmingham Museums and Art Gallery, Munich, Museum Villa Stuck and London, Ben Uri Gallery, *Love Revealed: Simeon Solomon and the Pre-Raphaelites*, 2005–2006 (cat. 74)

Solomon's father ran the family hat business and was a prominent member of the Jewish community in the City of London. Simeon trained as a painter in the studio of his older brother Abraham, until he started at the Royal Academy Schools in 1856. He showed his first painting at the Royal Academy in 1858, his second in 1860 and from then on annually until 1872. Solomon's friendships with members of the Pre-Raphaelite circle were formative, and he was particularly close to Burne-Jones and Rossetti. The latter artist's influence can be seen in Solomon's watercolours from the late 1850s and early 1860s. Solomon contributed, along with other Pre-Raphaelites, to the commission by the Dalziel brothers to produce drawings for their Bible project, as well as undertaking decorative work for William Burges and William Morris.

LL 3881 is one of Solomon's watercolours of single-figure classically draped women from the 1860s. *Girl at a Fountain* shows the influence of Rossetti's pictorial style during this period, with its concentration on female beauty as a subject and its abandonment of narrative. As with many of Rossetti's pictures of female beauties from the early 1860s, only the figure's head and shoulders are depicted and her proportions are large relative to the picture surface; she is viewed in close-up, a fact emphasised by the squarer proportions of the paper. Flowers are employed as a decorative device in the background.

F. G. Stephens, one of the original members of the Pre-Raphaelite Brotherhood and from 1865 art critic for the *Athenaeum*, emphasised the languorous aspect of the piece. He described the work in 1885 as

> one of the best instances of that artist's powers. It is the figure of a sweet-faced damsel in classical draperies, filling a vase of pale opal colour with water at a fountain flowing on our left from a wall of stone. Her pale and passion-worn features retain their sculpturesque character and choice forms; her hazel eyes

and full lips seem charged with memories of happiness. Their expression is in keeping with the motives of the design, the colour, and the soft low tones of the picture as a whole.[974]

William Coltart (c. 1823–1903), who owned both Lady Lever Solomon watercolours, lived in Birkenhead, near Liverpool, and owned the iron merchants Henry Wood & Co. Together with his wife, Eleanor Tong Coltart (c. 1829–1917), he collected works by artists of the Pre-Raphaelite and Aesthetic movements as well as those representing more standard Victorian taste.[975]

### The Mystery of Faith
LL 3997 (LP 71)

Watercolour with gum arabic and gouache on paper laid down on board
51.3 x 38.8 cm
Date: 1870

Inscr: SS [monogram] / 1870 (watercolour, lower left)

Prov: W. W. Warren; his sale, Christie's, 20–25 January 1886 (lot 734); bt. by Sedgefield (£27 6s); William Coltart, 1896; bequeathed by Clyde Birkmyre Coltart of Chester to the Trustees, 1950[976]

Exh: London, Dudley Gallery, *Seventh General Exhibition of Water-Colour Drawings*, 1871 (cat. 89); London, Royal Academy, *Winter Exhibition*, 1906 (cat. 191); Birmingham, Birmingham Museums and Art Gallery, Munich, Museum Villa Stuck and London, Ben Uri Gallery, *Love Revealed: Simeon Solomon and the Pre-Raphaelites*, 2005–2006 (cat. 88)

Lit: *The Art Journal* (1896), illus. p. 100 as *A Priest elevating the Host*

Solomon addressed religious subject-matter in his work throughout his career. His early drawings and paintings drew on his Jewish background, depicting Old Testament subjects; he also received commissions to produce illustrations of Jewish rituals and customs from *Once a Week* (1862) and *The Leisure Hour* (1866). In Solomon's later work he used both Jewish and Christian ritual subject-matter to express an all-embracing kind of spiritualism.

The Lady Lever watercolour depicts a young priest holding up a crystal monstrance containing the Eucharistic wafer or 'Host'; it has been suggested that the ceremony is that of Benediction of the Blessed Sacrament, where the congregation are blessed with the Host, rather than the sacrifice of the Mass.[977] Benediction

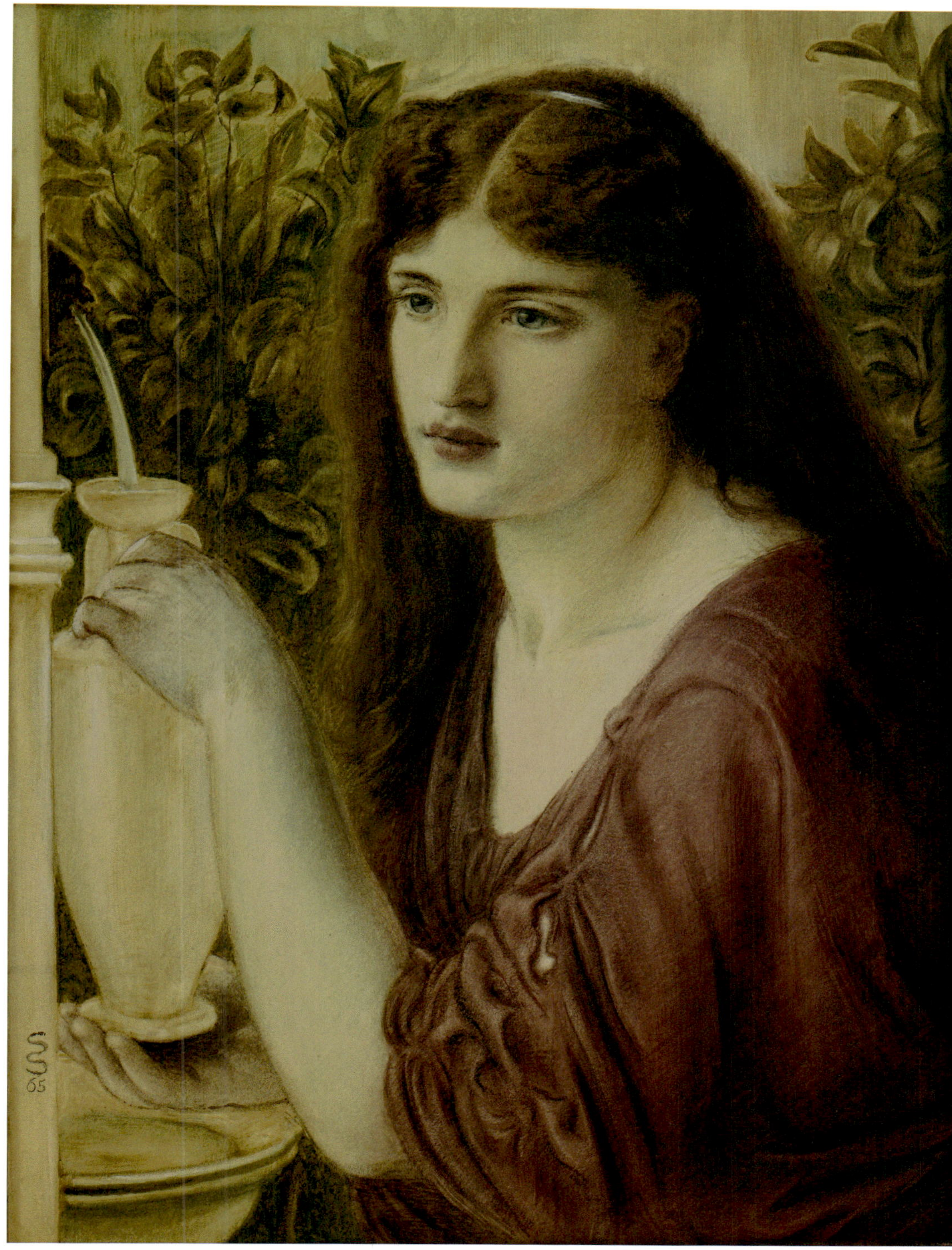


LL 3881

was practised in Roman Catholic churches and occasionally in some High Anglican services.

*The Mystery of Faith* may be seen in the context of contemporary debates within the Church of England about the function of ritual objects, vestments and ceremony in religious practice; these issues prompted heated argument among Anglicans, but were wholly accepted by Roman Catholics. In this sense, this piece (and others by the artist) depicting priests performing rites at the altar could be deemed as inflammatory. Colin Cruise has suggested that a passage from 1 Timothy 3:9–11, 'Deacons ... must be grave, not double-tongued, not given to much wine, not greedy of filthy lucre; holding the mystery of faith in a pure conscience', might have inspired Solomon, in particular to create a visual pun in this work based on Timothy's advice to hold the faith.[978]

LL 3997 was exhibited at the progressive Dudley Gallery in 1871, where Solomon had been showing his works since the late 1860s. The work was widely reviewed and generally praised,

974 F. G. Stephens, 'The Private Collections of England. No. LXXXI: Mr W. Coltart's, Woodleigh, Birkenhead', *Athenaeum* (26 September 1885), pp. 407–08.

975 For an article on William Coltart's collection, see *The Art Journal* (April 1896), pp. 97–101. For details about William and Eleanor Tong Coltart, see Macleod, *Art and the Victorian Middle Class*, pp. 401–02.

976 LLAG files.

977 Colin Cruise, *Love Revealed: Simeon Solomon and the Pre-Raphaelites* (exh. cat., Birmingham, Birmingham Museums and Art Gallery, Munich, Museum Villa Stuck, and London, Ben Uri Gallery, 2005–2006), p. 131 (cat. 88).

978 Cruise, *Love Revealed*, p. 61.

with commentators responding to the doctrinal readings, but also to the aesthetic qualities of the watercolour. The reviewer in *The Art Journal* wrote:

> Once again his genius oscillates between medievalism and classicism. *The Mystery of Faith* pertains to the religion and ritual of the Romish church. A priest, robed richly, elevates the Eucharist; his eye fixed as in a trance, his countenance that of an ascetic, reveal a soul steadfastly set on 'the mystery of faith' – the Real Presence. The execution is worthy of the conception; the artist has achieved a triumph.[979]

979 *The Art Journal* (March 1871), p. 85.

*The Mystery of Faith* was composed almost entirely in white and gold watercolour, giving the work a magnificence, as well as an abstract quality in line with Whistler's experiments in colour harmonies from a decade before.

*The Mystery of Faith* can instructively be compared to Solomon's slightly earlier watercolour of a young Jewish man holding the Torah in *Carrying the Scrolls of the Law* (1867, Whitworth Art Gallery, Manchester, fig. 52). Both works depict young men performing religious rituals and there is a poignancy in contrasting youth with religious tradition. What also unites the two is the beauty of the young men; there is an understated homo-erotic charge to these watercolours, which may reflect the artist's attempt to declare his own sexuality.

The positive reaction to LL 3997 represented a high point in Solomon's career. In 1873 the artist was arrested and charged with buggery. His public career practically came to an end and he never exhibited again at the Royal Academy or the Dudley Gallery. Although he continued to work sporadically, he lived in poverty throughout the 1880s and 1890s dependent on the charity of his family and died at St Giles's workhouse in 1905.

LL 3997

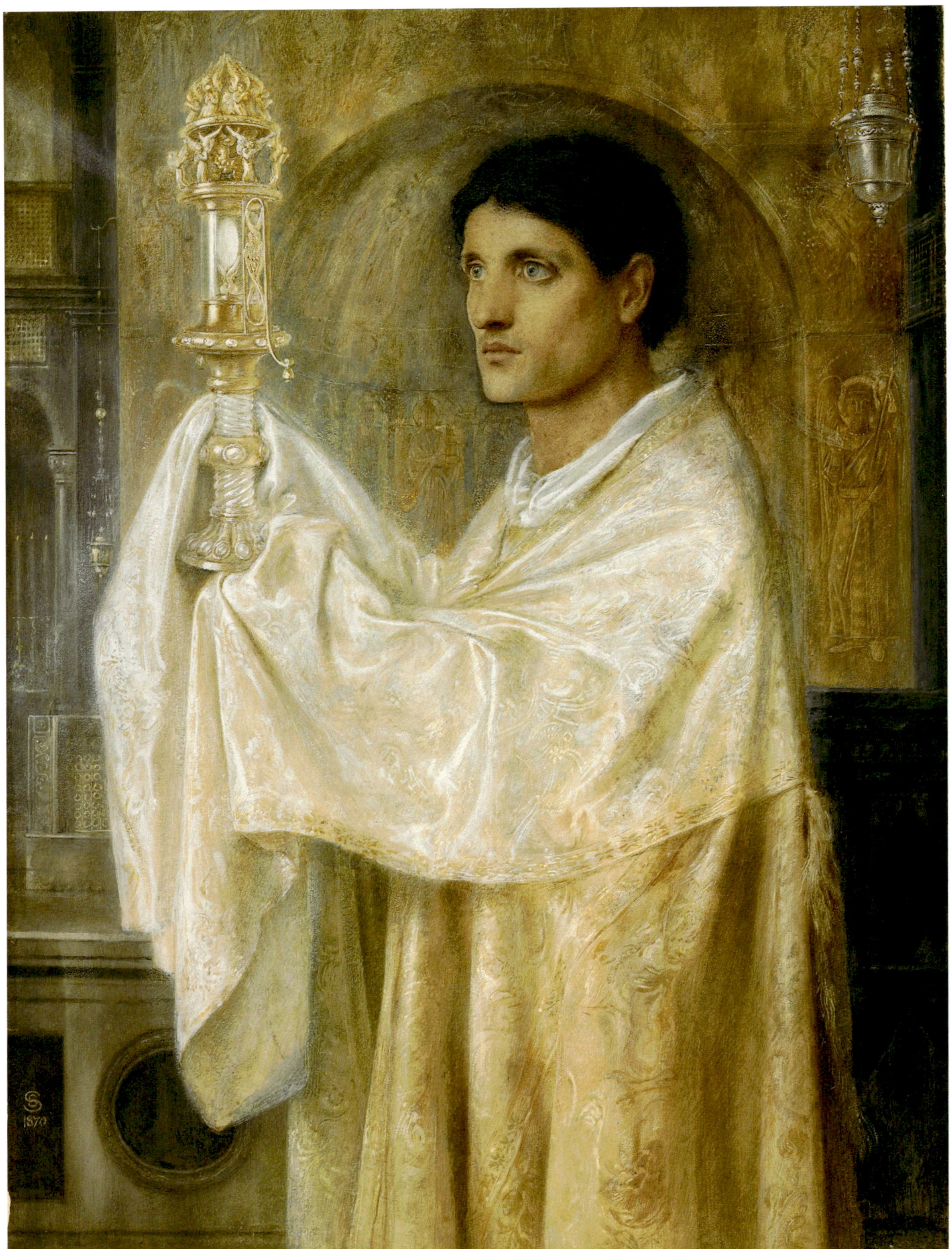

fig. 52. Simeon Solomon, *Carrying the Scrolls of the Law*, 1867, watercolour and gouache on paper laid on canvas, 35.7 x 25.5 cm, Whitworth Art Gallery, Manchester

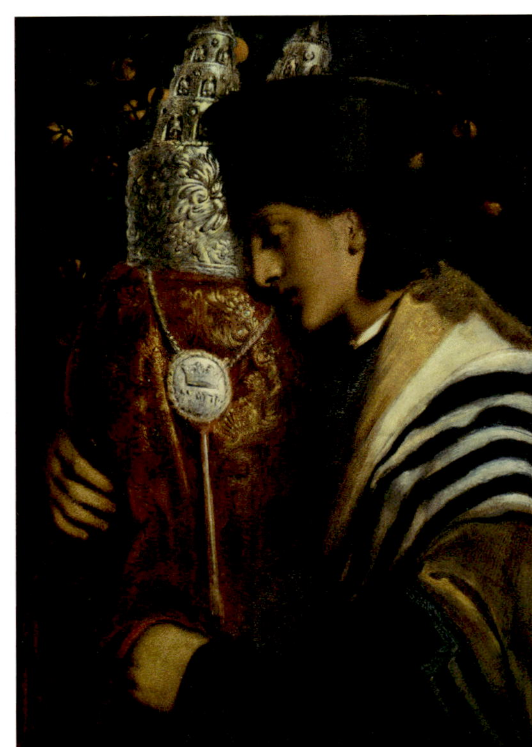

## AFTER CLARKSON STANFIELD

1793 Sunderland–1867 London

### Two Continental Scenes

LL 3874, 3878

Date: c. 1833–70

Prov: A. Sargent; Christie's, 16 May 1918 (lot 23); bt. by Gooden and Fox for Lever (34 gns with LL 3872-73 and LL 3875-77)

### Ehrenbreitstein, from Coblenz

LL 3874 (WHL 3526)

Watercolour and white gouache over pencil on wove paper
8 x 5.2 cm (sight)

This and the following work are part of a group of seven topographical watercolours of continental views framed together. For the other five works in the set, see above under Bonington (pp. 10–12) and Prout (pp. 155–57); Tatlock catalogued them as by the latter's nephew John Skinner Prout (1806–76).[980] Now that sources of most have been identified, it appears that all are anonymous copies of engravings from the popular *Landscape Annuals* of the 1830s.

Stanfield was christened in honour of Thomas Clarkson, the famous abolitionist admired by his father, a one-time sailor, wine-merchant and actor. In 1806 Stanfield moved from his home in Sunderland to be apprenticed to a painter in Edinburgh, a position he soon abandoned to go to sea. Press-ganged into the navy, he sustained an injury; after his discharge he joined a ship bound for China. Back in London in 1816 he began work as a scene painter, the career in which he first rose to prominence. In 1823 Stanfield was a founder member of the Society of British Artists, but after 1830 he set his sights on the Royal Academy, to which he was elected associate in 1832, and a full Academician in 1835. He first contributed topographical illustrations to Cooke's *London and its vicinity* in 1827. A tour along the Rhine and to Venice in 1830 provided material for the first of the three *Picturesque Annuals* he illustrated for Charles Heath, beginning in 1832. Several other ambitious travel books followed. With his speed of execution honed in the scene painter's workshop, Stanfield completed large commissions for William IV, the Marquess of Lansdowne and other noble patrons. During the 1840s he completed several canvases for Queen Victoria. Through his connections in the theatre, Stanfield came to know Charles Dickens; despite their age difference of nearly twenty years, the two remained close friends until Stanfield's death.

LL 3874 is a copy of the steel engraving by Robert Brandard after Clarkson Stanfield, published in Charles Heath's *Picturesque Annual for 1833, Travelling sketches on the Rhine and in Belgium and Holland*. The published engraving measures 13.5 x 9.5 cm, and includes areas to top, bottom and right not included in the copy. Despite its loose rendition of the original, and the spatial compression to which the source is subjected, the copy possesses considerable fluency and seems to have been made by a professional, rather than an amateur hand.

The medieval castle of Ehrenbreitstein, on the Rhine at its junction with the Mosel opposite Koblenz, fell to Napoleon in 1799. After the departure of the French in 1801, it was destroyed. Rebuilt after 1815, it became the largest fortification in Europe, excepting Gibraltar.
TW

### Strasbourg

LL 3878 (WHL 3530)

Watercolour, pen and ink and white gouache over pencil on wove paper
7.1 x 5.1 cm (sight)

LL 3878 is copied from a steel engraving by J. Carter after Clarkson Stanfield, published as the first plate in Charles Heath's *Picturesque Annual for 1833, Travelling sketches on the Rhine and in Belgium and Holland*. The engraving measures 14.2 x 9.7 cm, so the copy has been drawn at almost exactly half scale. The engraving reverses Stanfield's original watercolour, which is in the Victoria & Albert Museum.[981] Understanding the needs of his engraver, Stanfield painted his original in reverse, with the spire above the right-hand tower of the façade; in the engraving it is in its correct position, over the left tower. At 142 metres, the spire made the cathedral the tallest building in the world at the time.
TW

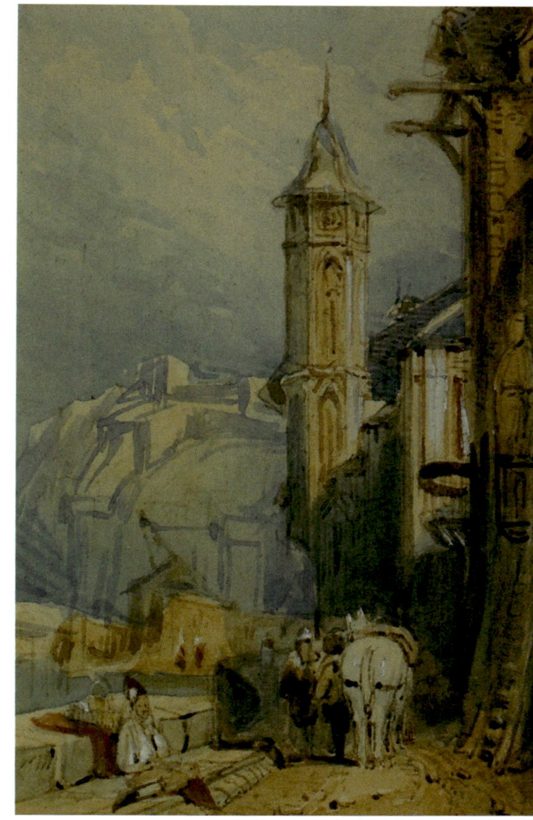

LL 3874

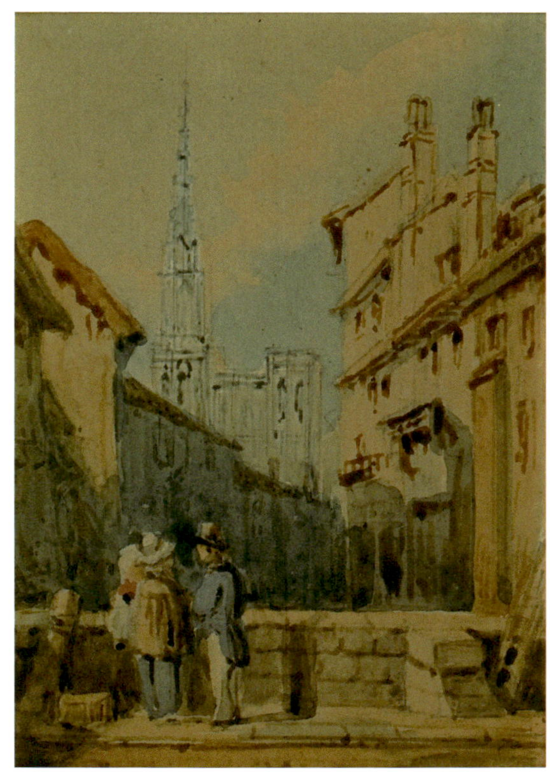

LL 3878

980 Tatlock, p. 135.

981 Peter van der Merwe, *Clarkson Stanfield 1793–1867* (exh. cat., Newcastle upon Tyne, Tyne and Wear County Council Museums, 1979), pp. 120–21 (cat. 191).

## PHILIP WILSON STEER
1860 Birkenhead–1942 London

### Hawes Bridge, Wensleydale
LL 3882 (LP 52)

Watercolour over pencil on paper, laid down on white board
25.3 x 36.6 cm
Date: 1904

Inscr: PW Steer / 1904 (watercolour, bottom right)

Prov: bt. from Lockett Thomson of Barbizon House by the Trustees, 24 May 1939 (£37, including purchase of copyright)[982]

Exh: London, Barbizon House, *Watercolours by P. Wilson Steer*, 1939 (cat. 27)

Lit: D. S. MacColl, *The Life, Work & Setting of Philip Wilson Steer* (London, 1945), p. 225

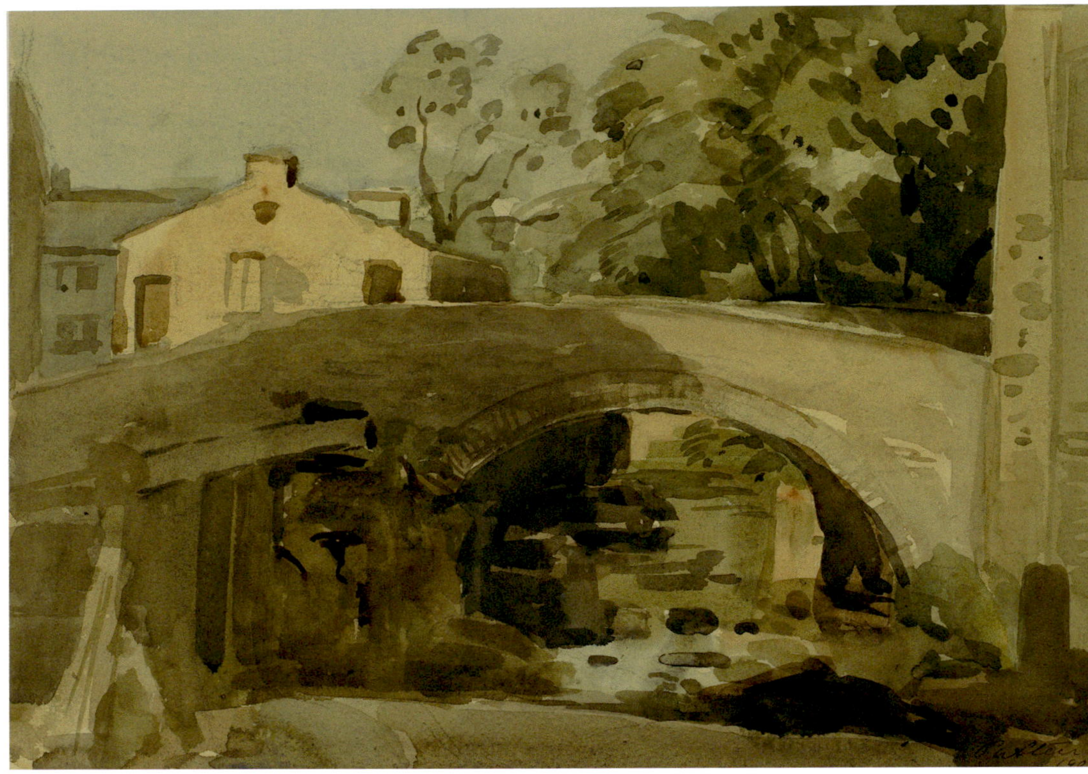

LL 3882

Steer was the son of a landscapist and portrait painter, Philip Steer (1810–71). He was educated at Hereford Cathedral School before attending Gloucester School of Art from 1878 to 1880. Although he spent a year at the South Kensington Drawing School, he was not accepted as a student at the Royal Academy Schools. Instead he moved to Paris where he studied with William Bouguereau at the Académie Julian between 1882 and 1883 and with Alexandre Cabanel at the Ecole des Beaux Arts in 1883. Back in London, Steer took a studio in Chelsea and began a lifetime practice of summer painting expeditions in *plein-air*, first of all visiting the Suffolk coastal village of Walberswick, where he produced some of his most memorable pictures. His early work was influenced by Bastien-Lepage, Corot and Whistler. For a short while Steer adopted a style akin to pointillism, more advanced than any other contemporary artist working in Britain. In 1886 he became a founder-member of the French-oriented New English Art Club. Three years later Steer joined the London Impressionists; their driving force was Walter Sickert, who became a lifelong friend.

In the 1890s Steer turned to Whistler and Manet for inspiration. In 1893 he was appointed to the Slade School of Art, where he taught for twenty-seven years, becoming a major influence on several generations of students. Following criticism of his work at his 1894 one-man show at the Goupil Gallery, Steer abandoned exhibiting his more innovative paintings. Instead he began to execute 'fancy pictures' and paintings of interiors. Steer collected eighteenth-century engravings and Chelsea figurines, and his interest in the rococo manifested itself in his pictures. Landscapes became an increasingly important part of his oeuvre. Claude Lorrain, Turner and Constable provided models for capturing the atmosphere in what could be considered Steer's neo-Romantic approach to representing the English countryside. In watercolour, too, his experiments reflected his study of the late works of Turner. His position as the 'Grand Old Man' of English landscape painting was recognised by the award in 1931 of the Order of Merit, very rarely granted to artists.

Steer must have extracted this sheet from a sketchbook, as all the watercolours that he painted at Hawes are of the same size. Other works painted there in 1904 include watercolours in the Walker Art Gallery, Liverpool, the Ulster Museum, Belfast, and the Scottish National Gallery of Modern Art, Edinburgh.[983] Several more were sold in the artist's studio sale at Christie's, 16 July 1942. Steer also painted oils at Hawes, among them *Landscape, sunshine and shadows*, now in Dublin City Gallery: The Hugh Lane.[984]

The main business of the small and remote market town of Hawes, 'the capital of the West Dales', 900 feet above sea level in Wensleydale, North Yorkshire, was the manufacture of knitted hosiery and woollen goods. In 1872 the etcher R. S. Chattock described the town as presenting 'little or no beauty or interest in itself, but being the centre of much the finest scenery of upper Wensleydale, it is well adapted for the headquarters of the tourist, who desires to explore this part of the valley; and comfortable quarters can be obtained at the "White Hart" at very moderate rates'.[985] Several guidebooks to Wensleydale and to Hawes were issued in the late nineteenth century, and Frank J. Nash's *Wensleydale and Swaledale: their advantages and attractions to holiday-makers* was published in 1904,[986] although not certainly before Steer's visit. Hawes itself in 1904 was 16 miles from the nearest railway station, and so, not surprisingly, it had seldom been painted by artists, but c. 1800 Thomas Girtin had painted two versions of a watercolour of a different bridge in the middle of the town, *Cottages at Hawes from the River Ure*,[987] which includes a spectacular waterfall. It was characteristic of Steer to avoid painting this dramatic view, and to choose the relatively insignificant bridge over the Duerley Beck at the east end of the town. A recent photograph has been taken by Robin Derngate of the bridge that Steer painted.[988] This shows that Steer very much played down the picturesque possibilities of the subject.

MH

982 This was a discounted price, as the watercolour was priced at £42 in the exhibition catalogue.

983 The inventory numbers of these three works are, respectively 936, 360 and 1149.

984 Bruce Laughton, *Philip Wilson Steer 1860–1942* (Oxford, 1971), p. 144, who also discusses Steer's oils and watercolours made in Hawes in general on pp. 95, 108.

985 R. S. Chattock, *Wensleydale. Fourteen etchings, with descriptive text* (London, 1872). The frontispiece was an etching of Hawes.

986 Frank Nash, *Wensleydale and Swaledale: their advantages and attractions to holiday-makers* (Leeds, 1904).

987 Smith (ed.), *Thomas Girtin*, p. 108 (cat. 82) and p. 174 (cat. 135), of which the latter, in Birmingham Museums and Art Gallery is vastly superior in quality.

988 http://www.scenicbritain.co.uk/coppermine/displayimage.php?album=search&cat=03&pos=3, consulted 12 January 2008.

## FRANCIS PHILIP STEPHANOFF[989]

1787/8 London–1860 Hanham, Gloucestershire

### Falstaff, Bardolph and Dame Quickly

LL 3998 (WHL 1515, TM 99)

Watercolour with extra gum arabic on wove paper
19.1 x 23.3 cm (sight)
Date: 1820–c. 1845

Inscr: F.P Stephanoff (watercolour, bottom right)

### Prince Hal and the Hostess[990]

LL 3999 (WHL 1516, TM 100)

Watercolour with extra gum arabic and touches of gouache on wove paper
19.4 x 23.8 cm (sight)
Date: 1820–c. 1845

Inscr: FP Stephanoff (watercolour, bottom centre)

Prov: [?] Christie's, 20 February 1869 (lots 6 and 11); bt. by Drake (£3 10s and £2 8s);[991] in Lever's collection by 1906 (acquired as a pair)[992]

Stephanoff entered the Royal Academy Schools at the age of 13 in 1801. Along with his older brother James (c. 1786–1874), he specialised in paintings of historical and genre subjects in oil and watercolour. He exhibited at the Royal Academy and the British Institution from 1807 to 1845, with the Associated Artists in Water-Colours in 1809 and at the SPWC between 1813 and 1820. Many of his works depict figures in elaborate historical costumes and were designed to be engraved. In 1850, following his wife's death, he moved to Bristol to live with his brother; he gave up painting many years before his own death a decade later.

In the early decades of the nineteenth century Stephanoff was one of a number of artists who depicted Shakespearean subjects. LL 3998 and LL 3999 are small, intimate pieces, stemming from a tradition of Dutch seventeenth-century genre painting as well as the humorous narratives and moralising pictures of David Wilkie (1785–1841). The style of these works is consistent with finished watercolours by the artist dating from the 1820s and 1830s.[993] However, Stephanoff's style appears to have remained remarkably similar throughout his career. LL 3998 and LL 3999 could equally date from later, with their style being similar to designs by Stephanoff that were engraved for the publication *Finden's Tableaux* in the early 1840s.[994]

LL 3998 depicts the character of Sir John Falstaff (in the chair), accompanied by his friend Bardolph and hostess of the Boar's Head tavern, Mistress Quickly. All these characters appear in Shakespeare's plays *Henry IV Part I*, *Henry IV Part II* and *The Merry Wives of Windsor*, but the work may be based on *Henry IV Part I*, Act III, Scene iii. In this scene, set in the tavern, the slovenly but lovable rogue Falstaff engages in comic insults with his friend Bardolph, while Mistress Quickly reminds the former of the money he owes (possibly represented in LL 3998 by the bill she holds). LL 3999 is referred to in the WHL Inventory as the companion to LL 3998 and it is only at a later date that it received its current title;[995] the characters depicted could be Prince Hal and Mistress Quickly, but it has not been possible to relate the narrative to a precise scene in any of the three plays. Stephanoff appears to have enjoyed the opportunity presented by Shakespeare's plays to present comic episodes; at least one other watercolour is known depicting a scene with Falstaff and Mistress Quickly from the *Merry Wives of Windsor* (Sotheby's, New York, 10 November 1998 [lot 129]).[996]

Lever had acquired the two works by 1906 and they are typical of the small and cheap watercolour purchases he had made up to that date.[997]

989 The name given on the artist's death certificate was Philip Francis Stephanoff; see Annette Peach, 'Stephanoff, Philip Francis (1787/8–1860)', *ODNB*, vol. 52, pp. 407–08; however, he signed his name 'F. P. Stephanoff' and has generally been known by this name.

990 LL 3999 is referred to in the WHL Inventory as 'the companion pair' to LL 3998. The current title is written on the accession card. It is not clear when or by whom it was ascribed.

991 This sale contained several works by Stephanoff including lot 6, *Falstaff*, bt. by Drake (£3 10s) and lot 11, *An Illustration to Shakespeare*; bt. by Drake (£2 11s).

992 LL 3998 and LL 3999 are listed in the 1906 TM Inventory but are not recorded in the 1905 TM Inventory.

993 See, for example, *Meeting of James I and Sir Henry Lee*, watercolour, 9¾ x 6¾ in., signed and dated F.P. Stephanoff. 1826, Royal Albert Memorial Museum, Exeter, and *The Last Moments of Cardinal Wolsey*, watercolour, 24 x 31.5 cm, signed, exhibited at the Liverpool Academy 1836 (cat. 203), Sotheby's, 10 April 1980 (lot 96).

994 In 1843–45 at a competition to design frescoes for Westminster Hall, Stephanoff won a prize of £100 for a scene from *Milton's Comus* (exh. RA 1844). He produced little work from the mid-1840s onwards.

995 See n. 990.

996 *Falstaff and Mistress Quickly from the Merry Wives of Windsor*, watercolour on paper, 24.5 x 34.3 cm, signed.

997 In the 1906 TM Inventory, the majority of watercolours are valued at no more than £10.

LL 3998

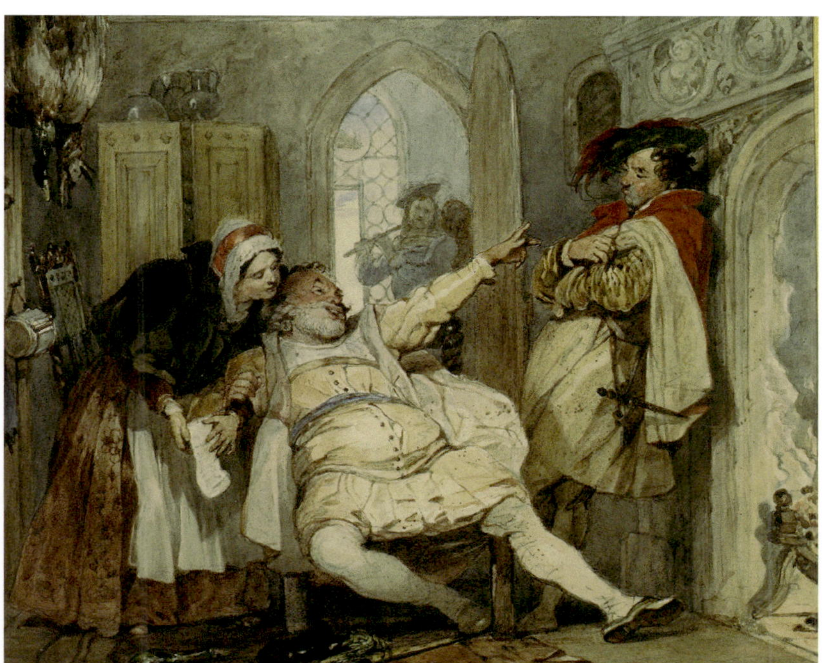

LL 3999

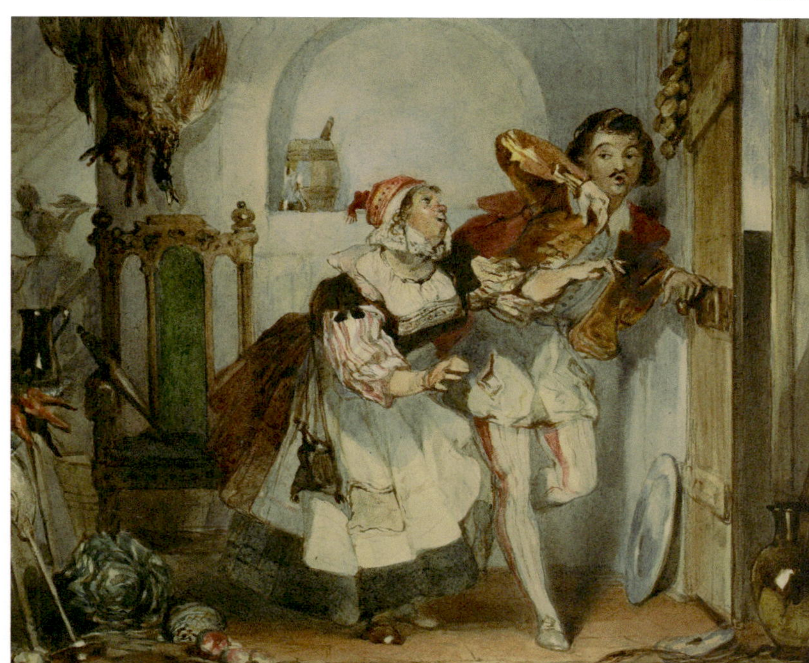

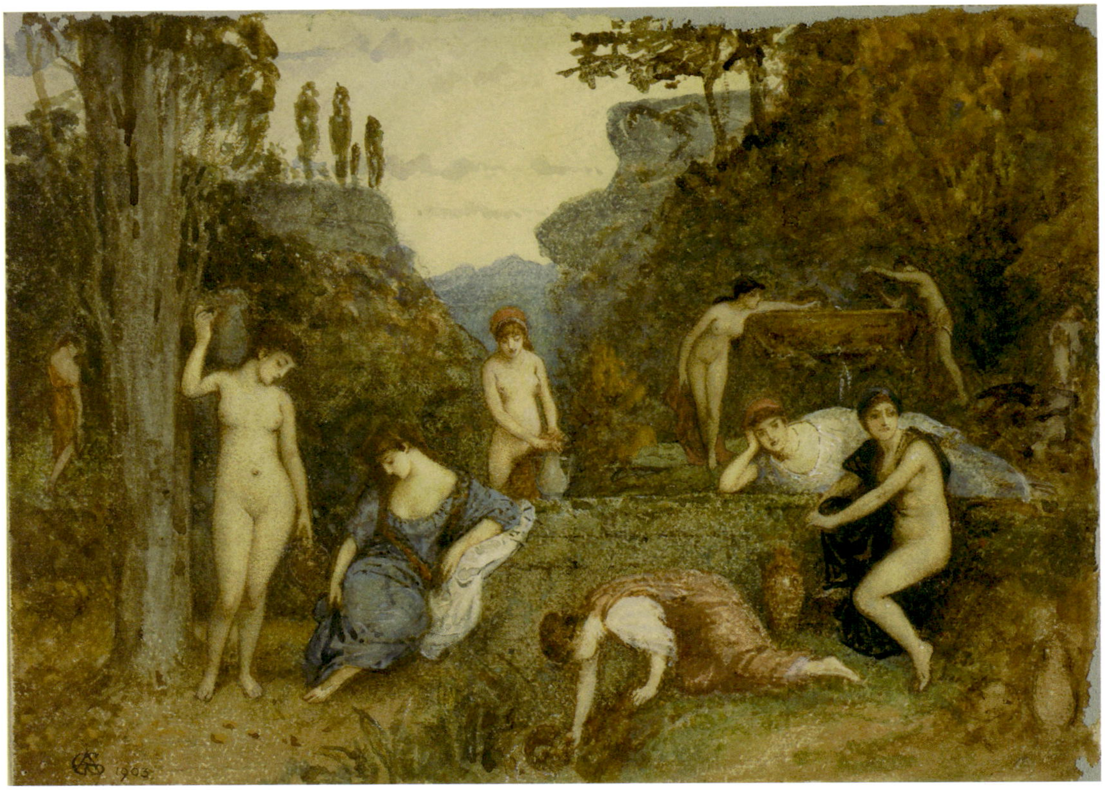

LL 3798

## GEORGE ADOLPHUS STOREY

1834 London–1919 Hampstead, London

### The Lost Labour of the Danaïdes

LL 3798 (WHL 4279)

Watercolour with gouache on paper
25.8 x 35.8 cm
Date: 1903

Inscr: GAS [monogram] 1903 (ink, bottom left)

Prov: Mrs Emily Storey (widow of the artist); bt. by Lever, 30 August 1920 (£105)

Exh: Port Sunlight, Lady Lever Art Gallery, *The Pre-Raphaelites – Their Friends and Followers*, 1948 (cat. 196)

The watercolour *The Lost Labour of the Danaïdes* is dated 1903 and seems to have been completed three years after an oil version of the subject exhibited at the Royal Academy in 1900. The drawing may have originated as a sketch for the oil, but was perhaps made as a variant replica of it. There are considerable differences between the two works, particularly in the treatment of the landscape and in the scale of the figures (in the oil they seem closer to the spectator), which argues against the drawing being a mere copy of the oil.[998]

When exhibited in 1900 the oil version of the subject was given the expanded title *The Lost Labour of the Danaïdes – Typical of Human Life.* A further quotation in the catalogue explained the subject: 'The lost Danaïdes drag their endless round / In dismal Hades, there to expiate / Their nuptial crime, etc.' The Danaids were the 50 daughters of Danaus, each of whom was unwillingly betrothed to a cousin, the 50 sons of Aegyptus. They attempted to escape the planned marriage, first by travelling with their father to Argos where they applied to King Pelasgus for protection. This part of the story is told by Aeschylus in his play *The Suppliants*. Pelasgus would not, or could not, assist them, so Danaus commanded them to go through with their forced weddings, but also told them to murder their husbands on their wedding night, and all but one – Hypermestra, who thus became the ancestress of all the future kings of Argos – did so. All of this is described in the *Odes* of Horace and Ovid's *Heroides* 14. The conclusion to the story, which is told frequently in Latin literature, tells how the 49 murderesses were condemned to an eternal fate in the Underworld where they were compelled to carry water to, and attempt to fill, a leaking vessel. Storey shows the girls drawing water from a stream, which they then carry in pitchers to the basin that stands a short distance beyond, and from which a torrent is seen to flow.

Born in London, Storey took up painting and sculpting as a child, and was then – aged 14 and for a period of two years – sent to study painting under Jean-Louis Dulong in Paris. Back in London, he attended classes at Leigh's school and later enrolled in the Royal Academy Schools. His circle of friends consisted principally of artists who were later to form the so-called St John's Wood Clique, including P. H. Calderon, H. S. Marks and G. D. Leslie; he himself was a member of this group. In the 1850s he exhibited works that demonstrate the powerful influence of contemporary Pre-Raphaelitism on his developing style. Percy Bate cites three works, *The Annunciation*, *A Song of the Past* and *The Burial of the Bride* as representative of this formative period.[999] In his later career Storey turned to historical subjects and then to genre, often showing attractive young people in contemporary or old-fashioned settings, and portraits.[1000] Subjects from ancient literature, such as the present, occur only infrequently among his exhibited works. One previous example, *Paris and Œnone*, was shown at the Royal Academy in 1890.

CN

998 Present location unknown, illus. *Royal Academy Pictures* (London, 1900), p. 7 (cat. 107).

999 P. Bate, *The English Pre-Raphaelite Painters* (London, 1899), p. 90.

1000 Biographical information for G. A. Storey derives from two principal sources, his own *Sketches from Memory* (London, 1899), and James Dafforne, 'The Works of George Adolphus Storey', *The Art Journal* (June 1875), pp. 173–76.

## JOHN FREDERICK TAYLER
1802 Borehamwood, Hertfordshire–1889 London

### A Highland Cottage Farm
LL 3768 (WHL 719, HH 407)

Watercolour over pencil on wove paper
12 x 18.4 cm (sight)
Date: late 1860s or 1870s–1889

Inscriptions: F.T (watercolour, bottom left)
Prov: bt. from James Orrock by Lever, 1910

Tayler attended both Eton and Harrow before studying at Sass's Academy in London and then at the Royal Academy Schools, completing his training in Paris and Rome. He exhibited at the Royal Academy between 1830 and 1865. He was principally a watercolourist; he became an associate of the SPWC in 1831 and a member in 1834. In 1858 he became president of the Society, holding the position until his retirement in 1871. Tayler's handling of watercolour, with his free, fluid strokes, was strongly influenced by David Cox (pp. 59–65) and to a lesser extent, George Cattermole (p. 42). His work was admired by Queen Victoria and John Ruskin, although the latter expressed doubts in the 1850s about the increasing slickness of his style.

Tayler is best known for his hunting and hawking subjects, often set in historic times. However, LL 3768 is one of his great number of pastoral scenes with rustic figures and animals, based on his frequent visits to the homes of his aristocratic friends and patrons in Scotland. It is difficult to date this work as with Tayler's watercolours generally there is not much overall development in style; however, the 'feathery' nature of the brushwork in LL 3768 is consistent with other works that are signed and dated from the late 1860s and early 1870s onwards.

LL 3768

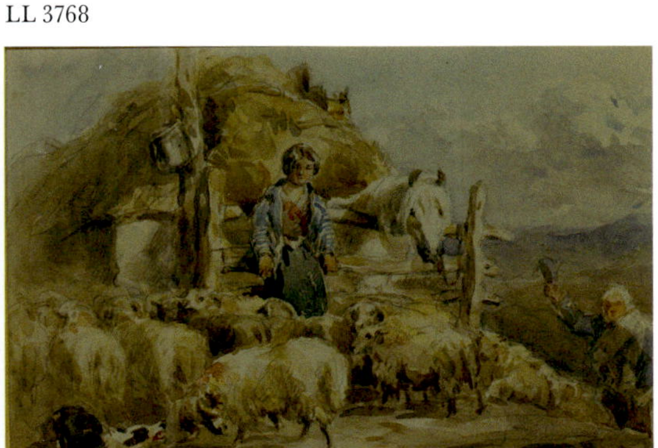

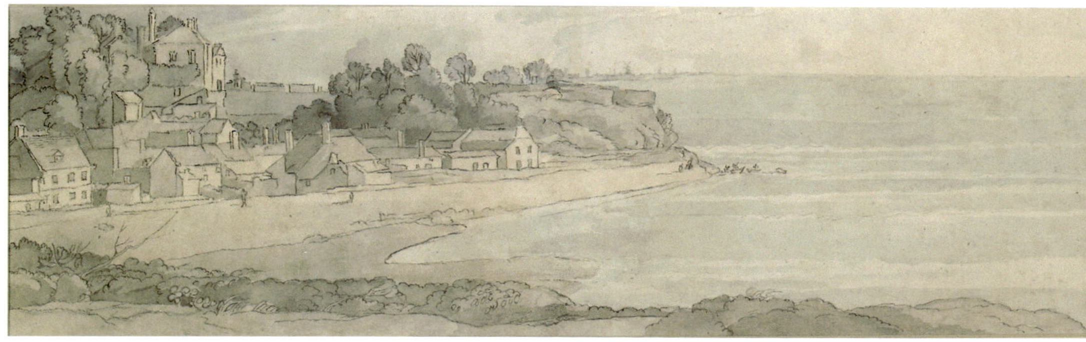

LL 3769

## FRANCIS TOWNE
1739 Isleworth, near London–1816 London

### From the Heathfields Seat, Lympstone
LL 3769 (LP 63)

Watercolour, with pen and ink outlines on two sheets of wove paper, joined vertically at the centre
10.8 x 35.8 cm (whole), 10.8 x 18.1 cm (left sheet), 10.8 x 17.7 cm (right sheet)
Date: probably 1813

Inscr: From Heathfields Seat Lympstone (pen and ink, verso, lower left)
Prov: bequeathed to James White, 1816;[1001] bequeathed to John Herman Merivale, 1825; by descent to Maria Sophia and Judith Ann Merivale, 1915; probably sold by Judith Merivale to the Squire Gallery, 1945;[1002] bt. from the Fine Art Society by the Trustees, 7 March 1946 (£70 18s 6d with LL 3977)
Exh: London, Fine Art Society, *Winter Exhibition of Early English Watercolours and Drawings*, 1945–46 (cat. 2, as *From Heathfield Spar, Lympstone*)

Francis Towne, the son of a corn chandler, was apprenticed in 1752, while still a young boy, to a London coach-painter. When his indenture came to an end, Towne is believed to have studied under the court portraitist John Shackleton, but he also continued to earn his living as a coach-painter. He had begun to exhibit landscapes at the Society of Artists in 1762, and soon after this he left London for Exeter, where he was to make his living as a drawing master. Towne's most successful pupil was the Exeter surgeon, John White Abbott (see pp. 2–3), whose reputation even superseded his teacher's. Towne seems to have retired from teaching in Exeter around 1800 and taken up permanent residence in London from then on. Although Towne had little commercial success as a painter, he had made a considerable fortune by 1809 through his teaching practice and consistent frugality, and he was able to spend the remaining years of his life pursuing his art, making annual sketching excursions in Wales, Scotland and the West Country. Little recognised during his lifetime, Towne's original genius and distinctive style only emerged with the rediscovery of a large quantity of his sketches in 1915, and the publication in 1920 of an article by the scholar-collector, Paul Oppé.

LL 3769 belonged to a sketchbook that Towne used between 1812 and 1815 that contained around 19 or 20 images.[1003] From 1809 Towne, now living in London, made almost annual excursions in late summer to the West Country to see friends. The Lady Lever drawing is a view of the village of Lympstone taken from Nutwell Court or 'the Heathfields Seat', and looking out on the Exe Estuary. Now a man of leisure, Towne no longer had to depict the great country seats of Devon as he had done for so much of his professional career, but could, as with LL 3769, depict more intimate views of a town, sketched as he walked along a road, the portability of the tiny 1812–15 sketchbook making it ideal for this purpose. The 1812–15 sketchbook differs from Towne's other late sketchbooks in that it was used sporadically over the course of four years, and so unlike many of Towne's sketches its contents do not form part of a numbered series.

Richard Stephens has suggested that the drawing may date from the summer of 1813.[1004] That year Towne visited Oxford, Warwick and Kenilworth in late August before reaching the north Devon coast in early September. Although Towne used a separate and larger sketchbook for this excursion, he also would have carried the 1812–15 sketchbook with him. Another sketch from the book, of the Topsham Road (the road which ran between the port town of Topsham and Exeter), is dated 1813 (now in the Rhode Island School of Design, Providence).[1005] LL 3769, as with the Topsham Road sketch, but unlike the other 1812–15 sketches which are fully coloured, has

1001 The Exeter lawyer James White (1744–1825) was a close friend of the artist and also the executor of his will.
1002 The information about the provenance of LL 3769 down to 1945 is derived from Richard Stephens, email correspondence, June 2007. His information is based on a checklist kept by Judith Merivale of the drawings she sold and donated from the early 1920s to her death (the original copy of this is lost but there is a photocopy in Agnew's Archives). LL 3769 was probably among the 'two small sketchbooks and five small drawings late in date' which Judith Merivale sold to the Squire Gallery in 1945 for £50.

1003 Richard Stephens, email correspondence, 7 June 2007.
1004 Ibid.
1005 The Rhode Island sketch is inscribed on the verso: On the Topham (crossed out) (Topsham) / road / Devonshire / 1813 / Francis Towne (pencil). The work is a single-page view, with dimensions 11.2 x 18.3 cm. The Lady Lever work is a double-page view.

a preliminary shading of greys and blues. LL 3769 exhibits Towne's characteristic technique of pen-and-ink outline and flat washes of colour. This was built up in the following way: he would have started with the drawing in pencil or ink (or sometimes ink over pencil) taken direct from nature and some time later he would have added the watercolour, and then drawn over the outlines again in pen and ink. It is this particular use of outline that makes Towne's drawings so distinctive, even among his contemporaries.

Stephens has suggested that Towne's inscribed title, with its slightly odd phrasing 'From the Heathfields Seat, Lympstone', provides additional circumstantial evidence for an 1813 date.[1006] Following the death of the 2nd Baron Heathfield in January 1813 the ownership of Nutwell Court, or 'the Heathfields Seat', inherited by Thomas Trayton Fuller, Heathfield's nephew, was contested by the Drakes (Heathfield's uncle had been Sir Francis Drake [1723-94], a descendant of the famous Elizabethan). Towne's inscription suggests that the drawing was made after Lord Heathfield's death (otherwise 'Lord Heathfield's Seat') and before he was aware of the identity of the new owner. As Stephens has also pointed out, the 2nd Baron Heathfield was notoriously inhospitable to people who wanted to look around his grounds and Towne may have taken the opportunity following his death to visit Nutwell.[1007]

1006 Richard Stephens, email correspondence, 7 June 2007.

1007 Ibid. The Revd John Swete criticised Heathfield at length in his journal of topographical descriptions of Devon: M. Rowe and T. Gray (eds), *Travels in Georgian Devon: The Illustrated Journals of the Reverend John Swete (1789-1800)* (Exeter, 4 vols, 1997-2000), vol. IV, pp. 143-49.

## JOSEPH MALLORD WILLIAM TURNER

1775 London-1851 London

### Wells Cathedral

LL 3780 (WHL 327, H 417)

Watercolour over pencil on paper
42.4 x 54.7 cm
Date: probably 1795-96

Inscr: W Turner (ink, smudged, bottom right)

Prov: [?] Joseph Shepherd Munden;[1008] John Alnutt; his sale, Christie's, 18 June 1863 (lot 25); bt. by Crofts (£27 6s); B. J. Windus; his sale, Christie's, 15 February 1868 (lot 264); bt. by Haghe (£105); A. P. Haig; his sale, Christie's, 27 May 1910 (lot 47); bt. by Wallis (£210); Agnew's, 1912; bt. from James Orrock by Lever, 1912[1009]

Exh: [?] London, Soho Square, W. B. Cooke Gallery, exhibition title unknown, 1822 (cat. 95);[1010] Liverpool, Walker Art Gallery, *Turner's Journeys of the Imagination*, 2002 (cat. 16)

Lit: Andrew Wilton, *J.M.W. Turner: His Art and Life* (New Jersey, 1979), p. 314 (cat. 134); Frank Milner, *Turner: Paintings in Merseyside Collections* (Liverpool, 1990), p. 10, illus. p. 17

Considered to be the foremost British landscape painter of the first half of the nineteenth century, Turner and his friend and rival Thomas Girtin (see p. 102) led the revolution in watercolour painting of the 1790s. Having gained some experience in the office of the architect Thomas Hardwick and with Thomas Malton, an architectural draughtsman, Turner entered the Royal Academy Schools in 1789 and exhibited his first watercolour, an architectural subject, the following year. Although Turner's early watercolours were firmly rooted within the topographical tradition, his training at Dr Thomas Monro's 'academy' (1794-97), his tours to Wales in the 1790s and his experience with oil painting contributed, along with his experimental technical processes, to the development of his powerful, atmospheric landscapes in watercolour. Turner was an indefatigable traveller and as a young man he toured widely in England and Scotland. After 1815 he travelled frequently on the Continent, visiting Italy for the first time in 1819. Some of his last trips were to Switzerland in the early 1840s, which resulted in arguably some of his finest finished watercolours. Turner's large output in watercolour and gouache (he rarely mixed the media) was of two types: a great number of spontaneous sketches in watercolour, some of which were associated with engraving projects such as the *Picturesque Views in England and Wales* (1827-38); and highly worked watercolours which were more often intended for sale than exhibition. Turner exhibited at the Royal Academy throughout his life, as well as at his own gallery in his house on the corner of Harley Street and Queen Anne Street. He never joined any of the watercolour societies. He was elected an associate of the Royal Academy in 1799 and a full member in 1802, and held the post of the Academy's Professor of Perspective from 1807 to 1837. At his death, Turner bequeathed around 100 pictures to the nation; the Turner Bequest now includes his sketchbooks, preliminary drawings and watercolours as well as oil sketches and is held at the Clore Gallery in the Tate and at the National Gallery.

Although Turner may have visited the cathedral city of Wells in Somerset, near Bristol, on his 1791 tour to the area, no sketches of the city have been found from this trip.[1011] There is, however, strong evidence to suggest that the Lady Lever watercolour is based on his tour to South Wales in the summer of 1795. A sketchbook that is now generally believed to date from this trip includes two drawings of Wells Cathedral and one of these is a study of the architecture of the west front, relating closely to the final work.[1012] On the basis of this sketch, LL 3780, which is a fully worked up watercolour, is likely to have been made over the autumn or winter of 1795-96.[1013]

Turner has depicted one of the best-known features of the cathedral, its west front, dating from the first half of the thirteenth century and completed by the addition of towers in the late fourteenth and early fifteenth centuries. He has paid great attention to the architectural details of the magnificent façade, showing its many niches containing figure sculptures. In the background and given more cursory treatment are several medieval buildings built for the use of the junior clergy.

1008 There is a reference to a Turner drawing of Wells Cathedral in Thomas Shepherd Munden, *Memoirs of Joseph Shepherd Munden, by His Son* (London, 1844), p. 56: 'He got together a valuable collection of drawings by Turner, in his earlier and best style, Girtin, Cousins [*sic*], Cipriani, and Bartolozzi. Two companion drawings, on a large scale, which he possessed - Wells Cathedral, by Turner, and Durham Castle, by Girtin - were works of extraordinary merit ... An intimacy with the artists, and a ready admittance to their studios, enabled him to obtain these drawings at moderate prices.' LL 3780 appears to be the only known candidate for this drawing. The comic actor J. S. Munden (1758-1832) is recorded as taking lessons from Turner, but it has not been possible to trace sales of works from his collection. I am grateful to Greg Smith for this reference.

1009 1912 Inventory, p. 4 (no. 49), valued at £250.

1010 Walter Armstrong records that a *Wells Cathedral - West Front* was exhibited at Cooke's gallery in 1822. See Walter Armstrong, *Turner* (London and New York, 2 vols, 1902), vol. II, p. 284. The work may also have been exhibited at the French Gallery at an unknown date. LLAG files: a note on the accession card records that 'the frame is said to have borne a small label reading "French Gallery, No. 6296, Turner, Wells Cathedral"'.

1011 In the summer of 1791 Turner paid a visit to Bristol to stay with the Narraway family who appear to have been old family friends.

1012 The 'South Wales sketchbook', Tate, contains *Wells Cathedral: The West Front* (TB XXVI 2) which relates closely to LL 3780. The same sketchbook contains another view made in the city, *Penniless Porch and Bishop's Eye Gateways from the Market Place, Wells* (TB XXVI 1). The smaller 'South Wales sketchbook', Tate, contains *Wells Cathedral: The South-West Tower from the Cloisters* (TB XXV 4) but this has no relationship to the Lady Lever work.

1013 Turner, like other artists, was in the practice of making his sketching tours during the summer, spending the autumn and winter in the studio working up his finished paintings and watercolours.

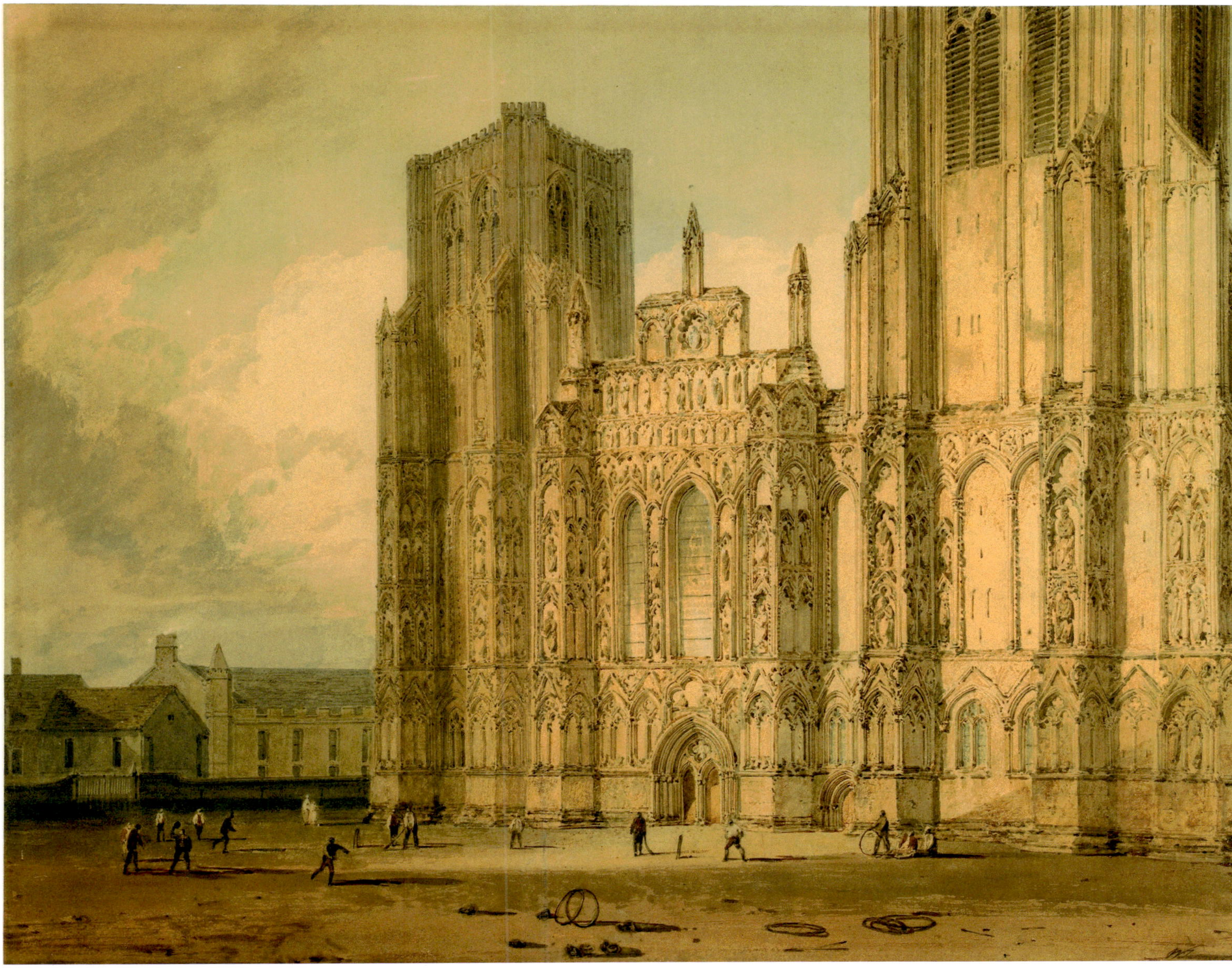

LL 3780

Turner has chosen to emphasise the monumental scale of the cathedral, deciding not to paint the façade face-on but instead from an angle at the side, adjacent to its near or south-western tower. This choice of viewpoint means that the near tower appears much larger than its north-western neighbour. This is an effect achieved by techniques of foreshortening and perspective, with the furthermost tower receding into the shadows in the background and the nearer tower appearing to loom massively over the composition, its top seemingly too large to be contained within the picture. The grandeur of the cathedral is also emphasised by the contrast with the tiny figures below, who are the same if not smaller in size than some of the sculptures on the façade.

The Lady Lever watercolour is one of many that Turner made of ecclesiastical subjects from the early 1790s onwards. In common with other early watercolours, Turner has included incidental detail in the form of figures to enliven the composition. Here the foreground figures are occupied in a game of cricket; a few are playing with hoops. The inclusion of figures engaged in a sociable pursuit is repeated in another watercolour from the same period, *Ely from the South East* (c. 1796, private collection) which includes a number of fashionably dressed figures strolling, as well as young men playing with hoops.[1014] Turner's intention in both works may have been to contrast the secular pursuits of the figures with the religious connotations of the buildings.

Although somewhat faded overall, in its precise style the work is typical of Turner's watercolours of architectural subjects from the mid-1790s. Here, extensive pencil under-drawing is overlaid with wash, with the line then strengthened with fine brushstrokes to represent detail. Turner's careful attention to the nuances of the architecture as well as his use of complex perspective techniques suggests the quality of the training that he had received in Hardwick's architectural practice. *Wells Cathedral*, with its bold viewpoint and use of light and shadow, was on the cusp of the stylistic development that Turner's architectural subjects would show in the second half of the 1790s. The watercolour is not in the same vein as the straightforward views of the topographical work of earlier draughtsmen such as Paul and Thomas Sandby and Thomas Malton. However, nor does it exhibit the more muscular watercolour techniques or dramatic composition and lighting effects seen in Turner's watercolours of Salisbury Cathedral from the late 1790s and early 1800s.[1015]

1014 Wilton, p. 179 (cat. 193).

1015 See, for example, *Choir of Salisbury Cathedral*, 1797, Salisbury and South Wiltshire Museum, Salisbury, Wilton, p. 321 (cat. 197); *South view from the cloisters, Salisbury Cathedral*, c. 1802, Victoria & Albert Museum, Wilton, p. 322 (cat. 202).

## Hafod

LL 3778 (WHL 328, H 416)

Watercolour over pencil on paper
61 x 91.5 cm
Date: c. 1798-99

Prov: bt. from James Orrock by Lever, 1912[1016]

Exh: Swansea, Glynn Vivian Art Gallery, *Art in Wales*, 1964 (cat. 92); London, Tate Gallery, *Landscape in Britain c.1750–1850*, 1973 (cat. 141); Cardiff, National Museum of Wales and Aberystwyth, National Library of Wales, *Plans and Prospects, Architecture in Wales 1780–1914*, 1975 (cat. 2); Liverpool, Walker Art Gallery, *Turner's Journeys of the Imagination*, 2002 (cat. 17); Birmingham, Birmingham Museums and Art Gallery, *Turner's Britain*, 2003–2004 (cat. 19)

Lit: Andrew Wilton, *J.M.W. Turner: His Art and Life* (New Jersey, 1979), p. 337 (cat. 331); Frank Milner, *Turner: Paintings in Merseyside Collections* (Liverpool, 1990), pp. 15–16

In 1780 Thomas Johnes (1748–1816) inherited the estate of Hafod, located in the mountains to the south-east of Aberystwyth, Cardiganshire, and quickly set about transforming its ruinous state.[1017] He commissioned the architect Thomas Baldwin of Bath to design a new Gothic-style house, which was completed between 1786 and 1788.[1018] The house, with its huge library, planned Picturesque gardens and estate, quickly became a favourite stop on the Welsh tourist circuit and was popular with eminent visitors.[1019] The estate also became famous for its agricultural improvements and model forestry.[1020]

Turner may have visited Hafod on his trip to Wales in the summer of 1798 but no drawings of the house can be found in the sketchbooks for this tour or any other trips to Wales.[1021] Two drawings for the composition are known but their attribution is not certain. The poor handling of an ink-and-watercolour drawing in the Tate strongly suggests it is not by the artist;[1022] the attribution of a further drawing in the Hickman Bacon collection is not conclusive.[1023]

Although LL 3778 has long been titled *Hafod*, it bears only a limited resemblance to the design by Baldwin, as represented in a watercolour by John 'Warwick' Smith.[1024] It is now generally thought that the Lady Lever work represents an unrealised scheme for a new frontage for the house.[1025] Following the completion of Baldwin's scheme, from the early 1790s Johnes began to plan extensions to the house. Andrew Wilton has quoted John Harris as being 'fairly certain that [the watercolour] represents a scheme by John Nash' which was rejected.[1026] The architect John Nash (1752–1835) had made some small changes to the house in 1793–94 and may have felt qualified to put forward more ambitious additions and alterations. The design for the house as represented in LL 3778 does bear a strong similarity to Nash's scheme for Corsham Court, Wiltshire, and may have been reconstituted for this purpose by 1797.[1027] LL 3778 may have been commissioned by John Nash to present to his potential client Thomas Johnes.

Turner could have met Nash in the same way that he met and worked for other architects such as James Wyatt and Joseph Bonomi and LL 3778 is one of a number of architectural presentation drawings that Turner made in the period c. 1796–99.[1028] LL 3778 is unusual among these works, however, in combining an atmospheric sublime landscape with a formal architectural drawing. As James Hamilton has argued recently, it 'reveals that Turner was perfectly prepared to use the profound experience of landscape form and mood that he had gained on his travels to enhance a workaday drawing'.[1029]

The work's traditional dating of c. 1798–99 is based presumably on Turner's trip to North Wales and is probably correct.[1030] However, given the uncertainty over whether Turner visited Hafod on this trip, this dating can also be made on stylistic grounds. In style, LL 3778 relates closely to an architectural drawing made for James Wyatt, *North-west view of Fonthill Abbey*, exhibited at the Royal Academy in 1798 (Yale Center for British Art).[1031]

Wilton has suggested that the drawing of the architecture in LL 3778, from its mechanical quality, may not be Turner's hand.[1032] However, although Wilton is right to point out the different quality in the drawing style, it is difficult to dismiss the possibility of Turner's authorship of the whole work.[1033] It is worth remembering that at this early period in Turner's career he would have been fully versed in making such plain drawings, having executed them for the architect Thomas Hardwick. If we are to see LL 3778 as a presentation drawing of a proposed architect's scheme, then it seems possible that Turner may have altered his style to suit the purpose, changing from the more fluent style of drawing architecture in works such as *Wells Cathedral* (LL 3780 above).

The watercolour includes three figures standing in the portico of the house, which are unusual certainly among Turner's architectural drawings in adding more than incidental detail to the work. Two of these are dressed in classical costume; they are saluting with raised arms the third figure who wears tights, a three-quarter cloak and what may be a plumed hat. One of the classical figures holds what appears to be a crown or laurel wreath over the head of the third figure. As Frank Milner has convincingly suggested, these figures may have a symbolic connection with Hafod and Thomas Johnes.[1034] For example, they may represent the idea of ancient learning saluting more recent contemporary poetry (perhaps referring to Johnes's setting up of the Hafod press for his translations of the medieval French writer Froissart).[1035] It is not hard to see how the addition of such symbolic figures may have been intended subtly to flatter a potential client like Johnes.

1016 1912 Inventory, p. 4 (no. 42), valued at £750.

1017 Johnes's father (also Thomas Johnes) died in 1780, leaving him the estate of Croft Castle, Herefordshire as well as Hafod.

1018 For information on Thomas Johnes and Hafod, see E. Inglis Jones, *Peacocks in Paradise* (London, 1990); William Condry, 'Last Look at Hafod?', *Country Life* (6 February 1958), pp. 252–53. See also David S. Yerburgh, *An Attempt to Depict Hafod: An Artistic Impression* (Salisbury, 2000).

1019 For details of Johnes's book collecting and publishing activities, see James A. Dearden, 'Thomas Johnes and the Hafod Press 1803–10', *The Book Collector*, vol. 22, no. 3 (autumn 1973). Hafod was included in a number of guidebooks to Wales from the 1790s onwards, with George Cumberland's *An Attempt to Describe Hafod* (London, 1796) being the first to be solely dedicated to the house and estate. Yerburgh, *An Attempt to Depict Hafod*, p. 77, lists many of these guidebooks.

1020 By the late 1790s Hafod was in decline and in a precarious financial state; in 1807 it was burnt down in a serious fire. By 1811 the house had been built again but Johnes never recovered financially and in 1813 was forced to offer the reversion of Hafod for sale. After a series of owners, the house was demolished in 1955.

1021 Turner described Hafod in a letter dated 1847 to W. H. Fawkes in connection with a sketching tour that Fawkes intended to make. Turner wrote: 'In the neighbourhood of Havord or Hawvorford known by being the seat of Esquire Jones, ... I do not think you could have hit a more desirable spot for your pencil'; quoted by J. Gage, *Turner's Correspondence* (London, 1980), p. 218, letter 307. As Milner has pointed out, Turner made no mention of having stayed at Hafod or having sketched the house.

1022 *A Landscape with a Proposed Elevation of Hafod*, c. 1798, catalogued as British School, eighteenth century, ink wash, pencil and watercolour on paper, 16.2 x 28 cm, Tate (TB CCCLXXX 4).

1023 Wilton, p. 337 (cat. 331) has doubted the attribution of the Hickman/Bacon work to Turner, but even if this work were securely attributed to Turner, it does not necessarily prove that Turner ever visited Hafod.

1024 This watercolour is dated 1795, but is based on sketches of 1792 (National Library of Wales, Aberystwyth).

1025 This was first suggested by Wilton, p. 337.

1026 Ibid.

1027 Ibid.

1028 It is not known when exactly Turner might have met Nash but they certainly knew one another by 1827 when Turner stayed at Nash's house at Cowes. For other examples of Turner's early architectural drawings, see Wilton, pp. 337–38 (cats. 327–34).

1029 James Hamilton, *Turner's Britain* (exh. cat., Birmingham, Birmingham Museums and Art Gallery, 2003–2004), p. 65.

1030 LL 3778 is dated to c. 1798 by Wilton, p. 337 (cat. 331). Milner dates the work to c. 1795 on the basis of stylistic similarity to *Wells Cathedral* (LL 3780). However, the latter work demonstrates a more fluid handling of the architecture than the diagrammatic clarity shown in *Hafod*.

1031 Wilton, p. 338 (cat. 333).

1032 Wilton, p. 337 (cat. 331).

1033 See Hamilton, *Turner's Britain*, p. 198, n. 42. Here, Hamilton says that he sees 'no reason to doubt' that the façade is by Turner's hand. This is also the opinion of Ian Warrell, verbally, April 2008.

1034 Milner, p. 16.

1035 Ibid. Milner also offers other suggestions.

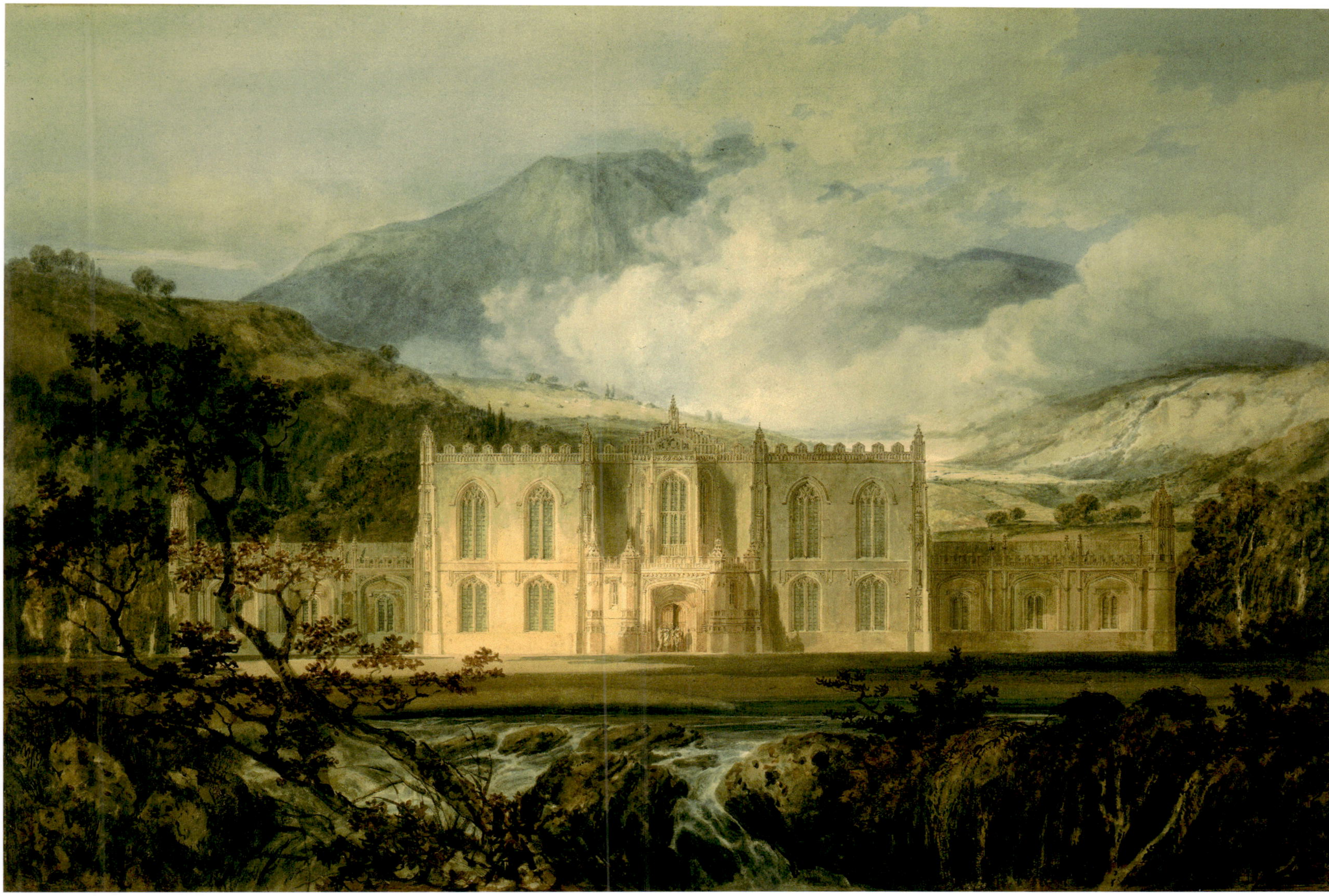

LL 3778

### Falmouth Harbour, Cornwall[1036]
LL 3771 (WHL 3507)

Watercolour with touches of gouache and scratching out on wove paper
15.6 x 23.2 cm
Date: c. 1812–14

Prov: Mrs C. Molyneux; her sale, Christie's, March 1910 (lot 53); bt. by Wallis (£199 10s); Royal Institute of Painters in Water-Colours; their sale, Christie's, 3 May 1918 (lot 62); bt. by Gooden and Fox (£262 10s) for Lever (£275 12s 6d)[1037]

Exh: London, Royal Academy, *Turner, 1775–1851*, 1974–75 (cat. 160); London, Royal Academy, *Turner: The Great Watercolours*, 2000–2001 (cat. 26); Liverpool, Walker Art Gallery, *Turner's Journeys of the Imagination*, 2002 (cat. 26); Birmingham, Birmingham Museums and Art Gallery, *Turner's Britain*, 2003–2004 (cat. 61)

Lit: Andrew Wilton, *J.M.W. Turner: His Art and Life* (New Jersey, 1979), p. 351 (cat. 455); Eric Shanes, *Turner's Rivers, Harbours and Coasts* (London, 1981), p. 24; Frank Milner, *Turner: Paintings in Merseyside Collections* (Liverpool, 1990), pp. 35–36

LL 3771 was one of 39 watercolours made by Turner to be engraved as part of the *Picturesque Views of the Southern Coast of England*.[1038] It is one of three from this series purchased by Lever (see also LL 3782 and LL 3783). In 1811 the engravers, William Bernard Cooke and his brother George Cooke, invited Turner to take part in creating a set of engravings of views in southern England. Although other artists also contributed images it was Turner, having become somewhat of a celebrity by this date, who was crucial to the publication's success. The project suited Turner who had begun around 1806 to commission and make engravings of his own work and was well aware of the potential commercial success this could bring. However, unlike Turner's own series of engraved landscapes, the *Liber Studiorum*, which was a private venture, the Cookes' invitation had the advantage that he did not have to take any financial risk.[1039] The *Southern Coast* project was published in parts between 1814 and 1826. Although the engravings provide a topographical record of the locations visited, they also reveal Turner's keen interest in a wide variety of aspects of English life, including the effect of the Napoleonic wars on the nation.

Turner set about making sketches for *Southern Coast* subjects in the summer of 1811 when he toured the West Country. He visited Falmouth on this occasion and a number of drawings of the harbour appear in two sketchbooks used on this tour, although none appears to be directly related to this composition.[1040] *Falmouth Harbour, Cornwall* was engraved by W. B. Cooke in 1816 and was one of the earliest images to be made for the series.[1041] The watercolours were by and large engraved in the order that they were made, and on this basis the work has been dated to c. 1812–14.[1042]

LL 3771 is typical of many of the *Southern Coast* subjects in showing a view of the coast from the land. Turner's view was probably taken from the steep hill north-west of Falmouth town centre and looks out across its roofs and chimneys over the harbour.[1043] Pendennis Castle is pictured directly opposite on the tip of the peninsula that stretches round to the right. Mawes Castle is just visible on the shoreline in the far distance of the watercolour. Both castles were built in the mid-sixteenth century by Henry VIII as defensive fortifications against France and Spain.

In 1811, when Turner was sketching in Falmouth, the port was particularly busy with naval vessels involved in protecting the country against the French. It is these boats, along with some civilian ones, that can be seen in the harbour. In the foreground Turner has depicted sailors on shore leave in a variety of stages of drunkenness, their revelry accompanied by music played by a wooden-legged fiddler. They are shown cavorting with women and, as Eric Shanes has suggested, the smoking chimney on the right may be a 'Hogarthian visual pun' which would seem appropriate in this 'sexually charged context'.[1044] It is unlikely that Turner actually saw this drunken revelry, as this type of imagery turns up in many of the artist's depictions of naval bases and is typical of his concern to reflect the broad range of human activity.[1045] Although the work was painted before the final allied victory at Waterloo in 1815, Lord Nelson's victory at Trafalgar in 1805 made an invasion after this point unlikely. James Hamilton has suggested that *Falmouth Harbour*, in showing naval ships in the far distance and resting sailors under tranquil skies, 'shows a nation at peace with itself' and intimates an awareness that the war was nearly over.[1046]

### Minehead and Dunster Castle, Somerset[1047]
LL 3782 (WHL 225, H 209)

Watercolour with extra gum arabic and scratching out on wove paper
15.3 x 22.3 cm
Date: c. 1818

Prov: J. Morley; his sale, Christie's, 16 May 1896 (lot 21); bt. by Agnew's (£168);[1048] Francis Stevenson; Agnew's, 1903; James Orrock; his sale, Christie's, 4 June 1904 (lot 46); bt. by A. Smith (£399);[1049] Agnew's; from whom bt. by Lever, 22 February 1907 (£4,000 with five other works)[1050]

Exh: London, Soho Square, W. B. Cooke Gallery, exhibition title unknown, 1822 (cat. 94);[1051] London, Agnew's, *37th Annual Exhibition of Selected High Class Watercolour Drawings*, 1903 (cat. 223); Liverpool, Walker Art Gallery, *Turner's Journeys of the Imagination*, 2002 (cat. 27)

Lit: Andrew Wilton, *J.M.W. Turner: His Art and Life* (New Jersey, 1979), p. 353 (cat. 469); Eric Shanes, *Turner's Rivers, Harbours and Coasts* (London, 1981), p. 35; John Gage, *J.M.W. Turner: 'A Wonderful Range of Mind'* (New Haven and London, 1987), p. 195, illus. fig. 271; Frank Milner, *Turner: Paintings in Merseyside Collections* (Liverpool, 1990), pp. 38, 41

*Minehead*, like two other works in Lever's collection (*Falmouth Harbour*, LL 3771 and *Portsmouth*, LL 3783) was made to be engraved as part of Turner's first and largest collaborative project with the Cooke brothers, in which he was engaged to make views of the southern coast of England. Originally commissioned around 1811, the *Picturesque Views of the Southern Coast of England* was published in parts between 1814 and 1826 (for further details see LL 3771 above).

The watercolour shows on the left hill in the middle distance Dunster Castle, which was owned by the Luttrell family from the late fourteenth century to the late twentieth. The conical hill to its right probably shows the distinctive Conygar Tower, a folly commissioned by the family in the late eighteenth century. The village of Minehead is on the right beyond these hills and in the far distance looms the massive bulk of Porlock Hill. Turner's view was made from the south-east of Minehead, probably from the site of the Blue Anchor inn, which Eric Shanes has identified in the foreground of this work.[1052]

Turner visited Minehead towards the end of his 1811 tour to the West Country following time spent in Devon and Cornwall.[1053] He made several sketches of Minehead and Dunster Castle on this trip but none relates directly to the

1036 This is the title under which LL 3771 was engraved.

1037 LLAG files: invoice.

1038 Forty subjects in total by Turner were engraved for the *Southern Coast* project. Turner made 39 watercolours specifically for the series between 1811 and 1825. Another drawing of *Martello Towers, near Bexhill, Sussex*, made for the *Liber Studiorum*, was also engraved for the *Southern Coast* (Wilton, p.352, cat. 460). For further details of the project see Wilton, p. 350 and cats. 445–84, and Eric Shanes, *Turner's Rivers, Harbours and Coasts* (London, 1981), pp. 6–8, 11. See also Hamilton, *Turner's Britain*, pp. 99–109.

1039 Turner's *Liber Studiorum* or 'Book of Studies' was based partly on the model of Richard Earlom's mezzotints after Claude's *Liber Veritatis* published in 1777. The prints after Turner's work were issued at regular intervals between 1807 and 1819. Ultimately, the *Liber Studiorum* was a financial failure and 5000 unsold *Liber* prints were found in Turner's studio after his death (see James Hamilton, *Turner: A Life* [London, 1997], p. 133). For the most recent survey of the *Liber Studiorum*, see Gillian Forrester, *Turner's 'Drawing Book' The Liber Studiorum* (exh. cat., London, Tate Gallery, 1996).

1040 Drawings of the subject of Falmouth Harbour appear in the 'Devonshire Coast No. 1 sketchbook', Tate (TB CXXIII) and the 'Ivy Bridge to Penzance sketchbook', Tate (TB CXXV), both dating from the 1811 tour.

1041 W. G. Rawlinson, *The Engraved Work of J.M.W. Turner* (London, 2 vols, 1908, 1913), vol. I, p. 53 (cat. 98). There are four impressions of this print in the Tate's collection.

1042 Wilton dates LL 3771 to c. 1812–14. More recently, Hamilton, *Turner's Britain*, p. 202, has dated the work to c. 1812–13 but it is not clear on what basis he made this marginally earlier dating.

1043 LLAG files: this is the opinion of John Irons, letter, August 2002. This is different from the opinion expressed by Milner, p. 35, that the view is taken from the hill behind the village of Flushing. The view of both Pendennis Castle and Mawes Castle would not have been possible from this point.

1044 Eric Shanes, *Turner: The Great Watercolours* (exh. cat., London, Royal Academy, 2000–2001), p. 100 (cat. 26).

1045 Ibid.

1046 Hamilton, *Turner's Britain*, p. 105.

1047 LL 3782 was engraved under the title *Minehead and Dunster Castle, Somersetshire*. See Rawlinson, *Engraved Work of J.M.W Turner*, vol. I, p. 59 (cat. 112). See also A. J. Finberg, *An Introduction to Turner's Southern Coast with a catalogue of the engravings etc...* (London, 1929), p. 46.

1048 LLAG files: note on accession card.

1049 Ibid. The note also states '? nominally sold for £399'.

1050 The group included two works by George Morland and three other watercolours by Turner: *Bolton Abbey*, *Portsmouth* and *Lancaster from the Aqueduct*. Although Lever's invoice from Agnew's was dated 1907, the works were in his possession by 1905 as they are listed in the 1905 TM Inventory.

1051 LLAG files: note on accession card.

1052 Shanes, *Turner's Rivers*, p. 26.

1053 Hamilton, *Turner: A Life*, p. 146.

composition in LL 3782.[1054] The work was engraved by W. B. Cooke in 1821 and on this basis has previously been dated to c. 1820.[1055] However, Shanes has pointed out that the drawing was with the engraver in July 1818 and a note on a page of the 'Hints River sketchbook' of 1818 also suggests that it was made that year.[1056]

In common with many of the other *Southern Coast* views (including *Falmouth*), Turner has depicted a view of the sea from the land, but here he has particularly emphasised the forms and structure of the hills beyond the stretch of water. As Frank Milner has pointed out, Turner has adapted a composition long used by artists to depict the bay of Naples.[1057] Turner had already used it in one of his own watercolours of the subject (c. 1817, Williamson Art Gallery, Birkenhead) where, as with LL 3782, the land curves round to the right, and in place of the distant hills is the volcano Vesuvius.[1058]

In the foreground of LL 3782 Turner has depicted two seated figures with their backs to the viewer; the bundle beside one suggests that they are travellers. In a similar vein to other *Southern Coast* views, the figures are shown relaxing (one has a pipe in his hand), although here in comparison to *Falmouth* the atmosphere is more serene, with the long shadows cast by the late afternoon sun contributing to the sense of repose.[1059] By the time of the 1821 engraving Turner had added a dog adjacent to the seated figures as well as three further figures in the middle distance, two on horseback, perhaps believing that the relatively spartan composition needed more incidental detail.

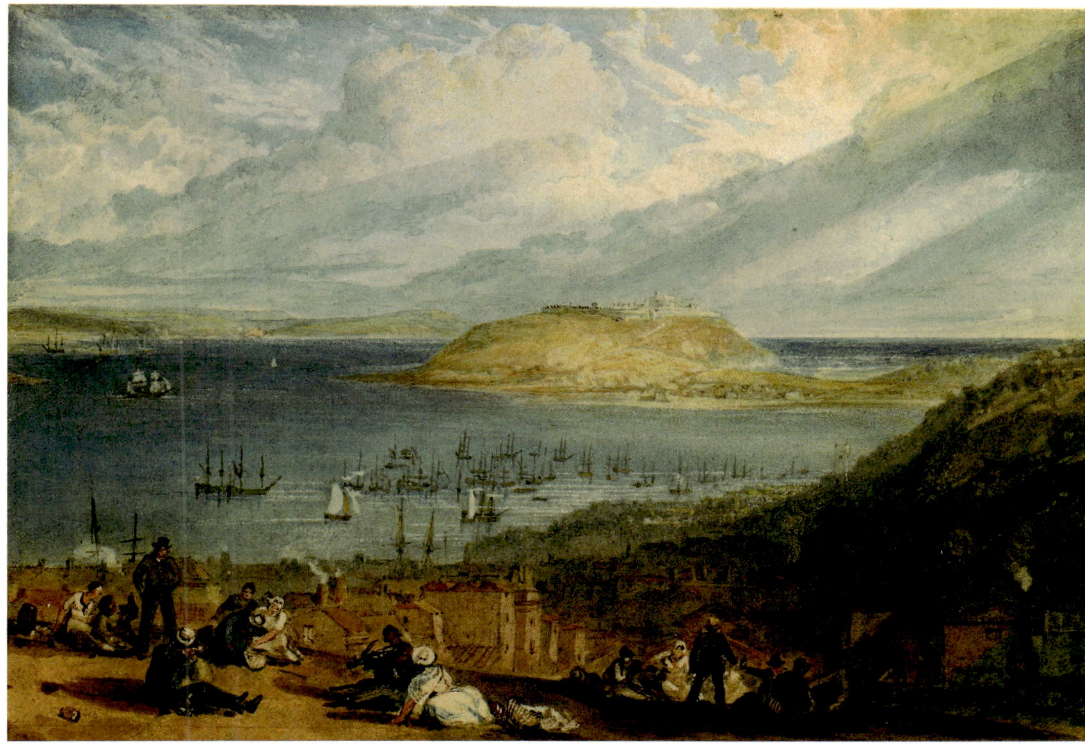

LL 3771

LL 3782

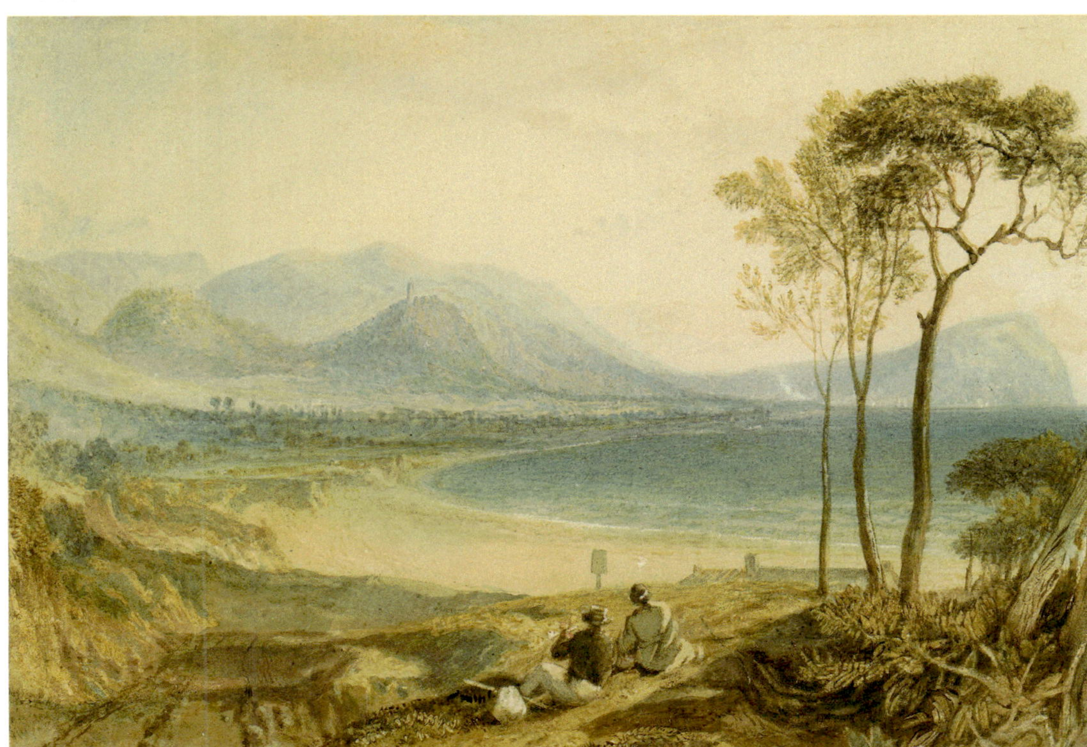

1054 The 'Somerset and North Devon sketchbook' which dates from 1811 contains a drawing which appears to be of Minehead, Tate (TB CXXVI 10). The same sketchbook contains two sketches which are definitely of Dunster Castle, Tate (TB CXXVI 9 and CXXVI 7). A drawing on a sheet in the 'Devonshire Coast no.1 sketchbook', from 1811 may also be of the castle, Tate (TB CXXIII 167 (a)).

1055 Wilton, p. 353, dated LL 3782 to c. 1820. Shanes's suggestion is presumably the basis of Frank Milner's dating of the work to c. 1818 (Milner, p. 38).

1056 The 'Hints River sketchbook', Tate (TB CXLI 35); see Shanes, *Turner's Rivers*, p. 26.

1057 Milner, p. 38.

1058 *Bay of Naples*, c. 1817, watercolour, 17.6 x 28.4 cm; see Milner, p. 30, pl. 9 (illus.).

1059 However, not all the figures in the *Southern Coast* series were of people at rest and play; many also show men and women at work. See, for example, *Bow and Arrow Castle, Island of Portland*, c. 1815, University of Liverpool Art Collections (Wilton, p. 352, cat. 459), which shows men at work in a quarry.

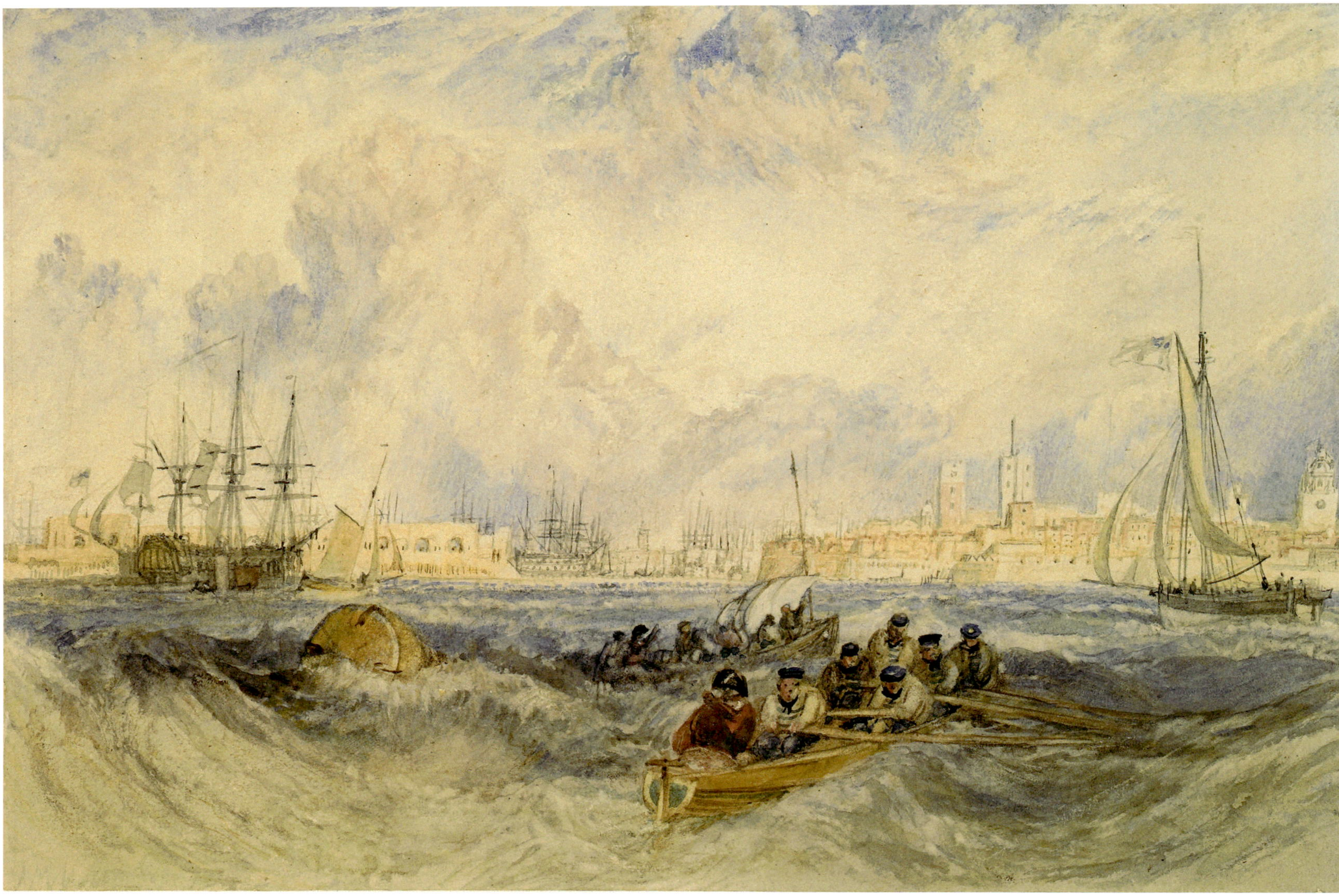

LL 3783

**Portsmouth, Hampshire**[1060]
LL 3783 (WHL 226, H 211)

Watercolour with touches of gouache on wove paper
15.4 x 23.5 cm
Date: c. 1824

Annot: JMW Turner (pencil, bottom left, by a later hand)[1061]

Prov: James Vine; his sale, Christie's, 25 April 1838 (lot 491); bt. by D. White; [?] E. Rodgett, 1857;[1062] C. F. Huth; his sale, Christie's, 6 July 1895 (lot 59); bt. by Agnew's (240 gns);[1063] Francis Stevenson; Agnew's, 1903; James Orrock; his sale, Christie's, 4 June 1904 (lot 45); bt. by A. Smith (£462);[1064] Agnew's; from whom bt. by Lever, 22 February 1907 (£4,000 with five other works)[1065]

Exh: [?] Manchester, Art Treasures Palace, *Exhibition of Art Treasures of the United Kingdom*, 1857 (cat. 328); London, Agnew's, *37th Annual Exhibition of Selected High Class Watercolour Drawings*, 1903 (cat. 221); Liverpool, Walker Art Gallery, *Turner's Journeys of the Imagination*, 2002 (cat. 28)

Lit: A. J. Finberg, *An Introduction to Turner's Southern Coast* (London, 1929), p. 59; Andrew Wilton, *J.M.W. Turner: His Art and Life* (New Jersey, 1979), p. 354 (cat. 477); Eric Shanes, *Turner's Rivers, Harbours and Coasts* (London, 1981), p. 28; Frank Milner, *Turner: Paintings in Merseyside Collections* (Liverpool, 1990), pp. 42–43

This watercolour, in common with two others in Lever's collection (see *Falmouth Harbour*, LL 3771 and *Minehead*, LL 3782) was engraved as part of the *Southern Coast* project. Turner contributed 40 subjects to this topographical publication over the period c. 1811–24, 39 of which were made specifically for the series.[1066] The work was engraved by William

1060 This is the title under which LL 3783 was engraved. See Rawlinson, *Engraved Work of J.M.W. Turner*, vol. I, pp. 64–65 (cat. 120) and Finberg, *Turner's Southern Coast*, pp. 59–60.

1061 LLAG files: a note records that LL 3783 is signed and dated JMW Turner, 1825. The date is no longer visible on the watercolour. The engraving, bottom left is signed: J MW TUR [with the remainder illeg.]. This was visible in an impression from the reprinted M. A. Nattali, *An Antiquarian and Picturesque Tour round the Southern Coast of England* (London, 1849).

1062 A *Portsmouth* was exhibited at Manchester's *Art Treasures* exhibition of 1857 (cat. 328), lent by E. Rodgett. The only other known Turner watercolours showing Portsmouth (from the *Ports of England and Wales* series) were with the National Gallery and Ruskin, respectively, in 1857; neither owner lent to this exhibition. Furthermore, the *Portsmouth* shown at this exhibition is listed alongside other *Southern Coast* subjects. It is possible that the *Portsmouth* shown at the *Art Treasures* was not a genuine work. However, Rodgett lent two further Turners to the exhibition, at least one of which was genuine: another *Southern Coast* subject, *Dartmouth*. I am grateful to Andrew Loukes, formerly of Manchester Art Gallery, for supplying me with this information.

1063 LLAG files: price given on accession card.

1064 Ibid.

1065 The group included two works by George Morland and three other watercolours by Turner: *Bolton Abbey*, *Lancaster from the Aqueduct* and *Minehead*. Although Lever's invoice from Agnew's was dated 1907, the works were in his possession by 1905 as they are listed in the 1905 TM Inventory.

1066 See entry on *Falmouth Harbour*, LL 3771, for details of the *Picturesque Views of the Southern Coast of England*, particularly n. 1038.

Miller in 1826 and it is partially on this basis that it has been dated to c. 1824.[1067]

LL 3783 is a distant view of Portsmouth Harbour from the sea; in this sense it is unusual among the *Southern Coast* subjects, which mainly show the sea from the land. On the left is the neighbouring town of Gosport; its blockhouse used for observation is clearly visible. On the right is Portsmouth, with its cathedral (formerly the parish church of St Thomas of Canterbury) on the far right;[1068] closer to the harbour are the towers of Burridge's Folly and the Admiralty Semaphore, part of a new signalling system between London and Portsmouth which was only operational from 1822 and would have appealed to Turner's keen interest in technology.

According to his sketchbooks, Turner visited Portsmouth in 1807, 1814 and 1823–24. The city probably appealed to him because of its important historical associations, most recently as the port from which Admiral Nelson had embarked to fight the Battle of Trafalgar, its link with new technologies as well as the opportunity it gave him to study one of his favourite subjects, the sea. A number of drawings of the buildings on the skyline and different sailing vessels in the 1823–24 sketchbook relate closely to details in the final work, although there are drawings in the 1814 sketchbook of similar vessels and it is quite possible that Turner, who was used to making paintings in the studio from sketches made many years before, drew on a mixture of images from both sketchbooks.[1069]

In the watercolour Turner has depicted the strong naval presence at Portsmouth; on the left are two frigates and in the harbour behind is a man-of-war. On the far right is a Royal Navy longboat (with the flag) while in the two gigs in the foreground naval officers give orders to sailors. Eric Shanes has suggested that the composition reinforces this message of naval control.[1070] He has pointed out that the forms of the cumulus cloud in the sky are repeated by the round buoy immediately below it. In the far distance the tower of the dockyard semaphore that controlled the entrance of ships to the harbour by signals is mirrored by an image of the naval officer in a gig waving his orders to his men. Exactly underneath him is the rudder of the gig in the foreground. In this way, Shanes has argued, the idea of naval control is repeated three times in one concise line.

Turner made two similar views of Portsmouth harbour viewed from the sea for other engraving projects. One watercolour of c. 1825 was engraved for the *Ports of England* series in 1828 and another dating to c. 1829 was engraved for the *England and Wales* series in 1831.[1071] In common with these two other watercolours, the viewpoint in LL 3783 is low so that Turner places his viewer at the eye level of the sailors rowing against the waves in the foreground. This allowed the artist to demonstrate his real understanding of the motion of water and his ability to recreate this in watercolour.

## Off Dover
LL 3781 (WHL 4698)

Watercolour, with extra gum arabic and scratching out on wove paper
17.7 x 27.8 cm
Date: c. 1820–27

Prov: Pawsey and Payne; their sale, Christie's, 22 June 1923 (lot 24); bt. by Gooden and Fox (300 gns) for Lever (£322 17s 6d)[1072]

Exh: Liverpool, Walker Art Gallery, *Turner's Journeys of the Imagination*, 2002 (cat. 30)

Lit: Andrew Wilton, *J.M.W. Turner: His Art and Life* (New Jersey, 1979), p. 355 (cat. 485); Eric Shanes, *Turner's Rivers, Harbours and Coasts* (London, 1981), p. 39; Frank Milner, *Turner: Paintings in Merseyside Collections* (Liverpool, 1990), p. 45

Although the work was purchased by Lever with the title *Off Dover*, the location shown in LL 3781 is not certain.[1073] Eric Shanes has suggested that the topography depicted is only loosely related to this title and that Turner 'seems to have moved the castle across the valley in which Dover is situated'.[1074] He has also pointed out that this 'cavalier approach' to topography was not uncommon for Turner, who was to repeat this treatment of the town in his watercolour of the *Straits of Dover* (c. 1827) for the *Picturesque Views in England and Wales* series.[1075] No sketches have been found relating to the Lady Lever composition.

Despite the uncertainty regarding its topography, LL 3781 has the appearance of a finished work that was intended for engraving. Andrew Wilton linked the watercolour with works produced c. 1820 for the *Southern Coast* project, although the size of the Lady Lever watercolour is much larger than that of the works for this series.[1076] Shanes has associated it in size and style with drawings made for the *Ports of England* series (c. 1825–28), although the re-measuring of LL 3781 without its old mount has demonstrated that it was again substantially larger.[1077] As Frank Milner has pointed out, compositionally the Lady Lever work differs from both the *Southern Coast* and *Ports of England* watercolours of the subject, which show a busier view of Dover and its port from the other side of Dover Castle.[1078] In compositional terms it is closest to the c. 1827 watercolour made for the *England and Wales* series referred to above but is much smaller than the rest of the subjects for this project.

More recently, Ian Warrell has raised the possibility that the work may be related to an unfinished project on the English Channel, for which no engravings were ever published.[1079] This series, which was advertised in 1827, grew out of Turner's 1826 trip to France and was intended to consist of views taken on both sides of the Channel. A group of finished watercolours of both English and French subjects have been identified as relating to this project which, at around 18 x 28 cm, are of similar dimensions to LL 3781. It is on this basis that Warrell has suggested that this work may relate to this project and could even be an unknown French subject. However, the context for the work's production remains inconclusive, even if on stylistic grounds it is in keeping with Turner's finished watercolours made for engraving between c. 1820–27.

In the foreground Turner has depicted the remains of a ship, wrecked as a result of a storm. He has captured the movement of the sea and the storm-laden sky with his customary mastery. The work has suffered considerably from fading, demonstrated by the difference in pigment at the edges of the work which were covered by an earlier mount. The colour overall would have originally been much richer.

1067 The date on the engraving's publication line is 15 February 1825. On this basis Rawlinson, *Engraved Work of J.M.W. Turner*, vol. I, pp. 64–65, dated the engraving to 1825. However, Finberg, *Turner's Southern Coast*, p. 60, cited evidence of a postmark on a final proof of the print sent through the post which was dated 1826. LL 3783 has been dated to c. 1824 by Wilton and Milner. Along with the date of the engraving, LL 3783 has also been dated to c. 1824 because of its close links to sketches in the 'London Bridge and Portsmouth sketchbook' of c. 1823–24.

1068 The medieval church was given the status of cathedral in the twentieth century. It is not visible in previous reproductions of LL 3783 as it was obscured behind the picture's frame.

1069 Shanes, *Turner's Rivers*, p. 28, relates LL 3783 to the following drawings in the 'London Bridge and Portsmouth sketchbook', c. 1823–24, Tate (TB CCVI 1, 2, 2a, 3, 3a, 4a, 5a, 6a, 7, 7a, 9). Sketches of Portsmouth harbour and of various sailing vessels also appear in the 'Review at Portsmouth sketchbook', c. 1814, Tate (TB CXXXVI).

1070 Shanes, *Turner's Rivers*, p. 28.

1071 *Portsmouth*, c. 1825, watercolour, engraved for Thomas Lupton's *Ports of England*, 1828, Tate, Wilton, p. 387 (cat. 756); *Gosport, entrance to Portsmouth harbour*, c. 1829, watercolour, engraved for Charles Heath's *England and Wales*, 1831, Portsmouth City Museum, Wilton, p. 397 (cat. 828).

1072 LLAG files: invoice.

1073 Tatlock, p. 139, titled the work as *Off Dover, Storm Clearing*.

1074 Shanes, *Turner's Rivers*, p. 39.

1075 Ibid. Wilton, p. 393 (cat. 797), as untraced; engraved by Willliam Miller, 1828 for *England and Wales*. See Rawlinson, *Engraved Work of J.M.W Turner*, vol. I, p. 125 (cat. 221). For details of the *England and Wales* series, see entry on *Lancaster from the Aqueduct* (LL 3774).

1076 For details of Turner's *Southern Coast* series, see entry on *Falmouth Harbour, Cornwall* (LL 3771).

1077 Shanes, *Turner's Rivers*, p. 39, has described the 'free-handling' in LL 3781 as suggesting that this was probably a preparatory study taken to an advanced stage for a *Ports of England* drawing that was never made. However, LL 3781 has every appearance of being a finished drawing.

1078 Milner, p. 45. See Wilton, pp. 355 and 387 (cats. 483 and 753).

1079 Ian Warrell, verbally, April 2008. For details of the English Channel project, see Ian Warrell, *Turner on the Loire* (exh. cat., London, Tate Gallery, 1997), pp. 158–71.

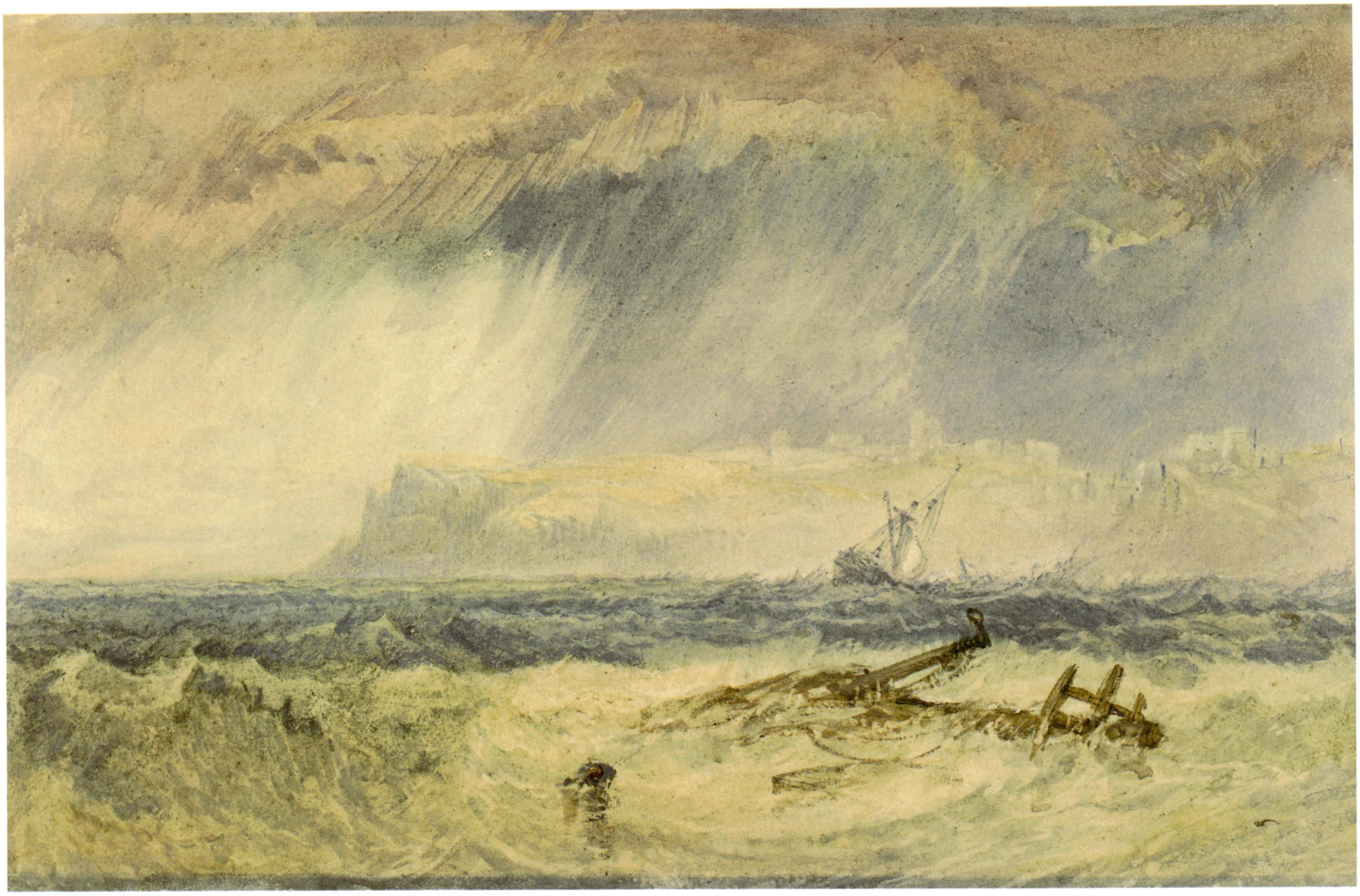

LL 3781

LL 10329

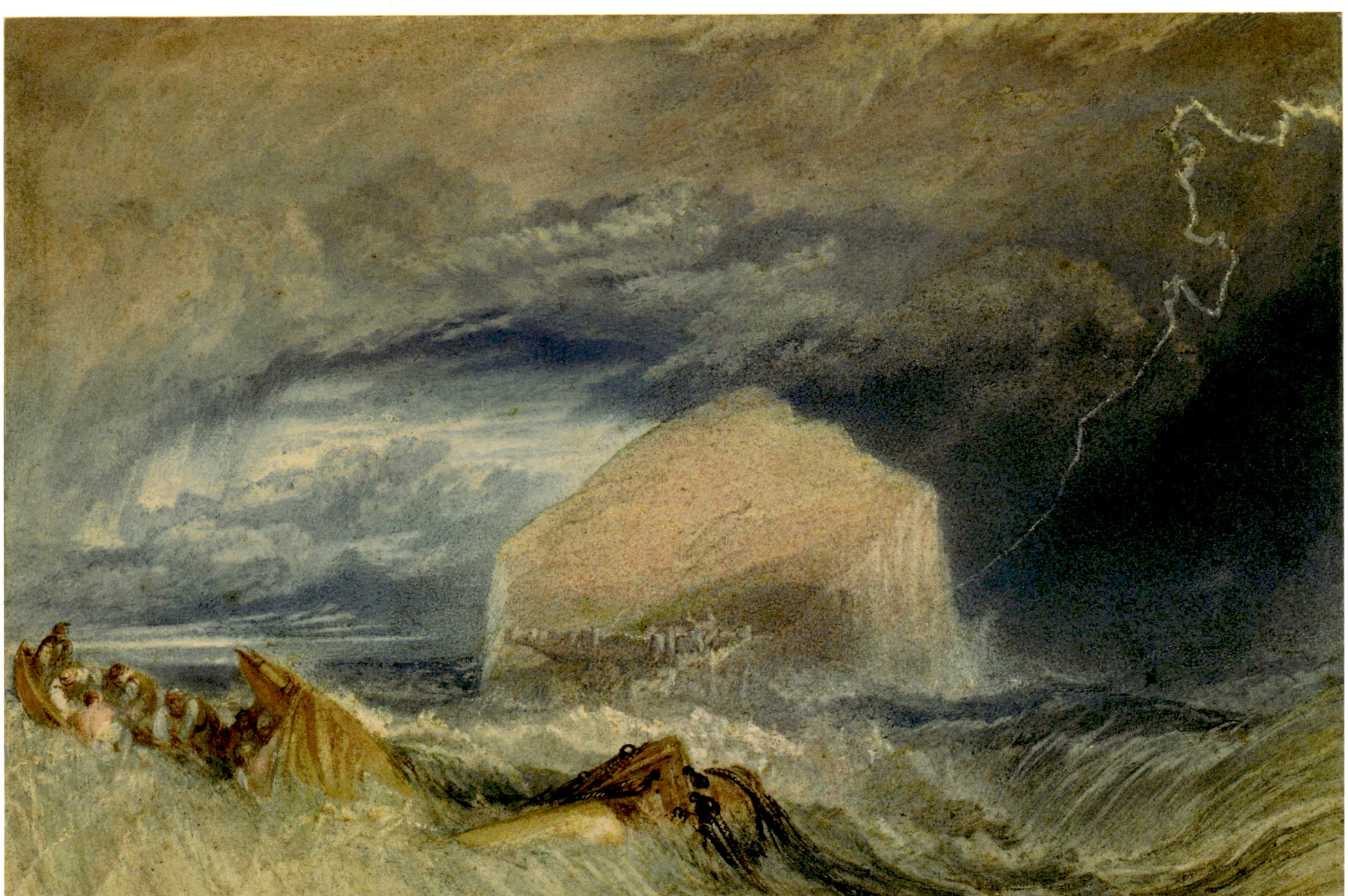

## The Bass Rock
LL 10329 (WHL 4696)

Watercolour over pencil with scratching out and stopping out on paper
17 x 25.4 cm
Date: c. 1824

Prov: Matthew Uzielli; his sale, Christie's, 12 April 1861 (lot 235); bt. by J. & W. Vokins; C.F. Huth; his sale, Christie's, 6 July 1895 (lot 57); bt. by J. & W. Vokins; Charles Maw, 1920; Pawsey and Payne; their sale, Christie's, 22 June 1923 (lot 22); bt. by Gooden and Fox (330 gns) for Lever (£335 3s 3d)

Exh: London, Royal Academy, *Turner 1775–1851*, 1974–75 (cat. 205); Aberdeen, Aberdeen Art Gallery, *Turner in Scotland*, 1982 (cat. 47); Canberra, National Gallery of Australia, *Turner*, 1996 (cat. 57); Edinburgh, National Gallery of Scotland, *Turner and Sir Walter Scott*, 1999–2000 (cat. 36); Liverpool, Walker Art Gallery, *Turner's Journeys of the Imagination*, 2002 (cat. 41); Washington, National Gallery of Art, Dallas, Dallas Museum of Art, New York, Metropolitan Museum of Art, *J.M.W. Turner*, 2007–2008 (cat. 64)

Lit: Andrew Wilton, *J.M.W. Turner: His Art and Life* (New Jersey, 1979), p. 426 (cat. 1069); Gerald Finley, *Landscapes of Memory: Turner as an Illustrator to Scott* (London, 1980), p. 85; Frank Milner, *Turner: Paintings in Merseyside Collections* (Liverpool, 1990), pp. 57–59; Eric Shanes, *Turner's Watercolour Explorations* (exh. cat., London, Tate Gallery, 1997), pp. 56–57; Sam Smiles, *J.M.W. Turner* (London, 2000), p. 40

LL 10329 was one of ten subjects, together with two title-page vignettes, which Turner produced to accompany Sir Walter Scott's text in *The Provincial Antiquities and Picturesque Scenery of Scotland*, issued in parts between 1819 and 1826.[1080] The project was probably conceived in the winter of 1817–18 and Turner's contribution was assured by October 1818. The prestige that Turner's name added to the publication is suggested by the terms of his contract; he was to be paid twice as much as the two other main contributing illustrators, who were similarly shareholders in the scheme. From Turner's point of view, the considerable weight of his workload in the autumn of 1818 (he was already contracted to make illustrations for the Cooke brothers' *Southern Coast* project, for Thomas Whitaker's *The History of Richmondshire* and for Hakewill's *A Picturesque Tour in Italy*) suggests the extent to which the artist wanted to be associated with Scott, who was by 1818 one of Scotland's most celebrated poets and novelists. *Bass Rock* was engraved by William Miller for the last number of *The Provincial Antiquities* series in 1826 and on this basis it has been dated to c. 1824.[1081]

The large volcanic outcrop known as the Bass Rock is located off the coast near Edinburgh and opposite Tantallon Castle, which also featured as one of Turner's designs for the *Provincial Antiquities* project.[1082] Despite the island's bleakness, the strategic importance of the rock meant that it had played an important part in Scottish history. By the early fourteenth century it was owned and occupied by the Lauder family, and in the seventeenth century it was acquired by Charles II and used as a royal fortress and prison. The subject of the Bass Rock, as with all the designs for the *Provincial Antiquities*, was chosen by Scott, but it was left up to Turner to select the viewpoint and manner of treatment. In his depiction, Turner emphasised the dramatic incident taking place in the dangerous and potentially fatal waters surrounding the rock. The watercolour shows the remains of a broken mast and a boat rescuing survivors of a shipwreck. The inclusion of a sole streak of lightning (made here by scratching away pigment so that the white paper shows through) was relatively rare among Turner's subjects and accentuates the sense of drama in the scene.[1083] Scott's text that accompanied the subject in its engraved form was only loosely connected to Turner's watercolour and described the pleasures to be had in a dawn trip to watch the mass flight of the island's many seabirds. Although the original scheme had envisaged that the text would be written around the illustrations, the difficulties of getting the plates ready on time meant that in practice this rarely happened after 1821.[1084]

Turner sketched the rock on his visit to Edinburgh and the Scottish lowlands in November 1818, when he took the opportunity to study it both from land and from the sea. He made further sketches of the rock on his return to Scotland in August 1822, before completing the watercolour. Turner based the final work on pencil studies contained in two sketchbooks used on the 1818 tour as well as a further book from the 1822 trip.[1085] Additionally, before making the final composition, Turner made at least two experimental colour sketches, known as 'colour beginnings', where he explored the effects of different weather conditions or times of the day.[1086] In one he depicted an alternative view from the final work, showing the rock looking towards the west at sunset, with a foundering vessel just visible in the rough waters before the centre of the rock.[1087] The second colour sketch correlates with the view chosen for the final design, where the rock is viewed from the south in the early morning sunlight.[1088] As in the final watercolour, the less threatening weather appears on the left-hand side of the subject, suggesting that the storm is moving off eastwards. Like the completed composition the rock is viewed across a heavy swell, although it is marginally more heightened than in the finished work.

The *Provincial Antiquities* project was a financial failure, with Turner's unwillingness to contribute to his share of the losses causing animosity between him and Scott. Despite this unpromising beginning, Turner was to work on further literary projects associated with Scott, providing illustrations for Scott's *Poetical Works* from 1832–34; even after Scott's death in 1832, Turner produced illustrations for books by the author, most importantly an edition of his *Miscellaneous Prose Works* (published 1834–36).

1080 Wilton, pp. 425–26 (cats. 1058–69). For the most recent consideration of the series, see Katrina Thomson, *Turner and Sir Walter Scott* (exh. cat., Edinburgh, National Gallery of Scotland, 1999–2000), pp. 94–95.

1081 See Rawlinson, *Engraved Work of J.M.W Turner*, vol. I, p. 112 (cat. 200). This is the date given in Wilton and Thomson. More recently Ian Warrell, *J.M.W. Turner* (exh. cat., Washington, National Gallery of Art, Dallas, Dallas Museum of Art, New York, Metropolitan Museum of Art, 2007–2008), p. 105, has suggested that the work may have been begun in the winter of 1823. This is plausible, given Turner's known working pattern of completing works in the winter months.

1082 *Tantallon Castle*, signed and dated 1821, watercolour, scratching out and gouache on paper, 17.4 x 25.7 cm, Manchester Art Gallery, Wilton, p. 426 (cat. 1067).

1083 Another occasion when Turner depicted lightning in a finished watercolour was *Stonehenge*, c. 1827, watercolour on paper, 27.9 x 40.4 cm, Salisbury and South Wiltshire Museum, Wilton, p. 394 (cat. 811). This was engraved for the *England and Wales* series, 1829.

1084 Gerald Finley, *Landscapes of Memory: Turner as an Illustrator to Scott* (London, 1980), pp. 56–61.

1085 These sketches are listed by Eric Shanes, *Turner's Watercolour Explorations* (exh. cat., London, Tate Gallery, 1997), pp. 56–57, as the following: pp. 3v, 5, 5v, 7, 8, 8v of the 'Bass Rock and Edinburgh sketchbook' of 1818, Tate (TB CLXV); pp. 3, 6 and 31 of the 'Scotch Antiquities sketchbook' of 1818, Tate (TB CLXVII); and pp. 5, 78v, 79, 79v and 80 of the 'King's Visit to Scotland sketchbook' of 1822, Tate (TB CC).

1086 The term 'colour beginnings' was coined by A. J. Finberg to describe these loose, rapid and experimental colour studies. Both these sketches are illustrated and catalogued in Shanes, *Turner's Watercolour Explorations*, p. 57 (cats. 36 and 37). Also see Thomson, *Turner and Sir Walter Scott*, p. 94 (cats. 37 and 38). Thomson (p. 94) listed a third 'colour beginning' in an American private collection which Wilton, p. 389 (cat. 768), had 'mistakenly recognised as *A Storm off Margate*'. The association of this sketch with *Bass Rock* was made by Ian Warrell and stemmed from his identification of Wilton cat. 768 with the work sold by Ruskin at Christie's, 15 April 1869 (lot 8), described as 'sketch for or more probably commencement of drawing for the *Bass Rock*. Most characteristic of Turner's execution in the middle time, impetuously deliberate'; bt. by Agnew's. Wilton cat. 768 has been identified as a study for *Bass Rock* in Warrell, *J.M.W. Turner*, p. 105, fig. 25 and also in Christie's sale catalogue of 4 June 2008 (lot 26). However, David Hill has recently pointed out that the sketch in fact shows the Mew Stone off Plymouth. In support of this more recent and plausible suggestion, Warrell has pointed out that the sketch shows the stone from the shore and corresponds with sketches in the 'Plymouth, Hamoaze sketchbook', c. 1812–13, Tate (TB CXXXI); Warrell, email correspondence, May 2008. It probably relates to *A Ship against the Mew-Stone, at the entrance of Plymouth Sound*, c. 1814, watercolour on paper, 15.1 x 23.2 cm, National Gallery of Ireland, Wilton, p. 351 (cat. 454), engraved for the *Southern Coast* series, 1816. A further study showing the rock by moonlight was sold by Louis Huth, Christie's, 20 May 1905 (lot 23); bt. by Agnew's (untraced).

1087 *Colour study for the Bass Rock*, watercolour on paper, 21.9 x 29.4 cm, Tate (TB CCCLXIV 130).

1088 *Colour study for the Bass Rock*, watercolour on paper, 20 x 26.4 cm, Tate (TB CCLXIII 205).

**Richmond Hill**[1089]
LL 3773 (WHL 743, HH 392)

Watercolour over pencil, with extra gum arabic, gouache and scratching out on paper
30.5 x 49.1 cm
Date: c. 1825

Prov: John Knowles; his sale, Christie's, 19 May 1877 (lot 97, as *Richmond Hill – Boy and Kite*); bt. by Agnew's; Agnew's, 1902; James Orrock; from whom bt. by Lever 1910[1090]

Exh: [?] Windsor, Eton College, exhibition title unknown, 1933 (cat. 11);[1091] London, Royal Academy, *Turner 1775–1851*, 1974–75 (cat. 257); Paris, Grand Palais, *J. M. W. Turner*, 1983–84 (cat. 202); London, Royal Academy, *Turner: The Great Watercolours*, 2000–2001 (cat. 72); Liverpool, Walker Art Gallery, *Turner's Journeys of the Imagination*, 2002 (cat. 10)

Lit: Andrew Wilton, *J.M.W. Turner: His Art and Life* (New Jersey, 1979), p. 359 (cat. 518); Eric Shanes, *Turner's Picturesque Views in England and Wales* (London, 1979), pp. 35–36; Frank Milner, *Turner: Paintings in Merseyside Collections* (Liverpool, 1990), p. 46

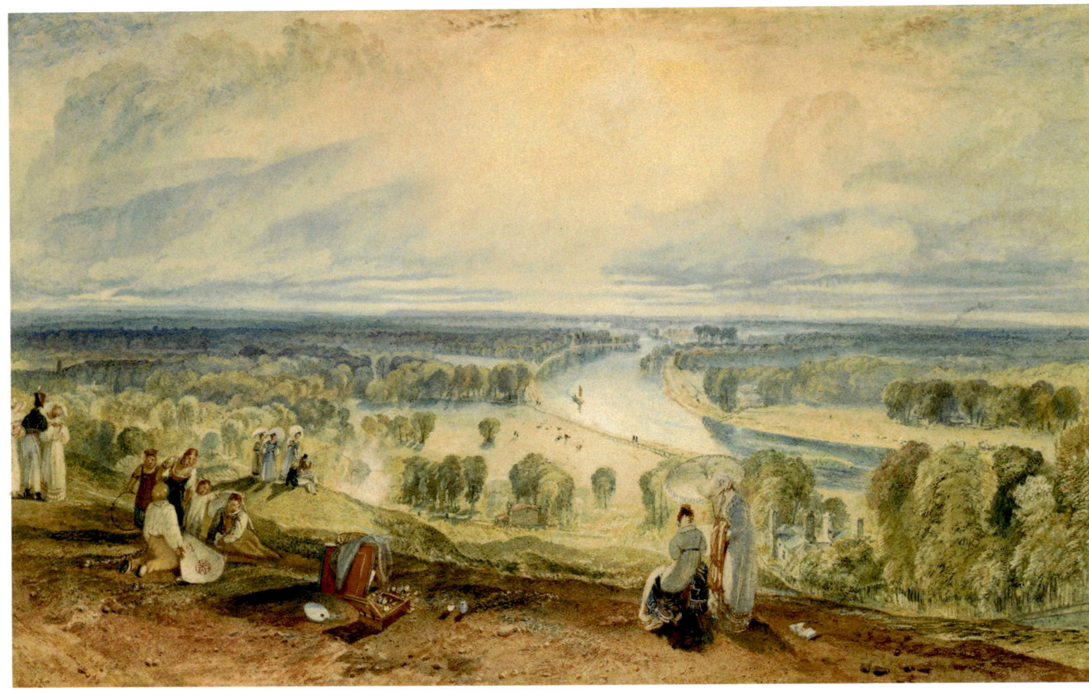

LL 3773

This watercolour shows the celebrated view from Richmond Hill, Surrey, looking west towards Twickenham. Turner had known this stretch of the river from childhood when he had first stayed with his uncle at Brentford.[1092] He made an early watercolour view of the subject in c. 1794–95[1093] and the vista recurred in his art throughout his career. From 1807 he began building a house for himself at Twickenham (shown here, to the right of the view), a town which since the seventeenth century had attracted wealthy, famous and artistic residents, including the poet Alexander Pope (1688–1744) who built a Palladian villa there.[1094] Turner sold the Twickenham house in 1826, returning to a property in Queen Anne Street, London.

By the mid-eighteenth century this vista was overlaid with literary and artistic connotations, which invoked a wistful, Arcadian idyll. In particular, James Thomson, who lived at Richmond, was highly influential in eulogising this view with his poem *The Seasons* of 1727, which is a panegyric to the Thames valley and is full of references to the great English statesmen, poets and authors who lived in the area. Turner alluded directly to Thomson in an earlier oil painting of the same view, *Thomson's Aeolian Harp* (1809, Manchester Art Gallery), one of the artist's most overtly Claudian paintings.[1095] Another classical treatment of this river view was *England: Richmond Hill, on the Prince Regent's Birthday* (exh. RA 1819, Tate), and Turner appended a quotation from Thomson's *Seasons* to the title of the work in the Royal Academy catalogue.[1096]

LL 3773 was engraved by Edward Goodall for the *Literary Souvenir*, a venture by the publisher Charles Heath in 1826 and on stylistic grounds has previously been dated to c. 1820–25.[1097] More recently, Eric Shanes has suggested that based on its size and detail the work may originally have been intended for *Picturesque Views in England and Wales* which was another of Charles Heath's projects commissioned around 1825 but that it was diverted to the *Literary Souvenir*.[1098] It is presumably on this basis that Shanes has suggested the slightly later dating for the watercolour of c. 1825.[1099] It is not entirely clear that *Richmond Hill* should be linked to the *England and Wales* series on the basis of its size; at 30.5 x 49.1 cm, LL 3773 is a good 10 cm wider than most of the early *England and Wales* views.[1100] Nevertheless, on stylistic grounds the work does have similarities with the handling of other watercolours dating from the mid-1820s such as *Lancaster* (LL 3774) from the *England and Wales* series and a date of c. 1825 seems reasonable.

By the time he made LL 3773, Turner appears to have been less concerned with the classical and literary associations of the view. In contrast with the earlier *England: Richmond Hill* from 1819 which is treated in an overtly classical manner, with trees framing the view, the Lady Lever work has a far more open composition. The difference should not be overstated, as Jean Golt has pointed out that LL 3773 in fact represents the view as seen from higher up Richmond Hill, at its crest, above the trees.[1101] Moreover, Turner returned to the more overtly Claudian format in a watercolour of c. 1836 depicting the view from even further up Richmond Hill (Walker Art Gallery, Liverpool).[1102]

Eric Shanes has suggested that the smoke on the right of the picture on the horizon may indicate the site of Turner's house in Twickenham.[1103] The viewer's attention is drawn to this by a top-hatted gentleman looking through a telescope on the left towards the view. Turner's presence may also be suggested by the paintbox, palette and pots of paint in the foreground, although this could equally be intended to suggest a more general artistic enthusiasm for the view.[1104]

1089 In Tatlock, p. 138, LL 3773 is described as being from the Novar collection and as being engraved in Turner's *England and Wales* publication. This description actually refers to *Richmond Terrace*, now in the Walker Art Gallery, Liverpool (see n. 1102).

1090 1910 Inventory, p. 50, valued at £1,500.

1091 This exhibition is cited in the LLAG files, but there is no record of it in Eton College's archives. The exhibition may have been held in the Drawing Schools (the school's art department) but it is not recorded in the *Eton Chronicle* (the school's magazine) for 1933 . I am grateful to Penny Hatfield, Eton College's archivist, for providing this information.

1092 The young Turner was sent to stay with his uncle, a butcher in New Brentford, near Kew in 1785; he probably stayed there for a year. It is not clear why he was sent, but it has generally been assumed that it was because the family's youngest child was mortally ill. See Hamilton, *Turner: A Life*, p. 14.

1093 *View of the Thames from Richmond Hill*, gouache, pencil and watercolour, 14.6 x 21.4 cm, Tate (TB XXVII K).

1094 Turner named his house at Twickenham Sandycombe Lodge; it is not known when exactly it was given this name but it was at least by 1814. See Hamilton, *Turner: A Life*, p. 135.

1095 See Wilton, p. 310 (cat. P86).

1096 Wilton, p. 315 (cat. P140).

1097 Rawlinson, *Engraved Work of J.M.W Turner*, vol. II, p. 219 (cat. 314). Wilton dated LL 3773 to c. 1820–25.

1098 Eric Shanes, *Turner's Picturesque Views in England and Wales* (London, 1979), pp. 35–36.

1099 Ibid. Shanes has linked LL 3773 to preliminary pencil drawings in the 'Thames sketchbook' (Tate, TB CCXII, pp. 5v, 6, 6v, 9v, 82, 88 and 88v). He has dated this sketchbook to c. 1825, although it is not clear whether this date is reliant on his dating of LL 3773 or is based on other evidence.

1100 See Wilton, pp. 391–403 (cats. 785–880).

1101 Jean Golt, 'Beauty and meaning on Richmond Hill: New Light on Turner's Masterpiece of 1819', *Turner Studies*, vol. 7, no. 2 (1987), p. 13.

1102 *Richmond Terrace*, c. 1836, watercolour and gouache, 28 x 43.5 cm; Wilton, p. 403 (cat. 879). See also Milner, p. 47 (cat. 24), illus. p. 40, pl. 12.

1103 Shanes, *Turner: The Great Watercolours*, p. 180 (cat. 72).

1104 Milner, p. 46 (cat. 23).

## Lancaster from the Aqueduct[1105]
LL 3774 (WHL 227, H 202)

Watercolour, with extra gum arabic, scratching out and stopping out on paper
28.3 x 39.7 cm
Date: c. 1825

Inscr: LANCASTER (watercolour, on boat, lower right)

Prov: Charles Langton, Liverpool; his sale, Christie's, 17 May 1862 (lot 104); bt. by Agnew's (£326);[1106] William Leech; his sale, Christie's, 21 May 1887 (lot 67); bt. by Agnew's (£640 10s);[1107] [?] Francis Stevenson;[1108] James Orrock; his sale, Christie's, 4 June 1904 (lot 42); bt. by Boswell; Agnew's; from whom bt. by Lever, 22 February 1907 (£4,000 with five other works)[1109]

1105 LLAG files: this is the title as recorded in Agnew's invoice, 22 February 1907.
1106 WHL Inventory, p. 42.
1107 Ibid.
1108 This provenance is given in Tatlock, p. 138.
1109 The group included two works by George Morland and three other watercolours by Turner: *Bolton Abbey*, *Portsmouth* and *Minehead*. Although Lever's invoice from Agnew's is dated 1907, the works were in his possession by 1905 as they are listed in the 1905 TM Inventory.

Exh: Manchester, Art Treasures Palace, *Exhibition of Art Treasures of the United Kingdom*, 1857 (cat. 336); South Kensington, *International Exhibition*, 1862 (cat. 1022); Lancaster, Storey Institute Art Gallery, *Summer Exhibition of Oils and Watercolours*, 1929 (cat. 61); Liverpool, Walker Art Gallery, *Turner's Journeys of the Imagination*, 2002 (cat. 21); Birmingham, Birmingham Museums and Art Gallery, *Turner's Britain*, 2003–2004 (cat. 95)

Lit: Andrew Wilton, *J.M.W. Turner: His Art and Life* (New Jersey, 1979), p. 391 (cat. 786); Eric Shanes, *Turner's Picturesque Views in England and Wales* (London, 1979), p. 24; David Hill, *In Turner's Footsteps* (London, 1984), pp. 84–99; Frank Milner, *Turner: Paintings in Merseyside Collections* (Liverpool, 1990), pp. 47–48, illus. pl. 13

*Lancaster from the Aqueduct* was one of the earliest subjects to be designed for the *Picturesque Views in England and Wales*, Turner's most ambitious and longest-running watercolour engraving project.[1110] The series was commissioned in 1824 by the print publisher Charles Heath and was issued in parts between 1827 and 1838. By this latter date 96 of a planned 120 images had been published. The project was ended prematurely at this juncture as the costs had proved to be financially disastrous for Heath. The commercial failure of the series was in part due to the market being flooded with topographical engravings and to changing taste. It was also due to Turner's insistence on copper rather than steel plates being used for the engravings; the former were softer and so created a more atmospheric impression but were consequently less hard-wearing and produced fewer prints. LL 3774 was engraved by Robert Wallis in 1827 and on this basis has been dated to c. 1825.[1111]

The scope of the *England and Wales* series was all-embracing (unlike other engraving projects

1110 See Wilton, pp. 391–404 (cats. 785–895), which includes details of unused designs and related 'colour beginnings'. For a full discussion of the series see Shanes, *Turner's Picturesque Views*, pp. 10–23.

1111 Rawlinson, *Engraved Work of J.M.W Turner*, vol. I, p. 119 (cat. 210).

LL 3774

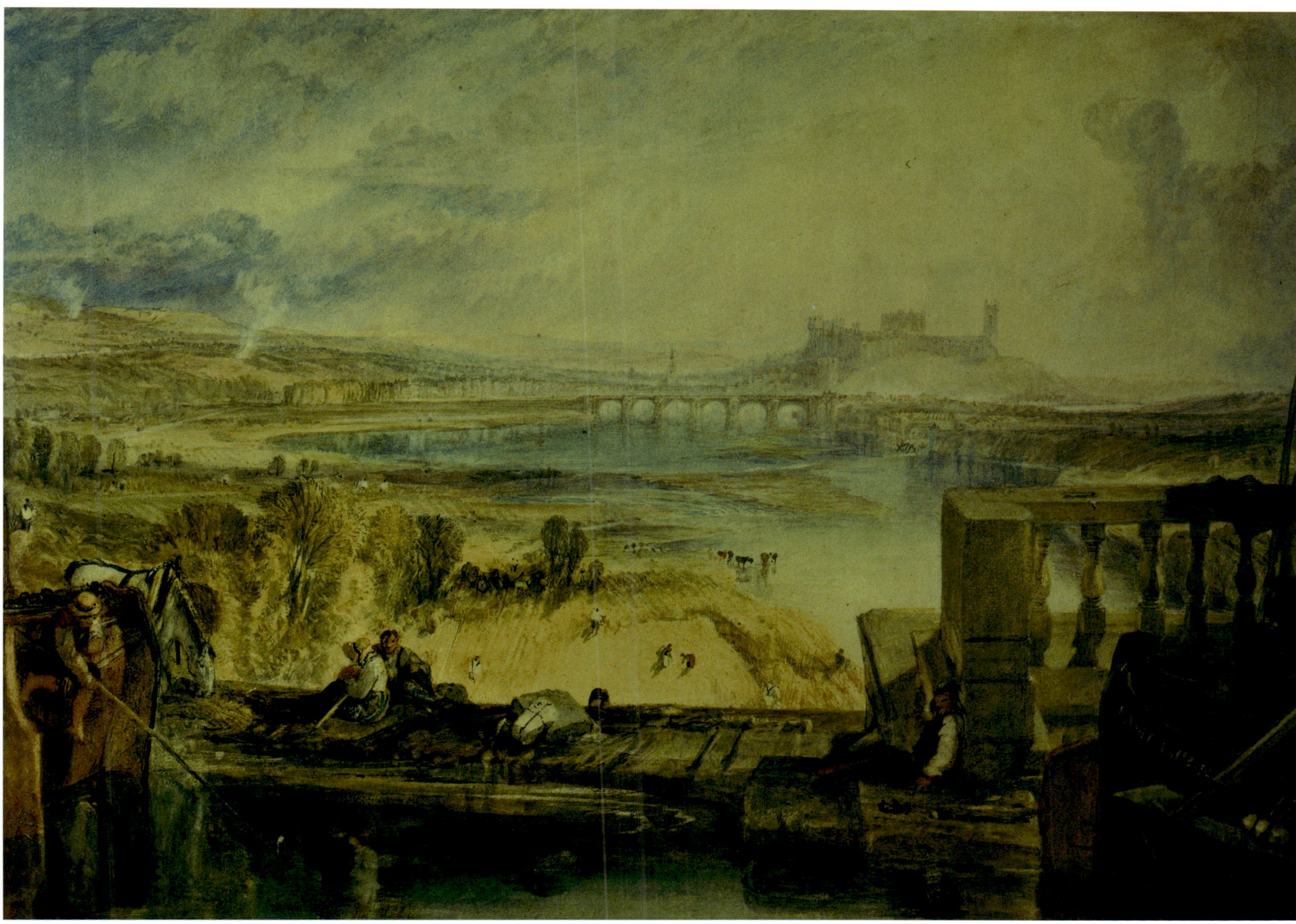

by Turner which were limited to specific geographical regions or themes). Its subjects included simple, landscape views but also scenes such as a horse fair at Louth and festive inebriation at Dartmouth.[1112] This work depicting the town of Lancaster viewed from the River Lune aqueduct reflects Turner's long-standing interest in the new navigable canals and the heroic structures that had been designed for them.[1113] This aqueduct, designed by John Rennie (1761–1821) in a classical style, was begun in 1794 and opened in 1797. The structure was an impressive feat of civil engineering, carrying the Lancaster Canal on five huge arches for a distance of 221 yards, 53 feet above the River Lune.

Turner had sketched the aqueduct in close-up on his first tour of the north of England in 1797, the year it had opened.[1114] However, the Lady Lever watercolour is based on a drawing he had made on his 1816 tour of Yorkshire and Lancashire.[1115] Both works depict the view from the aqueduct, with Lancaster Castle in the far background and Skerton bridge in the middle distance. Frank Milner has suggested that by placing the aqueduct in the foreground Turner has emphasised the new rather than the old.[1116] This is also the argument of Eric Shanes who has contrasted the 'busy canal' with the 'pre-industrial agricultural countryside' in the background.[1117] On the other hand, David Hill has pointed out that by the time of the 1816 sketch and the later watercolour, the aqueduct has been used only as a viewpoint for the old town, suggesting that perhaps by this point Turner's interest in the modern had faded.[1118]

The watercolour is typical of Turner's topographical work from the 1810s onwards in showing his keen interest in all classes of human beings and all aspects of their activity. In the foreground, canal and barge workers lie around at leisure and the composition is set up so that they are contrasted with the workers in the fields directly behind them. A touch of narrative incident is created by the figure of a young boy in the left foreground, who, in fishing for something with his pole, appears as if he is about to fall off the barge into the canal. In style, LL 3774 is typical of Turner's work in oil and watercolour from the 1820s onwards in its strong luminosity. This was a new-found understanding of colour and light which had been acquired in part as a result of his first trip to Italy in 1819–20.

There is a very good copy of the Lady Lever watercolour in the Cecil Higgins Art Gallery, Bedford.[1119] This copy is slightly larger, having been extended on both sides.

### Bolton Abbey[1120]
LL 3777 (WHL 228, H 203)

Watercolour with extra gum arabic and scratching out on paper
28.1 x 40cm
Date: c. 1825

Inscr: J.M.W. Turner RA (watercolour, bottom left)

Prov: bt. by John Ruskin, May 1851; James Orrock, 1878; his sale, Christie's, 4 June 1904 (lot 40); bt. by Agnew's; from whom bt. by Lever, 22 February 1907 (£4,000 with five other works)[1121]

Exh: London, Fine Art Society, *Drawings by JMW Turner from Ruskin's Collection, with works by himself and others*, 1878 (cat. 44); London, Fine Art Society, *[Ruskin's] Drawings by J.M.W. Turner*, 1900 (cat. 37); Manchester, Manchester Art Gallery, *Ruskin*, 1904 (cat. 166); London, Arts Council, *Ruskin and his Circle*, 1964 (cat. 107); London, Tate Gallery, *Landscape in Britain, c.1750–1850*, 1973–74 (cat. 209); London, Tate Gallery, *Ruskin, Turner and the Pre-Raphaelites*, 2000 (cat. 58); Liverpool, Walker Art Gallery, *Turner's Journeys of the Imagination*, 2002 (cat. 7); Birmingham, Birmingham Museums and Art Gallery, *Turner's Britain*, 2003–2004 (cat. 94)

Lit: E. T. Cook and A. Wedderburn (eds), *The Works of John Ruskin* (London and New York, 39 vols, 1903–12), vol. III, p. 586, vol. V, pp. 161–64, vol. VI, pp. 305–07, vol. XIII, p. 444; A. J. Finberg, *The Life of J.M.W. Turner, R.A.* (Oxford, 1961), p. 297; J. L. Bradley, *Ruskin's Letters from Venice, 1851–1852* (New Haven, 1955), p. 199; Andrew Wilton, *J.M.W. Turner: His Art and Life* (New Jersey, 1979), p. 391 (cat. 788); Eric Shanes, *Turner's Picturesque Views in England and Wales* (London, 1979), p. 24; Frank Milner, *Turner: Paintings in Merseyside Collections* (Liverpool, 1990), pp. 23–24, illus. pl. 6

*Bolton Abbey*, in common with *Lancaster from the Aqueduct* (LL 3774), was one of the earlier designs for the *Picturesque Views in England and Wales*, Turner's most ambitious and longest-running watercolour-engraving project. The series was commissioned in 1824 by the print publisher Charles Heath and was issued in parts between 1827 and 1838. By this latter date, 96 of a planned 120 images had been published. Owing to financial losses, the project was ended prematurely at this juncture.[1122] LL 3777 was engraved in 1827 by Robert Wallis and on this basis has been dated to c. 1825.[1123]

Bolton Abbey near Skipton in Yorkshire was founded in the mid-twelfth century by the Augustinian order on land given by the de Romillè family. The abbey had originally been established at Embsay but (according to local folklore) had been moved by Alice de Romillè so that it was nearer the river Wharfe where her only son William had been drowned while out hunting. Following the dissolution of the abbey in 1540, part of the nave was retained as a parish church but the rest of the building was allowed to fall into ruins. The ruined abbey situated in a picturesque natural setting became a celebrated sight on the tourist circuit in the late eighteenth and early nineteenth centuries, with William Wordsworth encouraging popular enthusiasm for the valley through poems such as *The Force of Prayer*, published in 1815.

Turner first visited the abbey on his extensive tour of the north of England in 1797 and a watercolour from c. 1798 is based on a sketch made from this trip.[1124] He returned in 1808 to stay with Walter Fawkes at nearby Farnley Hall; sketches from this trip formed the basis of two finished watercolours painted in 1809.[1125] However, LL 3777 was based on one particular study made on another trip to Yorkshire in c. 1815.[1126] The Lady Lever view contrasts dramatically with earlier views of the subject; in particular, its brilliance of colouring differs from the muted palette of his two 1809 views. LL 3777 demonstrates the changes that occurred in Turner's use of colour from the 1820s onwards, in part because of his experience of the stronger light in Italy on his 1819–20 trip. Additionally Turner presents a different view of the abbey from any of his other watercolours of the subject. Here, the abbey is barely visible and the focus of the piece is the landscape, with the bank opposite being exaggerated in scale both in the watercolour and the earlier study.

---

1112 *Louth, Lincolnshire*, Wilton, p. 394, cat. 809 and *Dartmouth Cove*, Wilton, p. 391 (cat. 787).

1113 The first navigable canal, the Duke of Bridgewater's canal from the mines at Worsley into Manchester, was completed in 1760.

1114 *Lancaster Aqueduct, with the Church and Castle seen through the right-hand arch*, 1797, from 'Tweed and Lakes sketchbook', pencil on paper, 36.8 x 26.2 cm, Tate (TB XXXV 65).

1115 Study for *Lancaster from the Aqueduct*, from 'Yorkshire 5 sketchbook', c. 1816, pencil on paper, 17.3 x 26 cm, Tate (TB CXLVIII 35a). This is illustrated in Milner, p. 48.

1116 Milner, p. 48.

1117 Shanes, *Turner's Picturesque Views*, p. 24.

1118 David Hill, *Turner in the North* (New Haven and London, 1996), p. 141.

1119 *Lancaster from the Aqueduct Bridge*, after J. M. W. Turner, watercolour on paper, 32.9 x 48.1 cm, illus. col. in Evelyn Joll, *Cecil Higgins Art Gallery Watercolours and Drawings* (Bedford, 2002), p. 275. The work is described by Wilton, p. 391, under cat. 786, as 'a very close copy ... apparently accepted by Finberg (MS Index), but is perhaps a drawing in the same category as the elaborate copy of the 1843 *Faido* in the Rhode Island School of Design executed by a member of Ruskin's circle'.

1120 LLAG files: this is the title as recorded on Agnew's invoice, 22 February 1907.

1121 The group included two works by George Morland and three other works by Turner: *Lancaster from the Aqueduct*, *Portsmouth* and *Minehead*. Although Lever's invoice from Agnew's is dated 1907, the works were in his possession by 1905 as they are listed in the 1905 TM Inventory.

1122 For more details see entry on *Lancaster from the Aqueduct*, LL 3774.

1123 Rawlinson, *Engraved Work of J.M.W Turner*, vol. I, pp. 120–21 (cat. 212).

1124 *Bolton Abbey*, private collection, c. 1798, watercolour, pencil and gouache, 27 x 39 cm, Tate, not in Wilton, illus. on *Turner Worldwide* (see tate.org.uk). There is a sketch of the abbey from this view in the 'Tweed and Lakes sketchbook' from Turner's 1797 tour, pencil on paper, 36.8 x 26.2, Tate (TB XXXV 68).

1125 *Bolton Abbey*, c. 1809, watercolour on paper, 27.8 x 38.7 cm, University of Liverpool Art Collections, Wilton, p. 360 (cat. 531); *Bolton Abbey*, 1809, watercolour and gouache on paper, 27.8 x 39.5 cm, British Museum, Wilton, p. 360 (cat. 532).

1126 *Study for Bolton Abbey* from the 'Devonshire Rivers, No. 3, and Wharfedale sketchbook', c. 1812–15, pencil on paper, Tate (TB CXXXIV 81a–82).

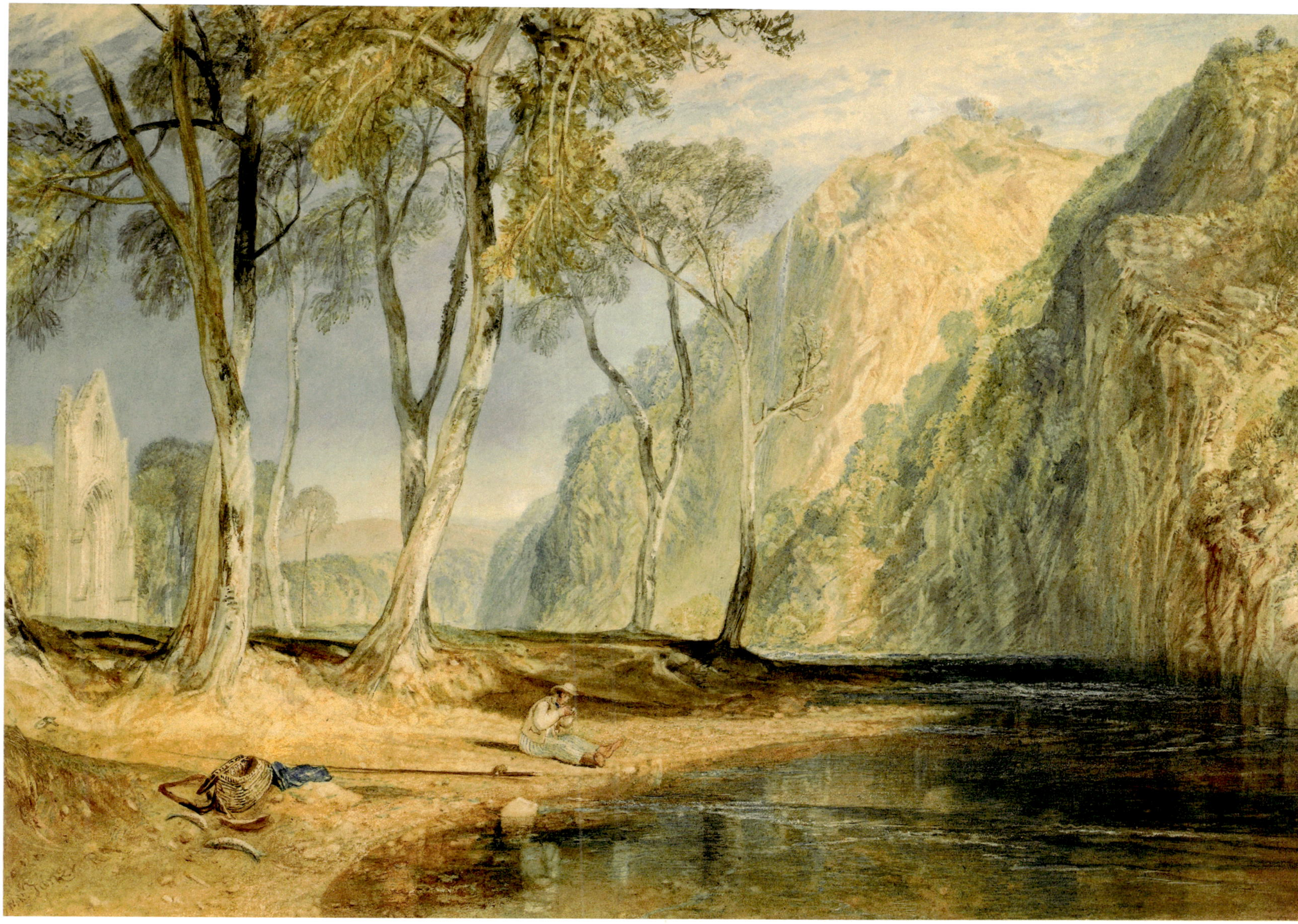

LL 3777

*Bolton Abbey* has become one of Turner's best-known Yorkshire subjects, largely because it is mentioned frequently in Ruskin's writings. Ruskin's opinions about the watercolour became increasingly complex as he himself developed, and were compounded by the fact that he acquired it in May 1851. In *Modern Painters* he singled out Turner's representations of trees as far superior in their accuracy to those of other artists. In particular, he compared the ash trees in *Bolton Abbey* to examples in two of Constable's paintings, which he described as 'wholly barbarous'.[1127] In a later volume of *Modern Painters*, Ruskin argued that the exaggerations in Turner's topography were informed by the surrounding scenery:

> But the scene in reality does affect the imagination strongly, and in a way wholly different from lowland hill scenery ... Noble moorlands extend above, purple with heath, and broken into scars and glens; and around every soft tuft of wood, and gentle extent of meadow, throughout the dale, there floats a feeling of this mountain power, and an instinctive apprehension of the strength and greatness of the wild northern land.[1128]

However, later on Ruskin came to disapprove of his original enthusiasm, writing in 1878: 'Glorious as the rock drawing is, and beautiful as the flow of the dark stream, I regret the exaggeration of mountain scale which he admitted to fulfil the strength of his mental impression'.[1129] Nevertheless, Ruskin never lost his appreciation of the piece, which he kept in his bedroom at Brantwood. In his diary for June 1884 he wrote: '*Bolton* so bright in last night's sunset!'[1130]

The figure of the fisherman tying bait in the foreground also appears in another *England and Wales* subject, *Rievaulx Abbey* (c. 1825). As both works portray ruined Yorkshire abbeys in morning light, it has been suggested that they might have been conceived as a pair.[1131]

1127 Cook and Wedderburn (eds), *Works of John Ruskin*, vol. V, p. 162.

1128 Ibid., vol. VI, p. 305.

1129 Ibid., vol. XIII, p. 444.

1130 J. Evans and J. H. Whitehouse (eds), *The Diaries of John Ruskin* (Oxford, 3 vols, 1959), vol. III, p. 1072 (entry for 29 June 1884).

1131 *Rievaulx Abbey*, c. 1825, watercolour, 28 x 40 cm, private collection on loan to York City Art Gallery, Wilton, p. 391 (cat. 785). See Shanes, *Turner: The Great Watercolours*, p. 198 (cat. 85), illus. col.

## Dudley, Worcestershire[1132]

LL 3923 (WHL 4030)

Watercolour, with extra gum arabic, scratching and stopping out on paper
29.3 x 43.2 cm
Date: 1830–33

Inscr: DUDL (watercolour, bottom right, on barge)

Watermark: C ANSELL / 1828 (right edge)[1133]

Prov: Charles Heath, 1833; John Ruskin, 1843 to 1878;[1134] Sir George A. Drummond, Montreal; his sale, Christie's, 26–27 June 1919 (lot 131); bt. Gooden and Fox (£2,310) for Lever (£2,367 15s including commission)

Exh: London, Moon, Boys and Graves Gallery, exhibition title unknown, 1833 (cat. 77); London, Fine Art Society, *Drawings by JMW Turner from Ruskin's Collection, with works by himself and others*, 1878 (cat. 32); London, Fine Art Society, *[Ruskin's] Drawings by J.M.W. Turner*, 1900 (cat. 28); Perth, Art Gallery of Western Australia and Australian tour, *Exhibition of Early British Water-colours*, organised by the Empire Art Loans Exhibition Society, 1948–49 (cat. 71); London, Royal Academy, *Turner 1775–1851*, 1974–75 (cat. 426); Manchester, Whitworth Art Gallery, *The Most Beautiful Art of England*, 1983 (cat. 31); Paris, Grand Palais, *J.M.W. Turner*, 1983–84 (cat. 205); London, Tate Gallery, *Turner: The Fifth Decade, Watercolours 1830–1840*, 1992 (cat. 16); Liverpool, Walker Art Gallery, *Turner's Journeys of the Imagination*, 2002 (cat. 22); Birmingham, Birmingham Museums and Art Gallery, *Turner's Britain*, 2003–2004 (cat. 107)

Lit: E. T. Cook and A. Wedderburn (eds), *The Works of John Ruskin* (London and New York, 39 vols, 1903–12), vol. XIII, pp. 435–36, vol. XXII, p. 64, illus. pl. 10; A. J. Finberg, *The Life of J.M.W. Turner, R.A.* (Oxford, 1961), p. 497; Andrew Wilton, *J.M.W. Turner: His Art and Life* (New Jersey, 1979), p. 400 (cat. 858), p. 187, illus. pl. 195; Eric Shanes, *Turner's Picturesque Views in England and Wales* (London, 1979), pp. 21, 23, 43, illus. pl. 66; Frank Milner, *Turner: Paintings in Merseyside Collections* (Liverpool, 1990), pp. 53–55, illus. pl. 16

Turner visited and made sketches of Dudley during his summer 1830 trip to the Midlands when he was searching for further subjects for the *Picturesque Views in England and Wales* series.[1135] LL 3923 was engraved in 1835 by Robert Wallis and was published three years later in the collected two-volume edition of the entire series.[1136] Interestingly, *Dudley* was the only design for the *England and Wales* series to feature industrialisation as its sole subject, although the theme was not unusual among Turner's work as a whole.[1137] The work was exhibited at Moon, Boys and Graves in 1833 and on this basis must have been produced some time between late 1830 and 1833.

By Turner's day Dudley in the West Midlands was a rapidly expanding industrial town at the heart of England's so-called Black Country, a district conspicuous for its concentration of heavy industry. Turner's depiction captures the dramatic intensity of a town caught in the throes of industrial and technological change against the backdrop of a traditional landscape. Here, the architectural symbols of tradition and faith (the ruins of Dudley castle on the hillside and two churches) are pictured alongside the furnaces, chimneys, boilers and canal boats of the modern industrial age.

On his 1830 visit to Dudley, Turner made many pencil studies of the town and surveyed the scene from various spots throughout the area.[1138] LL 3923 is closest to a detailed two-page sketch of the castle and town seen from the north-east, although this study does not include the canal pool and furnaces seen in the foreground of the final watercolour.[1139] William Rodner has suggested that the total view of the canal basin as well as the castle and church spires could have been seen from Dudley Port, an area slightly further south and closer in towards the castle.[1140] On the other hand, Frank Milner has argued that given the close resemblance of the two-page sketch to the final watercolour, LL 3923 is most likely to be based upon a conflation of this study with parts of detailed drawings of the canalsides and pool half a mile away at Tipton.[1141]

When the work first appeared before the public, its subject-matter attracted little comment. *The Spectator*, for example, only mentioned it briefly, praising Turner's skill in capturing the luminescent effect of 'the moon and … the furnace-fires'.[1142] To subsequent critics, however, primarily John Ruskin, who owned the work for a period, *Dudley* symbolised the disquieting effects of industrial change. In 1878 Ruskin wrote that it represented 'one of Turner's first expressions of his full understanding of what England was to become', with its 'ruined castle on the hill, and the church spire scarcely discernible among the moon-lighted clouds, as emblems of the passing away of the baron and the monk'.[1143] It seems clear that Ruskin's comments had little to do with Turner's intent and are more associated with his own increasing antipathy towards industrialisation.

In fact more recently it has been argued that *Dudley* shows Turner's excitement and fascination with industrialisation, a mood that characterises other works made by him along a similar theme such as the watercolour *Shields on the River Tyne* (c. 1823) and the oil painting *Keelmen Heaving in Coals by Moonlight* from the mid-1830s.[1144] In all these works Turner chose to depict a nocturnal setting, a device that allows him to contrast the warmth of firelight with more muted moonlight.[1145] Furthermore, the nocturnal setting helps to emphasise the intense efforts needed to fuel these industries. In *Dudley*, for example, the labourers are shown working through the night with the help of artificial light. However, the exact source of this light is never revealed lending a deep sense of mystery to the piece.[1146] This sense of mystery is reinforced by Turner's composition and technique. In applying washes into soaked paper, and with little linear structure to the piece, Turner created a hazy, atmospheric effect. Andrew Wilton has suggested that this feeling of 'excitement' for industrialism as expressed in *Dudley* is based on the eighteenth-century theory of the Sublime.[1147] In a slightly different vein, William Rodner has argued that the work can also be read 'as an expression of [Turner's] positive attitudes' towards the industrialisation of the 1820s and 1830s.[1148]

---

1132 This is the title under which LL 3923 was engraved. See n. 1136.

1133 Wove watercolour paper with an Ansell watermark was used by Turner throughout his career. The brothers Charles and James Ansell ran two paper mills, Lower Mill and the Paper Mill at Carshalton, Surrey. However, despite the Ansell name in the watermark, no members of the family were still making paper in 1828. The Paper Mill at Carshalton was run between 1820 until 1894 by different members of the Muggeridge family who always used the C ANSELL watermark in their papers. For more details see Peter Bower, *Turner's Later Papers: A Study of the Manufacture, Selection and Use of his Drawing Papers 1820–1851* (exh. cat., London, Tate Gallery, 1999), p. 81.

1134 *Dudley* was purchased in March 1843, according to an entry in his father's account book. See H. Shapiro (ed.), *Ruskin in Italy: Letters to his Parents 1845* (Oxford, 1972), p. 83, n. 1.

1135 For details of the *Picturesque Views in England and Wales*, see the entry on *Lancaster from the Aqueduct* (LL 3774).

1136 Rawlinson, *Engraved Work of J.M.W Turner*, vol. I, p. 158 (cat. 282).

1137 The work which was closest in content to *Dudley*, although less dramatic in mood, was Turner's 1816 watercolour *Leeds*, 29.2 x 43.2 cm, Yale Center for British Art, New Haven, Wilton, p. 362 (cat. 544). For details of Turner's engagement with the subject of industry more generally, see John Gage, *Turner: Rain, Steam and Speed* (London, 1972); Judy Egerton, *Turner: The Fighting Temeraire* (exh. cat., London, National Gallery, 1995); William S. Rodner, *J. M. W. Turner, Romantic Painter of the Industrial Revolution* (Berkeley, 1997).

1138 Studies of the town appear in two sketchbooks: the larger 'Kenilworth sketchbook', c. 1829–30, Tate (TB CCXXXVIII) used generally for more panoramic views and the pocket-sized 'Birmingham and Coventry sketchbook', Tate (TB CCXL) used for more detailed studies.

1139 *Ruined castle on hill, with town in distance*, 1829–30, pencil, 12 x 20.3 cm from the 'Kenilworth sketchbook', Tate (TB CCXXXVIII 65a and 66). This study is illustrated in full in William S. Rodner, 'Turner's Dudley: Continuity, Change and Adaptability in the Industrial Black Country', *Turner Studies*, vol. 8, no. 1 (1988), p. 36. Milner, p. 54, identified the viewpoint as from the old Birmingham Road.

1140 Rodner, 'Turner's Dudley', p. 36.

1141 Milner, p. 54.

1142 *The Spectator*, 16 April 1836, p. 374 quoted in Rodner, 'Turner's Dudley', p. 32.

1143 Ruskin, 'Notes by Mr Ruskin, Part I. On His Drawings by the late J.M.W Turner, R.A', in Cook and Wedderburn (eds), *Works of John Ruskin*, vol. XIII, p. 435.

1144 *Shields on the River Tyne*, 1823, watercolour on paper, 15.4 x 21.6 cm, Tate (TB CCVIIIV). *Keelmen Heaving in Coals by Moonlight*, exh. RA 1835, oil on canvas, 92.3 x 128.8 cm, National Gallery of Art, Washington, DC. Martin Butlin and Evelyn Joll, *The Paintings of J.M.W. Turner* (New Haven and London, 2 vols, 1977), vol. I, pp. 210–11 (cat. 360).

1145 This point is made in Anne Lyles, *Turner: The Fifth Decade, Watercolours 1830–1840* (exh. cat., London, Tate Gallery, 1992), p. 53 (cat. 16).

1146 Rodner, 'Turner's Dudley', p. 37.

1147 Andrew Wilton, *Turner and the Sublime* (exh. cat., Toronto, Art Gallery of Ontario, New Haven, Yale Center for British Art, and London, British Museum, 1980–81), pp. 168–69.

1148 Rodner, 'Turner's Dudley', p. 32.

## Fort Bard, Val d'Aosta
LL 3775 (WHL 4697)

Watercolour over pencil and scratching out on paper
25.6 x 27.9 cm
Date: probably 1836

Prov: F. Stevenson;[1149] Pawsey and Payne; their sale, Christie's, 22 June 1923 (lot 23 as *A Swiss Valley Scene*); bt. by Gooden and Fox (170 gns) for Lever (£182 19s 3d)

Exh: Aosta, Musée Archéologique Régional, *Joseph Mallord William Turner: Le Mont-Blanc et la Vallée d'Aoste*, 2000 (cat. 71); Liverpool, Walker Art Gallery, *Turner's Journeys of the Imagination*, 2002 (cat. 43)

Lit: Andrew Wilton, *J.M.W. Turner: His Art and Life* (New Jersey, 1979), p. 481 (cat. 1515); Frank Milner, *Turner: Paintings in Merseyside Collections* (Liverpool, 1990), p. 65

The subject of LL 3775 has been identified by David Hill as Fort Bard in the lower Val d'Aosta region.[1150] Its composition closely relates to a number of small and rapidly made pencil studies in Turner's so-called 'Fort Bard sketchbook' which was used during the artist's 1836 Swiss tour.[1151] On this trip, Turner and his friend and patron, the Scottish landowner Hugh Munro of Novar (1797–1864), retraced much of the same route taken by Turner on his first tour to Switzerland in 1802 which had marked the beginning of a lifetime appreciation of the sublime character of alpine scenery. After travelling through France to Geneva and making a circuit of the lake embracing Lausanne, Vevey and Chillon, the two men travelled south through Bonneville and Cluse to Chamonix and then through the Val d'Aosta to Turin where they went their separate ways. The principal focus of the 1836 trip was, however, the area of Mont Blanc and the Val d'Aosta.

Although Turner made no finished watercolours as a result of his 1836 tour, a large number of colour studies of mountainous scenery have long been associated with the trip.[1152] The identification of the location strongly suggests that LL 3775 is one of these works. Evidence that Turner did make colour sketches on this tour is supplied by his companion Munro's comment that 'I don't remember colouring coming out till we got into Switzerland'.[1153] It is possible that Turner made many of these colour sketches *en plein air*. Hill has suggested, given the lack of exact correspondence between the pencil

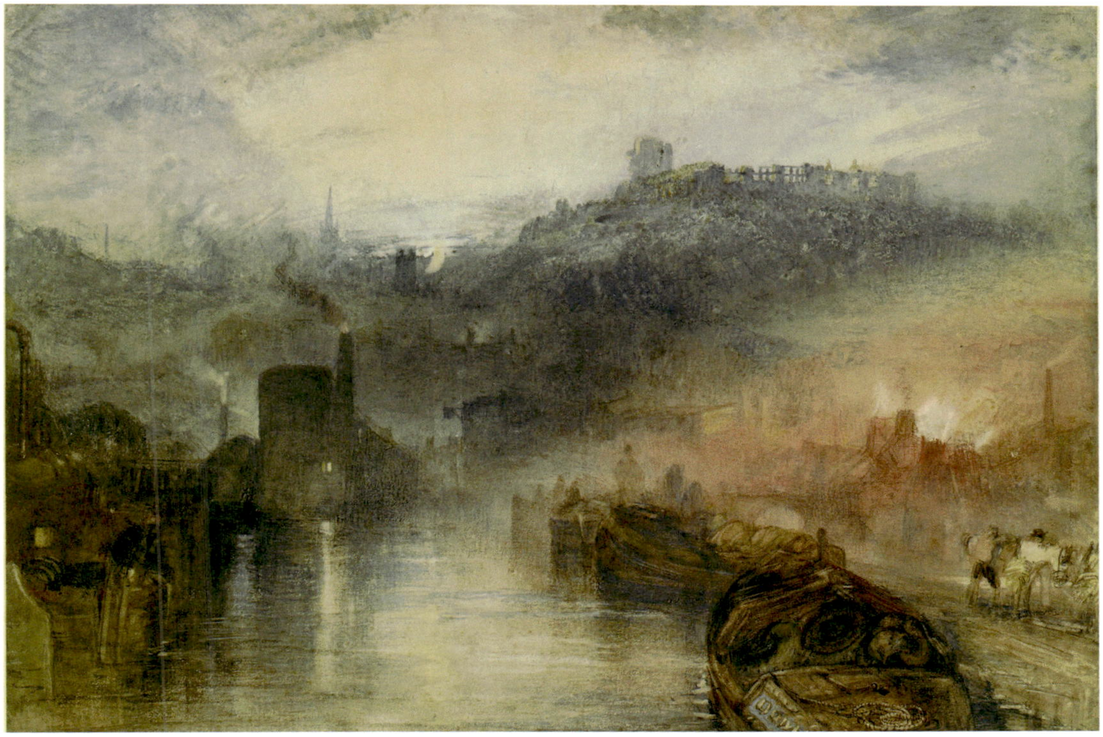

LL 3923

LL 3775

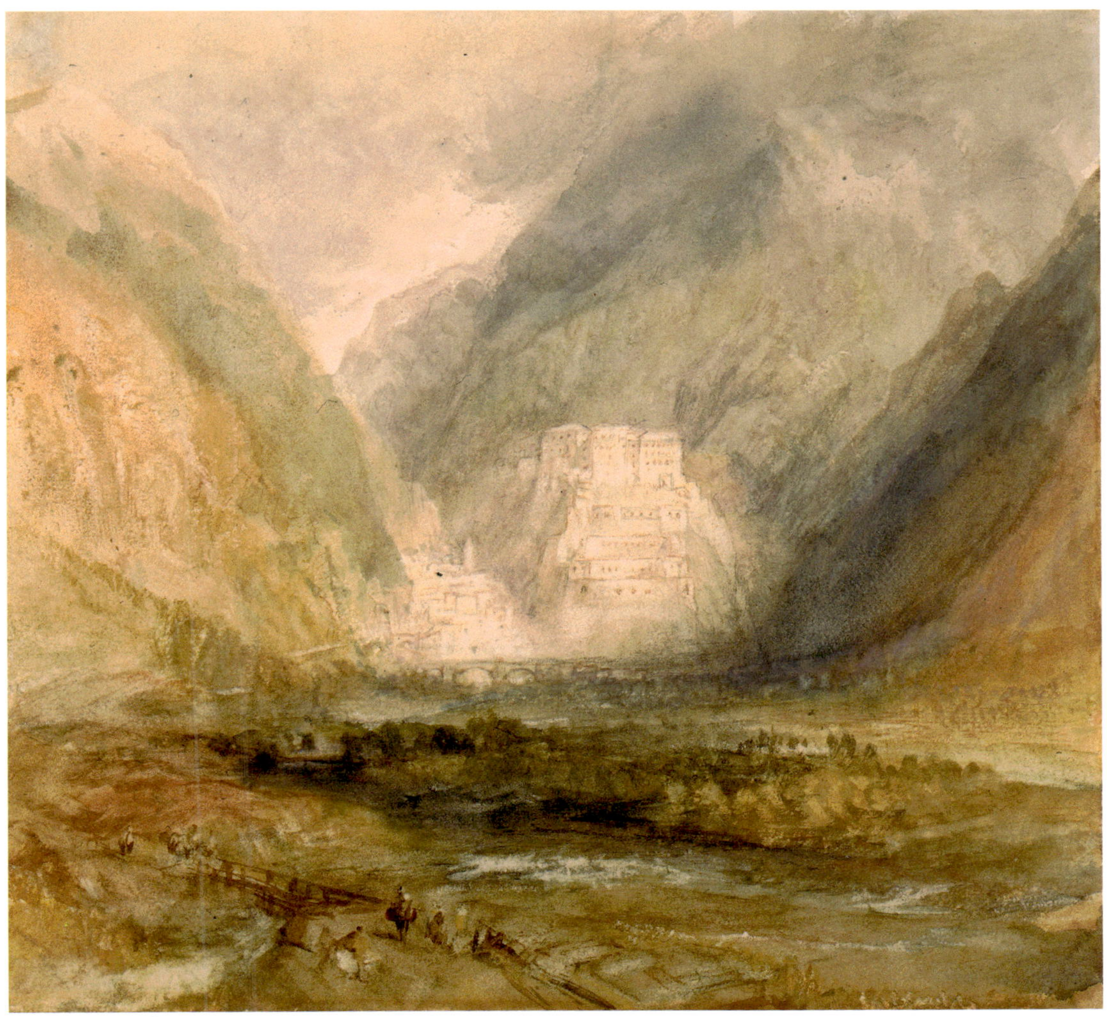

1149 This provenance derives from Wilton, p. 481 (cat. 1515).
1150 LLAG files: David Hill, letter to Frank Milner, 9 December 1997. This identification is also made in Hill, *Joseph Mallord William Turner: Le Mont Blanc et la Vallée d'Aoste* (exh. cat., Aosta, Musée Archéologique Régional, 2000), p. 291 (cat. 71). LL 3775 was titled by Wilton *Swiss valley scene*. As the location was then unidentified, the work was grouped with others made in Switzerland during 1841–44. However, Wilton also suggested that like other late Swiss drawings (see pp. 471–74, cats. 1430–56) the work seemed to belong stylistically to the 1836 Swiss tour.
1151 'Fort Bard sketchbook', Tate (TB CXCIV). For illustrations of a number of these sketches, see Hill, *Joseph Mallord William Turner*, p. 236.
1152 These include Wilton, pp. 471–74 (cats. 1430–56) as well as others in the Turner Bequest.
1153 A. J. Finberg, *The Life of J.M.W. Turner, R.A.* (Oxford, 1961), p. 360.

sketches in the 'Fort Bard sketchbook' and LL 3775 as well as the large amount of pencil on the final work, that the watercolour was begun on site, at least in pencil.[1154] He has also pointed out that the breadth of handling at least in some areas of the work may indicate that it was coloured in part in situ.[1155] The suggestion that LL 3775 was made *en plein air* is reinforced by the argument that it is one of a group of works deriving from the so-called 'Dora Baltea roll sketchbook', named after the river that runs through the Aosta valley.[1156] This group, consisting of works in the Turner Bequest, Tate, and several other public collections, share their dimensions and square format with LL 3775.

The colour studies associated with Turner's 1836 tour are often described as characterised by strong colours.[1157] However, the subtle colour palette of LL 3775, combining soft pinks and greys with darker greens and purples, is not unusual among these watercolours. For example, a similar colour palette is employed in *Sion, Rhône*, in the National Gallery of Scotland, Edinburgh.[1158] LL 3775 also demonstrates Turner's use of scratching out to create highlights with the blunt end of a brush, a feature of many of the works made on the 1836 trip.

In common with many of Turner's subjects, LL 3775 combines a depiction of natural landscape with historical allusion. In 1800 the massive fortifications of Fort Bard, by far the strongest in the valley, had been famously captured by Napoleon prior to his crossing the Great St Bernard Pass into Italy. Turner would have known about this campaign as it was reported in Brockedon's *Excursions in the Alps*, and the military associations of the site would have been clear to contemporaries.[1159] In the Lady Lever watercolour Turner, who had sketched the Fort from every angle, finally selected a view from up the valley, on the road from Verres.[1160] This was a view of Fort Bard as it would have been seen by Napoleon and his army as they approached.[1161]

1154 LLAG files: David Hill, letter to Frank Milner, 9 December 1997.
1155 Ibid.
1156 This is proposed by Nicholas Serota, 'J.M.W. Turner's Alpine Tours' (unpublished MA thesis, Courtauld Institute of Art, 1970), pp. 124–25. Aside from LL 3775, the other two works in public collections that are included in this group are *Verrès in the Val d'Aosta*, watercolour and pen and red ink and scratching out on paper, 25.6 x 27.8 cm, Wilton, p. 472 (cat. 1435), and *Tête Noire*, watercolour, 25.6 x 28.3 cm, Wilton, p. 473 (cat. 1441).
1157 See Wilton, p. 471.
1158 *Sion, Rhône*, c. 1836, watercolour with scratching out on paper, 24.5 x 27.7 cm, National Gallery of Scotland, Edinburgh (D NG 876). Wilton, p. 473 (cat. 1446); Christopher Baker, *J.M.W. Turner, The Vaughan Bequest* (exh. cat., Edinburgh, National Gallery of Scotland, 2006), pp. 68–69, illus. col.
1159 Hill, *Joseph Mallord William Turner*, p. 291.
1160 Ibid.
1161 Ibid.

## Margate
LL 3440 (WHL 4398)

Watercolour over pencil on white wove paper
21.6 x 16.6 cm
Date: possibly c. 1840

Annot: Mar (pencil, lower centre); 4 (pencil, lower right, in same hand)

Prov: Charles Stokes;[1162] [?] T. S. Kennedy, 1895;[1163] Thomas Hughes; by descent to Mrs F. Hughes; her sale, Sotheby's, 28 November 1922 (lot 123); bt. by Gooden and Fox for Lever (£168)[1164]

Exh: Liverpool, Walker Art Gallery, *Turner's Journeys of the Imagination*, 2002 (cat. 32)

Lit: Andrew Wilton, *J.M.W. Turner: His Art and Life* (New Jersey, 1979), p. 419 (cat. 1004); Craig Hartley, *Turner Watercolours in the Whitworth Art Gallery* (Manchester, 1984), p. 54; Frank Milner, *Turner: Paintings in Merseyside Collections* (Liverpool, 1990), p. 60, illus. p. 61

This watercolour has traditionally been titled *Margate* on the basis of its abbreviated inscription.[1165] Andrew Wilton has described LL 3440 as one of four studies for *Light-towers of la Hève*, the title vignette of *Turner's Annual Tour* (or *Wanderings by the Seine* as it was also known) published in 1834 (fig. 53).[1166] However, he has noted that both the Lady Lever work and a further watercolour in the Whitworth Art Gallery, Manchester (fig. 54), with a similar composition 'may possibly represent a different location'.[1167] Frank Milner has argued that there seems to be no reason to believe that LL 3440 relates to Turner's views of la Hève.[1168] There is no evidence of the steep cliffs and lighthouse towers that characterise Turner's view of the Cap de la Hève in both his title vignette for the *Annual Tour* as well as two more realistic colour studies of the topography in the Turner Bequest at the Tate.[1169] More positive identifications of the view as Margate have been made by Milner and Ian Warrell.[1170] Milner has pointed out that the relationship between the jetty and the light tower and Margate Church (just to the left of the moon) is replicated in another view of Margate (Yale Center for British Art, New Haven, fig. 55).[1171]

LL 3440 appears to be an incomplete study for a vignette, in relation to a more finished illustration like the *Light-towers of la Hève* also in the Lady Lever Art Gallery (LL 3779, pp. 202–203). No sketches or more finished designs are known for LL 3440. The closest design is the less finished watercolour in the Whitworth Art Gallery, referred to above.[1172] In this latter work, the composition is similar although Turner has introduced buildings behind the lighthouse and the moon is higher up in the sky. It is possible that both the Lady Lever and the Whitworth works were unused studies for a vignette that was never realised.

The Lady Lever watercolour has generally been dated to c. 1832 on the basis of its relationship to the title vignette of *Turner's Annual Tour* (or *Wanderings by the Seine*) published in 1834.[1173] However, as it seems likely that the work is not linked to the la Hève subjects, there is reason to question this dating. It is now known that Turner was making vignettes such as the six owned by Elhanan Bicknell as late as the early 1840s (for details see *Light-towers of la Hève*, LL 3779). The style of Turner's later vignettes (defined here as from the late 1830s onwards) is more linear than the fine stippling of earlier designs from the early 1830s (see, for example, Turner's 33 watercolour designs for Samuel Rogers's *Poems* published in 1834).[1174] LL 3440, with its numerous short lines placed parallel to one another, appears to be from this more mature period. Warrell has suggested that Margate may date from c. 1840.[1175] This dating is certainly in keeping with Turner's frequent visits to Margate in the late 1830s and early 1840s.

1162 Charles Stokes FSA (1785–1853) was Turner's stockbroker. He collected the artist's work.
1163 Tatlock, p. 139.
1164 LLAG files: invoice.
1165 Ian Warrell, verbally, April 2008, has suggested that this inscription may be by Charles Stokes.
1166 Wilton, p. 418 (cats. 1001–04). The title vignette is *Light-towers of la Hève*, c. 1832, gouache and watercolour with pen on blue paper, 18.9 x 13.7 cm, Tate (TB CCLIX 136); Wilton, p. 412 (cat. 951). See also Ian Warrell, *Turner on the Seine* (exh. cat., London, Tate Gallery, Paris, Pavillon des Arts and Le Havre, Musée Malraux, 1999–2000), p. 273 (cat. 115), illus. col. fig. 53. *Turner's Annual Tour* of 1834 was part of an ongoing series of travel books on which Turner collaborated with his publisher Charles Heath. The *Annual Tours* for 1834 and 1835 were dedicated to views of the Seine. An earlier volume, his *Annual Tour* of 1833 was dedicated to views by the Loire. Each work had 20 engravings based on Turner's designs, one of which appeared as a vignette on the title page. The engravings from all three were reissued as *The Rivers of France* in 1837. See Warrell, *Turner on the Seine* and the same author's *Turner on the Loire*.
1167 *A vignette study of a lighthouse*, watercolour over pencil on thin board, 19.8 x 15.5 cm, Whitworth Art Gallery, Manchester; Wilton, p. 418 (cat. 1003). See Craig Hartley, *Turner Watercolours in the Whitworth Art Gallery* (Manchester, 1984), p. 54 (cat. 44), illus. Wilton, p. 418.
1168 Milner, p. 60.
1169 *A ship under sail below the light-towers of la Hève*, c. 1832, gouache and watercolour with pen on blue paper, Tate (TB CCLIX 80) and *The Cap de la Hève*, c. 1832, gouache and watercolour on blue paper, Tate (TB CCLIX 29). See Warrell, *Turner on the Seine*, pp. 92–93 (cats. 59 and 60), illus. figs. 54 and 55. Warrell has pointed out, *Turner on the Seine*, p. 94, that Turner has exaggerated the proportions of the cliffs in the frontispiece vignette for his *Annual Tour* of 1834 in an effort to give the lighthouse towers an exaggerated significance, and that a truer impression of the cliffs at la Hève is given in his remaining colour sketches.

1170 Milner, p. 60. Ian Warrell, verbally, April 2008.
1171 Milner, p. 60. *Margate*, c. 1822, watercolour, engraved 1824 for *Southern Coast*, Yale Center for British Art, New Haven; Wilton, p. 353 (cat. 470).
1172 Although Hartley, *Turner Watercolours*, p. 54, emphasised the closeness of the compositions of the Whitworth and Lady Lever watercolours, he did not re-title the former as *Margate*.
1173 It has been dated to c. 1832 by Wilton, p. 419 (cat. 1004). Milner, pp. 59–60, also dated the work to c. 1832.
1174 For details of Turner's illustrations to Rogers's *Poems*, see Jan Piggott, *Turner's Vignettes* (exh. cat., London, Tate Gallery, 1994), pp. 39–44 and 82–85.
1175 Ian Warrell, verbally, April 2008.

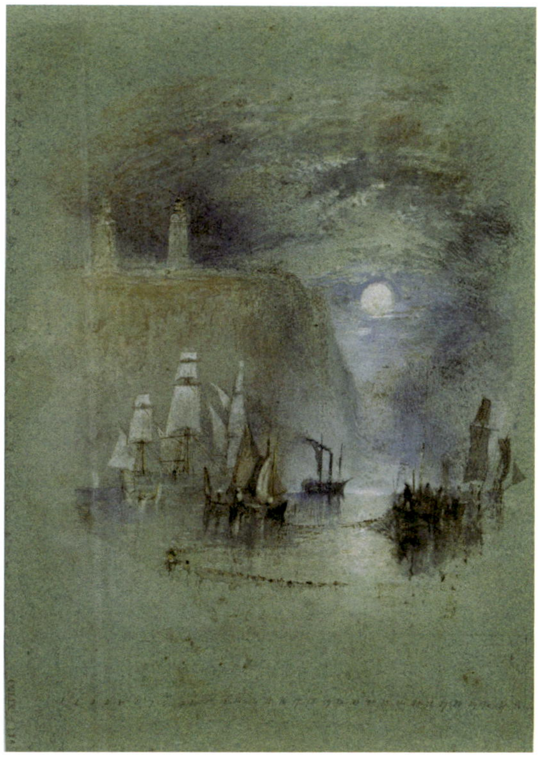

fig. 53. Joseph Mallord William Turner, *Light-Towers of La Hève* (title vignette from *Turner's Annual Tour: The Seine*, 1834), c. 1832, gouache and watercolour on paper, 18.9 x 13.7 cm, © Tate, London, 2008

fig. 54. Joseph Mallord William Turner, *Vignette Study of a Lighthouse*, ?1833–35, watercolour over pencil on thin board, 19.8 x 15.5 cm, Whitworth Art Gallery, Manchester

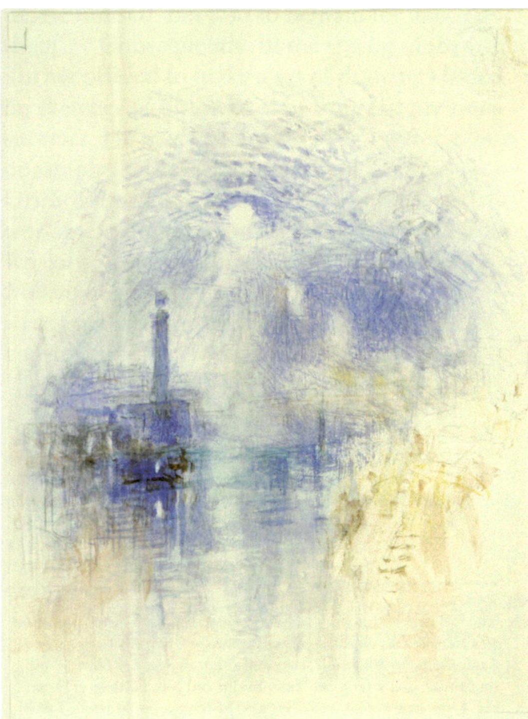

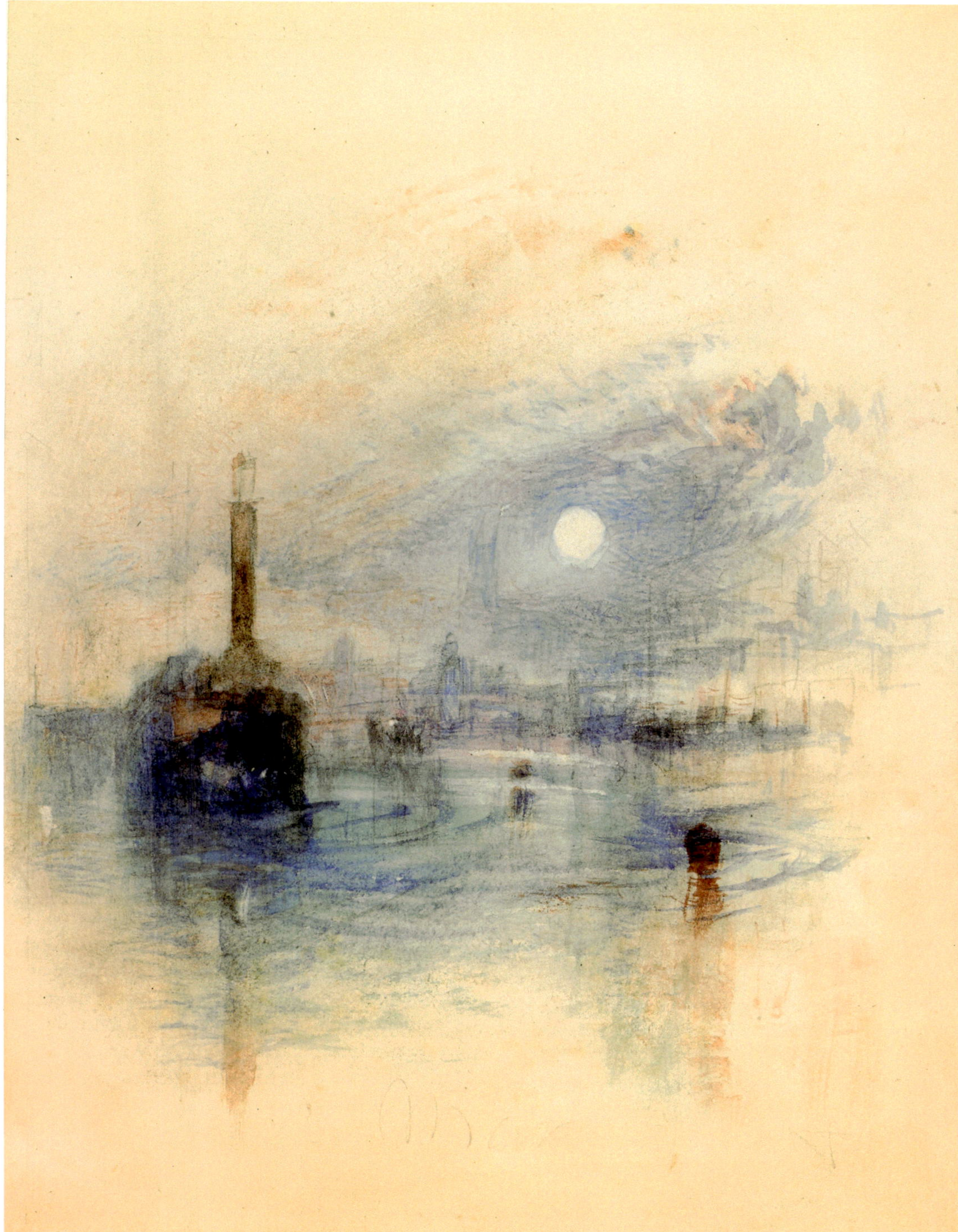

LL 3440

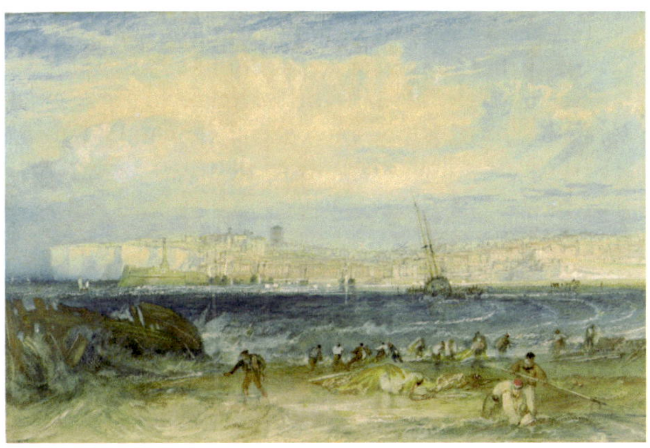

fig. 55. Joseph Mallord William Turner, *Margate*, c. 1822, watercolour on paper, 15.7 x 23.7 cm, Yale Center for British Art/Bridgeman

he had been disillusioned by the insensitive developments that had occurred in the town since his earlier visit in 1854. When he returned in 1866 he described the following: 'Round by Turner's old view, all destroyed by barracks below, now, and Restaurants *every*where'.[1201]

Turner's late Swiss finished watercolours are generally characterised by the artist's concern to depict the play of light on buildings, water and landscape. This is seen in LL 3772 in the dramatic contrast between the bright sunshine over the town and the shadows in the foreground. *Lucerne from the Walls* is also typical of these late watercolours in its haziness of execution, seen particularly in areas of the town and the indistinct Rigi in the background. Turner has used a variety of techniques to obtain these effects, which are typical of his mature watercolours, combining loose feathery brushstrokes and scratching out and in some areas, such as the roofs of buildings, overlaid with a fine watercolour line obtained by using a nibbed pen to give greater definition to the detail.

Although many of the late Swiss watercolours were transformed as Turner worked on them, LL 3772 is very close to the 'sample study' for the subject (Tate).[1202] In the final work, Turner has replaced the single figure climbing the walls with two sets of figures: a family group on the left and a young man and a woman reading or drawing on the right. He has also added further small details such as the shooting contest in the foreground.

## Light-towers of la Hève[1203]
LL 3779 (WHL 4715)

Watercolour over pencil on white wove paper
20.2 x 15.8 cm
Date: c. 1844

Prov: Elhanan Bicknell; his sale, Christie's, 29 April–1 May 1863 (lot 118); bt. by Colnaghi (£108 3s);[1204] [?] F.R Leyland; [?] his sale, Christie's, 9 March 1872 (lot 43); bt. by White (£168); Mrs Newall of Croxley Green, Rickmansworth, Hertfordshire, 1899; bt. from Phillips and MacConnal by Lever, 10 August 1923 (with LL 3770 for £400)[1205]

Exh: London, Guildhall Art Gallery, *Turner*, 1899 (cat. 154);[1206] Paris, Centre Culturel du Marais, *Turner en France: Aquarelles, Peintures, Dessins, Gravures, Carnets de Croquis*, 1981 (cat. 157); London, Tate, Paris, Pavillon des Arts and Le Havre, Musée Malraux, *Turner on the Seine*, 1999–2000 (cat. 176); Liverpool, Walker Art Gallery, *Turner's Journeys of the Imagination*, 2002 (cat 31)

Lit: Andrew Wilton, *J.M.W. Turner: His Art and Life* (New Jersey, 1979), p. 418 (cat. 1001); Frank Milner, *Turner: Paintings in Merseyside Collections* (Liverpool, 1990), pp. 59–60 (cat. 29)

This watercolour was described by Andrew Wilton as a study for the title vignette of *Turner's Annual Tour* (or *Wanderings by the Seine*), published in 1834 (see fig. 53).[1207] On this basis he dated the work to c. 1832. Frank Milner has pointed out that the work is in fact a highly finished treatment of the subject with a number of differences from the title vignette and he has suggested that LL 3779 may represent an alternative treatment.[1208] More recently, Ian Warrell has included the Lady Lever watercolour in a group of six vignettes that were first owned by the whaling entrepreneur Elhanan Bicknell (1788–1861).[1209] Bicknell probably acquired these works in the early 1840s, the period during which he acquired a substantial group of oil paintings as well as two late Swiss watercolours by the artist.[1210] Warrell has argued for a date of the early 1840s for the production of these vignettes as it is now known that Turner continued to make vignette designs well into that decade.[1211] He has pointed to the stylistic qualities of these Bicknell vignettes, which with their numerous short lines placed in parallel, are markedly different from the designs for this type of illustration from the early 1830s.[1212] Additionally, one of the six subjects is alleged to have been Burg Eltz, a site that Turner did not visit until 1840.[1213] On this evidence, Warrell's dating of *Light-towers of la Hève* to c. 1844 does not seem problematic. In this context, it seems that Turner repeated the c. 1832 motif around a decade later, with some alterations. It was not unknown for Turner to make repeat versions of subjects in this manner; on a few occasions during the 1830s he had repeated in oil other engraved subjects at the request of patrons.[1214] The popularity of Turner's *The Rivers of France* of 1837 (which included his *Annual Tours* of 1834 and 1835) would have made it the kind of material with which a patron like Bicknell might be familiar and from which he might select a work to be repeated.[1215] Another design from the same group, *Château Gaillard*, incorporates some elements from the abandoned title vignette from *Turner's Annual Tour* of 1835.[1216]

In addition to being on a piece of white paper rather than a blue sheet, LL 3779 has some more substantial differences from the title vignette. Although Turner repeated many of the same elements of the earlier scene, including the fishermen and some of the boats, he included an old building to the left of the lighthouses, and on the far right added a streak of white to suggest a church tower. It has been argued that the old building is similar to the church of St Mary and St Eanswythe at Folkestone, which Turner had depicted on a number of occasions.[1217] It has also been pointed out that the distant church tower on the far right of the drawing resembles Margate Church as seen in the Lady Lever vignette of *Margate* (LL 3440). The reasons for Turner's apparent combination of places on the Kent coast with a view of Cap de la Hève near Le Havre, on the north bank of the Seine estuary, remain unclear. However, by the early 1840s he was a frequent visitor to Margate and the surrounding area and it is not hard to imagine that he might have impressed current experiences on an older composition. Warrell has suggested that the most significant change is the movement of the steamboat from its central position to the left foreground.[1218] In this position, the steamboat

1201 Evans and Whitehouse (eds), *Diaries of John Ruskin*, vol. II, p. 591 (entry for 19 June 1866).

1202 *Lucerne from the Walls: Sample Study*, c. 1841–42, pencil and watercolour on paper, 23.4 x 31.2 cm, Tate (TB CCCLXIV 290), inscribed in pencil: J Ruskin Jnr Esqr, and in red chalk, 17. Warrell, *Through Switzerland with Turner*, p. 60 (cat. 23), illus. col. This study would have been based on pencil sketches: the 'Lucerne and Berne sketchbook' contains various pencil notes of the city and its medieval fortifications, Tate (TB CCCXXVIII, pp. 3v, 4r).

1203 LLAG files: this is the title as recorded on the invoice.

1204 Sold as *Lighthouse of the Hève: mouth of the Seine. Painted for Mr. Bicknell.* Warrell, *Turner on the Seine*, p. 280, has noted that 'according to notes in the family copy of the sale catalogue, it was bought by Colnaghi for a Mr Smith of Edinburgh for £103 [*sic*] 3s. – then possibly resold at Fosters on 9 May 1866 with the vignette of Geneva from the same Bicknell group (however the Foster catalogue makes no reference to the Hève drawing, and does not specifically state that the Geneva work was a vignette)'.

1205 LLAG files: invoice; LL 3779 was purchased with another Turner watercolour, *A Steamer off Ostend*, previously described as *Yarmouth Roads* (WHL 4716, now LL 3770).

1206 Lent by Mrs Newall.

1207 Wilton, p. 418 (cat. 1001). Wilton described LL 3779 as well as LL 3440 as two of four studies for this title vignette (see *Margate* LL 3440 for further details).

1208 Milner, p. 60.

1209 See Warrell, *Turner on the Seine*, pp. 87–88 for a discussion of this.

1210 Ibid.

1211 Ibid.

1212 See also Piggott, *Turner's Vignettes*, p. 60.

1213 Warrell, *Turner on the Seine*, p. 87.

1214 Butlin and Joll, *Paintings of Turner*, vol. I, pp. 188–89 (cat. 358), 191–92 (cat. 360), 194 (cat. 363), cited in Warrell, *Turner on the Seine*, p. 88.

1215 *The Rivers of France* of 1837 included the engravings from all three of *Turner's Annual Tours*, including his *Wanderings by the Seine* from 1834 and 1835 as well as his *Wanderings by the Loire* of 1833. See also *Margate* LL 3440 for further details.

1216 Warrell, *Turner on the Seine*, p. 88. *Château Gaillard*, c. 1844, watercolour, private collection, not in Wilton (see Warrell, *Turner on the Seine*, p. 280 [cat. 178], illus. col. fig. 182); *Château Gaillard and Les Andelys: Nicholas Poussin's Birth-Place*, c. 1832, watercolour on blue paper, Indianapolis Museum of Art, Wilton, p. 419 (cat. 1006) (Warrell, *Turner on the Seine*, p. 198, illus. col., fig. 181).

1217 *Folkestone, Kent*, c. 1823, watercolour, engraved for *Southern Coast*, 1826, Taft Museum of Art, Cincinnati, Ohio. See also Warrell, *Turner on the Seine*, p. 96; Wilton, p. 335 (cat. 480).

1218 Warrell, *Turner on the Seine*, p. 97.

LL 3779

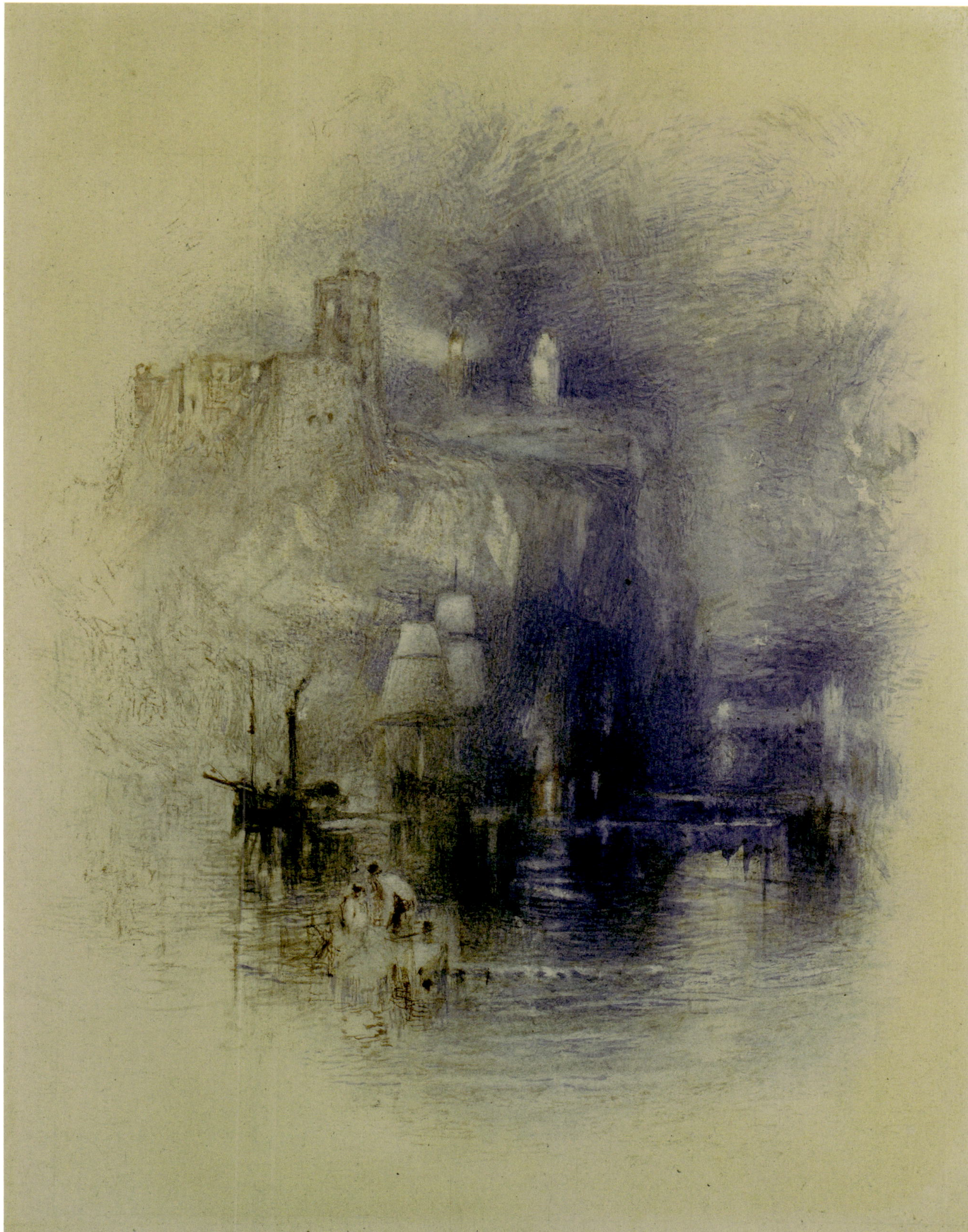

appears, like the tug in Turner's painting *The Fighting Temeraire* (1839, National Gallery, London), to tow the boat behind it. In this context, the placement of the steamboat underneath the church may be symbolic, with the church intended to represent the passing of the old order and the steamboat and lighthouses as icons of technology, representing the modern and the new.

## AFTER JOSEPH MALLORD WILLIAM TURNER

### Hackfall
LL 3776 (WHL 754, HH 391)

Watercolour over pencil with extra gum arabic and scratching out on wove paper
28.2 x 39.9 cm
Date: after 1816; possibly late nineteenth century

Prov: bt. from James Orrock by Lever, 1910[1219]

Exh: London, Tate Gallery, *The Romantic Movement*, 1959 (cat. 441); Liverpool, Walker Art Gallery, *Turner's Journeys of the Imagination*, 2002 (cat. 8)

Lit: Andrew Wilton, *J.M.W. Turner: His Art and Life* (New Jersey, 1979), p. 361 (cat. 537); Frank Milner, *Turner: Paintings in Merseyside Collections* (Liverpool, 1990), pp. 24–25

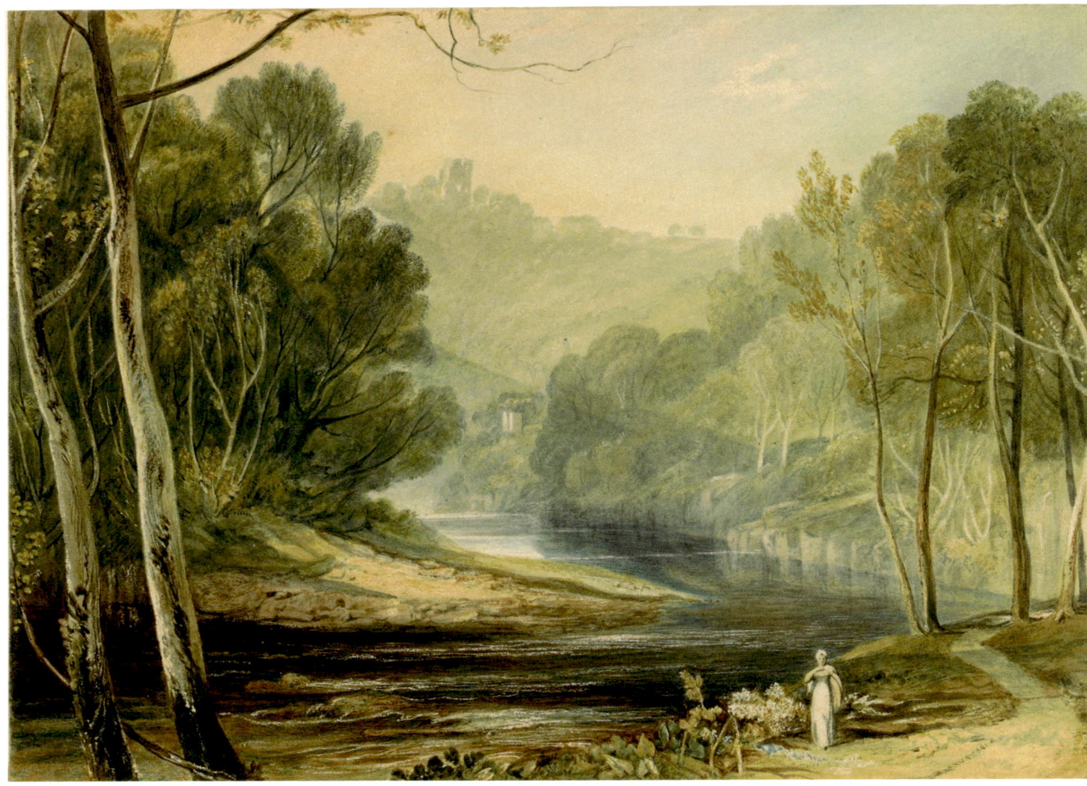

LL 3776

*Hackfall* was purchased by Lever as by Turner, but is now thought to be a copy by an unknown artist after a watercolour in the Wallace Collection, London (fig. 56).[1220] The two works are almost identical in composition and size. Although LL 3776 was included in Andrew Wilton's 1979 catalogue as a genuine work, he pointed out it was 'most unusual for Turner to have repeated a subject so literally' and suggested that the Lady Lever work was the replica.[1221] It was quite common for Turner to make variants of the same design in his watercolours; for example, he made a much larger and later version of the Wallace Collection's *Scarborough Castle: Boys Crab Fishing* of 1809.[1222] By contrast, however, LL 3776 is almost identical in size to the Wallace watercolour. Additionally, there are stylistic grounds for rejecting the attribution of LL 3776 to Turner. David Hill has argued that the harder style of paint application is uncharacteristic of the artist.[1223] He has suggested that it is a copy by another artist in the later nineteenth century; the context for its production remains unknown but one possibility is that it was copied from the Wallace Collection version when that was exhibited at Bethnal Green between 1872 and 1875.[1224]

Hackfall, near Ripon, North Yorkshire is a richly wooded valley of the river Ure. John Aislabie bought the land in c. 1730 and began to develop it as a planned Picturesque landscape, similar to that made by Thomas Johnes of Hafod (see LL 3778, pp. 184–85) with various riverside and woodland walks. However, it was Aislabie's son William, in the mid-eighteenth century, who added the various artificial ruins, grottoes, waterfalls and seats which were placed at points to take advantage of specific views. By the early nineteenth century Hackfall had become a firm fixture on the tourist's itinerary and descriptions of the delights to be had from this most romantic scenery featured in many guidebooks of the period.[1225]

LL 3776 shows the Fisher's Hut (or Hall) in the mid-distance, a riverside grotto with an octagonal structure made of petrified stone and named after William Fisher, the Aislabies' head gardener. The building in the far distance on the hill is probably Mowbray Castle, an artificial ruined castle.

The Wallace Collection watercolour has been dated to c. 1816, as it is based on a sketch made on Turner's tour of central Yorkshire late in August that year.[1226] Hill has suggested that the Wallace Collection work and a companion piece were probably among the 120 drawings commissioned from Turner in 1816 by Longmans for Whitaker's *History of Yorkshire* but which were unused when the contract lapsed in 1819.[1227]

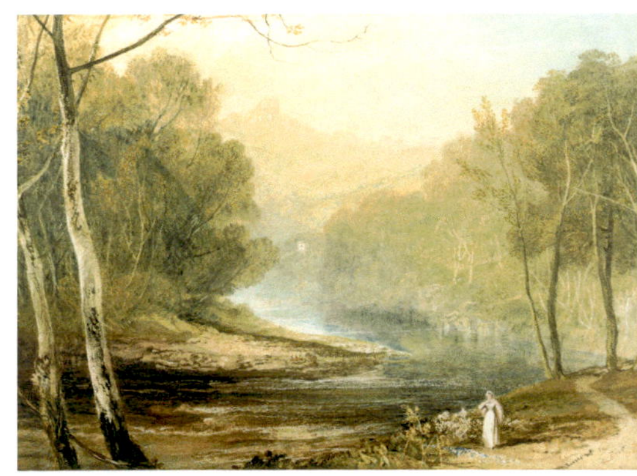

fig. 56. Joseph Mallord William Turner, *Hackfall, near Ripon*, c. 1816, watercolour and gum arabic on paper, 27.9 x 39.6 cm, © The Wallace Collection, London

1219 1910 Inventory, p. 50, valued at £200, titled *Mowbray Lodge, Ripon, Yorkshire*. This title presumably derives from the work in the Wallace Collection. Mowbray Lodge does not feature in contemporary descriptions of Hackfall. The 1910 Inventory records that LL 3776 was in the 'E.A Bicknell collection'. This is incorrect; the Bicknell provenance relates to the Wallace Collection work and was adopted by Orrock and accepted for the Inventory.

1220 *Hackfall, near Ripon,* c. 1816, watercolour and gum arabic on paper, 27.9 x 39.6 cm, Wallace Collection, London. Provenance: Sir William Pilkington; Elhanan Bicknell; his sale, Christie's, 30 April 1863 (lot 269) as *Mowbray Lodge, Ripon, Yorkshire: Earl Ripon's Seat;* bt. by Wells (510 gns) for the 4th Marquess of Hertford. See also Wilton, p. 361 (cat. 536); Ingamells, *Wallace Collection Catalogue*, vol. I, p. 188.

1221 Wilton, p. 361. As LL 3776 was included in Wilton's catalogue, it seems clear that he meant that the work was a replica by Turner and not by another artist. This is also the view taken by Milner, p. 25.

1222 *Scarborough Castle: Boys Crab Fishing*, signed and dated 1809, 27.9 x 39.8 cm, Wallace Collection, London, Wilton, p. 360 (cat. 527). Another version of this work was commissioned by Walter Fawkes: *Scarborough Town and Castle: Morning: Boys catching crabs*, c. 1811, watercolour, 68.7 x 101.6 cm, on long-term loan to the Art Gallery of South Australia, Adelaide, Wilton, p. 360 (cat. 528).

1223 Quoted by Milner. Hill's opinion remains the same to date, email correspondence, May 2008. Ian Warrell has also voiced doubt about the authenticity of LL 3776, verbally, April 2008.

1224 David Hill, email correspondence, May 2008.

1225 See, for example, T. Langdale, *The Tourist's Companion; being A Concise Description and History of Ripon, Studley park, Fountains Abbey, Hackfall, Brimham Craggs, Boroughbridge, Aldborough, Newby Hall, Knaresbrough, Plumpton, Harrogate, & Harewood House; & Intended as A Guide to Persons Visiting Those Places* (Ripon, 1817).

1226 The Wallace's *Hackfall* is based on a pencil study in the 'Large Farnley sketchbook', Tate (TB CXXVIII 37). This sketchbook was most recently dated by Hill to 1816. See Ingamells, *Wallace Collection Catalogue*, vol. I, p. 188, for details.

1227 See Hill's entry on *The River Ure at Hackfall, near Ripon* in the catalogue of Sotheby's sale of 7 July 1983, lot 171.

## WILLIAM TURNER OF OXFORD

1789 Black Bourton, Oxfordshire–1862 Oxford

**Distant View of Windsor Castle**[1228]
LL 3441 (LP 68)

Watercolour and gum arabic, with pencil and touches of gouache on paper
58.7 x 98.7 cm (sight)
Date: mid-1820s–1830s

Annot: D 920 / W. Turner (of Oxford) 1789-1862 LGD (pencil, on mount, verso; by Leonard Duke)

Prov: T. J. Nicholson; bt. by Leonard Duke, June 1946 (12 gns); sold to the Fine Art Society, June 1946 (£15);[1229] bt. from the Fine Art Society by the Trustees, 11 March, 1947 (£56 14s)

Exh: [?] London, SPWC, 1826 (cat. 246, as *Windsor Castle, from Near Salt Hill*)

Lit: *Antique Collector*, vol. 21 (September-October 1950), pp. 195–96 (illus. p. 195, as *Windsor Castle from the Park*)

Turner may have received early training from the drawing master William Delamotte (1775–1863) in Oxford, but in 1804 he left for London, becoming a pupil of John Varley (see pp. 206–207). In 1808 he was elected an associate of the SPWC, and later that year became its youngest full member. He exhibited there annually until his death, with 455 exhibits over a period of fifty-five years. Around 1812, despite gaining critical acclaim for his work in London, Turner returned to Oxford where he established a teaching practice. He remained in Oxford for the rest of his life, a move which may explain the gradual decline in his contemporary reputation (Ruskin, for example, only included him in the fifth edition of *Modern Painters*). Turner specialised in landscape and he travelled widely around Britain, visiting the Lake District in 1814, Wales in 1817, and making an extended tour of Scotland in 1838.

Leonard Duke recorded T. J. Nicholson's attribution of LL 3441 to Edmund Morison Wimperis (see p. 218), but gave it little credence, writing: 'There is a spurious monogram of Wimperis on the dead tree in [*sic*] foreground'.[1230] It has not been possible to find even a 'spurious monogram', and there does not seem to be any other foundation for Nicholson's attribution. The work was reattributed to Turner by the time it was purchased from the Fine Art Society by the Trustees.[1231]

The work can be dated on stylistic grounds to Turner's middle period, from the mid-1820s and 1830s following his return to Oxford.[1232] Windsor Castle, depicted here in the far distance, was the subject of seven watercolours exhibited by Turner at the SPWC during the period 1814–53. Both the size and high finish of LL 3441 suggest that it may have been an exhibition work. The location of the view has not been resolved, although it may be from the north, from Salt Hill (the area to the west of what is now Slough).[1233] If this is the case, the work could be *Windsor Castle from near Salt Hill*, exhibited at the SPWC in 1826.[1234]

The foreground of the scene is dominated by a tree stump and a fallen tree. These motifs were part of the visual language of the Picturesque and possessed the irregular qualities of nature deemed to be beautiful by the Revd William Gilpin in his *Remarks on Forest Scenery* (1791). In this sense the watercolour belongs to an eighteenth-century tradition of landscape painting which combined the topographical with the Picturesque. Nevertheless, it is also highly expressive, with a sense of drama created by the focus on a craggy tree stump and a thundery sky.

1228 LLAG files: the work was known as *Windsor Castle from the Park* when it was purchased by the Trustees in 1947, *Annual Report of the Trustees*, 30 June 1947.

1229 L. G. Duke, MS *Catalogue of my collection of early English drawings and watercolours… begun in 1924* (photocopy in Department of Prints and Drawings, British Museum), unpag.

1230 Ibid.

1231 LLAG files: described as Turner of Oxford in *Annual Report of the Trustees*, 30 June 1947.

1232 Tim Wilcox, verbally, March 2007.

1233 Jane Roberts, Royal Collection, email correspondence, February 2007.

1234 Sold for 15 gns. This identification is confused by the identification of a view of Windsor Castle in Oxford City Council's collection as *Windsor Castle from near Salt Hill*, which shows the castle much closer up and from a different viewpoint (illus. in T. Wilcox and C. Titterington, *William Turner of Oxford, 1789–1862* [exh. cat., Woodstock, Oxfordshire County Museum, 1984], p. 48 [cat. 40]). The alternative, that LL 3441 is *Windsor from the Brockhurst – Clearing Up After A Shower*, exhibited at the SPWC in 1832 (cat. 62), 25 gns but unsold, seems possible to discount. The Brockhurst is what is now called 'the Brocas', a meadow on the Eton side of the River Thames; this is immediately under the castle and therefore too close up to be the Lady Lever view.

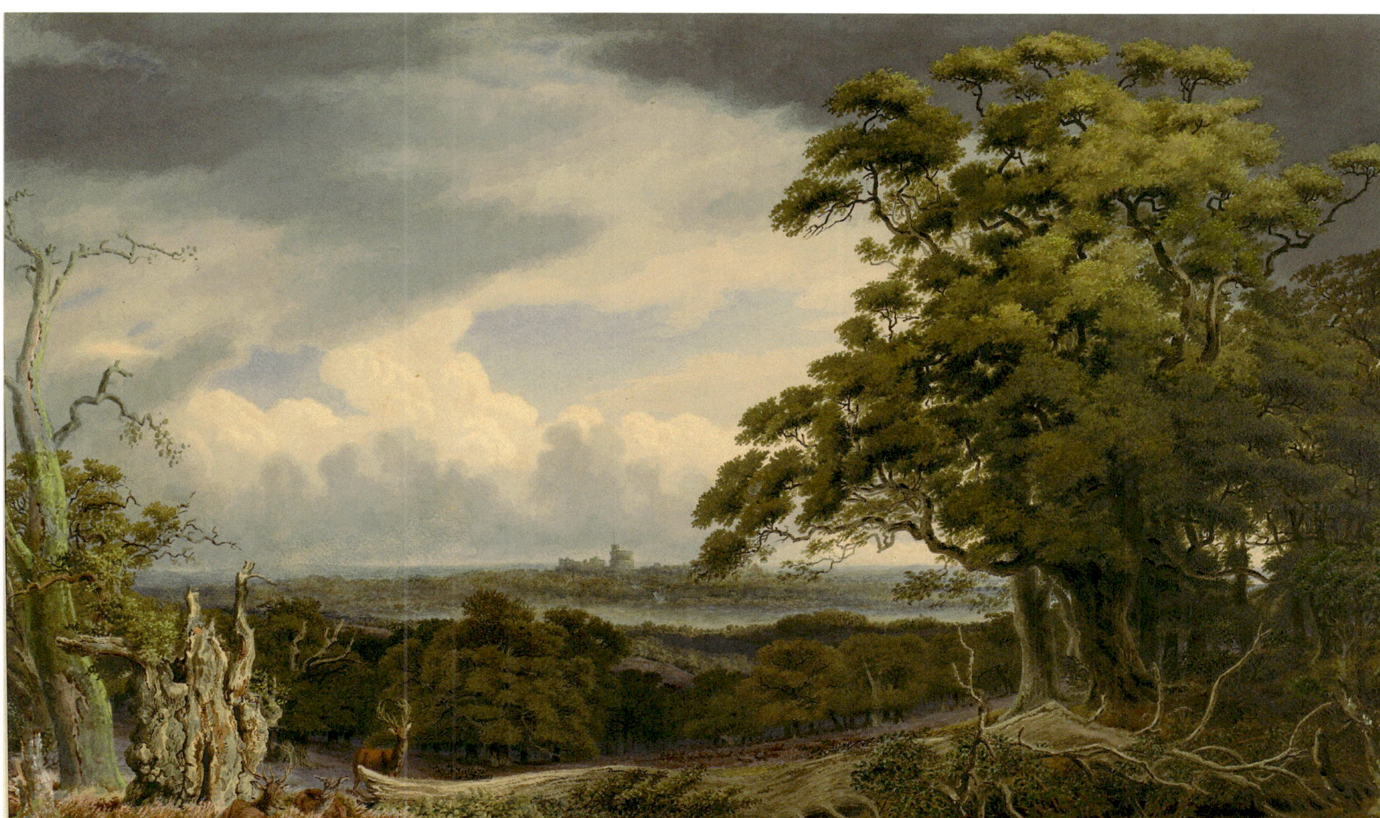

LL 3441

## JOHN VARLEY

1778 Hackney, London–1842 Westminster, London

### Swiss Mountains and Lake

LL 3442 (WHL 366, H 424)

Watercolour over pencil with scratching out on wove paper
38.6 x 50.1 cm
Date: 1824

Inscr: J Varley. 1825 (ink, bottom centre, below rock)

Prov: bt. from James Orrock by Lever, 1912[1235]

Exh: [?] London, SPWC, 1825 (cat. 141); [?] Windsor, Eton College, exhibition title unknown, 1933 (cat. 22);[1236] [?] Bedford, Cecil Higgins Art Gallery, *English watercolours from the Hickman Bacon and other collections*, 1952 (cat. no. unknown)[1237]

Varley was the eldest of five children, all but one of whom became artists. When their father died in 1791 John found employment at a stationer's but also began taking drawing lessons from John Charles Barrow. He exhibited a sketch of Peterborough Cathedral at the Royal Academy in 1798, following a sketching trip to the city with Barrow, and later that year, or possibly in 1799, Varley made a tour of Wales. He received encouragement from Dr Thomas Monro, who took him to Surrey to sketch from nature and may have introduced him to an earlier protégé, Thomas Girtin. After Girtin's death in 1802 Varley became one of the most noted exponents of his style. As a teacher of many of the generation of watercolour painters who would dominate the SPWC for the first half of the nineteenth century, including David Cox, Peter DeWint and Copley Fielding, Varley also became the conduit through which Girtin's breadth of handling and sensitivity to subtle effects of light were preserved as the bedrock of the national technique. Varley was one of the founders of the SPWC in 1804, and the first fully to exploit the market thus created, showing up to 60 watercolours in a single year. He codified his approach to composition in his *Treatise on the principles of landscape drawing*, published 1816–18. Despite being highly sought after as a teacher, though in the latter part of his life more by amateurs than aspiring professionals, Varley was permanently short of money and was more than once imprisoned for debt. His interest in astrology and other occult sciences brought him into a creative relationship with William Blake, who drew the *Visionary heads* and painted the *Ghost of a flea* for him.

This watercolour is likely to be based on a sketch by John Rennie (1794–1874), who made a lengthy tour of Europe, which extended to Greece and also to Turkey and Egypt in 1819–21.[1238] Rennie was the son of engineer John Rennie (1761–1821), builder of Southwark and Waterloo bridges in London and the aqueduct at Lancaster (see pp. 193–94), and designer of London Bridge, work on which was to be undertaken by the son after his death. Construction began in 1824; on its completion in 1831, Rennie was knighted. 1824 was also the year in which Varley exhibited at the SPWC a number of watercolours 'From a sketch by J. Rennie, Esq.'[1239] A further group followed in 1825, including (cat. 141), *View in Switzerland*, which may well be LL 3442. It was accompanied by (cat. 225), *View of Pisa*. A view of the Italian town, inscribed on the back from a sketch by J. Rennie Esq and also dated 1824 was sold at Sotheby's, 26 June 1980 (lot 73).

During the second and third decades of the nineteenth century, Varley often exhibited watercolours based on the sketches of travelling amateurs. He never travelled abroad himself, and these subjects allowed him to extend his range at a time when foreign travel was a major pursuit of the leisured classes. All of the amateurs thus associated with Varley were men, several in the military; at a time of enormous expansion in the ranks of lady amateurs, Varley may also have wanted to assert the value of drawing as more than a purely leisure activity, and suggest his willingness and experience in teaching gentlemen as well as lady pupils.

TW

### Harlech Castle, North Wales

LL 3884 (WHL 201, H 190)

Watercolour with gouache and gum arabic, with scratching out and stopping out on wove paper
12.7 x 18.9 cm
Date: probably later 1820s

Prov: bt. from James Orrock by Lever, 1912[1240]

Exh: London, Earl's Court, *Victorian Era Exhibition*, 1897 (cat. 250)

Lit: Adrian Bury, *John Varley of the Old Society* (Leigh-on-Sea, 1946), pl. 2; C. M. Kauffmann, *John Varley 1778–1842* (London, 1984), p. 160

Varley made a tour of North Wales in the summer of 1802, accompanied by his brother Cornelius and the architect Thomas Webster.[1241] A drawing of Harlech Castle by Cornelius dated August 1802 was made just beneath the walls, looking away to the coast as it extends to the south.[1242] John Varley's treatment in LL 3884 views the building from the other direction, with the Snowdon range to the north. It presumably corresponded in some respects with a watercolour he exhibited at the Royal Academy in 1803, no. 560, *View of Harlech Castle, with Snowdon*. Over the course of his career Varley exhibited more than 20 further variations on this subject. A version in the Victoria & Albert Museum has the same frame of trees, with a central clump and pool of water with cattle in the foreground.[1243] With its brilliant colours of green and yellow as well as blue, the Victoria & Albert Museum's version is probably a work of around 1820, or the decade following, though caution is always necessary when dating watercolours by Varley. LL 3884, with its slightly more muted palette, extensive use of stopping out, and displacement of the trees to confine the castle more tightly to the right third of the composition, has much in common with a version of the subject in the National Museum of Wales.[1244] These are more likely to date from nearer to 1830, when Varley's treatment of foliage, in particular, was often heavily textured and sculptural, achieved through a succession of lifting and layering techniques.

Harlech Castle was built between 1283 and 1289 as one of a string of fourteen strongholds ordered by Edward I to maintain his dominance of the Welsh. The castles at Conway and Caernarvon, on similarly strategic coastal locations, were commenced at the same time. It was besieged for a final time by the

1235 1912 Inventory.

1236 This exhibition is cited in the LLAG files, but there is no record of it in Eton College's archives. The exhibition may have been held in the Drawing Schools (the school's art department) but it is not recorded in the *Eton Chronicle* (the school's magazine) for 1933 . I am grateful to Penny Hatfield, Eton College's archivist, for providing this information.

1237 This reference is cited in the LLAG files. It has not been possible to check this as there does not appear to have been a catalogue for this exhibition. Information supplied by Tom Perrett, Cecil Higgins Art Gallery, Bedford, verbally, March 2009.

1238 Andrew Saint, 'Rennie, John (1794–1874)', *ODNB*, vol. 46, pp. 486–87.

1239 C. M. Kauffmann, *John Varley 1778–1842* (London, 1984), pp. 81–82.

1240 1912 Inventory.

1241 Kauffmann, *John Varley*, p. 15. On 5 June Webster had been a visitor at a meeting of the Sketching Society attended by Varley, when Cotman presided; see S. D. Kitson, *The Life of John Sell Cotman* (London, 1937), p. 33.

1242 *Cornelius Varley: The Art of Observation* (exh. cat., London, Lowell Libson, 2005), pp. 76–77 (cat. 12).

1243 Victoria & Albert Museum, no. 1735-1900; Kauffmann, *John Varley*, p. 137 (cat. 36).

1244 *A Picturesque tour through Wales 1675–1855* (exh. cat., Gifu, Japan, The Museum of Fine Arts, 1998), pp. 115–16 (cat. 51).

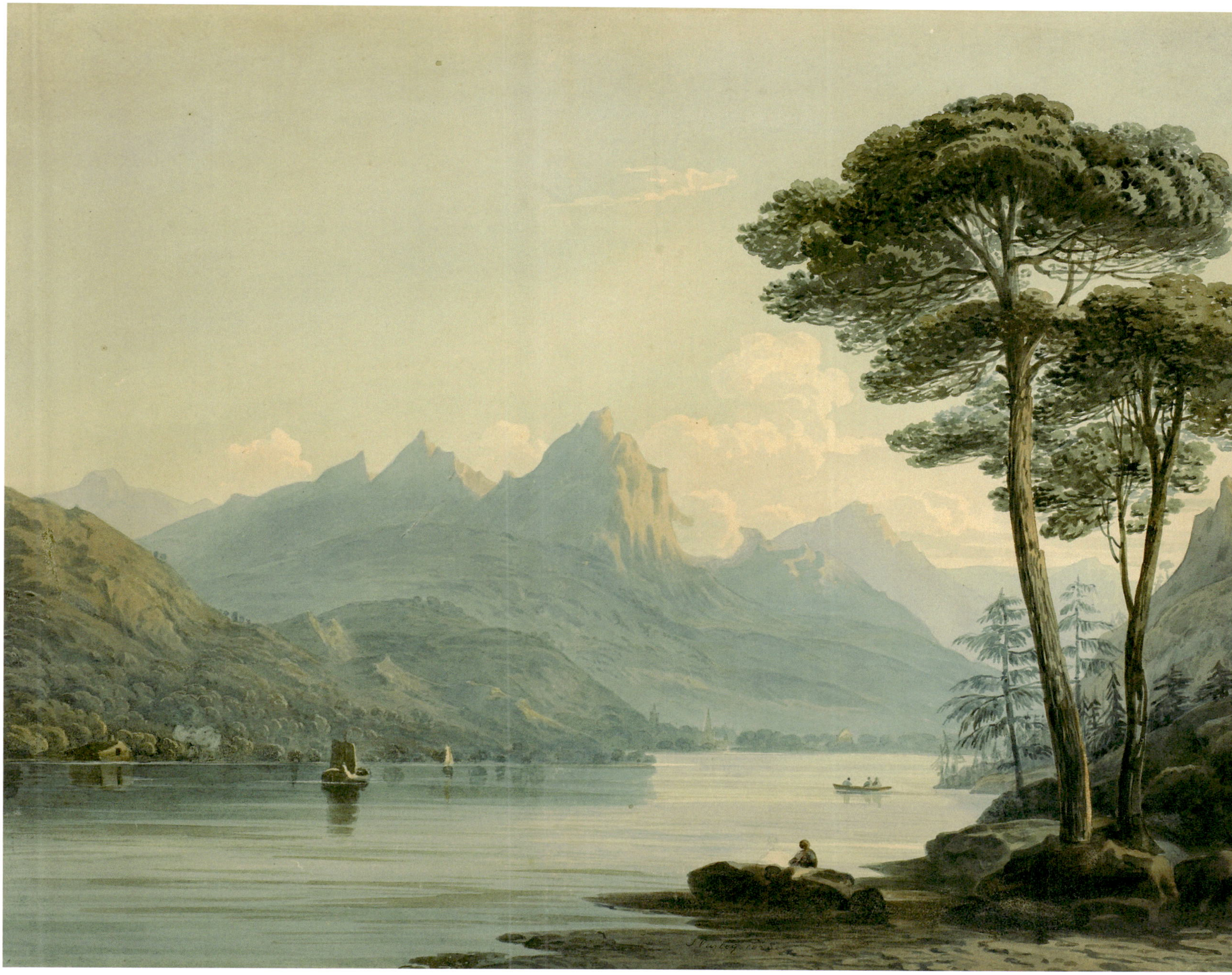

LL 3442

LL 3884

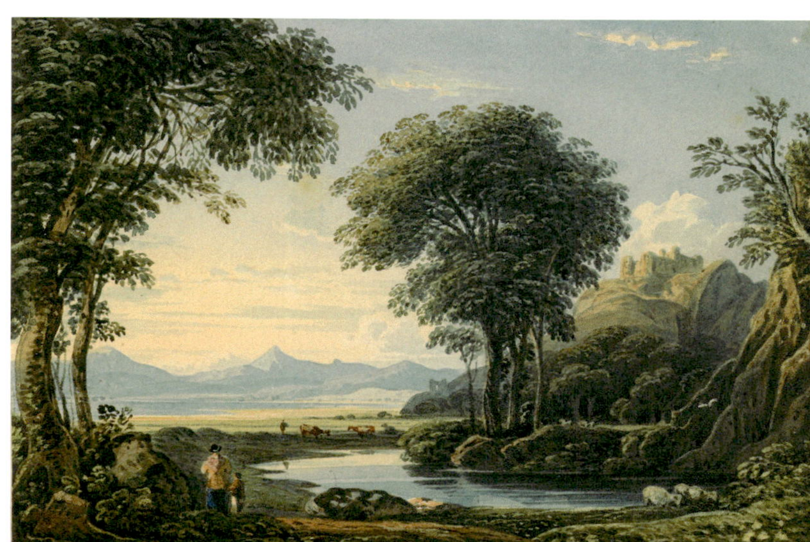

parliamentarians in 1646–47; the surrender on 15 March 1647 of the small royalist force effectively marked the end of the English Civil War.[1245] TW

1245 Arnold Taylor, *Harlech Castle* (Cardiff, 1980, 2nd rev. edn, 1988), pp. 5–13.

## 'JOHN VARLEY'

**Landscape with Bridge and Cattle**
LL 3883 (WHL 755, HH 378)

Watercolour and gouache with scratching out on wove paper
9 x 15 cm (sight)
Date: c. 1820–50

Prov: bt. from James Orrock by Lever, 1910[1246]

This landscape seems to depict an English scene, but one composed in the manner of Claude Lorrain, and bathed in a soft, warm light. John Varley was a lifelong admirer of Claude, but the variety of touch and the richly textured surface of this watercolour are not typical of his style at any period of his career. There is a sensitivity in the way the light bathes and dissolves the distances and catches sharp highlights in the foreground which are not consistent with Varley's interests, which lay much more in the direction of composition. This watercolour may be a more mature work of an artist who came under Varley's influence, but outgrew it, such as William Havell (1782–1857), much of whose later work is still unidentified.[1247]
TW

1246 1910 Inventory, p. 49, titled *A Landscape with bridge and cattle, mountains in distance*, valued at £10.
1247 *William Havell 1782–1857* (exh. cat., London, Spink, 1981), pp. 23–24.

LL 3883

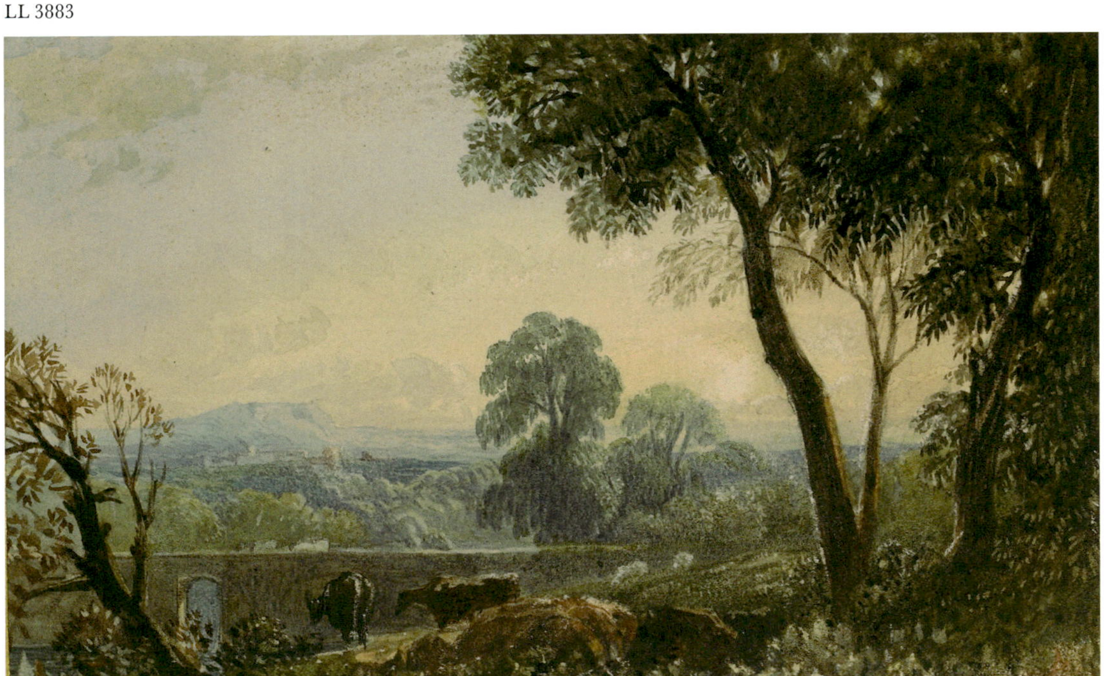

## SYDNEY CURNOW VOSPER

1866 East Stonehouse, Plymouth–1942 Shaldon, Devon

**Salem**
LL 3446 (WHL 1500, TM 81)

Watercolour on paper
71.1 x 73.7 cm (sight)
Date: 1908

Inscr: S. CURNOW VOSPER (watercolour, bottom left)

Prov: bt. from the artist at the Royal Society of Painters in Water-Colours, 15 June 1909 (£105)[1248]

Exh: London, Royal Society of Painters in Water-Colours, 1909 (cat. 174); London, Victoria & Albert Museum, *Change and Decay: the Future of our Churches*, 1977 (cat. no. unknown)

Lit: Tal Williams, *Salem Y Llun a'r Llan Painting and Chapel* (Cyhoeddiadau Barddas, 1991)

Vosper was educated at King's College, Taunton, and Plymouth College. He trained as an architect for three years before leaving to study art in Paris at the Colarossi Academy. After three years he returned to London where he made a living doing illustration work while continuing to train as a watercolour artist. He later painted regularly in Brittany, the West Country and Wales. In 1902 he married Constance James, the daughter of a solicitor from Methyr Tydfil. His images of Wales often focus on the daily life of local people.

Vosper painted this image while visiting Llanbedr, near Harlech, North Wales in 1908, possibly during one of his many cycling tours. It shows the interior of the Baptist chapel Salem Cefncymerau, built in 1850. The church-goers are in quiet contemplation before the service begins. The clock shows it is just before ten o'clock. The elderly woman, arriving just in time for the service, walks towards her pew.

The artist asked people from the local area to sit for him, paying them sixpence per hour.[1249] Thirty years later, when describing the process of painting this picture, the artist was a little vague on the identity of his models but noted that, 'the one thing I do remember is how modest and how eager to help me everyone was, and how interested they were in the picture's progress'.[1250] The figures have been identified as, from left to right, Robert Williams, a carpenter; Laura Williams, a shopkeeper; Sian Owen; William Sion; Leusa Jones, a dummy used in place of Sian Owen when the artist was making lengthy studies of the paisley shawl; Evan Edward Lloyd aged 6; Mary Rowlands and Owen Sion.[1251] Vosper made mostly individual studies of these characters. The women all wear traditional Welsh dress with

1248 LLAG files: invoice.
1249 Einion Evans, 'The Story of Mr. Curnow Vosper's Picture', *Y Fordd Gron* (April 1933), p. 125.
1250 Ibid.
1251 The sitters are described in detail in Tal Williams, *Salem Y Llun a'r Llan Painting and Chapel* (Cyhoeddiadau Barddas, 1991), pp. 25–33.

the distinctive steeple hats. In fact all the women modelled in the same steeple hat and cap, which belonged to the mother of Mary Rowlands. The shawl was borrowed from Mrs Williams of the Vicarage, Harlech.[1252] Vosper found it difficult to paint this garment accurately:

> I remember I had trouble with the shawl, as every moment the old woman would alter the folds of the shawl and I had to begin all over. Finally I had to get a lay figure from London Town and pin the shawl to it and stick it up in the chapel, but I dared not ask the minister if I could do this. The lay figure went by the name of Eliza Jones. She had to be cleared out for the Wednesday eve service and on Saturdays for the Sunday services.[1253]

The shawl has been the focus of much discussion. It has been suggested that an image of the Devil's face is hidden among its folds and pattern at the right as we look at the picture. Indeed some descriptions of this imagery go into considerable detail.[1254] But it is clear that the artist never intended his work to have some secret message about the omnipresence of evil. Understandable frustration about this 'myth' surfaces in Vosper's letter to the curator of the Lady Lever Art Gallery in 1940: 'There has been quite a lot of correspondence from time to time in Welsh papers, some accusing me of having put the Devil in the picture; in fact the Editor of *Cymro* wrote and asked if this was deliberate on my part, of course it was not!'[1255] The picture was purchased by Lever in 1909 to use as a promotional print for Sunlight Soap. The image had a mass circulation, which has no doubt contributed to its iconic status. Vosper was obviously unaware that his work was to be used in this way as his son's recollections suggest:

> Whether Lord Leverhulme realised the commercial possibilities of the picture before or after the purchase - we shall never know ... but about six months later my father happened to enter a little village shop in North Wales. He was amazed to see a very good coloured reproduction of *Salem* in the room behind the shop. As calmly as he could he asked the old lady where she had got hold of such a nice picture. 'Oh', she replied excitedly, 'the Lever salesman was round last week and anybody who buys 7lbs of soap at one time gets one of those.'[1256]

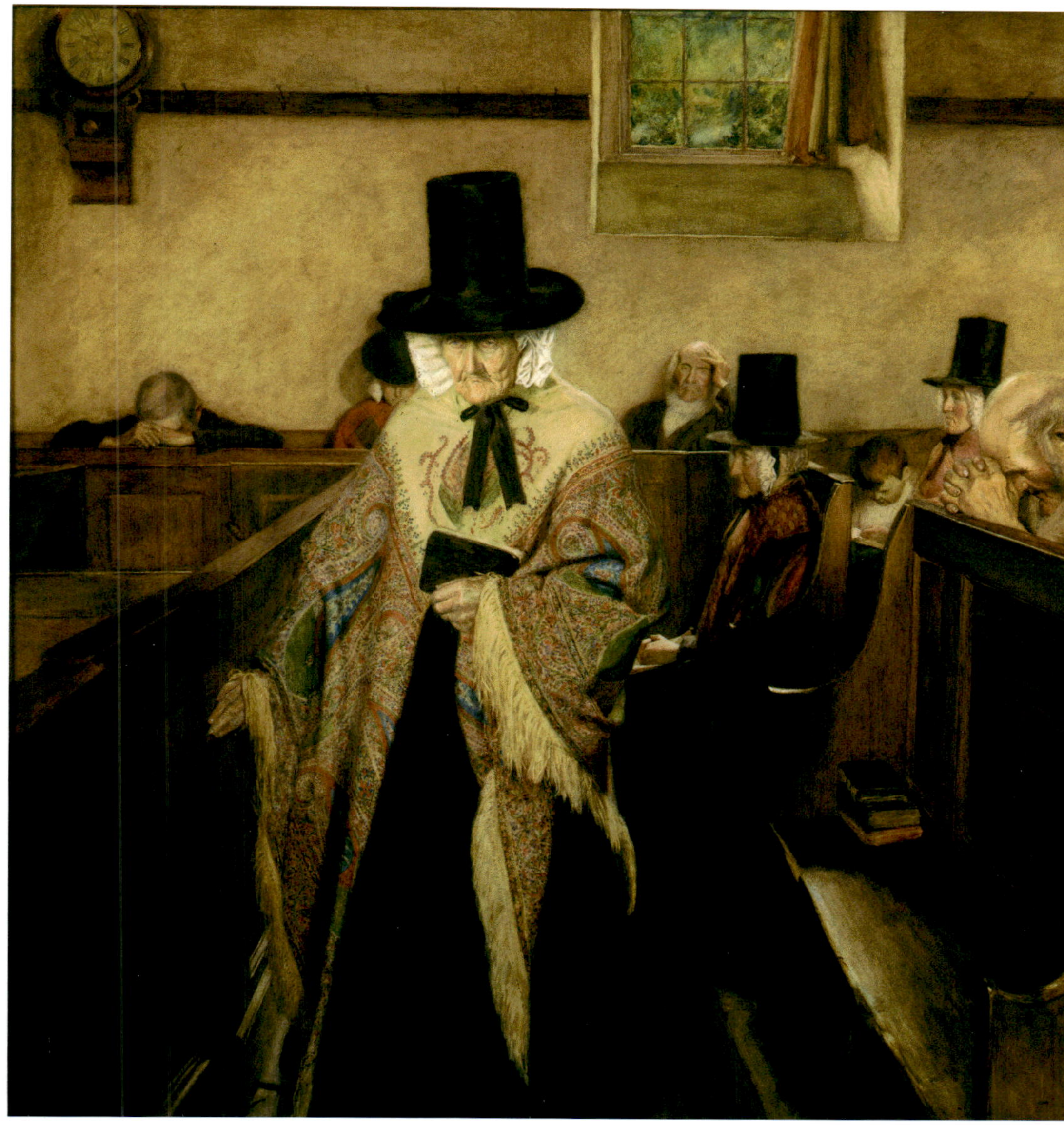

LL 3446

The popularity of the picture was perpetuated by further reproductions. In 1937 Ifan ab Owen Edwards purchased large numbers of prints to distribute through the Urdd Gobaith Cymru - the Welsh League of Youth. *Salem* was also reproduced as the cover of the Cymru Fydd Calendar in 1950, 1956 and 1957. But the true reason for the picture's huge popularity is bound up with feelings of nationality and historicism. For many Welsh people it has become a symbol of Welshness. In a single image Vosper has represented pre-industrial 'old Wales', faith and the family (the latter represented by the matriarchal figure of Sian Owen).[1257] The popularity of the work is such that it has even been immortalised in poetry.[1258]

There is a second, half-size version of this subject on loan to the National Museum of Wales[1259] and a preparatory drawing for the figure of Sian Owen in Cyfartha Castle Museum and Art Gallery. A related work, *Market Day in Old Wales*, also in the National Museum of Wales, includes the same principal sitter Sian Owen.
SP

1252 Ibid.
1253 LLAG files: letter from the artist to the Gallery's curator S. L. Davison, 12 March 1940.
1254 Williams, *Salem Y Llun*, p. 15.
1255 LLAG files: letter from the artist to the Gallery's curator S. L. Davison, 12 March 1940.
1256 LLAG files: copy of letter from D. F. C. Vosper, 21 December 1956, addressed to the Editor of the *Western Mail*.
1257 See Williams, *Salem Y Llun*, p. 19.
1258 For example *Salem* by T. Rowland Hughes.
1259 This smaller version, from a private collection, was commissioned by Frank James, brother-in-law of the artist. Some details are different: the sitter Owen Sion is missing as are the clock and clothes rail on the back wall.

## WILLIAM WALCOT

1874 Lutsdorf, near Odessa, Russia–1943 Hurstpierpoint, West Sussex

### The Palace of Justice, Brussels

LL 3890 (WHL 2667)

Watercolour over pencil, with touches of gouache, gum arabic and stopping out on paper
90.4 x 70.5 cm
Date: 1914

Inscr: W. WALCOT 1914 (green ink, lower right)

Prov: bt. from the Maddox Street Galleries, London, by Lever, 1915 (£60)[1260]

Exh: London, Maddox Street Galleries, *Artists' War Relief Exhibition of The Royal Institute of British Architects and The Imperial Arts League*, 1915 (cat. 81)

1260 LLAG files: the price asked for LL 3890 is recorded in the Maddox Street Galleries' catalogue as £105. The price paid is recorded on the accession card for LL 3890. No invoice can be located.

LL 3890

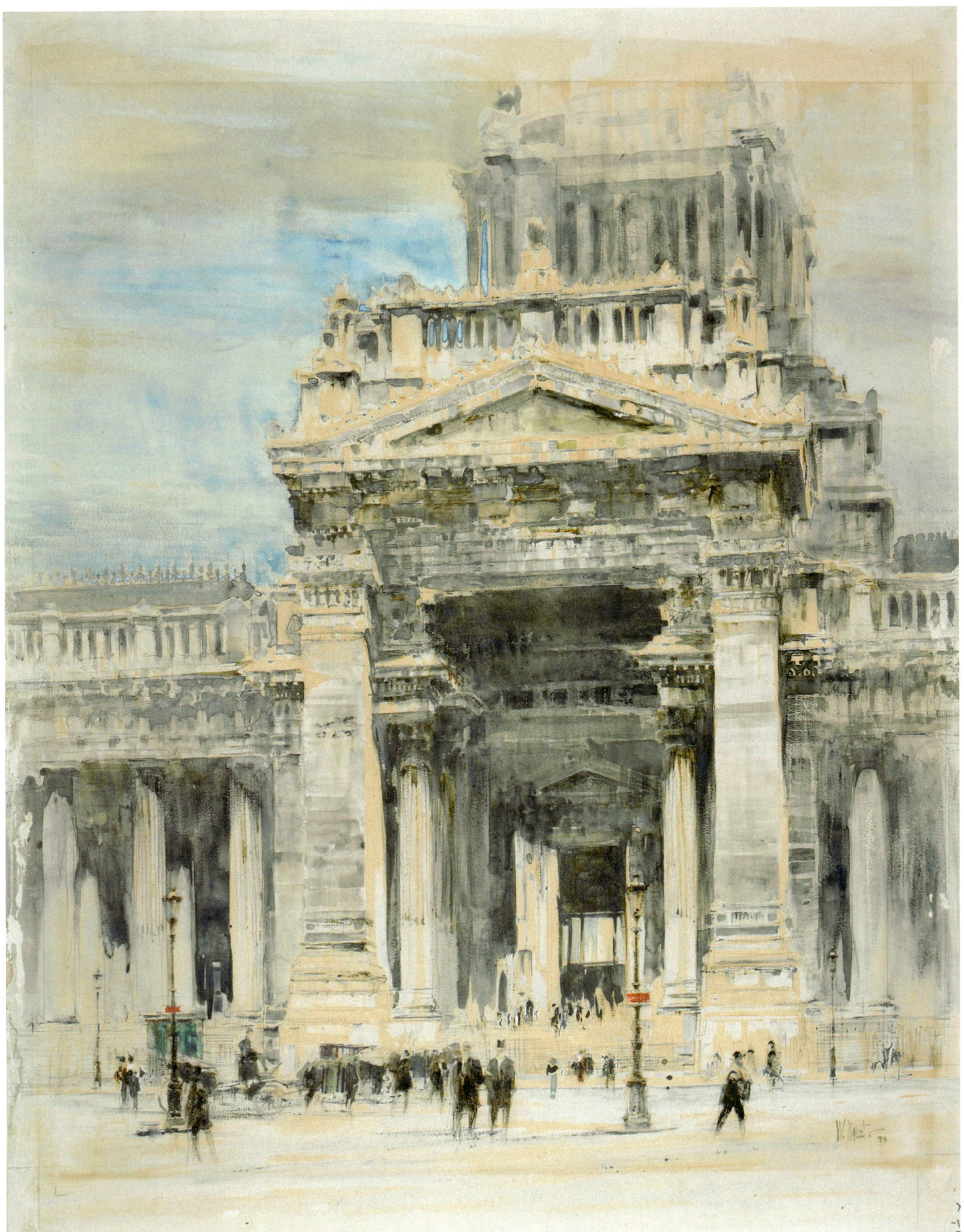

William Walcot's father was an English businessman and his mother the daughter of a Russian landowner. He studied architecture at the Imperial Academy of Fine Arts, St Petersburg, and subsequently practised briefly as an architect in Moscow, designing the Hotel Metropol (1898–1902). He settled in London from 1907, where he was celebrated for his main activity as an architectural draughtsman, producing presentation watercolours for architects to show to their clients. He was also a successful printmaker, noted for his etched modern cityscapes and his imaginative reconstructions of daily life in the temples and palaces of the ancient world. In 1913 Walcot became a member of the Royal Society of British Artists and in 1916 an associate of the Royal Society of Painter-Etchers and Engravers. In 1922 he was elected a fellow of the Royal Institute of British Architects.

LL 3890 depicts the entrance to the Palace of Justice, Brussels, built between 1866 and 1883 and designed by architect Joseph Poelaert (1817–79). The watercolour may have been a commission; Walcot's work in all media became highly sought after in the early 1900s, with The Fine Art Society, his agents, sending him to Rome and Venice between c. 1908 and 1928 to produce work to be sold at their exhibitions. The Lady Lever work, as with all Walcot's watercolours, contrasts with the precise linear style of his prints; the watercolours are impressionistic in approach, the paint is laid on in broad areas of colour, with detail being sacrificed to the larger effect. Lever also owned at least four etchings of imaginary classical scenes by Walcot, purchased from the Fine Art Society in 1915.[1261]

1261 WHL 2202-06. These were at Thornton Manor until sold in 2001. See Leverhulme Collection sale, Thornton Manor, Sotheby's, 26–28 June 2001 (lots 463, 464, 468 and 470).

## FREDERICK WALKER
1840 London–1875 St Fillans, Perthshire

**Fisherman and Boy**
LL 3445 (WHL 4101)

Watercolour with extra gum arabic and gouache over pencil, on wove paper laid down on board
52.2 x 39.2 cm (sight)
Date: 1866

Inscr: F W (watercolour, lower right)

Prov: William Leech, 1876;[1262] his sale, Christie's, 21 May 1887 (lot 95); bt. by Agnew's (£451 10s); [?] George James, 1896; Dame Amy Tate, 1920; her house sale, Streatham, 17 February 1920 (lot 430A) (560 gns);[1263] bt. by Gooden and Fox for Lever (£617 8s)

Exh: London, SPWC, 1867 (cat. 245); London, Deschamps' Gallery, *Walker Memorial Exhibition*, 1876 (cat. 47)

Lit: J. G. Marks, *Life and Letters of Frederick Walker, A.R.A.* (London and New York, 1896), pp. 81–88

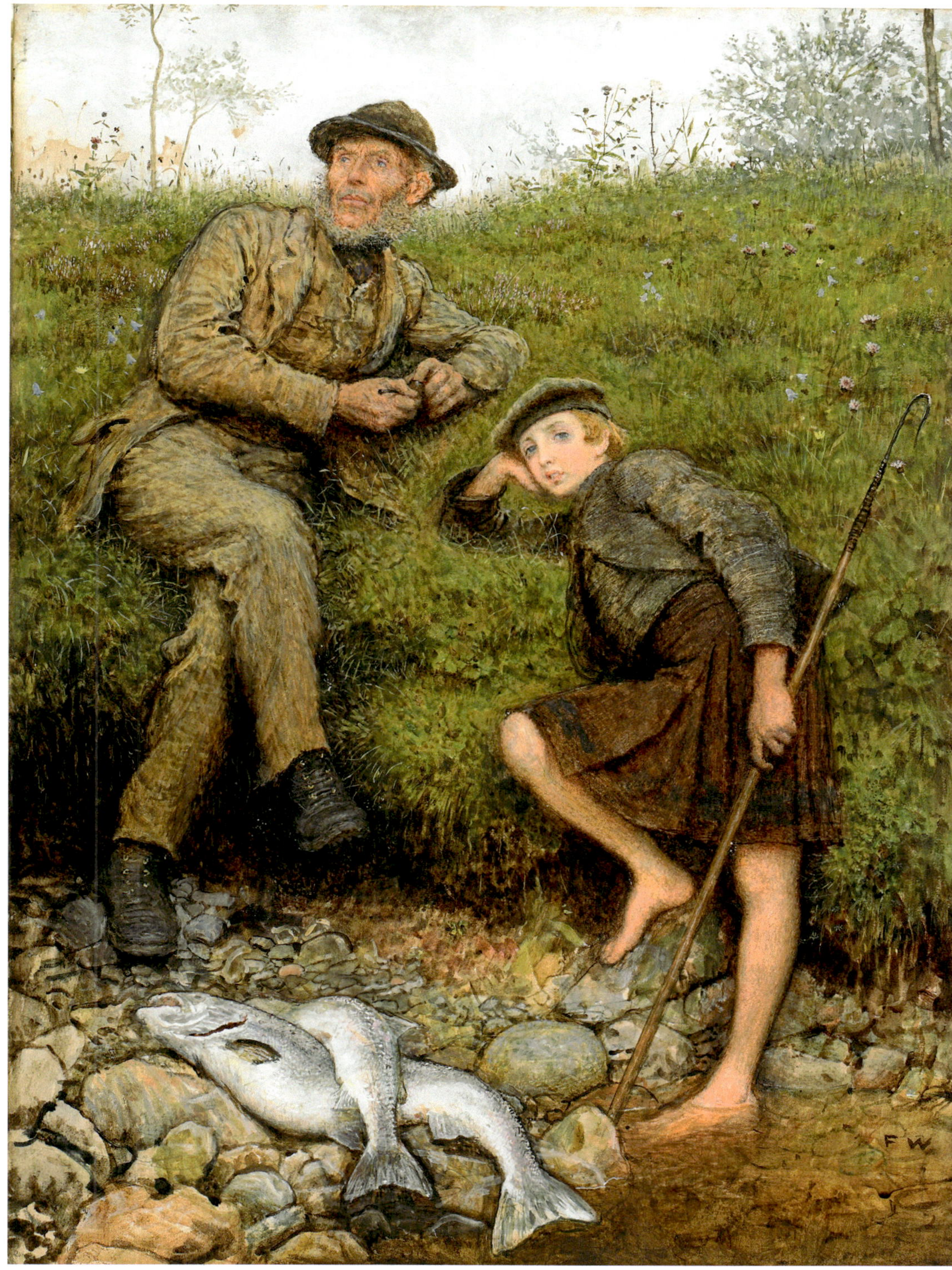

LL 3445

Walker gained his artistic training by drawing intensively from the antique in the British Museum and from life classes at Leigh's School. He began his career in the 1860s as an illustrator, making drawings for magazines including *Cornhill*, *Good Words* and *Once a Week*. As a painter in watercolours and oils, Walker began to enjoy success from about 1863 onwards. He was one of a number of artists, including John William North and George John Pinwell (see pp. 152–54), whose figurative and mainly rustic subject-matter showed a concern for a more poetic and idealised art rather than the naturalism pioneered by the Pre-Raphaelites. Walker's watercolours were well received at the SPWC and he was elected associate in 1864 and member in 1866.

LL 3445 dates from 1866, when Walker had already established himself as a watercolourist of some note. In the summer of that year he went on one of the first of several visits to the home of his friend, the artist Richard Ansdell, on the river Spean in the highlands of Scotland. Here, Walker was initiated into the pleasures of salmon fishing and his letters that summer are filled with excitement about the sublime Scottish landscape.[1264] On 12 August he wrote to his brother, describing the two characters who were later to become the subject of the Lady Lever watercolour: 'The head keeper lives in a cottage behind the house, and is a tall, well-made fellow; always wears rough knickerbocks. He has two boys, the elder with a face perfectly beautiful – would be on a girl's shoulders. He is very tall, and always goes about in a kilt, without shoes and stockings.'[1265] Later that month Walker began a study of this boy although he left it unfinished. However, by the autumn of 1866 his letters describe how he had decided to 'raise a good thing out of the ashes' and had embarked on a watercolour of the father and son, finishing the work in London in October of that year.[1266]

LL 3445 was exhibited at the SPWC in 1867, where one reviewer, Mr Hodgson, described it as an 'exquisite drawing' and a 'gem'.[1267] It is typical of Walker's watercolours with its liberal use of Chinese white to create a heavily worked stippling effect, a technique influenced by the watercolours of William Henry Hunt (see pp. 120–27) and Myles Birket Foster (see pp. 98–99).

1262 LLAG files: note on accession card.
1263 LLAG files: invoice.
1264 See, for example, the letter dated 5 August 1866 to his mother, in J. G. Marks, *Life and Letters of Frederick Walker, A.R.A.* (London and New York, 1896), pp. 83–84.
1265 Ibid., pp. 84–85.
1266 Ibid., pp. 86–88.
1267 Quoted in ibid., p. 86.

## Study for *The Harbour of Refuge*
LL 3443 (WHL 4648)

Watercolour, gum arabic and gouache on wove paper
25 x 41.5 cm
Date: 1871–72

Inscr: F W (watercolour, lower left)

Prov: artist's sale, Christie's, 17 July 1875 ([?] lot 91); bt. by Agnew's (£22 1s);[1268] R. Dunthorne and Son; Christie's, 17 May 1923 (lot 62); bt. by Gooden and Fox (£28 7s) for Lever (£29 1s)

Exh: Brisbane, Queensland Art Gallery and tour of Australia and New Zealand, *Exhibition of British Watercolours 1850–1914*, organised by the Empire Art Loan Exhibitions Society, 1952–53 (cat. 100)

This work is one of several known preliminary studies for Walker's celebrated painting *The Harbour of Refuge* (Tate, fig. 57), which was exhibited at the Royal Academy in 1872.[1269] The painting's subject, a group of elderly people in the grounds of an almshouse, is full of symbolism. One Victorian description of it was typical:

> It is not merely an almshouse with its few poor occupants. Youth and age, vigour and decrepitude, are placed in opposition one to the other. The health and bloom of the young girl, strong of frame, are fresh as the blooming may-tree opposite. She turns her eyes towards the vigorous young mower, and thinks, it may be, as she gives her support to the bowed and aged inmate who leans upon her arm, of that reaper whose name is Death. The swing of the scythe is heard, and the gentle murmur of engaging talk by the monument, where welcome news to cheer the monotony of the day has just arrived; and the sunset, against which the old roofs darken and the last lights play, means too the sunset of life for the peaceful souls who have found this harbour of refuge. To what higher teaching could painting be put?[1270]

The painting was well received when it was shown at the Royal Academy, *The Times* describing it as 'most exquisite and complete', and the *Pall Mall Gazette* as a 'powerful and elevated piece of colour and design'.[1271]

Walker may have had the initial idea for part of the composition of the painting in 1870. Early that year he was reported to have seen 'one Sunday in church, a group of old, bent labourers on a long bench in front of the pulpit, reposing in the gleams of sunlight that lightened the gloom of the place'.[1272] It was from this motif that the oil painting was developed. Over the next year Walker struggled to find a backdrop for his figures, although by July 1871 he was reported to be making trips to Bray, near Maidenhead, Berkshire, whose almshouses provided the setting for the painting.[1273]

As a study for the final composition LL 3443 closely resembles the painting. It incorporates the changes Walker had decided to make to the composition in the interval since making an earlier watercolour (Tate, fig. 58).[1274] In LL 3443 Walker has added a statue of the founder of the almshouses, reported to be loosely based on a statue of Charles II in period dress once in Soho Square, London.[1275] He has also moved the figures of the old men further back, to beside the founder's statue, replacing them in the foreground with the reaper with the scythe. On the left-hand side of the sketch, the stoop of the elder woman has become more emphasised and the dress and aspect of the young girl has been idealised, closely resembling the painting. The Lady Lever sketch must have been made some time between July 1871 (when Walker was making sketches of the almshouses) and early 1872 when for the first three months of that year he worked on the final painting.[1276]

F. W. Fox of Gooden and Fox, who sold the work to Lever, allegedly thought that LL 3443 'was left as a very slight outline sketch and [that] somebody has since worked on it'.[1277] He also suggested that the work may have been finished by Walker's close friend John William North.[1278] Both these suggestions are unlikely to be right. It is true that LL 3443 is notable for its broad style in comparison to the highly finished technique of Walker's earlier watercolour *Fisherman and Boy* (above), but this may be explained by the fact that the later work was not intended for exhibition, as well as by changes in Walker's later watercolour style.

In addition to the Lady Lever and Tate works, Walker made at least two other sketches for the painting.[1279] He also made a three-foot long watercolour replica of the painting which was completed in 1873 and exhibited at the SPWC in the same year.[1280] The painting was engraved by J.M. Johnstone[1281] and Robert Walker Macbeth.[1282]

---

1268 Lot 91 is titled in the sale catalogue *Study for 'The Harbour of Refuge'*. Another possibility is lot 102, *The Harbour of Refuge – the original design*, bt. by Agnew's (£210); this, however, seems more likely to be the earlier watercolour in the Tate (see n. 1274).

1269 *The Harbour of Refuge*, oil on canvas, 117 x 197.5 cm, Tate (N01391), presented by Sir William Agnew to the National Gallery, 1893, transferred to the Tate 1897. For more details on the evolution of this painting, see Marks, *Life and Letters of Frederick Walker*, pp. 208, 227, 231, 237–38, 240–45. For an interpretation of the painting see Julian Treuherz, *Hard Times: Social Realism in Victorian art* (exh. cat., Manchester, Manchester City Art Gallery and New Haven, Yale Center for British Art, 1987–88), pp. 51–52.

1270 A. G. Temple, *Painting in the Queen's Reign* (London, 1896), pp. 251–52, quoted in Treuherz, *Hard Times*, p. 51.

1271 Marks, *Life and Letters of Frederick Walker*, p. 241.

1272 Ibid., p. 238.

1273 Ibid., p. 231.

1274 Watercolour on paper, 24.8 x 45.4 cm, Tate (N02762), bequeathed by Sir William Agnew 1911.

1275 Marks, *Life and Letters of Frederick Walker*, pp. 240–41.

1276 Ibid., p. 237.

1277 LLAG files: curatorial note whose source is not specified.

1278 LLAG files: curatorial note whose source is not specified.

1279 A sketch for the figures on the terrace is listed by Marks, *Life and Letters of Frederick Walker*, p. 309; there is also a watercolour for the composition in the collection of Lee Edwards, New York.

1280 Sold at Christie's, 13 March 1973 (lot 128); its location is now unknown.

1281 Illus. *The Magazine of Art* (1894), p. 13.

1282 See *The Art Journal* (1893), p. 278.

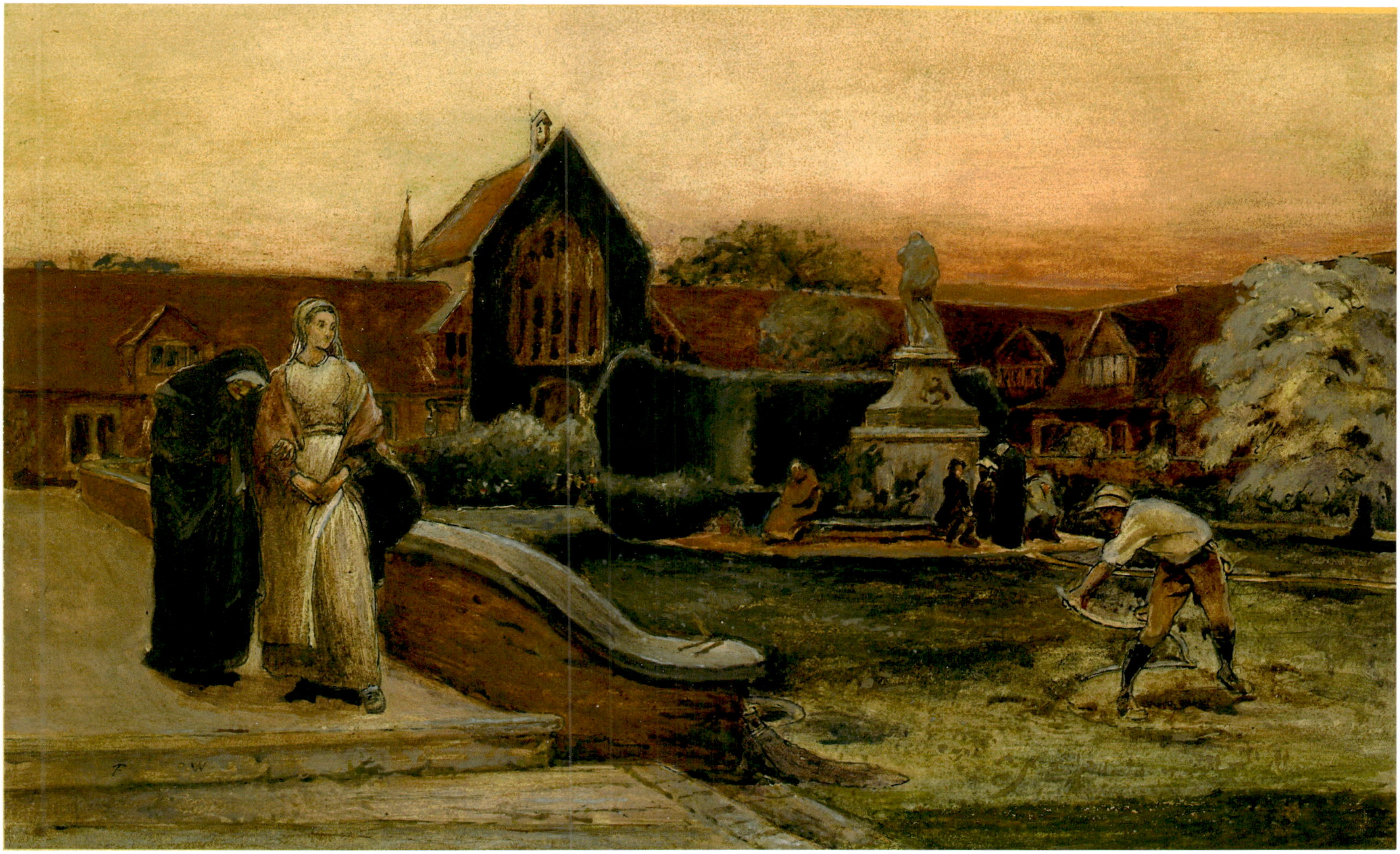

LL 3443

fig. 57. Frederick Walker, *The Harbour of Refuge*, 1871–72, oil on canvas, 117 x 197.5 cm, © Tate, London, 2007

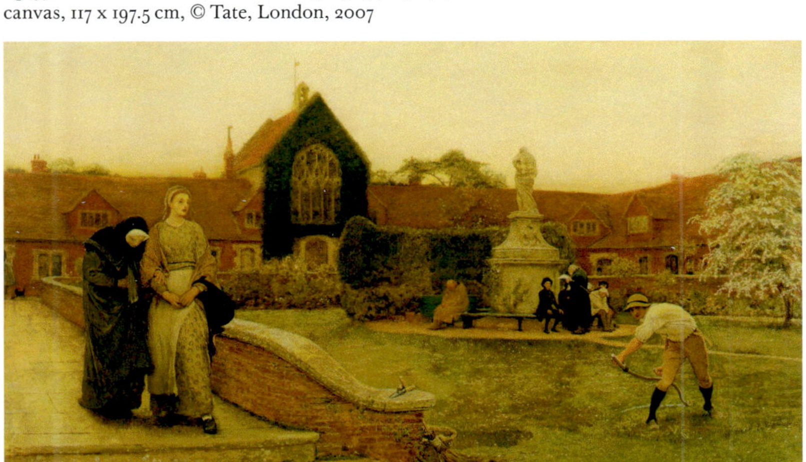

fig. 58. Frederick Walker, Study for *The Harbour of Refuge*, 1870–71, watercolour and gouache over pencil on paper, 24.8 x 45.4 cm, © Tate, London, 2007

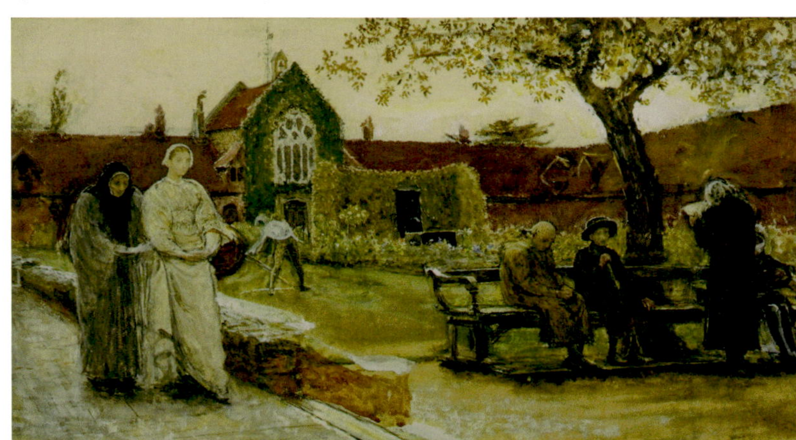

## The Fishmonger's Shop
LL 3444 (WHL 3690)

Watercolour and gum arabic, with touches of gouache and scratching out on wove paper
37.5 x 59.1 cm
Date: 1872

Prov: bt. from the artist by Frederick Lehmann, 1872 (600 gns);[1283] his sale, Christie's, 19 March 1892 (lot 801); bt. by J. & W. Vokins (600 gns); Stephen G. Holland, 1896; his sale, Christie's, 26 June 1908 (lot 269); bt. by Joseph Beecham (1,600 gns);[1284] his sale, Christie's, 29 November 1918 (lot 89); bt. by Gooden and Fox (1,000 gns) for Lever, November 1918 (£1,076 5s)[1285]

Exh: London, SPWC, *Winter Exhibition*, 1872–73 (cat. 330); London, Deschamps' Gallery, *Walker Memorial Exhibition*, 1876 (cat. 62); Paris, *Exposition Universelle Internationale*, 1878 (cat. 144); London, Burlington House, *Exhibition of Works by the Old Masters, and by Deceased Masters of the British School; including a Collection of Watercolour Drawings illustrating the Progress of the Art of Watercolour in England*, 1891 (cat. 159); London, Burlington House, *Exhibition of Works by British Artists Deceased since 1850*, 1901 (cat. 157); Perth, Art Gallery of Western Australia and Australian tour, *Exhibition of Early British Water-colours*, organised by the Empire Art Loans Exhibition Society, 1948–49 (cat. 157); China and East Berlin, British-China Friendship Association, *British Watercolour Painting during Three Centuries*, 1963 (cat. 112)

Lit: C. Phillips, *Frederick Walker and his works* (London, 1894), pp. 59–61; J. G. Marks, *Life and Letters of Frederick Walker, A.R.A.* (London and New York, 1896), pp. 30, 252–54, 264, illus. p. 252; C. Newall, *Victorian Watercolours* (London, 1987), pp. 88–92, illus. p. 91

Walker seems to have been interested in the subject of the fishmonger some ten years before he painted the Lady Lever watercolour. In 1862 he made a drawing as part of a series to be engraved for the Dalziel brothers depicting a fishmonger at the door of a cottage, receiving payment from a little boy.[1286] However, it was not until 29 October 1872, following years developing his watercolour technique, that he wrote to his friend, the artist John William North: 'I'm working hard at a fishmonger's shop, with a great slab of fish and a fair buyer!'[1287] In LL 3444, the narrative centres on a lady dressed in Regency costume, deliberating over her choice of purchase at the fishmonger's, and a small boy on the left-hand side of the work playing with his hoop, while looking into the contents of the pot at his feet.

Walker always placed an emphasis on working directly from nature and a description survives of him drawing his sister Mary as the model for the female figure from the inside of his carriage parked outside a shop.[1288] It is likely that Walker used various locations in and around London to furnish him with the material for this image; one source suggested that the slab of fish was taken from a shop in Bond Street, and that a shop at Hampton Court may have inspired the highly decorative cornice and balustraded entablature.[1289] Another source claimed that the shop was based on one in Paddington.[1290] Two studies for the fish on the slab suggest the effort to which Walker went to depict details of the watercolour with accuracy (Courtauld Institute of Art Gallery, figs. 59, 60).[1291]

The work was hailed as a masterpiece when it was exhibited at the SPWC in 1872–73. The *Saturday Review*, despite taking exception to the subject-matter, wrote that 'by skilful art treatment, dependent on a harmony of colour, on balance of composition, on illusive realism, and on cunning dexterity of pencil, a perfect triumph is gained'.[1292] *The Times*'s reviewer commented on Walker's use of Regency costume, notably for the figures of the young lady and the boy. He wrote that through this 'he escaped from the familiarity which often jars with artistic association'.[1293] The *Athenaeum* reviewer described 'The showboard ... loaded with superbly painted fish of all kinds, of all degrees of lustre and colour, an aggregate of senses, the splendour of which has rarely been approached ... a little masterpiece of colour both local and general'.[1294] *The Times* made the favourable comparison with the more typical Dutch versions of such subjects: 'The grace of the woman and boy is so much thrown in by the painter beyond the suggestion of the fishmonger's shop and is just what we should not have had in a Dutch version of such a subject'.[1295] Nevertheless, the work had its critics, notably John Ruskin, whom *The Art Journal* reported as objecting to the drawing, 'but only because the labour spent on it would have painted twenty instructive studies of fish of their real size'.[1296] *The Art Journal* retorted: 'One can scarcely understand the consistency of the objection from a critic usually so exigeant after "delicate completion"'.[1297]

Walker repeated LL 3444 on a smaller scale in a drawing of 1873, which was not publicly exhibited during his lifetime but was shown in the *Memorial Exhibition* of 1876 (cat. 9).[1298] The work was engraved by Robert Walker Macbeth in 1886.[1299]

1283 Marks, *Life and Letters of Frederick Walker*, p. 253.
1284 *The Connoisseur*, vol. 39 (June 1914), p. 83.
1285 LLAG files: invoice.
1286 This connection is made by Marks, *Life and Letters of Frederick Walker*, p. 30. The Victoria & Albert Museum has an impression of the engraving as well as the original drawing on woodblock.
1287 Ibid., p. 252.
1288 Newall, *Victorian Watercolours*, p. 92.
1289 Marks, *Life and Letters of Frederick Walker*, p. 253.
1290 LLAG files: curatorial note that Henry Raeburn-Macbeth stated in 1933 that his brother Robert Walker Macbeth believed that this was the case.
1291 It is notable that most of the fish on the slab can be identified and therefore were probably studied from life. They have been identified by Rachel Porter of World Museum Liverpool as including the following: porcupine pufferfish (hanging from the balustrade), turbot, lobster, edible crab, sprat or sardines, mackerel, gurnard, plaice, mullet. The Courtauld's watercolour studies relate to the mackerel in the centre of the slab (fig. 59), and the turbot that hangs on a hook from a rail, alongside the exotic pufferfish (fig. 60); *Study of mackerel*, watercolour on paper, 8.2 x 14.6 cm, Robert Witt bequest, 1952; *Study of turbot*, watercolour on paper, 9.7 x 12.7 cm, Robert Witt bequest, 1952.
1292 Quoted by Marks, *Life and Letters of Frederick Walker*, p. 253.
1293 Ibid.
1294 Ibid.
1295 Ibid.
1296 *The Art Journal* (1876), p. 299.
1297 Ibid.
1298 Marks, *Life and Letters of Frederick Walker*, p. 272, believed this small *Fishmonger's Shop* to have been completed by June 1873. It was in the collection of John Knowles; sold Christie's, 19 May 1877 (lot 68 as *The Fish Shop*); location now unknown.
1299 Victoria & Albert Museum: artist's proof.

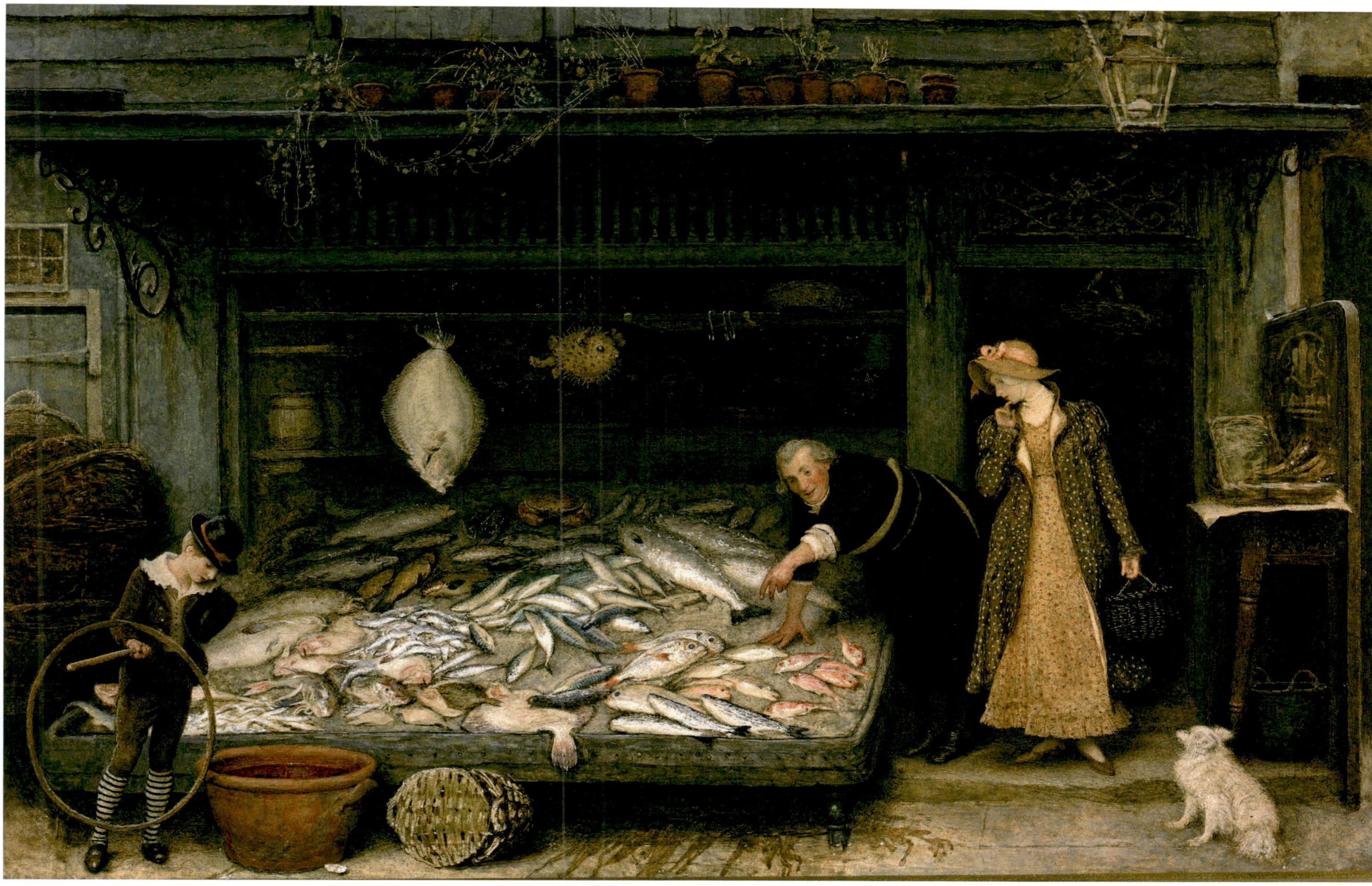

LL 3444

fig. 59. Frederick Walker, *Study of Mackerel*, c. 1872, watercolour on paper, 8.2 x 14.6 cm, Courtauld Institute of Art Gallery, London

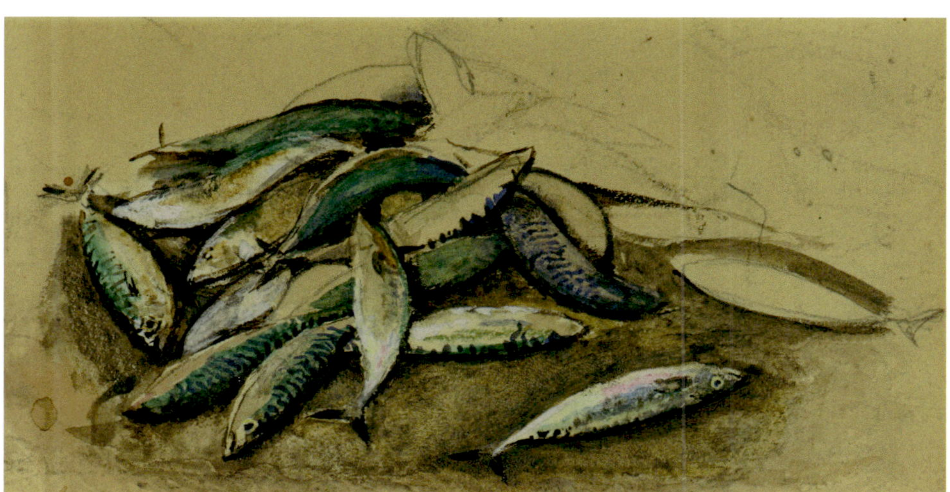

fig. 60. Frederick Walker, *Study of Turbot*, c. 1872, watercolour on paper, 9.7 x 12.7 cm, Courtauld Institute of Art Gallery, London

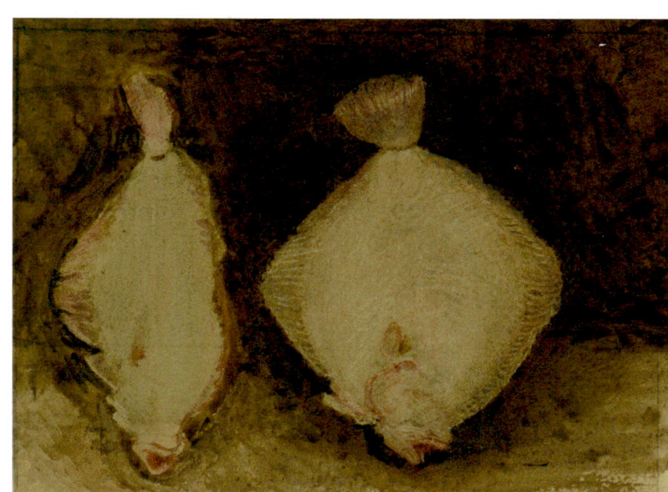

## FRANCIS WHEATLEY

1747 London–1801 London

### A Farmyard with Figures and Cattle[1300]

LL 3807 (WHL 3710)

Watercolour on wove paper
34.3 x 47.8 cm
Date: 1793

Inscr: F. Wheatley delt.1793 (watercolour, bottom left)

Prov: Pawsey and Payne; Christie's, 20 December 1918 (lot 10); bt. by Gooden and Fox (£36 15s) for Lever (£ 37 9s 6d)

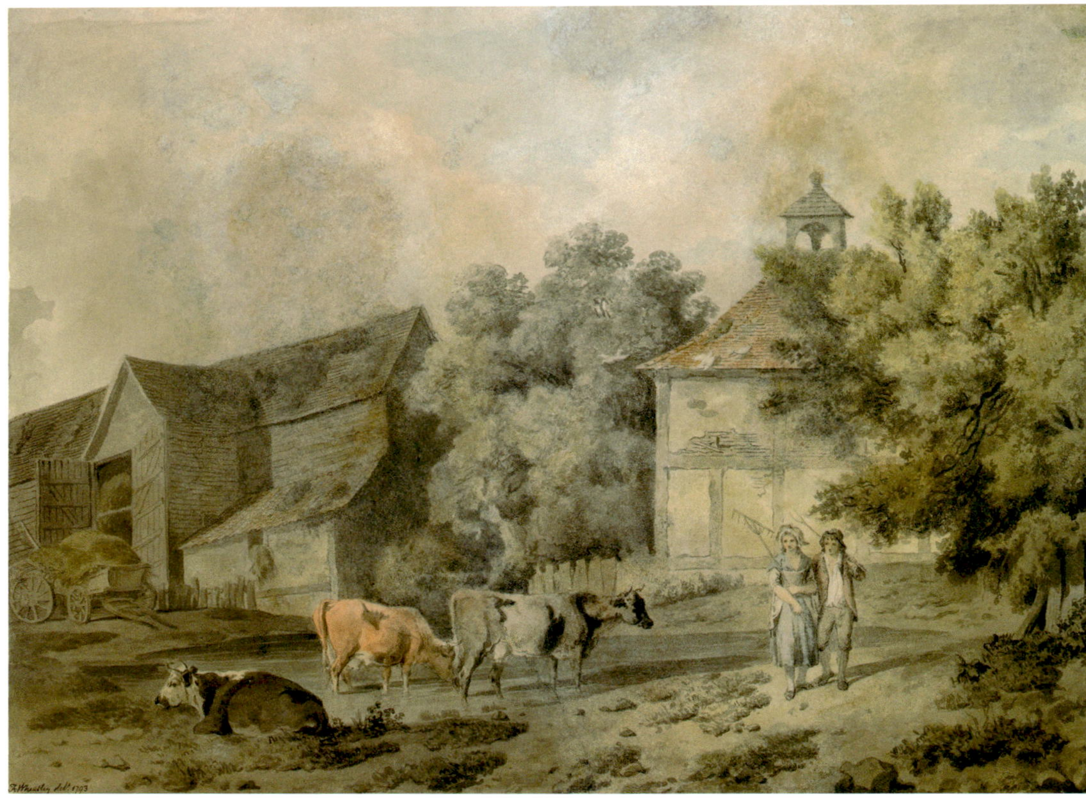

LL 3807

Wheatley studied at Shipley's drawing school and subsequently at the Royal Academy Schools and the Society of Artists. From 1774 he exhibited landscapes (and some portraits) at the Society of Artists and from 1778 at the Royal Academy. In 1779 he fled to Ireland to escape creditors, where he received commissions from aristocratic Irish families for large group portraits and informal conversation pieces. He returned to London at the end of 1783 and throughout the 1780s and early 1790s was engaged in producing a variety of compositions to be engraved: these included scenes from literature and contemporary poetry as well as fancy pictures. From 1793 Wheatley's series of *The Cries of London* was engraved and published in pairs. He was elected to membership of the Royal Academy in 1791. Wheatley's last years from 1796 onwards were a record of ill health and debt which affected the quality and quantity of his output.

LL 3807 is one of a number of watercolours by Wheatley from the 1790s where peasants are depicted alongside ramshackle cottages and farmyards – compare, for example, his *A farm on the outskirts of a village* (Christie's, 9 November 1976, lot 40). In the Lady Lever watercolour rural life is depicted in idyllic form; the cows that take centre stage are large in size, and the peasants are industrious (they carry farm tools) yet walk harmoniously side by side. Dated 1793, the work coincided with a period (c. 1790–1815) in which contemporary theorists of the Picturesque were advocating a return to older forms of rural life, at a time when these were felt to be threatened in the wake of agricultural revolution and industrialisation. In Wheatley's depiction of a farmyard, the decaying farm buildings embody elements of this Picturesque taste. For example, Uvedale Price, one of the main writers on this taste, described the Picturesque nature of 'hovels, cottages, mills and the insides of old barns'.[1301]

The Lady Lever drawing typifies Wheatley's skills as a draughtsman before his decline in the later 1790s. It is also an example of the change of style that occurred in his landscape watercolours following his return from Ireland. The use of outline in pen or pencil, which was so apparent in Wheatley's earlier watercolours, for example, his scenes of peasants and gypsies in Ireland produced during the 1780s (see, for example, *Palmerston Fair*, Huntington Art Collections, San Marino, and *Irish Fair Scene*, Birmingham Museums and Art Gallery, both dated 1782), has been softened. Unfortunately LL 3807 is in poor condition; its pigments have notably faded overall and there is evidence of retouching on the girl's clothes and also on the roofs of the farm buildings. There are also two substantial stain marks in the sky which appear to have been treated with chemicals.[1302]

1300 The title given in the WHL Inventory, p. 517.

1301 Uvedale Price, *Essay on the Picturesque* (London, 1810), p. 84 quoted by Ann Bermingham, *Landscape and Ideology: The English Rustic Tradition, 1740–1860* (London, 1987), p. 68.

1302 LLAG files: conservation report from Dr Plenderleith, British Museum, 29 July 1935.

## ATTRIBUTED TO CHARLES THOMAS WHEELER

1892 Codsall, Staffordshire -1974 Mayfield, Sussex

and

## ALFRED JAMES MUNNINGS

1875 Mendham, Suffolk-1959 Dedham, Essex

**Portrait of Alfred Munnings delivering a speech and Self-Portrait of Munnings painting in the open air**
LL 3990[1303]

Pencil on paper
22.5 x 16.5 cm
Date: 1947

Inscr: Munnings (pencil, lower left centre); "Rufus" (pencil, lower right)
Prov: acquired by the Trustees at an unknown date after 1947

Charles Wheeler was the son of a freelance journalist. After initially attending Wolverhampton School of Art, he won a scholarship to the Royal College of Art, where he studied with Edouard Lanteri. As Wheeler suffered from rheumatic fever, he was unfit for military service and he spent the First World War casting metals and making prosthetic limbs for amputees. He was taken up in the early 1920s by the architect Sir Herbert Baker, who regularly chose him to design and execute architectural sculpture for his buildings; their artistic partnership lasted until Baker's death. Wheeler's fame and fortune was made by the huge commission to make the exterior sculpture for the Bank of England, on which he worked from 1928 to 1937. Wheeler worked with several other leading architects, including Sir Edwin Lutyens. He practised direct carving and generally worked on site. The principal influences on his art were the sculpture of the Croatian Ivan Meštrović and the Swede Carl Milles. He worked in limewood as well as in stone, and executed many portraits in both stone and bronze. He was elected an associate of the Royal Academy in 1934 and a Royal Academician in 1940, and he was president of the Royal Society of British Sculptors from 1944 to 1949. Finally, in 1956, with the support of Sir Alfred Munnings, he was elected president of the Royal Academy, in which office he served until 1966. Wheeler's reign, in contrast to that of Munnings, was liberal, as he strove to maintain a balance between the modernists and the traditionalists. He received a knighthood in 1958.

Alfred Munnings, the son of a Suffolk miller, was brought up with a love of the countryside and of horses, which he drew from memory and imagination as a child. The daughter of a local vicar gave him his earliest drawing lessons. Aged 14 Munnings was apprenticed to the Norwich lithographers, Page Brothers, for whom he designed posters and advertisements, while attending Norwich School of Art in the evenings.

Munnings began to exhibit at the Royal Academy and the Royal Institute of Painters in Water-Colours in 1899. He overcame the loss of sight in one eye that year as a result of an accident, going to Paris to study on and off at the Académie Julian in 1902 and 1903. Munnings's other significant venture abroad was to Munich in 1909 where he was much impressed by the brushwork and feeling for movement in the work of Heinrich von Zügel (1850–1941). Two years later he joined the Newlyn School, associating particularly with Harold and Laura Knight. His subject-matter included hop-pickers, gypsies, country race meetings, horse fairs and hunting scenes, as well as studies of individual horses. Munnings was always a fast worker and he painted a large number of pictures.

Munnings's disability kept him out of the forces during the First World War, but eventually in 1918 he was attached as a civilian war artist to the Canadian cavalry in France. That year he was elected an associate of the Royal Academy and established himself in a studio in Chelsea. He became a full academician in 1925. Munnings improved his anatomical knowledge through visits to a local veterinary surgeon and by studying George Stubbs's *Anatomy of the Horse*. His immediate success in attracting patronage after the war enabled him to buy a Georgian house in Dedham in the heart of 'Constable country', which he renamed Castle House, and which his widow turned into the Sir Alfred Munnings Museum. Stubbs and Constable were his two principal models for the rest of his career. Munnings was the most successful horse painter of his day, but he himself preferred to paint landscapes. He kept a large number of horses on the 40 acres of his land.

In the Second World War Munnings retired to Exmoor, where he painted landscapes. In 1944 he was elected president of the Royal Academy, a position for which his irascible nature and his disdain for protocol made him an unsuitable choice. At a banquet in the Royal Academy in 1949 he delivered a notorious attack on modern art, Cézanne, Matisse and Picasso, the Arts Council, the Tate Gallery and Anthony Blunt, the Surveyor of the King's Pictures, before resigning his post at the end of the year.

These two drawings were made in the Lady Lever Art Gallery on 16 December 1947, when the artist made a speech – in response to a toast to the Royal Academy – at a lunch which was

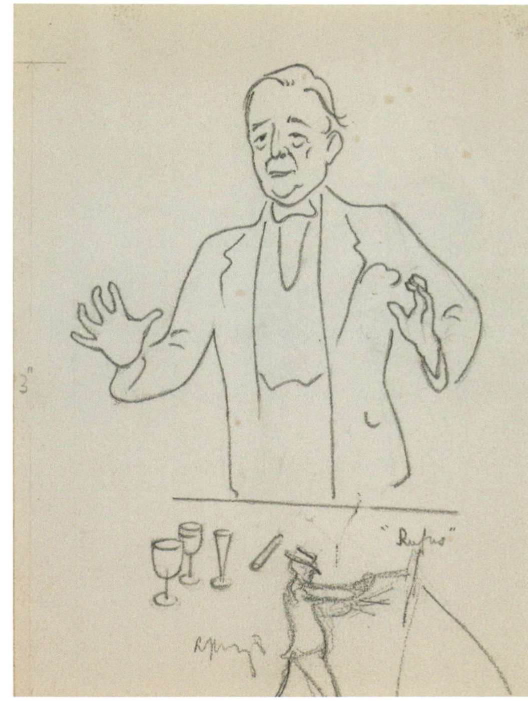

LL 3990

held to mark the twenty-fifth anniversary of the opening of the Gallery, as well as its reopening after the Second World War.[1304] Munnings is reported to have told the guests that 'there are now more experts on art, more teaching art, more folk broadcasting on art, than there are artists... Artists are being made too self-conscious, afraid of what certain types of critic will say about their work.'[1305]

The main drawing of Munnings addressing the 200 or so guests was drawn by an unidentified artist who was sitting opposite him at the table. Among the guests were the artists Will C. Penn; H.P. Huggill, Principal of Laird School of Art, Birkenhead; Geoffrey Heath Wedgwood; J. Coburn Witherop; H. T. Hoodless; and the sculptors William Reid Dick and Charles Wheeler.[1306] It is likely that the unknown draughtsman was one of these, with the sculptors, Reid Dick and Wheeler, being the best candidates. As Reid Dick seems to have sat on the same side of the table as Munnings, to judge by the clockwise listing of the guests in the commemorative brochure, that leaves Wheeler as the probable artist.[1307]

The smaller sketchier drawing of an artist painting at an easel is a characteristic work by

1303 Not previously inventoried.

1304 Sir Alfred Munnings, *The Finish* (London, 1952), pp. 129–30.
1305 Reginald Pound, *The Englishman. A Biography of Sir Alfred Munnings* (London, 1962), p. 156.
1306 A full list of guests was printed in *The Lady Lever Art Gallery Silver Jubilee 1922–1947* (Port Sunlight, 1948), p. 12. This commemorative brochure also publishes Munnings's speech at length.
1307 The attribution must remain tentative in the absence of any scholarly study of Wheeler's drawings. For the ups and downs of his relations with Munnings, see Charles Wheeler, *High Relief. The Autobiography of Sir Charles Wheeler: Sculptor* (Feltham, 1968), pp. 57, 67–70, 72, 74–75, 120.

Munnings himself. It was previously thought that Rufus was the signature of an unknown artist;[1308] in fact, this was the name of the hunter that Munnings regularly borrowed from his neighbour, Mrs C. S. Myers, when he went hunting on Exmoor.[1309] Munnings executed at least two pictures of this horse, a fifteen and a half hands chestnut, about 1943,[1310] and presumably it is the subject of the painting on the easel visible in the sketch. Munnings prided himself on being a *plein-air* painter and made several other similar sketches of himself at work in the open air.[1311] Nearly all of them appear to be connected with his plans for illustrating the first volume of his autobiography, but the Lady Lever sketch, which seems to be the first in the series, may have been done as a gift for the 2nd Lord and Lady Leverhulme, who had put him up before the lunch. Lord Leverhulme had bought Munnings's oil *The Friesian Bull* (Lady Lever Art Gallery, LL 3915) earlier that year.[1312]
MH

1308 This error first occurred in the caption to the illustration of the drawing in *The Lady Lever Art Gallery Silver Jubilee*, p. 11.
1309 Sir Alfred Munnings, *An Artist's Life* (London, 1950), p. 13 and *The Finish*, pp. 66-67.
1310 *'Rufus' held by a groom in the stable yard*. The property of Brigadier E. C. V. Myers, Christie's, 17 November 1978 (lot 244) and *'Rufus' and Jimmy Delaney*, Sotheby's New York, 4 June 1987 (lot 385) as well as the triple portrait *Anarchist, Rufus and Cherrybourne at exercise*. Munnings, *An Artist's Life*, p. 18.
1311 Another in pen is in the National Portrait Gallery, no. 4136 and other sketches of the artist at his easel are reproduced on pp. 47, 203, 286 and on the endpapers of *An Artist's Life*. Photographs of nine further drawings are in the Munnings box in the National Portrait Gallery Archive.
1312 Painted 1920, exhibited at the Royal Academy in 1921, reworked 1946-47, before it was re-exhibited at the Royal Academy in 1947; see Morris, *Victorian and Edwardian Paintings*, pp. 90-92.

## EDMUND MORISON WIMPERIS
1835 Chester-1900 Southbourne, Hampshire

### A Surrey Gravel Pit
LL 3891 (LP 31)

Watercolour over pencil on wove paper
23 x 33 cm (sight)
Date: late 1870s-1900

Inscr: EMW [monogram] (watercolour, bottom left)

Prov: bt. from Charles Nicholls and Son, Manchester by E. A. Behrend;[1313] bt. from the Bluecoat Society of Arts, Liverpool, by the Trustees, 11 July 1930 (£10)[1314]

Wimperis trained as a wood engraver in London under Mason Jackson and Myles Birket Foster. He subsequently produced illustrations for the *Illustrated London News*. From the 1860s he turned from engraving to painting landscapes in watercolour, favouring bleak, unpopulated moorland subjects. He went abroad only once, preferring to spend time sketching around the Thames Valley and the South Downs, Wales and East Anglia. Wimperis exhibited with the Institute of Painters in Water-Colours from 1866, becoming a member in 1875 and vice-president in 1895.

Wimperis's early watercolour landscapes from the 1860s are highly finished, revealing the influence of his former teacher Myles Birket Foster (see pp. 98-99). LL 3891 by contrast displays the change of technique found in his watercolours from the late 1870s onwards. During this period, Wimperis and his friend and sketching colleague Thomas Collier (see pp. 44-46) were attracted to the loose brushwork and broad treatment of David Cox senior's late work (see, for example, LL 3833, and LL 3948, pp. 64-65). With its colour palette of greens and browns and barely painted sky, the Lady Lever work also shows the influence of Peter DeWint (see pp. 76-89). Although LL 3891 was exhibited with the title *A Surrey Gravel Pit* at the Bluecoat Society of Arts, there is little evidence from the topography that this is the location,[1315] nor is it clear that a gravel pit actually is the subject of the work.

1313 LLAG files: dealers' label on back of frame. The gold mount bears the information 'From the collection of E. A. Behrend, Esq.'
1314 LLAG files: Purchases and Acquisitions, 1923-45.

1315 LLAG files: 'Purchases by Trustees 1925-1945'.

LL 3891

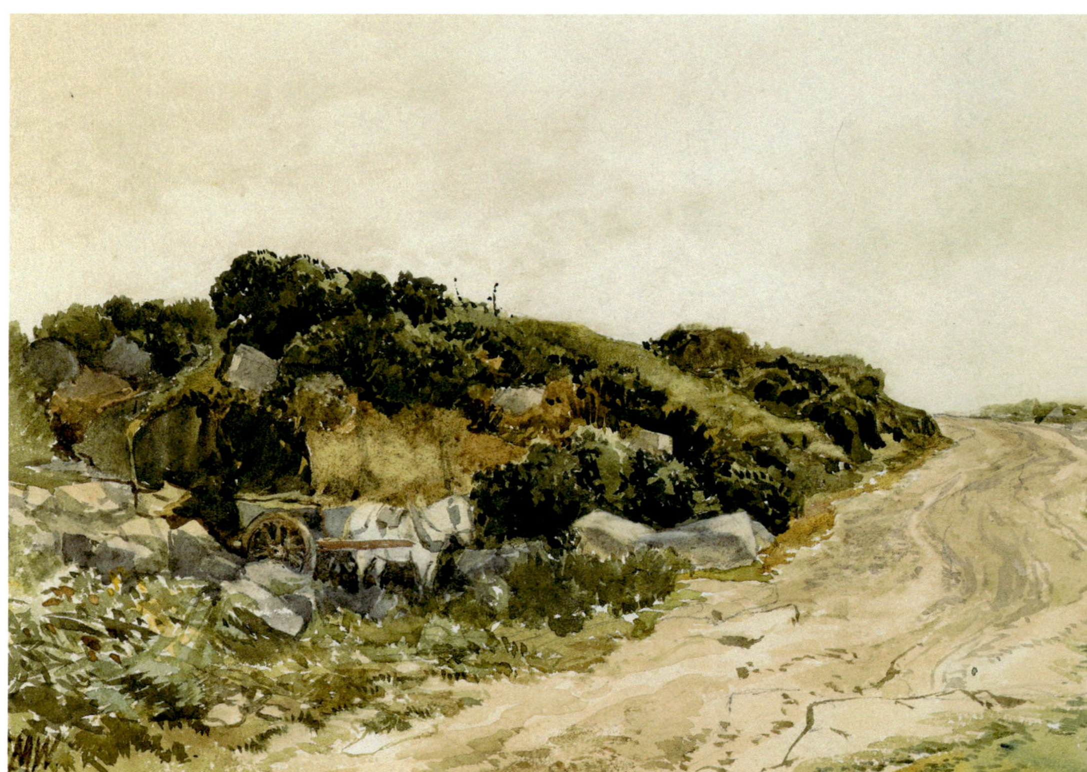

## Appendices

The following appendices contain all the British watercolours and drawings as listed in all known sales from Lever's private collection and from the Lady Lever Art Gallery. An asterisk indicates that the work in question has been bought back by the Gallery and is catalogued above. The final appendix records those works stolen from the Gallery.

The term 'British' has been applied here to those works by artists born in Britain but also includes those artists who were born abroad but spent much of their career in Britain, or established prominence there, or became naturalised British citizens. Where it has not been possible to establish the nationality of an artist, the decision has been taken to include their work.

The works have been transcribed as far as possible as listed in the sales catalogues, with the precise medium given where available. When it has been recorded, the lot number is given in brackets after the work.

The majority of works would have been allocated a William Hesketh Lever (WHL) number and where this is cited in the sale catalogue it has been transcribed along with the various numbers relating to Lever's homes and properties. These items do not possess LL numbers either because they were not part of Lever's original gift to the Gallery or because they were sold or stolen from the Gallery prior to the re-accessioning that began in the 1980s.

Where available, all dimensions are as stated in the original sales catalogues.

## Appendix 1[1]

**1915: Works of Art presented to the British Red Cross Society and the Order of the Hospital of Jerusalem in England to be sold for the benefit of their funds**

**Christie's, London, 12–27 April 1915**

**George Cattermole**
*Defending the Tower*, 9 x 12½ in.

**Thomas Collier**
*Hillside Stream*, 6½ x 9½ in.

*Arundel*, 5 x 8½ in.

**Henry Dawson**
*A Peasant Seated, with a Jug*, 6 x 8¼ in. (614)

**Peter DeWint**
*The Undercliffe, Isle of Wight*, 6 x 10 in. (627)

**Myles Birket Foster**
*A View in Rouen, with market figures near a church*, 5¾ x 4 in. (629)

**William Henry Hunt**
*Oyster-Shell and Onion*, 4¾ x 6½ in. (615)

**Augustus Edwin John**
*A Study of a Female Figure*, pencil, 13¾ x 6¾ in. (628)

**John Leech**
*"DOOSED AGGRAVATING FOR YOUNG CORNET FLINDERS YOU KNOW!"*; and an illustration of same – two in one frame (616)

**James Orrock**
*Tyburn Hill, Bradgate Park, Leicestershire*, 1896, 28½ x 44 in. (618)

*The Wharfe, Yorkshire*, 1890, 13½ x 20½ in.

*Holy Island: Low Water*, 10¾ x 14¾ in.

*Clouds on Criffel*, 9¾ x 13½ in.

*Weston-on-Trent, Derbyshire*, 1883, 9¾ x 13½ in.

*Jedburgh Abbey*, 9¾ x 13½ in.

*Doune Castle, near Stirling*, 5½ x 8¾ in.

**John Frederick Tayler**
*Drawing Cover*, 1873, 3¼ x 6¼ in. (625)

**Joseph Mallord William Turner**
*A Hilly Landscape with Cattle and Figures*, 6¾ x 9 in. (626)

1 The following list is compiled from a catalogue of works sold from Lever's personal collection in 1915.

## Appendix 2[2]

**1925 / 1926: The Leverhulme Collection Sale**

**Abbreviations**

KFR 1: Knight, Frank and Rutley at the Bungalow and Rivington Hall, Horwich, Lancashire, 9–17 November 1925

KFR 4: Knight, Frank and Rutley, London, 15–18 June 1926 (pictures removed from Cheshire)

AG 6 & 7: Anderson Galleries, New York, 2–4 March 1926

**Anna Airy**
*Three and Twenty Damsons* (WHL 2833), 24 x 17 in., KFR 4 (193)

**Henry Alken**
*Fox Hunting* (WHL 3836, 3837), a pair, 10½ x 15½ in., AG 6 & 7 (1), pencil and wash drawings

**Lawrence Alma-Tadema**
*'Strigills and Sponges': An Interior in a Roman Therma, with a Figure reclining on a Couch, and another standing reading a Manuscript* (WHL 3533), 15½ x 10½ in., KFR 4 (194). Exh: *Jubilee Exhibition* 1886; *Loan Exhibition*, Walker Art Gallery, 1887

**Angell**
*Roses* (WHL 3013), 13½ x 11 in., KFR 4 (195)

**C. Arumin**
*Foreign Street Scene, with a Minaret of a Mosque* (WHL 1544), 14 x 7 in., KFR 4 (196)

**Edmund Ashfield**
*Portrait of John, 4th Duke of Somerset and Marquess of Hertford* (WHL 4252), seventeenth century, 13 x 9 in., AG 6 & 7 (2), black crayon drawing

**Austen**
*River Scene, with Hay Barge and Boat* (WHL 268), 9 x 9 in., KFR 4 (197)

**J. H. Bacon**
*Reading Aloud* (WHL 1150), 16½ x 12½ in., AG 6 & 7 (3), chalk on olive-coloured paper

**Bruce Bairnsfather**
*Other Times, Other Manners*; *The Communication* (WHL 3067, 3068), 13 x 9 in., AG 6 & 7 (5), two wash drawings

2 The following two appendices have been compiled from the catalogues of works sold by Lever's executors after his death in 1925. These works had not been part of Lever's gift to the Lady Lever Art Gallery in 1922 but had remained in his private collection.

*The Historical Touch – Well Alfred, ow are the cakes?*; *Old Saws and New Meaning* (WHL 3071, 3069), 15 x 14 in., AG 6 & 7 (6), two wash drawings

**E. Bale**
*Flower Painting* (WHL 4701), 12¾ x 9¾ in., AG 6 & 7 (7), watercolour, from the collection of Sir Cuthbert Quilter

**T. Barnard**
*A Dispute over Cards* (WHL 1725), KFR 4 (198), pen drawing

**R. Barnes**
*A set of six wash drawings in three frames, for the 'Mayor of Casterbridge' when appearing in serial form in the Graphic* (WHL 1672, 1686, 1773), KFR 4 (199)

**Bernard Baron**
*Charles I and Henrietta Maria, with Prince Charles and Princess Mary* (WHL 4254), 19 x 15 in., AG 6 & 7 (8), wash drawing, from the collection of Francis Wellesley

**George Barrett**
*Sunset, Isle of Wight* (WHL 300), 6 x 8¾ in., AG 6 & 7 (9), watercolour

*Classic Ruins* (WHL 285), 3¾ x 5¾ in., AG 6 & 7 (10), watercolour

**Max Beerbohm**
*One Fine Morning, or How They Might Undo Me* (WHL 8458), a pair, 12½ x 15¾ in., AG 6 & 7 (12), watercolour and pen and ink drawing

**John Hodges Benwell**
*Jenny* (WHL 2881), 8 x 6½ in., AG 6 & 7 (13), watercolour

**Richard Parkes Bonington**
*Two Sketches: Street Scene in a City of Southern Europe*; *Barges, City and Shipping, in one frame* (WHL 2705), KFR 4 (200)

*Rouen from the Seine* (WHL 4156), 8 x 11 in., AG 6 & 7 (18), pencil drawing, from the collection of J. P. Heseltine

**Basil Bradley**
*Excelsior* (WHL 1539), 25 x 18 in., KFR 4 (201)

**Eleanor Fortescue Brickdale**
*Kate, Queen of Cyprus* (2) (WHL 4644, 4645), 20 x 9¾ in., AG 6 & 7 (168), watercolour

**Ford Madox Brown**
*Eight small designs for stained glass: Saints, etc.* (WHL 2639), 9¾ x 27½ in., KFR 4 (203)

*Chaucer reading his Poems at the Court of Edward III* (WHL 3742), 20 x 13½ in., KFR 4 (204), pencil drawing, signed in ink

**Hablot Knight Browne ('Phiz')**
*Mr. Ralph Nickleby's First Visit to his Poor Relations* (WHL 421), 5 x 4 in., AG 6 & 7 (19), watercolour and pencil drawing

*Pat and his Pig* (WHL 465), 3¼ x 4½ in., AG 6 & 7 (20), watercolour

*Drawing for the engraved Title-page of 'Martin Chuzzlewit'* (WHL 425), 7½ x 5 in., AG 6 & 7 (21), pencil drawing

*Frontispiece sketch and six finished drawings entitled 'Norfolk Howard's Ride to the Row'* (WHL 429–35), 7½ x 10½ in., AG 6 & 7 (22), pencil and watercolour

**Adam Buck**
*Portrait of John Philpot Curran (Irish Orator and Judge)* (WHL 4257), 13½ x 10½ in., AG 6 & 7 (23), pencil and sepia drawing

**Edward Burne-Jones**
*The Stoning of St Stephen, three large crayon drawings in one frame, designed for stained glass window* (WHL 3334), KFR 4 (206), from the collection of Mrs Humphrey Ward

*Two Female Figures* (WHL 3813), KFR 4 (207), pencil drawing

*David and Solomon, a large design in black and white for window in Trinity Church, Boston* (WHL 3863), 76½ x 74 in., KFR 4 (208)

*Two pencil drawings in one panel: Study of Heads* (WHL 3884), 10¼ x 6¼ in., KFR 4 (209)

*Female Head* (WHL 3886), 13¾ x 9½ in., KFR 4 (210)

*Four small studies in one frame: 'Daphne Turned into a Laurel'; 'Spes' draped female figure; 'Spes and winged female figure'* (2) (WHL 3912), KFR 4 (211)

*Unfinished Landscape, Lake and Sky, blue tones* (WHL 3925), 35½ x 84 in., KFR 4 (212), pastel

*Female Head, with head-dress* (WHL 3930), 7¾ x 8½ in., KFR 4 (213), pastel

*'The Flaming Sword', draped Angel with sword of flame* (WHL 3946), 50 x 18 in., KFR 4 (214)

*Study for Arthur in Avalon* (WHL 3951), 21 x 75¾ in., KFR 4 (215), chalk on brown paper

*Study for 'Phyllis and Demophoön'* (WHL 3952), 47 x 23 in., KFR 4 (216), pastel on brown paper

*Study for 'The Car of Love' or 'Love's Wayfaring'* (WHL 3953), 64 x 35 in., KFR 4 (217), charcoal drawing

*'St Margaret', design in black chalk for left hand stained glass window at Rottingdean* (WHL 3960), 84 x 23½ in., KFR 4 (218), pastel

*'St Margaret', Study for right hand stained glass window at Rottingdean* (WHL 3961), 84 x 23½ in., KFR 4 (219), pastel

*Study of a King for 'The Adoration'* (WHL 3963), 14 x 6¾ in., KFR 4 (220), black and white chalk on dark brown paper

*Study for figure of the Beggarmaid in King Cophetua* (WHL 3967), 16 x 11¾ in., KFR 4 (221), white chalk

*A Draped figure about to descend a flight of stairs* (WHL 3972), 9¾ x 6½ in., KFR 4 (222)

*Three Heads, Studies in chalk for Sleeping Women in Briar Rose series* (WHL 3973), 15¾ x 11¾ in., KFR 4 (233)

*The Fall of Lucifer, Lucifer accompanied by his host of rebel angels, cast out from the gates of Heaven, is seen descending to the infernal regions* (WHL 3981), 97 x 46½ in., KFR 4 (224), watercolour in bluish tones. Exh: New Gallery, *Winter Exhibition*, 1898–99; *Japan-British Exhibition*, 1910

*Study for picture 'The Passing of Venus'* (WHL 3988), 15½ x 38 in., KFR 4 (225)

*'If Hope were Not, Heart would Break'* (WHL 3992), 66 x 35 in., KFR 4 (226)

*'The Battle of Flodden', design for bas relief at Naworth Castle* (WHL 3993), 20½ x 39 in., KFR 4 (227)

*A Study for the Prince in Briar Rose series* (WHL 3994), 47 x 20 in., KFR 4 (228)

*A Study for the Prince in Briar Rose series* (WHL 3994A), 47 x 20 in., KFR 4 (229)

*A Female figure in hood and cloak* (WHL 3867), 47½ x 23½ in., KFR 4 (230),[3] black chalk

*A Study for the Death of King Arthur* (WHL 3938), 23½ x 35½ in., KFR 4 (231)

*A Study for the Briar Rose* (WHL 3936), 23½ x 35½ in., KFR 4 (232), pastel

*Figures in a Landscape* (WHL 3990), 22 x 35 in., KFR 4 (233), pastel

3 Lots 230–49 had previously been consigned in KFR1 (lots 9–18, 1178–87) but were withdrawn and sent to London for sale in KFR4.

*Four Angels in a Landscape* (WHL 3934), 15½ x 23½ in., KFR 4 (234), pastel

*The Sirens: a study for a picture, unfinished* (WHL 3991), 19½ x 17½ in., KFR 4 (235)

*The Departure of the Knight* (WHL 3933), 20 x 14 in., KFR 4 (236), pastel

*Three Heads in one frame* (WHL 3890), 18 x 33 in., KFR 4 (237), pencil study

*Sea and Sunset: seashore strewn with black rocks, hills in the distance* (WHL 3949), KFR 4 (238)

*The Masque of Cupid* (WHL 3914), 13¾ x 34 in., KFR 4 (239), pencil sketch

*'The Wizard': a study for the picture* (WHL 3927), 35½ x 21½ in., KFR 4 (240), pastel

*St Paul preaching at Athens: A design for a stained glass window for church at Morton*, and *the companion drawing to above* (WHL 3852, 3853), 87 x 17 in., KFR 4 (241/2), black chalk

*'The Briar Rose': A study of an old man* (WHL 3935), 35½ x 23½ in., KFR 4 (243), pastel

*A Study for 'The Nativity'* (WHL 3968), 26½ x 16½ in., KFR 4 (244), red chalk

*'Fortitude'* (WHL 3984), 16½ x 7½ in., KFR 4 (245)

*'By the Rivers of Babylon': A design in black chalk for a stained glass window* (WHL 3856), 84 x 25 in., KFR 4 (246)

*'St Christopher'* (WHL 3864), 85 x 24½ in., KFR 4 (247), black chalk

*'The Raising of Lazarus'* (WHL 3939), 23½ x 22½ in., KFR 4 (248), pastel

*'The Briar Rose'* (WHL 3948), 11½ x 42 in., KFR 4 (249), pastel

*Polar Bear* (WHL 4649), 8¾ x 14 in., AG 6 & 7 (28), black and white chalk

*Study of a Girl's Head* (WHL 3908), 7¾ x 6¾ in., AG 6 & 7 (29), pencil, from sale of remaining works of the artist, Christie's 1919

*Study of a Young Woman's Head* (WHL 3887), 9½ x 7 in., AG 6 & 7 (30), pencil, from sale of remaining works of the artist, Christie's 1919

*The Field of Boaz* (WHL 3316), 15½ x 9 in., AG 6 & 7 (31), watercolour, from the collection of James Gresham. Exh: watercolour exhibition at Manchester, Whitworth Institute, 1912

*Study of a Female Figure* (WHL 3970), 14 x 7¾ in., AG 6 & 7 (32), gold and white on pink paper. Exh: *Fine Arts Exhibition*, Berlin, 1898; Burlington Fine Arts Club, London, 1899; *Japan-British Exhibition*, 1910

*Study for a King in 'The Star of Bethlehem'* (WHL 3964), 13½ x 6½ in., AG 6 & 7 (33), black and white chalk, from sale of remaining works of the artist, Christie's, 1919

*Study of three young women* (WHL 3699), 11½ x 9½ in., AG 6 & 7 (34), red chalk on white paper, from the collection of F. S. Ellis, Torquay, 1918

*The Meeting* (WHL 3944), 6½ x 9¾ in., AG 6 & 7 (35), watercolour and pastel

*St Michael* (WHL 3965), 14½ x 7½ in., AG 6 & 7 (36), black and white chalk on brown paper

*Studies of Angels* (WHL 3943), 20 x 17½ in., AG 6 & 7 (37), pastel on brown paper, from sale of remaining works of the artist, Christie's, 1919

*Two Studies of Male Figures* (WHL 3905), 10½ x 7 in., AG 6 & 7 (38), pencil, two in one frame, from sale of remaining works of the artist, Christie's, 1919

*Two studies of hair* (WHL 3892), 8¾ x 6¾ in., AG 6 & 7 (39), pencil

*Five studies of hair and head-dresses* (WHL 3889), 10 x 7 in., AG 6 & 7 (40), pencil, from sale of remaining works of the artist, Christie's, 1919

*Two Portrait Studies of Miss May Morris* (WHL 688), 12½ x 9½ in., AG 6 & 7 (41), pencil

*Day and Night* (WHL 1156), 6 in. diameter, AG 6 & 7 (42), watercolour

*Four Studies of Heads* (WHL 3880, 3881), 12½ x 9½, 10 x 6 in., AG 6 & 7 (43), pencil

*Study for the Head of Fortune* (WHL 3903), 9¾ x 9½ in., AG 6 & 7 (44), pencil

*Study for Perseus* (WHL 3915), 11¾ x 9½ in., AG 6 & 7 (45), pencil

*Ganymede* (WHL 3942), 12¾ x 9 in., AG 6 & 7 (46), pastel

*Six Intaglio designs* (WHL 3981), 3½ in. diameter, AG 6 & 7 (47), black and white chalk on brown paper

*Two studies for Cophetua* (WHL 3943, 3974), 12 x 7½ in., AG 6 & 7 (48), pencil

*Study of a Male Figure* (WHL 3941), 31 x 19½ in., AG 6 & 7 (49), black and white chalk on brown paper

*Study of a Wing* (WHL 3893), 13 x 10 in., AG 6 & 7 (50), watercolour on brown paper

*Study for Briar Rose* (WHL 3937), 24 x 36 in., AG 6 & 7 (51), pastel on brown paper

*Head of a Man* (WHL 3391), 17¾ x 16 in., AG 6 & 7 (52), black and white chalk

*Study of a Woman's Head* (WHL 3962), 16 x 12 in., AG 6 & 7 (53), red chalk

*Martyrdom* (WHL 3865), 30 x 22 in., AG 6 & 7 (54), pencil cartoon

*Study for Perseus* (WHL 3940), 28 x 25½ in., AG 6 & 7 (55), pastel on brown paper

*'Spes': Figure draped* (WHL 3743), 81 x 31 in., AG 6 & 7 (55a), pastel

*Blind Love* (WHL 3945), 41 x 14 in., AG 6 & 7 (56), pastel on brown paper

*Wood Nymphs* (WHL 3866), 48 x 24 in., AG 6 & 7 (57), charcoal on brown paper

*Two Studies for 'The Car of Love'* (WHL 3957), 42 x 24 in., AG 6 & 7 (58), charcoal on brown paper

*Three Studies for 'The Car of Love'* (WHL 3825–27), 42 x 24 in., AG 6 & 7 (59), charcoal on brown paper

*St Michael* (WHL 3862), 89 x 31 in., AG 6 & 7 (60), charcoal

*St Paul preaching at Athens* (WHL 3854), 98 x 24 in., AG 6 & 7 (61), charcoal

**W. G. Burn-Murdoch**
*Washing Day at Carcasson* (WHL 4374), 18¾ x 27 in., AG 6 & 7 (62), charcoal

*Clearing Stones out of the Crede* (WHL 4815), 10¼ x 14¾ in., AG 6 & 7 (62A), watercolour

**L. T. Butcher**
*Piccadilly Circus*, 18½ x 13½ in., AG 6 & 7 (63), coloured chalk

**Randolph Caldecott**
*May-day offerings* (WHL 466), 4¼ x 6¾ in., AG 6 & 7 (64), pen and ink

*Three Pencil drawings* (WHL 422), AG 6 & 7 (65), pen and wash sketches

**William Callow**
*Cottage in the Snow* (WHL 2999), 10½ x 14½ in., KFR 4 (250)

**George Cattermole**
*Entrance to an Abbey, with numerous Figures* (WHL 2303), KFR 4 (252)

*Starting for the Wars* (WHL 368), 12 x 19½ in., AG 6 & 7 (67), watercolour

*The Armoury (WHL 321), 18 x 26 in., AG 6 & 7 (68), watercolour*

**G. Chambers**
*Off the Nore* (WHL 351), 9 x 12 in., AG 6 & 7 (69), watercolour

**J. Charlton**
*Riding Sketch, in town* (WHL 1738), KFR 4 (253)

**Coleman**
*'The Guitar'* (WHL 2994), 9½ x 6½ in., KFR 4 (254)

*'The Flower Seller'* (WHL 2995), 9½ x 6½ in., KFR 4 (255)

*Water Lilies* (WHL 2996), 7½ x 10 in., KFR 4 (256)

*'Oranges'* (WHL 2997), 9½ x 6½ in., KFR 4 (257)

*'The Fan'* (WHL 2998), 7½ x 10 in., KFR 4 (258)

**Thomas Collier**
*The Sussex Downs* (WHL 364), 14¾ x 21½ in., KFR 4 (259)

*A Moorland* (WHL 339), 6¾ x 9¾ in., AG 6 & 7 (76), watercolour

*Seashore with Cliffs* (WHL 3788), 7¾ x 11¾ in., AG 6 & 7 (76A), watercolour

**John Constable**
*Salisbury Cathedral* (WHL 3383), 10 x 7½ in., AG 6 & 7 (77), pen and wash drawing, from the artist's sale, 1892, Fairfax Murray sale, 1917

*Salisbury Cathedral* (WHL 4158), 6½ x 9 in., AG 6 & 7 (78), pencil drawing, from the Captain Constable and J. P. Heseltine collections

*The Close at Salisbury* (WHL 4163), 4½ x 7 in., AG 6 & 7 (79), pencil, from the Captain Constable and J. P. Heseltine collections

*Ploughing* (WHL 4159), 4 x 8 in., AG 6 & 7 (80), pencil, from the collections of Mrs MacKinnon (née Constable) and J. P. Heseltine

*A Lugger, Brighton Beach, 1824* (WHL 4161), 7 x 10½ in., AG 6 & 7 (81), pencil, from the Captain Constable and J. P. Heseltine collections

*Landscape* (WHL 3814), 6½ x 10¼ in., AG 6 & 7 (82), charcoal

*Brighton Beach* (WHL 4137), 7 x 10½ in., AG 6 & 7 (83), pen and wash, from the Captain Constable and J. P. Heseltine collections

*Harrow, from the fields at Child's Hill* (WHL 4160), 6 x 9 in., AG 6 & 7 (84), pencil, from the Captain Constable and J. P. Heseltine collections

*Old Sarum from Durnford Downs* (WHL 4162), 6½ x 9½ in., AG 6 & 7 (85), pencil, from the Captain Constable and J. P. Heseltine collections

*Elstree* and *Near Goring* (WHL 283, 282), 3 x 4 in., AG 6 & 7 (86), watercolours

**T. Corbella**
*A series of six cartoons in colour 'German Kulture'* (WHL 3048–53), KFR 4 (260)

**Matthew Ridley Corbet**
*Haystacks in France* (WHL 1153), 5 x 14 in., AG 6 & 7 (88), watercolour

**Richard Cosway**
*Kitty Fisher* (WHL 4260), AG 6 & 7 (89), pen and ink drawing, from the collection of Francis Wellesley

*Frances Abington, The Actress* (WHL 4262), 6 x 4¾ in., AG 6 & 7 (90), pencil, from the collection of Francis Wellesley

*Portrait of Mrs. Delaney* (WHL 4261), 9 x 7¼ in., AG 6 & 7 (91), pencil, from the collection of Francis Wellesley

*John and Frederick Ponsonby* (WHL 4259), 9 x 7 in., AG 6 & 7 (92), India ink drawing, from the collection of Francis Wellesley. Exh: Bath, 1909

**John Sell Cotman**
*A View of a Gravel Pit* (WHL 4165), 9 x 13 in., AG 6 & 7 (93), pencil on buff paper, from the collection of J. P. Heseltine

*Landscape with Figures* (WHL 4164), 6½ x 9¾ in., AG 6 & 7 (94), watercolour, from the collections of Dr Percy and J. P. Heseltine

*Loddon, Norfolk* (WHL 4166), 6 x 11 in., AG 6 & 7 (95), pencil and wash, from the collection of J. P. Heseltine. *Engraved in Excursions through Norfolk in 1818*, by E. Roberts

**David Cox**
*Fish Market on Hastings Beach, with numerous figures and fishing markets* (WHL 749), KFR 4 (262)

*Pastoral Landscape, with Sheep and Flowers* (WHL 2064), KFR 4 (263)

*Haddon Hall in the olden time* (WHL 332), 13½ x 19½ in., AG 6 & 7 (96), watercolour, from the collection of James Orrock. Exh: *Victorian Era Exhibition*, 1897

**Alexander Cozens**
*A Mountainous Landscape* (WHL 4167), 9 x 12 in., AG 6 & 7 (97), sepia wash

**John Robert Cozens**
*Bay near Harlech* (WHL 354), 10 x 14 in., AG 6 & 7 (98), watercolour

**Joshua Cristall**
*A Country Girl in a Sunbonnet* (WHL 4168), 12½ x 9 in., AG 6 & 7 (99), watercolour, from the collection of J. P. Heseltine

**Shaw Crompton**
*The Night Watch* (WHL 3039), KFR 1 (1189)

**George Cruikshank**
*A Pair – Before and After Dinner* (WHL 2409, 2410), KFR 1 (19)

*'St Bernard', original pencil drawing for the Ingoldsby legends, representing the Devil with a bundle on his shoulders* (WHL 1919), KFR 4 (264)

*A Midsummer Night's Dream* (WHL 3698), 13½ x 17 in., AG 6 & 7 (100), watercolour

*The Triumph of Cupid: A Reverie* (WHL 882), 7¼ x 7½ in., AG 6 & 7 (101), pencil

*Killing Time* (WHL 450), 9 x 11 in., AG 6 & 7 (102), sepia wash

*Time Thrown Away* (WHL 451), 8½ x 11 in., AG 6 & 7 (103), wash drawing

*A Pretty Time to Come Home* (WHL 411), 8½ x 11 in., AG 6 & 7 (104), sepia wash

*Working Overtime Making Military Clothes* (WHL 414), 8½ x 11 in., AG 6 & 7 (105), pencil

*The Elves and the Shoemaker* (WHL 429), 6 x 4½ in., AG 6 & 7 (106), pencil

*Tom Puss, After his Master is dressed, introduces him to the King* (WHL 386), 8 x 5 in., AG 6 & 7 (107), watercolour and pencil

*Hop-o'-my-Thumb and the Seven-league Boots* (WHL 390), 9 x 7 in., AG 6 & 7 (108), pencil

*Hop-o'-my-Thumb and the Seven-league Boots* (WHL 389), 8½ x 6¾ in., AG 6 & 7 (109), pencil

*Sketches* (WHL 396), 7 x 4½ in., AG 6 & 7 (110), pencil

*Timothy's Shoes* (WHL 400), 6½ x 4½ in., AG 6 & 7 (111), watercolour

*Tom Puss and the King* (WHL 394), 8½ x 5¼ in., AG 6 & 7 (112), watercolour

*The Last Scene in the Life of Sir John Falstaff* (WHL 388), 7¾ x 11¾ in., AG 6 & 7 (113), pencil

*Jack Falstaff breaking Skogan's Head at the Court Gate* (WHL 422), 6¾ x 8½ in., AG 6 & 7 (114), pen, ink and pencil

*Sir John Falstaff receiving a most unexpected Rebuke from King Henry V* (WHL 424), 4½ x 7 in., AG 6 & 7 (115), watercolour and pencil

*Sir John Falstaff stepping into the Buck Basket* (WHL 387), 8 x 12½ in., AG 6 & 7 (116), pencil

*Sir John Falstaff in the Buck Basket* (WHL 393), 4½ x 7 in., AG 6 & 7 (117), pencil

*'Men of all sorts take a pride to gird at me'* (WHL 391), 9¾ x 6¾ in., AG 6 & 7 (118), pencil

*Falstaff at the Boar's Head Tavern* (WHL 392), 7¾ x 11½ in., AG 6 & 7 (119), pencil

*Sketches of the Heads of Falstaff and Bardolph* (WHL 399), 4¼ x 3½ in., AG 6 & 7 (120), watercolour and pencil

*Attack upon the Brass Mount by Lord Guilford Dudley* (WHL 376), 4 x 5½ in., AG 6 & 7 (121), pen and watercolour

*Masque in the Palace Garden of the Tower* (WHL 378), 4 x 5½ in., AG 6 & 7 (122), pen and watercolour

*Herne the Hunter appearing to Henry on the Terrace* (WHL 408), 5¼ x 4¼ in., AG 6 & 7 (123), watercolour

*Sir Bulkeley Price bringing the mortgage money to Mr. Scarve* (WHL 407), 5 x 4½ in., AG 6 & 7 (124), watercolour

*The Discovery of the Mysterious packet* (WHL 381), 5 x 4¼ in., AG 6 & 7 (125), watercolour

*The Procession of Jack Sheppard from Newgate to Tyburn* (WHL 401), 5½ x 4 in., AG 6 & 7 (126), pencil and watercolour

*A Night of Horror* (WHL 397), 9½ x 7¼ in., AG 6 & 7 (127), pencil

*The Rival Fountains, or Gin and Water* (WHL 413), 8 x 6 in., AG 6 & 7 (128), watercolour

*Figures of Two Men* (WHL 383), 5 x 4 in., AG 6 & 7 (129), watercolour and pencil

*The British Bee-Hive* (WHL 405), 9½ x 8 in., AG 6 & 7 (130), pencil

*The Golden Spoon* (WHL 406), 8¾ x 7 in., AG 6 & 7 (131), pencil

*Portraits* (WHL 409), 7 x 4 in., AG 6 & 7 (132), pencil

*Fairies and Sundial* (WHL 428), 6½ x 6½ in., AG 6 & 7 (133), pencil

*Between the Devil and the Deep Sea: Candlemas Day* (WHL 404), 8½ x 7¼ in., AG 6 & 7 (134), pencil

*Carving the Chicken* (WHL 380), 2¼ x 4¾ in., AG 6 & 7 (135), watercolour and pencil

*A Most Adorable Lady* (WHL 385), 7 x 9½ in., AG 6 & 7 (136), watercolour and pencil

*Going A-Courting* (WHL 398), 4½ x 3½ in., AG 6 & 7 (137), watercolour and pencil

**Frank Dadd**
*Food for Powder* (WHL 1746), 12 x 12 in., KFR 1 (20), pen and ink

*'Fine Feathers make Fine Birds': The Highwaymen* (WHL 1534), 18 x 24 in., KFR 4 (265)

*'The Meet'* (WHL 2991), 14 x 19 in., KFR 4 (266)

*'Waiting for the Coach'* (WHL 3037), 17 x 13 in., KFR 4 (267)

*'John Peel': A set of three incidents from the song* (WHL 3001, 3002, 3005), 16 x 13 in., KFR 4 (268)

*A set of four illustrations to 'Tom Pearse'* (WHL 3006–09), 16 x 17½ in., KFR 4 (269)

*A set of four illustrations to 'The Harvest Home'* (WHL 3010-13), 16 x 13 in., KFR 4 (270)

*A set of three illustrations to ballad 'To all you Ladies at Land'* (WHL 3015-17), 18 x 11 in., KFR 4 (271)

*'Jester at Fireside'* (WHL 3022), 19 x 14 in., KFR 4 (272)

*Coach in Village* (WHL 3023), 14 x 10 in., KFR 4 (273)

*'Christmas Dinner in Olden Days'* (WHL 3024), 14 x 11 in., KFR 4 (274)

**L. Davis**
*Girl's Head* (WHL 2992), 12 x 9½ in., KFR 4 (275)

**Thomas Raffles Davison**
*Westminster Abbey* (WHL 2145), 14 x 9 in., AG 6 & 7 (141), pen and ink

*Landscapes and Ships* (3) (WHL 3624, 3634, 3827), 8½ x 9½, 13 x 12½, 13½ x 9 in., AG 6 & 7 (142), coloured chalk

*Landscapes* (3) (WHL 3629, 3632, 3628), 6 x 9, 13½ x 11½, 13½ x 9½ in., AG 6 & 7 (143), coloured chalk

*Landscapes* (3) (WHL 3642, 3643, 3645), 9 x 13 in., AG 6 & 7 (144), coloured chalk

*Landscapes* (3) (WHL 3666, 3630, 3631), 9 x 13 in., AG 6 & 7 (145), coloured chalk

**Henry Dawson**
*A Study of Trees in October* (WHL 330), 12¾ x 18¾ in., AG 6 & 7 (146), watercolour

**Peter DeWint**
*A dark landscape, with a ruined castle* (WHL 803), KFR 4 (276)

*London from Greenwich* (WHL 204), 5 x 7½ in., AG 6 & 7 (147), watercolour, from the collection of James Orrock. Exh: *Manchester Fine Art Exhibition*

*Landscape with Cattle* (WHL 365), 8 x 12 in., AG 6 & 7 (148), watercolour

*A Village Scene with Cottages and Barns* (WHL 308), 12 x 18 in., AG 6 & 7 (149), watercolour, from the collection of James Orrock

*A Road Scene with Cottages* (WHL 288), 9½ x 13½ in., AG 6 & 7 (150), watercolour, from the collection of James Orrock

**J. Dewitt**
*Children and Flower* (WHL 1747), KFR 4 (277)

**Frank Dicksee**
*The Magic Crystal* (WHL 3303), 12 x 7¾ in., AG 6 & 7 (151), watercolour, from the collection of James Gresham

**H. Dodd**
*Crewe Hall, before restoration* (WHL 236), KFR 4 (278)

**George Haydock Dodgson**
*Cathedral Interior* (WHL 363), 5¼ x 8¼ in., AG 6 & 7 (152), watercolour

*The Ferry* (WHL 331), 16 x 27 in., AG 6 & 7 (153), watercolour

**W. C. Dollman**
*Humours of Christmastide* (WHL 1697), KFR 4 (279)

**John Downman**
*Miss Andrews as Cupid* (WHL 4143), 14 x 11½ in., AG 6 & 7 (154), coloured chalk

*Portrait of a Young Lady* (WHL 411), 9½ x 7½ in., AG 6 & 7 (155), watercolour

*Portrait of a Young Lady* (WHL 4494), 7½ x 6 in., AG 6 & 7 (156), crayon drawing, from the collection of Admiral Lord Walter Talbot Kerr, Brocket Hall, New Hatfield, Hertfordshire, England, 1923

*Portrait of a Lady with powdered hair* (WHL 412), 7 x 5¾ in., AG 6 & 7 (157), crayon

*Portrait of Miss Storace, noted singer* (WHL 4170), 8 x 6 in., AG 6 & 7 (158), black chalk and wash, from the collection of J. P. Heseltine, 1920

*Portrait of a Young Woman in a mob-cap* (WHL 4169), 8 x 6¾ in., AG 6 & 7 (159), black chalk and wash, from the collection of J. P. Heseltine, 1920

*A Lady in a white dress and white mob-cap* (WHL 410), 8½ x 6¾ in., AG 6 & 7 (160), pastel

**Du Maurier**
*'Personal Experience Better than Book Learning'* (WHL 1719), KFR 4 (280), pen drawing

**Maud Earl**
*A Dog Begging* (WHL 3000), 20 x 16 in., KFR 1 (1190), an oval

**William Etty**
*Study of two nude women* (WHL 4171), 13 x 14 in., AG 6 & 7 (162), black and white chalk on buff paper, from the collection of J. P. Heseltine

**F. M. Evans**
*'For Home Defence'* (WHL 3020), KFR 4 (281)

**Anthony Vandyke Copley Fielding**
*Scarborough* (WHL 4511), 25 x 38½ in., AG 6 & 7 (163), watercolour, from the collection of T. W. Wright, Edinburgh, 1923

**John Flaxman**
*Aurora and the Pleiades* (WHL 3818), 19½ x 28½ in., KFR 1 (23), Indian ink and wash

*Eleven pen and ink studies* (WHL 3818, 3820, 3821, 3821A, 3827), various sizes, in three frames, AG 6 & 7 (164)

*The Day of Judgment* (WHL 3819), 17½ x 7½ in., AG 6 & 7 (165), sepia, from the collection of Richard Norton, Boston, Mass.

*Studies for Bas Reliefs* (2) (WHL 3822, 3823), AG 6 & 7 (166), pencil and wash

*Three Pen and Ink Sketches* (WHL 3824, 3825, 3826), AG 6 & 7 (167), from the collection of Richard Norton, Boston, Mass.

**(after) Myles Birket Foster**
*Landscape with Cows at a Stream* (WHL 347), 7 x 12 in., KFR 4 (282)

**Franklin**
*An Interior with Six Figures in Georgian Costume* (WHL 1538), KFR 4 (283)

**Annie French**
*Autumn Leaves* (WHL 4424), 10 x 14½ in., KFR 1 (1191)

*Three Girls in a Garden* (WHL 4795), 11½ x 11½ in., AG 6 & 7 (170), pen, ink and watercolour, Exh: Royal Academy, 1924

*The Scent of Roses* (WHL 4370), 6 x 9¾ in., AG 6 & 7 (171), pen, ink and watercolour

*The Spirit of the Rose* (WHL 4372), 10 x 6 in., AG 6 & 7 (172), pen, ink and watercolour

**Harry Furniss**
*Lady in Evening Dress with head through picture frame* (WHL 1705), KFR 4 (284), pen drawing

*'Jubilee Shadows'* (WHL 1716), KFR 4 (285), pen drawing

*Mr. Gladstone, gracefully persuasive* (WHL 1717), KFR 4 (286), wash drawing

*Mr. Gladstone seated on the Bench* (WHL 1742), KFR 4 (288), wash drawing

*Mr. Gladstone writing in the House* (WHL 1744), KFR 4 (289)

**Thomas Gainsborough**
*A Woody Landscape, Lane with children playing in front of a cottage* (WHL 3833), 19¼ x 25½ in., KFR 1 (24), sepia and chalk drawing

*A Valley Scene* (WHL 4096), 17½ x 23½ in., AG 6 & 7 (173), watercolour, from the collection of Fairfax Murray

*Cattle in a Water Meadow* (WHL 3557), 7¼ x 9½ in., AG 6 & 7 (174), sepia wash

*A Market Cart on a Country Road* (WHL 453), 7¾ x 9¾ in., AG 6 & 7 (175), wash drawing with tints of colour

**Daniel Gardner**
*Marquess of Cholmondeley* (WHL 4635), 33½ x 23½ in., AG 6 & 7 (176), gouache

**Thomas Girtin**
*A River Scene* (WHL 334), 5 x 7½ in., AG 6 & 7 (177), watercolour

*River Scene, showing village in the distance* (WHL 362), 3¼ x 7½ in., AG 6 & 7 (178), watercolour

*Landscape with Clumps of Trees* (WHL 359), 4 x 6¾ in., AG 6 & 7 (179), watercolour

**Countess F. Gleichen**
*On the Simplon Route* (WHL 4376), 9½ x 13¾ in., AG 6 & 7 (180), watercolour

**Francis Carruthers Gould**
*'Down the Rapids'* (WHL 1163), KFR 4 (291), pen and ink drawing

*John Bull in Wonderland* (WHL 1164), KFR 4 (292), pen and ink drawing

*'Sowing Tares'*, KFR 4 (293), pen and ink drawing

*The Chaplin Toby Jug*, KFR 4 (301), pen and ink cartoon

*The Redmond Toby Jug*, KFR 4 (302), pen and ink cartoon

*A Solemn Warning: Caricature*, KFR 4 (303)

*The Art of Taking Things Quietly*, KFR 4 (304), cartoon

*A South African Melody*, KFR 4 (305)

*Wilfully Deaf*, KFR 4 (306), cartoon

*Why Won't he Play*, KFR 4 (307)

*Tying the Flag to the Weather Cock*, KFR 4 (294), pen and ink drawing

*The Wind of Adversity*, KFR 4 (295), pen and ink drawing

*One-Sided View*, KFR 4 (296), pen and ink drawing

*Not the Sebastian This Time*, KFR 4 (297), pen and ink cartoon

*A Gentle Think*, KFR 4 (298), pen and ink cartoon

*Won't Run Away*, KFR 4 (299), pen and ink cartoon

*An Interested Observer*, KFR 4 (300), pen and ink cartoon

*The Children of Gibeon*, KFR 4 (308)

*Muddling and Meddling*, KFR 4 (309)

*The Lyre Bird*, KFR 4 (310)

*Direct Cause and Definite Effect*, KFR 4 (311)

*'The Unionists' Pre-Historic Museum'*, KFR 4 (312)

*Caricature of the Earl of Durdans*, KFR 4 (313)

*Caricature of Sir Arthur Balfour, playing Golf*, KFR 4 (314)

*'Consolation'. The Kaiser and Von Tirpitz*, KFR 4 (315)

*Macbeth's Excuse; The Path of Glory; The Lusitania* (3) (WHL 2869, 2867, 2868), 14 x 11 in., AG 6 & 7 (181), pencil

**Charles Green**
*Sir Roger de Coverley, dancing in an old fashioned room* (WHL 2904), 22 x 30 in., KFR 4 (316)

*Charity* (WHL 278), 5½ x 6½ in., AG 6 & 7 (182), watercolour

**C. Griffiths**
*St Tudwell's Island* (WHL 4430), 7 x 8½ in., AG 6 & 7 (183), watercolour

**Ernest Griset**
*Primeval Man* (WHL 2985), 56 x 34 in., KFR 1 (1192), 1890

**William Hamilton**
*Study of a Nude Model* (WHL 4172), 14½ x 11½ in., AG 6 & 7 (184), pencil and coloured chalks, from the collection of J. P. Heseltine

**Dudley Hardy**
*Three black and white drawings in one frame: 'All's Well That Ends Well', 'In Maiden Meditation, Fancy Free' and 'Holiday Scene'* (WHL 1694), KFR 4 (318)

*The Indian Level at the Wild West Show* (WHL 1663), KFR 4 (317), pen and ink sketch

*The Fish Market* (WHL 1692), 10½ x 15 in., AG 6 & 7 (185), pen, ink and charcoal

**Thomas Bush Hardy**
*On the Medway* (WHL 4646), 8¾ x 27½ in., KFR 1 (1193)

*The Pool of London* (WHL 4647), 8¾ x 27½ in., KFR 1 (1194)

**Hare**
*So There* (WHL 3036), 28 x 19 in., KFR 1 (1195)

*The Reply* (WHL 3019), 26 x 20 in., KFR 1 (1196), pastel

**Hector Hareau**
*Hall of Columns, Karnak* (WHL 830), KFR 4 (340), formerly in Alma-Tadema collection

**Gertrude Hayes (Mrs. A. K. Morgan)**
*Algiers* (WHL 4375), 10½ x 14½ in., AG 6 & 7 (186), watercolour

**William Heath**
*The Frost Fair on the Thames in 1814* (WHL 4779), 13 x 19 in., AG 6 & 7 (187), watercolour

*Blackfriars Bridge* (WHL 4775), 11¼ x 16¾ in., AG 6 & 7 (188), watercolour

*The Approach to Blackfriars Bridge, Surrey side* (WHL 4778), 11 x 16½ in., AG 6 & 7 (188A), watercolour

**Robert Hills**
*A Shepherd resting with his Dog* (WHL 877), 4 x 3 in., KFR 4 (319)

**Hobson**
*Undine* (WHL 3026), 12 x 6½ in., KFR 4 (320)

**William Hoggatt**
*The Magic of the Glen* (WHL 3351), KFR 4 (321)

**James Holland**
*A Sketch in Town* (WHL 732), KFR 4 (322)

*Rialto Bridge; Lighthouse and rough Sea; Seascape and Ship* (WHL 2850, 2851, 2851A) (3), 6 in. diameter, AG 6 & 7 (189), watercolour

*Venice* (WHL 2851B), 3 x 10 in., AG 6 & 7 (190), watercolour, from the collection of Alexander Huth, 1916

*Landscapes* (3) (WHL 2851C, D, E), height, 3 and 4 in., width, 5 and 6¾ in., AG 6 & 7 (191), pen and watercolour, from the collection of Alexander Huth, 1916

**R. Holyoake**
*A Study – Lady in White Empire Costume* (WHL 1540), 10½ x 5 in., KFR 4 (337)

**William Holyoake**
*Head of a Spanish Girl*, 12 x 9 ½ in., AG 6 & 7 (192), sketch in oils on paper

**A. Hopkins**
*A Cornish Fisher Lad* (WHL 1546), KFR 4 (339)

**Ozias Humphry**
*Portrait of the Rev. Mr. Penneck* (WHL 3415), 23 x 19 in., AG 6 & 7 (194), pastel

**William Henry Hunt**
*Study of a Man's Head* (WHL 319), 8½ x 6½ in., AG 6 & 7 (195), watercolour

*A Negro Boy with a Tambourine* (WHL 210), 11 x 7¾ in., AG 6 & 7 (196), watercolour, from the John Morley and James Orrock collections. Exh: Royal Academy, 1908

**William Holman Hunt**
*Portrait of W. Etty, at work* (WHL 2647), 4¾ x 4 in., KFR 4 (341)

**William Hunt**
*An Interior: Study of Furniture* (WHL 720), KFR 4 (342)

**G. P. Jacomb-Hood**
*Hospital Saturday* (WHL 1775), KFR 4 (338), pen drawing

**Charles Samuel Keene**
*'Here's A pretty Discovery Indeed'* (WHL 419), 7½ x 6¼ in., AG 6 & 7 (199), watercolour

*'Hold Tight, Yer 'Oner'* (WHL 2840), 4½ x 7 in., AG 6 & 7 (200), pen and ink

*A Note and Query*; *A Good Listener* (2) (WHL 453, 455), 6½ x 4¼ in., AG 6 & 7 (201), pen and ink

*A Misconception*; *Officer's Grievances*; *Picture Hanging* (3) (WHL 457, 456, 454), AG 6 & 7 (202), pen drawings

*Jubilee Time* (WHL 2841), 9 x 5¾ in., AG 6 & 7 (203), pen and wash, from the collection of E. F. J. Deprez, St Amands, Hampshire

*Put to the Rout* (WHL 2839), 5 x 7 in., AG 6 & 7 (204), pen and ink, from the collection of E. F. J. Deprez

**G. G. Kilburne**
*'Here's to the Maiden'* (WHL 3042), 24 x 32 in., KFR 4 (345)

**O'Neil Latham**
*Boy smoking a Cigar, with other Children looking on, a slum scene* (WHL 1755), 25 x 32 in., KFR 4 (346), pen drawing

**John Leech**
*Hunting Scene. Horsemen on the Downs* (WHL 1533), KFR 4 (347)

*'What a terrible Turk': a small sketch for 'Punch'* (WHL 1743), KFR 4 (348)

*A Family Group: Baby stirring the Pudding* (WHL 470), 7 x 8 in., AG 6 & 7 (208), pencil drawing

*Set of five original illustrations for Haliburton's 'The Clockmaker': 'Only a remarkable development, says I'; 'Behind the Scenes'; The Black Brother; Patriotism; 'What do you think of Socialism?'* (5) (WHL 4271), 5 x 4 in., AG 6 & 7 (209), pencil and watercolour

*Where Ignorance is Bliss, 'Tis Folly to be Wise* (WHL 469), 9 x 7 in., AG 6 & 7 (210), pencil

*A Brilliant Idea* (WHL 379), 6 x 4½ in., AG 6 & 7 (211), watercolour

*Donkey Racing* (WHL 438), 3 x 6½ in., AG 6 & 7 (212), pencil

*On the Sands at Sunset* (WHL 415), 4¾ x 7¼ in., AG 6 & 7 (213), crayon

*A Reflection* (WHL 417), 7 x 5 in., AG 6 & 7 (214), pencil

*A Great Liberty* (WHL 473), 4½ x 6½ in., AG 6 & 7 (215), watercolour

*The March of Speculation* (WHL 467), 9 x 7 in., AG 6 & 7 (216), pencil

*Ophelia* (WHL 445), 9 x 7 in., AG 6 & 7 (217), pen and pencil

**John Leighton**
*'Youth at the Prow and Pleasure at the Helm'* (WHL 1777), KFR 4 (349), black and white drawing

**William Leighton Leitch**
*View in the Isle of Wight* (WHL 3121), 3 x 4½ in., AG 6 & 7 (221A), watercolour, with one other French painting

**George Dunlop Leslie**
*The Valentine* (WHL 1701), 19 x 13 in., KFR 4 (323)

**John Frederick Lewis**
*A Cavalcade in the Desert* (WHL 3789), 14 x 20 in., KFR 1 (1197)

**James Dromgole Linton**
*Interior with Lady carrying a Basket* (WHL 778), 15 x 11 in., KFR 4 (324)

*Study in gold and crimson, lady holding flower* (WHL 844), KFR 4 (325)

*The Bravo* (WHL 855), 20 x 16 in., KFR 4 (326)

*Head of a Lady* (WHL 879), KFR 4 (327)

*The Letter* (WHL 2821), KFR 4 (328)

*Off Guard* (WHL 374), 14¼ x 10¼ in., AG 6 & 7 (225), watercolour. Exh: Grosvenor Gallery, Paris *Universal*, Manchester and *Victorian Era* exhibitions

*Lady with a Spinning Wheel* (WHL 297), 8¾ x 11 in., AG 6 & 7 (226), watercolour

*The Reverie* (WHL 295), 14¼ x 10½ in., AG 6 & 7 (227), watercolour. Exh: Grosvenor Gallery, Manchester and *Victorian Era* exhibitions

**Mabel Lipscomb**
*Mercery Lane, Canterbury* (WHL 4203), 8½ x 10¾ in., AG 6 & 7 (228a), watercolour

*Interior of 'The Beeches', Tring* (WHL 4204), 8½ x 10¾ in., AG 6 & 7 (228b), watercolour

**James MacWhirter**
*Alpine Stream* (WHL 1151), 4¾ x 6¾ in., AG 6 & 7 (232), watercolour

**Hamilton McClure**
*Spring, Summer* and *Autumn* (3) (WHL 2762, 2763, 2764), 32 x 8 in., AG 6 & 7 (231), pastels. Exh: Liverpool, 1916

**H. Magenis**
*A pair – The Port at Liverpool and the Customs House, Liverpool, 17th century*, 1891 (WHL 4720, 4721), 7½ x 12½ in., KFR 1 (25)

**Henry Stacy Marks**
*Three Teal, water fowl* (WHL 1499), 9¾ x 14 in., KFR 4 (330)

*Edwin and Angelina* (WHL 3162), 18½ x 8½ in., AG 6 & 7 (233), watercolour

*Darby and Joan* (WHL 3163), 18½ x 8½ in., AG 6 & 7 (234), watercolour

**Phil May**
*Out of Work* (WHL 489), 29 x 21 in., KFR 4 (331)

*'Arriet* (WHL 490), 29 x 21 in., KFR 4 (332)

*Hospitality* (WHL 1722), KFR 4 (333), pen sketch

*Statue of Robert Raikes: Boys casting Snowballs at it* (WHL 1731), KFR 4 (334), pen drawing

**John Everett Millais**
*A Visit to the Dungeon* (WHL 1665), 7 in., KFR 4 (335)

*Mary Queen of Scots* (WHL 3062), 4 x 5 in., AG 6 & 7 (236), watercolour. Exh: *Irish International Exhibition*, 1907; *Franco-British Exhibition*, 1908

*The Romans carrying off the Sabine Women* (WHL 4785), 12½ x 16 in., AG 6 & 7 (237), Indian ink

**E. J. Enraught Mooney**
*'The Hours of the Morning': Figures in Clouds with Stars* (WHL 758), KFR 4 (336). Exh: Royal Academy, 1913

**George Morland**
*Head of a Soldier* (WHL 4174), 11½ x 8½ in., AG 6 & 7 (240), black and red chalk

**Attributed to George Morland**
*The Farmer's Family* (WHL 4781), 14 x 19 in., AG 6 & 7 (241), pen and watercolour

**David Murray**
*Stornoway Harbour* (WHL 4084A), 9½ x 14 in., AG 6 & 7 (243), watercolour

*By the Lake Side* (WHL 3197), 14½ x 17½ in., AG 6 & 7 (244), watercolour and pastel

**Joseph Nash**
*A Series of 26 drawings of Windsor Castle, interior and exterior, executed by special command of Queen Victoria, from 1846 onward* (WHL 4442–67), KFR 1 (26), from collection of Mr J. H. Naylor of Welshpool

*Staircase at Burleigh* (WHL 237), 12 x 15 in., KFR 4 (350)

*The Long Gallery, Lanhydroc, Cornwall* (WHL 3217), 13 x 19¼ in., AG 6 & 7 (245), watercolour

*The Great Bedchamber, Knole* (WHL 3216), 13½ x 18 in., AG 6 & 7 (246), watercolour

*Baronial Interior* (WHL 3203), 12 x 19½ in., AG 6 & 7 (247) watercolour

**M. L. Nisbet**
*Autumn Festival* (WHL 4667), 23½ x 39½ in., AG 6 & 7 (249), watercolour. Exh: Royal Institute of Painters in Water Colours, 1923

**Miss T. O'Halloran**
*Sun-Worshippers* (WHL 4470), 10½ x 14 in., AG 6 & 7 (250), watercolour

**William Quiller Orchardson**
*Napoleon at St Helena dictating his Memoirs to Comte Las Casas* (WHL 4817), 49 x 85 in., AG 6 & 7 (251), crayon, from the collection of the Rt. Hon. Lord Blyth, 1925

**James Orrock**
*Stirling: Cattle in River and two Figures Fishing* (WHL 211), 11½ x 17½ in., KFR 4 (351)

*Arundel Castle* (WHL 438), 8½ x 13½ in., KFR 4 (352)

*On the Border of Lochar Moss, Dumfriesshire* (WHL 723), 30 x 44 in., KFR 4 (353)

*Sawley on the Trent* (WHL 726), 19 x 33 in., KFR 4 (354)

*Off Arran: Herring Boats* (WHL 730), 14 x 21 in., KFR 4 (355)

*On the Border of Lochar Moss, Dumfriesshire* (WHL 731), KFR 4 (356)

*Men and Women Potato Picking* (WHL 781), 8 x 18 in., KFR 4 (357)

*View in Warwickshire: Old Windmill on Hill with Sheep* (WHL 785), 8 x 19 in., KFR 4 (358). Exh: Royal Institute of Painters in Water Colours.

*Kegworth* (WHL 786), 14 x 30 in., KFR 4 (359). Exh: Manchester Art Gallery

*Canal near Danbury* (WHL 800), 5 x 13 in., KFR 4 (360)

*Zouch Mill* (WHL 812), 16 x 30 in., KFR 4 (361)

*Rough Sea on the Coast* (WHL 831), 8 x 13 in., KFR 4 (362)

*Sligachan, Isle of Skye* (WHL 846), 14 x 22 in., KFR 4 (370). Exh: Royal Institute of Painters in Water Colours

*Near Worthing: Carrying Corn* (WHL 848), 8 x 12 in., KFR 4 (371)

*Craigmillar Castle* (WHL 851), 20 x 42 in., KFR 4 (372)

*Ratcliffe on the Soar* (WHL 852), 13½ x 29 in., KFR 4 (373)

*Old Dutch Windmill* (WHL 856), 13 x 19 in., KFR 4 (374)

*Dumbarton Castle* (WHL 857), 3 x 13 in., KFR 4 (375)

*Peterborough from River Nene, Cathedral in distance* (WHL 858), 5 x 8½ in., KFR 4 (356)

*View of Bradgate Park* (WHL 832), 12 x 20 in., KFR 4 (363)

*Fishing Boats off Holy Island* (WHL 833), 13 x 20 in., KFR 4 (364)

*Warkworth, with village and castle on hill* (WHL 834), 14 x 17 in., KFR 4 (365)

*Tutbury Castle, Derbyshire* (WHL 838), KFR 4 (366)

*Du Nottar Castle* (WHL 839), 14 x 20 in., KFR 4 (367)

*Dunstanborough Castle* (WHL 843), 12 x 19 in., KFR 4 (368)

*Silverton Mills, Sussex* (WHL 845), 8 x 17 in., KFR 4 (369)

*Normanton on Soar* (WHL 859), 14 x 30 in., KFR 4 (377)

*Craigmillar Castle* (WHL 860), 17 x 22½ in., KFR 4 (378)

*Dumbarton Castle* (WHL 861), 5 x 13 in., KFR 4 (379)

*Cathcart Castle, near Glasgow* (WHL 867), 5 x 8 ½ in., KFR 4 (380)

*Bolton Castle, with cattle in foreground* (WHL 873), 5½ x 8½ in., KFR 4 (381)

*Off Arran Coast, a Sea Scene with rocks* (WHL 878), 12 x 20 in., KFR 4 (382). Exh: Royal Institute of Painters in Water Colours

*The Juncture of the Tees and Greta* (WHL 880), 8 x 11 in., KFR 4 (383)

*Dunstanborough Castle, Northumberland* (WHL 882), 10 x 16 in., KFR 4 (384). Exh: Royal Institute of Painters in Water Colours

*Loch Leven Castle, with mountains behind* (WHL 883), 11 x 16 in., KFR 4 (385)

*Stirling Castle, Farm and Sheep in foreground* (WHL 884), 10½ x 16 in., KFR 4 (386)

*Near Dalmeny* (WHL 885), 10¾ x 18 in., KFR 4 (387). Exh: Royal Institute of Painters in Water Colours

*Off Brighton, a seascape* (WHL 872), KFR 4 (388)

*A Common in Essex, with cottages, sand dunes and bracken (probably Danbury)* (WHL 1404), 12 x 18 in., KFR 4 (389)

*An Old Farm near Elsted, Surrey* (WHL 1405), 21 x 18 in., KFR 4 (390)

*Oystermouth Castle and Mumbles Lighthouse* (WHL 1406), 20 x 30 in., KFR 4 (391)

*An Old Watermill, Essex* (WHL 1407), 20 x 30 in., KFR 4 (392)

*Normanton on Soar, Leicestershire* (WHL 2075), 32 x 50 in., KFR 4 (393)

*The Ferry, Hoveringham* (WHL 2077), 20 x 30 in., KFR 4 (394)

*Footbridge at Danbury, Essex, cowherds cooking* (WHL 2078), 20 x 30 in., KFR 4 (395)

*Hoveringham Ferry* (WHL 2079), 20 x 30 in., KFR 4 (396)

*Lochar Moss, Dumfries* (WHL 2080), 20 x 30 in., KFR 4 (397)

*Wensleydale and Bolton Castle from the Moors* (WHL 2083), 24 x 36 in., KFR 4 (398)

*Off Skye: Coast and Gulls, Sounds of Sleet* (WHL 2084), 13 x 20 in., KFR 4 (399)

*Arundel Castle and Park* (WHL 2085), 13 x 20 in., KFR 4 (400)

*Woodhouse Mill, Leicestershire* (WHL 2086), 13 x 21 in., KFR 4 (401)

*Skye: Coast Scene with Gulls* (WHL 2087), 13 x 20 in., KFR 4 (402)

*Lake Monteith: Island and Castle* (WHL 2088), 13 x 20 in., KFR 4 (403)

*Rain at Sea: Lincolnshire Castle* (WHL 2089), 13 x 20 in., KFR 4 (404)

*Wallace Monument, Stirling* (WHL 2090), 13 x 20 in., KFR 4 (405)

*Seascape with Seafield Tower, Fife* (WHL 2091), 13 x 20 in., KFR 4 (406)

*Nappa Hall and Park with Cattle, Wensleydale* (WHL 2092), 13 x 20 in., KFR 4 (407)

*Duddingston and Craigmillar: Church and cattle in stream* (WHL 2093), 13 x 20 in., KFR 4 (408)

*Dunblane Cathedral: Man Fishing* (WHL 2094), 13 x 20 in., KFR 4 (416)

*On the Soar, Keyworth Church in distance* (WHL 2096), 13 x 20 in., KFR 4 (410)

*Off Iona: Sea Swell on the Atlantic* (WHL 2097), 13 x 22 in., KFR 4 (411)

*Solway Moss* (WHL 2099), 13 x 22 in., KFR 4 (442)

*Aysgarth Falls, Yorkshire* (WHL 2100), 13 x 22 in., KFR 4 (413)

*Barnard Castle from the River* (WHL 2101), 13 x 22 in., KFR 4 (414)

*Borthwick Castle, river, bridge and cottage in foreground* (WHL 2102), 13 x 22 in., KFR 4 (415)

*Dunblane Cathedral* (WHL 2103), 13 x 22 in., KFR 4 (416)

*Criffel on the Nith: Ship and cottages* (WHL 2104), 7 x 19 in., KFR 4 (417)

*Amberley Castle, Sussex* (WHL 2105), 7 x 19 in., KFR 4 (418)

*Worthing Beach with Fishing Boats* (WHL 2106), 7 x 19 in., KFR 4 (419)

*Worthing Beach: Fishermen drying Sail* (WHL 2107), 7 x 19 in., KFR 4 (420)

*Smailholm Tower, near Kelso, Eildon Hills in distance* (WHL 2108), 11 x 17 in., KFR 4 (421)

*Solway Moss, with cattle and hills in background* (WHL 2109), 11 x 17 in., KFR 4 (422)

*Libberton Tower, near Edinburgh* (WHL 2110), 11 x 17 in., KFR 4 (423)

*Near Milford, Surrey* (WHL 2111), 7 x 19 in., KFR 4 (424)

*Village Green, near Danbury, Essex* (WHL 2112), 7½ x 19 in., KFR 4 (425)

*Near Milford, Surrey; Wooded Valley with Cottages and Figures* (WHL 2114), 30½ x 53 in., KFR 4 (426)

*Donnington Park, Leicestershire* (WHL 2116), 30½ x 53 in., KFR 4 (427)

*Solway Sands: Fishermen in danger of the bore tide* (WHL 2117), 30½ x 53 in., KFR 4 (428)

*Holy Island Castle, Longstone Light and Farne Island in distance* (WHL 2118), 30½ x 53 in., KFR 4 (429)

*Bradgate Park, Leicestershire* (WHL 2119), 30 x 45 in., KFR 4 (430)

*Solway Sand, Criffel in background* (WHL 2120), 30 x 45 in., KFR 4 (431)

*Estuary of the Nith* (WHL 2121), 30 x 45 in., KFR 4 (432)

*Woodhouse Mill, Leicestershire* (WHL 2122), 20 x 30 in., KFR 4 (433)

*Near Kidderminster* (WHL 2123), 6 x 9 in., KFR 4 (434)

*Small Seascape, with gulls round a buoy and distant ship* (WHL 2124), 5 x 6½ in., KFR 4 (435)

*View at Newark* (WHL 2125), 6 x 9 in., KFR 4 (436)

*Off Hastings* (WHL 2126), 7 x 10 in., KFR 4 (437)

*Near Danbury, Essex* (WHL 326), 11½ x 17½ in., AG 6 & 7 (252), watercolour

*Near Danbury* (WHL 373), 7½ x 18½ in., AG 6 & 7 (253), watercolour

*Sketch at Warkworth, Durham* (WHL 154), 7¾ x 12¾ in., AG 6 & 7 (254), watercolour

*Hastings* (WHL 153), 7 x 9¾ in., AG 6 & 7 (255), watercolour

**J. H. P.**
*A Yacht Race*, 1882 (WHL 1661), 14 x 25 in., KFR 4 (482)

**A. Parsons**
*'Cottage on the Hill': Autumn* (WHL 2810), 8 x 11 in., KFR 1 (1199)

**Bernard Partridge**
*Lady in hammock with parasol by the side of a river* (WHL 1771), KFR 4 (439)

*Le Grand Penseur* (WHL 2785), KFR 4 (440), pen and ink cartoon

**Bernard Partridge and J. V. Selb**
*Three black and white drawings in one frame: 'The Secondhand Stuff'; 'The Swing Door'; and 'Dogs Fighting'*, KFR 4 (438)

**Elizabeth Petrie**
*Back Street in Florence* (WHL 1543), 14 x 9¼ in., KFR 4 (441)

**Henry Pilleau**
*A Halt in the Desert* (WHL 1524), 4½ x 7½ in., KFR 4 (442)

**Samuel Prout**
*An Ancient Bridge, with statue, boats and figures* (WHL 735), 12 x 8½ in., KFR 4 (443)

*A Gothic Church Porch with figures* (WHL 745), 10 x 8 in., KFR 4 (444)

*Gothic Architecture, with sculpted figure* (WHL 766), 12 x 9½ in., KFR 4 (445)

*A Village Crucifix with ruined Abbey, Normandy* (WHL 772), 11 x 9 in., KFR 4 (446)

*A Row of Almshouses with Figures* (WHL 2082), 9 x 19 in., KFR 4 (447)

*Street Scenes* (2) (WHL 263, 264), 9¾ x 7½ in., AG 6 & 7 (258), watercolours

*The Well* (WHL 269), 10 x 7¾ in., AG 6 & 7 (259), watercolour

**Thomas Pyne**
*Cattle in the Meadows* (WHL 4377), 13½ x 20 in., AG 6 & 7 (260), watercolour. Exh: Royal Institute of Painters in Water Colours, 1922

**Rainey**
*The Christening* (WHL 2993), KFR 4 (451)

**William Rainey**
*'An International Conference': Children by the Sea* (WHL 1740), KFR 1 (31), sepia

**Mrs. A. Rathbone**
*'Ragtime'* (WHL 2649, 2650), a pair, 9 x 13½ in., KFR 4 (452), pen and ink

**Louise Rayner**
*High Street, Eton* (WHL 4510), 9¾ x 15½ in., AG 6 & 7 (262), watercolour

**E. T. Reed**
*A Cartoon for Punch – 'Essence of Parliament': His Majesty starts the Marionettes* (WHL 2403), 21 x 17½ in., KFR 1 (28), pen and ink

**Joshua Reynolds**
*The Mask and the Ghost* (2) (WHL 4670, 4671), 7¼ x 9 in., AG 6 & 7 (264), coloured chalk, from the Cremetti collection

**Charles James Richardson**
*South West Gateway, Nantwich* (WHL 234), KFR 4 (454)

**Thomas Miles Richardson**
*Old Houses in Holborn* (WHL 4776), 9¾ x 13¾ in., AG 6 & 7 (265), watercolour

**William Blake Richmond**
*The Feast of Bacchus* (WHL 4432), 11½ x 24½ in., KFR 1 (29)

*'La Vierge Consolatrice': a study for the picture* (WHL 4433), 47 x 36 in., KFR 1 (1201), coloured chalks

**Miss E. Robinson**
*The Beacons, Brecon* (WHL 2700), 6¾ x 21 in., KFR 4 (455)

**George F. Robson**
*Loch Achray* (WHL 4427), 29 x 53 in., AG 6 & 7 (266), watercolour

**Dante Gabriel Rossetti**
*The Magdalen with the Pot of Ointment* (WHL 4195), 30 x 22 in., KFR 1 (30), pastel

*A Fight for a Woman* (WHL 3153), 13½ x 11 in., AG 6 & 7 (267), watercolour, from the collection of George Rae, 1917

*Woman holding a Crystal* (WHL 4097), 35 x 22½ in., AG 6 & 7 (268), pastel, from the collections of Charles W. Mills and Fairfax Murray. Exh: Burlington Fine Arts Club, London

*Portrait Head of a Lady* (WHL 4098), 21 x 17 in., AG 6 & 7 (269), red chalk, from the collection of Fairfax Murray

*Death of Breuse* (WHL 3152), 19 x 13½ in., AG 6 & 7 (270), watercolour, from the collection of George Rae, 1917

*Head of Miss Wilding* (WHL 3700), 16½ x 13½ in., AG 6 & 7 (271), red and black chalk, from the collection of F. S. Ellis. Exh: *Irish International Exhibition*, 1907

*Dante and Beatrice* (WHL 3154), 14½ x 25½ in., AG 6 & 7 (272), pen and ink, from the collection of George Rae, 1917. Exh: Burlington Fine Arts Club, London

**S. Rothwell**
*Little Bolton Hall* (WHL 3343), 22 x 32 in., KFR 1 (1200), pastel

**Thomas Rowlandson**
*Ploughing Time* (WHL 2734), 8½ x 11¼ in., AG 6 & 7 (273), watercolour

*The Village Alehouse* (WHL 2737), 11 x 8½ in., AG 6 & 7 (274), pen and watercolour

*Outside a Country Carriage Workshop* (WHL 2733), 8 x 12 in., AG 6 & 7 (275), pen and watercolour

*The Freight Wagon* (WHL 2735), 6 x 9¾ in., AG 6 & 7 (276), pen and watercolour

*Nymphs Bathing* (WHL 4177), 5¾ x 9½ in., AG 6 & 7 (277), pen and watercolour, from the collection of J. P. Heseltine

*A Port Admiral, or a Snug Cabin* (WHL 462), 7 x 10½ in., AG 6 & 7 (278), pen and watercolour

*The Landing at Margate, 1792* (WHL 2738), 7½ x 10 in., AG 6 & 7 (279), pen and watercolour

*The Lecture* (WHL 460), 7½ x 5½ in., AG 6 & 7 (280), pen and watercolour

*Oxford – The Sheldonian Theatre* (WHL 4788), 8½ x 12 in., AG 6 & 7 (281), pen and watercolour

*The Dead Horse* (WHL 446), 7 x 10½ in., AG 6 & 7 (282), pen and watercolour

*Village Scene, with Huntsmen* (WHL 2736), 6 x 9 in., AG 6 & 7 (283), pen and watercolour

*Flirtation* (WHL 4789), 6½ x 10 in., AG 6 & 7 (284), pen and watercolour

*A Game of Cribbage* (WHL 452), 9½ x 14 in., AG 6 & 7 (285), pen and watercolour

*A Cabriolet with Figures* (WHL 464), 3½ x 4¾ in., AG 6 & 7 (286), watercolour

**Salomon**
*A Girl's Head* (WHL 2987), 30 x 19½ in., KFR 1 (1202)

**Linley Sambourne**
*A set of six designs for Christmas number at 'Punch': Aesop's Fables up to date* (WHL 2406), in one frame, 29 x 32½ in., KFR 1 (32)

*The Microscope* (WHL 1715), KFR 4 (456), pen drawing

*Huntsmen and Hounds* (WHL 1720), KFR 4 (457)

*'In the Shade'* (WHL 1721), KFR 4 (458)

*Women's Liberal Federation* (WHL 1730), KFR 4 (459)

**Paul Sandby**
*Landscape* (WHL 357), 5 x 7½ in., AG 6 & 7 (287), watercolour

**J. Sargent**
*A Study of Trees* (WHL 1554), KFR 4 (460)

**Charles Sarjent**
*In the Woods* (WHL 3840), 17½ x 23½ in., AG 6 & 7 (288), gouache, from the collection of Viscount Canterbury

*Two New Recruits* (WHL 3839), 17½ x 23½ in., AG 6 & 7 (289), gouache, from the collection of Viscount Canterbury

*Ratting in a Farmyard* (WHL 3841), 17½ x 23½ in., AG 6 & 7 (290), gouache, from the collection of Viscount Canterbury

*Poachers* (WHL 3842), 17½ x 23½ in., AG 6 & 7 (291), gouache, from the collection of Viscount Canterbury

*Pheasant Shooting in the Woods* (WHL 3843), 17½ x 23½ in., AG 6 & 7 (292), gouache, from the collection of Viscount Canterbury

**Eva Savory**
*Flower Painting* (WHL 4499), 13½ x 19½ in., AG 6 & 7 (293), watercolour

*Flower Painting* (WHL 4300), 19 x 17 in., AG 6 & 7 (294), watercolour. Exh: Grieves Art Gallery, London, 1923

*Japonica* (WHL 4498), 19½ x 23½ in., AG 6 & 7 (295), watercolour. Exh: Grieves Art Gallery, London, 1923

**F. H. Seddon**
*Village Scene with lych gate* (WHL 1442), 10 x 14 in., KFR 4 (461)

**J. V. Selb (see Partridge)**

**V. Selb**
*A Night of Horror* (WHL 1700), KFR 4 (462)

**Byam Shaw**
*Three Blind Mice*; *Patriotism*; *Special Etiquette* (3) (WHL 1157, 3765, 3764), 12 x 10 in., AG 6 & 7 (296), pen and ink

*'She Shall Not Strike Dame Eleanor Unavenged'* (WHL 3763), 19½ x 30 in., AG 6 & 7 (296a), watercolour

**W. Small**
*Mr. Gladstone in Midlothian* (WHL 1741), KFR 4 (463)

**Austin O. Spare**
*Three Studies: chalk study of a female head*; *chalk study of a female head*; *chalk study of a female nude figure* (3) (WHL 4756-58), 19 x 14, 19 x 14, 18 x 22 in., AG 6 & 7 (298), coloured chalks. Exh: Society of Independent Artists, London, 1924

**Clarkson Stanfield**
*Interior with Monk reading and other figures* (WHL 1521), 13 x 17 in., KFR 4 (464), from Sir W. Drake's collection

**John Roddam Spencer Stanhope**
*Cupid's Surprise* (WHL 4108), 14½ x 16 in., AG 6 & 7 (299), watercolour, from the collection of the Rt. Hon. the Earl of Wiltshire

**Helen Stiebel**
*Woman with Veil* (WHL 4373), 14½ x 10 in., AG 6 & 7 (300), pencil and wash

**George Adolphus Storey**
*Stirring the Christmas Pudding* (WHL 4299), 19 x 14 in., KFR 4 (465)

*A Kitchen Interior* (WHL 4591), 9½ x 13½ in., AG 6 & 7 (301), watercolour

*Farm Cottages* (WHL 4591), 11 x 17 in., AG 6 & 7 (302), watercolour

*Rocks at Sunderland; Tajus at Toledo* (2) (WHL 4584, 4586), AG 6 & 7 (303), watercolour

*Maid carrying Dish* (WHL 4607), AG 6 & 7 (304), watercolour

*Near Hampton Court; Dollis Hill, Hendon* (2) (WHL 4598, 4588), AG 6 & 7 (305), watercolour

*Girl in Green*; *Lady Bet*; *A Music Lesson* (3) (WHL 4614, 4593, 4624), AG 6 & 7 (306), watercolour and charcoal

*Costume and Character Sketches* (3) (WHL 4615, 4618, 4620), AG 6 & 7 (307), watercolour

*Costume and Character Sketches* (3) (WHL 4613, 4621, 4623), AG 6 & 7 (308), watercolour

*Girl in Red*; *At the Orphanage*; *Kilburn Gate* (3) (WHL 4597, 4619, 4602), AG 6 & 7 (309), watercolour

*Gateway, Canterbury; In the Garden, 12 Marlborough Place* (2) (WHL 4601, 4609), AG 6 & 7 (310), watercolour

*Near Pegwell; Courtyard, Casa Abad, Toledo* (2) (WHL 4627, 4595), AG 6 & 7 (311), watercolour

*The City of Toledo; Pootings* (2) (WHL 4616, 4599), AG 6 & 7 (312), watercolour

*Near Willesden; Verulam* (2) (WHL 4630, 4589), AG 6 & 7 (313), watercolour

*Bridge at Toledo; High Road, Kilburn; Baker's House, Toledo* (3) (WHL 4590, 4622, 4583), AG 6 & 7 (314)

**J. M. Swan**
*Leopards in a Jungle* (WHL 3795), 15½ x 19½ in., KFR 1 (1203)

**Taylor**
*Preparing for Christmas* (WHL 3031), 20 x 27½ in., KFR 1 (1205)

**Frederick Taylor**
*Rio Harbour at Night* (WHL 3806), 13 x 40 in., KFR 1 (1207)

*Three Huntsmen (Going to Cover with the Hounds)* (WHL 286), 3¼ x 6½ in., AG 6 & 7 (315), watercolour

*A Lady with Horse and Dogs* (WHL 284), 4 x 6¼ in., AG 6 & 7 (316), watercolour

**John Tenniel**
*In the Tantrums* (WHL 3167), 8 x 6½ in., AG 6 & 7 (317), pencil

*John Morley, Diogenes* (1899); *Rubbing it in* (1900) (2) (WHL 3166, 3168), 7 x 7 in., AG 6 & 7 (318), pencil

**H. J. Theaker**
*Love's Minstrelsie* (WHL 4055), 19½ x 13½ in., KFR 1 (1208)

**Thompson**
*A Canter on the Heath* (WHL 2989), KFR 1 (1206)

**Hugh Thompson**
*A set of five – Hunting Subjects: 'The Meet'; Gone Away'; 'Taking the Fence'; 'The Brush' and 'The Wedding'* (WHL 2977-81), KFR 4 (466)

*Coach leaving Inn Yard* (WHL 2990), 14 x 19 in., KFR 4 (467)

**Joseph Mallord William Turner**
*The Soap Works* (2) (WHL 2789, 2790), 15½ x 21½ in., AG 6 & 7 (321), watercolour

**John Varley**
*North Wales: Evening* (WHL 336), 9¾ x 13¾ in., AG 6 & 7 (330), watercolour

*Folkestone* (WHL 360), 5 x 8 in., AG 6 & 7 (331), watercolour, from the collection of James Orrock. Exh: Burlington House, London, 1891

*Preston, near Brighton* (WHL 280), 3¼ x 5½ in., AG 6 & 7 (332), watercolour

*Windsor* (WHL 281), 3½ x 5½ in., AG 6 & 7 (333), watercolour

*River Scene, Surrey* (WHL 279), 4½ x 6 in., AG 6 & 7 (334), watercolour

**John Varley Junior**
*A distant view of the inland sea and great plains of Osaka, Japan* (WHL 1506), 28½ x 21 in., KFR 4 (468)

**W. J. Wadham**
*Evening on the Murray* (WHL 1504), 19 x 29 in., KFR 4 (469)

**W. H. Walker**
*The Bird Fancier* (WHL 4818), 10¾ x 7 in., AG 6 & 7 (336), watercolour

*True and False* (WHL 4820), 9 x 6¾ in., AG 6 & 7 (337), watercolour

*On the Trail* (WHL 4819), 9¾ x 6 in., AG 6 & 7 (338), watercolour

**F. Ward**
*A Bit of Burton, Cheshire, 1891* (WHL 1753), KFR 4 (470), a miniature pencil drawing

**James Ward**
*Milking Time* (WHL 4180), 7½ x 11 in., AG 6 & 7 (340), pencil, from the collection of J. P. Heseltine, 1920

*Study of Two Calves* (WHL 4181), 5½ x 9 in., AG 6 & 7 (341), watercolour, from the collection of J. P. Heseltine, 1920

**Warren**
*How do you spell Soap* (WHL 2986), 54 x 40 in., KFR 1 (1209), red and white

**Aston Webb**
*A Gateway at Bruges, Porte d'Ostende* (WHL 2668), KFR 4 (471)

**D. S. Sanderson Wells**
*'Where are you going to?'* (WHL 3035), 19 x 30 in., KFR 4 (472)

**Richard Westall**
*Portrait of a Young Man* (WHL 3377), 8½ x 6½ in., AG 6 & 7 (347), coloured chalk

*Portrait of a Lady* (WHL 3377E), 8½ x 6½ in., AG 6 & 7 (348), coloured chalk

*Portrait of a Gentleman* (WHL 3377D) 8½ x 6½ in., AG 6 & 7 (349), coloured chalk

*Portrait of a Gentleman* (WHL 3377C), 8½ x 6½ in., AG 6 & 7 (350), coloured chalk

*Portrait of a Boy* (WHL 3377A), 8½ x 5½ in., AG 6 & 7 (351), coloured chalk

*Portrait of A Boy* (WHL 3377B), 8½ x 5½ in., AG 6 & 7 (352), coloured chalk

**Clarence H. Whaite**
*Conway Castle, by moonlight* (WHL 2643), 10½ x 14½ in., KFR 4 (473)

**Francis Wheatley**
*Haymakers at Rest* (WHL 4039), 13 x 16 in., AG 6 & 7 (353), watercolour

**Mrs M. Whyte**
*The Shoulders of Ben Cruachan: Wintry field by a riverside* (WHL 2669), KFR 4 (474)

**C. Williams**
*Château de Bouillon* (WHL 1172), 30 x 38 in., KFR 4 (475), imitation of mosaic

**Arthur W. Willmer**
*Autumn, near Llangollen* (WHL 1541), 11½ x 14 in., KFR 4 (476)

**Richard Wilson**
*Remains of Circus Maximus, Rome* (WHL 3817), 6¼ x 15 in., AG 6 & 7 (355), pencil, from the collection of Professor Charles Eliot Norton, Harvard and Richard Norton, Boston, Mass.

**T. W. Wilson**
*A set of five, in one frame: 'Life in Poonah'* (WHL 1673), KFR 4 (477)

**Edmund Morison Wimperis**
*Cottages near Ringwood* (WHL 3803), 6 x 9¾ in., AG 6 & 7 (356), watercolour

**Wright**
*A set of four: 'Arriving at Xmas'; 'Snowballing'; 'The Doorman' and 'Horseman Departing'* (WHL 3027-30), 7½ x 12 in., KFR 4 (478)

**Unknown**
*An Old House, Stibbington, formerly the Haycroft Inn* (WHL 1215), 8 x 14 in., KFR 4 (479)

*Mr. Crosthwaite's House, Boundary Lane, 1862* (WHL 1545), KFR 4 (480)

*Equestrian portraits of a gentleman and groom riding in a park* (WHL 1547), KFR 4 (481)

*Head of a Girl* (WHL 1669), KFR 4 (483)

*John Falstaff, and several other figures* (WHL 1792), KFR 4 (484)

*Back view of a Lady in Evening Dress looking through a picture frame* (WHL 1760), KFR 4 (485)

*Three pen drawings in one frame: 'Unintentional Candour'; 'A Night on Shore' and 'A Social Distinction'* (WHL 1772), KFR 4 (486)

*Mr. Cobden seated at a table with a document in his hand* (WHL 1996), KFR 4 (487)

*Duchess of Bedford* (WHL 3411), 7 x 5 in., AG 6 & 7 (322), pencil and watercolour

*Landscape with Figures* (WHL 461), 5 x 7 in., AG 6 & 7 (323), black chalk on grey paper

*Liverpool from the Mersey* (WHL 447), AG 6 & 7 (324)

*Coffee Stall; Promenade; Dog's Head* (3) (WHL 3810–12), AG 6 & 7 (325), pen, ink and watercolour

*The Rialto; The Grand Canal, Venice* (2) (WHL 3820), 9 x 11½ in., AG 6 & 7 (326), pencil

*War Cartoons; A Champagne Victory, and others* (4) (WHL 4046, 3045, 3047, 3044), 17 x 14 in., AG 6 & 7 (339), two watercolours and two chalk

## Appendix 3

**1926: Additional and Unclaimed Pictures from the Leverhulme Collection**

**Anderson Galleries, New York, 11 May 1926**

**Edward Burne-Jones**
*Ganymede*, 12¾ x 9 in. (94), pastel

*Polar Bear*, 8¾ x 14 in. (103), black and white chalk

**George Aldolphus Storey**
*Three Studies* (3) watercolour (1)

**Medieval Illuminations**
*Christ and Two Apostles* (2), initial 'H'

## Appendix 4[4]

**1958: Modern Pictures and Drawings mainly of the British School of the nineteenth century, the property of The Trustees of the Lady Lever Art Gallery, Port Sunlight, coming from the collection of the 1st Lord Leverhulme**

**Christie's, London, 6 June 1958**

**George Owen Wynne Apperley**
**The Death of Procris*, 1915 (WHL 2820), 31 x 53 in. (1)

**George Barret**
*Walton Bridge, sunset* (WHL 3802), 19½ x 39½ in. (2)

*A Landscape with Shepherds and Sheep* (WHL 372), 16 x 20½ in. (3)

*A Classical Landscape, with figures and goats* (WHL 323), 12½ x 19½ in. (4)

*A Classical Landscape* (WHL 361), 12½ x 18½ in. (5)

*A Classical Landscape*, 1841 (WHL 775), 12½ x 16½ in. (6)

**Ford Madox Brown**
*Jacopo Foscari in Prison, with his wife Marina, who has come to visit him*, 1870 (WHL 4703), 37 x 24 in. (8)

**Edward Burne-Jones**
*Saint Michael – a design for the East Window of St Margaret's Church, Rottingdean* (WHL 3921), 118 x 29 in. (9), coloured chalks

'*Spes*' (WHL 2637), 84 x 21 in. (10), charcoal

*Love and the Pilgrim – a study for 'The Romance of the Rose'* (WHL 3926), 29½ x 60 in. (11), coloured chalks

*Spes and Daphne* (WHL 3872), 36 x 48 in. (12), pencil

*A Study for Figures in 'The Car of Love'* (WHL 3954), 35½ x 35½ in. (13), charcoal and white

*A Study for 'the Wizard'* (WHL 3989), 34½ x 20 in. (14), grey wash and white

*Saint Agnes* (WHL 3947), 37 x 15 in. (15), coloured chalks

*Design for an Illuminated Border to Virgil's Aeneid* (WHL 3985), 28 x 16 in. (16), gouache

'*The Nativity*' *– a study for a stained glass window at Hawarden – arched top* (WHL 3983), 16½ x 11½ in. (17)

*Two Girls Dancing* (WHL 3976), 9¾ x 6½ in. (18), gold on black

4 The following five appendices are compiled from the catalogues of works of art sold from the Lady Lever Art Gallery by its Trustees between 1958 and 1961.

*Studies for 'The Golden Stairs'* (WHL 3969), four in one frame (19), pencil and white

*Draped Female Figures* (WHL 3966), red chalk and white; *A Group of Robed Suppliant Figures* (WHL 3982), gouache (two) (20)

*A Girl's Head – a study for the first of the three graces in 'Venus Concordia'*, 1895 (WHL 3873); *A Girl's Head*, 1897 (WHL 3876), pencil (two) (21)

*Gawain – a study for the 'Round Table' in the 'Morte d'Arthur' tapestry series* (WHL 3868); *A Female Head – a study for 'The Sirens'* (WHL 3875), pencil (two) (22)

*Study of a Girl's Head for 'The Car of Love'*, 1895 (WHL 3878), pencil; *Study of a Girl's Head* (WHL 718), red chalk (two) (23)

*Richesse – a study for 'The Romance of the Rose'*, 1896 (WHL 3980); *A Female Figure with a Shield* (WHL 3978), gold on black (two) (24)

*A Figure Study*, 1864 (WHL 3929), red chalk; *A Draped Female Figure* (WHL 3899), pencil (two) (25)

*Seated Female Figures – a study for 'The Sirens'* (WHL 3900); *A Male Head* (WHL 3919), pencil (two) (26)

*The Forbidding Angel* (WHL 1782); *The Failure of Sir Gawaine and Sir Ywaine – studies for 'The Holy Grail' tapestry series* (WHL 1783), coloured chalks (two) (27)

*Girls Dancing* (WHL 3986), sepia; *A Female Figure* (WHL 3971), red chalk and white (two) (28)

**Elizabeth Butler**
*The Charge of the Inniskillings at Waterloo*, 1914 (WHL 2227); *The Last Sight of Waterloo* (WHL 2232) (two) (29)

**Randolph Caldecott**
*How Tankerville Smith Took a Country Cottage – drawn for 'The Graphic'* (WHL 1734, 1735) (14 in two frames) (30), pen and ink, and colour

**George Cattermole**
*Divine Service in the Baron's Chapel* (WHL 222), 12 x 20½ in. (31)

*Macbeth and Lady Macbeth* (WHL 799); *Reading the Warrant* (WHL 779) (two) (32)

*A Baronial Kitchen* (WHL 218); *A Mediaeval Castle* (WHL 716) (two) (33)

*Arming for the Wars* (WHL 722); *Arming the Young Knight* (WHL 1494) (two) (34)

**J. J. Chalon**
*Souvenir D'Italie*, 7 x 9¾ in. (35)

**Thomas Collier**
*The South Downs* (WHL 276); *A Moorland Loch near Loch Awe, stormy weather* (WHL 774) (two) (36)

**Alfred Heaton Cooper**
*Wild Daffodils*, 1911 (WHL 748) (37 part)

**John Sell Cotman**
*A Picnic in the Alps*, 13½ x 17½ in. (38)

**David Cox**
*A Welsh Cottage, with children and figures*, 1850 (WHL 824), 9 x 12 in. (39)

*The Cart Shed*, 1841 (WHL 290), 8¾ x 12¾ in. (40)

*The Coming Storm, Stokesay Castle*, 1846 (WHL 814), 7½ x 10½ in. (41)

*A Man Sowing* (WHL 205), 7 x 10 in. (42)

*Bolton Abbey* (WHL 272), 7¼ x 10 in. (43)

*Crossing the Moor*, 1858 (WHL 356), 7 x 9½ in. (44)

*A Fisher Boy with a Creel* (WHL 820), 6 x 9 in. (45)

*Boys Fishing*, 1847 (WHL 793), 6¼ x 8½ in. (46)

*A Cornfield* (WHL 791), 5¼ x 8½ in. (47)

*Dover from the Sea; The Tuileries, Paris; Port Rouge, Calais* (WHL 827) (three in one frame) (48)

**Frank Dadd**
*The Rivals*, 1909 (WHL 2167), 11 x 17½ in. (49)

**Peter DeWint**
*Deer in a Park* (WHL 219), 20½ x 34½ in. (92)

**George Dodgson**
*Carol Singers*, 1860 (WHL 215) (85 part)

**Alfred East**
*Segovia Castle* (WHL 1219); *Rivington Pike from the Bungalow* (WHL 1510) (two) (50)

*Whitby, Yorkshire* (WHL 3054), 20½ x 26 in. (51)

**W. B. Fortescue**
*Cowslip Gatherers* (WHL 2822) (37 part)

**John Fulleylove**
*Versailles*, 1882–83 (WHL 353), 19½ x 30 in. (52)

*The Great Avenue, Hampton Court* (WHL 3183), 19½ x 29½ in. (53)

*Hampton Court*, 1879 (WHL 214), 17½ x 29½ in. (54)

**Charles Green**
*The Sailor's Hornpipe*, 1878 (WHL 2906), 15 x 30 in. (55)

**Charles Gregory**
*Near Runswick, Yorkshire* (WHL 3064) (62 part)

**Edward John Gregory**
*Last Touches* (WHL 491), 23 x 16½ in. (56), charcoal

**F. L. B. Griggs**
*The Bell Tower, Pembridge Church, Herefordshire; Feering Church, Essex; Marston Moretaine Church, Bedfordshire* (three) (57), pencil

**Carl Haag**
*Head of a Negro*, 1874 (WHL 829), 19½ x 13½ in. (58)

**James Holland**
*Spanish Ladies at their Devotions*, 1844 (WHL 1542), 14 x 11½ in. (59)

**William Henry Hunt**
*The Wanderer* (WHL 312), 14¾ x 11¼ in. (60), coloured chalks

*A Boy Kneeling in Prayer* (WHL 744); *A Girl Seated, Sewing* (WHL 733) (two) (61)

**Yeend King**
*Clifton Hampden, on the Thames* (WHL 1507) (62 part)

**William Leighton Leitch**
*The Bass Rock*, 1870 (WHL 783) 15 x 23½ in. (63)

**James Dromgole Linton**
*Off Guard* (WHL 787), 22½ x 44 in. (65)

*The Rose* (WHL 2223), 19½ x 13½ in. (66)

*Lord Lindsay*, 1888 (WHL 780); *Lord Darnley*, 1888 (WHL 837) (two) (67)

*Beatrice* (WHL 267); *Lady in a Red Dress* (WHL 304) (two) (68)

*Mary Seton*, 1889 (WHL 784); *Earl Murray*, 1889 (WHL 847) (two) (69)

**W. H. Margetson**
*A Friendly Chat*, 1907 (WHL 3025) (70 part)

**Henry Stacy Marks**
*The Sentinels, two cranes* (WHL 1498) (70 part)

**Herbert Marshall**
*The Top of Waterloo Place*, 1909 (WHL 1517), 19 x 26 in. (71)

**John Everett Millais**
*Preaching to the Roundheads – a scene from Sir Walter Scott's 'Peveril of the Peak', chap. 43*, 1841 (LP 28), 35 x 47 in. (72), oil and watercolour

**William James Müller**
*Fishing Smacks in a Breeze*, 1838 (WHL 742), 11¾ x 17 in. (73)

**James Orrock**
*Worthing Beach*, 1895 (WHL 869); *Lincoln Cathedral* (WHL 782) (two) (74)

*Warkworth Castle* (WHL 2115); *Durham Cathedral*, 1893 (WHL 2095) (two) (75)

**Harry Sutton Palmer**
*Tantallon Castle*, 14 x 21 in. (76)

**Edward John Poynter**
*A Surrey Arcadia*, 1883 (WHL 322), 15½ x 23½ in. (77)

**Samuel Prout**
*A View in Metz* (WHL 309), 20 x 14 in. (78)

**Arthur Rackham**
*Andromeda* (WHL 17), 21 x 14½ in. (79)

**Charles James Richardson**
*The Entrance, Montacute* (WHL 229); *Park Hall, Oswestry, the dining room* (WHL 231); *The White Hart Inn, Shoale, Norfolk* (WHL 235), pencil and colour (three) (80)

**Dante Gabriel Rossetti**
*Heads of Ladies*, 1873 & 1874 (WHL 2886, 2887), coloured chalks (two) (81)

**Simeon Solomon**
*The Angel of Death* (WHL 3353), 12½ x 10½ in. (82)

**John Roddam Spencer Stanhope**
*The Mill* (WHL 2642); *The White Rabbit* (WHL 2765) (two) (83)

**John M. Swan**
*A Leopard* (WHL 1160), 5¾ x 8½ in. (84), coloured chalks

**John Frederick Tayler**
*Border Reivers, A Cattle Raid*, 1858 (WHL 747) (85 part)

**William Makepeace Thackeray**
*Mr and Mrs Caudle – drawn for 'Punch'* (WHL 414), 9½ x 8½ in. (86), pencil and colour

**John Varley**
*A River Scene, with shepherds and sheep on a road* (WHL 764), 9½ x 14 in. (87)

*A Tidal River* (WHL 352), 8 x 15 in. (88)

*A River Scene, with a Castle in the distance* (WHL 1519); *A Lake Scene* (WHL 738) (two) (89)

**Ernest Albert Waterlow**
*Clayton Mills, Sussex Downs* (WHL 1536), 21½ x 30 in. (90)

**William Harris Weatherhead**
*Chelsea Pensioners: 'Though aged the frame, yet still untamed the fire that oft had lead to victory'*, 1886 (WHL 2224), 30 x 47 in. (91)

**1958: Water-Colour Drawings by Samuel Prout, the Property of the Late Miss A. G. Wigram of Chestnut Lodge, Cobham Surrey [and] Ancient and Modern Pictures and Drawings, also a few bronzes from other sources**

**Christie's, London, 31 July 1958**

**David Cox**
*The Cart Shed*, 6¼ x 9½ in. (96)

*The Windmill, Moseley Common*, 7½ x 10¾ in. (97)

*An Open Landscape, with Figures*, 7½ x 9¾ in. (98)

**Peter DeWint**
*The Fresh Greens of Early Spring*, 9 x 13 in. (95)

## Appendix 6

### 1961: English Pictures and Drawings 1700–1900

Christie's, London, 17 March 1961

**Edward Burne-Jones**
*'Spes'*, 84½ x 21½ in. (72), charcoal, annotated and squared for transfer

**David Cox**
*Harvest Time*, 17 x 23 in. (73), watercolour

## Appendix 7

### 1961: Old and Modern Engravings and Etchings including Topographical and Portrait Prints; also Sporting and Coaching Prints; and Old and Modern Watercolours and Drawings, Books etc.

Sold by Bonham & Sons Ltd., Tooth & Tooth and Robinson & Foster at the Montpellier Galleries, London, 14 April 1961

**John Sell Cotman**
*Fishermen with a Stranded Boat*, 6½ x 9 in.; and two others (13), watercolour

**James Dromgole Linton**
*Lady in a Red Dress*, 8 x 7 in.; and another by the same artist (14), watercolour

**Stannard**
*Boatmen by a Pier*, 4 x 6 in.; and another (12), watercolour

**Nineteenth-century English School**
*A View of Tewkesbury Abbey*, 23 x 34 in. (11), watercolour

## Appendix 8

### 1961: Pictures and Drawings of the Nineteenth Century from various sources

Christie's, London, 21 April 1961

**David Cox**
*The Coming Storm, Stokesay Castle*, 1839, 5½ x 8¾ in.; and another (two) (15), watercolour

**John Fulleylove**
*Versailles*, 1882–83, 19½ x 30 in. (11), watercolour

**Thomas Girtin**
*A Pastoral Landscape*, 3¾ x 7¾ in.; and another (two) (16), watercolour

**George Harvey**
*A Paddle Steamer off Point Judith*, 9 x 13 in. (17), watercolour

**William Leighton Leitch**
*The Bass Rock*, 1870, 15 x 23½ in. (12), watercolour

**James Orrock**
*Falkland; White Horse Close, Edinburgh; Bolton Castle; Crookston Castle*, 1888, 5¼ x 8½ in. (four) (13), watercolour

*Leicester Cathedral; Kegsworth Church; An Old Windmill, Sussex*, watercolour (three) (14)

**E. A. Waterlow**
*Clayton Mills, Sussex Downs*, 21 x 30 in. (10), watercolour

## 2001: The Leverhulme Collection Sale

**Sold by Sotheby's at Thornton Manor, Wirral, Merseyside, 26–28 June 2001**

**Lawrence Alma-Tadema**
*A Votive Offering*, 47.3 x 39.4 cm (403), watercolour

**Robert Baden Powell**
*A Sketch of Soldiers in the Trenches*, 16.5 x 21.5 cm (358), pen and ink

**Henry Mayo Bateman**
*Forbidding the Banns*, 33 x 25 cm (447), pen and ink

**Edward Frederick Brewtnall**
*Little Red Riding Hood*, 47.5 x 24 cm (406), watercolour

**Leonard Leslie Brooke**
*The Lion and The Crow*, 40.5 x 18 cm (434), pen and ink, watercolour

**Ford Madox Brown**
*The Supper at Emmaus "And how it was known of them by breaking of bread"* (WHL 4745), 53.3 x 48.2 cm (396), watercolour

**G. E. C. (twentieth century)**
*Cheerio Everyone – Marion, Lady Leverhulme Driving from Chester to Birkenhead*, 26.5 x 77.5 cm (499), watercolour

**Hector Caffieri**
*Waiting* (WHL 1508, TM 91), 34.5 x 24 cm (427), watercolour

**John Charlton**
*The Meet* (WHL 1779, TM 441), 33 x 54.5 cm (364), ink and wash

**Ellen Gertrude Cohen**
*Moments of Inquietude*, 39 x 28 cm (429), watercolour

**Thomas Collier**
*Landscapes* (2) (WHL 223, H 474), both 10 x 16.5 cm (389 a-b), watercolour

**Alick Cooper**
*Late* (WHL 1527, TM 111), 34.5 x 25 cm (425), watercolour

**David Cox**
*Crossing the Ford* (WHL 370, H 422), 25 x 34.5 cm (390), watercolour

**George Cruikshank**
*Original sketch illustrating Guy Fawkes interrogated by James I* (WHL 406, H 278), 20 x 17 cm (349), pen and ink

*Study for Guy Fawkes* (WHL 403, H 275), 21.5 x 16.5 cm (350)

**Isaac Robert Cruikshank**
*Punch and Judy* (WHL 463, H 230), 15 x 10 cm (348), pen and ink

**Frank Dadd**
*Claret and Small Beer* (WHL 1522, TM 106), 39.5 x 58.5 cm (412), watercolour

**Thomas Raffles Davison**
**Portrait of Sir David Murray, R.A. Sketching* (WHL 3667), 33 x 24 cm (449), pencil and crayon

*A Black House at Uig, Lewis* (WHL 4077), 24 x 34 cm (450), coloured chalks

*Approach to Moraghail Lodge, Lewis* (WHL 3627), 24 x 34.5 cm (451), coloured chalks

*Evening Light, Hey Tor, Devon* (WHL 4822), 19 x 30.5 cm (452), coloured chalks

*Cheddar Gorge, Somerset* (probably one of the untitled drawings listed WHL 3646–66), 34 x 22 cm (453), pencil and wash

*The Village Street, Rockford, Devon* (WHL 4823), 19 x 28 cm (454), pencil and coloured chalks

*Horsley, Near the Church at Dusk* (WHL 4824), 16 x 26 cm (455), coloured chalks

**Attributed to Peter DeWint**
*A Windy Day* (WHL 261, H 208), 22.75 x 32.5 cm (385), watercolour

**Frank Bernard Dicksee**
*Paolo and Francesca* (WHL 3160), 21 cm (circular) (400), watercolour

**Richard Doyle**
*Gnomes*, 16 x 23 cm (398), watercolour

**George du Maurier**
*Aggravating Flippancy* (WHL 1727, TM 370), 23 x 18 cm (362), pen and ink

*Queen Prima Donna at Home* (WHL 1726, TM 369), 17.5 x 28 cm (363), pen and ink

**Alfred East**
*Woodland Path*, 24 x 33 cm (393), watercolour

**Harry Furniss**
*Gladstone at the Dispatch Box* (WHL 1742, TM 386), 24 x 18 cm (360) ink and wash

**Matthew Gosset**
*A Country House*, 48 x 23.5 cm (428), watercolour

**Kate Greenaway**
*Apple Pie Alphabet, F Fought for it*, 23.5 x 35 cm (417), pen and ink, watercolour

*Apple Pie Alphabet, T Took it*, 26 x 37 cm (418), pen and ink, watercolour

**William Hoggatt**
*Cottagers*, 26.5 x 26.5 cm (432), watercolour

**Will Houghton**
*Portrait of the Hon. Miss Lever*, 49.5 x 34 cm (500), black and white chalks

**William Henry Hunt**
*Sunday Morning* (WHL 3201), 23 x 33 cm (384), watercolour

*The Pet Lamb* (WHL 310, H 406), 28.5 x 43 cm (386), watercolour

**William Holman Hunt**
*The Mosque of Assakreh Jerusalem – The Dome of the Rock*, 25 x 35 cm (395), watercolour

**Charles Samuel Keene**
*Relief* (WHL 2842), 14 x 20 cm (351), pen and ink

**O'Neill Latham**
*A Young Swag* (WHL 1755), 57 x 54.5 cm (354), pen and ink

**John Leighton**
*The First Rehearsal* (WHL 1778, TM 440), 24 x 41 cm (355), pen and ink

**Henry Stacy Marks**
*Of Making Many Books There is no end: Design for the Bookplate of W. H. Lever*, 25.5 x 29 cm (445), pen and ink

*A Gull* (WHL 1514, TM 98), 12 x 14 cm (446), watercolour

**Phillip William May**
*A letter to Lord Cross, with sketch of Lord Cross and Mr. Chamberlain below* (WHL 1754, TM 400), 13 x 9 cm (359), pencil and ink

5 The following list is compiled from the catalogue of the sale of the works of art belonging to the 3rd Viscount Leverhulme following his death in 2000. The majority of these items were acquired by William Hesketh Lever, the 1st Lord Leverhulme, and were subsequently retained by the family at Thornton Manor.

*You Never Come to Church Noo, Sandy!* (WHL 1704, TM 347), 23.5 x 18 cm (365), pen and ink

**Joseph Nash**
*Great Hall at Parham, Sussex* (WHL 341, H 487), 33.5 x 51 cm (343), watercolour

*The Long Gallery at Haddon Hall, Derbyshire* (WHL 348), 33.5 x 51 cm (344), watercolour

*Drawing Room at Broughton Castle, Oxfordshire* (WHL 4041), 33.5 x 51 cm (345), watercolour

*The Hall at Penshurst, Kent* (WHL 333, H 486), 33.5 x 51 cm (346), watercolour

**James Orrock**
*Old Mill near Danbury, Essex*, 49 x 79 cm (419), watercolour

*Aberdovey Castle, North Wales* (WHL 2113, HH 75), 15.5 x 26 cm (420), watercolour

*Carnarvon Castle, North Wales* (HH 714, TM 273), 12.75 x 16.25 cm (421), watercolour

*Carnarvon Castle, North Wales* (TM 272), 15.25 x 22.75 cm (422), watercolour

*Criccieth Castle, North Wales* (HH 732), 12.75 x 16.25 cm (423), watercolour

**George John Pinwell**
**Study for 'A Seat in St James's Park'* (WHL 4381), 23.4 x 31.9 cm (414), watercolour

**Samuel Gillespie Prout**
*Barge on a Canal* (WHL 263), 30.5 x 21.5 cm (391), watercolour

*Street Scene in Italy* (WHL 264), 34 x 23.5 cm (392), watercolour

**Louise Rayner**
*Eton College Chapel* (WHL 4509), 55 x 47 cm (430), watercolour

**Frank Reynolds**
*After Act 1*, 29 x 20 cm (356), black chalk

**Follower of Paul Sandby**
*In the Grounds of a Palladian House* (WHL 344, H 219), 20 x 31 cm (387), watercolour

**Charles W. Sharpe**
*The Ash Tree*, 37.5 x 27 cm (433), watercolour

*Wonder Lake*, 27.5 x 37 cm (435), watercolour

**Sidney Starr**
*Lords Cricket Ground July 8th & 9th 1887* (WHL 1691, TM 295), 33 x 47.75 cm (352), pen and ink

**Alfred William Strutt**
*Welcome Home Mother* (WHL 1535, TM 119), 51 x 34 cm (409), watercolour

**Charles Sykes**
*Caricature*, 33 x 58.5 cm (361), pen and ink

**Leonard Campbell Taylor**
*The First Steam Boat on the Mersey – Sunset, Liverpool Beyond* (WHL 4435), 48.25 x 64 cm (436), watercolour and oil

**Hugh Thomson**
*The Father whose Return is Greeted by Young Voices* (WHL 2208), 32 x 21.5 cm (443), pen and ink, watercolour

**Frederick Henry Townsend**
*Hyde Park Corner* (WHL 1687), 25.5 x 33 cm (353), pen and ink

*On the Bank of the River* (WHL 1774, TM 431), 21.5 x 25.5 cm (357), pen and ink

**Joseph Mallord William Turner**
*Fishing Boats at Sea, Boarding a Steamer off Cowes, Isle of Wight* (WHL 4179) 13 x 19 cm (383), ink

*View of East Cowes, Isle of Wight* (WHL 4178), 13 x 19 cm (382), ink

**Charles Paget Wade**
*Outside Mistress Lavinia Vane's Shop* (WHL 2198), 24 x 36 cm (444), watercolour

**Frederick Walker**
*The Wayfarers* (WHL 4704), 35.3 x 49.2 cm (399), watercolour

**E. J. Whineray**
*Bradford-Upon-Avon, Wiltshire*, 27.25 x 38 cm (426), watercolour

### Works formerly transferred to the Lady Lever Art Gallery but subsequently stolen while on loan

**William Henry Hunt**
*Peaches, purple grapes and filberts* (WHL 292), 7½ x 11 in., watercolour

*Chaffinch's Nest and primroses* (WHL 299), 7¾ x 10¾ in., watercolour

*Bird's nest and primroses* (WHL 338), 9 x 11¾ in., watercolour

Allingham, H. and M. B. Huish, *Happy England* (London, 1903)

B[urne]-J[ones], G[eorgiana], *Memorials of Edward Burne-Jones* (London, 2 vols, 1904)

Beckett, R. B. (ed.), *John Constable's Correspondence* (Ipswich, 6 vols, 1962–68)

Bendiner, Kenneth, *The Art of Ford Madox Brown* (Pennsylvania, 1998)

Bennett, Mary, *Artists of the Pre-Raphaelite Circle: The First Generation* (London, 1988)

Bury, Adrian, *The Life and Art of Thomas Collier, R. I.* (Leigh-on-Sea, 1944)

Butlin, Martin and Evelyn Joll, *The Paintings of J. M. W. Turner* (New Haven and London, 2 vols, 1977)

Christian, John, *Burne-Jones* (exh. cat., London, Hayward Gallery and tour organised by the Arts Council, 1975–76)

Christian, John (ed.), *The Last Romantics: The Romantic Tradition in British Art, Burne-Jones to Stanley Spencer* (exh. cat., London, Barbican Art Gallery 1989)

Christian, John, 'La Roue de Fortune de Burne-Jones', *Revue du Louvre et des musées de France* (March 1984), pp. 204–11

Cook, E. T. and A. Wedderburn (eds), *The Works of John Ruskin* (London and New York, 39 vols, 1903–12)

Cox, Trenchard, *David Cox* (London, 1947)

Doughty, Oswald and John Robert Wahl (eds), *Letters of Dante Gabriel Rossetti* (Oxford, 4 vols, 1965)

Duffy, S., *Richard Parkes Bonington* (London, 2003)

Engen, Rodney, *Kate Greenaway, A Biography* (London and Sydney, 1981)

Evans, J. and J. H. Whitehouse (eds), *The Diaries of John Ruskin* (Oxford, 3 vols, 1959)

Finberg, A. J., *An Introduction to Turner's Southern Coast with a catalogue of the engravings etc...* (London, 1929)

Finberg, A. J., *The Life of J.M.W. Turner, R.A.* (Oxford, 1961)

Finley, Gerald, *Landscapes of Memory: Turner as an Illustrator to Scott* (London, 1980)

Fleming-Williams, Ian and Leslie Parris, *The Discovery of Constable* (London, 1984)

Gage, J., *Turner's Correspondence* (London, 1980)

Greenacre, Francis and Sheena Stoddard, *W. J. Müller, 1812–1845* (exh. cat., Bristol, Museum and Art Gallery, 1991)

Hamilton, James, *Turner: A Life* (London, 1997)

Hamilton, James, *Turner's Britain* (exh. cat, Birmingham, Birmingham Museums and Art Gallery, 2003–2004)

Hardie, M., *Watercolour Painting in Britain* (London, 3 vols, 1979)

Harmsworth, G., *Exhibition of the Works of Peter DeWint* (exh. cat., Lincoln, Usher Gallery, 1937)

Harrison, Martin and Bill Waters, *Burne-Jones* (London, 1973)

Hartley, Craig, *Turner Watercolours in the Whitworth Art Gallery* (exh. cat., Manchester, Whitworth Art Gallery, 1984)

Hewison, R., *Ruskin, Turner and the Pre-Raphaelites* (exh. cat., London, Tate Gallery, 2000)

Hill, David, *Joseph Mallord William Turner: Le Mont Blanc et la Vallée d'Aoste* (exh. cat., Aosta, Musée Archéologique Régional, 2000)

Hill, David, *Turner in the North* (New Haven and London, 1996)

Hubbard, Edward and Michael Shippobottom, *A Guide to Port Sunlight Village* (Liverpool, 1988)

Ingamells, J., *The Wallace Collection. Catalogue of pictures, I: British, German, Italian, Spanish* (London, 1985)

Jones, T., *William Henry Hunt 1790-1864* (exh. cat., Wolverhampton, Wolverhampton Art Gallery, 1981)

Kauffmann, C. M., *John Varley 1778–1842* (London, 1984)

Kidson, Alex, *Earlier British Paintings in the Lady Lever Art Gallery* (Liverpool, 1999)

Kidson, Alex, *George Romney 1734–1802* (exh. cat., Liverpool, Walker Art Gallery, London, National Portrait Gallery, and San Marino, Huntington Art Collections, 2002)

Leverhulme, 2nd Viscount, *Viscount Leverhulme by His Son* (London, 1927)

Lloyd, Stephen, *Richard & Maria Cosway, Regency Artists of Taste and Fashion* (exh. cat., Edinburgh, Scottish National Portrait Gallery, 1995)

Lochnan, Katharine A., Douglas E. Schoenherr and Carole Silver (eds), *The Earthly Paradise: Arts and Crafts by William Morris and His Circle from Canadian Collections* (exh. cat., Toronto, Art Gallery of Ontario and tour, 1993–94)

Lord, John (ed.), *Peter DeWint 1784–1849: 'For the common observer of life and nature'* (exh. cat., Lincoln, The Collection, 2007)

Lyles, Anne (ed.), *Constable: The Great Landscapes* (exh. cat., London, Tate, Washington, DC, National Gallery of Art and San Marino, Huntington Art Collections, 2006–2007)

Lyles, Anne, *Turner: The Fifth Decade, Watercolours 1830–1840* (exh. cat., London, Tate, 1992)

Macleod, Dianne Sachko, *Art and the Victorian Middle Class: Money and the Making of Cultural Identity* (Cambridge, 1996)

Marks, J. G., *Life and Letters of Frederick Walker, A.R.A.* (London and New York, 1896)

Marsh, Jan and Pamela Gerrish Nunn, *Pre-Raphaelite Women Artists* (London, 1998)

Millais, John Guille, *The Life and Letters of Sir John Everett Millais* (London, 2 vols, 1899)

Milner, Frank, *Turner: Paintings in Merseyside Collections* (Liverpool, 1990)

Moore, Andrew W., *John Sell Cotman, 1782–1842* (exh. cat., Norwich, Castle Museum, 1982)

Morgan, Hilary, *Burne-Jones, The Pre-Raphaelites and Their Century* (exh. cat., London, Peter Nahum Gallery, 2 vols, 1989)

Morris, Edward, 'James Orrock, dentist, artist, patron, collector, dealer, curator, connoisseur, forger, propagandist', *Visual Culture in Britain*, vol. 6, no. 2 (2005), pp. 85–98

Morris, Edward (ed.), *Lord Leverhulme: Founder of the Lady Lever Art Gallery and Port Sunlight on Merseyside: A Great Edwardian Collector and Builder* (exh. cat., London, Royal Academy, 1980)

Morris, Edward, *Victorian and Edwardian Paintings in the Lady Lever Art Gallery* (London, 1994)

Morris, Edward and Timothy Stevens, *Early English Drawings and Watercolours in the Walker Art Gallery* (Liverpool, 1968)

National Museums Liverpool, *Lady Lever Art Gallery Guide* (Liverpool, 2007)

Newall, Christopher, *Victorian Watercolours* (London, 1987)

Noon, Patrick, *English Portrait Drawings and Miniatures* (exh. cat., New Haven, Yale Center for British Art, 1979–80)

Noon, Patrick, *Richard Parkes Bonington 'On the Pleasure of Painting'* (exh. cat., New Haven, Yale Center for British Art and Paris, Petit Palais, 1991–92)

Noon, Patrick, *Richard Parkes Bonington: The Complete Paintings* (New Haven and London, 2008)

Nugent, Charles., *British watercolours in The Whitworth Art Gallery, The University of Manchester. A summary catalogue of drawings and watercolours by artists born before 1880* (Manchester, 2002)

Nugent, Charles, 'David Cox Jr and the Problem of Cox Forgeries', in Scott Wilcox (ed.), *Sun, Wind, and Rain: The Art of David Cox* (exh. cat., New Haven, Yale Center for British Art and Birmingham, Birmingham Museums and Art Gallery, 2008–2009)

Parris, Leslie (ed.), *The Pre-Raphaelites* (exh. cat., London, Tate Gallery, 1984)

Parris, Leslie, *The Tate Gallery Constable Collection* (London, 1981)

Parris, Leslie and Ian Fleming-Williams, *Constable* (exh. cat, London, Tate Gallery, 1991)

Parris, Leslie, Ian Fleming-Williams and Conal Shields, *Constable: Paintings, Watercolours and Drawings* (exh. cat, London, Tate Gallery, 1976)

Parry, Linda (ed.), *William Morris* (London, 1997)

Piggott, Jan, *Turner's Vignettes* (exh. cat., London, Tate Gallery, 1994)

Rawlinson, W. G., *The Engraved Work of J.M.W. Turner* (London, 2 vols, 1908, 1913)

Reynolds, Graham, *Catalogue of the Constable Collection at the Victoria and Albert Museum* (London, 1960)

Reynolds, Graham, *The Early Paintings and Drawings of John Constable* (New Haven and London, 2 vols, 1996)

Reynolds, Graham, *The Later Paintings and Drawings of John Constable* (New Haven and London, 2 vols, 1984)

Reynolds, J., *William Callow R.W.S.* (London, 1980)

Rhyne, C., 'Constable Drawings and Watercolours in the Collections of Mr and Mrs Paul Mellon and the Yale Center for British Art', *Master Drawings* (winter 1987)

Roe, F. Gordon, *Cox The Master* (Leigh-on-Sea, 1946)

Roe, F. Gordon, *David Cox* (London, 1924)

Roget, J. L., *A History of the 'Old Water-Colour' Society now the Royal Society of Painters in Water-Colours* (London, 2 vols, 1891)

Rowlands, John, *Centenary Exhibition of the Works of David Cox 1783–1859* (exh. cat., Birmingham, Birmingham Museum and Art Gallery, 1959)

Scrase, David, *Drawings & Watercolours by Peter De Wint* (exh. cat., Cambridge, Fitzwilliam Museum, 1979)

Sewter, A. Charles, *The Stained Glass of William Morris and his Circle* (New Haven and London, 2 vols, 1974–75)

Shanes, Eric, *Turner: The Great Watercolours* (exh. cat., London, Royal Academy, 2000–01)

Shanes, Eric, *Turner's Picturesque Views in England and Wales* (London, 1979)

Shanes, Eric, *Turner's Rivers, Harbours and Coasts* (London, 1981)

Shanes, Eric, *Turner's Watercolour Explorations* (exh. cat., London, Tate Gallery, 1997)

Shirley, Andrew, *Bonington* (London, 1940)

Smith, Greg (ed.), *Thomas Girtin: The Art of Watercolour* (exh. cat., London, Tate, 2002)

Smith, Hammond, *Peter DeWint 1784–1849* (London, 1982)

Solly, N. Neal, *Memoir of the Life of David Cox* (London, 1873)

Solly, N. Neal, *Memoir of the Life of William James Müller* (London, 1875)

Spielmann, M. H. and G. S. Layard, *Kate Greenaway* (London, 1905)

Sumner, Anne, *Ruskin and the English watercolour from Turner to the Pre-Raphaelites* (exh. cat., Manchester, Whitworth Art Gallery, 1989)

Surtees, Virginia, *Dante Gabriel Rossetti 1828–1882: The Paintings and Drawings: A Catalogue Raisonné* (London, 2 vols, 1971)

Surtees, Virginia (ed.), *The Diary of Ford Madox Brown* (New Haven and London, 1981)

Tatlock, R. R., *English Painting of the XVIIIth to XXth Centuries with some examples of the Spanish, French and Dutch Schools, together with a collection of Historic and Modern Sculpture* (London, 1928)

Thomson, Katrina, *Turner and Sir Walter Scott* (exh. cat., Edinburgh, National Gallery of Scotland, 1999)

Tickner, Lisa, 'Messing About in Boats: E.J. Gregory's Boulter's Lock: Sunday Afternoon (R.A. 1897)', *Oxford Art Journal*, vol. 25, no. 2 (2002), pp. 1–28

Tromans, Nicholas, Peter Cormack et al., *Pre-Raphaelite and Other Masters: The Andrew Lloyd Webber Collection* (exh. cat., London, Royal Academy, 2003)

Walker, R. J. B., 'The Portraits of JMW Turner: A Check-List', *Turner Studies*, vol. 3, no. 1 (summer 1983)

Warrell, Ian, *J.M.W. Turner* (exh. cat., Washington, DC, National Gallery of Art, Dallas, Dallas Museum of Art, New York, Metropolitan Museum of Art, 2007–2008)

Warrell, Ian, *Through Switzerland with Turner* (exh. cat., London, Tate Gallery, 1995)

Warrell, Ian, *Turner and Venice* (exh. cat., London, Tate, 2004)

Warrell, Ian, *Turner on the Loire* (exh. cat., London, Tate Gallery, 1997)

Warrell, Ian, *Turner on the Seine* (exh. cat., London, Tate Gallery, Paris, Pavillon des Arts and Le Havre, Musée Malraux, 1999–2000)

Waywell, Geoffrey B., *The Lever and Hope Sculptures, Ancient Sculptures in the Lady Lever Art Gallery, Port Sunlight and A Catalogue of the Ancient Sculptures formerly in the Hope Collection, London and Deepdene* (Berlin, 1986)

Webber, Byron, *James Orrock, R.I.: Painter, Connoisseur, Collector* (London, 2 vols, 1903)

Wilcox, Scott and Christopher Newall, *Victorian Landscape Watercolors* (exh. cat., New Haven, Yale Center for British Art, Cleveland, Cleveland Museum of Art and Birmingham, Birmingham Museums and Art Gallery, 1992–93)

Wilcox, Tim, *The Triumph of Watercolour: The early years of the Royal Watercolour Society 1805–55* (exh. cat., London, Dulwich Picture Gallery and Manchester, Whitworth Art Gallery, 2005)

Wildman, Stephen (ed.), *David Cox 1783–1859* (exh. cat., Birmingham, Birmingham Museums and Art Gallery and London, Victoria & Albert Museum, 1983–84)

Wildman, Stephen, *Visions of Love and Life: Pre-Raphaelite Art From The Birmingham Collection, England* (exh. cat., Birmingham, Birmingham Museums and Art Gallery and US tour organised by Art Services International, 1995–96)

Wildman, Stephen and John Christian, *Edward Burne-Jones: Victorian Artist-Dreamer* (exh. cat., New York, Metropolitan Museum of Art, Birmingham, Birmingham Museums and Art Gallery, and Paris, Musée d'Orsay, 1998–99)

Wilton, Andrew, *J.M.W. Turner: His Art and Life* (New Jersey, 1979)

Wilton, Andrew, *Turner and the Sublime* (exh. cat., Toronto, Art Gallery of Ontario, New Haven, Yale Center for British Art, and London, British Museum, 1980–81)

Wilton, Andrew and Anne Lyles, *The Great Age of British Watercolours, 1750–1880* (exh. cat., London, Royal Academy of Arts, 1993)

Witt, J., *William Henry Hunt (1790–1864): Life and Work, with a Catalogue* (London, 1982)

## Provenance index

**Names asterisked are those of collectors, purchasers and vendors at sales, whose full names have not been cited in the text and are sometimes unknown.**

# Index

**Page references for the main entry for artists with a catalogue entry are in bold; those for illustrations are in *italics***